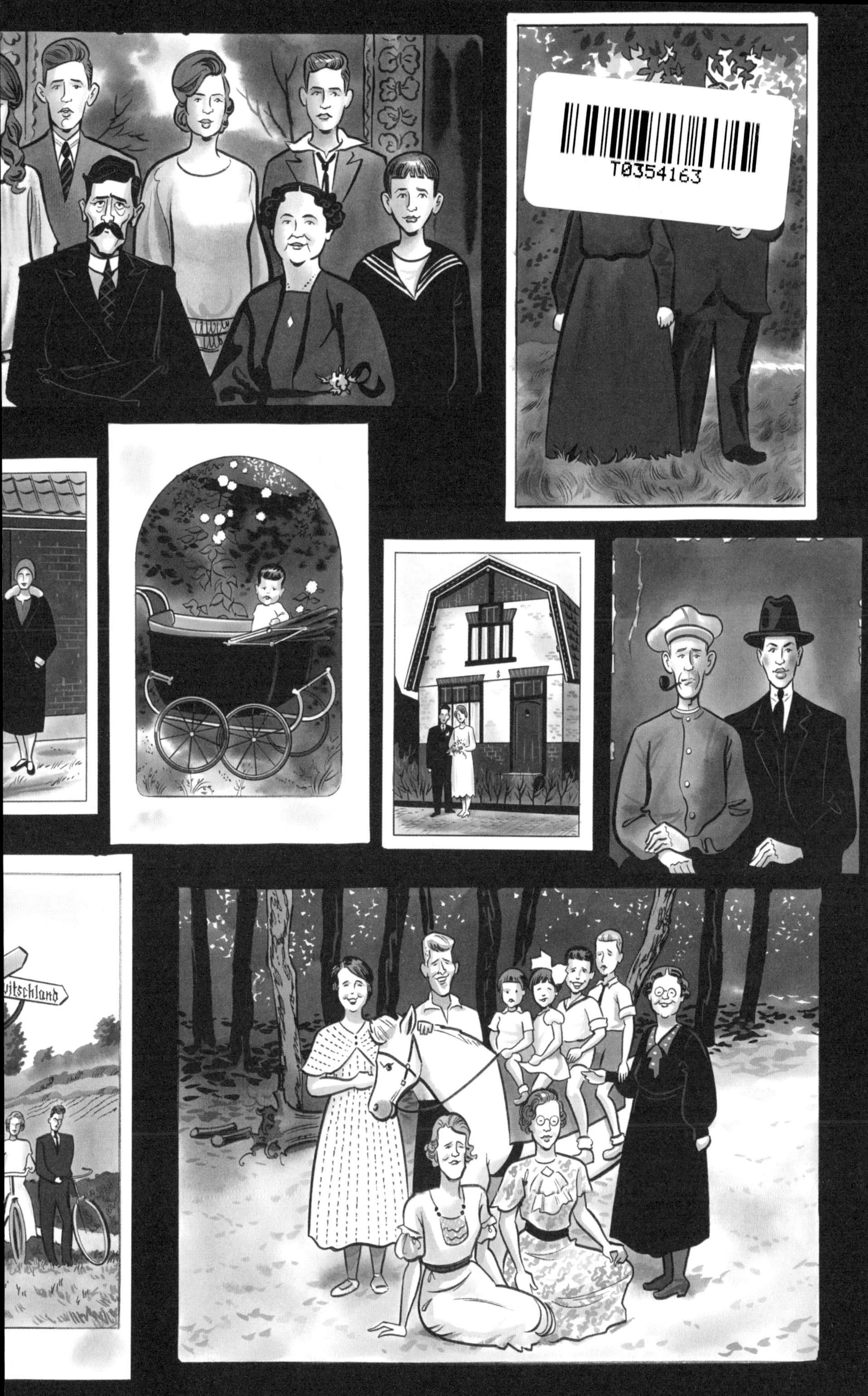

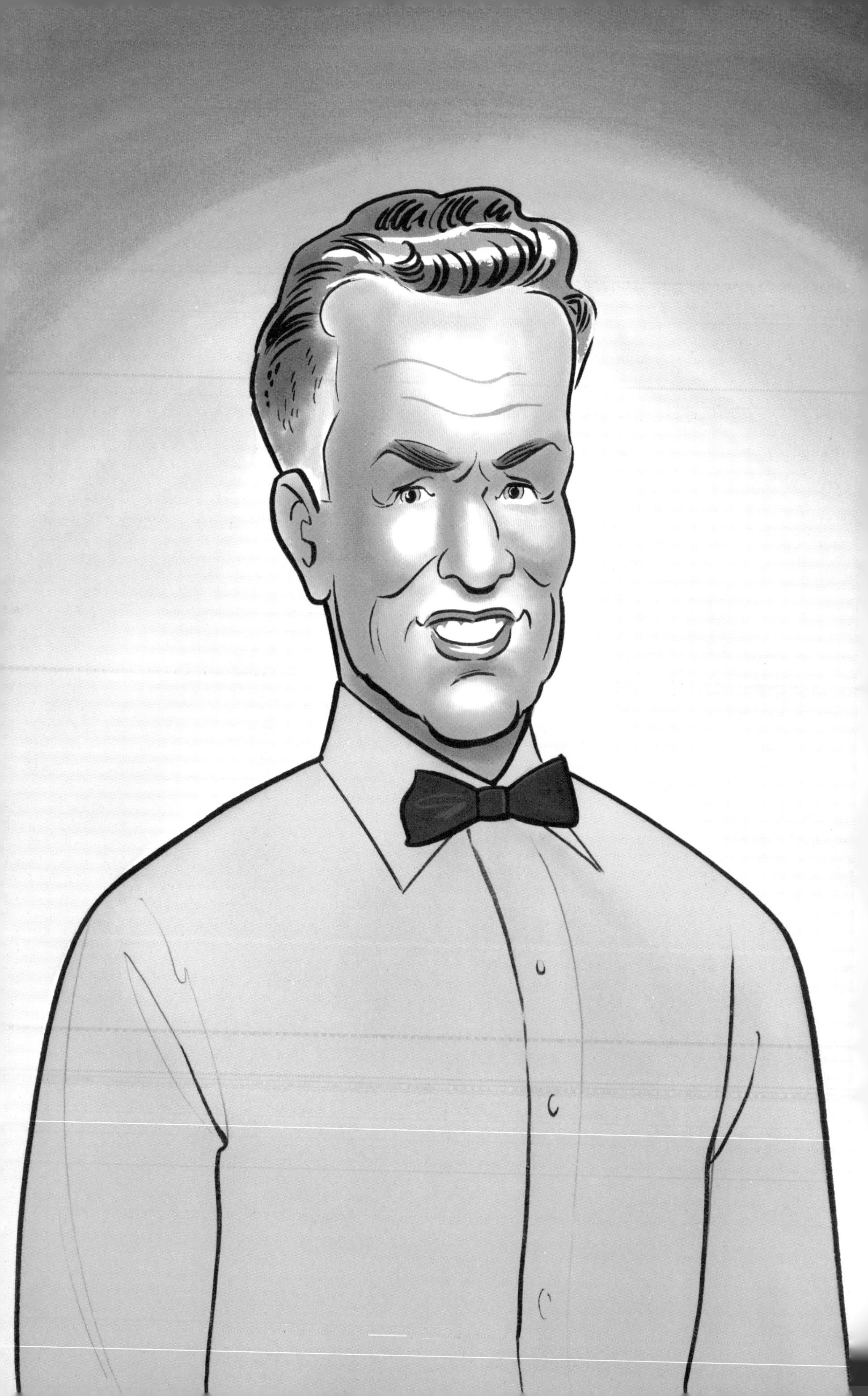

I'm So Glad We Had This Time Together

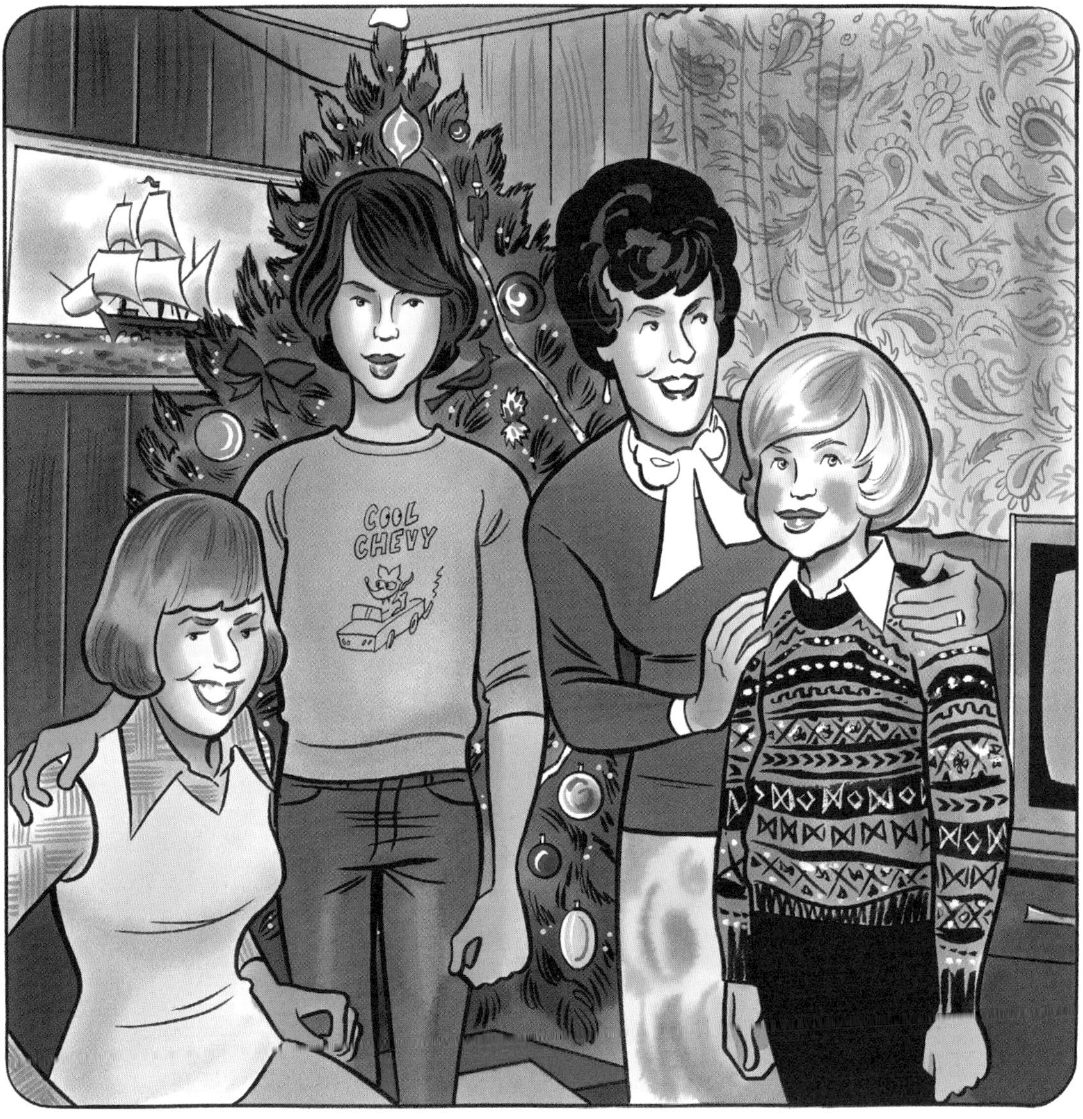
COOL CHEVY

A Memoir

I'm So Glad We Had Thi

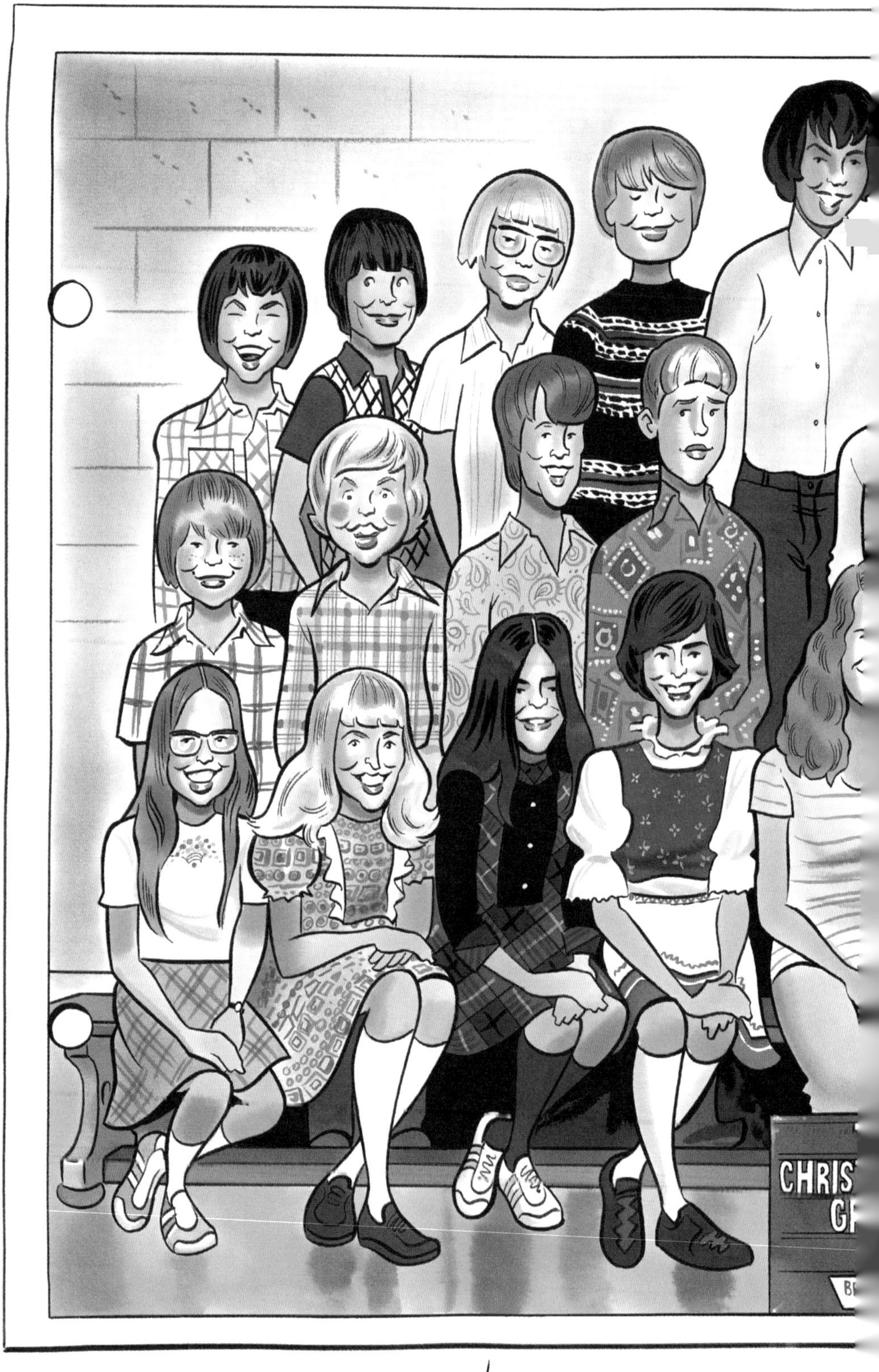

Maurice Vellekoop

Time Together: A Memoir

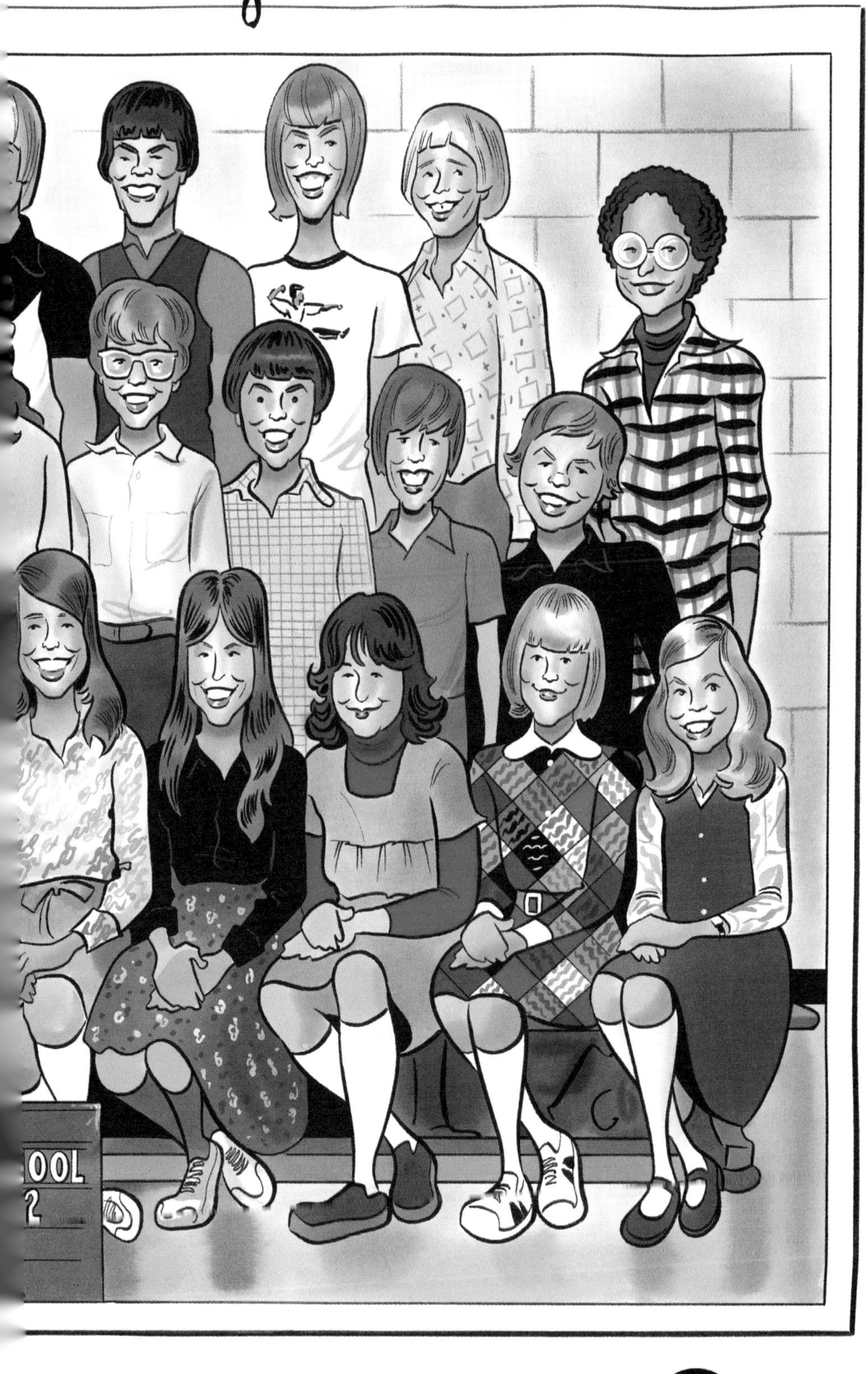

Pantheon Books, New York

All rights reserved. Published in the United States by Pantheon Books, a division of Penguin Random House LLC, New York.

Pantheon Books and colophon are registered trademarks of Penguin Random House LLC.

Grateful acknowledgment is made to Sony Music Publishing (US) LLC for permission to reprint lyrics from "I've Written a Letter to Daddy." © 1939 Colgems-EMI Music Inc. All rights administered by Sony Music Publishing (US) LLC, 424 Church Street, Suite 1200, Nashville, TN 37219. All rights reserved. Used by permission.

Library of Congress Cataloging-in-Publication Data
Name: Vellekoop, Maurice, author, illustrator.
Title: I'm so glad we had this time together / written and illustrated by Maurice Vellekoop.
Description: New York : Pantheon Books, 2024. Series: The Pantheon graphic library
Identifiers: LCCN 2023014393 (print) | LCCN 2023014394 (ebook) | ISBN 9780307908735 (hardcover) | ISBN 9780307908742 (ebook)
Subjects: LCSH: Vellekoop, Maurice. Gay cartoonists--Canada--Biography--Comic books, strips, etc. Cartoonists--Canada--Biography--Comic books, strips, etc. Self-realization--Comic books, strips, etc.
LCGFT: Coming-of-age comics. Gay comics. Autobiographies. Graphic novels.
Classification: LCC PN6733.V45 Z46 2024 (print) | LCC PN6733.V45 (ebook) | DDC 741.5/971 [B]--dc23/eng/20230410
LC record available at https://lccn.loc.gov/2023014393
LC ebook record available at https://lccn.loc.gov/2023014394

www.pantheonbooks.com

Jacket and case by Maurice Vellekoop with Reactor Art + Design

Printed in China
First Edition
10 9 8 7 6 5 4 3 2 1

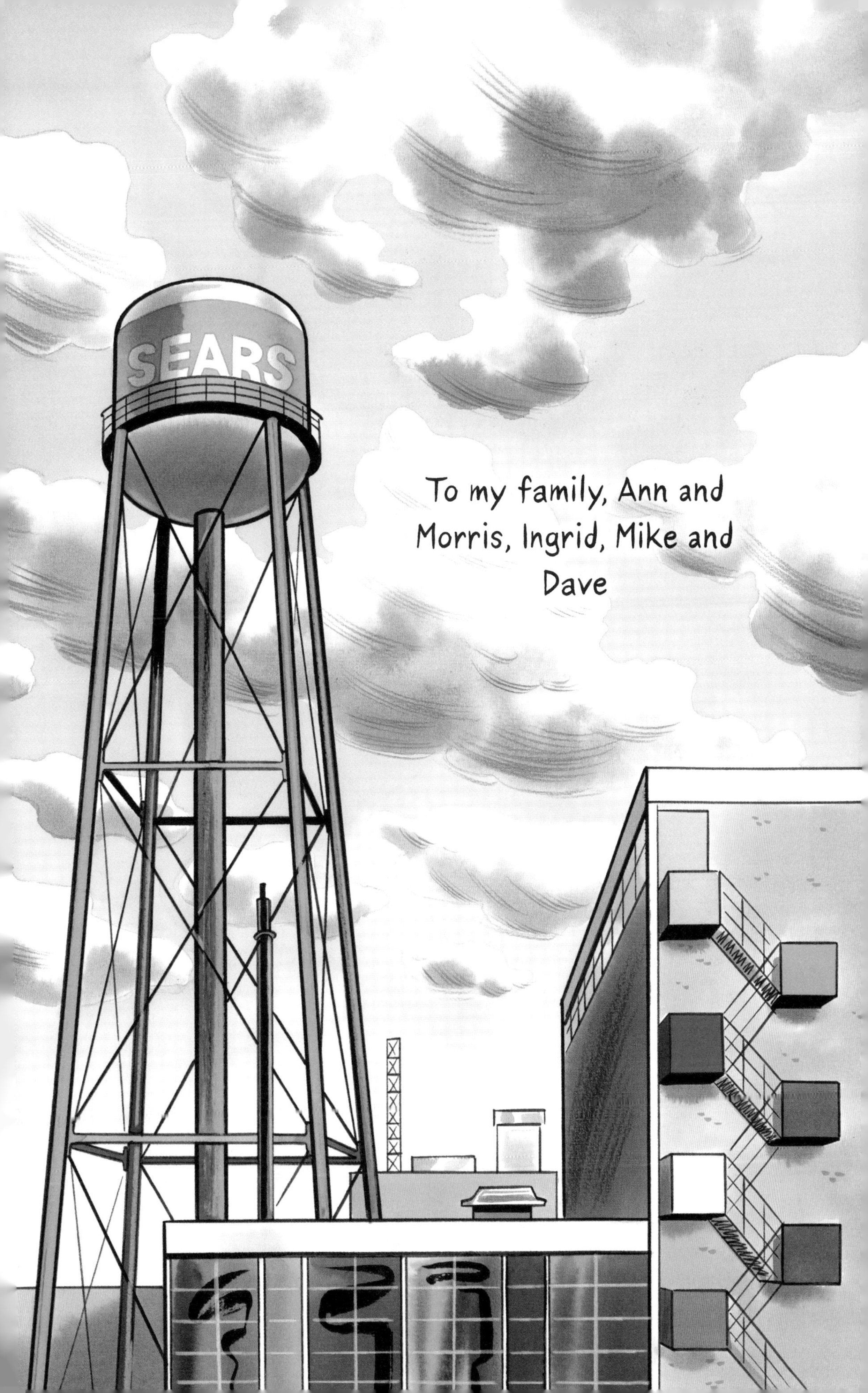
SEARS

To my family, Ann and Morris, Ingrid, Mike and Dave

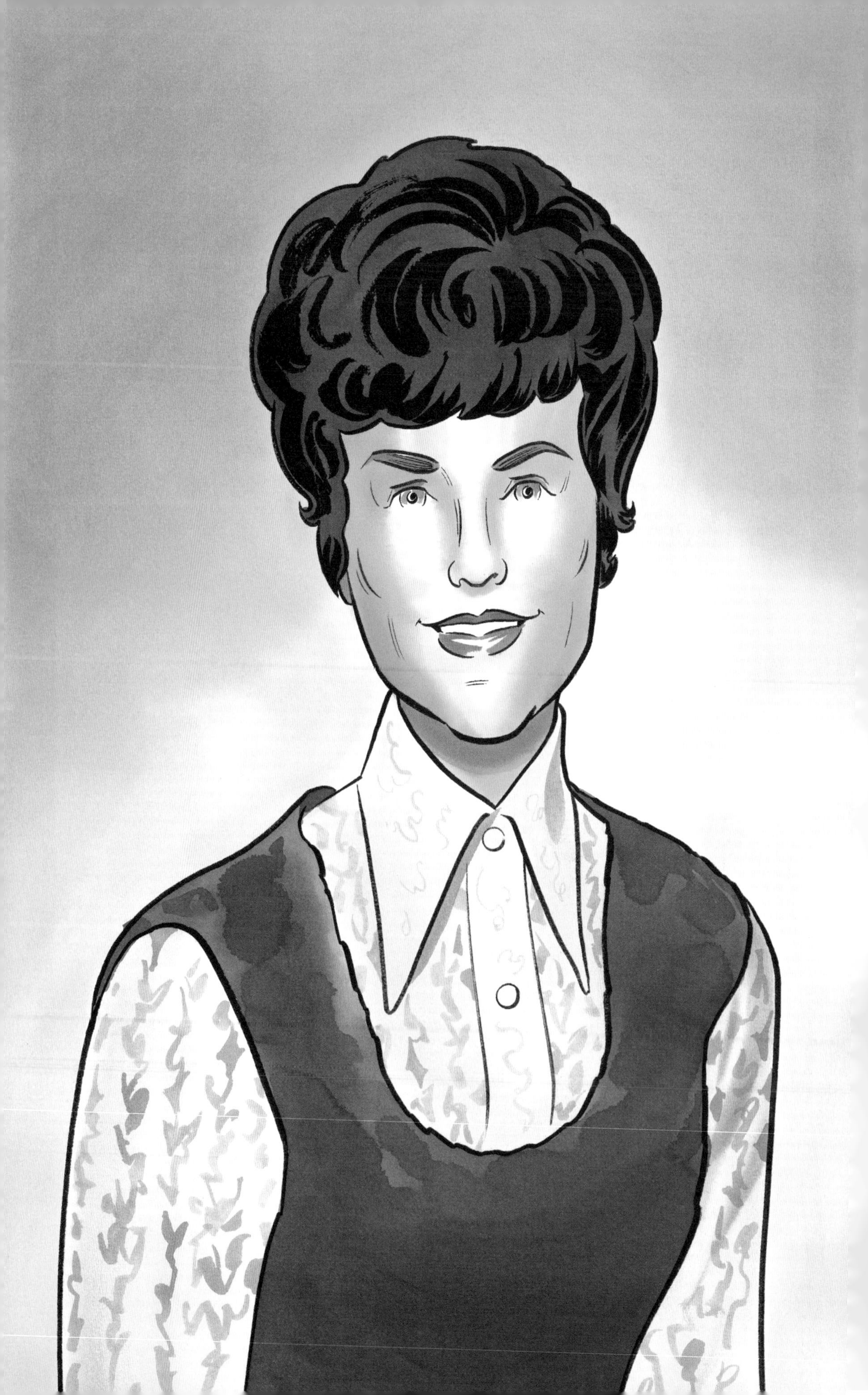

The untold want, by life and land ne'er granted,

Now, Voyager, sail thou forth to seek and find.

--Walt Whitman

Leaves of Grass

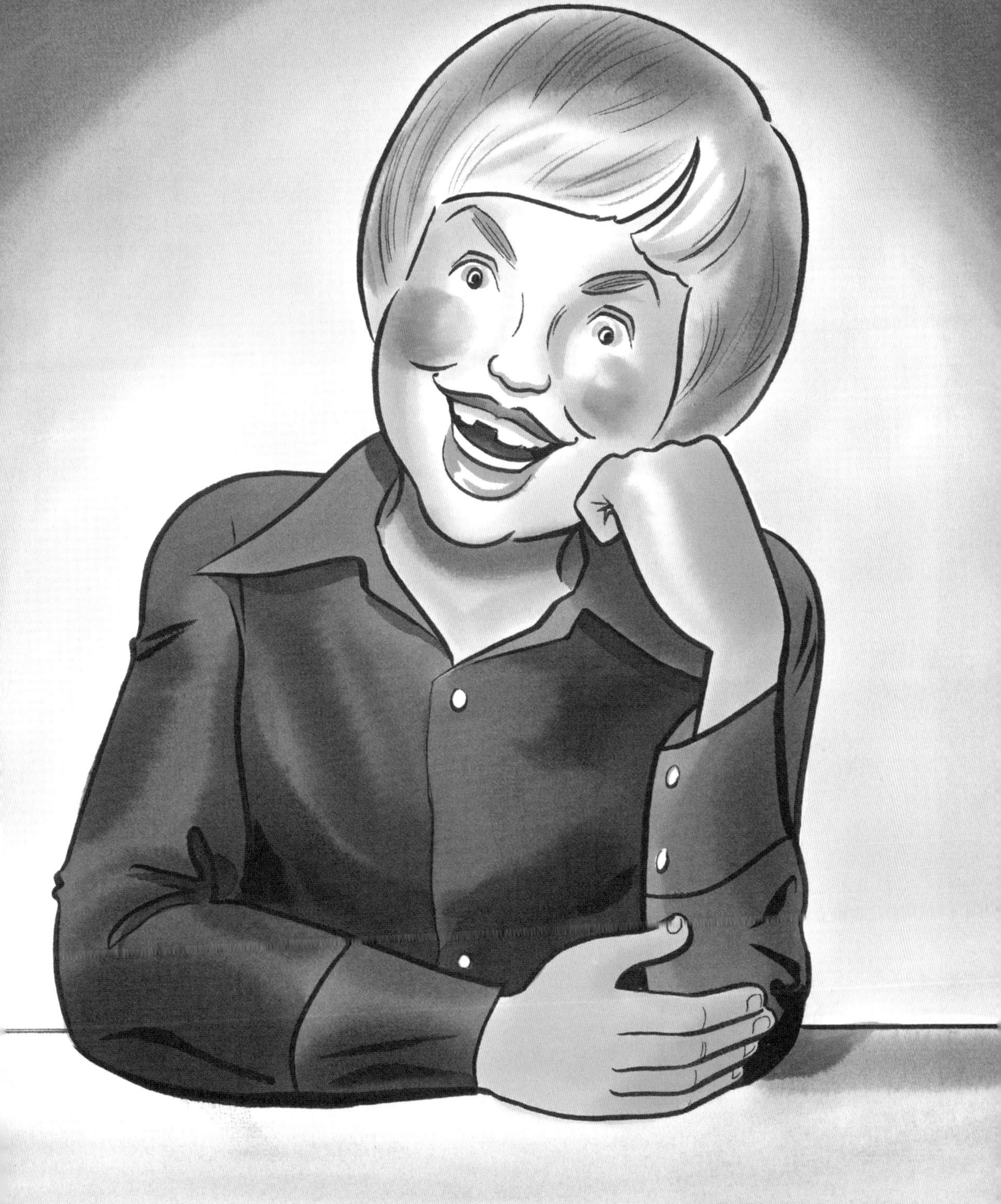

Contents

Part Three:
The Sleep

Part Four:
Wake Up!

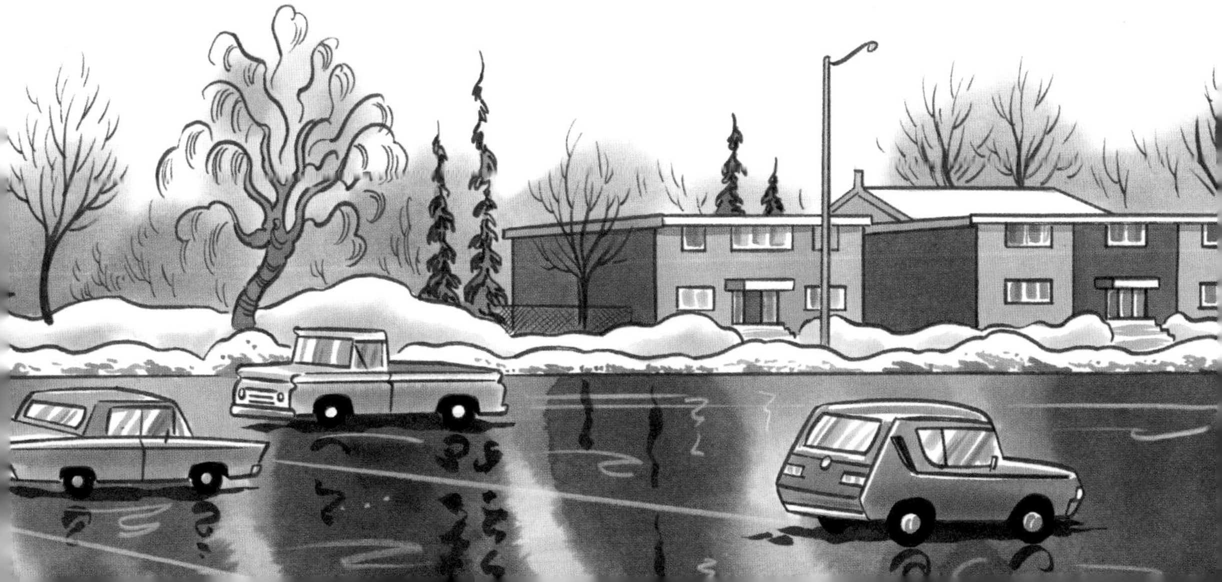

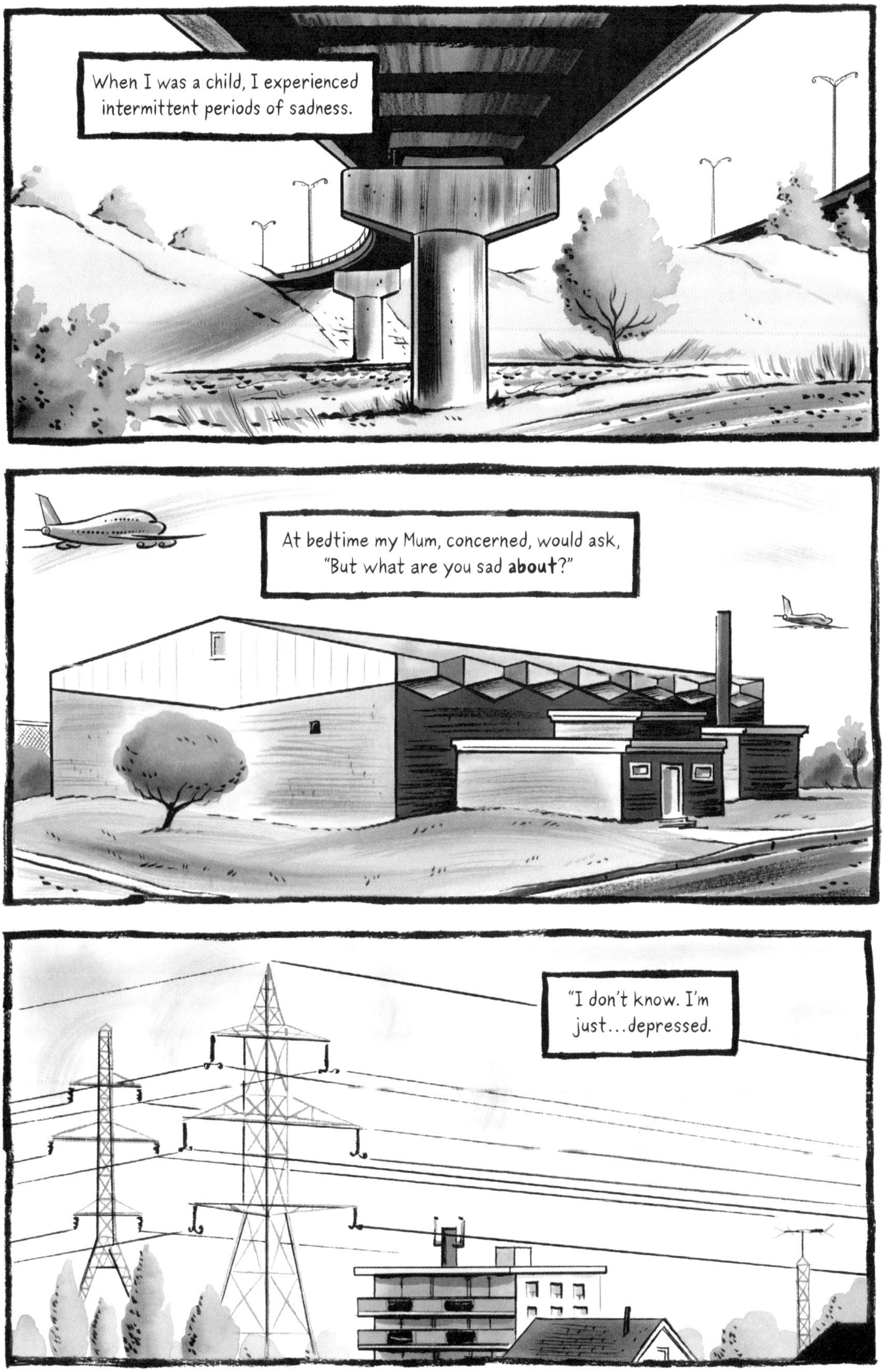
When I was a child, I experienced intermittent periods of sadness.
At bedtime my Mum, concerned, would ask, "But what are you sad **about**?"
"I don't know. I'm just…depressed.

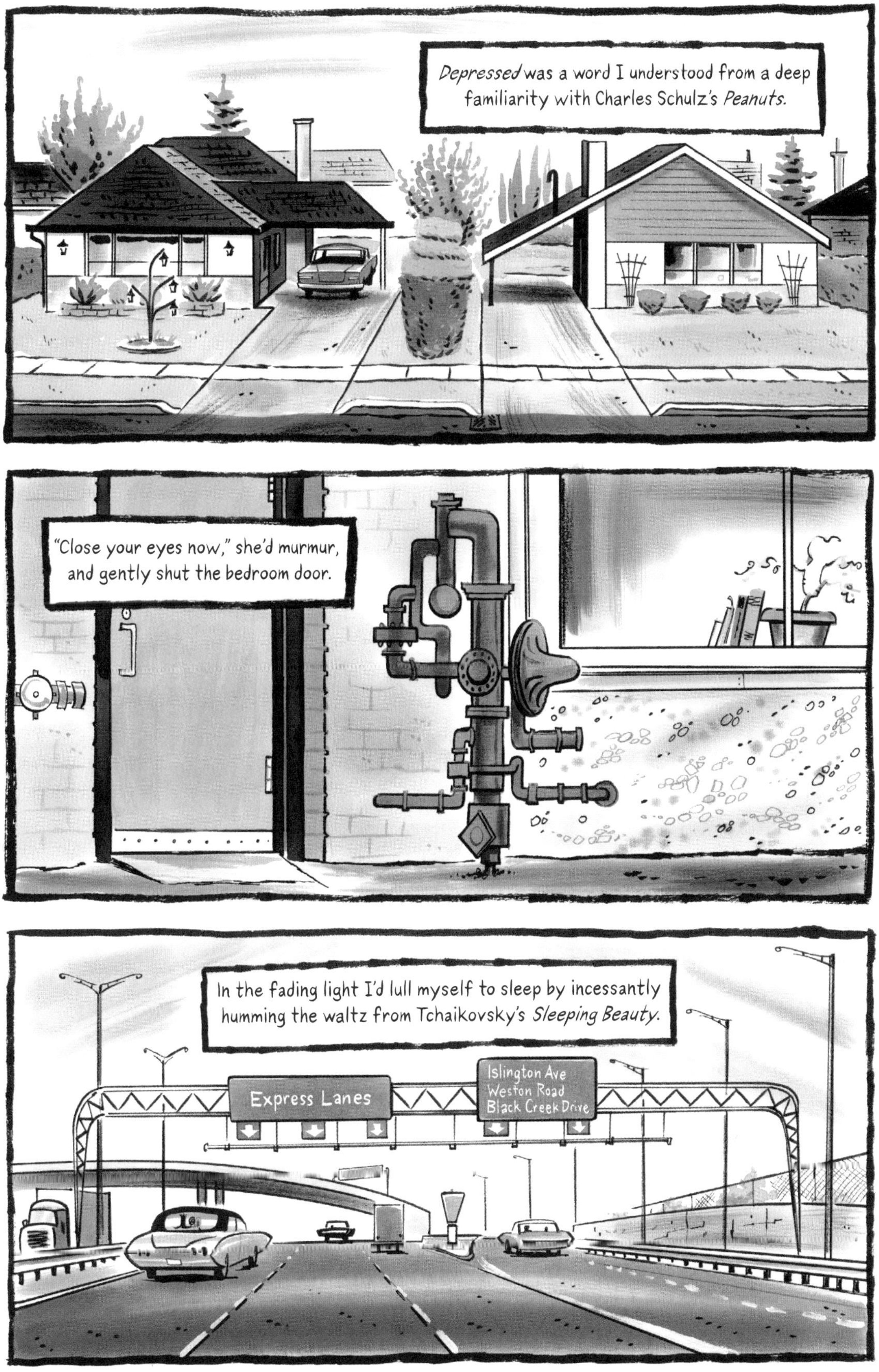
Depressed was a word I understood from a deep familiarity with Charles Schulz's *Peanuts.*
"Close your eyes now," she'd murmur, and gently shut the bedroom door.
In the fading light I'd lull myself to sleep by incessantly humming the waltz from Tchaikovsky's *Sleeping Beauty.*
Express Lanes
Islington Ave
Weston Road
Black Creek Drive

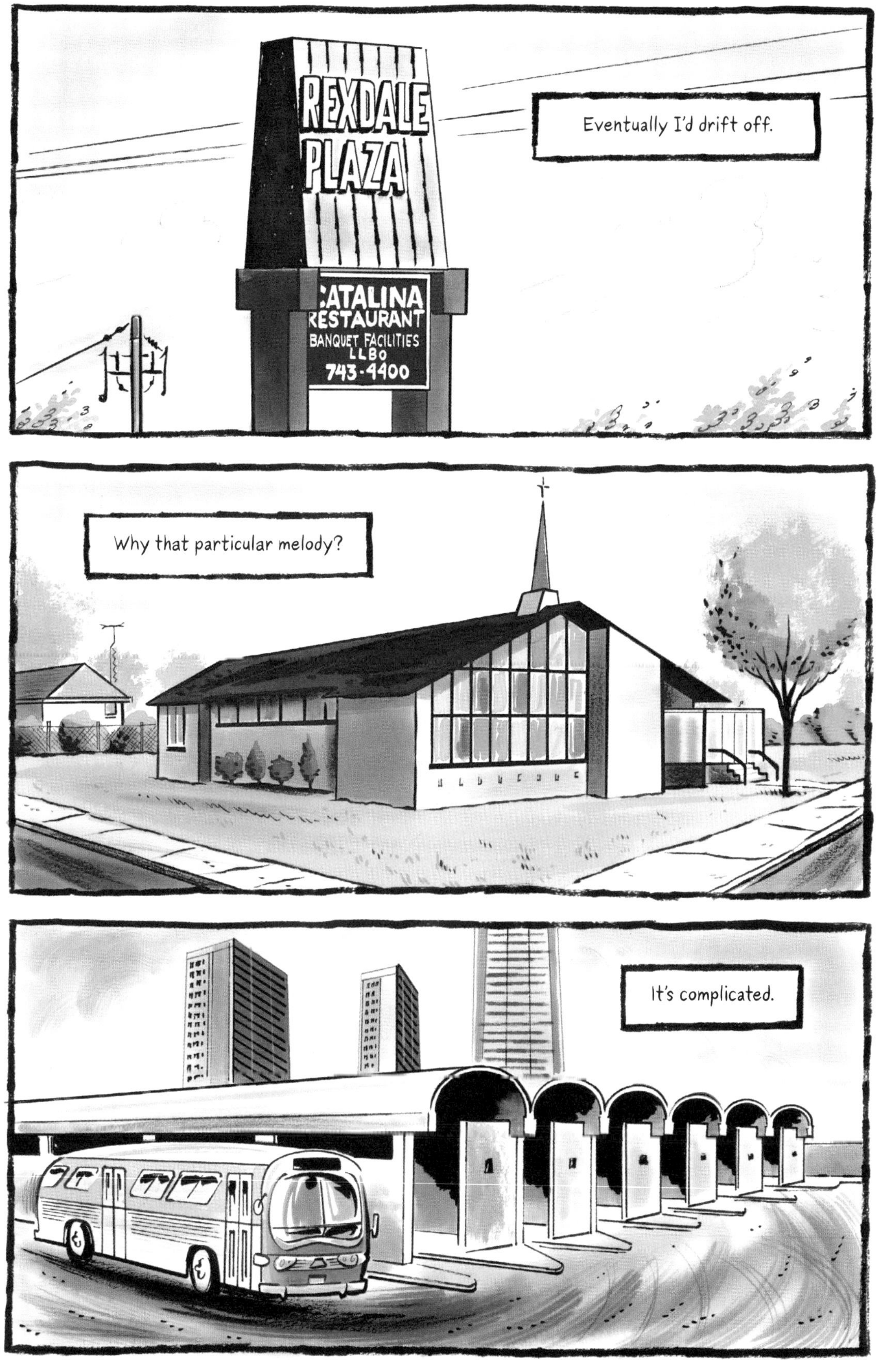
REXDALE PLAZA
CATALINA RESTAURANT
BANQUET FACILITIES
LLBO
743-4400
Eventually I'd drift off.
Why that particular melody?
It's complicated.

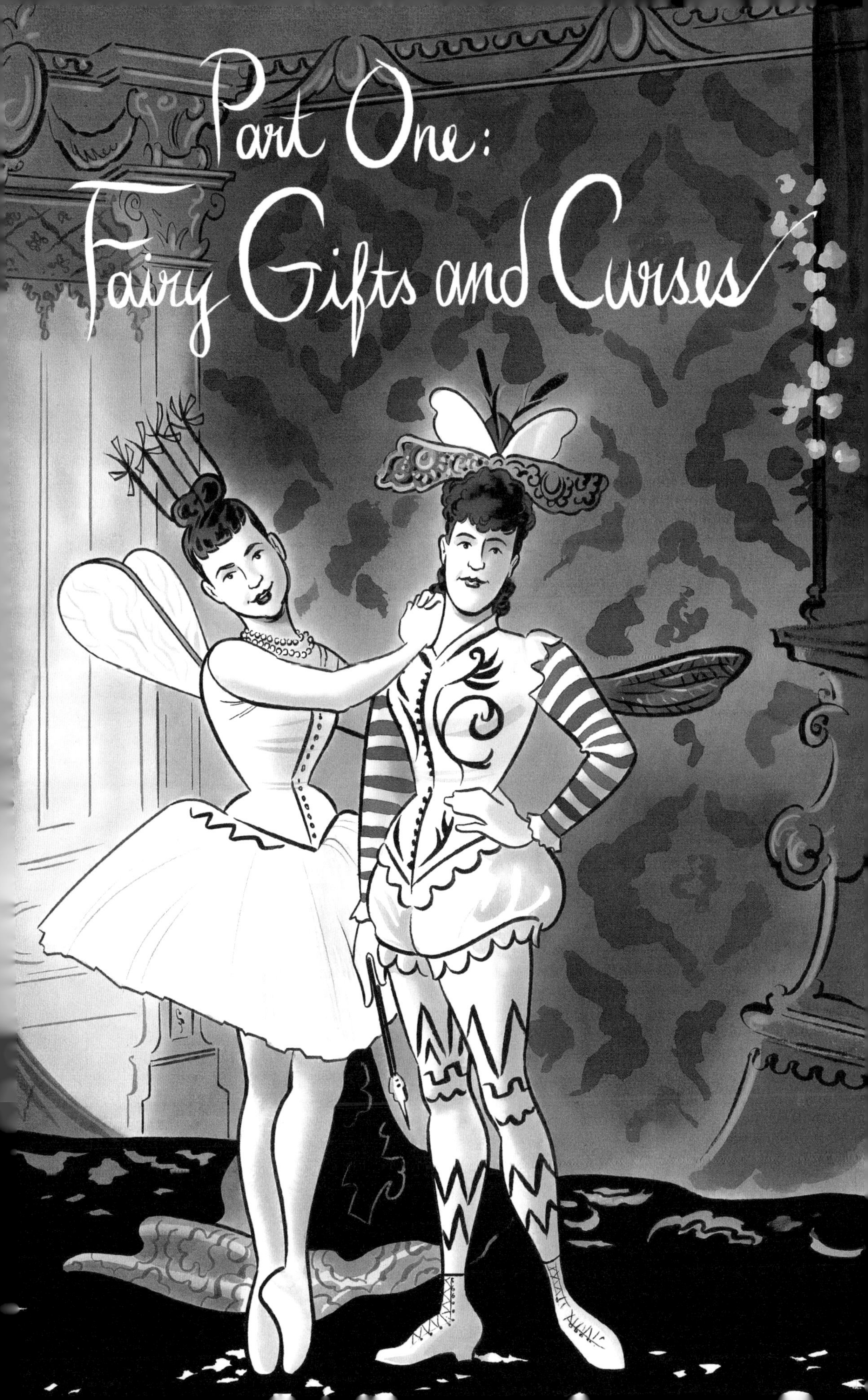
Part One:
Fairy Gifts and Curses

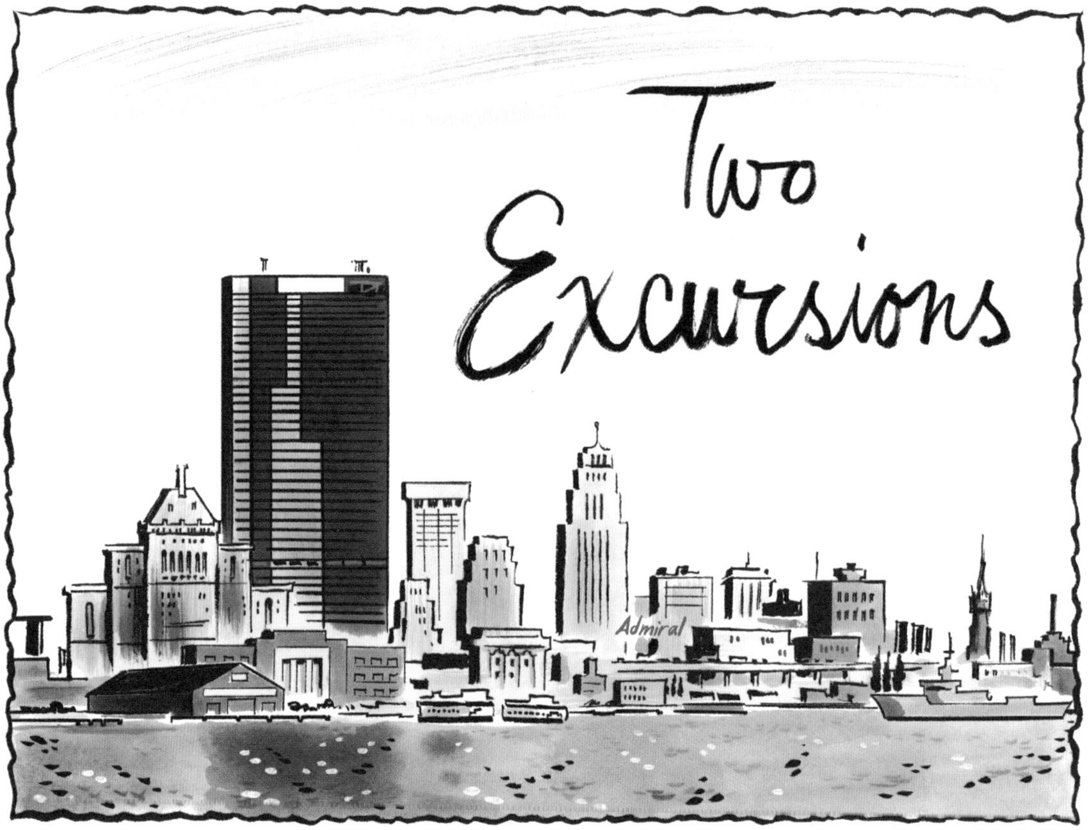
Two Excursions
Admiral

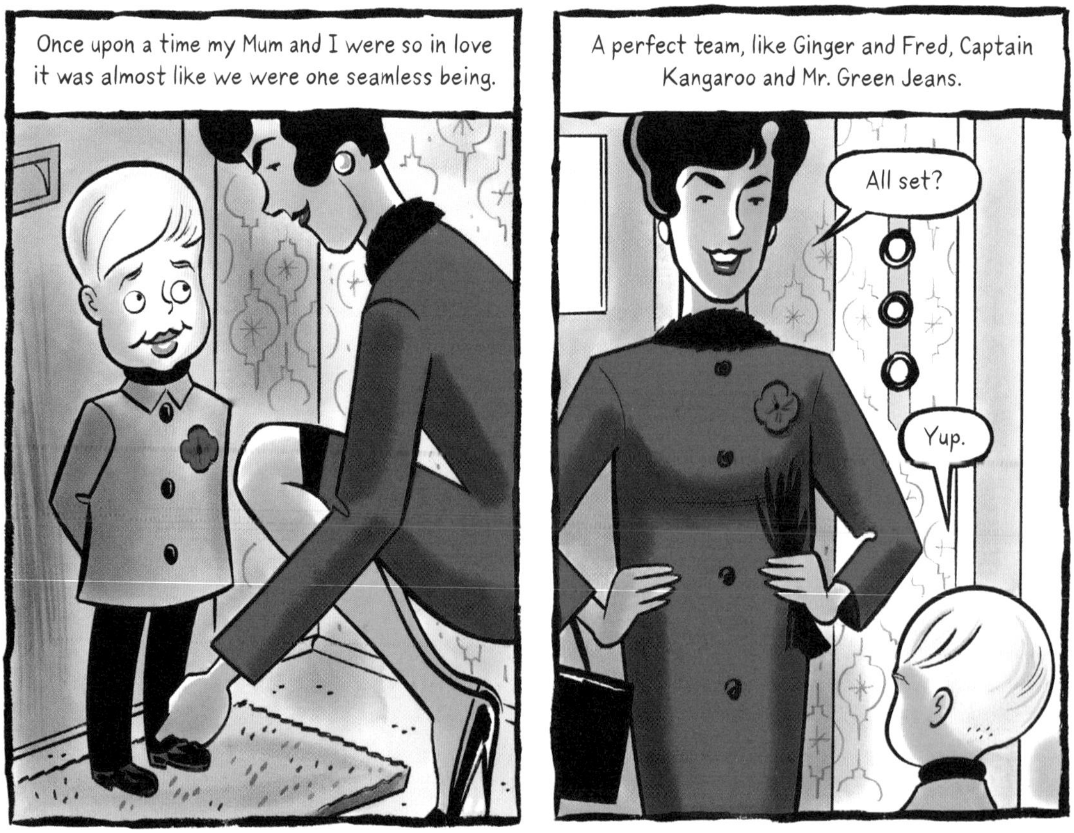
Once upon a time my Mum and I were so in love it was almost like we were one seamless being.
A perfect team, like Ginger and Fred, Captain Kangaroo and Mr. Green Jeans.
All set?
Yup.

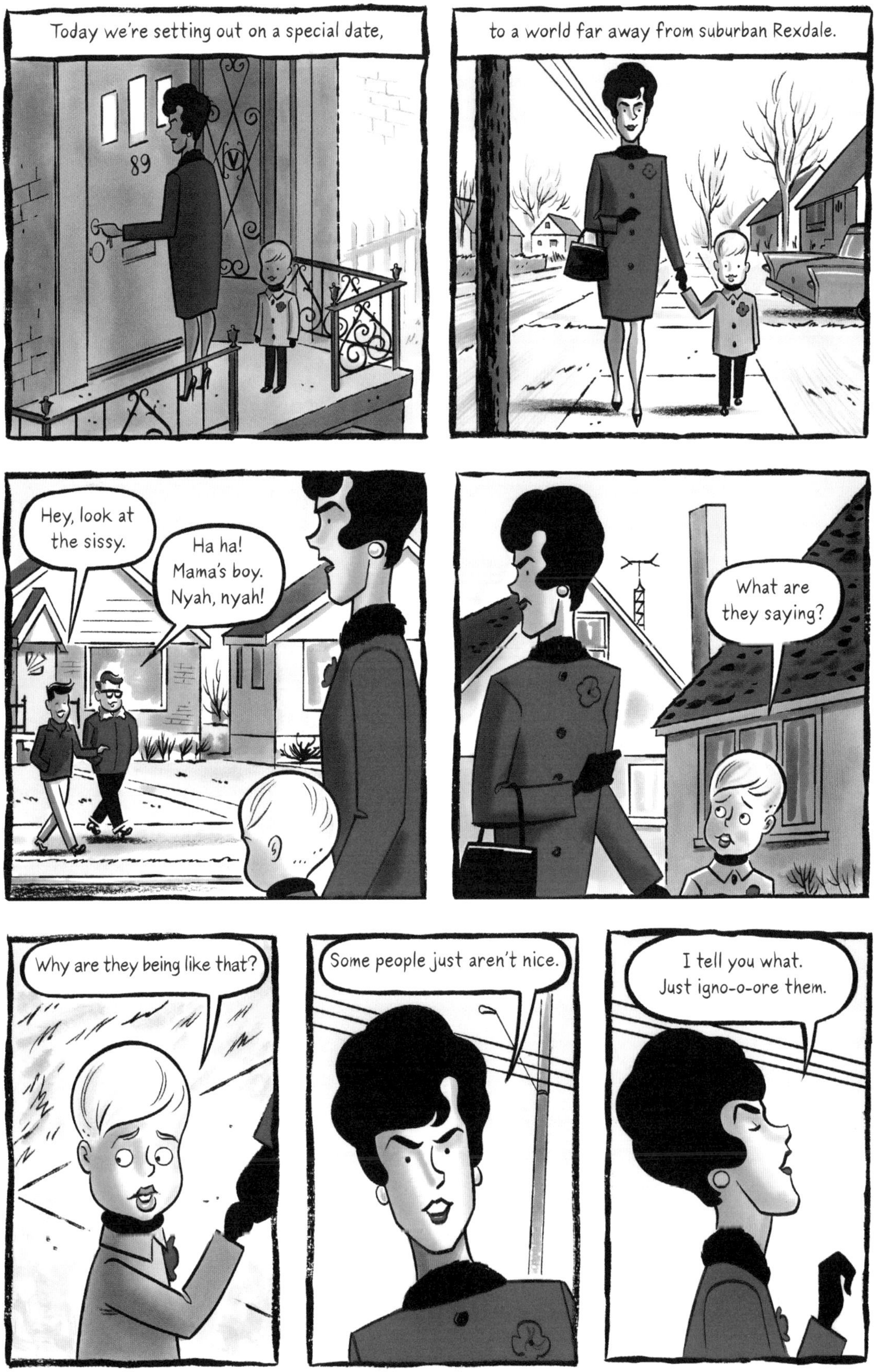
Today we're setting out on a special date,
to a world far away from suburban Rexdale.
89
Hey, look at the sissy.
Ha ha! Mama's boy. Nyah, nyah!
What are they saying?
Why are they being like that?
Some people just aren't nice.
I tell you what. Just igno-o-ore them.

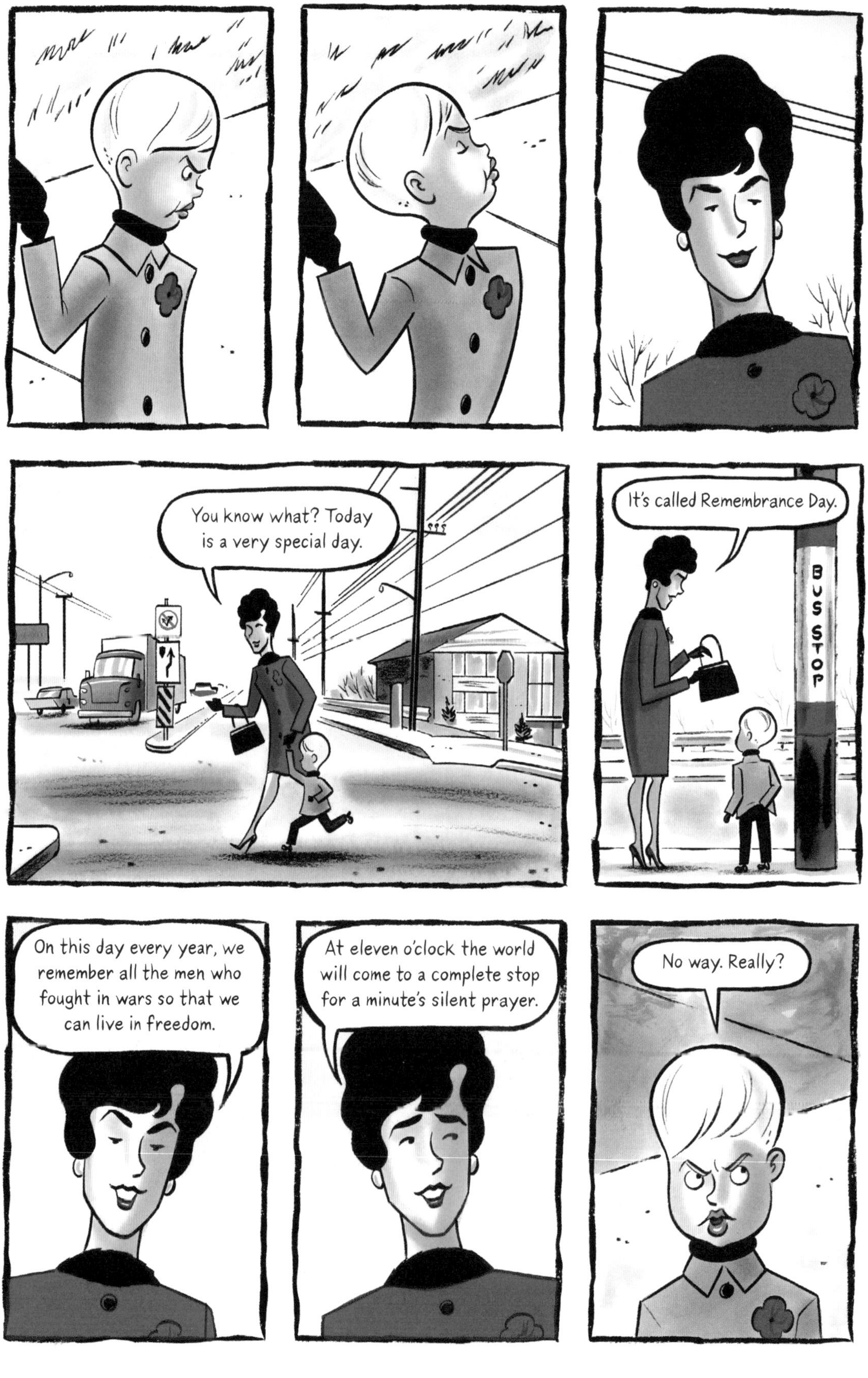
You know what? Today is a very special day.
It's called Remembrance Day.
BUS STOP
On this day every year, we remember all the men who fought in wars so that we can live in freedom.
At eleven o'clock the world will come to a complete stop for a minute's silent prayer.
No way. Really?

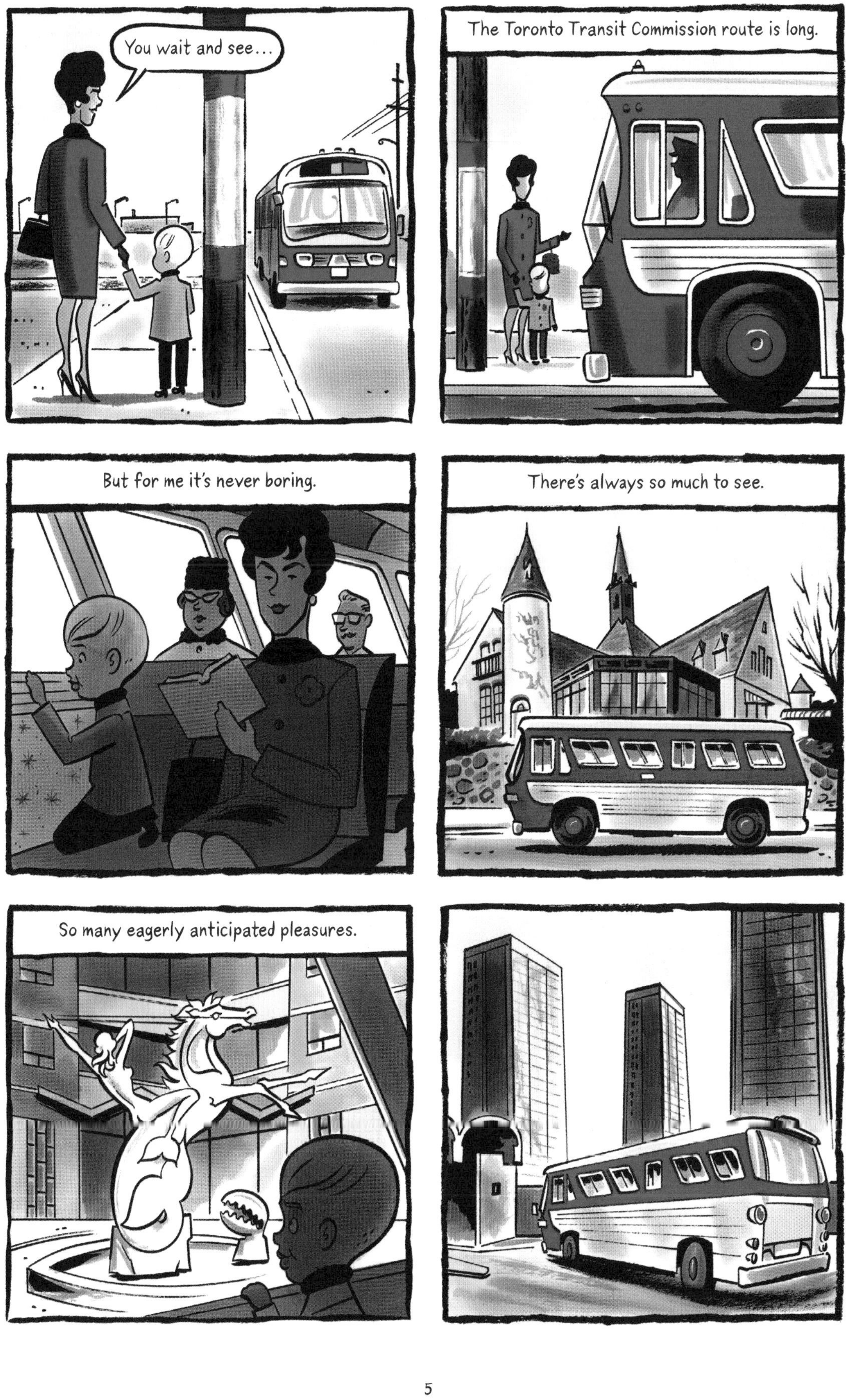
You wait and see...
The Toronto Transit Commission route is long.
But for me it's never boring.
There's always so much to see.
So many eagerly anticipated pleasures.

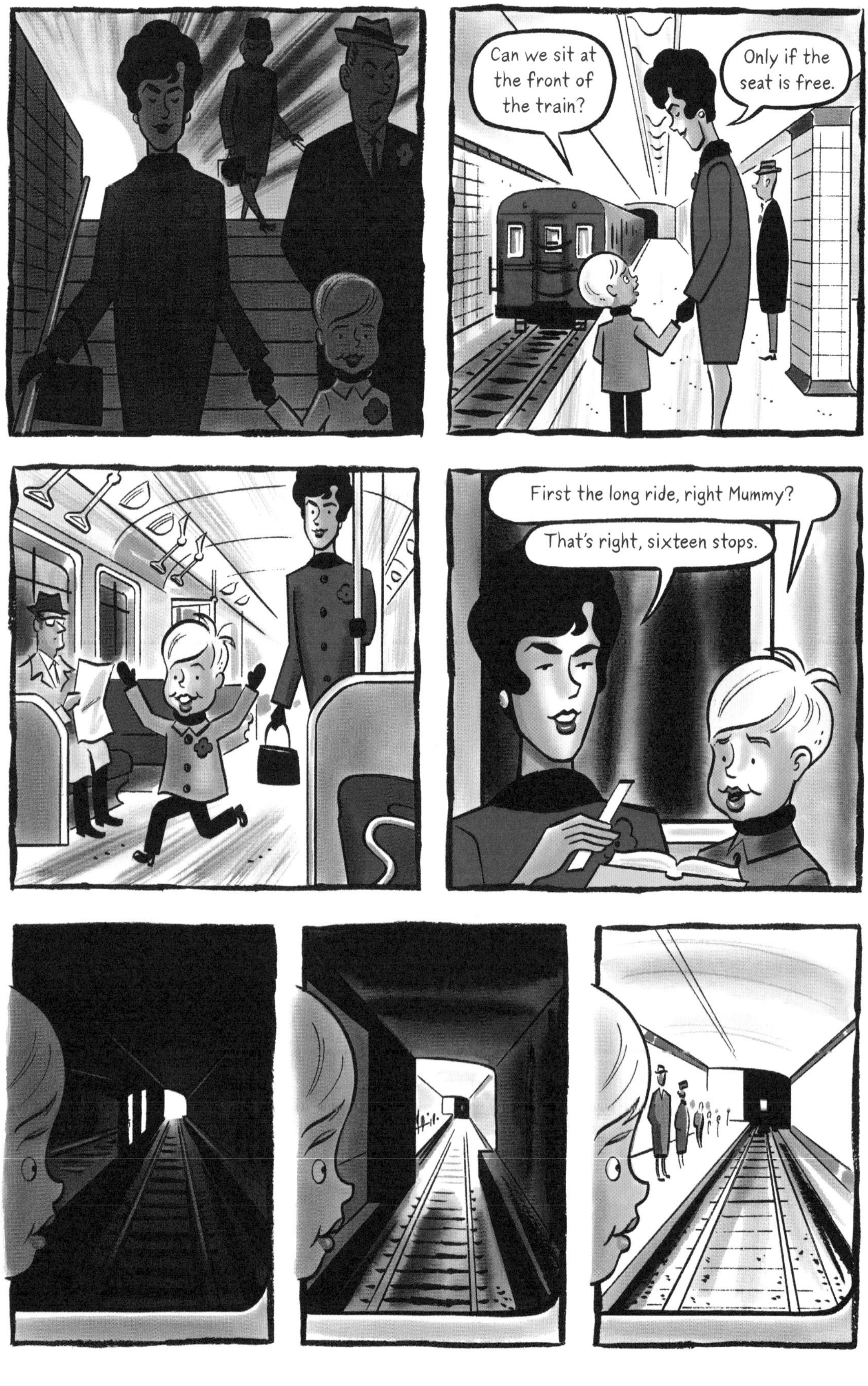
Can we sit at the front of the train?
Only if the seat is free.
First the long ride, right Mummy?
That's right, sixteen stops.

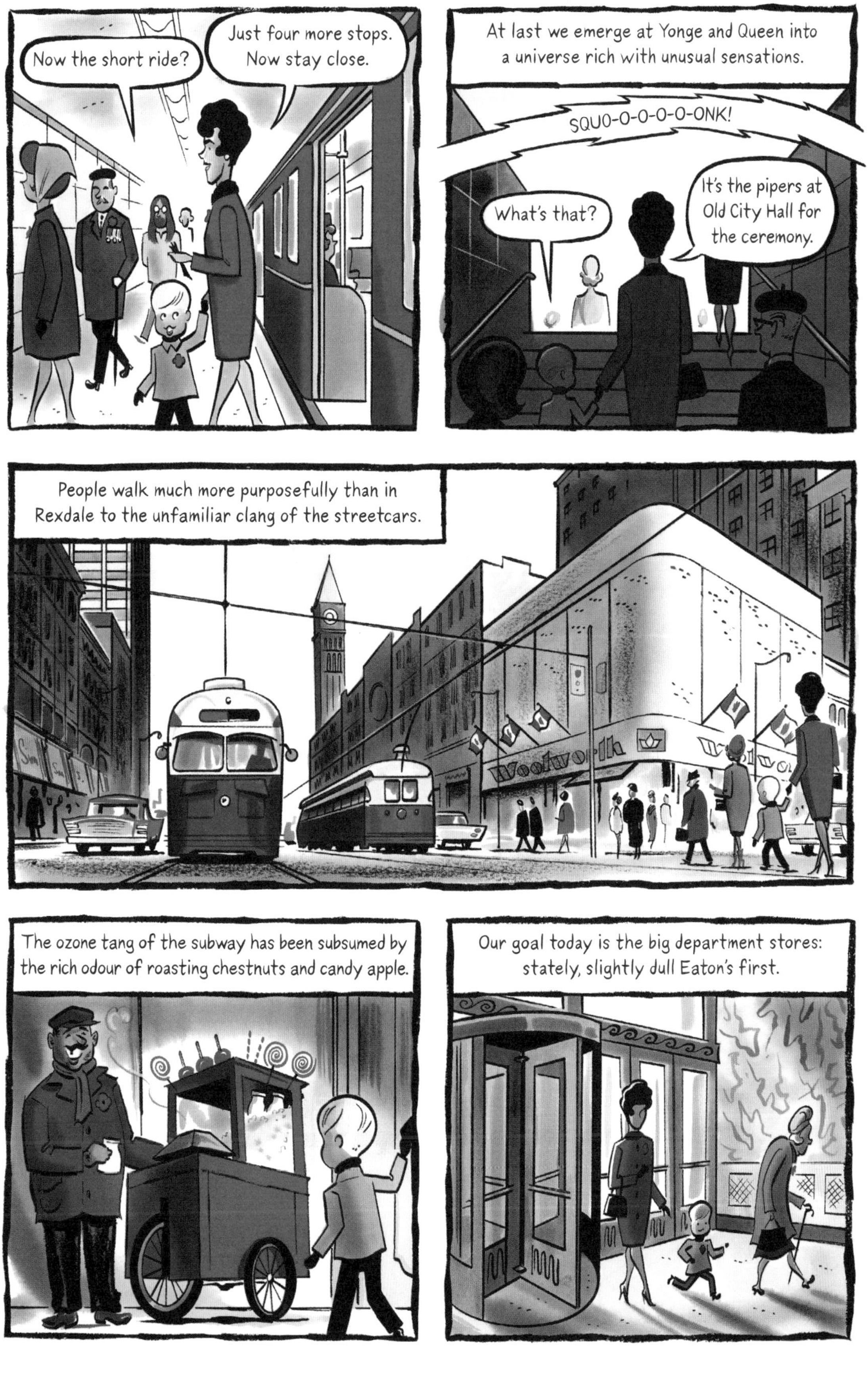

Now the short ride?
Just four more stops. Now stay close.
At last we emerge at Yonge and Queen into a universe rich with unusual sensations.
SQUO-O-O-O-O-ONK!
What's that?
It's the pipers at Old City Hall for the ceremony.
People walk much more purposefully than in Rexdale to the unfamiliar clang of the streetcars.
Woolworth
The ozone tang of the subway has been subsumed by the rich odour of roasting chestnuts and candy apple.
Our goal today is the big department stores: stately, slightly dull Eaton's first.

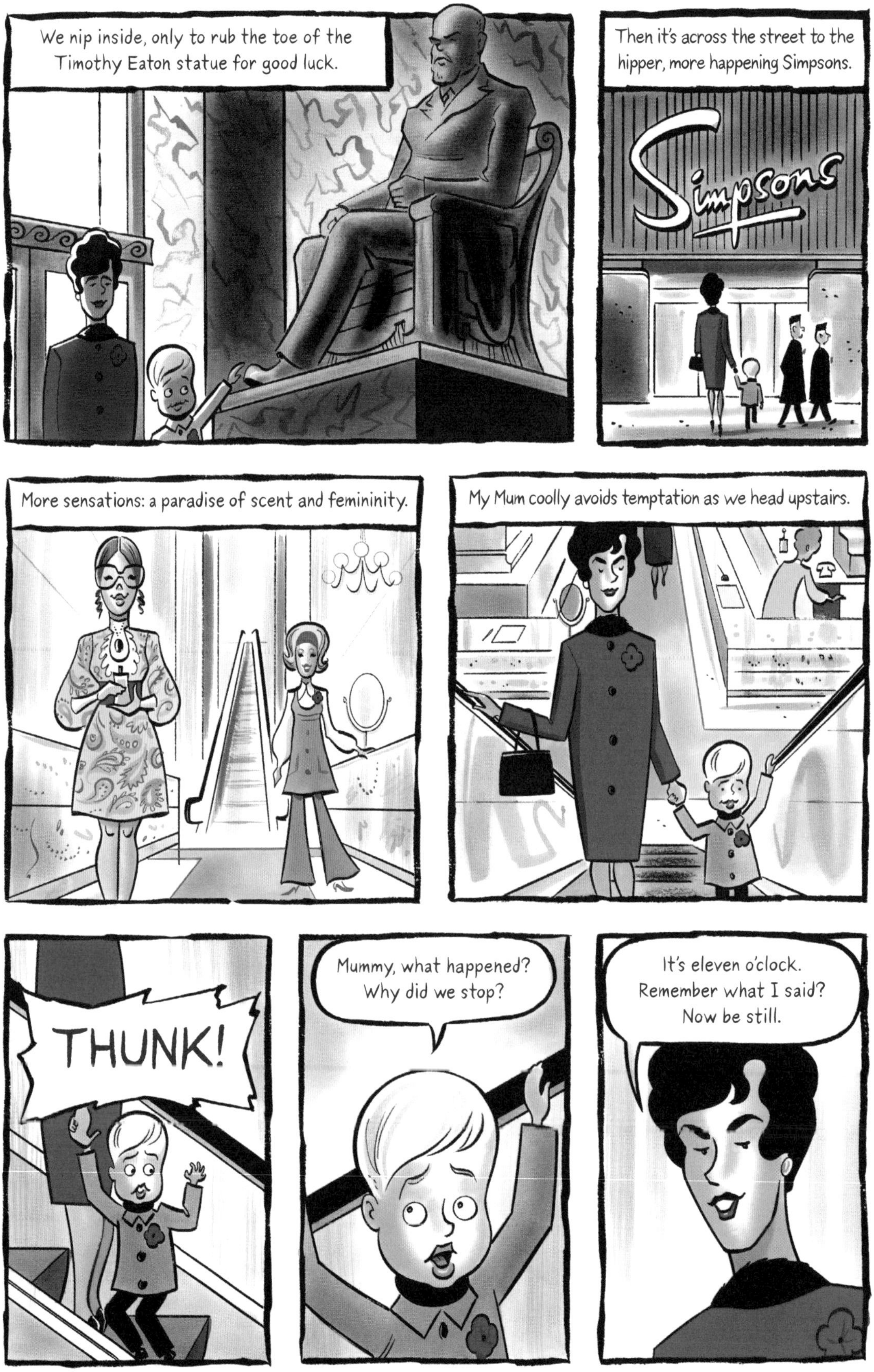
We nip inside, only to rub the toe of the Timothy Eaton statue for good luck.
Then it's across the street to the hipper, more happening Simpsons.
Simpsons
More sensations: a paradise of scent and femininity.
My Mum coolly avoids temptation as we head upstairs.
THUNK!
Mummy, what happened? Why did we stop?
It's eleven o'clock. Remember what I said? Now be still.

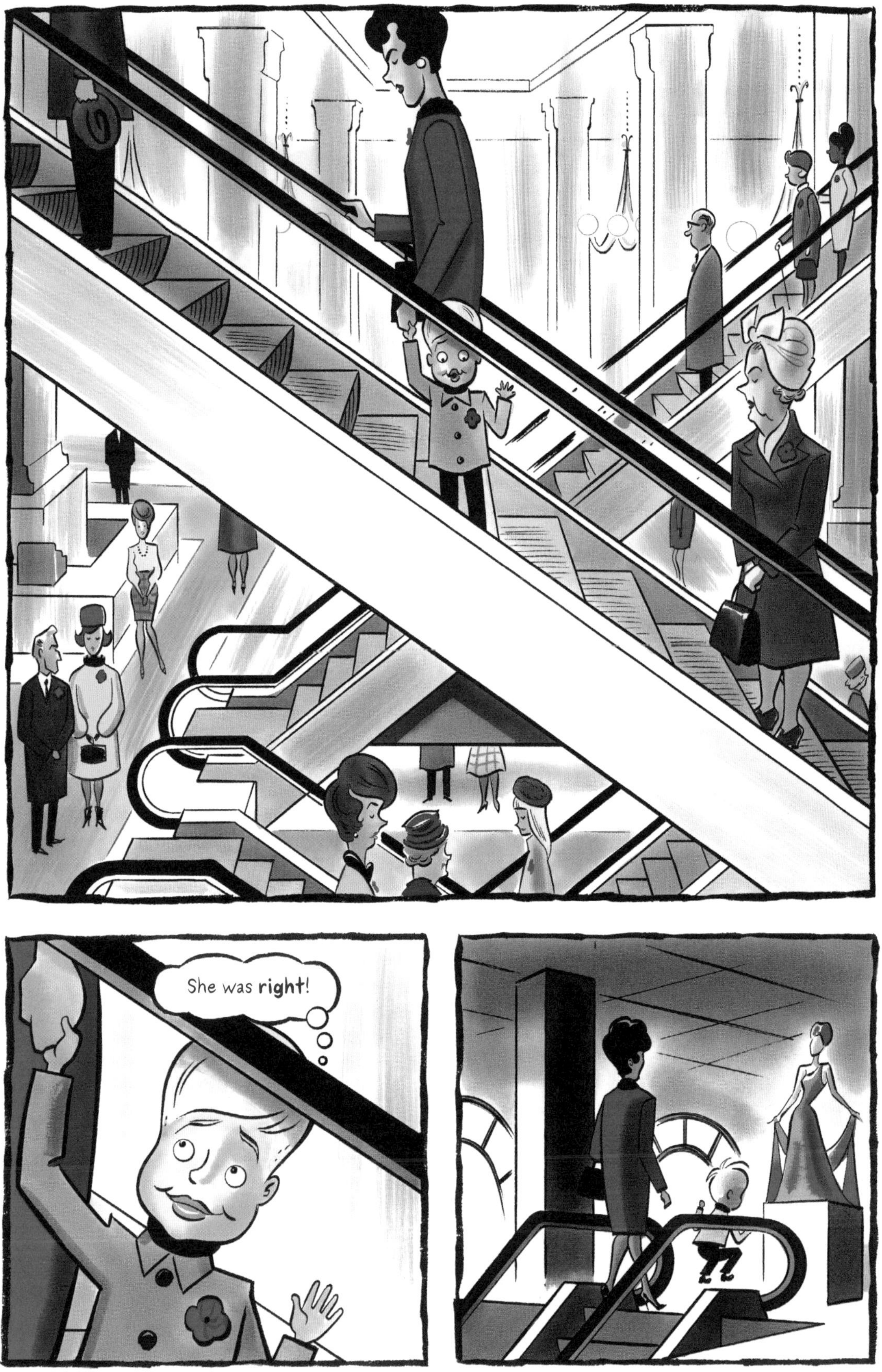
She was **right**!

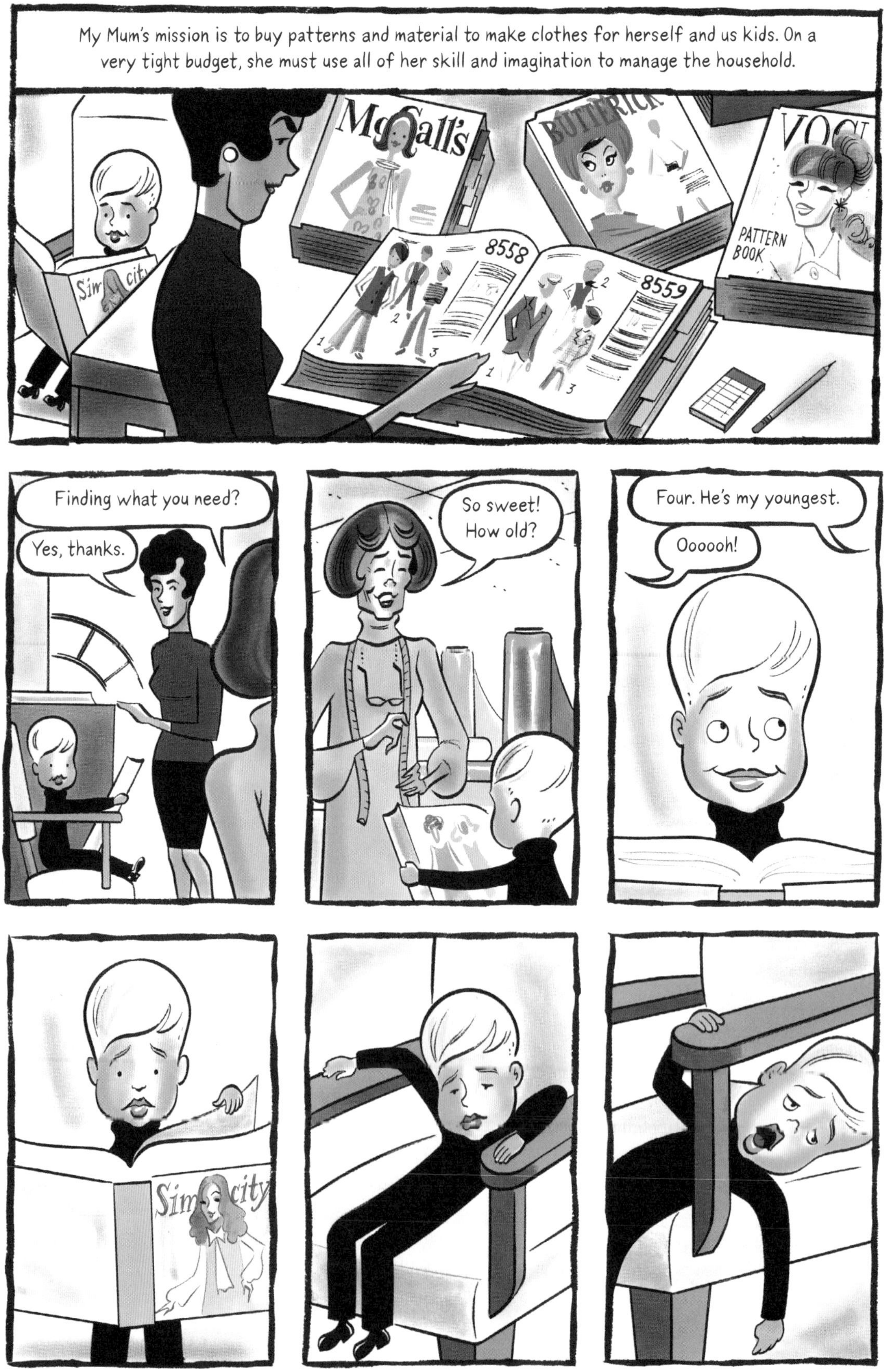

My Mum's mission is to buy patterns and material to make clothes for herself and us kids. On a very tight budget, she must use all of her skill and imagination to manage the household.
McCall's
BUTTERICK
VOGUE
PATTERN BOOK
8558
8559
Simplicity
Finding what you need?
Yes, thanks.
So sweet! How old?
Four. He's my youngest.
Oooooh!
Simplicity

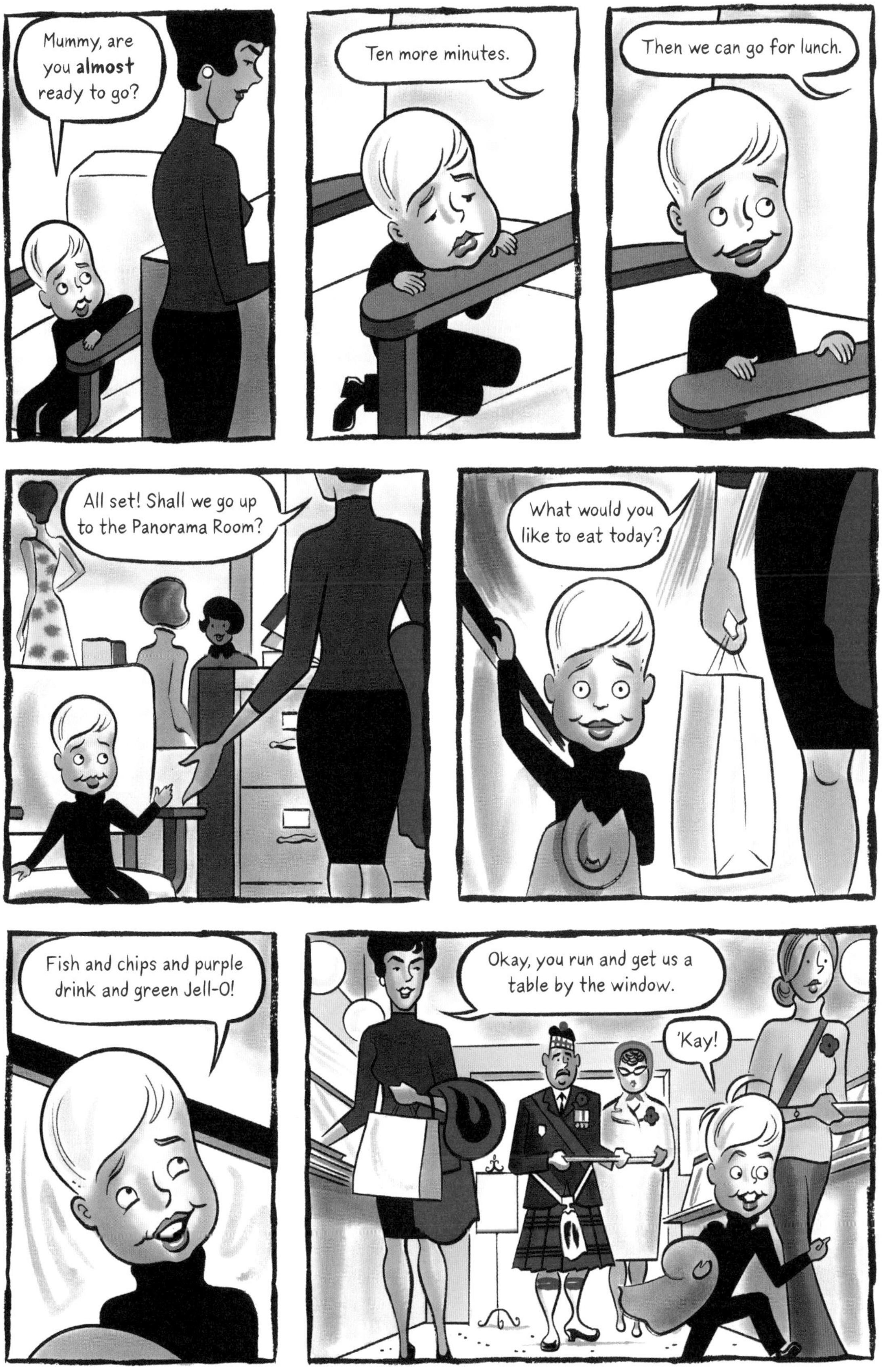
Mummy, are you **almost** ready to go?
Ten more minutes.
Then we can go for lunch.
All set! Shall we go up to the Panorama Room?
What would you like to eat today?
Fish and chips and purple drink and green Jell-O!
Okay, you run and get us a table by the window.
'Kay!

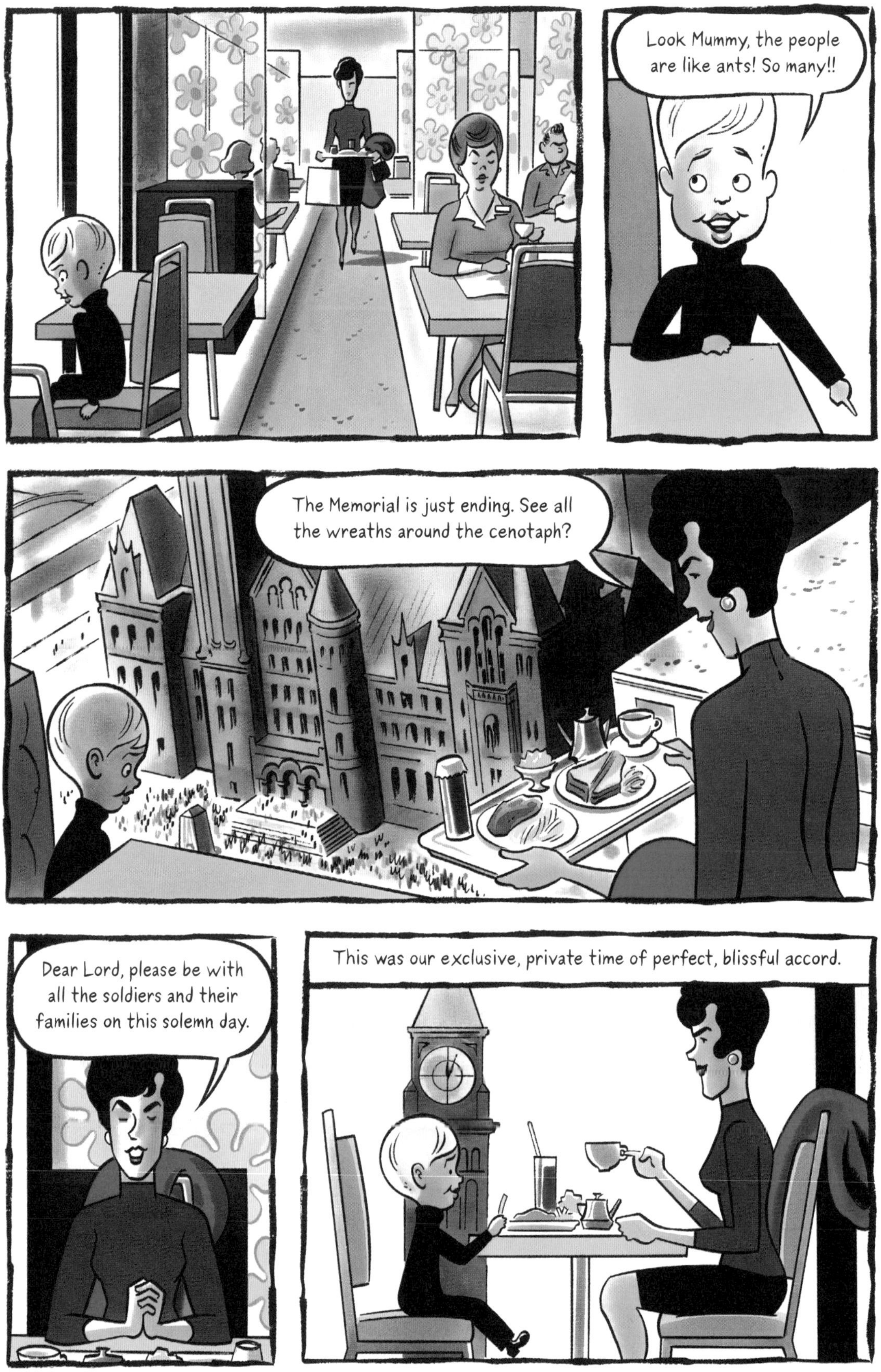
Look Mummy, the people are like ants! So many!!
The Memorial is just ending. See all the wreaths around the cenotaph?
Dear Lord, please be with all the soldiers and their families on this solemn day.
This was our exclusive, private time of perfect, blissful accord.

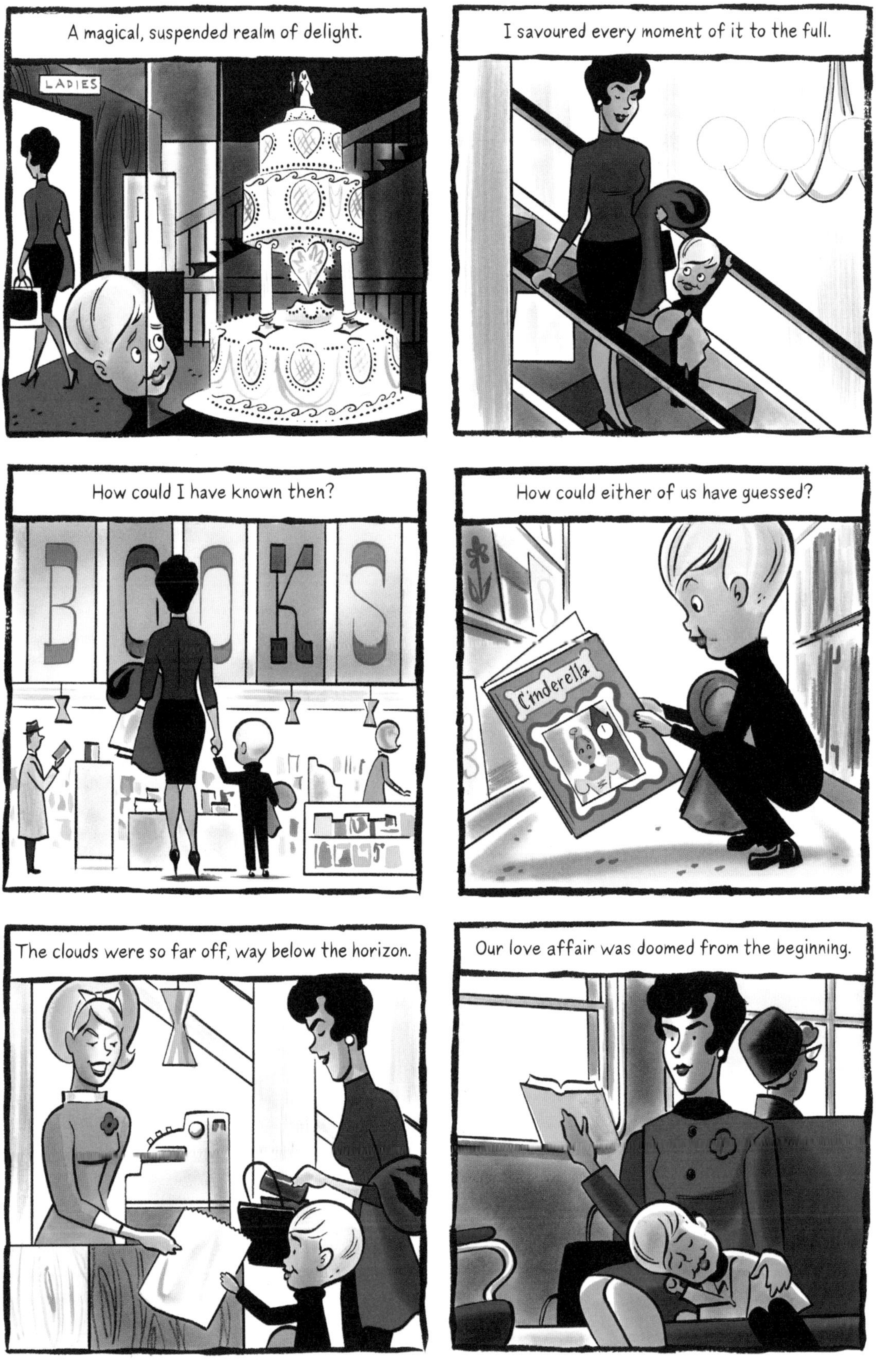
A magical, suspended realm of delight.
LADIES
I savoured every moment of it to the full.
How could I have known then?
BOOKS
How could either of us have guessed?
Cinderella
The clouds were so far off, way below the horizon.
Our love affair was doomed from the beginning.

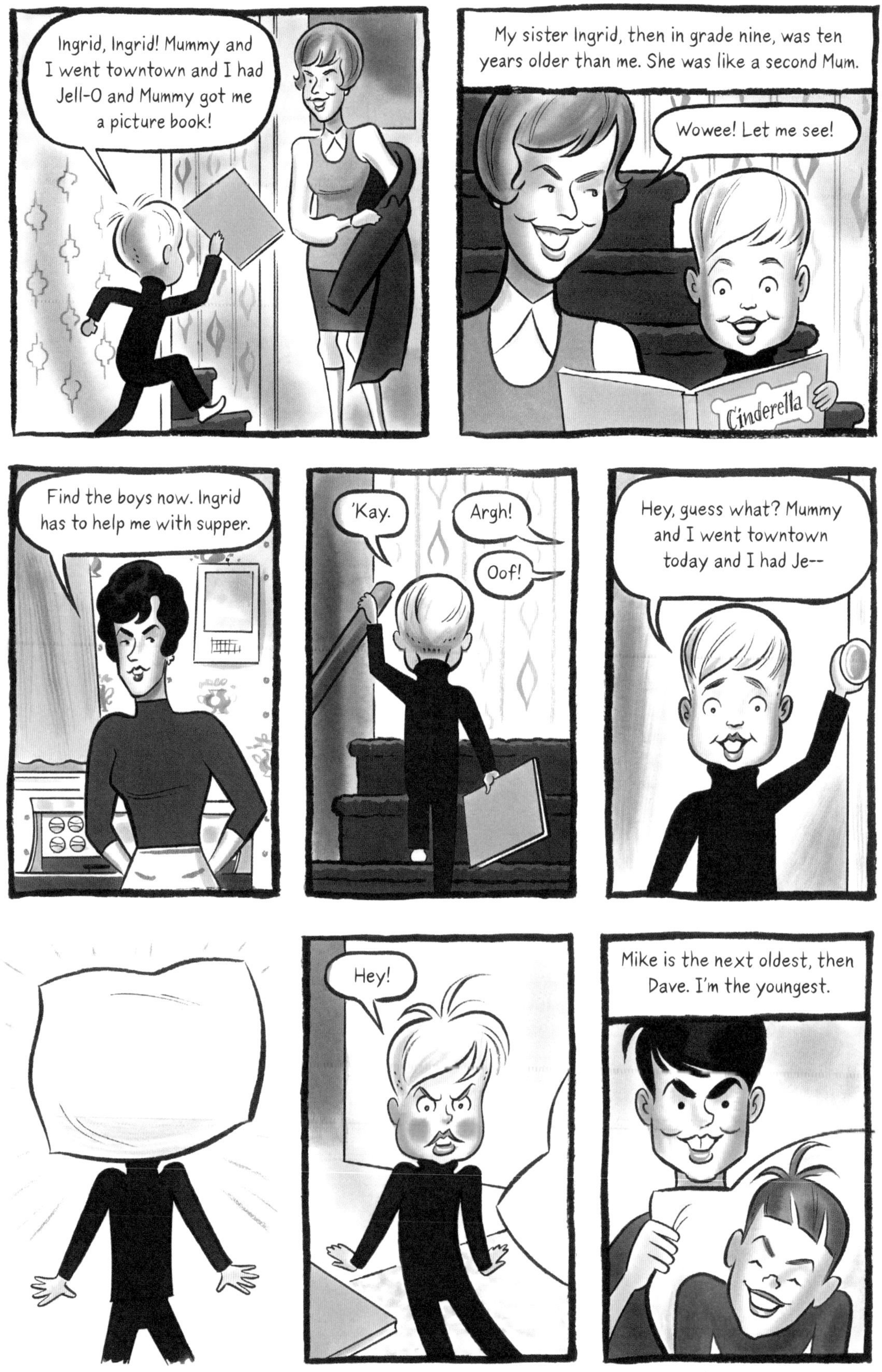

Ingrid, Ingrid! Mummy and I went towntown and I had Jell-O and Mummy got me a picture book!
My sister Ingrid, then in grade nine, was ten years older than me. She was like a second Mum.
Wowee! Let me see!
Cinderella
Find the boys now. Ingrid has to help me with supper.
'Kay.
Argh!
Oof!
Hey, guess what? Mummy and I went towntown today and I had Je--
Hey!
Mike is the next oldest, then Dave. I'm the youngest.

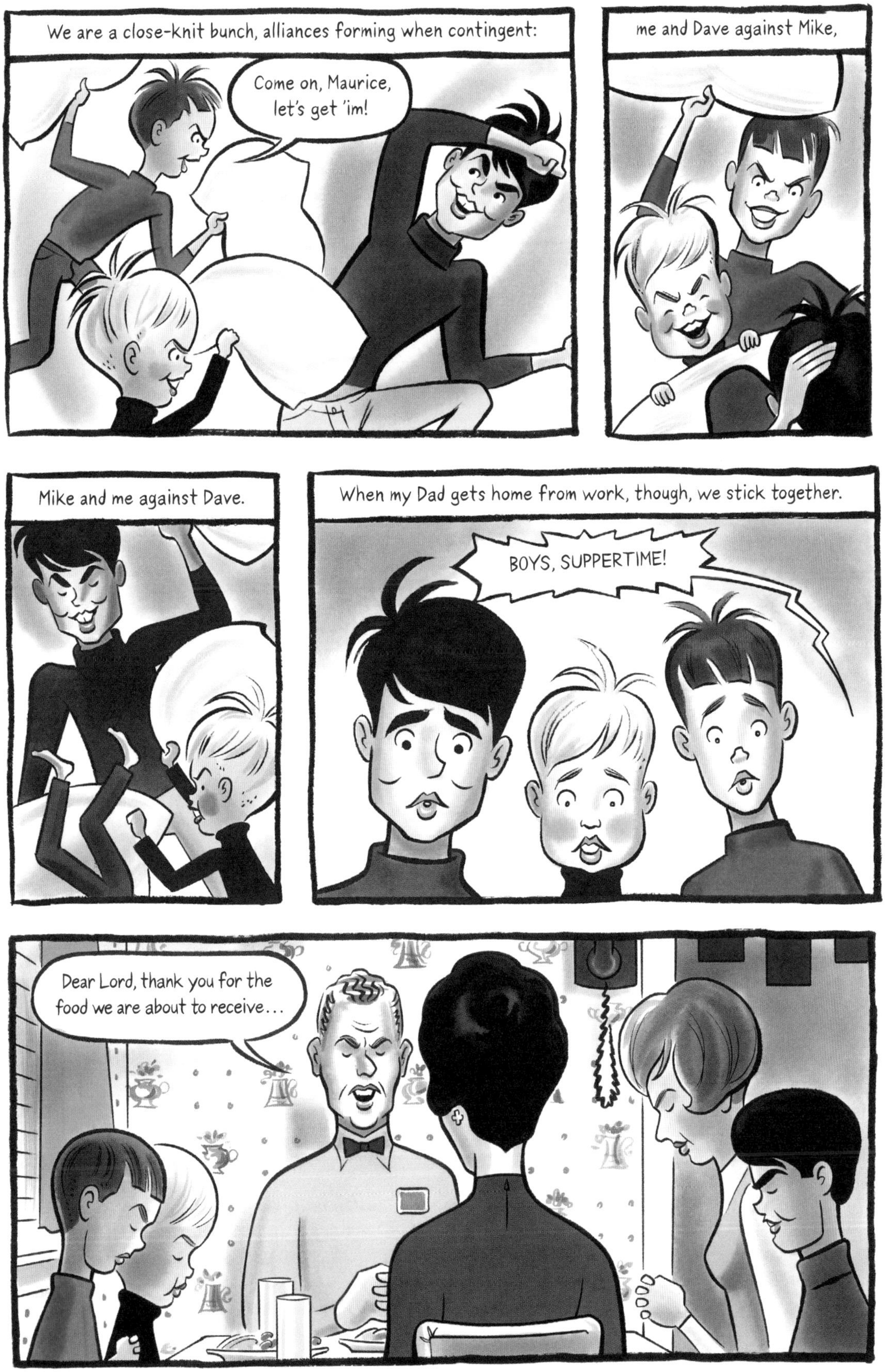
We are a close-knit bunch, alliances forming when contingent:
Come on, Maurice, let's get 'im!
me and Dave against Mike,
Mike and me against Dave.
When my Dad gets home from work, though, we stick together.
BOYS, SUPPERTIME!
Dear Lord, thank you for the food we are about to receive...

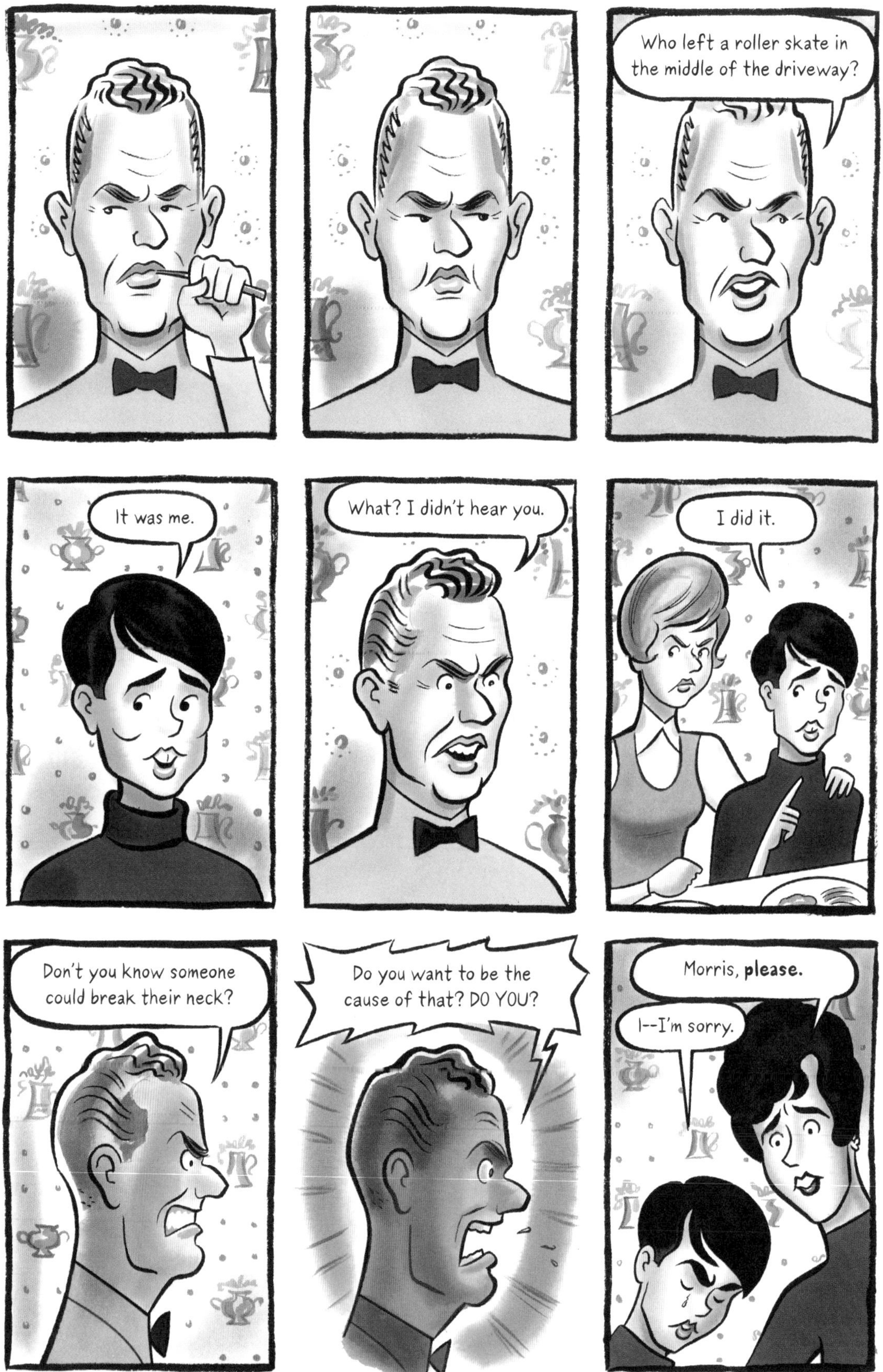
Who left a roller skate in the middle of the driveway?
It was me.
What? I didn't hear you.
I did it.
Don't you know someone could break their neck?
Do you want to be the cause of that? DO YOU?
Morris, **please.**
I--I'm sorry.

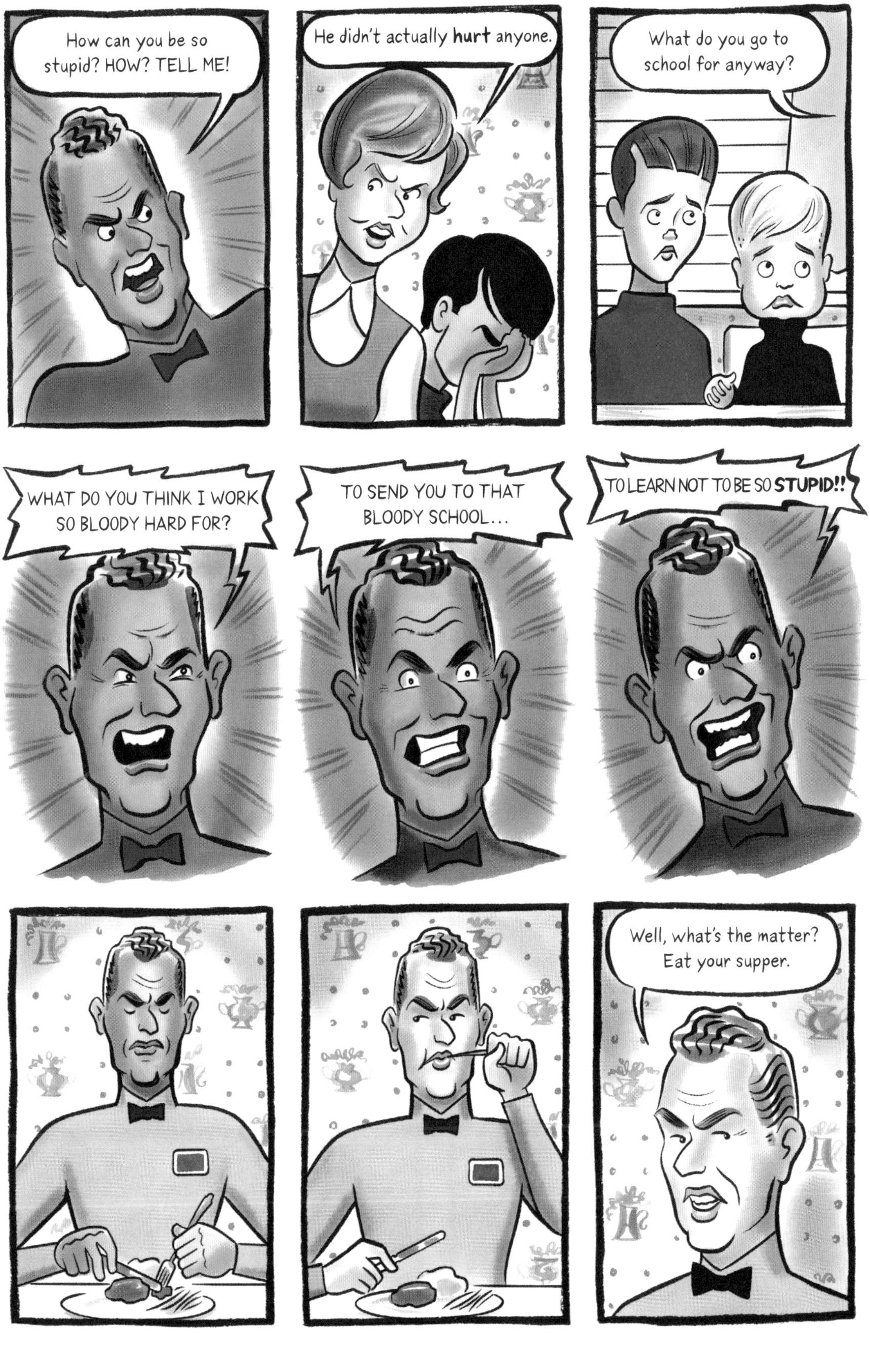
How can you be so stupid? HOW? TELL ME!
He didn't actually **hurt** anyone.
What do you go to school for anyway?
WHAT DO YOU THINK I WORK SO BLOODY HARD FOR?
TO SEND YOU TO THAT BLOODY SCHOOL...
TO LEARN NOT TO BE SO **STUPID!!**
Well, what's the matter? Eat your supper.

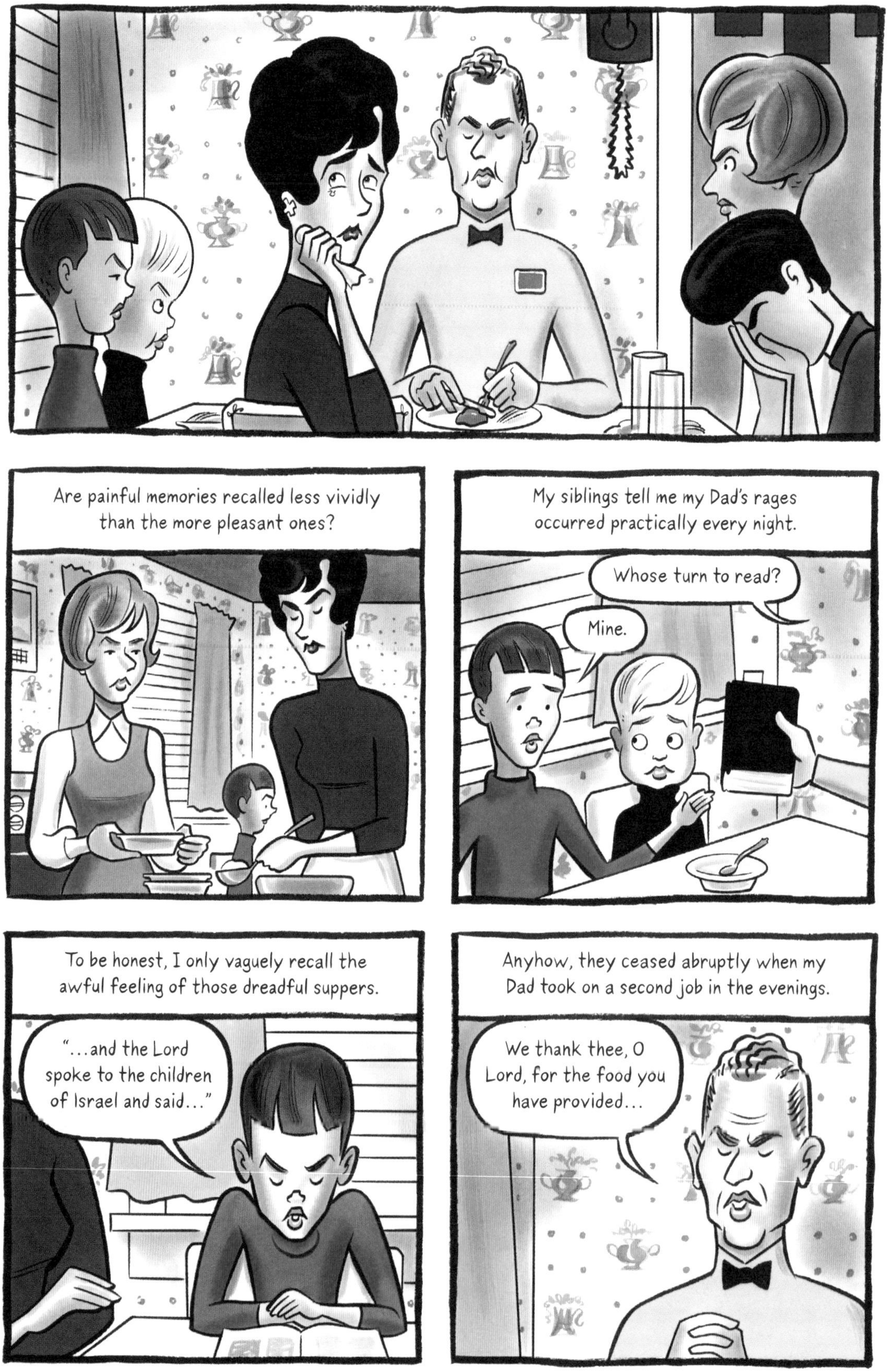
Are painful memories recalled less vividly than the more pleasant ones?
My siblings tell me my Dad's rages occurred practically every night.
Whose turn to read?
Mine.
To be honest, I only vaguely recall the awful feeling of those dreadful suppers.
"...and the Lord spoke to the children of Israel and said..."
Anyhow, they ceased abruptly when my Dad took on a second job in the evenings.
We thank thee, O Lord, for the food you have provided...

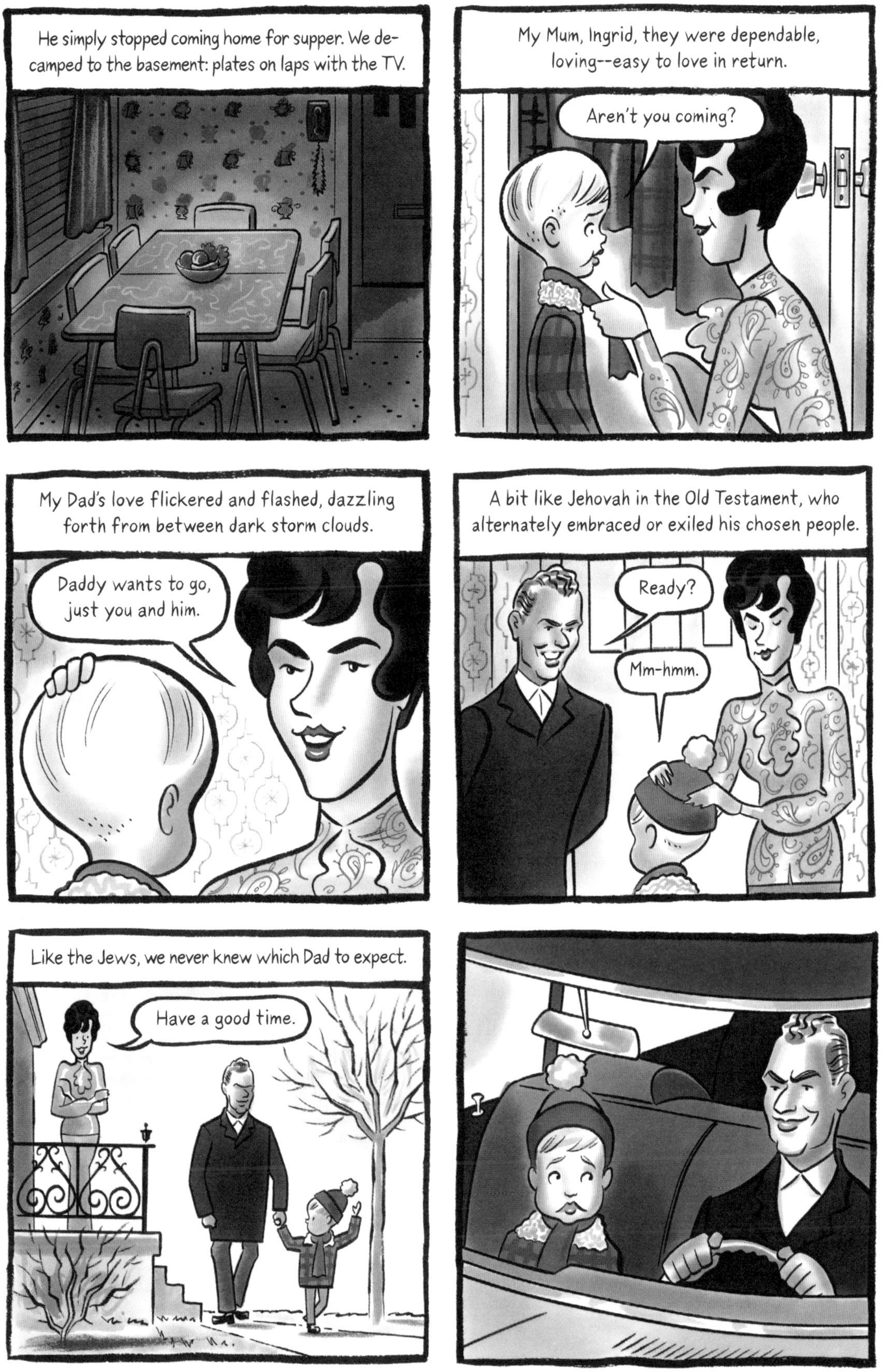

He simply stopped coming home for supper. We decamped to the basement: plates on laps with the TV.
My Mum, Ingrid, they were dependable, loving--easy to love in return.
Aren't you coming?
My Dad's love flickered and flashed, dazzling forth from between dark storm clouds.
Daddy wants to go, just you and him.
A bit like Jehovah in the Old Testament, who alternately embraced or exiled his chosen people.
Ready?
Mm-hmm.
Like the Jews, we never knew which Dad to expect.
Have a good time.

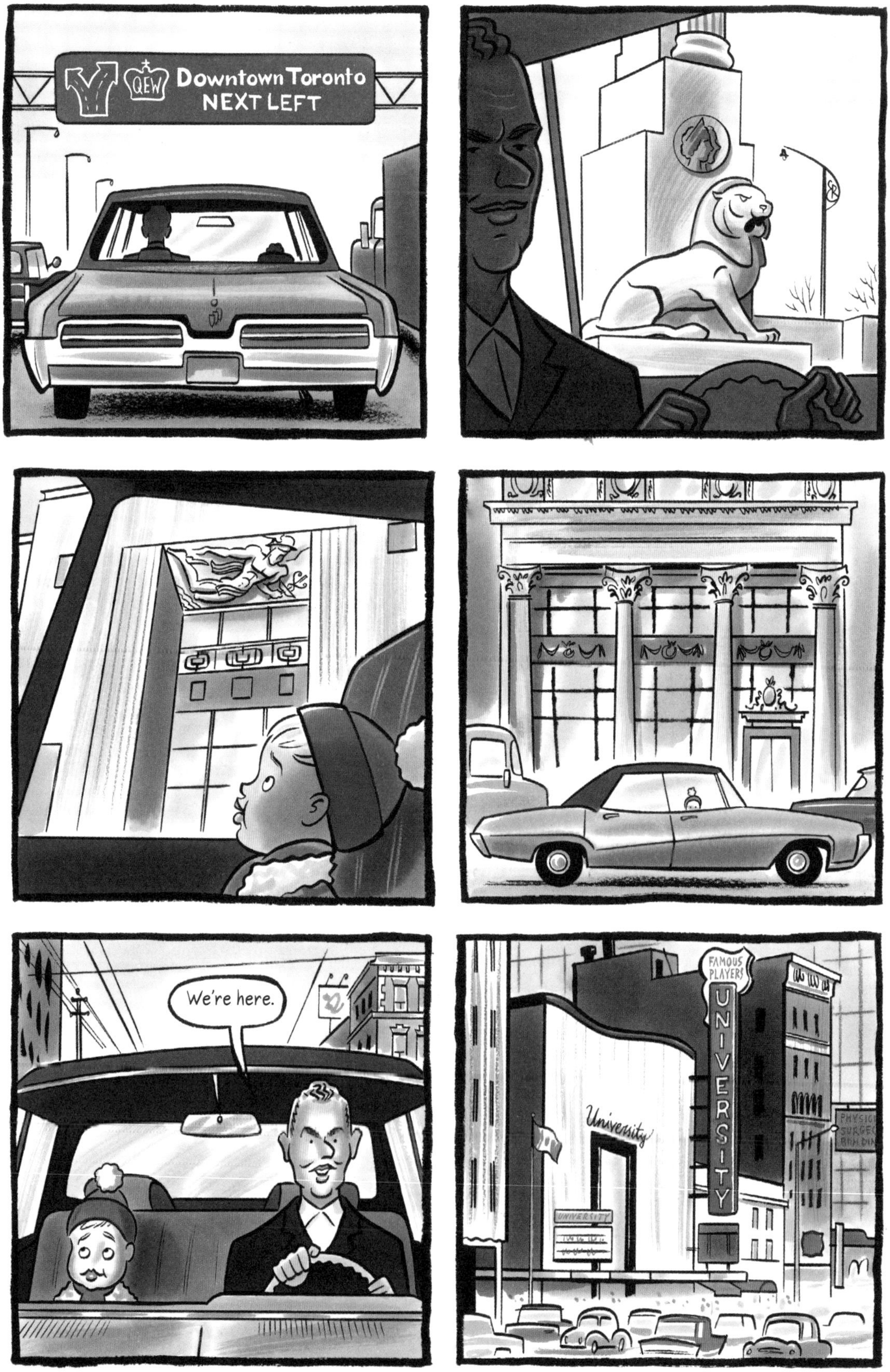
QEW
Downtown Toronto
NEXT LEFT
We're here.
FAMOUS PLAYERS
UNIVERSITY
University

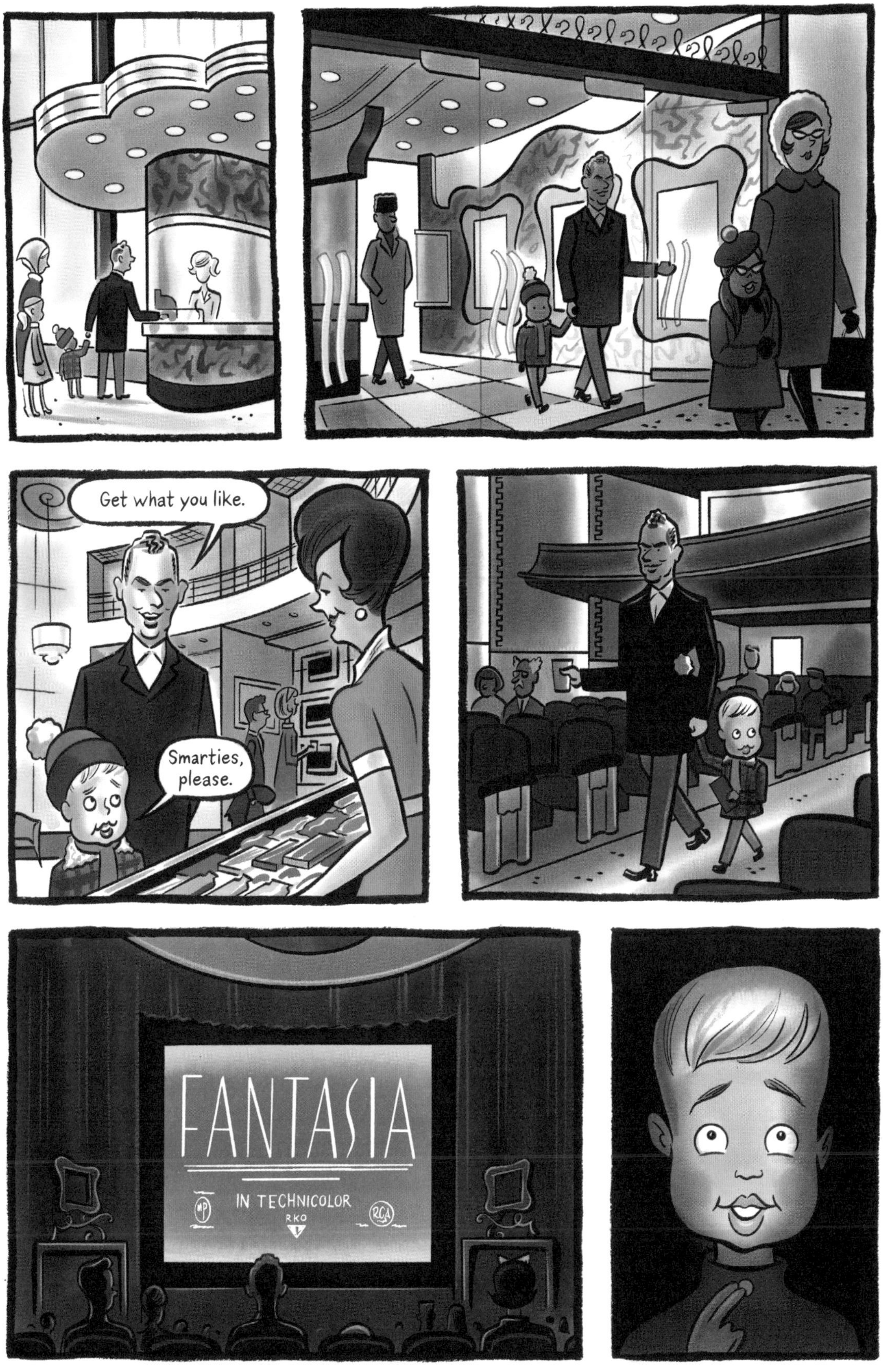
Get what you like.
Smarties, please.
FANTASIA
IN TECHNICOLOR
RKO

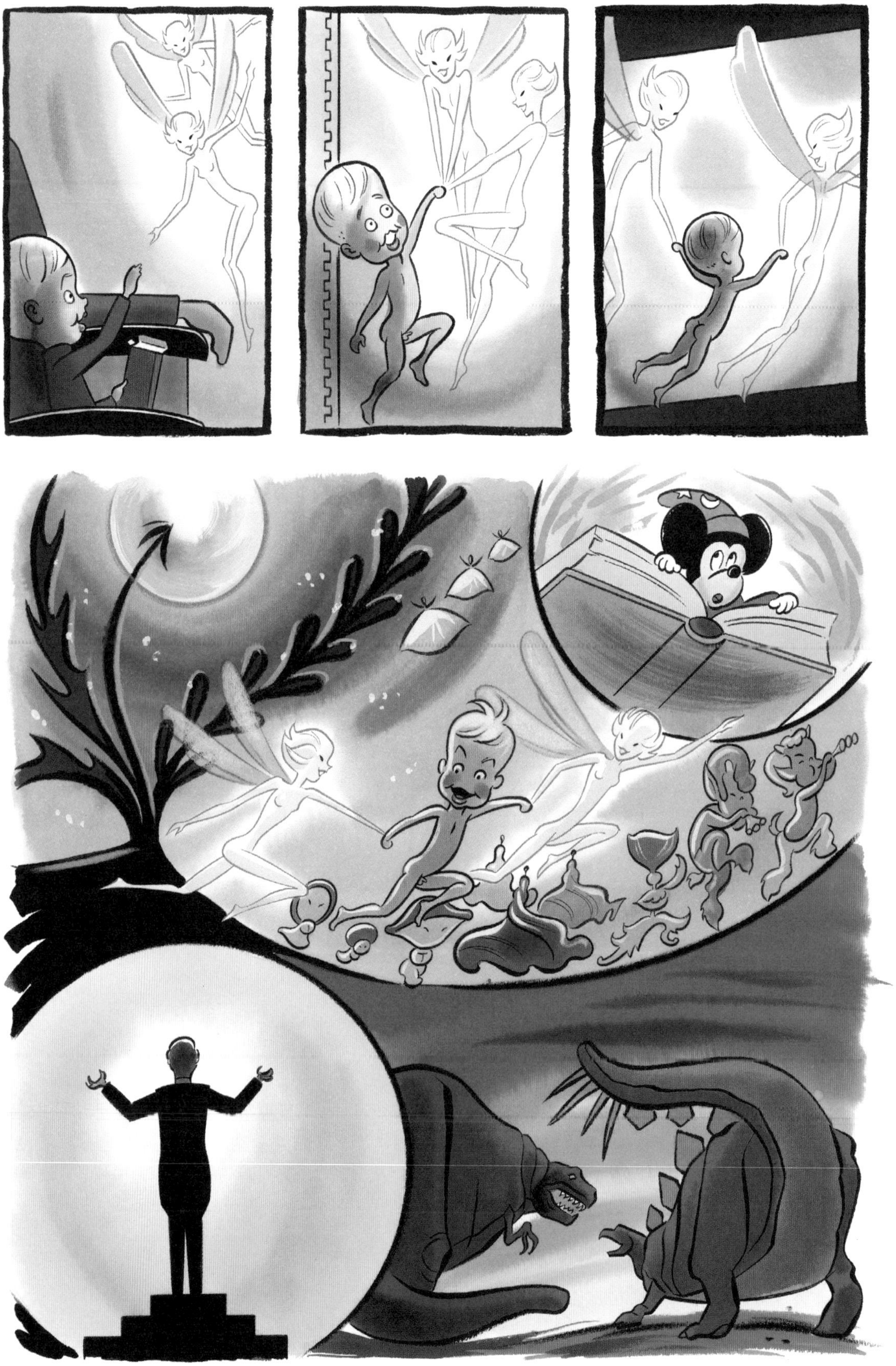

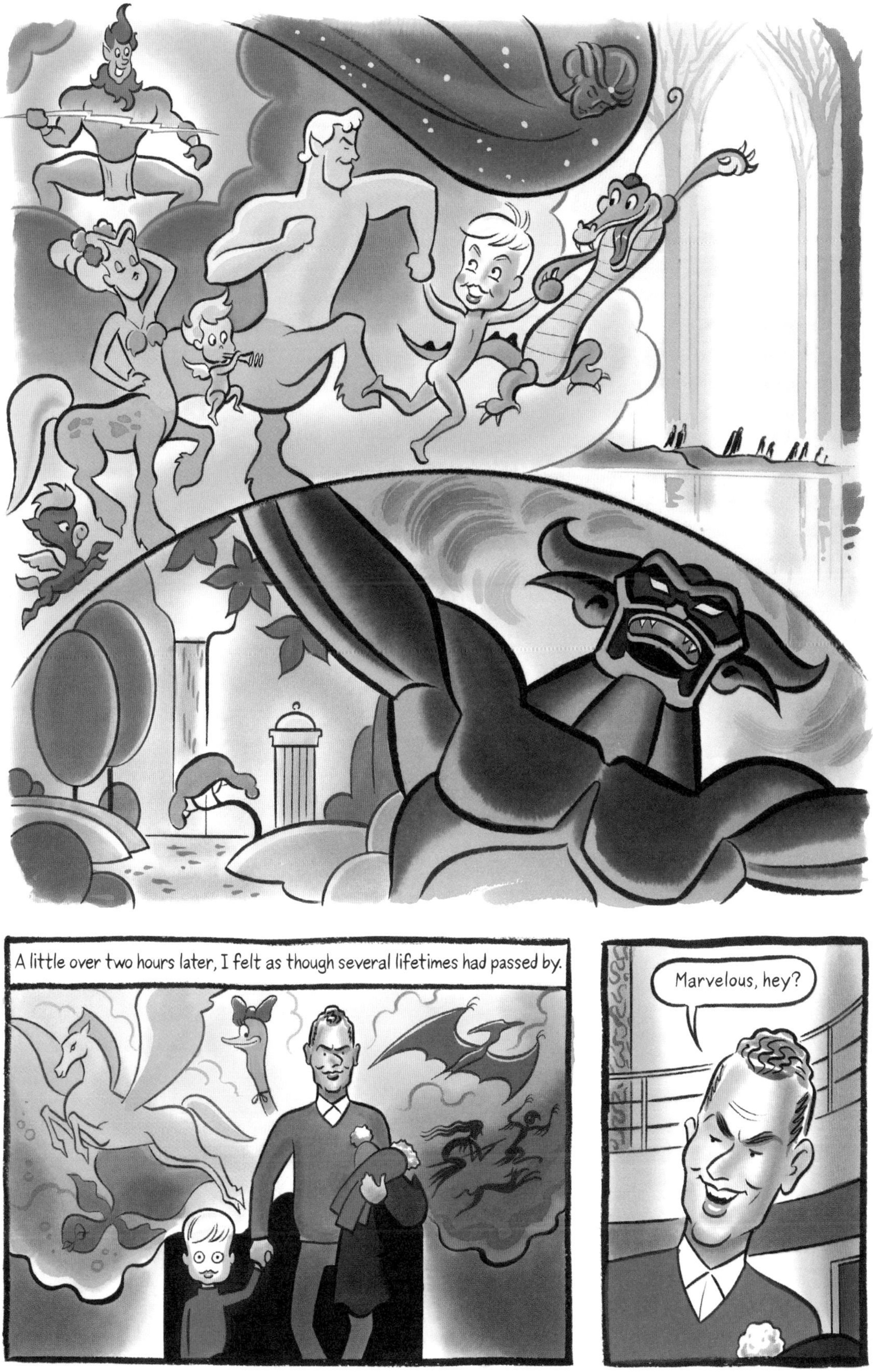
A little over two hours later, I felt as though several lifetimes had passed by.
Marvelous, hey?

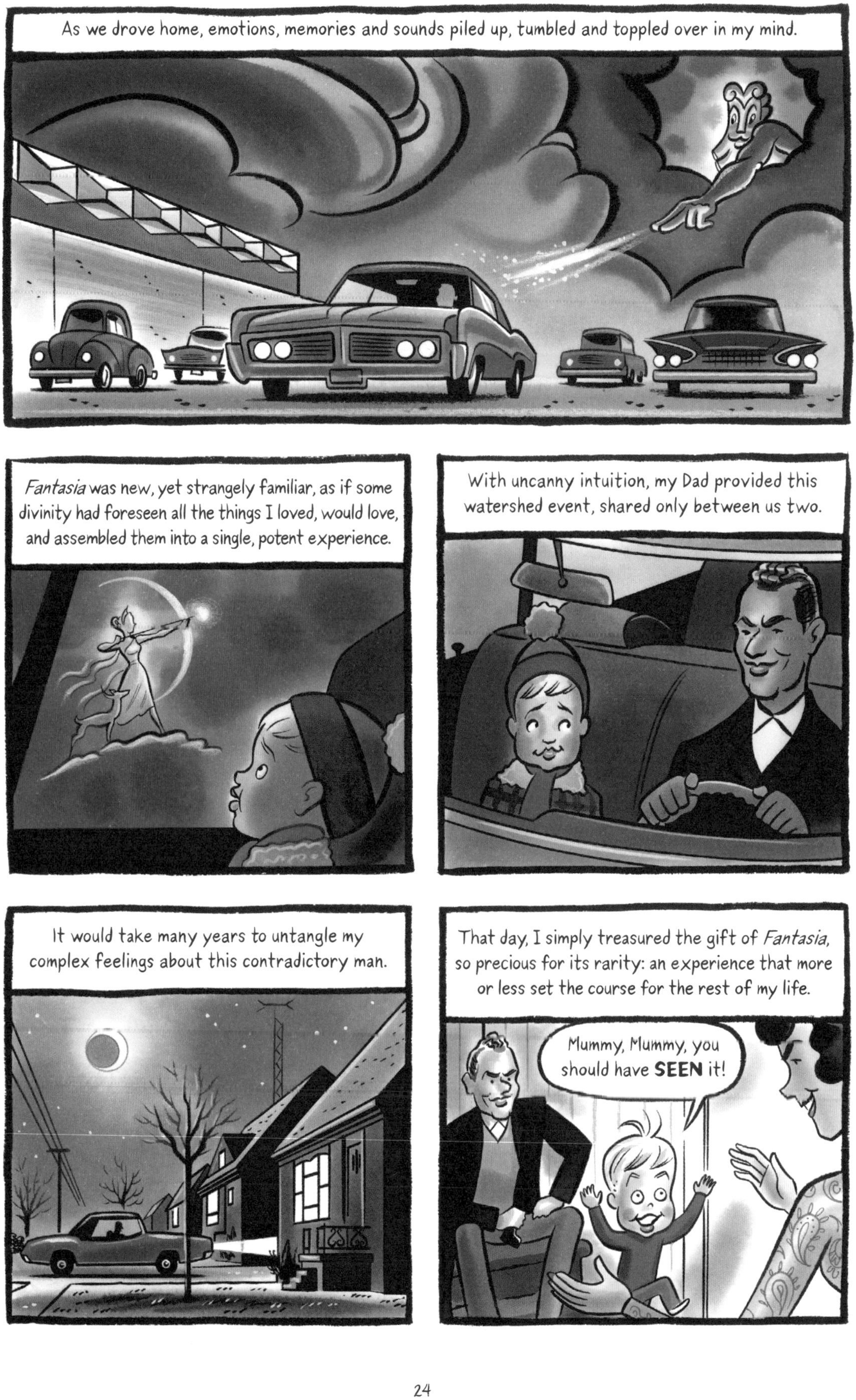
As we drove home, emotions, memories and sounds piled up, tumbled and toppled over in my mind.
Fantasia was new, yet strangely familiar, as if some divinity had foreseen all the things I loved, would love, and assembled them into a single, potent experience.
With uncanny intuition, my Dad provided this watershed event, shared only between us two.
It would take many years to untangle my complex feelings about this contradictory man.
That day, I simply treasured the gift of *Fantasia*, so precious for its rarity: an experience that more or less set the course for the rest of my life.
Mummy, Mummy, you should have **SEEN** it!

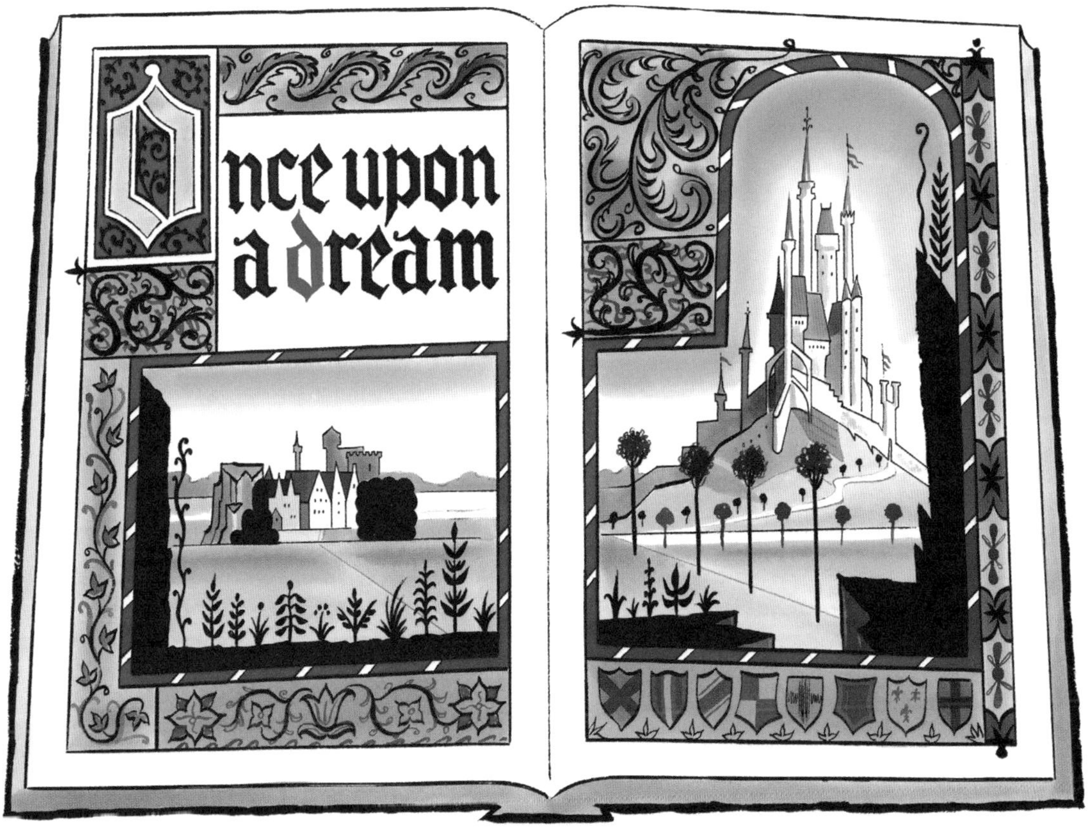
Once upon a dream

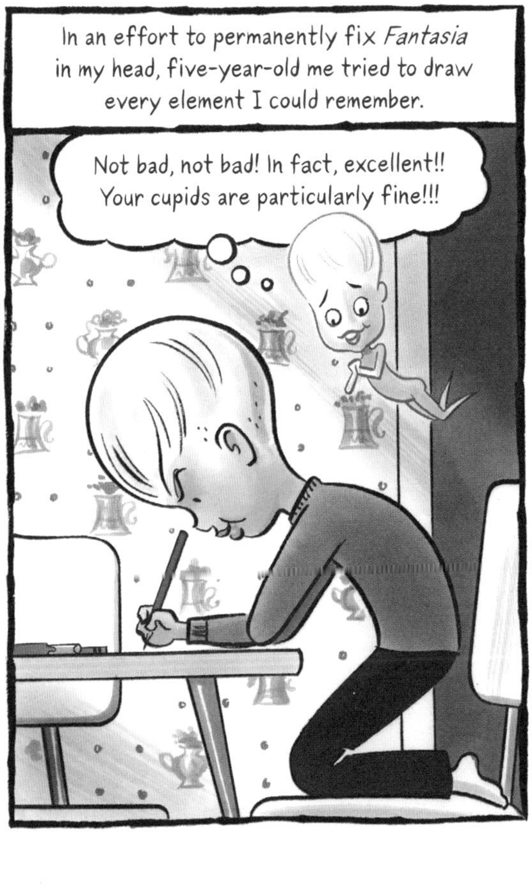
In an effort to permanently fix *Fantasia* in my head, five-year-old me tried to draw every element I could remember.
Not bad, not bad! In fact, excellent!! Your cupids are particularly fine!!!

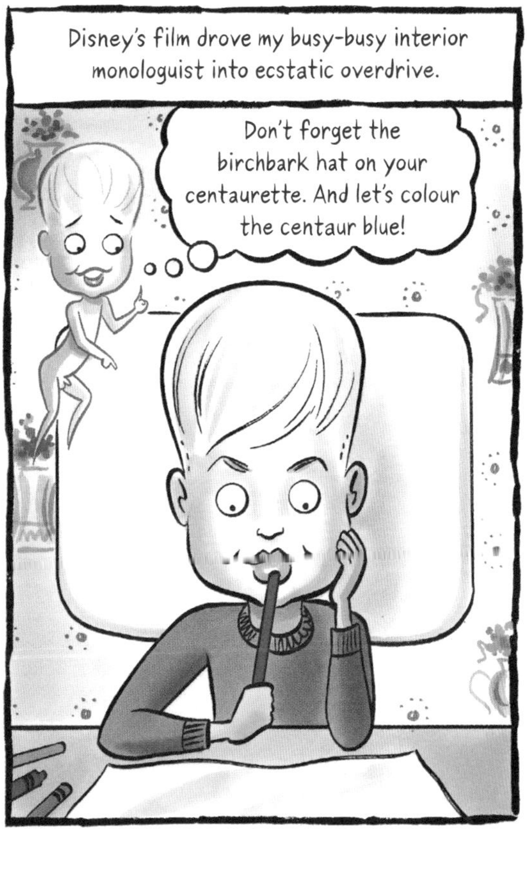
Disney's film drove my busy-busy interior monologuist into ecstatic overdrive.
Don't forget the birchbark hat on your centaurette. And let's colour the centaur blue!

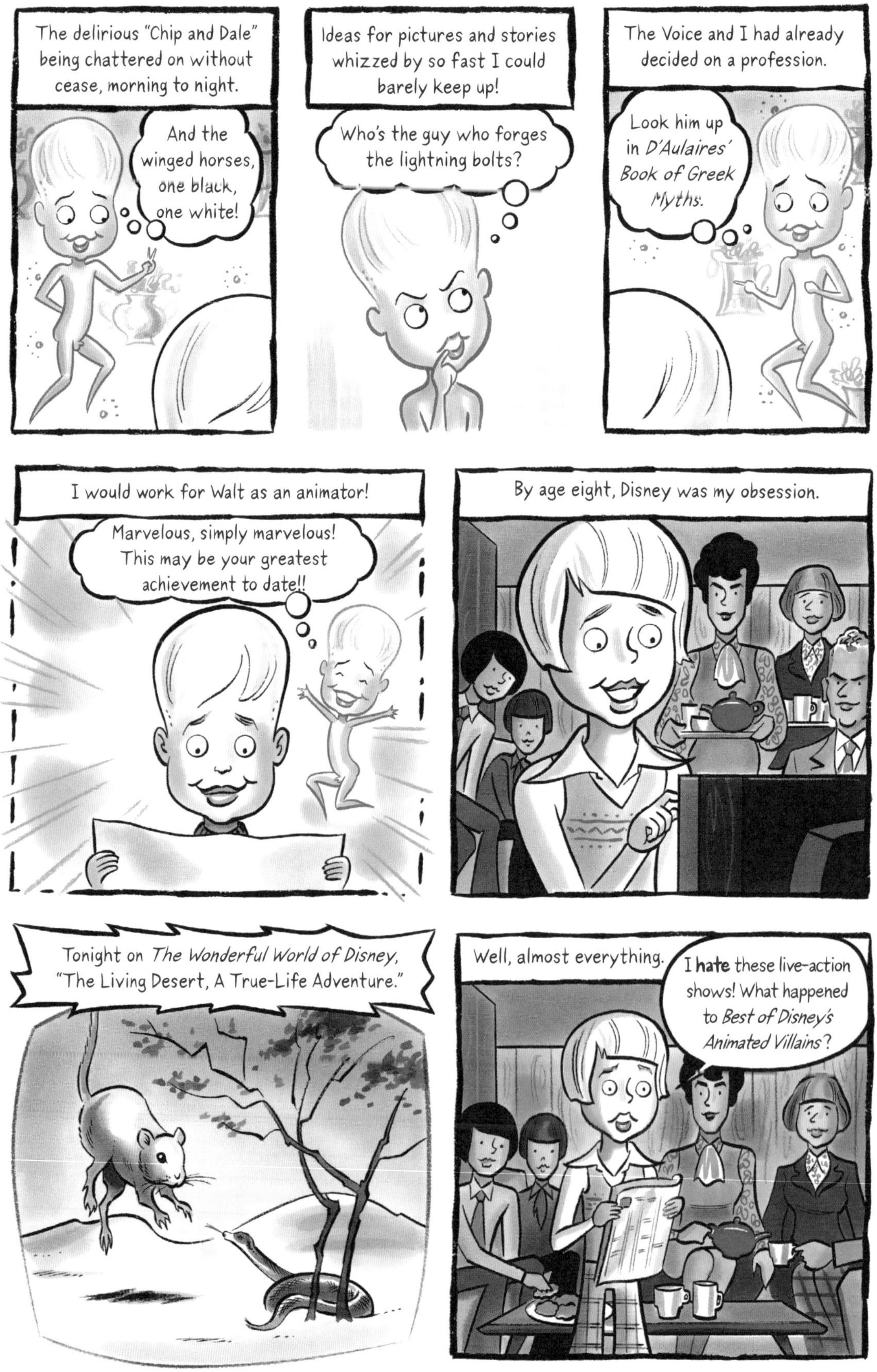
The delirious "Chip and Dale" being chattered on without cease, morning to night.
And the winged horses, one black, one white!
Ideas for pictures and stories whizzed by so fast I could barely keep up!
Who's the guy who forges the lightning bolts?
The Voice and I had already decided on a profession.
Look him up in D'Aulaires' Book of Greek Myths.
I would work for Walt as an animator!
Marvelous, simply marvelous! This may be your greatest achievement to date!!
By age eight, Disney was my obsession.
Tonight on The Wonderful World of Disney, "The Living Desert, A True-Life Adventure."
Well, almost everything.
I hate these live-action shows! What happened to Best of Disney's Animated Villains?

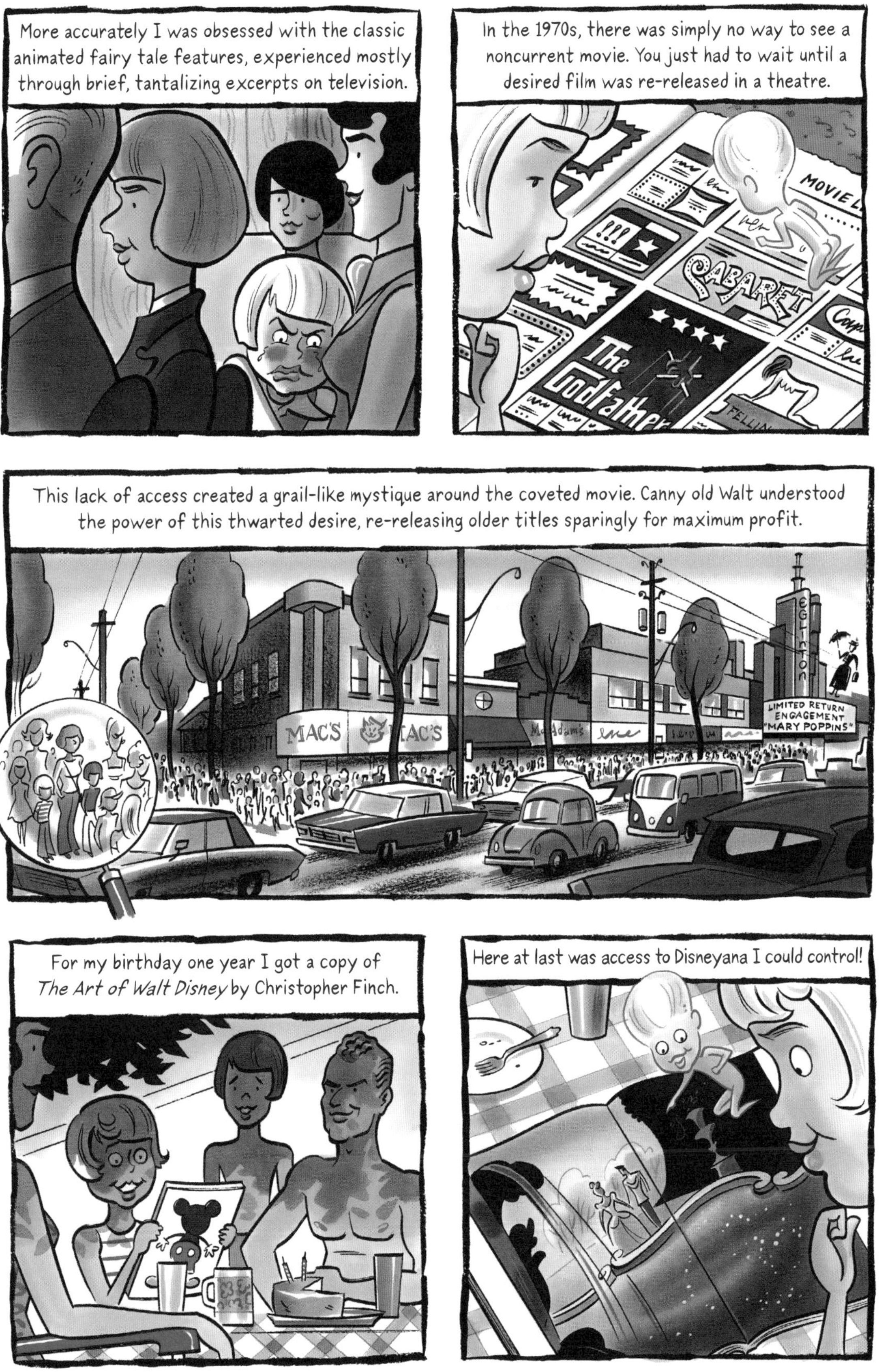
More accurately I was obsessed with the classic animated fairy tale features, experienced mostly through brief, tantalizing excerpts on television.
In the 1970s, there was simply no way to see a noncurrent movie. You just had to wait until a desired film was re-released in a theatre.
CABARET
The Godfather
This lack of access created a grail-like mystique around the coveted movie. Canny old Walt understood the power of this thwarted desire, re-releasing older titles sparingly for maximum profit.
MAC'S
MAC'S
McAdams
EGLINTON
LIMITED RETURN ENGAGEMENT "MARY POPPINS"
For my birthday one year I got a copy of *The Art of Walt Disney* by Christopher Finch.
Here at last was access to Disneyana I could control!

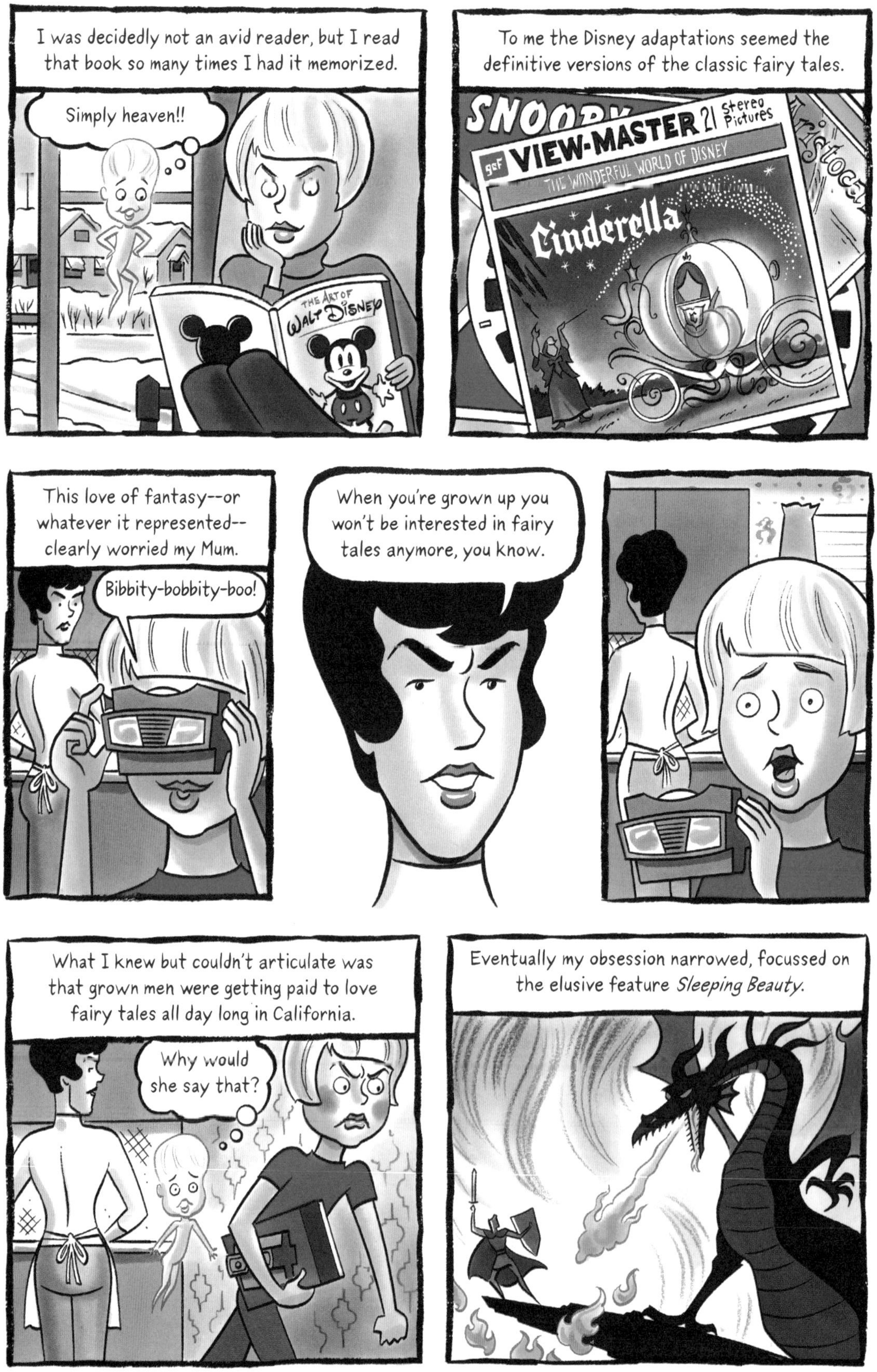
I was decidedly not an avid reader, but I read that book so many times I had it memorized.
Simply heaven!!
THE ART OF WALT DISNEY
To me the Disney adaptations seemed the definitive versions of the classic fairy tales.
VIEW-MASTER 21 Stereo Pictures
THE WONDERFUL WORLD OF DISNEY
Cinderella
This love of fantasy--or whatever it represented--clearly worried my Mum.
Bibbity-bobbity-boo!
When you're grown up you won't be interested in fairy tales anymore, you know.
What I knew but couldn't articulate was that grown men were getting paid to love fairy tales all day long in California.
Why would she say that?
Eventually my obsession narrowed, focussed on the elusive feature *Sleeping Beauty*.

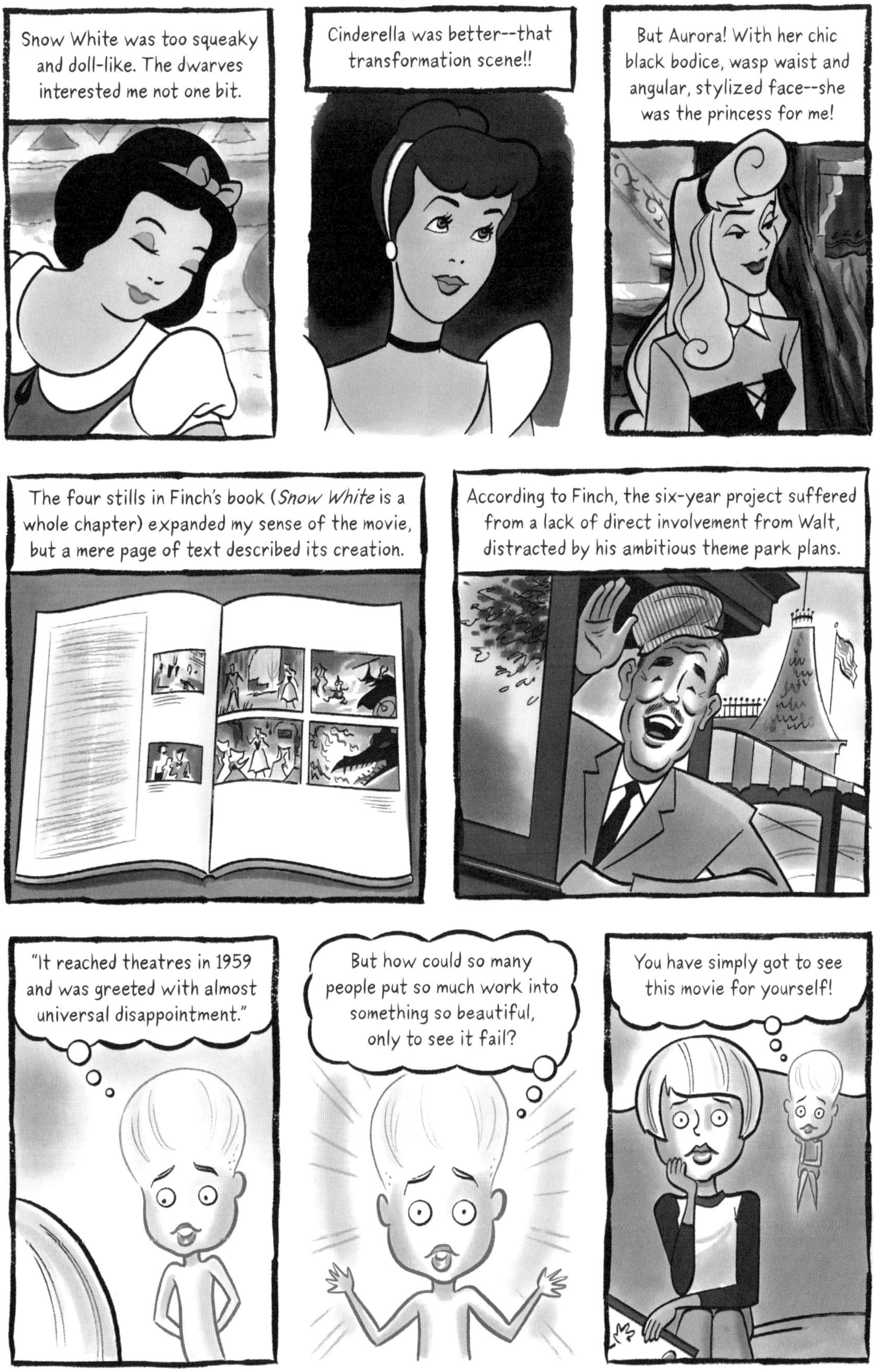

Snow White was too squeaky and doll-like. The dwarves interested me not one bit.
Cinderella was better--that transformation scene!!
But Aurora! With her chic black bodice, wasp waist and angular, stylized face--she was the princess for me!
The four stills in Finch's book (*Snow White* is a whole chapter) expanded my sense of the movie, but a mere page of text described its creation.
According to Finch, the six-year project suffered from a lack of direct involvement from Walt, distracted by his ambitious theme park plans.
"It reached theatres in 1959 and was greeted with almost universal disappointment."
But how could so many people put so much work into something so beautiful, only to see it fail?
You have simply got to see this movie for yourself!

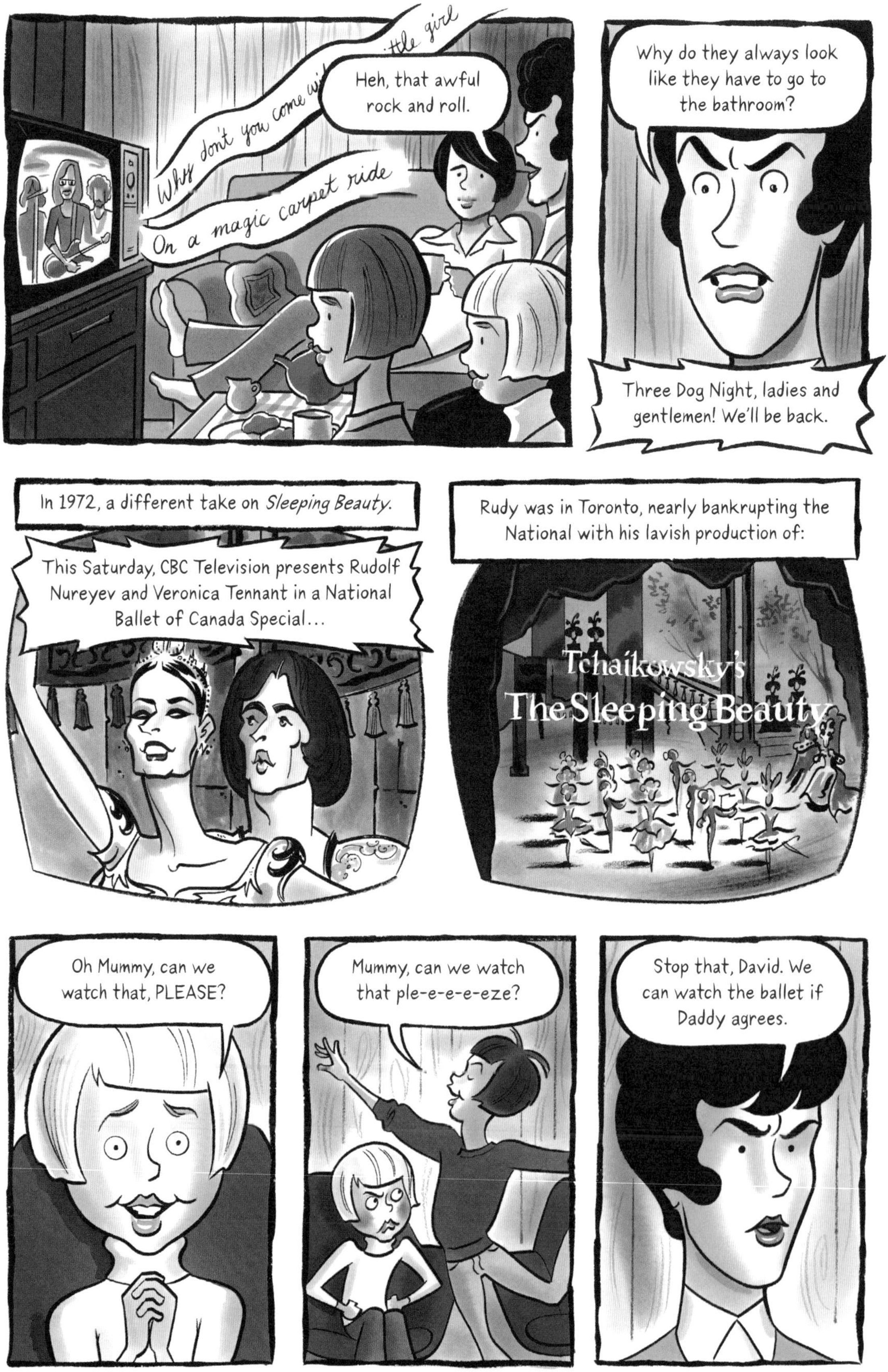
Why don't you come with me little girl
On a magic carpet ride
Heh, that awful rock and roll.
Why do they always look like they have to go to the bathroom?
Three Dog Night, ladies and gentlemen! We'll be back.
In 1972, a different take on *Sleeping Beauty*.
This Saturday, CBC Television presents Rudolf Nureyev and Veronica Tennant in a National Ballet of Canada Special…
Rudy was in Toronto, nearly bankrupting the National with his lavish production of:
Tchaikowsky's The Sleeping Beauty
Oh Mummy, can we watch that, PLEASE?
Mummy, can we watch that ple-e-e-e-eze?
Stop that, David. We can watch the ballet if Daddy agrees.

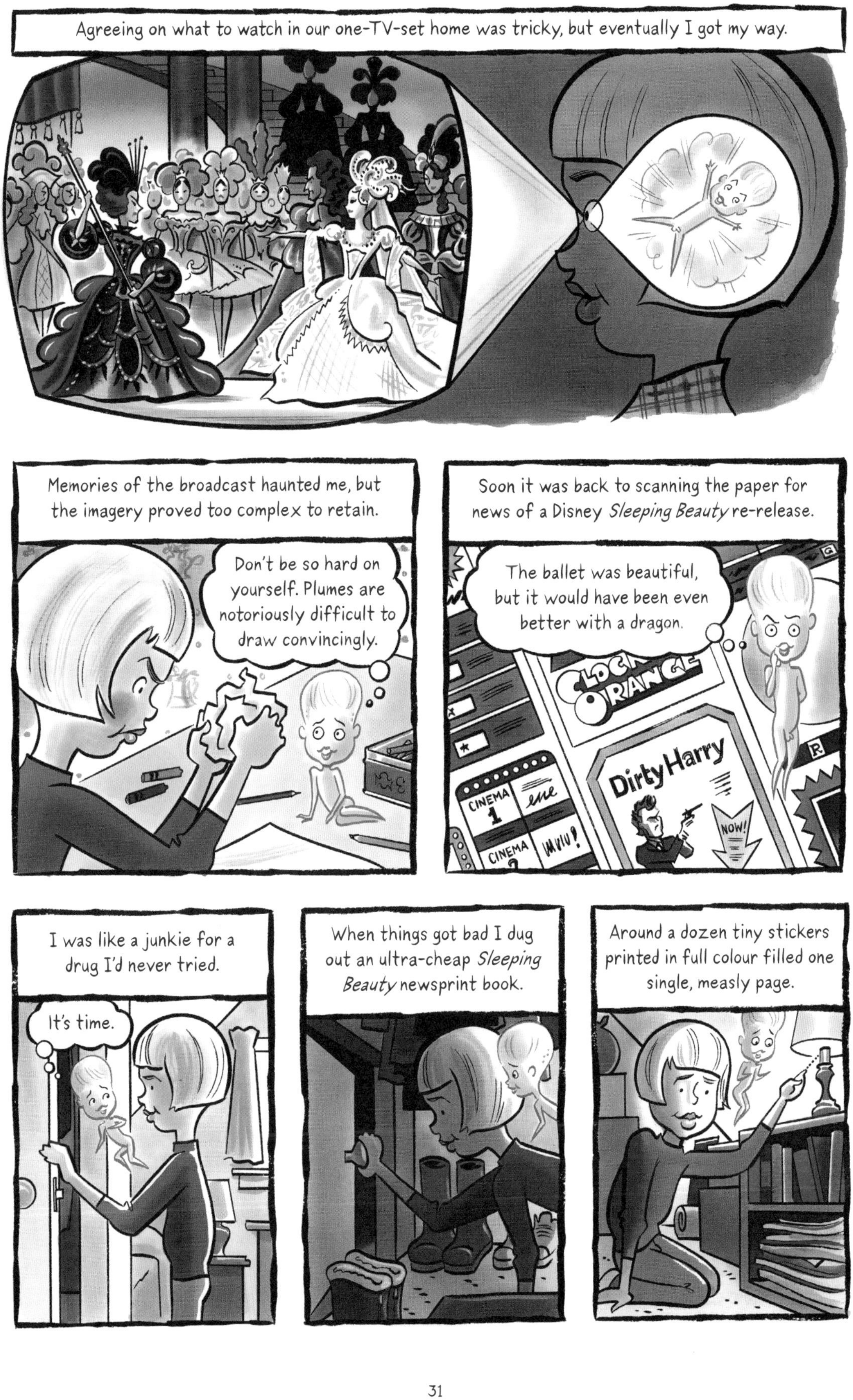
Agreeing on what to watch in our one-TV-set home was tricky, but eventually I got my way.
Memories of the broadcast haunted me, but the imagery proved too complex to retain.
Don't be so hard on yourself. Plumes are notoriously difficult to draw convincingly.
Soon it was back to scanning the paper for news of a Disney *Sleeping Beauty* re-release.
The ballet was beautiful, but it would have been even better with a dragon.
ORANGE
CINEMA 1
Dirty Harry
NOW!
CINEMA
R
I was like a junkie for a drug I'd never tried.
It's time.
When things got bad I dug out an ultra-cheap *Sleeping Beauty* newsprint book.
Around a dozen tiny stickers printed in full colour filled one single, measly page.

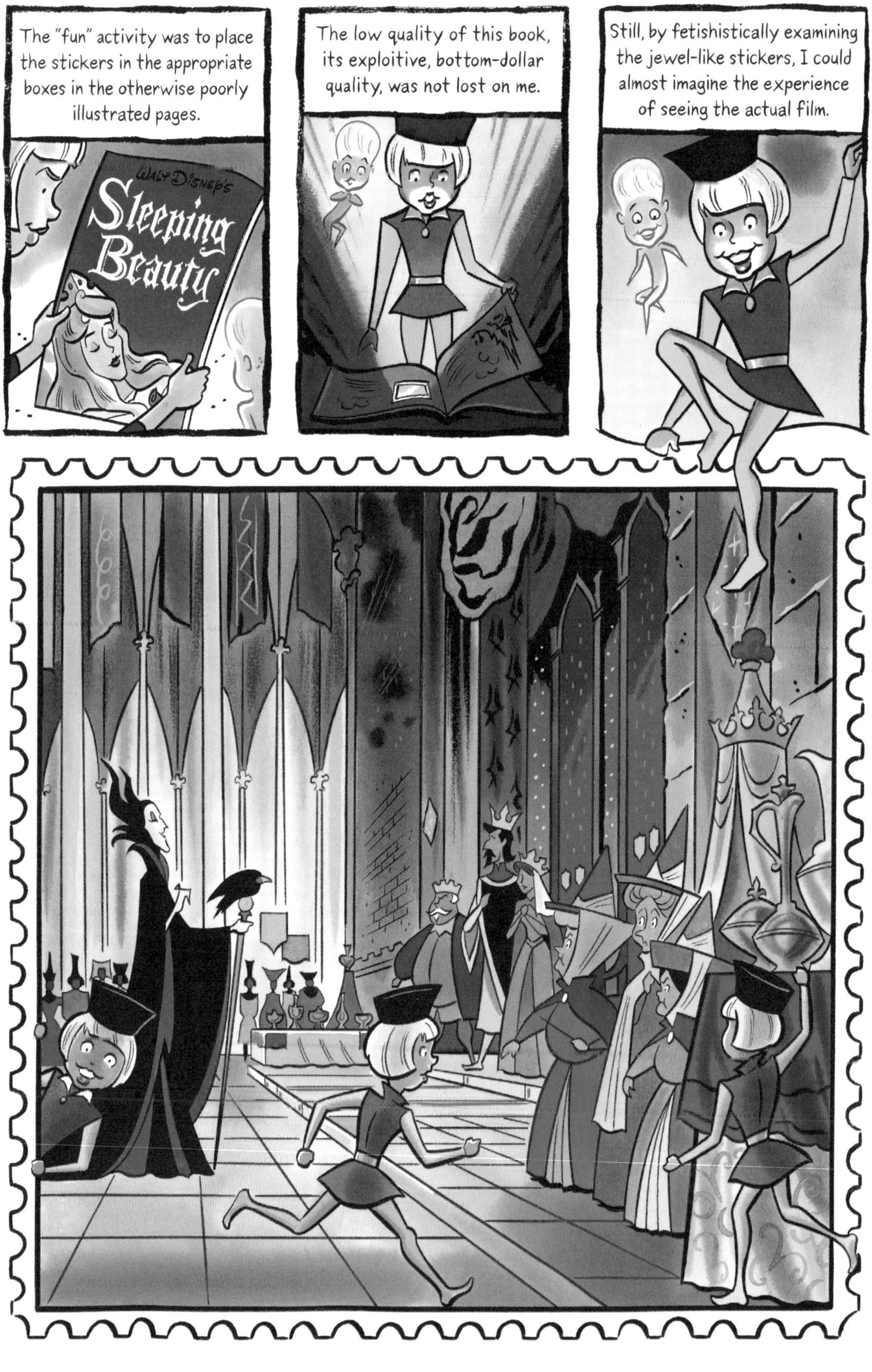
The "fun" activity was to place the stickers in the appropriate boxes in the otherwise poorly illustrated pages.
Walt Disney's
Sleeping Beauty
The low quality of this book, its exploitive, bottom-dollar quality, was not lost on me.
Still, by fetishistically examining the jewel-like stickers, I could almost imagine the experience of seeing the actual film.

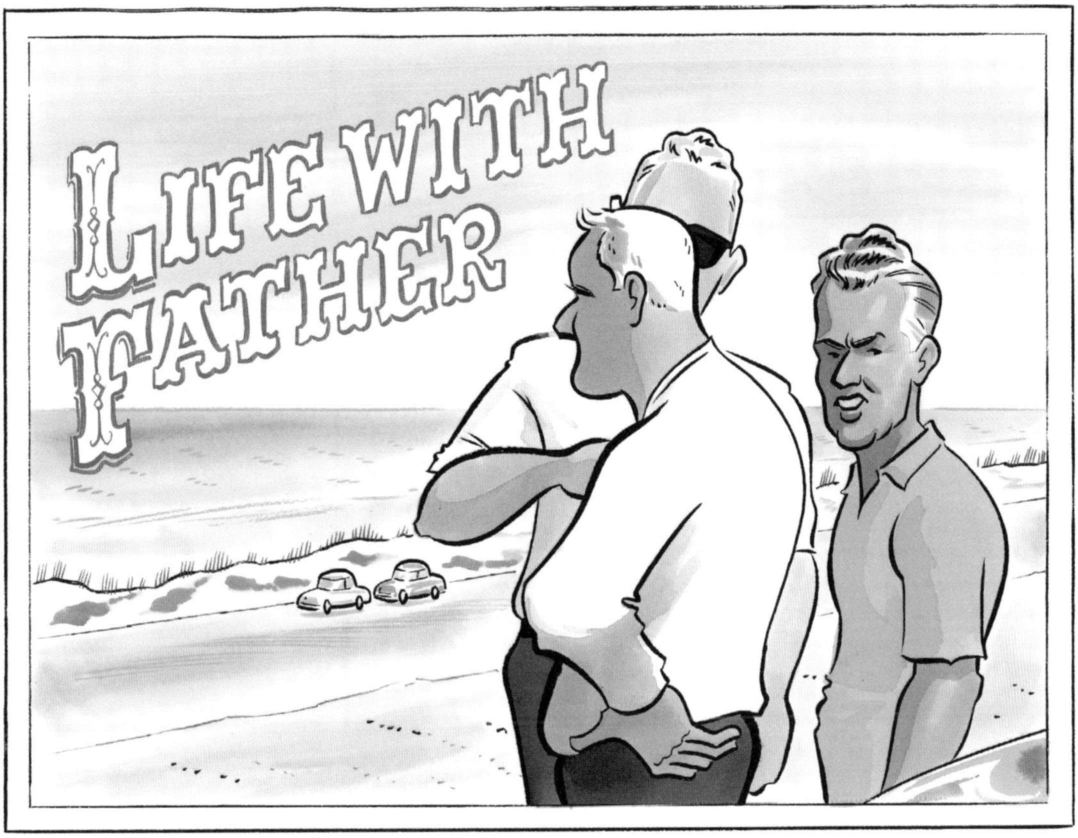
LIFE WITH FATHER

The source of my Dad's rage was a mystery; we knew so little about him or his folks, unlike my Mum's parents, Ari and Im Glas, my Oma and Opa.

They and their five children emigrated to Canada from Holland in 1950. Each one married and eventually raised seventeen children.

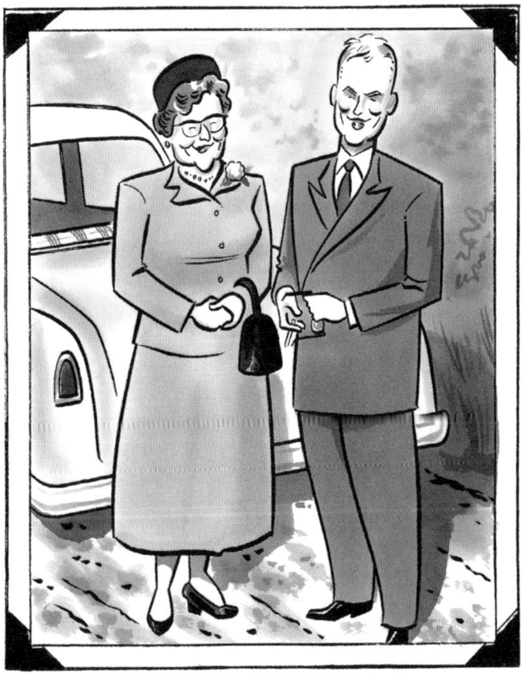

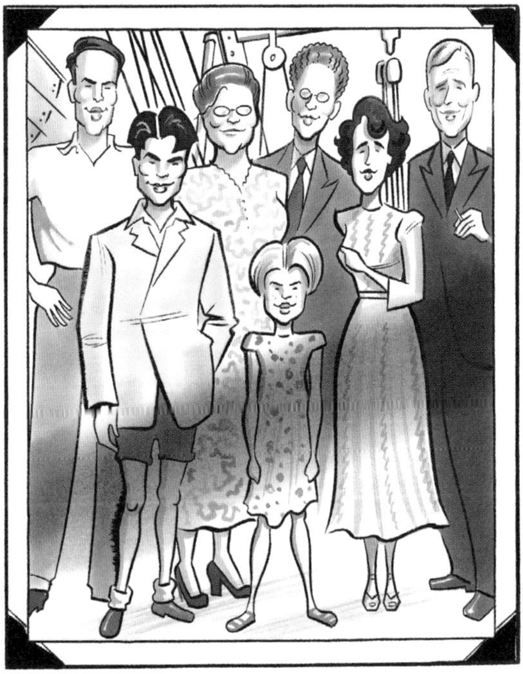

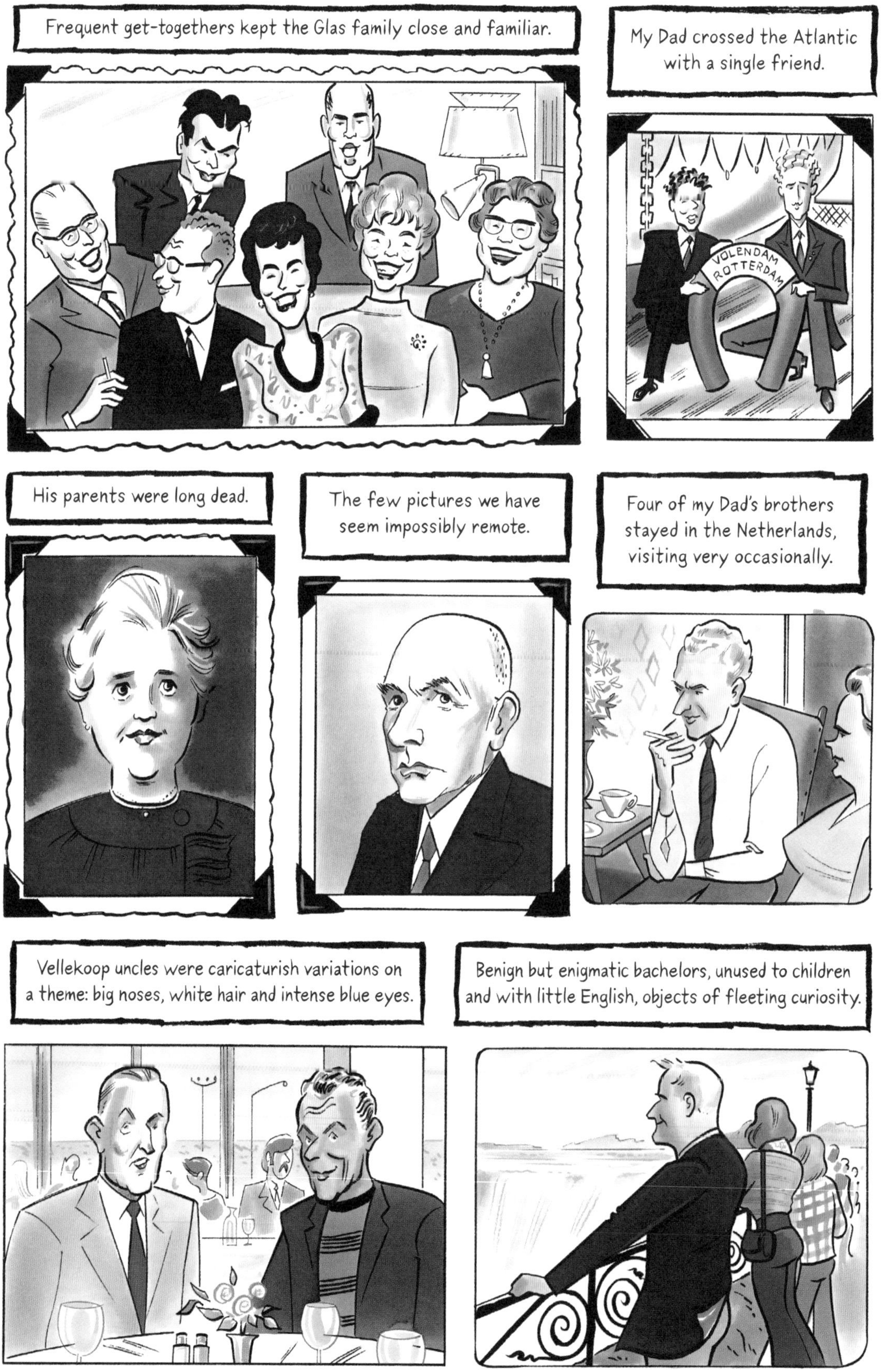
Frequent get-togethers kept the Glas family close and familiar.
My Dad crossed the Atlantic with a single friend.
VOLENDAM ROTTERDAM
His parents were long dead.
The few pictures we have seem impossibly remote.
Four of my Dad's brothers stayed in the Netherlands, visiting very occasionally.
Vellekoop uncles were caricaturish variations on a theme: big noses, white hair and intense blue eyes.
Benign but enigmatic bachelors, unused to children and with little English, objects of fleeting curiosity.

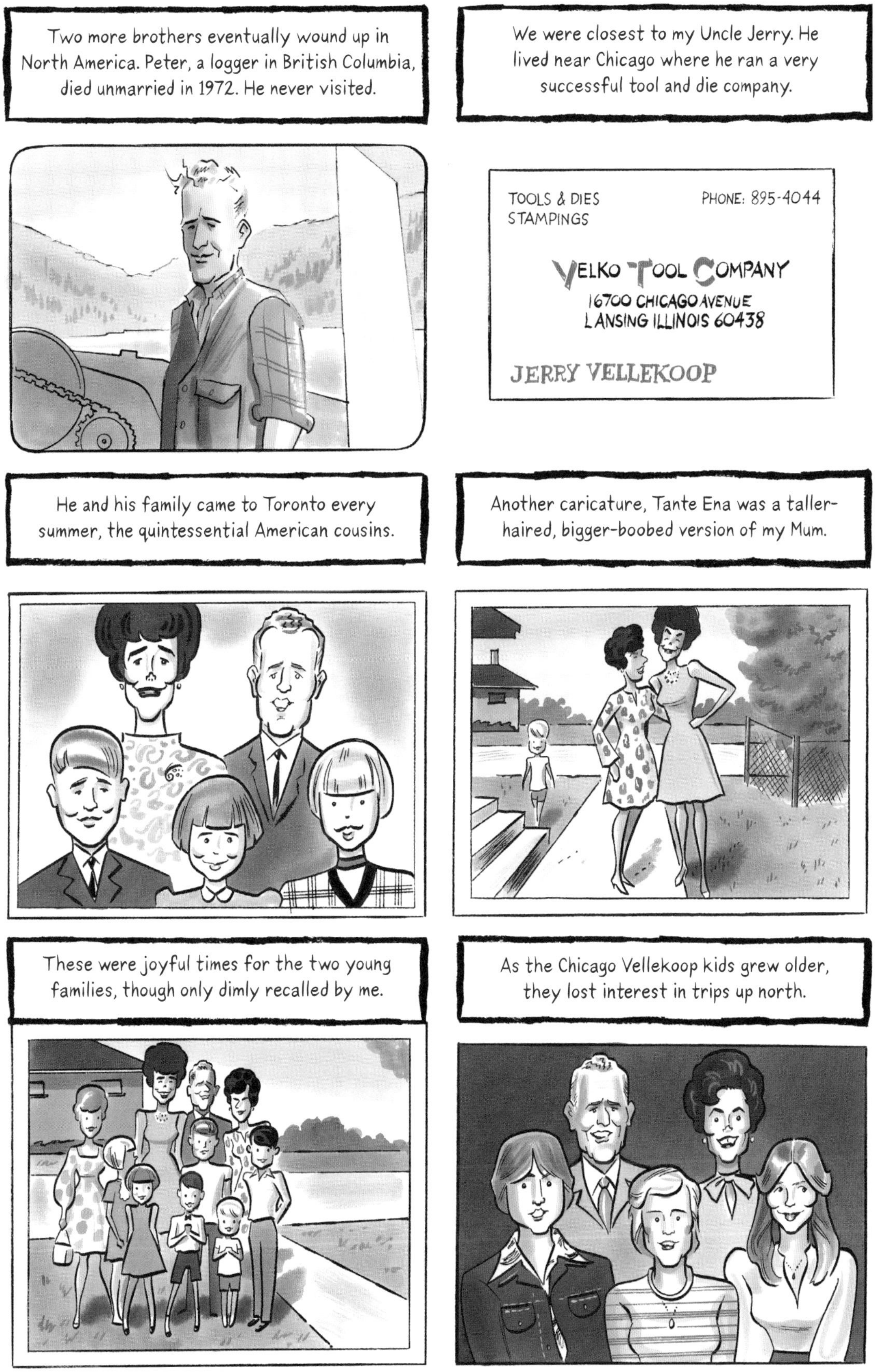

Two more brothers eventually wound up in North America. Peter, a logger in British Columbia, died unmarried in 1972. He never visited.
We were closest to my Uncle Jerry. He lived near Chicago where he ran a very successful tool and die company.
TOOLS & DIES
STAMPINGS
PHONE: 895-4044
VELKO TOOL COMPANY
16700 CHICAGO AVENUE
LANSING ILLINOIS 60438
JERRY VELLEKOOP
He and his family came to Toronto every summer, the quintessential American cousins.
Another caricature, Tante Ena was a taller-haired, bigger-boobed version of my Mum.
These were joyful times for the two young families, though only dimly recalled by me.
As the Chicago Vellekoop kids grew older, they lost interest in trips up north.

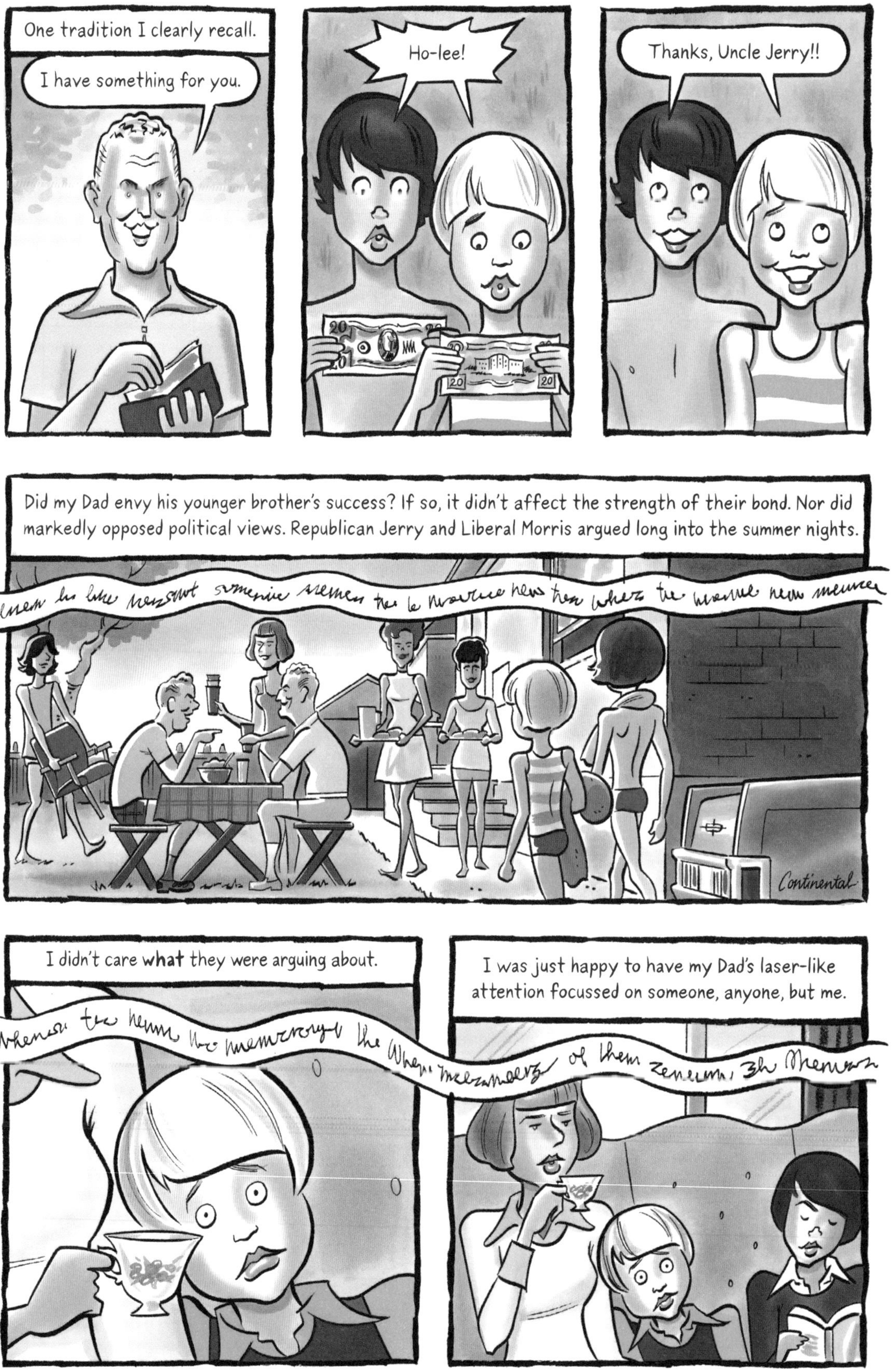

One tradition I clearly recall.
I have something for you.
Ho-lee!
Thanks, Uncle Jerry!!
Did my Dad envy his younger brother's success? If so, it didn't affect the strength of their bond. Nor did markedly opposed political views. Republican Jerry and Liberal Morris argued long into the summer nights.
Continental
I didn't care **what** they were arguing about.
I was just happy to have my Dad's laser-like attention focussed on someone, anyone, but me.

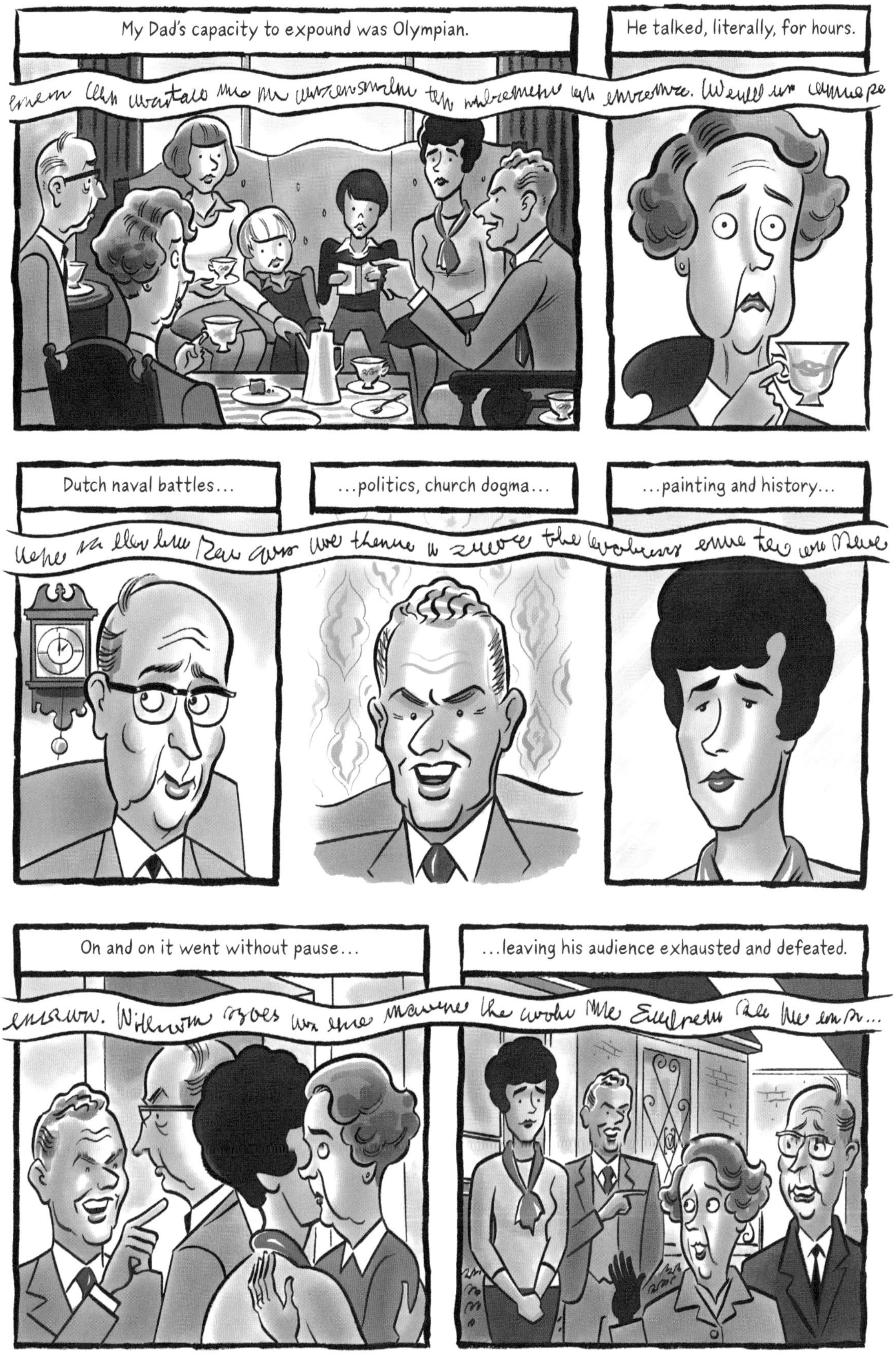
My Dad's capacity to expound was Olympian.
He talked, literally, for hours.
Dutch naval battles...
...politics, church dogma...
...painting and history...
On and on it went without pause...
...leaving his audience exhausted and defeated.

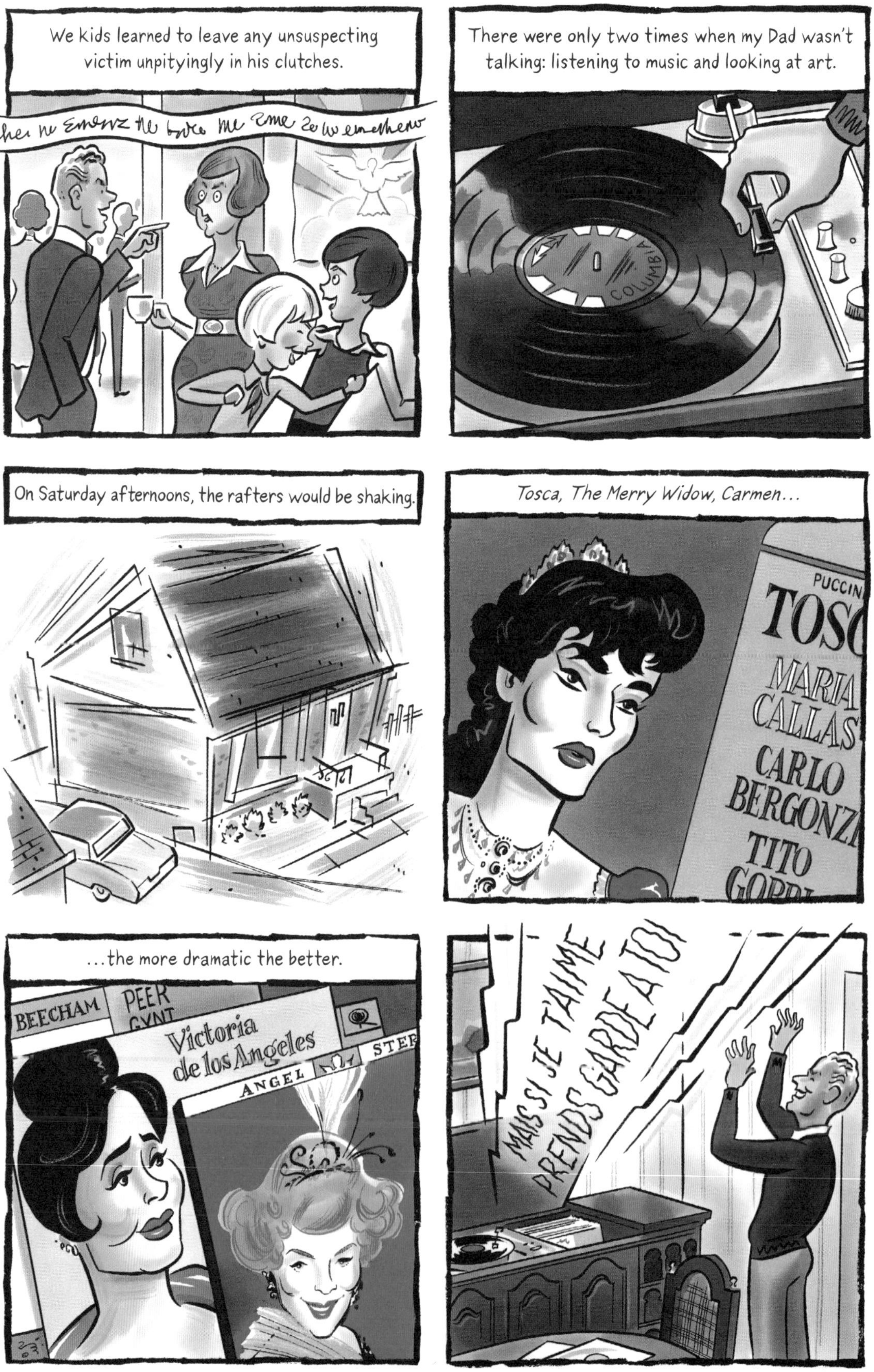
We kids learned to leave any unsuspecting victim unpityingly in his clutches.
There were only two times when my Dad wasn't talking: listening to music and looking at art.
COLUMBIA
On Saturday afternoons, the rafters would be shaking.
Tosca, The Merry Widow, Carmen...
MARIA CALLAS
CARLO
TITO
...the more dramatic the better.
BEECHAM
PEER
Victoria de los Angeles
ANGEL
MAIS SI JE T'AIME
PRENDS GARDE A TOI

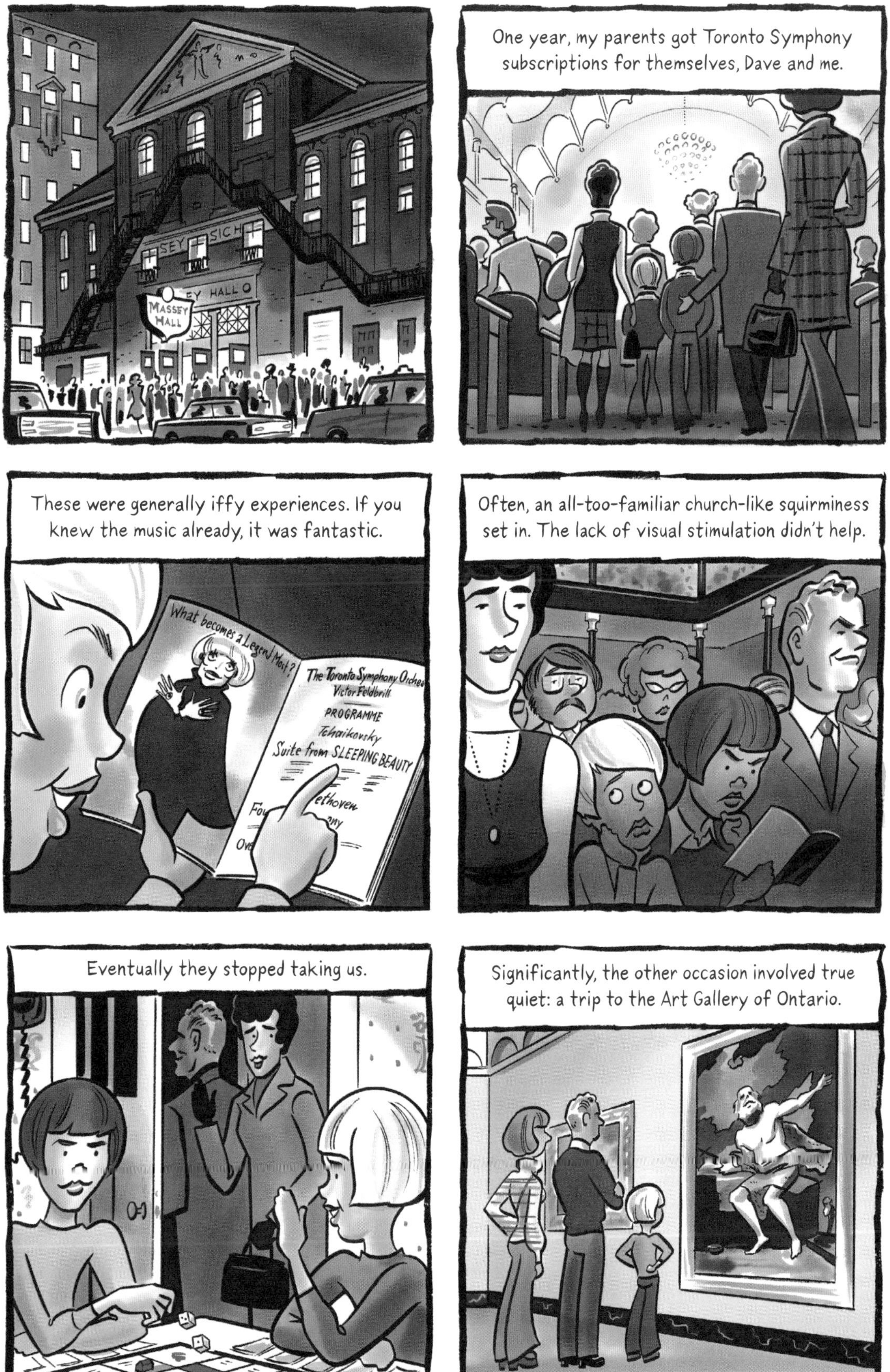
MASSEY HALL
One year, my parents got Toronto Symphony subscriptions for themselves, Dave and me.
These were generally iffy experiences. If you knew the music already, it was fantastic.
What becomes a Legend Most?
Victor Feldbrill
PROGRAMME
Tchaikovsky
Suite from SLEEPING BEAUTY
Often, an all-too-familiar church-like squirminess set in. The lack of visual stimulation didn't help.
Eventually they stopped taking us.
Significantly, the other occasion involved true quiet: a trip to the Art Gallery of Ontario.

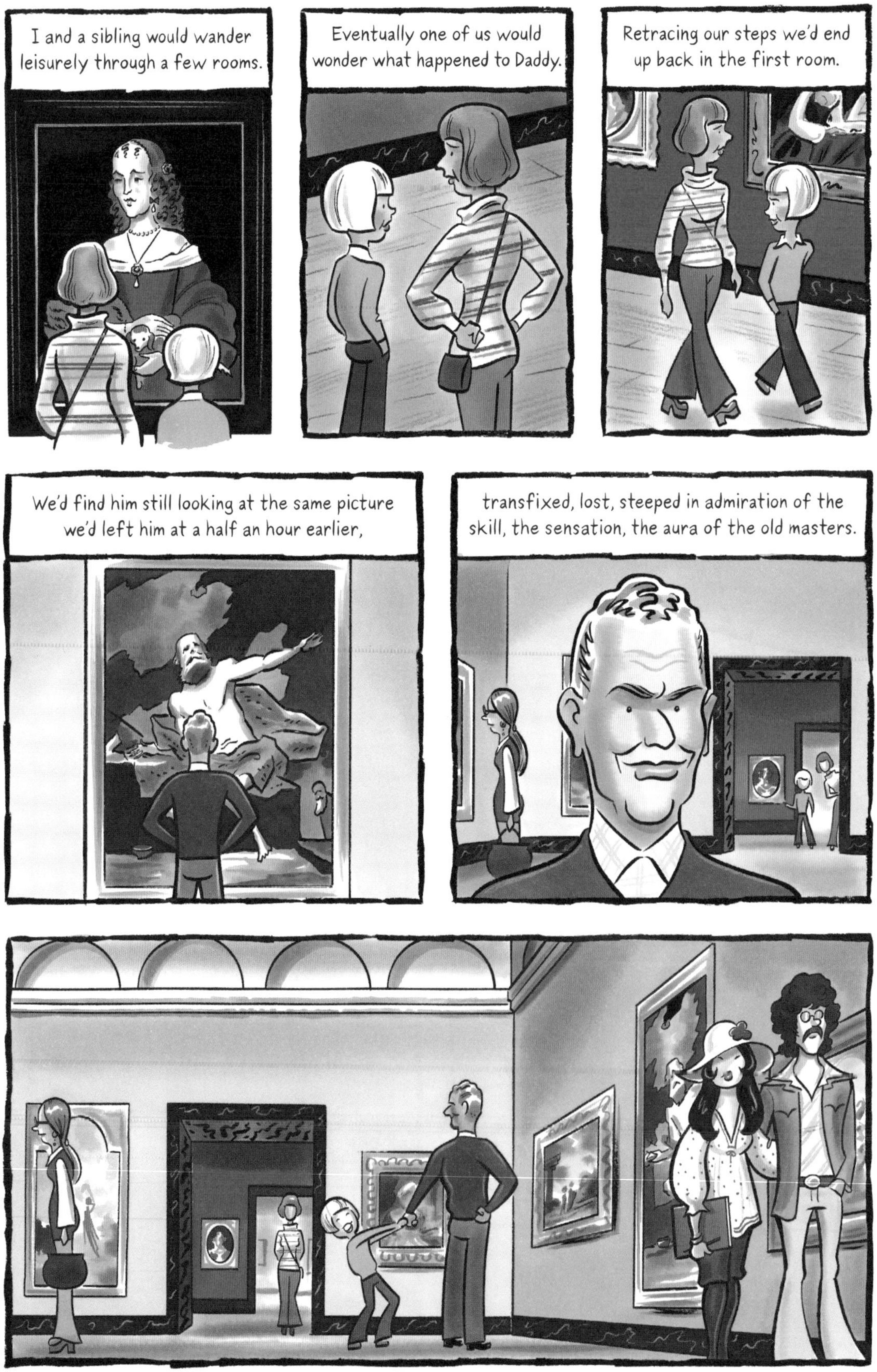
I and a sibling would wander leisurely through a few rooms.
Eventually one of us would wonder what happened to Daddy.
Retracing our steps we'd end up back in the first room.
We'd find him still looking at the same picture we'd left him at a half an hour earlier,
transfixed, lost, steeped in admiration of the skill, the sensation, the aura of the old masters.

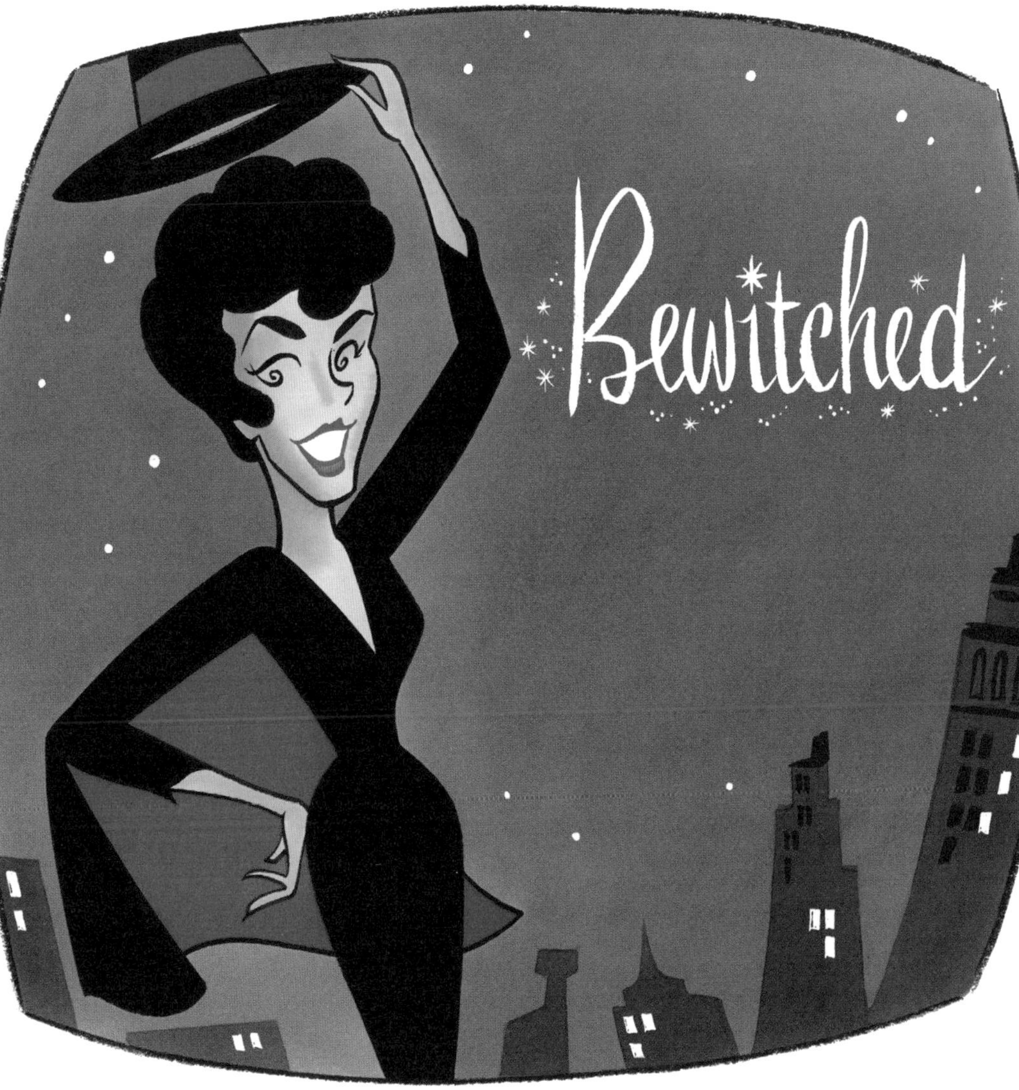
Bewitched

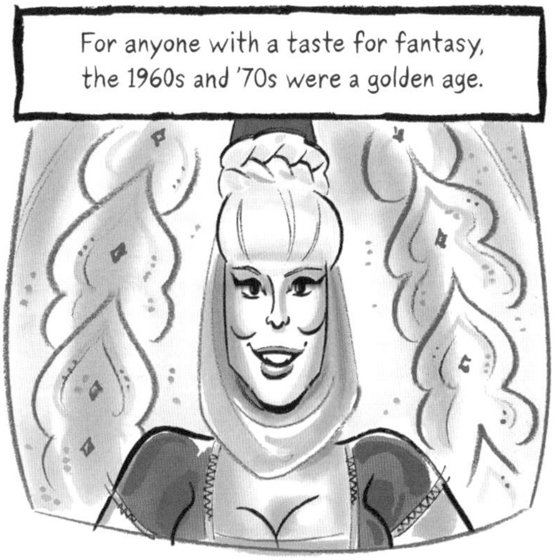
For anyone with a taste for fantasy,
the 1960s and '70s were a golden age.

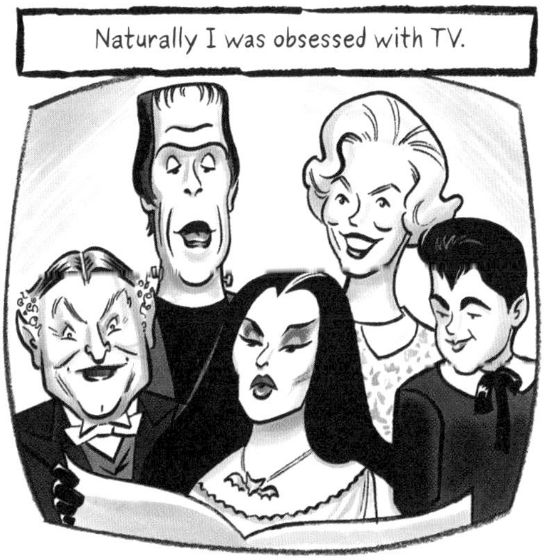
Naturally I was obsessed with TV.

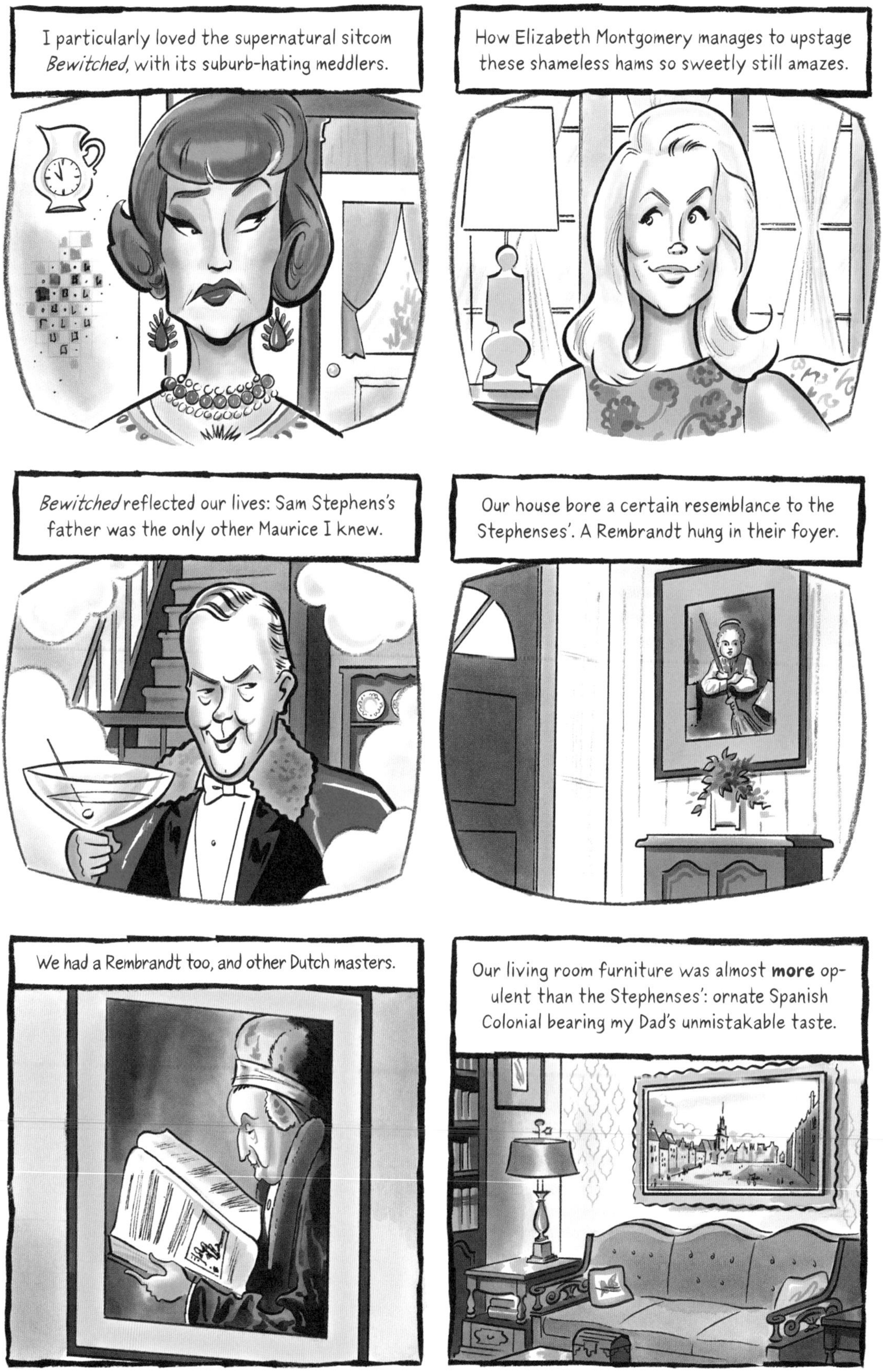
I particularly loved the supernatural sitcom *Bewitched*, with its suburb-hating meddlers.
How Elizabeth Montgomery manages to upstage these shameless hams so sweetly still amazes.
Bewitched reflected our lives: Sam Stephens's father was the only other Maurice I knew.
Our house bore a certain resemblance to the Stephenses'. A Rembrandt hung in their foyer.
We had a Rembrandt too, and other Dutch masters.
Our living room furniture was almost **more** opulent than the Stephenses': ornate Spanish Colonial bearing my Dad's unmistakable taste.

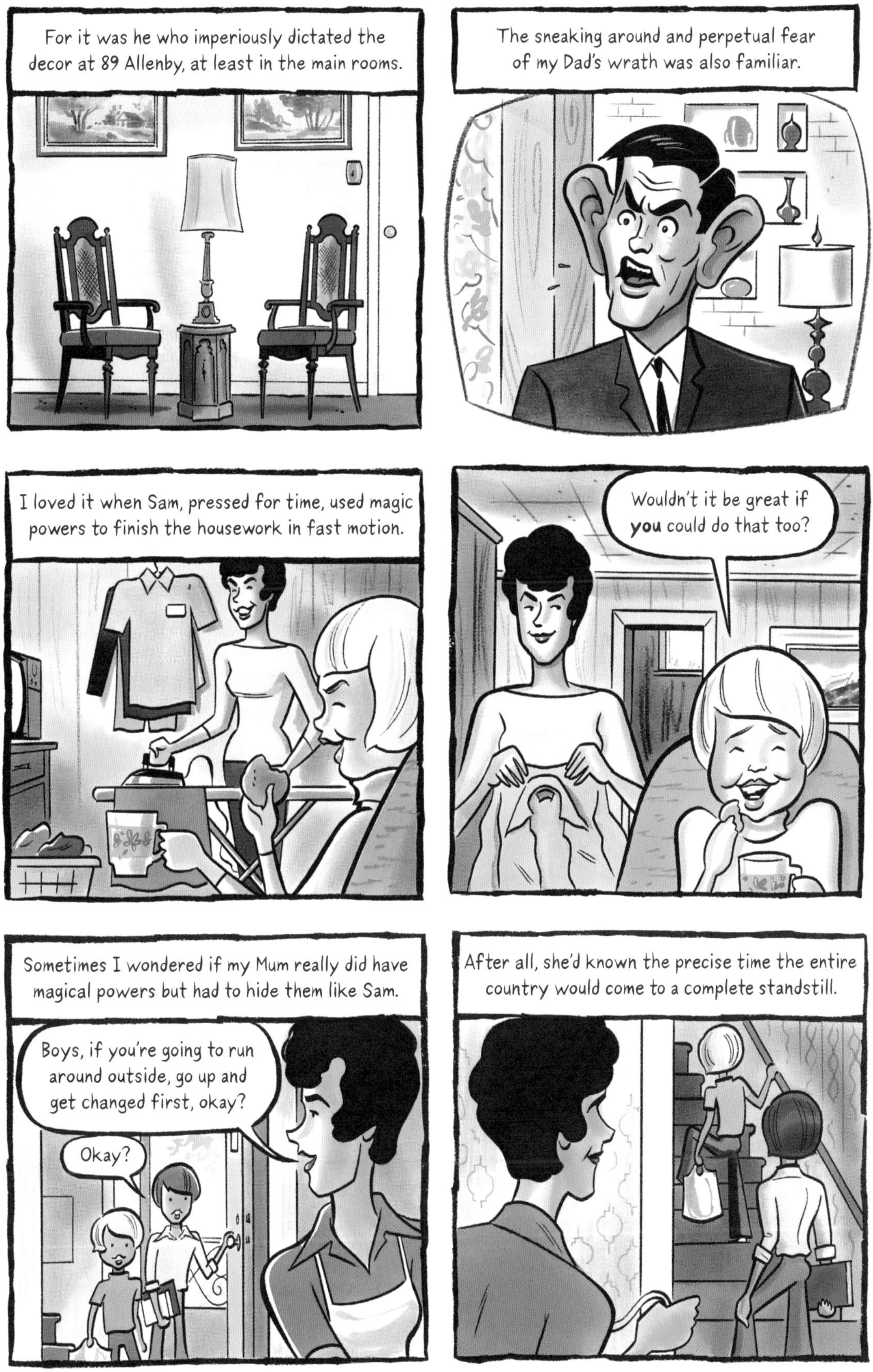
For it was he who imperiously dictated the decor at 89 Allenby, at least in the main rooms.
The sneaking around and perpetual fear of my Dad's wrath was also familiar.
I loved it when Sam, pressed for time, used magic powers to finish the housework in fast motion.
Wouldn't it be great if **you** could do that too?
Sometimes I wondered if my Mum really did have magical powers but had to hide them like Sam.
Boys, if you're going to run around outside, go up and get changed first, okay?
Okay?
After all, she'd known the precise time the entire country would come to a complete standstill.

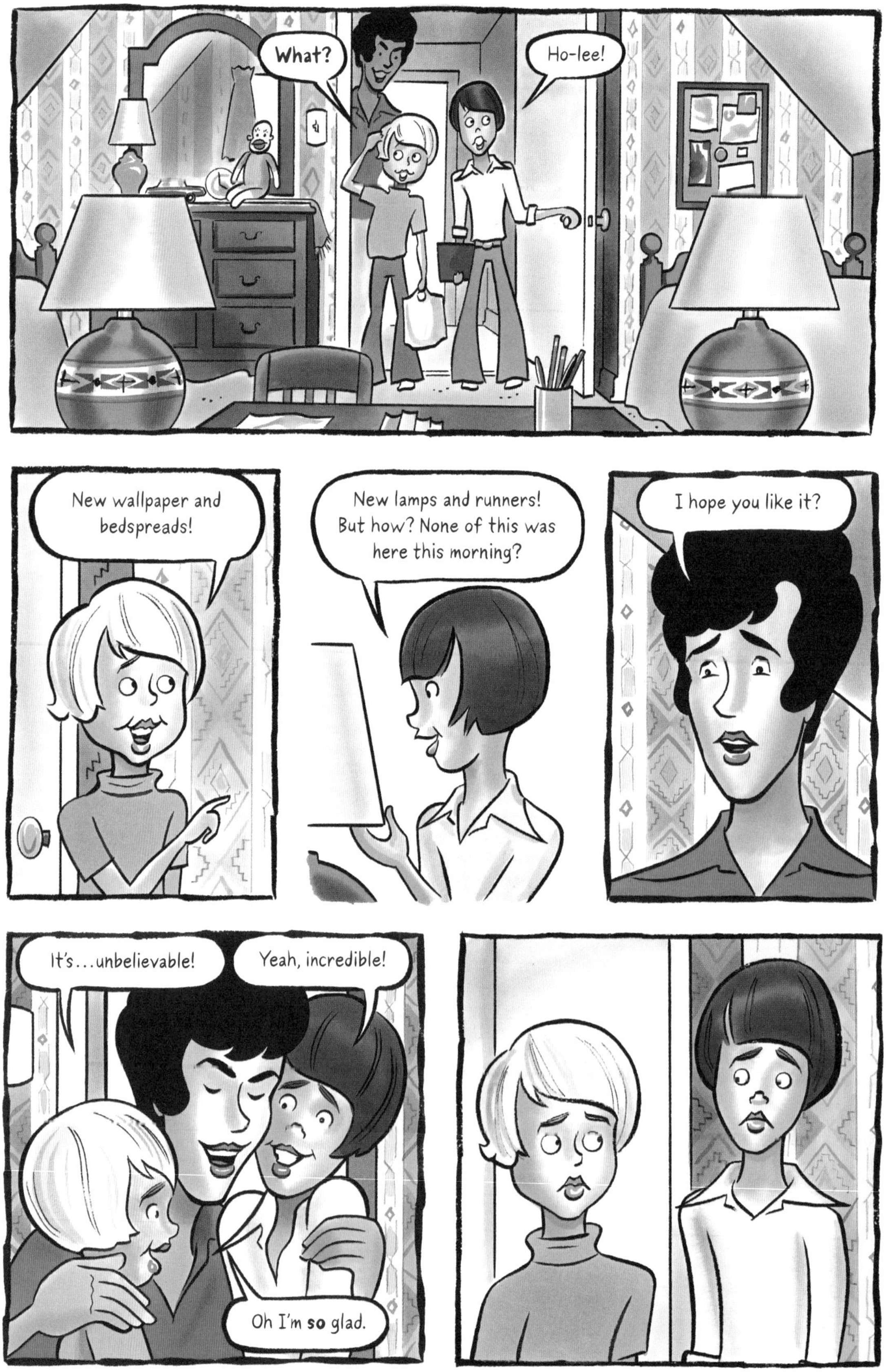
What?
Ho-lee!
New wallpaper and bedspreads!
New lamps and runners! But how? None of this was here this morning?
I hope you like it?
It's...unbelievable!
Yeah, incredible!
Oh I'm **so** glad.

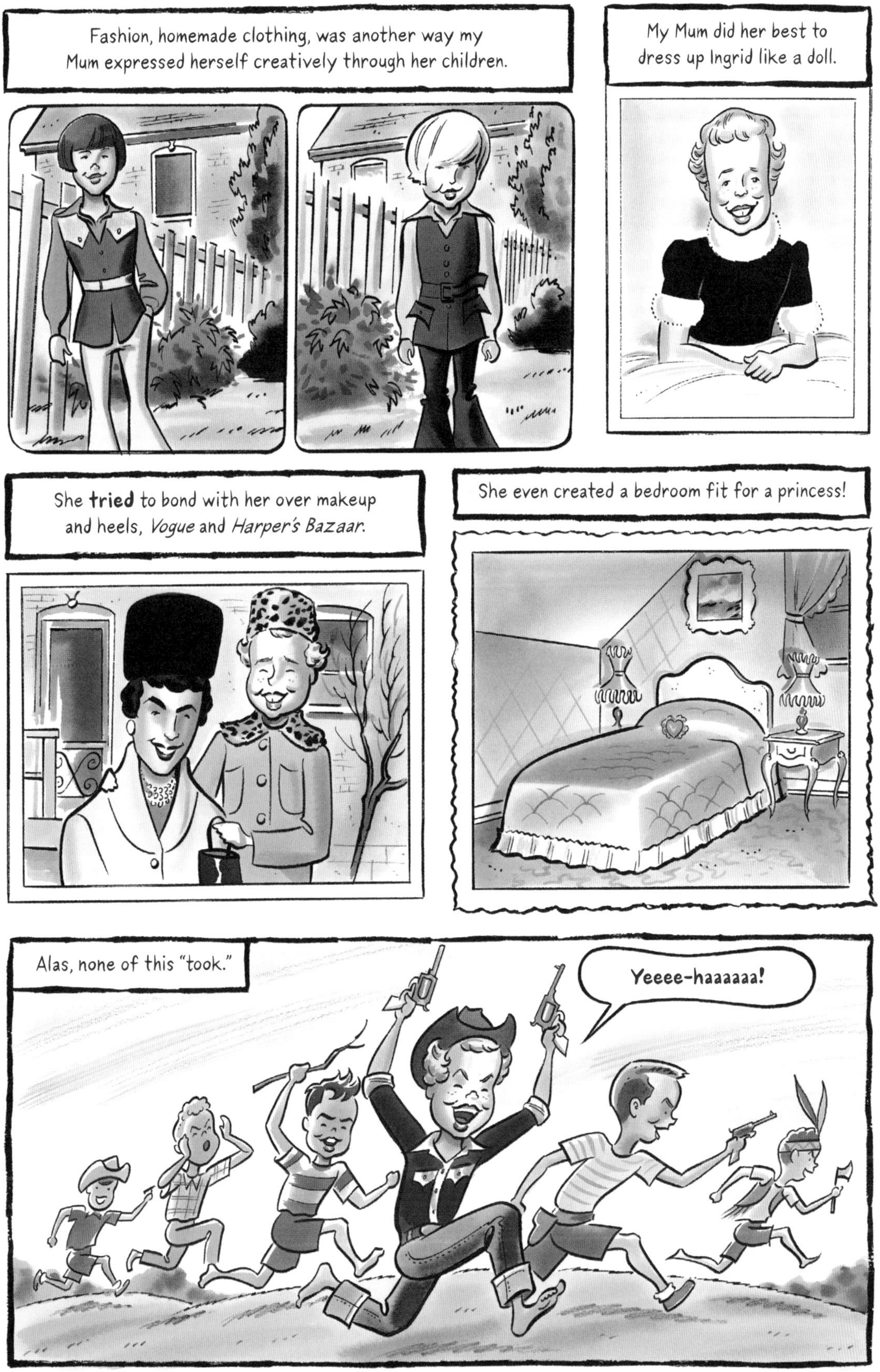
Fashion, homemade clothing, was another way my Mum expressed herself creatively through her children.
My Mum did her best to dress up Ingrid like a doll.
She **tried** to bond with her over makeup and heels, *Vogue* and *Harper's Bazaar*.
She even created a bedroom fit for a princess!
Alas, none of this "took."
Yeeee-haaaaaa!

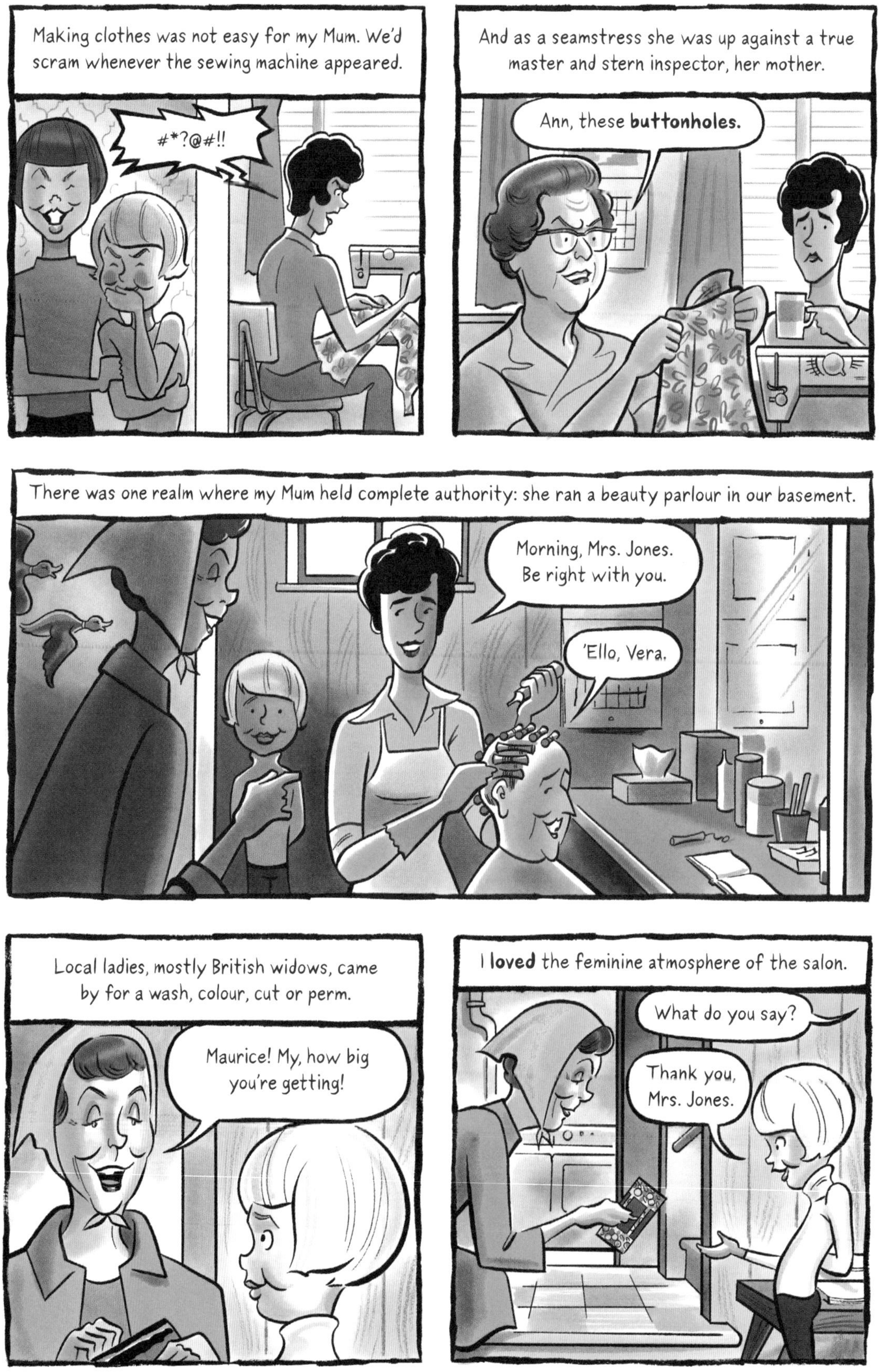

Making clothes was not easy for my Mum. We'd scram whenever the sewing machine appeared.
#*?@#!!
And as a seamstress she was up against a true master and stern inspector, her mother.
Ann, these **buttonholes.**
There was one realm where my Mum held complete authority: she ran a beauty parlour in our basement.
Morning, Mrs. Jones. Be right with you.
'Ello, Vera.
Local ladies, mostly British widows, came by for a wash, colour, cut or perm.
Maurice! My, how big you're getting!
I **loved** the feminine atmosphere of the salon.
What do you say?
Thank you, Mrs. Jones.

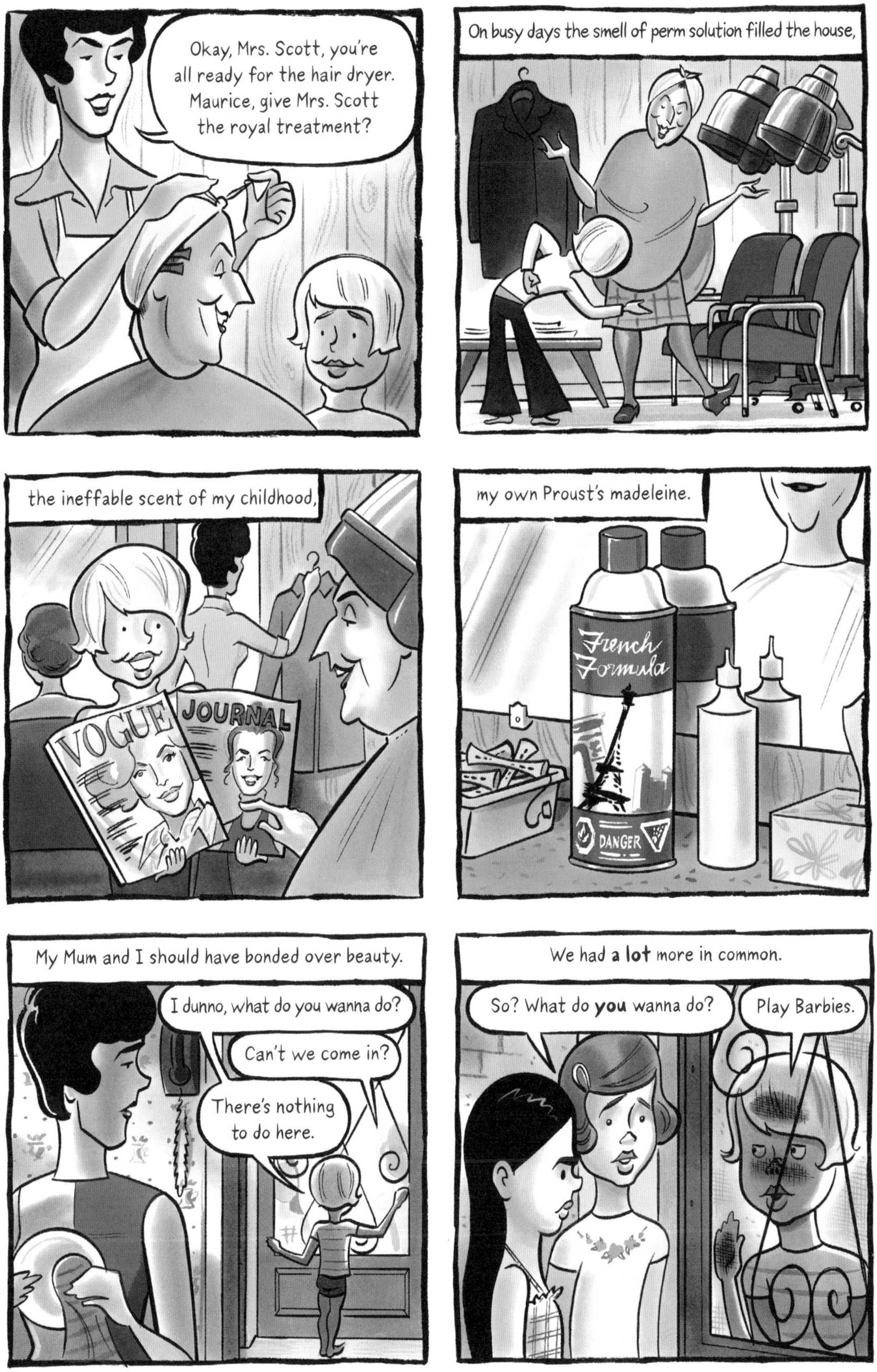
Okay, Mrs. Scott, you're all ready for the hair dryer. Maurice, give Mrs. Scott the royal treatment?
On busy days the smell of perm solution filled the house,
the ineffable scent of my childhood,
VOGUE
JOURNAL
my own Proust's madeleine.
French Formula
DANGER
My Mum and I should have bonded over beauty.
I dunno, what do you wanna do?
Can't we come in?
There's nothing to do here.
We had **a lot** more in common.
So? What do **you** wanna do?
Play Barbies.

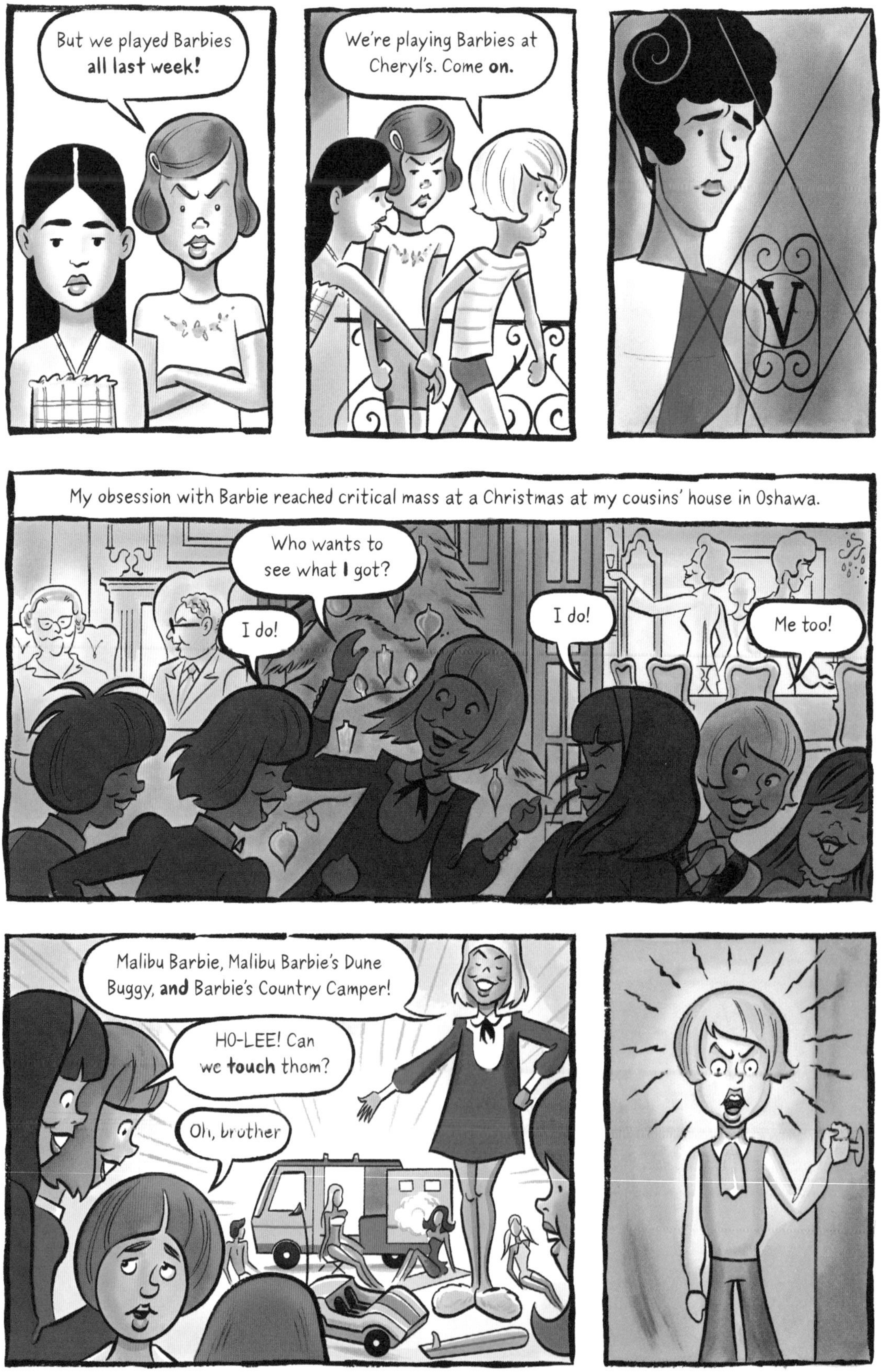

But we played Barbies **all last week!**
We're playing Barbies at Cheryl's. Come **on.**
My obsession with Barbie reached critical mass at a Christmas at my cousins' house in Oshawa.
Who wants to see what **I** got?
I do!
I do!
Me too!
Malibu Barbie, Malibu Barbie's Dune Buggy, **and** Barbie's Country Camper!
HO-LEE! Can we **touch** them?
Oh, brother

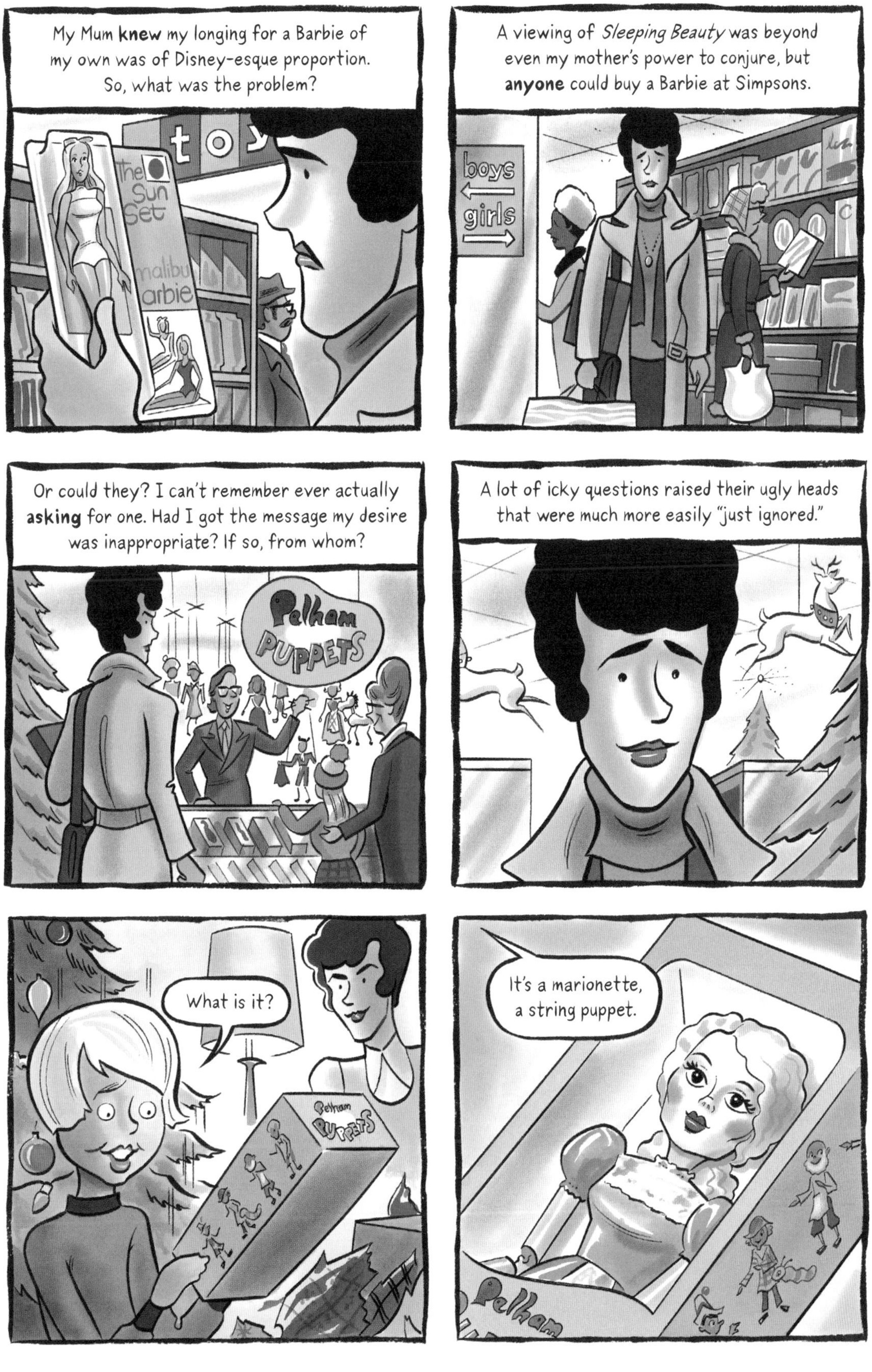
My Mum **knew** my longing for a Barbie of my own was of Disney-esque proportion. So, what was the problem?
toy
The Sun Set
malibu
arbie
A viewing of *Sleeping Beauty* was beyond even my mother's power to conjure, but **anyone** could buy a Barbie at Simpsons.
boys
girls
Or could they? I can't remember ever actually **asking** for one. Had I got the message my desire was inappropriate? If so, from whom?
Pelham PUPPETS
A lot of icky questions raised their ugly heads that were much more easily "just ignored."
What is it?
Pelham PUPPETS
It's a marionette, a string puppet.
Pelham

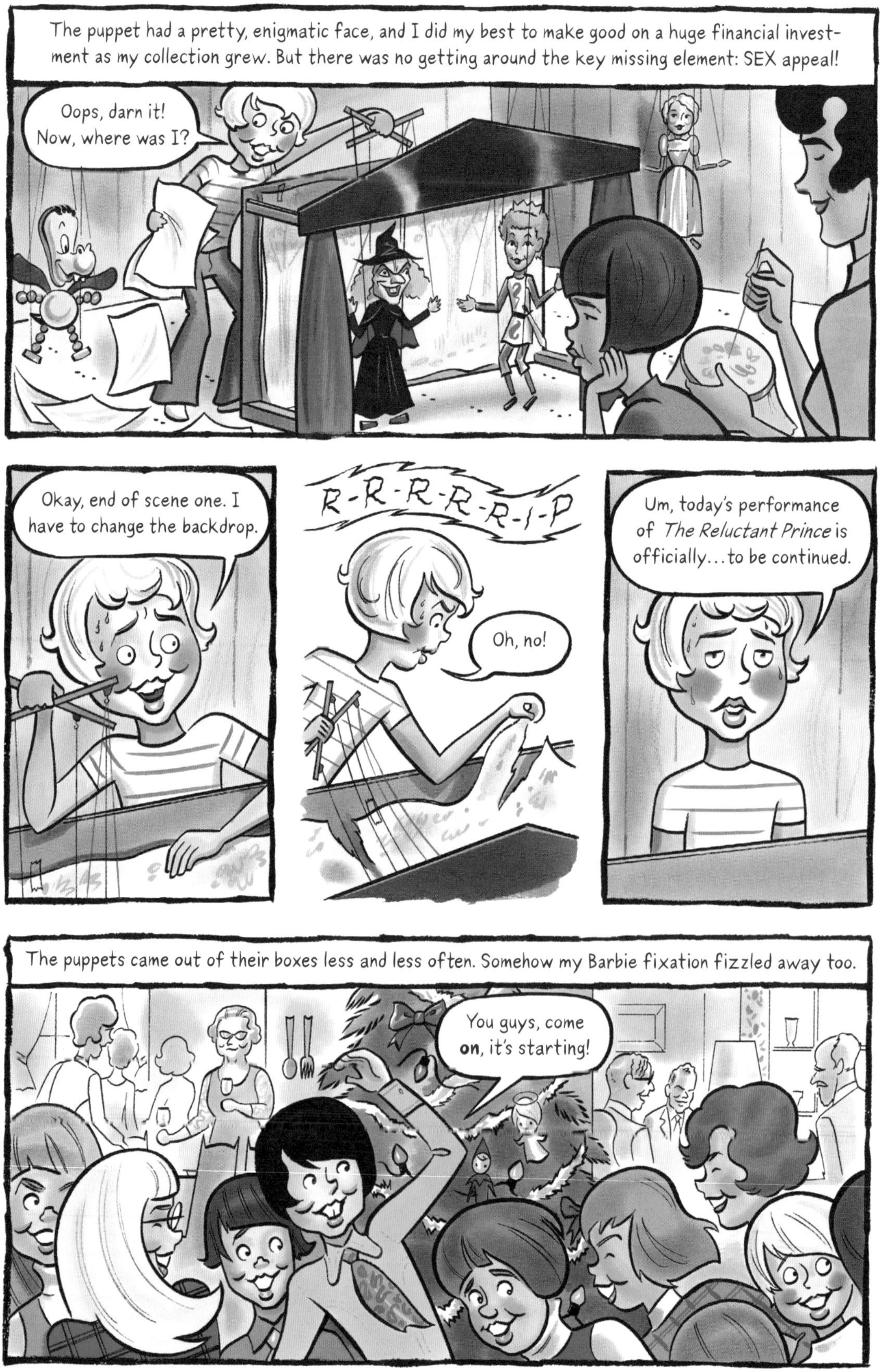

The puppet had a pretty, enigmatic face, and I did my best to make good on a huge financial investment as my collection grew. But there was no getting around the key missing element: SEX appeal!
Oops, darn it! Now, where was I?
Okay, end of scene one. I have to change the backdrop.
R-R-R-R-R-I-P
Oh, no!
Um, today's performance of *The Reluctant Prince* is officially... to be continued.
The puppets came out of their boxes less and less often. Somehow my Barbie fixation fizzled away too.
You guys, come **on**, it's starting!

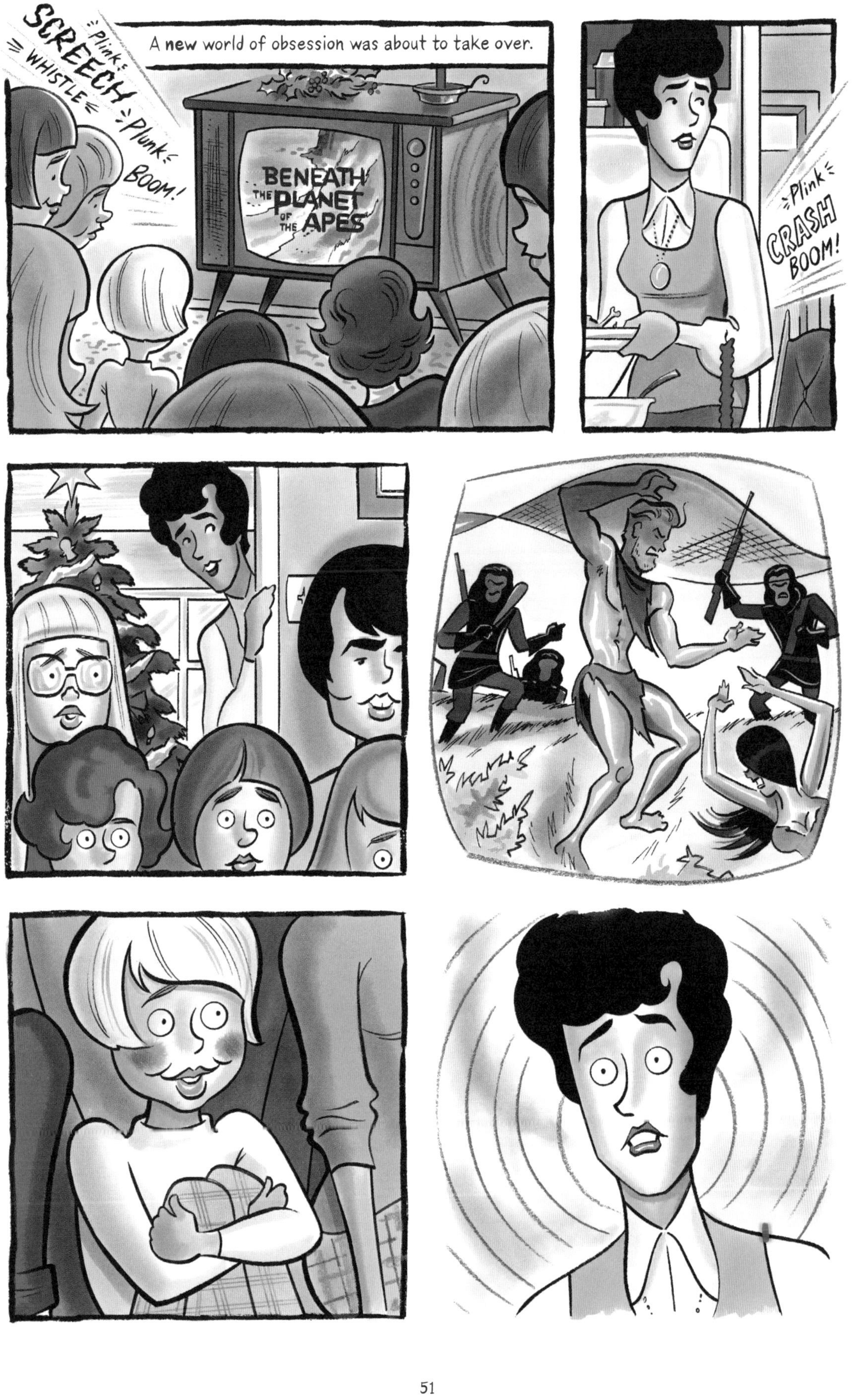

Plink
SCREECH
WHISTLE
Plunk
BOOM!
A new world of obsession was about to take over.
BENEATH THE PLANET OF THE APES
Plink
CRASH
BOOM!

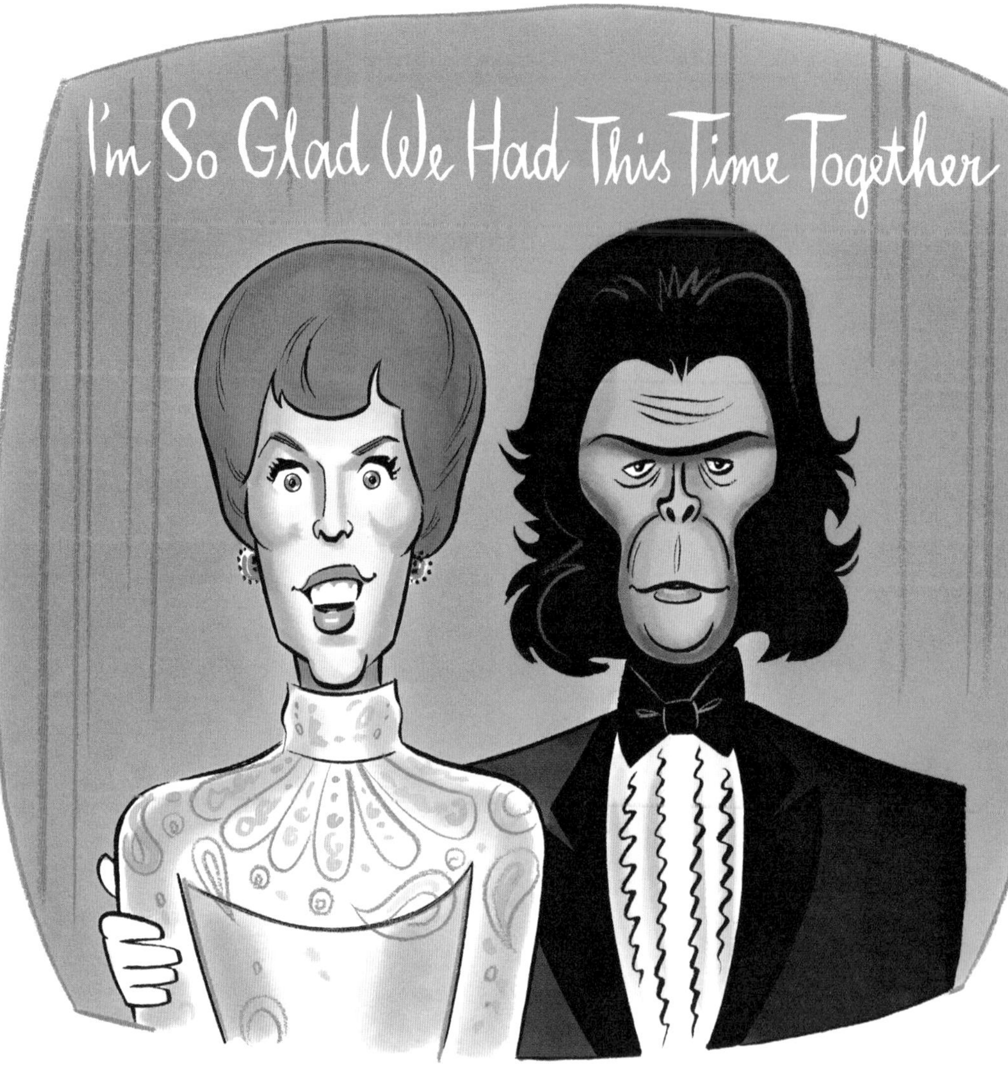
I'm So Glad We Had This Time Together

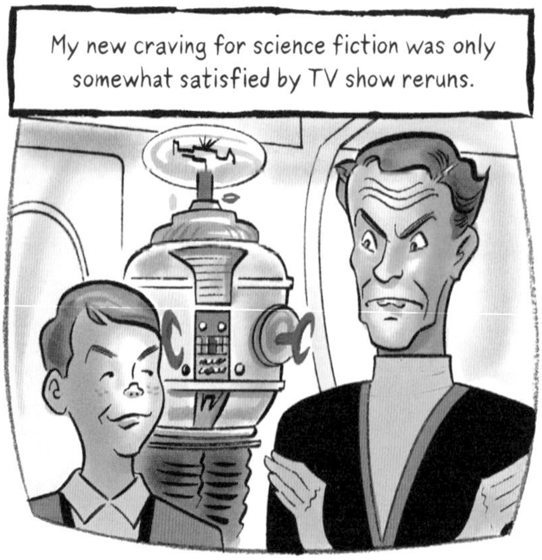
My new craving for science fiction was only somewhat satisfied by TV show reruns.

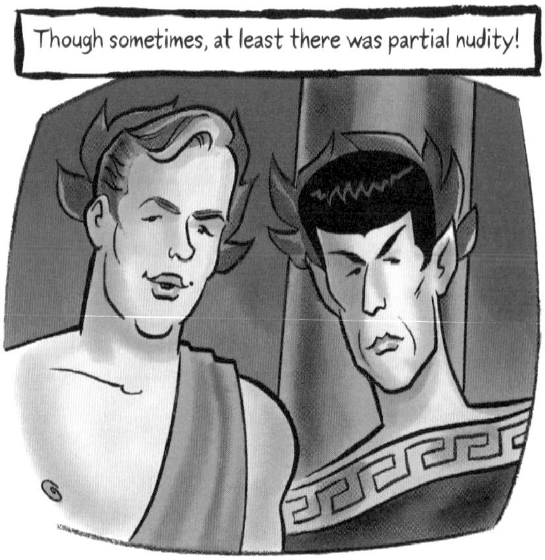
Though sometimes, at least there was partial nudity!

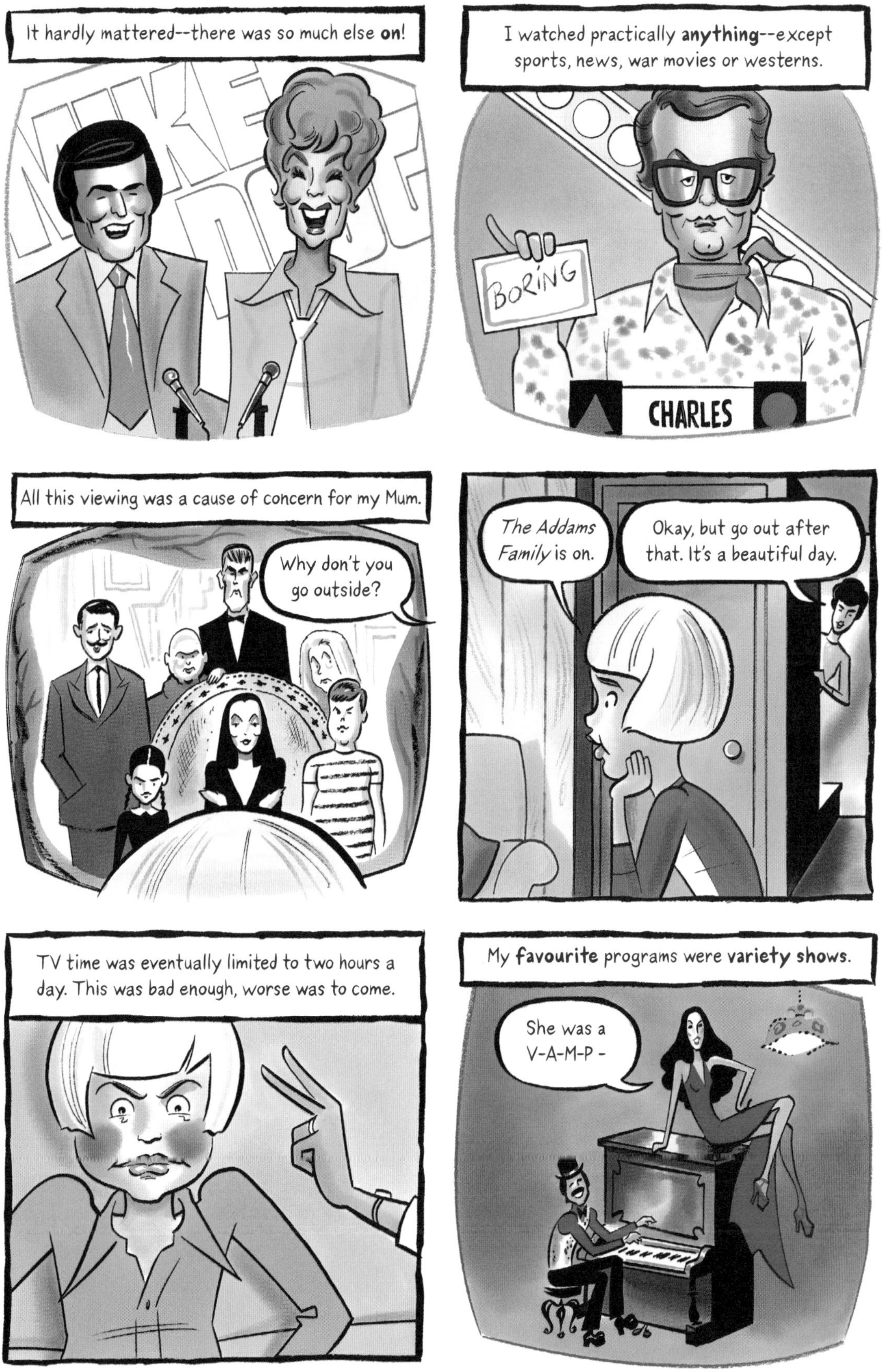
It hardly mattered--there was so much else **on**!
I watched practically **anything**--except sports, news, war movies or westerns.
BORING
CHARLES
All this viewing was a cause of concern for my Mum.
Why don't you go outside?
The Addams Family is on.
Okay, but go out after that. It's a beautiful day.
TV time was eventually limited to two hours a day. This was bad enough, worse was to come.
My **favourite** programs were **variety shows**.
She was a V-A-M-P -

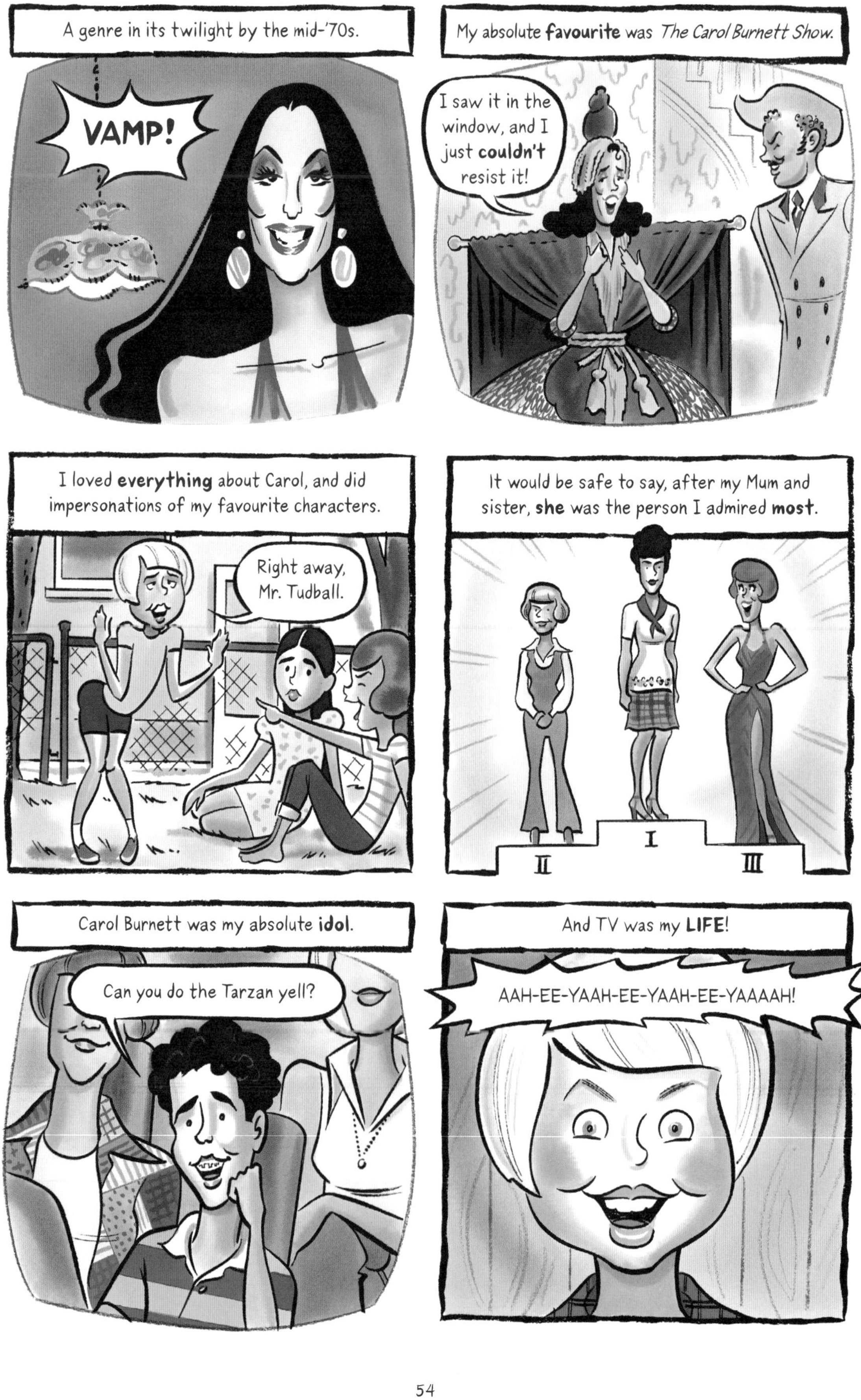
A genre in its twilight by the mid-'70s.
VAMP!
My absolute **favourite** was *The Carol Burnett Show.*
I saw it in the window, and I just **couldn't** resist it!
I loved **everything** about Carol, and did impersonations of my favourite characters.
Right away, Mr. Tudball.
It would be safe to say, after my Mum and sister, **she** was the person I admired **most**.
II
I
III
Carol Burnett was my absolute **idol**.
Can you do the Tarzan yell?
And TV was my **LIFE**!
AAH-EE-YAAH-EE-YAAH-EE-YAAAAH!

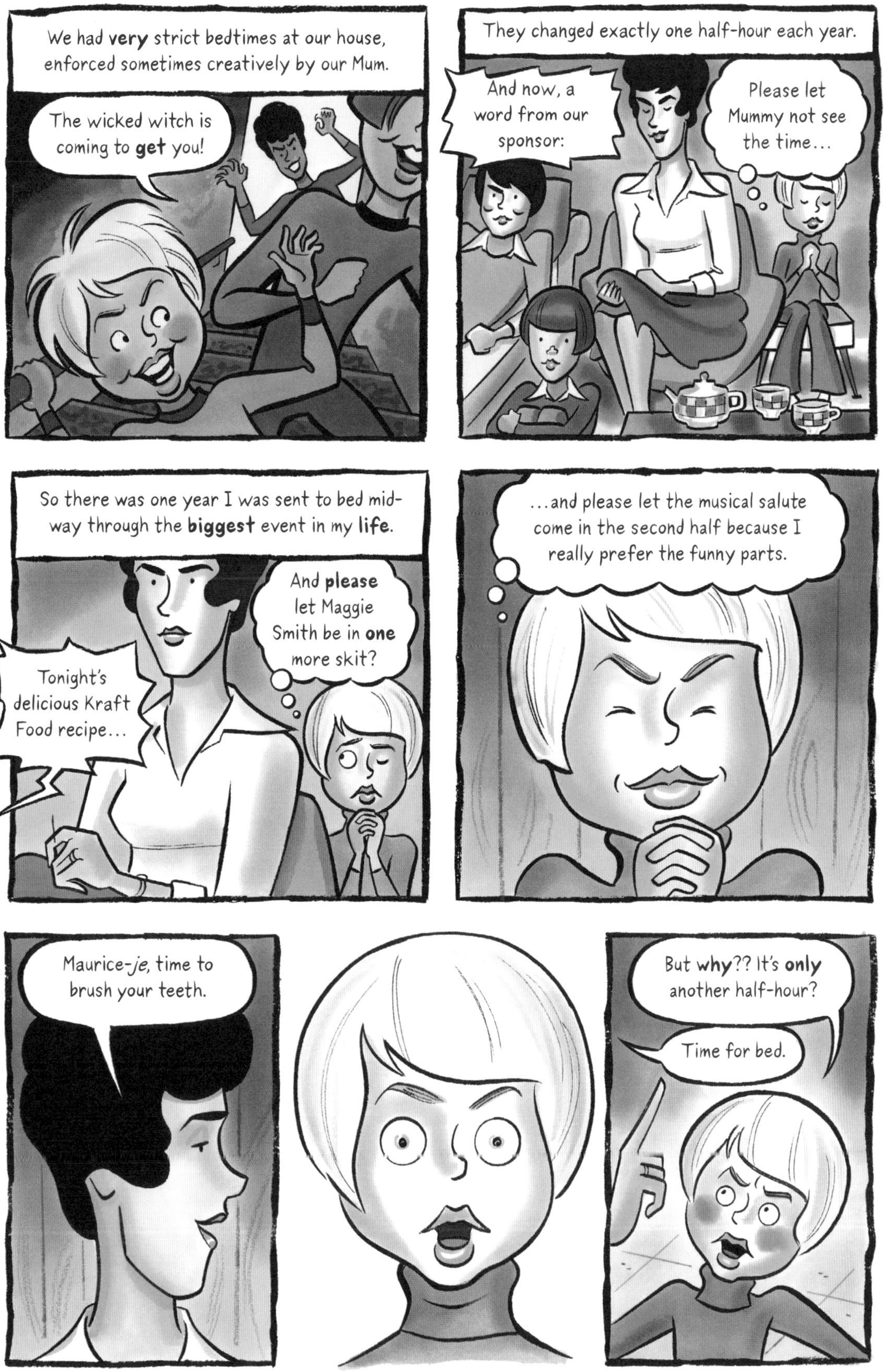
We had **very** strict bedtimes at our house, enforced sometimes creatively by our Mum.
The wicked witch is coming to **get** you!
They changed exactly one half-hour each year.
And now, a word from our sponsor:
Please let Mummy not see the time...
So there was one year I was sent to bed mid-way through the **biggest** event in my **life**.
Tonight's delicious Kraft Food recipe...
And **please** let Maggie Smith be in **one** more skit?
...and please let the musical salute come in the second half because I really prefer the funny parts.
Maurice-*je*, time to brush your teeth.
But **why**?? It's **only** another half-hour?
Time for bed.

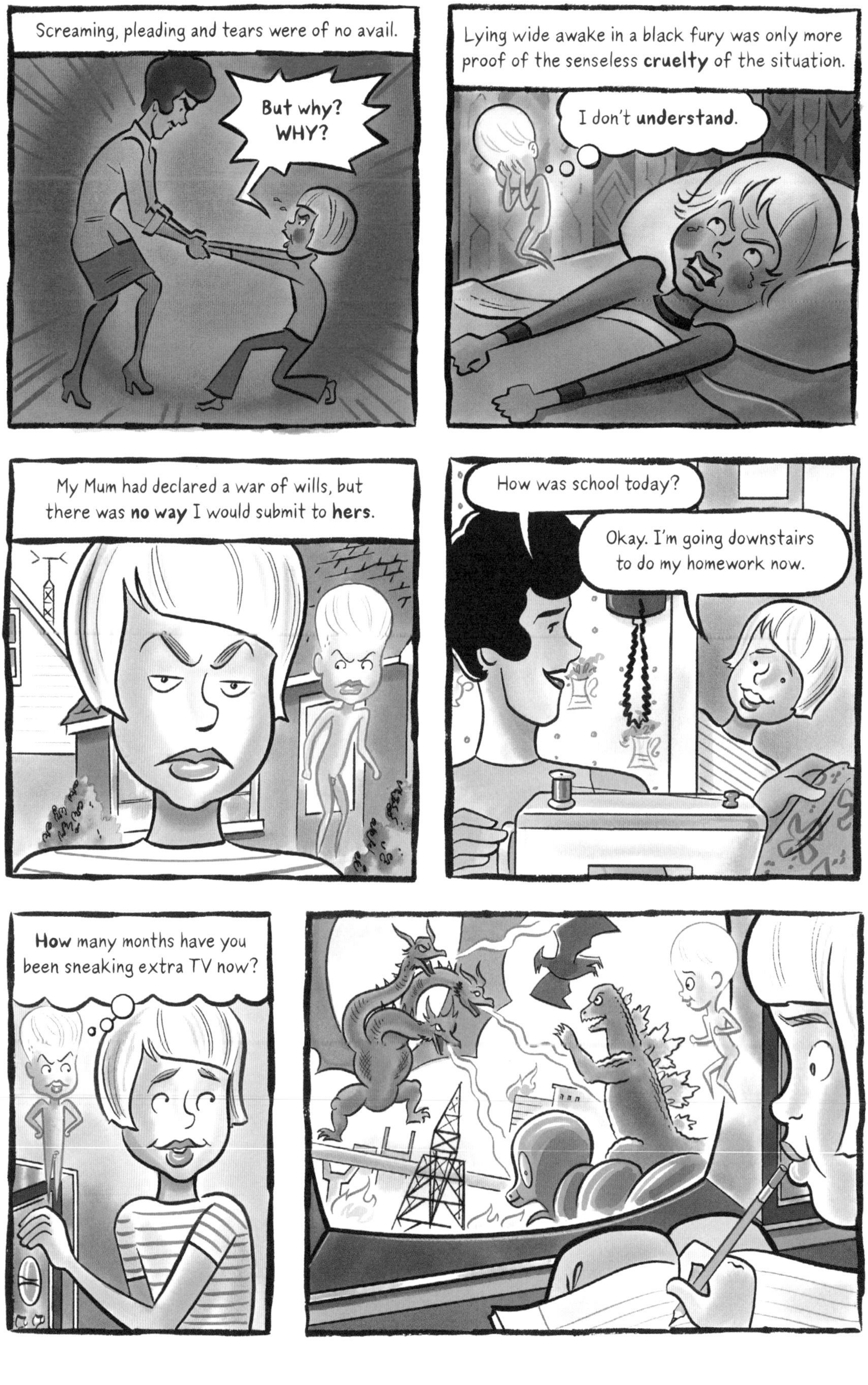
Screaming, pleading and tears were of no avail.
But why? WHY?
Lying wide awake in a black fury was only more proof of the senseless **cruelty** of the situation.
I don't **understand**.
My Mum had declared a war of wills, but there was **no way** I would submit to **hers**.
How was school today?
Okay. I'm going downstairs to do my homework now.
How many months have you been sneaking extra TV now?

It's incredible she **still** hasn't caught on to you.

THE END
RICAN INTERNATIONAL RELEASE

Supper's almost ready.

Just in time for *M*A*S*H*! And then *All in the Family* and *Ironside* and that will be my two hours, right?

Right. Now give me a hug.

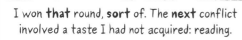

I won **that** round, **sort** of. The **next** conflict involved a taste I had not acquired: reading.

Books were everywhere! My Dad's history and art books, my Mum's biographies and historical fiction.

SIMENON
CHURCHILL
Needlepoint NOW!

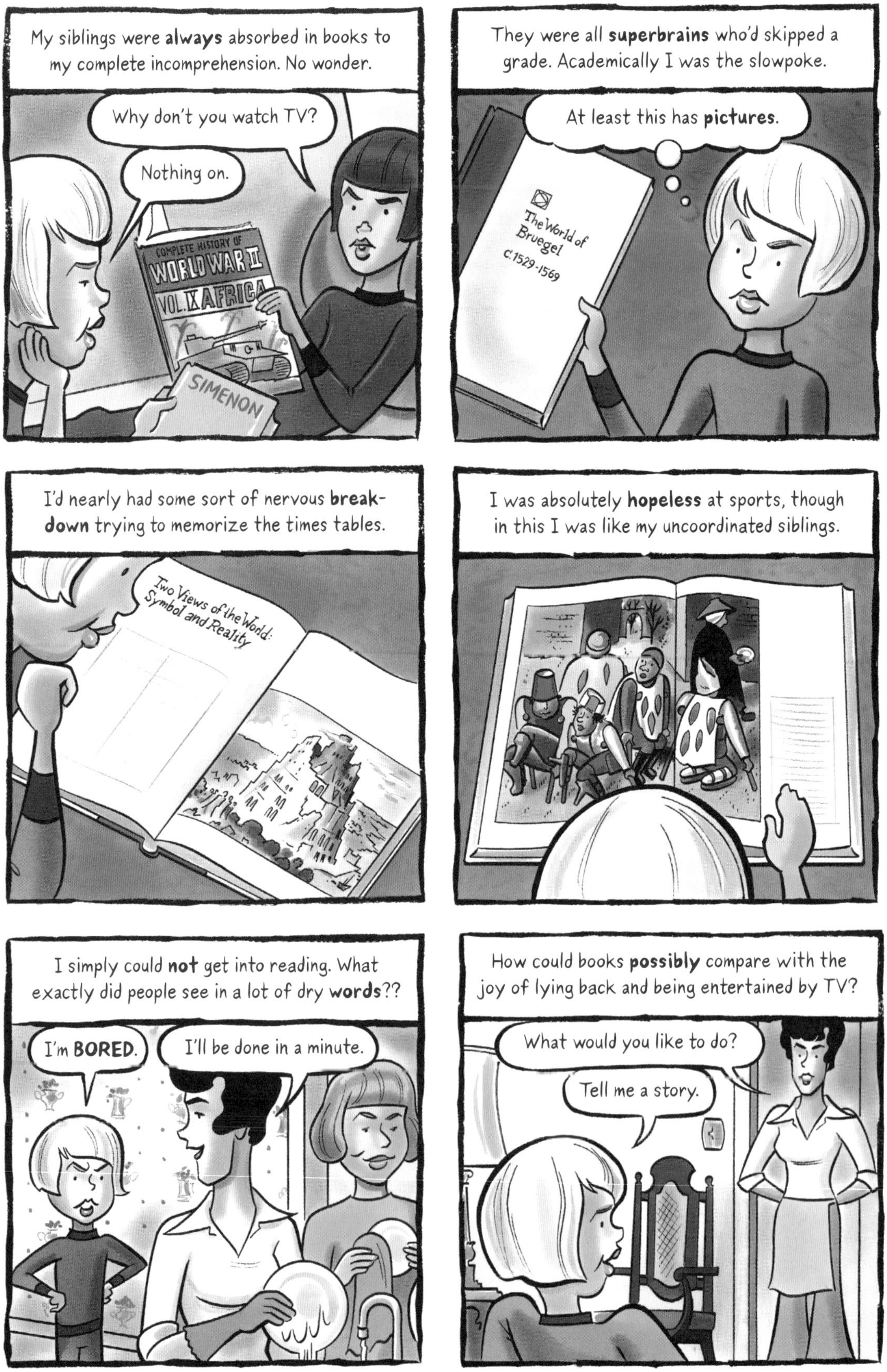
My siblings were **always** absorbed in books to my complete incomprehension. No wonder.
Why don't you watch TV?
Nothing on.
COMPLETE HISTORY OF WORLD WAR II VOL. X AFRICA
SIMENON
They were all **superbrains** who'd skipped a grade. Academically I was the slowpoke.
At least this has **pictures**.
The World of Bruegel c.1529-1569
I'd nearly had some sort of nervous **break-down** trying to memorize the times tables.
Two Views of the World: Symbol and Reality
I was absolutely **hopeless** at sports, though in this I was like my uncoordinated siblings.
I simply could **not** get into reading. What exactly did people see in a lot of dry **words**??
I'm **BORED**.
I'll be done in a minute.
How could books **possibly** compare with the joy of lying back and being entertained by TV?
What would you like to do?
Tell me a story.

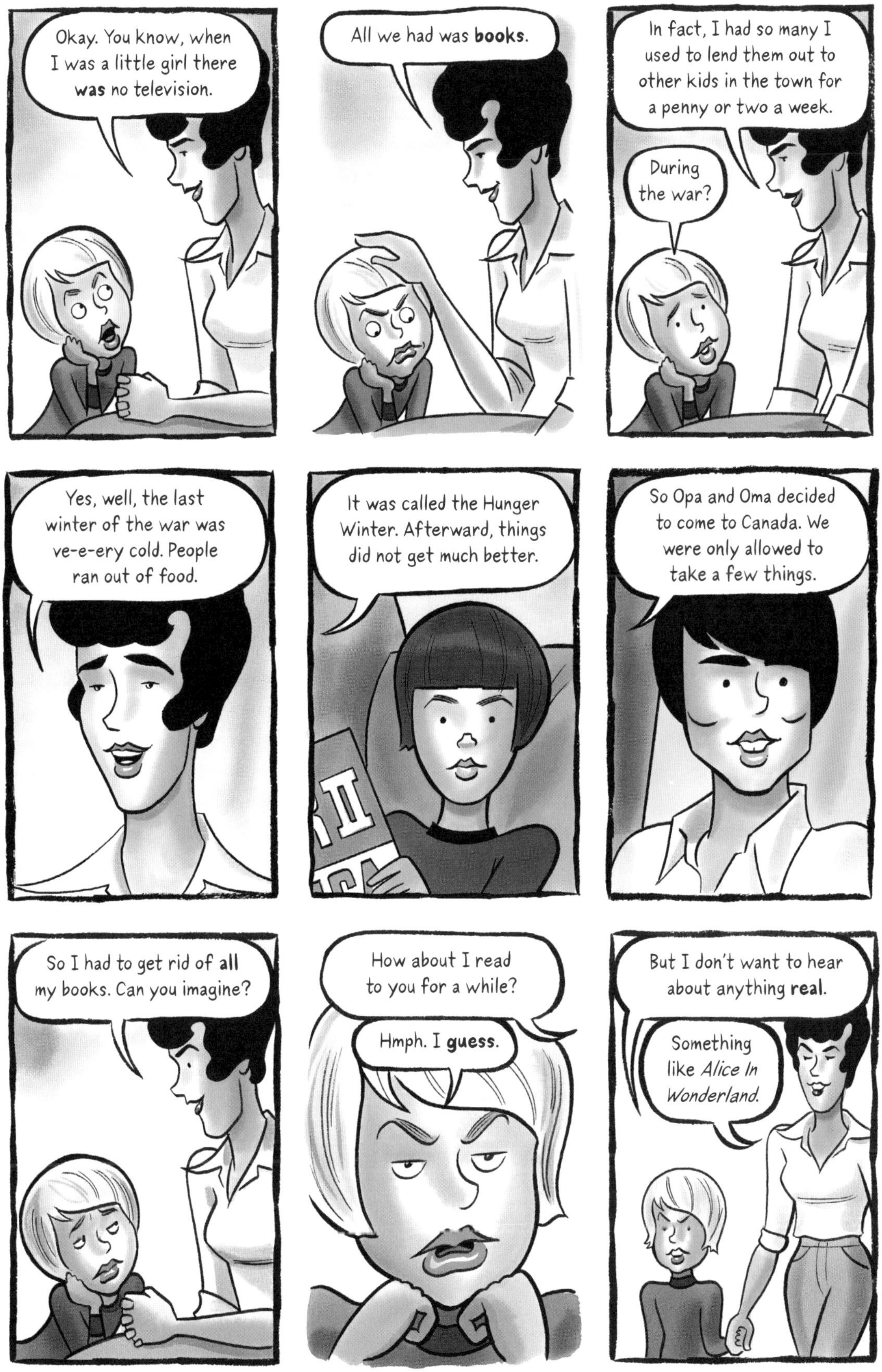
Okay. You know, when I was a little girl there **was** no television.
All we had was **books**.
In fact, I had so many I used to lend them out to other kids in the town for a penny or two a week.
During the war?
Yes, well, the last winter of the war was ve-e-ery cold. People ran out of food.
It was called the Hunger Winter. Afterward, things did not get much better.
So Opa and Oma decided to come to Canada. We were only allowed to take a few things.
So I had to get rid of **all** my books. Can you imagine?
How about I read to you for a while?
Hmph. I **guess**.
But I don't want to hear about anything **real**.
Something like *Alice In Wonderland*.

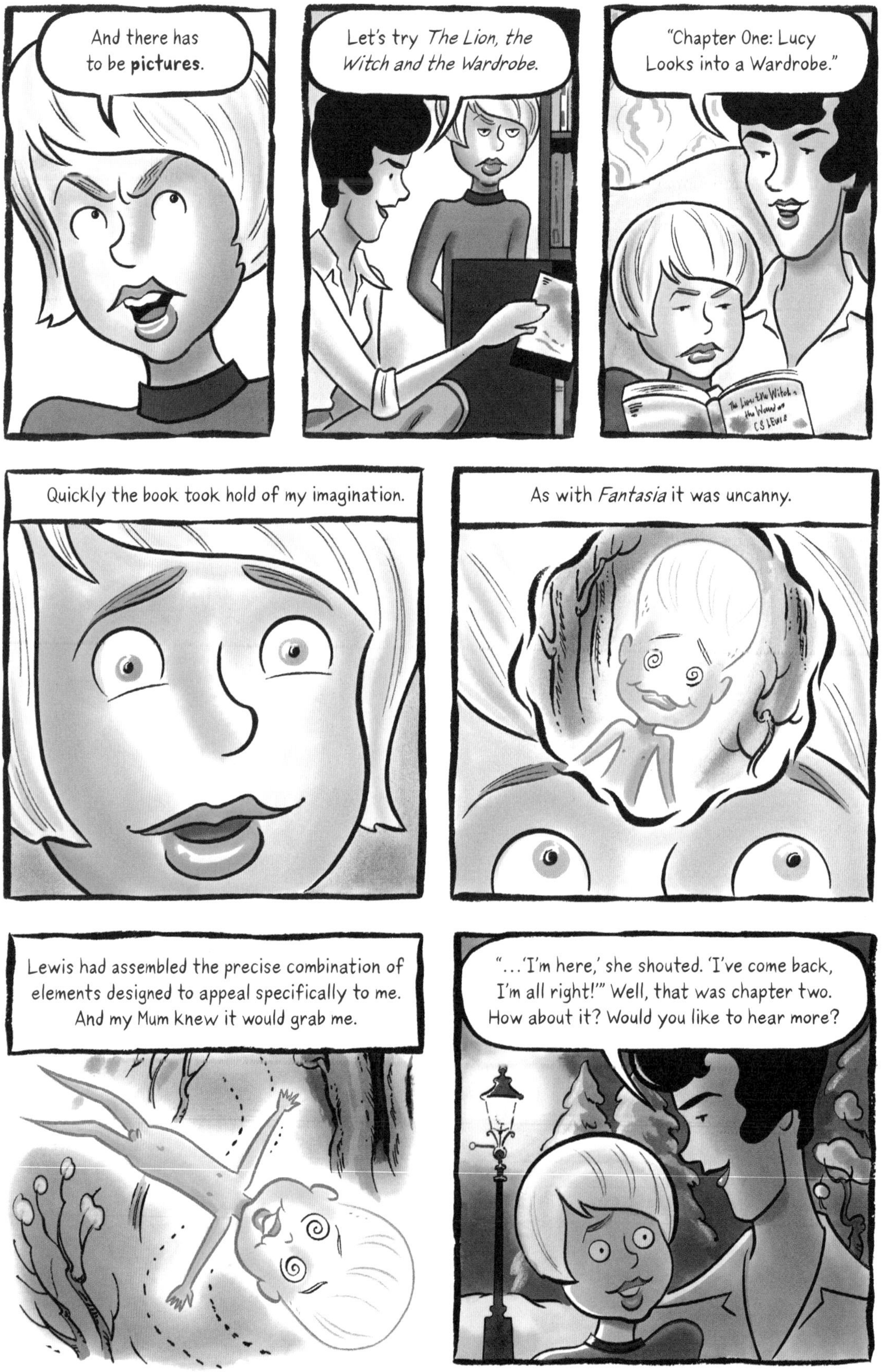

And there has to be **pictures**.
Let's try *The Lion, the Witch and the Wardrobe.*
"Chapter One: Lucy Looks into a Wardrobe."
Quickly the book took hold of my imagination.
As with *Fantasia* it was uncanny.
Lewis had assembled the precise combination of elements designed to appeal specifically to me. And my Mum knew it would grab me.
"...'I'm here,' she shouted. 'I've come back, I'm all right!'" Well, that was chapter two. How about it? Would you like to hear more?

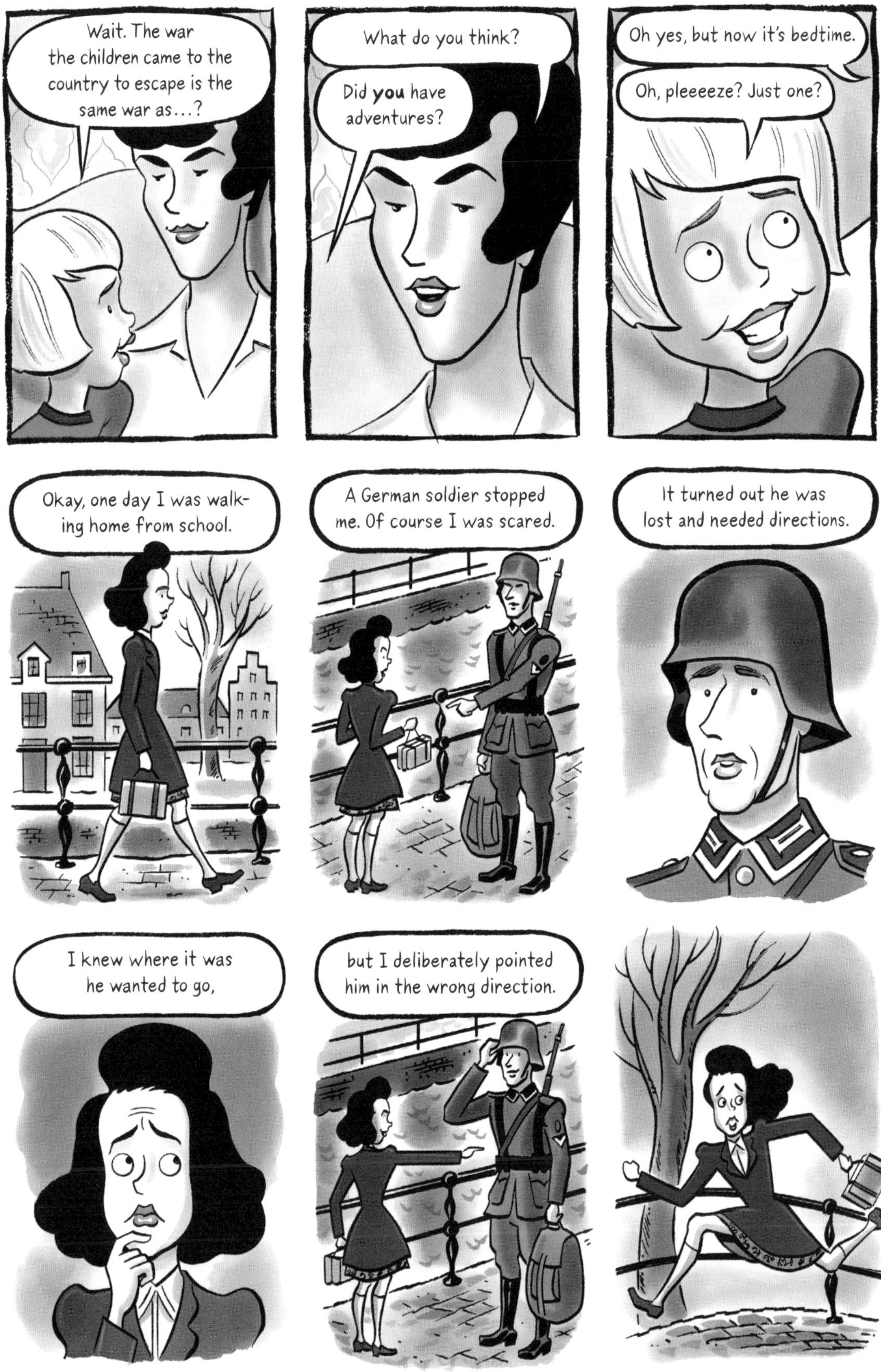
Wait. The war the children came to the country to escape is the same war as...?
What do you think?
Did **you** have adventures?
Oh yes, but now it's bedtime.
Oh, pleeeeze? Just one?
Okay, one day I was walk-ing home from school.
A German soldier stopped me. Of course I was scared.
It turned out he was lost and needed directions.
I knew where it was he wanted to go,
but I deliberately pointed him in the wrong direction.

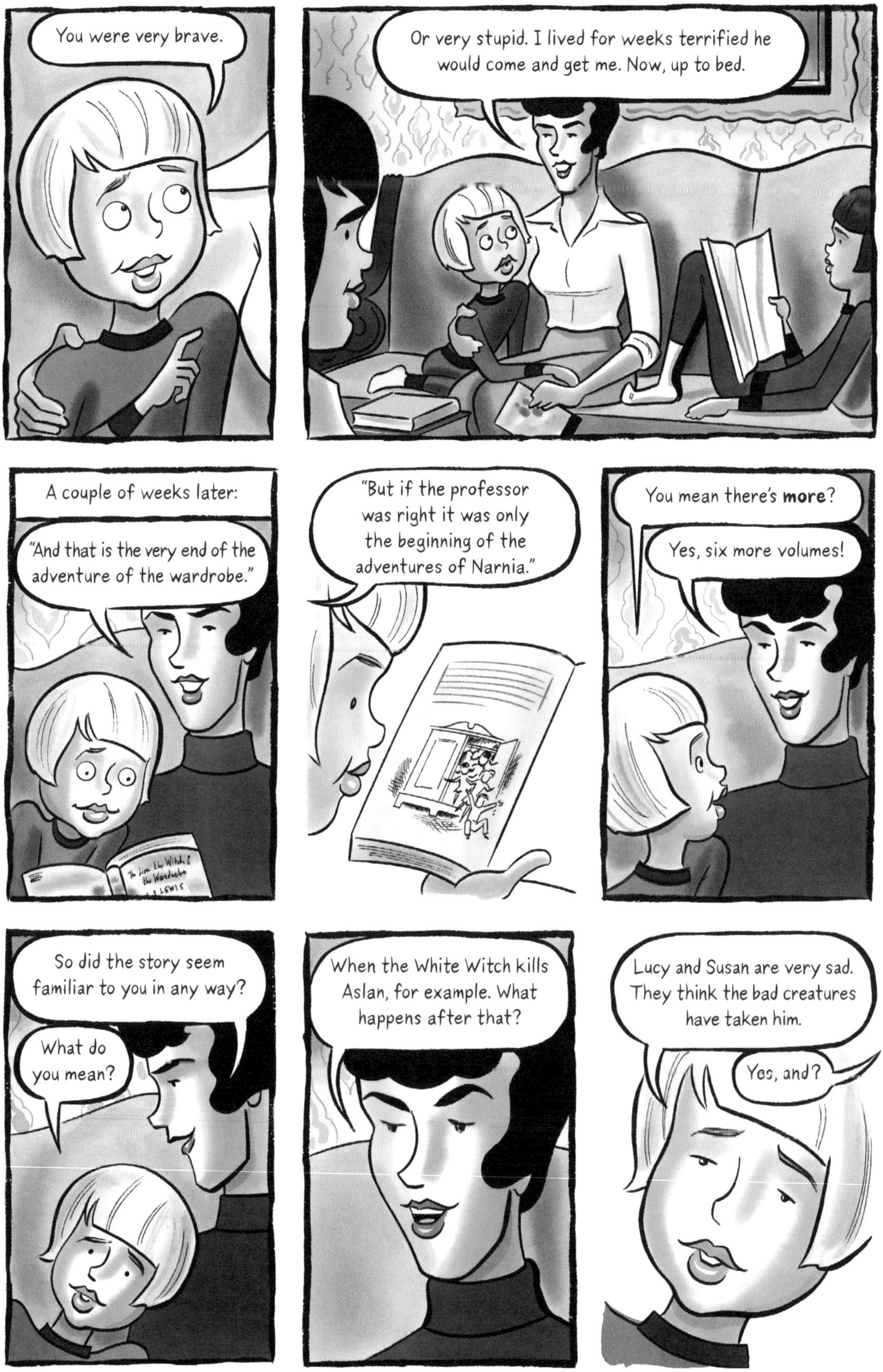
You were very brave.
Or very stupid. I lived for weeks terrified he would come and get me. Now, up to bed.
A couple of weeks later:
"And that is the very end of the adventure of the wardrobe."
"But if the professor was right it was only the beginning of the adventures of Narnia."
You mean there's **more**?
Yes, six more volumes!
So did the story seem familiar to you in any way?
What do you mean?
When the White Witch kills Aslan, for example. What happens after that?
Lucy and Susan are very sad. They think the bad creatures have taken him.
Yes, and?

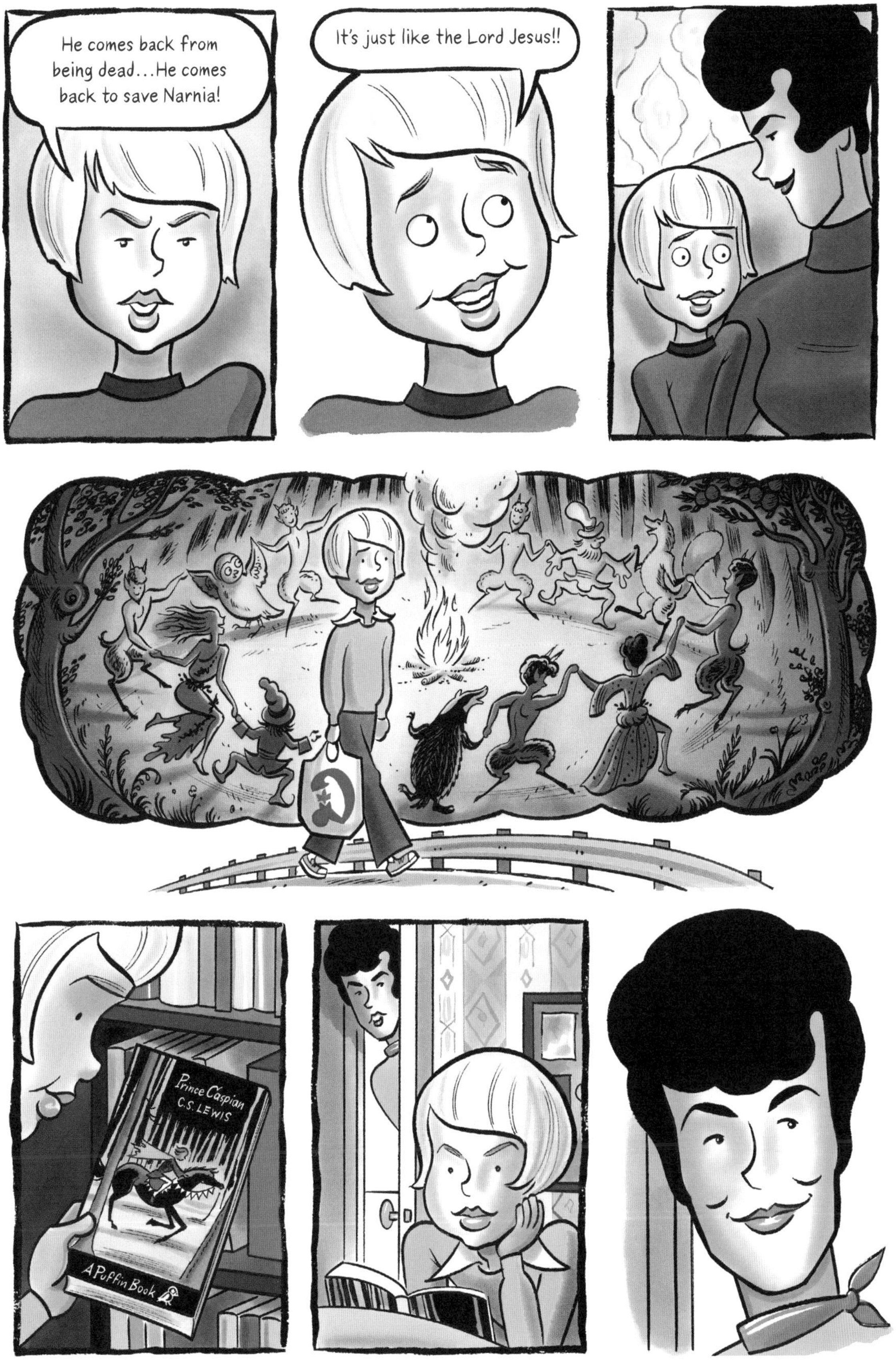
He comes back from being dead...He comes back to save Narnia!
It's just like the Lord Jesus!!
Prince Caspian
C.S. LEWIS
A Puffin Book

By introducing me to the Narnia books, my Mum had unwittingly created a monster.

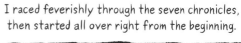

I raced feverishly through the seven chronicles, then started all over right from the beginning.

I'd been lucky enough to find my favourite books in the world--why explore anything else?

Yet the books created an uneasy tension inside of me. In the chronicles, Aslan is a complex creation.

At times playful as a kitten, at others ferocious, lofty, forbidding, terrible.

But he was lovable. I loved him. My feelings about Jesus Christ were less clear. At times I was moved by the stories:

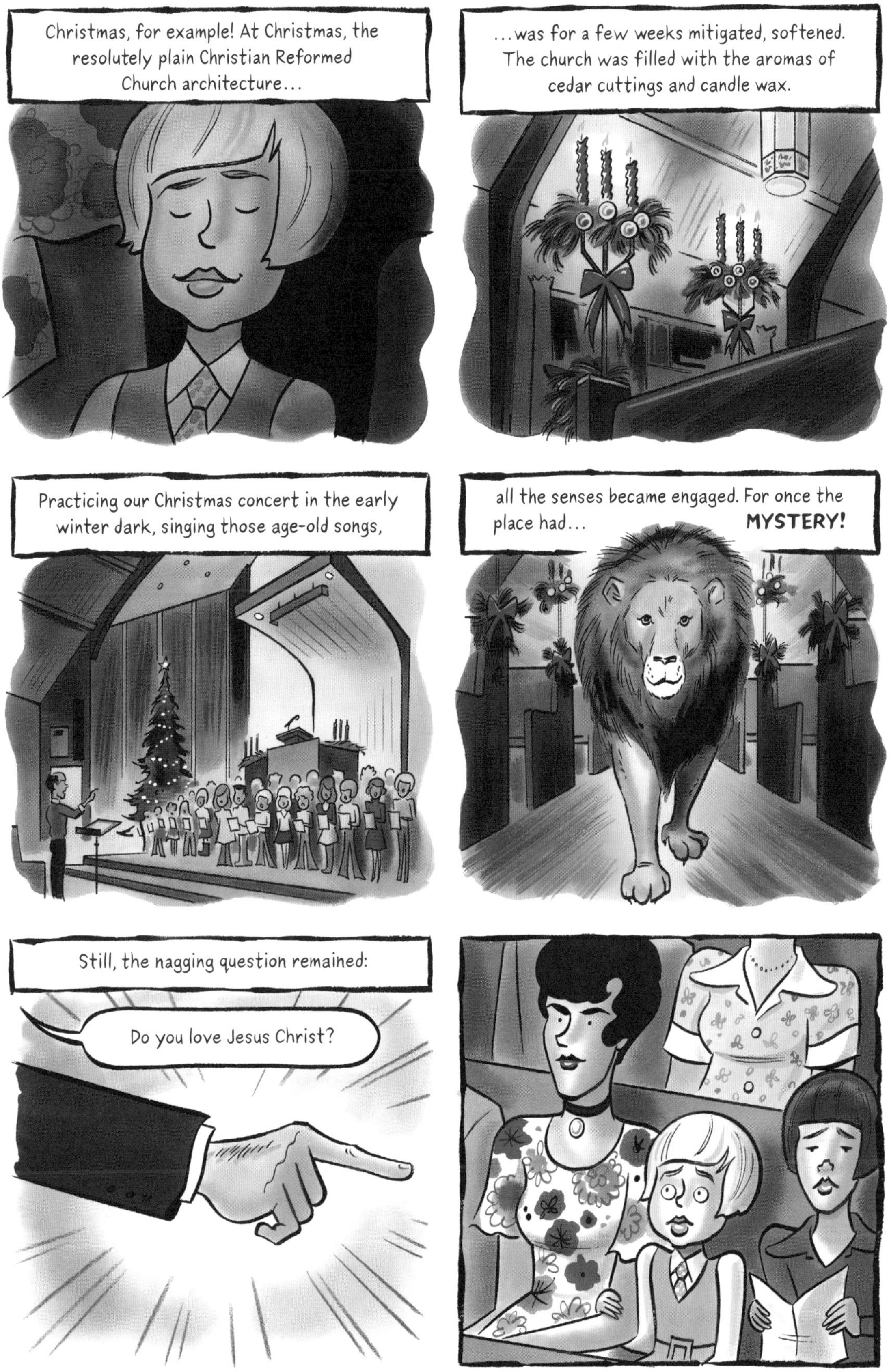
Christmas, for example! At Christmas, the resolutely plain Christian Reformed Church architecture...
...was for a few weeks mitigated, softened. The church was filled with the aromas of cedar cuttings and candle wax.
Practicing our Christmas concert in the early winter dark, singing those age-old songs,
all the senses became engaged. For once the place had... **MYSTERY!**
Still, the nagging question remained:
Do you love Jesus Christ?

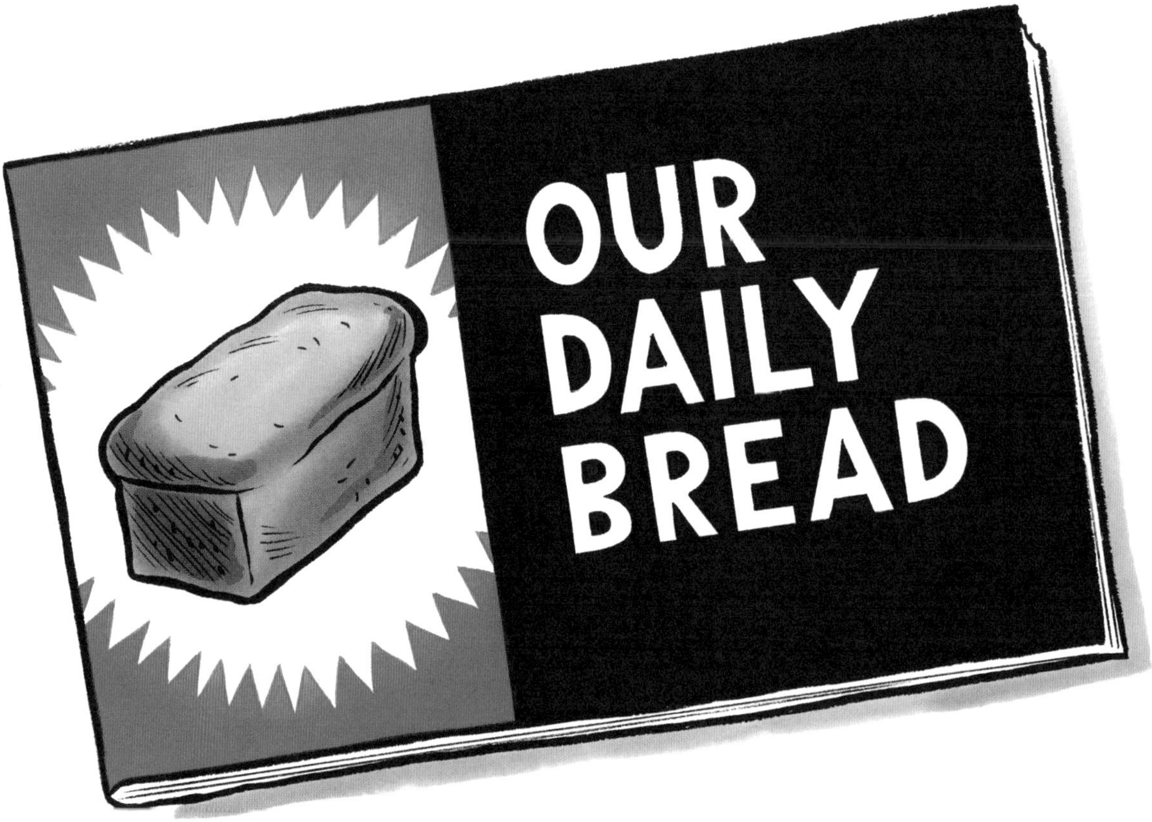
OUR DAILY BREAD

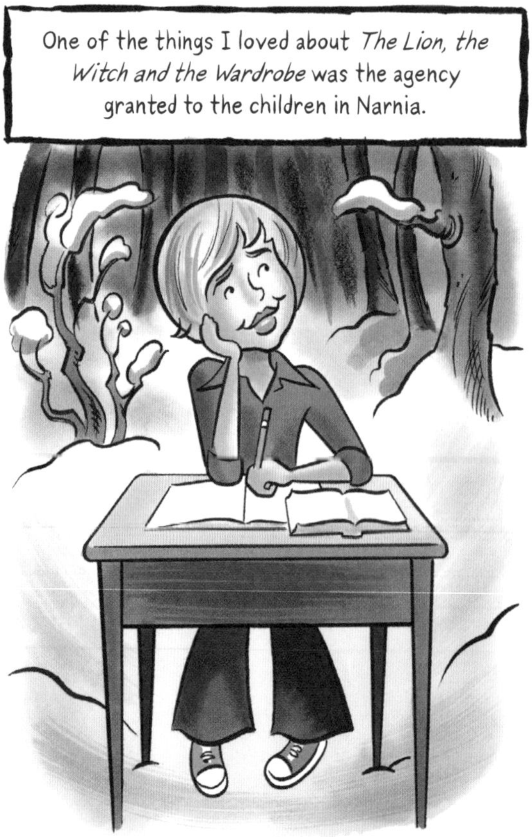
One of the things I loved about *The Lion, the Witch and the Wardrobe* was the agency granted to the children in Narnia.

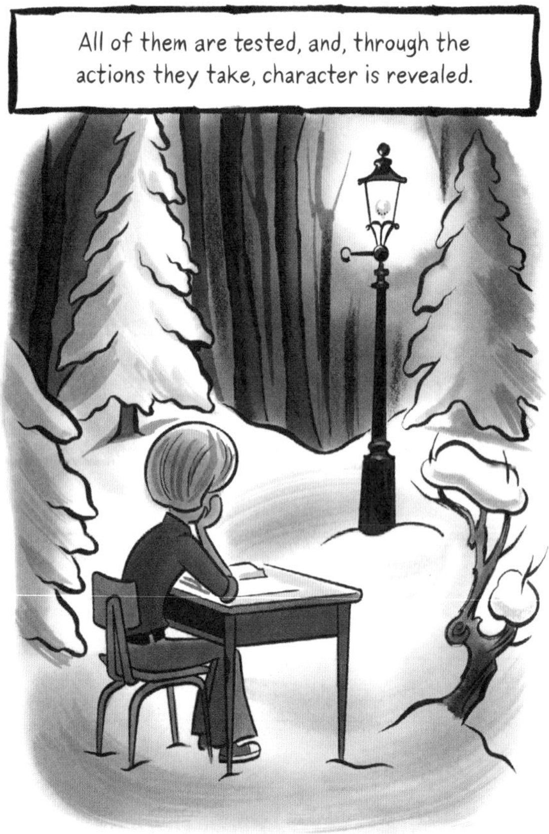
All of them are tested, and, through the actions they take, character is revealed.

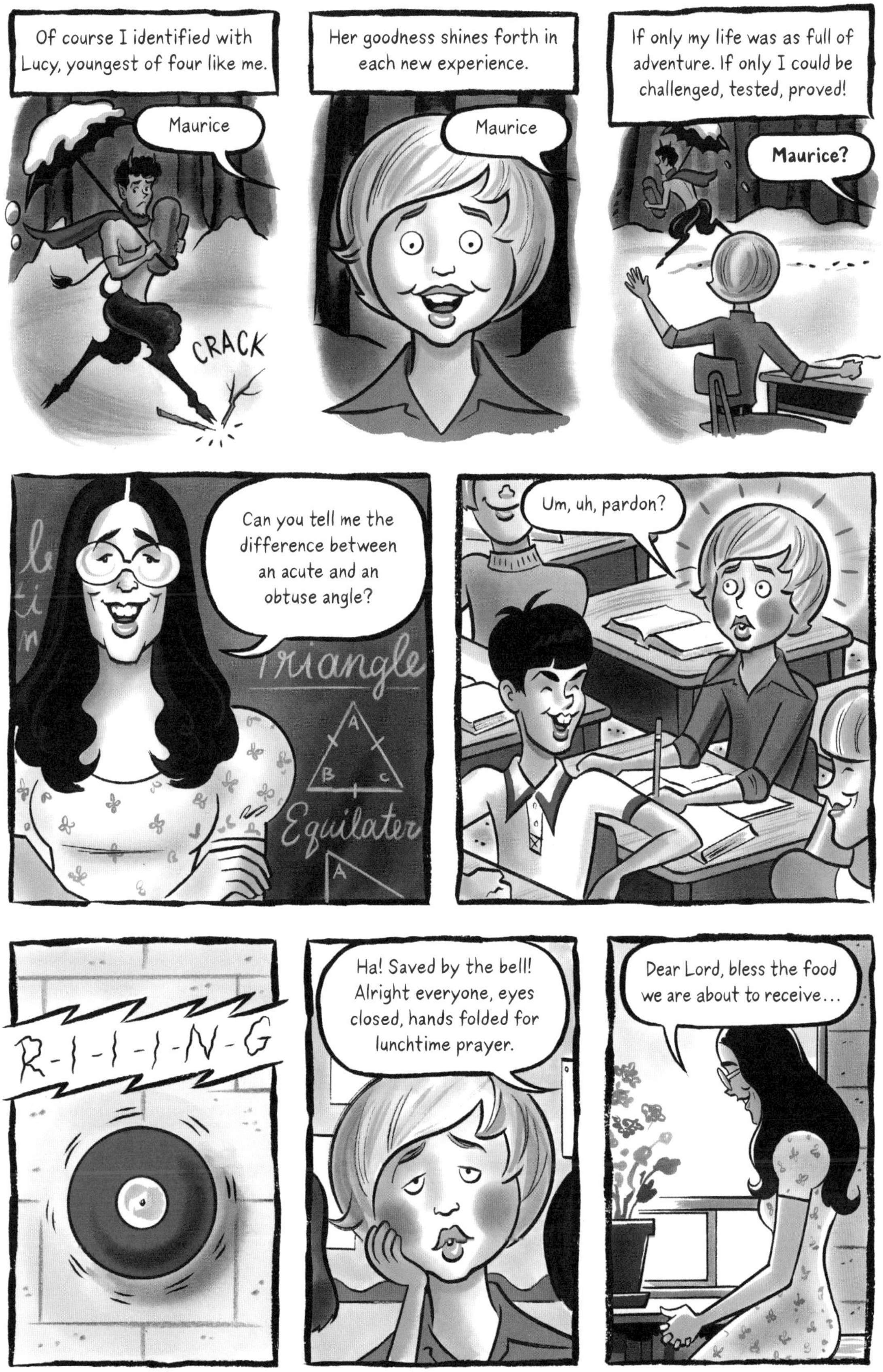
Of course I identified with Lucy, youngest of four like me.
Maurice
CRACK
Her goodness shines forth in each new experience.
Maurice
If only my life was as full of adventure. If only I could be challenged, tested, proved!
Maurice?
Can you tell me the difference between an acute and an obtuse angle?
Triangle
Equilater
Um, uh, pardon?
R-I-I-I-N-G
Ha! Saved by the bell! Alright everyone, eyes closed, hands folded for lunchtime prayer.
Dear Lord, bless the food we are about to receive...

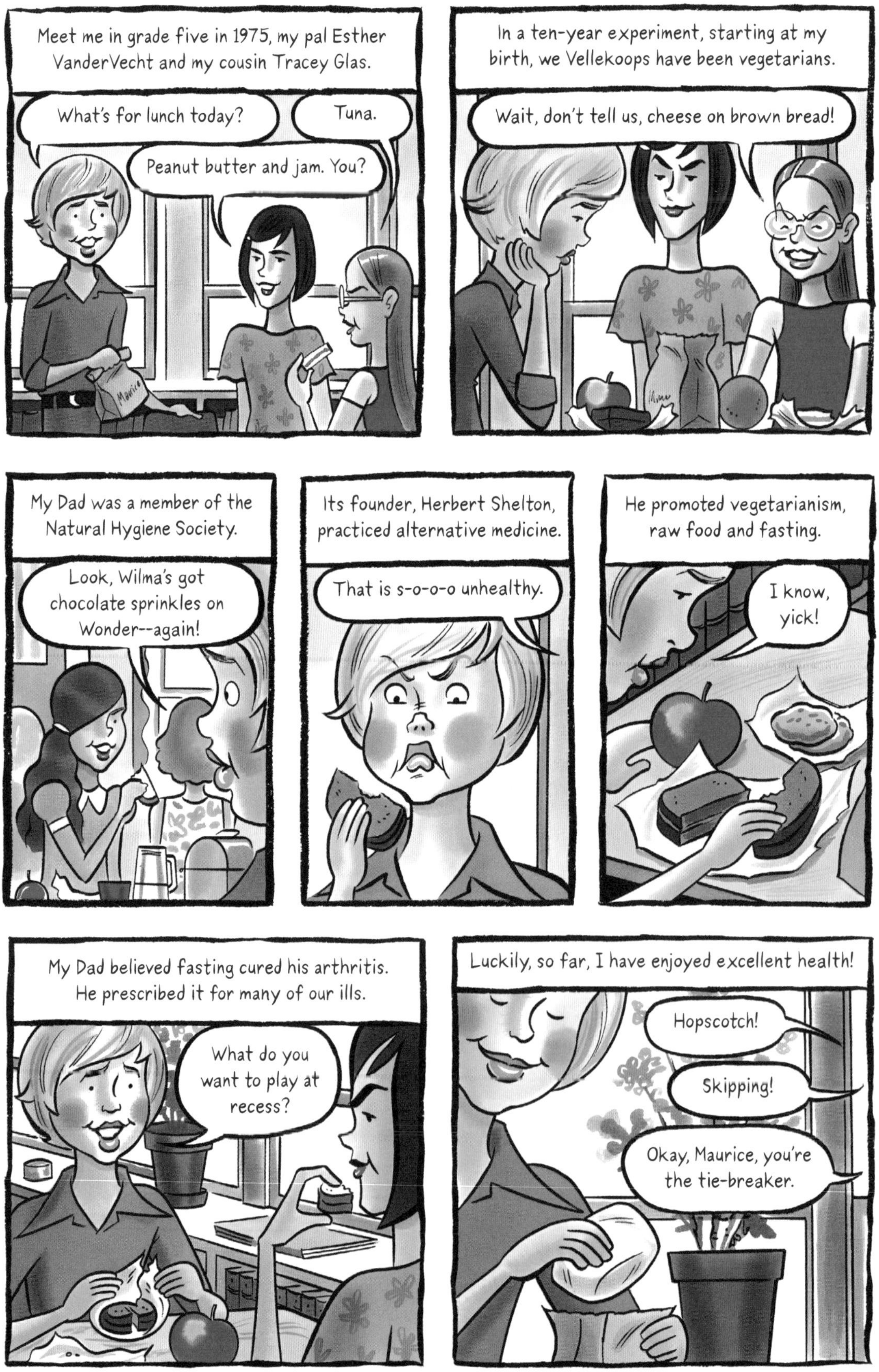
Meet me in grade five in 1975, my pal Esther VanderVecht and my cousin Tracey Glas.
What's for lunch today?
Tuna.
Peanut butter and jam. You?
Maurice
In a ten-year experiment, starting at my birth, we Vellekoops have been vegetarians.
Wait, don't tell us, cheese on brown bread!
My Dad was a member of the Natural Hygiene Society.
Look, Wilma's got chocolate sprinkles on Wonder--again!
Its founder, Herbert Shelton, practiced alternative medicine.
That is s-o-o-o unhealthy.
He promoted vegetarianism, raw food and fasting.
I know, yick!
My Dad believed fasting cured his arthritis. He prescribed it for many of our ills.
What do you want to play at recess?
Luckily, so far, I have enjoyed excellent health!
Hopscotch!
Skipping!
Okay, Maurice, you're the tie-breaker.

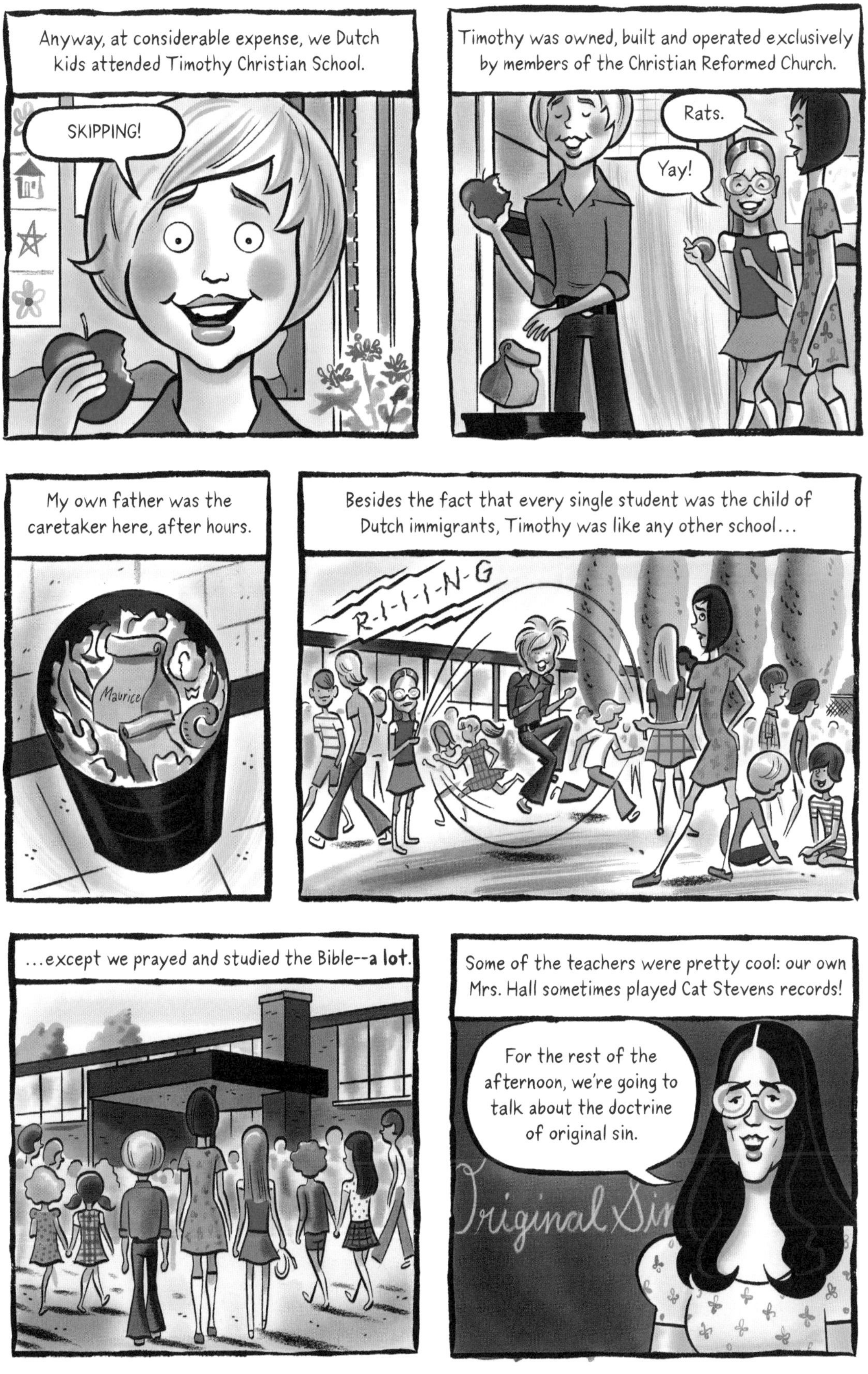
Anyway, at considerable expense, we Dutch kids attended Timothy Christian School.
SKIPPING!
Timothy was owned, built and operated exclusively by members of the Christian Reformed Church.
Rats.
Yay!
My own father was the caretaker here, after hours.
Maurice
Besides the fact that every single student was the child of Dutch immigrants, Timothy was like any other school...
R-I-I-I-N-G
...except we prayed and studied the Bible--**a lot**.
Some of the teachers were pretty cool: our own Mrs. Hall sometimes played Cat Stevens records!
For the rest of the afternoon, we're going to talk about the doctrine of original sin.

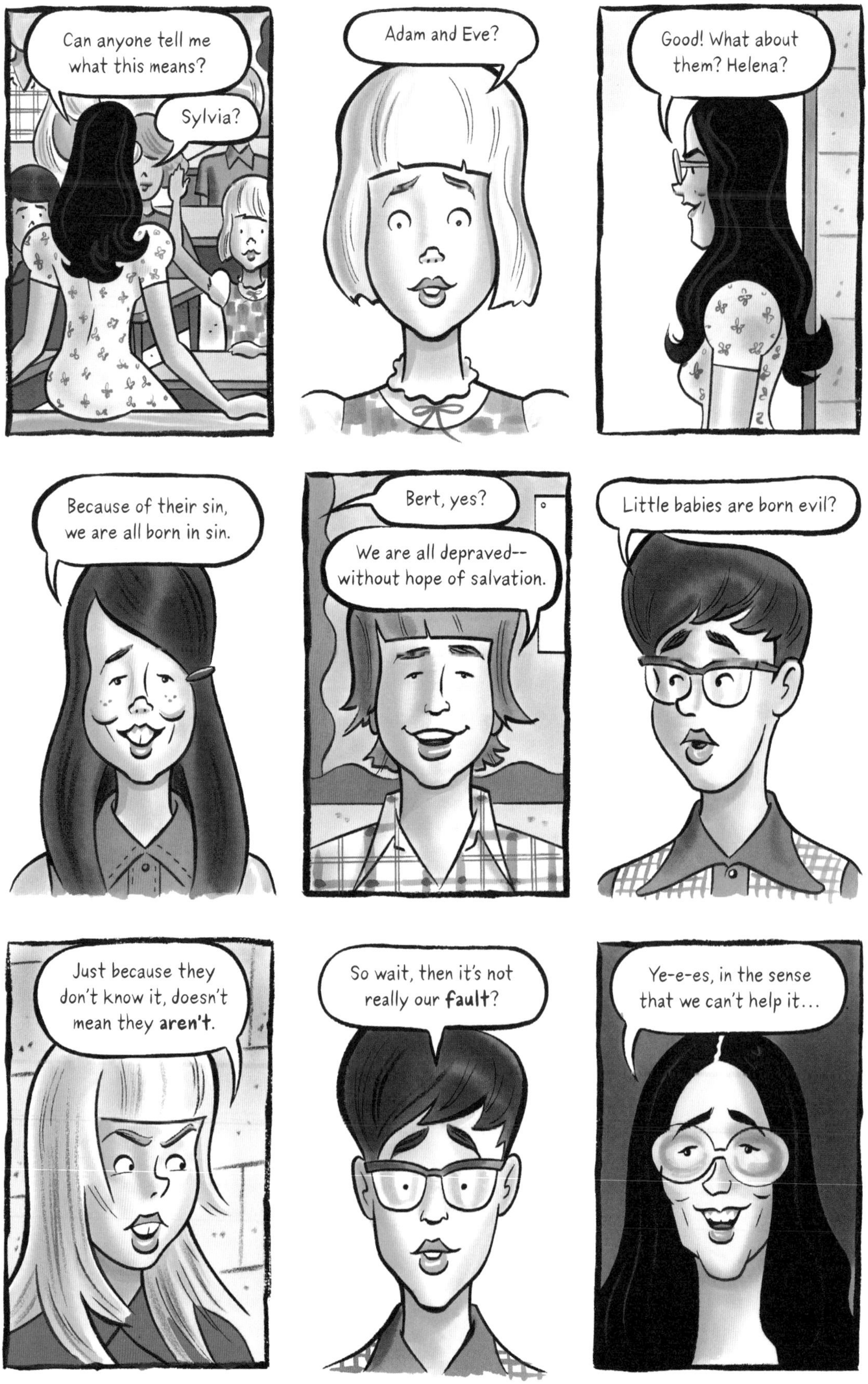
Can anyone tell me what this means?
Sylvia?
Adam and Eve?
Good! What about them? Helena?
Because of their sin, we are all born in sin.
Bert, yes?
We are all depraved-- without hope of salvation.
Little babies are born evil?
Just because they don't know it, doesn't mean they **aren't**.
So wait, then it's not really our **fault**?
Ye-e-es, in the sense that we can't help it...

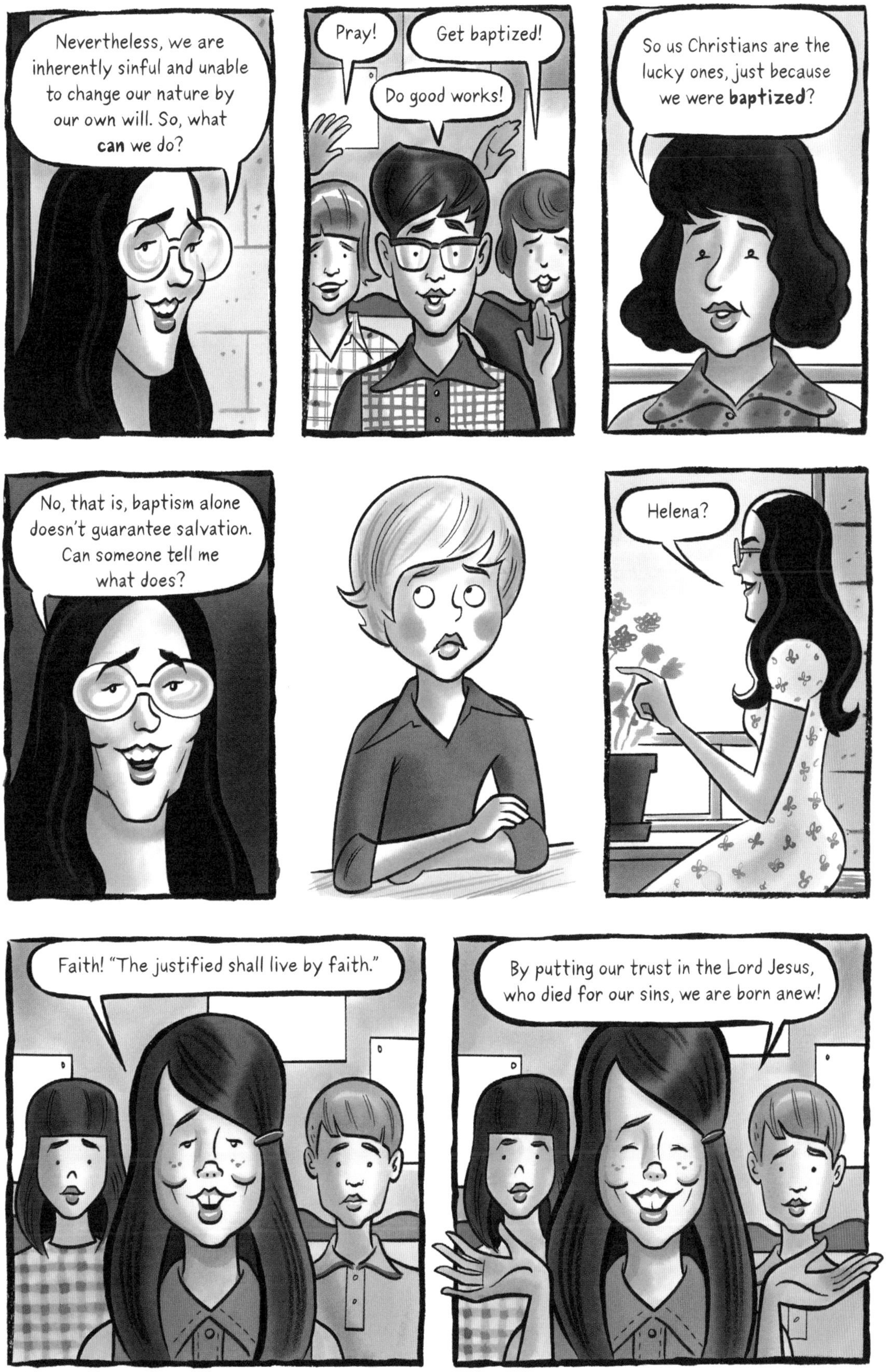
Nevertheless, we are inherently sinful and unable to change our nature by our own will. So, what **can** we do?
Pray!
Get baptized!
Do good works!
So us Christians are the lucky ones, just because we were **baptized**?
No, that is, baptism alone doesn't guarantee salvation. Can someone tell me what does?
Helena?
Faith! "The justified shall live by faith."
By putting our trust in the Lord Jesus, who died for our sins, we are born anew!

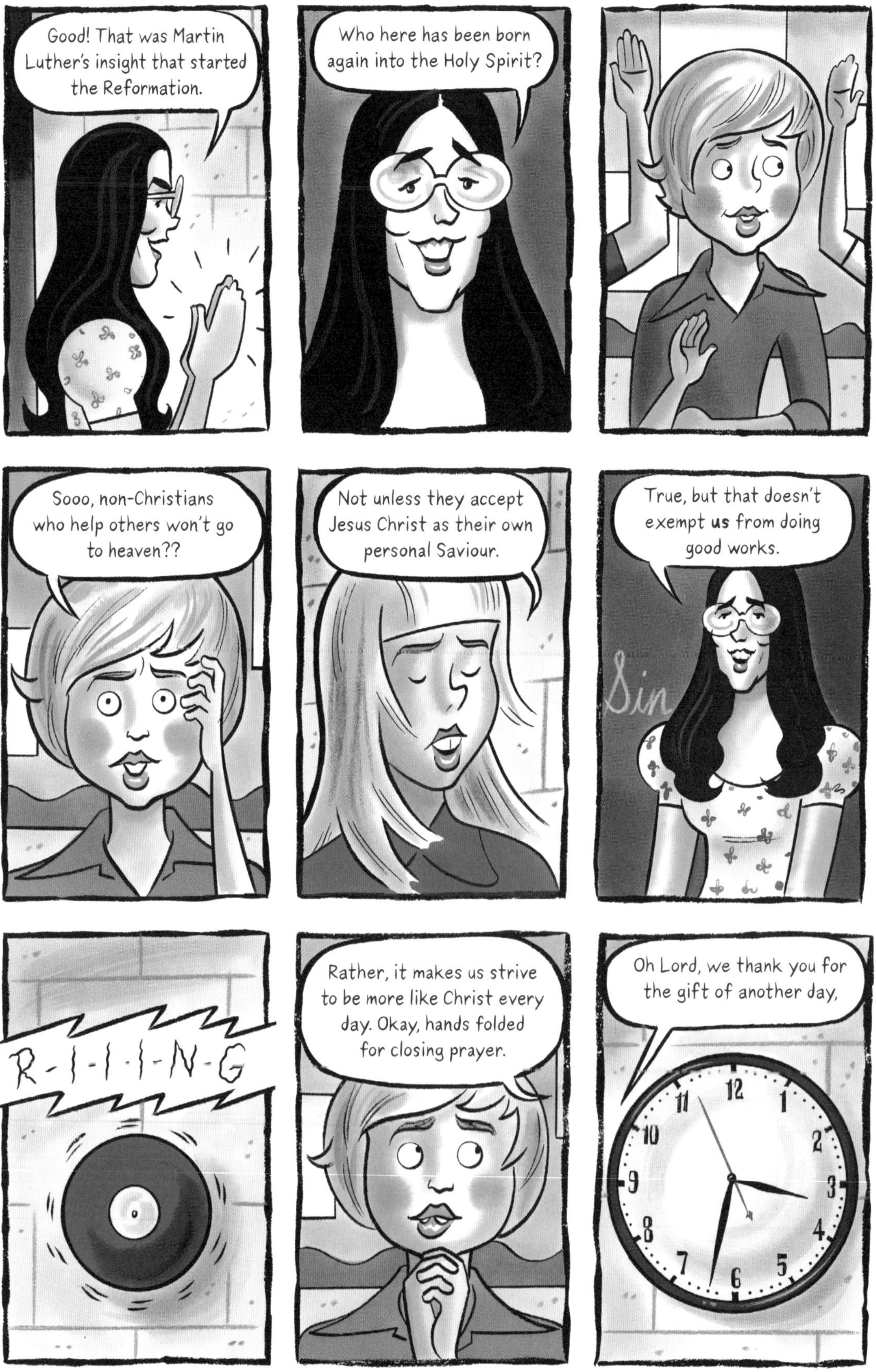

Good! That was Martin Luther's insight that started the Reformation.
Who here has been born again into the Holy Spirit?
Sooo, non-Christians who help others won't go to heaven??
Not unless they accept Jesus Christ as their own personal Saviour.
True, but that doesn't exempt **us** from doing good works.
Sin
R-I-I-I-N-G
Rather, it makes us strive to be more like Christ every day. Okay, hands folded for closing prayer.
Oh Lord, we thank you for the gift of another day,

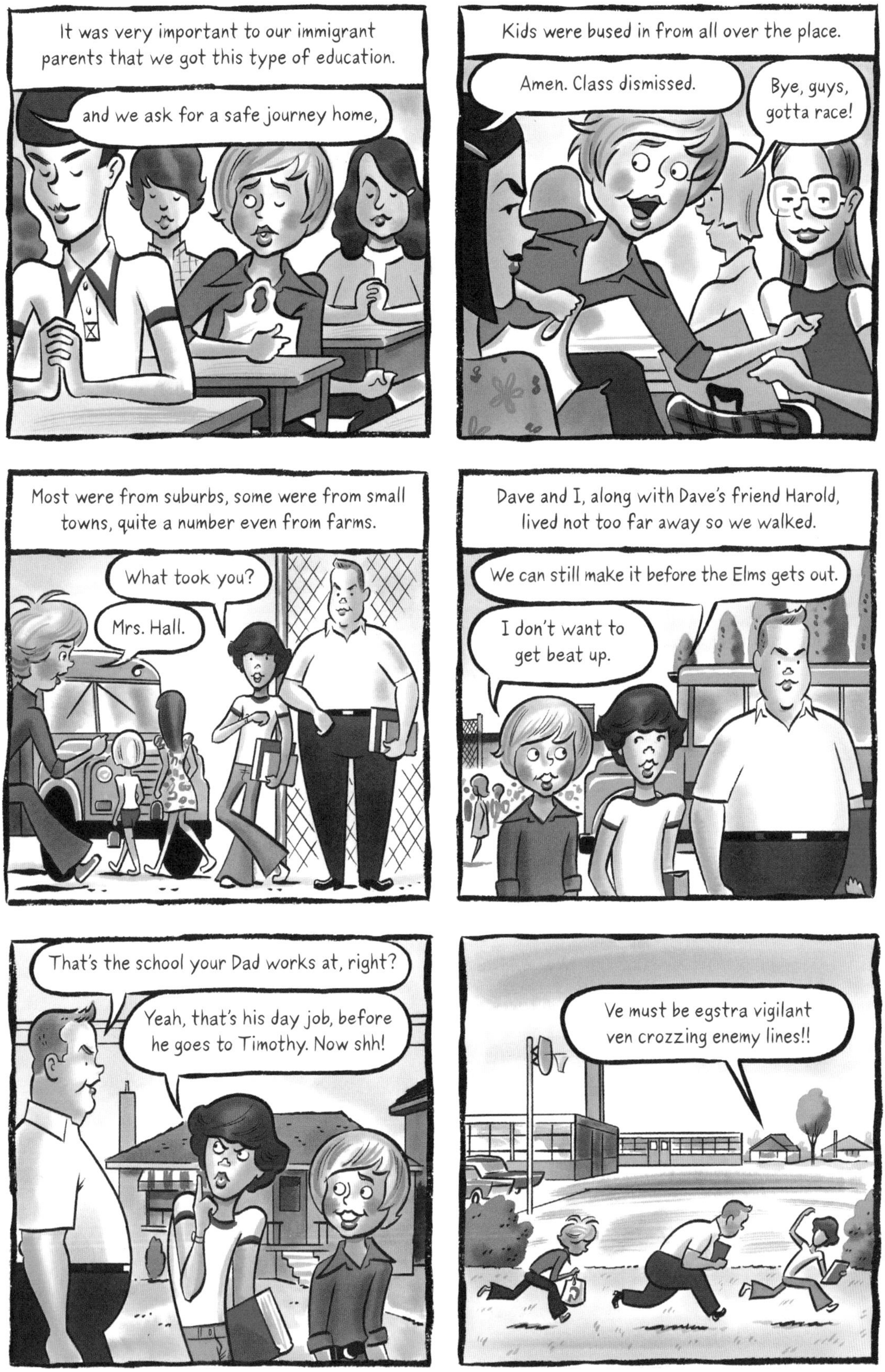
It was very important to our immigrant parents that we got this type of education.
and we ask for a safe journey home,
Kids were bused in from all over the place.
Amen. Class dismissed.
Bye, guys, gotta race!
Most were from suburbs, some were from small towns, quite a number even from farms.
What took you?
Mrs. Hall.
Dave and I, along with Dave's friend Harold, lived not too far away so we walked.
We can still make it before the Elms gets out.
I don't want to get beat up.
That's the school your Dad works at, right?
Yeah, that's his day job, before he goes to Timothy. Now shh!
Ve must be egstra vigilant ven crozzing enemy lines!!

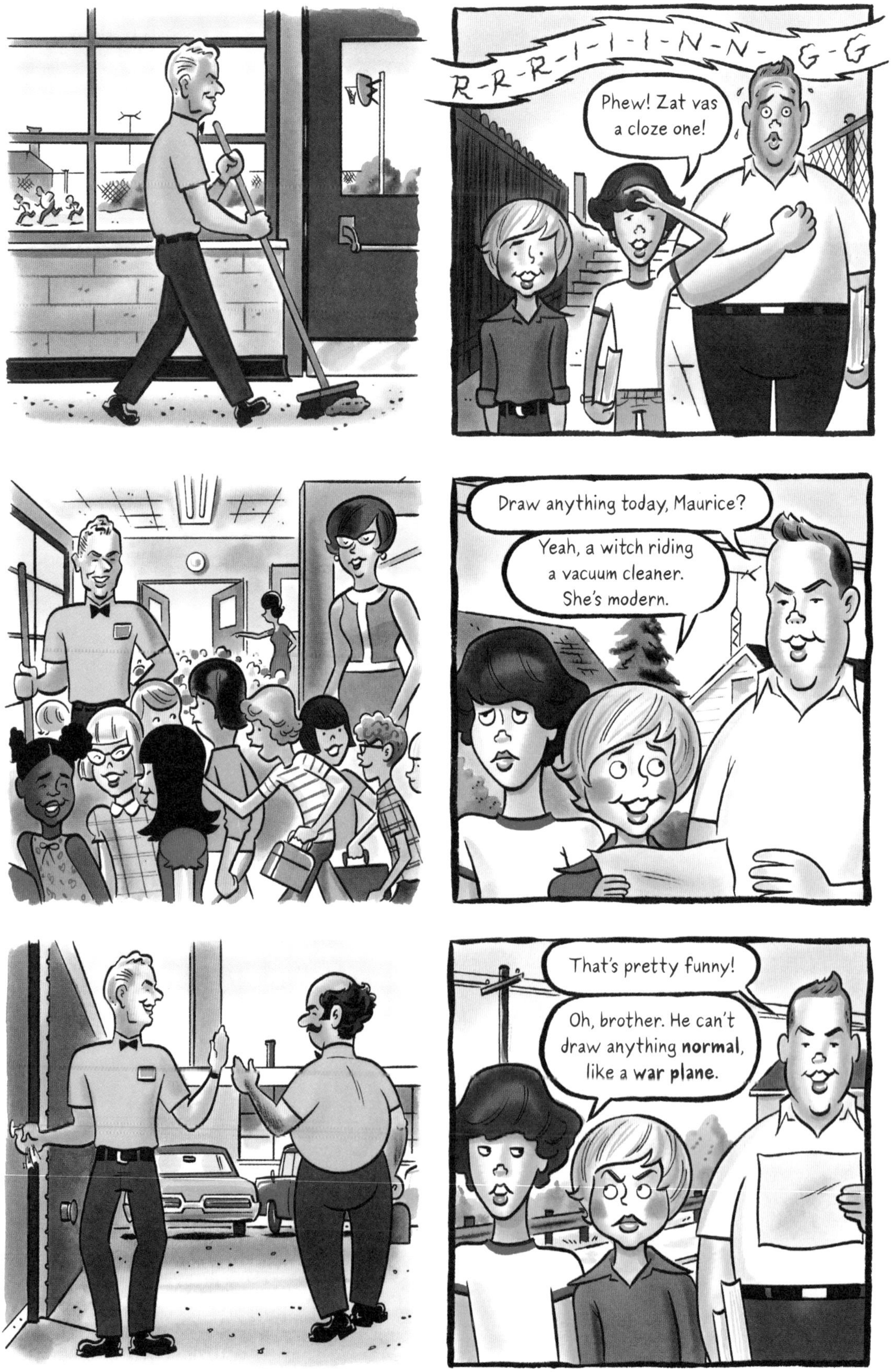
R-R-R-I-I-I-N-N-G-G
Phew! Zat vas a cloze one!
Draw anything today, Maurice?
Yeah, a witch riding a vacuum cleaner. She's modern.
That's pretty funny!
Oh, brother. He can't draw anything **normal**, like a **war plane**.

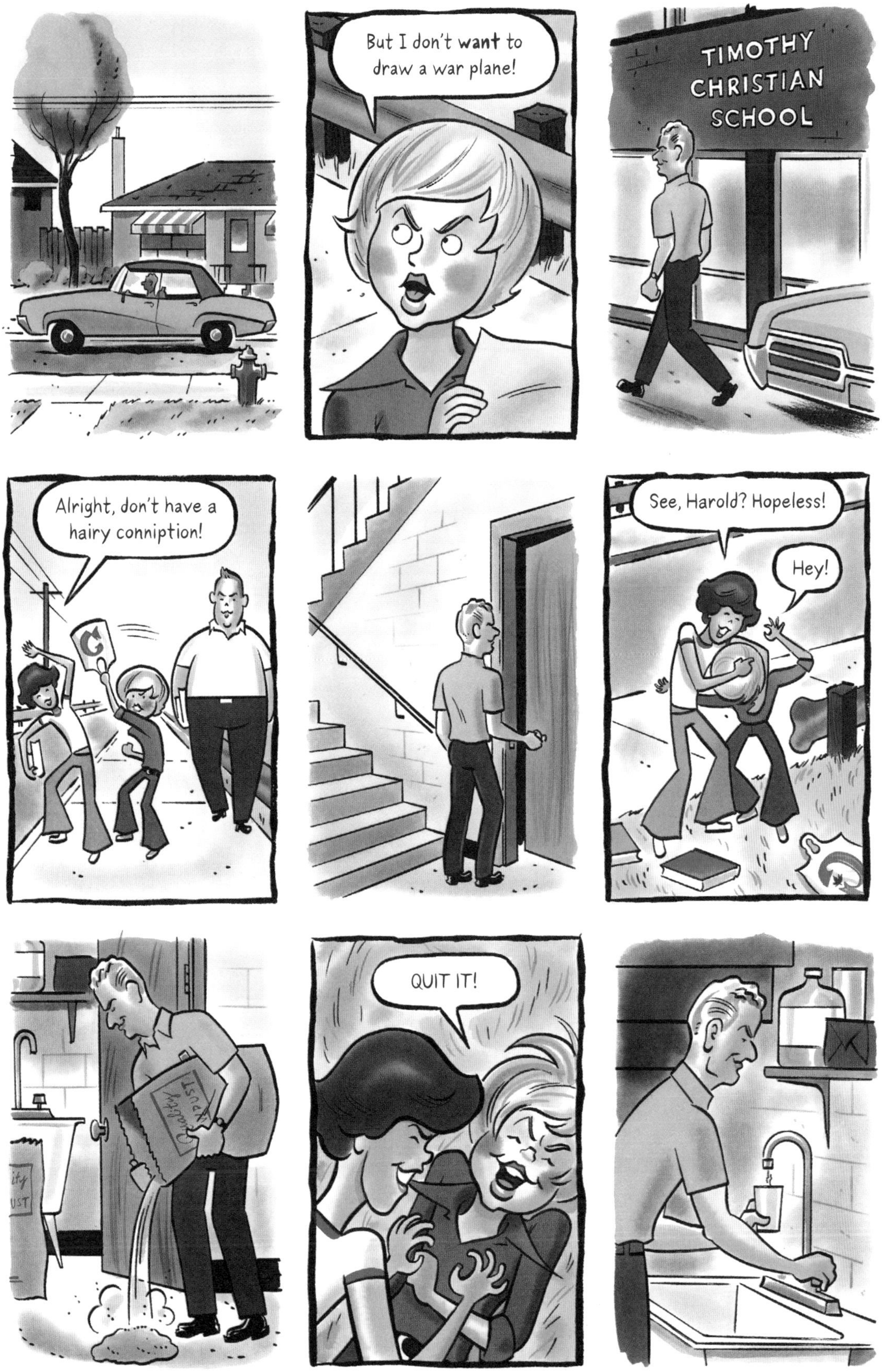
But I don't **want** to draw a war plane!
TIMOTHY CHRISTIAN SCHOOL
Alright, don't have a hairy conniption!
See, Harold? Hopeless!
Hey!
QUIT IT!

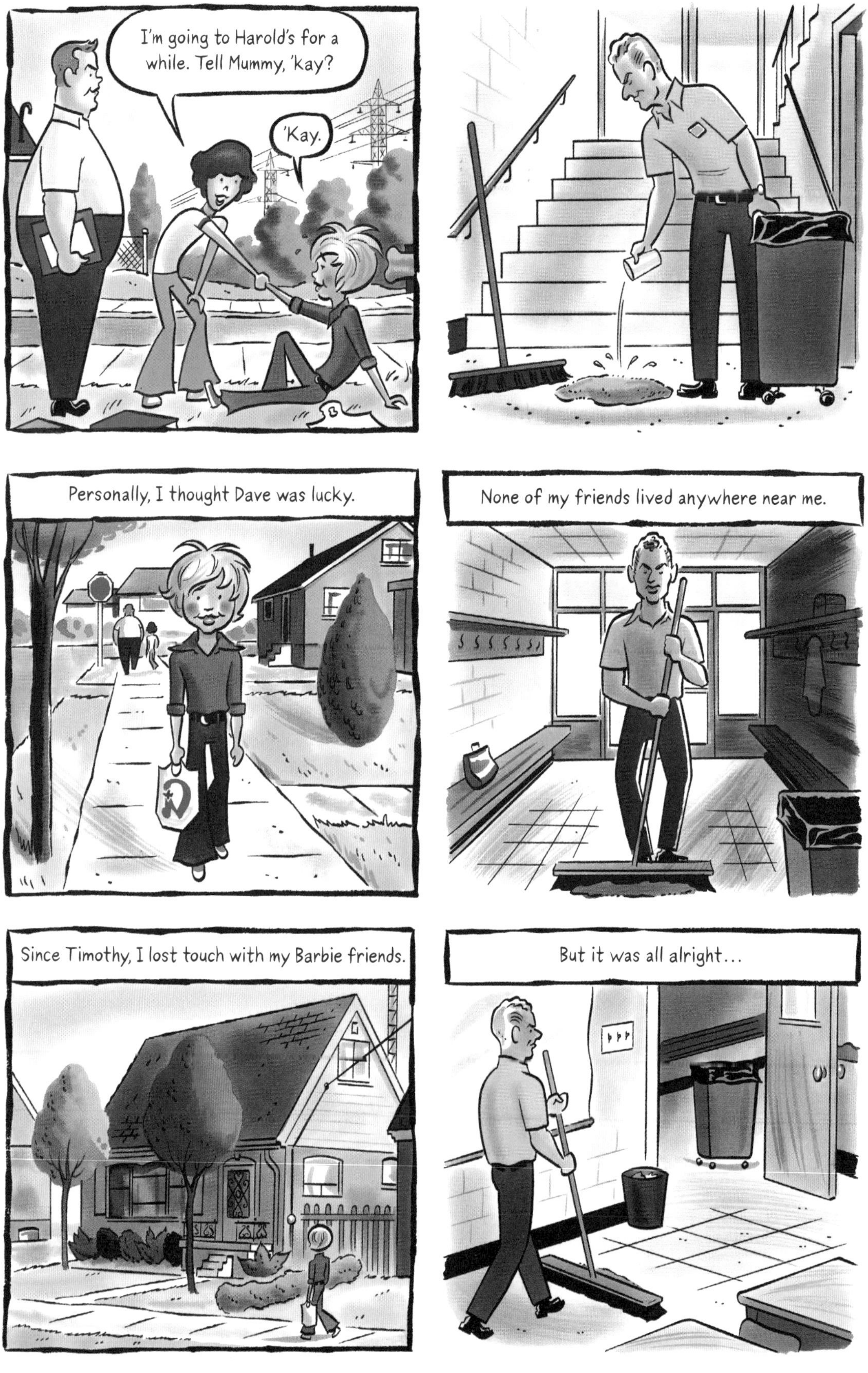
I'm going to Harold's for a while. Tell Mummy, 'kay?
'Kay.
Personally, I thought Dave was lucky.
None of my friends lived anywhere near me.
Since Timothy, I lost touch with my Barbie friends.
But it was all alright...

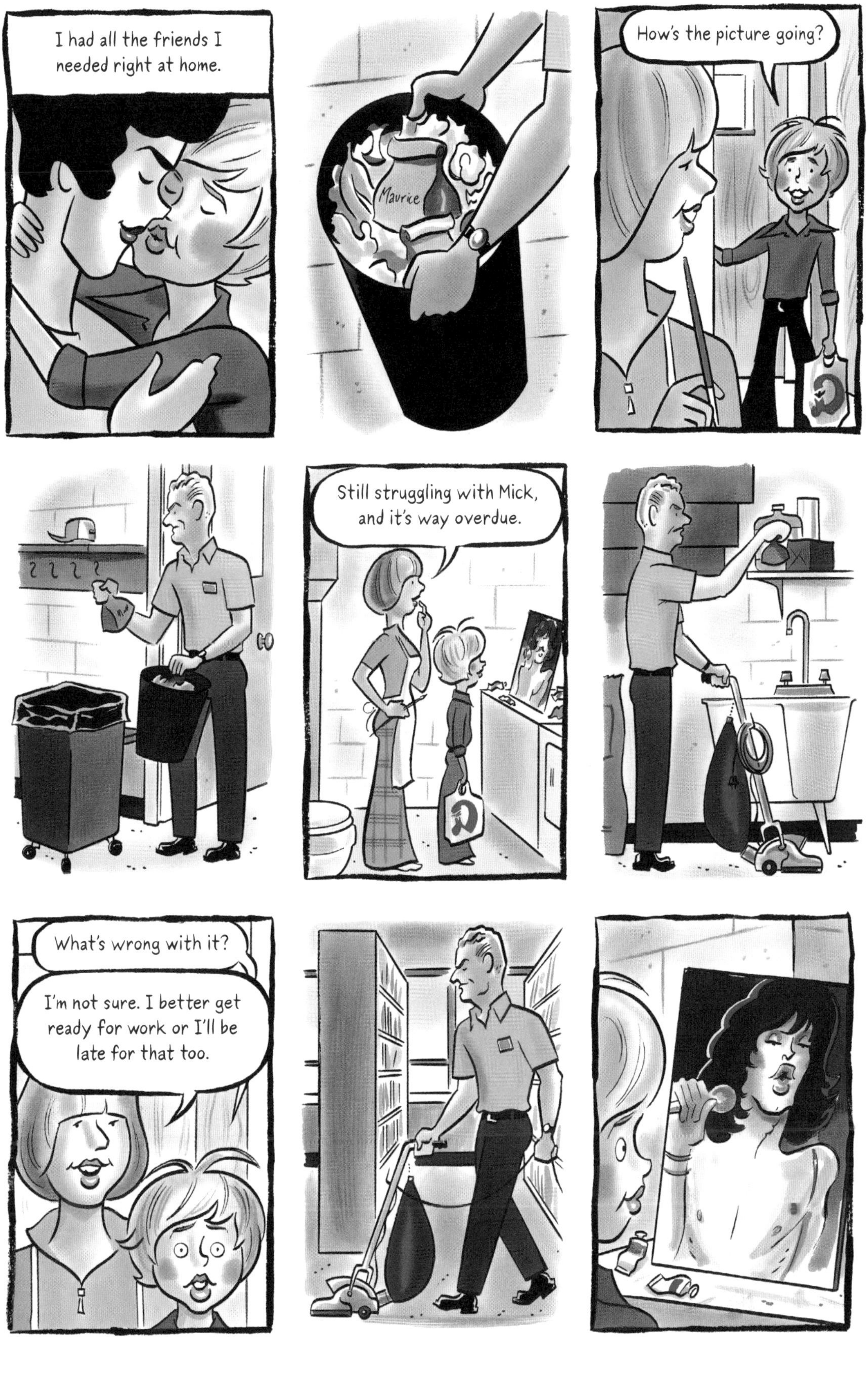
I had all the friends I needed right at home.
Maurice
How's the picture going?
Still struggling with Mick, and it's way overdue.
What's wrong with it?
I'm not sure. I better get ready for work or I'll be late for that too.

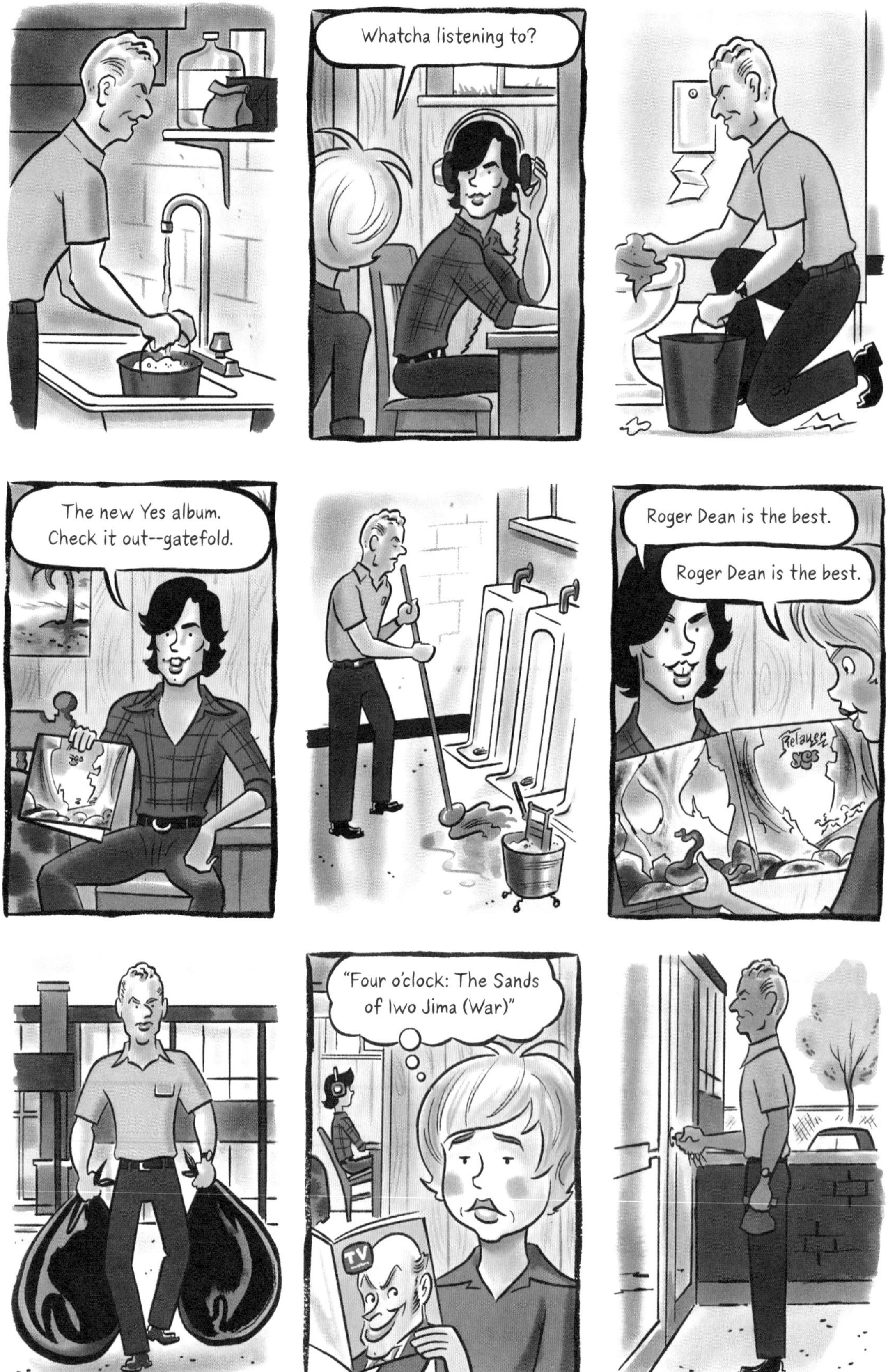
Whatcha listening to?
The new Yes album.
Check it out--gatefold.
Roger Dean is the best.
Roger Dean is the best.
"Four o'clock: The Sands of Iwo Jima (War)"

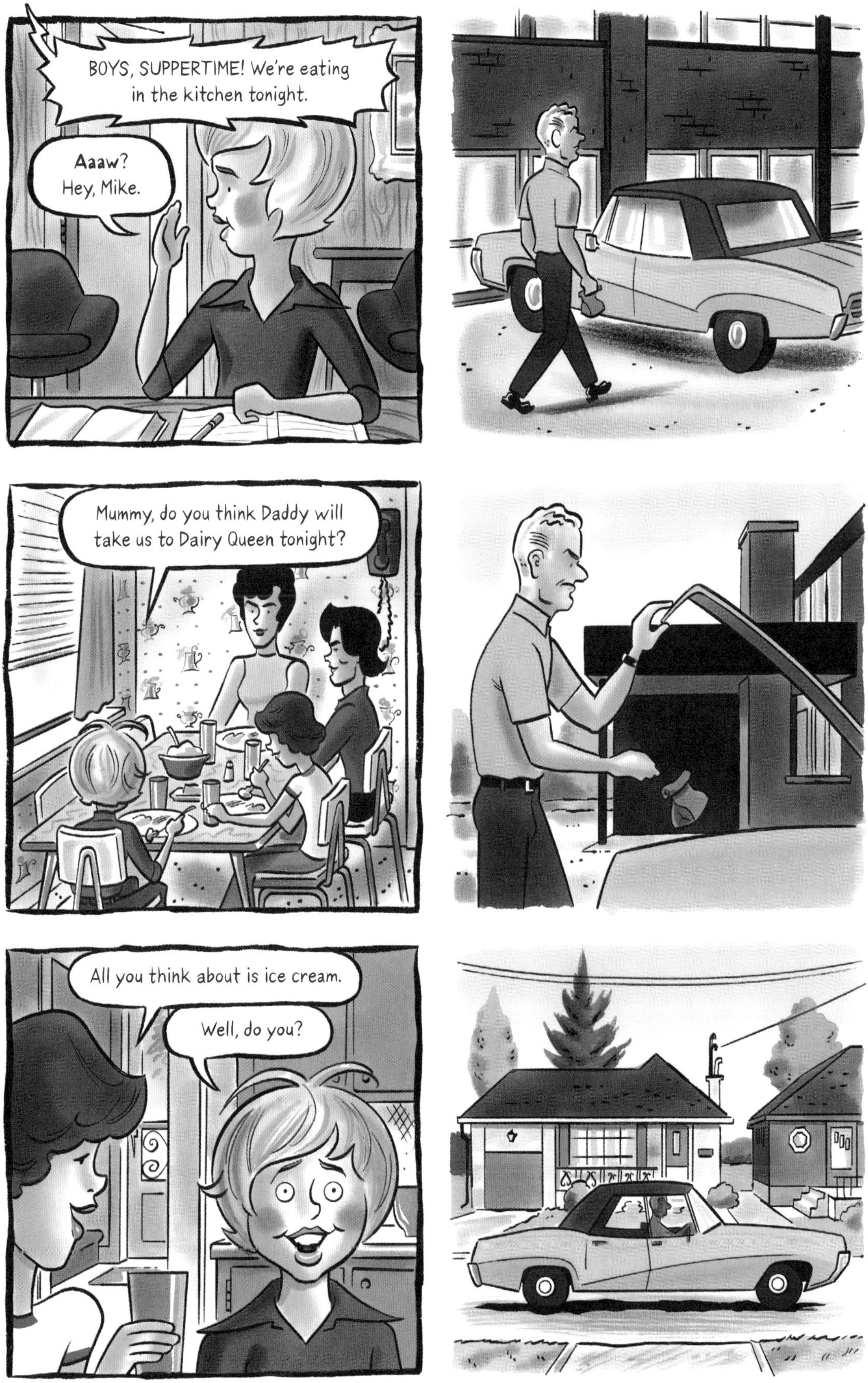
BOYS, SUPPERTIME! We're eating in the kitchen tonight.
Aaaw? Hey, Mike.
Mummy, do you think Daddy will take us to Dairy Queen tonight?
All you think about is ice cream.
Well, do you?

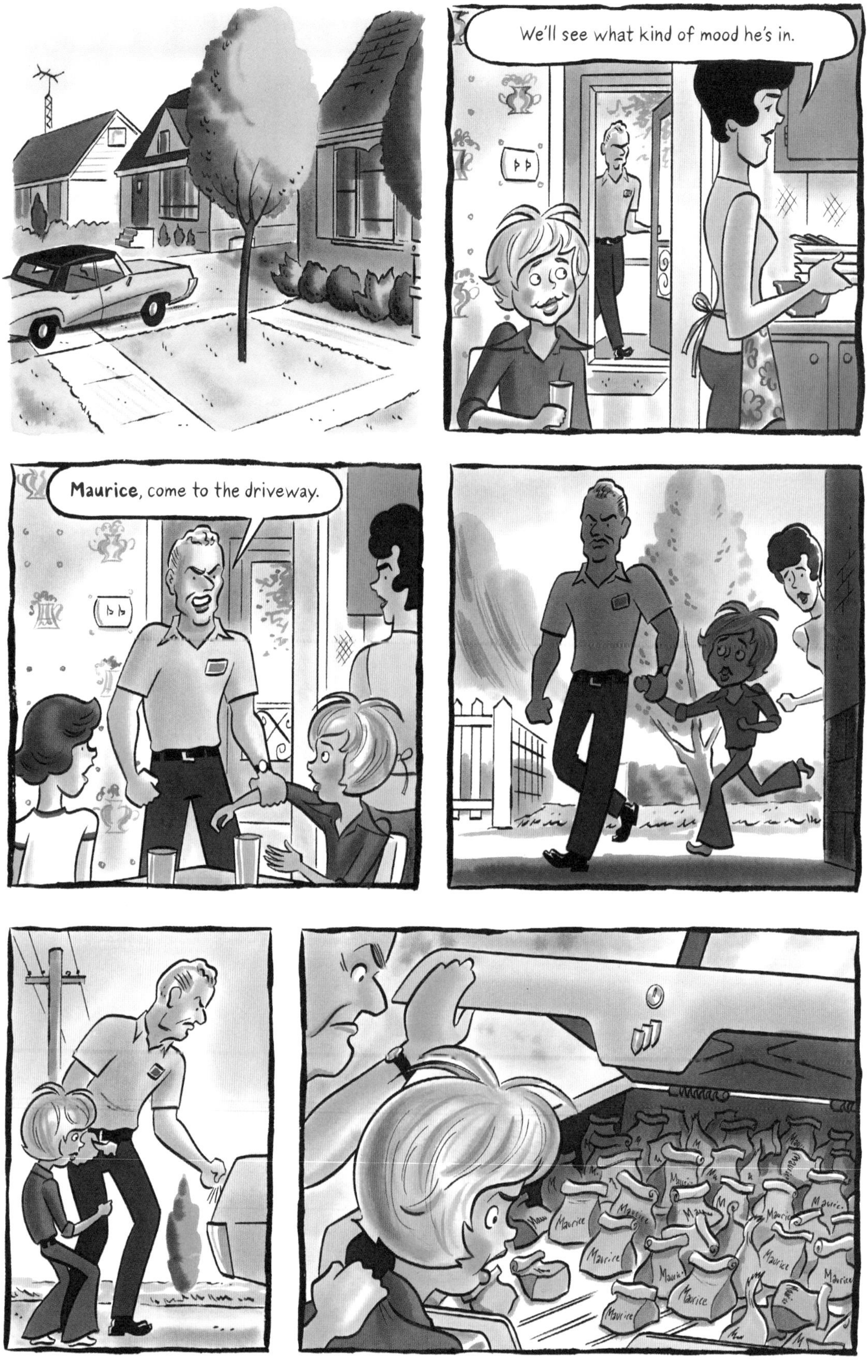
We'll see what kind of mood he's in.
Maurice, come to the driveway.

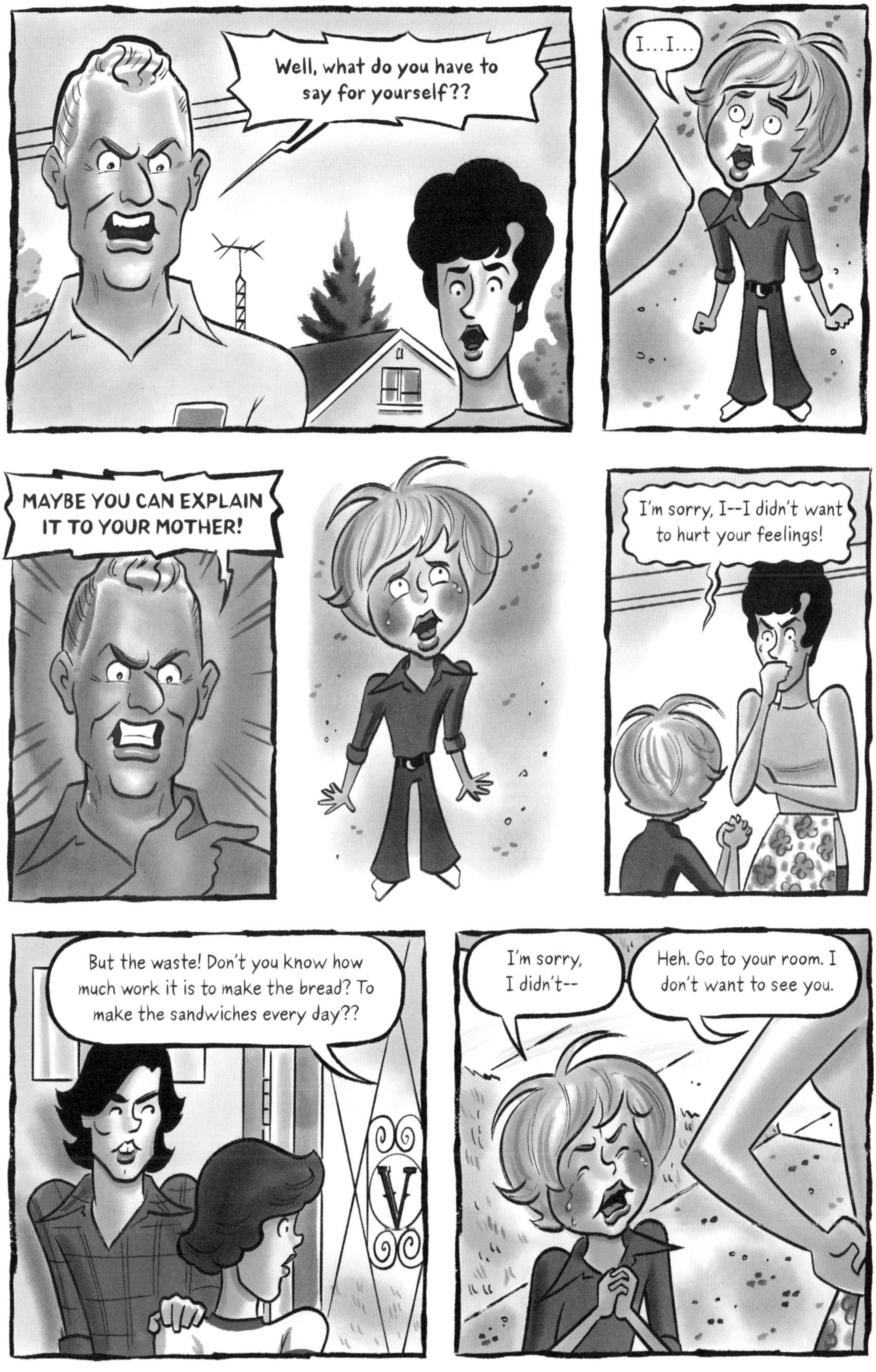
Well, what do you have to say for yourself??
I...I...
MAYBE YOU CAN EXPLAIN IT TO YOUR MOTHER!
I'm sorry, I--I didn't want to hurt your feelings!
But the waste! Don't you know how much work it is to make the bread? To make the sandwiches every day??
I'm sorry, I didn't--
Heh. Go to your room. I don't want to see you.

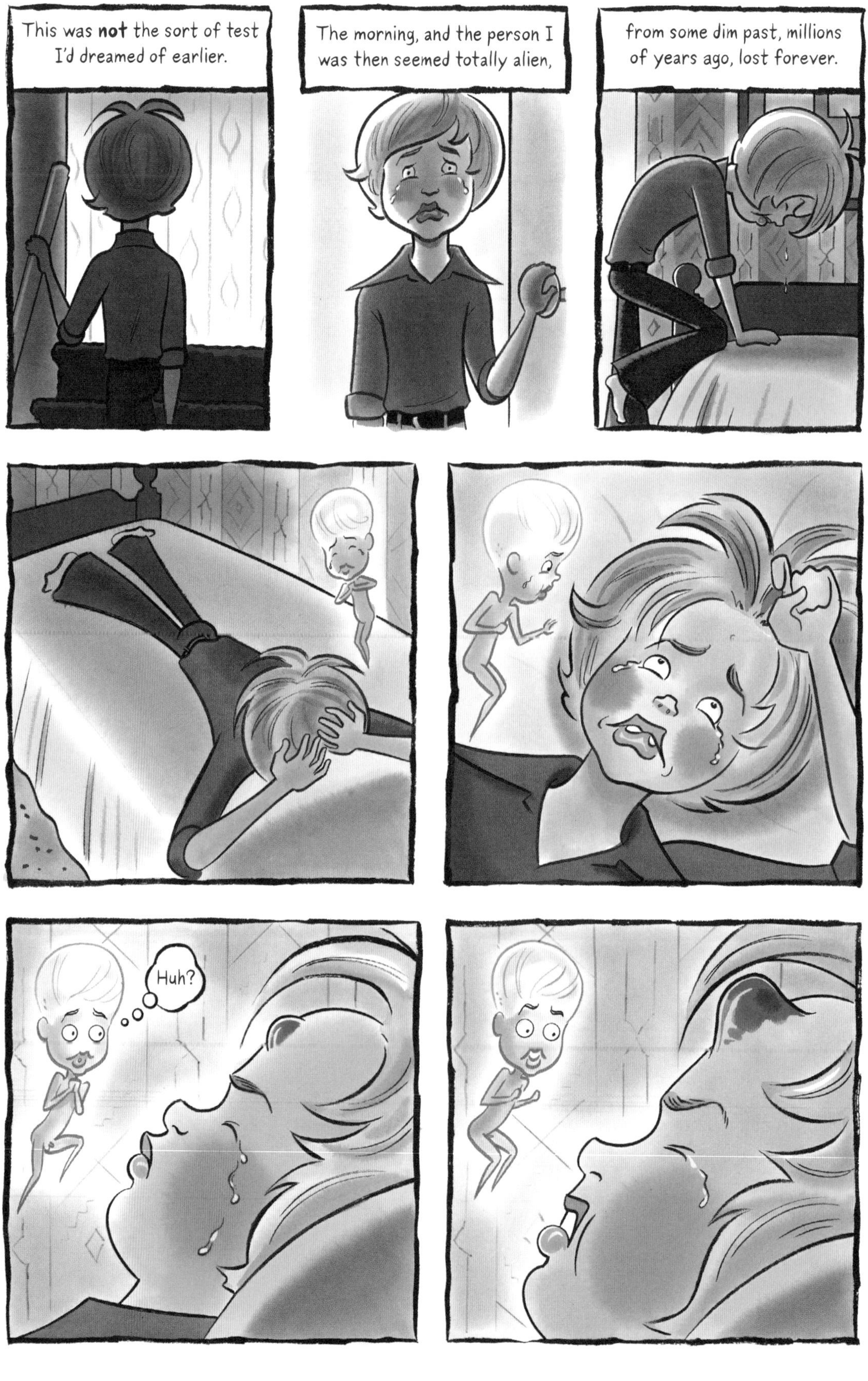
This was **not** the sort of test I'd dreamed of earlier.
The morning, and the person I was then seemed totally alien,
from some dim past, millions of years ago, lost forever.
Huh?

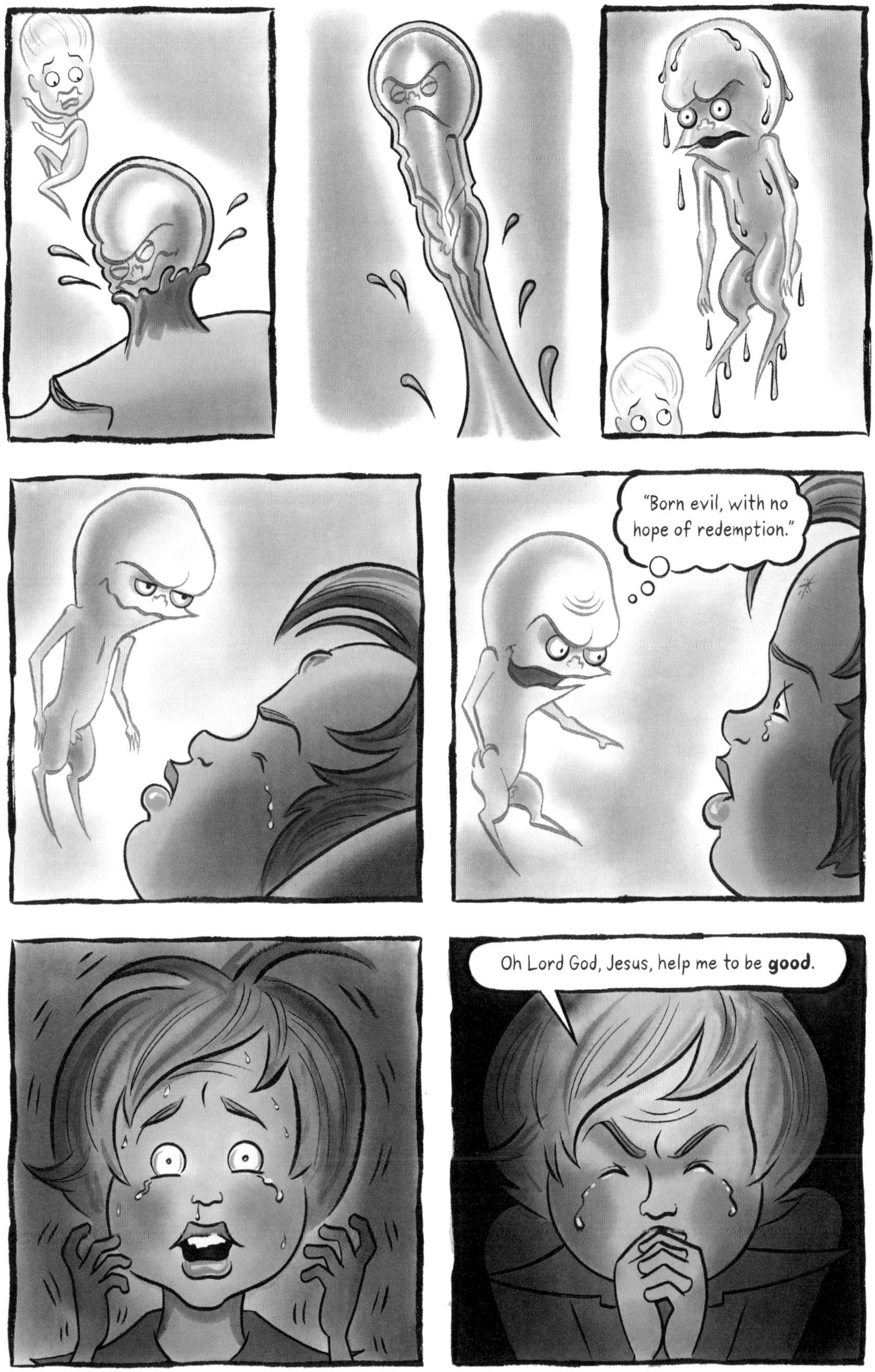
"Born evil, with no hope of redemption."
Oh Lord God, Jesus, help me to be **good**.

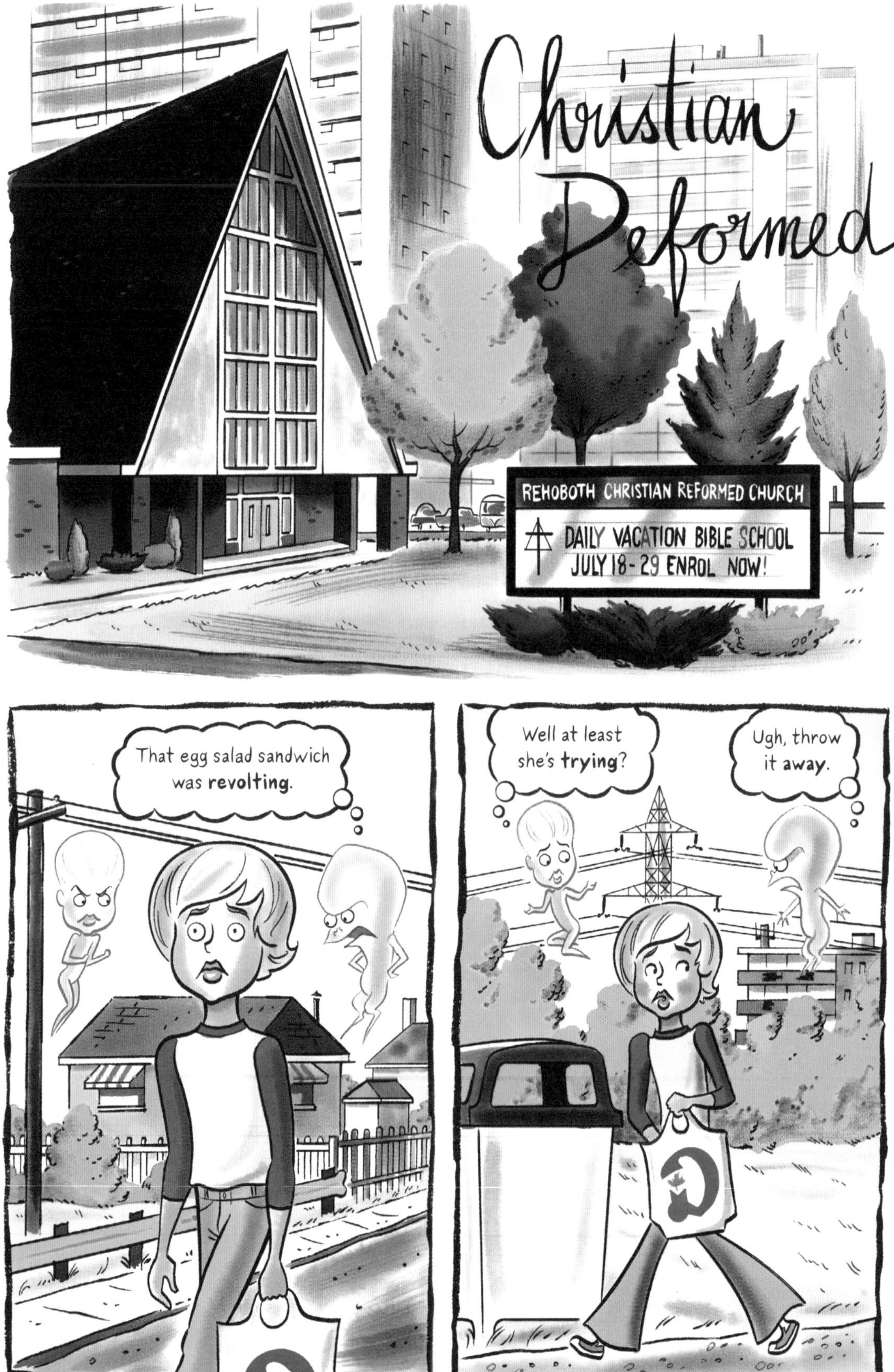

Christian Deformed
REHOBOTH CHRISTIAN REFORMED CHURCH
DAILY VACATION BIBLE SCHOOL
JULY 18-29 ENROL NOW!
That egg salad sandwich was **revolting**.
Well at least she's **trying**?
Ugh, throw it **away**.

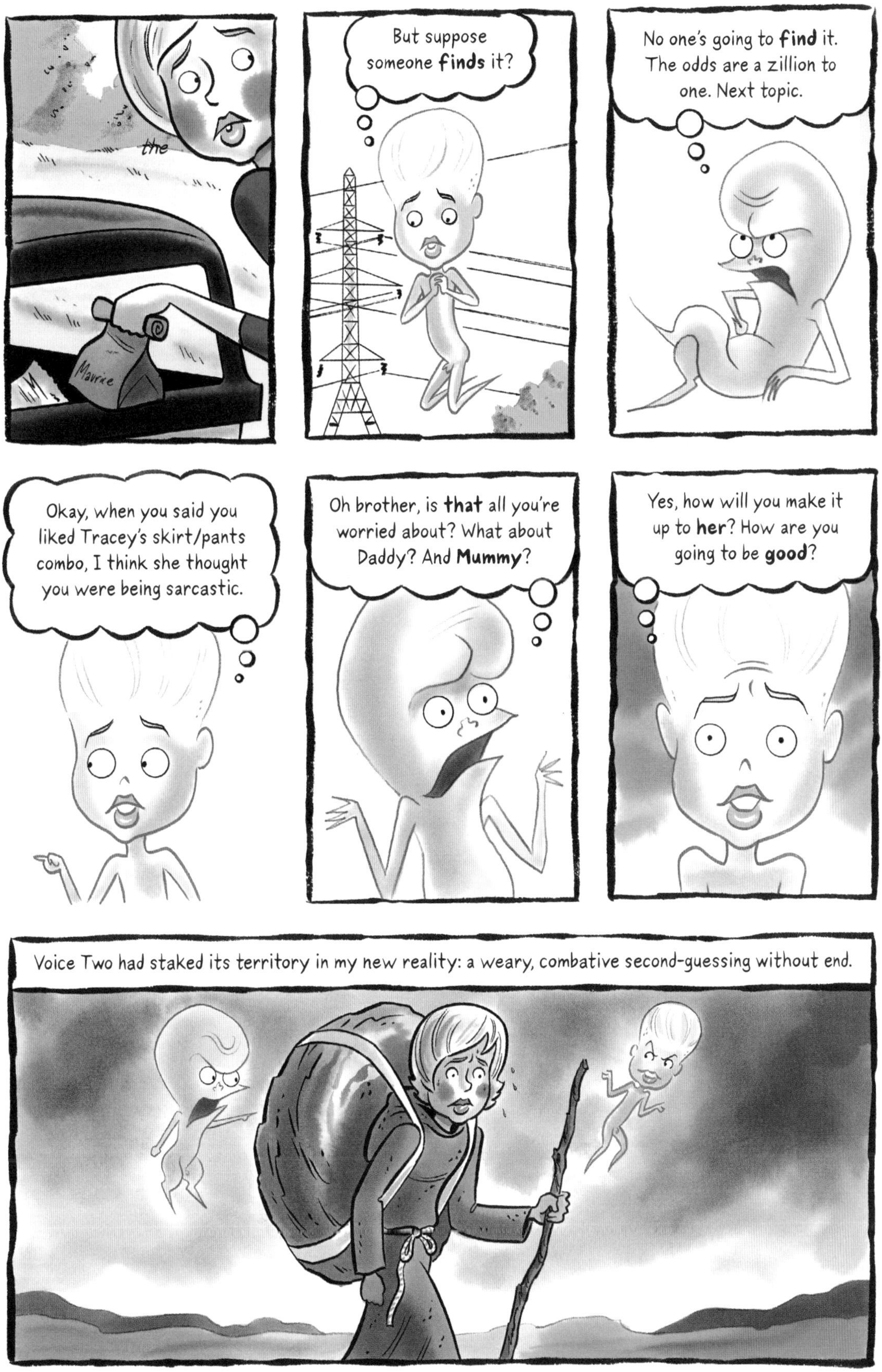
But suppose someone **finds** it?
No one's going to **find** it. The odds are a zillion to one. Next topic.
Okay, when you said you liked Tracey's skirt/pants combo, I think she thought you were being sarcastic.
Oh brother, is **that** all you're worried about? What about Daddy? And **Mummy**?
Yes, how will you make it up to **her**? How are you going to be **good**?
Voice Two had staked its territory in my new reality: a weary, combative second-guessing without end.

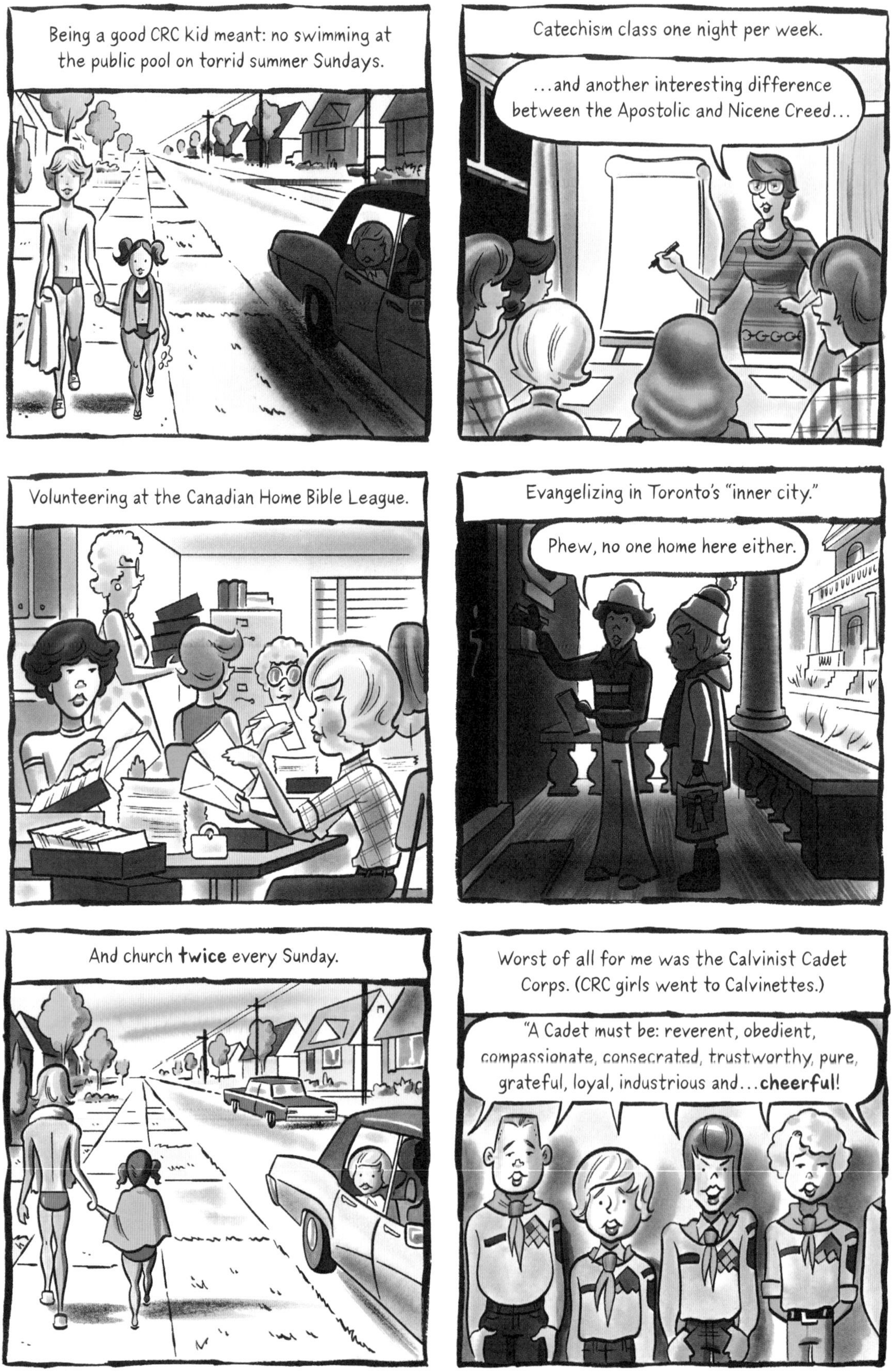
Being a good CRC kid meant: no swimming at the public pool on torrid summer Sundays.
Catechism class one night per week.
...and another interesting difference between the Apostolic and Nicene Creed...
Volunteering at the Canadian Home Bible League.
Evangelizing in Toronto's "inner city."
Phew, no one home here either.
And church **twice** every Sunday.
Worst of all for me was the Calvinist Cadet Corps. (CRC girls went to Calvinettes.)
"A Cadet must be: reverent, obedient, compassionate, consecrated, trustworthy, pure, grateful, loyal, industrious and...**cheerful**!

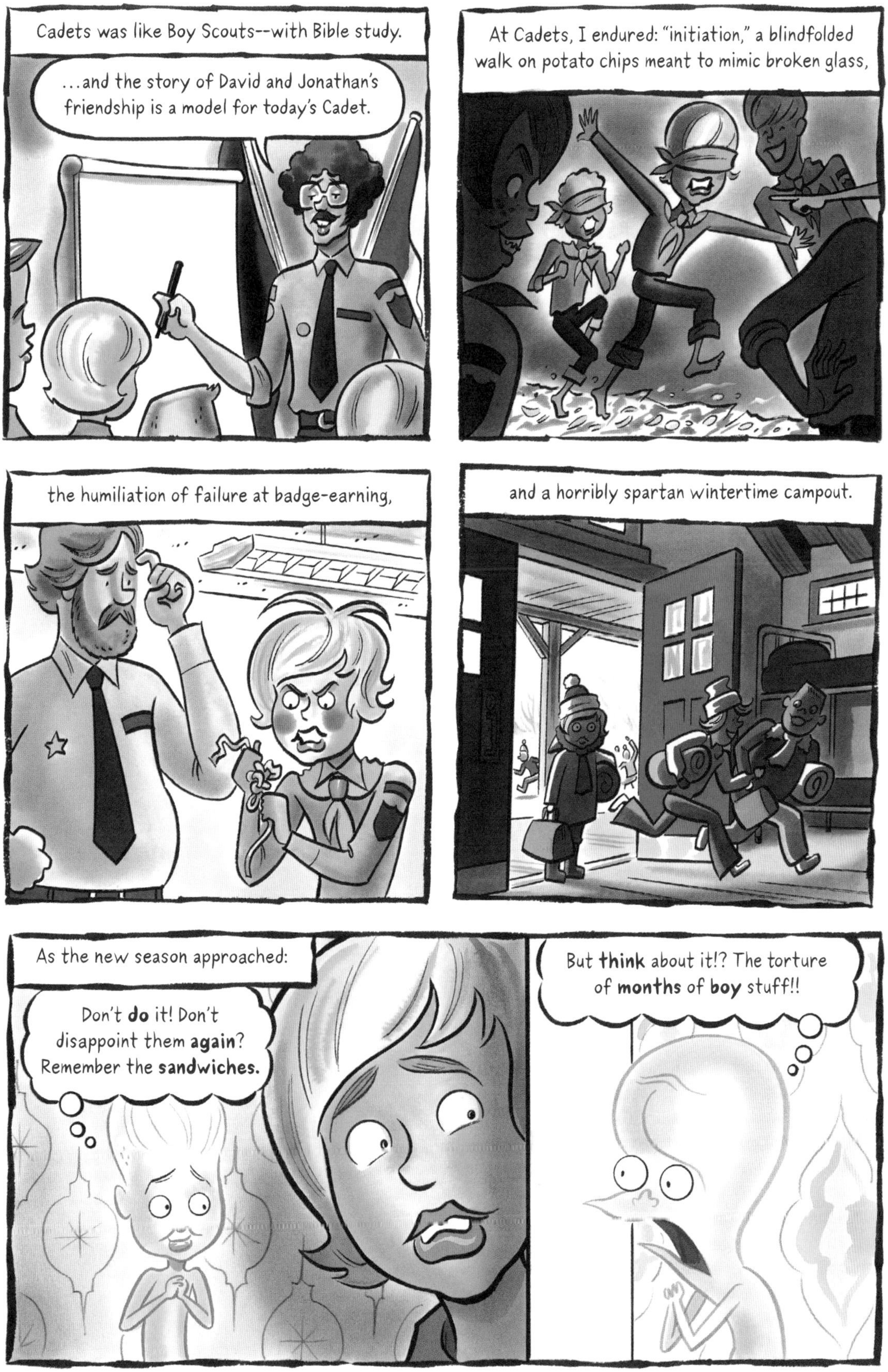
Cadets was like Boy Scouts--with Bible study.
...and the story of David and Jonathan's friendship is a model for today's Cadet.
At Cadets, I endured: "initiation," a blindfolded walk on potato chips meant to mimic broken glass,
the humiliation of failure at badge-earning,
and a horribly spartan wintertime campout.
As the new season approached:
Don't **do** it! Don't disappoint them **again**? Remember the **sandwiches.**
But **think** about it!? The torture of **months** of **boy** stuff!!

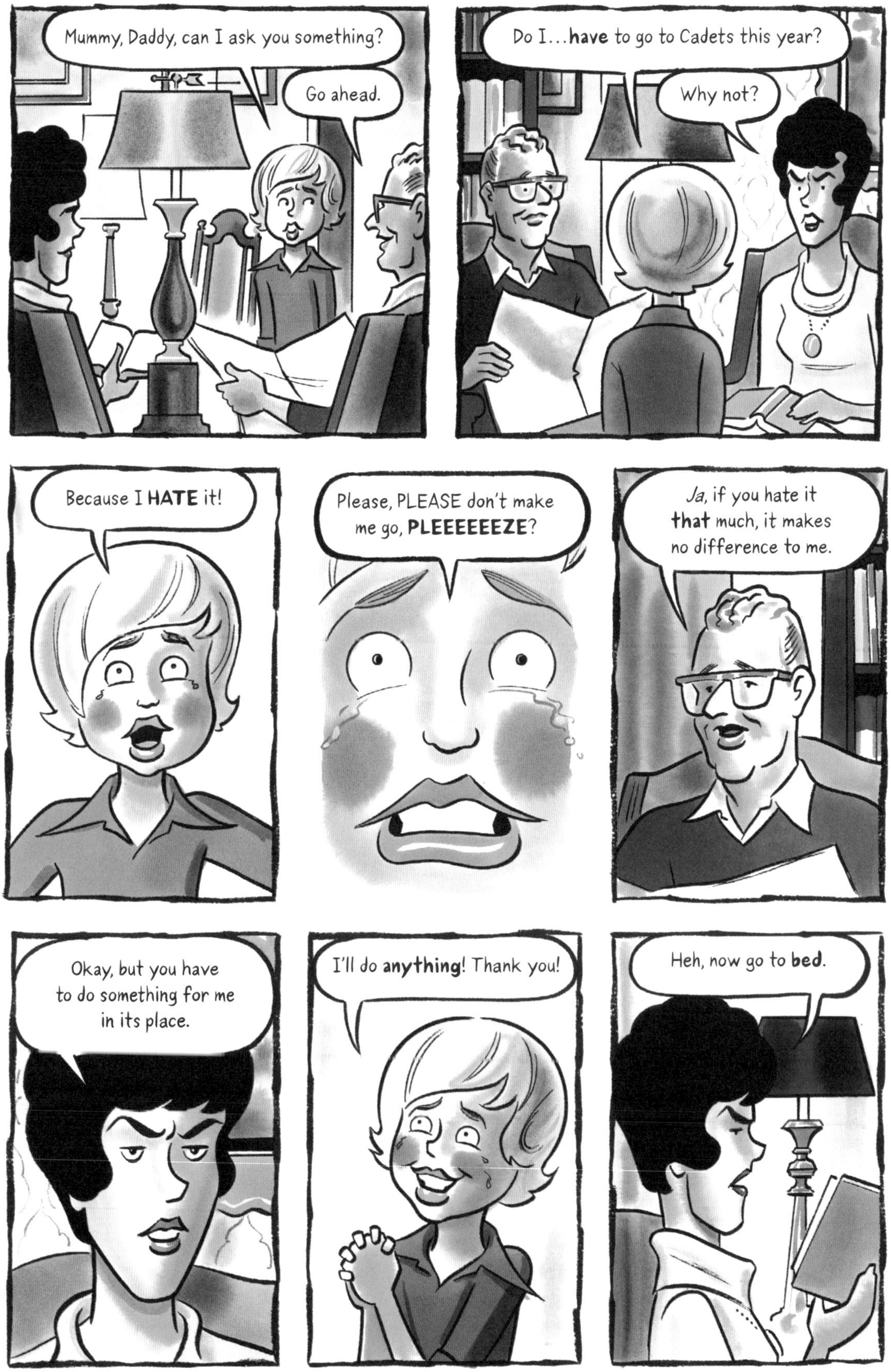
Mummy, Daddy, can I ask you something?
Go ahead.
Do I...**have** to go to Cadets this year?
Why not?
Because I **HATE** it!
Please, PLEASE don't make me go, **PLEEEEEEZE**?
Ja, if you hate it **that** much, it makes no difference to me.
Okay, but you have to do something for me in its place.
I'll do **anything**! Thank you!
Heh, now go to **bed**.

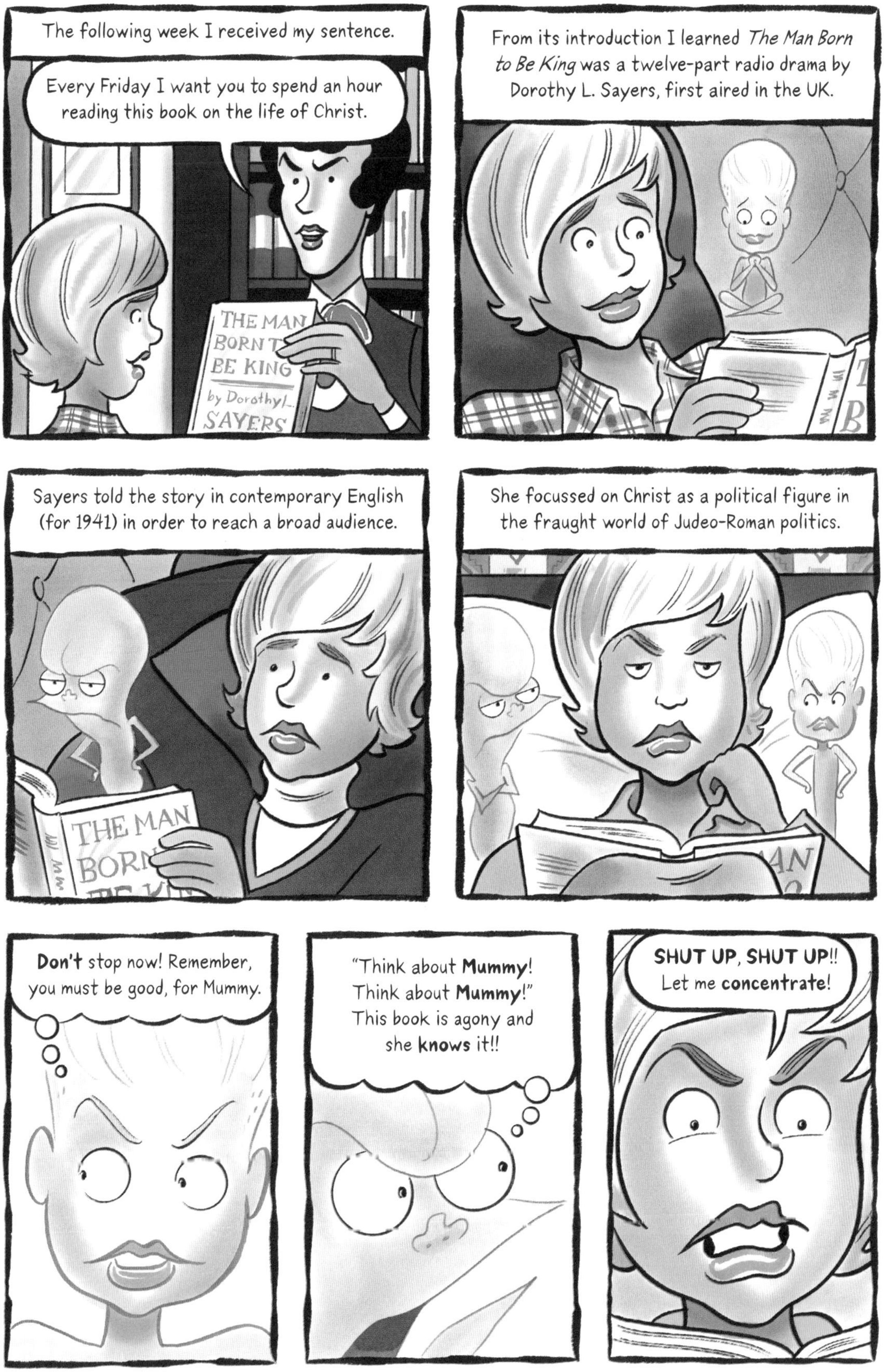
The following week I received my sentence.
Every Friday I want you to spend an hour reading this book on the life of Christ.
THE MAN BORN TO BE KING by Dorothy L. SAYERS
From its introduction I learned *The Man Born to Be King* was a twelve-part radio drama by Dorothy L. Sayers, first aired in the UK.
Sayers told the story in contemporary English (for 1941) in order to reach a broad audience.
THE MAN
She focussed on Christ as a political figure in the fraught world of Judeo-Roman politics.
Don't stop now! Remember, you must be good, for Mummy.
"Think about **Mummy**! Think about **Mummy**!" This book is agony and she **knows** it!!
SHUT UP, **SHUT UP**!! Let me **concentrate**!

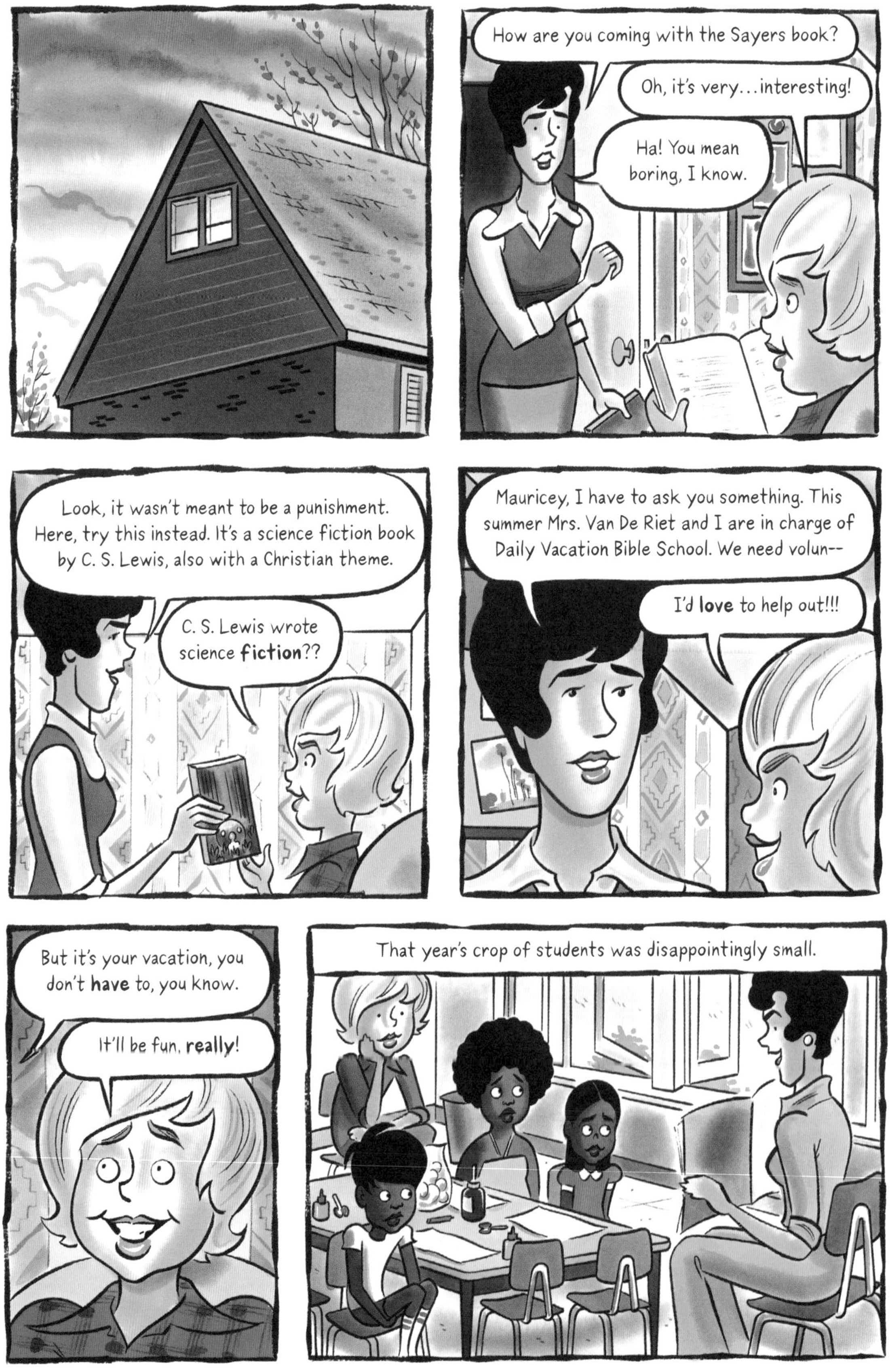
How are you coming with the Sayers book?
Oh, it's very...interesting!
Ha! You mean boring, I know.
Look, it wasn't meant to be a punishment. Here, try this instead. It's a science fiction book by C. S. Lewis, also with a Christian theme.
C. S. Lewis wrote science **fiction**??
Mauricey, I have to ask you something. This summer Mrs. Van De Riet and I are in charge of Daily Vacation Bible School. We need volun--
I'd **love** to help out!!!
But it's your vacation, you don't **have** to, you know.
It'll be fun, **really**!
That year's crop of students was disappointingly small.

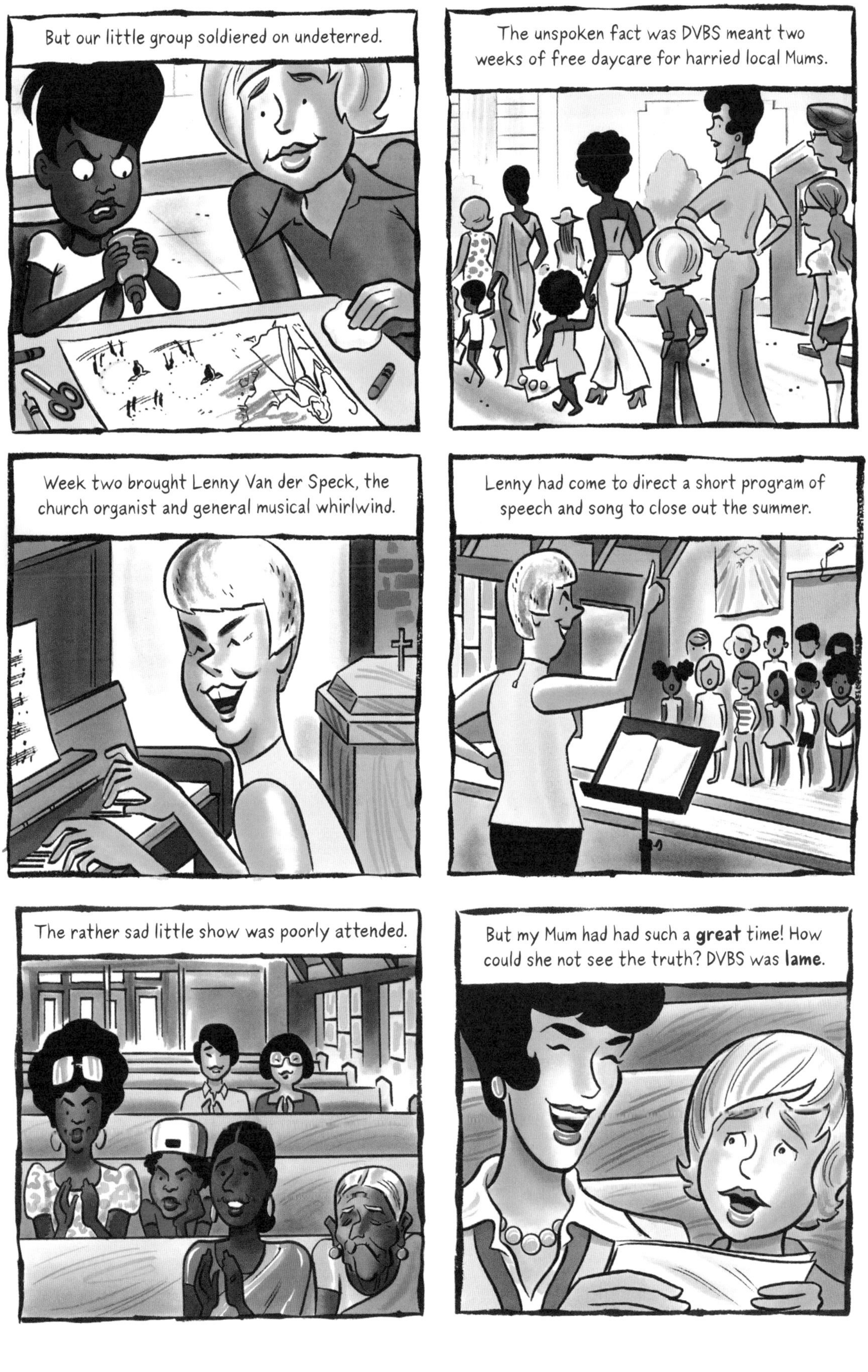
But our little group soldiered on undeterred.
The unspoken fact was DVBS meant two weeks of free daycare for harried local Mums.
Week two brought Lenny Van der Speck, the church organist and general musical whirlwind.
Lenny had come to direct a short program of speech and song to close out the summer.
The rather sad little show was poorly attended.
But my Mum had had such a **great** time! How could she not see the truth? DVBS was **lame**.

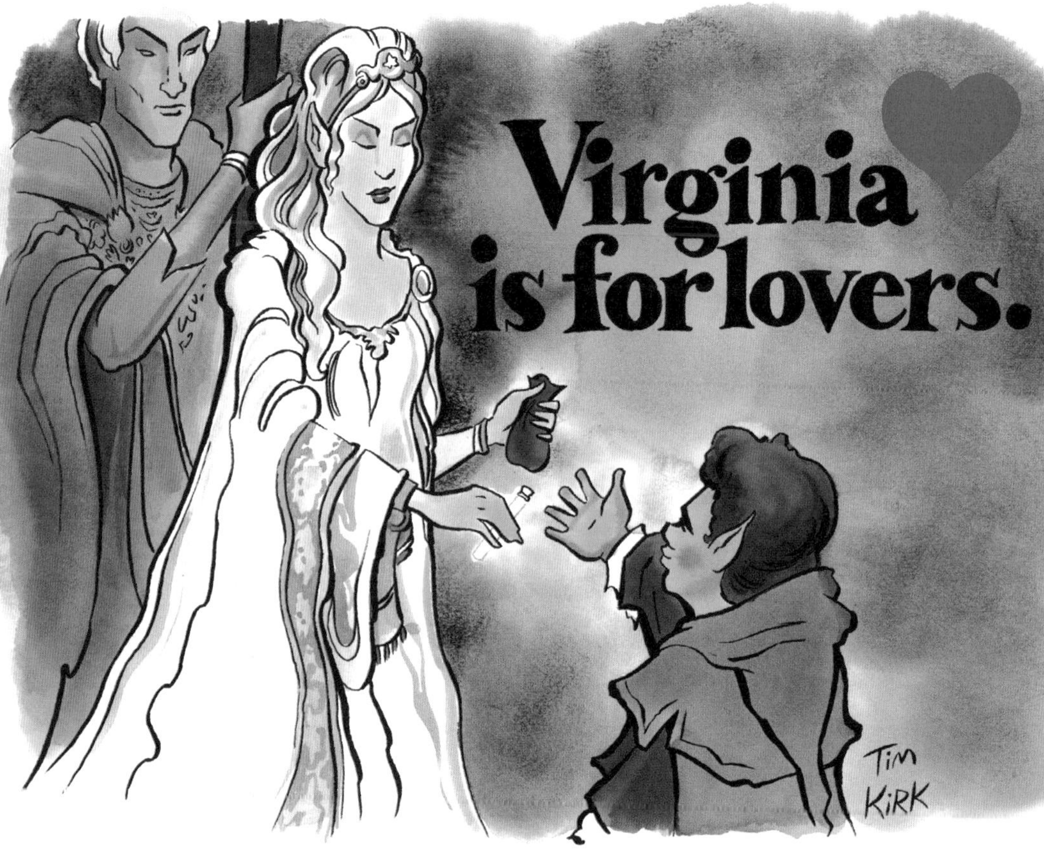
Virginia is for lovers.
TIM KIRK

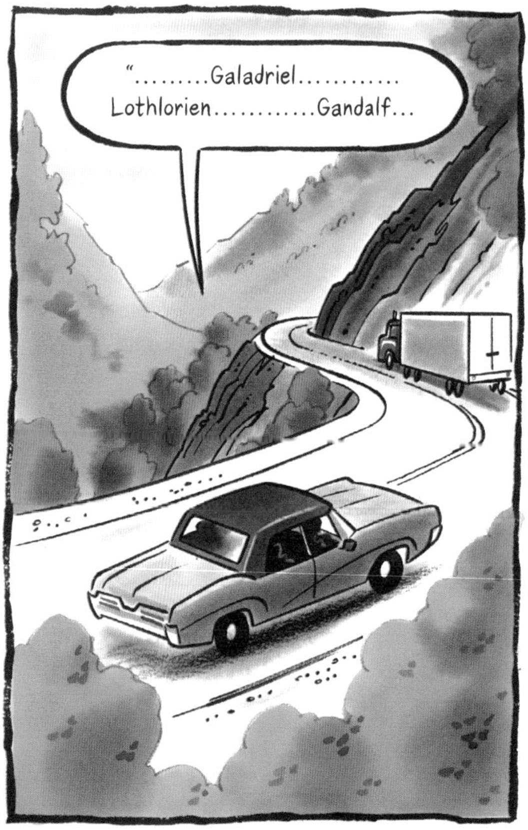
".........Galadriel...........
Lothlorien...........Gandalf...

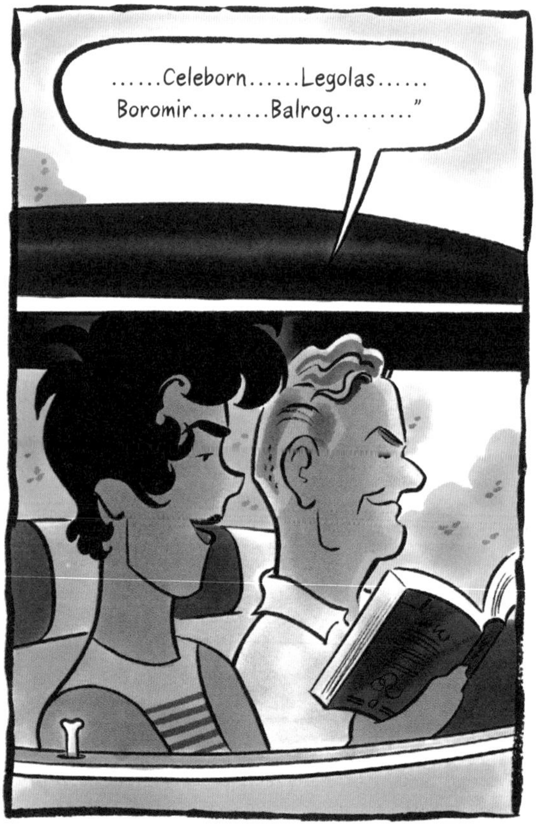
......Celeborn......Legolas......
Boromir.........Balrog........."

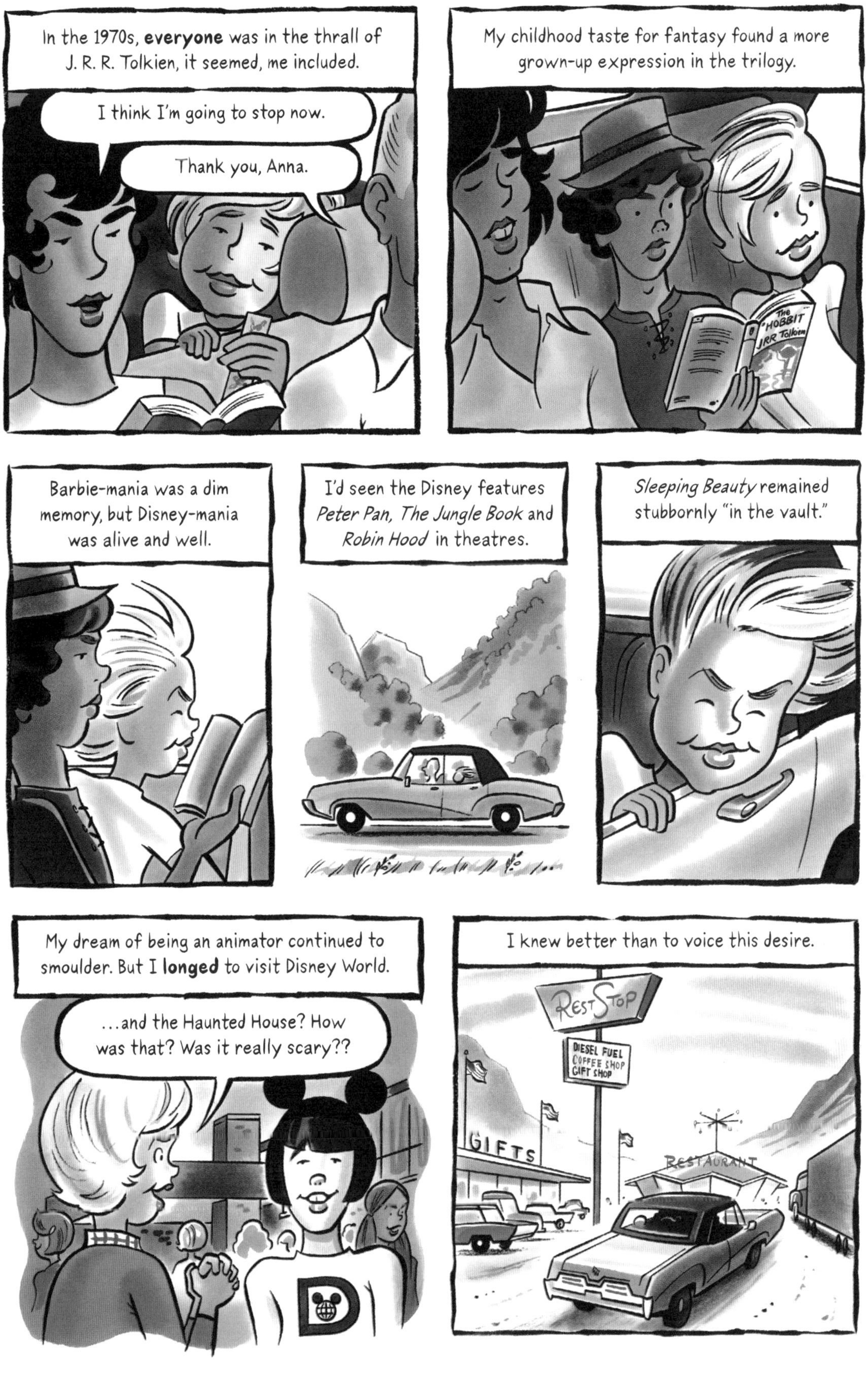

In the 1970s, **everyone** was in the thrall of J. R. R. Tolkien, it seemed, me included.
I think I'm going to stop now.
Thank you, Anna.
My childhood taste for fantasy found a more grown-up expression in the trilogy.
The HOBBIT
JRR Tolkien
Barbie-mania was a dim memory, but Disney-mania was alive and well.
I'd seen the Disney features *Peter Pan, The Jungle Book* and *Robin Hood* in theatres.
Sleeping Beauty remained stubbornly "in the vault."
My dream of being an animator continued to smoulder. But I **longed** to visit Disney World.
...and the Haunted House? How was that? Was it really scary??
I knew better than to voice this desire.
REST STOP
DIESEL FUEL
COFFEE SHOP
GIFT SHOP
GIFTS
RESTAURANT

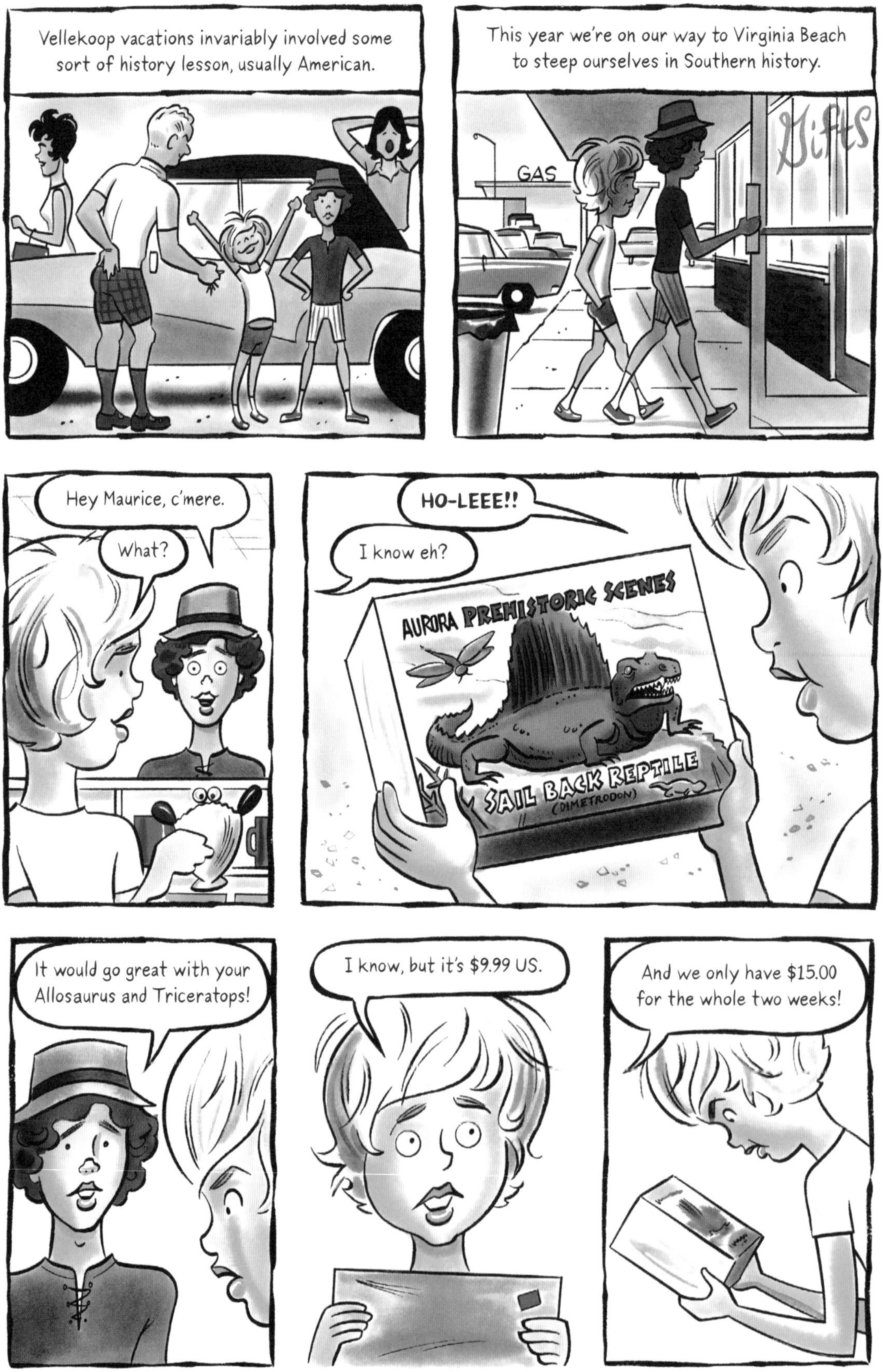
Vellekoop vacations invariably involved some sort of history lesson, usually American.
This year we're on our way to Virginia Beach to steep ourselves in Southern history.
GAS
Gifts
Hey Maurice, c'mere.
What?
HO-LEEE!!
I know eh?
AURORA PREHISTORIC SCENES
SAIL BACK REPTILE
(DIMETRODON)
It would go great with your Allosaurus and Triceratops!
I know, but it's $9.99 US.
And we only have $15.00 for the whole two weeks!

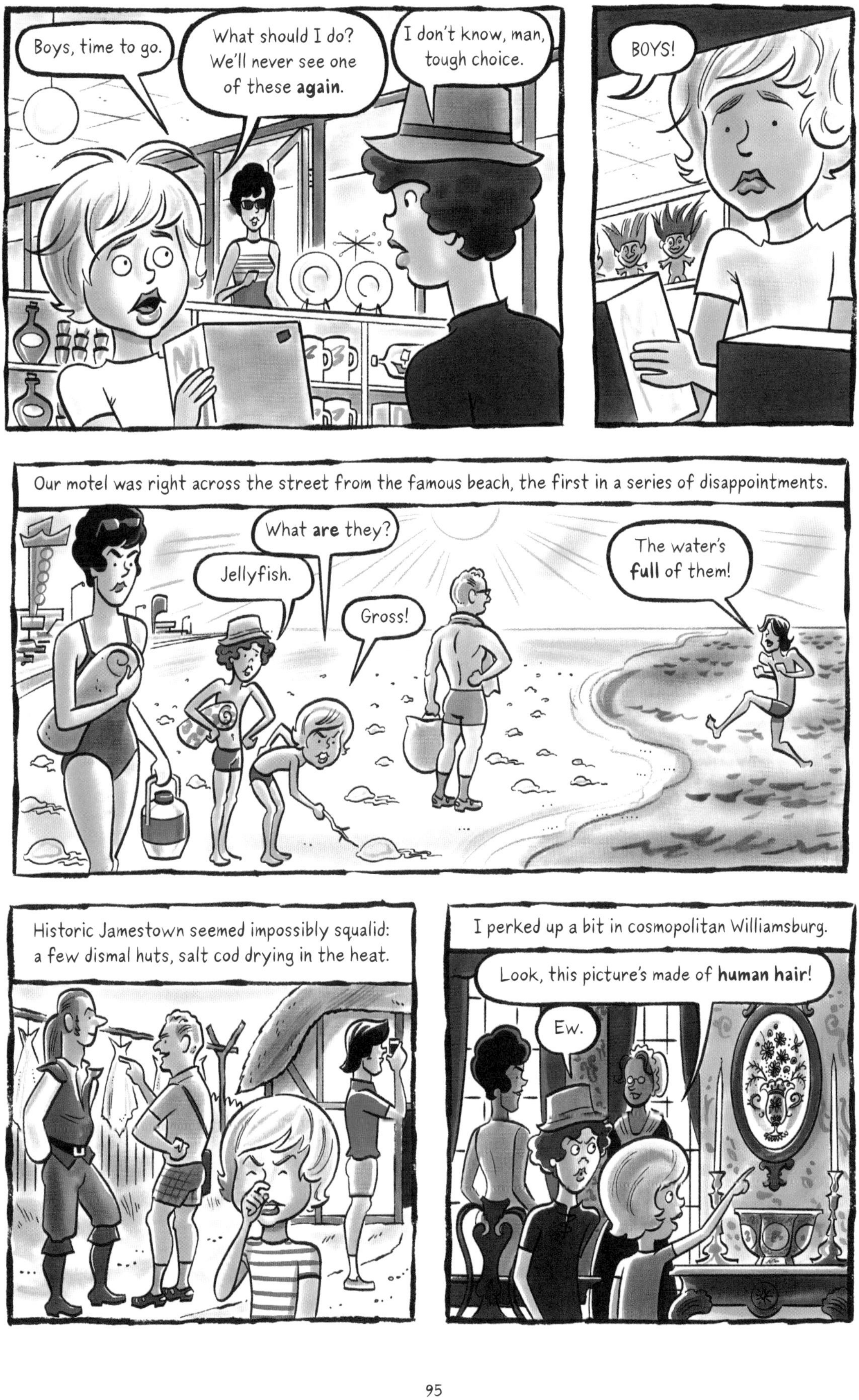
Boys, time to go.
What should I do? We'll never see one of these **again**.
I don't know, man, tough choice.
BOYS!
Our motel was right across the street from the famous beach, the first in a series of disappointments.
What **are** they?
Jellyfish.
Gross!
The water's **full** of them!
Historic Jamestown seemed impossibly squalid: a few dismal huts, salt cod drying in the heat.
I perked up a bit in cosmopolitan Williamsburg.
Look, this picture's made of **human hair**!
Ew.

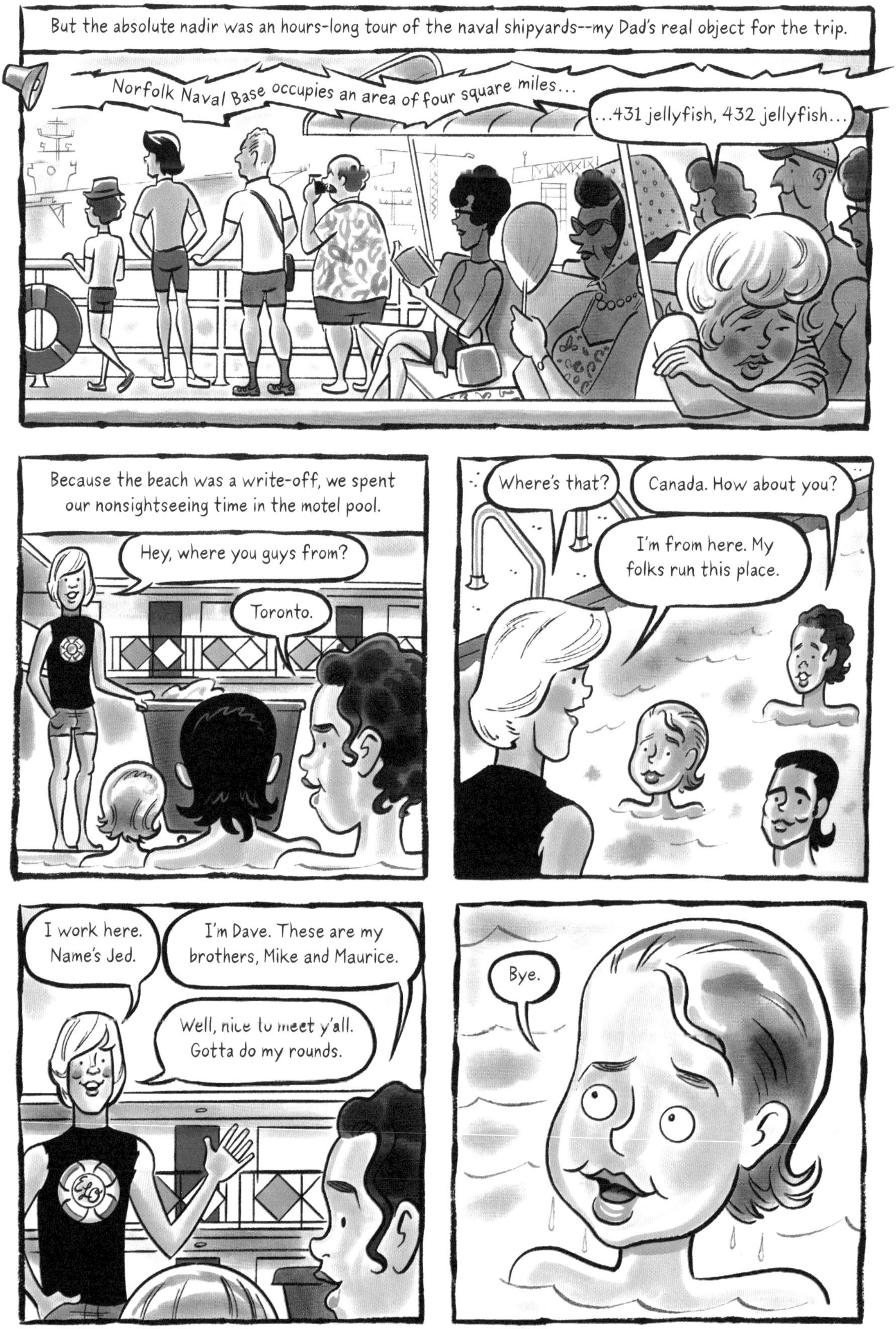

But the absolute nadir was an hours-long tour of the naval shipyards--my Dad's real object for the trip.
Norfolk Naval Base occupies an area of four square miles...
...431 jellyfish, 432 jellyfish...
Because the beach was a write-off, we spent our nonsightseeing time in the motel pool.
Hey, where you guys from?
Toronto.
Where's that?
Canada. How about you?
I'm from here. My folks run this place.
I work here. Name's Jed.
I'm Dave. These are my brothers, Mike and Maurice.
Well, nice to meet y'all. Gotta do my rounds.
Bye.

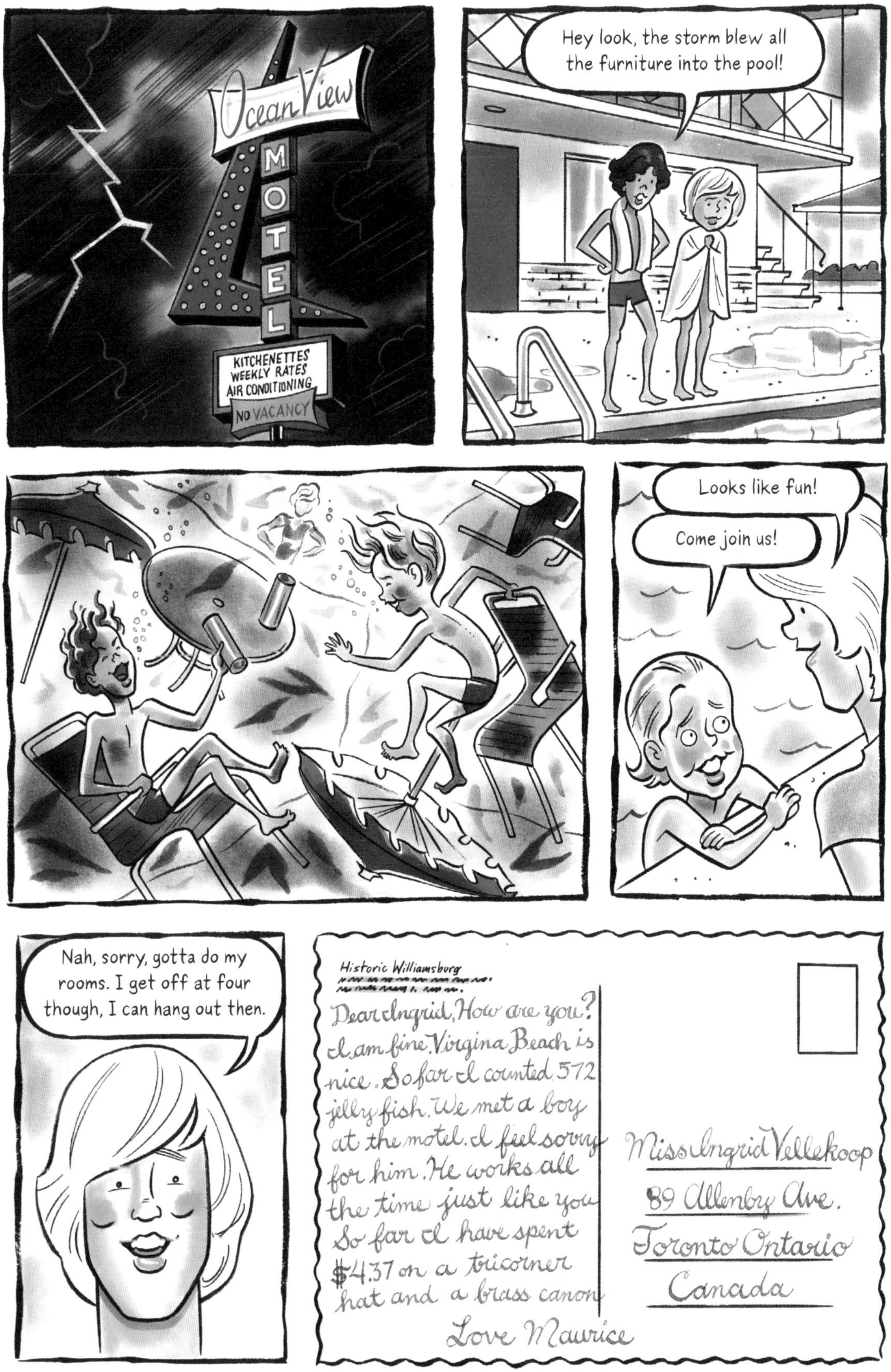
Ocean View
MOTEL
KITCHENETTES
WEEKLY RATES
AIR CONDITIONING
NO VACANCY
Hey look, the storm blew all the furniture into the pool!
Looks like fun!
Come join us!
Nah, sorry, gotta do my rooms. I get off at four though, I can hang out then.
Historic Williamsburg
Dear Ingrid, How are you? I am fine. Virgina Beach is nice. So far I counted 572 jelly fish. We met a boy at the motel. I feel sorry for him. He works all the time just like you. So far I have spent $4.37 on a tricorner hat and a brass canon
Love Maurice
Miss Ingrid Vellekoop
89 Allenby Ave.
Toronto Ontario
Canada

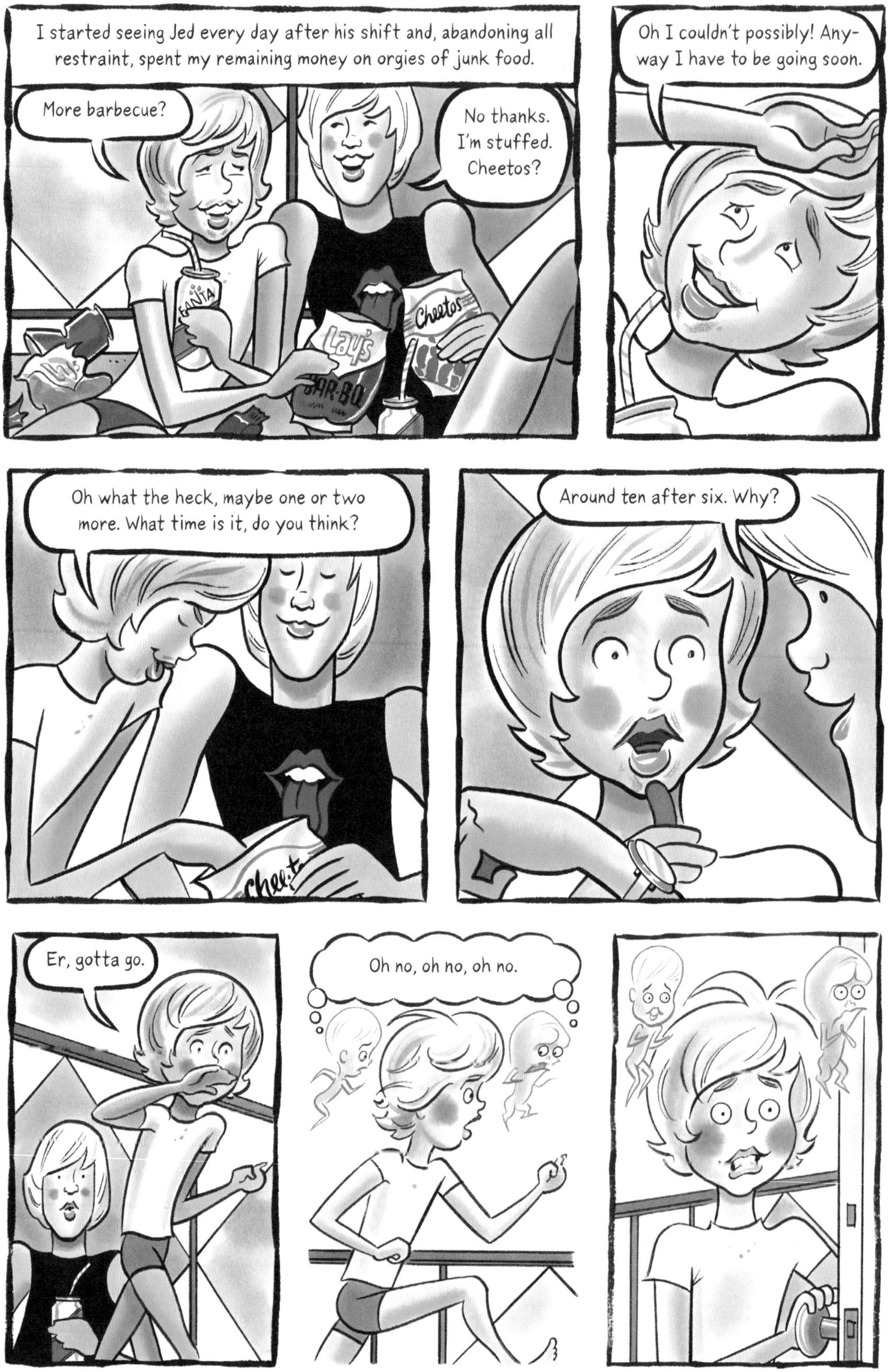
I started seeing Jed every day after his shift and, abandoning all restraint, spent my remaining money on orgies of junk food.
More barbecue?
No thanks. I'm stuffed. Cheetos?
Oh I couldn't possibly! Anyway I have to be going soon.
Oh what the heck, maybe one or two more. What time is it, do you think?
Around ten after six. Why?
Er, gotta go.
Oh no, oh no, oh no.

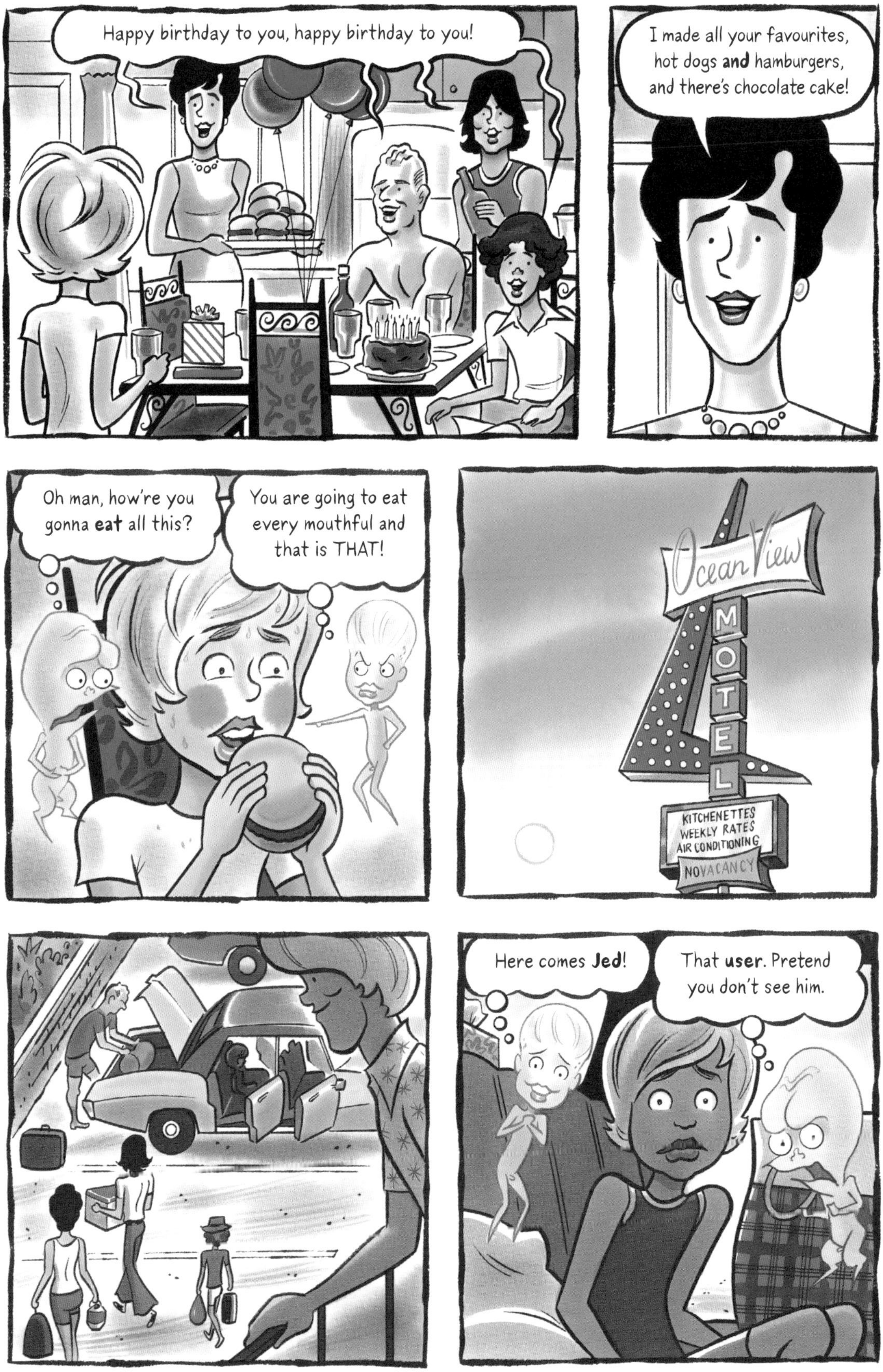
Happy birthday to you, happy birthday to you!
I made all your favourites, hot dogs **and** hamburgers, and there's chocolate cake!
Oh man, how're you gonna **eat** all this?
You are going to eat every mouthful and that is THAT!
Ocean View
MOTEL
KITCHENETTES
WEEKLY RATES
AIR CONDITIONING
NO VACANCY
Here comes **Jed**!
That **user**. Pretend you don't see him.

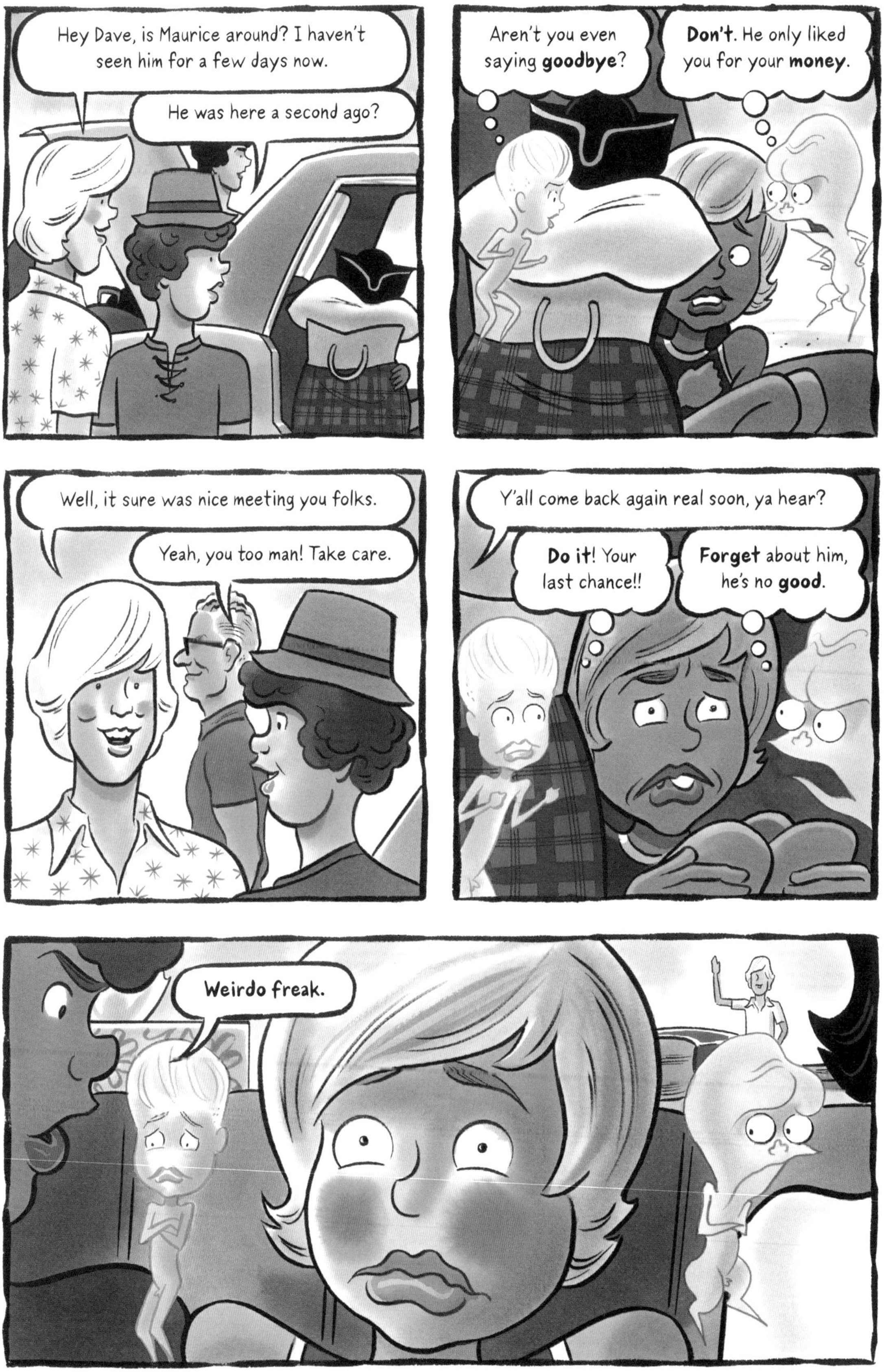
Hey Dave, is Maurice around? I haven't seen him for a few days now.
He was here a second ago?
Aren't you even saying **goodbye**?
Don't. He only liked you for your **money**.
Well, it sure was nice meeting you folks.
Yeah, you too man! Take care.
Y'all come back again real soon, ya hear?
Do it! Your last chance!!
Forget about him, he's no **good**.
Weirdo freak.

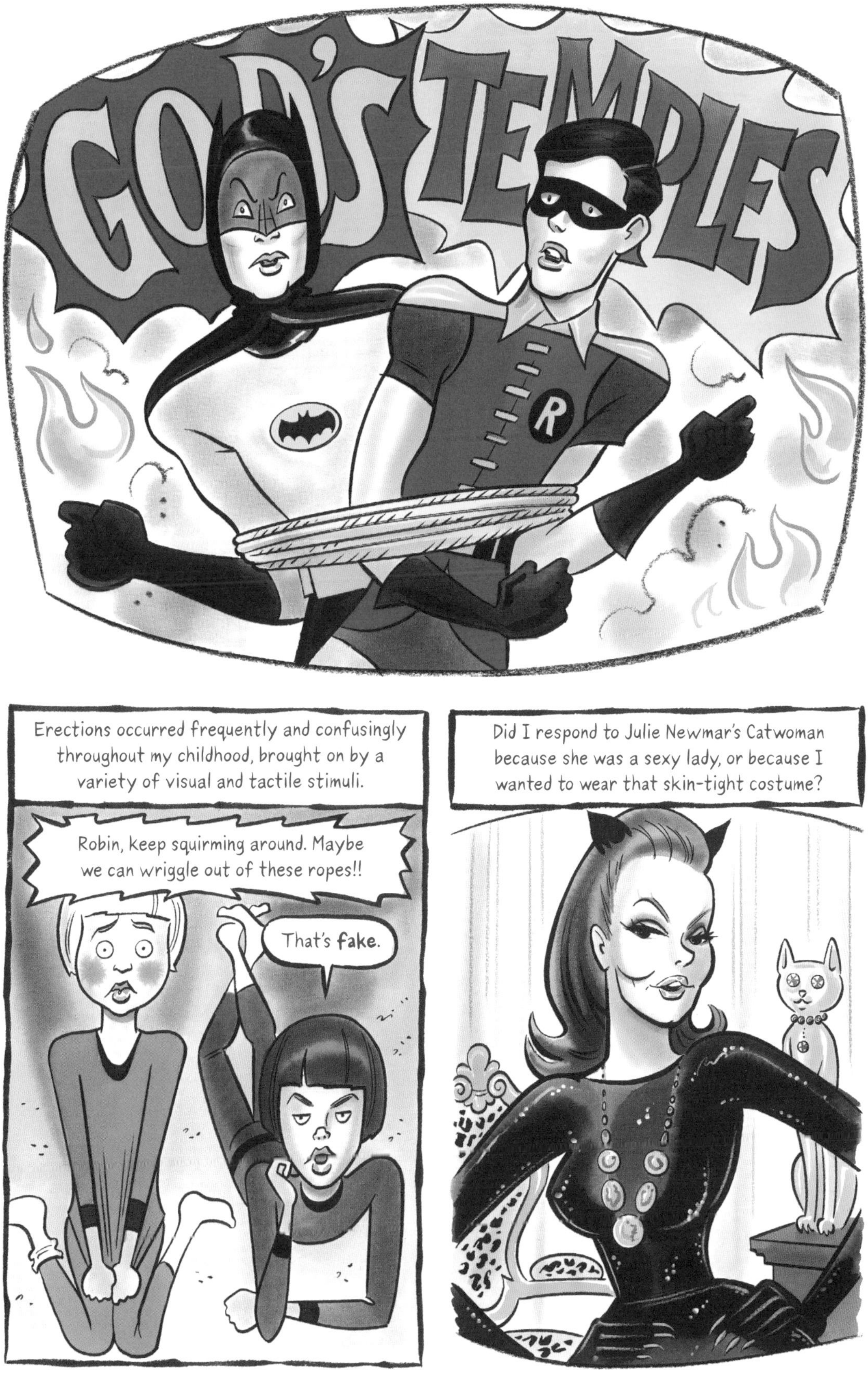
GOD'S TEMPLES
R
Erections occurred frequently and confusingly throughout my childhood, brought on by a variety of visual and tactile stimuli.
Robin, keep squirming around. Maybe we can wriggle out of these ropes!!
That's **fake**.
Did I respond to Julie Newmar's Catwoman because she was a sexy lady, or because I wanted to wear that skin-tight costume?

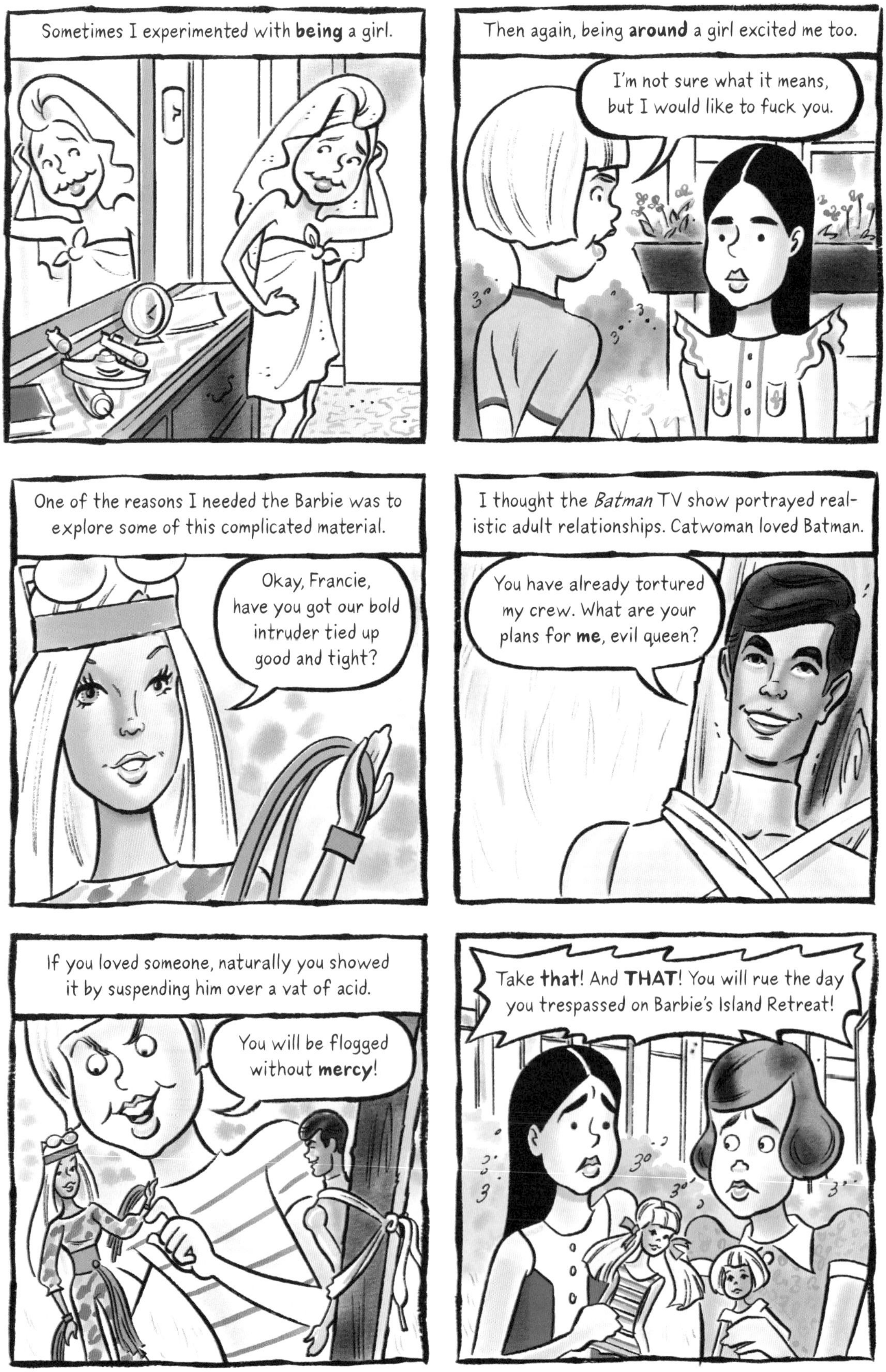
Sometimes I experimented with **being** a girl.
Then again, being **around** a girl excited me too.
I'm not sure what it means, but I would like to fuck you.
One of the reasons I needed the Barbie was to explore some of this complicated material.
Okay, Francie, have you got our bold intruder tied up good and tight?
I thought the *Batman* TV show portrayed realistic adult relationships. Catwoman loved Batman.
You have already tortured my crew. What are your plans for **me**, evil queen?
If you loved someone, naturally you showed it by suspending him over a vat of acid.
You will be flogged without **mercy**!
Take **that**! And **THAT**! You will rue the day you trespassed on Barbie's Island Retreat!

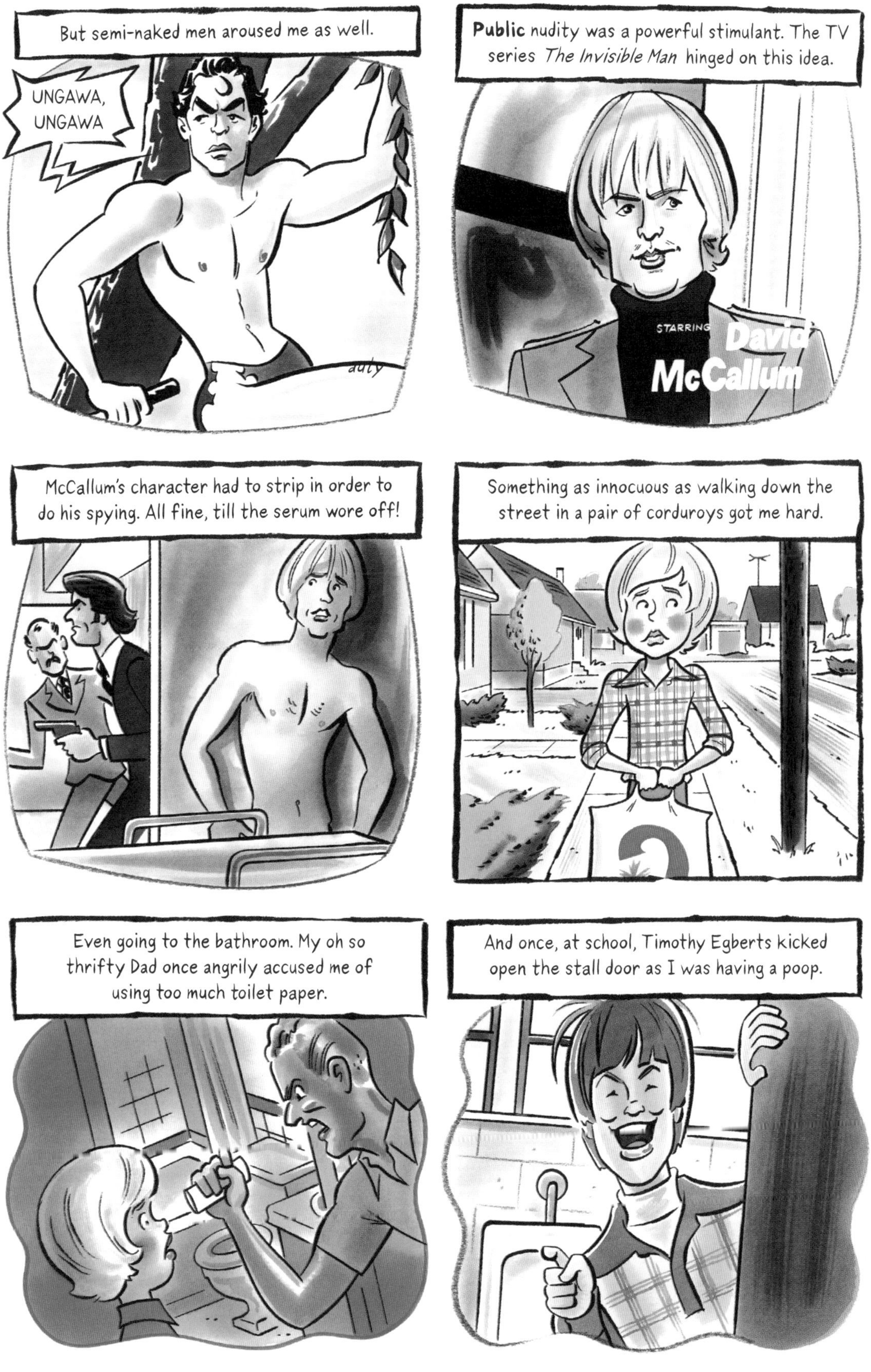
But semi-naked men aroused me as well.
UNGAWA, UNGAWA
Public nudity was a powerful stimulant. The TV series The Invisible Man hinged on this idea.
STARRING David McCallum
McCallum's character had to strip in order to do his spying. All fine, till the serum wore off!
Something as innocuous as walking down the street in a pair of corduroys got me hard.
Even going to the bathroom. My oh so thrifty Dad once angrily accused me of using too much toilet paper.
And once, at school, Timothy Egberts kicked open the stall door as I was having a poop.

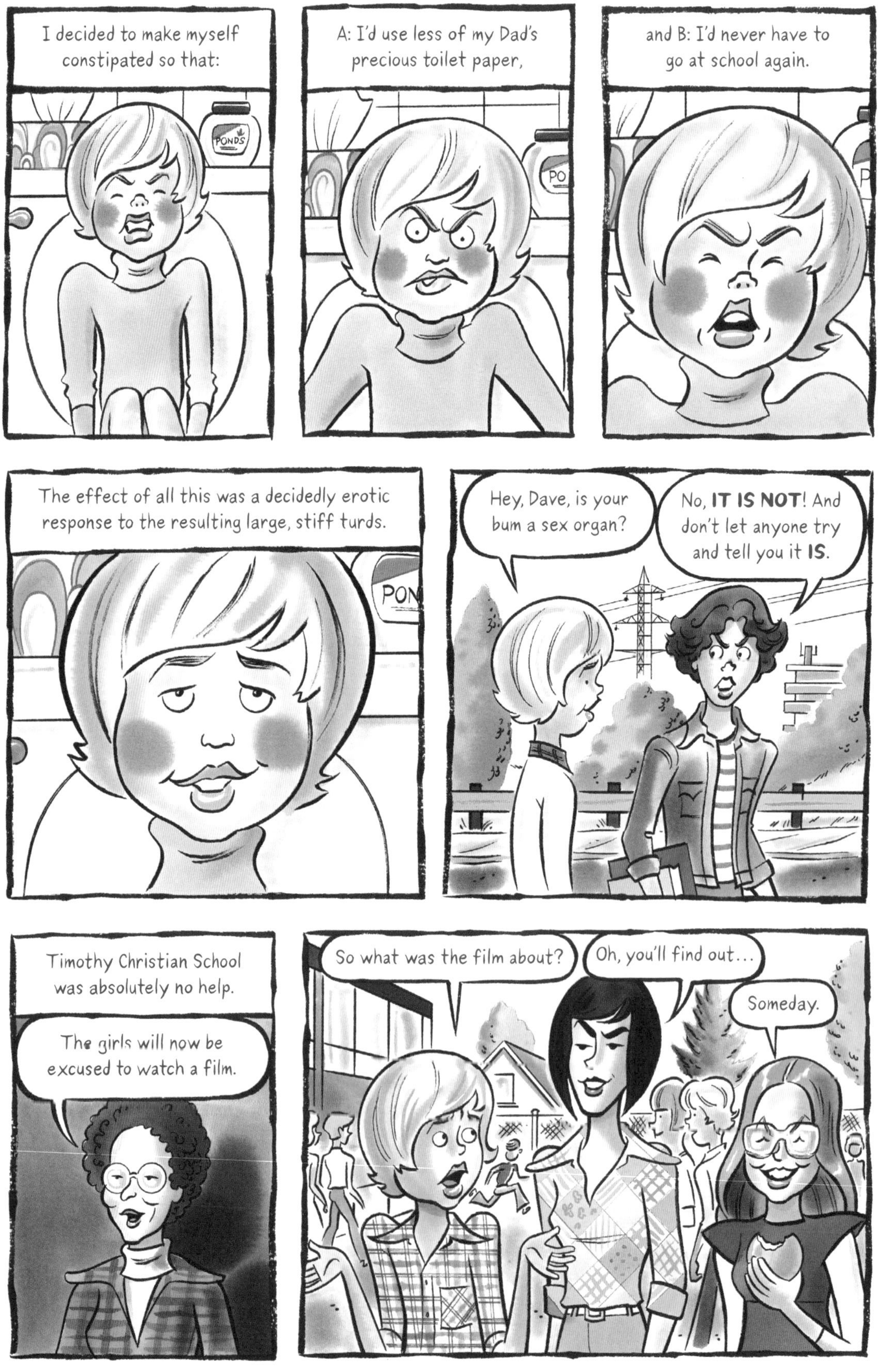
I decided to make myself constipated so that:
A: I'd use less of my Dad's precious toilet paper,
and B: I'd never have to go at school again.
PONDS
The effect of all this was a decidedly erotic response to the resulting large, stiff turds.
Hey, Dave, is your bum a sex organ?
No, **IT IS NOT**! And don't let anyone try and tell you it **IS**.
Timothy Christian School was absolutely no help.
The girls will now be excused to watch a film.
So what was the film about?
Oh, you'll find out...
Someday.

Around age thirteen my body started to change. Hair started to sprout in odd places, and the hair on my head turned dark. I touched myself down there whenever I could find privacy...

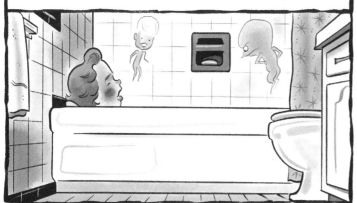

...until one day:

WHA-A-A-A?

What is it??   Smells salty-sweet.

This is so weird!   What should you do?

Maybe you should **tell** someone! What if something's **wrong**?

NO! Don't be an idiot!? **NOBODY** needs to know about this...aberration!

Okay, after all, it may never happen again.

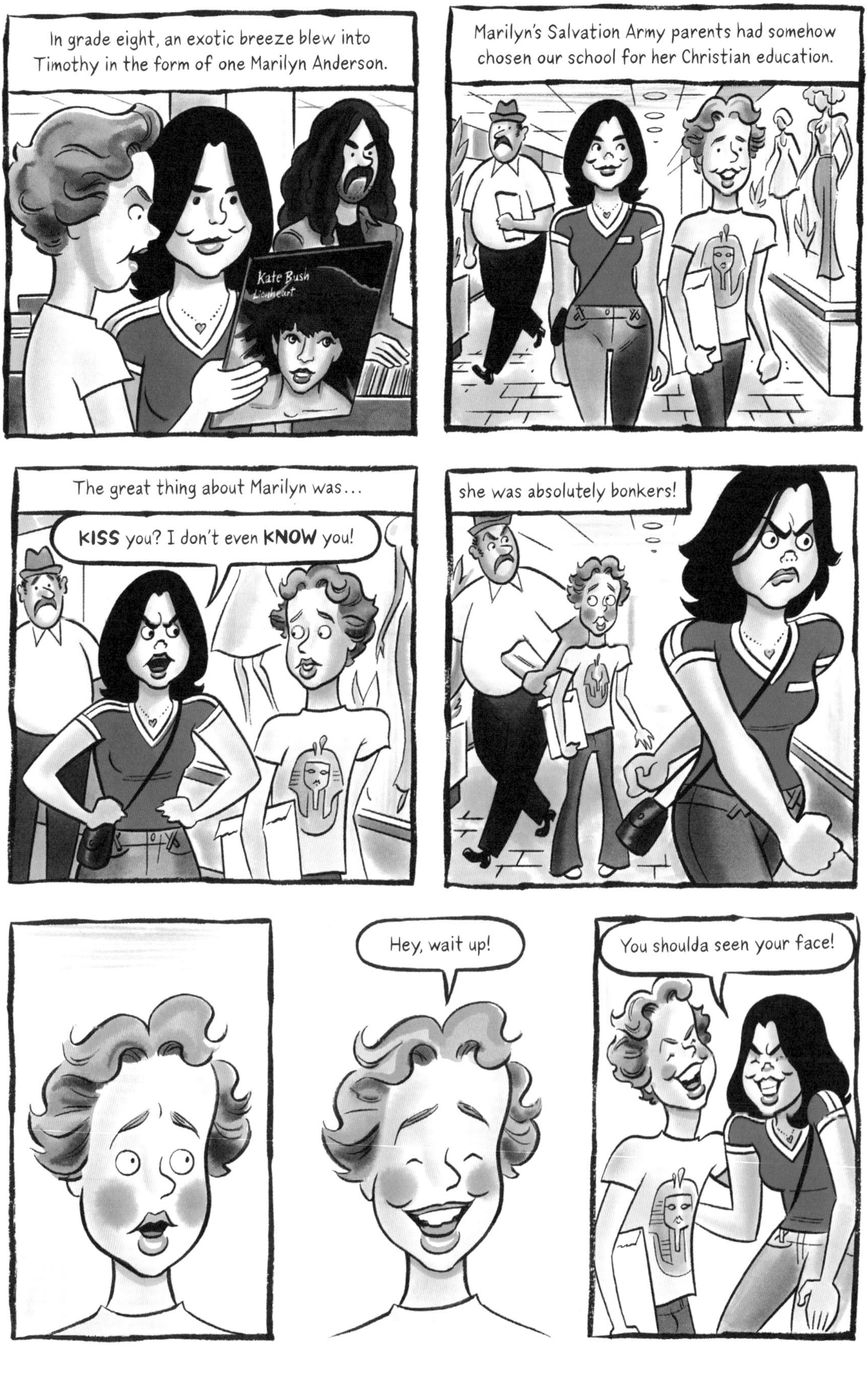
In grade eight, an exotic breeze blew into Timothy in the form of one Marilyn Anderson.
Kate Bush
Lionheart
Marilyn's Salvation Army parents had somehow chosen our school for her Christian education.
The great thing about Marilyn was...
KISS you? I don't even KNOW you!
she was absolutely bonkers!
Hey, wait up!
You shoulda seen your face!

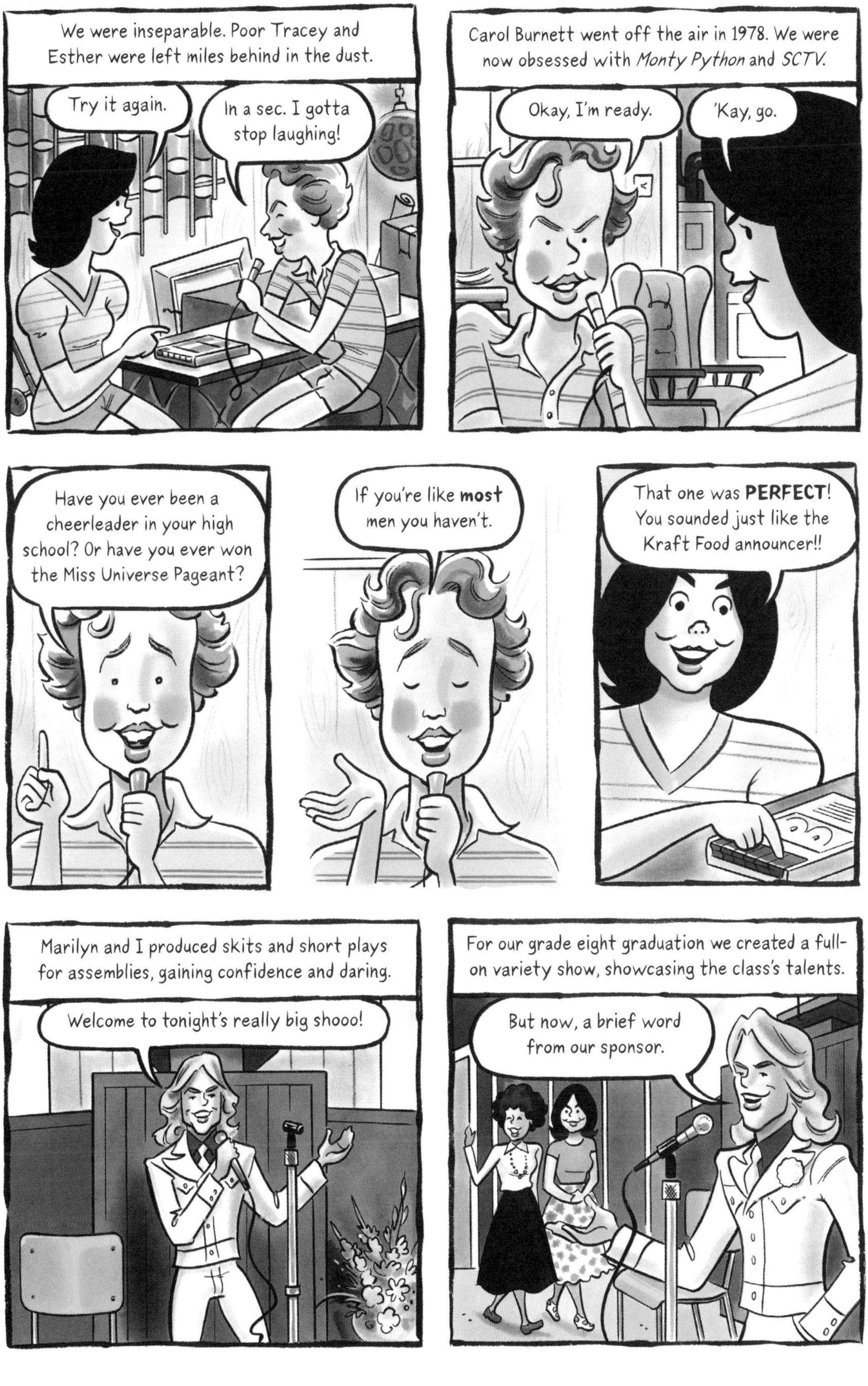

We were inseparable. Poor Tracey and Esther were left miles behind in the dust.
Try it again.
In a sec. I gotta stop laughing!
Carol Burnett went off the air in 1978. We were now obsessed with *Monty Python* and *SCTV*.
Okay, I'm ready.
'Kay, go.
Have you ever been a cheerleader in your high school? Or have you ever won the Miss Universe Pageant?
If you're like **most** men you haven't.
That one was **PERFECT**! You sounded just like the Kraft Food announcer!!
Marilyn and I produced skits and short plays for assemblies, gaining confidence and daring.
Welcome to tonight's really big shooo!
For our grade eight graduation we created a full-on variety show, showcasing the class's talents.
But now, a brief word from our sponsor.

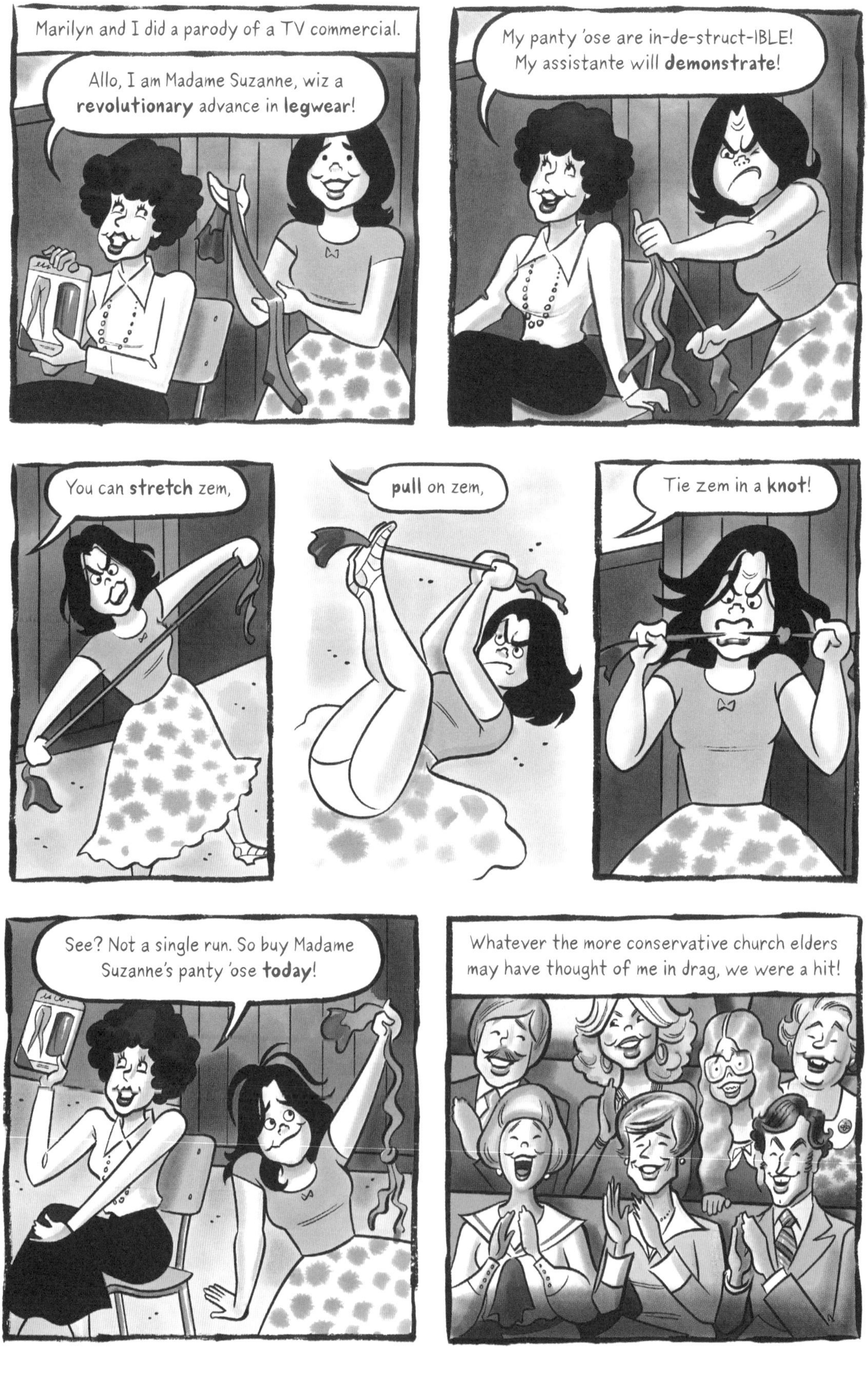
Marilyn and I did a parody of a TV commercial.
Allo, I am Madame Suzanne, wiz a **revolutionary** advance in **legwear**!
My panty 'ose are in-de-struct-IBLE! My assistante will **demonstrate**!
You can **stretch** zem,
pull on zem,
Tie zem in a **knot**!
See? Not a single run. So buy Madame Suzanne's panty 'ose **today**!
Whatever the more conservative church elders may have thought of me in drag, we were a hit!

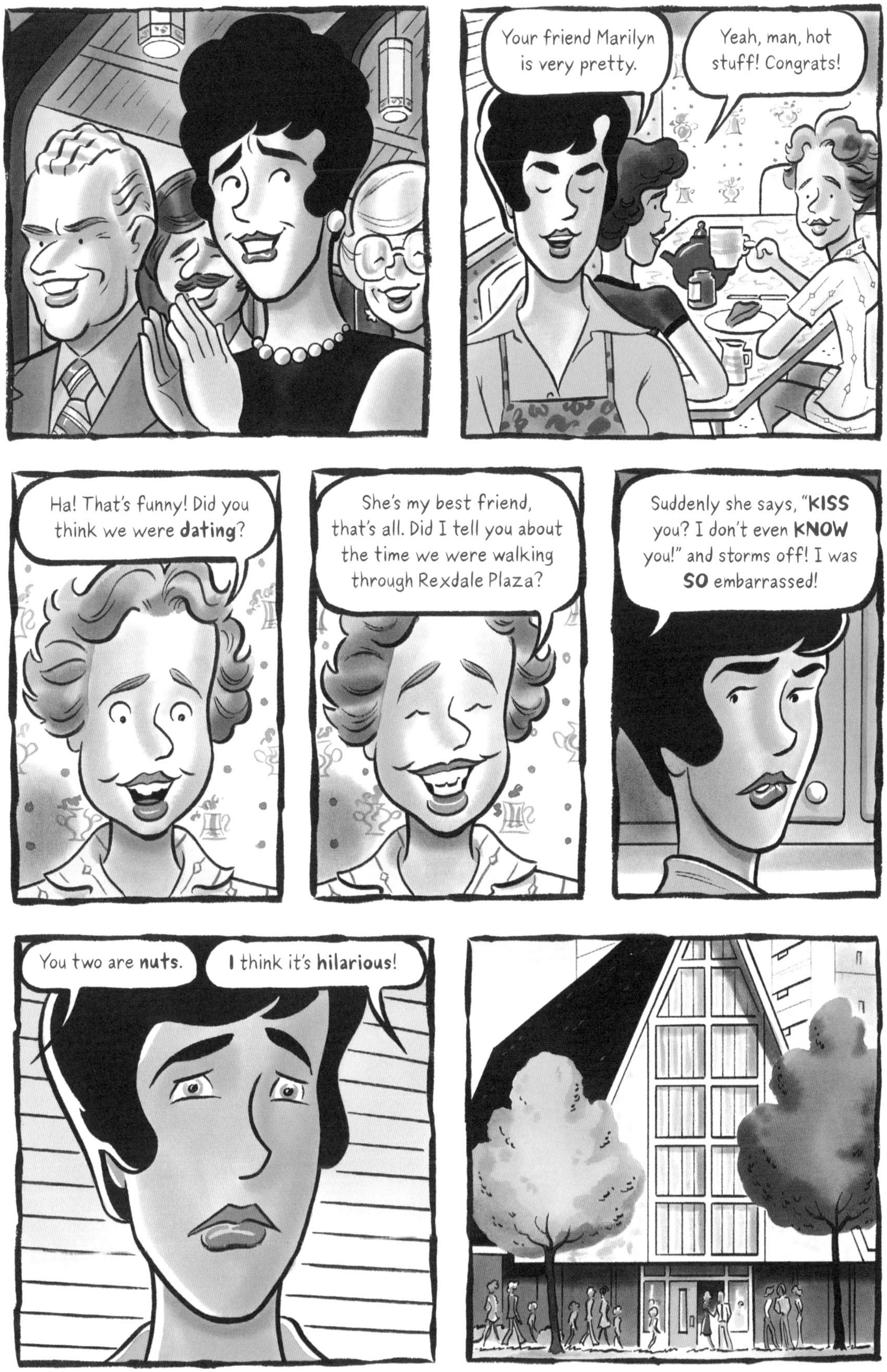
Your friend Marilyn is very pretty.
Yeah, man, hot stuff! Congrats!
Ha! That's funny! Did you think we were **dating**?
She's my best friend, that's all. Did I tell you about the time we were walking through Rexdale Plaza?
Suddenly she says, "**KISS** you? I don't even **KNOW** you!" and storms off! I was **SO** embarrassed!
You two are **nuts**.
I think it's **hilarious**!

So. Your friend's gorgeous and you never realized.

Haven't you noticed something else? I mean when you touch yourself?

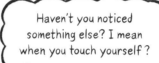

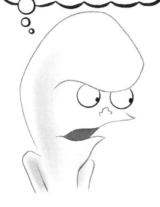

Before, it was just for the physical pleasure,

but lately **pictures** have begun to accompany the touching.

It's time to face the truth: you like **boys**.

Can I come in for a sec?
'Course!
Here, I thought you should have this.
Oh, uh, thanks.
GOD'S TEMPLES
A CHRISTIAN GUIDE TO SEXUALITY
Dr. Mark Van de Velde
If you have any questions...
TEMPLES
"The man puts his erect penis in the woman's vagina and ejaculates his sperm, thus fertilizing the eggs."
Hey, you were right, it's just as you guessed!
Big deal, now look up *homosexual.*
Herpes, p.
Heterosexual
Homosexuality,
Hormone, p.32
Hymen, p.22
Hysterectomy,
ntraurine, p.116
Labia, p.13
Mastitis, p.127

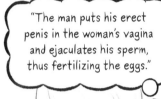

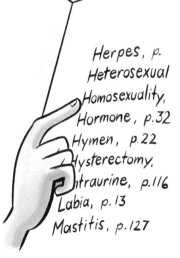

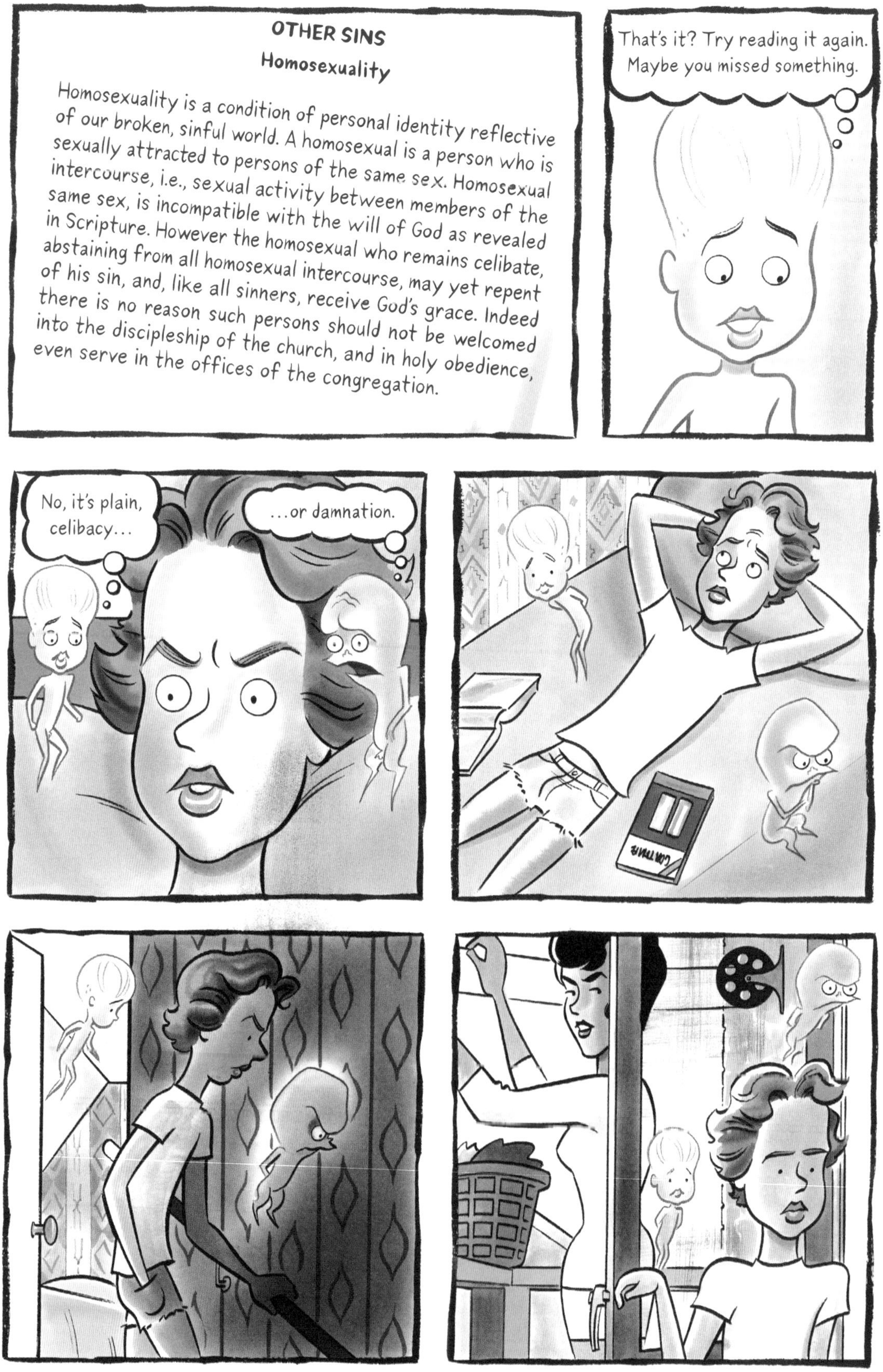
OTHER SINS
Homosexuality
Homosexuality is a condition of personal identity reflective of our broken, sinful world. A homosexual is a person who is sexually attracted to persons of the same sex. Homosexual intercourse, i.e., sexual activity between members of the same sex, is incompatible with the will of God as revealed in Scripture. However the homosexual who remains celibate, abstaining from all homosexual intercourse, may yet repent of his sin, and, like all sinners, receive God's grace. Indeed there is no reason such persons should not be welcomed into the discipleship of the church, and in holy obedience, even serve in the offices of the congregation.
That's it? Try reading it again. Maybe you missed something.
No, it's plain, celibacy...
...or damnation.

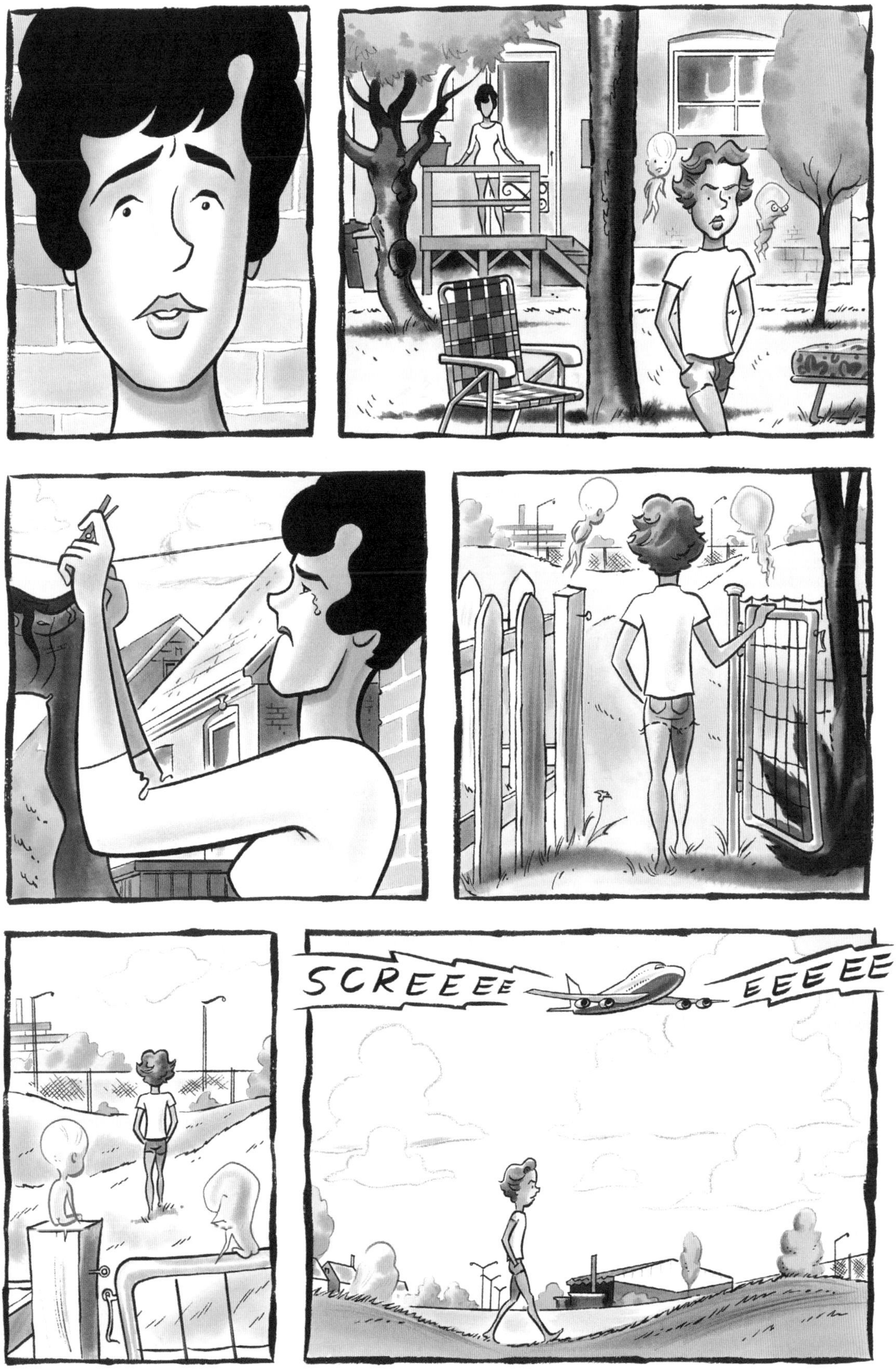
SCREEEEE
EEEEE

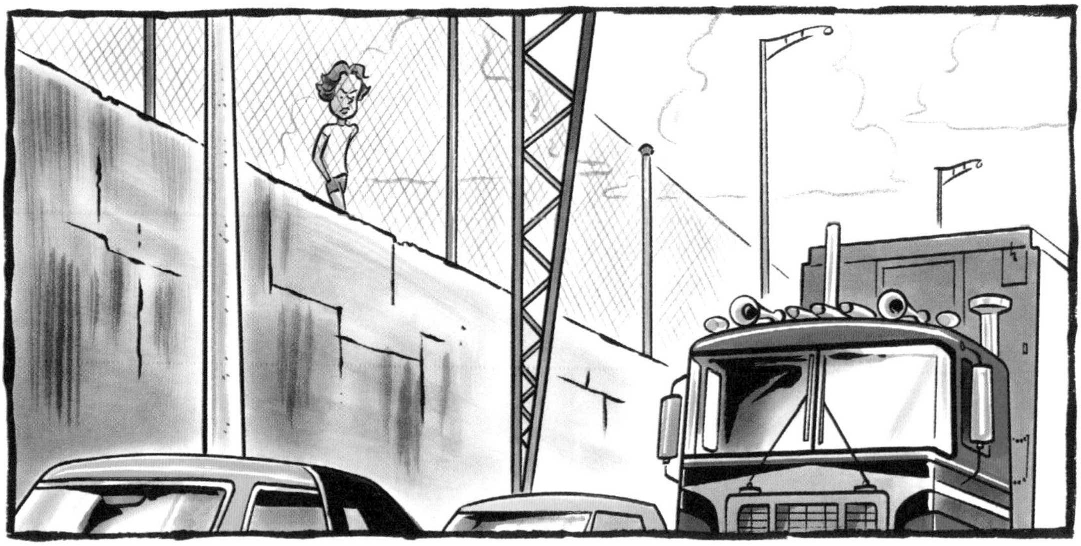

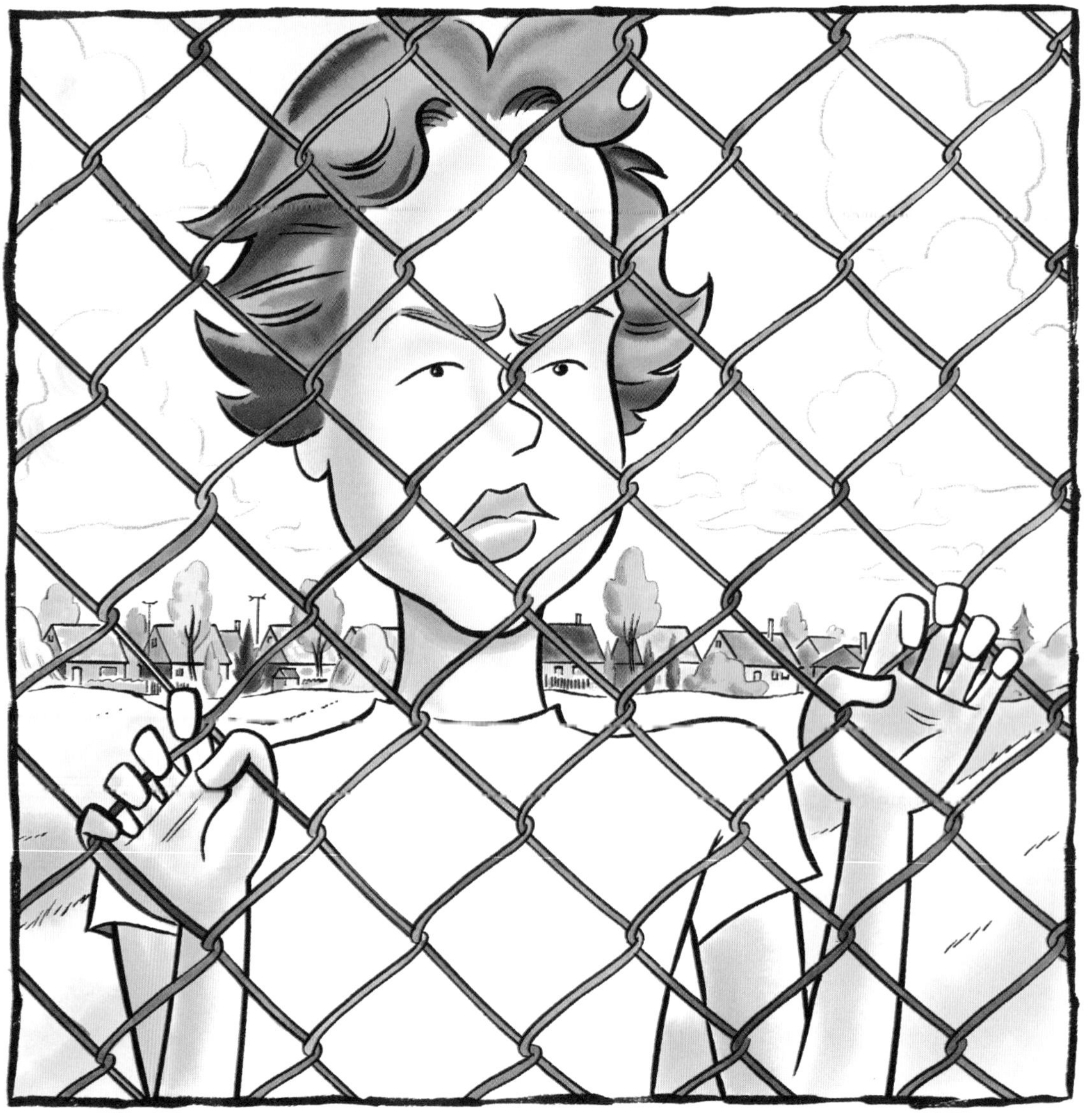

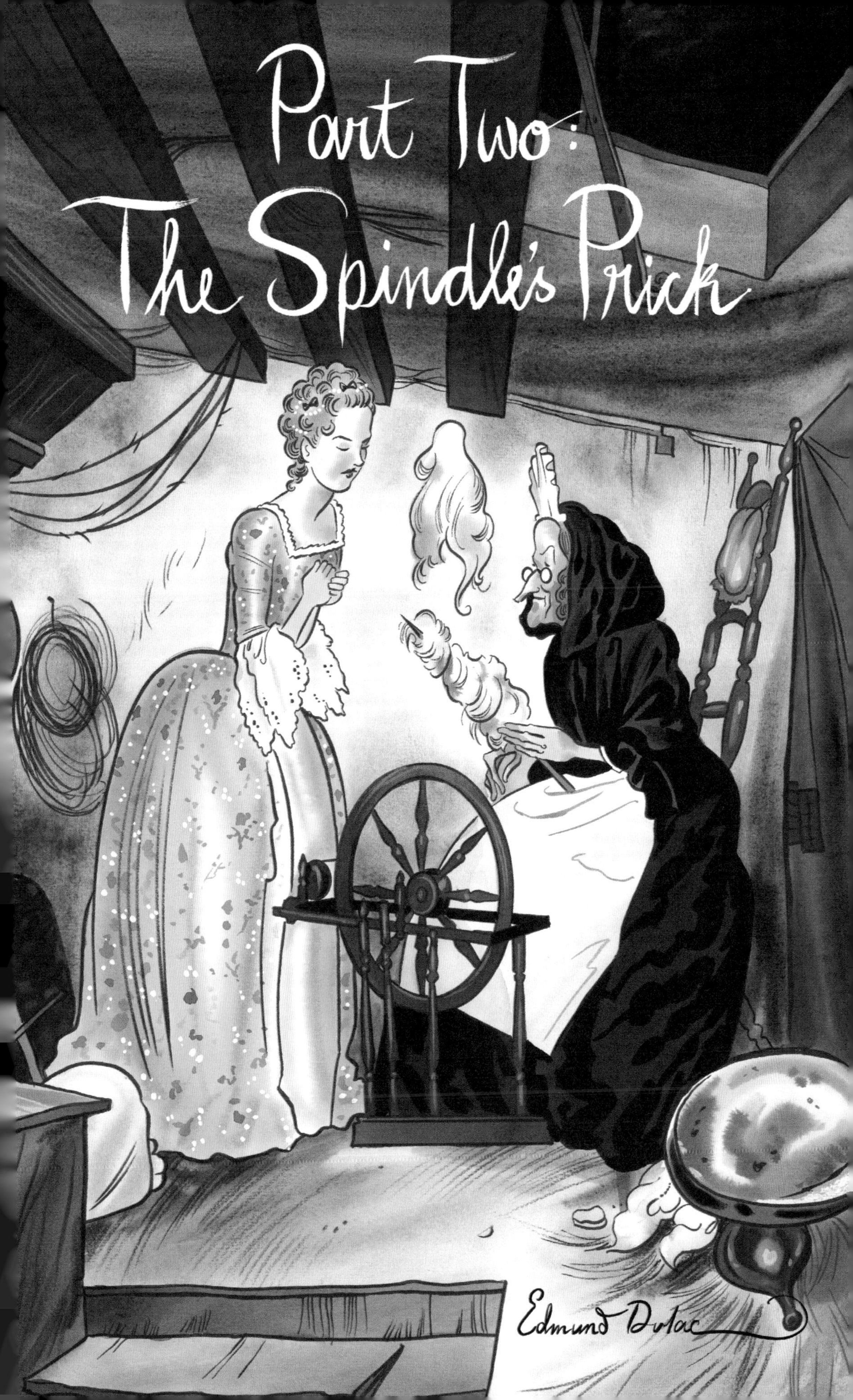
Part Two:
The Spindle's Prick
Edmund Dulac

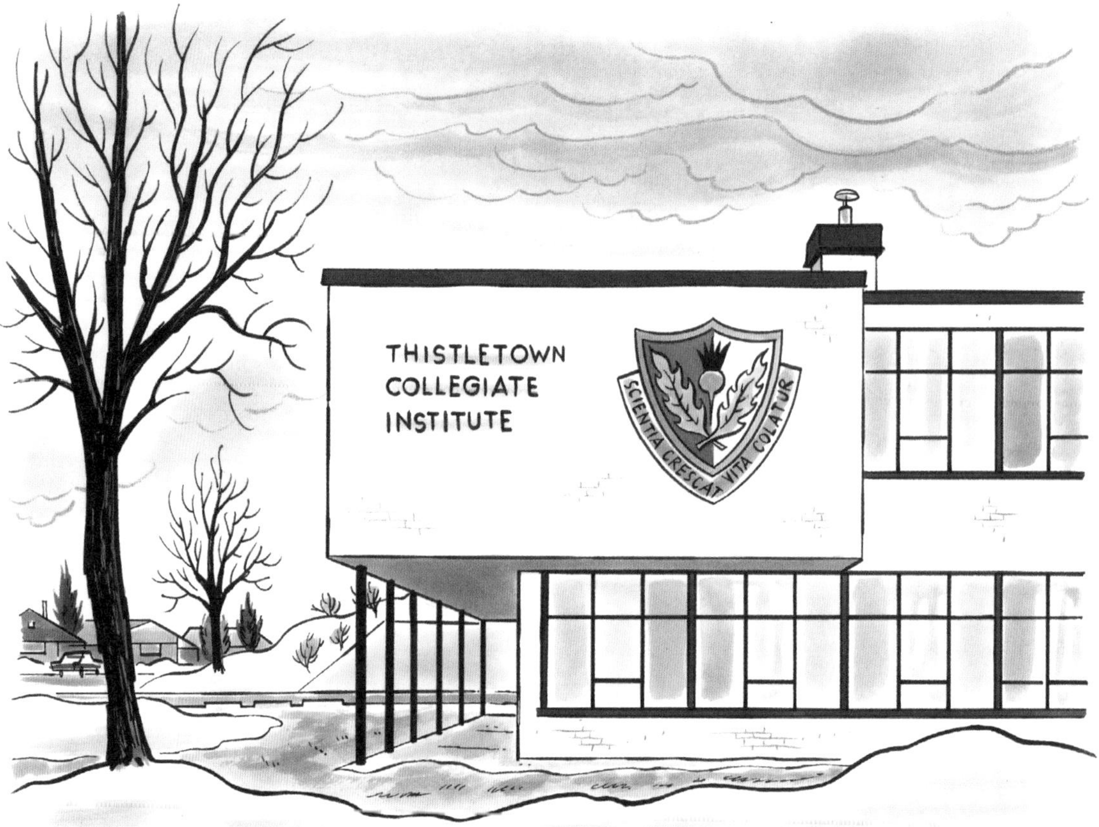
THISTLETOWN
COLLEGIATE
INSTITUTE
SCIENTIA CRESCAT VITA COLATUR

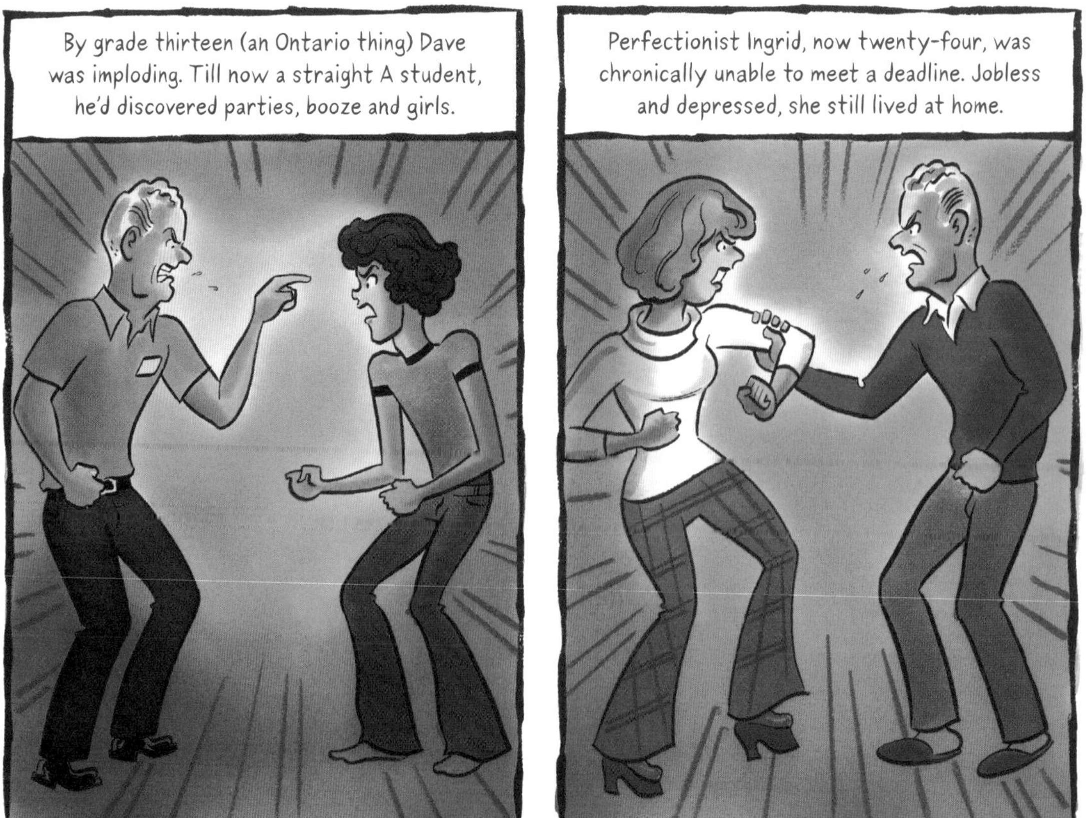
By grade thirteen (an Ontario thing) Dave was imploding. Till now a straight A student, he'd discovered parties, booze and girls.
Perfectionist Ingrid, now twenty-four, was chronically unable to meet a deadline. Jobless and depressed, she still lived at home.

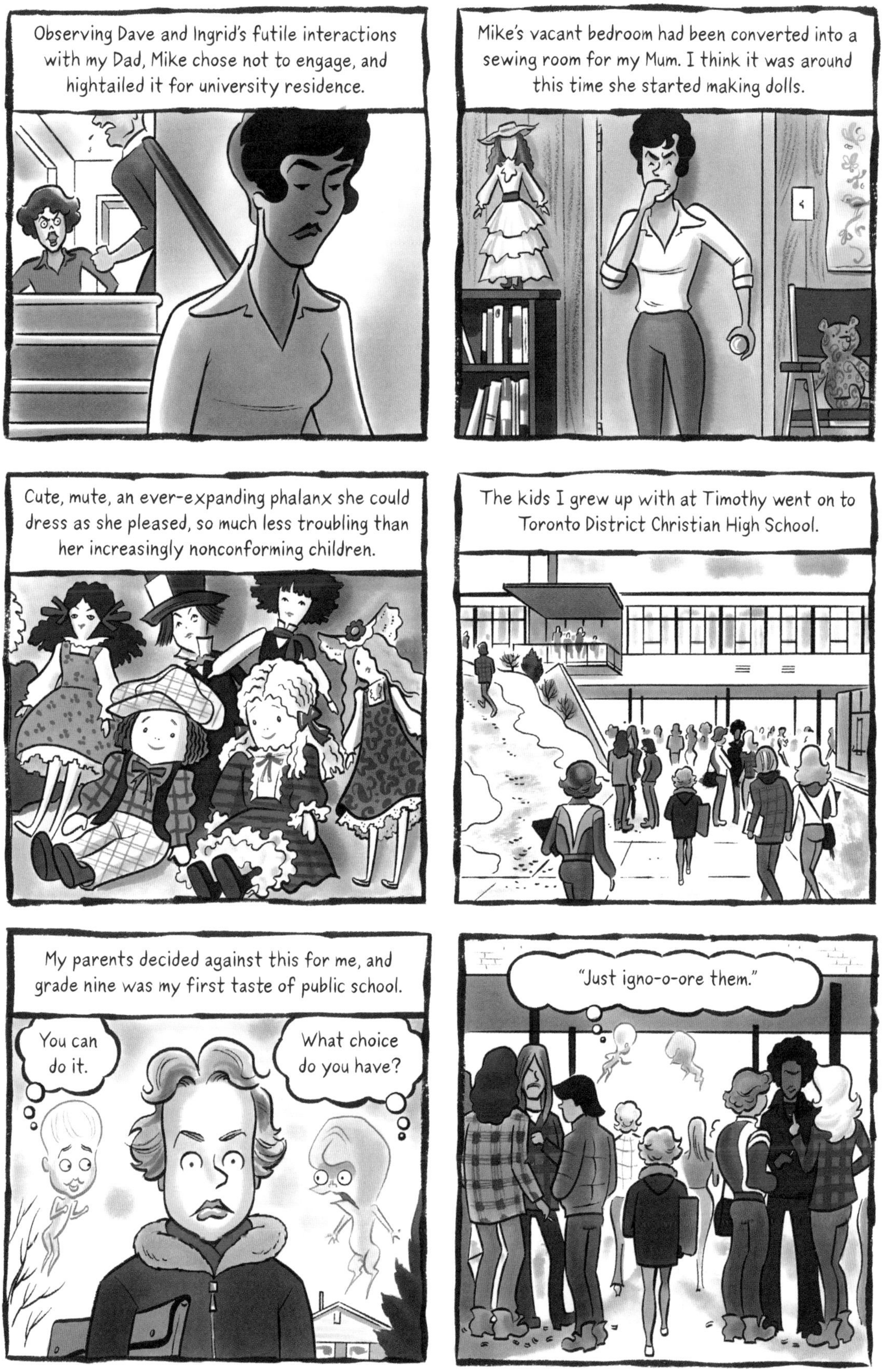
Observing Dave and Ingrid's futile interactions with my Dad, Mike chose not to engage, and hightailed it for university residence.
Mike's vacant bedroom had been converted into a sewing room for my Mum. I think it was around this time she started making dolls.
Cute, mute, an ever-expanding phalanx she could dress as she pleased, so much less troubling than her increasingly nonconforming children.
The kids I grew up with at Timothy went on to Toronto District Christian High School.
My parents decided against this for me, and grade nine was my first taste of public school.
You can do it.
What choice do you have?
"Just igno-o-ore them."

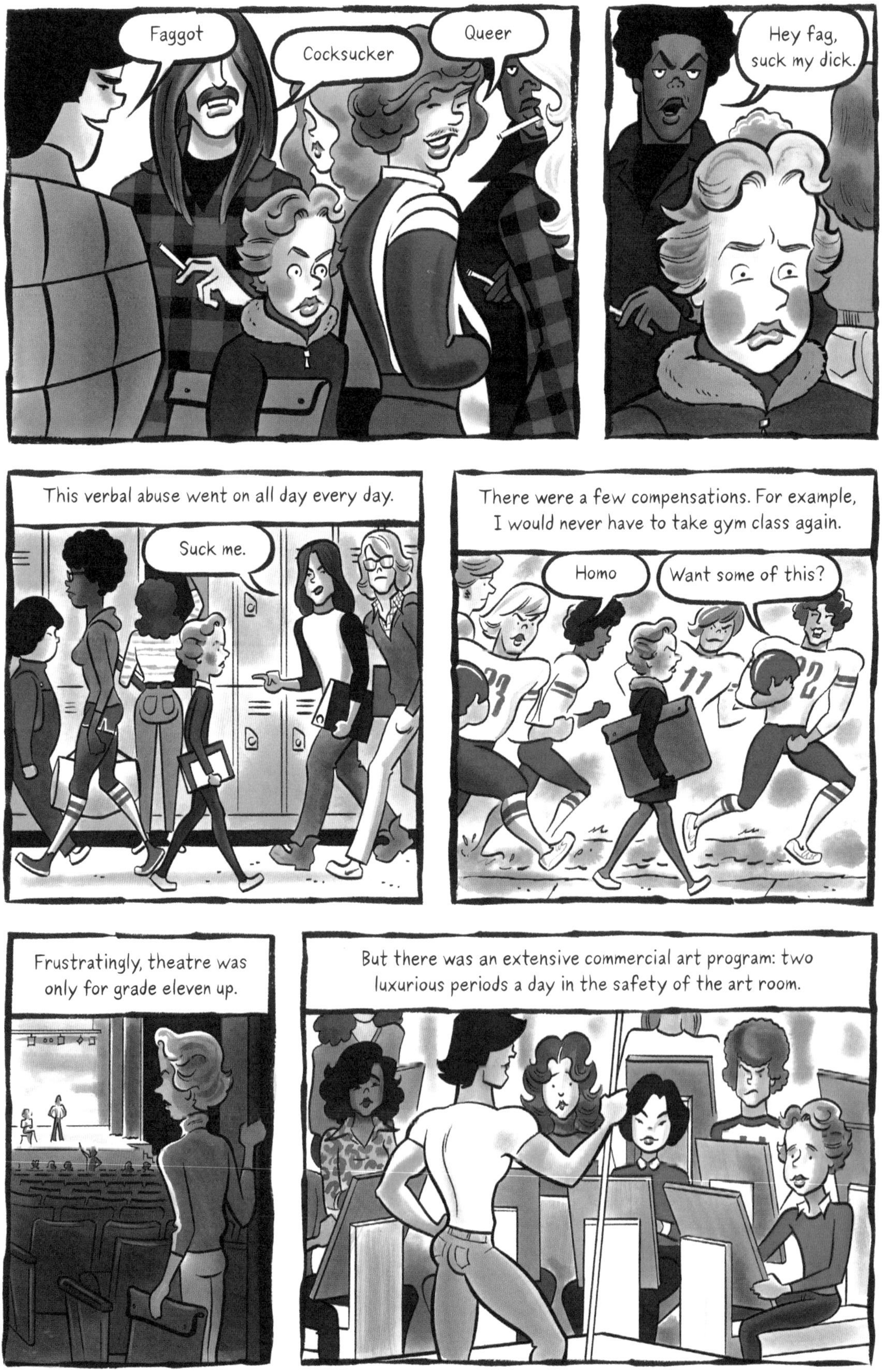
Faggot
Cocksucker
Queer
Hey fag, suck my dick.
This verbal abuse went on all day every day.
Suck me.
There were a few compensations. For example, I would never have to take gym class again.
Homo
Want some of this?
Frustratingly, theatre was only for grade eleven up.
But there was an extensive commercial art program: two luxurious periods a day in the safety of the art room.

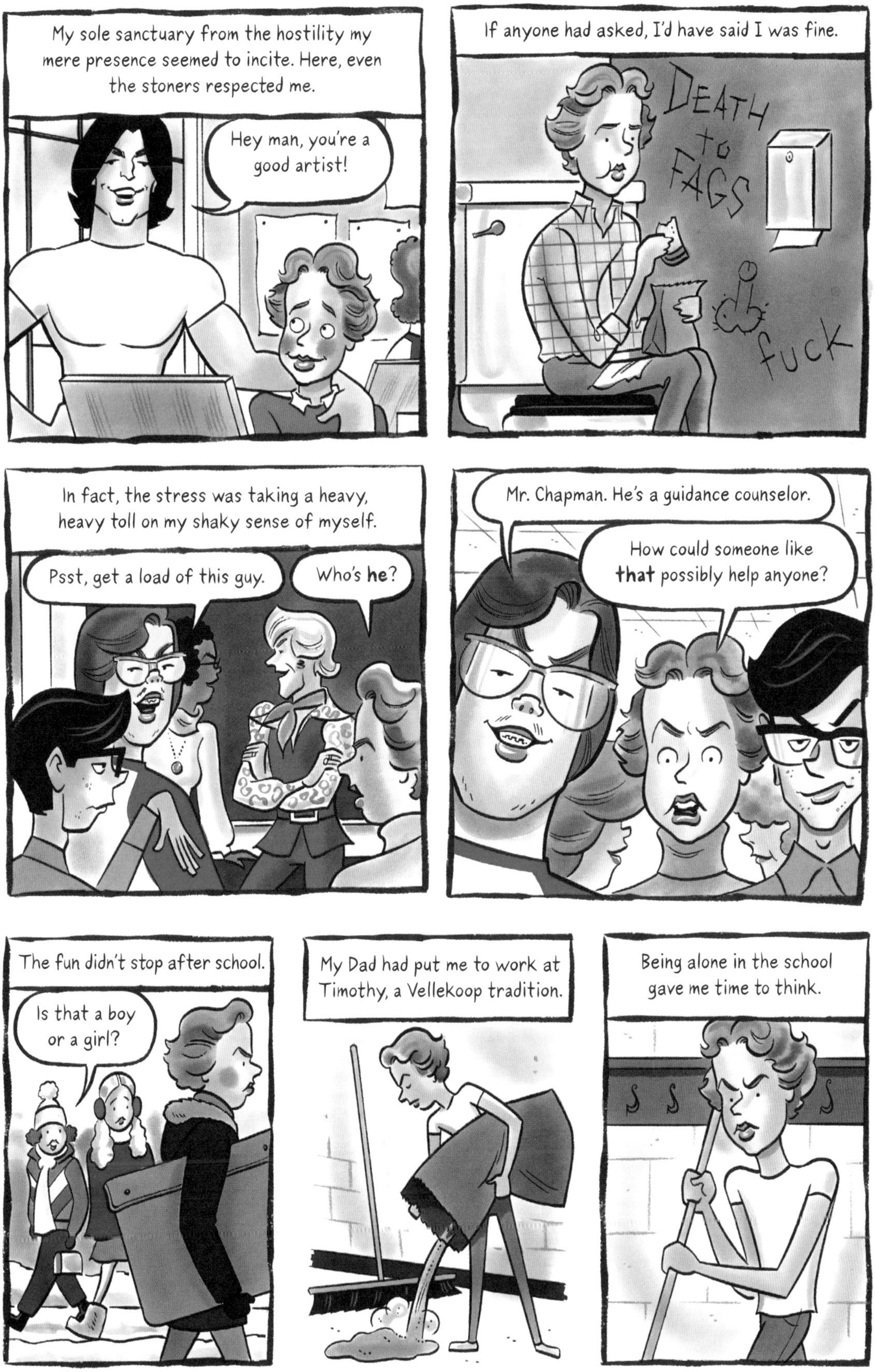
My sole sanctuary from the hostility my mere presence seemed to incite. Here, even the stoners respected me.
Hey man, you're a good artist!
If anyone had asked, I'd have said I was fine.
DEATH to FAGS
fuck
In fact, the stress was taking a heavy, heavy toll on my shaky sense of myself.
Psst, get a load of this guy.
Who's **he**?
Mr. Chapman. He's a guidance counselor.
How could someone like **that** possibly help anyone?
The fun didn't stop after school.
Is that a boy or a girl?
My Dad had put me to work at Timothy, a Vellekoop tradition.
Being alone in the school gave me time to think.

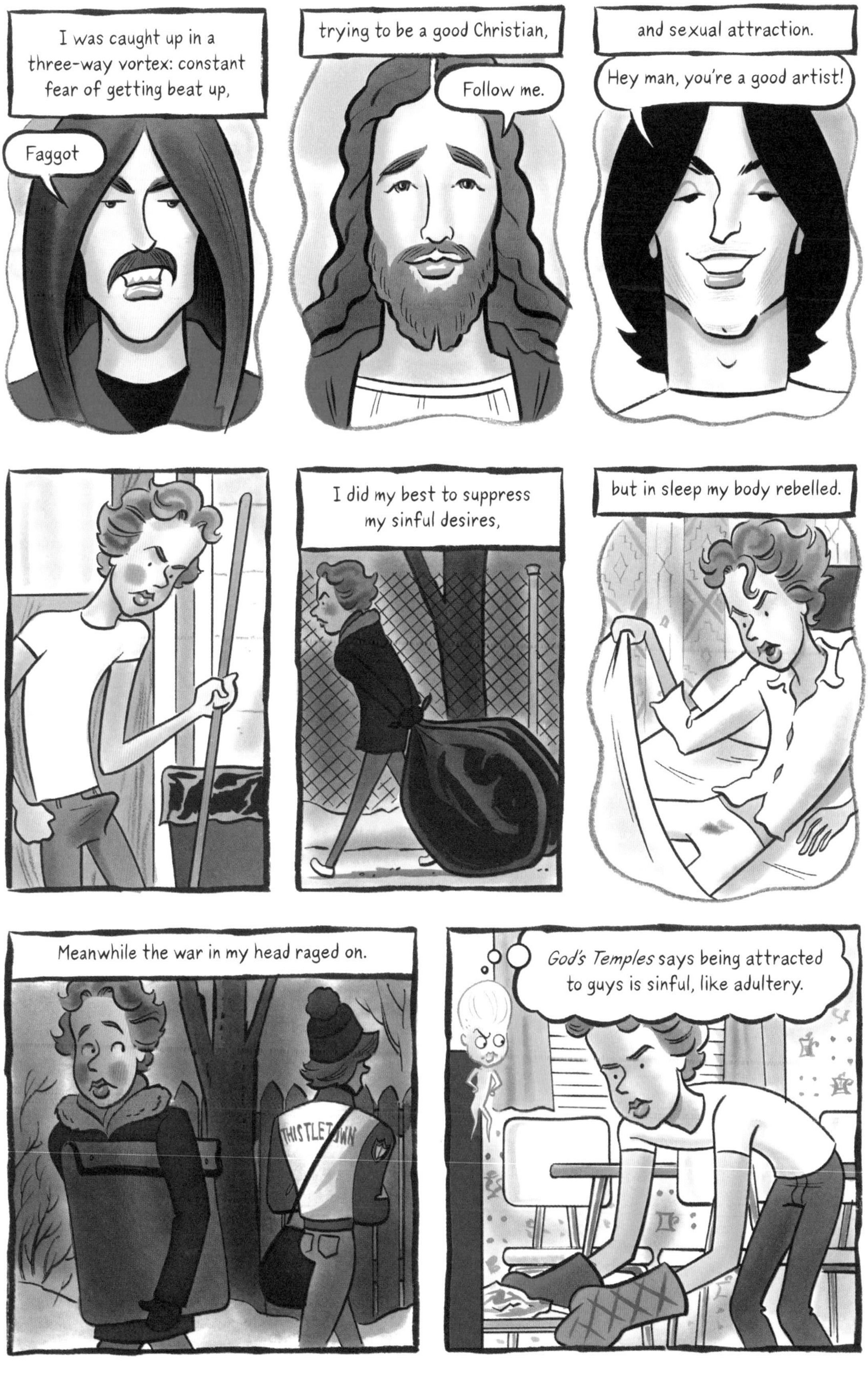
I was caught up in a three-way vortex: constant fear of getting beat up,
Faggot
trying to be a good Christian,
Follow me.
and sexual attraction.
Hey man, you're a good artist!
I did my best to suppress my sinful desires,
but in sleep my body rebelled.
Meanwhile the war in my head raged on.
THISTLETOWN
God's Temples says being attracted to guys is sinful, like adultery.

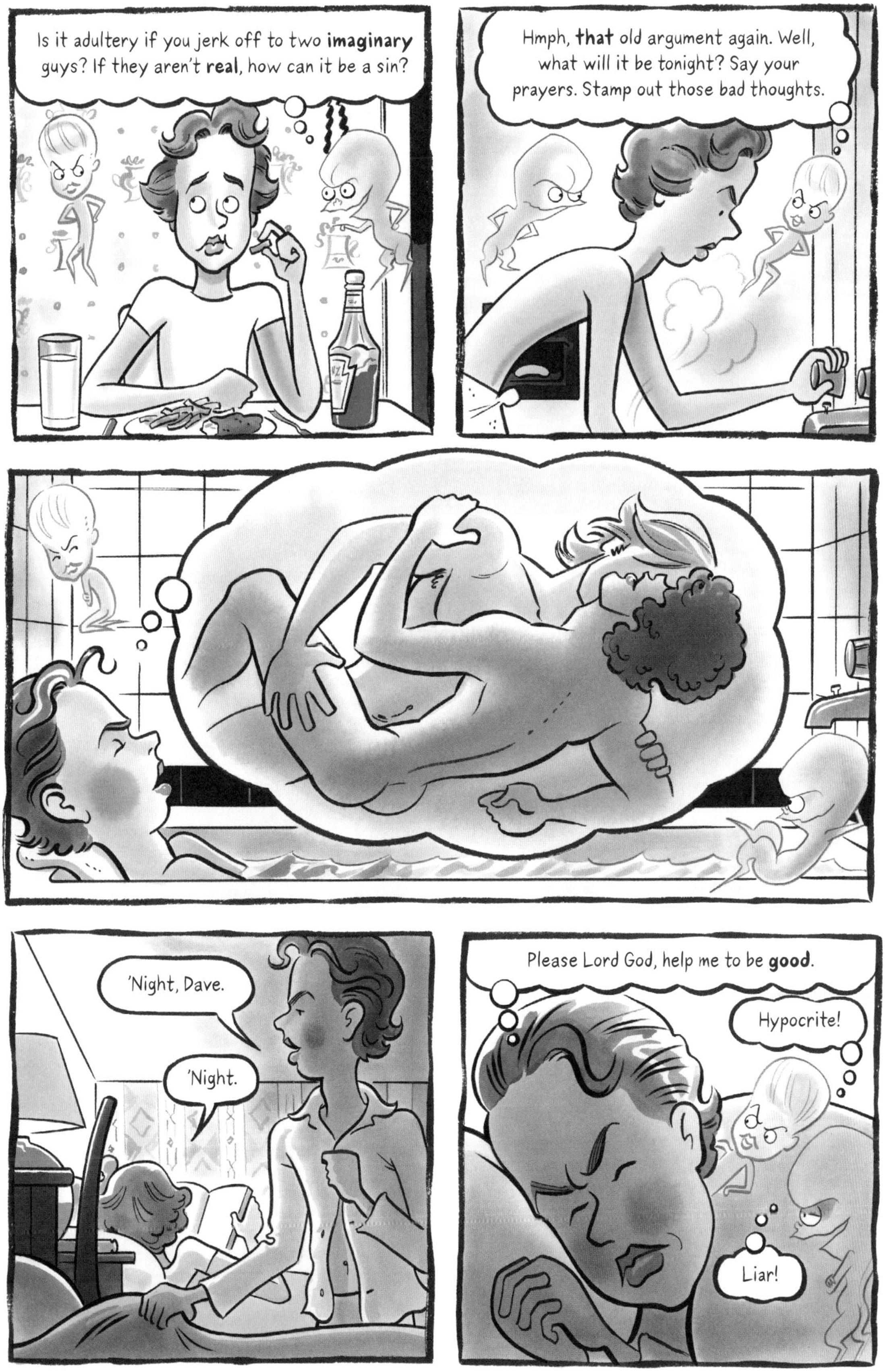
Is it adultery if you jerk off to two **imaginary** guys? If they aren't **real**, how can it be a sin?
Hmph, **that** old argument again. Well, what will it be tonight? Say your prayers. Stamp out those bad thoughts.
'Night, Dave.
'Night.
Please Lord God, help me to be **good**.
Hypocrite!
Liar!

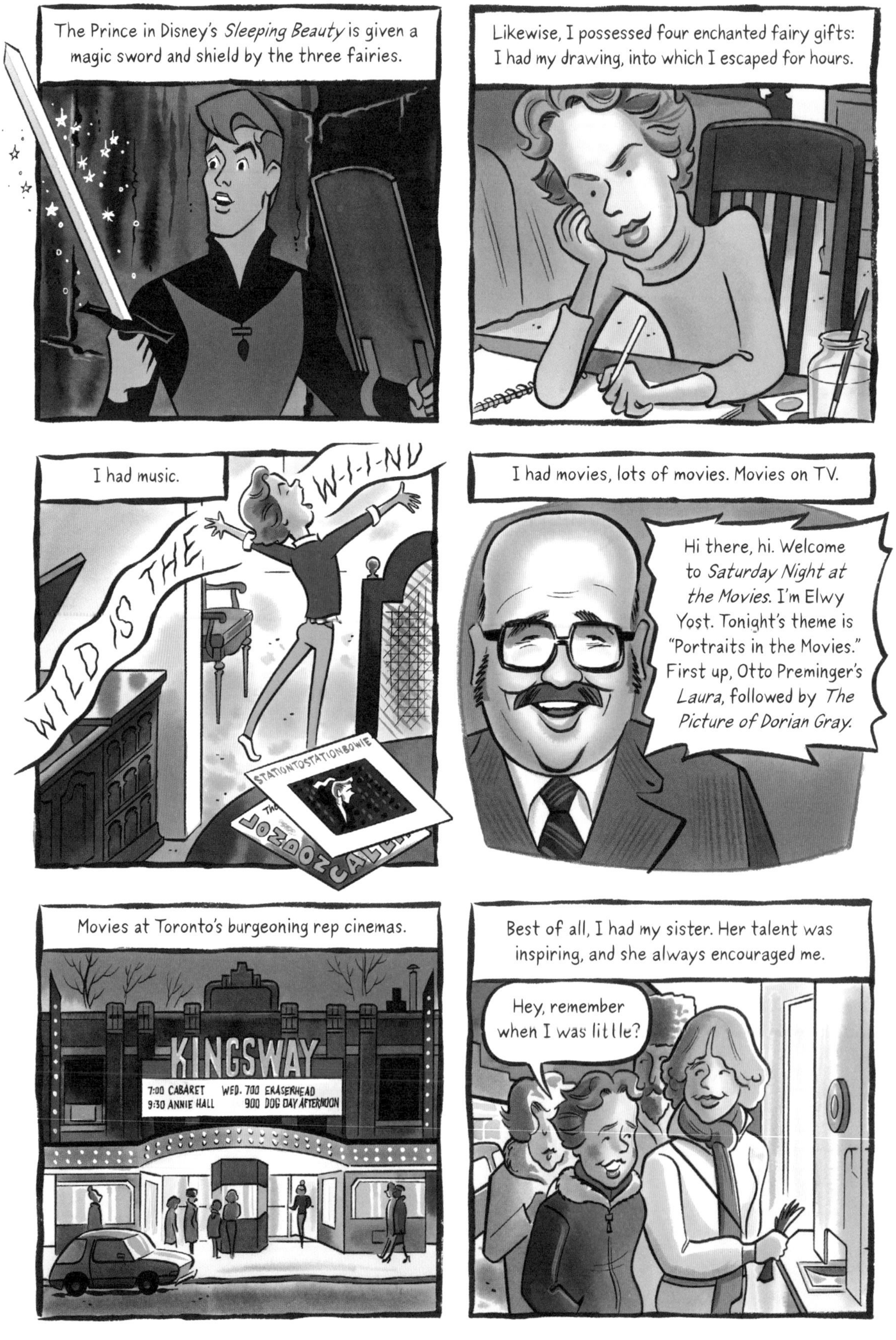
The Prince in Disney's *Sleeping Beauty* is given a magic sword and shield by the three fairies.
Likewise, I possessed four enchanted fairy gifts: I had my drawing, into which I escaped for hours.
I had music.
WILD IS THE W-I-I-ND
STATIONTOSTATIONBOWIE
I had movies, lots of movies. Movies on TV.
Hi there, hi. Welcome to *Saturday Night at the Movies*. I'm Elwy Yost. Tonight's theme is "Portraits in the Movies." First up, Otto Preminger's *Laura*, followed by *The Picture of Dorian Gray*.
Movies at Toronto's burgeoning rep cinemas.
KINGSWAY
7:00 CABARET WED. 700 ERASERHEAD
9:30 ANNIE HALL 900 DOG DAY AFTERNOON
Best of all, I had my sister. Her talent was inspiring, and she always encouraged me.
Hey, remember when I was little?

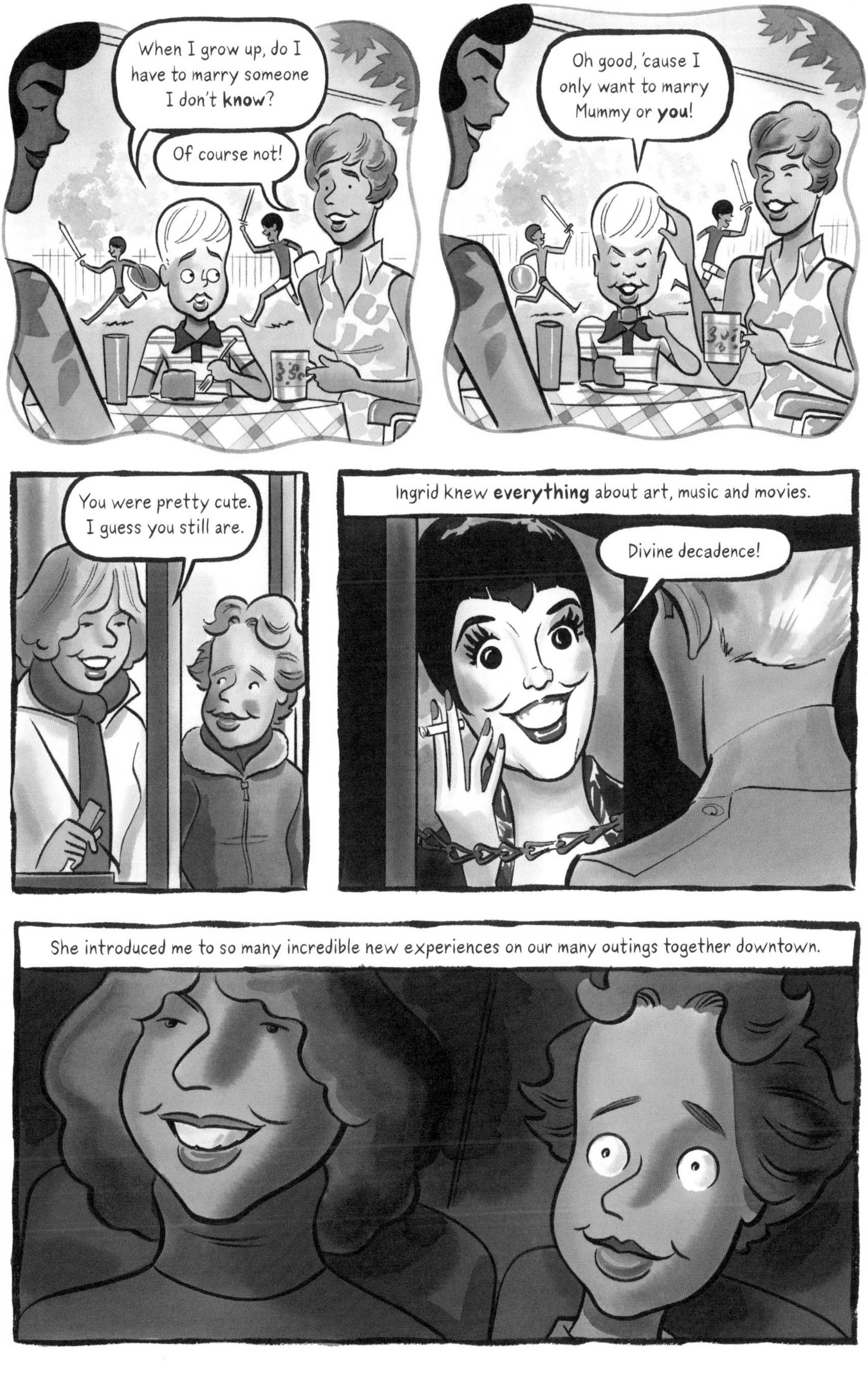
When I grow up, do I have to marry someone I don't **know**?
Of course not!
Oh good, 'cause I only want to marry Mummy or **you**!
You were pretty cute. I guess you still are.
Ingrid knew **everything** about art, music and movies.
Divine decadence!
She introduced me to so many incredible new experiences on our many outings together downtown.

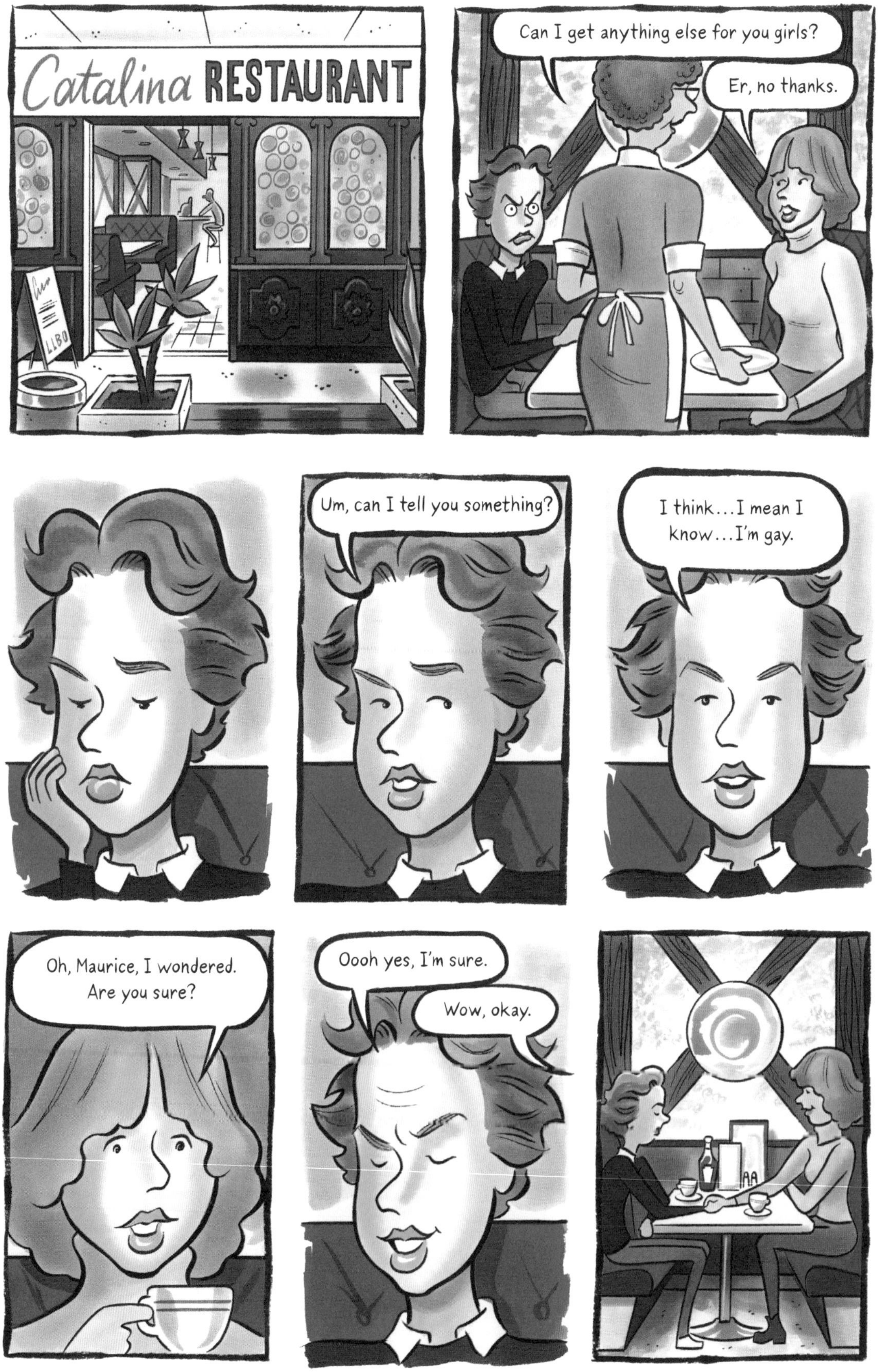
Catalina RESTAURANT
Can I get anything else for you girls?
Er, no thanks.
Um, can I tell you something?
I think... I mean I know... I'm gay.
Oh, Maurice, I wondered. Are you sure?
Oooh yes, I'm sure.
Wow, okay.

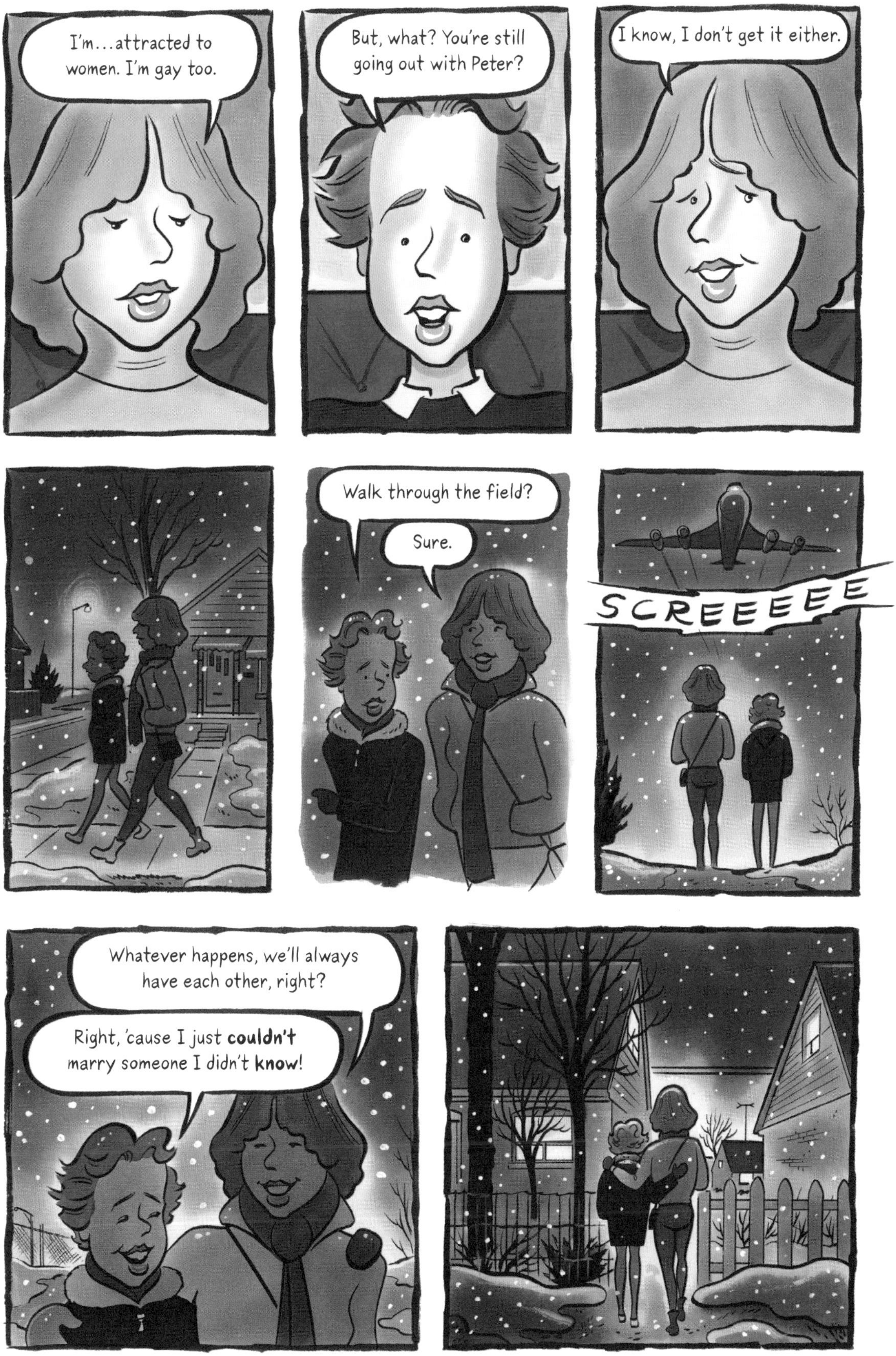
I'm...attracted to women. I'm gay too.
But, what? You're still going out with Peter?
I know, I don't get it either.
Walk through the field?
Sure.
SCREEEEEE
Whatever happens, we'll always have each other, right?
Right, 'cause I just **couldn't** marry someone I didn't **know**!

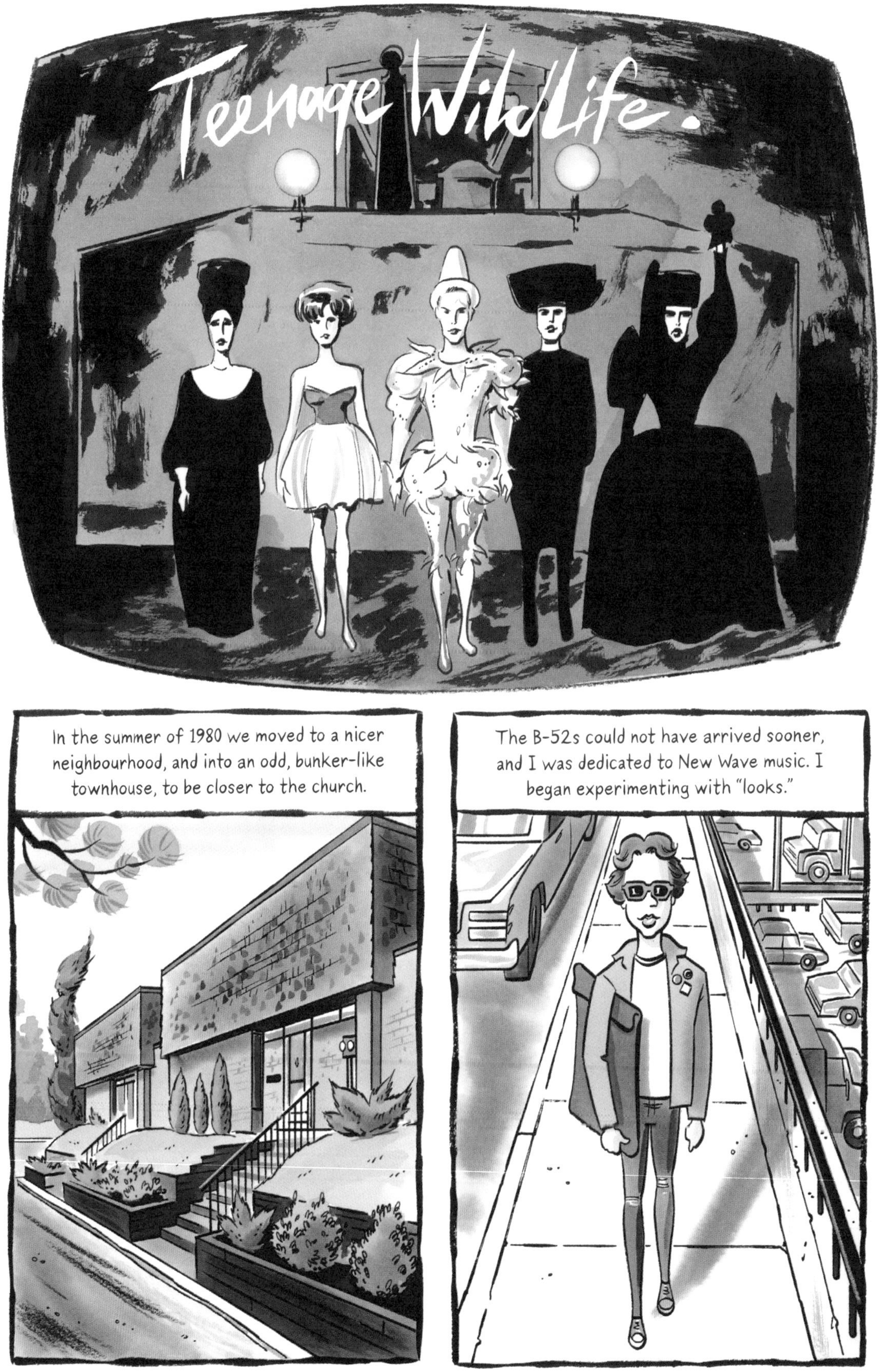
Teenage Wildlife.
In the summer of 1980 we moved to a nicer neighbourhood, and into an odd, bunker-like townhouse, to be closer to the church.
The B-52s could not have arrived sooner, and I was dedicated to New Wave music. I began experimenting with "looks."

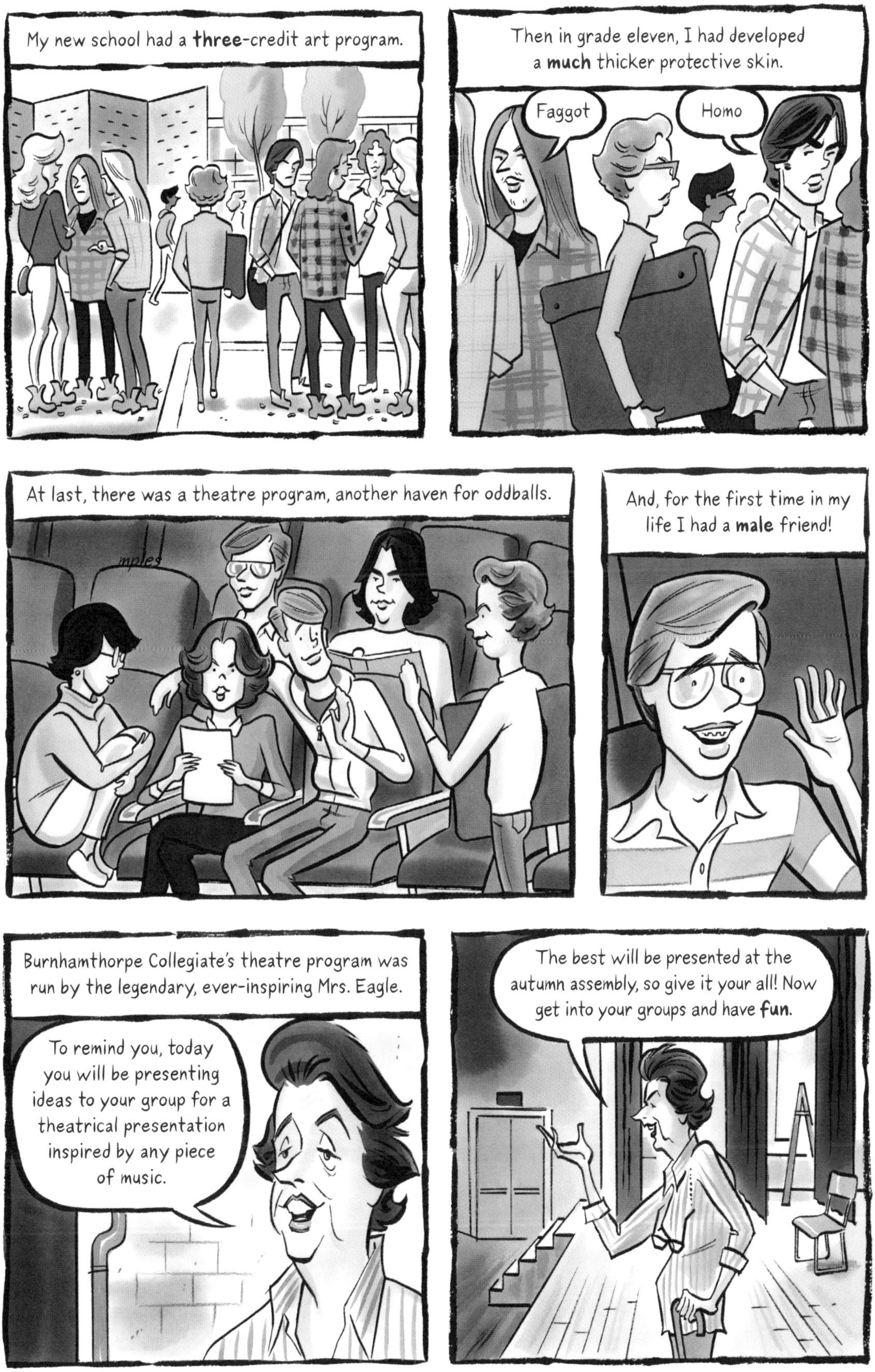
My new school had a **three**-credit art program.
Then in grade eleven, I had developed a **much** thicker protective skin.
Faggot
Homo
At last, there was a theatre program, another haven for oddballs.
And, for the first time in my life I had a **male** friend!
Burnhamthorpe Collegiate's theatre program was run by the legendary, ever-inspiring Mrs. Eagle.
To remind you, today you will be presenting ideas to your group for a theatrical presentation inspired by any piece of music.
The best will be presented at the autumn assembly, so give it your all! Now get into your groups and have **fun**.

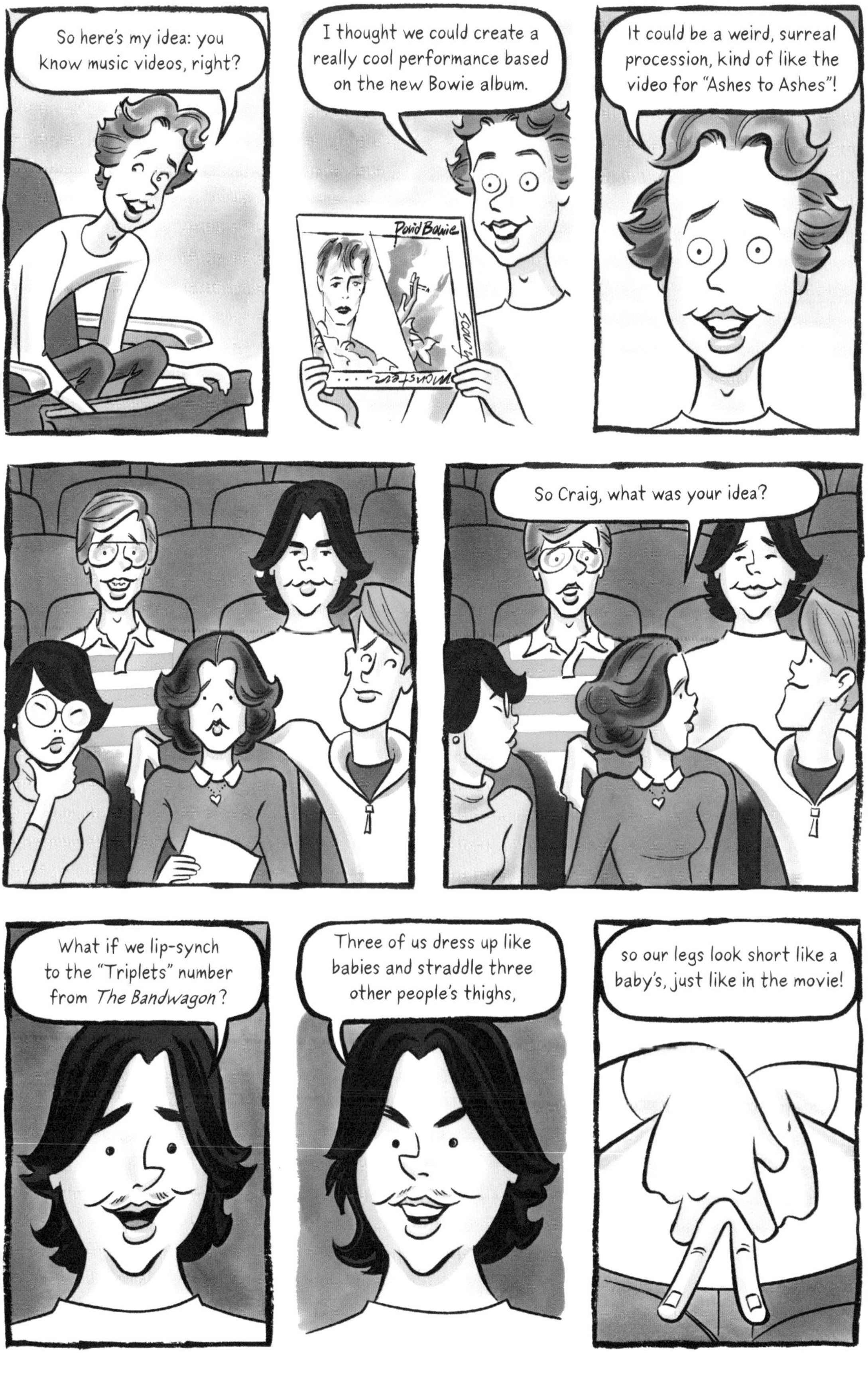
So here's my idea: you know music videos, right?
I thought we could create a really cool performance based on the new Bowie album.
David Bowie
Scary Monsters
It could be a weird, surreal procession, kind of like the video for "Ashes to Ashes"!
So Craig, what was your idea?
What if we lip-synch to the "Triplets" number from *The Bandwagon*?
Three of us dress up like babies and straddle three other people's thighs,
so our legs look short like a baby's, just like in the movie!

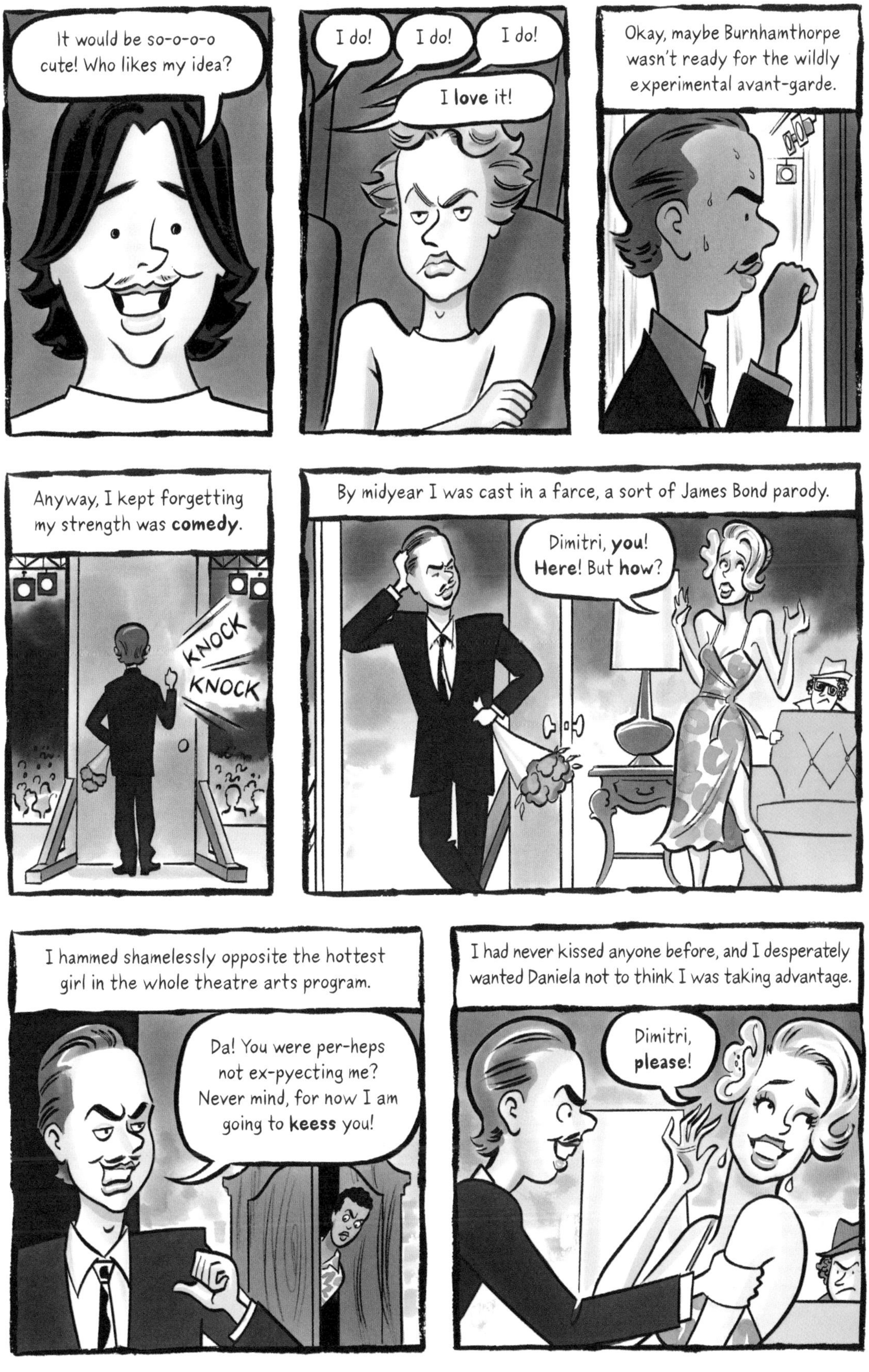
It would be so-o-o-o cute! Who likes my idea?
I do!
I do!
I do!
I **love** it!
Okay, maybe Burnhamthorpe wasn't ready for the wildly experimental avant-garde.
Anyway, I kept forgetting my strength was **comedy**.
KNOCK
KNOCK
By midyear I was cast in a farce, a sort of James Bond parody.
Dimitri, **you**! **Here**! But **how**?
I hammed shamelessly opposite the hottest girl in the whole theatre arts program.
Da! You were per-heps not ex-pyecting me? Never mind, for now I am going to **keess** you!
I had never kissed anyone before, and I desperately wanted Daniela not to think I was taking advantage.
Dimitri, **please**!

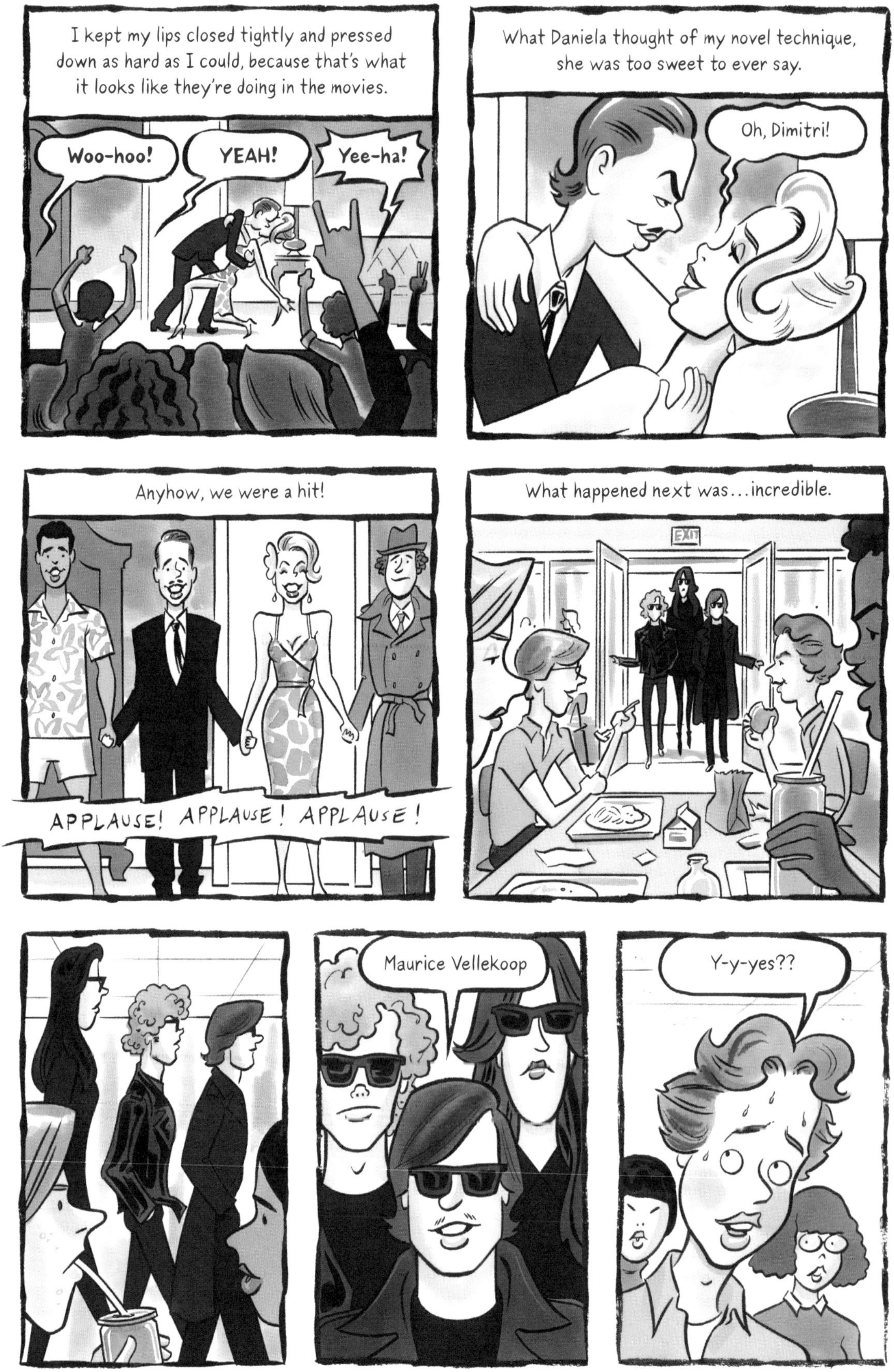
I kept my lips closed tightly and pressed down as hard as I could, because that's what it looks like they're doing in the movies.
Woo-hoo!
YEAH!
Yee-ha!
What Daniela thought of my novel technique, she was too sweet to ever say.
Oh, Dimitri!
Anyhow, we were a hit!
APPLAUSE! APPLAUSE! APPLAUSE!
What happened next was...incredible.
EXIT
Maurice Vellekoop
Y-y-yes??

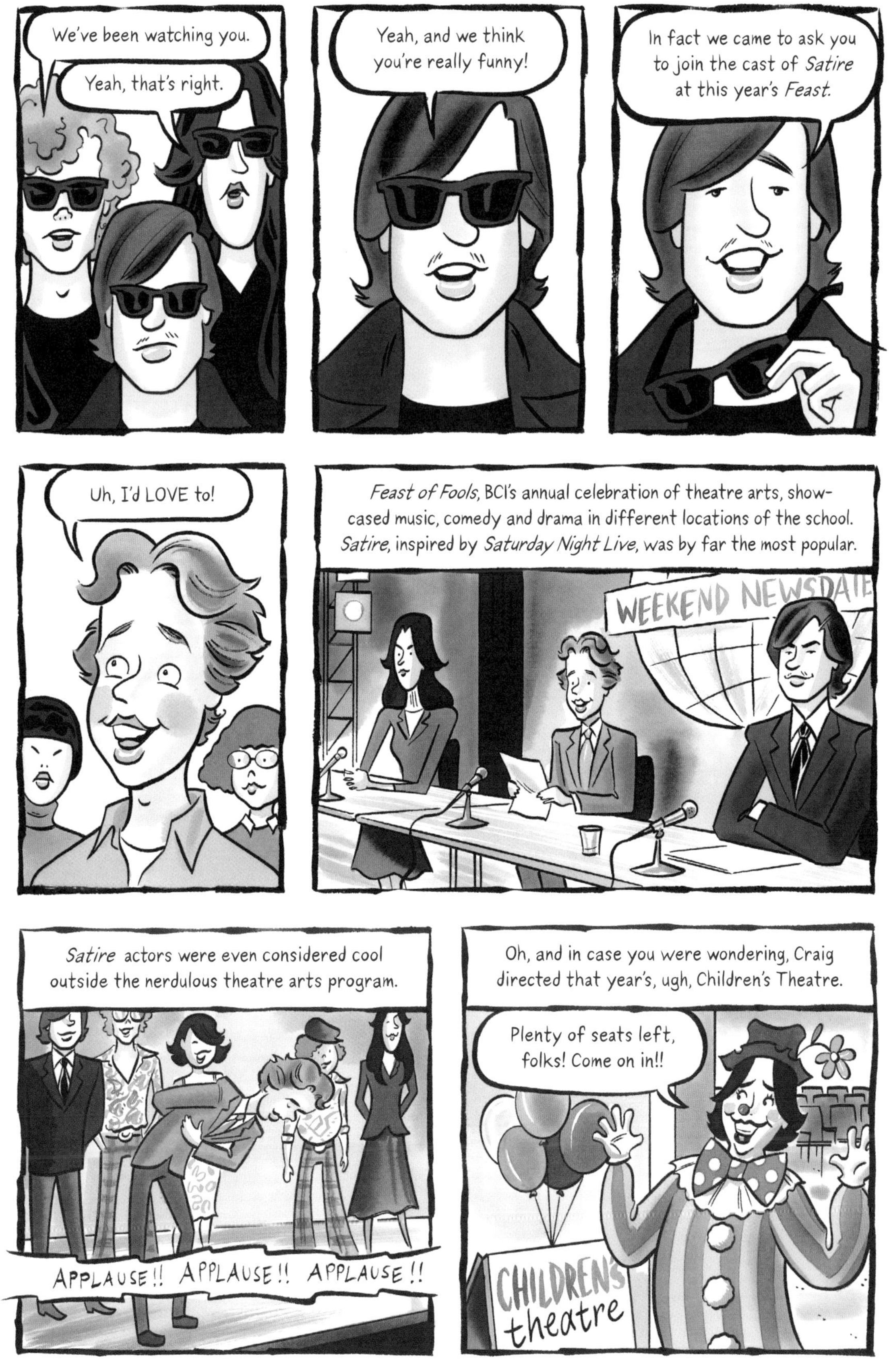

We've been watching you.
Yeah, that's right.
Yeah, and we think you're really funny!
In fact we came to ask you to join the cast of *Satire* at this year's *Feast.*
Uh, I'd LOVE to!
Feast of Fools, BCI's annual celebration of theatre arts, showcased music, comedy and drama in different locations of the school. *Satire,* inspired by *Saturday Night Live,* was by far the most popular.
WEEKEND NEWSDATE
Satire actors were even considered cool outside the nerdulous theatre arts program.
APPLAUSE!! APPLAUSE!! APPLAUSE!!
Oh, and in case you were wondering, Craig directed that year's, ugh, Children's Theatre.
Plenty of seats left, folks! Come on in!!
CHILDREN'S theatre

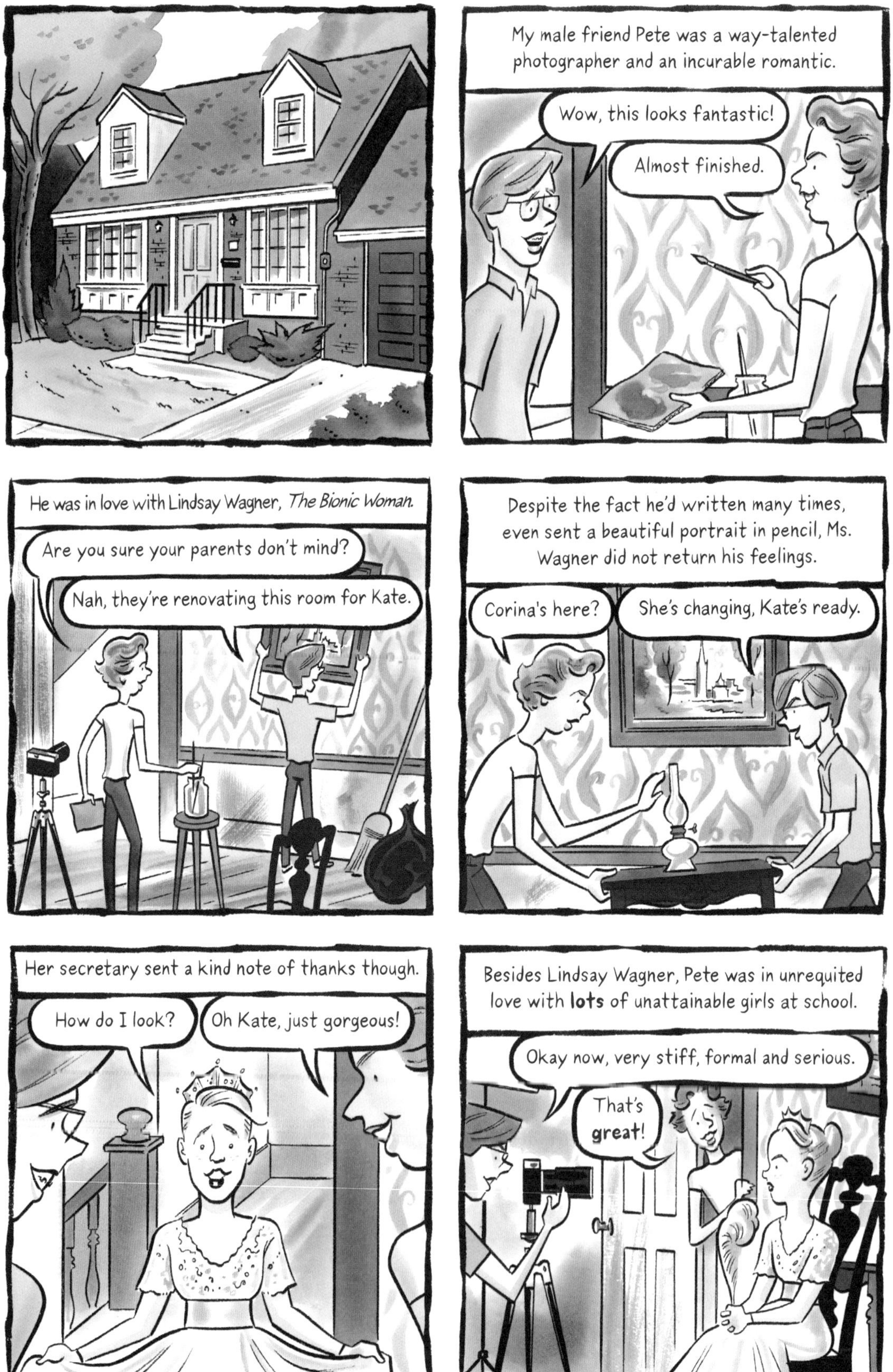
My male friend Pete was a way-talented photographer and an incurable romantic.
Wow, this looks fantastic!
Almost finished.
He was in love with Lindsay Wagner, *The Bionic Woman.*
Are you sure your parents don't mind?
Nah, they're renovating this room for Kate.
Despite the fact he'd written many times, even sent a beautiful portrait in pencil, Ms. Wagner did not return his feelings.
Corina's here?
She's changing, Kate's ready.
Her secretary sent a kind note of thanks though.
How do I look?
Oh Kate, just gorgeous!
Besides Lindsay Wagner, Pete was in unrequited love with **lots** of unattainable girls at school.
Okay now, very stiff, formal and serious.
That's **great!**

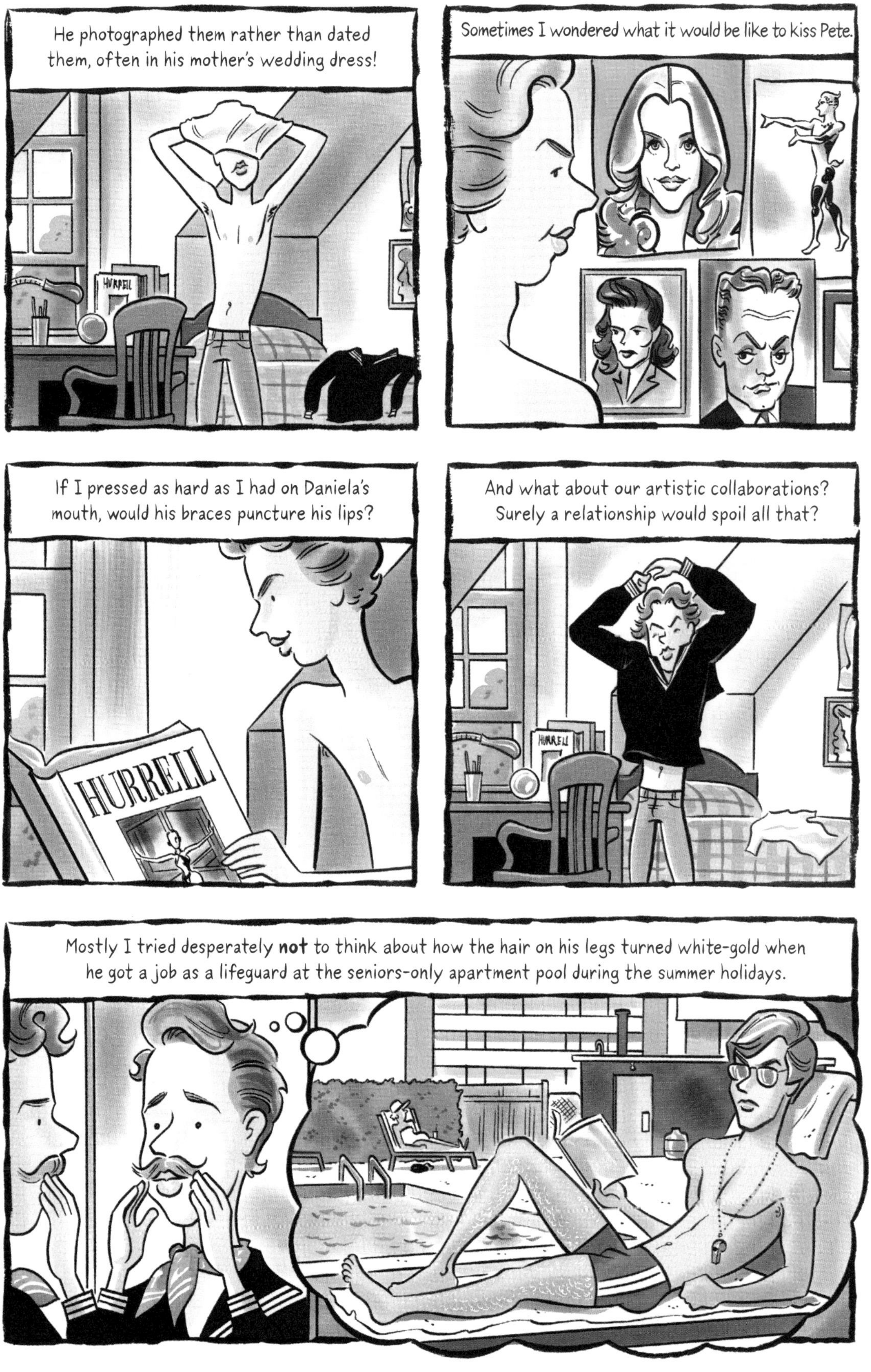
He photographed them rather than dated them, often in his mother's wedding dress!
Sometimes I wondered what it would be like to kiss Pete.
If I pressed as hard as I had on Daniela's mouth, would his braces puncture his lips?
HURRELL
And what about our artistic collaborations? Surely a relationship would spoil all that?
Mostly I tried desperately **not** to think about how the hair on his legs turned white-gold when he got a job as a lifeguard at the seniors-only apartment pool during the summer holidays.

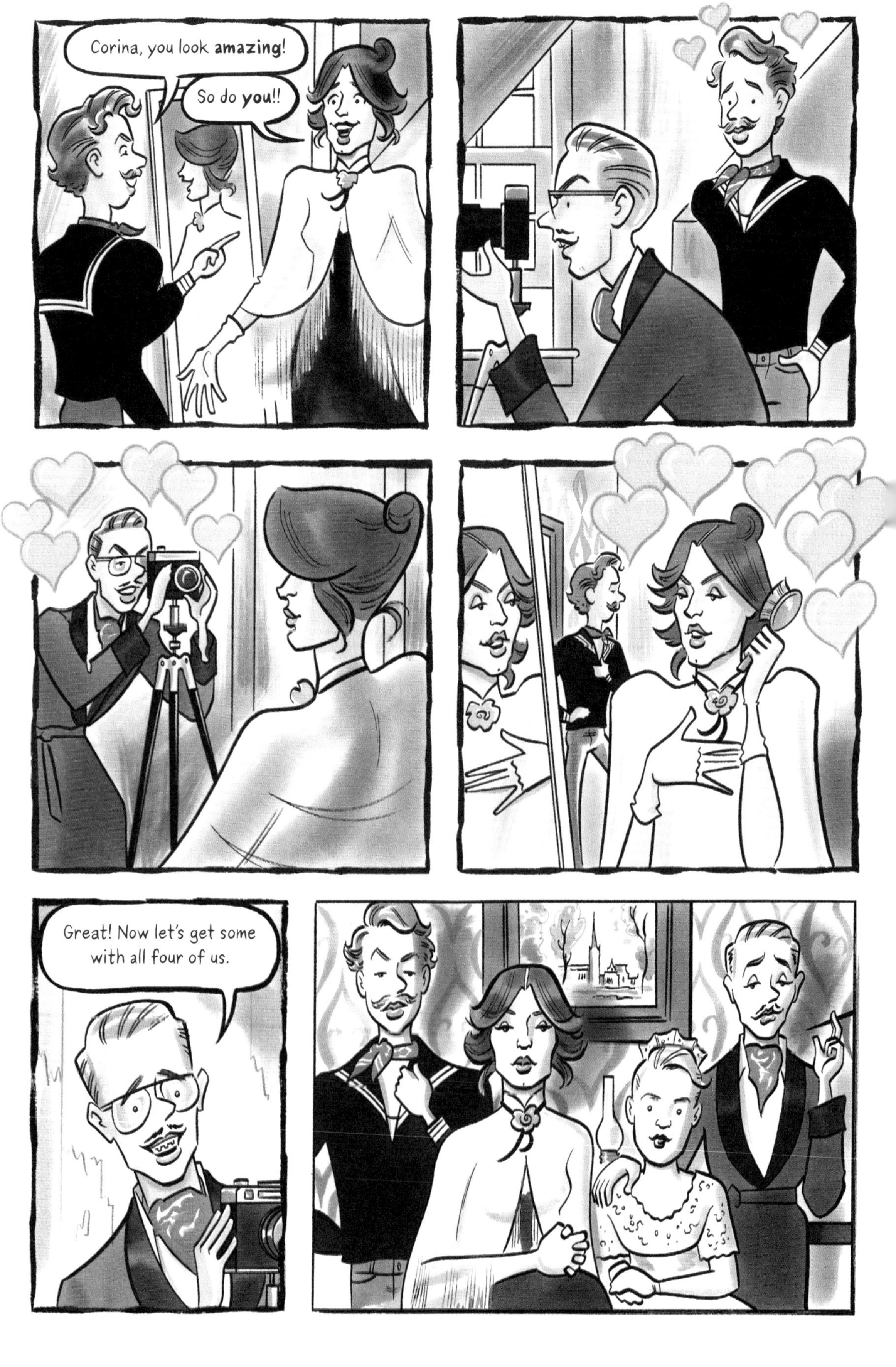
Corina, you look **amazing**!
So do **you**!!
Great! Now let's get some with all four of us.

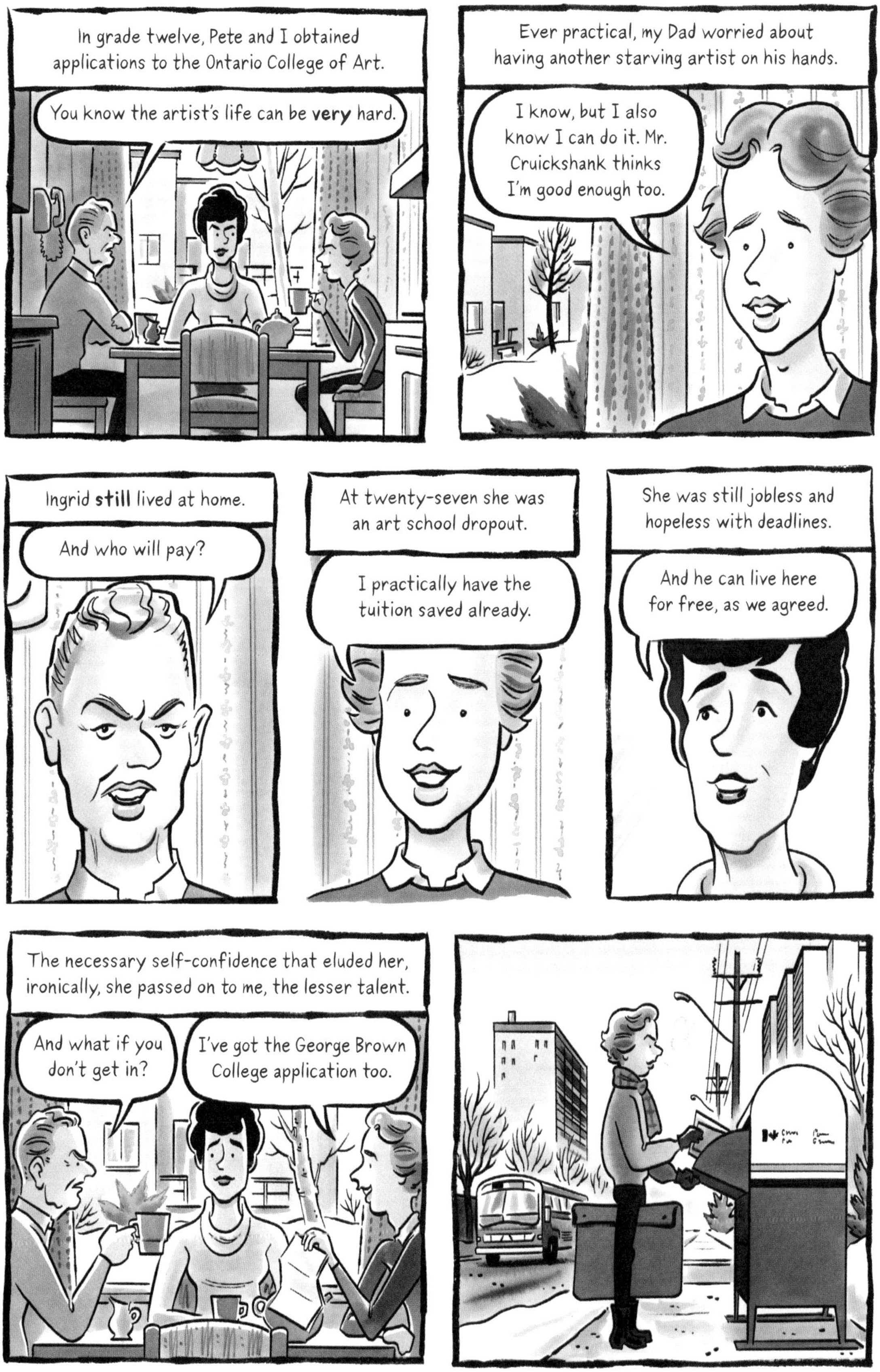
In grade twelve, Pete and I obtained applications to the Ontario College of Art.
You know the artist's life can be **very** hard.
Ever practical, my Dad worried about having another starving artist on his hands.
I know, but I also know I can do it. Mr. Cruickshank thinks I'm good enough too.
Ingrid **still** lived at home.
And who will pay?
At twenty-seven she was an art school dropout.
I practically have the tuition saved already.
She was still jobless and hopeless with deadlines.
And he can live here for free, as we agreed.
The necessary self-confidence that eluded her, ironically, she passed on to me, the lesser talent.
And what if you don't get in?
I've got the George Brown College application too.

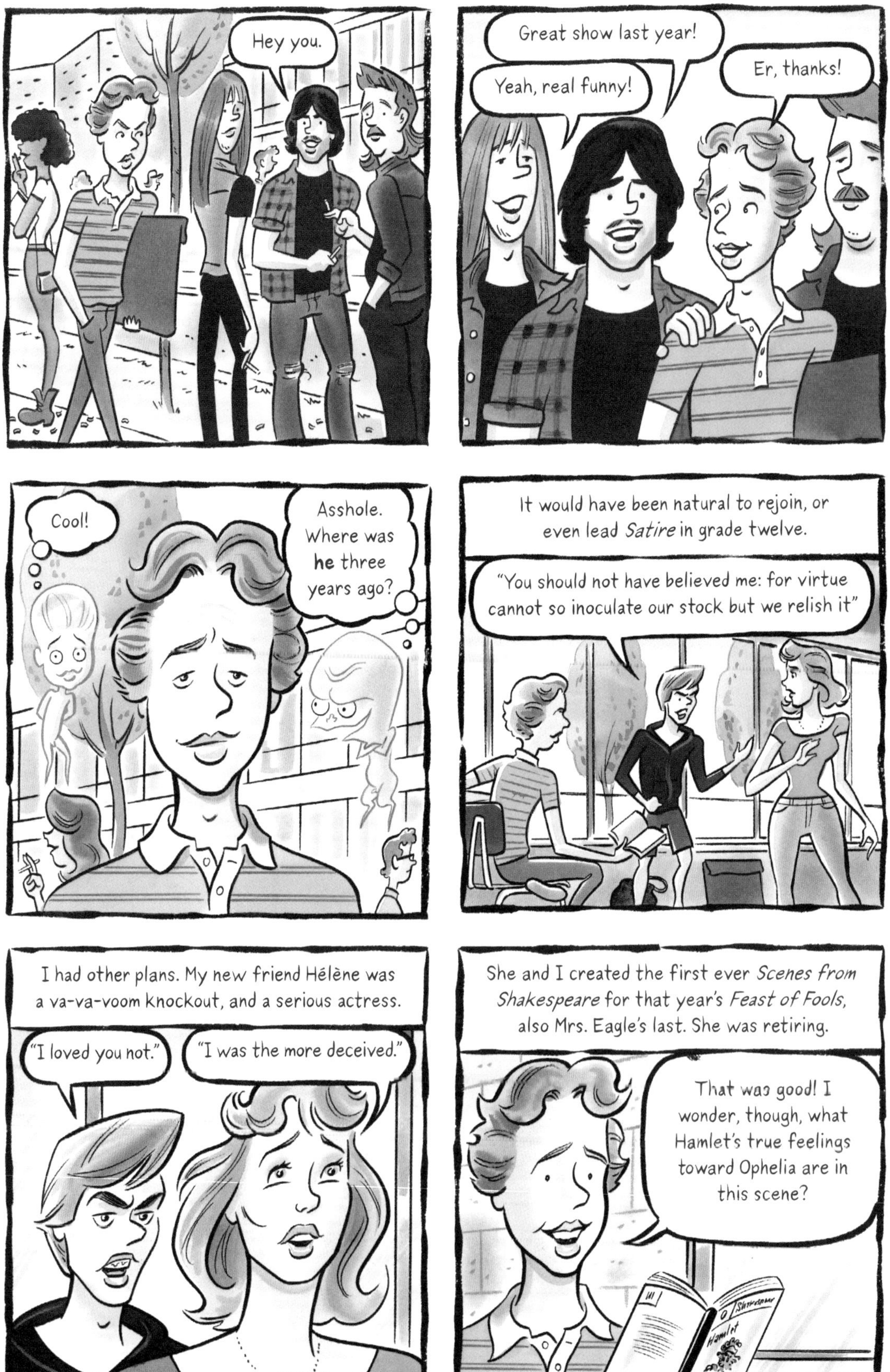
Hey you.
Great show last year!
Yeah, real funny!
Er, thanks!
Cool!
Asshole. Where was **he** three years ago?
It would have been natural to rejoin, or even lead *Satire* in grade twelve.
"You should not have believed me: for virtue cannot so inoculate our stock but we relish it"
I had other plans. My new friend Hélène was a va-va-voom knockout, and a serious actress.
"I loved you not."
"I was the more deceived."
She and I created the first ever *Scenes from Shakespeare* for that year's *Feast of Fools,* also Mrs. Eagle's last. She was retiring.
That was good! I wonder, though, what Hamlet's true feelings toward Ophelia are in this scene?
Hamlet

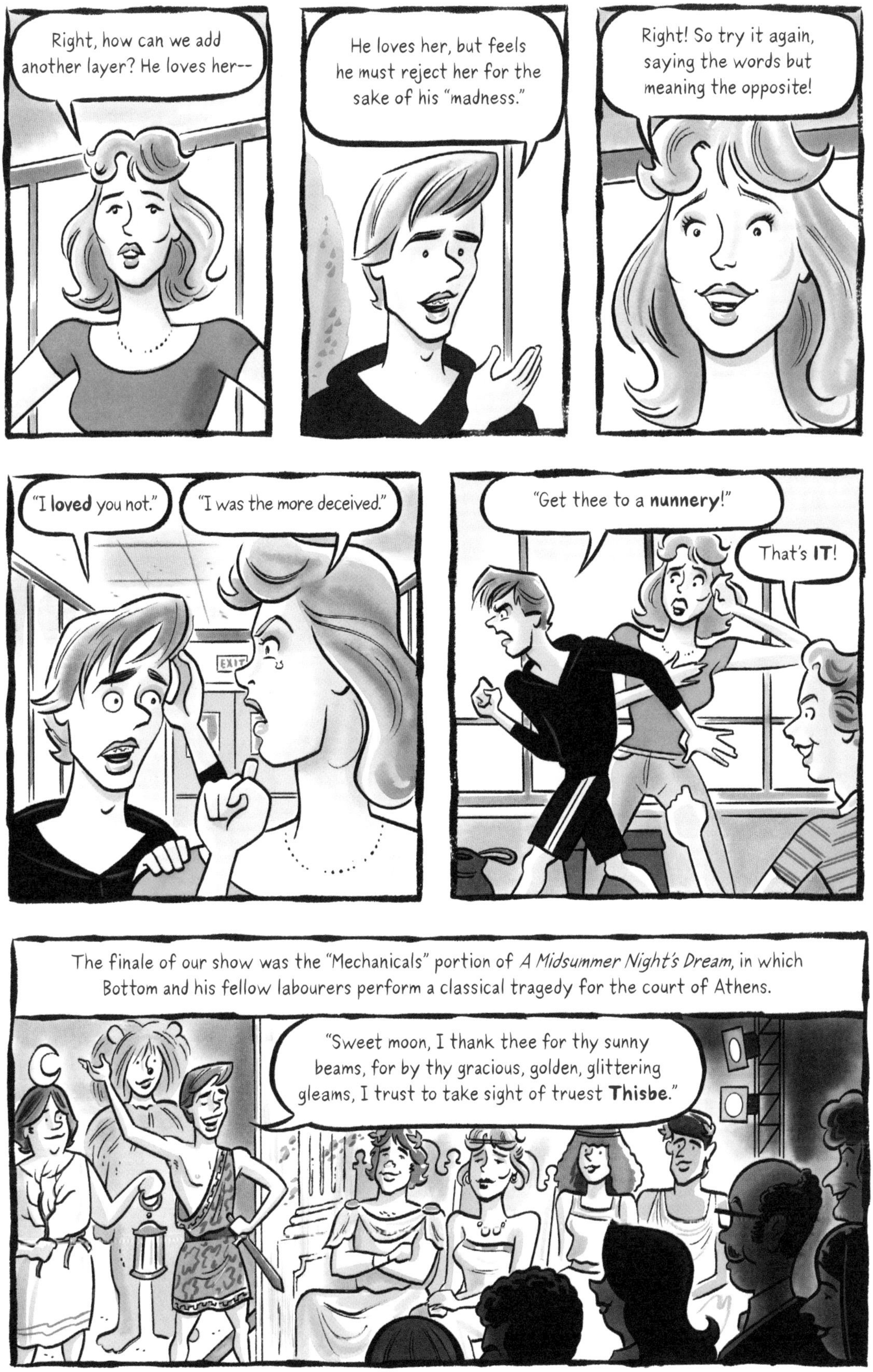

Right, how can we add another layer? He loves her--
He loves her, but feels he must reject her for the sake of his "madness."
Right! So try it again, saying the words but meaning the opposite!
"I **loved** you not."
"I was the more deceived."
EXIT
"Get thee to a **nunnery**!"
That's **IT**!
The finale of our show was the "Mechanicals" portion of *A Midsummer Night's Dream*, in which Bottom and his fellow labourers perform a classical tragedy for the court of Athens.
"Sweet moon, I thank thee for thy sunny beams, for by thy gracious, golden, glittering gleams, I trust to take sight of truest **Thisbe**."

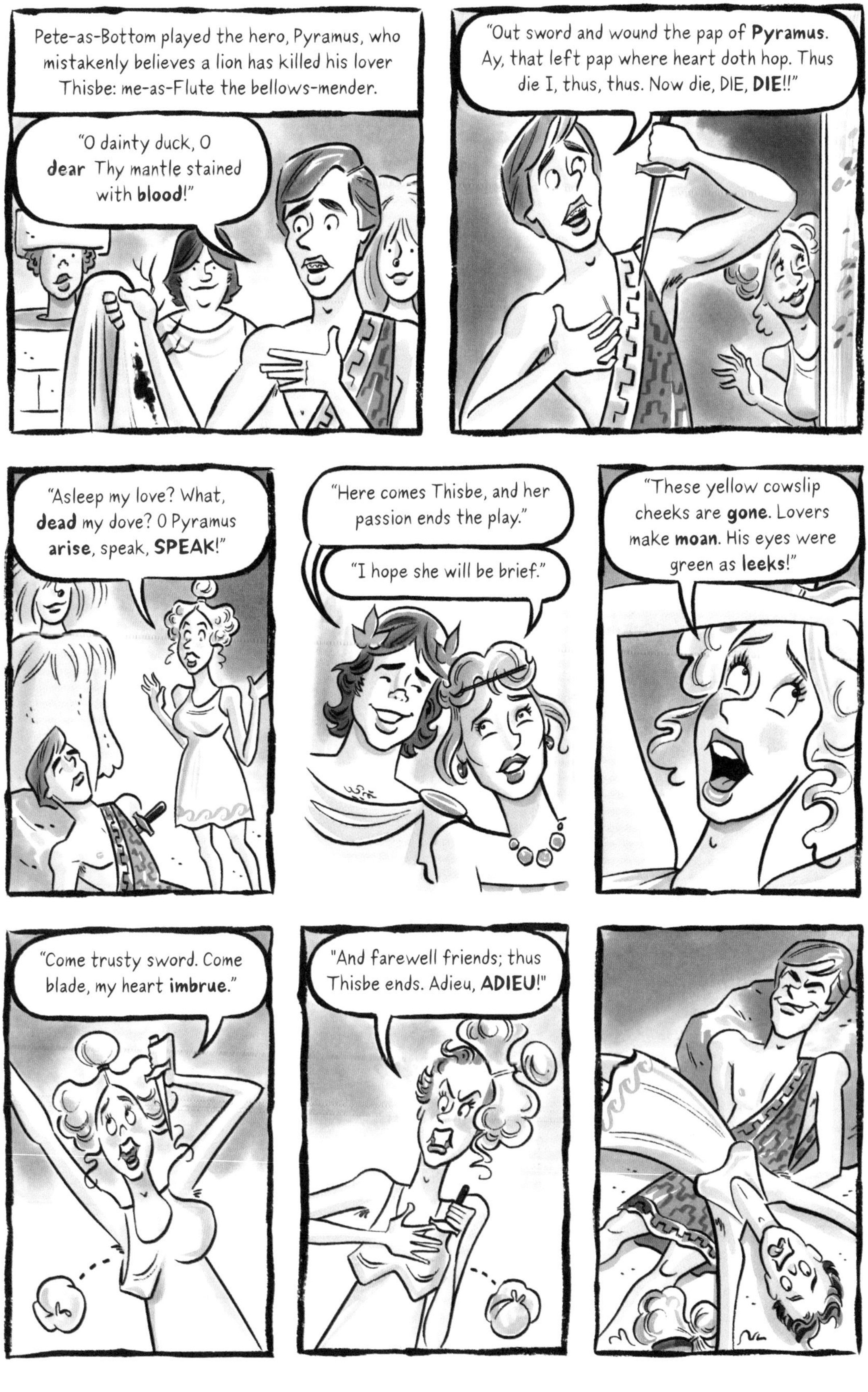
Pete-as-Bottom played the hero, Pyramus, who mistakenly believes a lion has killed his lover Thisbe: me-as-Flute the bellows-mender.
"O dainty duck, O dear Thy mantle stained with blood!"
"Out sword and wound the pap of Pyramus. Ay, that left pap where heart doth hop. Thus die I, thus, thus. Now die, DIE, DIE!!"
"Asleep my love? What, dead my dove? O Pyramus arise, speak, SPEAK!"
"Here comes Thisbe, and her passion ends the play."
"I hope she will be brief."
"These yellow cowslip cheeks are gone. Lovers make moan. His eyes were green as leeks!"
"Come trusty sword. Come blade, my heart imbrue."
"And farewell friends; thus Thisbe ends. Adieu, ADIEU!"

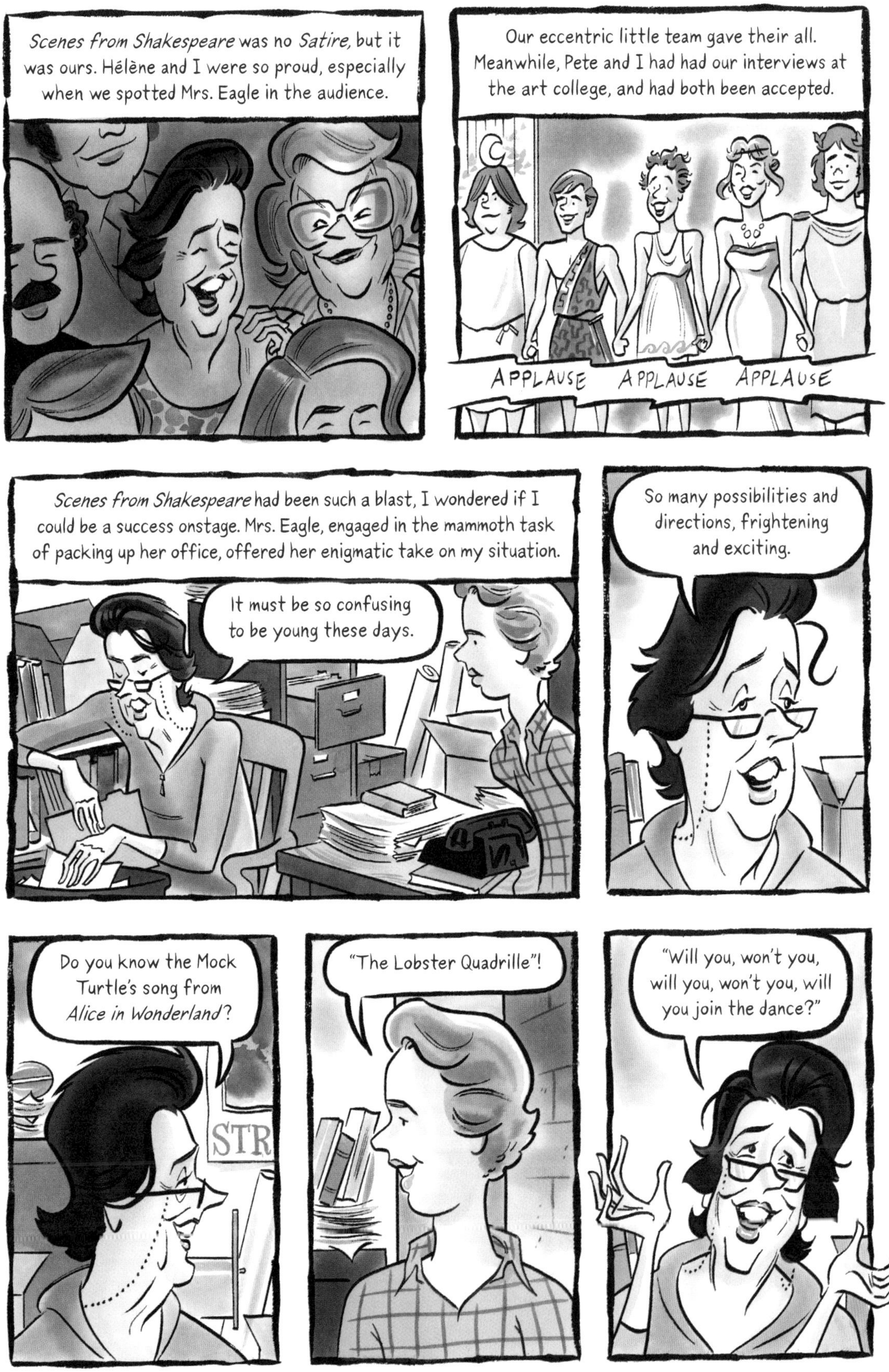
Scenes from Shakespeare was no Satire, but it was ours. Hélène and I were so proud, especially when we spotted Mrs. Eagle in the audience.
Our eccentric little team gave their all. Meanwhile, Pete and I had had our interviews at the art college, and had both been accepted.
APPLAUSE
APPLAUSE
APPLAUSE
Scenes from Shakespeare had been such a blast, I wondered if I could be a success onstage. Mrs. Eagle, engaged in the mammoth task of packing up her office, offered her enigmatic take on my situation.
It must be so confusing to be young these days.
So many possibilities and directions, frightening and exciting.
Do you know the Mock Turtle's song from Alice in Wonderland?
STR
"The Lobster Quadrille"!
"Will you, won't you, will you, won't you, will you join the dance?"

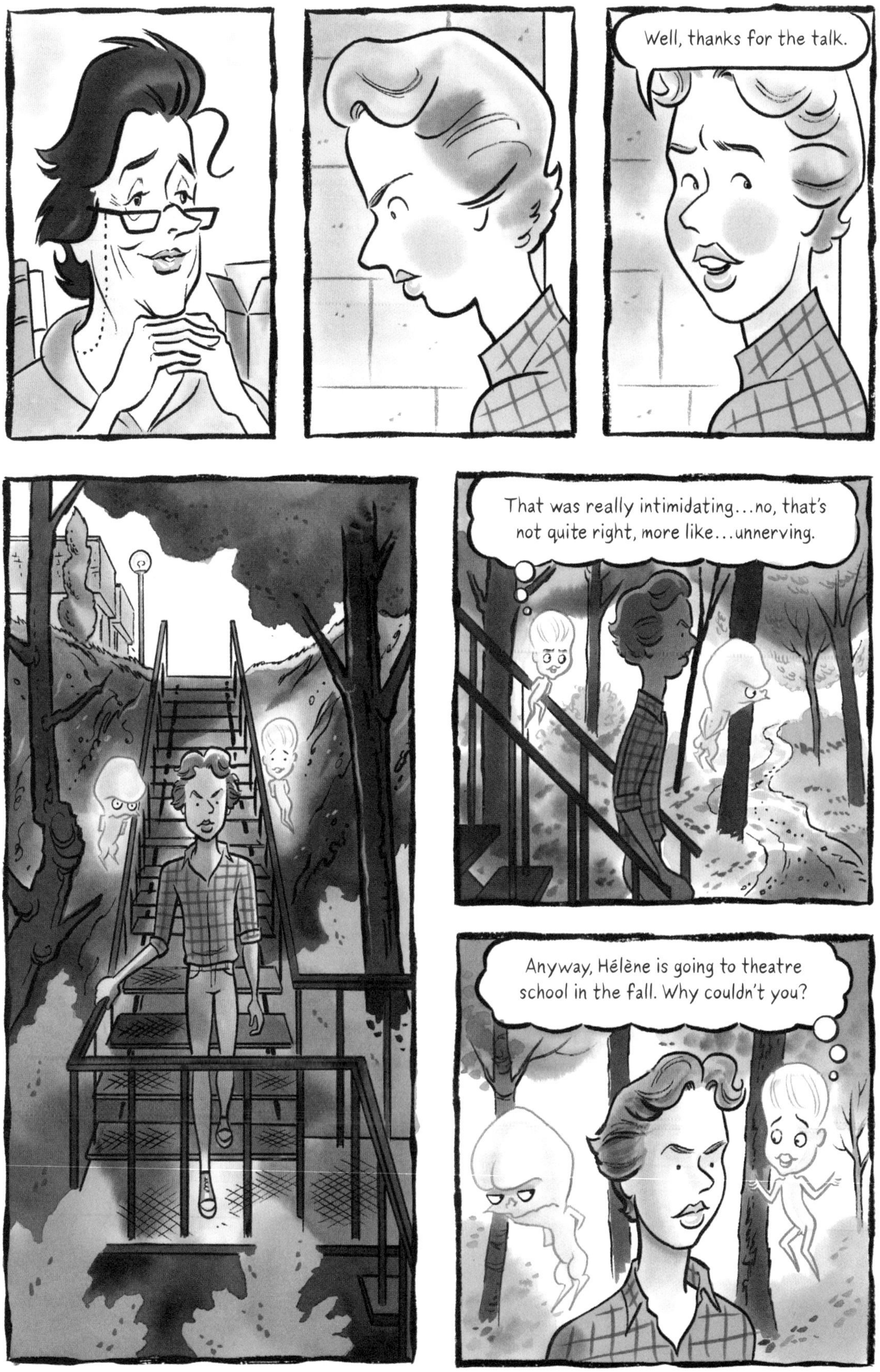
Well, thanks for the talk.
That was really intimidating...no, that's not quite right, more like...unnerving.
Anyway, Hélène is going to theatre school in the fall. Why couldn't you?

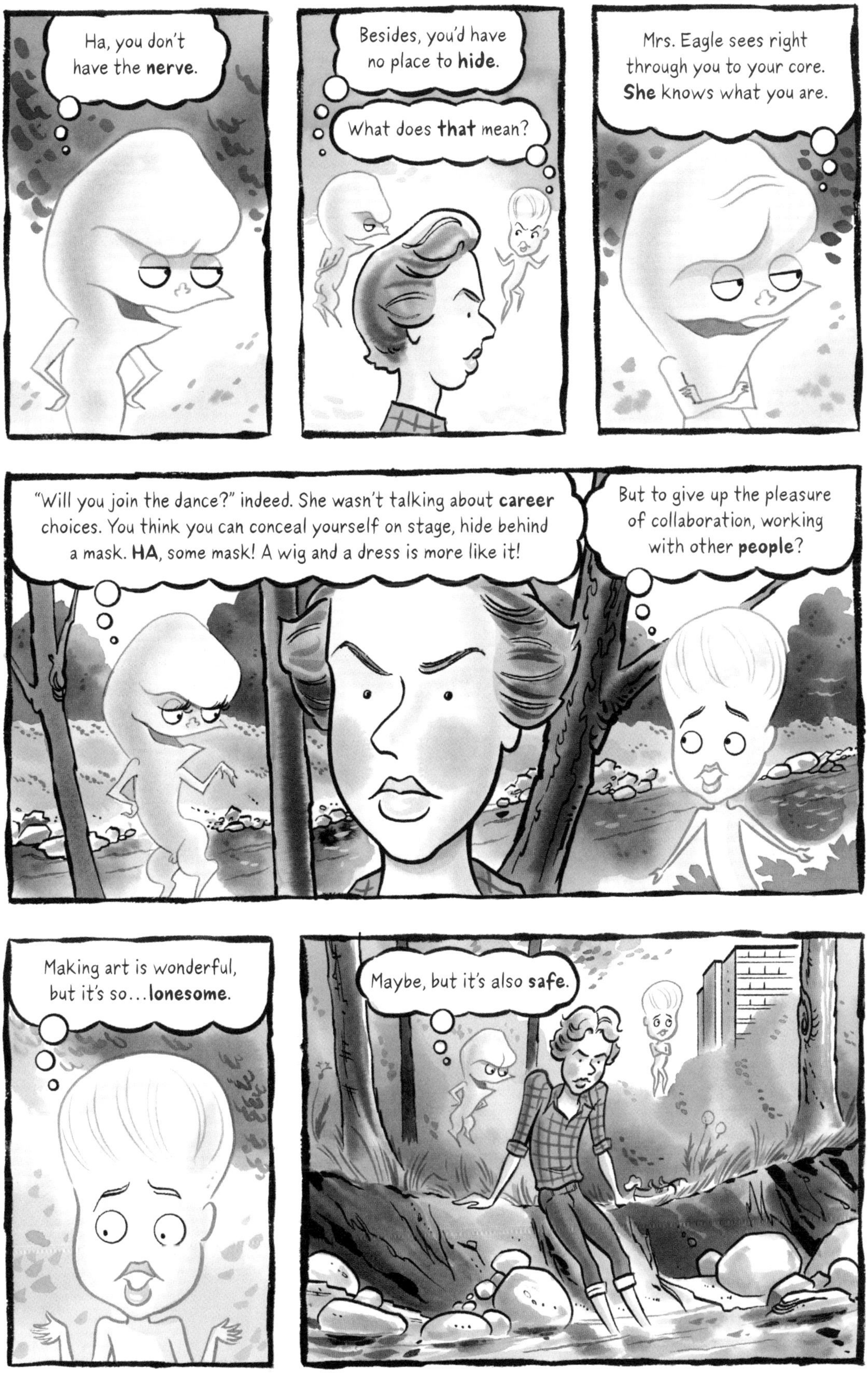
Ha, you don't have the **nerve**.
Besides, you'd have no place to **hide**.
What does **that** mean?
Mrs. Eagle sees right through you to your core. **She** knows what you are.
"Will you join the dance?" indeed. She wasn't talking about **career** choices. You think you can conceal yourself on stage, hide behind a mask. **HA**, some mask! A wig and a dress is more like it!
But to give up the pleasure of collaboration, working with other **people**?
Making art is wonderful, but it's so... **lonesome**.
Maybe, but it's also **safe**.

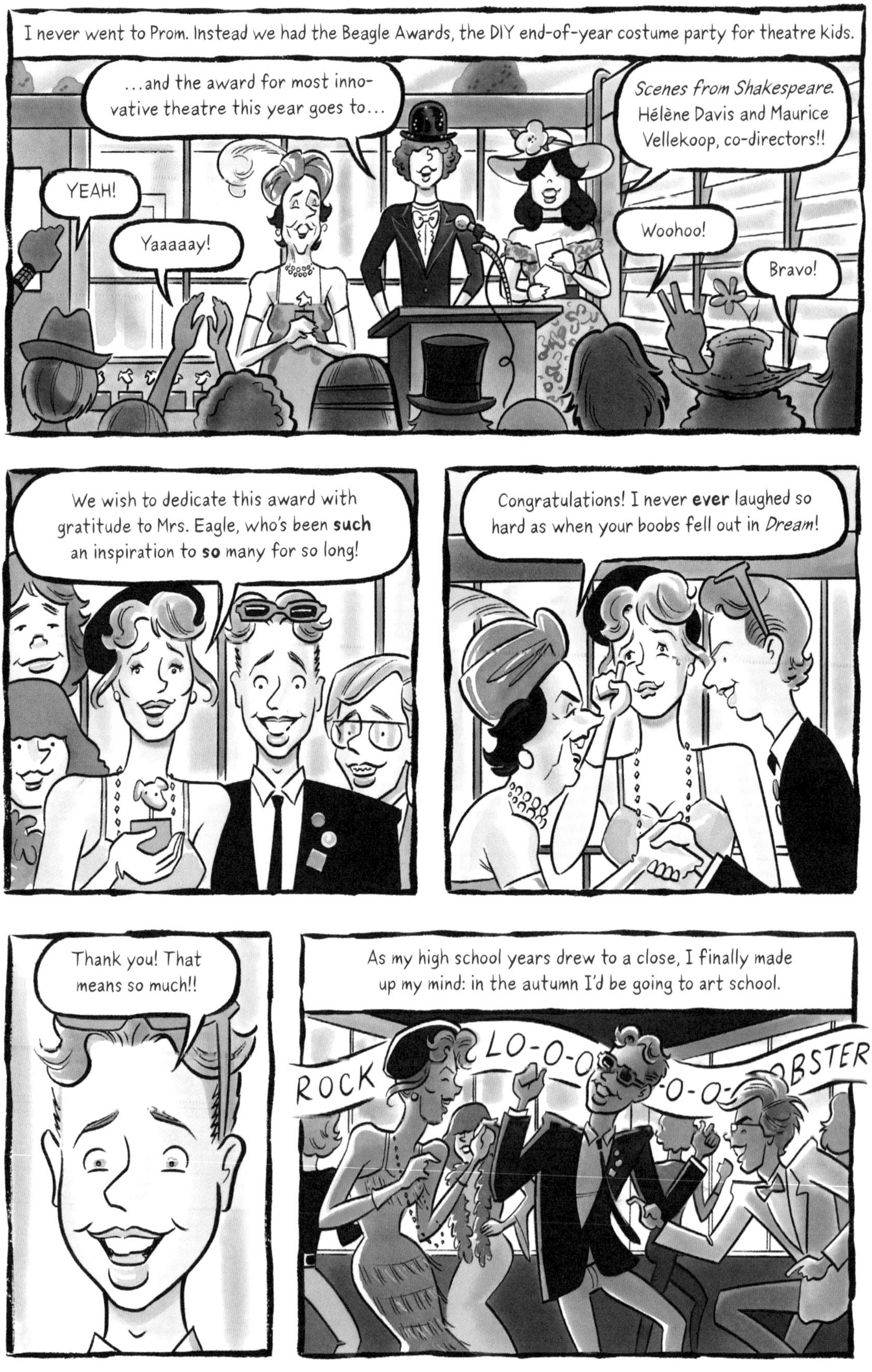

I never went to Prom. Instead we had the Beagle Awards, the DIY end-of-year costume party for theatre kids.
...and the award for most innovative theatre this year goes to...
Scenes from Shakespeare. Hélène Davis and Maurice Vellekoop, co-directors!!
YEAH!
Yaaaaay!
Woohoo!
Bravo!
We wish to dedicate this award with gratitude to Mrs. Eagle, who's been **such** an inspiration to **so** many for so long!
Congratulations! I never **ever** laughed so hard as when your boobs fell out in *Dream*!
Thank you! That means so much!!
As my high school years drew to a close, I finally made up my mind: in the autumn I'd be going to art school.
ROCK
LO-O-O
-O-O-
BSTER!

Paul Baker: an introduction

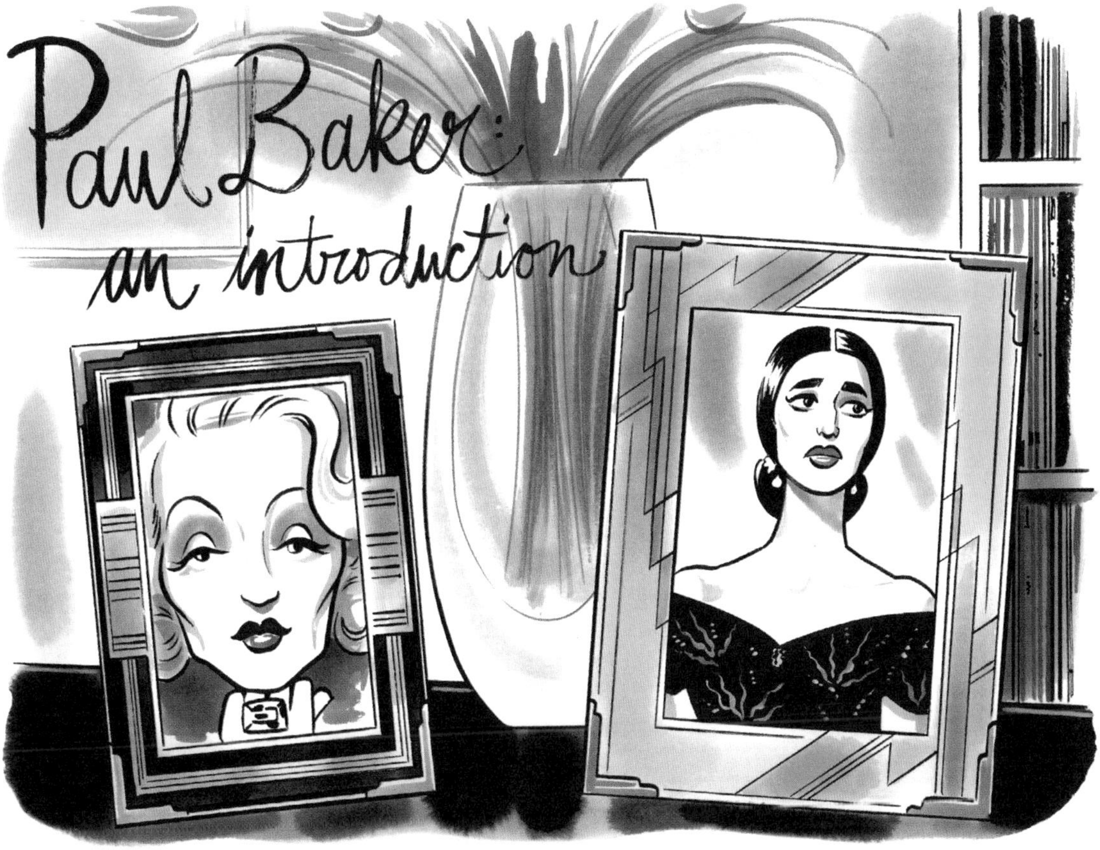

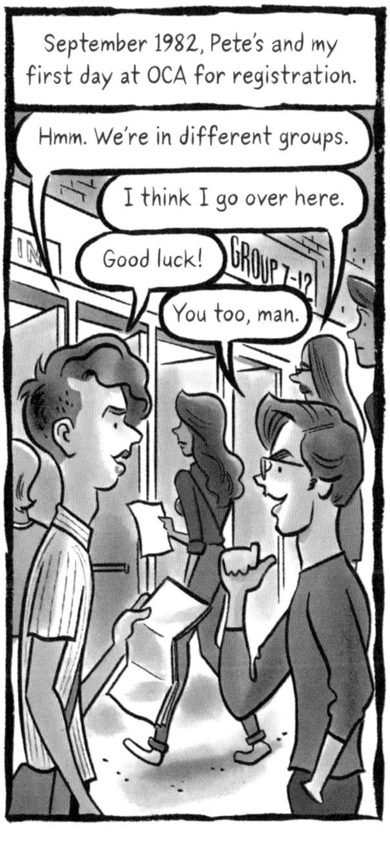
September 1982, Pete's and my first day at OCA for registration.
Hmm. We're in different groups.
I think I go over here.
Good luck!
You too, man.

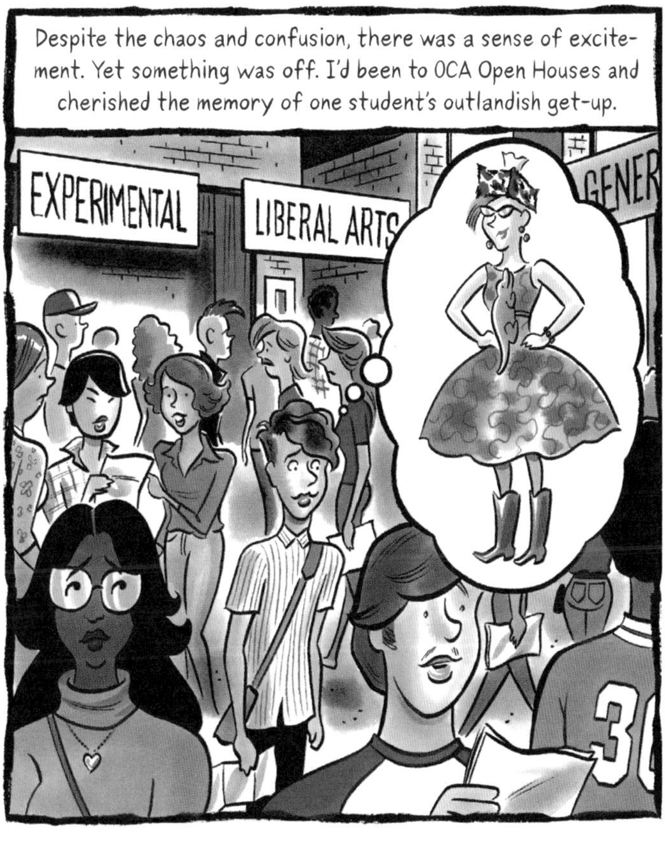
Despite the chaos and confusion, there was a sense of excitement. Yet something was off. I'd been to OCA Open Houses and cherished the memory of one student's outlandish get-up.
EXPERIMENTAL
LIBERAL ARTS

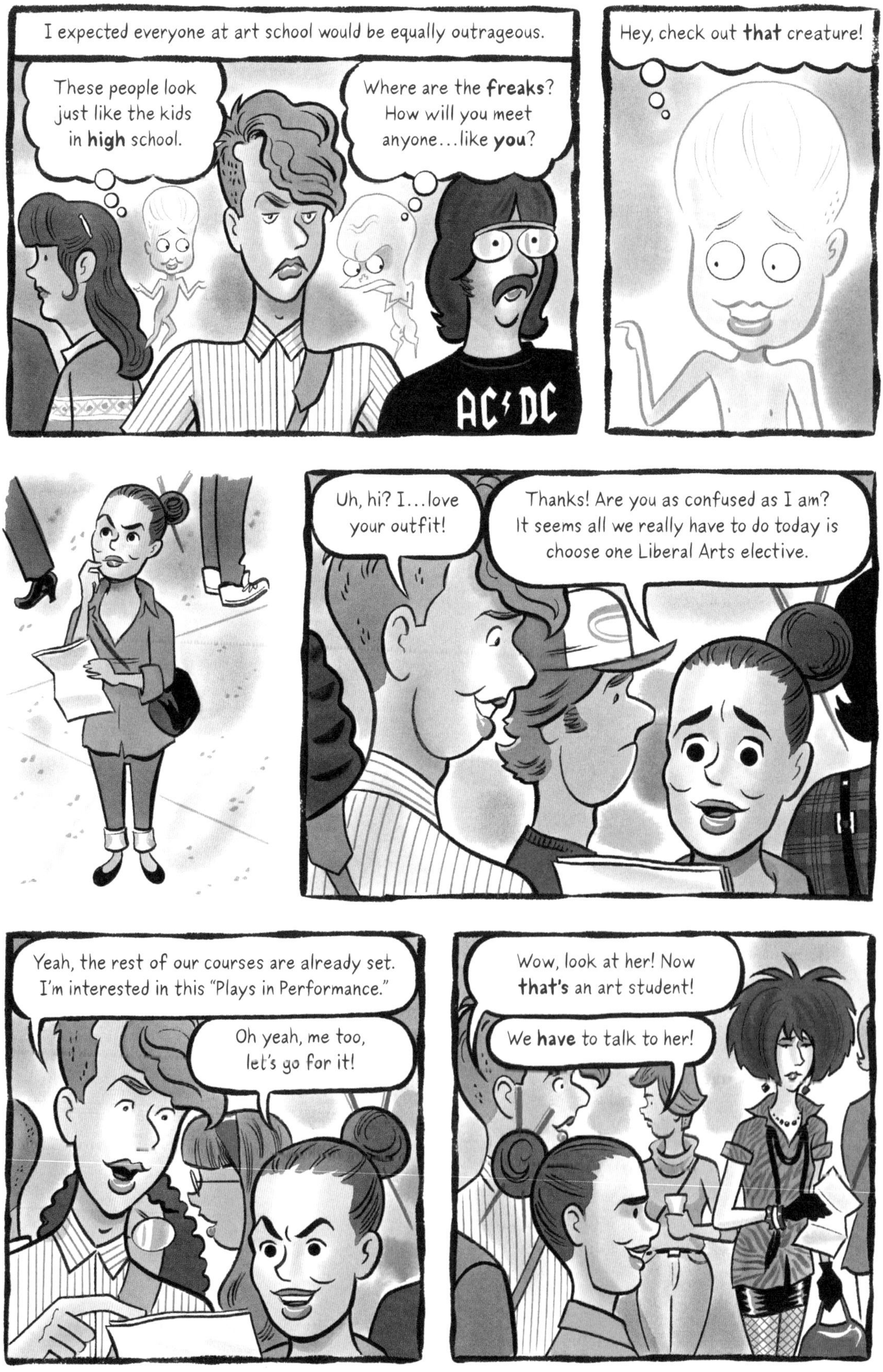
I expected everyone at art school would be equally outrageous.
These people look just like the kids in **high** school.
Where are the **freaks**? How will you meet anyone...like **you**?
AC/DC
Hey, check out **that** creature!
Uh, hi? I...love your outfit!
Thanks! Are you as confused as I am? It seems all we really have to do today is choose one Liberal Arts elective.
Yeah, the rest of our courses are already set. I'm interested in this "Plays in Performance."
Oh yeah, me too, let's go for it!
Wow, look at her! Now **that's** an art student!
We **have** to talk to her!

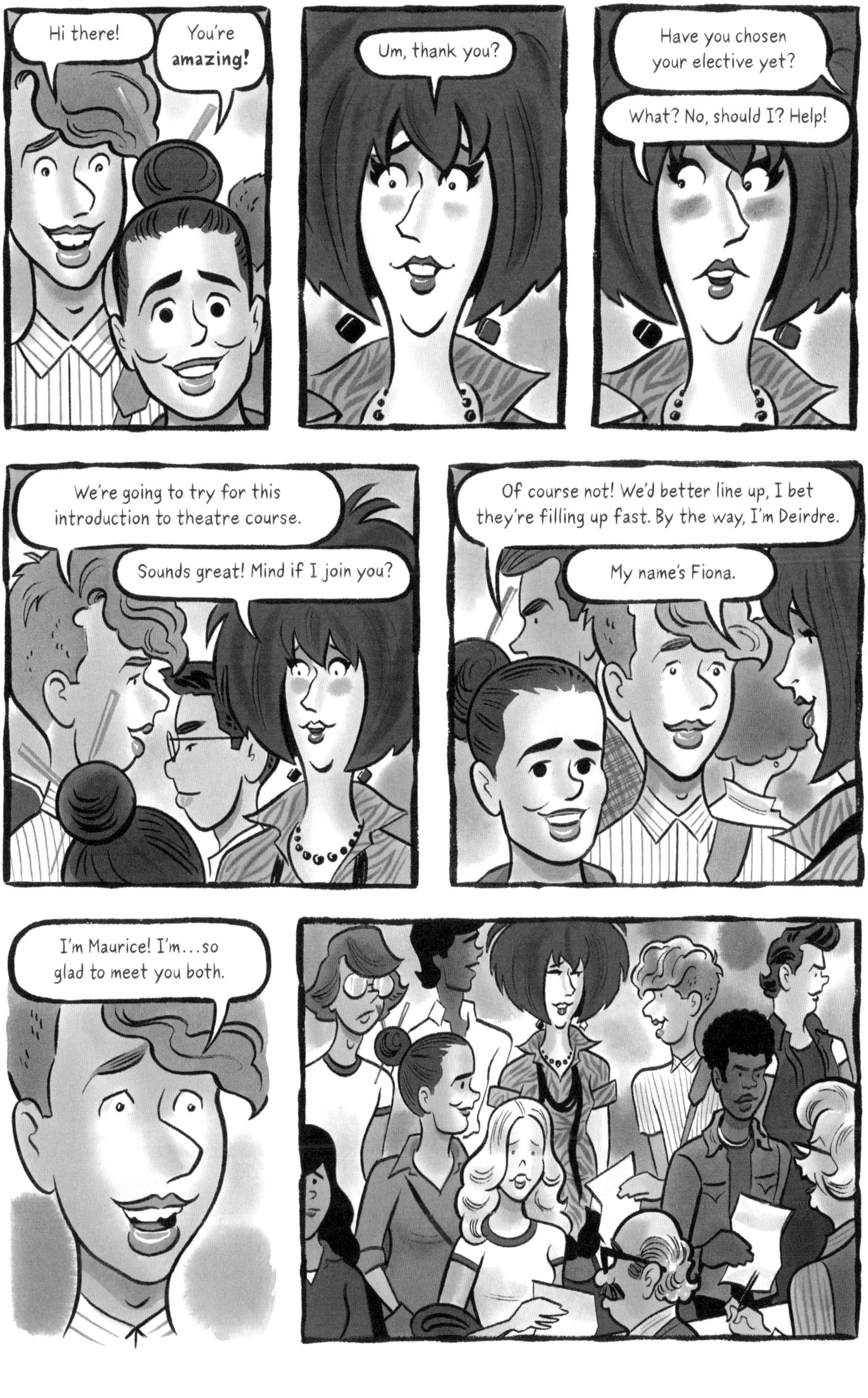
Hi there!
You're **amazing!**
Um, thank you?
Have you chosen your elective yet?
What? No, should I? Help!
We're going to try for this introduction to theatre course.
Sounds great! Mind if I join you?
Of course not! We'd better line up, I bet they're filling up fast. By the way, I'm Deirdre.
My name's Fiona.
I'm Maurice! I'm...so glad to meet you both.

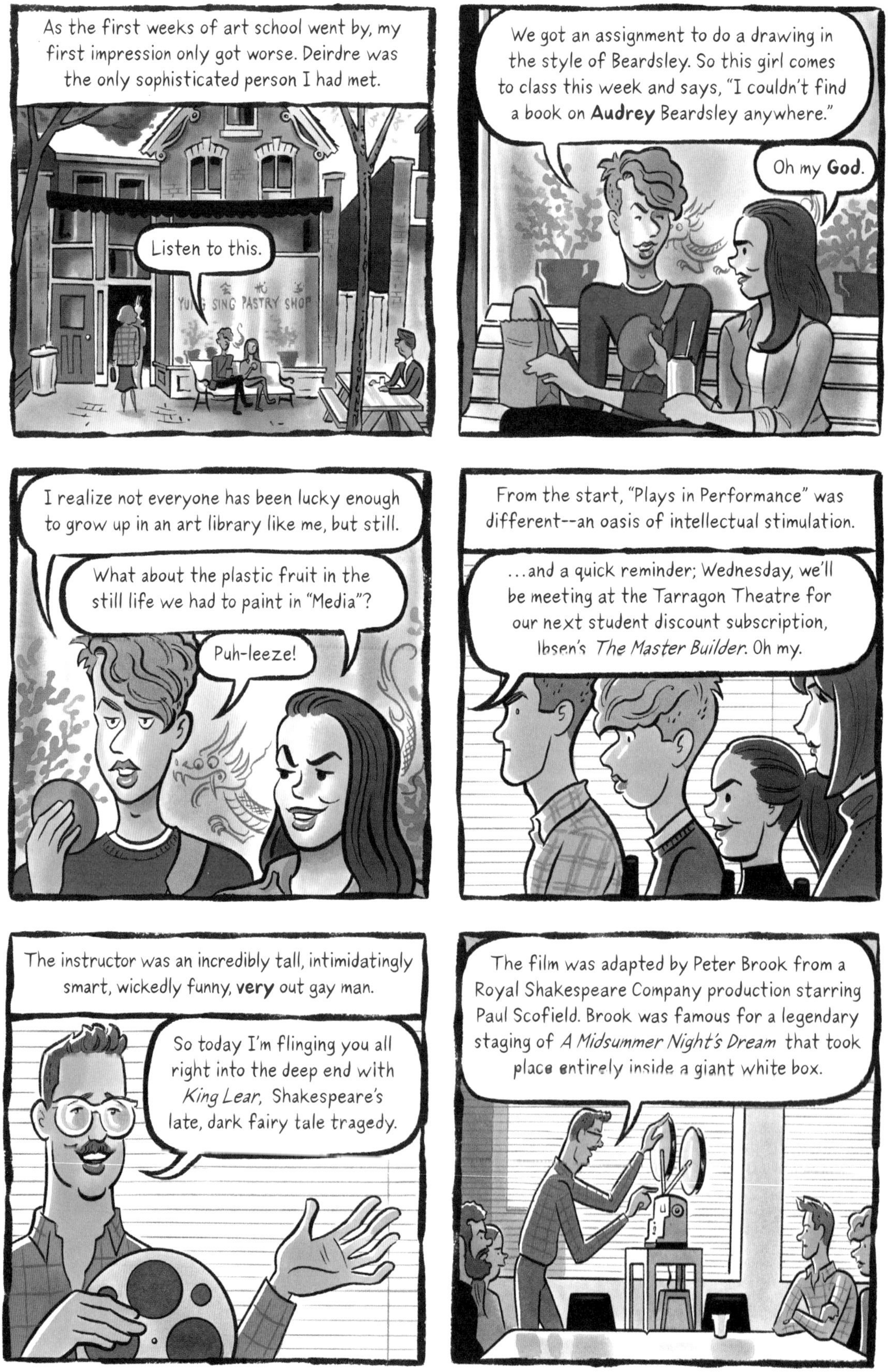
As the first weeks of art school went by, my first impression only got worse. Deirdre was the only sophisticated person I had met.
Listen to this.
YUNG SING PASTRY SHOP
We got an assignment to do a drawing in the style of Beardsley. So this girl comes to class this week and says, "I couldn't find a book on **Audrey** Beardsley anywhere."
Oh my **God**.
I realize not everyone has been lucky enough to grow up in an art library like me, but still.
What about the plastic fruit in the still life we had to paint in "Media"?
Puh-leeze!
From the start, "Plays in Performance" was different--an oasis of intellectual stimulation.
...and a quick reminder; Wednesday, we'll be meeting at the Tarragon Theatre for our next student discount subscription, Ibsen's *The Master Builder*. Oh my.
The instructor was an incredibly tall, intimidatingly smart, wickedly funny, **very** out gay man.
So today I'm flinging you all right into the deep end with *King Lear*, Shakespeare's late, dark fairy tale tragedy.
The film was adapted by Peter Brook from a Royal Shakespeare Company production starring Paul Scofield. Brook was famous for a legendary staging of *A Midsummer Night's Dream* that took place entirely inside a giant white box.

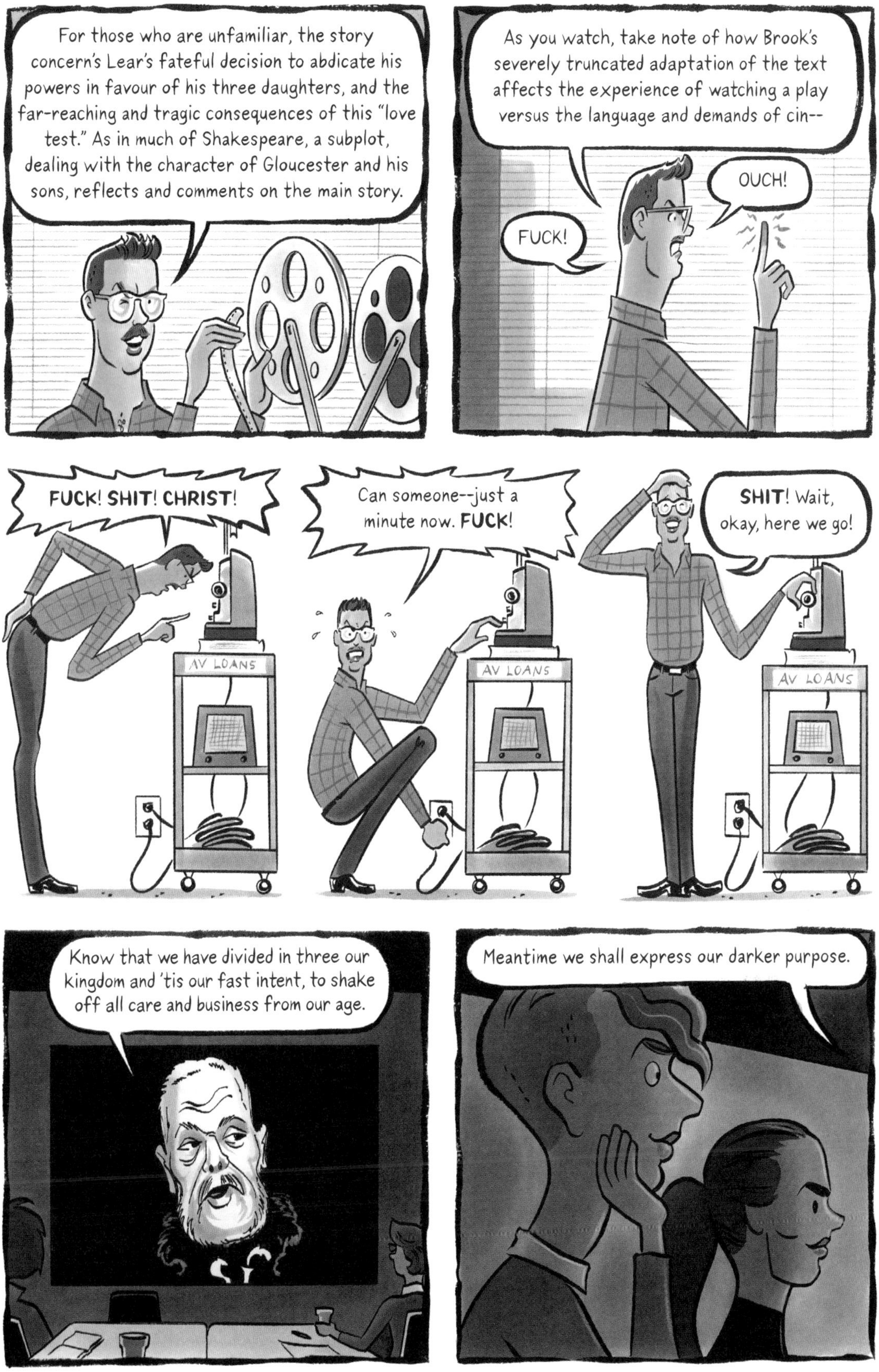
For those who are unfamiliar, the story concern's Lear's fateful decision to abdicate his powers in favour of his three daughters, and the far-reaching and tragic consequences of this "love test." As in much of Shakespeare, a subplot, dealing with the character of Gloucester and his sons, reflects and comments on the main story.
As you watch, take note of how Brook's severely truncated adaptation of the text affects the experience of watching a play versus the language and demands of cin--
FUCK!
OUCH!
FUCK! SHIT! CHRIST!
AV LOANS
Can someone--just a minute now. FUCK!
AV LOANS
SHIT! Wait, okay, here we go!
AV LOANS
Know that we have divided in three our kingdom and 'tis our fast intent, to shake off all care and business from our age.
Meantime we shall express our darker purpose.

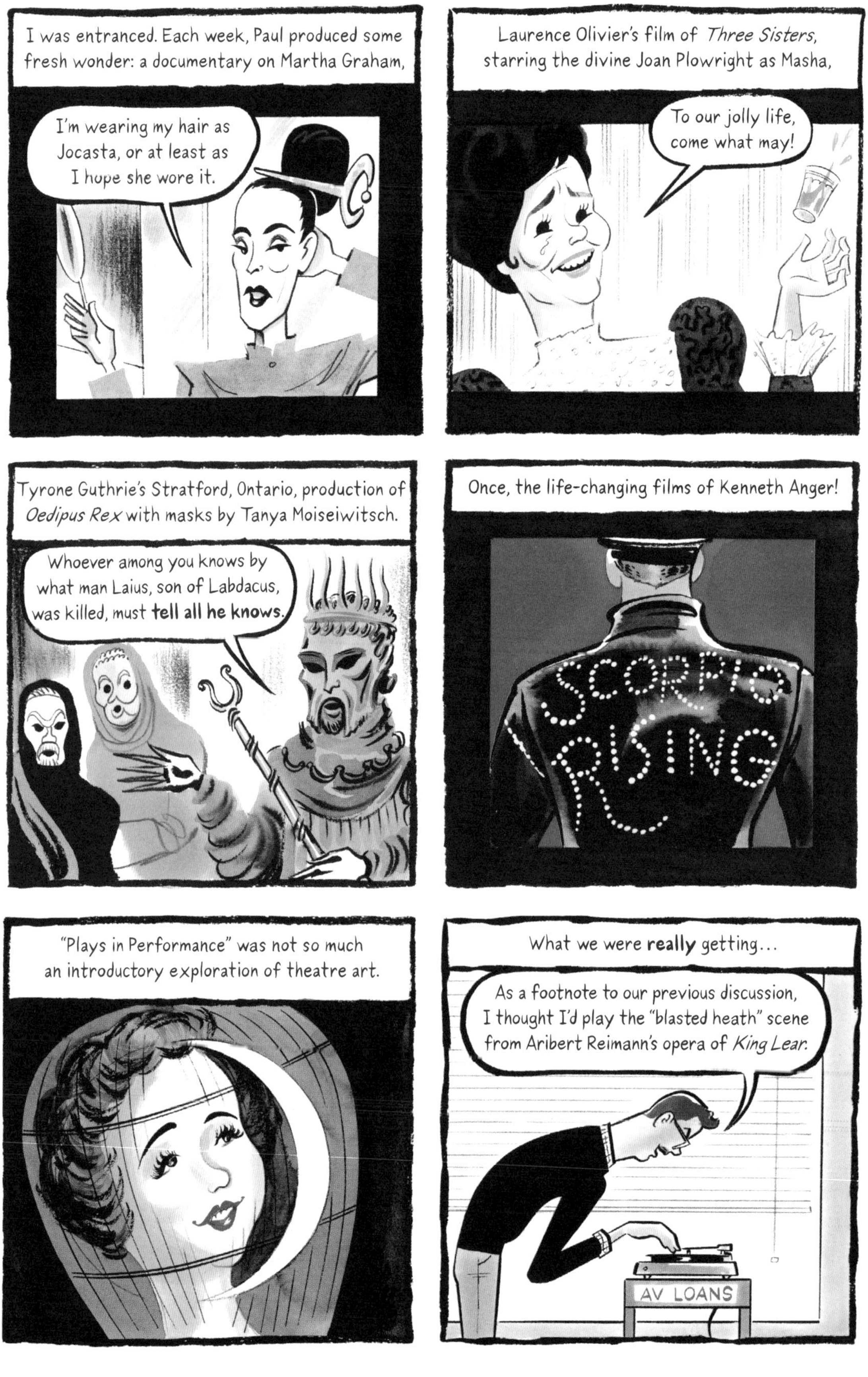
I was entranced. Each week, Paul produced some fresh wonder: a documentary on Martha Graham,
I'm wearing my hair as Jocasta, or at least as I hope she wore it.
Laurence Olivier's film of *Three Sisters*, starring the divine Joan Plowright as Masha,
To our jolly life, come what may!
Tyrone Guthrie's Stratford, Ontario, production of *Oedipus Rex* with masks by Tanya Moiseiwitsch.
Whoever among you knows by what man Laius, son of Labdacus, was killed, must **tell all he knows**.
Once, the life-changing films of Kenneth Anger!
SCORPIO RISING
"Plays in Performance" was not so much an introductory exploration of theatre art.
What we were **really** getting...
As a footnote to our previous discussion, I thought I'd play the "blasted heath" scene from Aribert Reimann's opera of *King Lear*.
AV LOANS

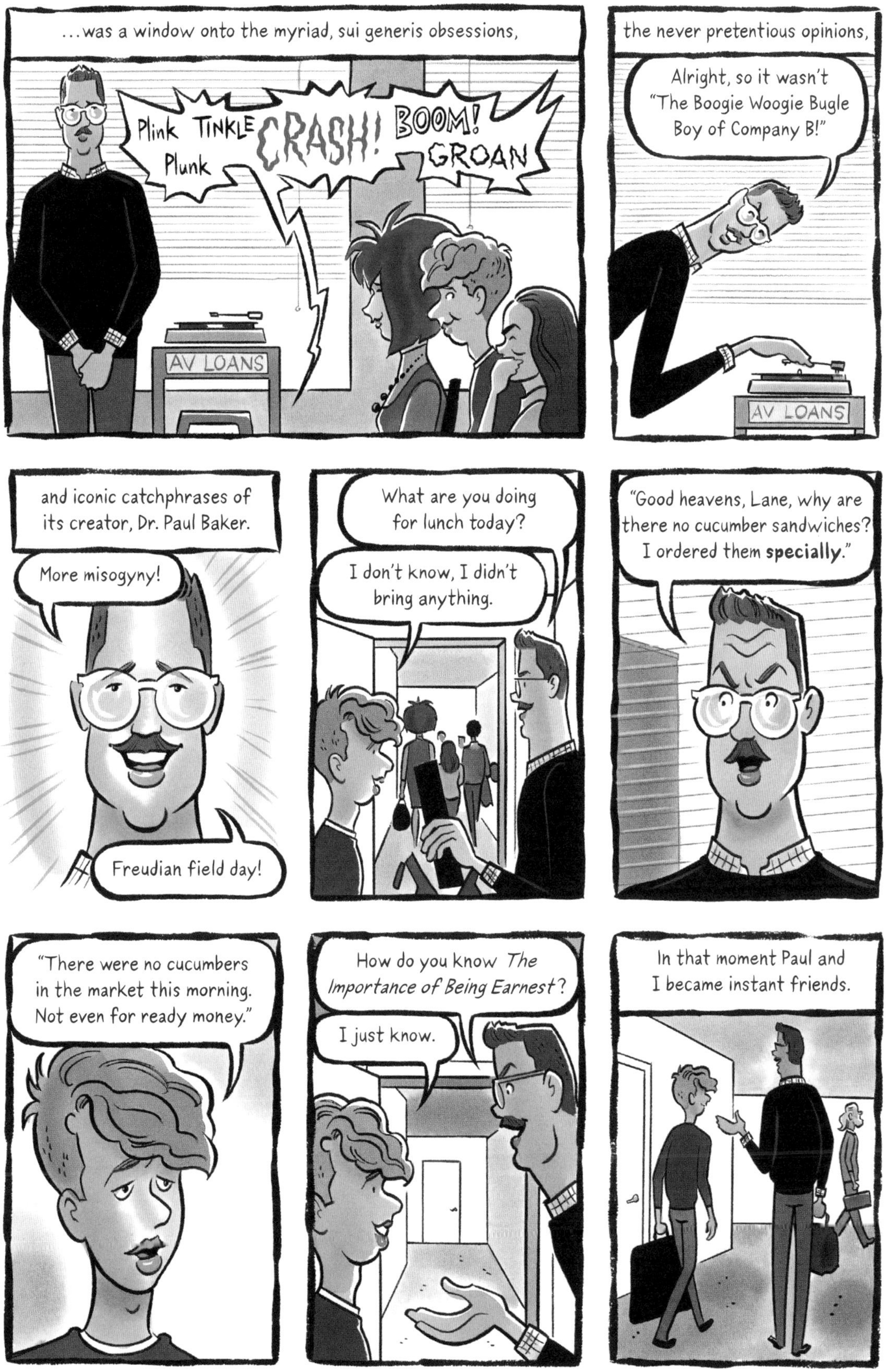
...was a window onto the myriad, sui generis obsessions,
Plink TINKLE Plunk CRASH! BOOM! GROAN
AV LOANS
the never pretentious opinions,
Alright, so it wasn't "The Boogie Woogie Bugle Boy of Company B!"
AV LOANS
and iconic catchphrases of its creator, Dr. Paul Baker.
More misogyny!
Freudian field day!
What are you doing for lunch today?
I don't know, I didn't bring anything.
"Good heavens, Lane, why are there no cucumber sandwiches? I ordered them **specially**."
"There were no cucumbers in the market this morning. Not even for ready money."
How do you know *The Importance of Being Earnest*?
I just know.
In that moment Paul and I became instant friends.

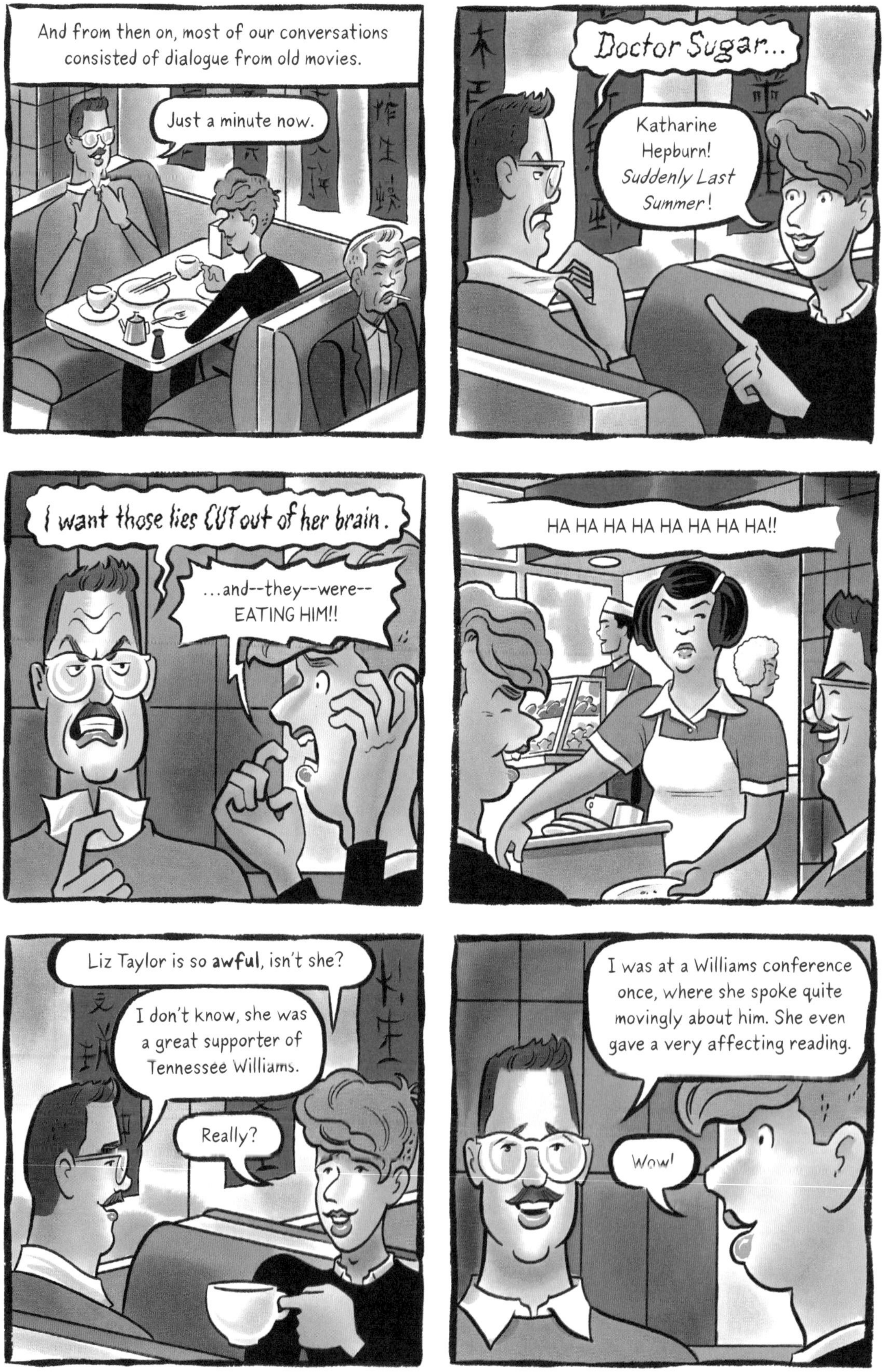
And from then on, most of our conversations consisted of dialogue from old movies.
Just a minute now.
Doctor Sugar...
Katharine Hepburn! *Suddenly Last Summer*!
I want those lies CUT out of her brain.
...and--they--were--EATING HIM!!
HA HA HA HA HA HA HA HA!!
Liz Taylor is so **awful**, isn't she?
I don't know, she was a great supporter of Tennessee Williams.
Really?
I was at a Williams conference once, where she spoke quite movingly about him. She even gave a very affecting reading.
Wow!

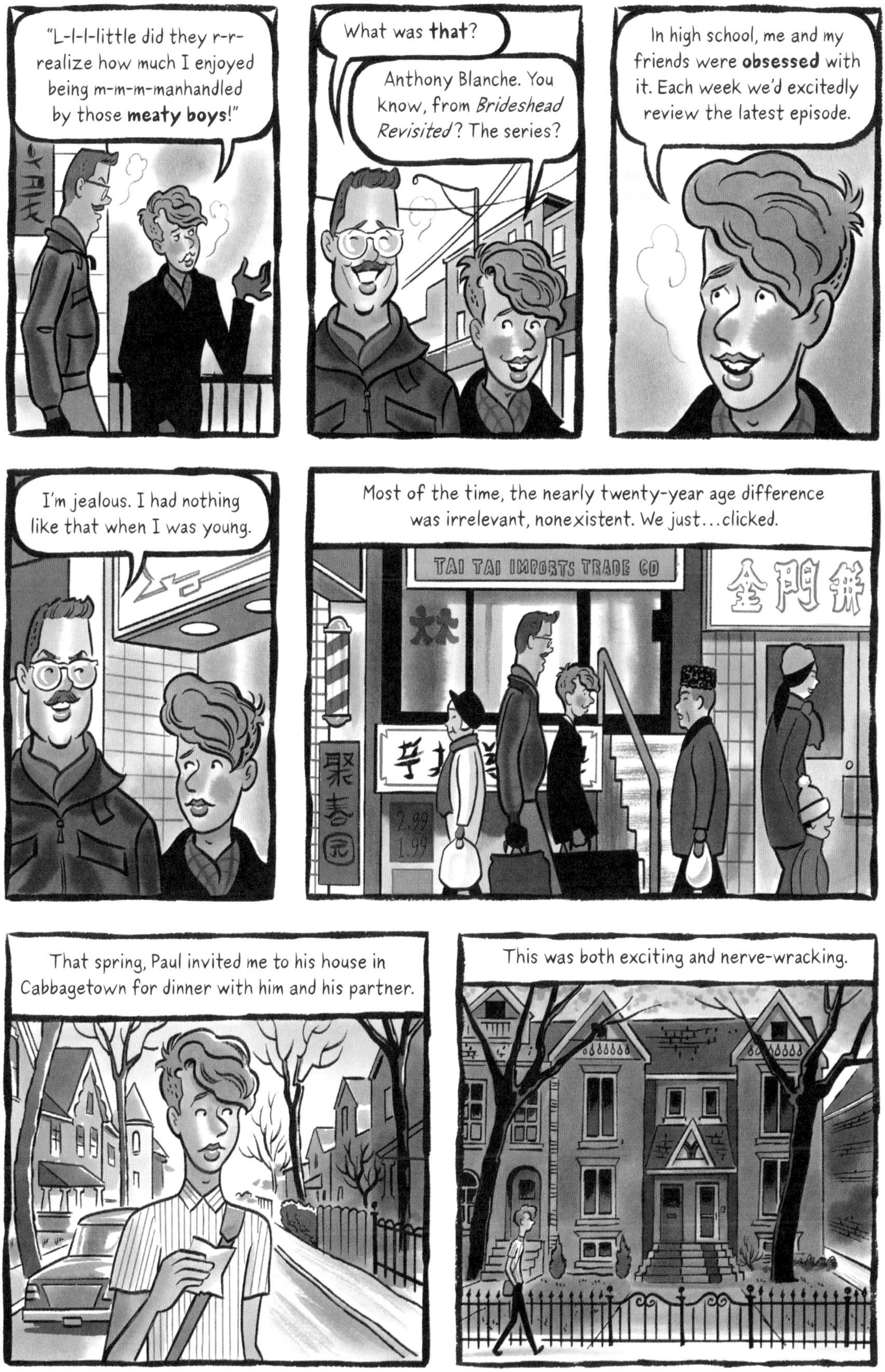
"L-l-l-little did they r-r-realize how much I enjoyed being m-m-m-manhandled by those **meaty boys**!"
What was **that**?
Anthony Blanche. You know, from *Brideshead Revisited*? The series?
In high school, me and my friends were **obsessed** with it. Each week we'd excitedly review the latest episode.
I'm jealous. I had nothing like that when I was young.
Most of the time, the nearly twenty-year age difference was irrelevant, nonexistent. We just...clicked.
TAI TAI IMPORTS TRADE CO
2.99
1.99
That spring, Paul invited me to his house in Cabbagetown for dinner with him and his partner.
This was both exciting and nerve-wracking.

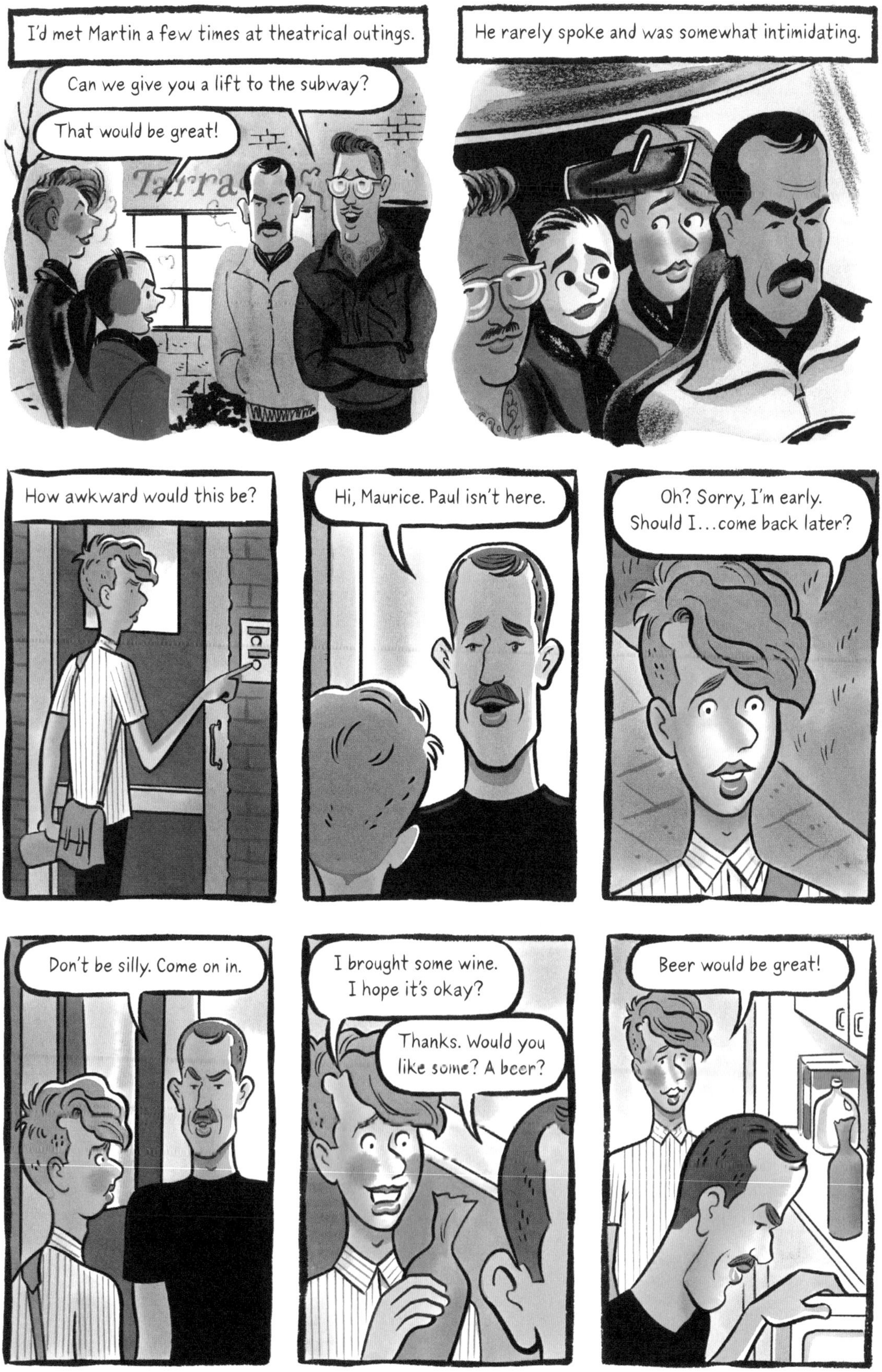
I'd met Martin a few times at theatrical outings.
Can we give you a lift to the subway?
That would be great!
Tarra
He rarely spoke and was somewhat intimidating.
How awkward would this be?
Hi, Maurice. Paul isn't here.
Oh? Sorry, I'm early. Should I...come back later?
Don't be silly. Come on in.
I brought some wine. I hope it's okay?
Thanks. Would you like some? A beer?
Beer would be great!

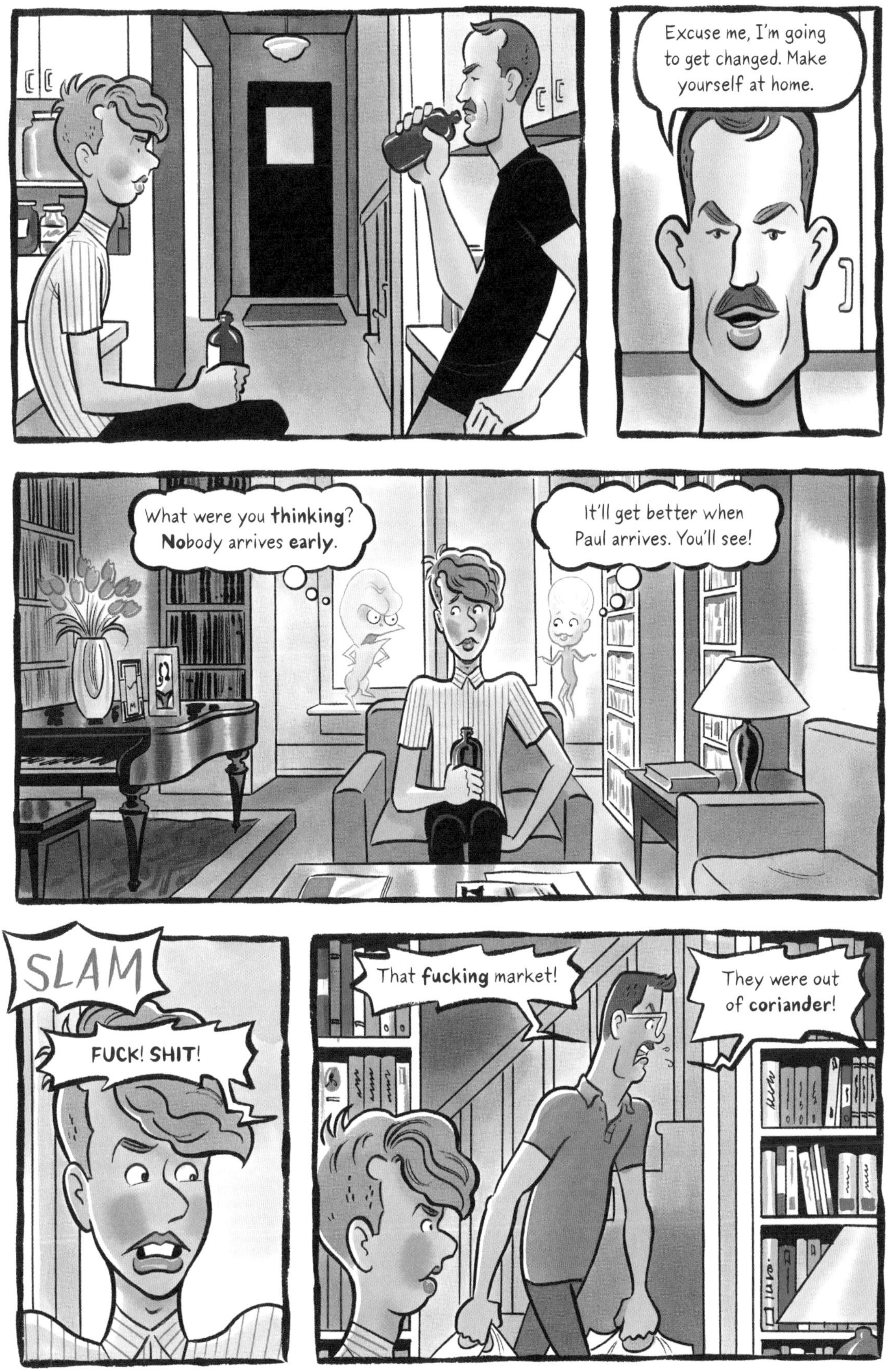
Excuse me, I'm going to get changed. Make yourself at home.
What were you **thinking**? **No**body arrives **early**.
It'll get better when Paul arrives. You'll see!
SLAM
FUCK! SHIT!
That **fucking** market!
They were out of **coriander**!

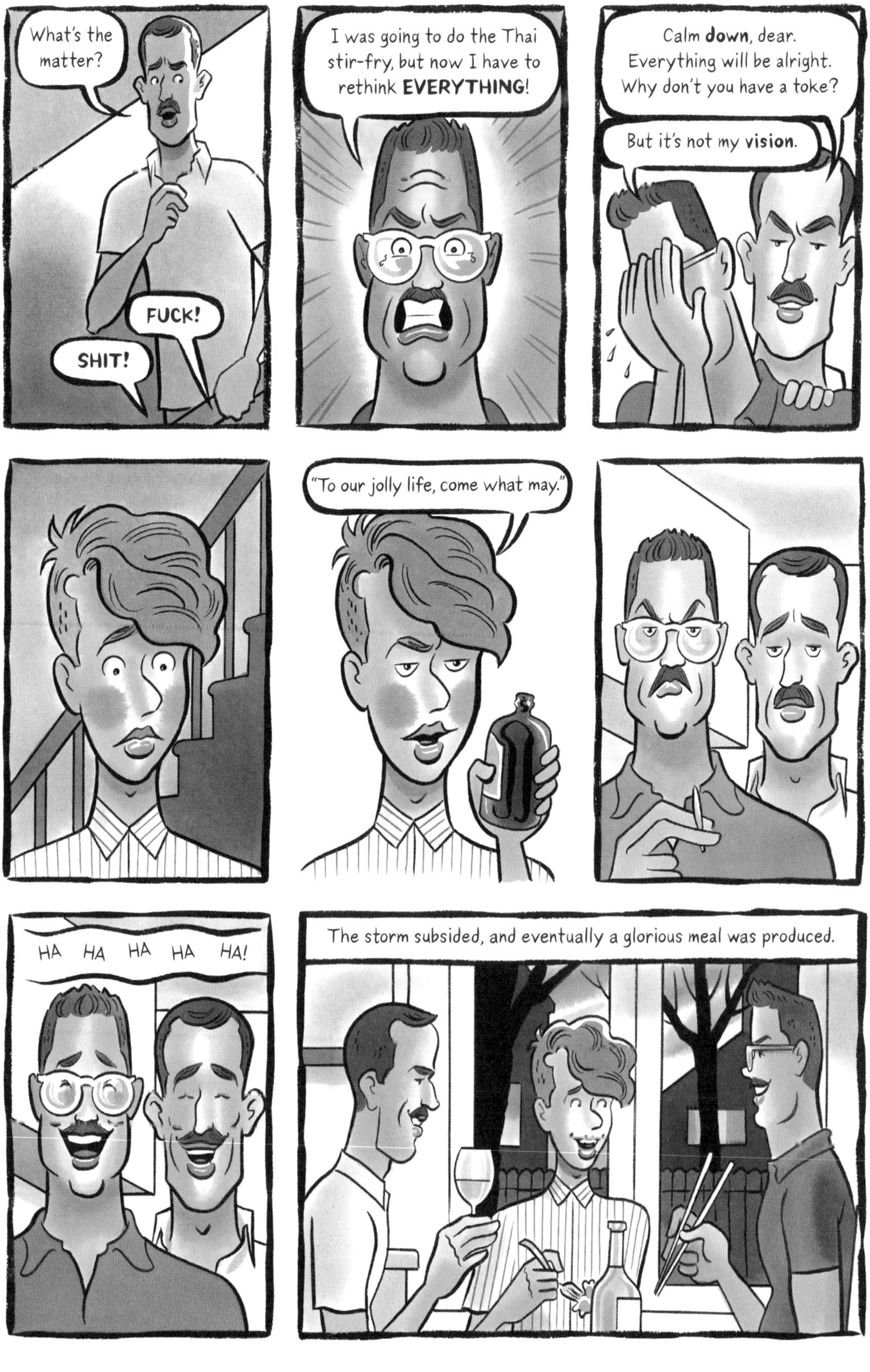
What's the matter?
FUCK!
SHIT!
I was going to do the Thai stir-fry, but now I have to rethink **EVERYTHING**!
Calm **down**, dear. Everything will be alright. Why don't you have a toke?
But it's not my **vision**.
"To our jolly life, come what may."
HA HA HA HA HA!
The storm subsided, and eventually a glorious meal was produced.

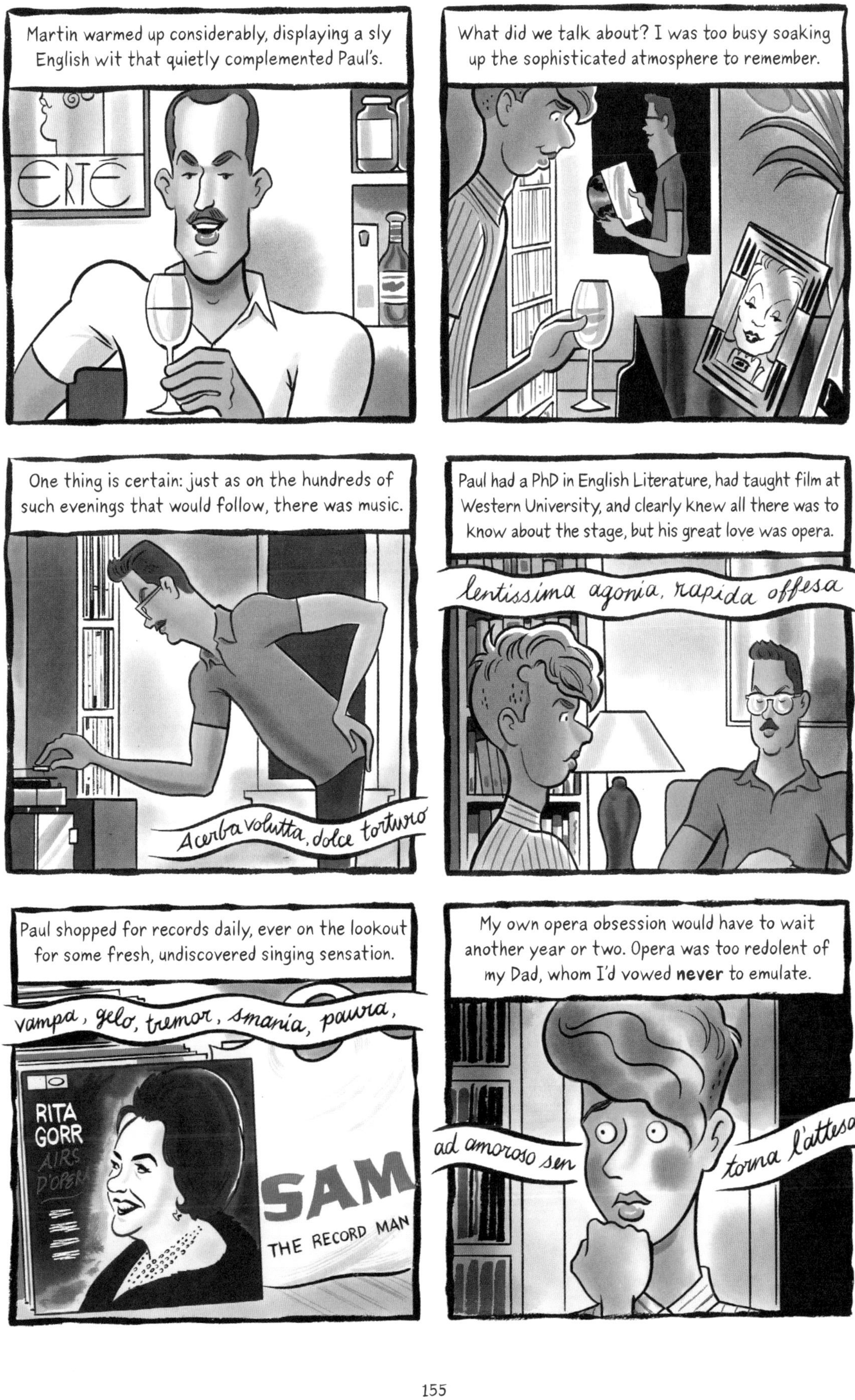
Martin warmed up considerably, displaying a sly English wit that quietly complemented Paul's.
ERTÉ
What did we talk about? I was too busy soaking up the sophisticated atmosphere to remember.
One thing is certain: just as on the hundreds of such evenings that would follow, there was music.
Acerba volutta, dolce torturo
Paul had a PhD in English Literature, had taught film at Western University, and clearly knew all there was to know about the stage, but his great love was opera.
lentissima agonia, rapida offesa
Paul shopped for records daily, ever on the lookout for some fresh, undiscovered singing sensation.
vampa, gelo, tremor, smania, paura,
RITA GORR
AIRS D'OPERA
SAM
THE RECORD MAN
My own opera obsession would have to wait another year or two. Opera was too redolent of my Dad, whom I'd vowed **never** to emulate.
ad amoroso sen
torna l'attesa

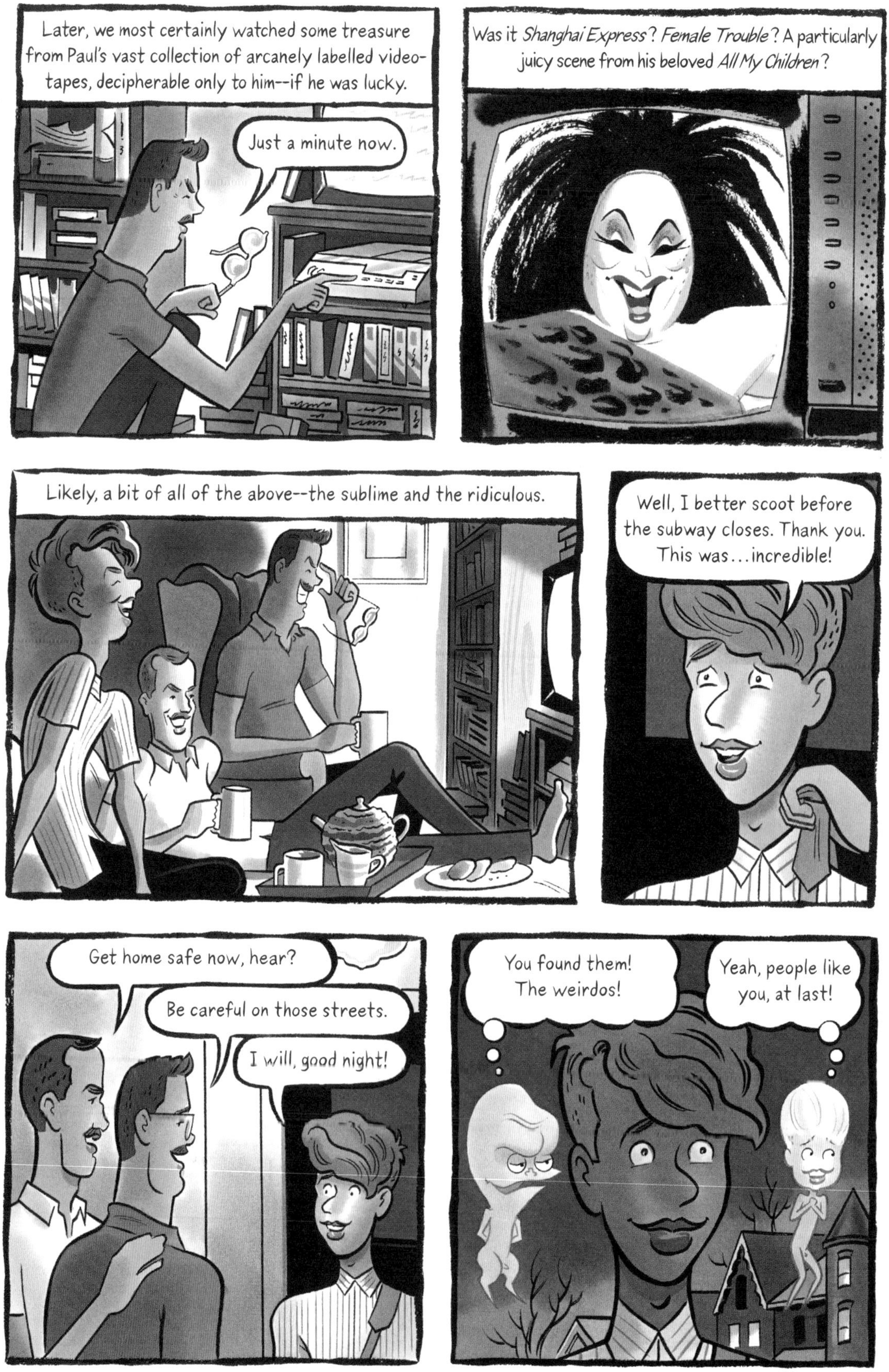
Later, we most certainly watched some treasure from Paul's vast collection of arcanely labelled videotapes, decipherable only to him--if he was lucky.
Just a minute now.
Was it *Shanghai Express*? *Female Trouble*? A particularly juicy scene from his beloved *All My Children*?
Likely, a bit of all of the above--the sublime and the ridiculous.
Well, I better scoot before the subway closes. Thank you. This was...incredible!
Get home safe now, hear?
Be careful on those streets.
I will, good night!
You found them! The weirdos!
Yeah, people like you, at last!

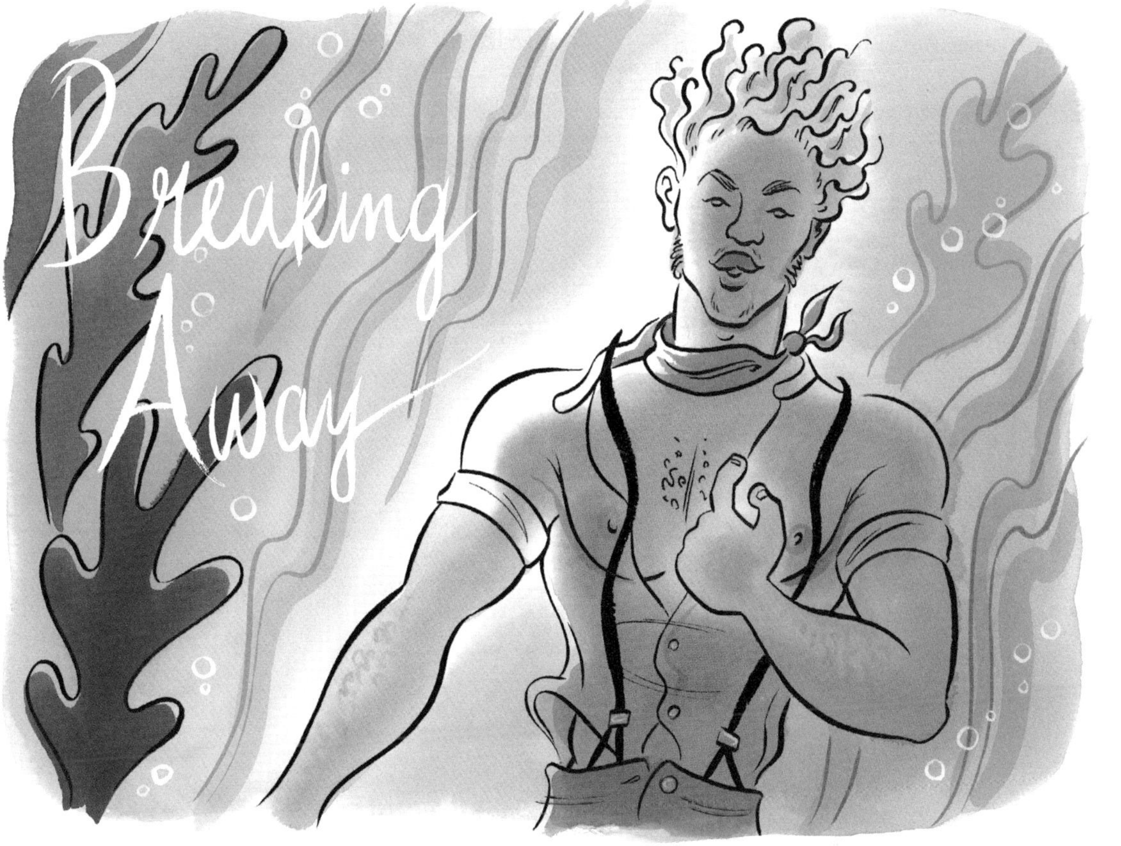
Breaking Away

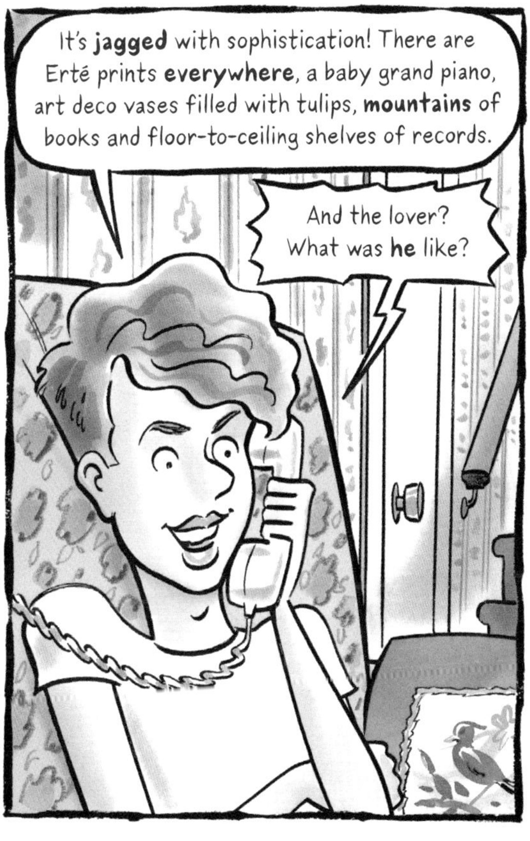
It's **jagged** with sophistication! There are Erté prints **everywhere**, a baby grand piano, art deco vases filled with tulips, **mountains** of books and floor-to-ceiling shelves of records.
And the lover? What was **he** like?

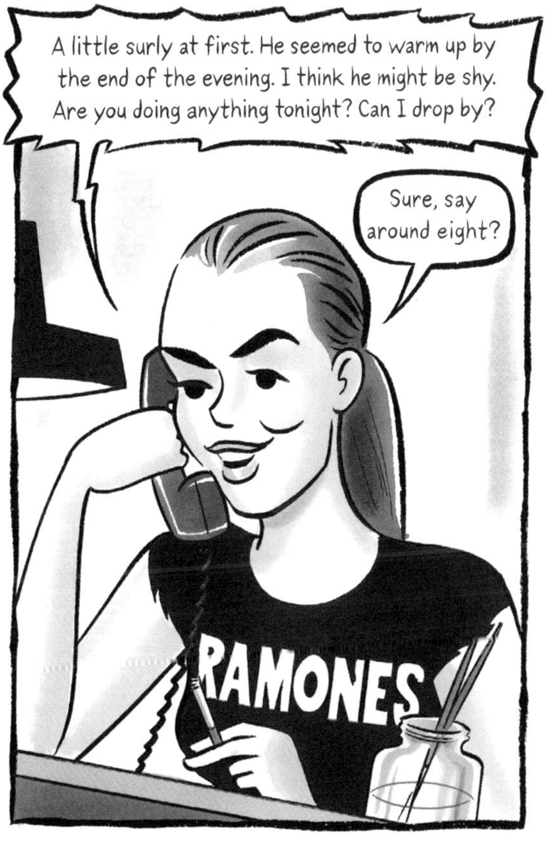
A little surly at first. He seemed to warm up by the end of the evening. I think he might be shy. Are you doing anything tonight? Can I drop by?
Sure, say around eight?
RAMONES

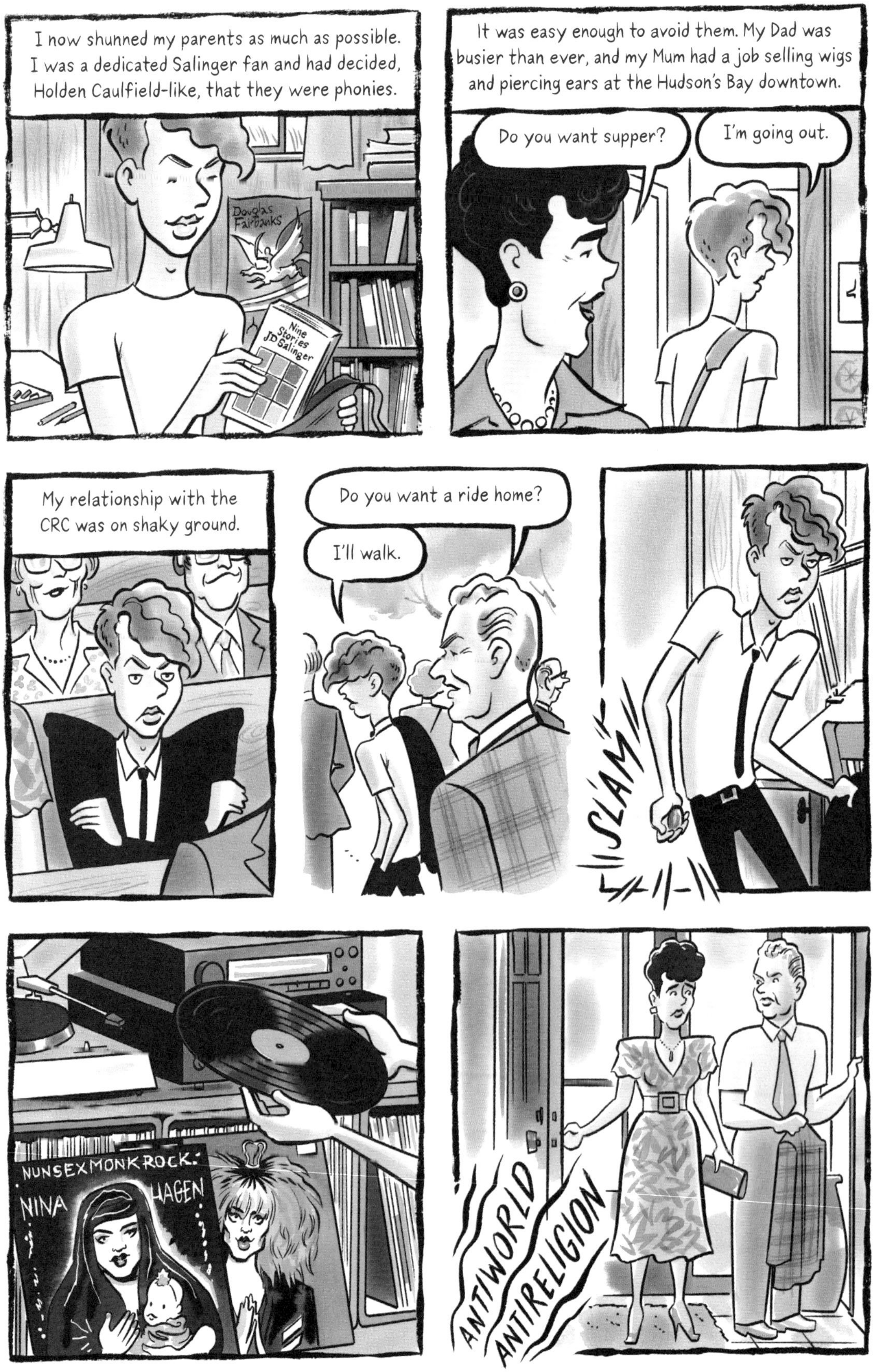
I now shunned my parents as much as possible. I was a dedicated Salinger fan and had decided, Holden Caulfield-like, that they were phonies.
Douglas Fairbanks
Nine Stories JD Salinger
It was easy enough to avoid them. My Dad was busier than ever, and my Mum had a job selling wigs and piercing ears at the Hudson's Bay downtown.
Do you want supper?
I'm going out.
My relationship with the CRC was on shaky ground.
Do you want a ride home?
I'll walk.
SLAM
NUNSEXMONKROCK.
NINA HAGEN
ANTIWORLD
ANTIRELIGION

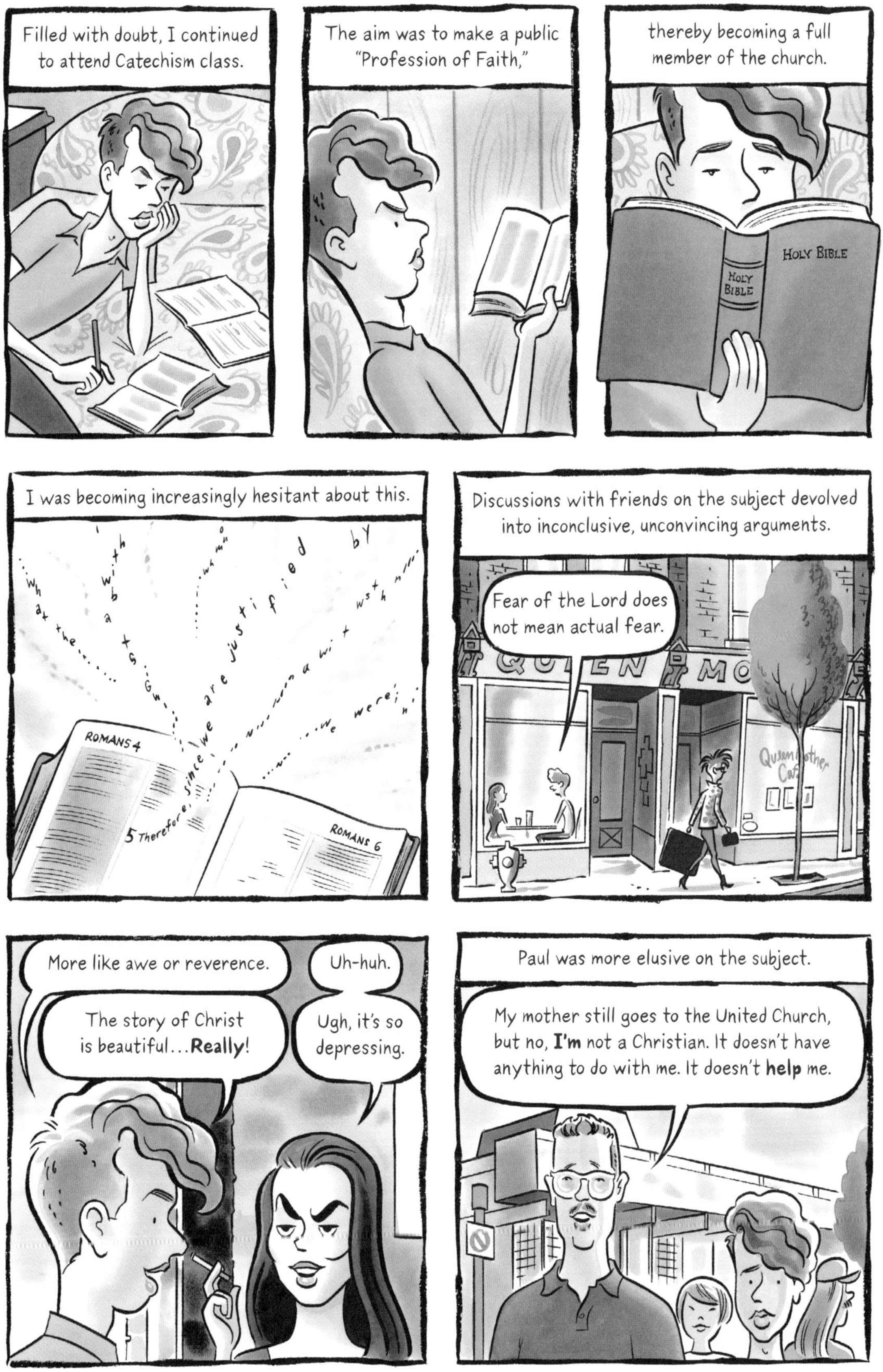

Filled with doubt, I continued to attend Catechism class.
The aim was to make a public "Profession of Faith,"
thereby becoming a full member of the church.
HOLY BIBLE
HOLY BIBLE
I was becoming increasingly hesitant about this.
ROMANS 4
5 Therefore, since we are justified by
ROMANS 6
Discussions with friends on the subject devolved into inconclusive, unconvincing arguments.
Fear of the Lord does not mean actual fear.
More like awe or reverence.
Uh-huh.
The story of Christ is beautiful... **Really**!
Ugh, it's so depressing.
Paul was more elusive on the subject.
My mother still goes to the United Church, but no, **I'm** not a Christian. It doesn't have anything to do with me. It doesn't **help** me.

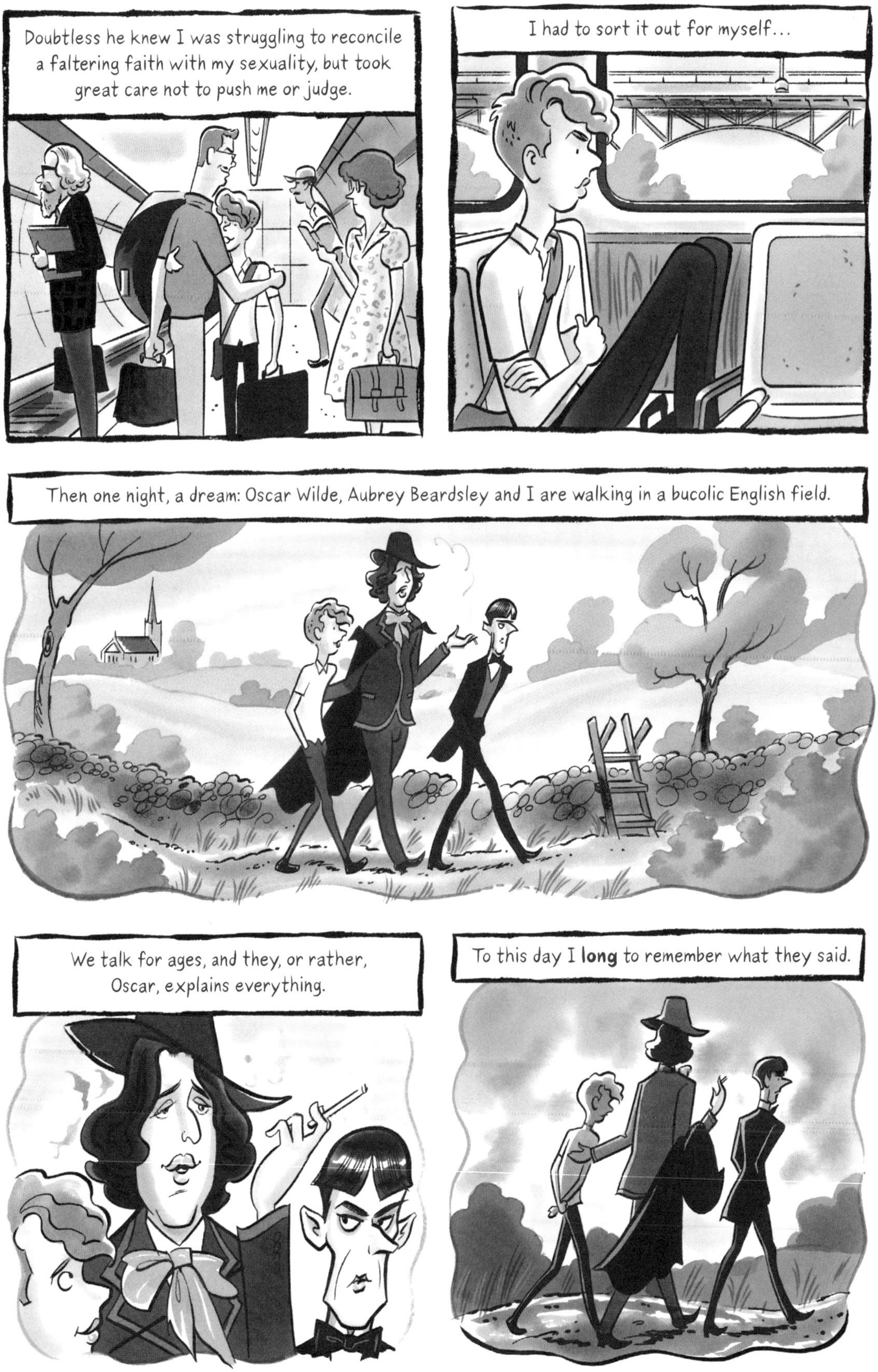
Doubtless he knew I was struggling to reconcile a faltering faith with my sexuality, but took great care not to push me or judge.
I had to sort it out for myself...
Then one night, a dream: Oscar Wilde, Aubrey Beardsley and I are walking in a bucolic English field.
We talk for ages, and they, or rather, Oscar, explains everything.
To this day I **long** to remember what they said.

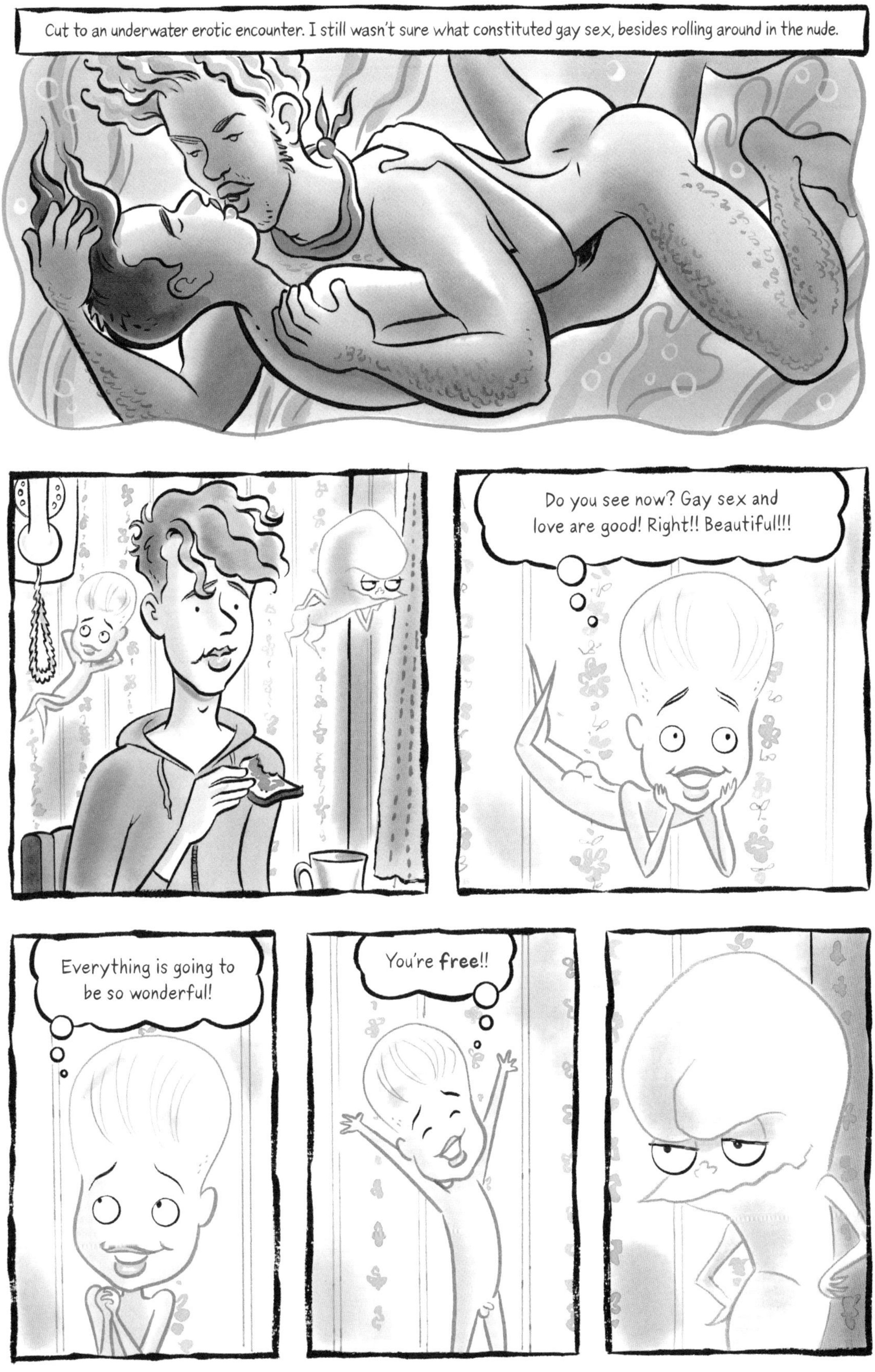
Cut to an underwater erotic encounter. I still wasn't sure what constituted gay sex, besides rolling around in the nude.
Do you see now? Gay sex and love are good! Right!! Beautiful!!!
Everything is going to be so wonderful!
You're **free**!!

A short time later:

Maurice, are you coming to church this morning?

Um, not today.

It's time.

I've made the coffee. Can we talk for a bit?

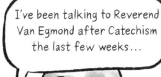
I've been talking to Reverend Van Egmond after Catechism the last few weeks...

and he agreed; I'm just not ready to do my Profession of Faith,

and I won't be going back.

I need time away from it, from the church. I don't know if it...fits me anymore.

Well, it's your decision. It's up to you.

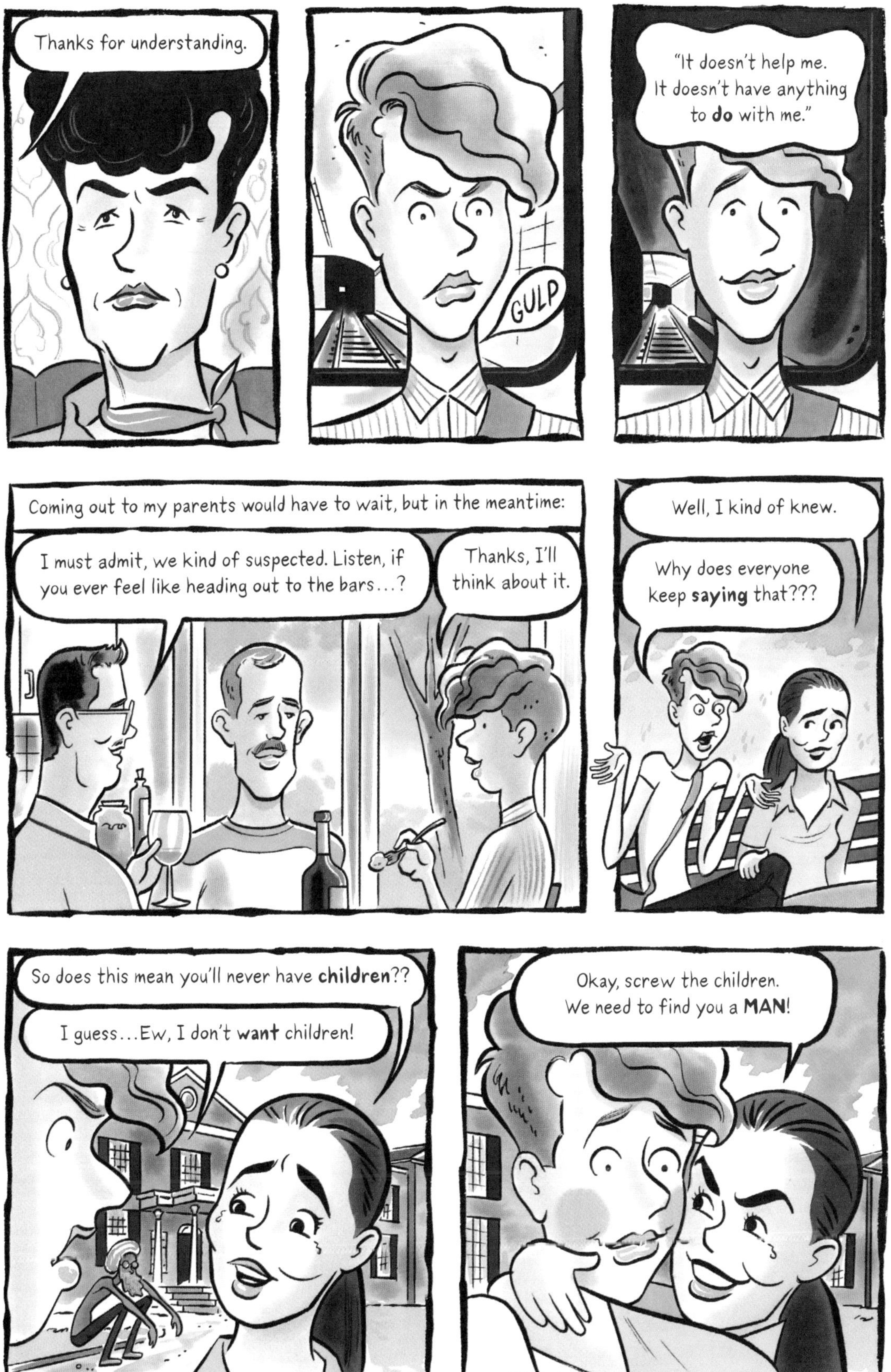
Thanks for understanding.
GULP
"It doesn't help me. It doesn't have anything to **do** with me."
Coming out to my parents would have to wait, but in the meantime:
I must admit, we kind of suspected. Listen, if you ever feel like heading out to the bars...?
Thanks, I'll think about it.
Well, I kind of knew.
Why does everyone keep **saying** that???
So does this mean you'll never have **children**??
I guess...Ew, I don't **want** children!
Okay, screw the children. We need to find you a **MAN**!

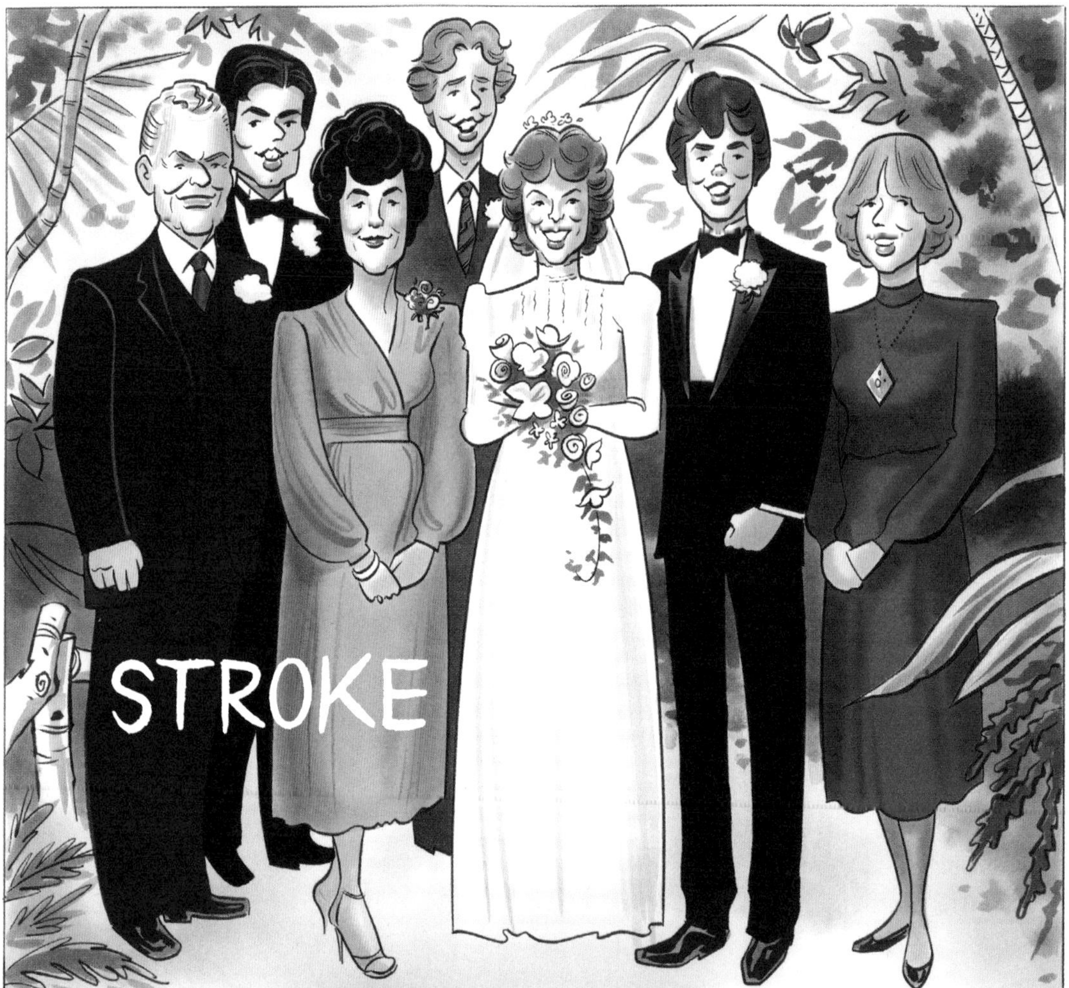
STROKE

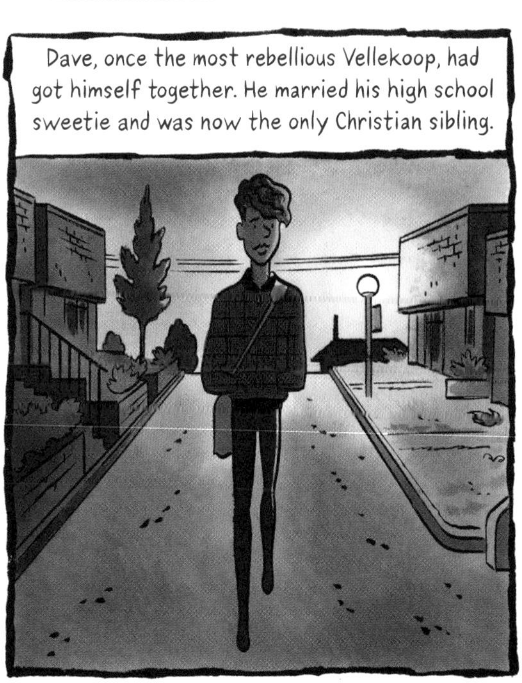
Dave, once the most rebellious Vellekoop, had got himself together. He married his high school sweetie and was now the only Christian sibling.

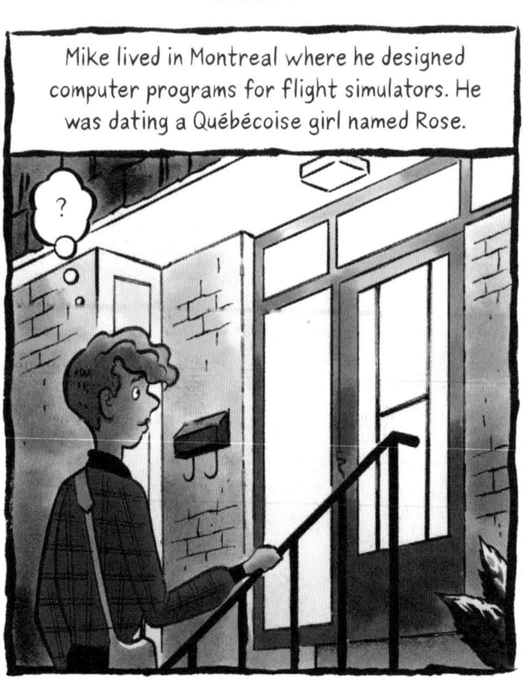
Mike lived in Montreal where he designed computer programs for flight simulators. He was dating a Québécoise girl named Rose.
?

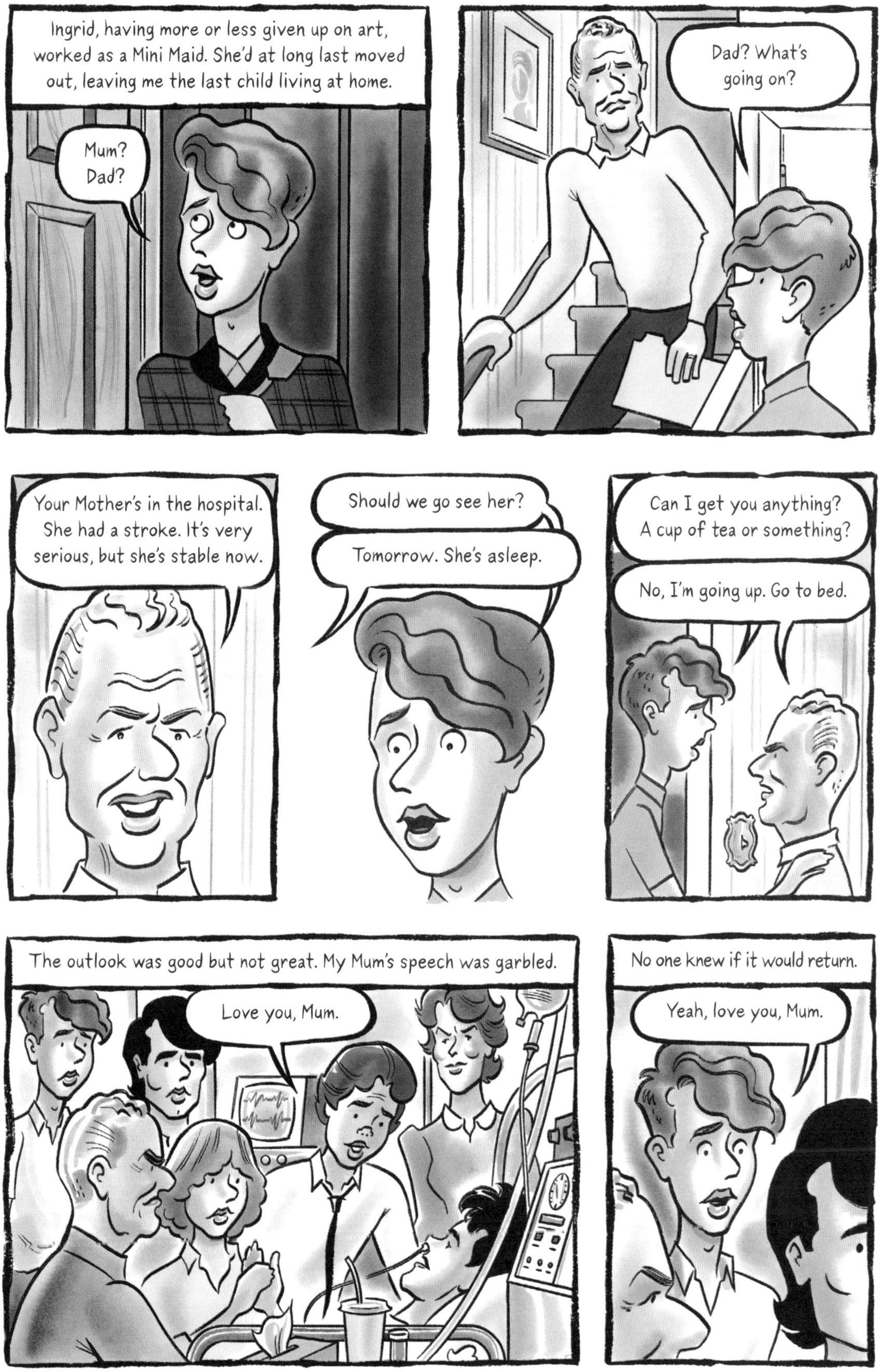
Ingrid, having more or less given up on art, worked as a Mini Maid. She'd at long last moved out, leaving me the last child living at home.
Mum? Dad?
Dad? What's going on?
Your Mother's in the hospital. She had a stroke. It's very serious, but she's stable now.
Should we go see her?
Tomorrow. She's asleep.
Can I get you anything? A cup of tea or something?
No, I'm going up. Go to bed.
The outlook was good but not great. My Mum's speech was garbled.
Love you, Mum.
No one knew if it would return.
Yeah, love you, Mum.

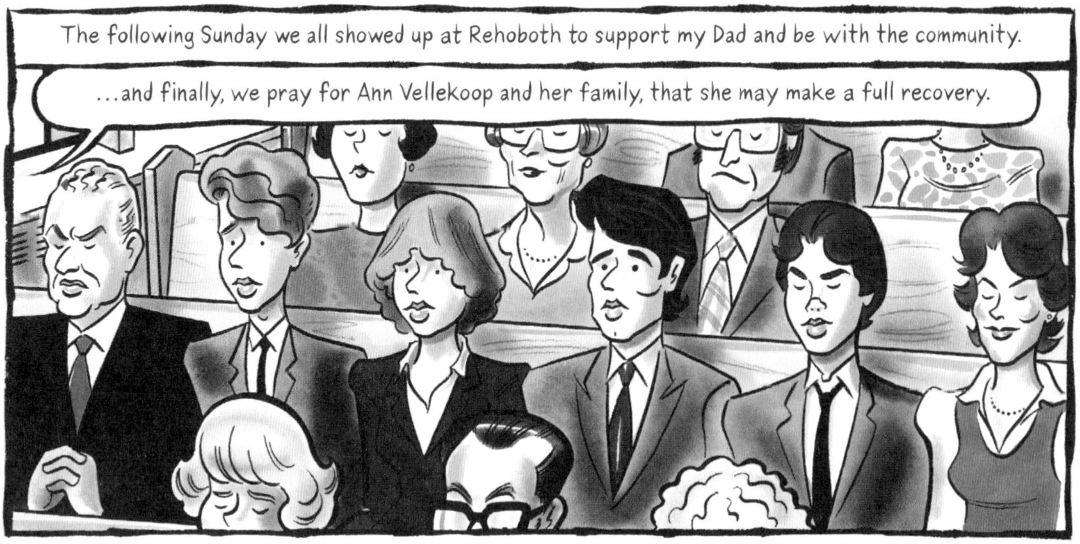
The following Sunday we all showed up at Rehoboth to support my Dad and be with the community.
...and finally, we pray for Ann Vellekoop and her family, that she may make a full recovery.

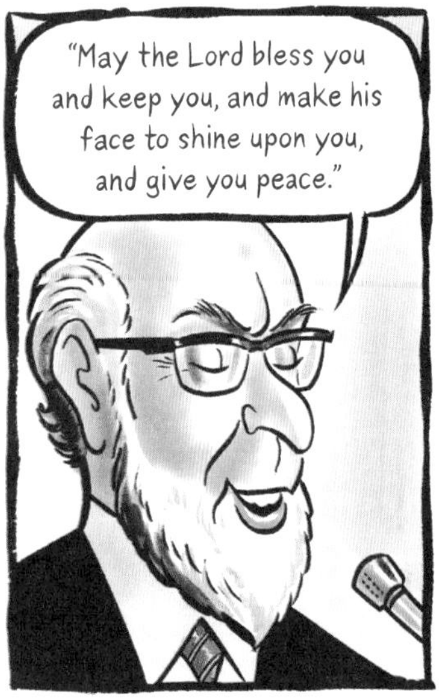
"May the Lord bless you and keep you, and make his face to shine upon you, and give you peace."

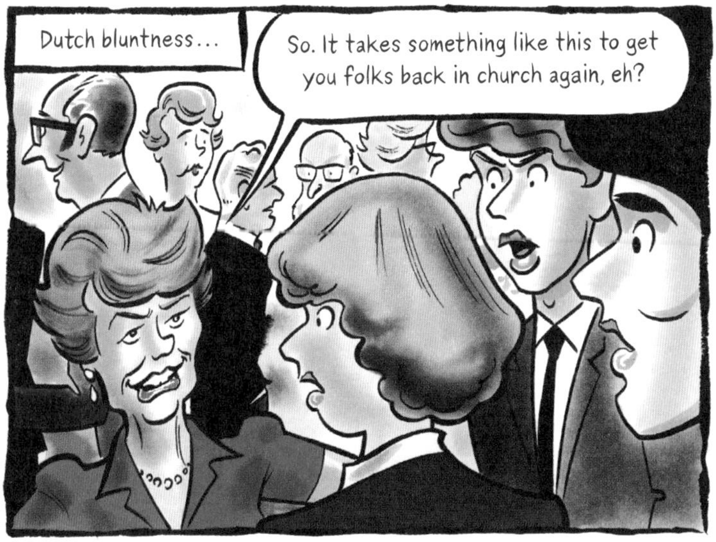
Dutch bluntness...
So. It takes something like this to get you folks back in church again, eh?

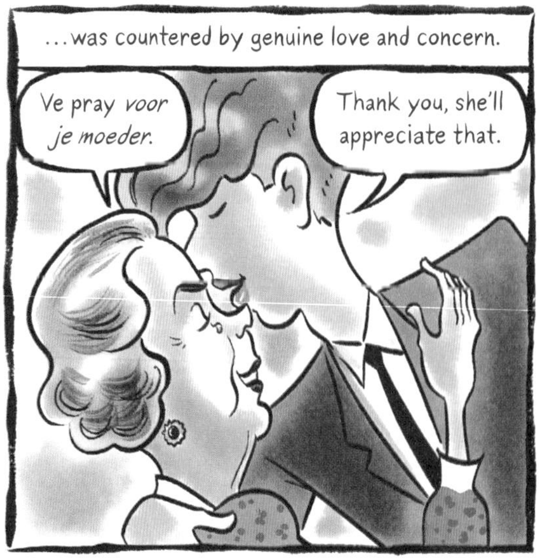
...was countered by genuine love and concern.
Ve pray *voor je moeder.*
Thank you, she'll appreciate that.

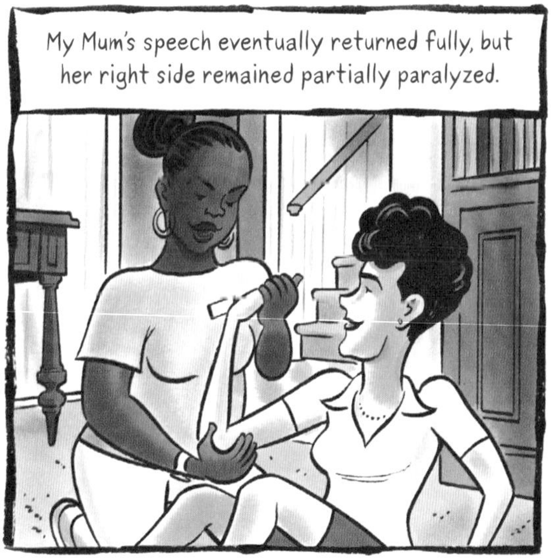
My Mum's speech eventually returned fully, but her right side remained partially paralyzed.

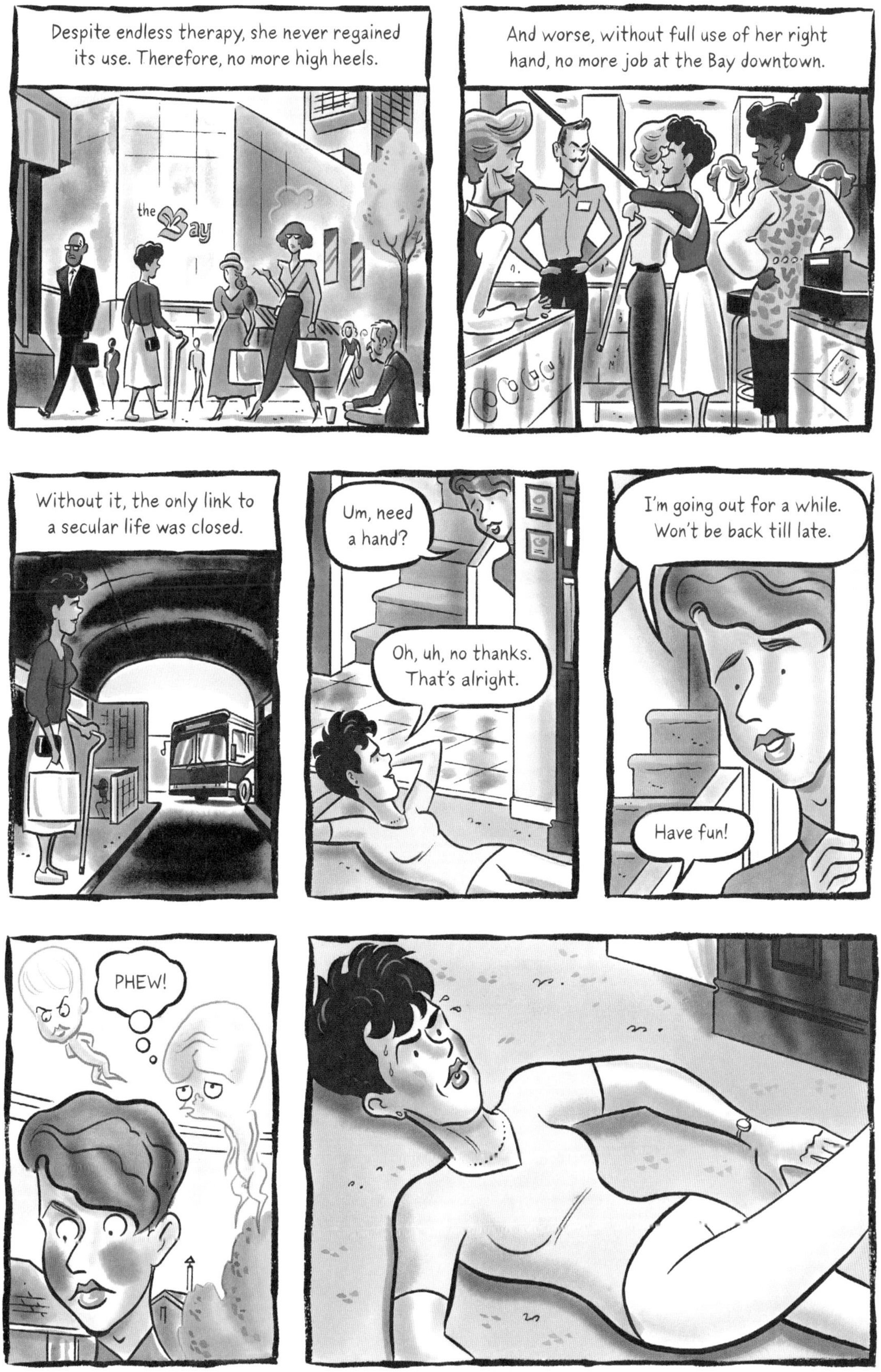
Despite endless therapy, she never regained its use. Therefore, no more high heels.
the Bay
And worse, without full use of her right hand, no more job at the Bay downtown.
Without it, the only link to a secular life was closed.
Um, need a hand?
Oh, uh, no thanks. That's alright.
I'm going out for a while. Won't be back till late.
Have fun!
PHEW!

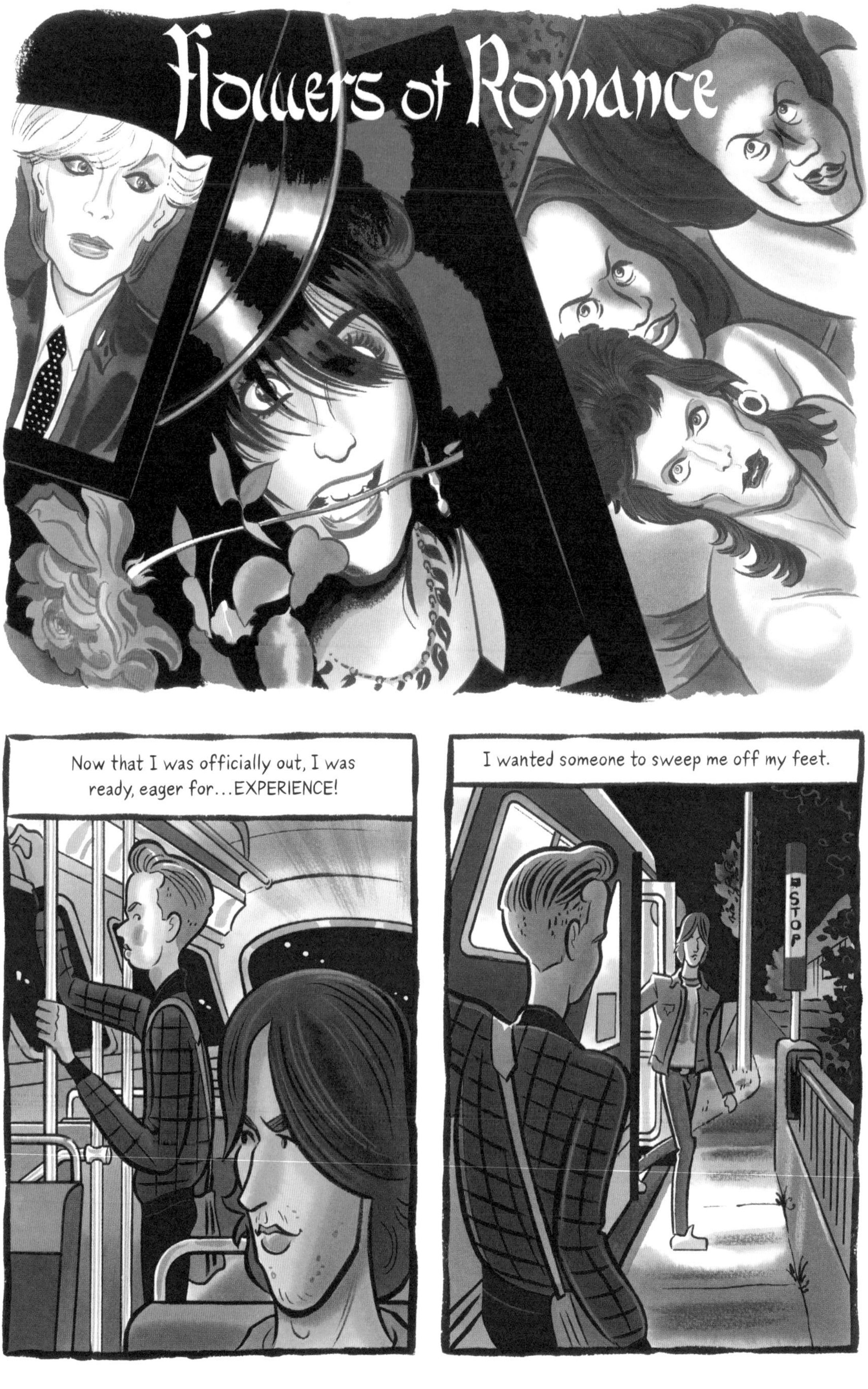
Flowers of Romance
Now that I was officially out, I was ready, eager for...EXPERIENCE!
I wanted someone to sweep me off my feet.
STOP

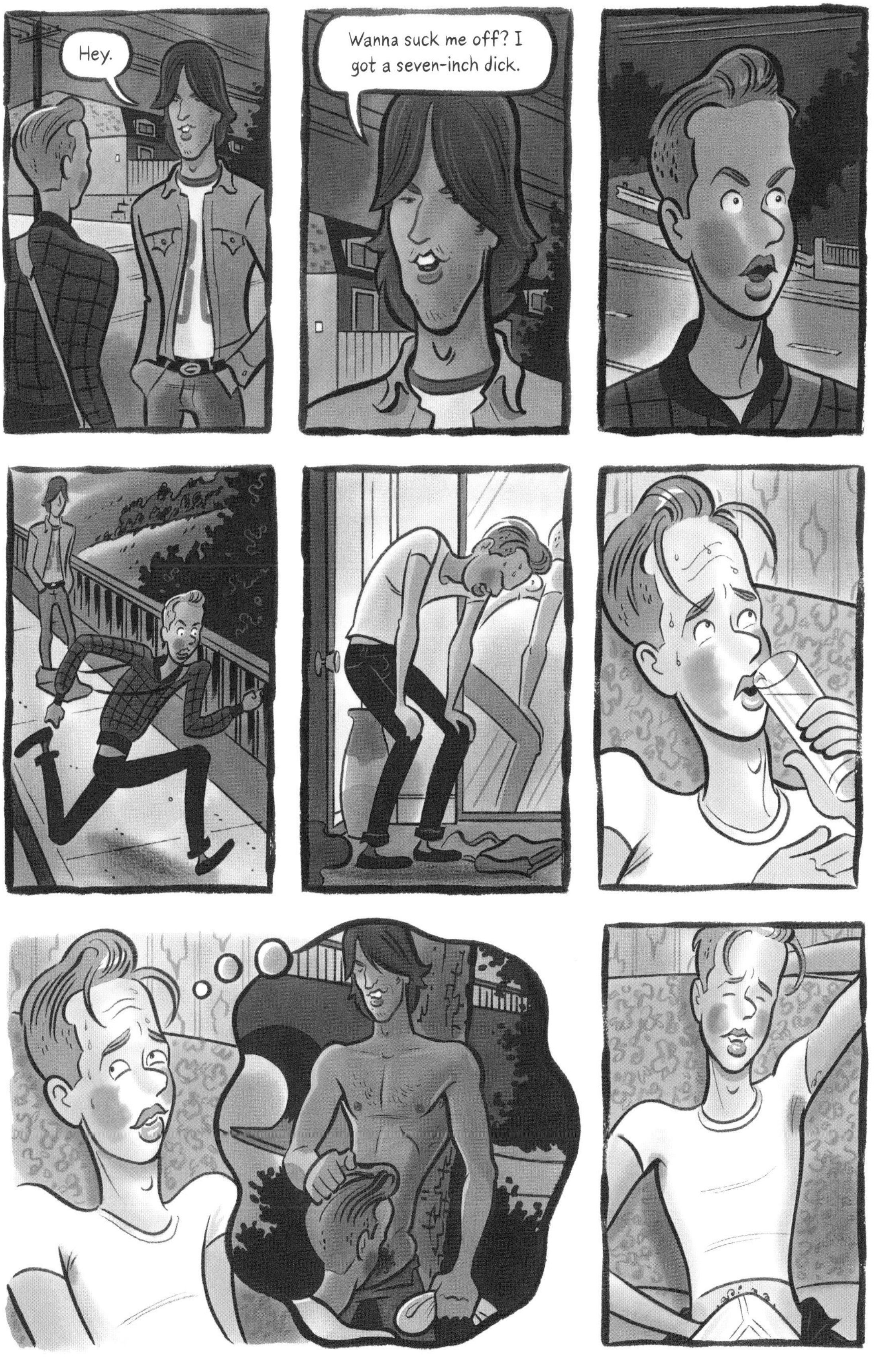
Hey.
Wanna suck me off? I got a seven-inch dick.

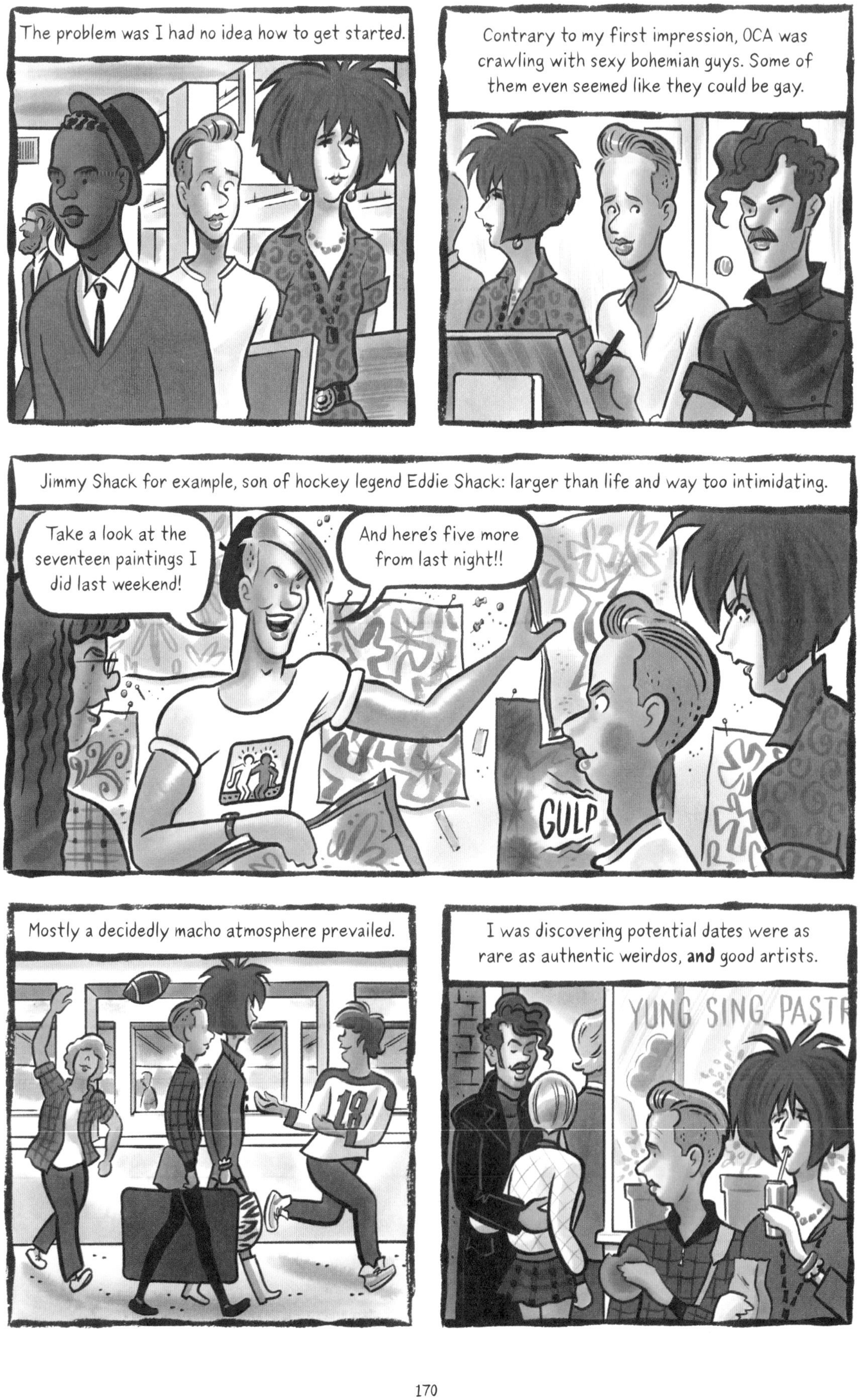
The problem was I had no idea how to get started.
Contrary to my first impression, OCA was crawling with sexy bohemian guys. Some of them even seemed like they could be gay.
Jimmy Shack for example, son of hockey legend Eddie Shack: larger than life and way too intimidating.
Take a look at the seventeen paintings I did last weekend!
And here's five more from last night!!
GULP
Mostly a decidedly macho atmosphere prevailed.
18
I was discovering potential dates were as rare as authentic weirdos, **and** good artists.
YUNG SING PASTR

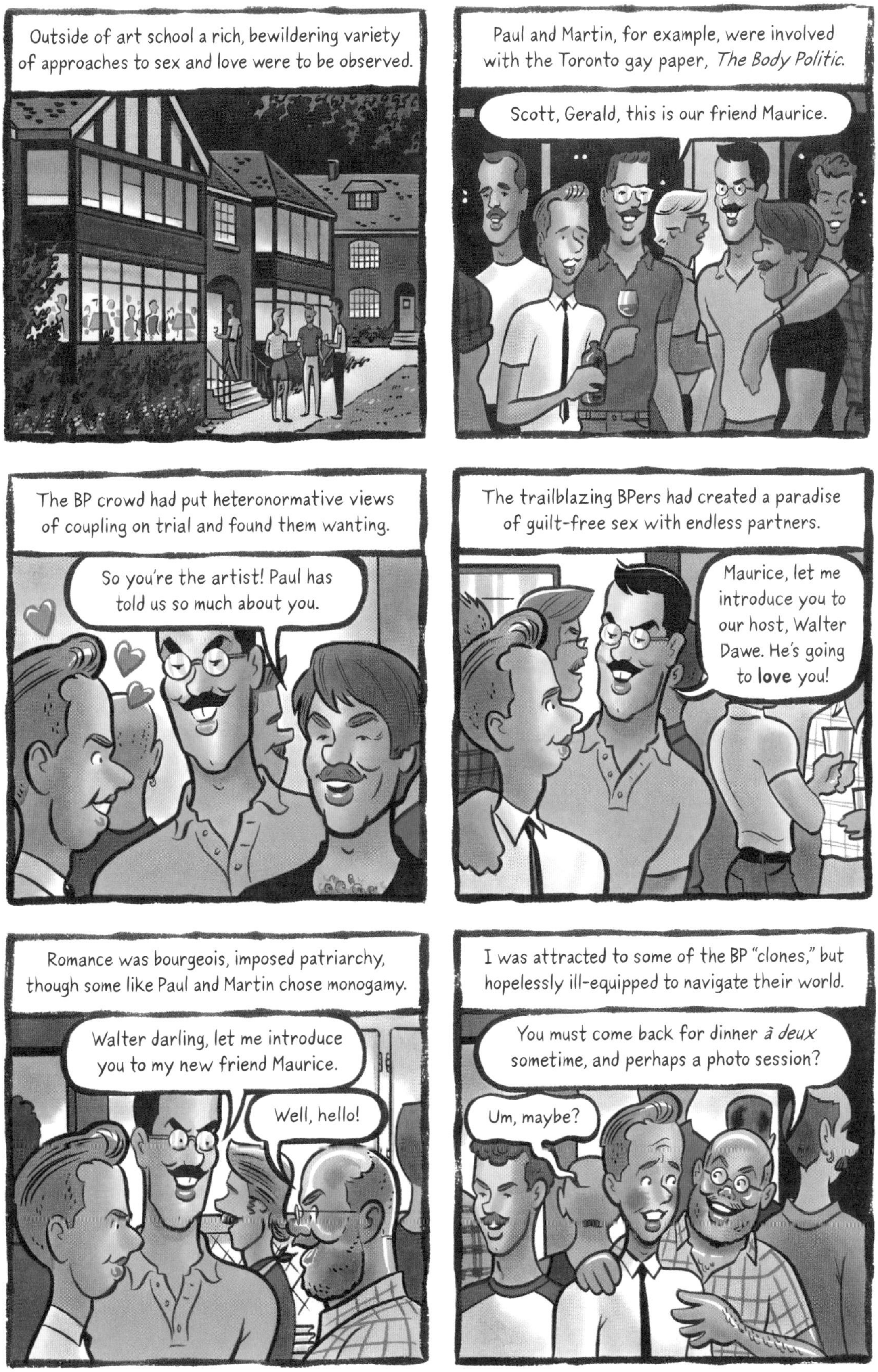
Outside of art school a rich, bewildering variety of approaches to sex and love were to be observed.
Paul and Martin, for example, were involved with the Toronto gay paper, *The Body Politic*.
Scott, Gerald, this is our friend Maurice.
The BP crowd had put heteronormative views of coupling on trial and found them wanting.
So you're the artist! Paul has told us so much about you.
The trailblazing BPers had created a paradise of guilt-free sex with endless partners.
Maurice, let me introduce you to our host, Walter Dawe. He's going to **love** you!
Romance was bourgeois, imposed patriarchy, though some like Paul and Martin chose monogamy.
Walter darling, let me introduce you to my new friend Maurice.
Well, hello!
I was attracted to some of the BP "clones," but hopelessly ill-equipped to navigate their world.
You must come back for dinner *à deux* sometime, and perhaps a photo session?
Um, maybe?

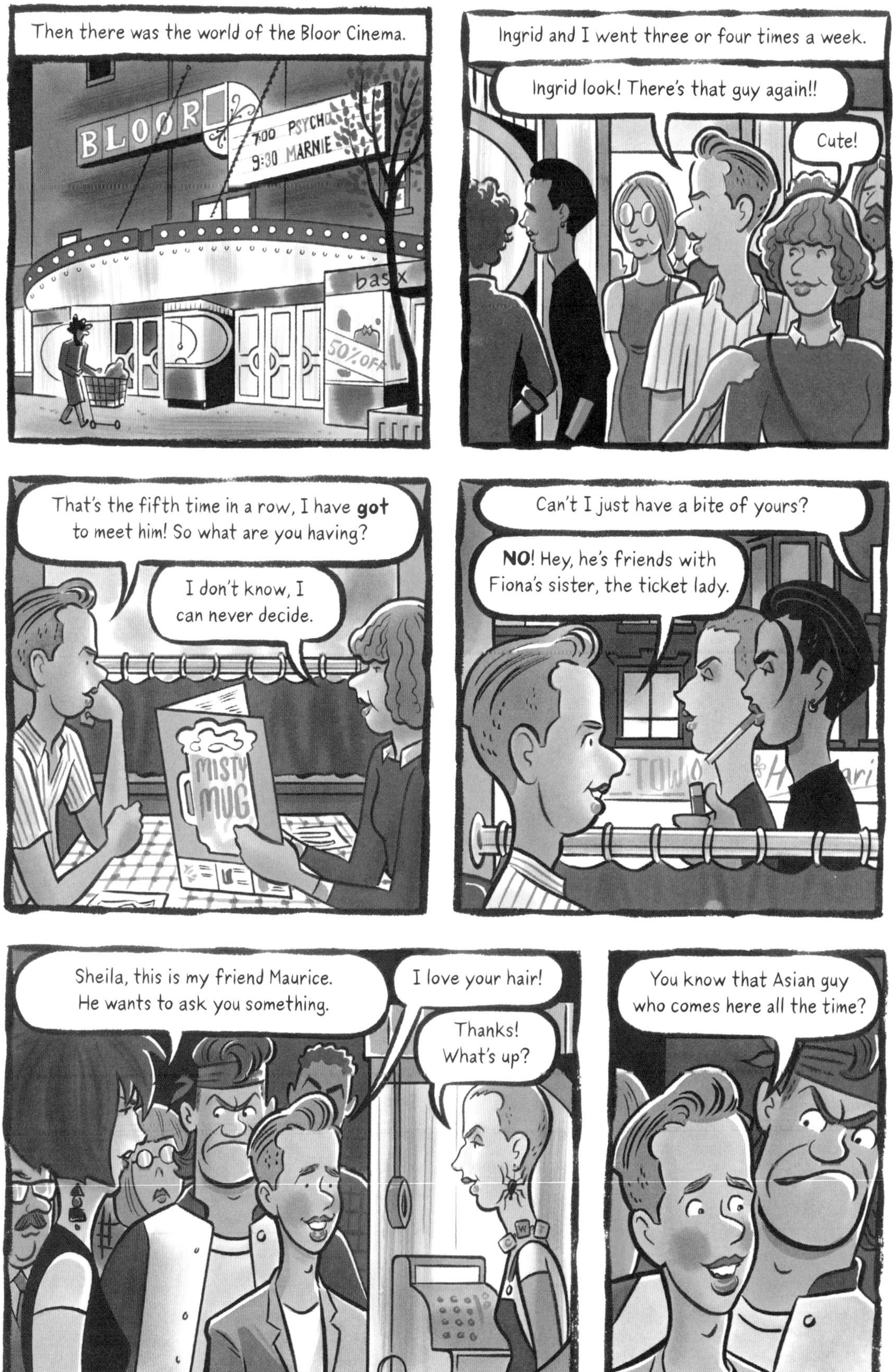
Then there was the world of the Bloor Cinema.
BLOOR
7:00 PSYCHO
9:30 MARNIE
50% OFF
Ingrid and I went three or four times a week.
Ingrid look! There's that guy again!!
Cute!
That's the fifth time in a row, I have **got** to meet him! So what are you having?
I don't know, I can never decide.
MISTY MUG
Can't I just have a bite of yours?
NO! Hey, he's friends with Fiona's sister, the ticket lady.
Sheila, this is my friend Maurice. He wants to ask you something.
I love your hair!
Thanks! What's up?
You know that Asian guy who comes here all the time?

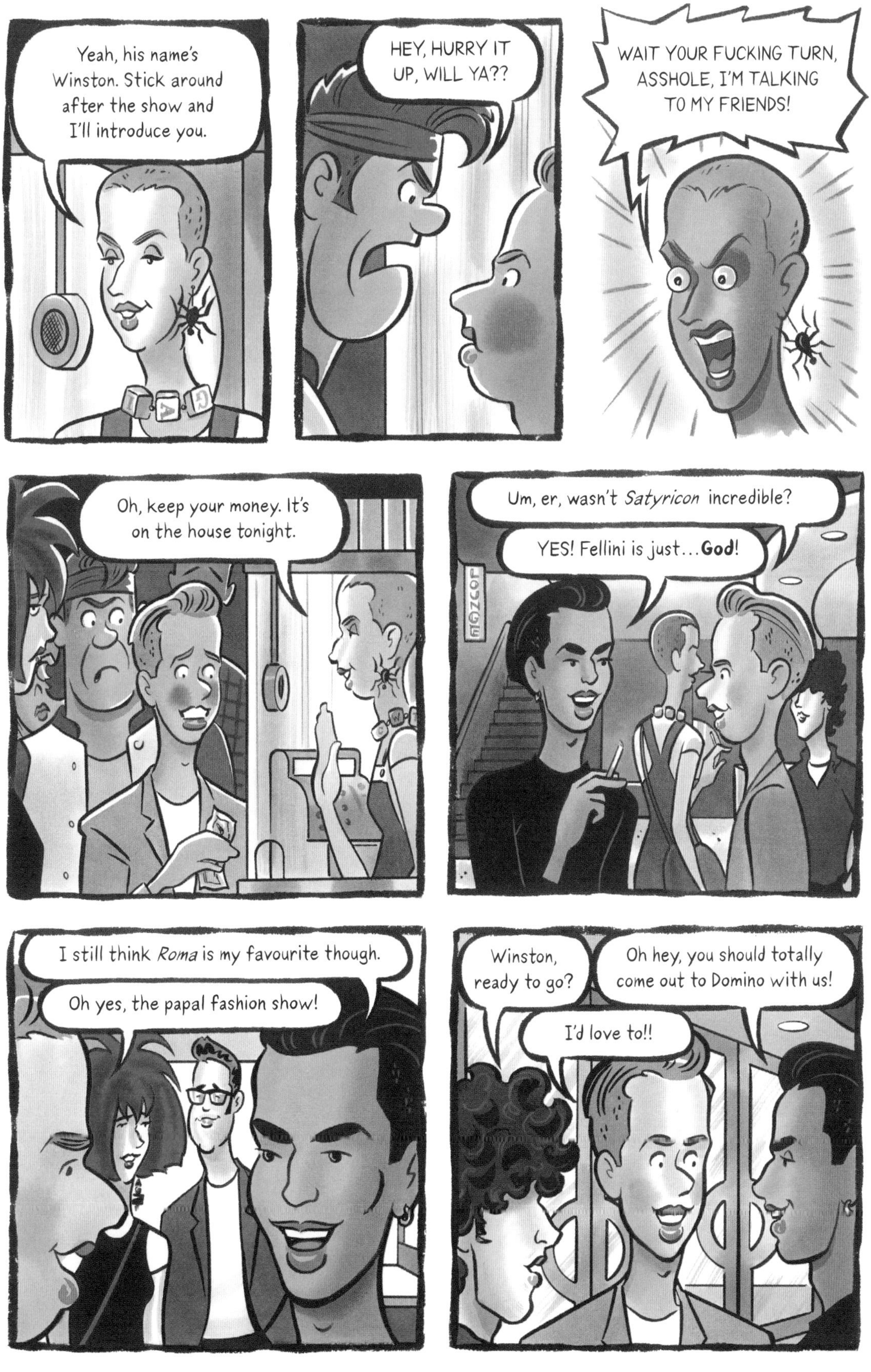
Yeah, his name's Winston. Stick around after the show and I'll introduce you.
HEY, HURRY IT UP, WILL YA??
WAIT YOUR FUCKING TURN, ASSHOLE, I'M TALKING TO MY FRIENDS!
Oh, keep your money. It's on the house tonight.
Um, er, wasn't *Satyricon* incredible?
YES! Fellini is just...**God**!
I still think *Roma* is my favourite though.
Oh yes, the papal fashion show!
Winston, ready to go?
Oh hey, you should totally come out to Domino with us!
I'd love to!!

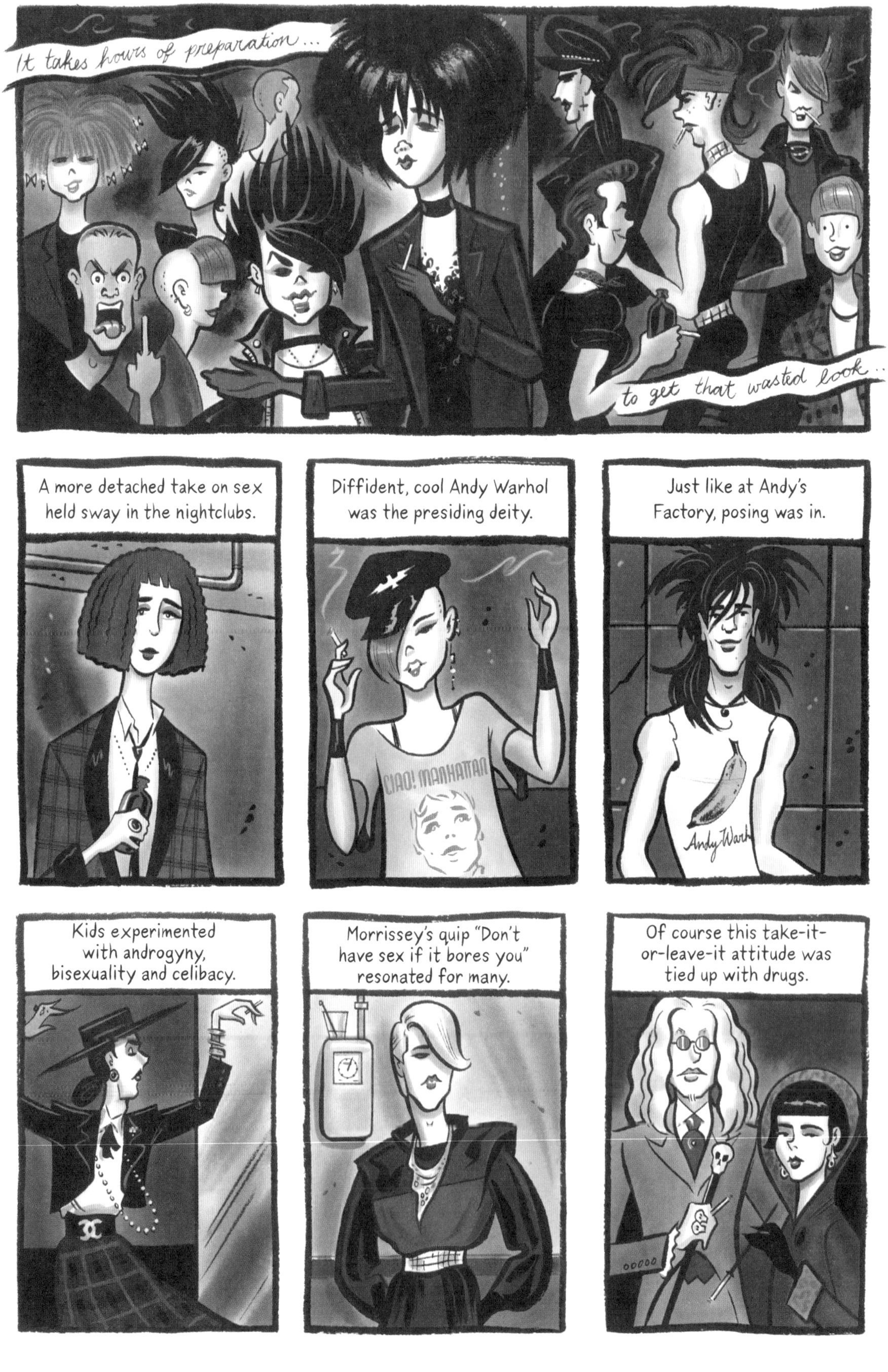
It takes hours of preparation...
to get that wasted look...
A more detached take on sex held sway in the nightclubs.
Diffident, cool Andy Warhol was the presiding deity.
CIAO! MANHATTAN
Just like at Andy's Factory, posing was in.
Andy Warh
Kids experimented with androgyny, bisexuality and celibacy.
Morrissey's quip "Don't have sex if it bores you" resonated for many.
Of course this take-it-or-leave-it attitude was tied up with drugs.

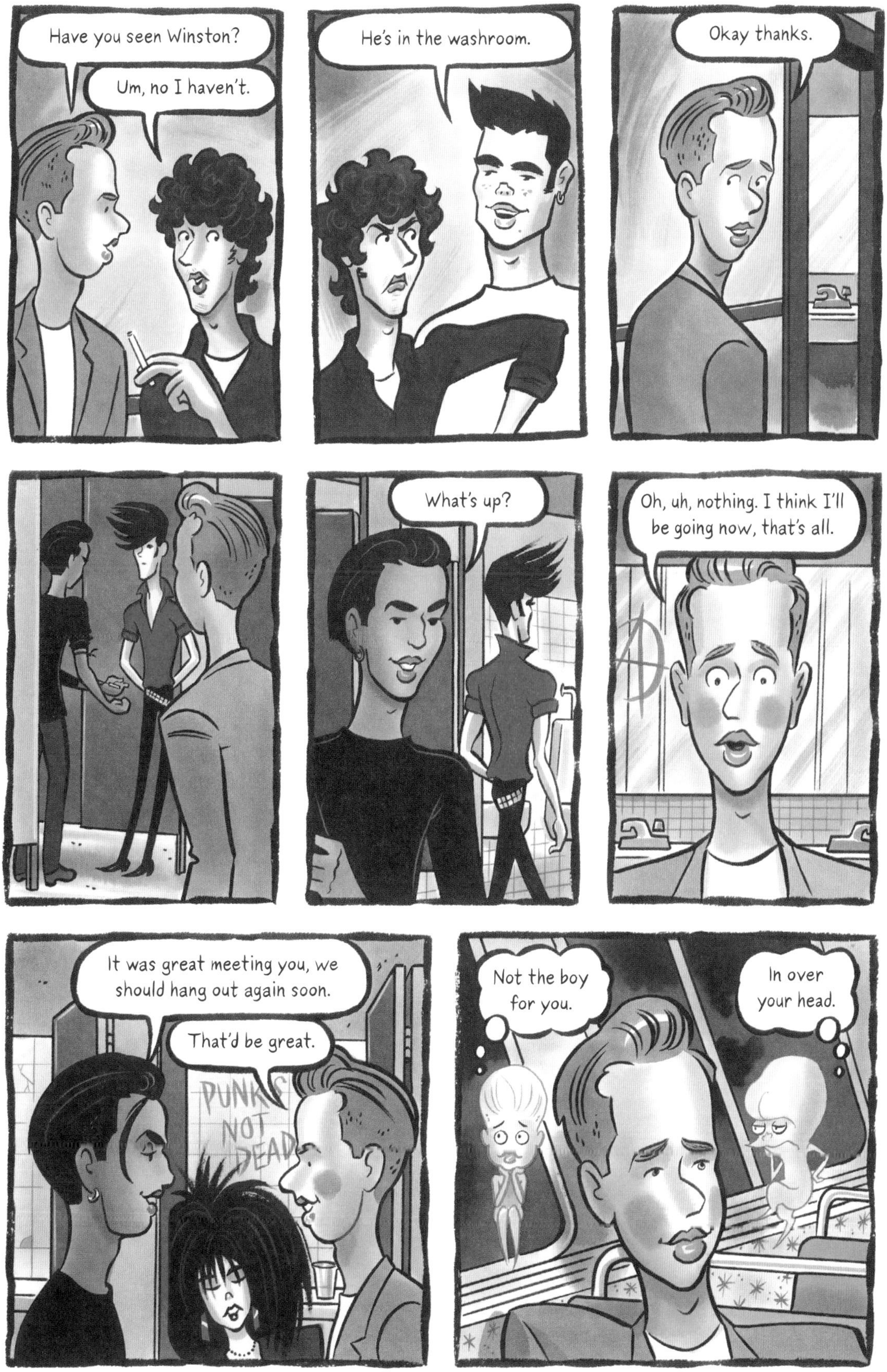
Have you seen Winston?
Um, no I haven't.
He's in the washroom.
Okay thanks.
What's up?
Oh, uh, nothing. I think I'll be going now, that's all.
It was great meeting you, we should hang out again soon.
That'd be great.
PUNKS NOT DEAD
Not the boy for you.
In over your head.

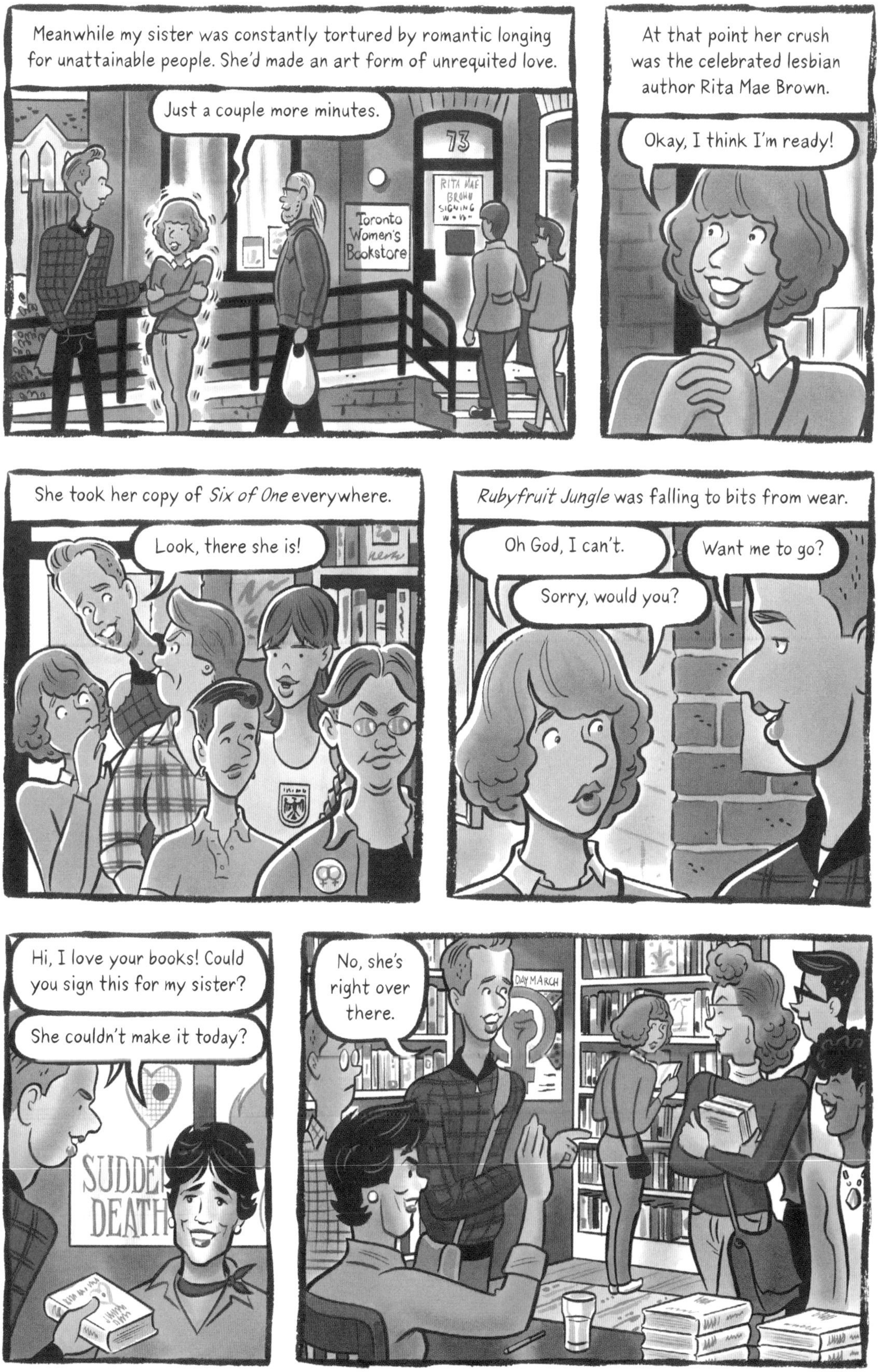
Meanwhile my sister was constantly tortured by romantic longing for unattainable people. She'd made an art form of unrequited love.
Just a couple more minutes.
73
Toronto Women's Bookstore
At that point her crush was the celebrated lesbian author Rita Mae Brown.
Okay, I think I'm ready!
She took her copy of *Six of One* everywhere.
Look, there she is!
Rubyfruit Jungle was falling to bits from wear.
Oh God, I can't.
Want me to go?
Sorry, would you?
Hi, I love your books! Could you sign this for my sister?
She couldn't make it today?
No, she's right over there.
DAY MARCH

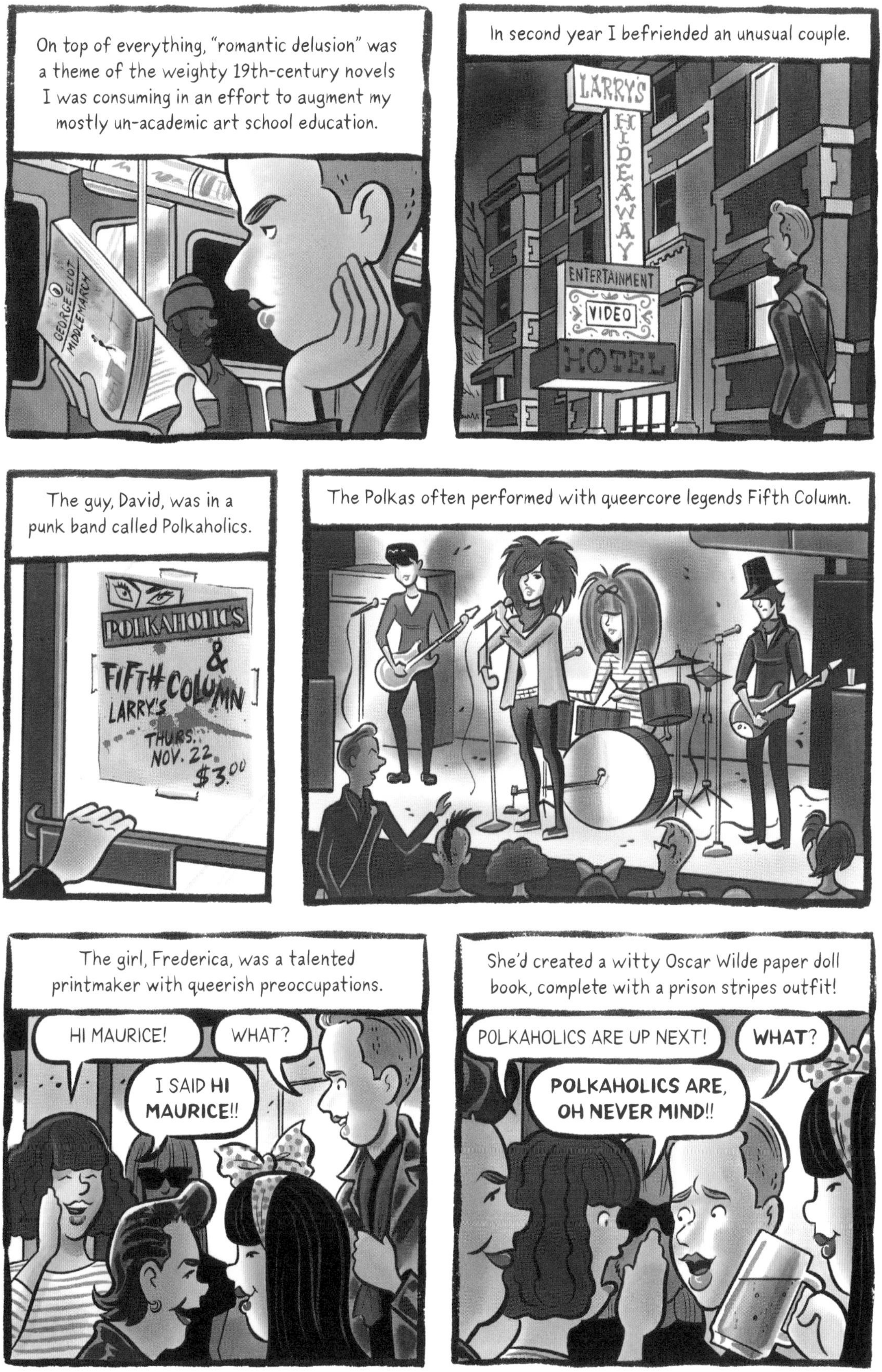
On top of everything, "romantic delusion" was a theme of the weighty 19th-century novels I was consuming in an effort to augment my mostly un-academic art school education.
GEORGE ELIOT
MIDDLEMARCH
In second year I befriended an unusual couple.
LARRY'S
HIDEAWAY
ENTERTAINMENT
VIDEO
HOTEL
The guy, David, was in a punk band called Polkaholics.
POLKAHOLICS
&
FIFTH COLUMN
LARRY'S
THURS.
NOV. 22
$3.00
The Polkas often performed with queercore legends Fifth Column.
The girl, Frederica, was a talented printmaker with queerish preoccupations.
HI MAURICE!
WHAT?
I SAID **HI MAURICE!!**
She'd created a witty Oscar Wilde paper doll book, complete with a prison stripes outfit!
POLKAHOLICS ARE UP NEXT!
WHAT?
POLKAHOLICS ARE, OH NEVER MIND!!

Fred and David lived together, but they were in an open relationship.

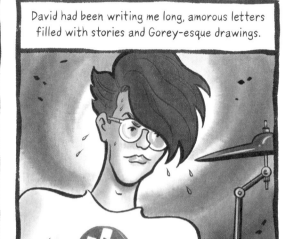

David had been writing me long, amorous letters filled with stories and Gorey-esque drawings.

Only dimly aware he wrote such letters to everyone, I was blindly swept off my feet.

Alas, just like in a novel, obstacles stood in our way: where to be alone for example.

I longed to swoon in his daylight-deprived arms, but not in a filthy Larry's Hideaway hotel room.

I lived in a constant, miserable state of unfulfilled longing, familiar from childhood.

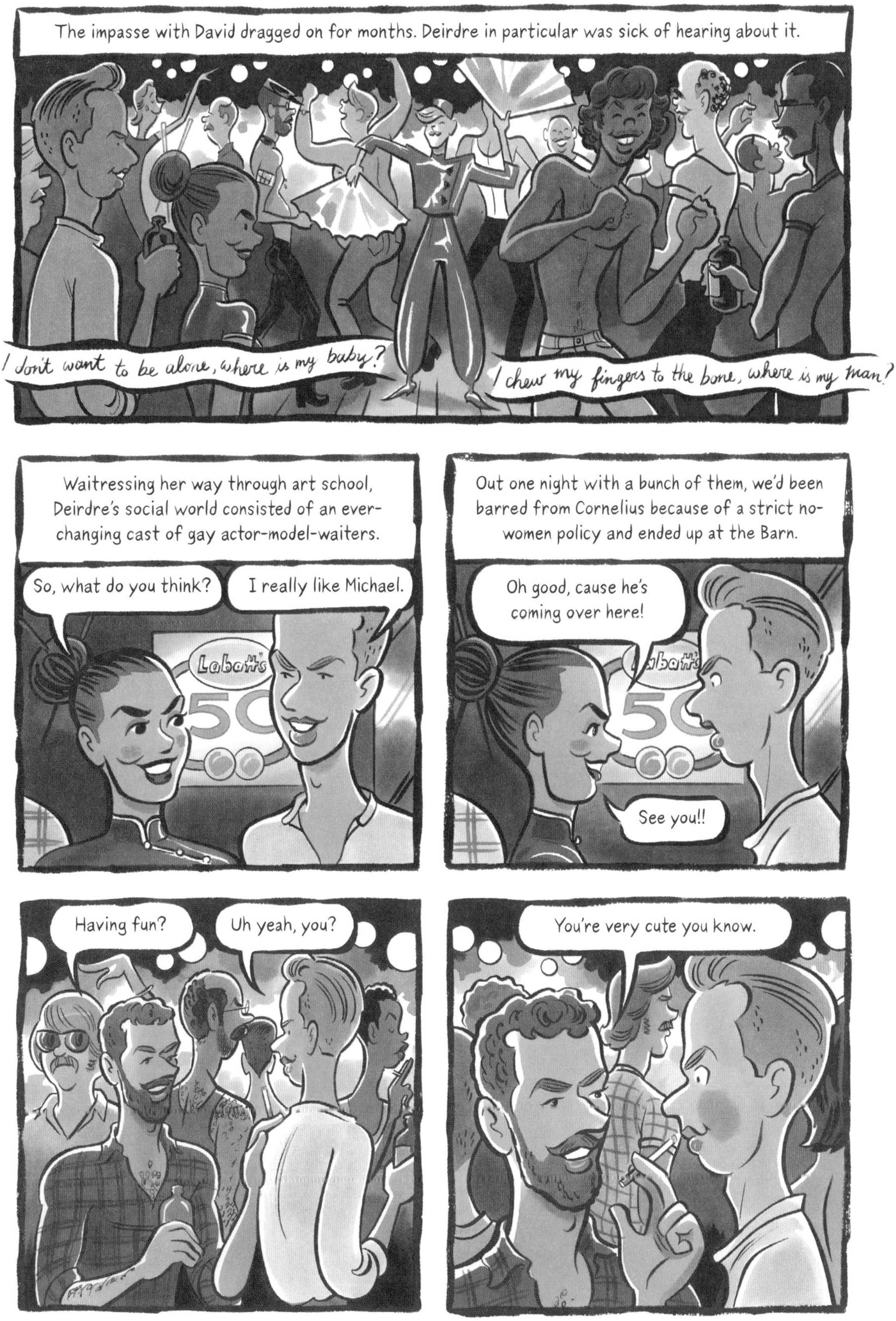
The impasse with David dragged on for months. Deirdre in particular was sick of hearing about it.
I don't want to be alone, where is my baby?
I chew my fingers to the bone, where is my man?
Waitressing her way through art school, Deirdre's social world consisted of an ever-changing cast of gay actor-model-waiters.
So, what do you think?
I really like Michael.
Labatt's
50
Out one night with a bunch of them, we'd been barred from Cornelius because of a strict no-women policy and ended up at the Barn.
Oh good, cause he's coming over here!
See you!!
Having fun?
Uh yeah, you?
You're very cute you know.

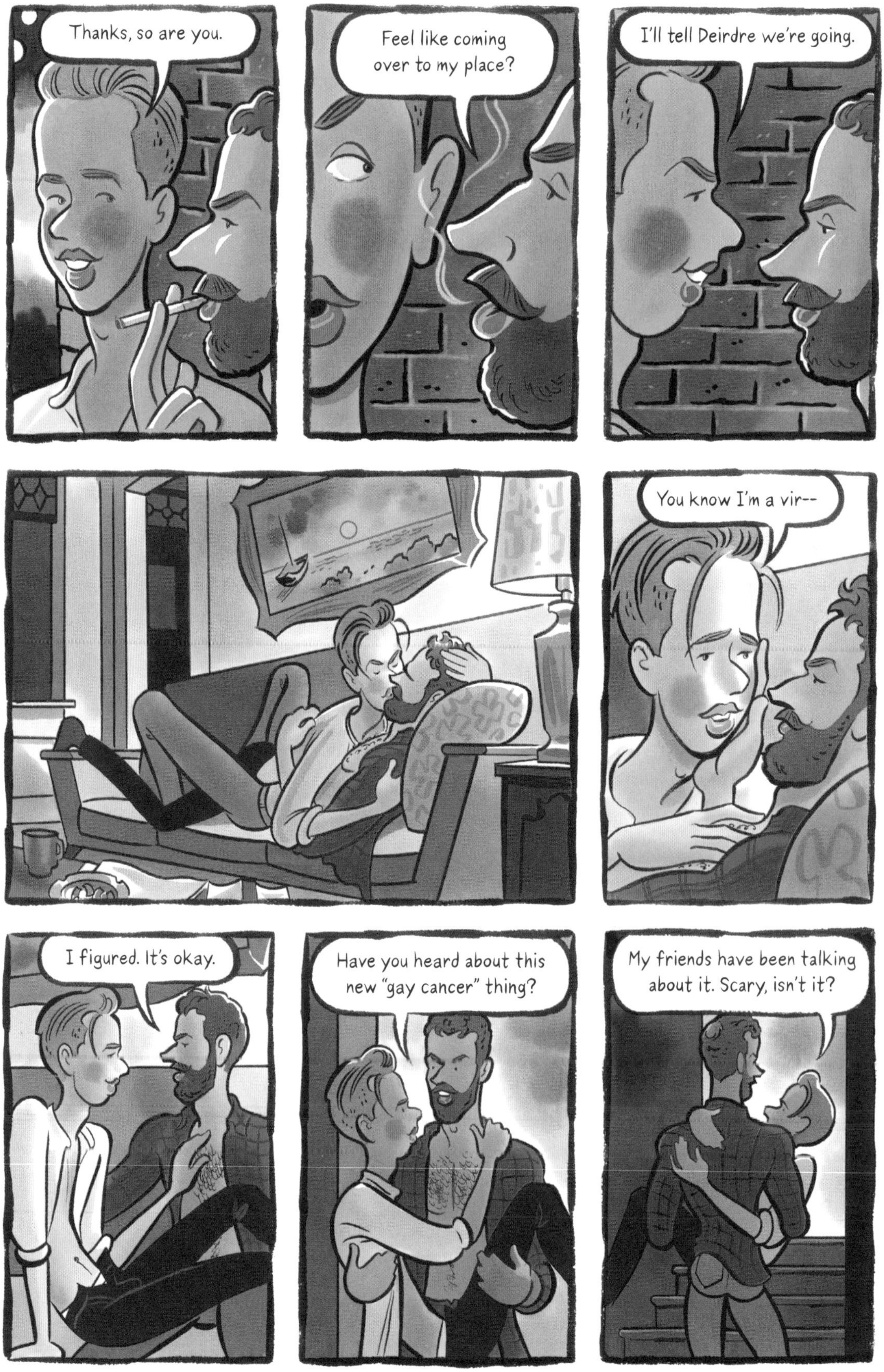
Thanks, so are you.
Feel like coming over to my place?
I'll tell Deirdre we're going.
You know I'm a vir--
I figured. It's okay.
Have you heard about this new "gay cancer" thing?
My friends have been talking about it. Scary, isn't it?

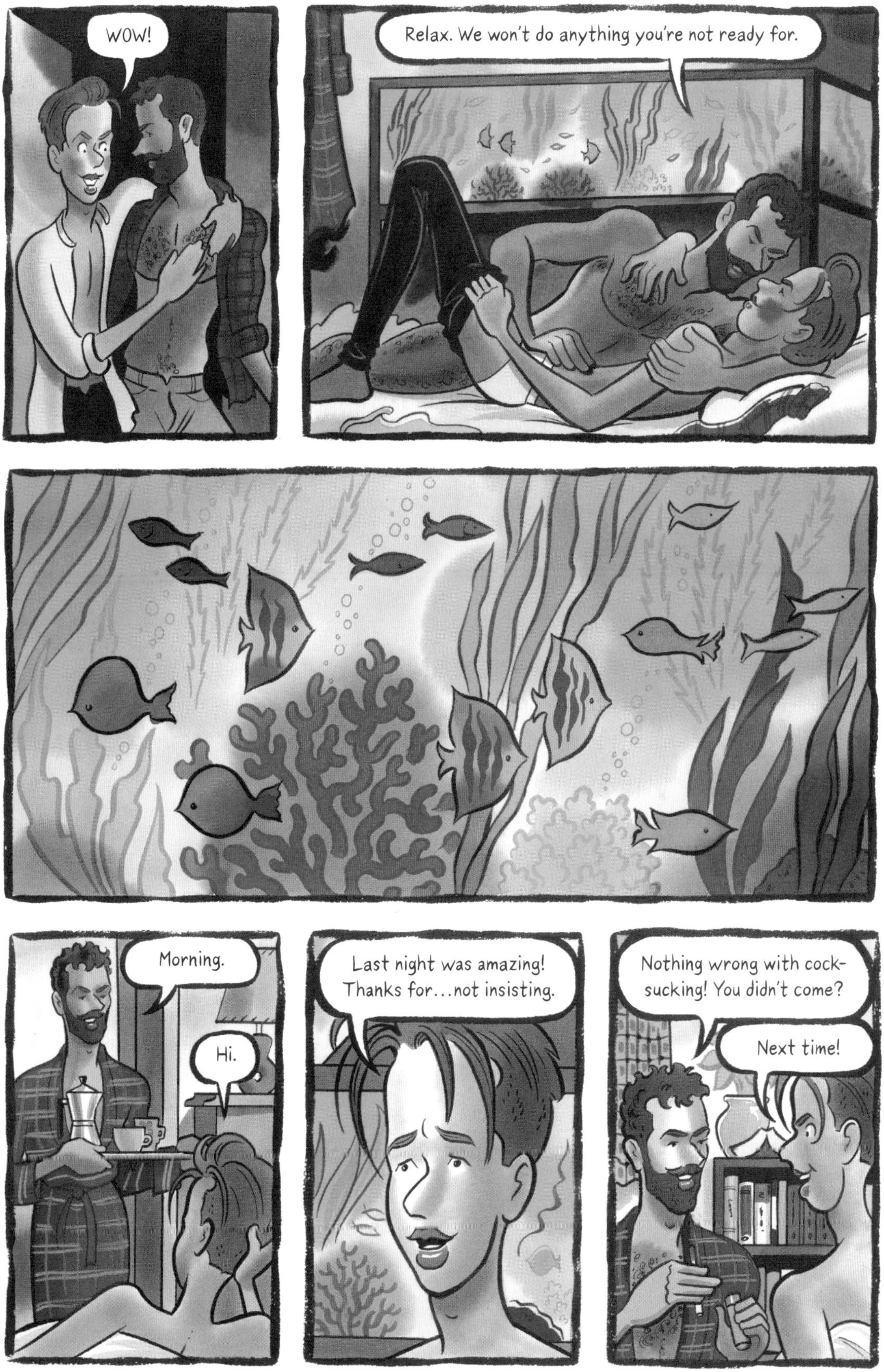
WOW!
Relax. We won't do anything you're not ready for.
Morning.
Hi.
Last night was amazing! Thanks for…not insisting.
Nothing wrong with cock-sucking! You didn't come?
Next time!

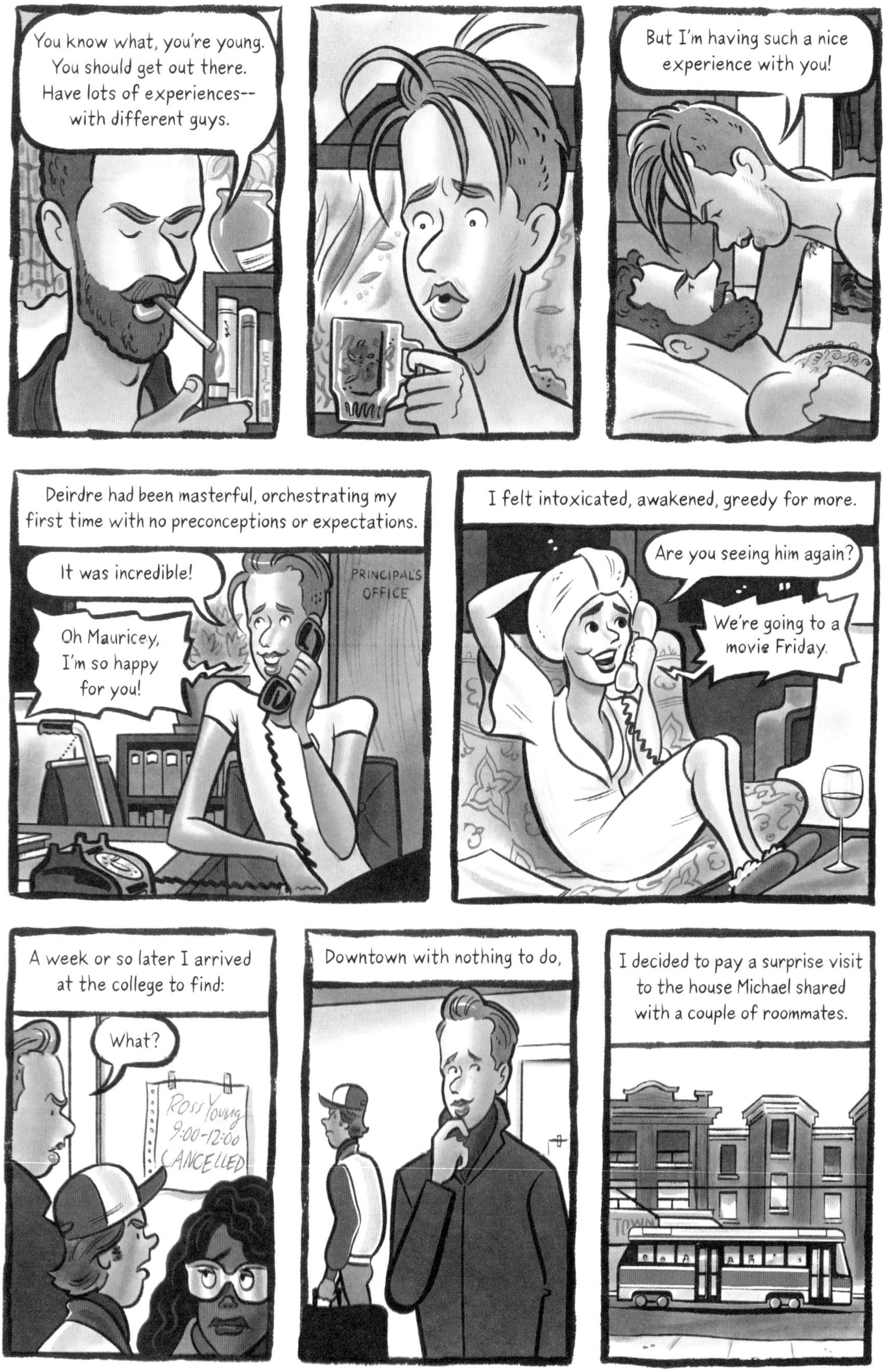
You know what, you're young. You should get out there. Have lots of experiences-- with different guys.
But I'm having such a nice experience with you!
Deirdre had been masterful, orchestrating my first time with no preconceptions or expectations.
It was incredible!
Oh Mauricey, I'm so happy for you!
PRINCIPAL'S OFFICE
I felt intoxicated, awakened, greedy for more.
Are you seeing him again?
We're going to a movie Friday.
A week or so later I arrived at the college to find:
What?
Ross Young 9:00-12:00 CANCELLED
Downtown with nothing to do,
I decided to pay a surprise visit to the house Michael shared with a couple of roommates.

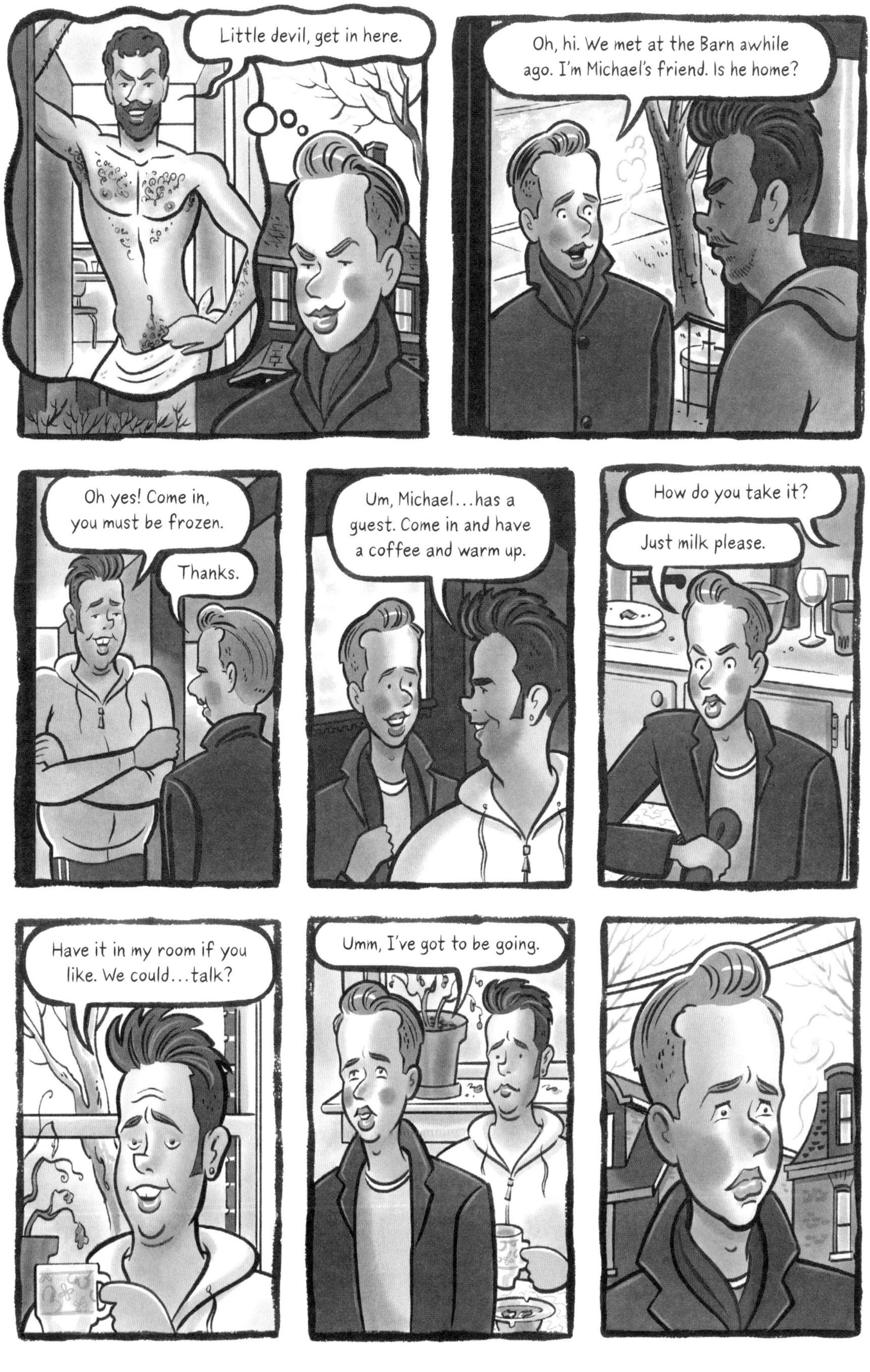
Little devil, get in here.
Oh, hi. We met at the Barn awhile ago. I'm Michael's friend. Is he home?
Oh yes! Come in, you must be frozen.
Thanks.
Um, Michael...has a guest. Come in and have a coffee and warm up.
How do you take it?
Just milk please.
Have it in my room if you like. We could...talk?
Umm, I've got to be going.

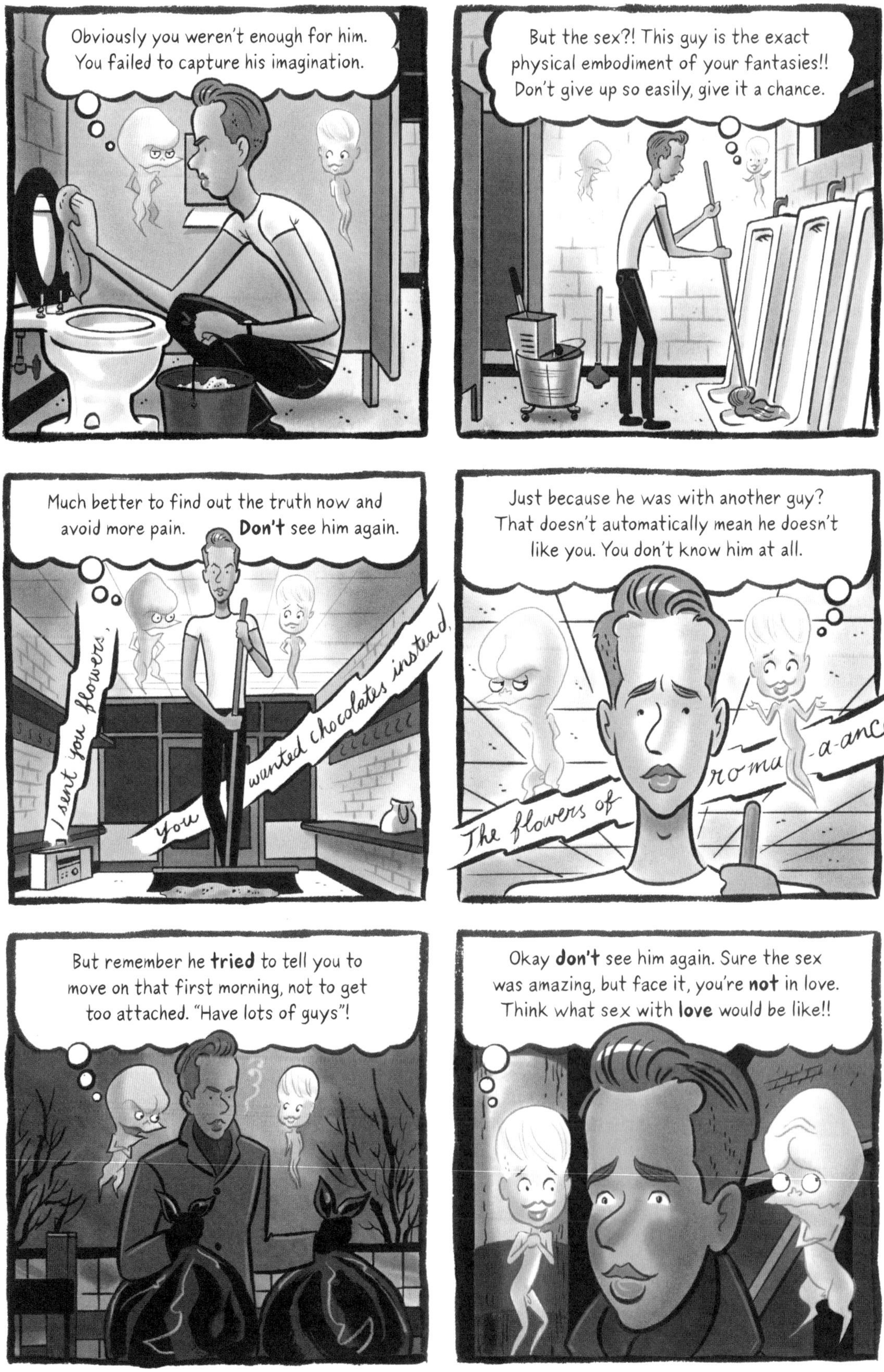
Obviously you weren't enough for him. You failed to capture his imagination.
But the sex?! This guy is the exact physical embodiment of your fantasies!! Don't give up so easily, give it a chance.
Much better to find out the truth now and avoid more pain. **Don't** see him again.
I sent you flowers, you wanted chocolates instead,
Just because he was with another guy? That doesn't automatically mean he doesn't like you. You don't know him at all.
The flowers of roma-a-ance
But remember he **tried** to tell you to move on that first morning, not to get too attached. "Have lots of guys"!
Okay **don't** see him again. Sure the sex was amazing, but face it, you're **not** in love. Think what sex with **love** would be like!!

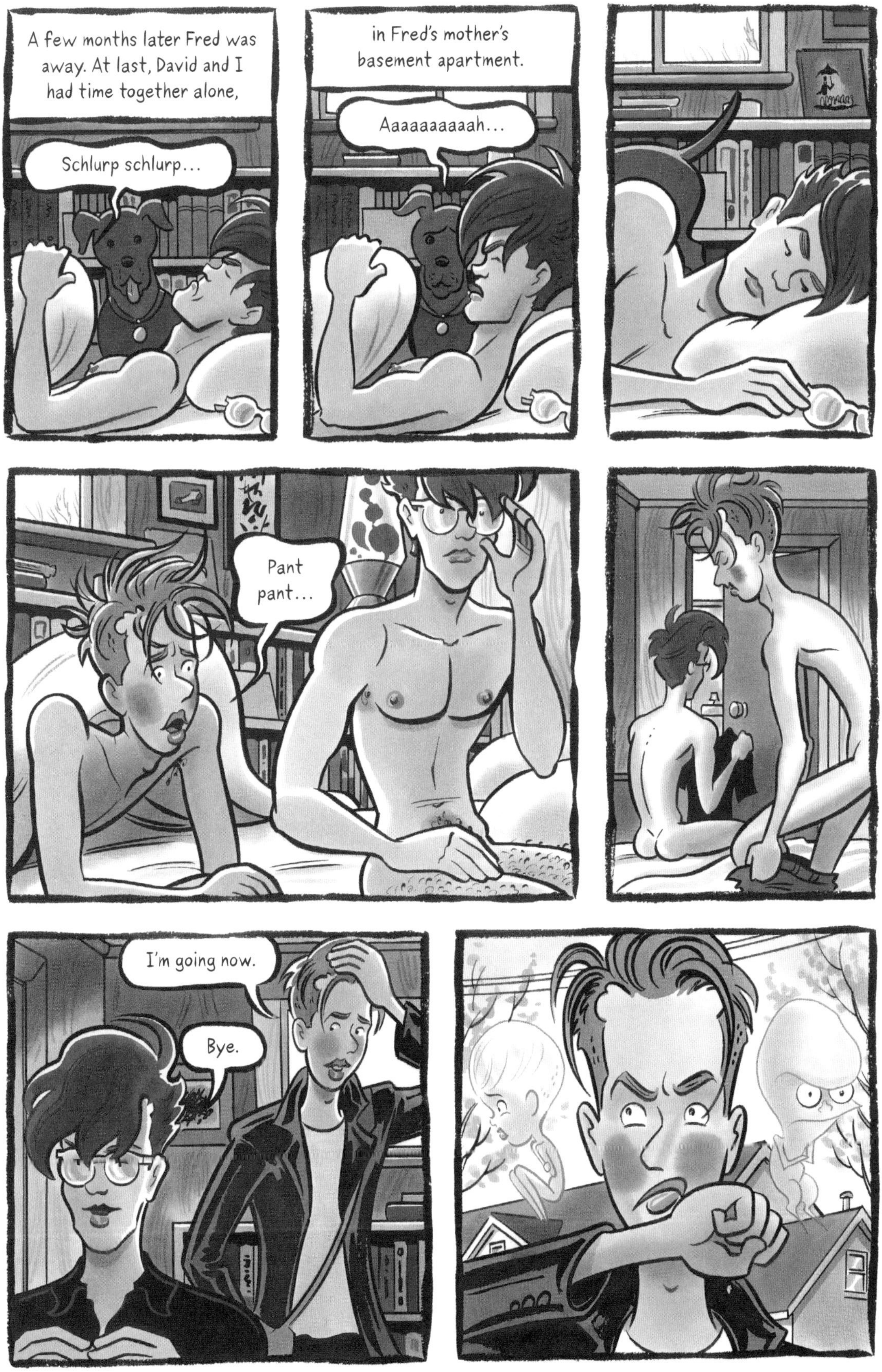
A few months later Fred was away. At last, David and I had time together alone,
Schlurp schlurp...
in Fred's mother's basement apartment.
Aaaaaaaaaah...
Pant pant...
I'm going now.
Bye.

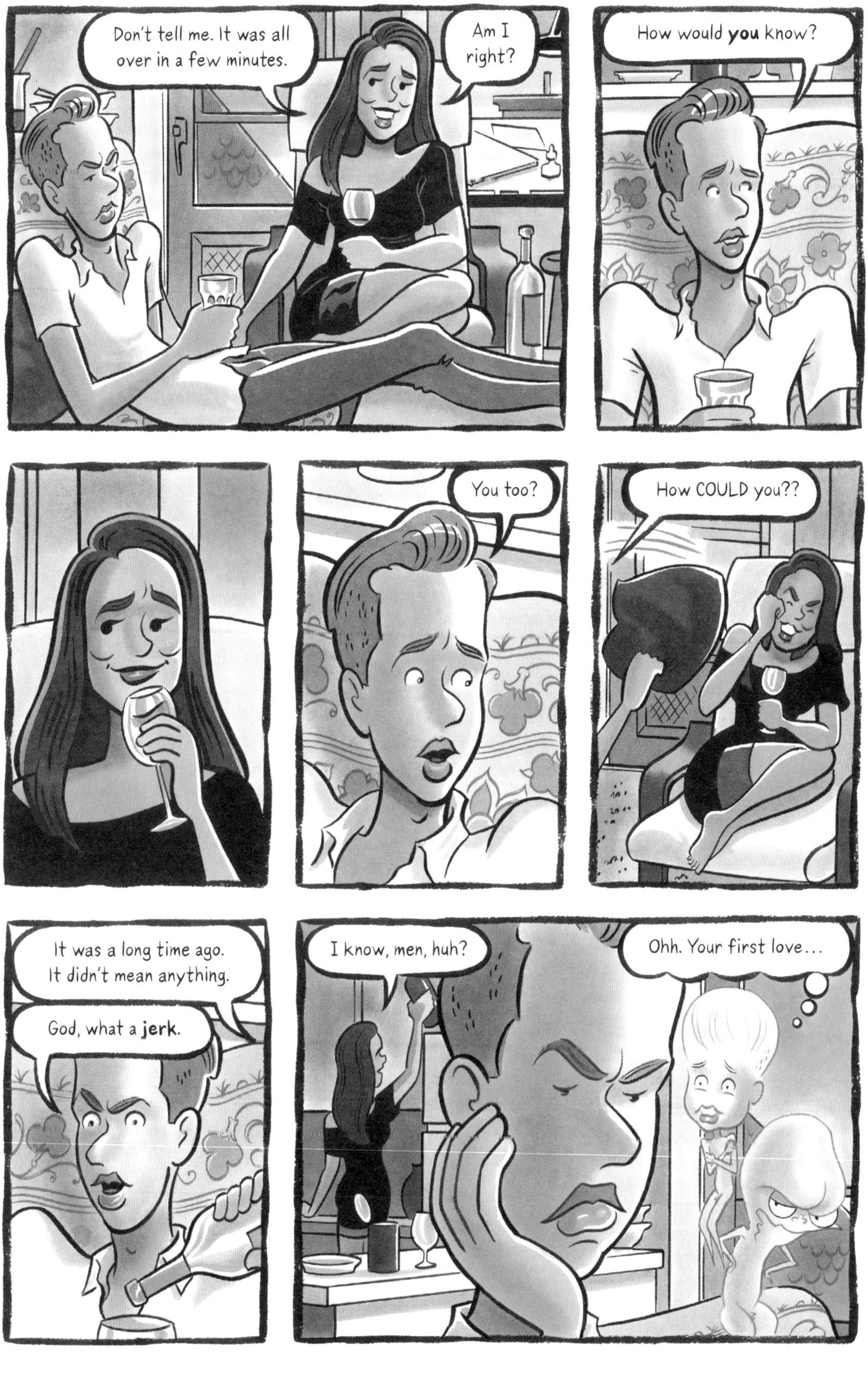
Don't tell me. It was all over in a few minutes.
Am I right?
How would **you** know?
You too?
How COULD you??
It was a long time ago. It didn't mean anything.
God, what a **jerk**.
I know, men, huh?
Ohh. Your first love...

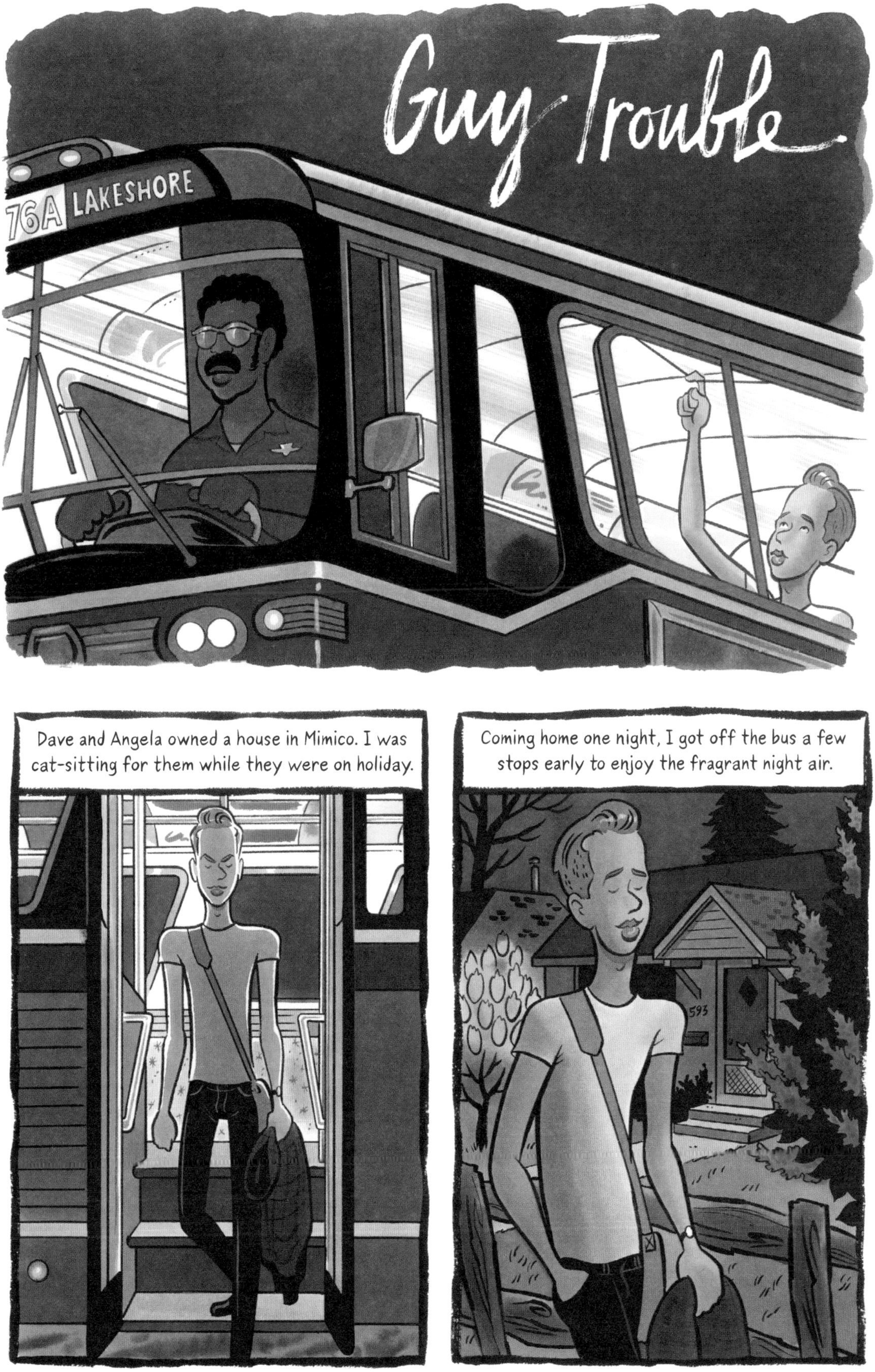
Guy Trouble
76A LAKESHORE
Dave and Angela owned a house in Mimico. I was cat-sitting for them while they were on holiday.
Coming home one night, I got off the bus a few stops early to enjoy the fragrant night air.
593

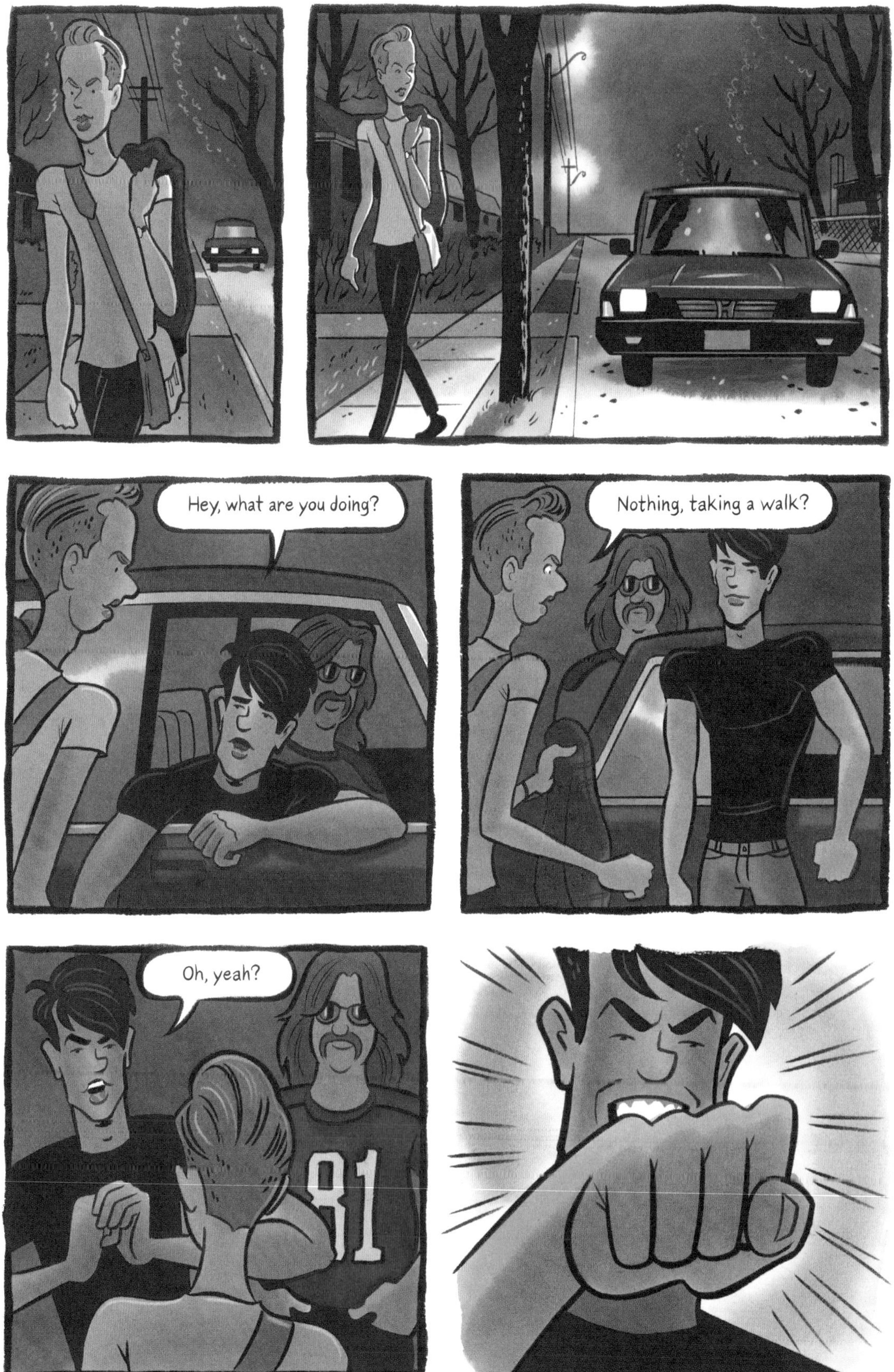
Hey, what are you doing?
Nothing, taking a walk?
Oh, yeah?
81

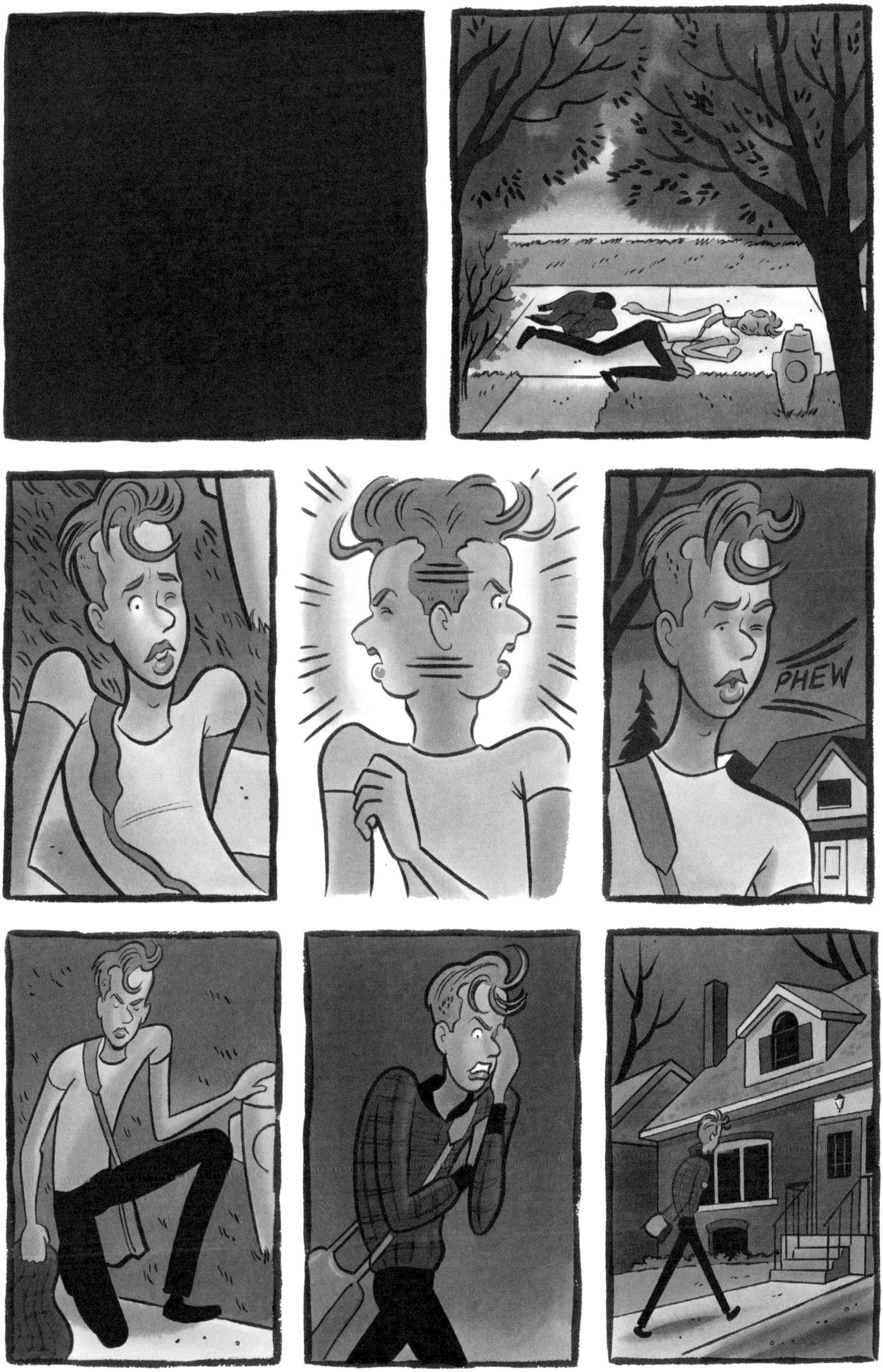
PHEW

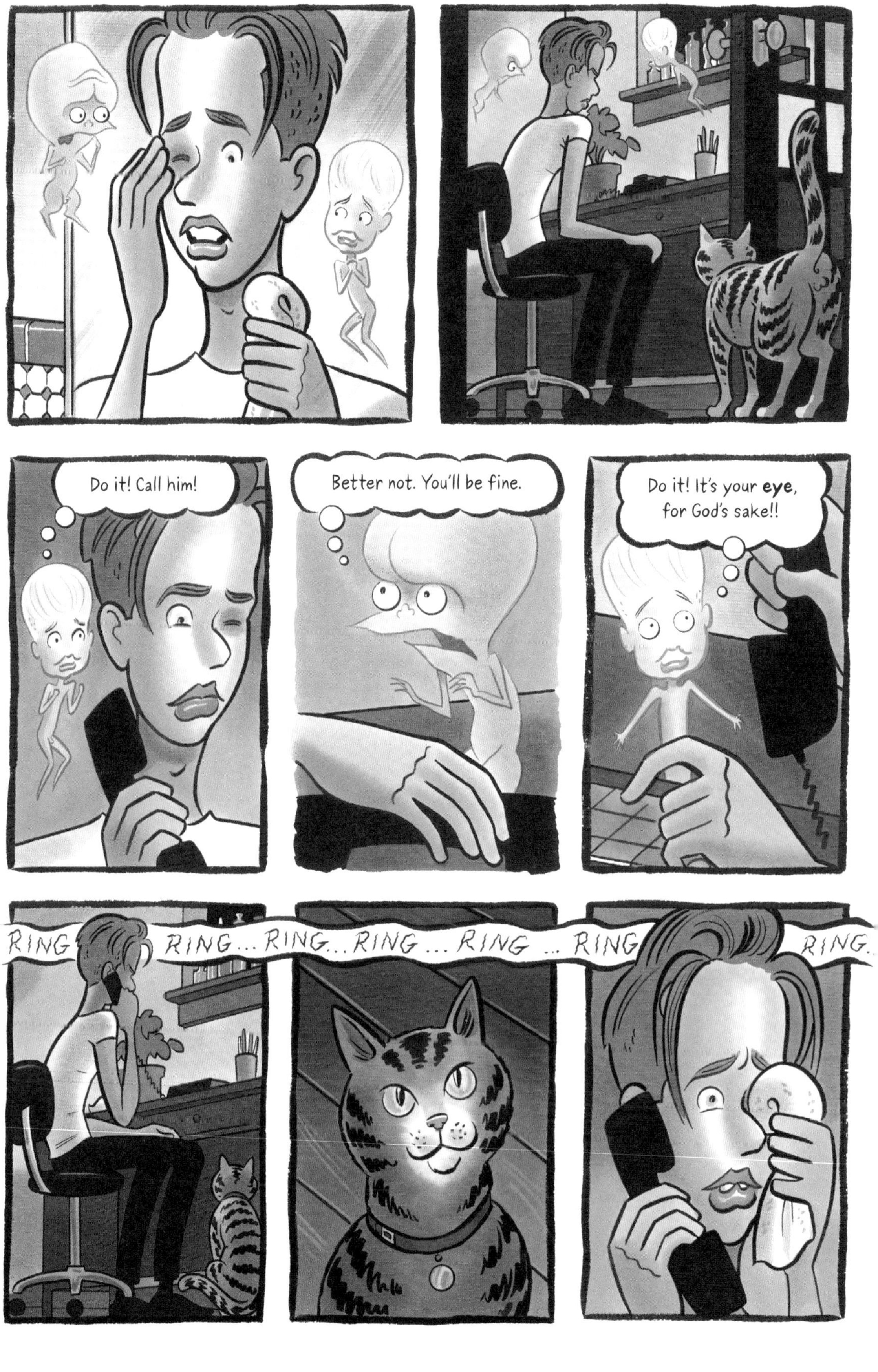
Do it! Call him!
Better not. You'll be fine.
Do it! It's your **eye**, for God's sake!!
RING RING... RING... RING... RING... RING RING...

Dad! **Finally!!** It's Maurice.

Huh? I'm here at Dave's in Mimico, remember?

Something bad happened. I was walking home... Two guys in a car stopped. One of them hit me. I think I was unconscious.

Uh-huh.

My left eye. It's all swollen.

Yes, I can still see out of it, but don't you think--

But--

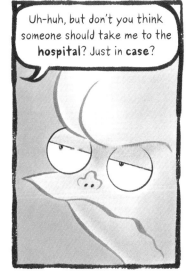

Uh-huh, but don't you think someone should take me to the **hospital**? Just in **case**?

Oh my **God**.

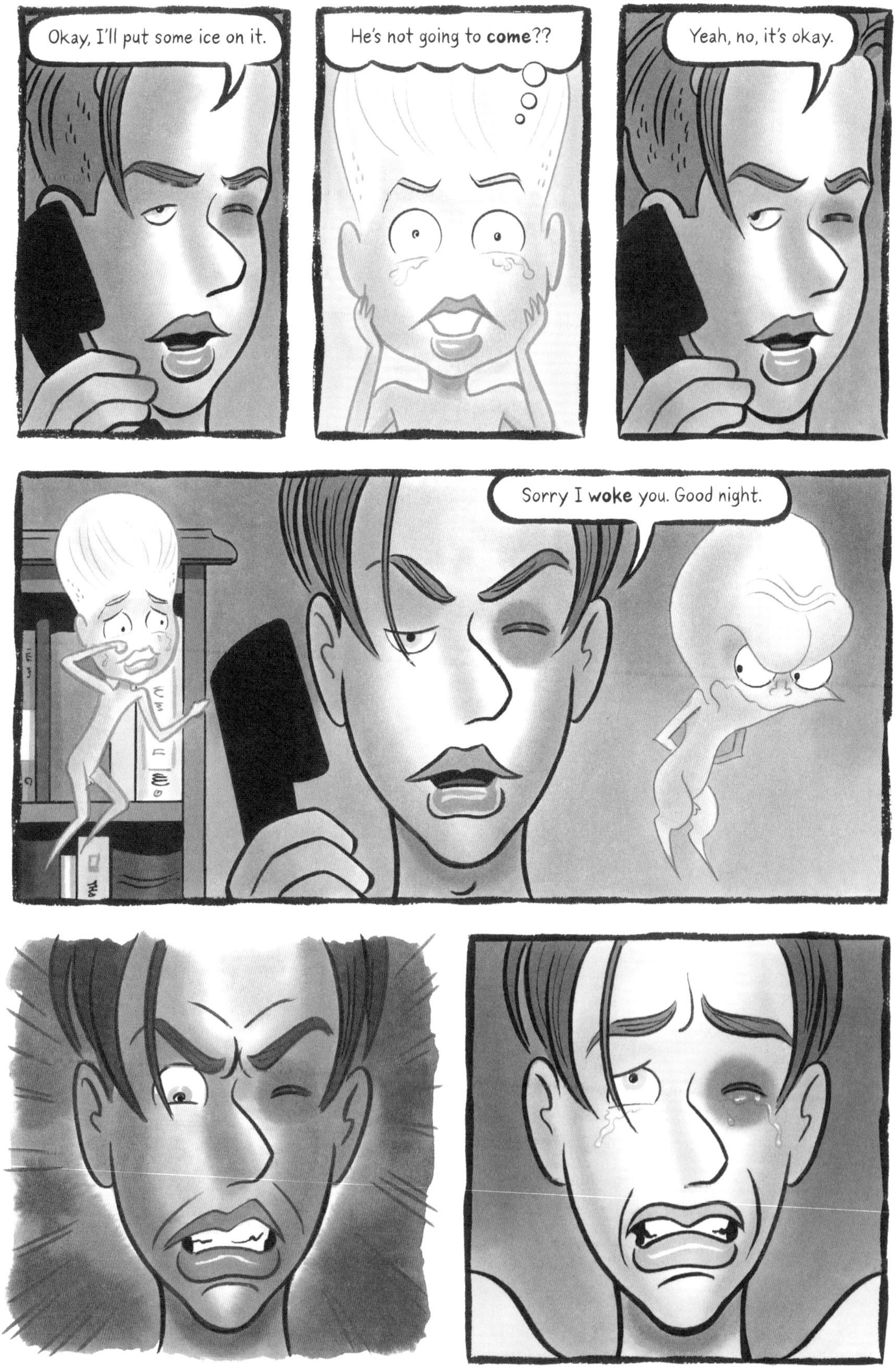
Okay, I'll put some ice on it.
He's not going to **come**??
Yeah, no, it's okay.
Sorry I **woke** you. Good night.

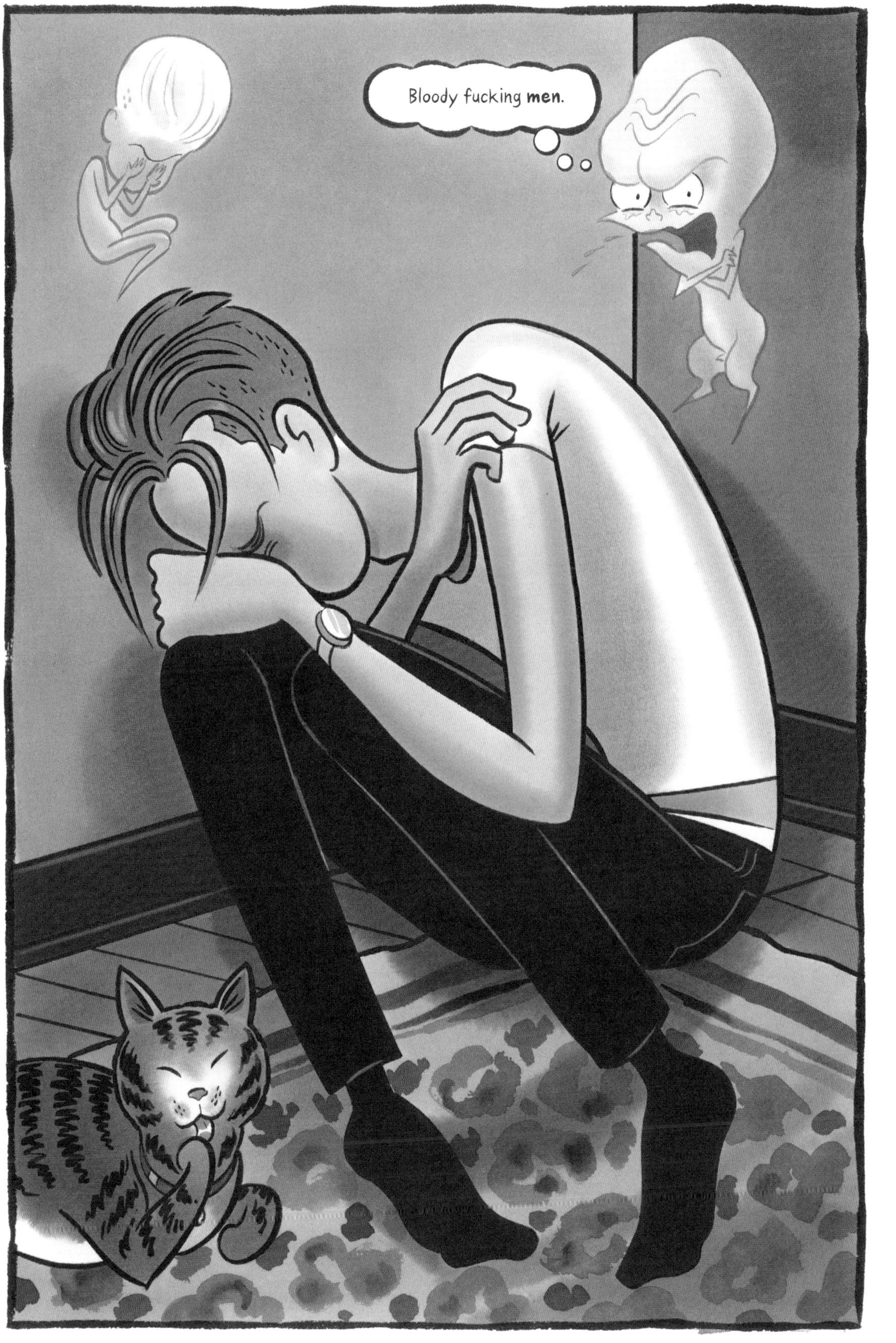
Bloody fucking **men**.

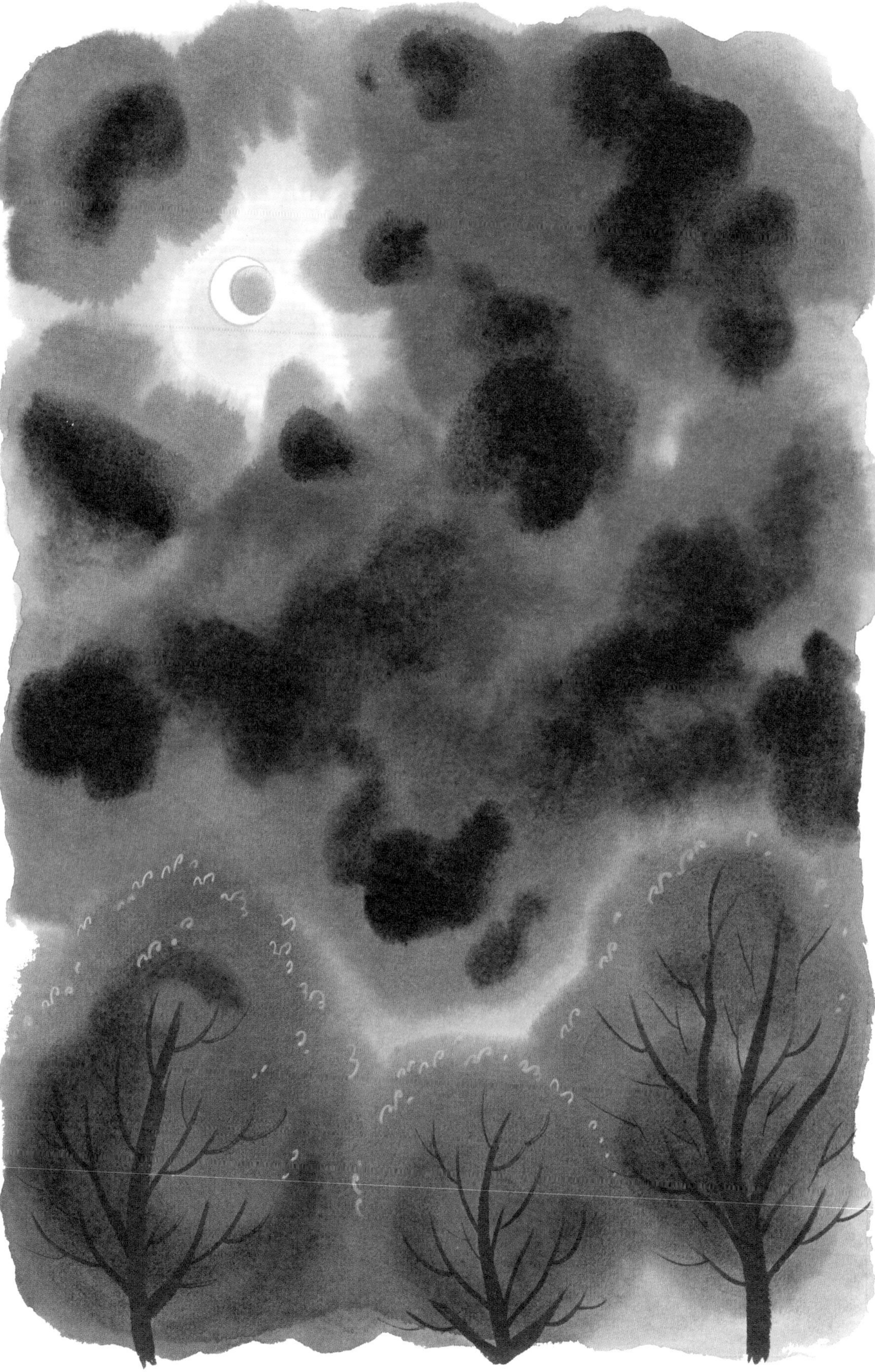

Part Three:
The Sleep

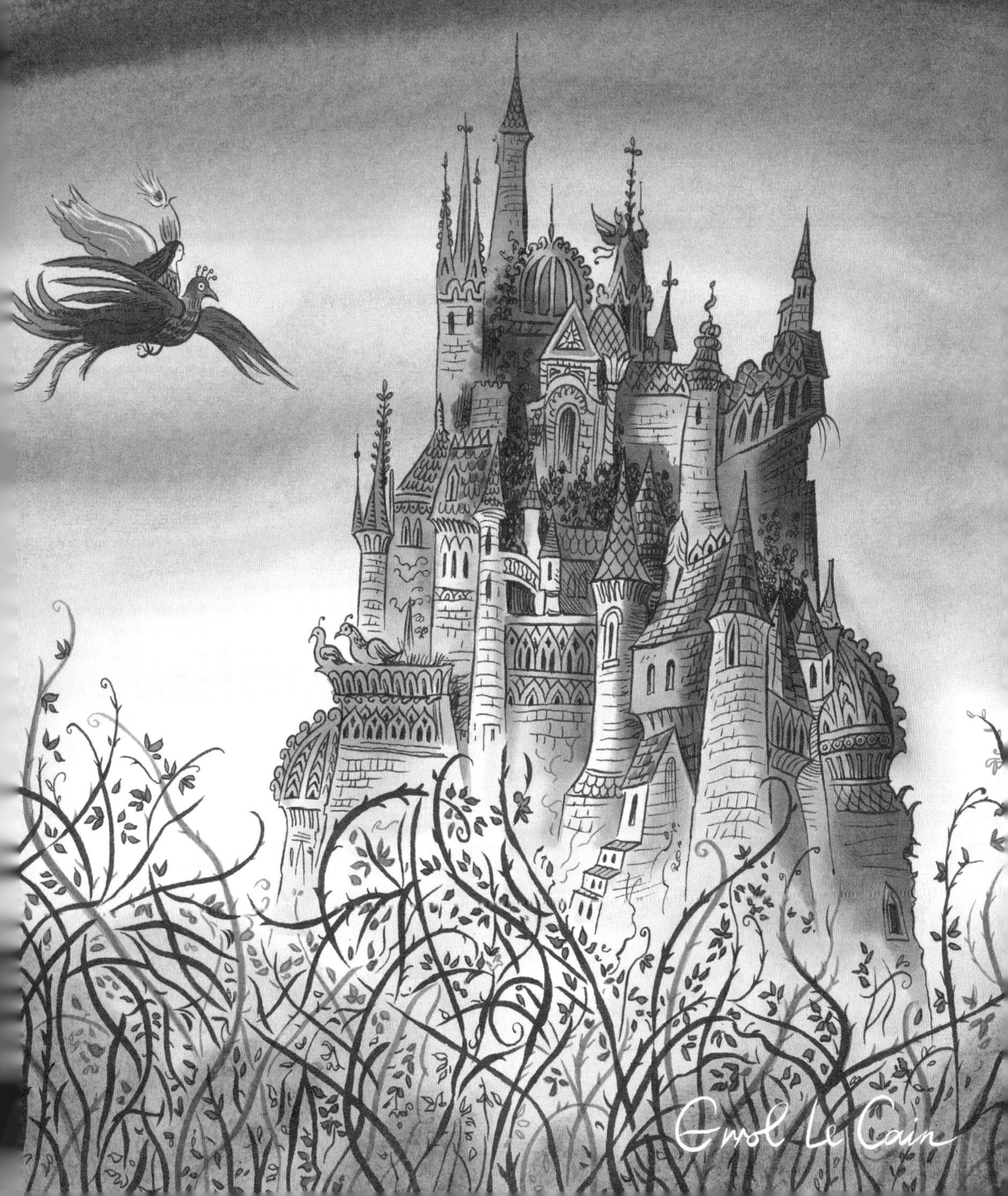
Errol Le Cain

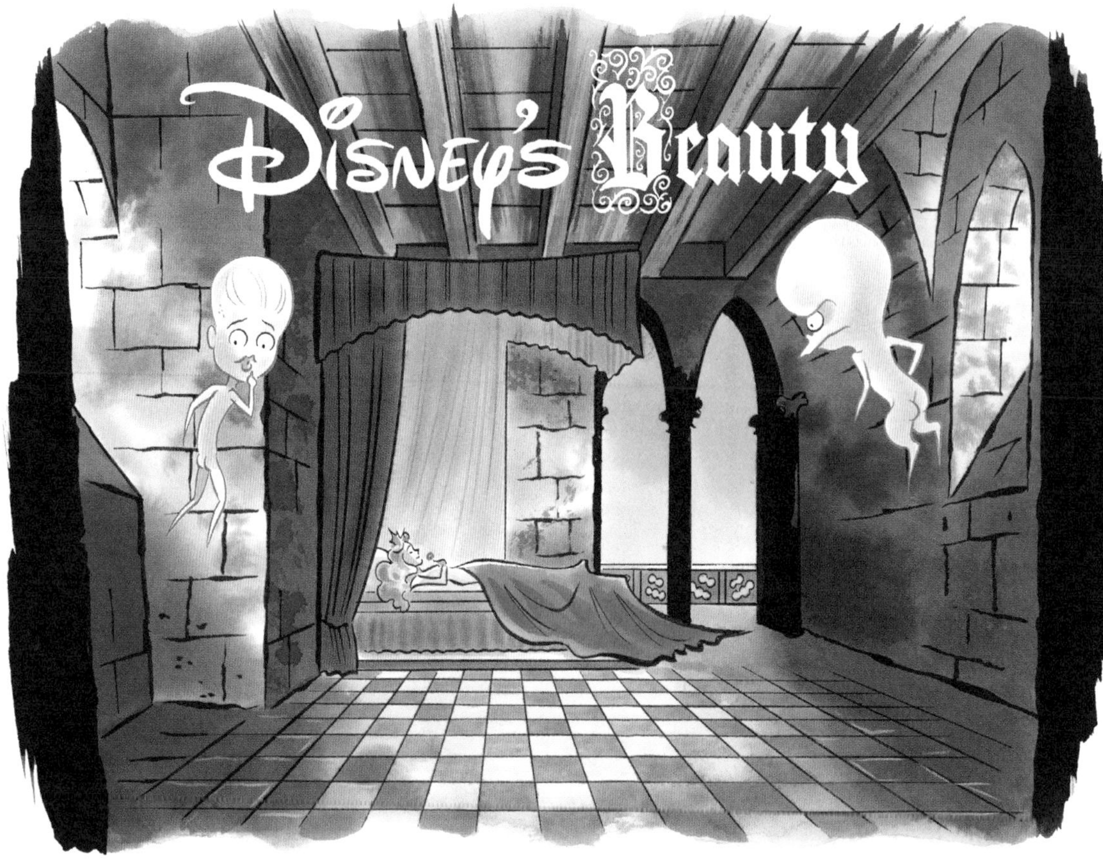
Disney's Beauty

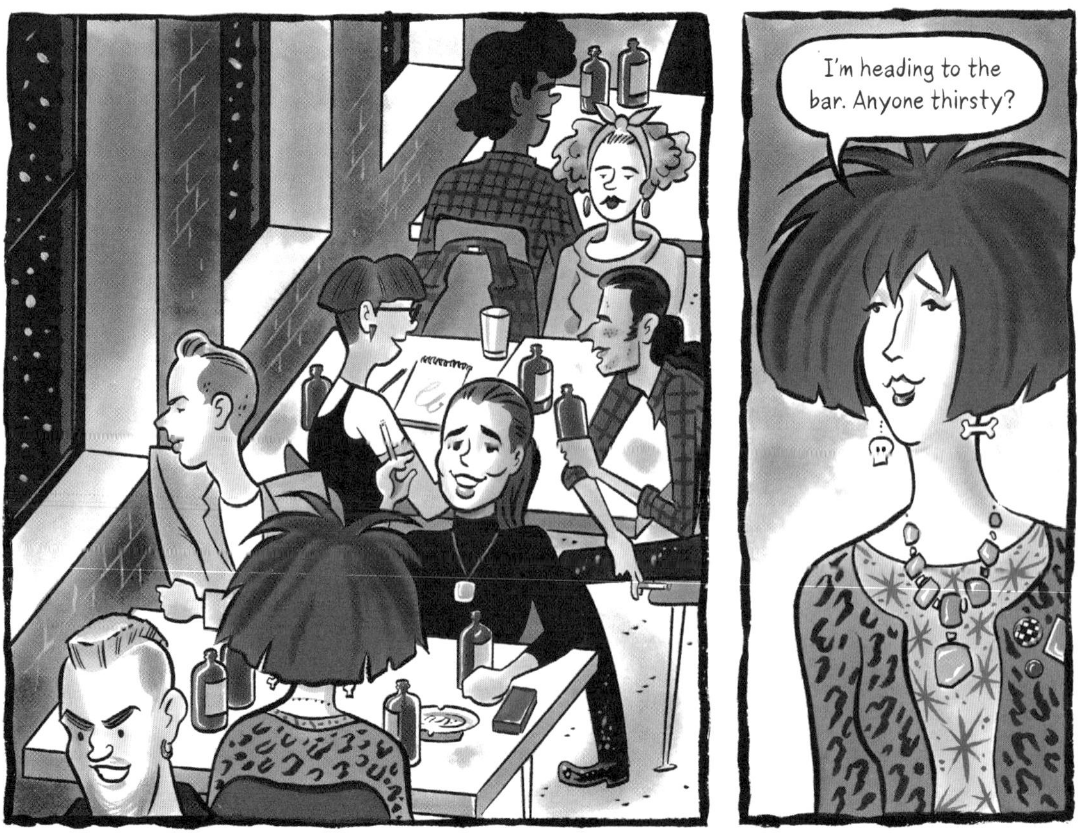
I'm heading to the bar. Anyone thirsty?

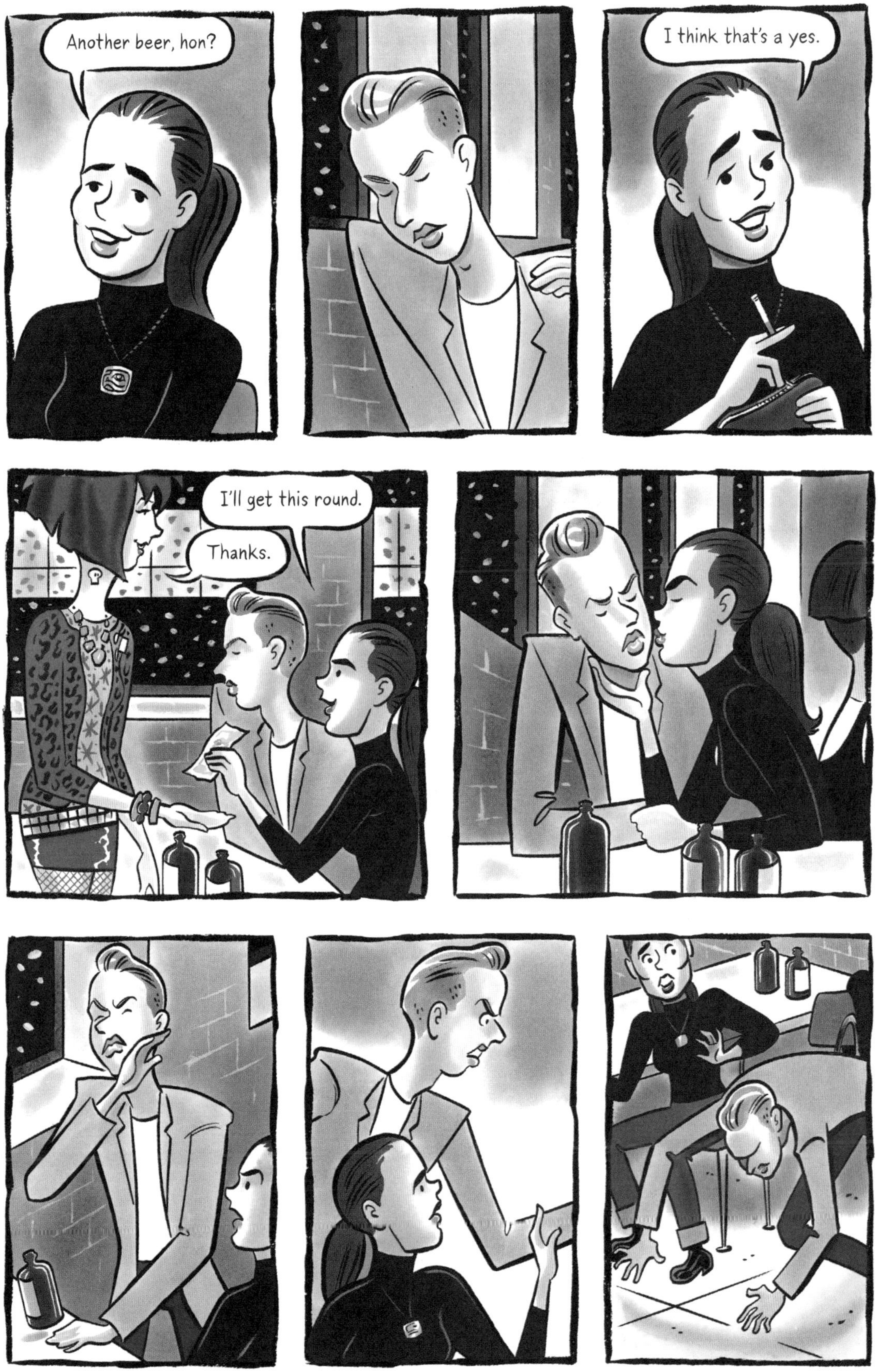
Another beer, hon?
I think that's a yes.
I'll get this round.
Thanks.

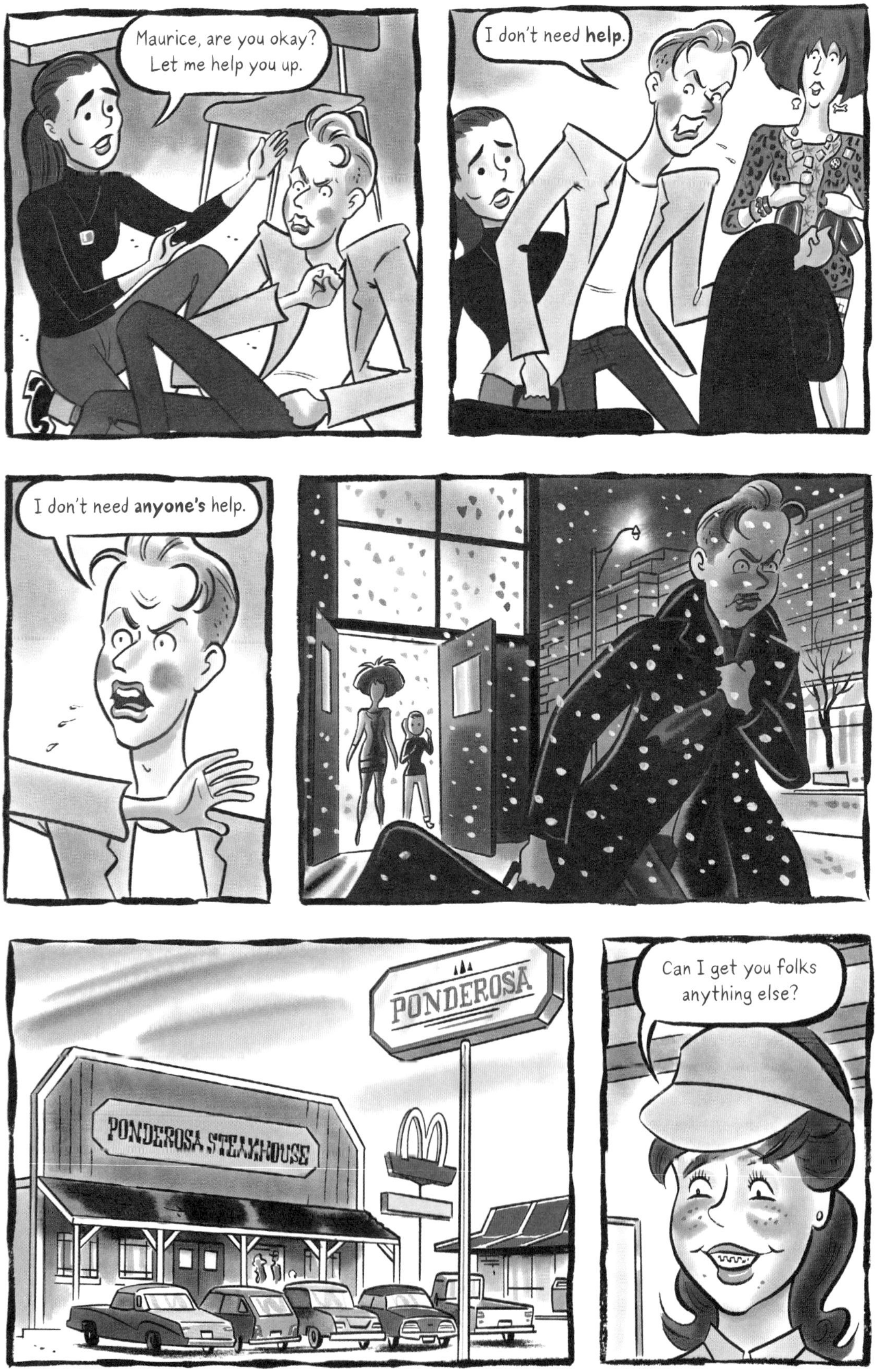
Maurice, are you okay? Let me help you up.
I don't need **help**.
I don't need **anyone's** help.
PONDEROSA
PONDEROSA STEAKHOUSE
Can I get you folks anything else?

Maurice once called himself a wimp.

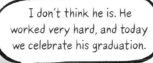

I don't think he is. He worked very hard, and today we celebrate his graduation.

To Maurice! We wish you all the best in your career.

In honour of his achievement, here is a gift.

What is it? A stereo?

An easel?

An Edsel?

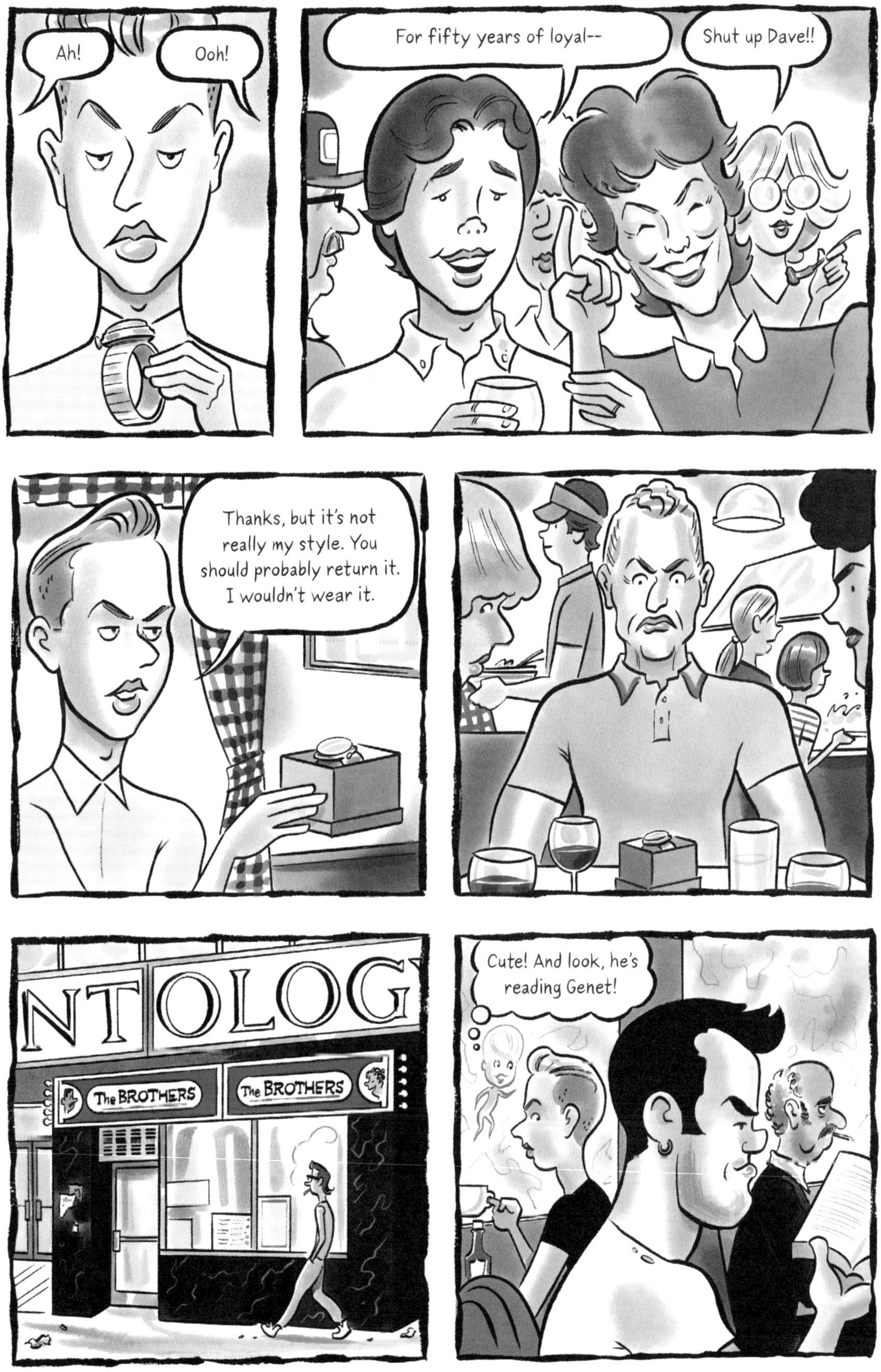
Ah!
Ooh!
For fifty years of loyal--
Shut up Dave!!
Thanks, but it's not really my style. You should probably return it. I wouldn't wear it.
NTOLOG
The BROTHERS
The BROTHERS
Cute! And look, he's reading Genet!

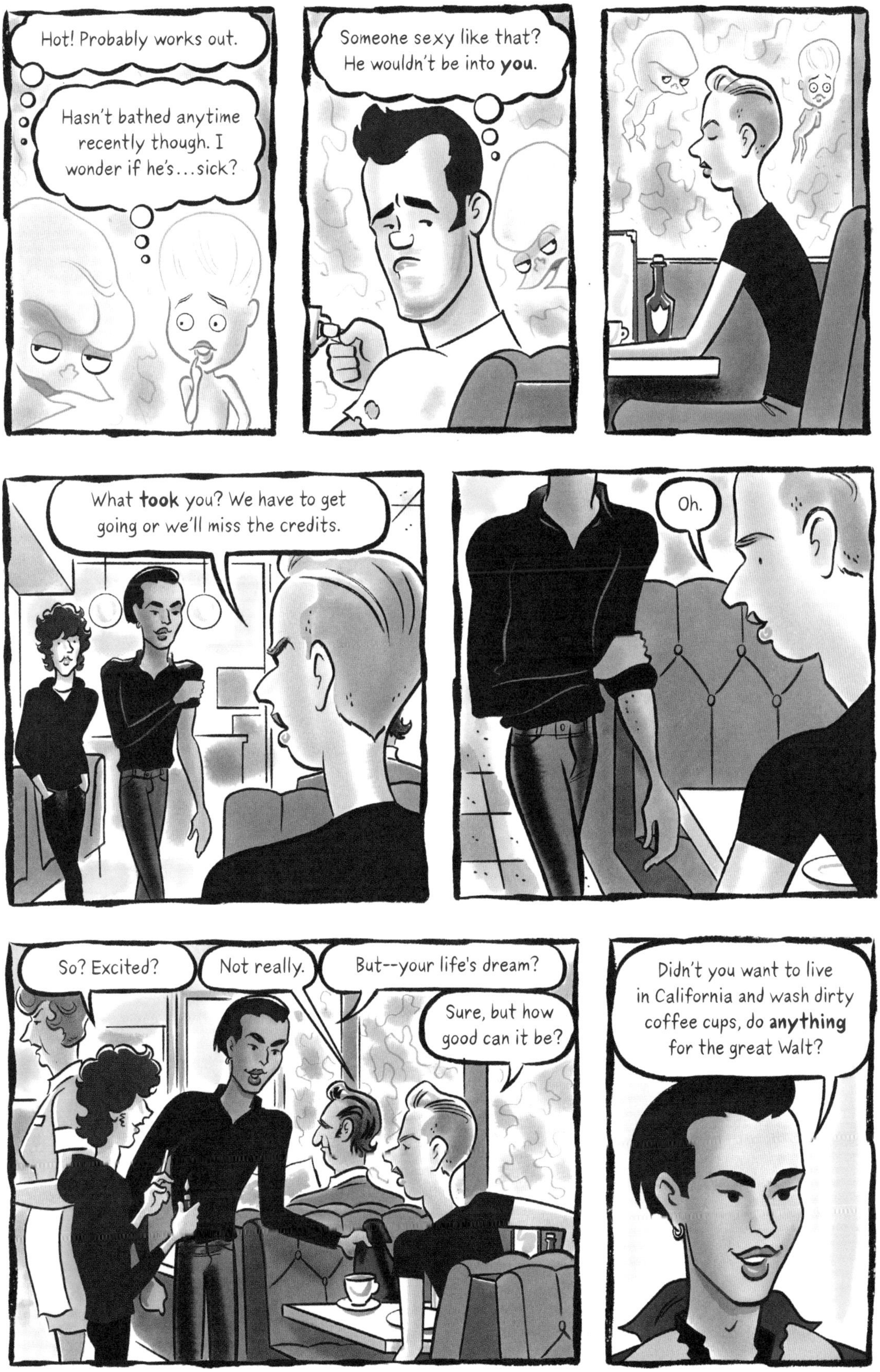
Hot! Probably works out.
Hasn't bathed anytime recently though. I wonder if he's...sick?
Someone sexy like that? He wouldn't be into **you**.
What **took** you? We have to get going or we'll miss the credits.
Oh.
So? Excited?
Not really.
But--your life's dream?
Sure, but how good can it be?
Didn't you want to live in California and wash dirty coffee cups, do **anything** for the great Walt?

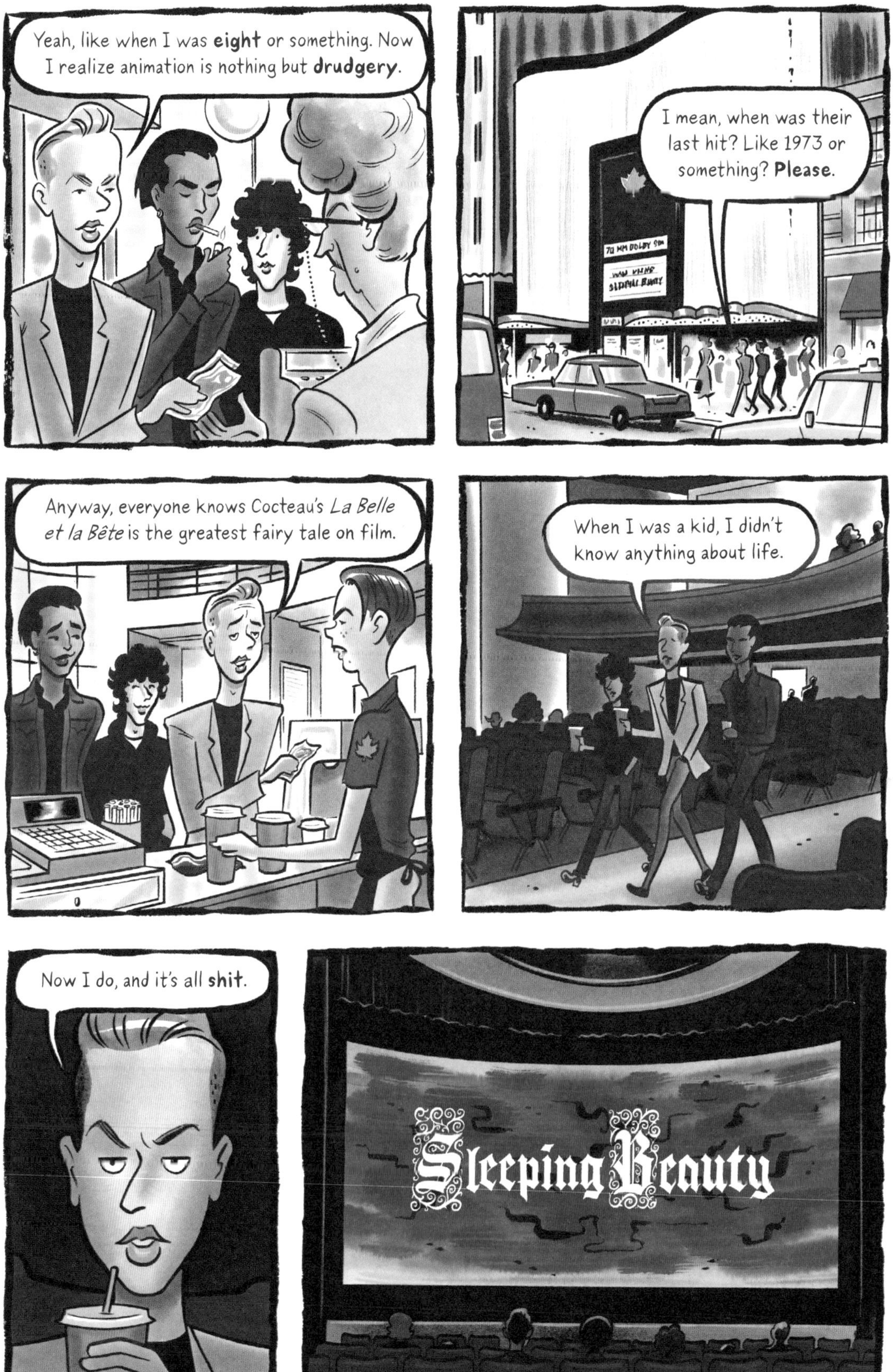
Yeah, like when I was **eight** or something. Now I realize animation is nothing but **drudgery**.
I mean, when was their last hit? Like 1973 or something? **Please**.
Anyway, everyone knows Cocteau's *La Belle et la Bête* is the greatest fairy tale on film.
When I was a kid, I didn't know anything about life.
Now I do, and it's all **shit**.
Sleeping Beauty

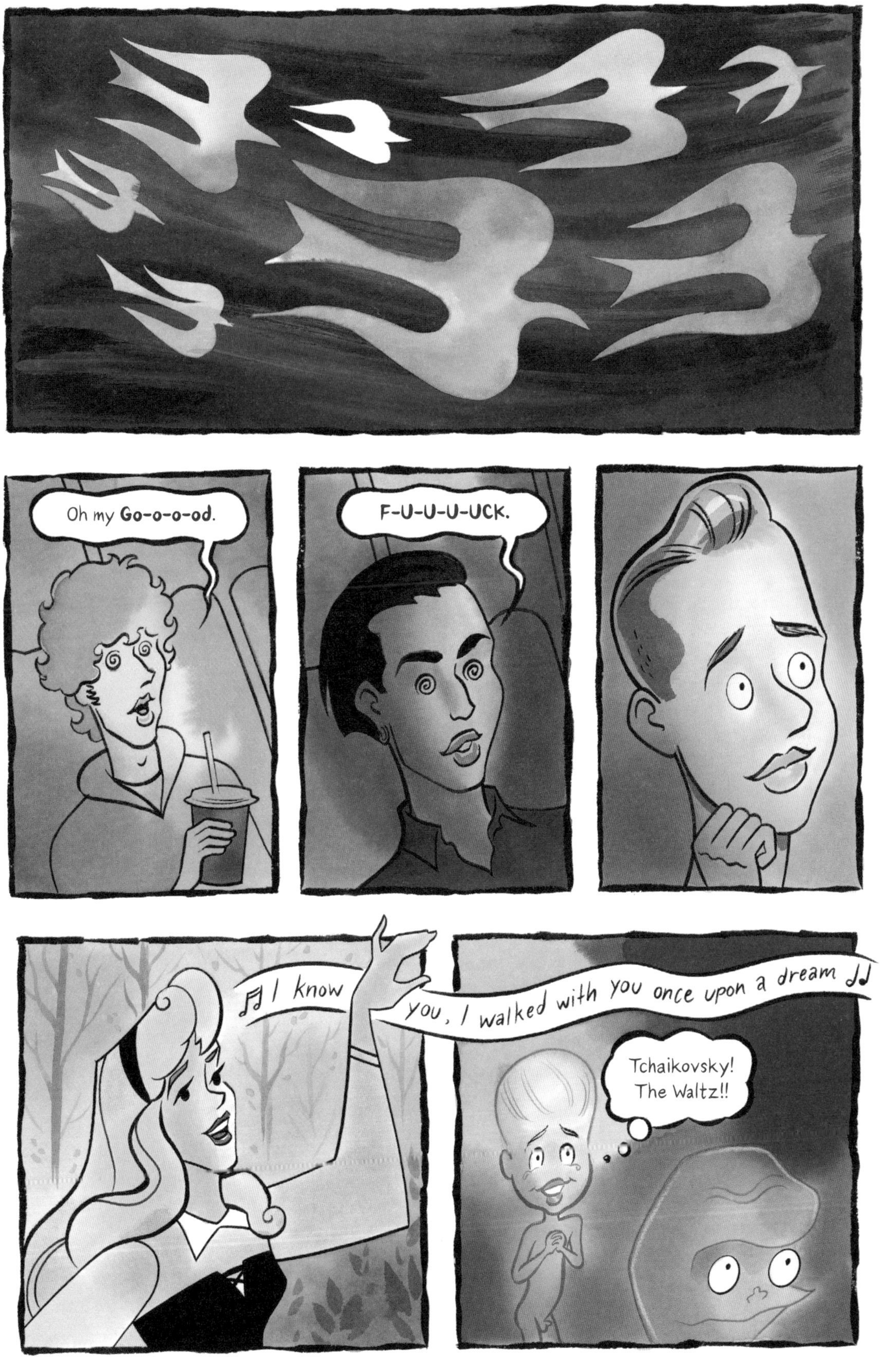
Oh my **Go-o-o-od.**
F-U-U-U-UCK.
♫ I know you, I walked with you once upon a dream ♫
Tchaikovsky! The Waltz!!

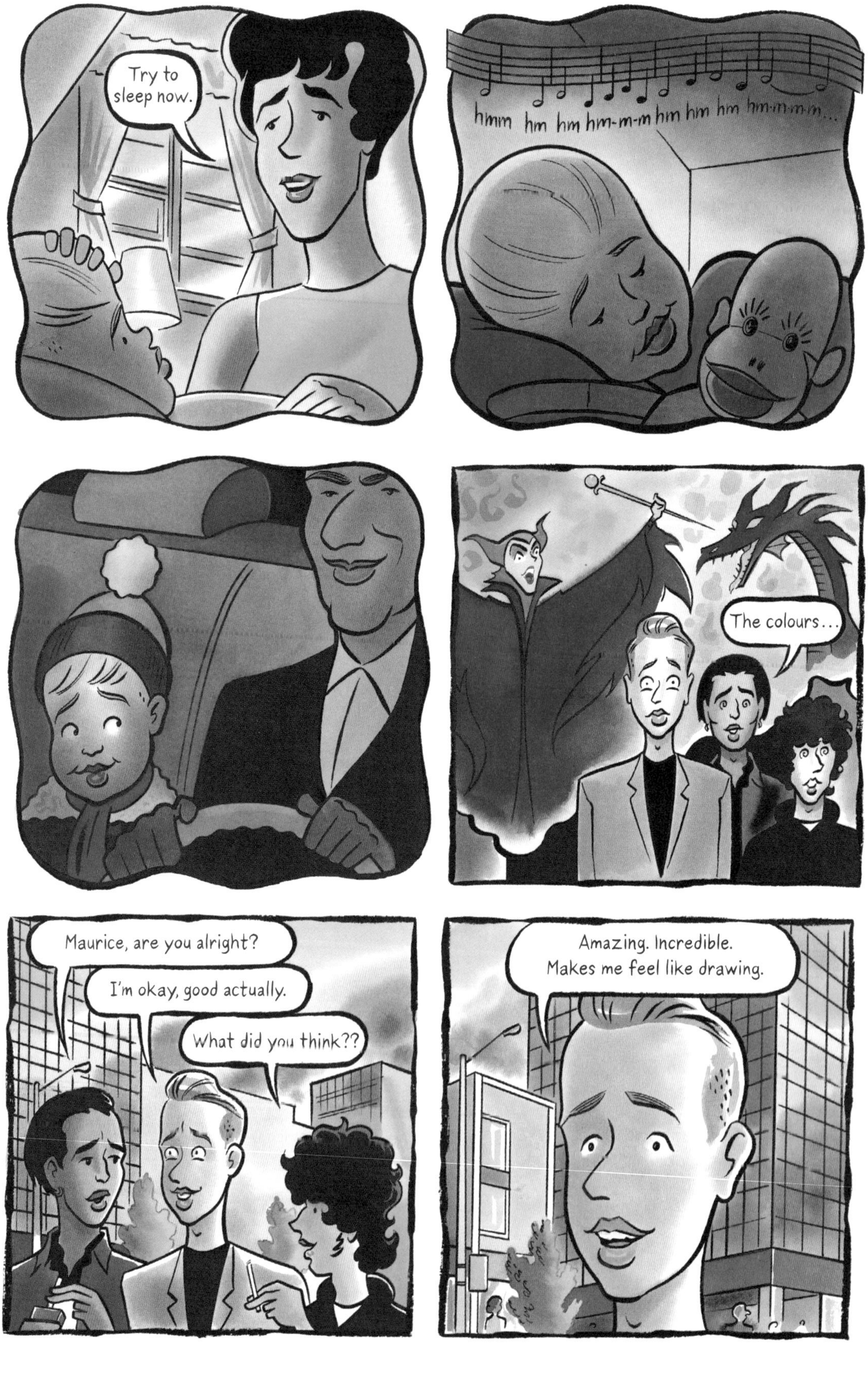
Try to sleep now.
hmm hm hm hm-m-m hm hm hm hm-m-m-m...
The colours...
Maurice, are you alright?
I'm okay, good actually.
What did you think??
Amazing. Incredible.
Makes me feel like drawing.

Tooty Fruity

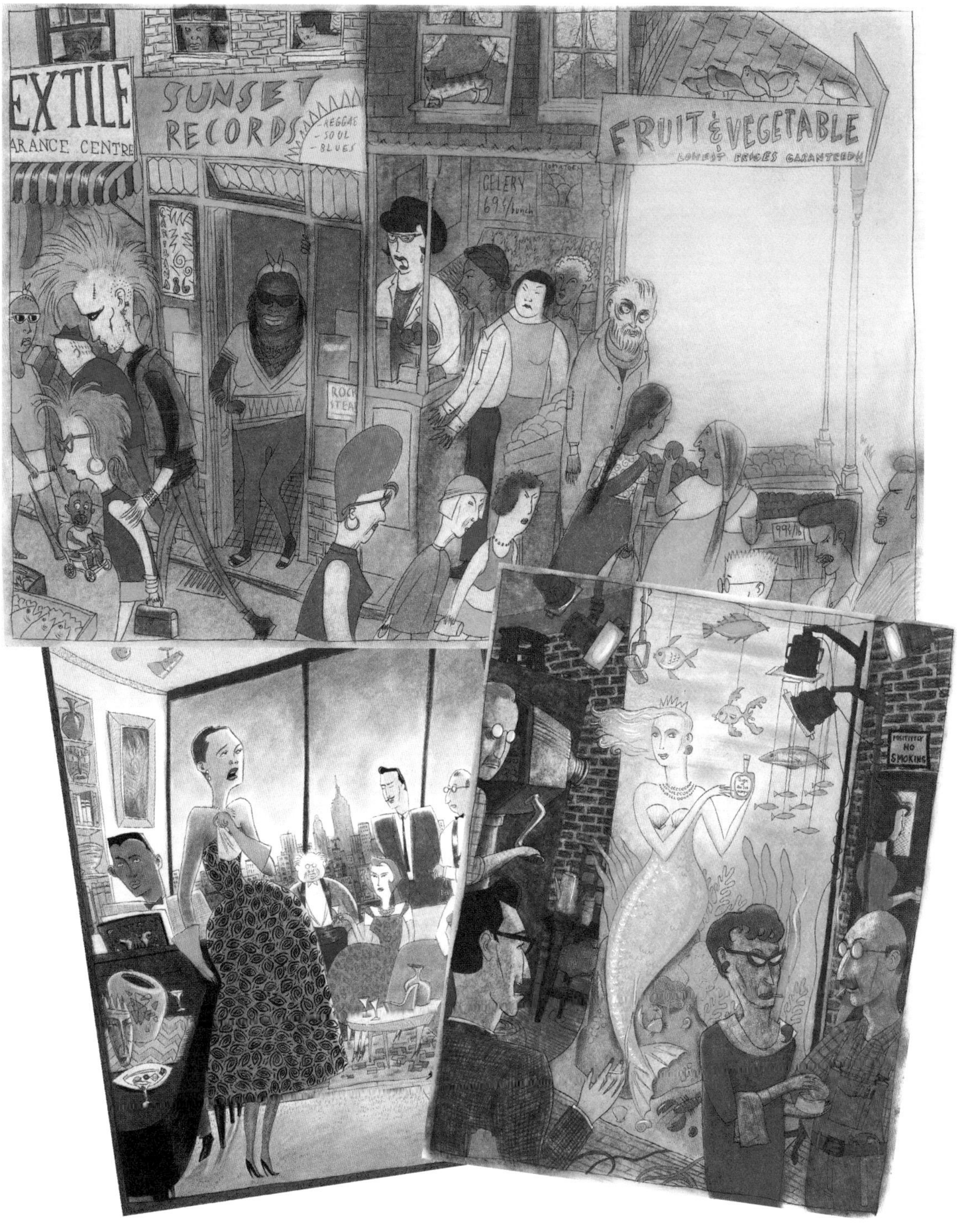
EXTILE
ARANCE CENTRE
SUNSET RECORDS
REGGAE
SOUL
BLUES
FRUIT & VEGETABLE
LOWEST PRICES GUARANTEED!!
CELERY
69¢/bunch
NO SMOKING

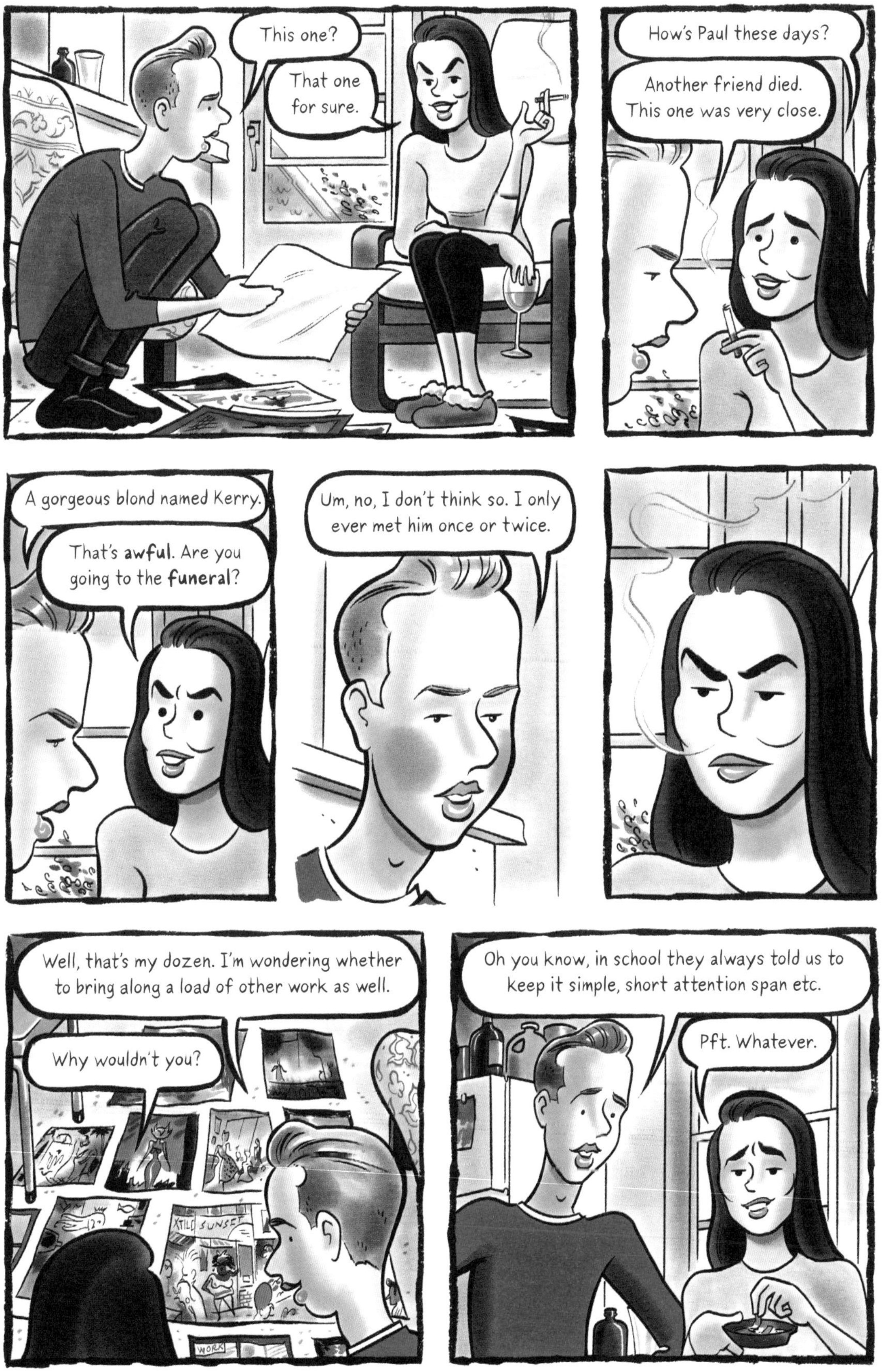
This one?
That one for sure.
How's Paul these days?
Another friend died. This one was very close.
A gorgeous blond named Kerry.
That's **awful**. Are you going to the **funeral**?
Um, no, I don't think so. I only ever met him once or twice.
Well, that's my dozen. I'm wondering whether to bring along a load of other work as well.
Why wouldn't you?
Oh you know, in school they always told us to keep it simple, short attention span etc.
Pft. Whatever.

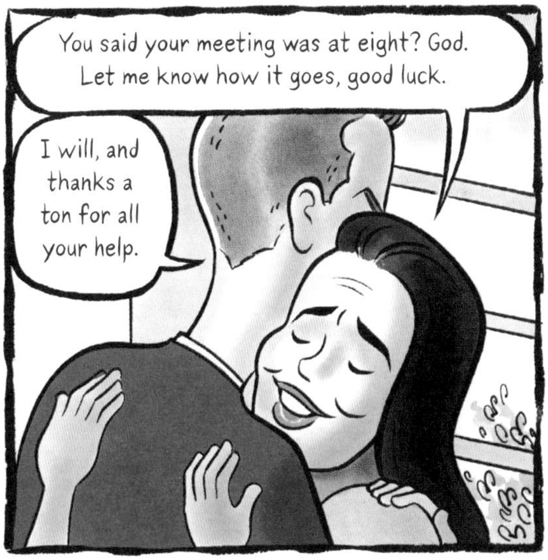
You said your meeting was at eight? God. Let me know how it goes, good luck.
I will, and thanks a ton for all your help.

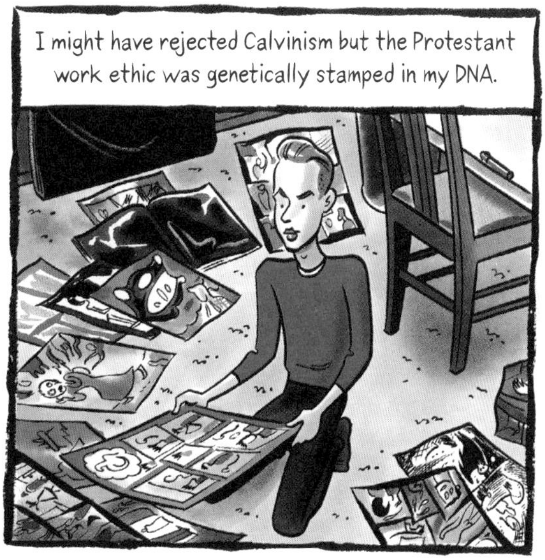
I might have rejected Calvinism but the Protestant work ethic was genetically stamped in my DNA.

In art school I dispatched my illustration assignments as quickly as possible, eager to get back to my more absorbing personal work. I discovered *RAW* magazine and with it the limitless potential of comics. Inspired by the absurdist vision of Jerry Moriarty, I created a series of single-page stories: slice-of-life moments that reflected life's banality, the fits and starts of art-making, and fumbled romance.

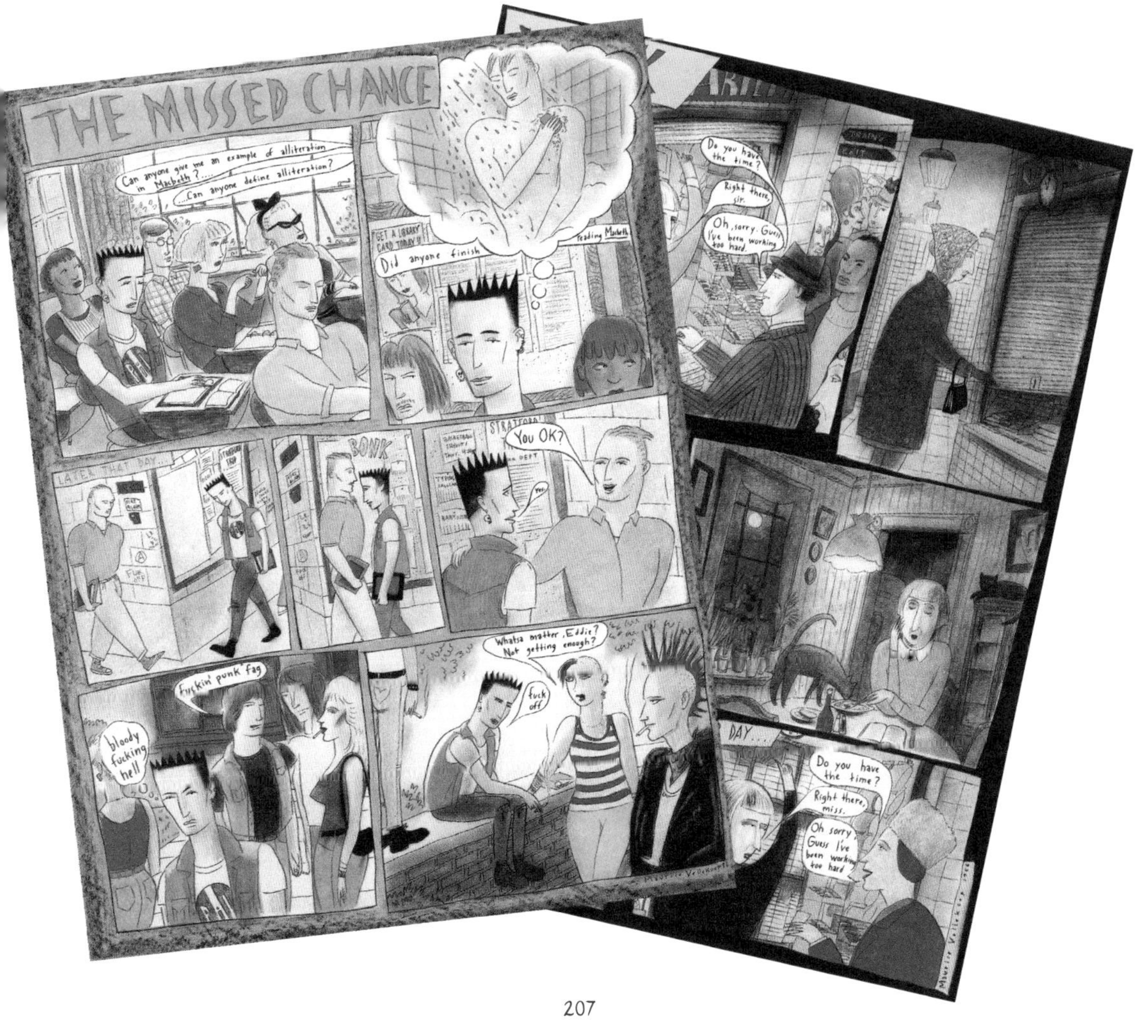
THE MISSED CHANCE
Can anyone give me an example of alliteration in Macbeth?....
...Can anyone define alliteration?
GET A LIBRARY CARD TODAY!!
Did anyone finish reading Macbeth
LATER THAT DAY...
BONK
STRATFORD
You OK?
Fuckin' punk fag
bloody fucking hell
Whatsa matter, Eddie? Not getting enough?
fuck off
Do you have the time?
Right there, sir.
Oh, sorry. Guess I've been working too hard.
DAY...
Do you have the time?
Right there, miss.
Oh sorry, Guess I've been working too hard

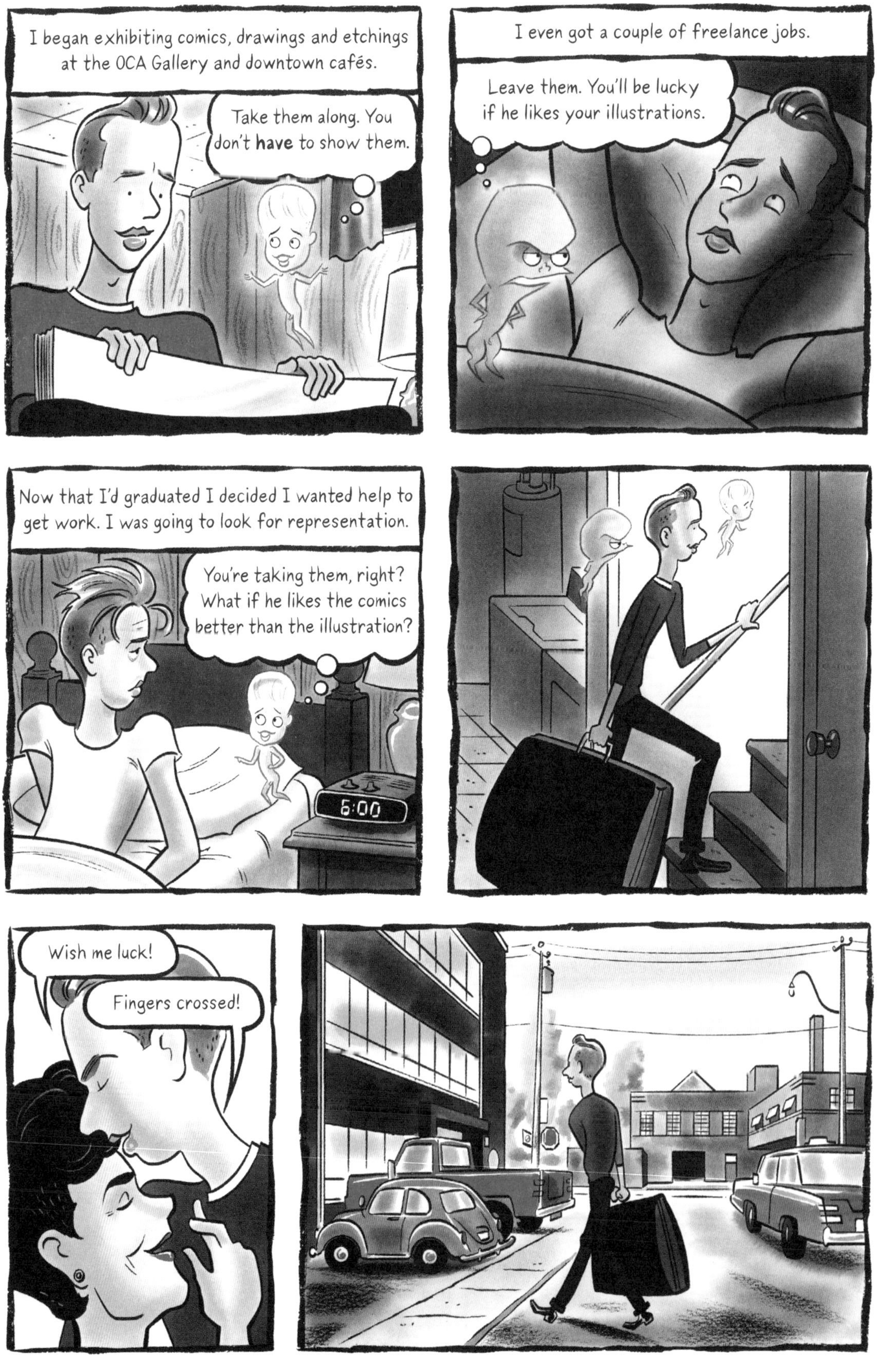
I began exhibiting comics, drawings and etchings at the OCA Gallery and downtown cafés.
Take them along. You don't **have** to show them.
I even got a couple of freelance jobs.
Leave them. You'll be lucky if he likes your illustrations.
Now that I'd graduated I decided I wanted help to get work. I was going to look for representation.
You're taking them, right? What if he likes the comics better than the illustration?
6:00
Wish me luck!
Fingers crossed!

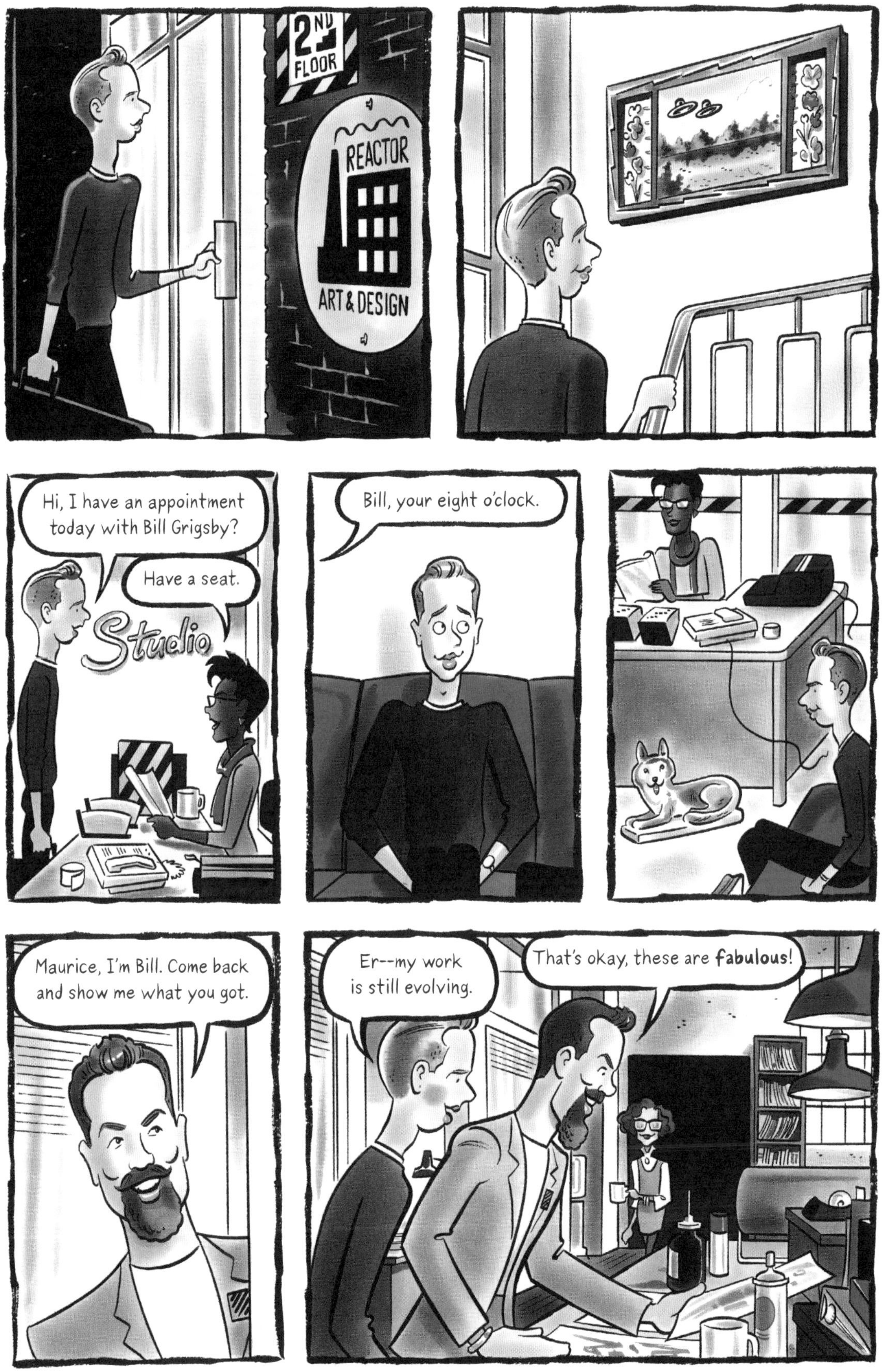
2ND FLOOR
REACTOR ART & DESIGN
Hi, I have an appointment today with Bill Grigsby?
Have a seat.
Studio
Bill, your eight o'clock.
Maurice, I'm Bill. Come back and show me what you got.
Er--my work is still evolving.
That's okay, these are **fabulous**!

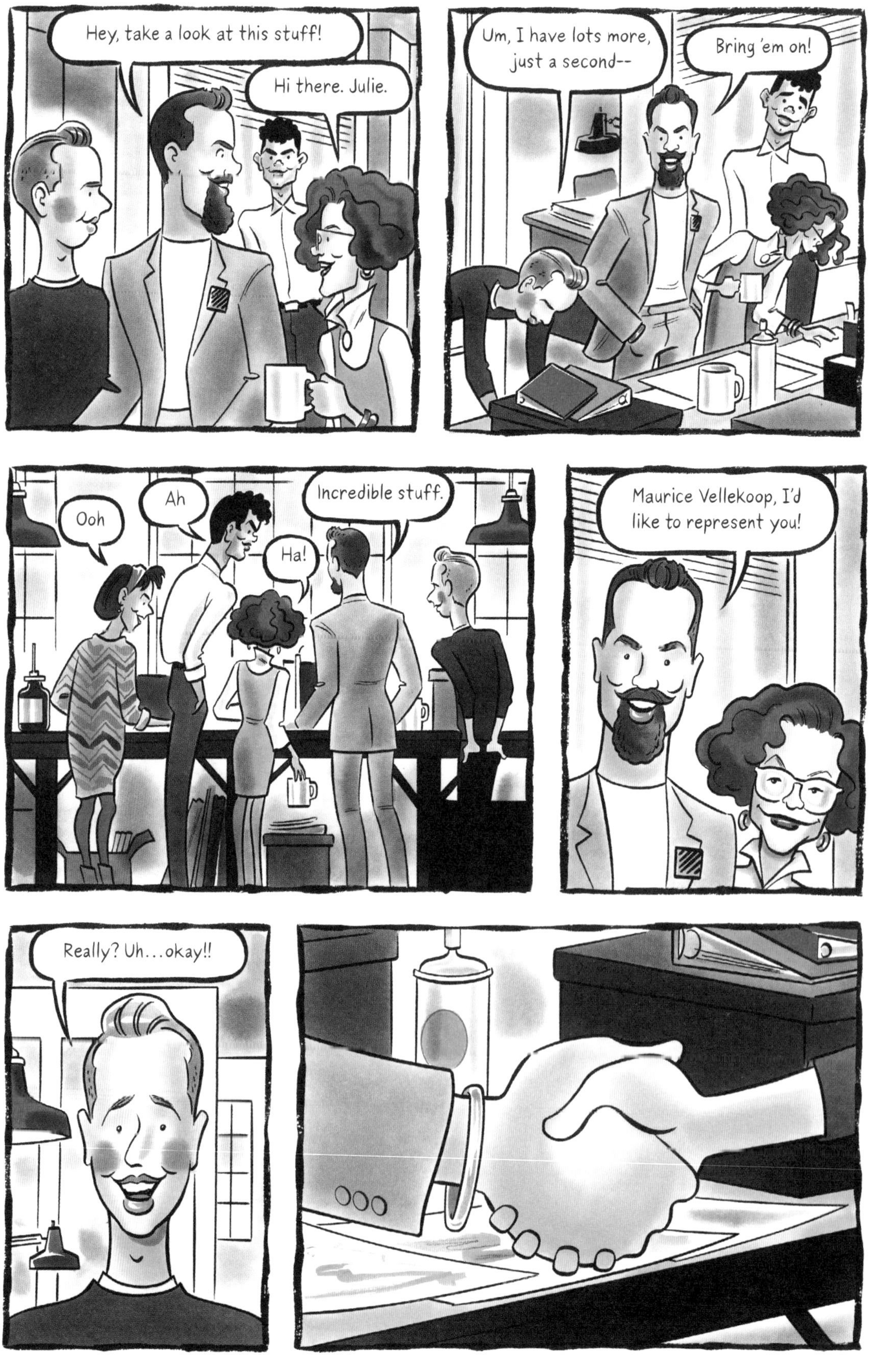
Hey, take a look at this stuff!
Hi there. Julie.
Um, I have lots more, just a second--
Bring 'em on!
Ooh
Ah
Ha!
Incredible stuff.
Maurice Vellekoop, I'd like to represent you!
Really? Uh...okay!!

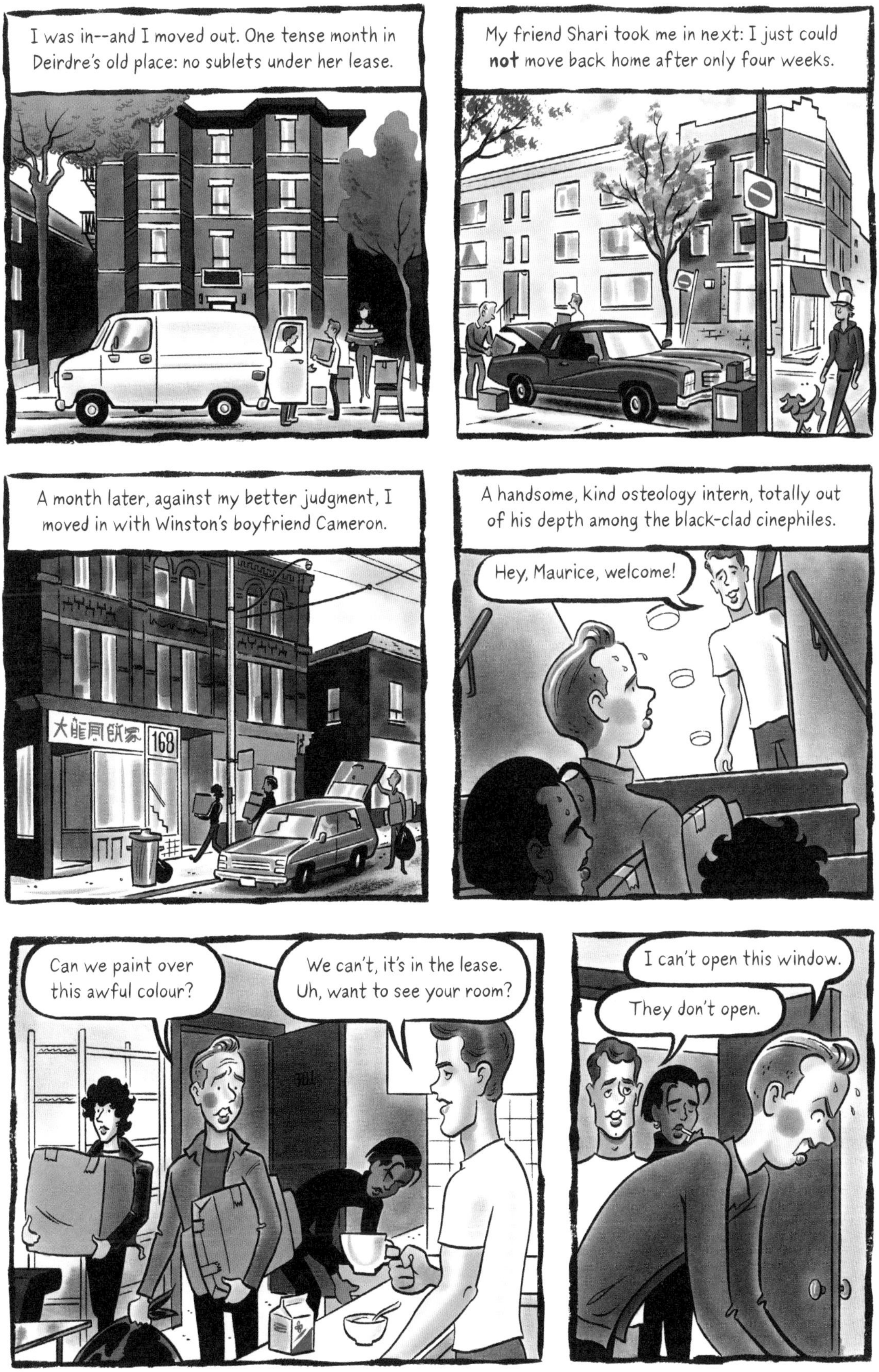
I was in--and I moved out. One tense month in Deirdre's old place: no sublets under her lease.
My friend Shari took me in next: I just could **not** move back home after only four weeks.
A month later, against my better judgment, I moved in with Winston's boyfriend Cameron.
168
A handsome, kind osteology intern, totally out of his depth among the black-clad cinephiles.
Hey, Maurice, welcome!
Can we paint over this awful colour?
We can't, it's in the lease. Uh, want to see your room?
301
I can't open this window.
They don't open.

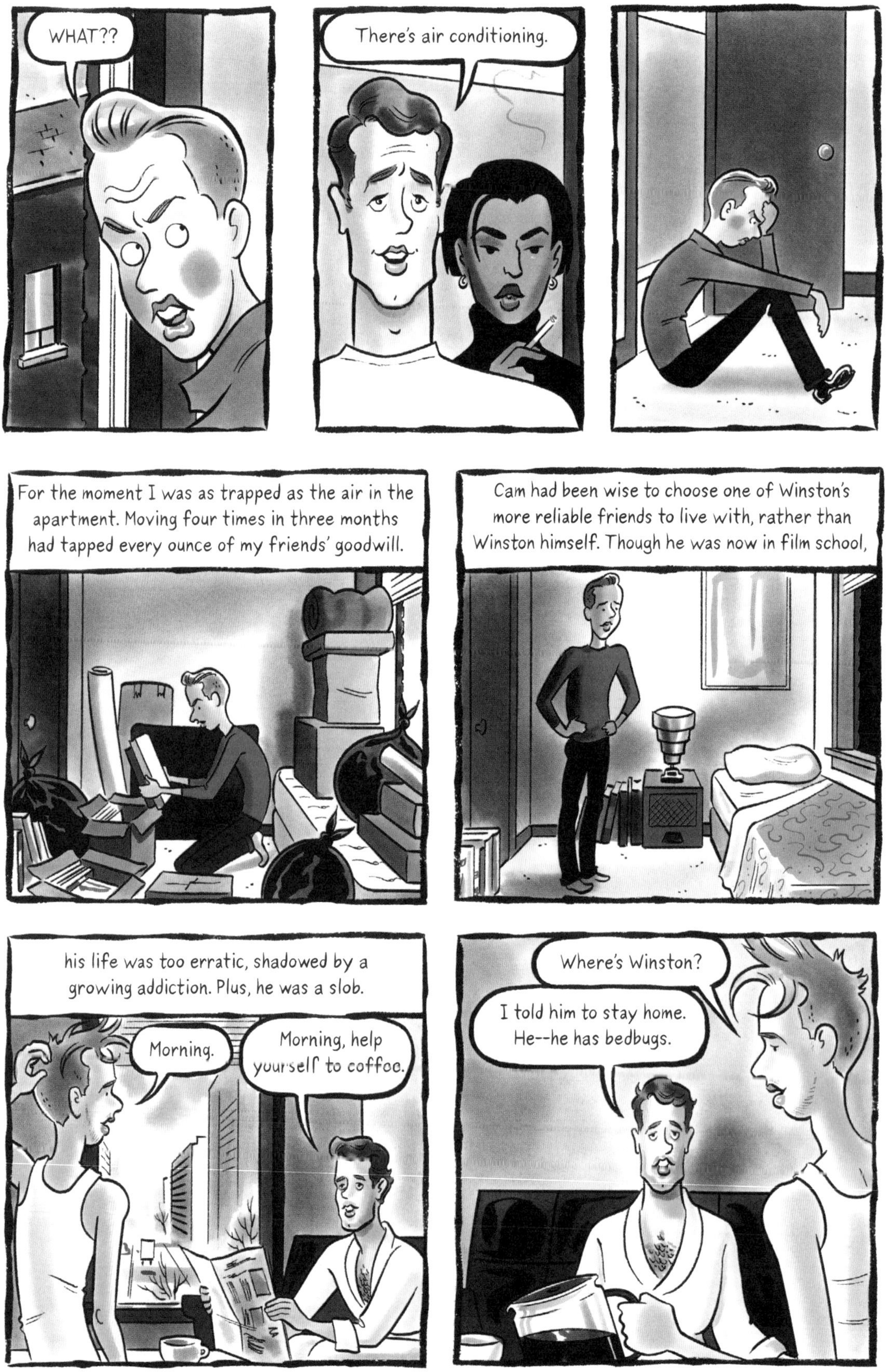
WHAT??
There's air conditioning.
For the moment I was as trapped as the air in the apartment. Moving four times in three months had tapped every ounce of my friends' goodwill.
Cam had been wise to choose one of Winston's more reliable friends to live with, rather than Winston himself. Though he was now in film school,
his life was too erratic, shadowed by a growing addiction. Plus, he was a slob.
Morning.
Morning, help yourself to coffee.
Where's Winston?
I told him to stay home. He--he has bedbugs.

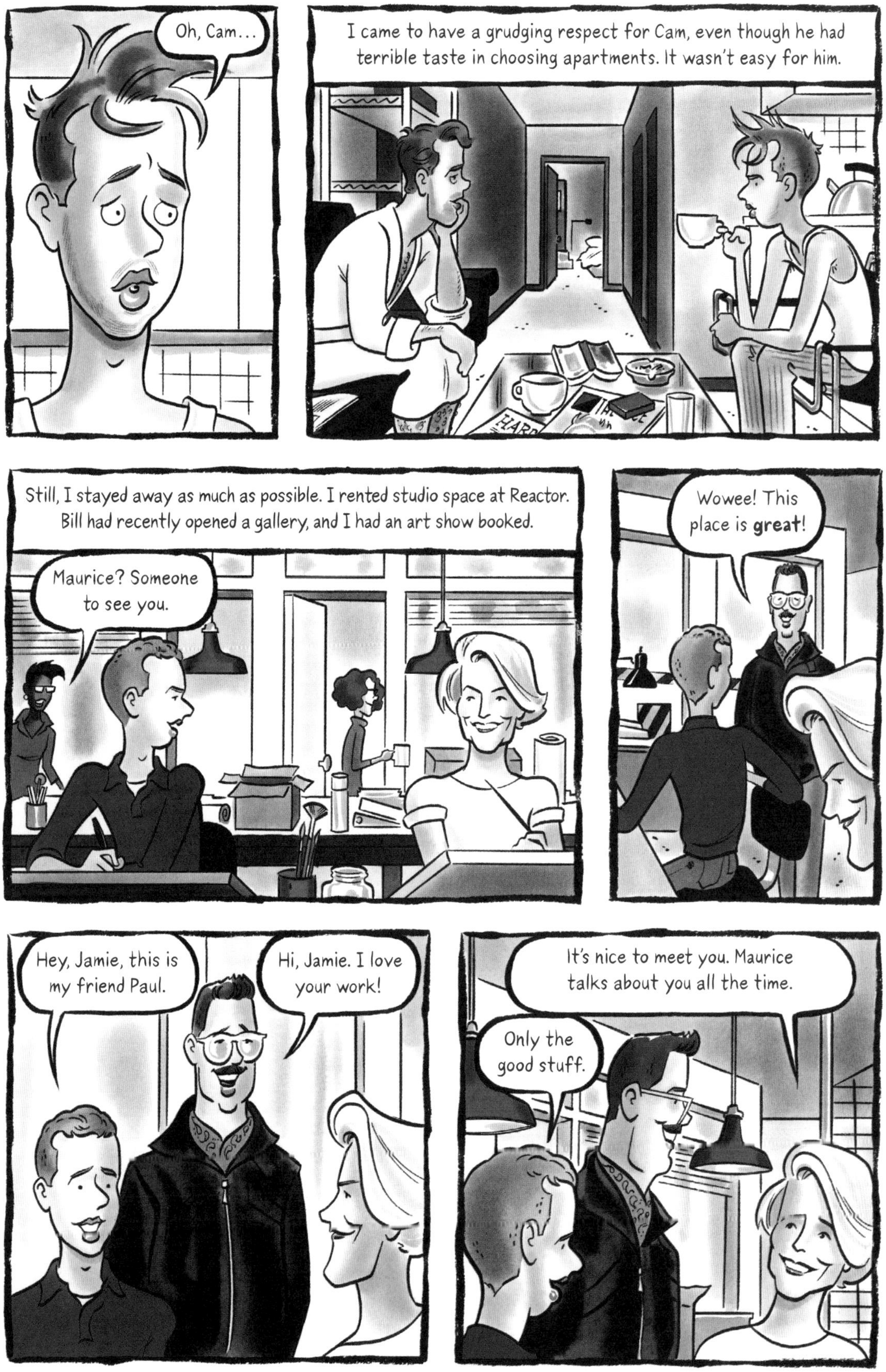
Oh, Cam...
I came to have a grudging respect for Cam, even though he had terrible taste in choosing apartments. It wasn't easy for him.
Still, I stayed away as much as possible. I rented studio space at Reactor. Bill had recently opened a gallery, and I had an art show booked.
Maurice? Someone to see you.
Wowee! This place is **great**!
Hey, Jamie, this is my friend Paul.
Hi, Jamie. I love your work!
It's nice to meet you. Maurice talks about you all the time.
Only the good stuff.

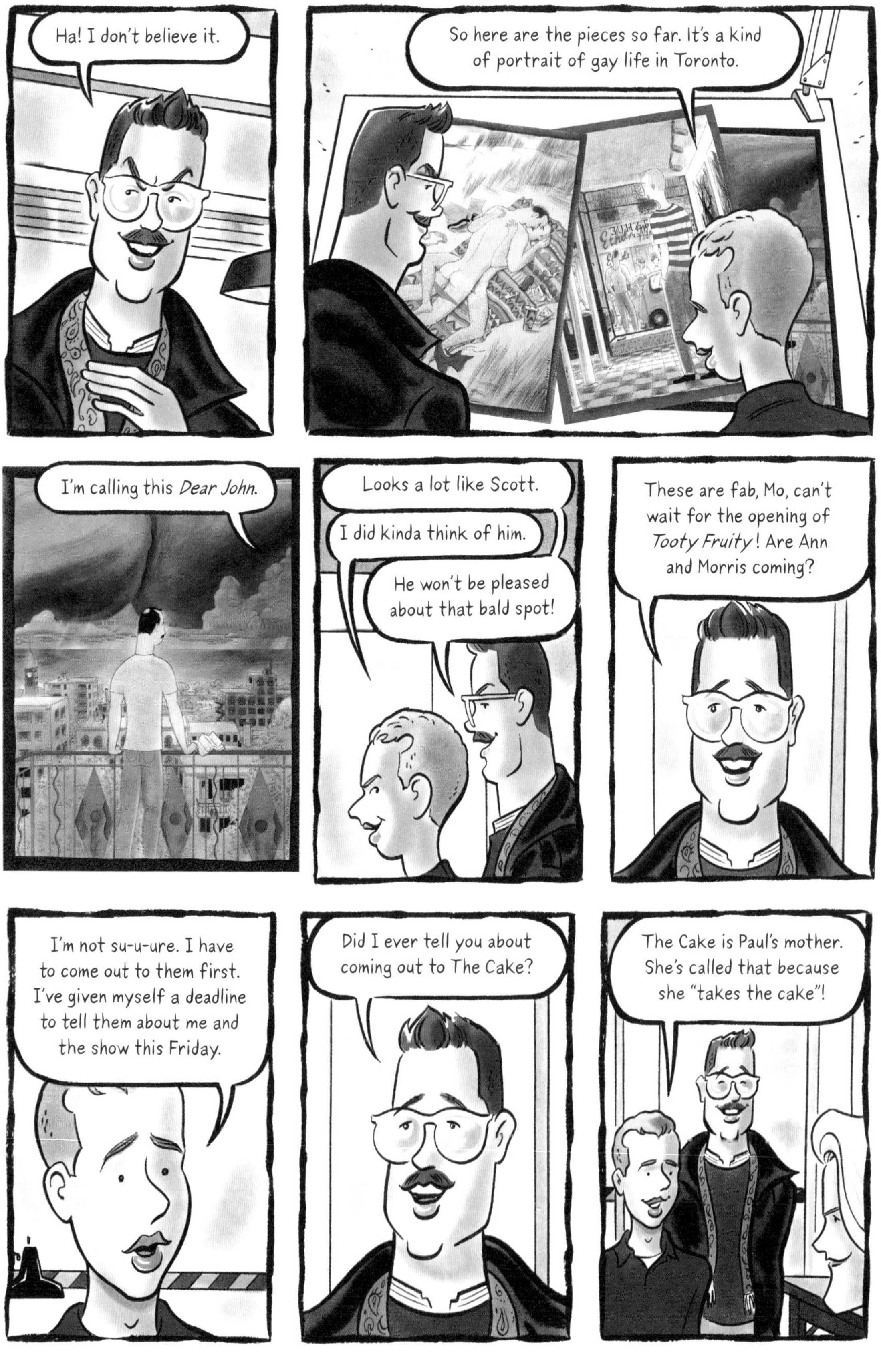
Ha! I don't believe it.
So here are the pieces so far. It's a kind of portrait of gay life in Toronto.
I'm calling this *Dear John*.
Looks a lot like Scott.
I did kinda think of him.
He won't be pleased about that bald spot!
These are fab, Mo, can't wait for the opening of *Tooty Fruity*! Are Ann and Morris coming?
I'm not su-u-ure. I have to come out to them first. I've given myself a deadline to tell them about me and the show this Friday.
Did I ever tell you about coming out to The Cake?
The Cake is Paul's mother. She's called that because she "takes the cake"!

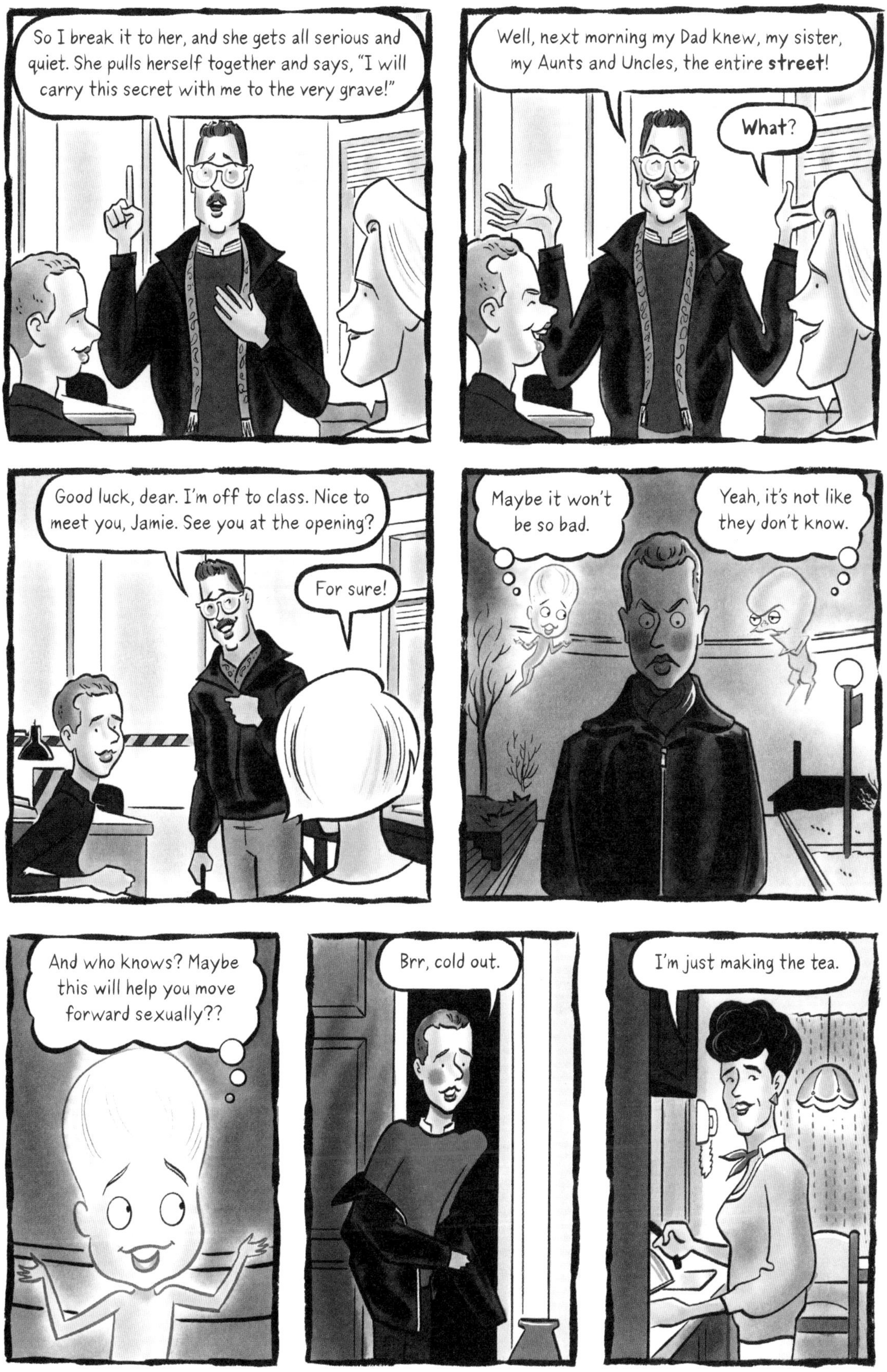
So I break it to her, and she gets all serious and quiet. She pulls herself together and says, "I will carry this secret with me to the very grave!"
Well, next morning my Dad knew, my sister, my Aunts and Uncles, the entire **street**!
What?
Good luck, dear. I'm off to class. Nice to meet you, Jamie. See you at the opening?
For sure!
Maybe it won't be so bad.
Yeah, it's not like they don't know.
And who knows? Maybe this will help you move forward sexually??
Brr, cold out.
I'm just making the tea.

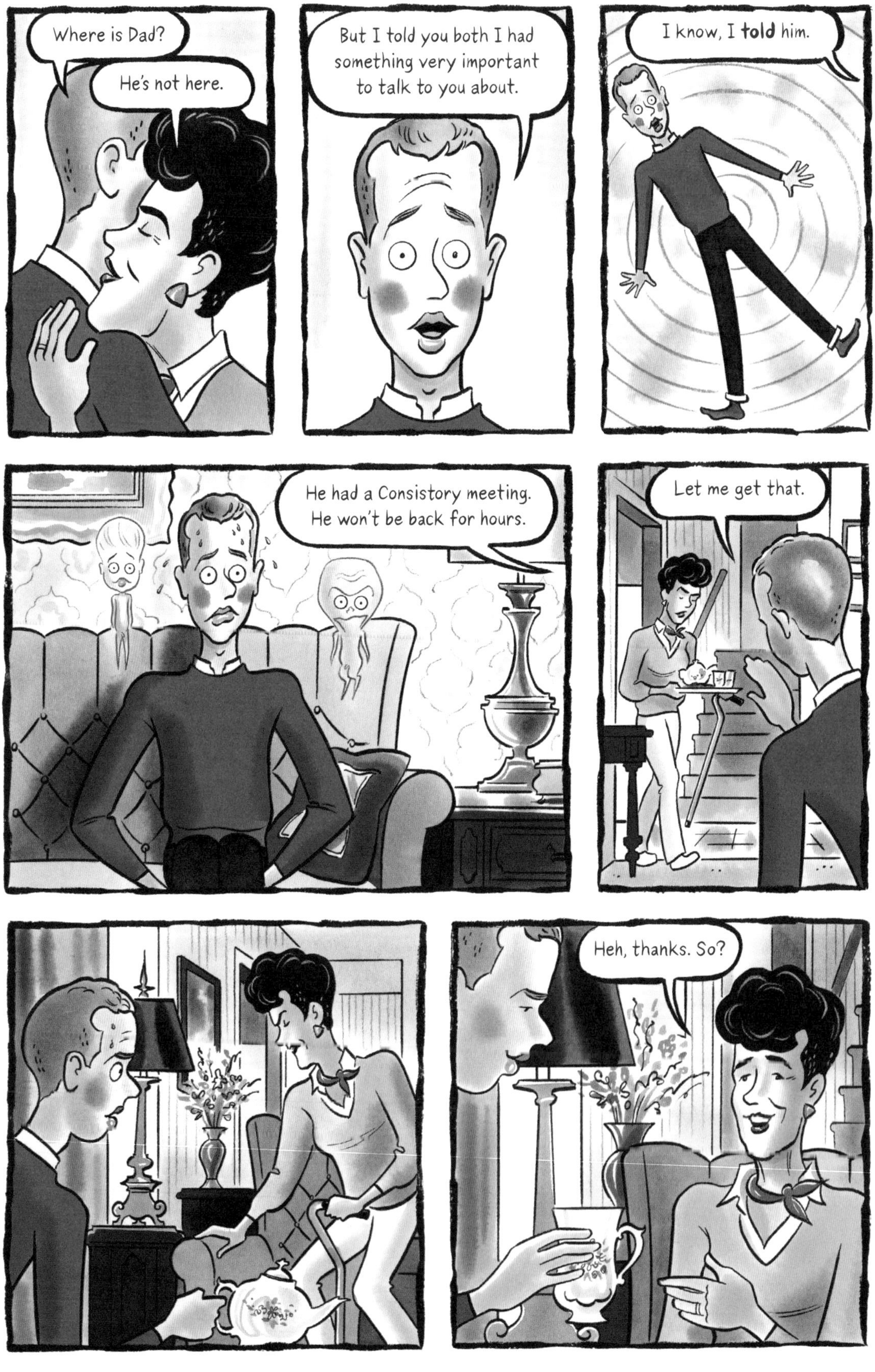
Where is Dad?
He's not here.
But I told you both I had something very important to talk to you about.
I know, I **told** him.
He had a Consistory meeting. He won't be back for hours.
Let me get that.
Heh, thanks. So?

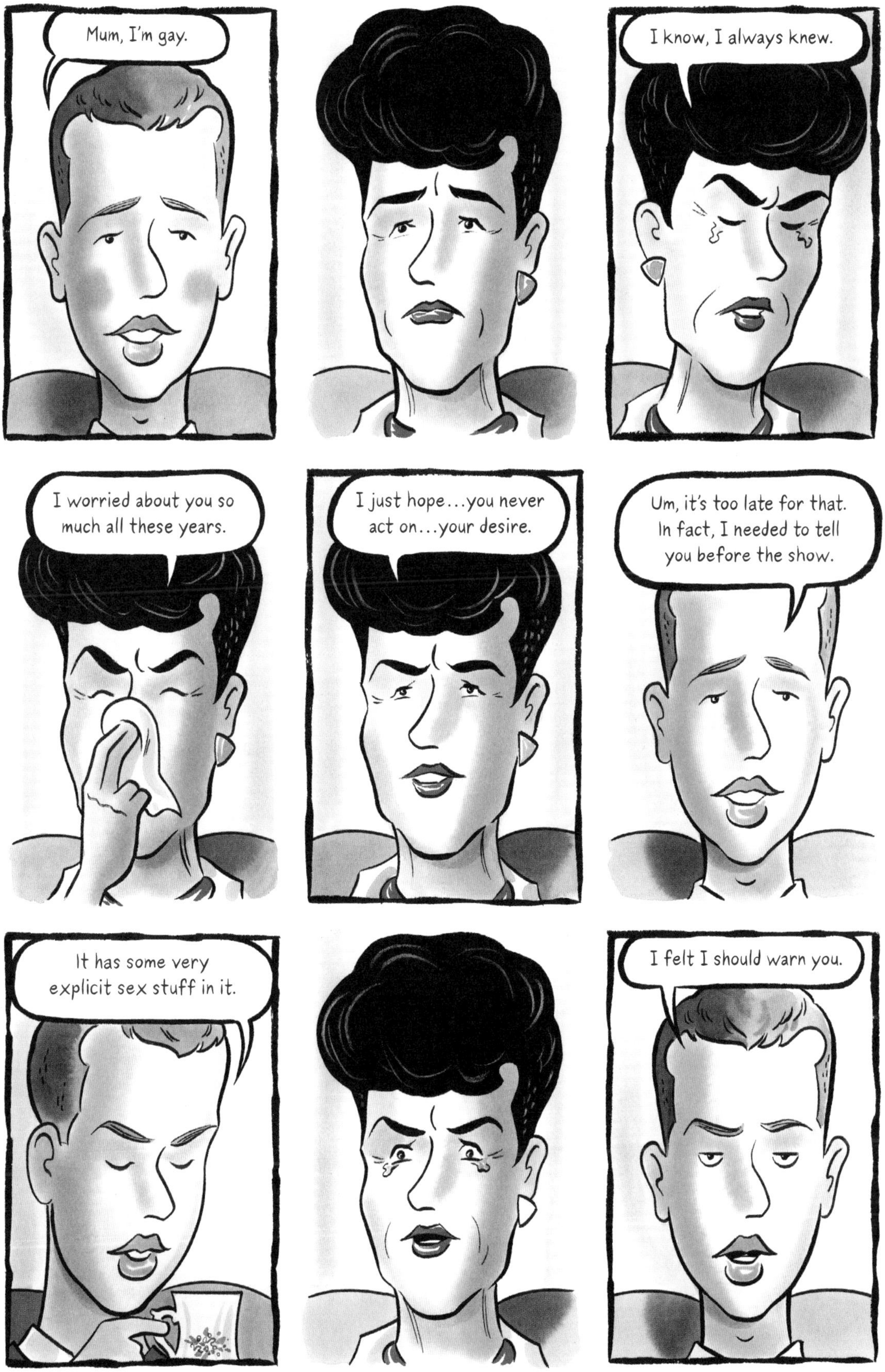

Mum, I'm gay.
I know, I always knew.
I worried about you so much all these years.
I just hope...you never act on...your desire.
Um, it's too late for that. In fact, I needed to tell you before the show.
It has some very explicit sex stuff in it.
I felt I should warn you.

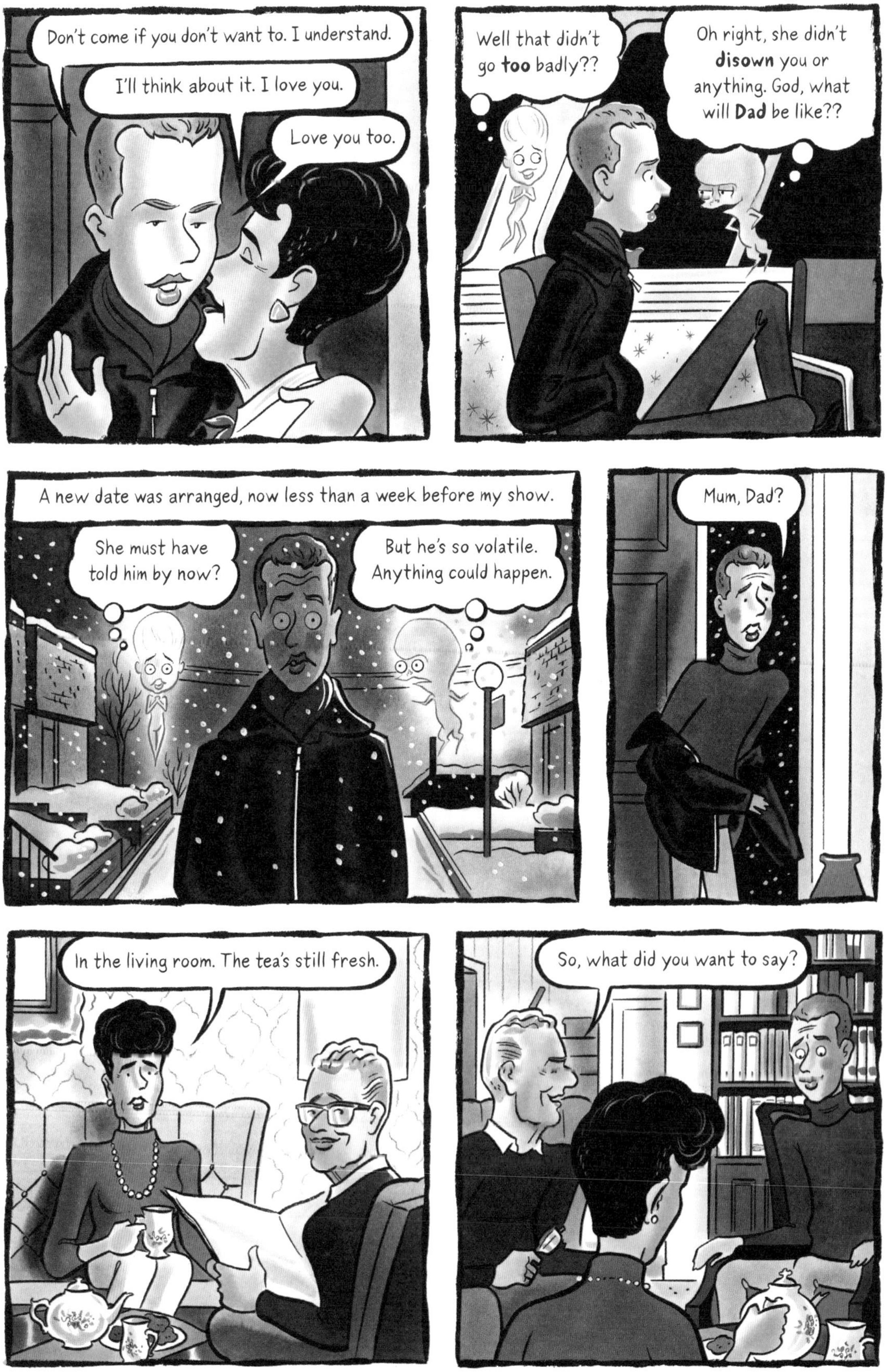
Don't come if you don't want to. I understand.
I'll think about it. I love you.
Love you too.
Well that didn't go **too** badly??
Oh right, she didn't **disown** you or anything. God, what will **Dad** be like??
A new date was arranged, now less than a week before my show.
She must have told him by now?
But he's so volatile. Anything could happen.
Mum, Dad?
In the living room. The tea's still fresh.
So, what did you want to say?

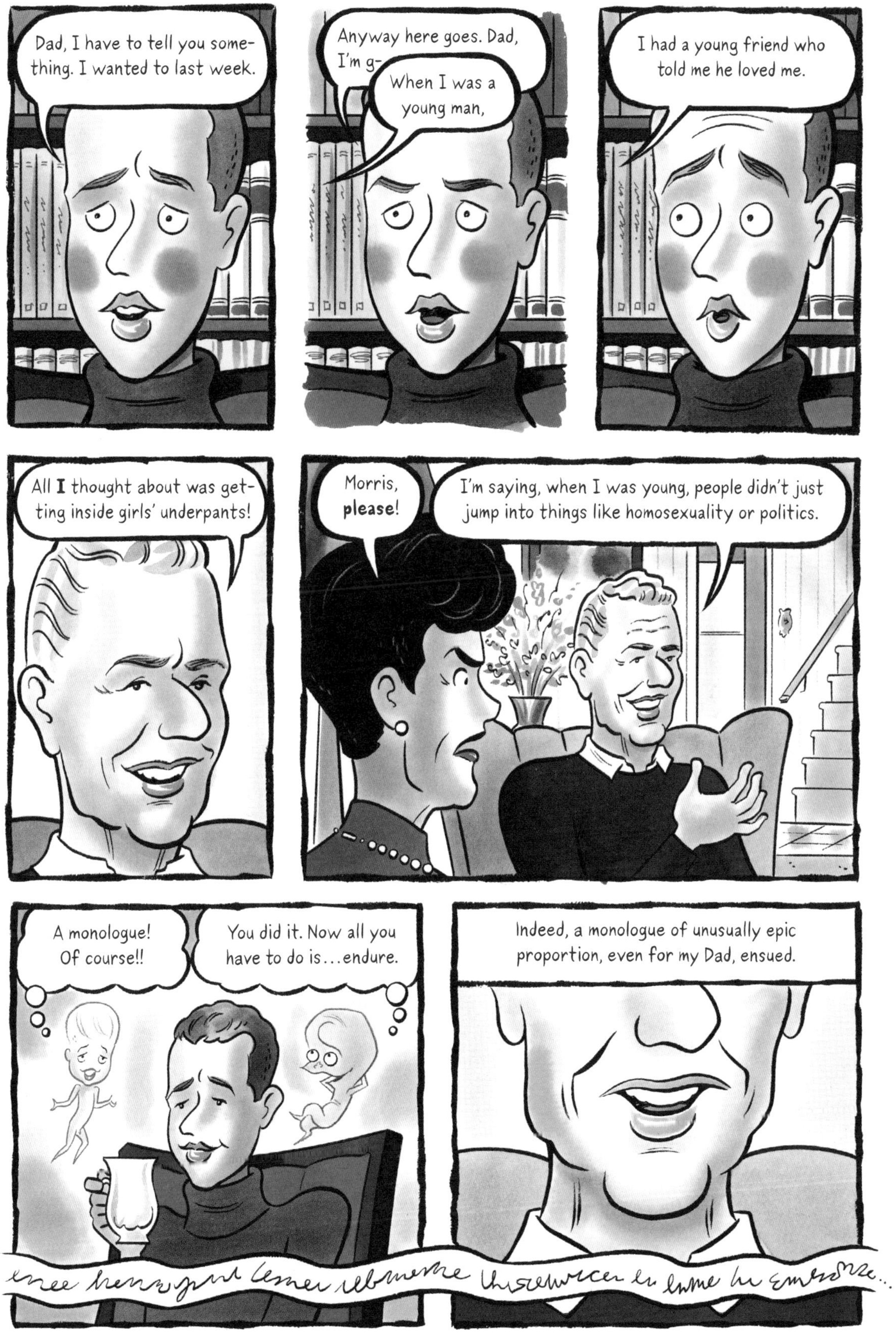

Dad, I have to tell you something. I wanted to last week.
Anyway here goes. Dad, I'm g-
When I was a young man,
I had a young friend who told me he loved me.
All **I** thought about was getting inside girls' underpants!
Morris, **please**!
I'm saying, when I was young, people didn't just jump into things like homosexuality or politics.
A monologue! Of course!!
You did it. Now all you have to do is...endure.
Indeed, a monologue of unusually epic proportion, even for my Dad, ensued.

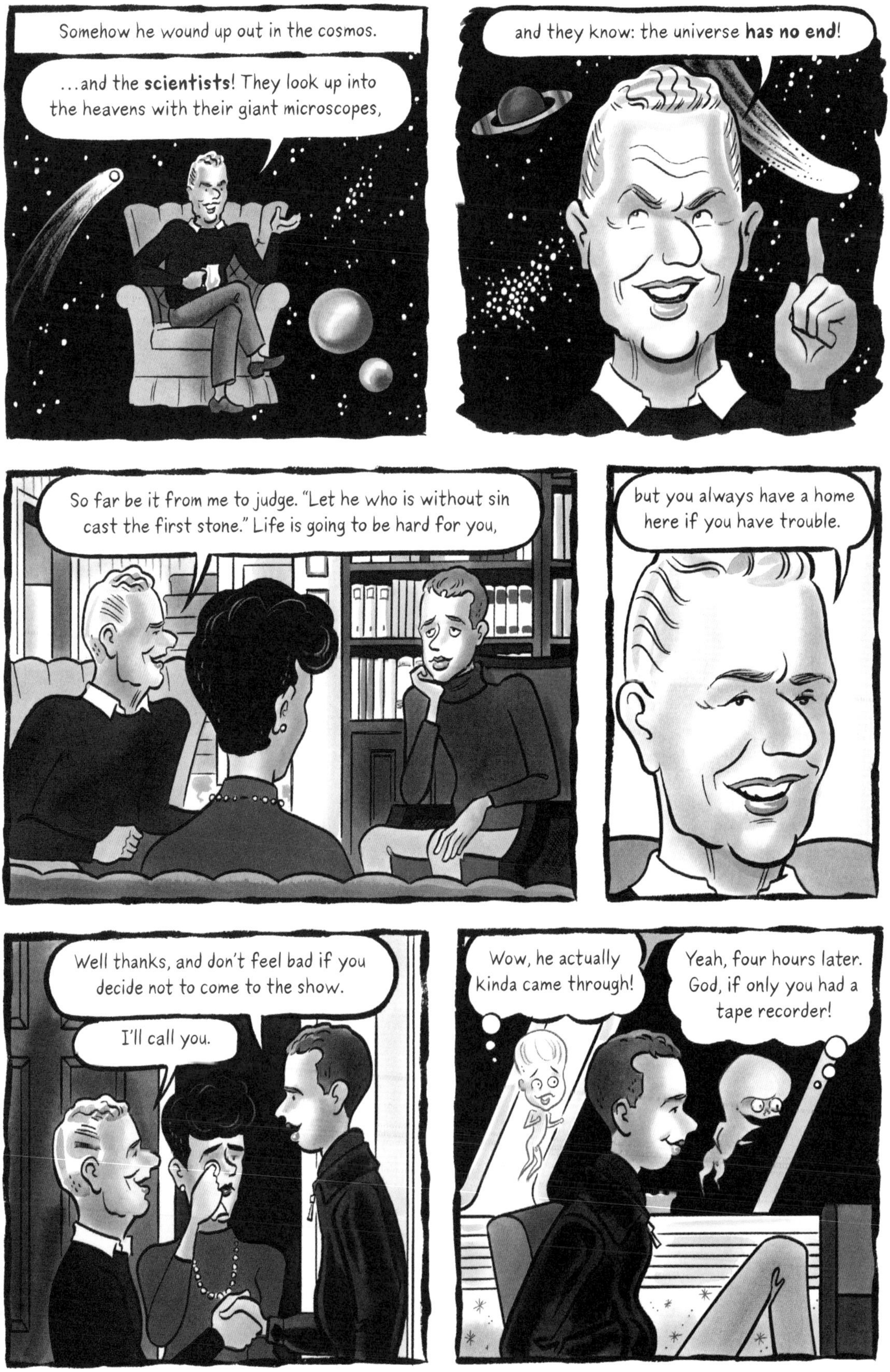
Somehow he wound up out in the cosmos.
...and the **scientists**! They look up into the heavens with their giant microscopes,
and they know: the universe **has no end**!
So far be it from me to judge. "Let he who is without sin cast the first stone." Life is going to be hard for you,
but you always have a home here if you have trouble.
Well thanks, and don't feel bad if you decide not to come to the show.
I'll call you.
Wow, he actually kinda came through!
Yeah, four hours later. God, if only you had a tape recorder!

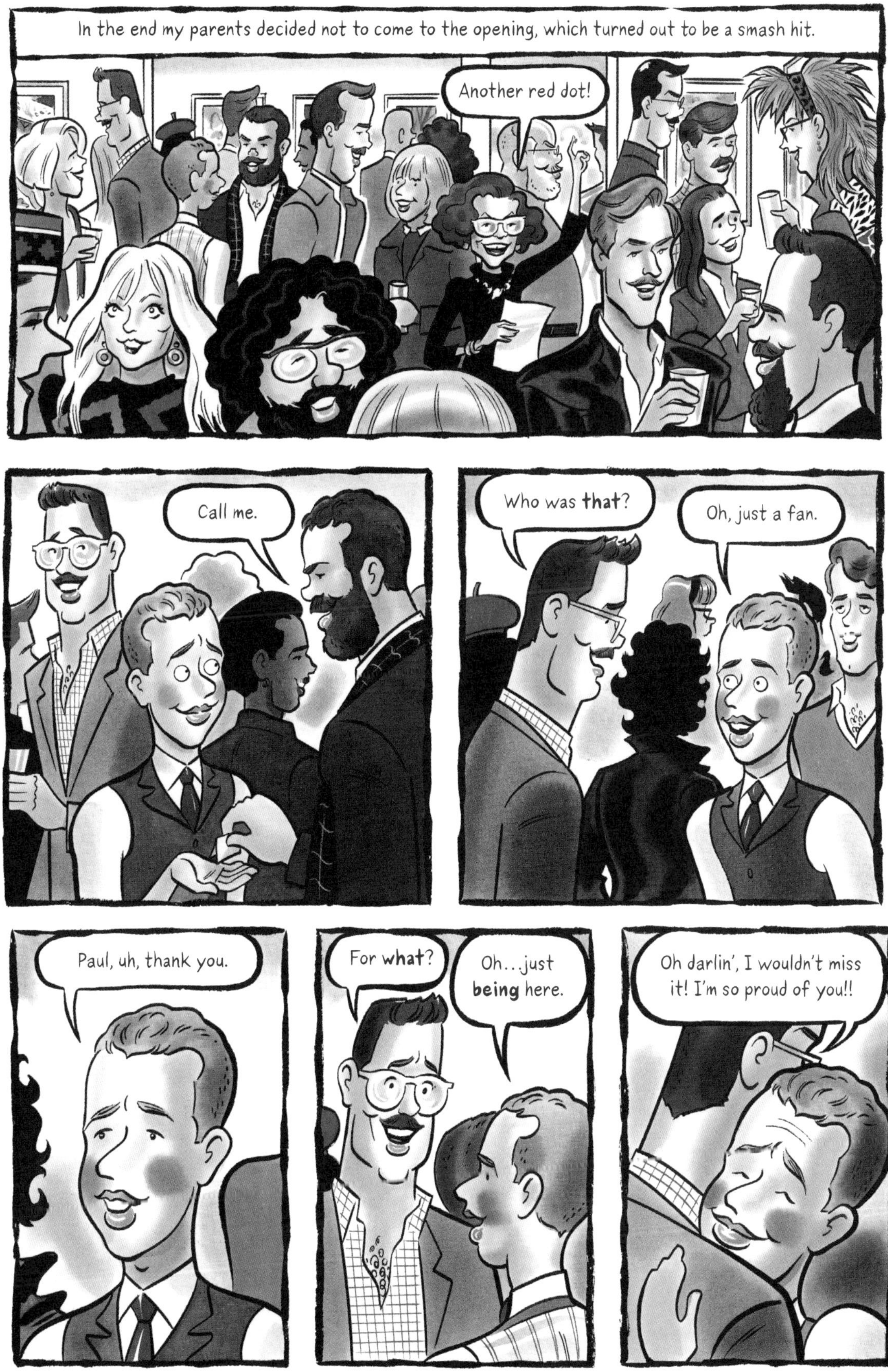

In the end my parents decided not to come to the opening, which turned out to be a smash hit.
Another red dot!
Call me.
Who was **that**?
Oh, just a fan.
Paul, uh, thank you.
For **what**?
Oh...just **being** here.
Oh darlin', I wouldn't miss it! I'm so proud of you!!

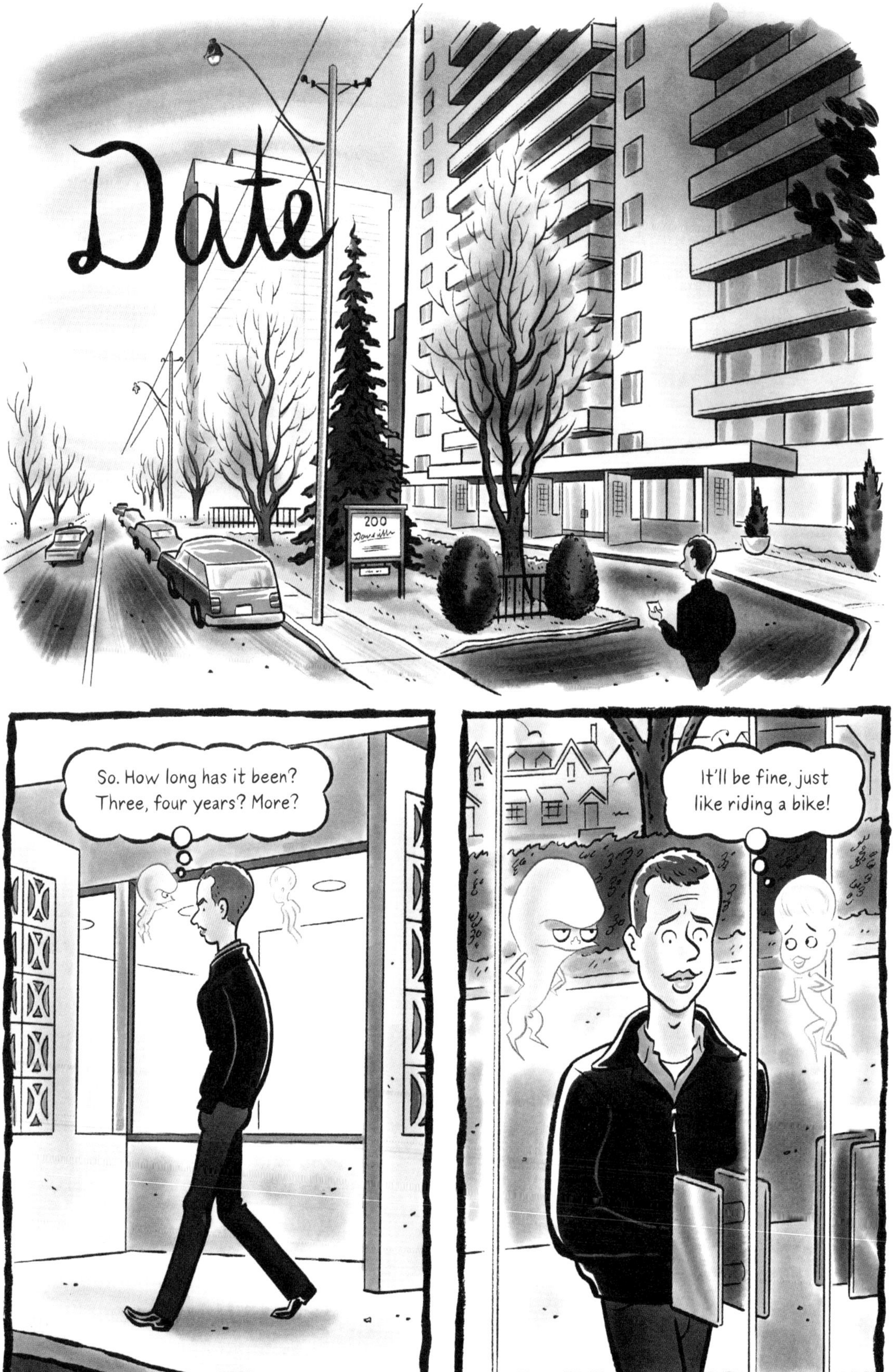
Date
200
So. How long has it been? Three, four years? More?
It'll be fine, just like riding a bike!

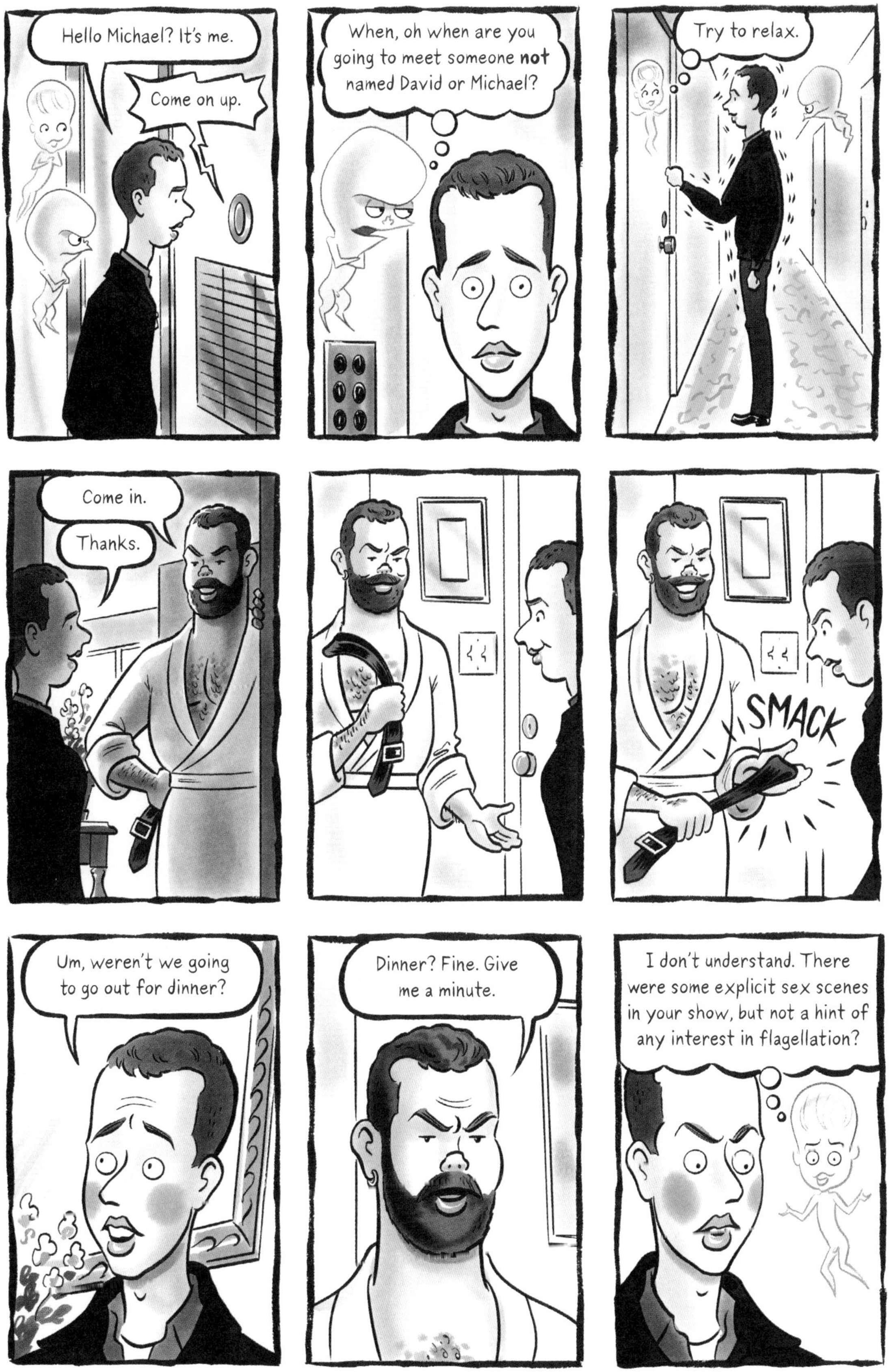
Hello Michael? It's me.
Come on up.
When, oh when are you going to meet someone **not** named David or Michael?
Try to relax.
Come in.
Thanks.
SMACK
Um, weren't we going to go out for dinner?
Dinner? Fine. Give me a minute.
I don't understand. There were some explicit sex scenes in your show, but not a hint of any interest in flagellation?

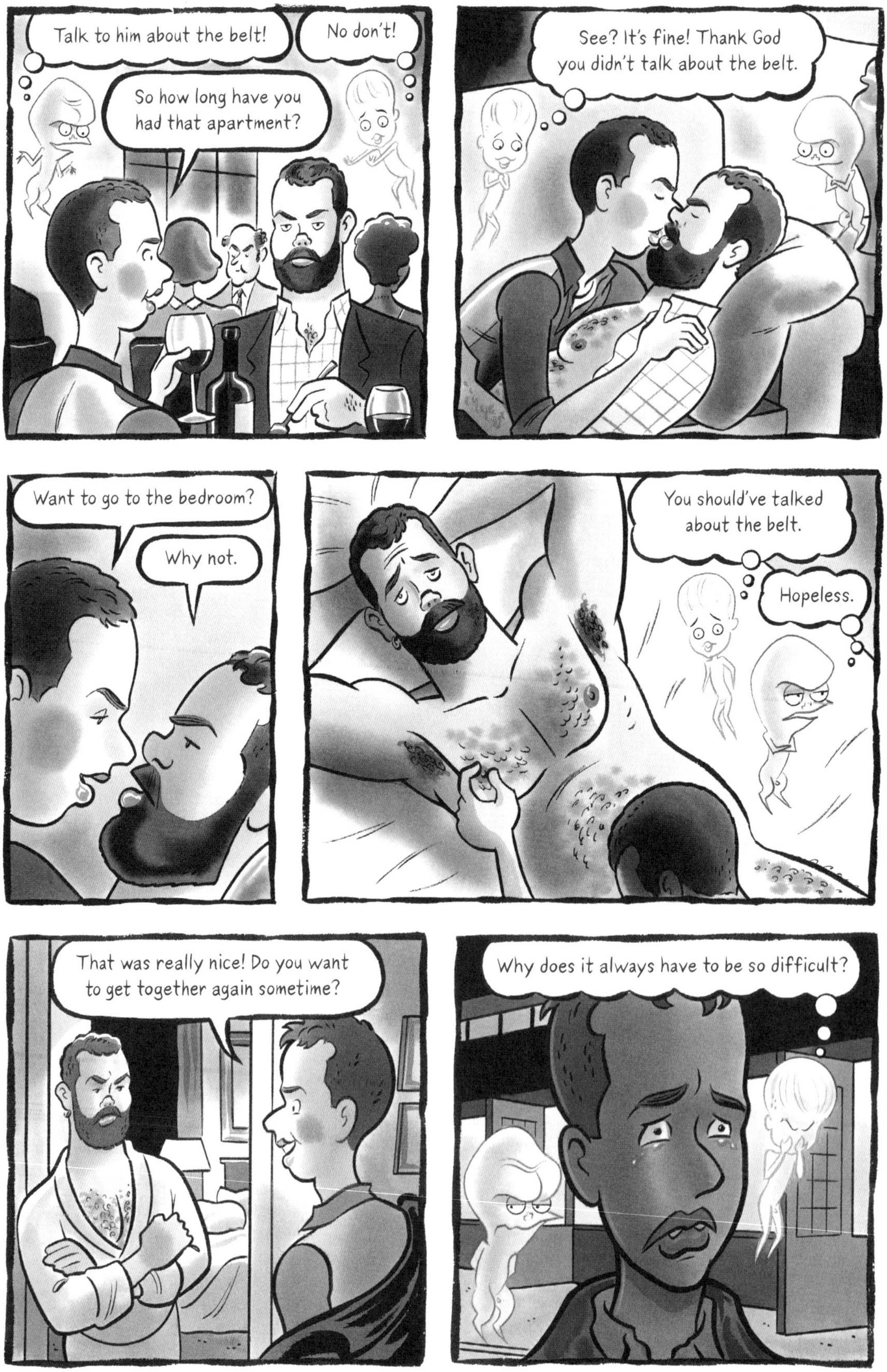
Talk to him about the belt!
No don't!
So how long have you had that apartment?
See? It's fine! Thank God you didn't talk about the belt.
Want to go to the bedroom?
Why not.
You should've talked about the belt.
Hopeless.
That was really nice! Do you want to get together again sometime?
Why does it always have to be so difficult?

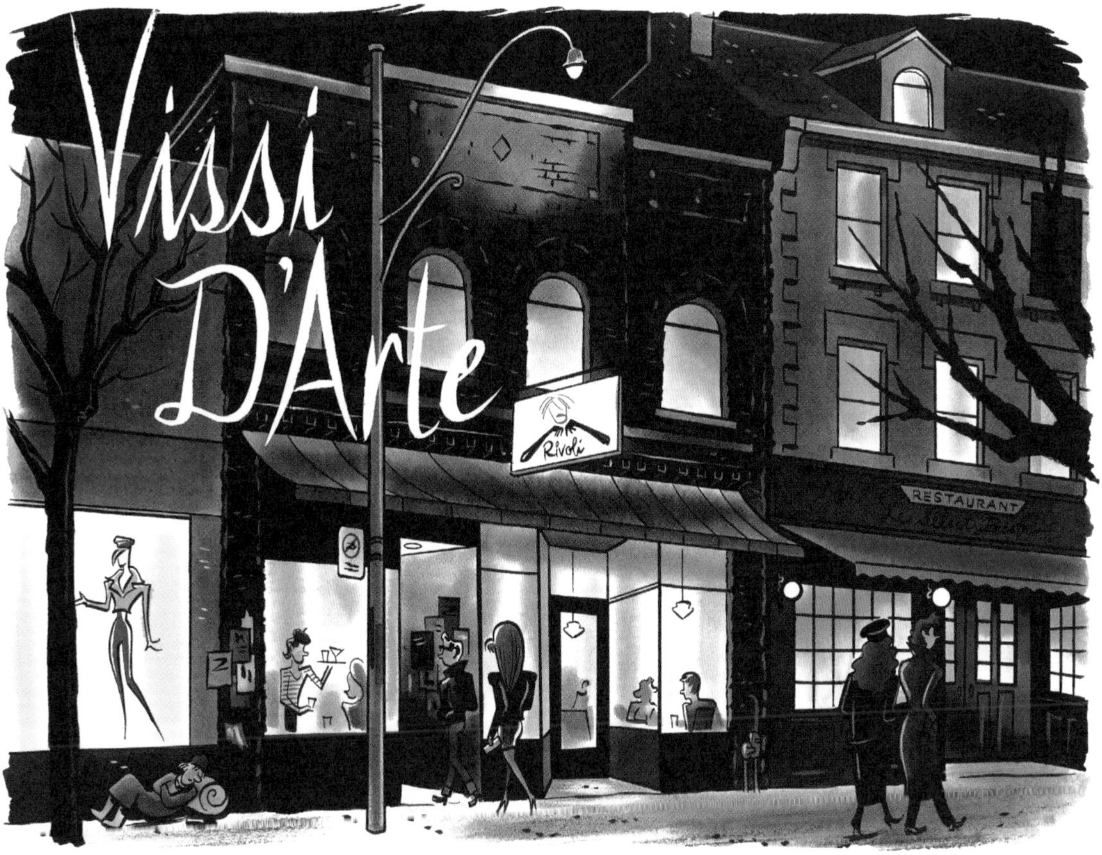
Vissi D'Arte
Rivoli
RESTAURANT

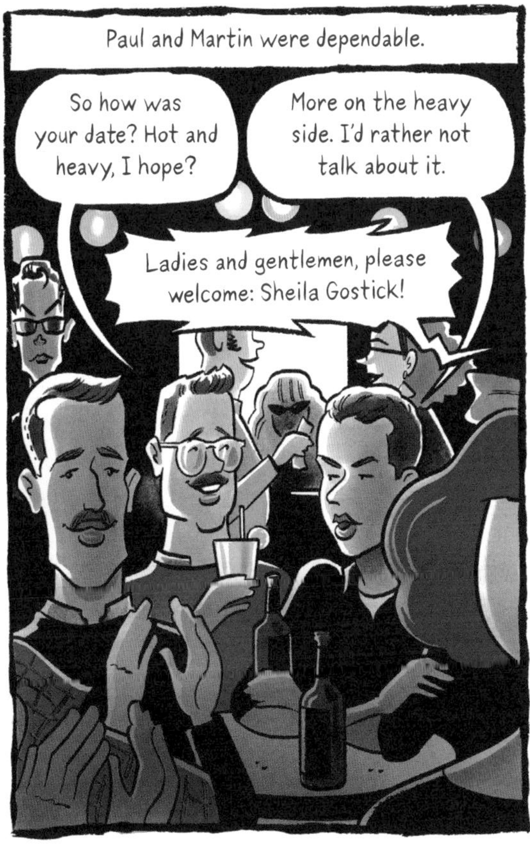
Paul and Martin were dependable.
So how was your date? Hot and heavy, I hope?
More on the heavy side. I'd rather not talk about it.
Ladies and gentlemen, please welcome: Sheila Gostick!

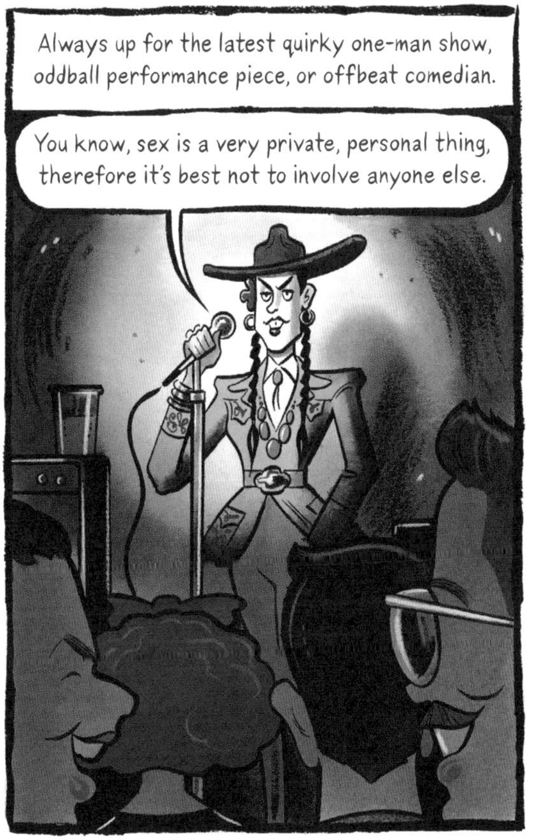
Always up for the latest quirky one-man show, oddball performance piece, or offbeat comedian.
You know, sex is a very private, personal thing, therefore it's best not to involve anyone else.

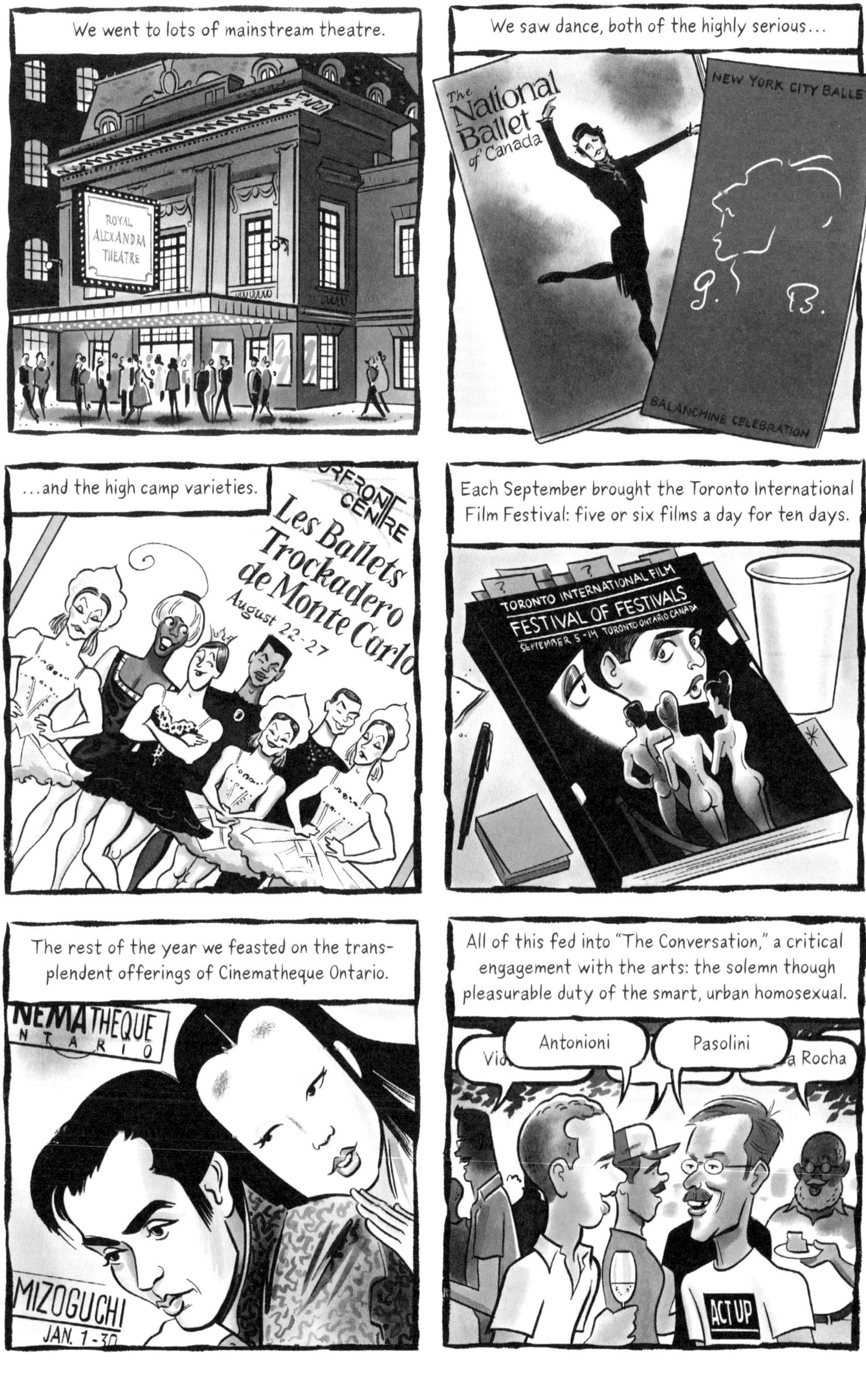
We went to lots of mainstream theatre.
ROYAL ALEXANDRA THEATRE
We saw dance, both of the highly serious...
The National Ballet of Canada
NEW YORK CITY BALLET
BALANCHINE CELEBRATION
...and the high camp varieties.
CENTRE
Les Ballets Trockadero de Monte Carlo
August 22-27
Each September brought the Toronto International Film Festival: five or six films a day for ten days.
TORONTO INTERNATIONAL FILM
FESTIVAL OF FESTIVALS
SEPTEMBER 5-14 TORONTO ONTARIO CANADA
The rest of the year we feasted on the transplendent offerings of Cinematheque Ontario.
MIZOGUCHI
All of this fed into "The Conversation," a critical engagement with the arts: the solemn though pleasurable duty of the smart, urban homosexual.
Antonioni
Pasolini
ACT UP

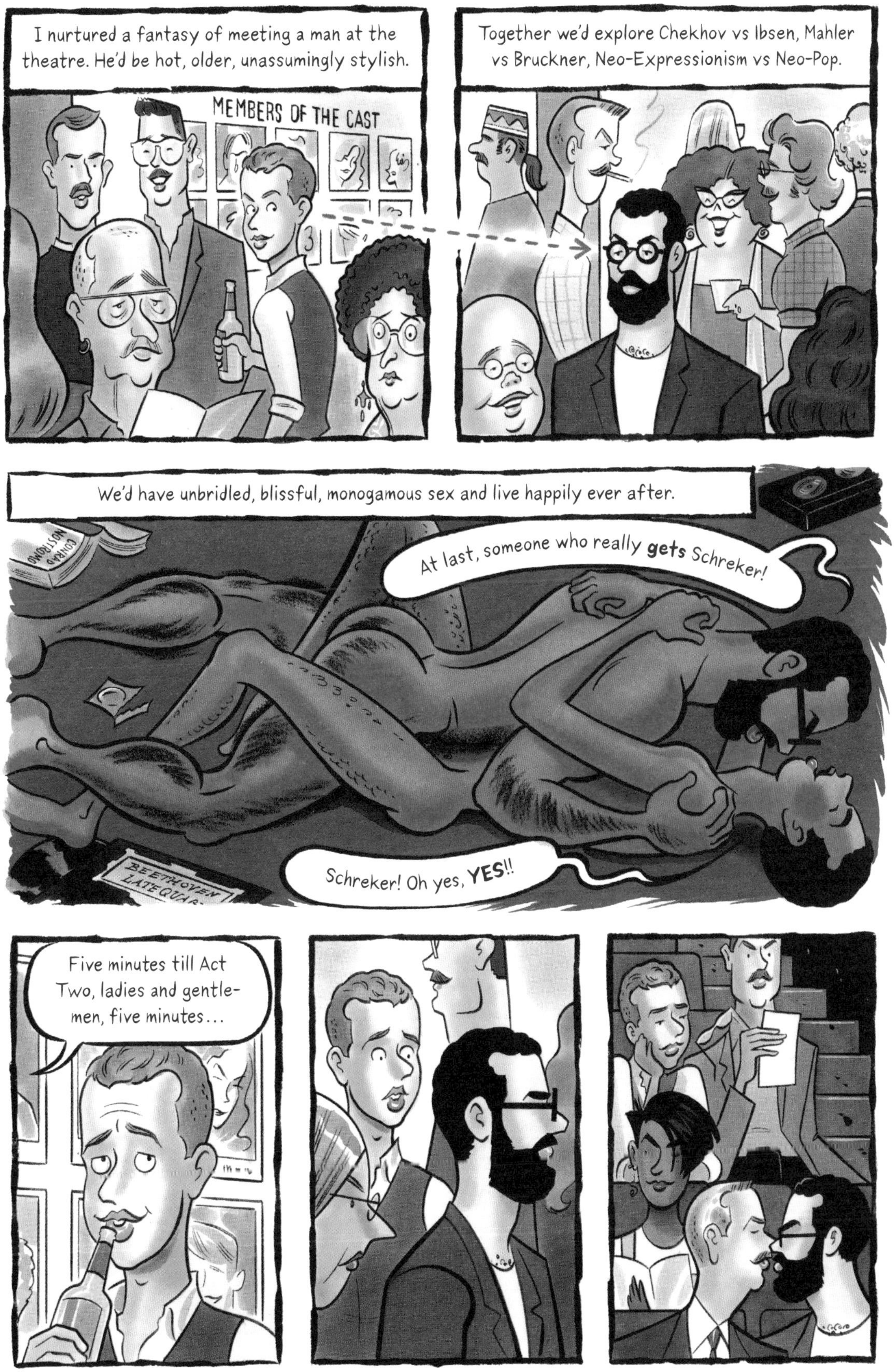
I nurtured a fantasy of meeting a man at the theatre. He'd be hot, older, unassumingly stylish.
MEMBERS OF THE CAST
Together we'd explore Chekhov vs Ibsen, Mahler vs Bruckner, Neo-Expressionism vs Neo-Pop.
We'd have unbridled, blissful, monogamous sex and live happily ever after.
CONRAD NOSTROMO
At last, someone who really **gets** Schreker!
Schreker! Oh yes, **YES**!!
Five minutes till Act Two, ladies and gentle-men, five minutes...

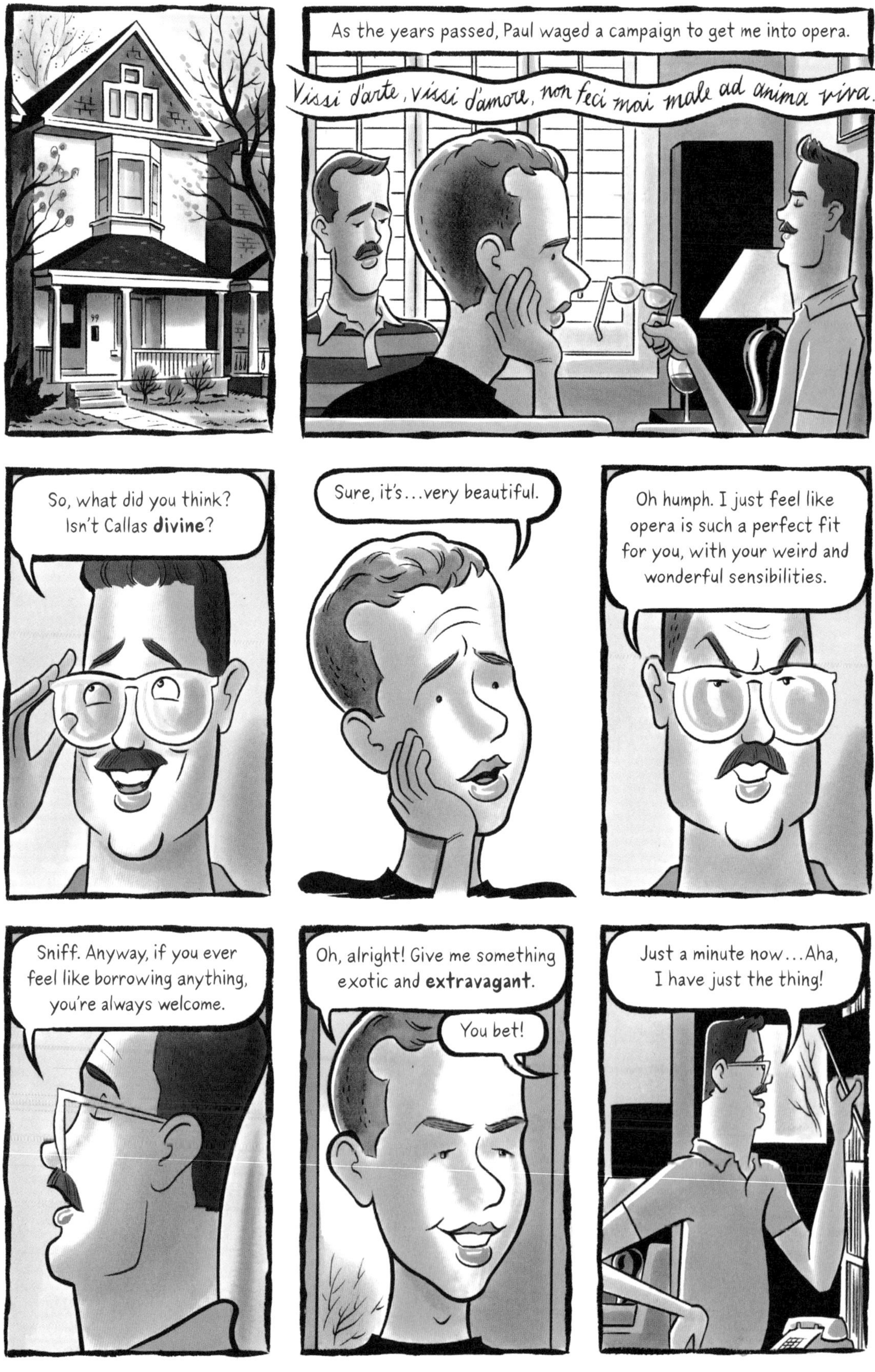
As the years passed, Paul waged a campaign to get me into opera.
Vissi d'arte, vissi d'amore, non feci mai male ad anima viva...
So, what did you think? Isn't Callas **divine**?
Sure, it's...very beautiful.
Oh humph. I just feel like opera is such a perfect fit for you, with your weird and wonderful sensibilities.
Sniff. Anyway, if you ever feel like borrowing anything, you're always welcome.
Oh, alright! Give me something exotic and **extravagant**.
You bet!
Just a minute now...Aha, I have just the thing!

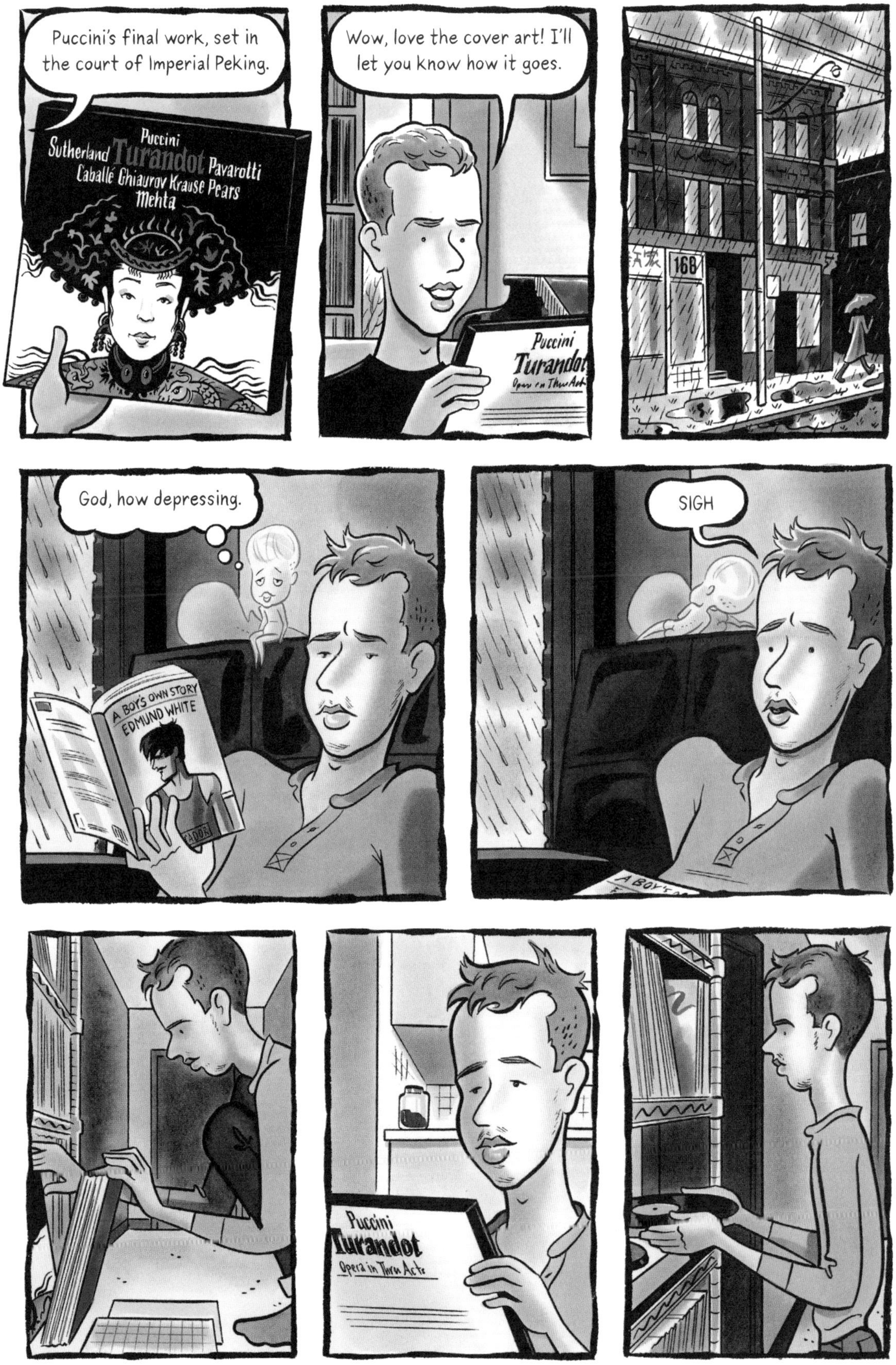
Puccini's final work, set in the court of Imperial Peking.
Puccini
Sutherland Turandot Pavarotti
Caballé Ghiaurov Krause Pears
Mehta
Wow, love the cover art! I'll let you know how it goes.
Puccini
Turandot
168
God, how depressing.
A BOY'S OWN STORY
EDMUND WHITE
SIGH
Puccini
Turandot
Opera in Three Acts

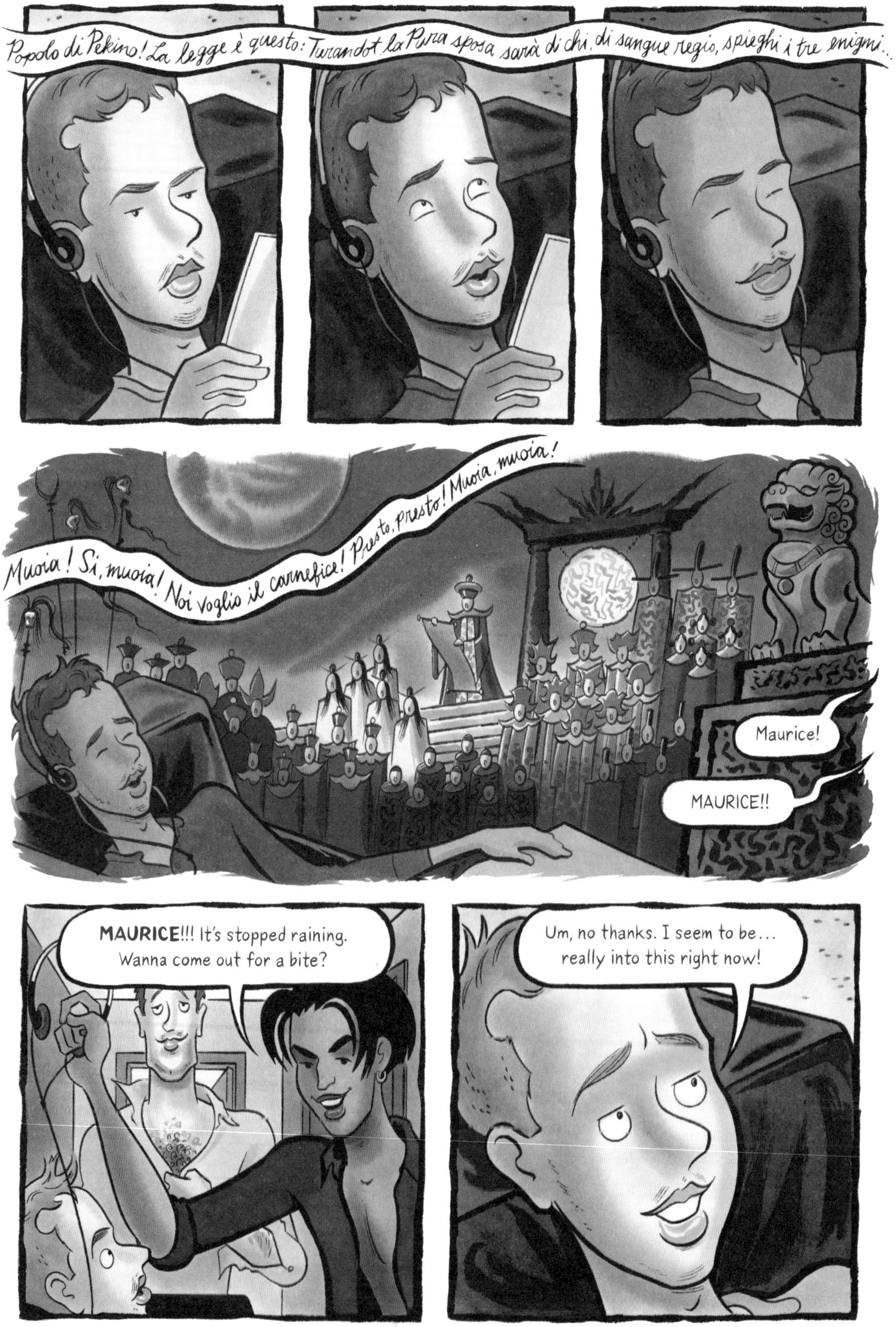
Popolo di Pekino! La legge è questo: Turandot la Pura sposa sarà di chi, di sangue regio, spieghi i tre enigmi...
Muoia! Sì, muoia! Noi voglio il carnefice! Presto, presto! Muoia, muoia!
Maurice!
MAURICE!!
MAURICE!!! It's stopped raining. Wanna come out for a bite?
Um, no thanks. I seem to be... really into this right now!

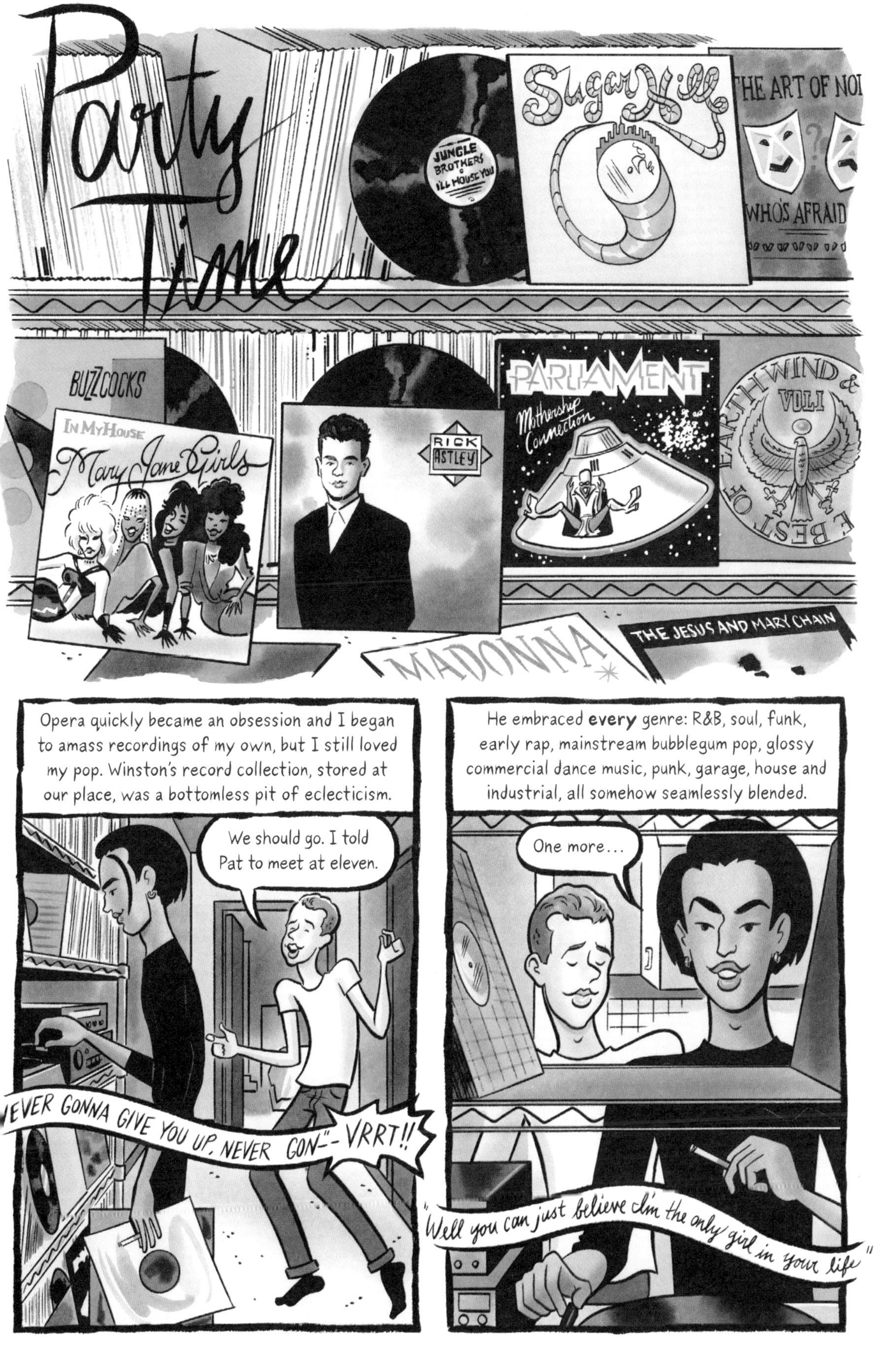

Party Time
JUNGLE BROTHERS
I'LL HOUSE YOU
Sugar Hill
THE ART OF NOI
WHO'S AFRAID
BUZZCOCKS
IN MY HOUSE
Mary Jane Girls
RICK ASTLEY
PARLIAMENT
Mothership Connection
VOL I
MADONNA
THE JESUS AND MARY CHAIN
Opera quickly became an obsession and I began to amass recordings of my own, but I still loved my pop. Winston's record collection, stored at our place, was a bottomless pit of eclecticism.
We should go. I told Pat to meet at eleven.
EVER GONNA GIVE YOU UP, NEVER GON–"- VRRT!!
He embraced **every** genre: R&B, soul, funk, early rap, mainstream bubblegum pop, glossy commercial dance music, punk, garage, house and industrial, all somehow seamlessly blended.
One more…
"Well you can just believe I'm the only girl in your life"

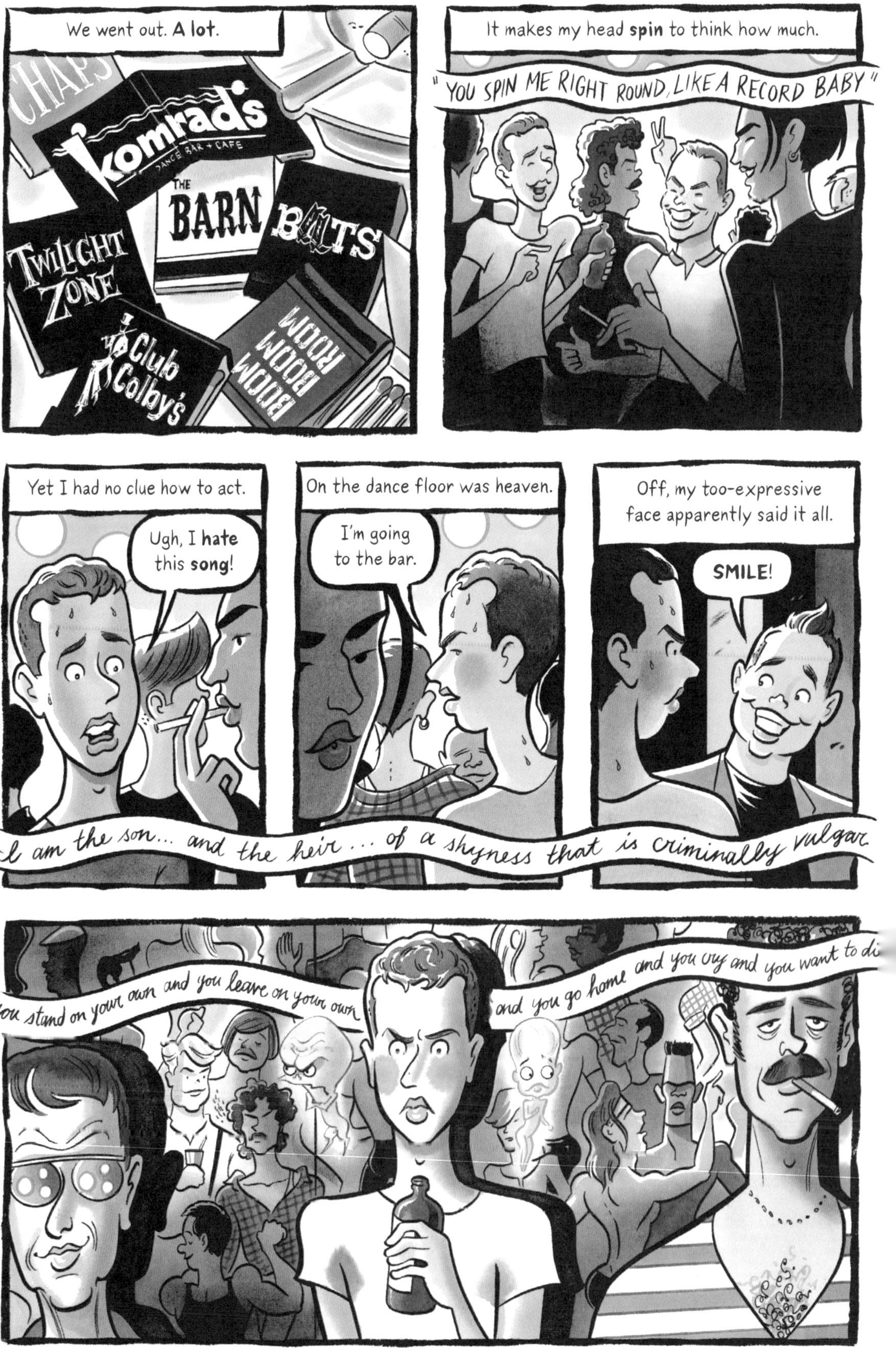

We went out. **A lot.**
CHAPS
komrad's
DANCE BAR + CAFE
THE BARN
TWILIGHT ZONE
Club Colby's
BOOM BOOM ROOM
It makes my head **spin** to think how much.
"YOU SPIN ME RIGHT ROUND, LIKE A RECORD BABY"
Yet I had no clue how to act.
Ugh, I **hate** this **song**!
On the dance floor was heaven.
I'm going to the bar.
Off, my too-expressive face apparently said it all.
SMILE!
"I am the son... and the heir... of a shyness that is criminally vulgar
you stand on your own and you leave on your own
and you go home and you cry and you want to di

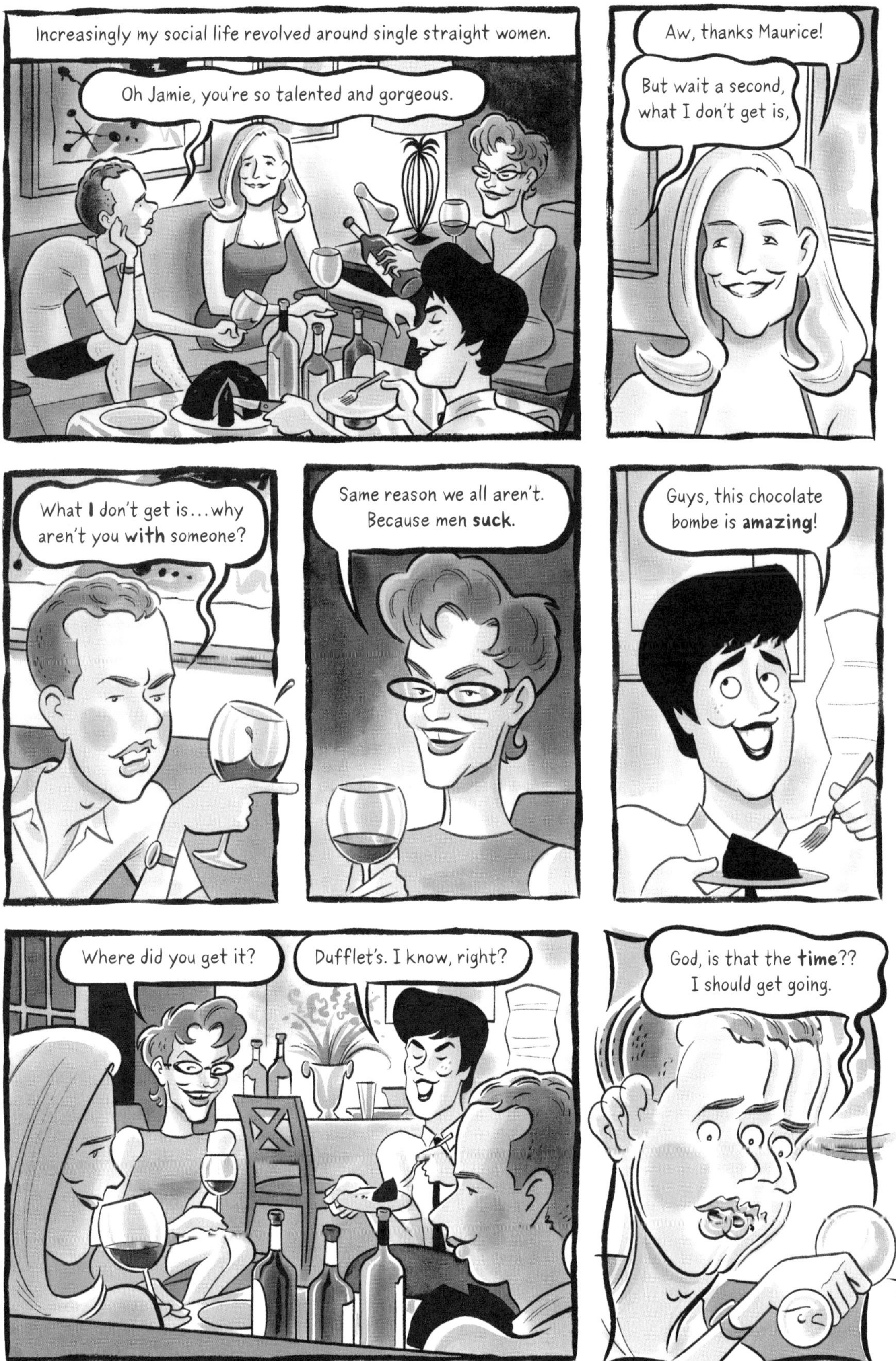
Increasingly my social life revolved around single straight women.
Oh Jamie, you're so talented and gorgeous.
Aw, thanks Maurice!
But wait a second, what I don't get is,
What **I** don't get is...why aren't you **with** someone?
Same reason we all aren't. Because men **suck**.
Guys, this chocolate bombe is **amazing**!
Where did you get it?
Dufflet's. I know, right?
God, is that the **time**?? I should get going.

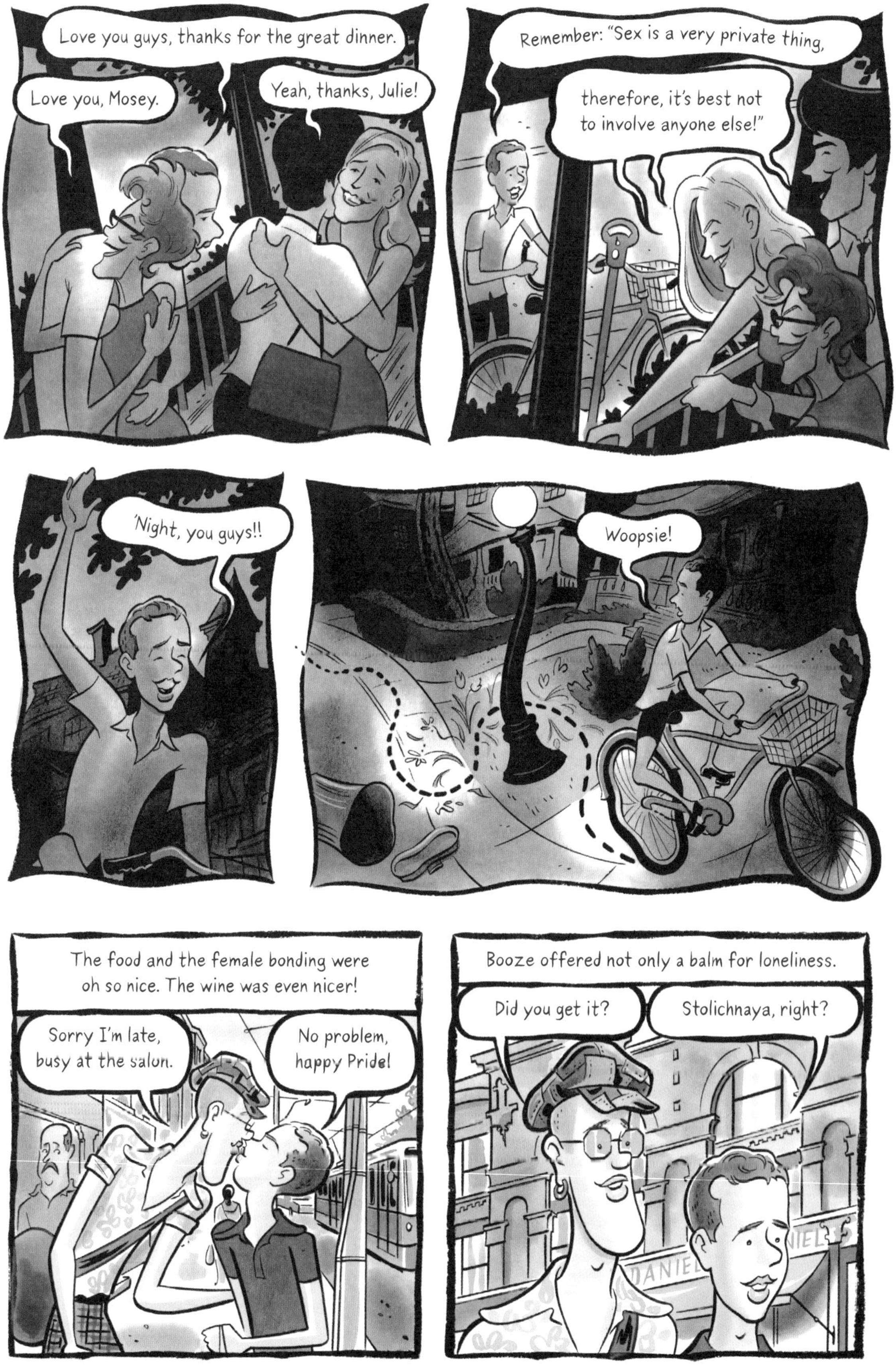

Love you guys, thanks for the great dinner.
Love you, Mosey.
Yeah, thanks, Julie!
Remember: "Sex is a very private thing,
therefore, it's best not to involve anyone else!"
'Night, you guys!!
Woopsie!
The food and the female bonding were oh so nice. The wine was even nicer!
Sorry I'm late, busy at the salon.
No problem, happy Pride!
Booze offered not only a balm for loneliness.
Did you get it?
Stolichnaya, right?

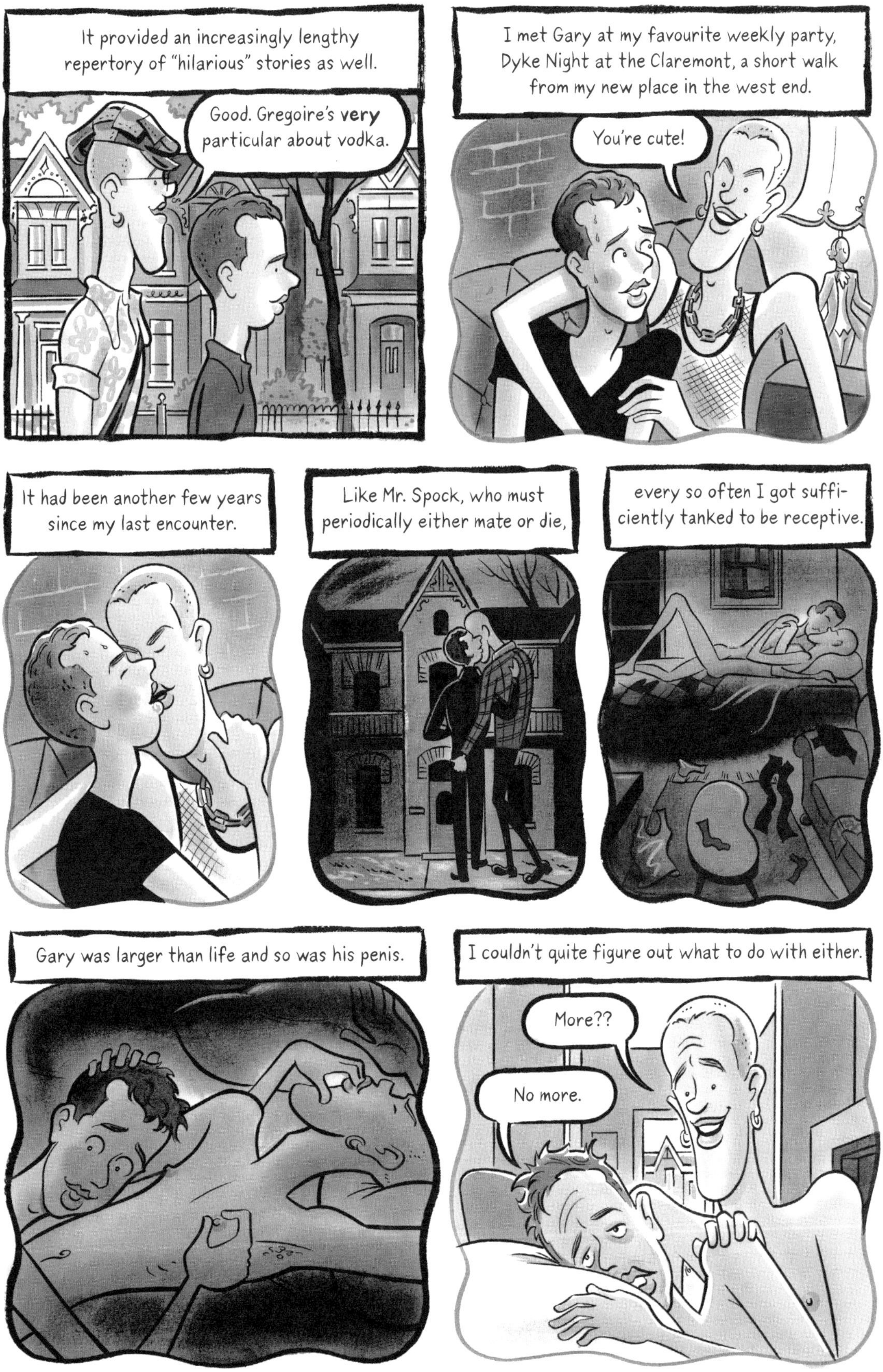
It provided an increasingly lengthy repertory of "hilarious" stories as well.
Good. Gregoire's **very** particular about vodka.
I met Gary at my favourite weekly party, Dyke Night at the Claremont, a short walk from my new place in the west end.
You're cute!
It had been another few years since my last encounter.
Like Mr. Spock, who must periodically either mate or die,
every so often I got sufficiently tanked to be receptive.
Gary was larger than life and so was his penis.
I couldn't quite figure out what to do with either.
More??
No more.

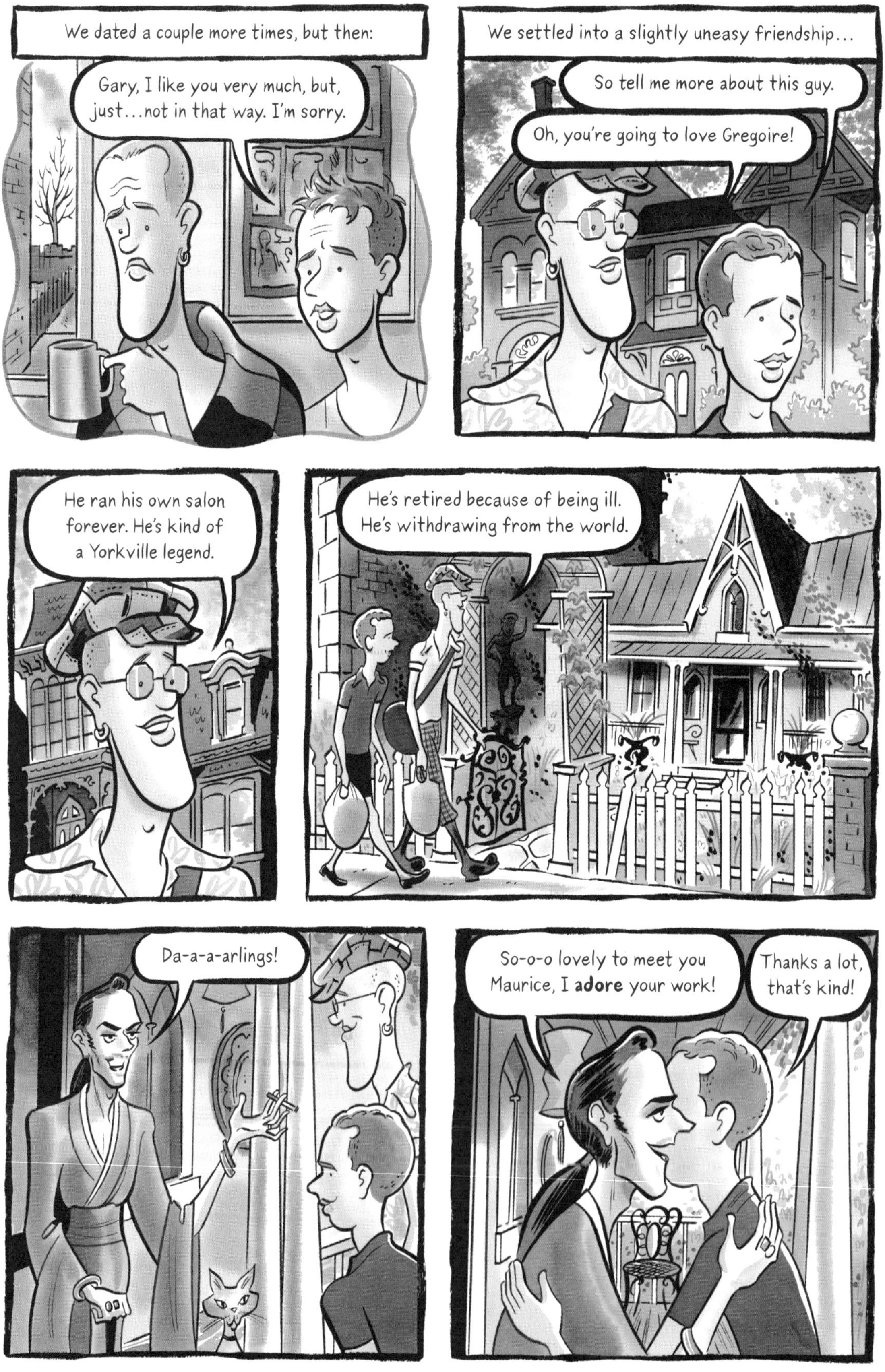
We dated a couple more times, but then:
Gary, I like you very much, but, just...not in that way. I'm sorry.
We settled into a slightly uneasy friendship...
So tell me more about this guy.
Oh, you're going to love Gregoire!
He ran his own salon forever. He's kind of a Yorkville legend.
He's retired because of being ill. He's withdrawing from the world.
Da-a-a-arlings!
So-o-o lovely to meet you Maurice, I **adore** your work!
Thanks a lot, that's kind!

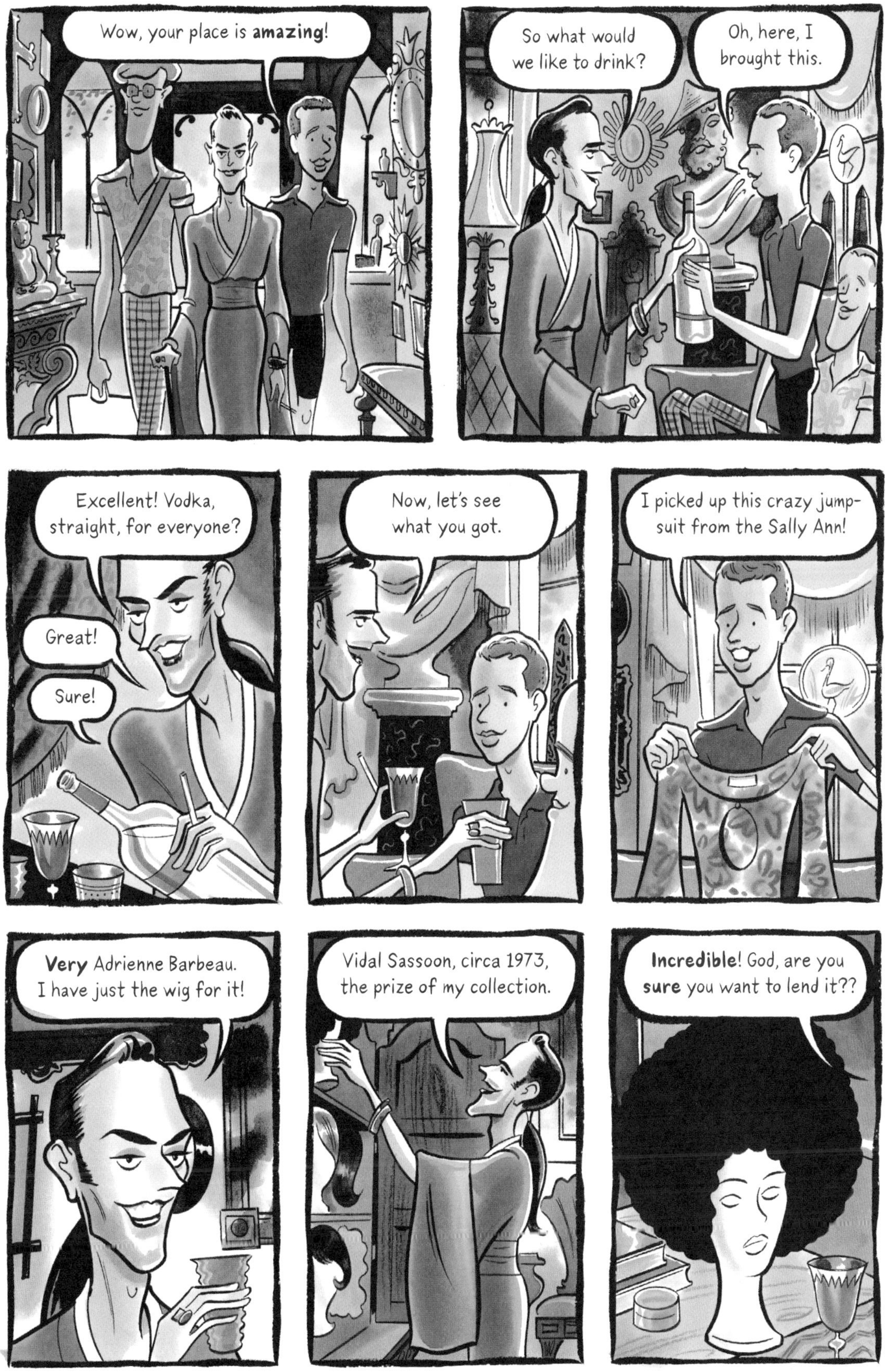
Wow, your place is **amazing**!
So what would we like to drink?
Oh, here, I brought this.
Excellent! Vodka, straight, for everyone?
Great!
Sure!
Now, let's see what you got.
I picked up this crazy jump-suit from the Sally Ann!
Very Adrienne Barbeau. I have just the wig for it!
Vidal Sassoon, circa 1973, the prize of my collection.
Incredible! God, are you **sure** you want to lend it??

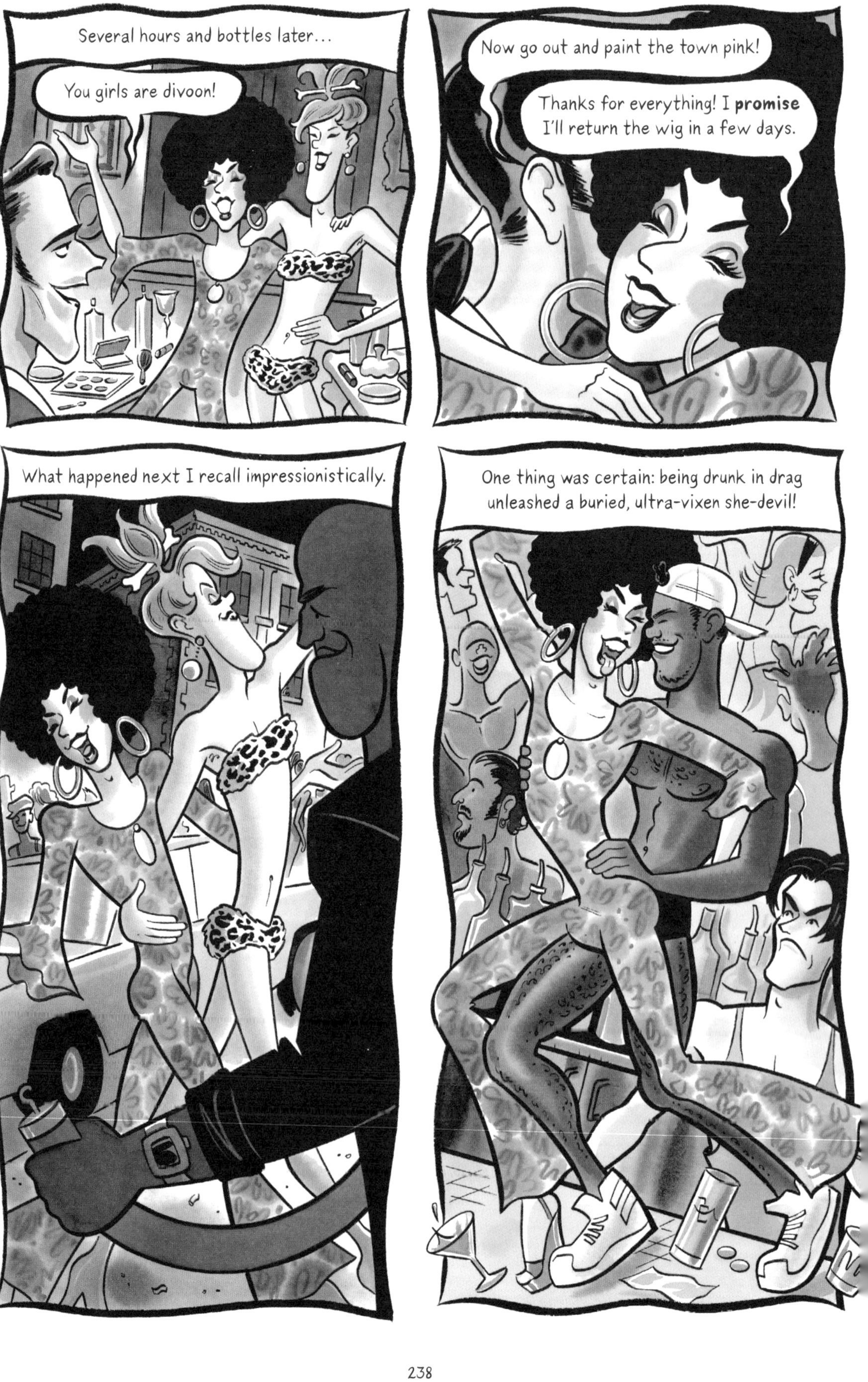
Several hours and bottles later...
You girls are divoon!
Now go out and paint the town pink!
Thanks for everything! I **promise** I'll return the wig in a few days.
What happened next I recall impressionistically.
One thing was certain: being drunk in drag unleashed a buried, ultra-vixen she-devil!

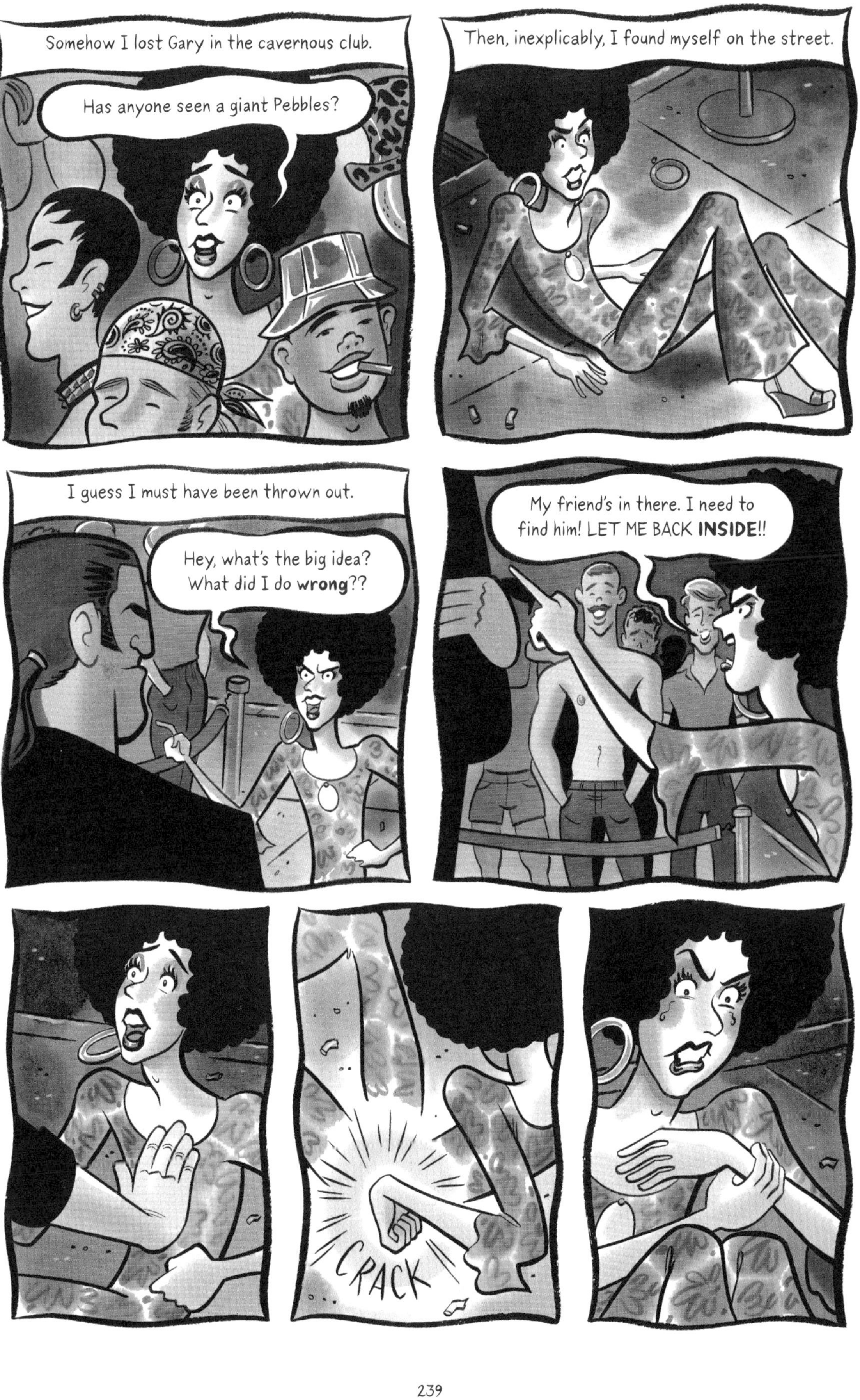
Somehow I lost Gary in the cavernous club.
Has anyone seen a giant Pebbles?
Then, inexplicably, I found myself on the street.
I guess I must have been thrown out.
Hey, what's the big idea? What did I do **wrong**??
My friend's in there. I need to find him! LET ME BACK **INSIDE**!!
CRACK

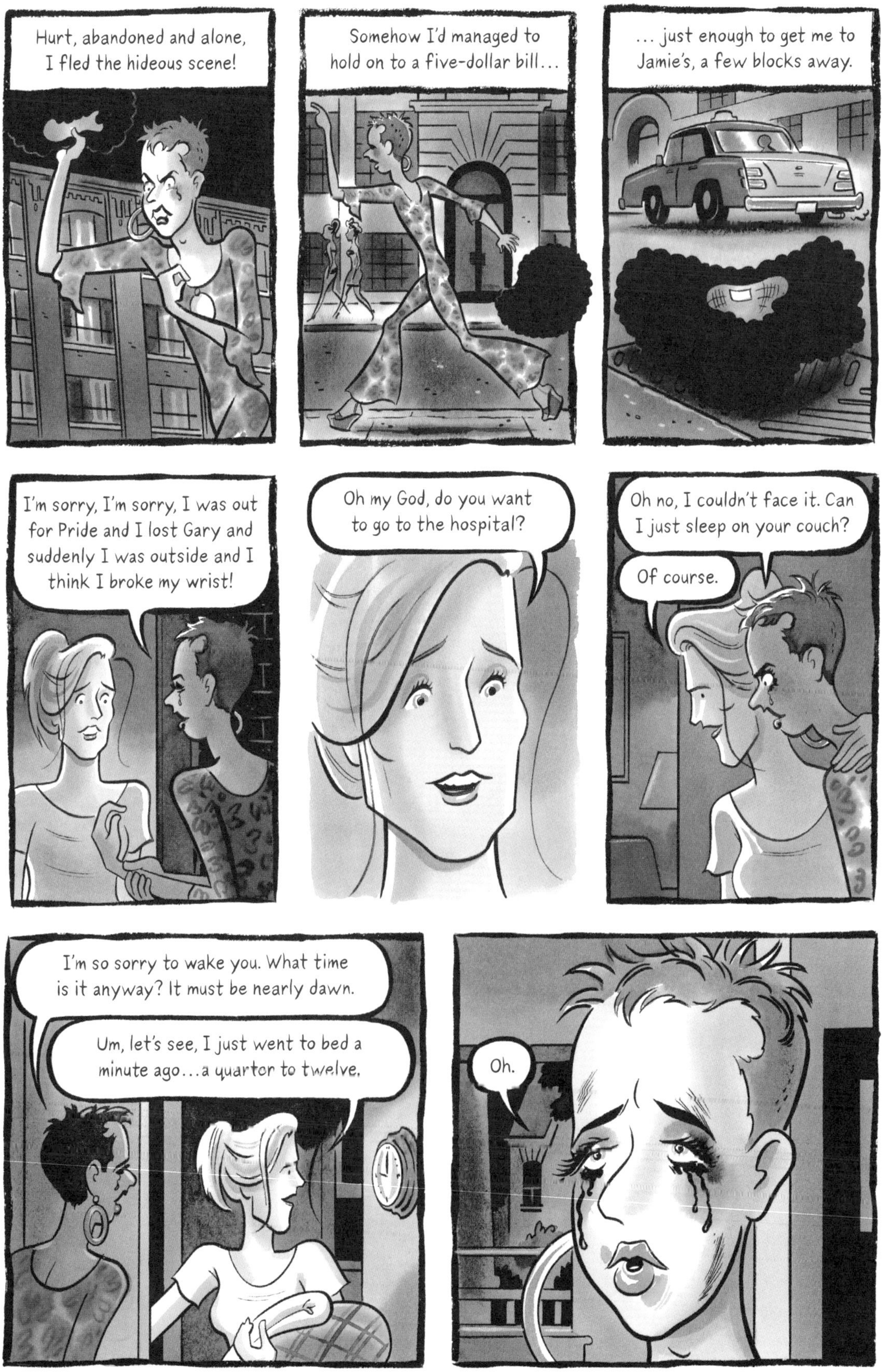
Hurt, abandoned and alone, I fled the hideous scene!
Somehow I'd managed to hold on to a five-dollar bill…
…just enough to get me to Jamie's, a few blocks away.
I'm sorry, I'm sorry, I was out for Pride and I lost Gary and suddenly I was outside and I think I broke my wrist!
Oh my God, do you want to go to the hospital?
Oh no, I couldn't face it. Can I just sleep on your couch?
Of course.
I'm so sorry to wake you. What time is it anyway? It must be nearly dawn.
Um, let's see, I just went to bed a minute ago…a quarter to twelve.
Oh.

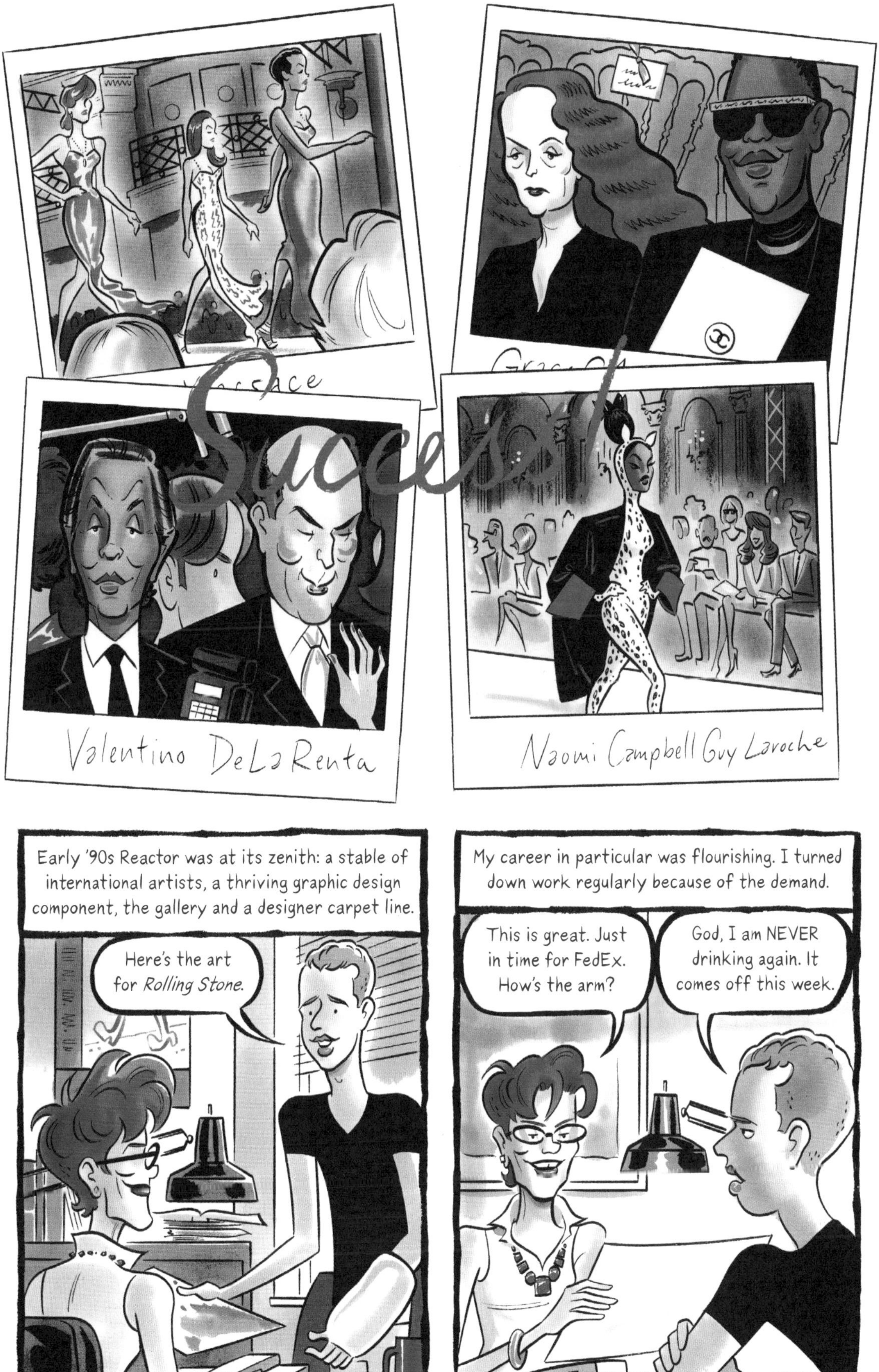
Success!
Valentino DeLaRenta
Naomi Campbell Guy Laroche
Early '90s Reactor was at its zenith: a stable of international artists, a thriving graphic design component, the gallery and a designer carpet line.
Here's the art for *Rolling Stone.*
My career in particular was flourishing. I turned down work regularly because of the demand.
This is great. Just in time for FedEx. How's the arm?
God, I am NEVER drinking again. It comes off this week.

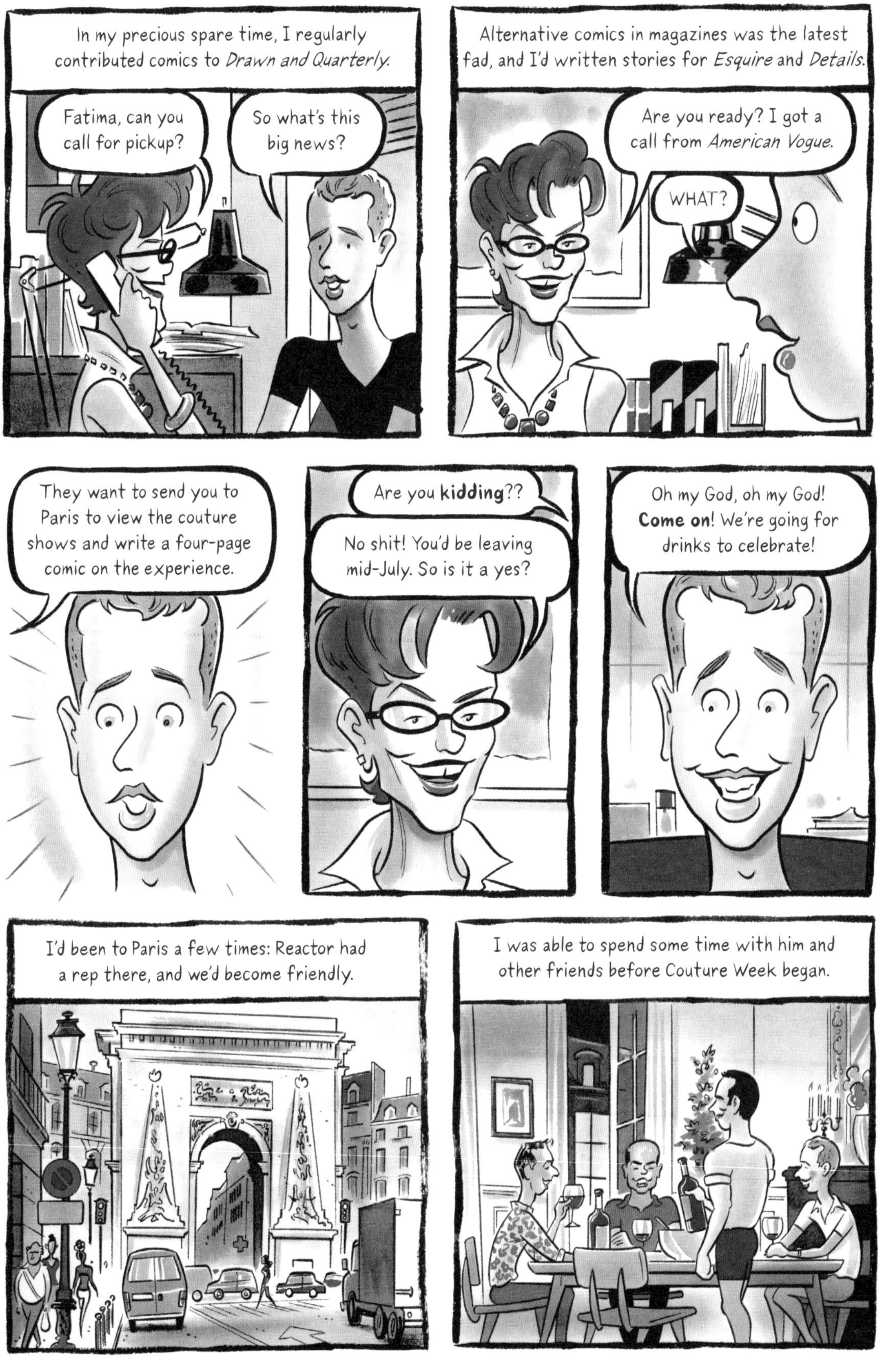
In my precious spare time, I regularly contributed comics to *Drawn and Quarterly*.
Fatima, can you call for pickup?
So what's this big news?
Alternative comics in magazines was the latest fad, and I'd written stories for *Esquire* and *Details*.
Are you ready? I got a call from *American Vogue*.
WHAT?
They want to send you to Paris to view the couture shows and write a four-page comic on the experience.
Are you **kidding**??
No shit! You'd be leaving mid-July. So is it a yes?
Oh my God, oh my God! **Come on**! We're going for drinks to celebrate!
I'd been to Paris a few times: Reactor had a rep there, and we'd become friendly.
I was able to spend some time with him and other friends before Couture Week began.

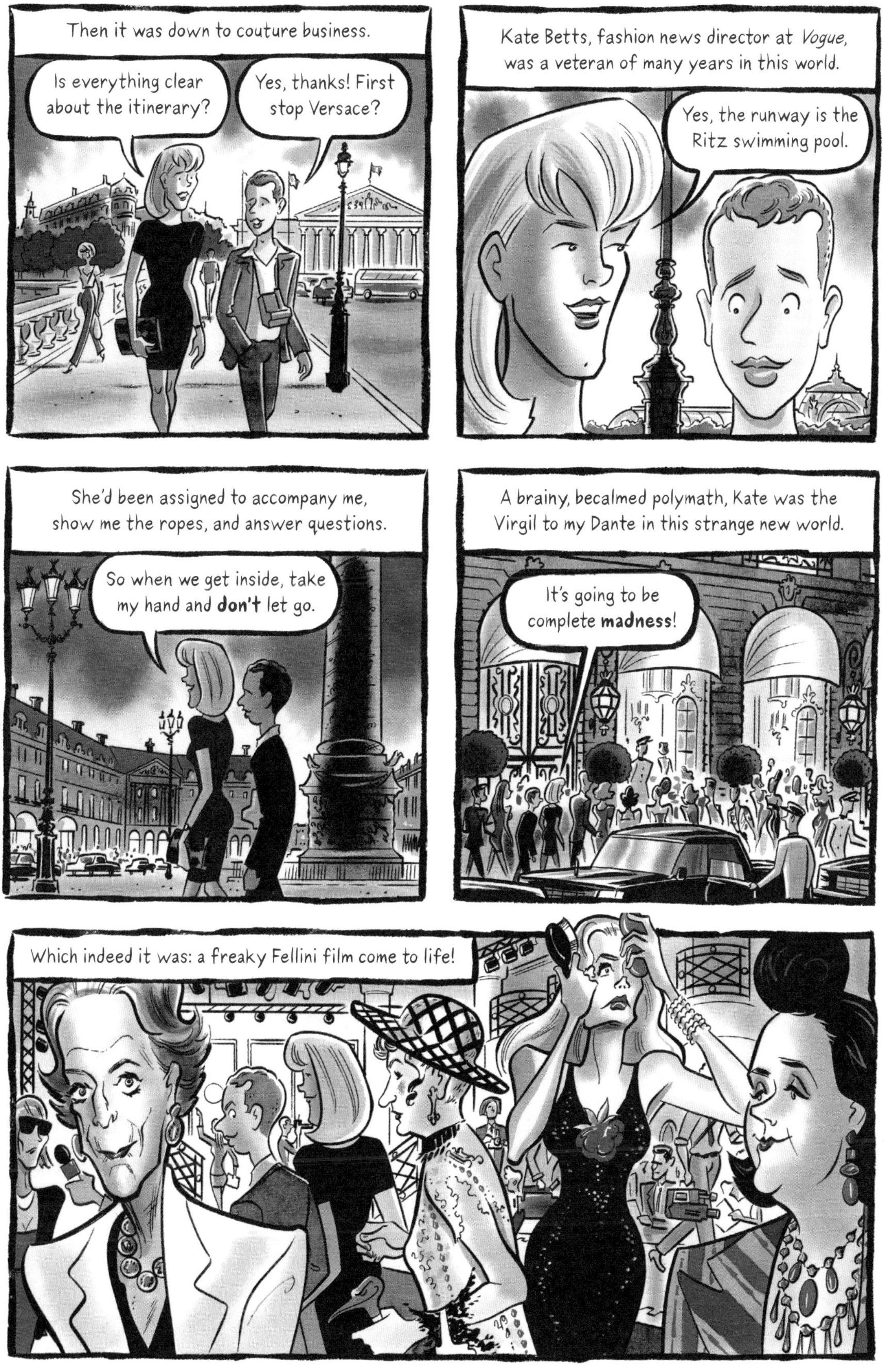
Then it was down to couture business.
Is everything clear about the itinerary?
Yes, thanks! First stop Versace?
Kate Betts, fashion news director at *Vogue*, was a veteran of many years in this world.
Yes, the runway is the Ritz swimming pool.
She'd been assigned to accompany me, show me the ropes, and answer questions.
So when we get inside, take my hand and **don't** let go.
A brainy, becalmed polymath, Kate was the Virgil to my Dante in this strange new world.
It's going to be complete **madness**!
Which indeed it was: a freaky Fellini film come to life!

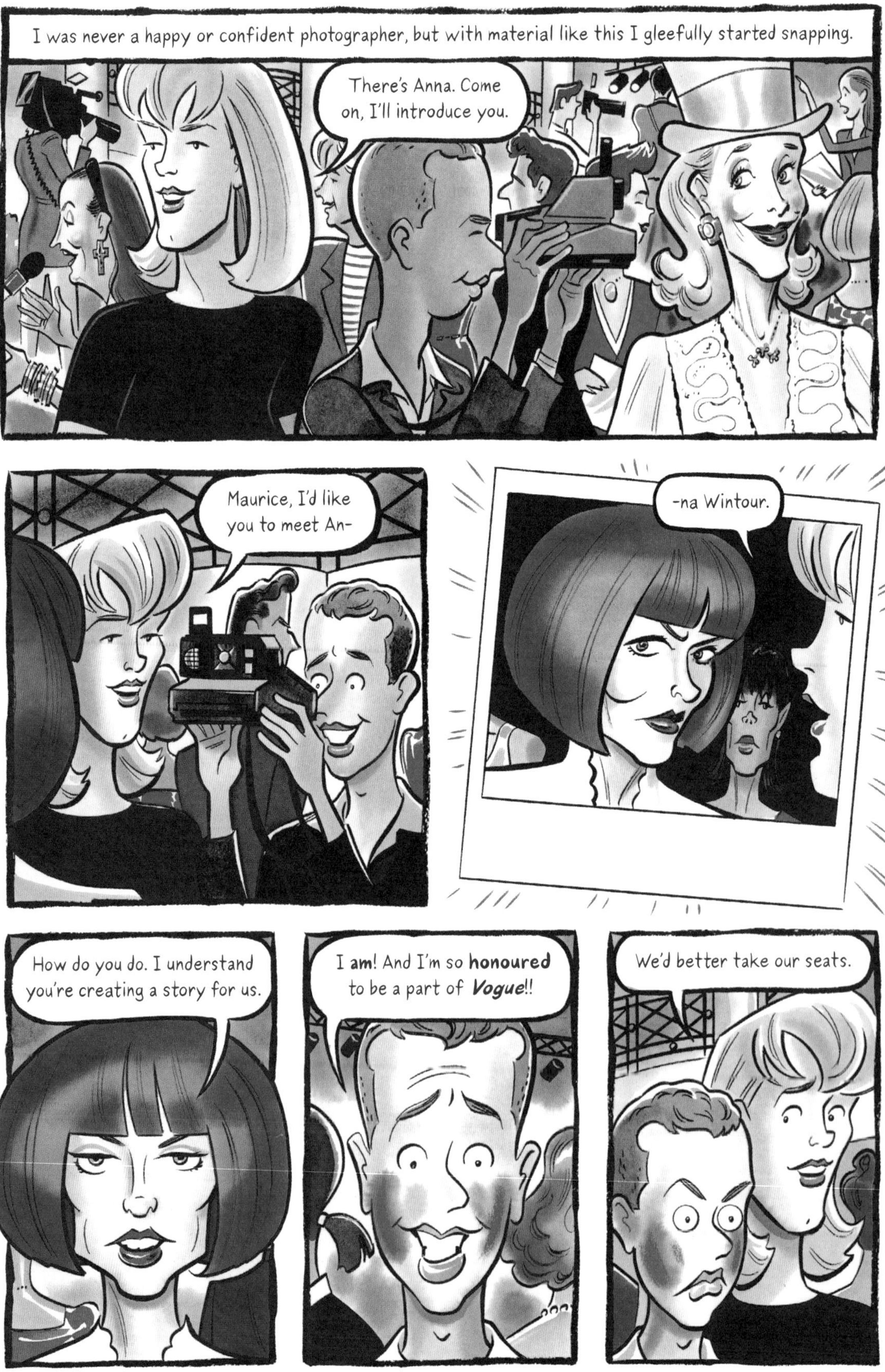
I was never a happy or confident photographer, but with material like this I gleefully started snapping.
There's Anna. Come on, I'll introduce you.
Maurice, I'd like you to meet An-
-na Wintour.
How do you do. I understand you're creating a story for us.
I **am**! And I'm so **honoured** to be a part of ***Vogue***!!
We'd better take our seats.

Couture Week was a dizzying whirl of meetings with designers, dinners with supermodels, parties...

Karl Lagerfeld, Joan Juliet Buck

...anel fans

Gian Franco Ferre

Caf...

emanuel ungar
PARIS
M. Maurice Villecoup
Vogue

Christy T., Naomi C., Linda E.

Versace party: Kirsty Hume, Donatella

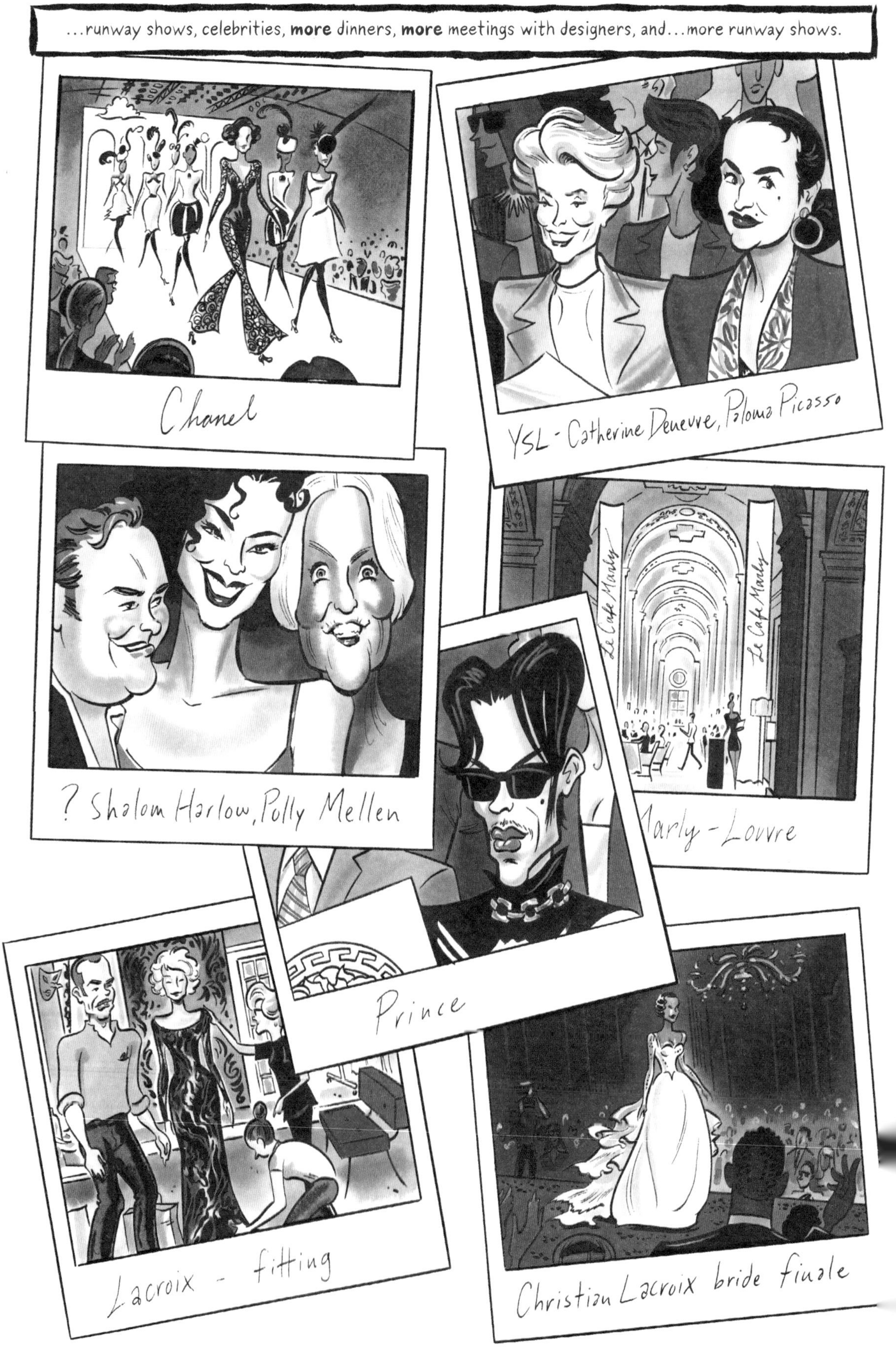
...runway shows, celebrities, **more** dinners, **more** meetings with designers, and...more runway shows.
Chanel
YSL - Catherine Deneuve, Paloma Picasso
? Shalom Harlow, Polly Mellen
Le Cafe Marly
Le Cafe Marly
arly - Louvre
Prince
Lacroix - fitting
Christian Lacroix bride finale

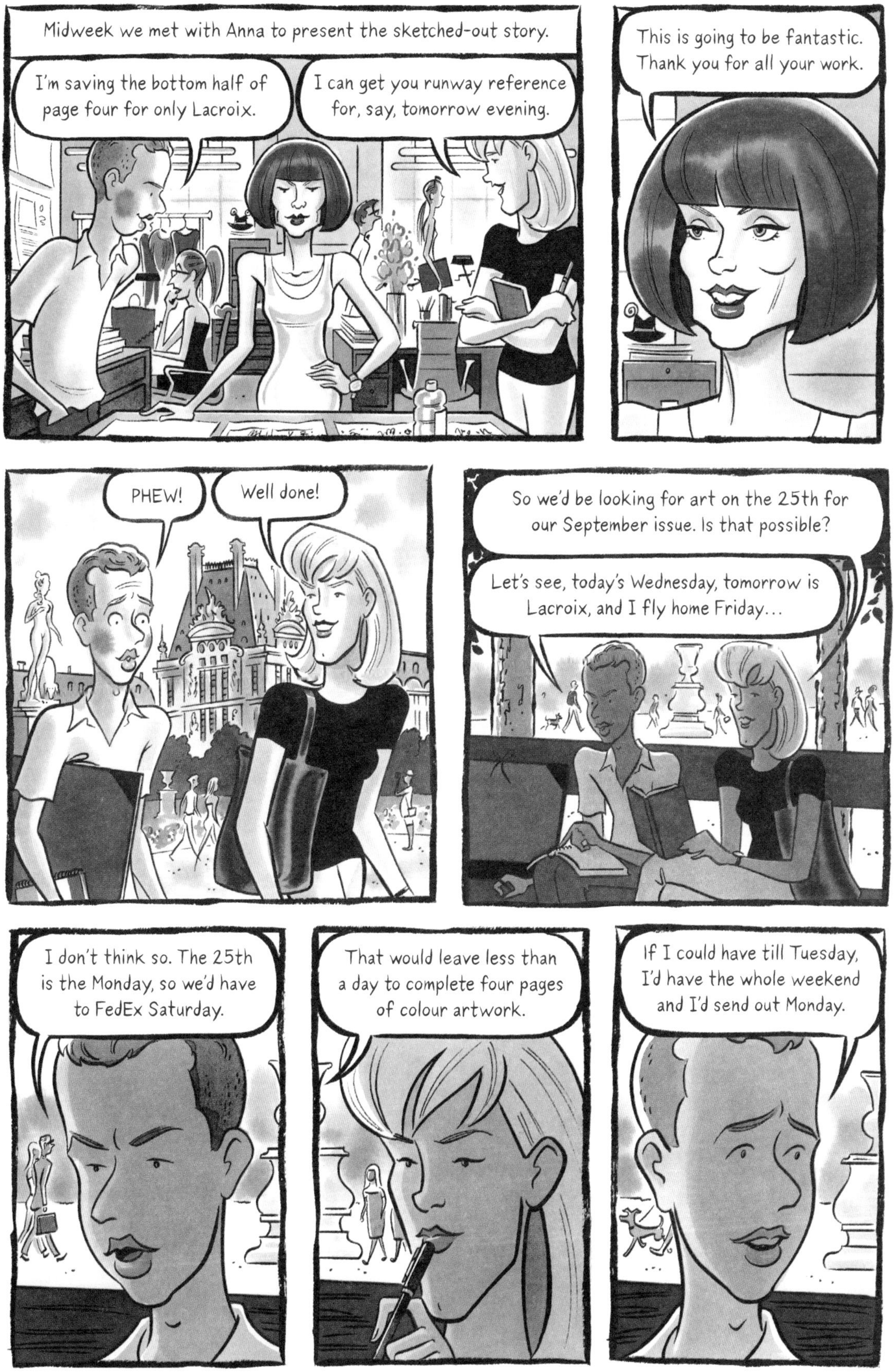
Midweek we met with Anna to present the sketched-out story.
I'm saving the bottom half of page four for only Lacroix.
I can get you runway reference for, say, tomorrow evening.
This is going to be fantastic. Thank you for all your work.
PHEW!
Well done!
So we'd be looking for art on the 25th for our September issue. Is that possible?
Let's see, today's Wednesday, tomorrow is Lacroix, and I fly home Friday...
I don't think so. The 25th is the Monday, so we'd have to FedEx Saturday.
That would leave less than a day to complete four pages of colour artwork.
If I could have till Tuesday, I'd have the whole weekend and I'd send out Monday.

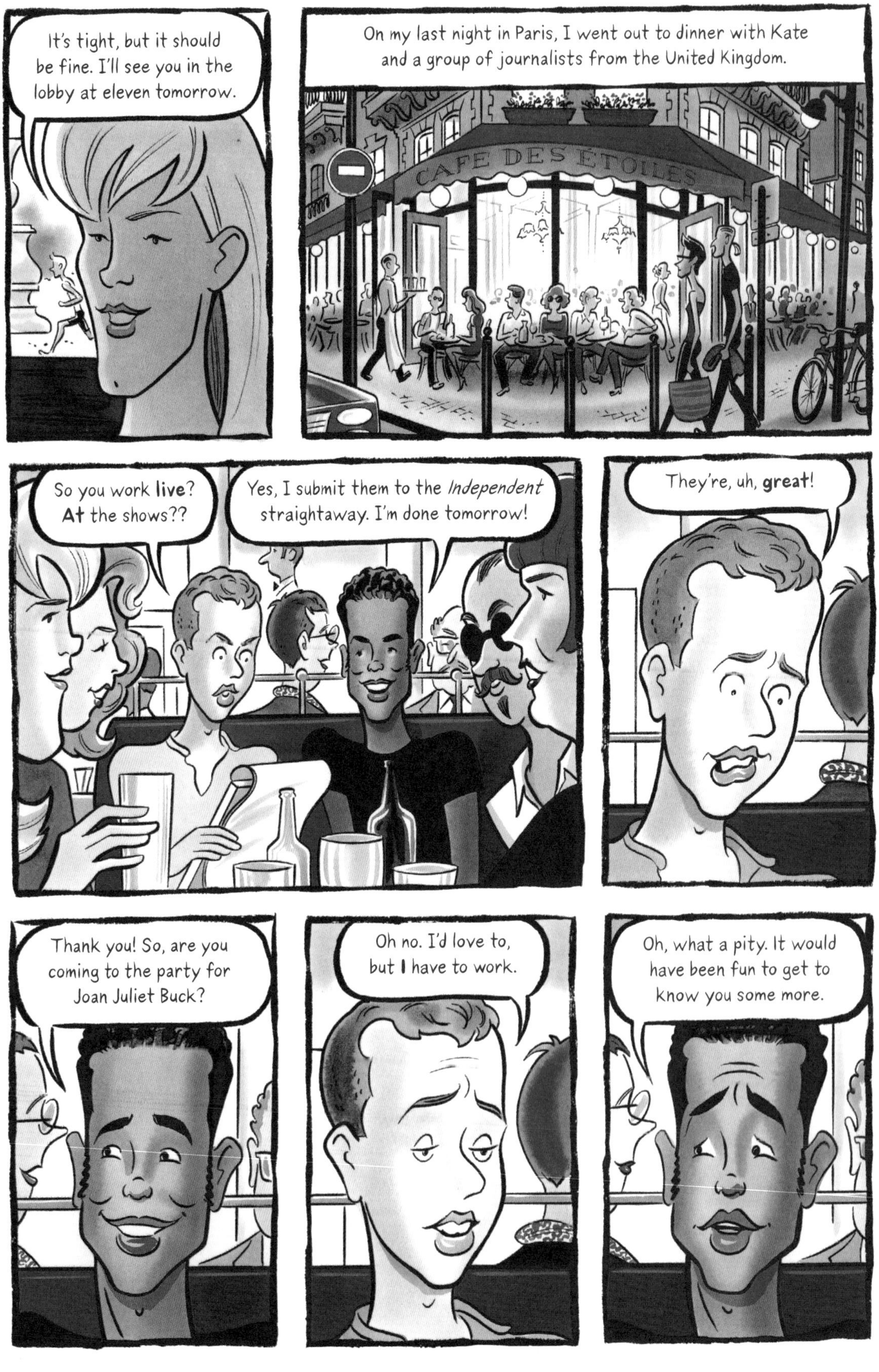
It's tight, but it should be fine. I'll see you in the lobby at eleven tomorrow.
On my last night in Paris, I went out to dinner with Kate and a group of journalists from the United Kingdom.
CAFE DES ETOILES
So you work **live**? **At** the shows??
Yes, I submit them to the *Independent* straightaway. I'm done tomorrow!
They're, uh, **great**!
Thank you! So, are you coming to the party for Joan Juliet Buck?
Oh no. I'd love to, but **I** have to work.
Oh, what a pity. It would have been fun to get to know you some more.

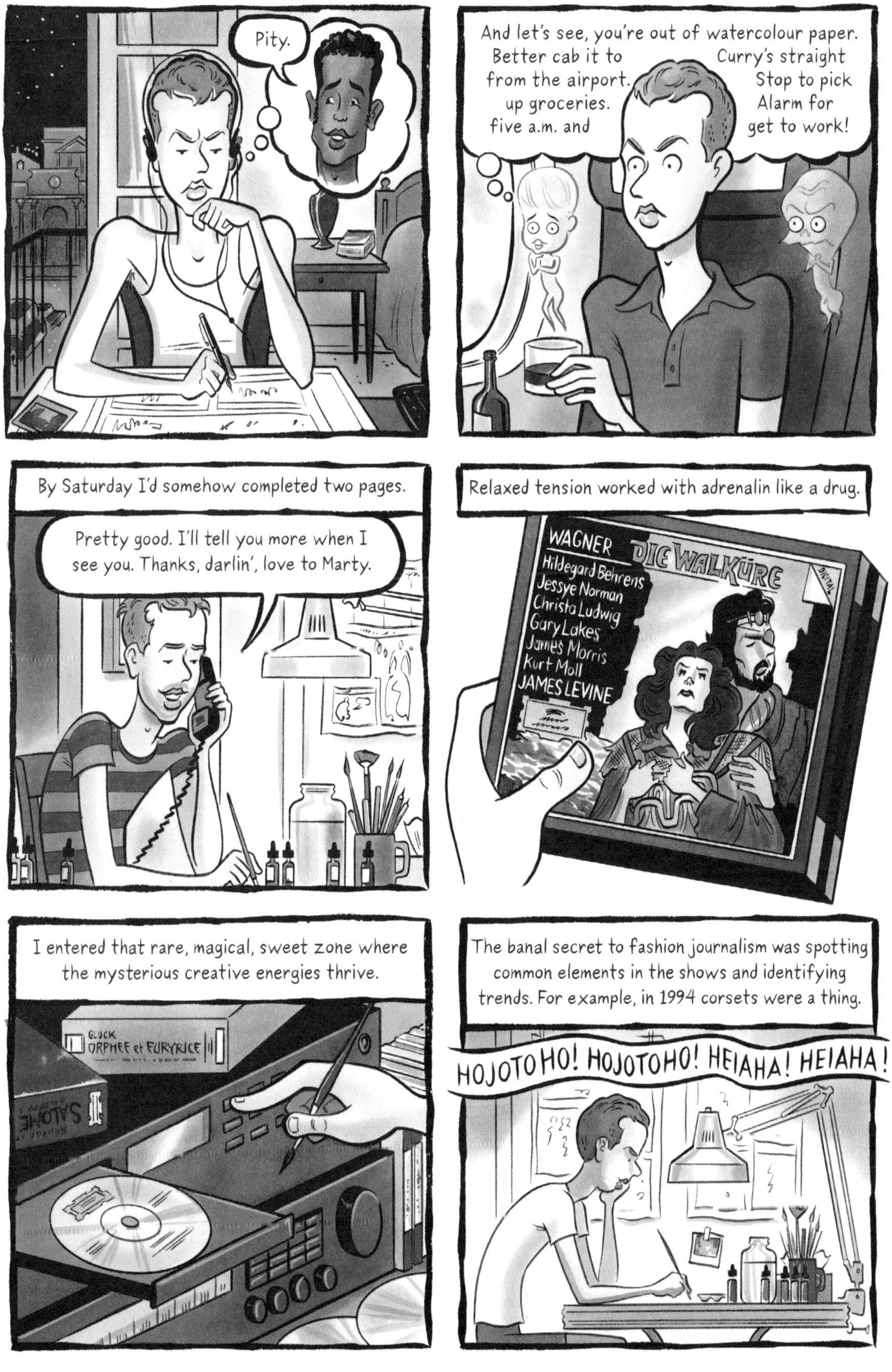
Pity.
And let's see, you're out of watercolour paper. Better cab it to Curry's straight from the airport. Stop to pick up groceries. Alarm for five a.m. and get to work!
By Saturday I'd somehow completed two pages.
Pretty good. I'll tell you more when I see you. Thanks, darlin', love to Marty.
Relaxed tension worked with adrenalin like a drug.
WAGNER
DIE WALKÜRE
Hildegard Behrens
Jessye Norman
Christa Ludwig
Gary Lakes
James Morris
Kurt Moll
JAMES LEVINE
DIGITAL
I entered that rare, magical, sweet zone where the mysterious creative energies thrive.
GLUCK
SALOME
The banal secret to fashion journalism was spotting common elements in the shows and identifying trends. For example, in 1994 corsets were a thing.
HOJOTOHO! HOJOTOHO! HEIAHA! HEIAHA!

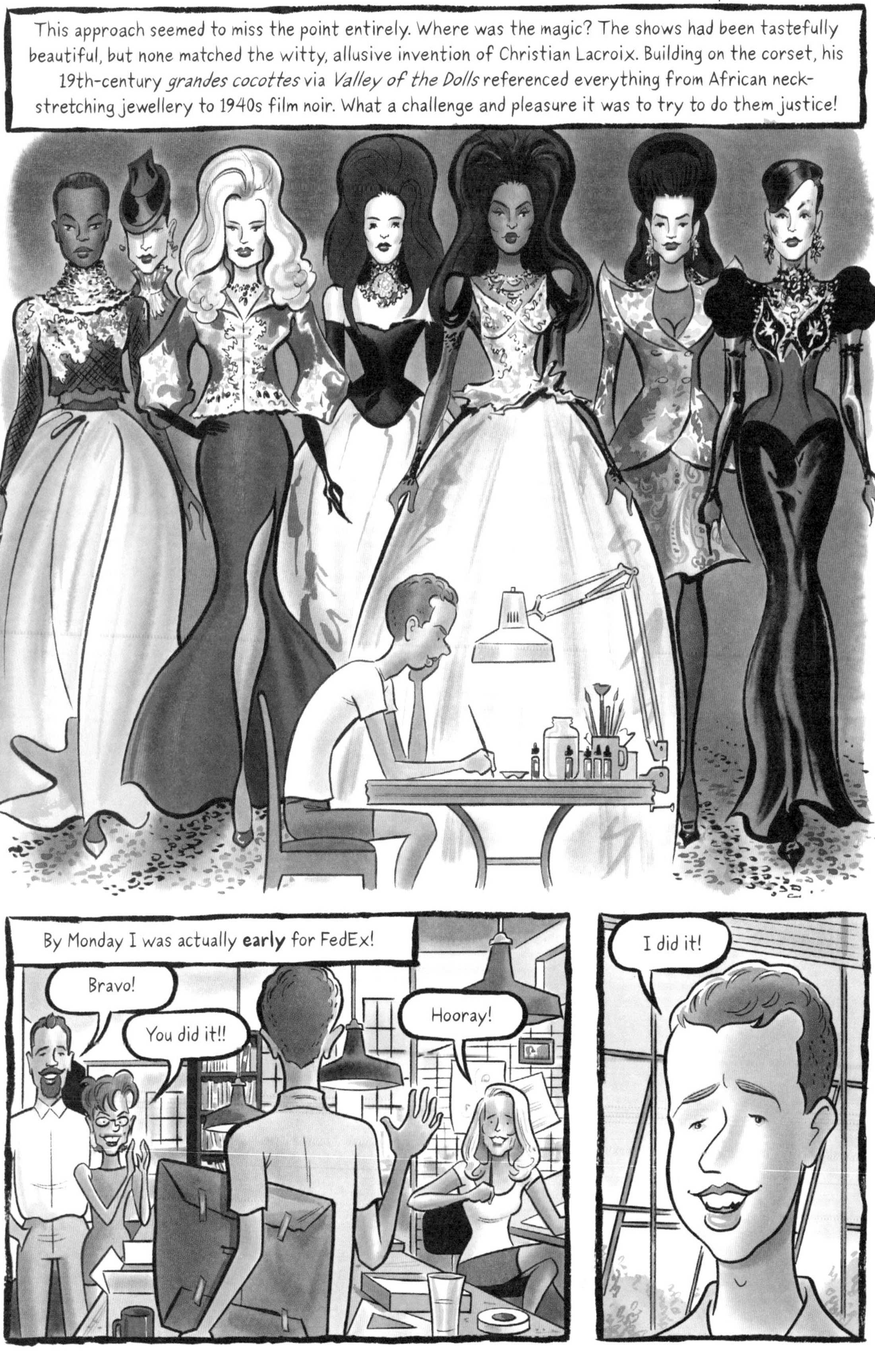
This approach seemed to miss the point entirely. Where was the magic? The shows had been tastefully beautiful, but none matched the witty, allusive invention of Christian Lacroix. Building on the corset, his 19th-century *grandes cocottes* via *Valley of the Dolls* referenced everything from African neck-stretching jewellery to 1940s film noir. What a challenge and pleasure it was to try to do them justice!
By Monday I was actually **early** for FedEx!
Bravo!
You did it!!
Hooray!
I did it!

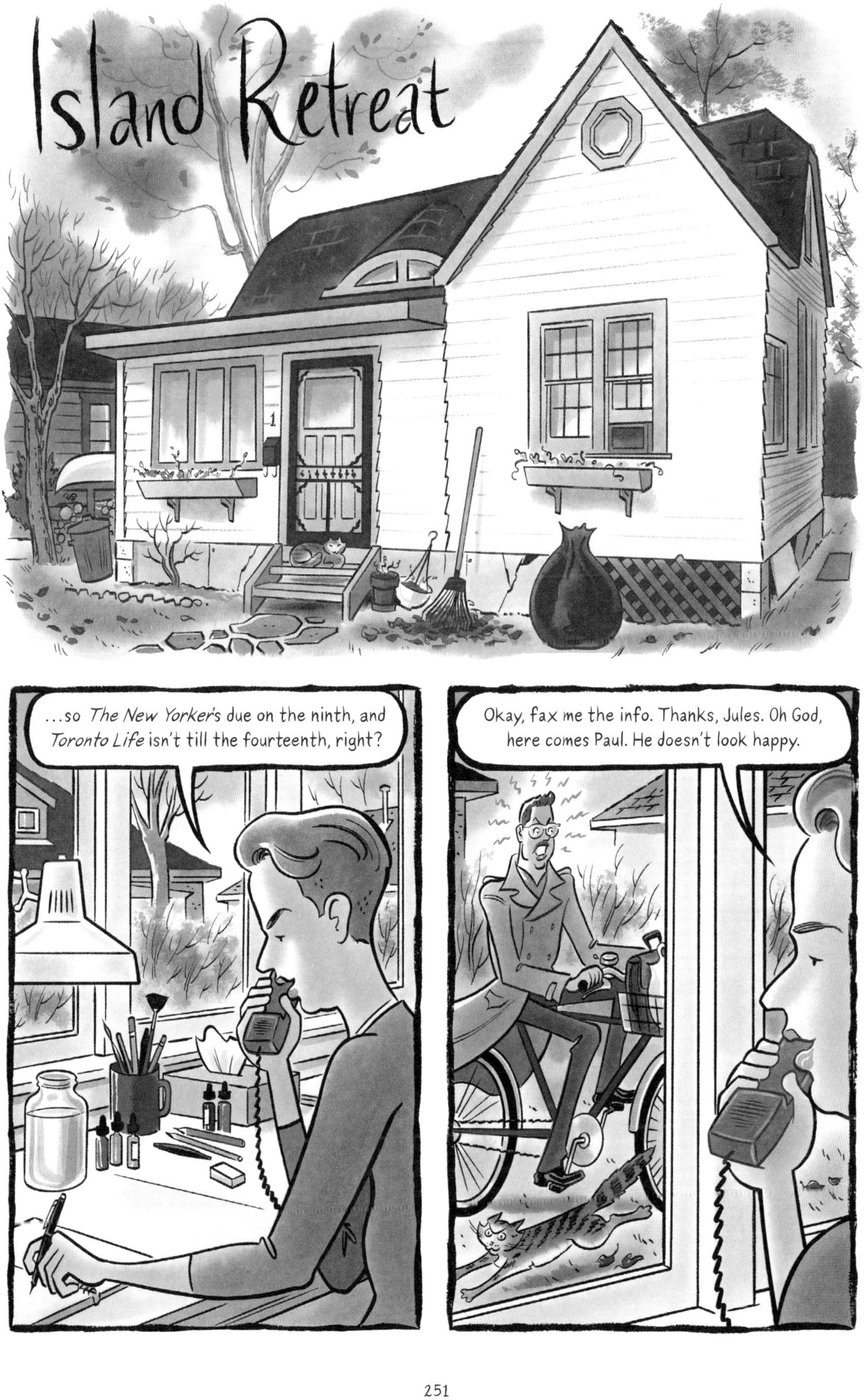
Island Retreat
...so *The New Yorker's* due on the ninth, and *Toronto Life* isn't till the fourteenth, right?
Okay, fax me the info. Thanks, Jules. Oh God, here comes Paul. He doesn't look happy.

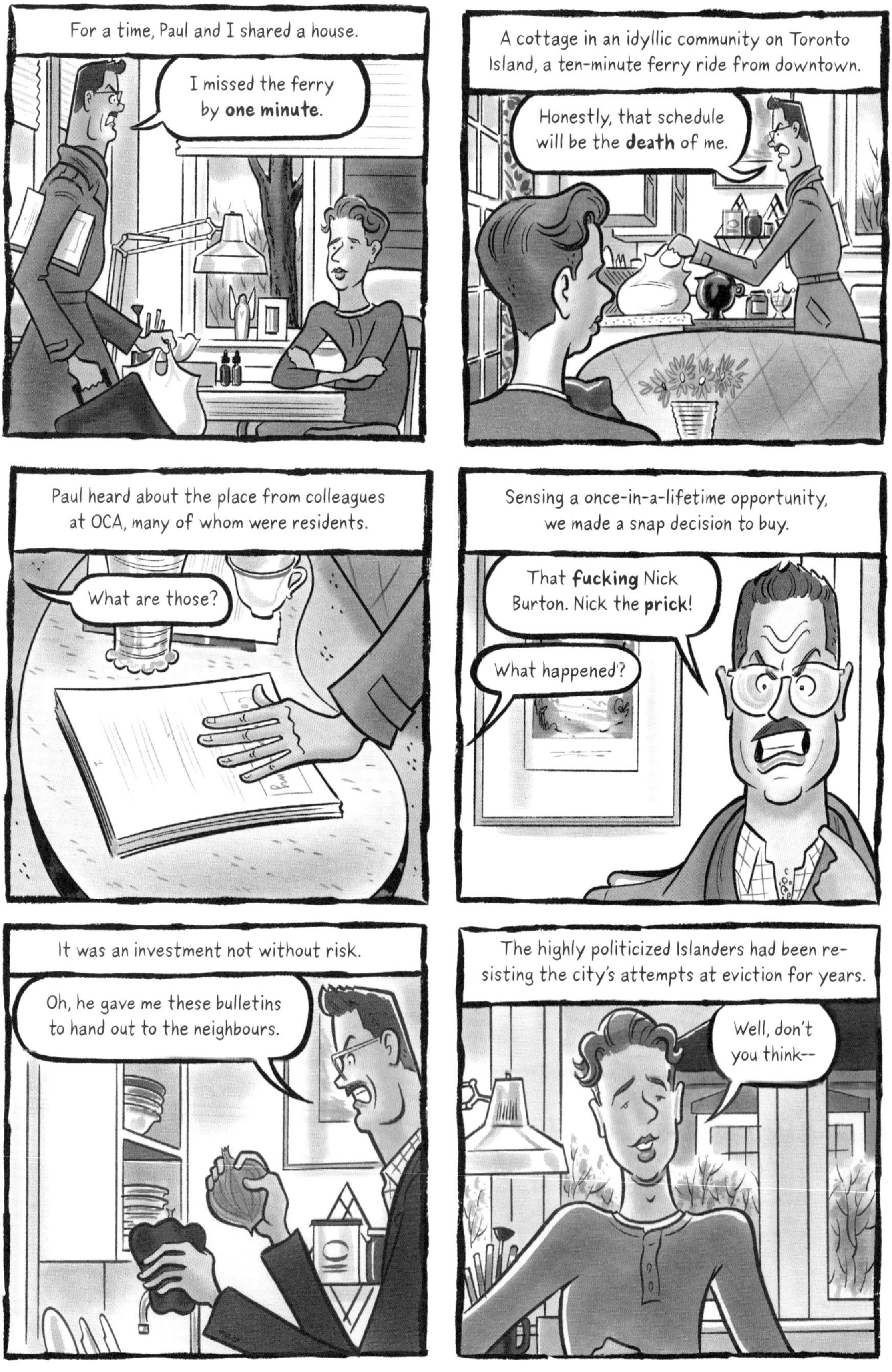
For a time, Paul and I shared a house.
I missed the ferry by **one minute**.
A cottage in an idyllic community on Toronto Island, a ten-minute ferry ride from downtown.
Honestly, that schedule will be the **death** of me.
Paul heard about the place from colleagues at OCA, many of whom were residents.
What are those?
Sensing a once-in-a-lifetime opportunity, we made a snap decision to buy.
That **fucking** Nick Burton. Nick the **prick**!
What happened?
It was an investment not without risk.
Oh, he gave me these bulletins to hand out to the neighbours.
The highly politicized Islanders had been resisting the city's attempts at eviction for years.
Well, don't you think--

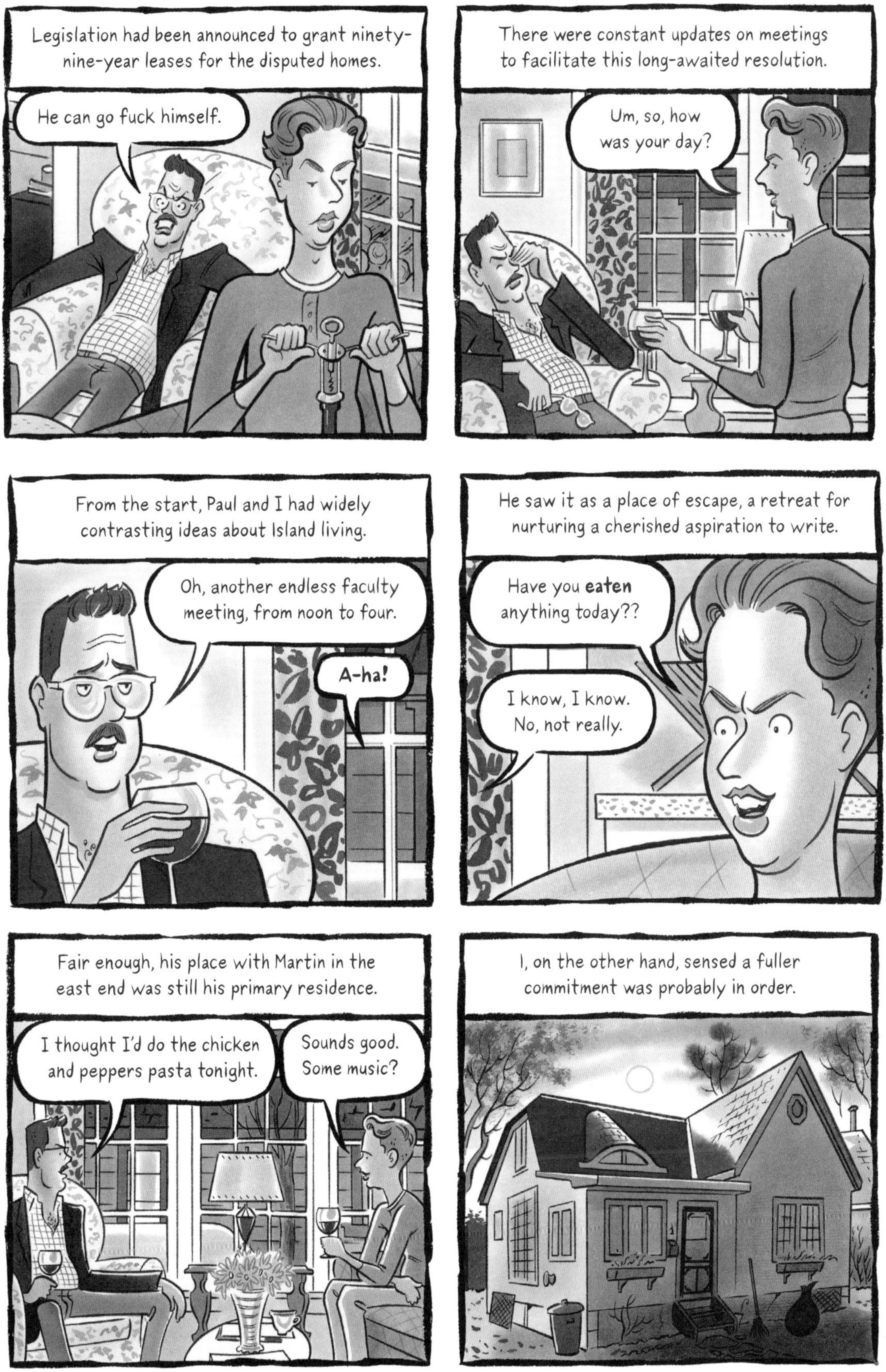
Legislation had been announced to grant ninety-nine-year leases for the disputed homes.
He can go fuck himself.
There were constant updates on meetings to facilitate this long-awaited resolution.
Um, so, how was your day?
From the start, Paul and I had widely contrasting ideas about Island living.
Oh, another endless faculty meeting, from noon to four.
A-ha!
He saw it as a place of escape, a retreat for nurturing a cherished aspiration to write.
Have you **eaten** anything today??
I know, I know. No, not really.
Fair enough, his place with Martin in the east end was still his primary residence.
I thought I'd do the chicken and peppers pasta tonight.
Sounds good. Some music?
I, on the other hand, sensed a fuller commitment was probably in order.

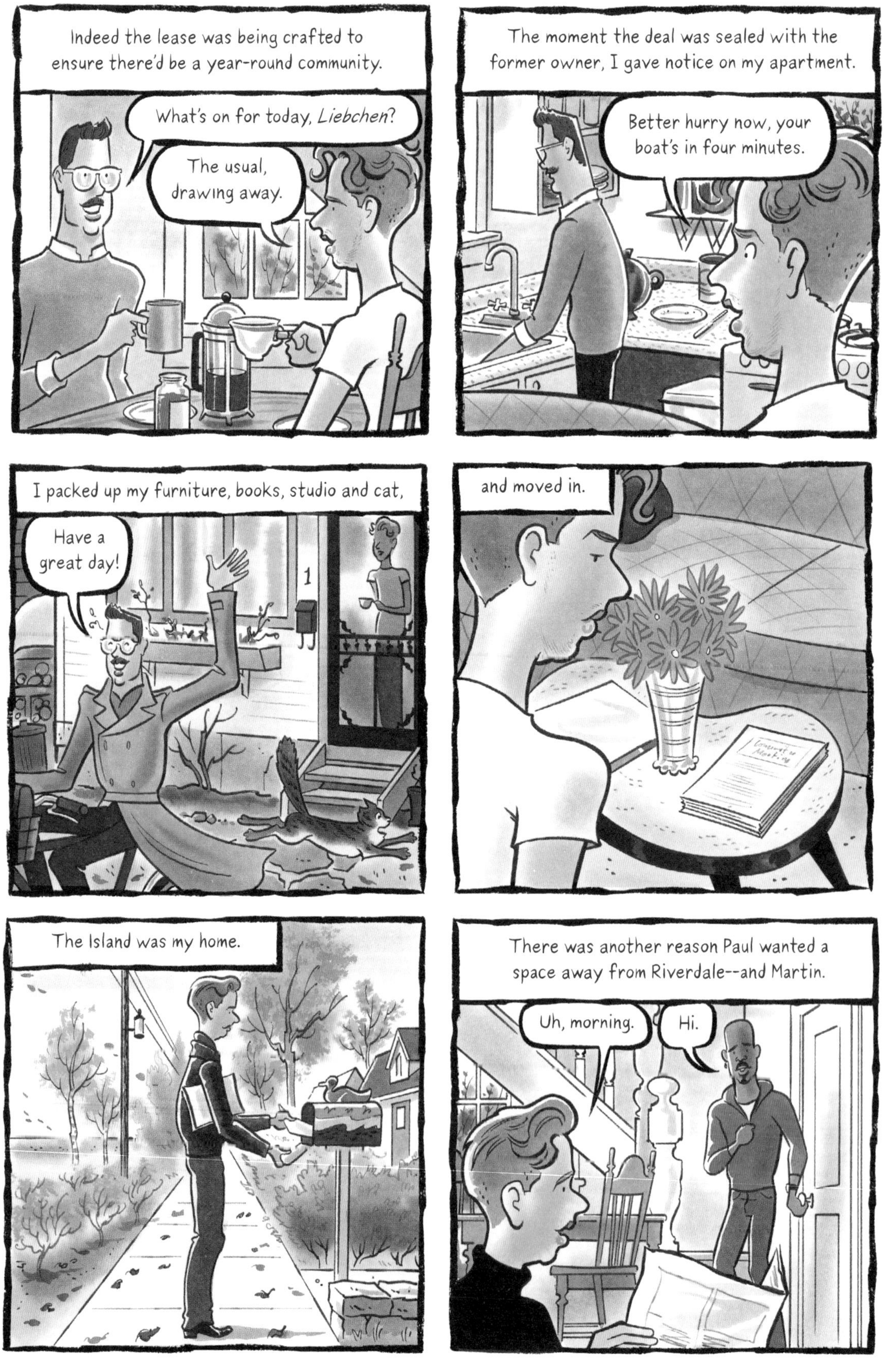
Indeed the lease was being crafted to ensure there'd be a year-round community.
What's on for today, *Liebchen*?
The usual, drawing away.
The moment the deal was sealed with the former owner, I gave notice on my apartment.
Better hurry now, your boat's in four minutes.
I packed up my furniture, books, studio and cat,
Have a great day!
1
and moved in.
The Island was my home.
There was another reason Paul wanted a space away from Riverdale--and Martin.
Uh, morning.
Hi.

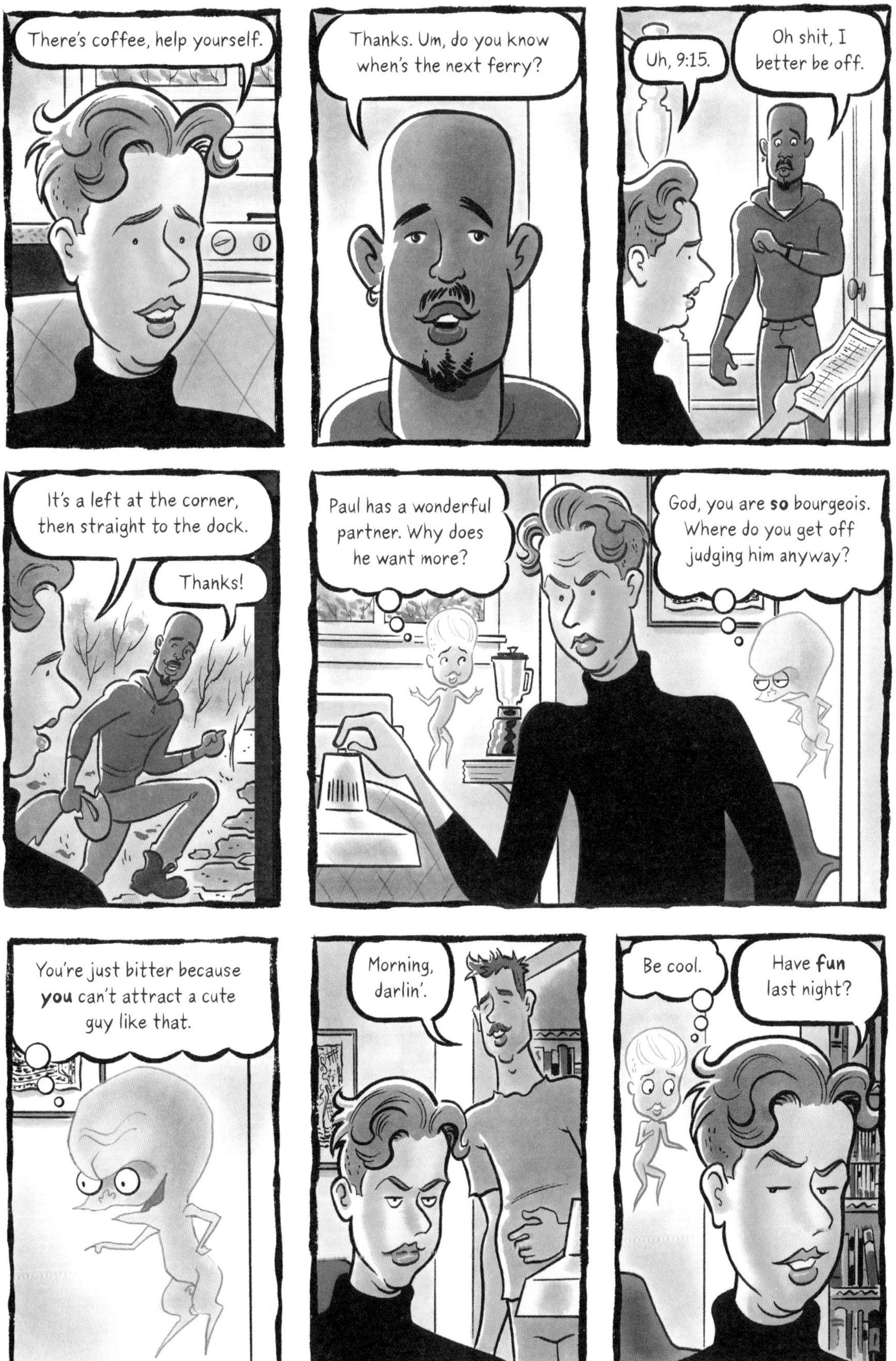
There's coffee, help yourself.
Thanks. Um, do you know when's the next ferry?
Uh, 9:15.
Oh shit, I better be off.
It's a left at the corner, then straight to the dock.
Thanks!
Paul has a wonderful partner. Why does he want more?
God, you are **so** bourgeois. Where do you get off judging him anyway?
You're just bitter because **you** can't attract a cute guy like that.
Morning, darlin'.
Be cool.
Have **fun** last night?

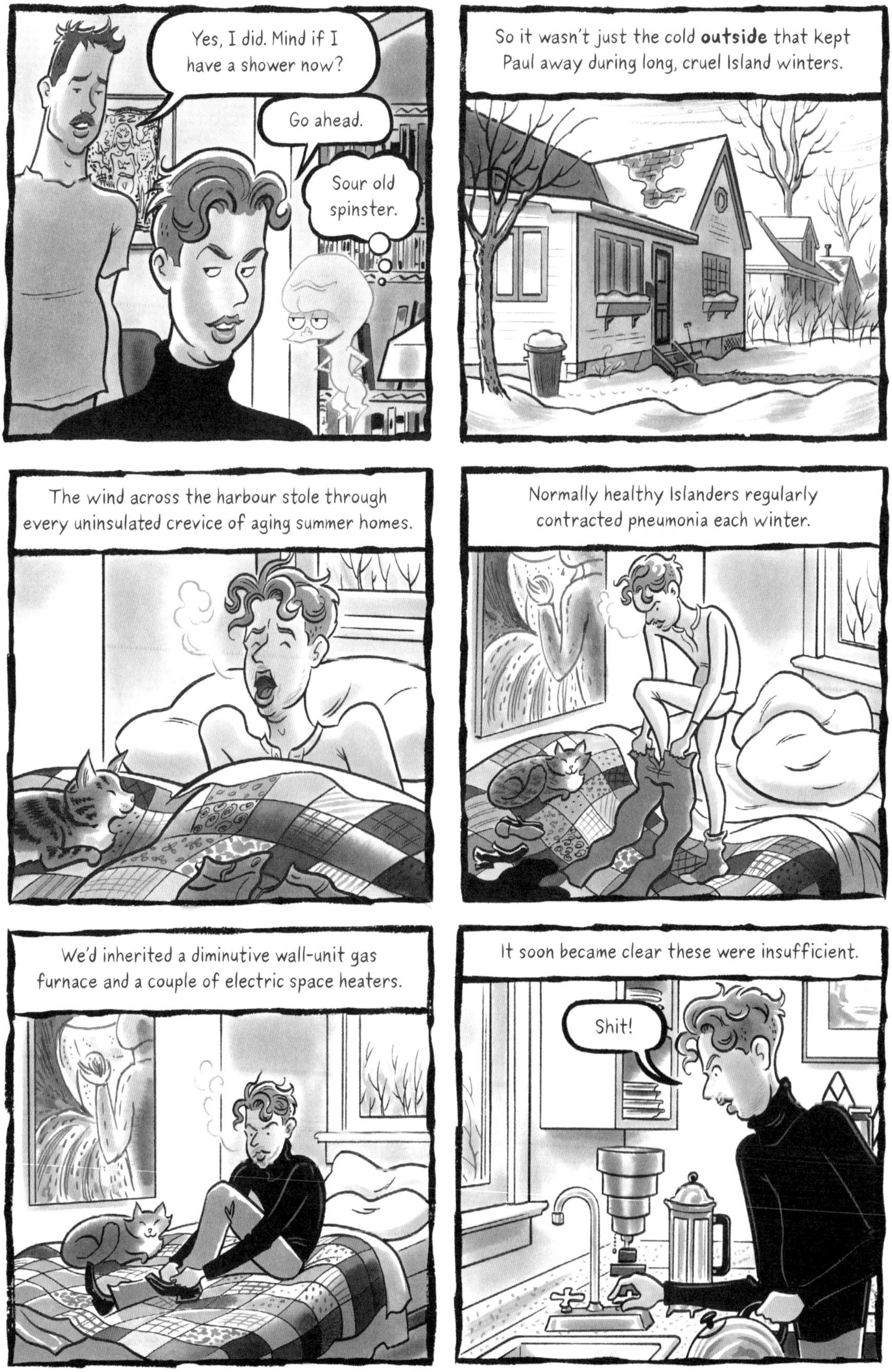
Yes, I did. Mind if I have a shower now?
Go ahead.
Sour old spinster.
So it wasn't just the cold **outside** that kept Paul away during long, cruel Island winters.
The wind across the harbour stole through every uninsulated crevice of aging summer homes.
Normally healthy Islanders regularly contracted pneumonia each winter.
We'd inherited a diminutive wall-unit gas furnace and a couple of electric space heaters.
It soon became clear these were insufficient.
Shit!

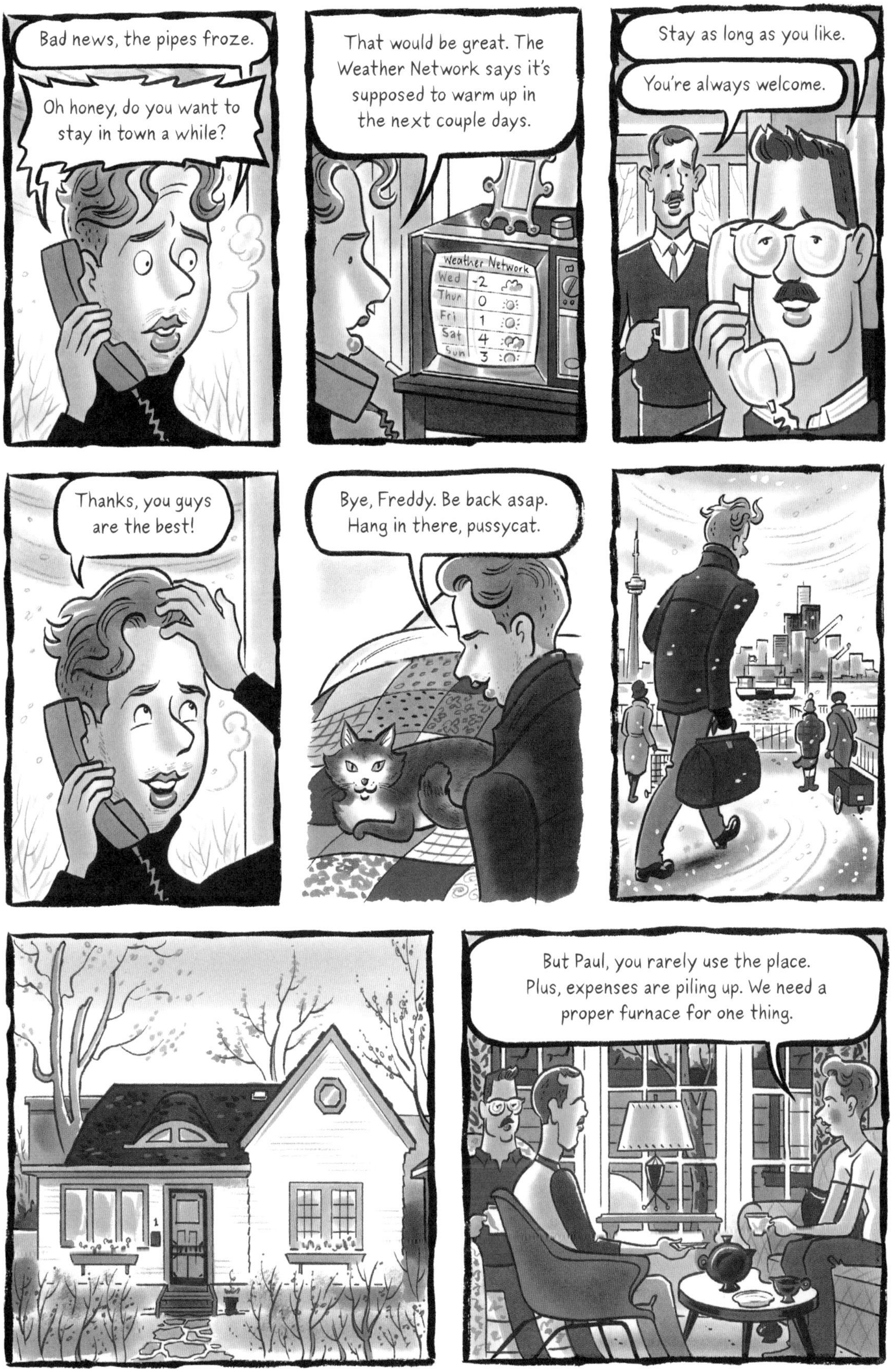
Bad news, the pipes froze.
Oh honey, do you want to stay in town a while?
That would be great. The Weather Network says it's supposed to warm up in the next couple days.
Weather Network
Wed -2
Thur 0
Fri 1
Sat 4
Sun 3
Stay as long as you like.
You're always welcome.
Thanks, you guys are the best!
Bye, Freddy. Be back asap. Hang in there, pussycat.
1
But Paul, you rarely use the place. Plus, expenses are piling up. We need a proper furnace for one thing.

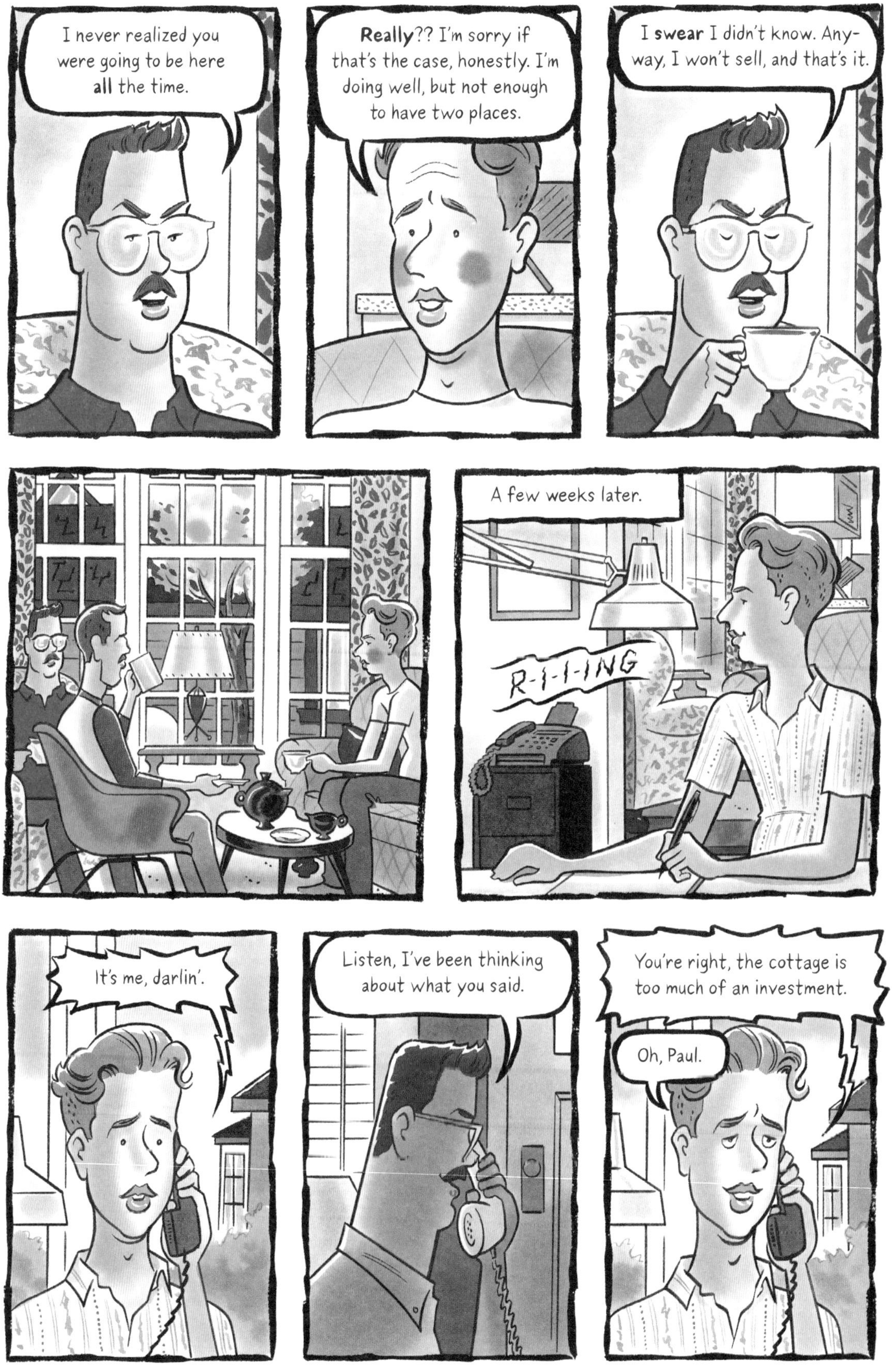
I never realized you were going to be here **all** the time.
Really?? I'm sorry if that's the case, honestly. I'm doing well, but not enough to have two places.
I **swear** I didn't know. Anyway, I won't sell, and that's it.
A few weeks later.
R-I-I-ING
It's me, darlin'.
Listen, I've been thinking about what you said.
You're right, the cottage is too much of an investment.
Oh, Paul.

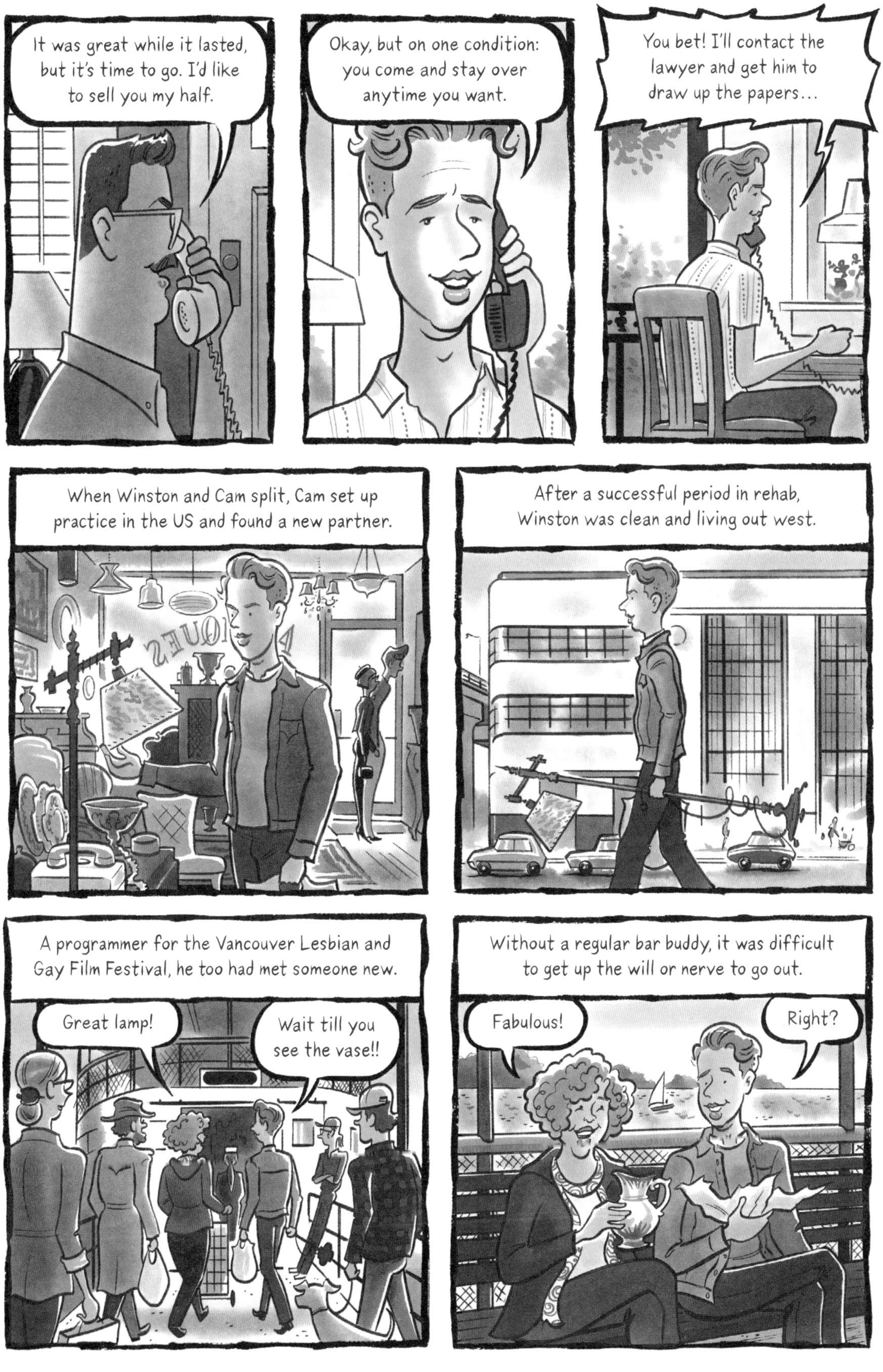
It was great while it lasted, but it's time to go. I'd like to sell you my half.
Okay, but on one condition: you come and stay over anytime you want.
You bet! I'll contact the lawyer and get him to draw up the papers...
When Winston and Cam split, Cam set up practice in the US and found a new partner.
After a successful period in rehab, Winston was clean and living out west.
A programmer for the Vancouver Lesbian and Gay Film Festival, he too had met someone new.
Great lamp!
Wait till you see the vase!!
Without a regular bar buddy, it was difficult to get up the will or nerve to go out.
Fabulous!
Right?

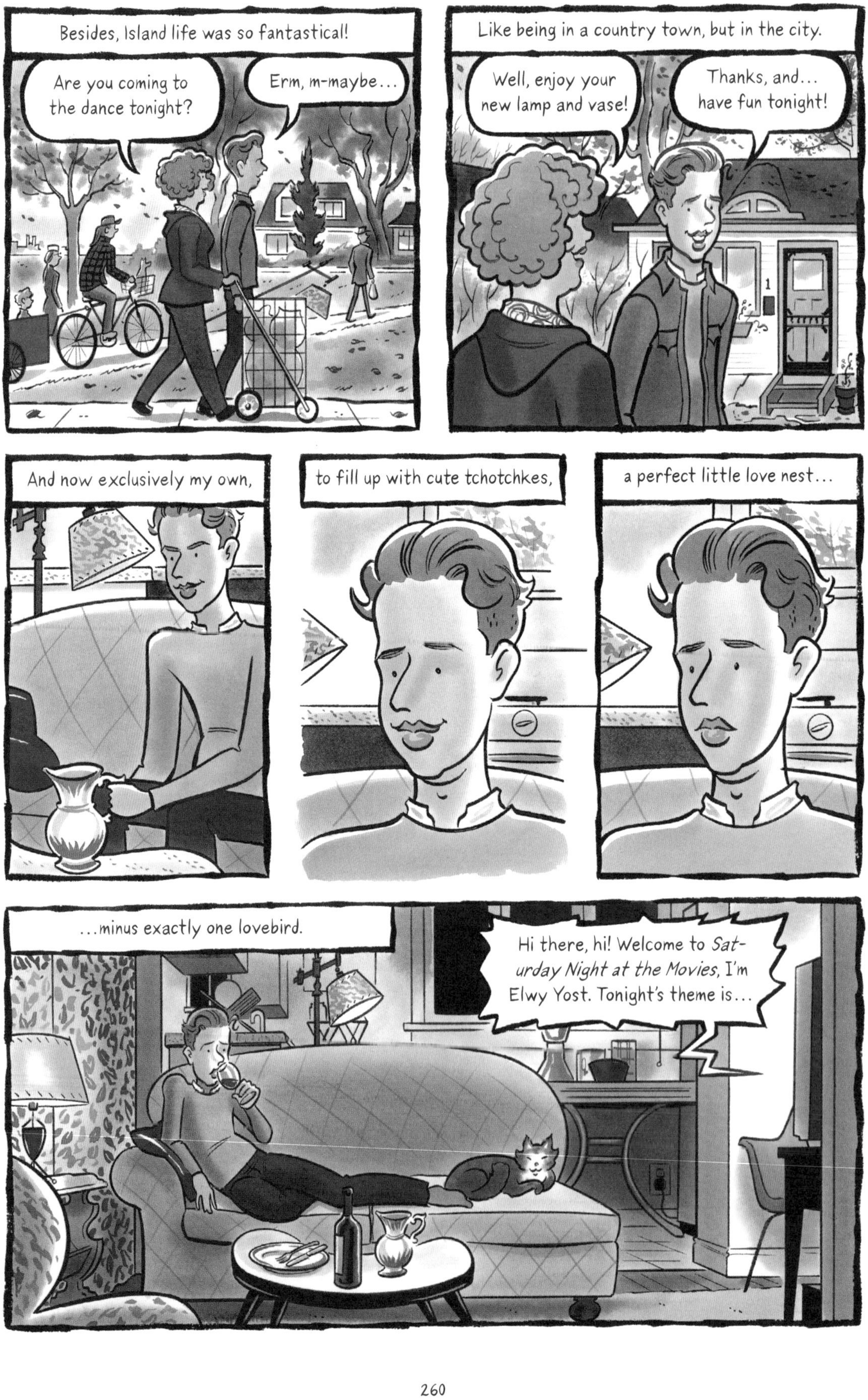
Besides, Island life was so fantastical!
Are you coming to the dance tonight?
Erm, m-maybe...
Like being in a country town, but in the city.
Well, enjoy your new lamp and vase!
Thanks, and... have fun tonight!
1
And now exclusively my own,
to fill up with cute tchotchkes,
a perfect little love nest...
...minus exactly one lovebird.
Hi there, hi! Welcome to *Saturday Night at the Movies*, I'm Elwy Yost. Tonight's theme is...

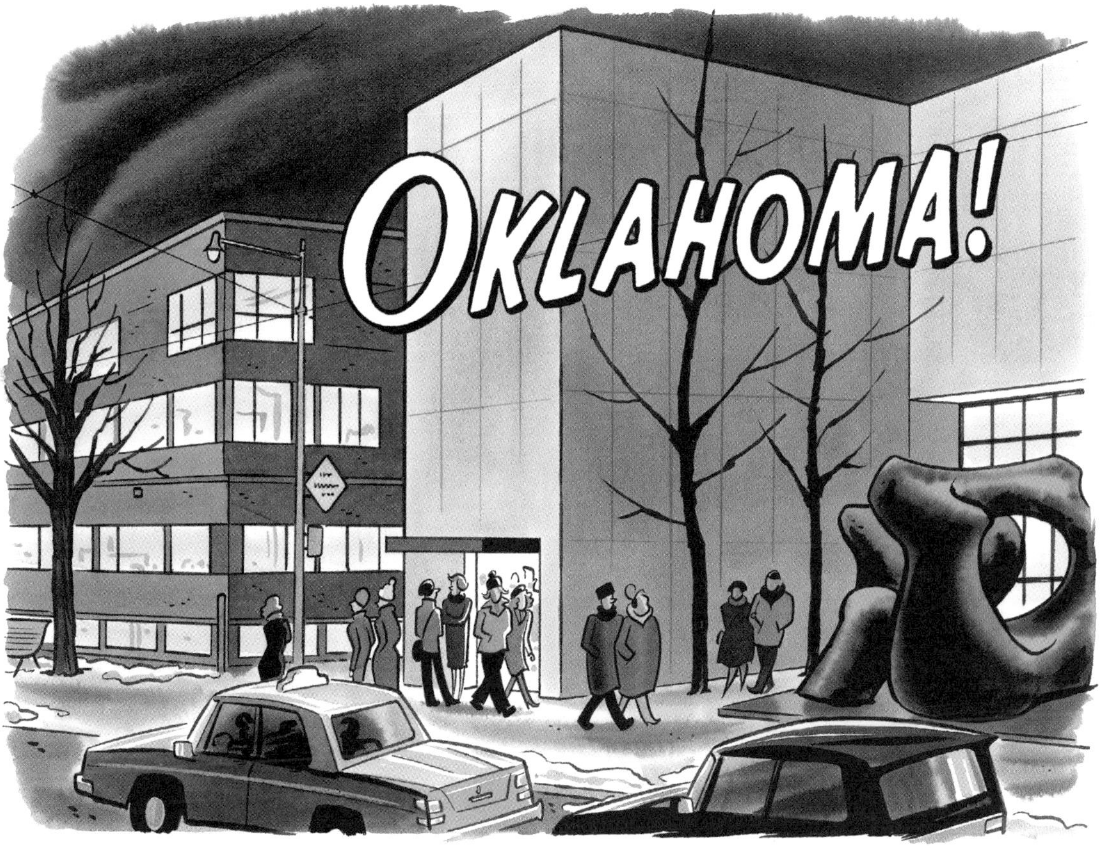
OKLAHOMA!

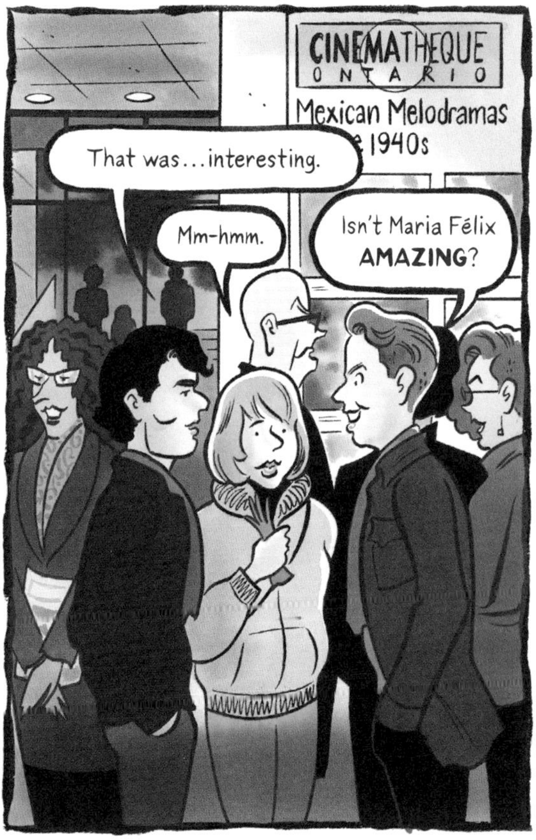
CINEMATHEQUE
ONTARIO
Mexican Melodramas
1940s
That was...interesting.
Mm-hmm.
Isn't Maria Félix **AMAZING**?

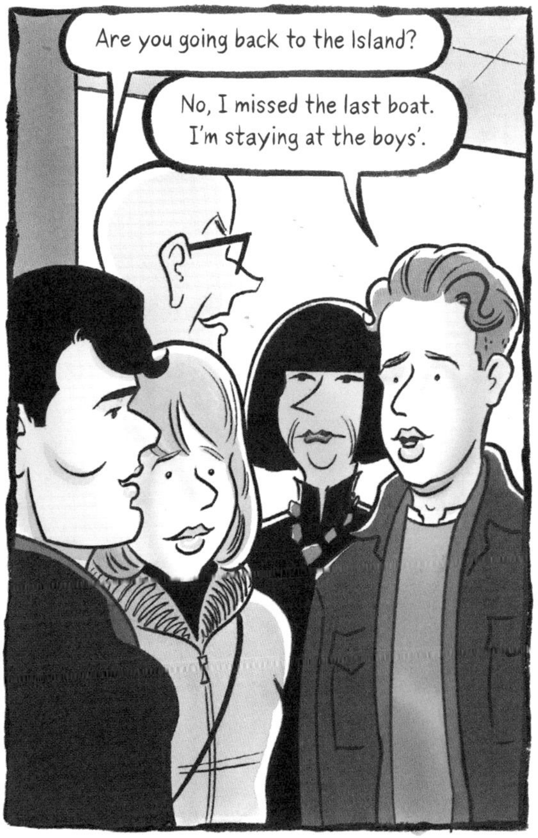
Are you going back to the Island?
No, I missed the last boat. I'm staying at the boys'.

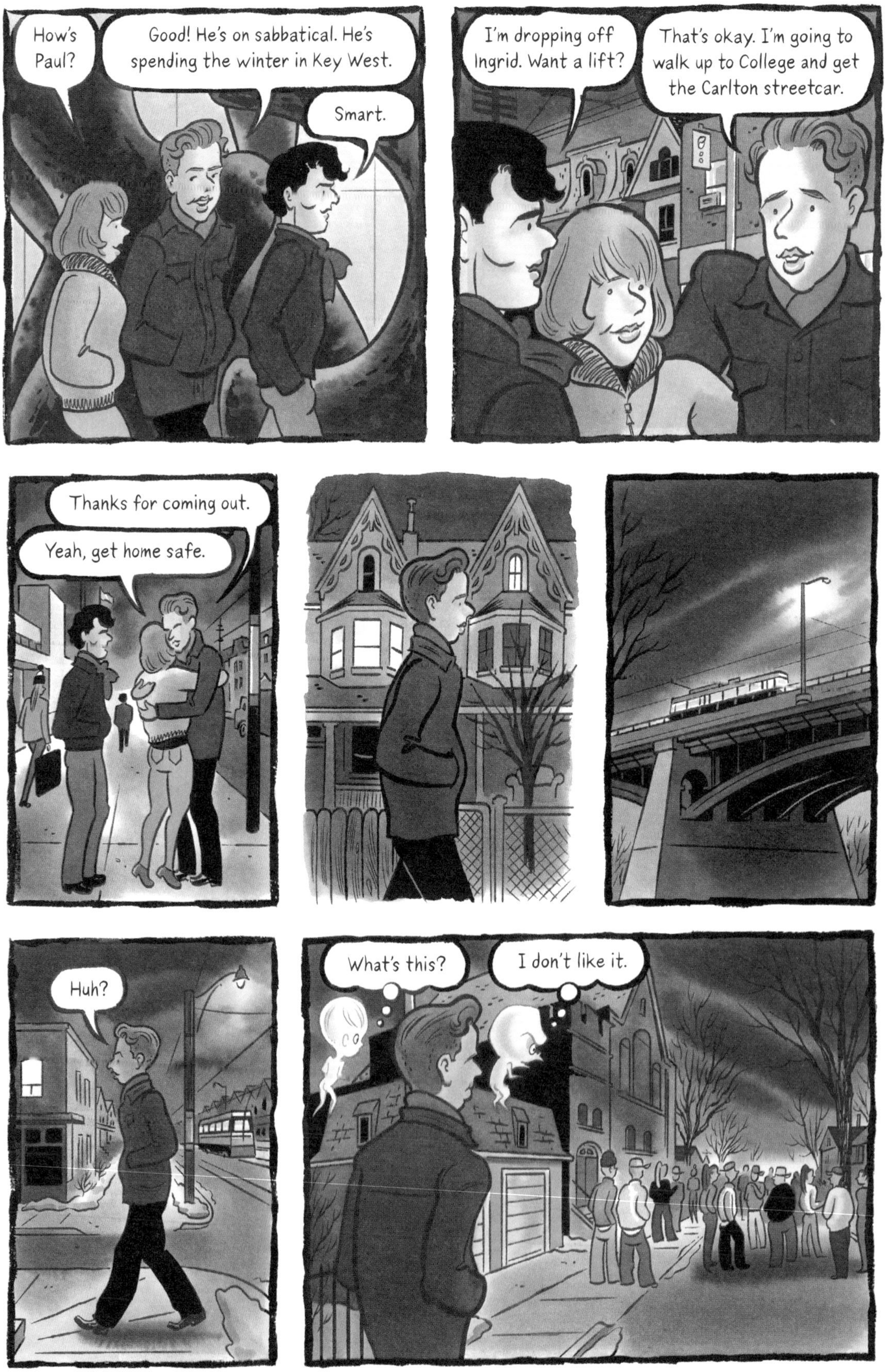
How's Paul?
Good! He's on sabbatical. He's spending the winter in Key West.
Smart.
I'm dropping off Ingrid. Want a lift?
That's okay. I'm going to walk up to College and get the Carlton streetcar.
Thanks for coming out.
Yeah, get home safe.
Huh?
What's this?
I don't like it.

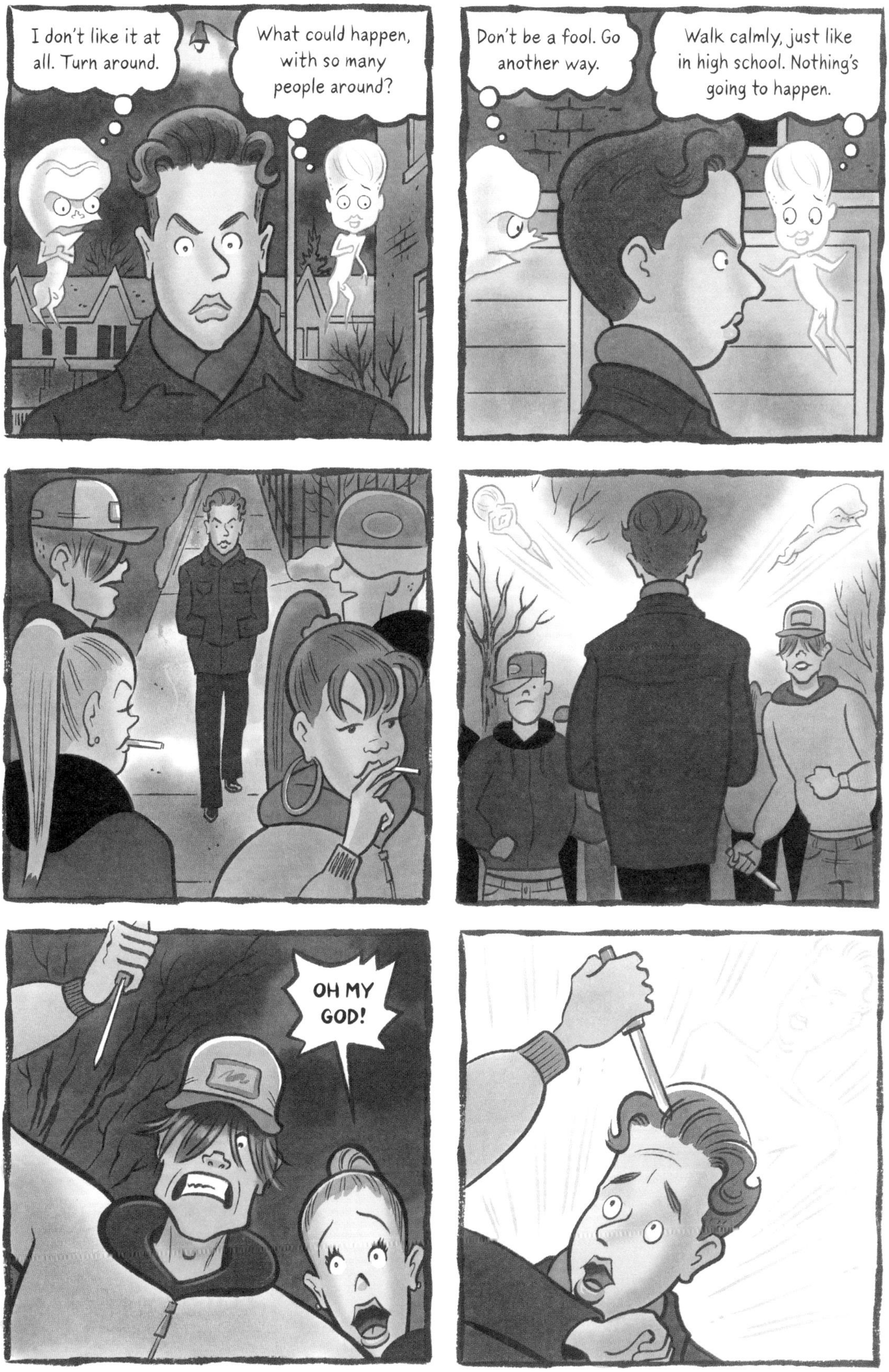
I don't like it at all. Turn around.
What could happen, with so many people around?
Don't be a fool. Go another way.
Walk calmly, just like in high school. Nothing's going to happen.
OH MY GOD!

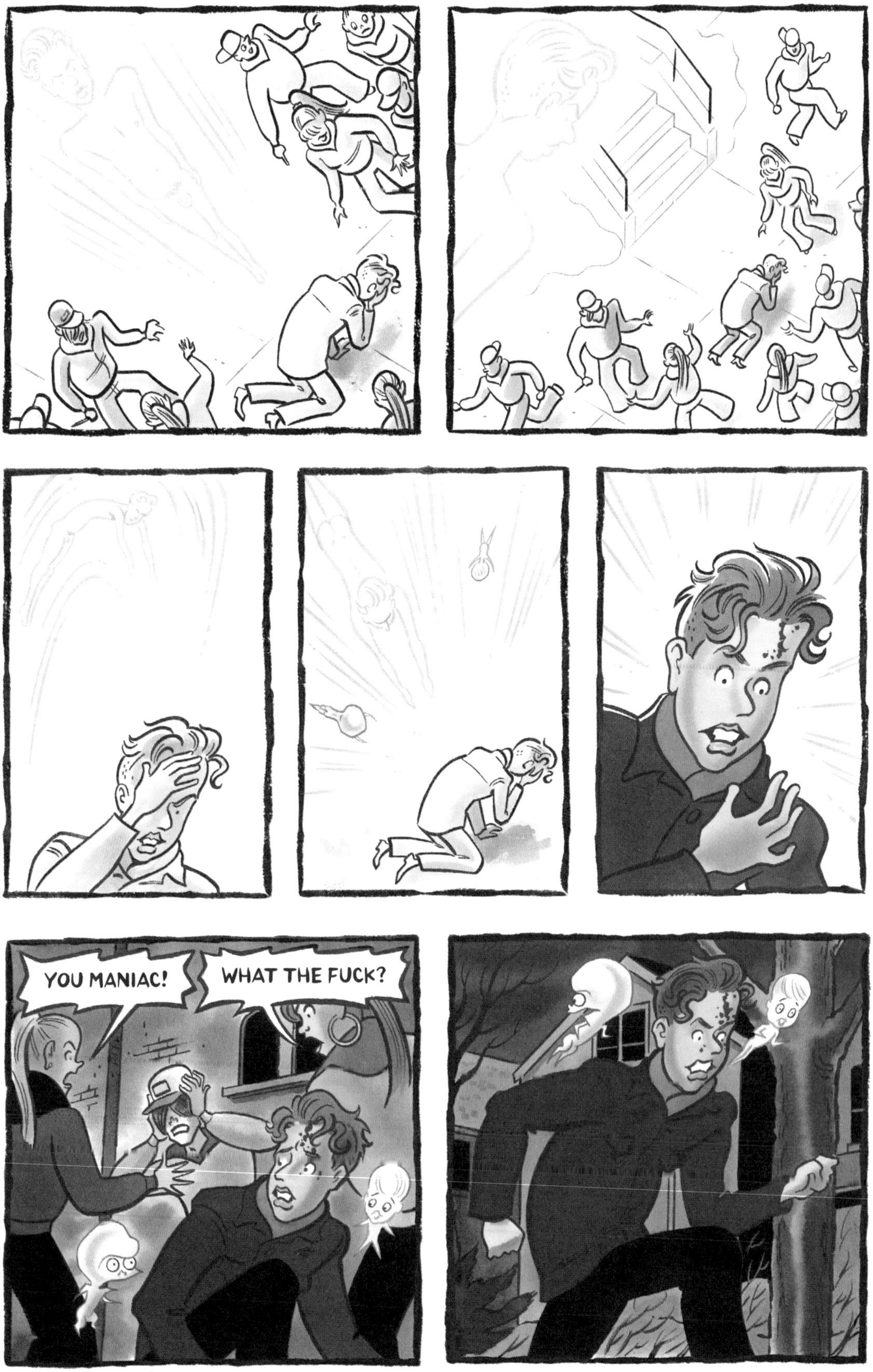

YOU MANIAC!
WHAT THE FUCK?

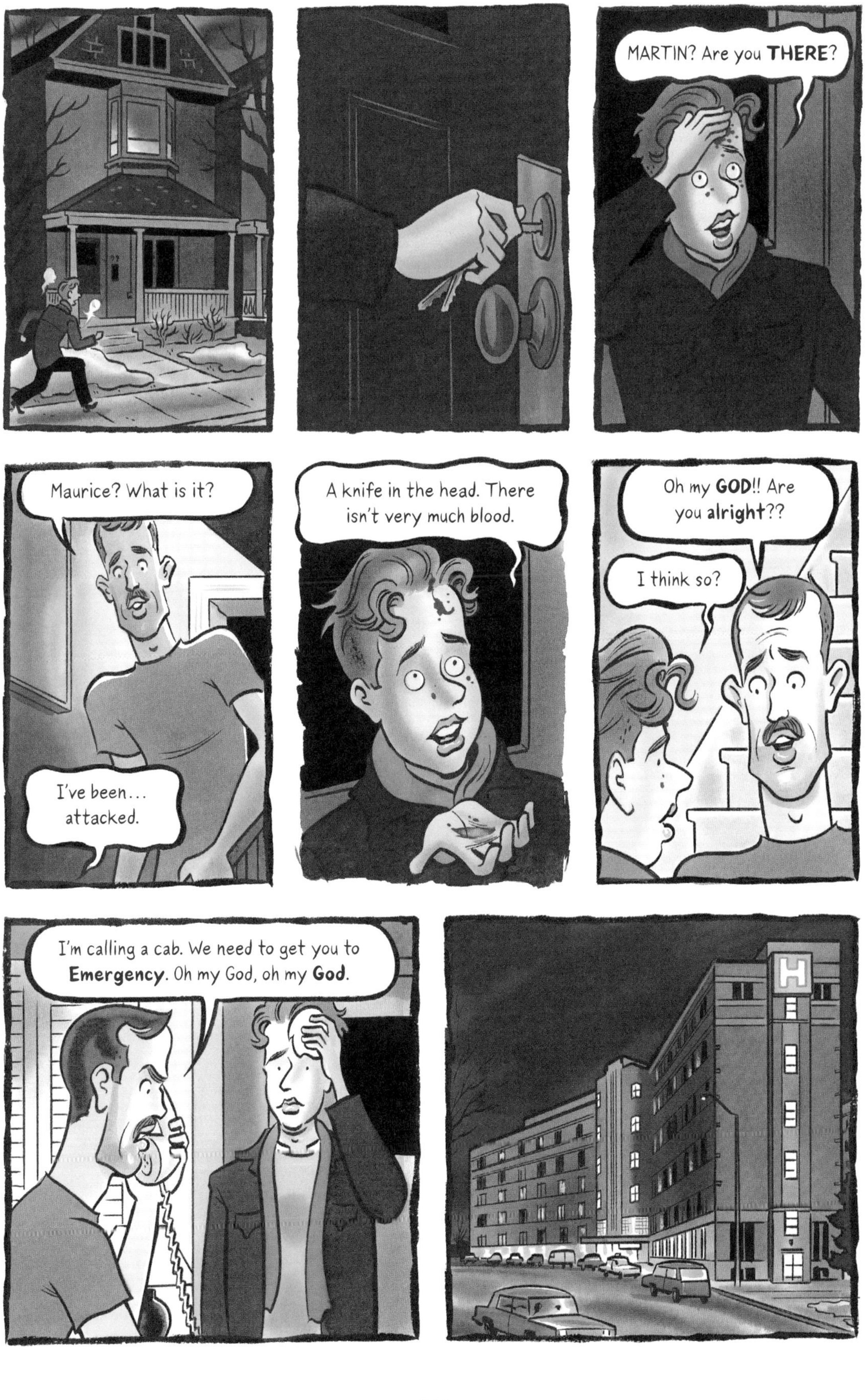
MARTIN? Are you **THERE**?
Maurice? What is it?
I've been... attacked.
A knife in the head. There isn't very much blood.
Oh my **GOD**!! Are you **alright**??
I think so?
I'm calling a cab. We need to get you to **Emergency**. Oh my God, oh my **God**.

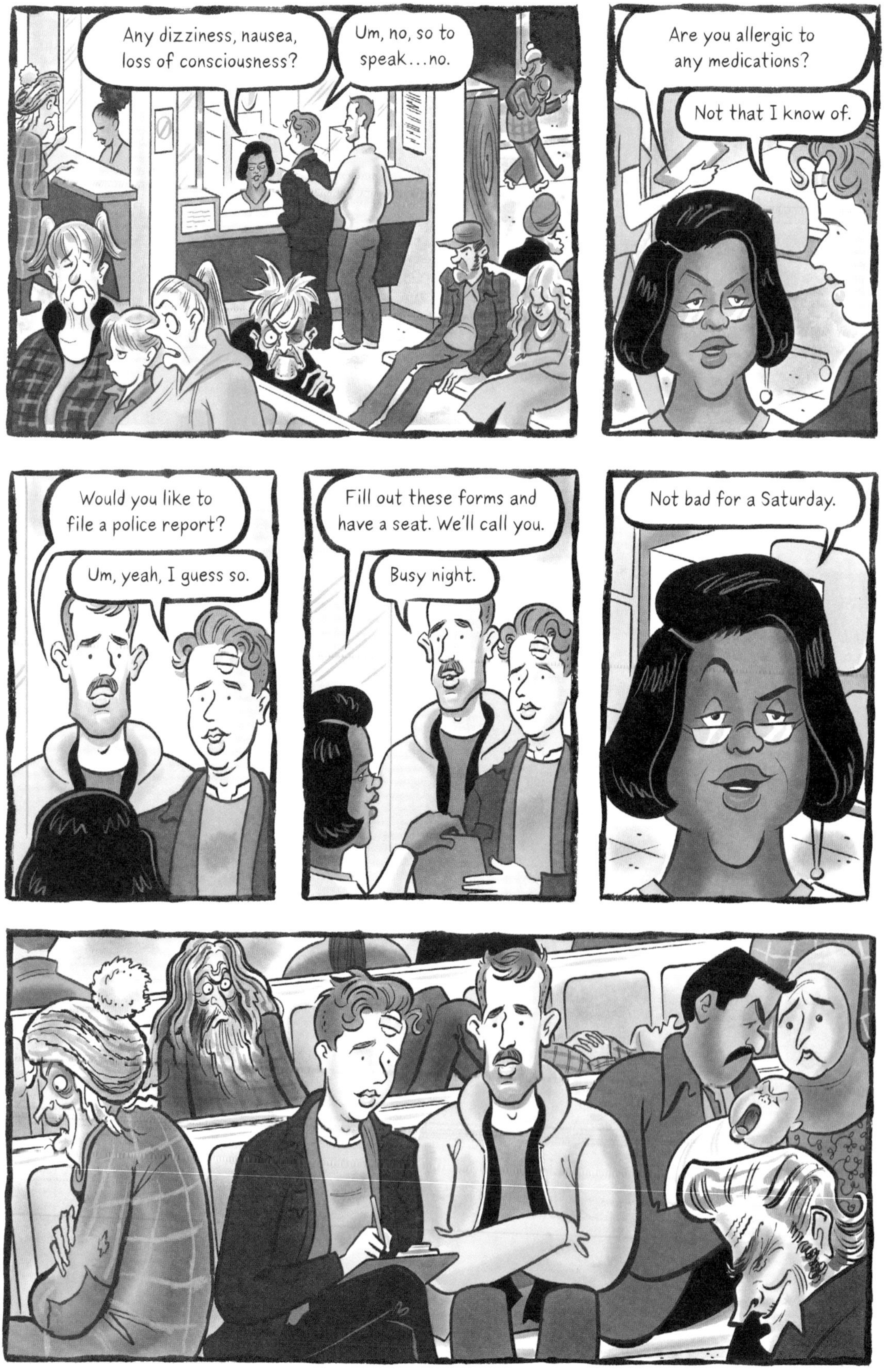
Any dizziness, nausea, loss of consciousness?
Um, no, so to speak...no.
Are you allergic to any medications?
Not that I know of.
Would you like to file a police report?
Um, yeah, I guess so.
Fill out these forms and have a seat. We'll call you.
Busy night.
Not bad for a Saturday.

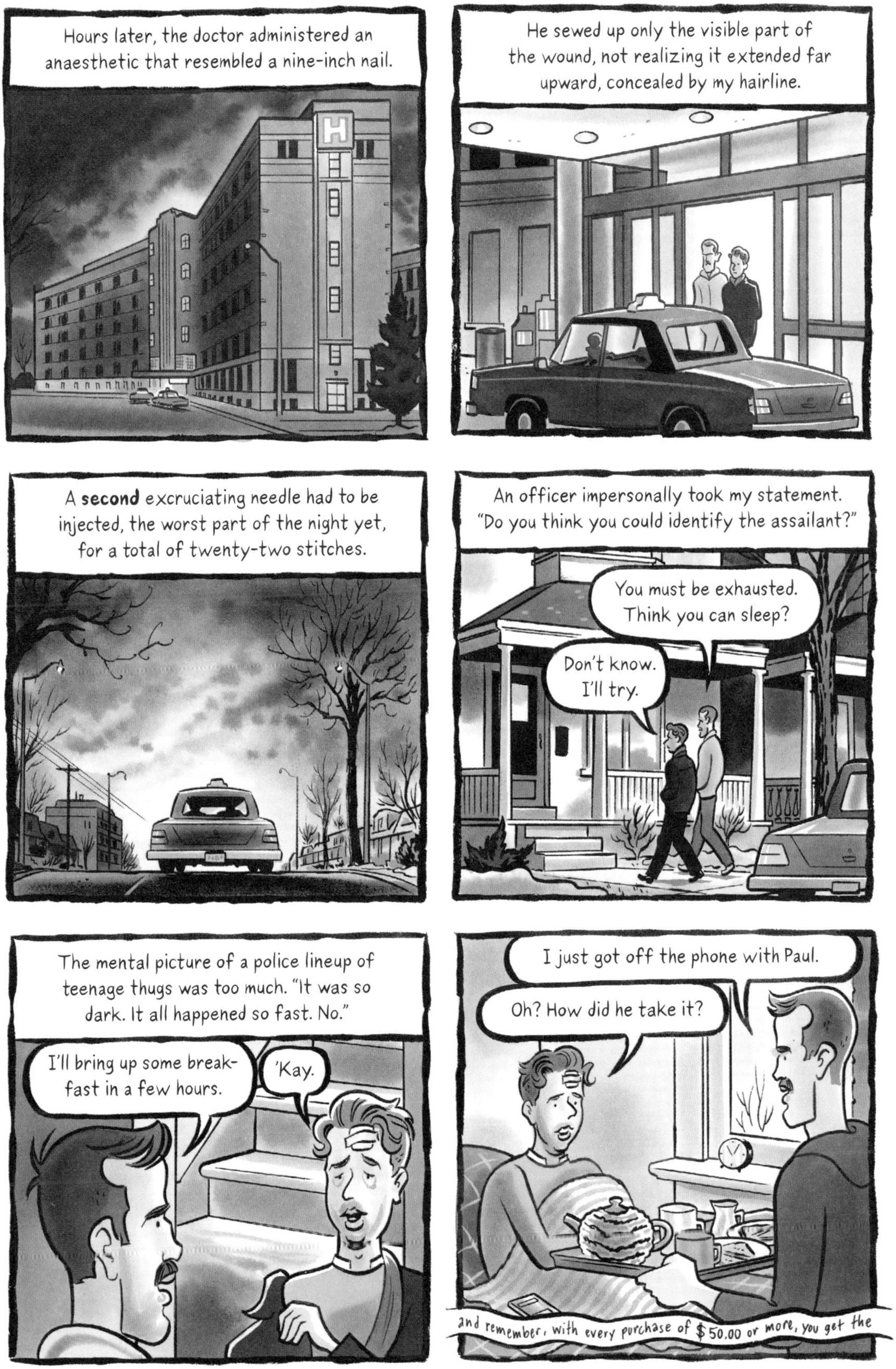
Hours later, the doctor administered an anaesthetic that resembled a nine-inch nail.
He sewed up only the visible part of the wound, not realizing it extended far upward, concealed by my hairline.
A **second** excruciating needle had to be injected, the worst part of the night yet, for a total of twenty-two stitches.
An officer impersonally took my statement. "Do you think you could identify the assailant?"
You must be exhausted. Think you can sleep?
Don't know. I'll try.
The mental picture of a police lineup of teenage thugs was too much. "It was so dark. It all happened so fast. No."
I'll bring up some breakfast in a few hours.
'Kay.
I just got off the phone with Paul.
Oh? How did he take it?
and remember, with every purchase of $50.00 or more, you get the

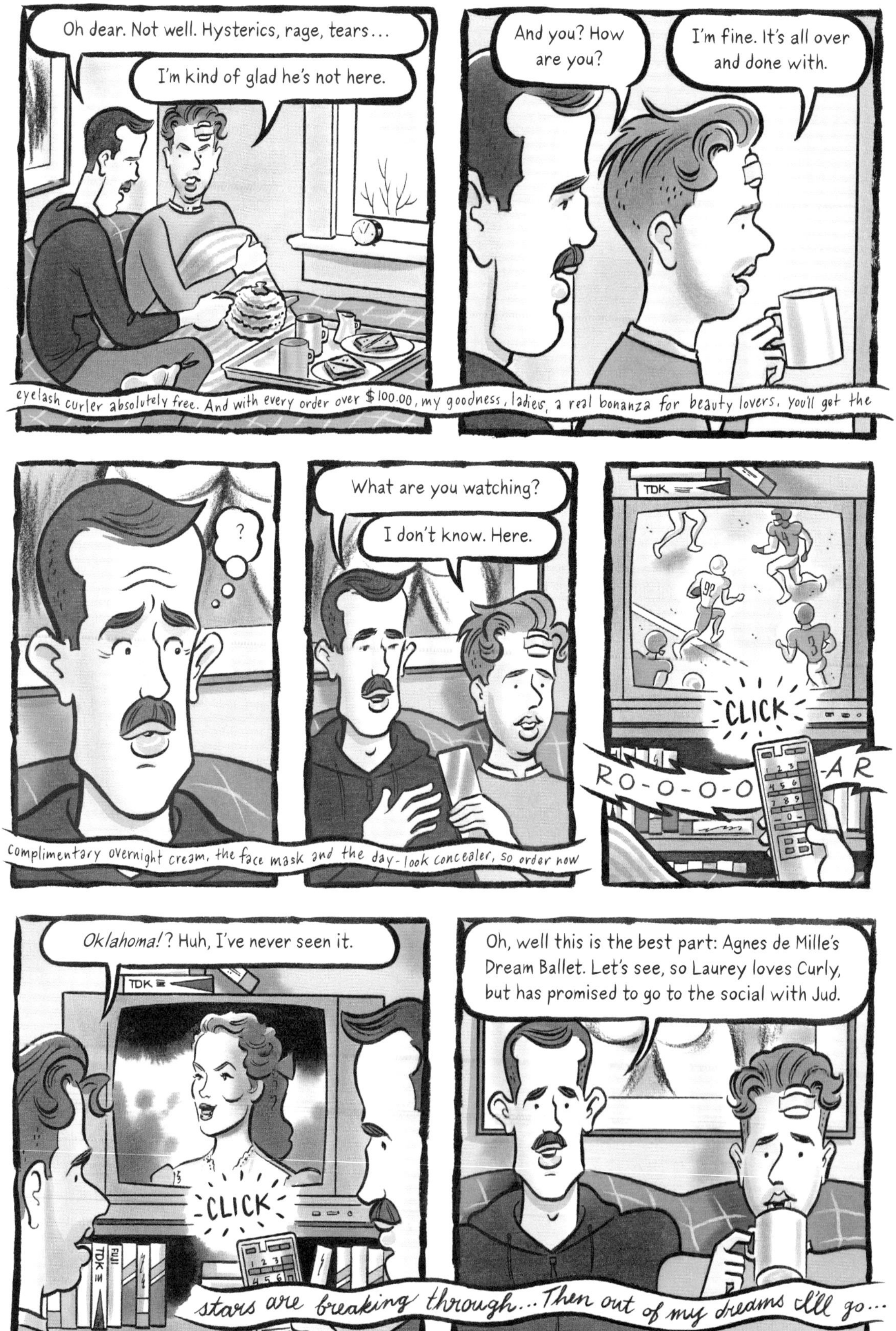
Oh dear. Not well. Hysterics, rage, tears...
I'm kind of glad he's not here.
And you? How are you?
I'm fine. It's all over and done with.
eyelash curler absolutely free. And with every order over $100.00, my goodness, ladies, a real bonanza for beauty lovers, you'll get the
?
What are you watching?
I don't know. Here.
TDK
CLICK
RO-O-O-O-O-AR
complimentary overnight cream, the face mask and the day-look concealer, so order now
Oklahoma!? Huh, I've never seen it.
TDK
CLICK
Oh, well this is the best part: Agnes de Mille's Dream Ballet. Let's see, so Laurey loves Curly, but has promised to go to the social with Jud.
stars are breaking through... Then out of my dreams I'll go...

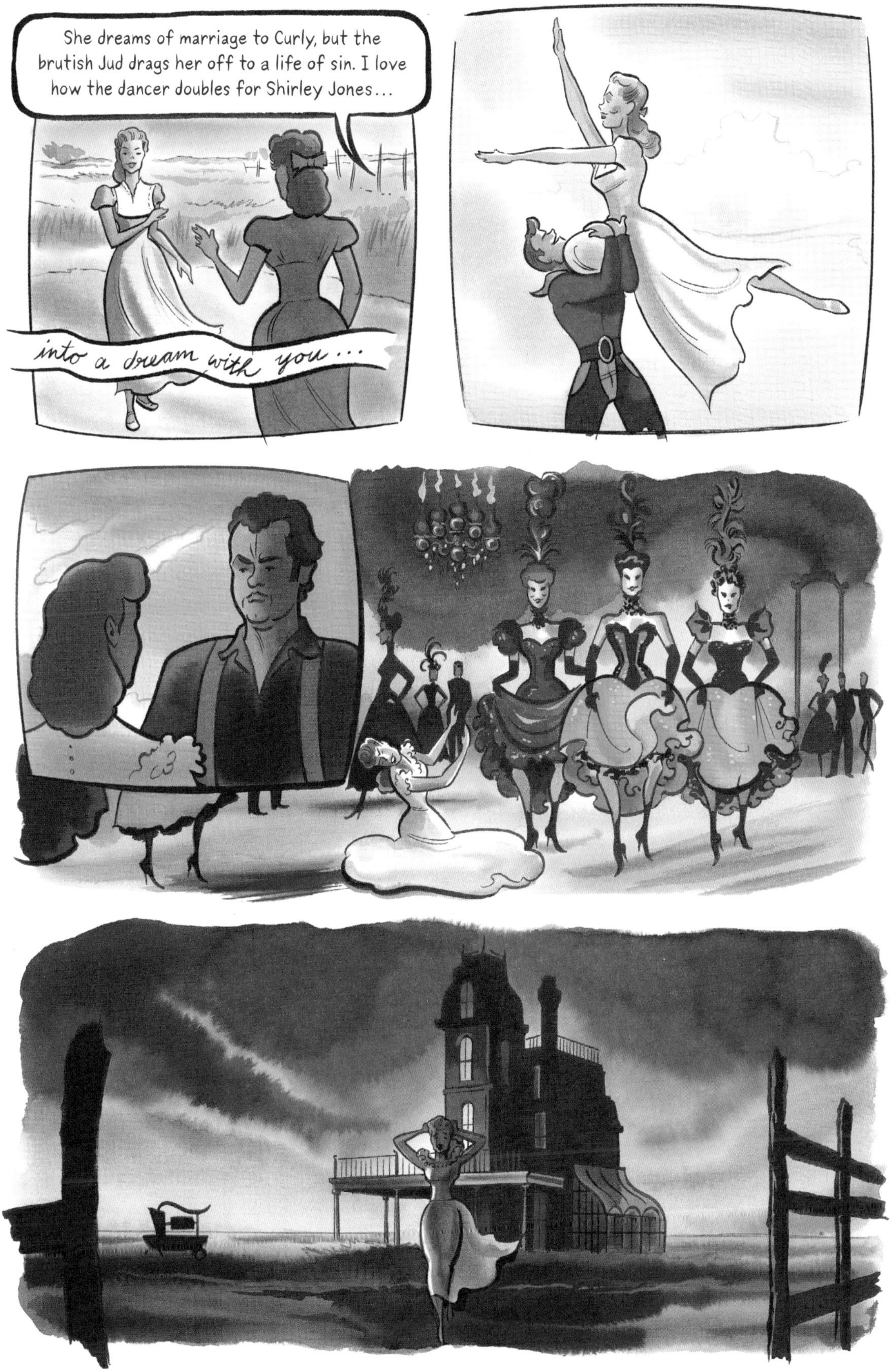
She dreams of marriage to Curly, but the brutish Jud drags her off to a life of sin. I love how the dancer doubles for Shirley Jones...
into a dream with you...

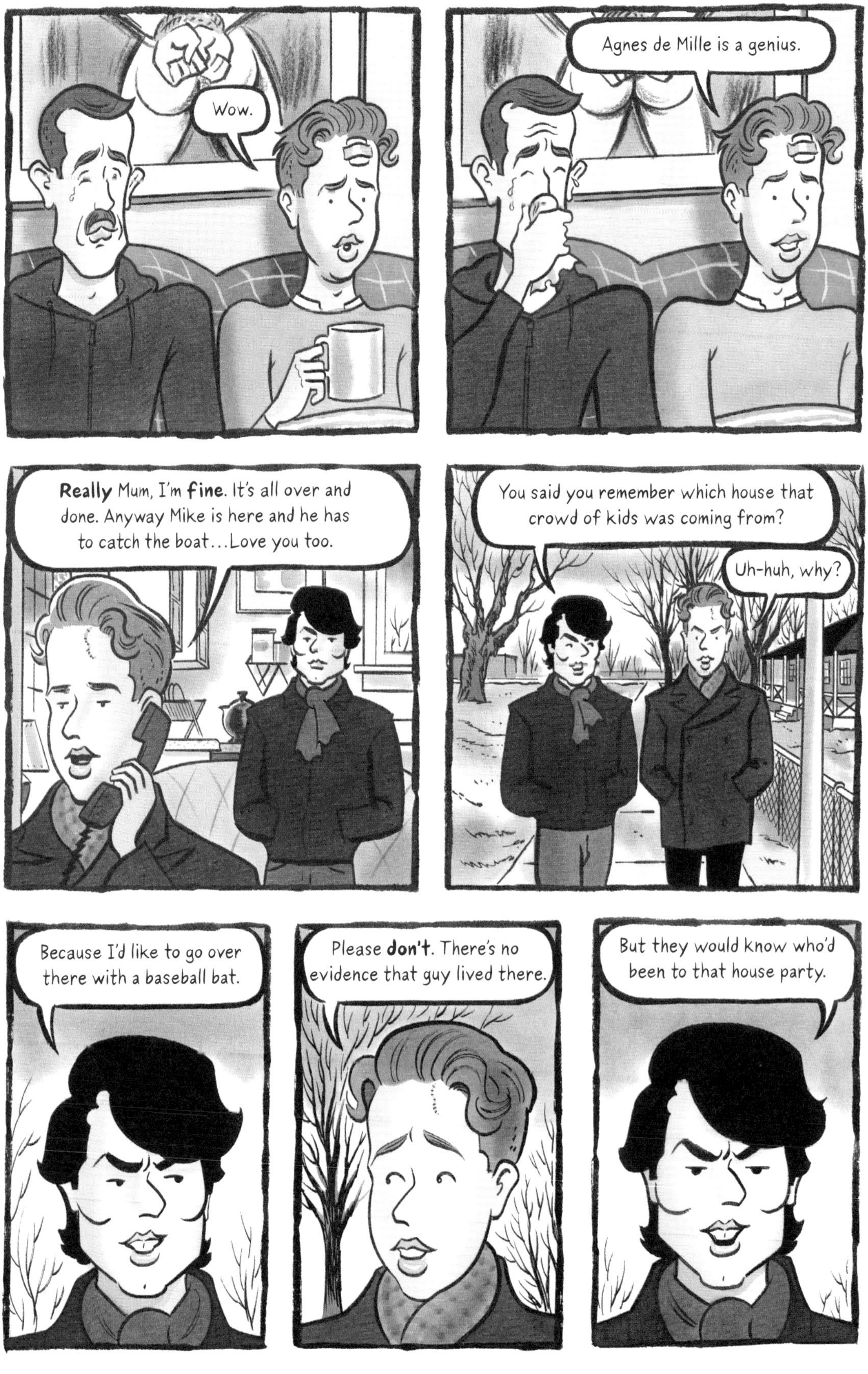

Wow.
Agnes de Mille is a genius.
Really Mum, I'm **fine**. It's all over and done. Anyway Mike is here and he has to catch the boat... Love you too.
You said you remember which house that crowd of kids was coming from?
Uh-huh, why?
Because I'd like to go over there with a baseball bat.
Please **don't**. There's no evidence that guy lived there.
But they would know who'd been to that house party.

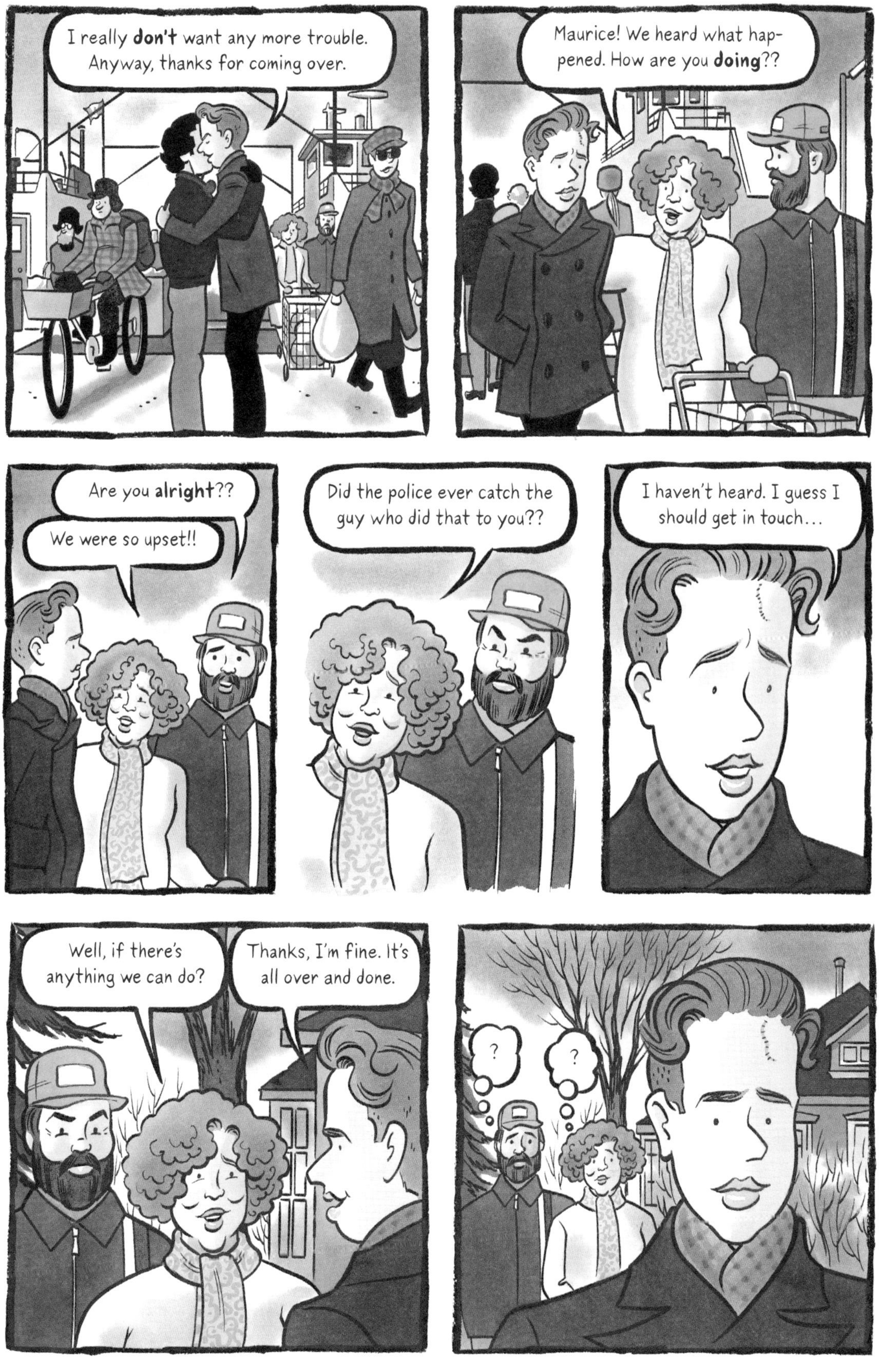
I really **don't** want any more trouble. Anyway, thanks for coming over.
Maurice! We heard what happened. How are you **doing**??
Are you **alright**??
We were so upset!!
Did the police ever catch the guy who did that to you??
I haven't heard. I guess I should get in touch...
Well, if there's anything we can do?
Thanks, I'm fine. It's all over and done.
?
?

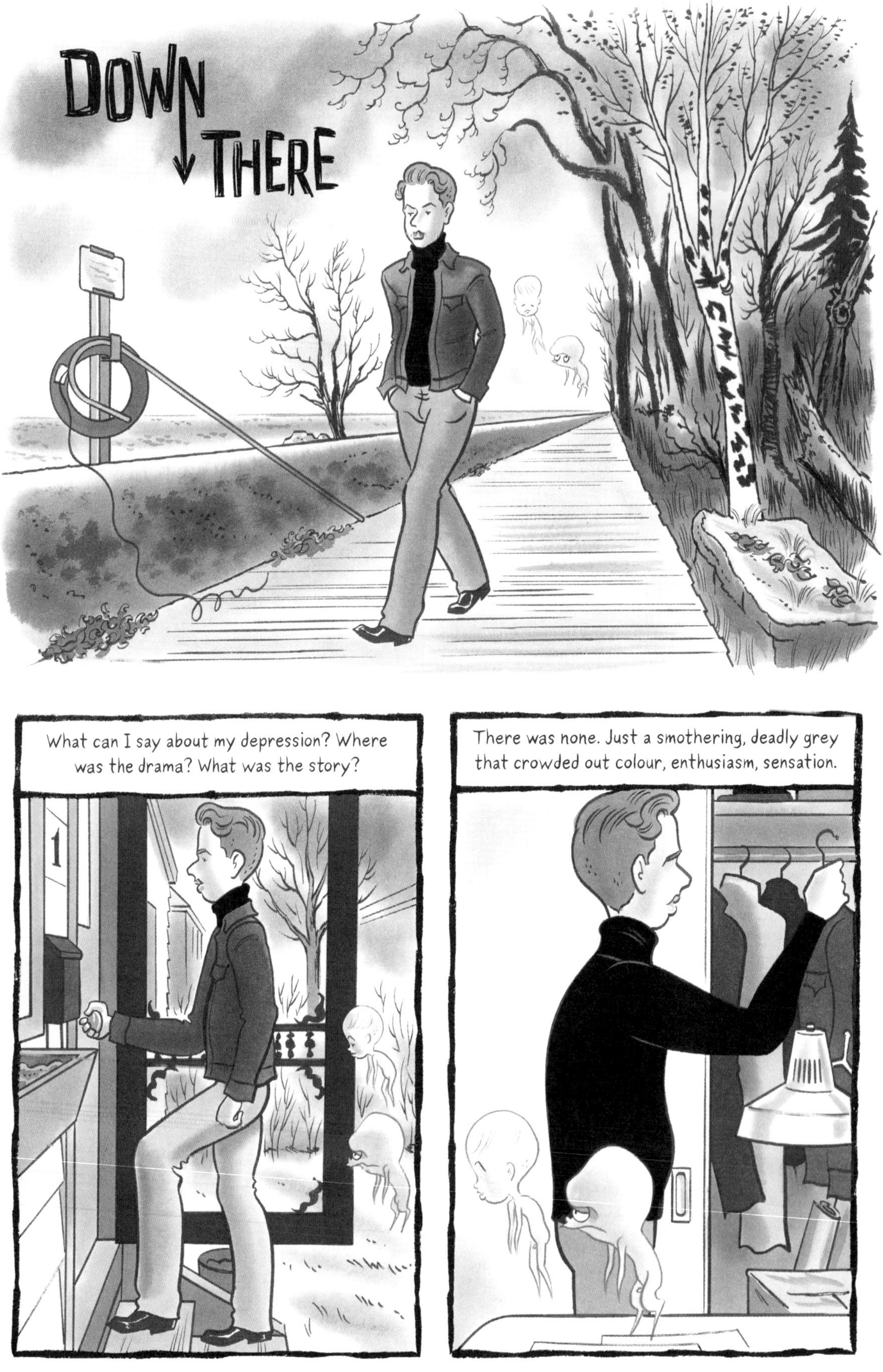
DOWN THERE
What can I say about my depression? Where was the drama? What was the story?
There was none. Just a smothering, deadly grey that crowded out colour, enthusiasm, sensation.

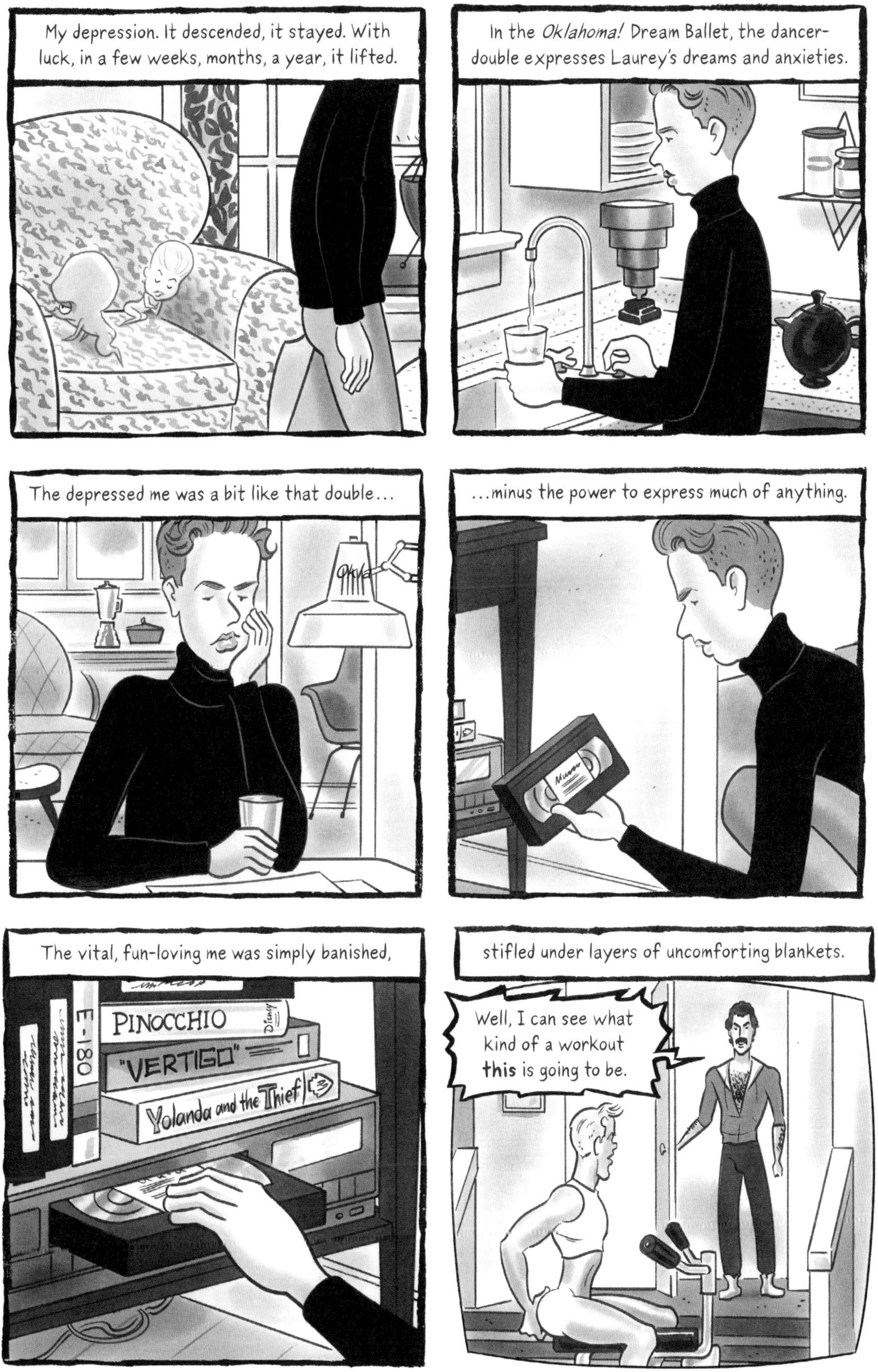

My depression. It descended, it stayed. With luck, in a few weeks, months, a year, it lifted.
In the *Oklahoma!* Dream Ballet, the dancer-double expresses Laurey's dreams and anxieties.
The depressed me was a bit like that double...
...minus the power to express much of anything.
The vital, fun-loving me was simply banished,
PINOCCHIO
"VERTIGO"
Yolanda and the Thief
E-180
stifled under layers of uncomforting blankets.
Well, I can see what kind of a workout **this** is going to be.

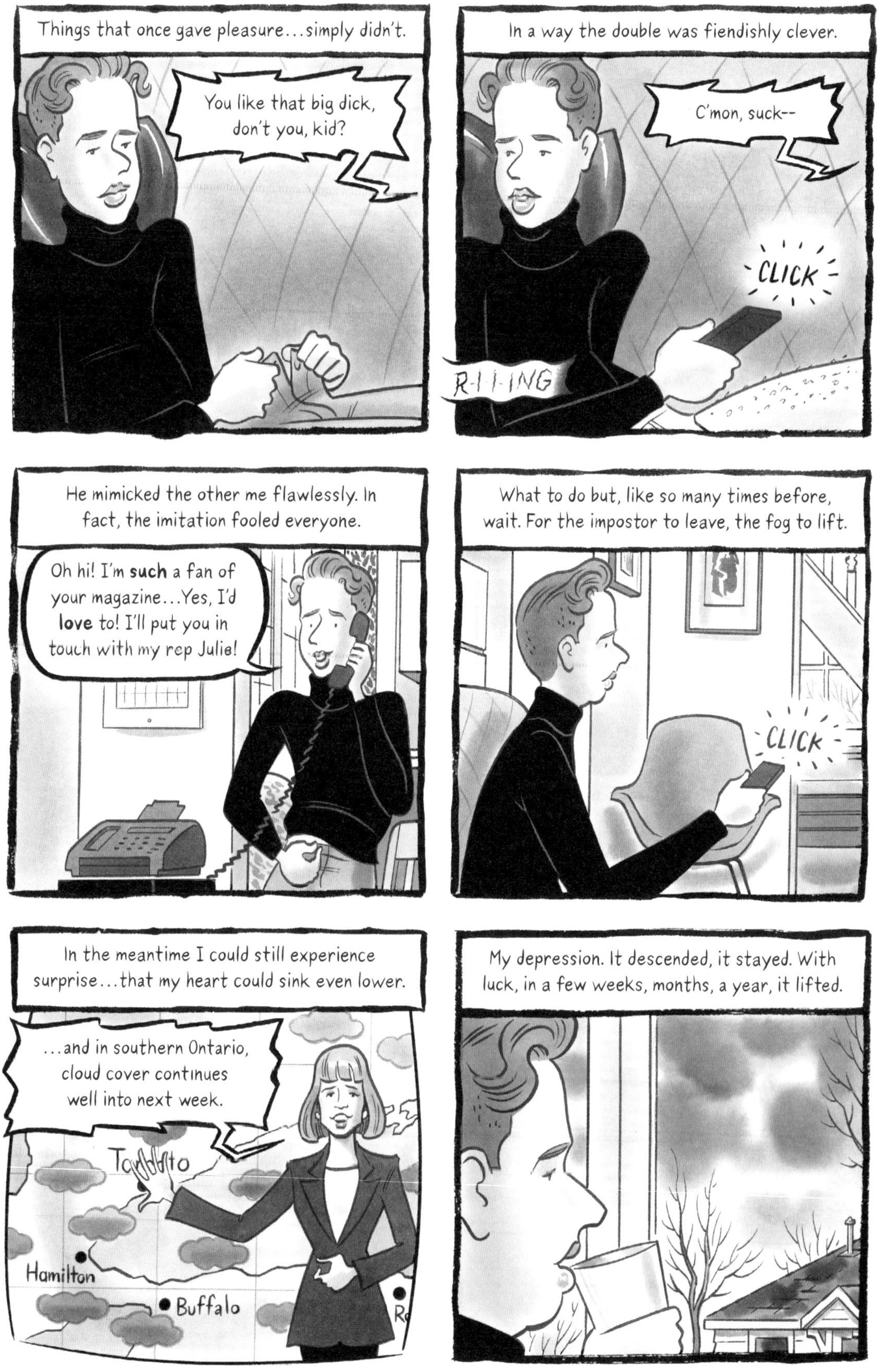
Things that once gave pleasure…simply didn't.
You like that big dick, don't you, kid?
In a way the double was fiendishly clever.
C'mon, suck--
CLICK
R-I-I-ING
He mimicked the other me flawlessly. In fact, the imitation fooled everyone.
Oh hi! I'm **such** a fan of your magazine…Yes, I'd **love** to! I'll put you in touch with my rep Julie!
What to do but, like so many times before, wait. For the impostor to leave, the fog to lift.
CLICK
In the meantime I could still experience surprise…that my heart could sink even lower.
…and in southern Ontario, cloud cover continues well into next week.
Hamilton
Buffalo
My depression. It descended, it stayed. With luck, in a few weeks, months, a year, it lifted.

Stendhal Syndrome

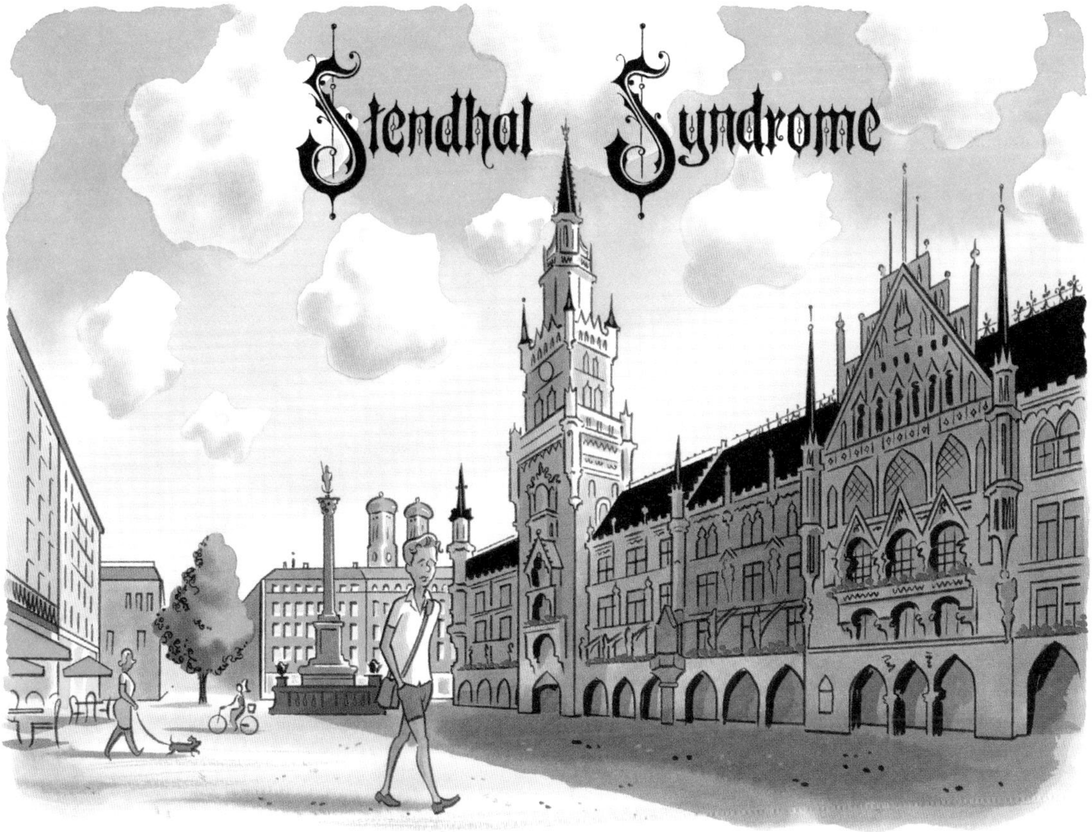

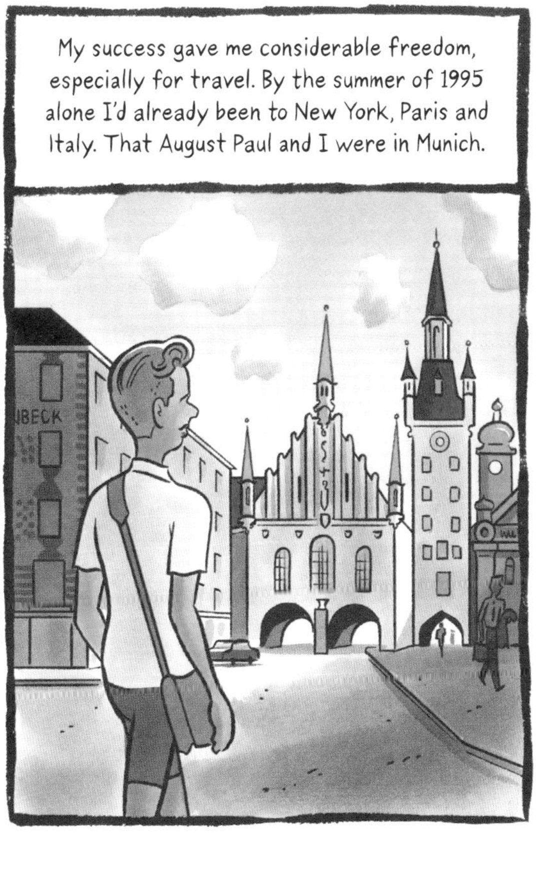
My success gave me considerable freedom, especially for travel. By the summer of 1995 alone I'd already been to New York, Paris and Italy. That August Paul and I were in Munich.

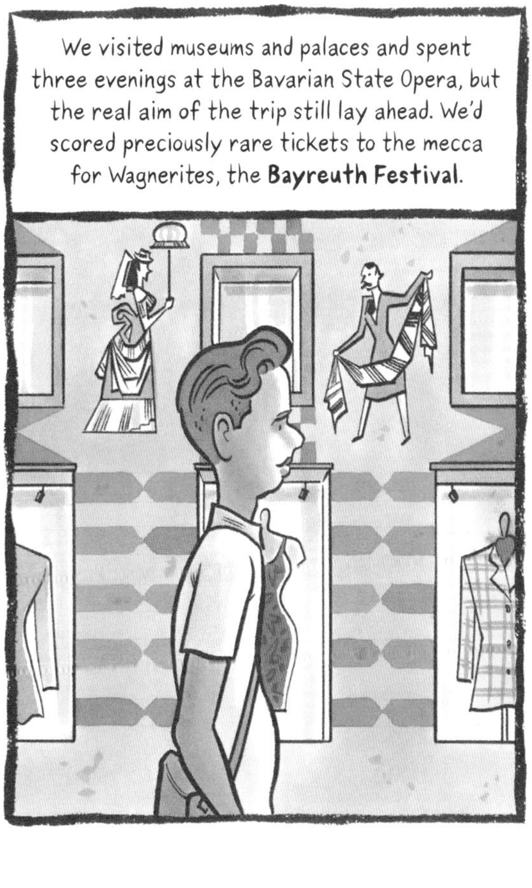
We visited museums and palaces and spent three evenings at the Bavarian State Opera, but the real aim of the trip still lay ahead. We'd scored preciously rare tickets to the mecca for Wagnerites, the **Bayreuth Festival**.

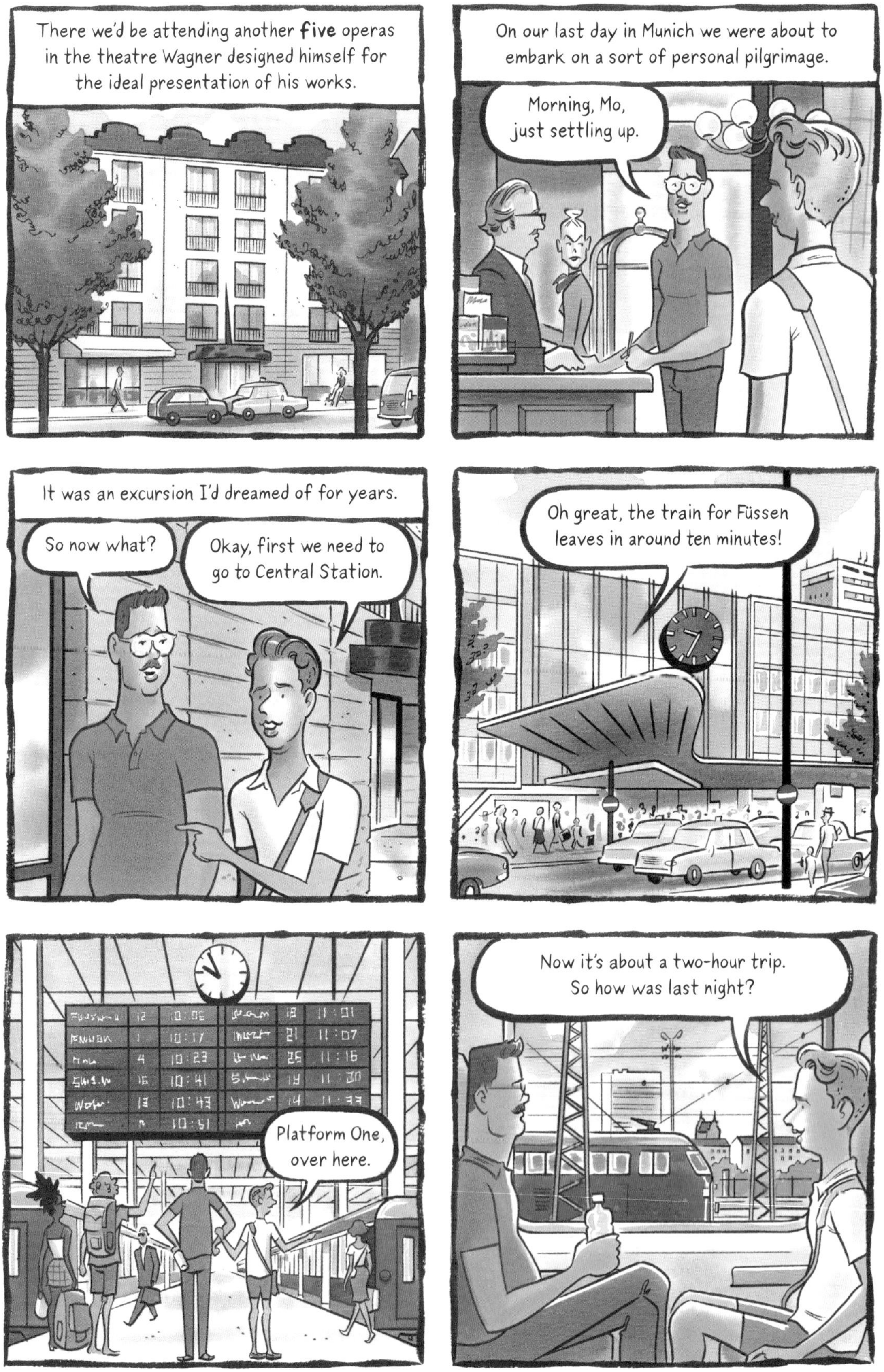
There we'd be attending another **five** operas in the theatre Wagner designed himself for the ideal presentation of his works.
On our last day in Munich we were about to embark on a sort of personal pilgrimage.
Morning, Mo, just settling up.
It was an excursion I'd dreamed of for years.
So now what?
Okay, first we need to go to Central Station.
Oh great, the train for Füssen leaves in around ten minutes!
Platform One, over here.
Now it's about a two-hour trip. So how was last night?

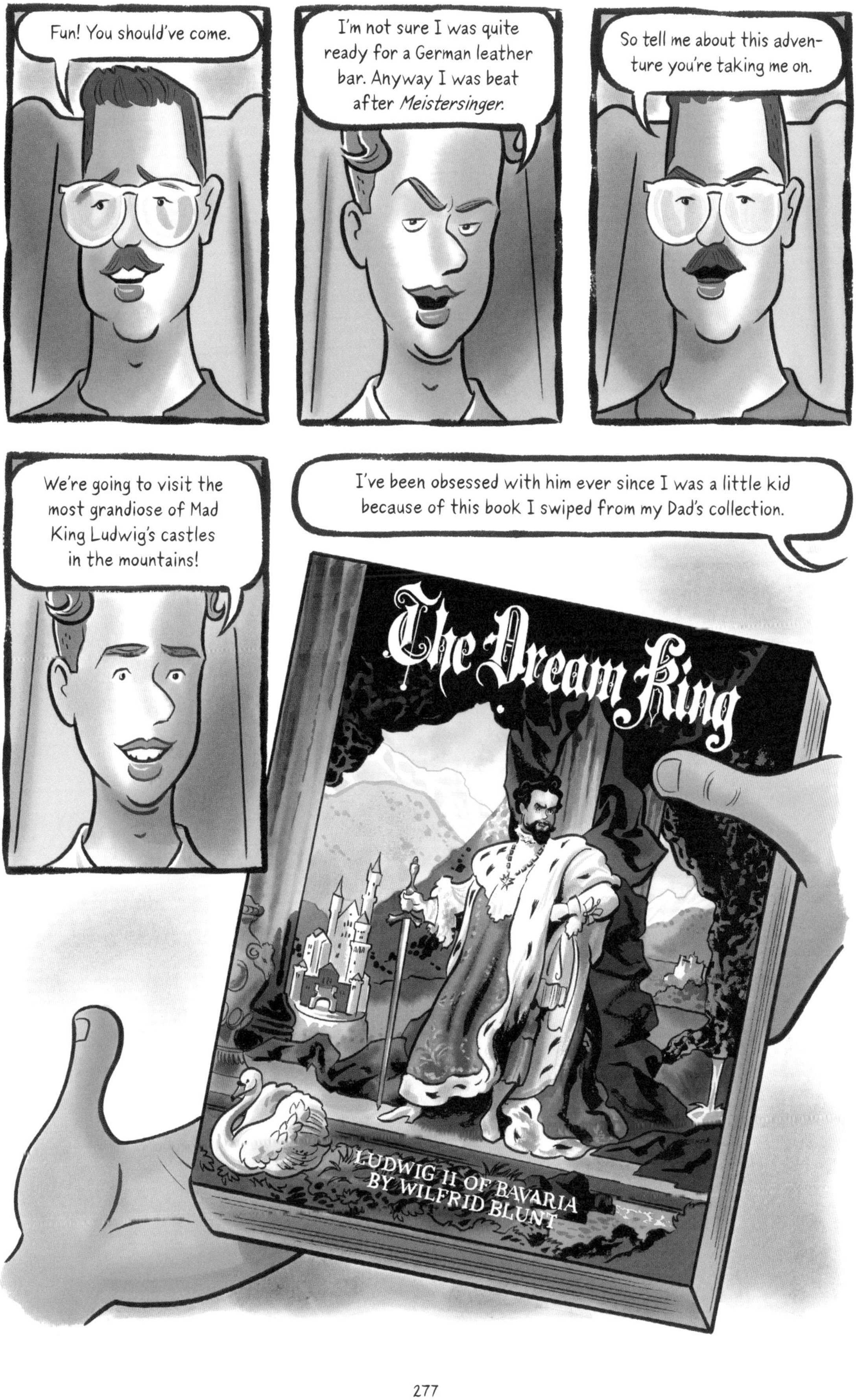
Fun! You should've come.
I'm not sure I was quite ready for a German leather bar. Anyway I was beat after Meistersinger.
So tell me about this adventure you're taking me on.
We're going to visit the most grandiose of Mad King Ludwig's castles in the mountains!
I've been obsessed with him ever since I was a little kid because of this book I swiped from my Dad's collection.
The Dream King
LUDWIG II OF BAVARIA
BY WILFRID BLUNT

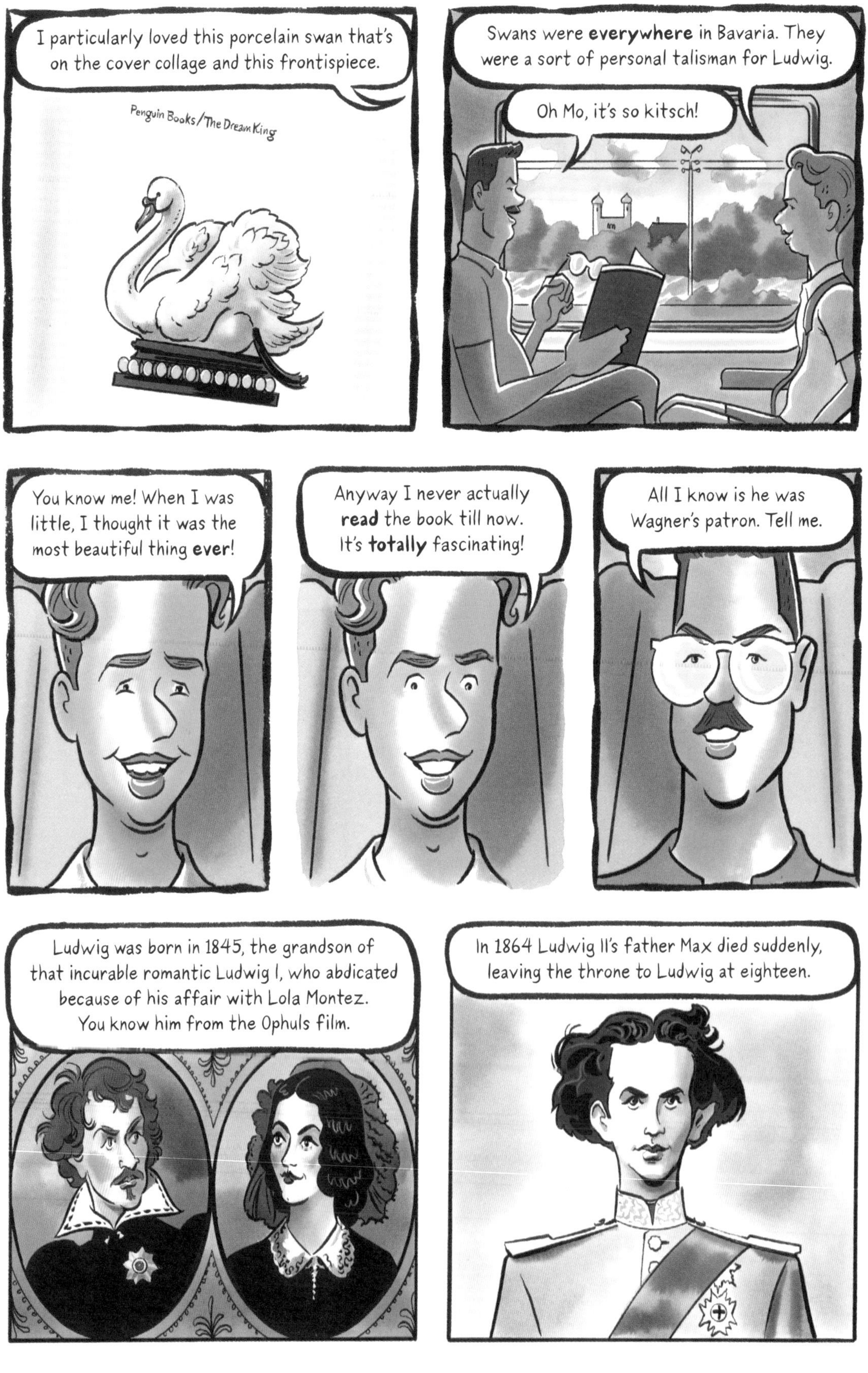
I particularly loved this porcelain swan that's on the cover collage and this frontispiece.
Penguin Books/The Dream King
Swans were **everywhere** in Bavaria. They were a sort of personal talisman for Ludwig.
Oh Mo, it's so kitsch!
You know me! When I was little, I thought it was the most beautiful thing **ever**!
Anyway I never actually **read** the book till now. It's **totally** fascinating!
All I know is he was Wagner's patron. Tell me.
Ludwig was born in 1845, the grandson of that incurable romantic Ludwig I, who abdicated because of his affair with Lola Montez. You know him from the Ophuls film.
In 1864 Ludwig II's father Max died suddenly, leaving the throne to Ludwig at eighteen.

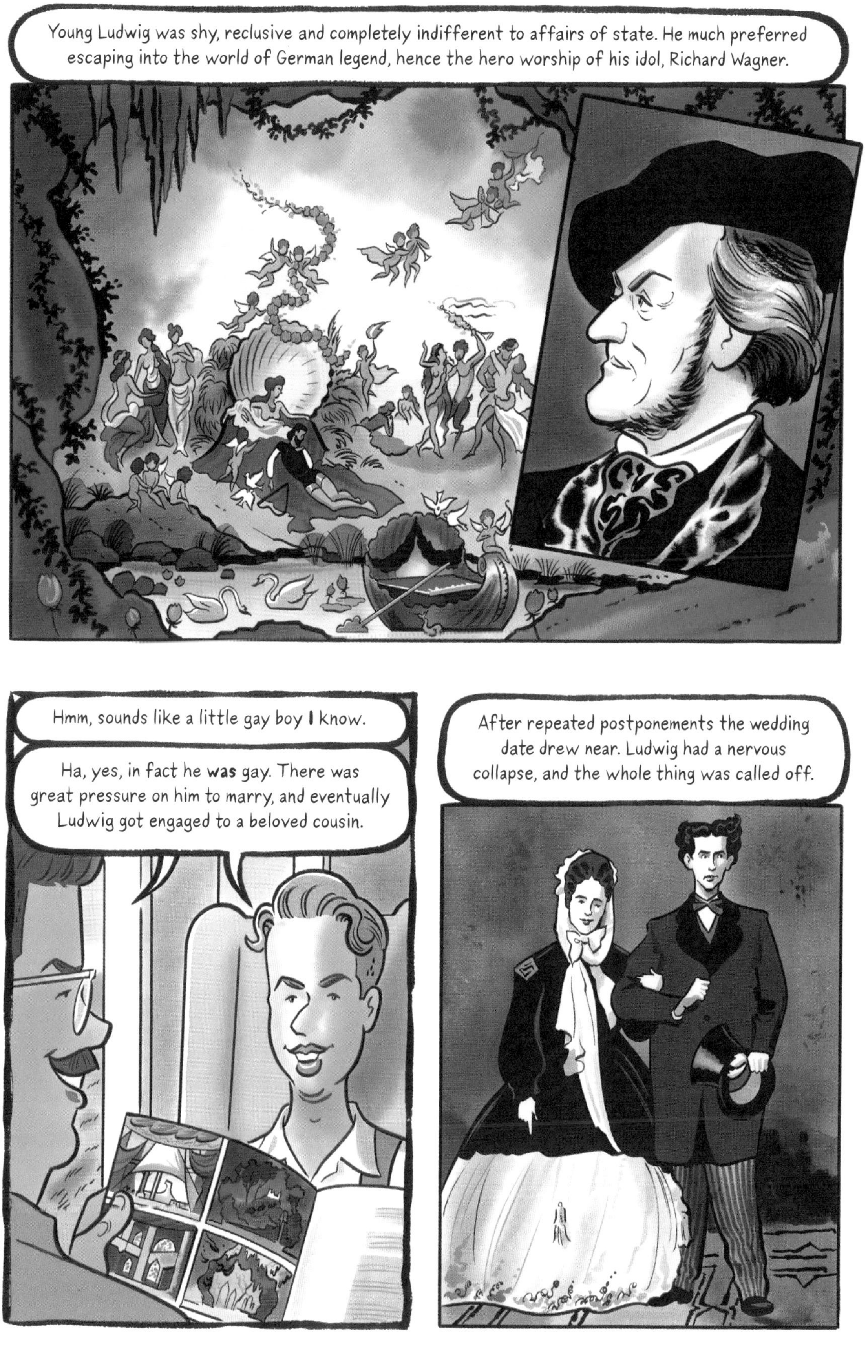
Young Ludwig was shy, reclusive and completely indifferent to affairs of state. He much preferred escaping into the world of German legend, hence the hero worship of his idol, Richard Wagner.
Hmm, sounds like a little gay boy **I** know.
Ha, yes, in fact he **was** gay. There was great pressure on him to marry, and eventually Ludwig got engaged to a beloved cousin.
After repeated postponements the wedding date drew near. Ludwig had a nervous collapse, and the whole thing was called off.

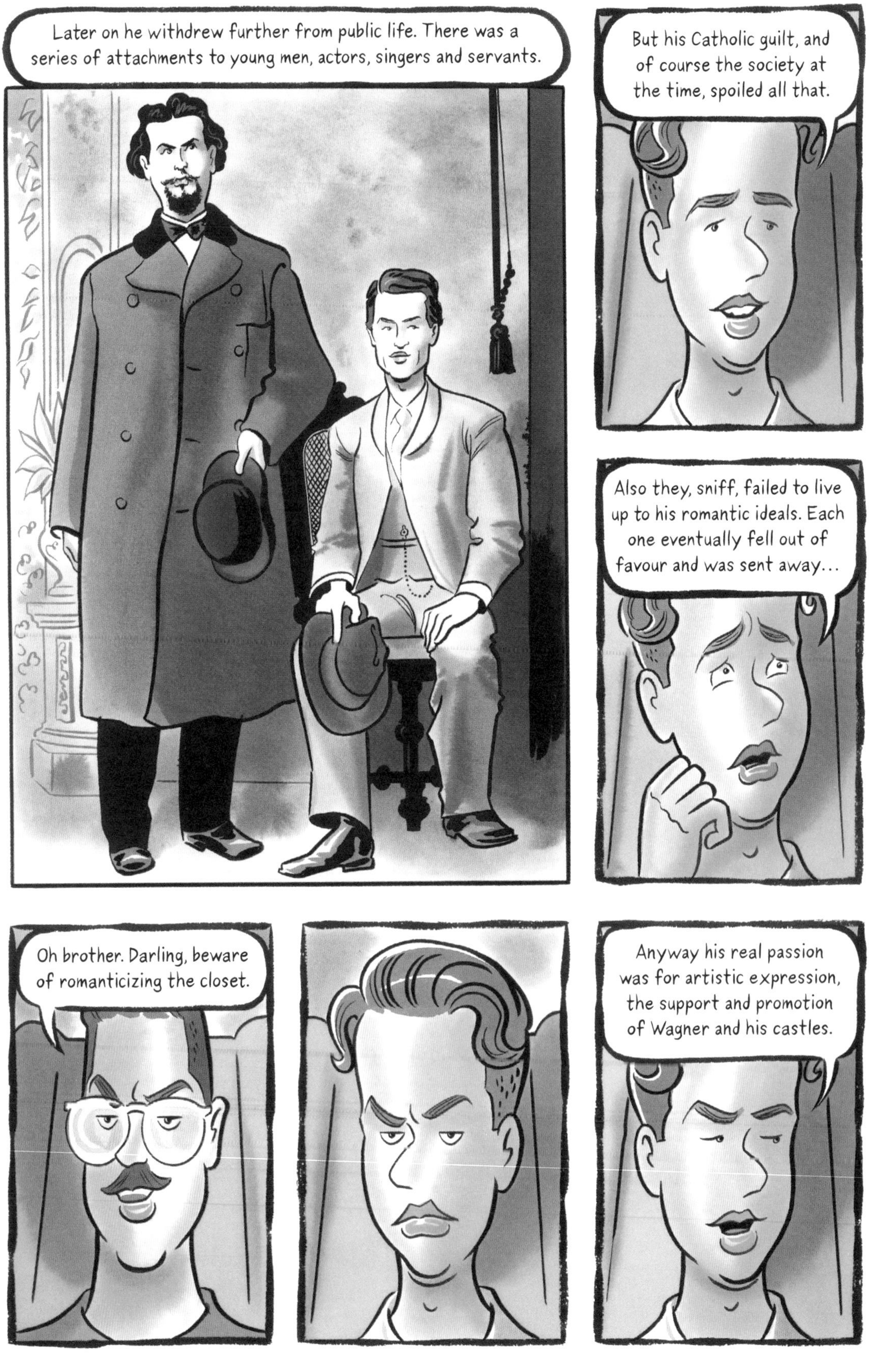
Later on he withdrew further from public life. There was a series of attachments to young men, actors, singers and servants.
But his Catholic guilt, and of course the society at the time, spoiled all that.
Also they, sniff, failed to live up to his romantic ideals. Each one eventually fell out of favour and was sent away...
Oh brother. Darling, beware of romanticizing the closet.
Anyway his real passion was for artistic expression, the support and promotion of Wagner and his castles.

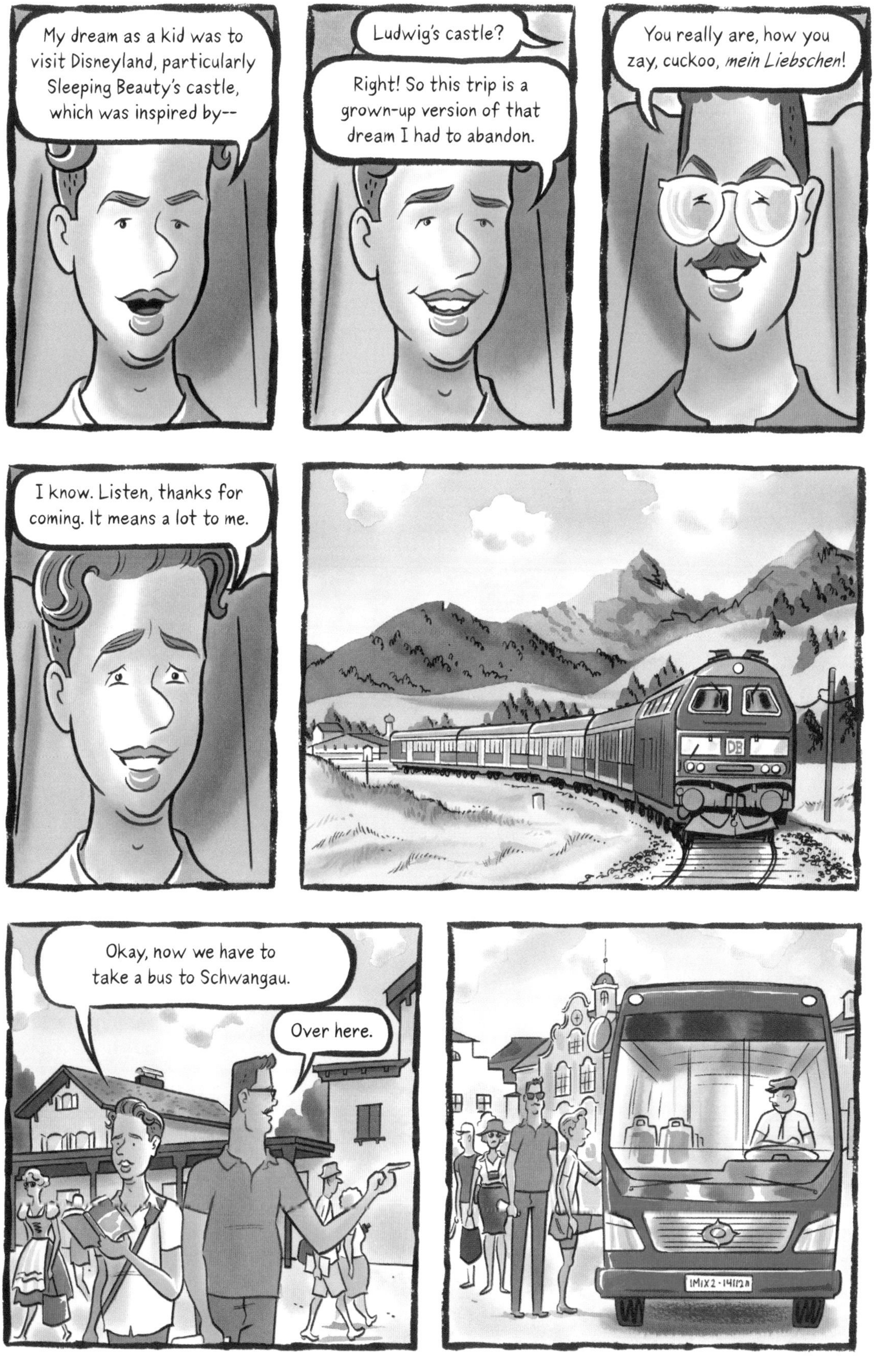

My dream as a kid was to visit Disneyland, particularly Sleeping Beauty's castle, which was inspired by--
Ludwig's castle?
Right! So this trip is a grown-up version of that dream I had to abandon.
You really are, how you zay, cuckoo, *mein Liebschen*!
I know. Listen, thanks for coming. It means a lot to me.
DB
Okay, now we have to take a bus to Schwangau.
Over here.

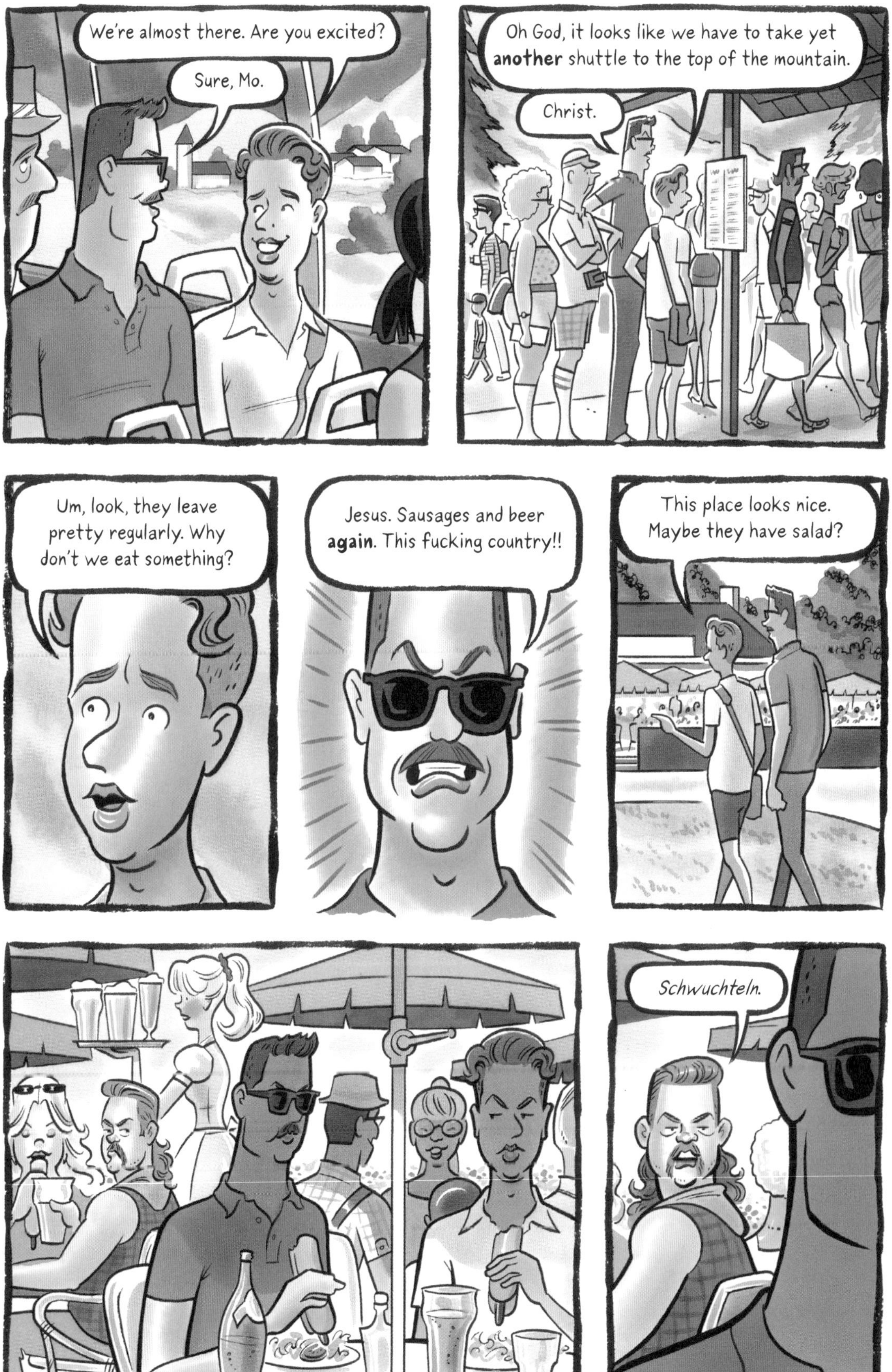
We're almost there. Are you excited?
Sure, Mo.
Oh God, it looks like we have to take yet **another** shuttle to the top of the mountain.
Christ.
Um, look, they leave pretty regularly. Why don't we eat something?
Jesus. Sausages and beer **again**. This fucking country!!
This place looks nice. Maybe they have salad?
Schwuchteln.

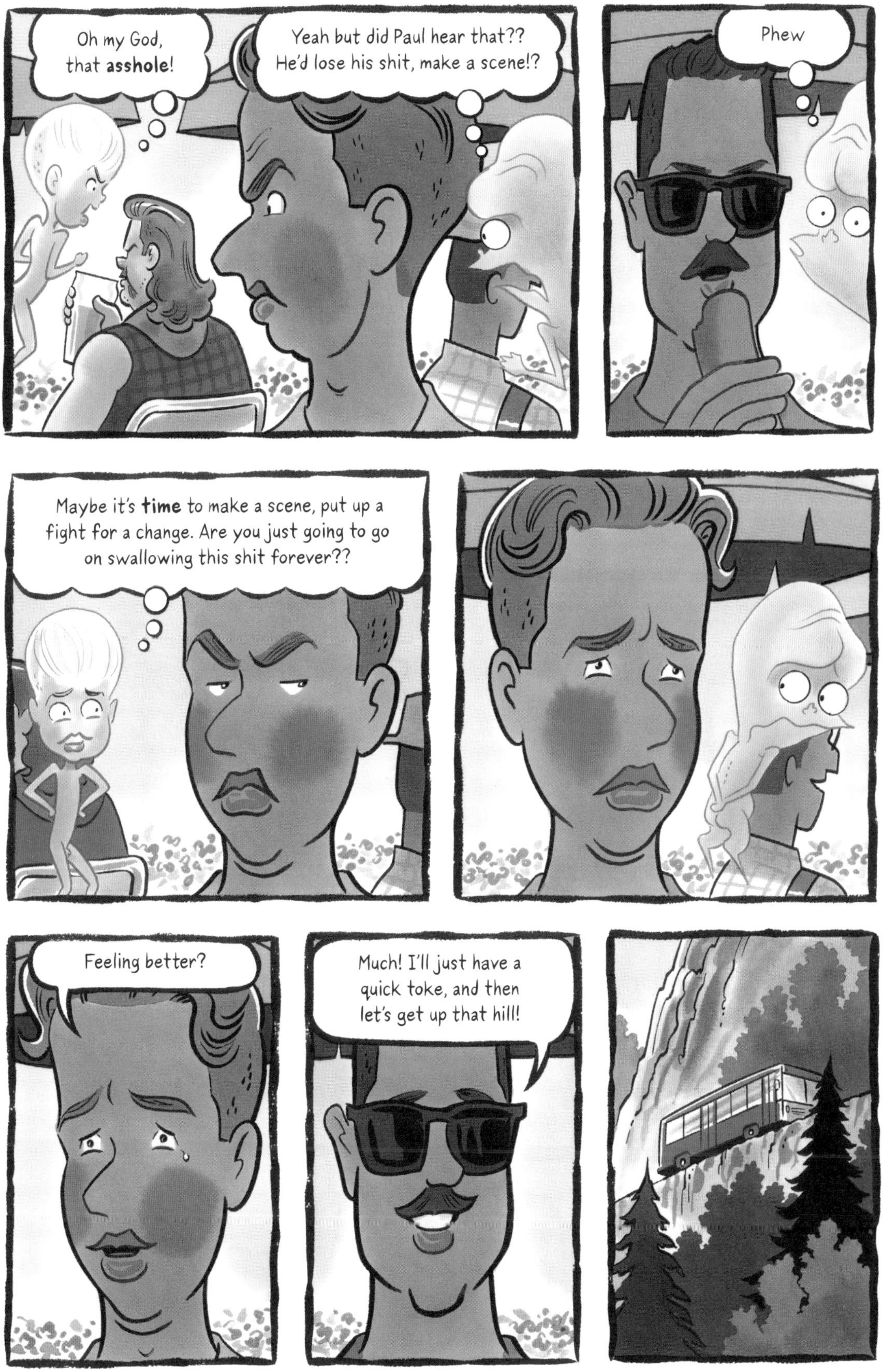
Oh my God, that **asshole**!
Yeah but did Paul hear that?? He'd lose his shit, make a scene!?
Phew
Maybe it's **time** to make a scene, put up a fight for a change. Are you just going to go on swallowing this shit forever??
Feeling better?
Much! I'll just have a quick toke, and then let's get up that hill!

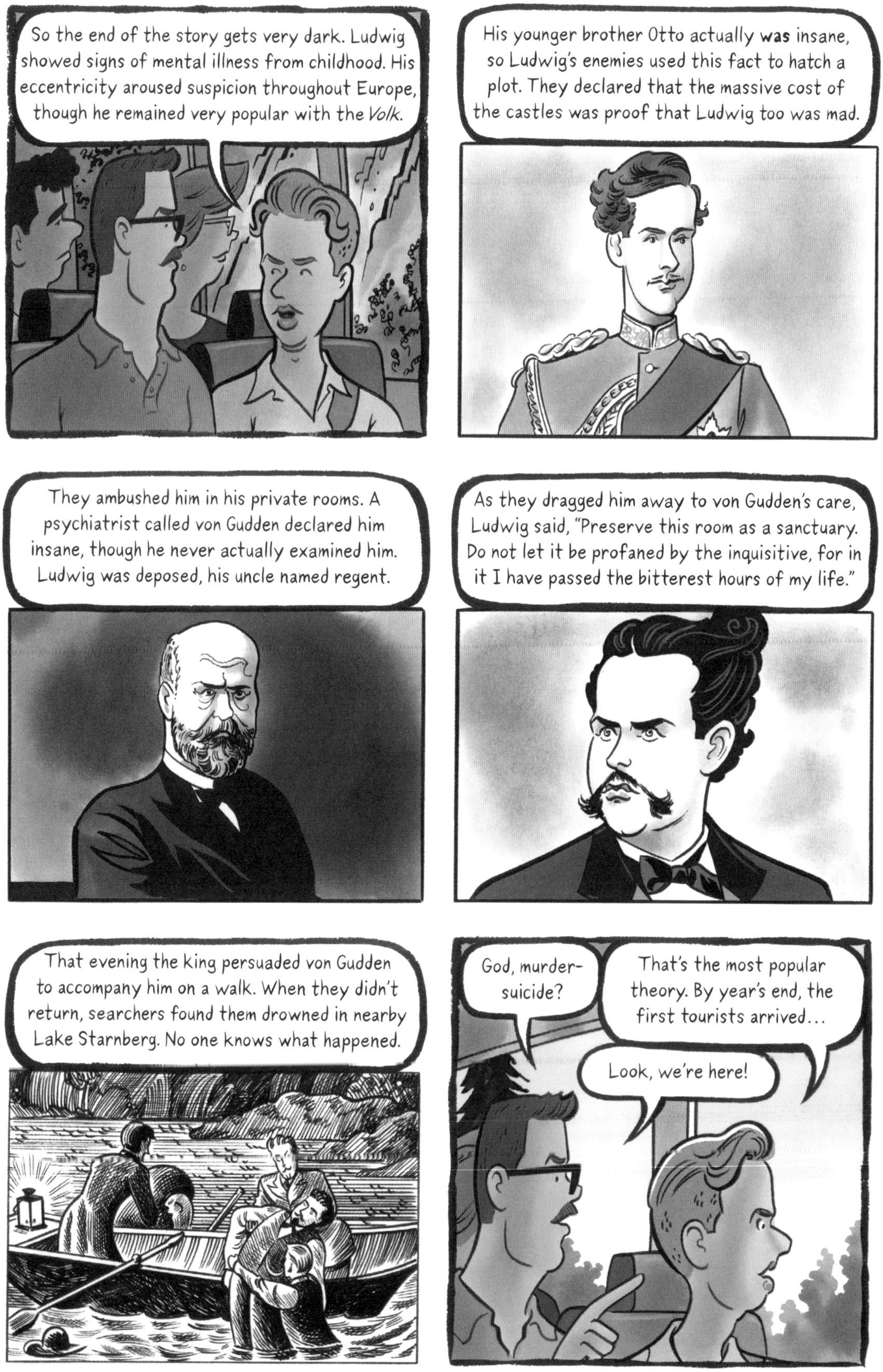
So the end of the story gets very dark. Ludwig showed signs of mental illness from childhood. His eccentricity aroused suspicion throughout Europe, though he remained very popular with the *Volk*.
His younger brother Otto actually **was** insane, so Ludwig's enemies used this fact to hatch a plot. They declared that the massive cost of the castles was proof that Ludwig too was mad.
They ambushed him in his private rooms. A psychiatrist called von Gudden declared him insane, though he never actually examined him. Ludwig was deposed, his uncle named regent.
As they dragged him away to von Gudden's care, Ludwig said, "Preserve this room as a sanctuary. Do not let it be profaned by the inquisitive, for in it I have passed the bitterest hours of my life."
That evening the king persuaded von Gudden to accompany him on a walk. When they didn't return, searchers found them drowned in nearby Lake Starnberg. No one knows what happened.
God, murder-suicide?
That's the most popular theory. By year's end, the first tourists arrived...
Look, we're here!

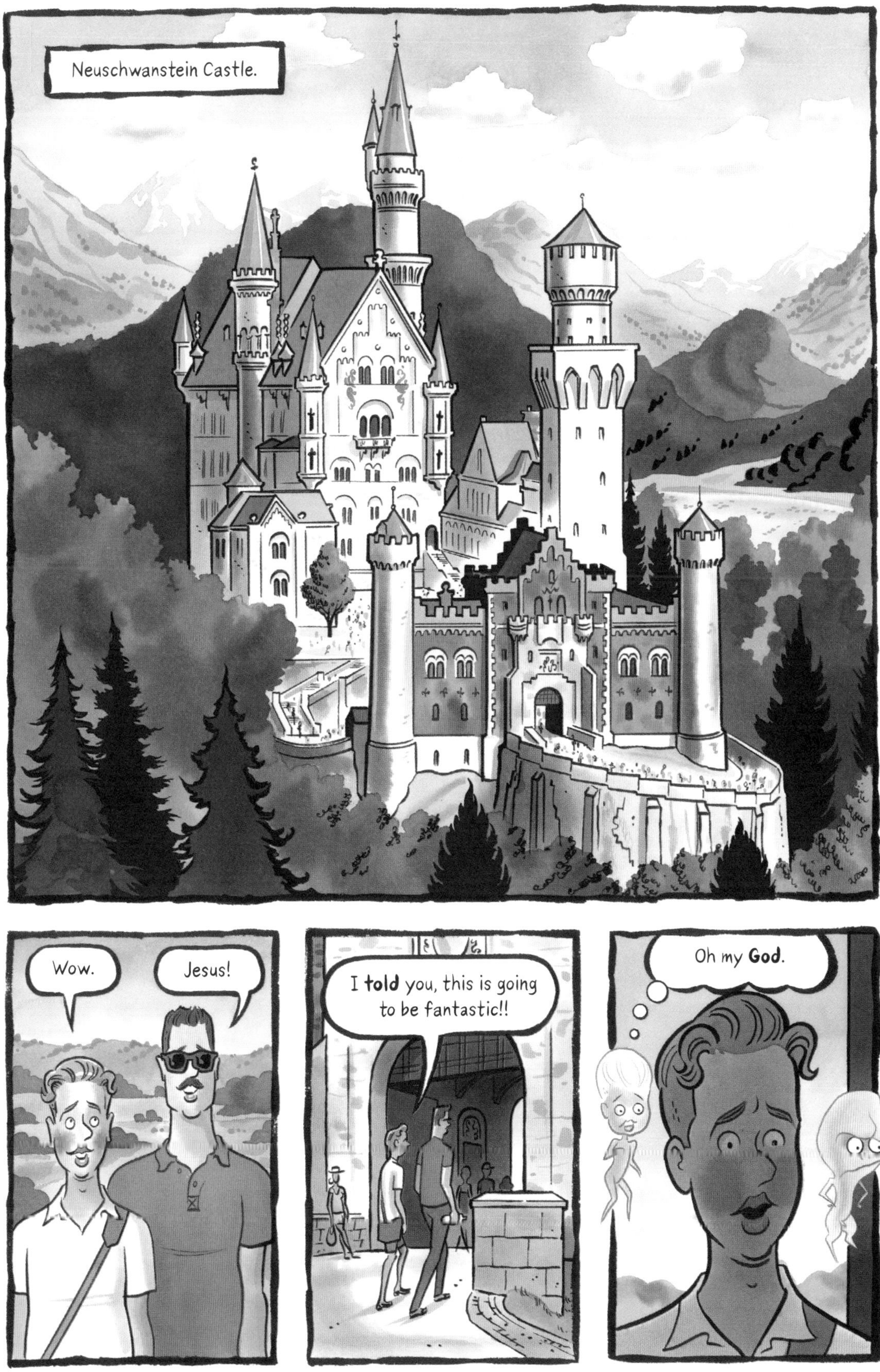
Neuschwanstein Castle.
Wow.
Jesus!
I **told** you, this is going to be fantastic!!
Oh my **God**.

Christ.

Actually the line is moving along pretty well, and look, tours start every few minutes.

You mean we have to take a **guided** tour?

Quick, let's join this group!

What!?

Hei!

ESPANOL

DEUTSC

ENGLISH

Hallo, my name is Josef. I will be your host today as we explore Schloss Neuschwanstein.

Cute!

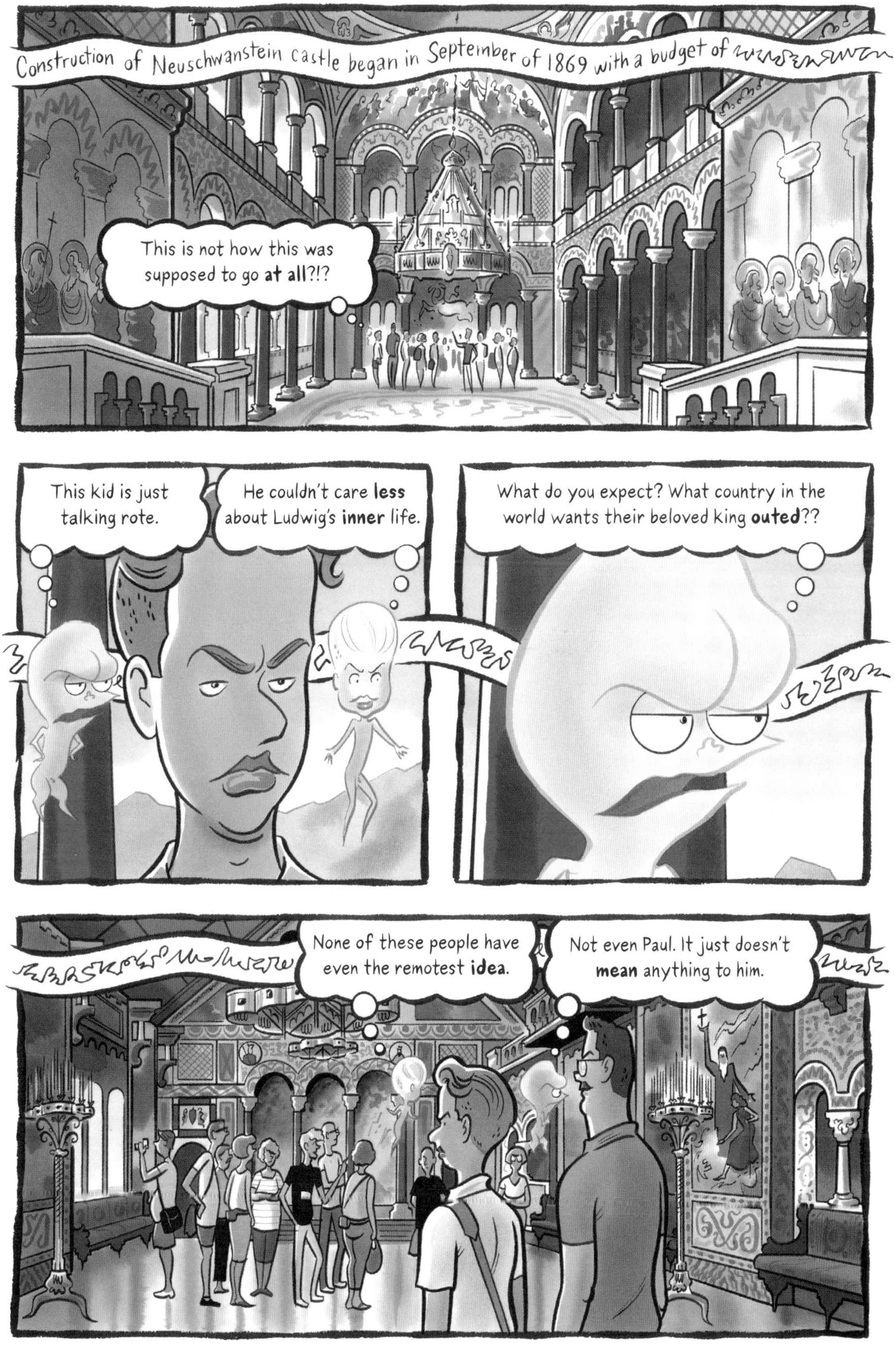

Construction of Neuschwanstein castle began in September of 1869 with a budget of
This is not how this was supposed to go **at all**?!?
This kid is just talking rote.
He couldn't care **less** about Ludwig's **inner** life.
What do you expect? What country in the world wants their beloved king **outed**??
None of these people have even the remotest **idea**.
Not even Paul. It just doesn't **mean** anything to him.

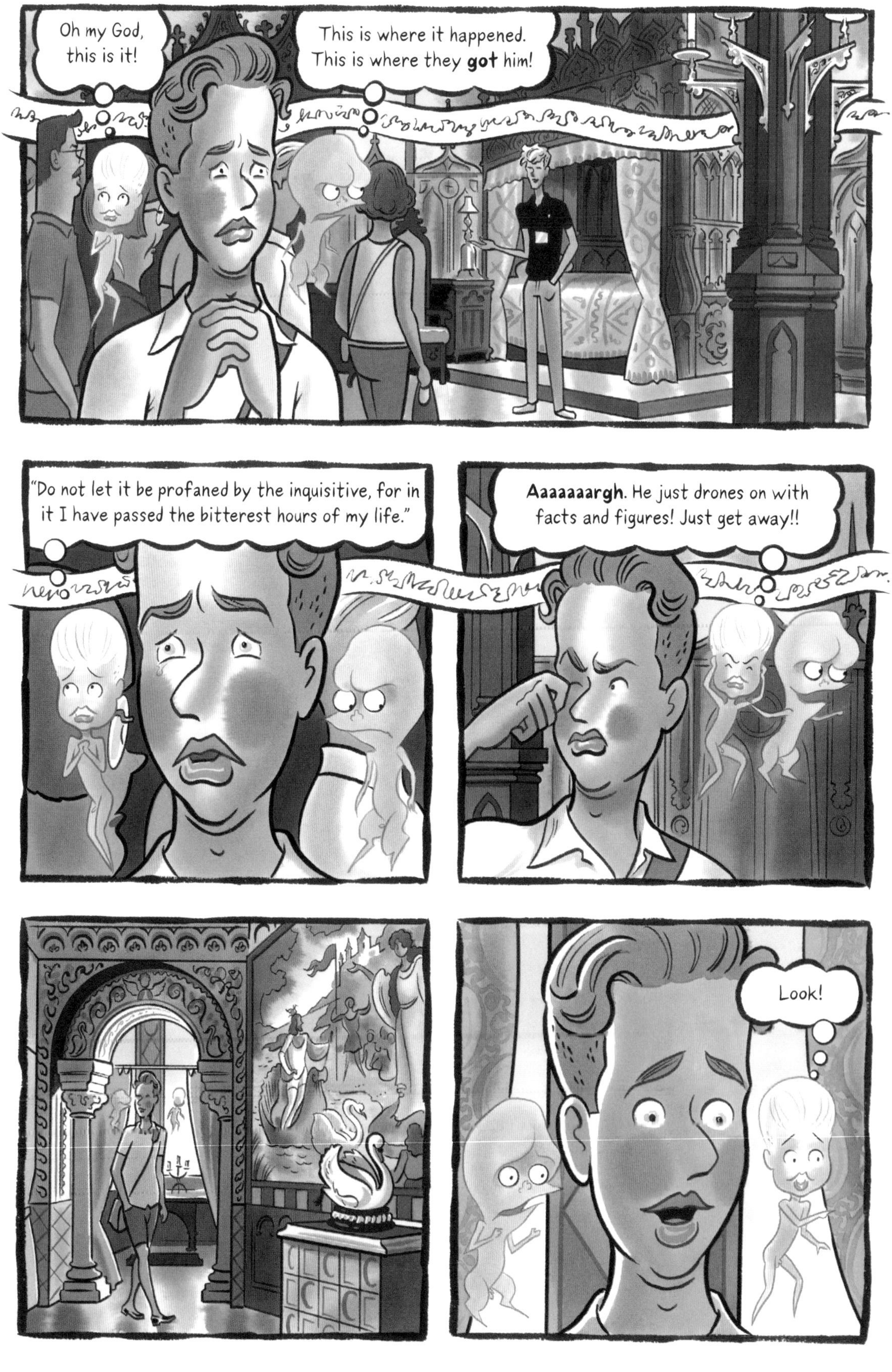
Oh my God, this is it!
This is where it happened. This is where they **got** him!
"Do not let it be profaned by the inquisitive, for in it I have passed the bitterest hours of my life."
Aaaaaaargh. He just drones on with facts and figures! Just get away!!
Look!

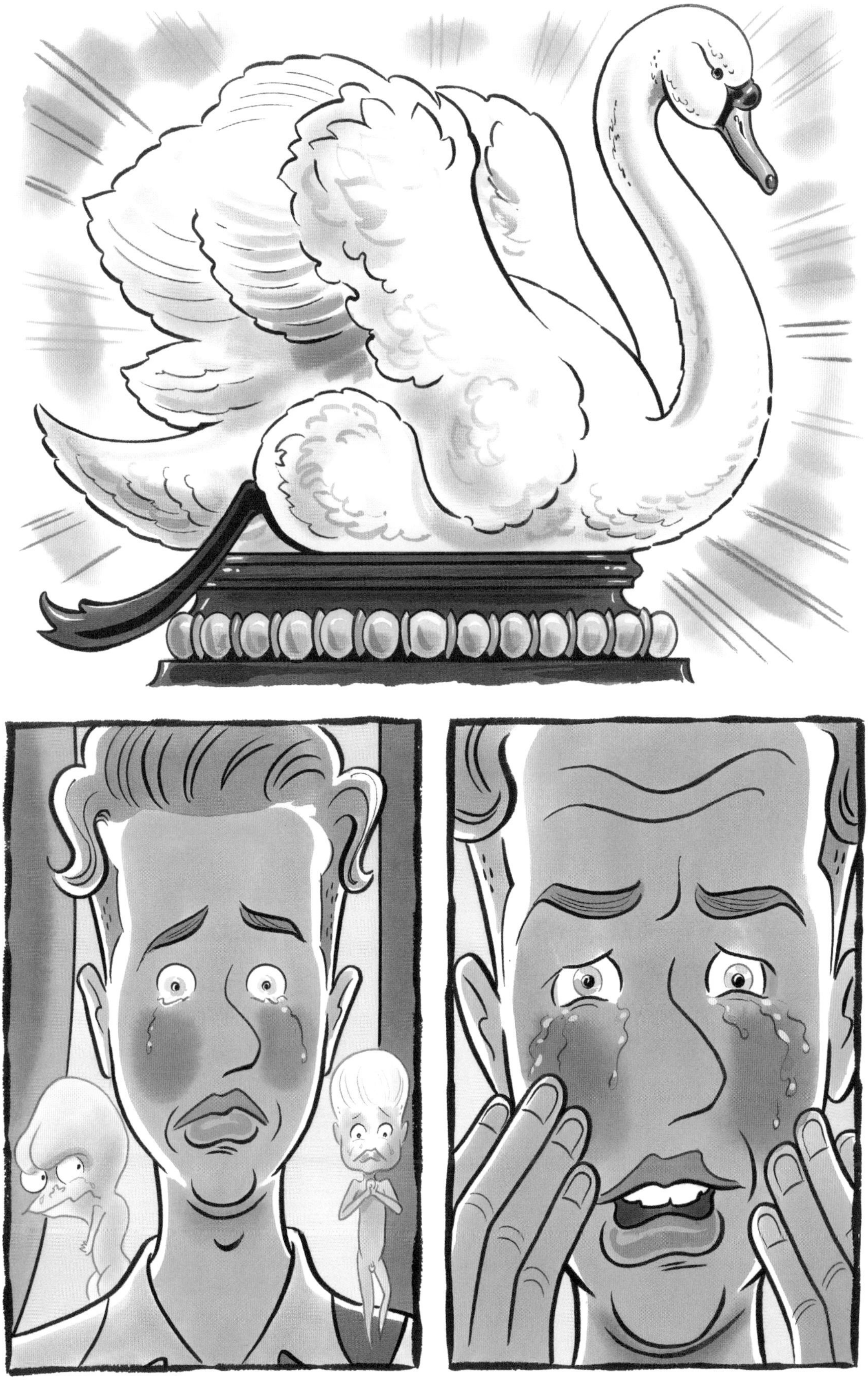

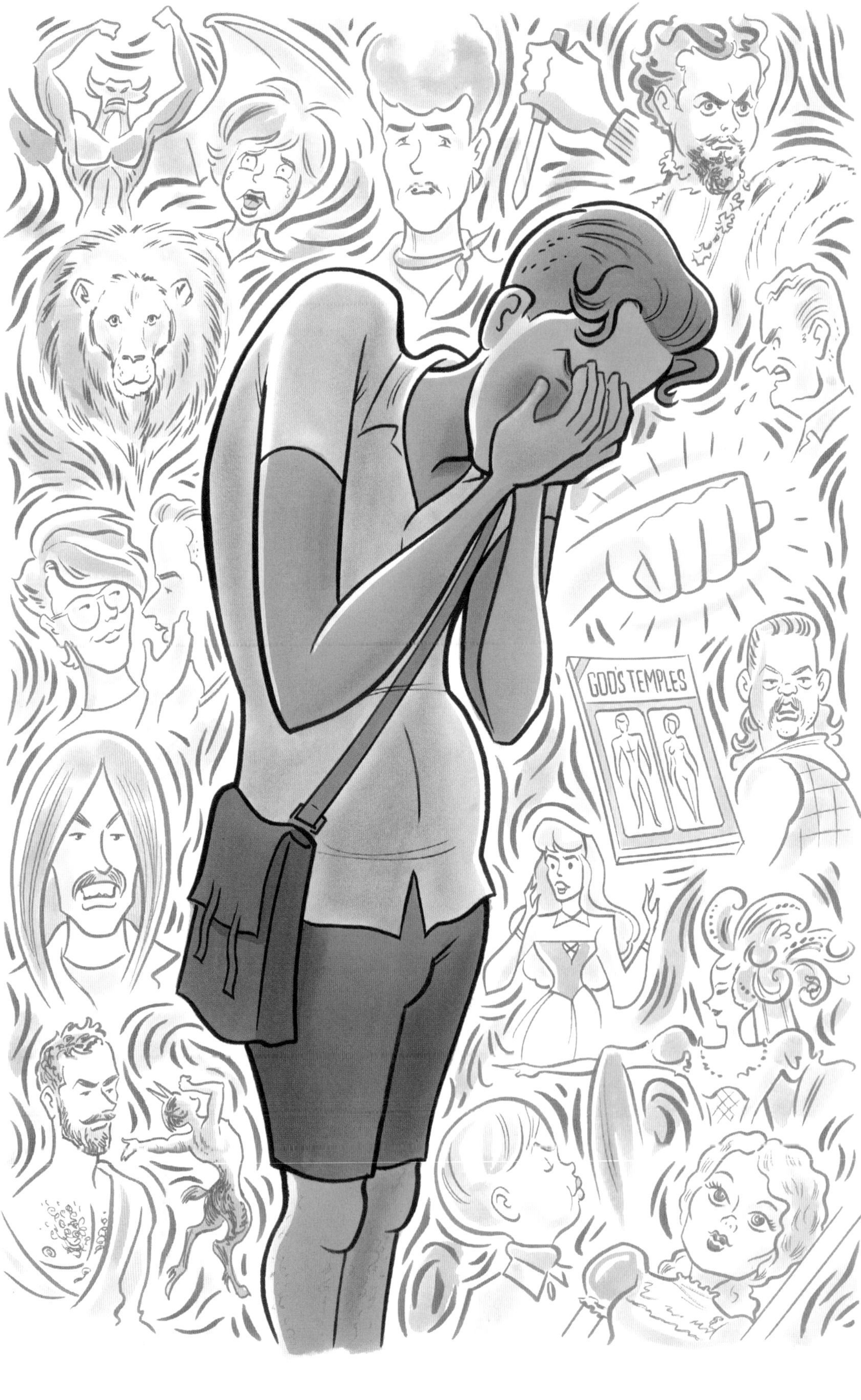
GOD'S TEMPLES

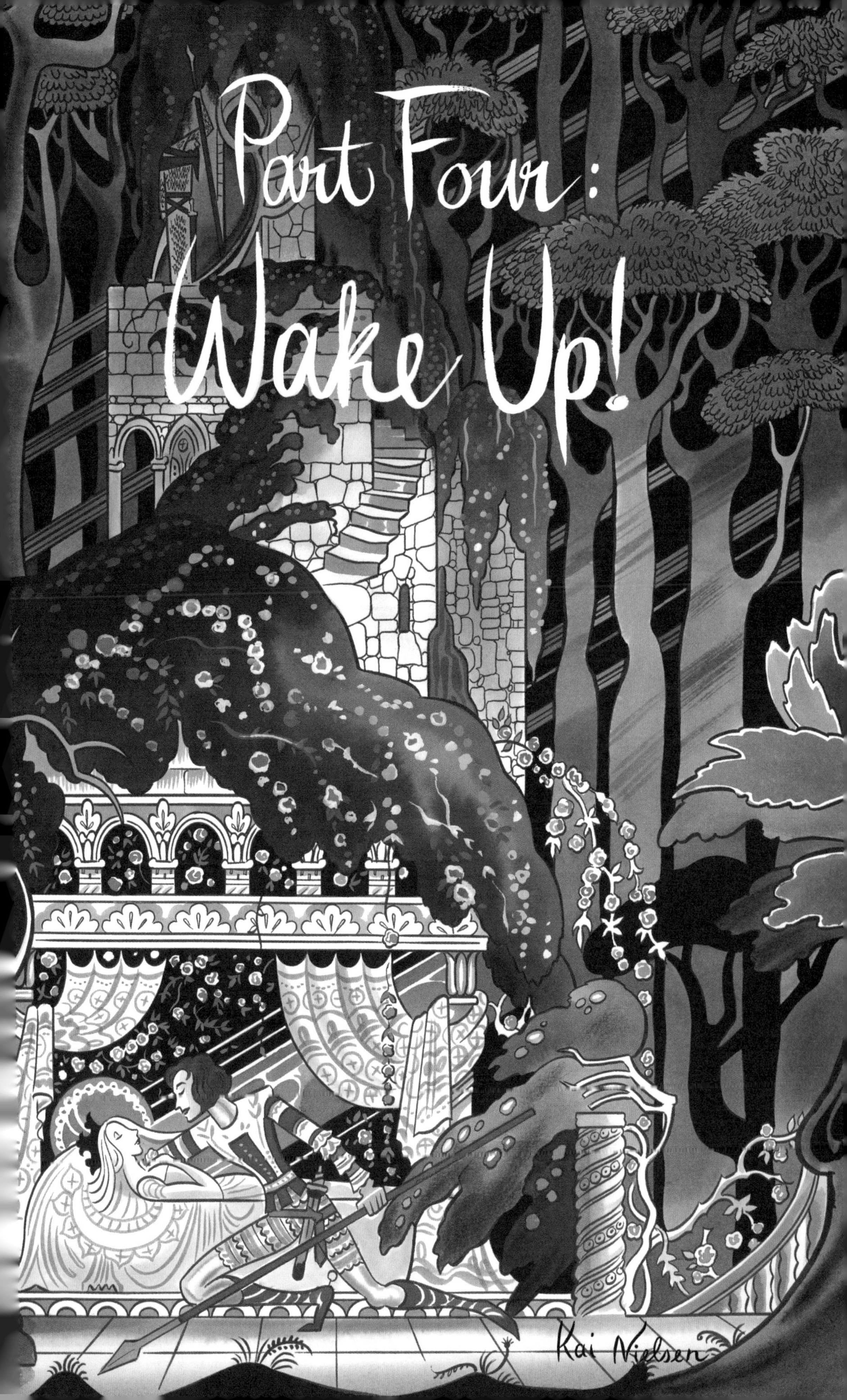
Part Four:
Wake Up!
Kai Nielsen

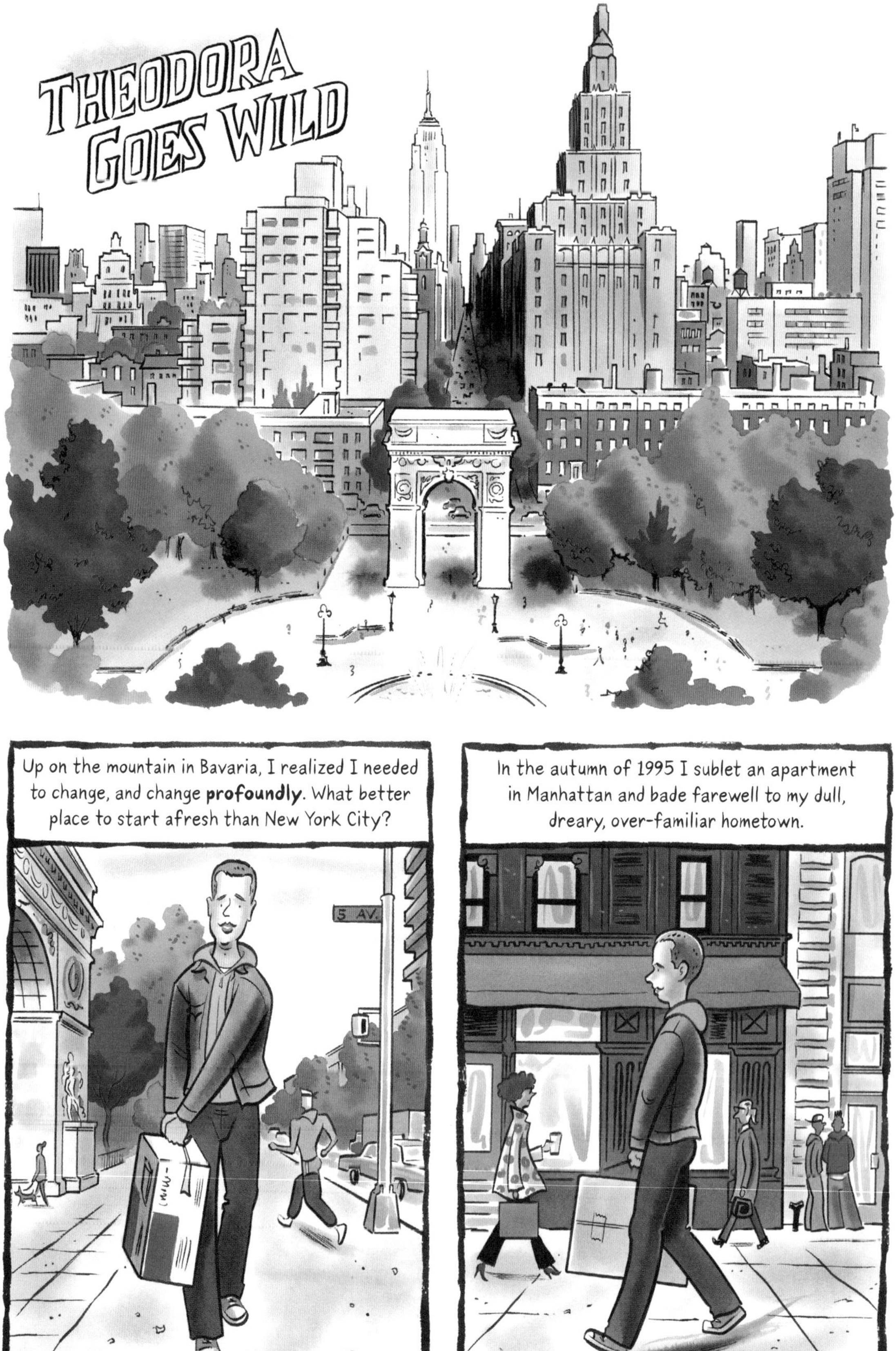
THEODORA GOES WILD
Up on the mountain in Bavaria, I realized I needed to change, and change **profoundly**. What better place to start afresh than New York City?
5 AV.
In the autumn of 1995 I sublet an apartment in Manhattan and bade farewell to my dull, dreary, over-familiar hometown.

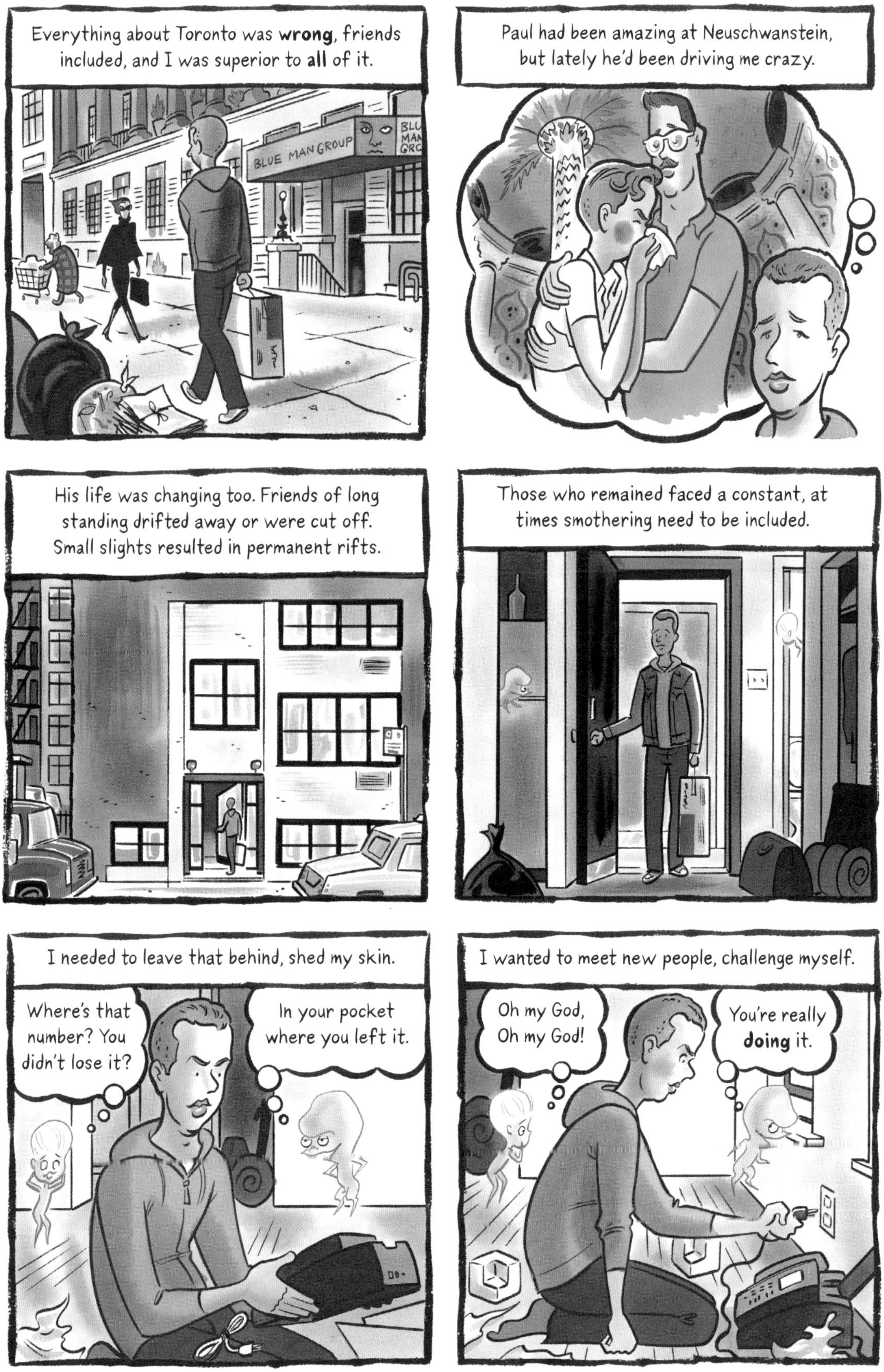
Everything about Toronto was **wrong**, friends included, and I was superior to **all** of it.
BLUE MAN GROUP
Paul had been amazing at Neuschwanstein, but lately he'd been driving me crazy.
His life was changing too. Friends of long standing drifted away or were cut off. Small slights resulted in permanent rifts.
Those who remained faced a constant, at times smothering need to be included.
I needed to leave that behind, shed my skin.
Where's that number? You didn't lose it?
In your pocket where you left it.
I wanted to meet new people, challenge myself.
Oh my God, Oh my God!
You're really **doing** it.

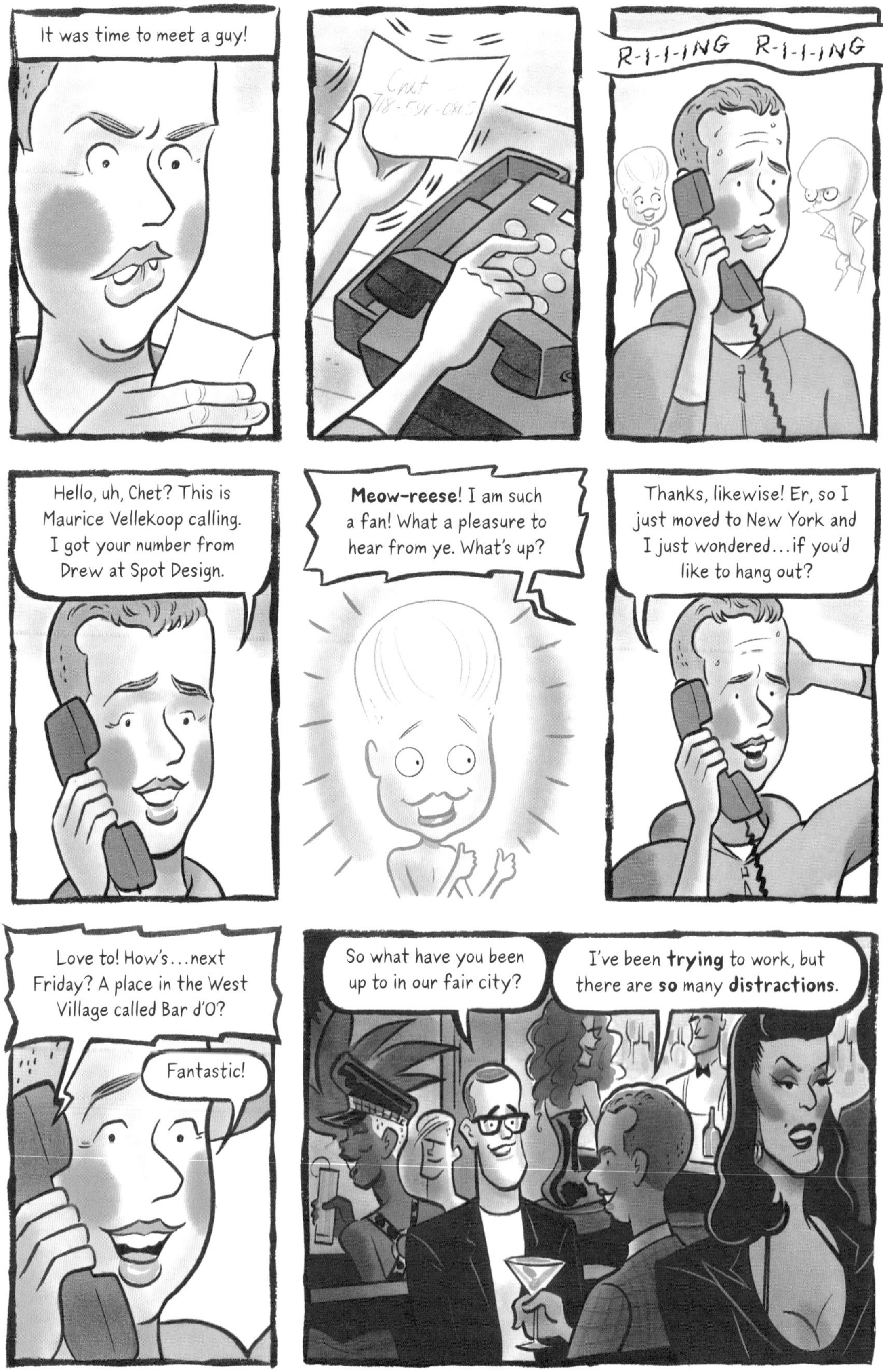
It was time to meet a guy!
R-I-I-ING R-I-I-ING
Hello, uh, Chet? This is Maurice Vellekoop calling. I got your number from Drew at Spot Design.
Meow-reese! I am such a fan! What a pleasure to hear from ye. What's up?
Thanks, likewise! Er, so I just moved to New York and I just wondered... if you'd like to hang out?
Love to! How's... next Friday? A place in the West Village called Bar d'O?
Fantastic!
So what have you been up to in our fair city?
I've been **trying** to work, but there are **so** many **distractions**.

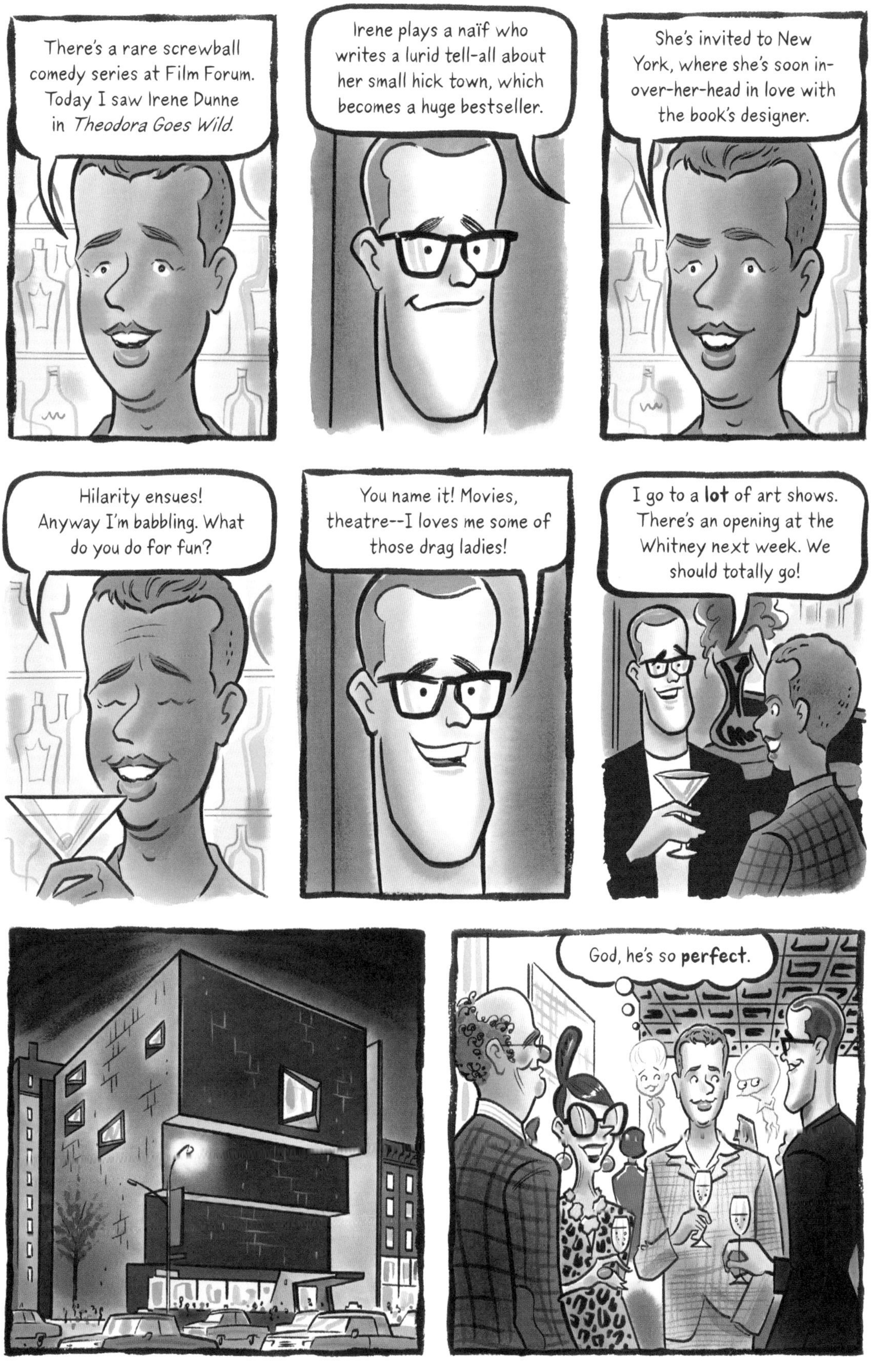
There's a rare screwball comedy series at Film Forum. Today I saw Irene Dunne in *Theodora Goes Wild.*
Irene plays a naïf who writes a lurid tell-all about her small hick town, which becomes a huge bestseller.
She's invited to New York, where she's soon in-over-her-head in love with the book's designer.
Hilarity ensues! Anyway I'm babbling. What do you do for fun?
You name it! Movies, theatre--I loves me some of those drag ladies!
I go to a **lot** of art shows. There's an opening at the Whitney next week. We should totally go!
God, he's so **perfect**.

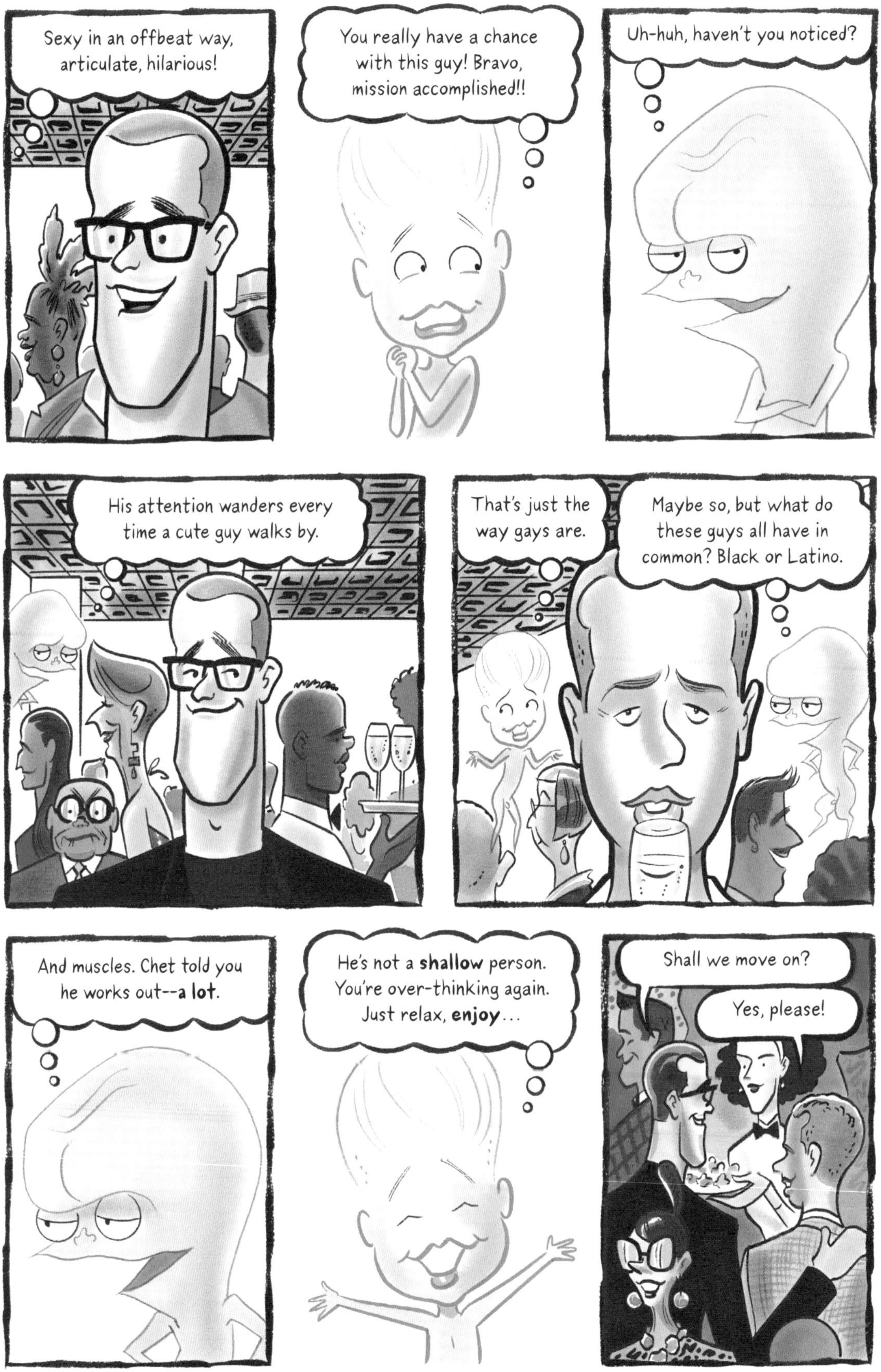
Sexy in an offbeat way, articulate, hilarious!
You really have a chance with this guy! Bravo, mission accomplished!!
Uh-huh, haven't you noticed?
His attention wanders every time a cute guy walks by.
That's just the way gays are.
Maybe so, but what do these guys all have in common? Black or Latino.
And muscles. Chet told you he works out--**a lot**.
He's not a **shallow** person. You're over-thinking again. Just relax, **enjoy**...
Shall we move on?
Yes, please!

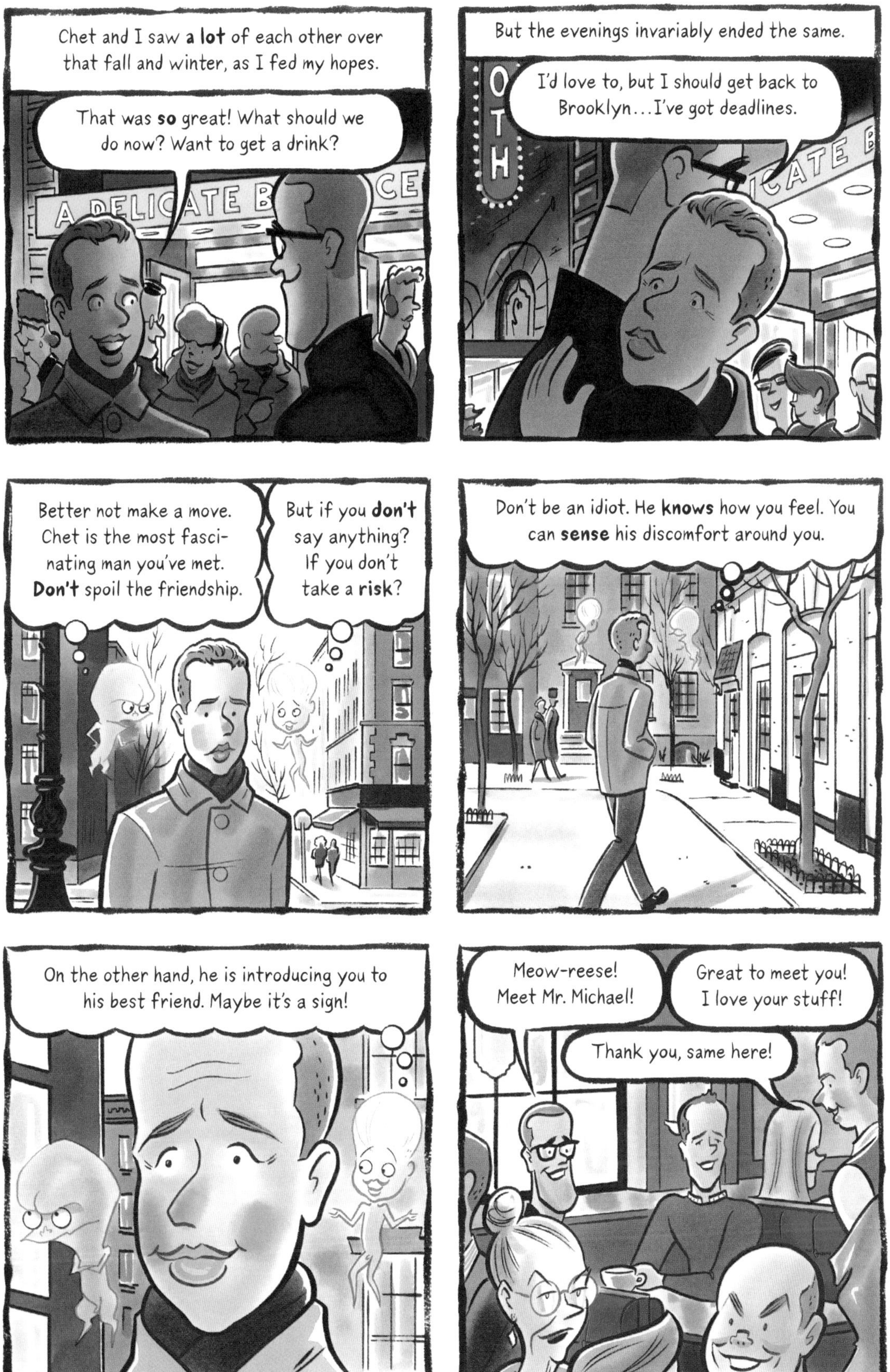
Chet and I saw **a lot** of each other over that fall and winter, as I fed my hopes.
That was **so** great! What should we do now? Want to get a drink?
But the evenings invariably ended the same.
I'd love to, but I should get back to Brooklyn. . . I've got deadlines.
Better not make a move. Chet is the most fascinating man you've met. **Don't** spoil the friendship.
But if you **don't** say anything? If you don't take a **risk**?
Don't be an idiot. He **knows** how you feel. You can **sense** his discomfort around you.
On the other hand, he is introducing you to his best friend. Maybe it's a sign!
Meow-reese! Meet Mr. Michael!
Great to meet you! I love your stuff!
Thank you, same here!

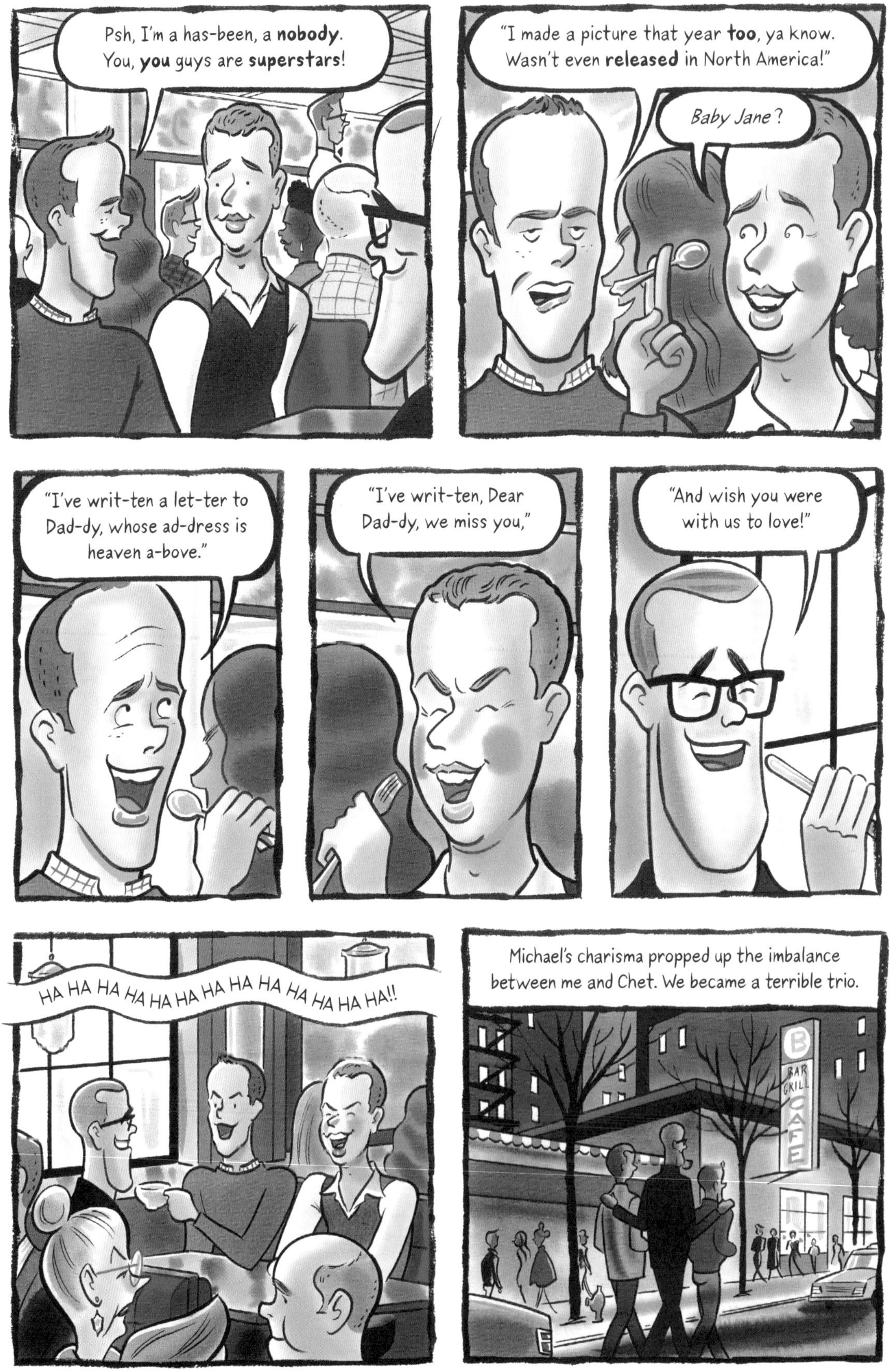
Psh, I'm a has-been, a **nobody**. You, **you** guys are **superstars**!
"I made a picture that year **too**, ya know. Wasn't even **released** in North America!"
Baby Jane?
"I've writ-ten a let-ter to Dad-dy, whose ad-dress is heaven a-bove."
"I've writ-ten, Dear Dad-dy, we miss you,"
"And wish you were with us to love!"
HA HA HA HA HA HA HA HA HA HA HA HA HA!!
Michael's charisma propped up the imbalance between me and Chet. We became a terrible trio.
B
BAR GRILL
CAFE

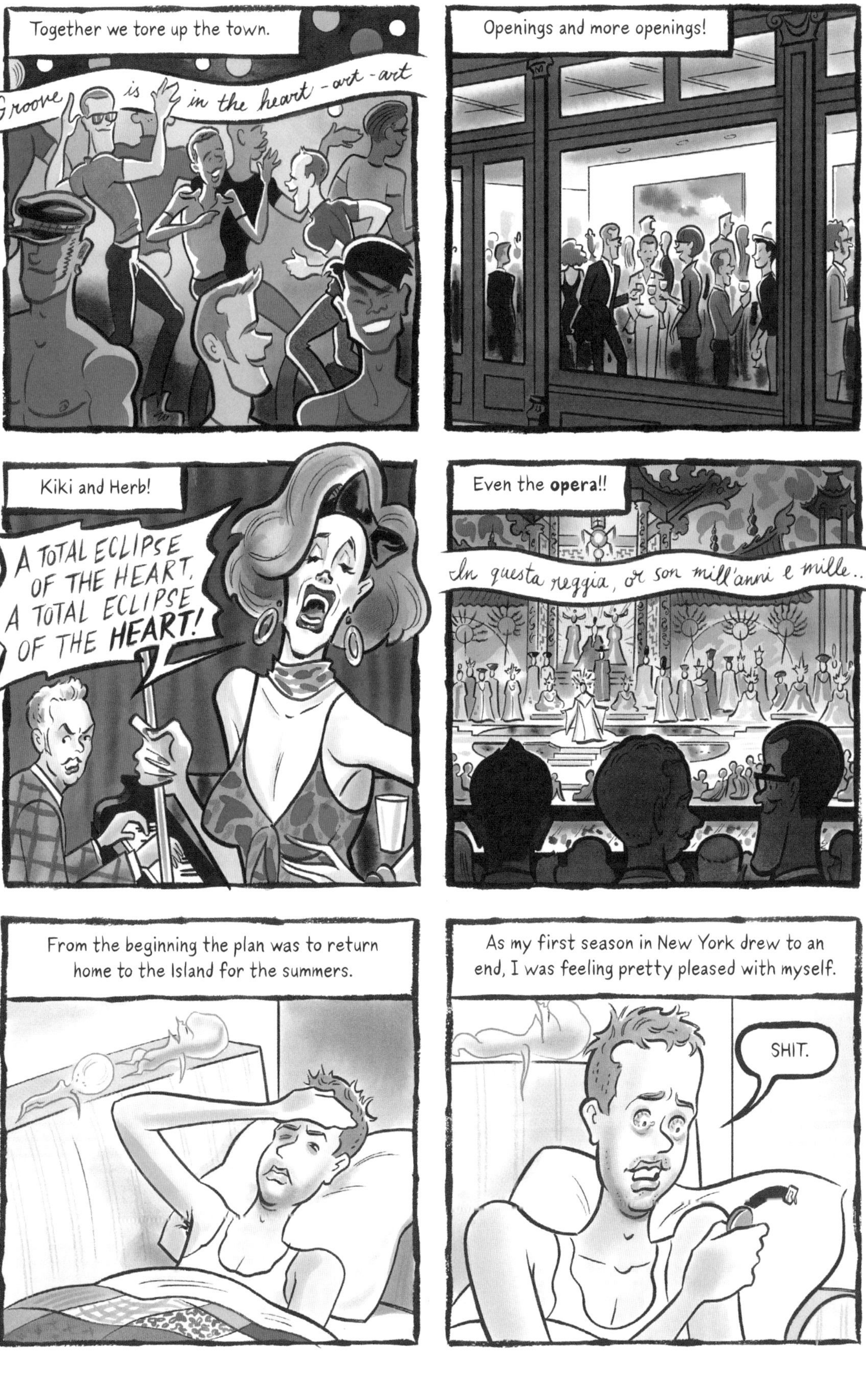

Together we tore up the town.
Groove is in the heart -art -art
Openings and more openings!
Kiki and Herb!
A TOTAL ECLIPSE OF THE HEART, A TOTAL ECLIPSE OF THE HEART!
Even the **opera**!!
In questa reggia, or son mill'anni e mille...
From the beginning the plan was to return home to the Island for the summers.
As my first season in New York drew to an end, I was feeling pretty pleased with myself.
SHIT.

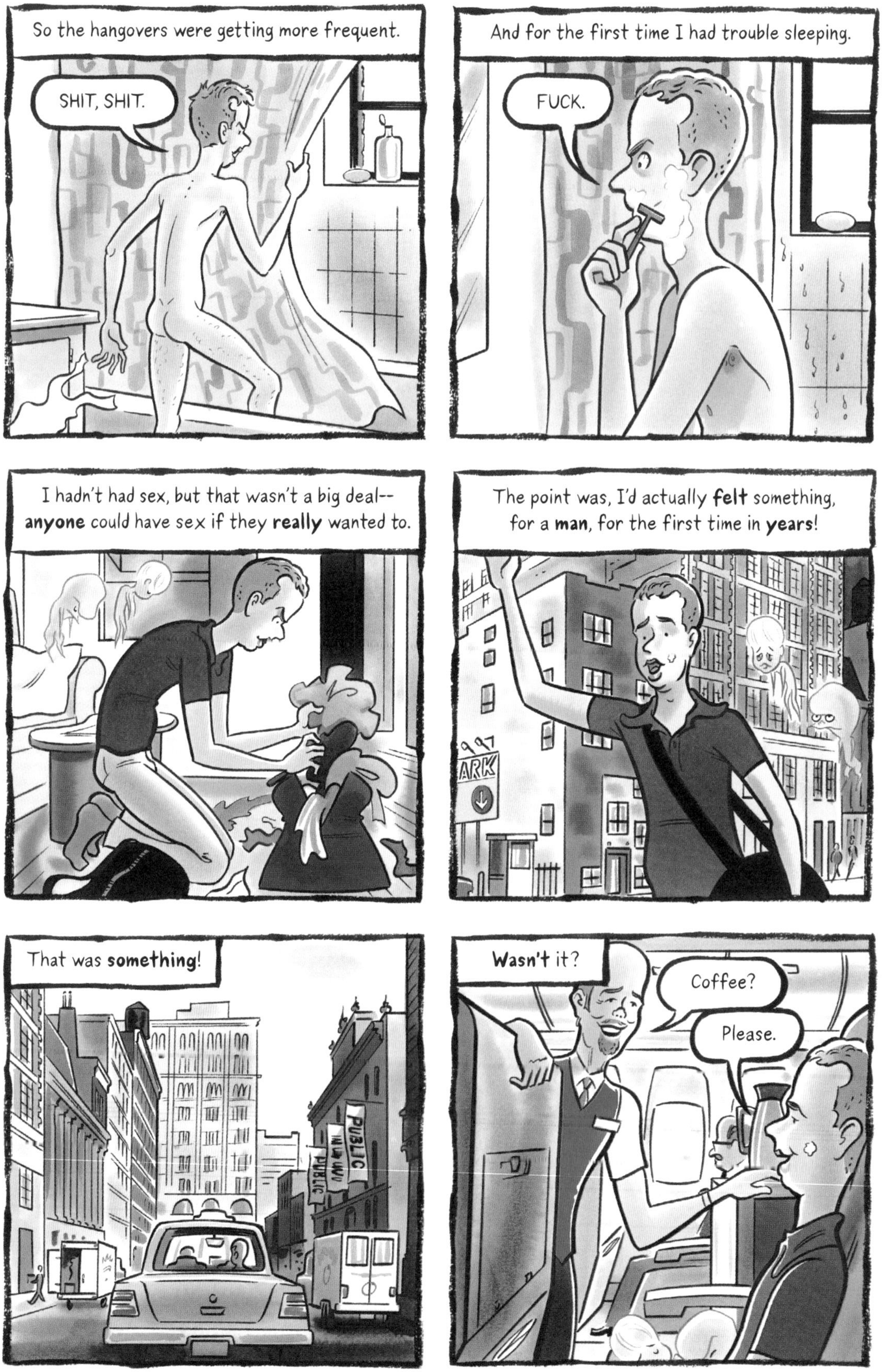
So the hangovers were getting more frequent.
SHIT, SHIT.
And for the first time I had trouble sleeping.
FUCK.
I hadn't had sex, but that wasn't a big deal-- **anyone** could have sex if they **really** wanted to.
The point was, I'd actually **felt** something, for a **man**, for the first time in **years**!
ARK
That was **something**!
PUBLIC
PUBLIC
Wasn't it?
Coffee?
Please.

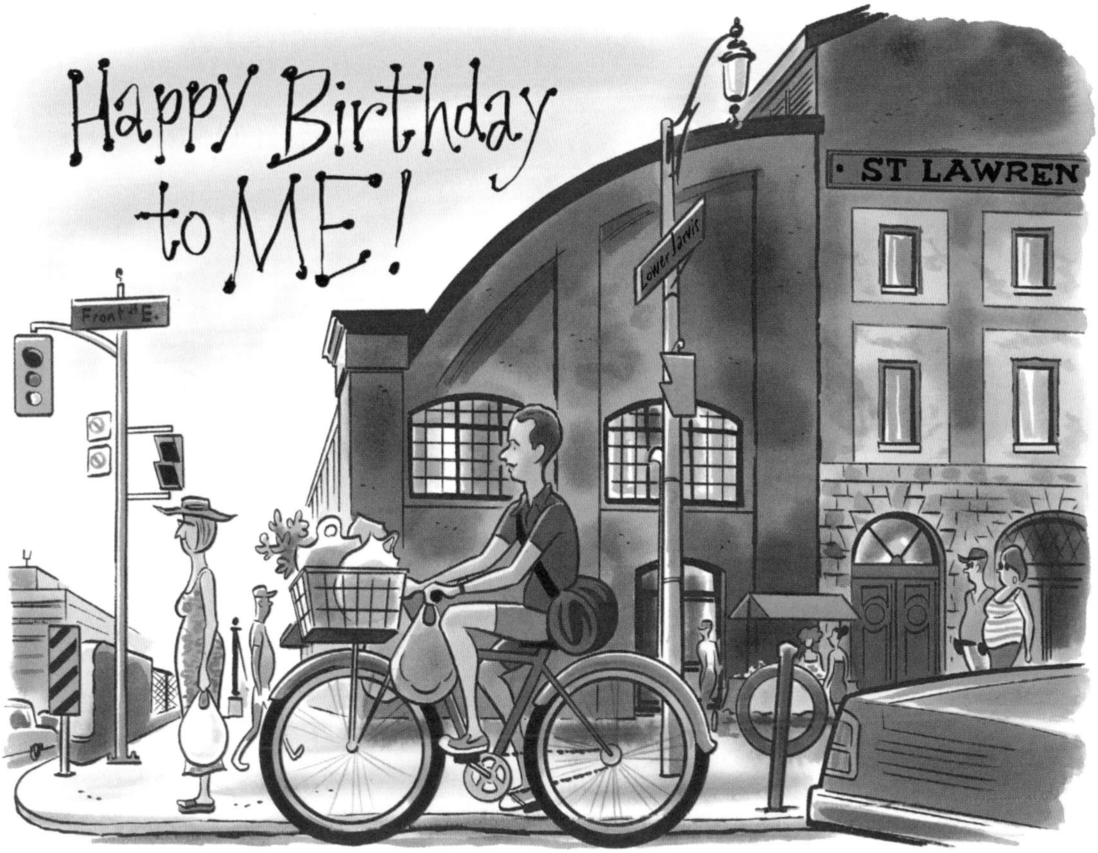
Happy Birthday to ME!
ST LAWREN
Front St E.
Lower Jarvis

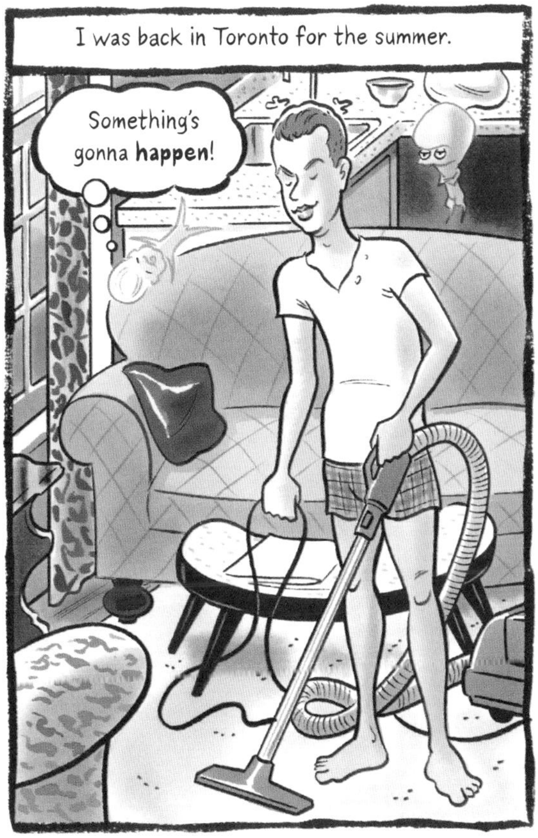
I was back in Toronto for the summer.
Something's gonna **happen**!

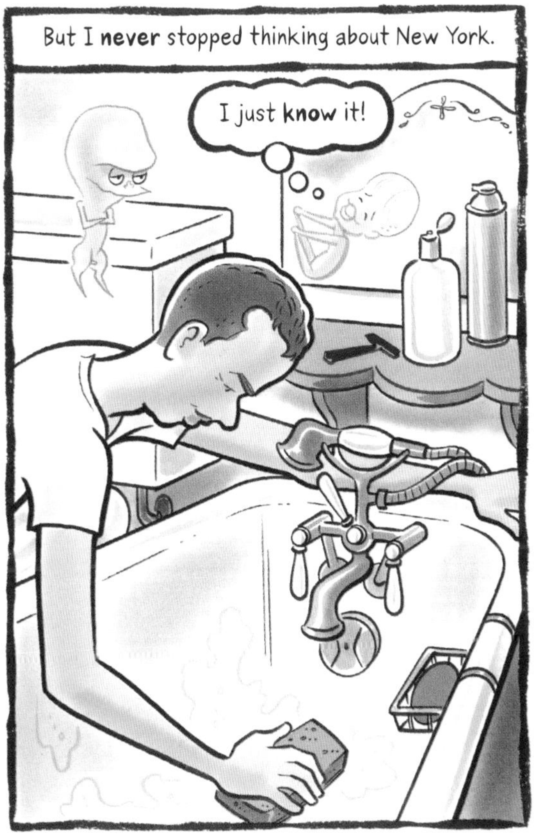
But I **never** stopped thinking about New York.
I just **know** it!

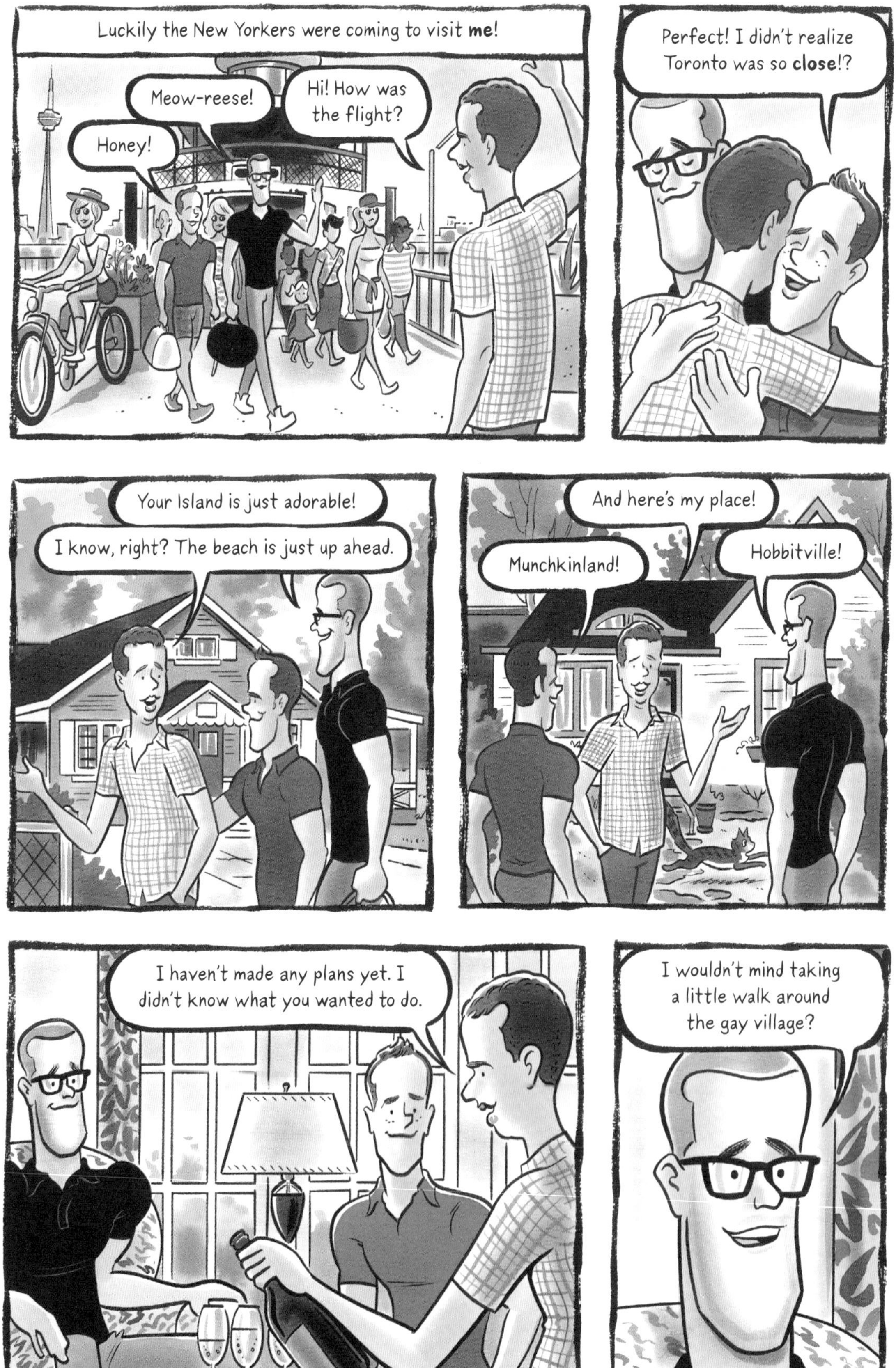
Luckily the New Yorkers were coming to visit **me**!
Honey!
Meow-reese!
Hi! How was the flight?
Perfect! I didn't realize Toronto was so **close**!?
Your Island is just adorable!
I know, right? The beach is just up ahead.
And here's my place!
Munchkinland!
Hobbitville!
I haven't made any plans yet. I didn't know what you wanted to do.
I wouldn't mind taking a little walk around the gay village?

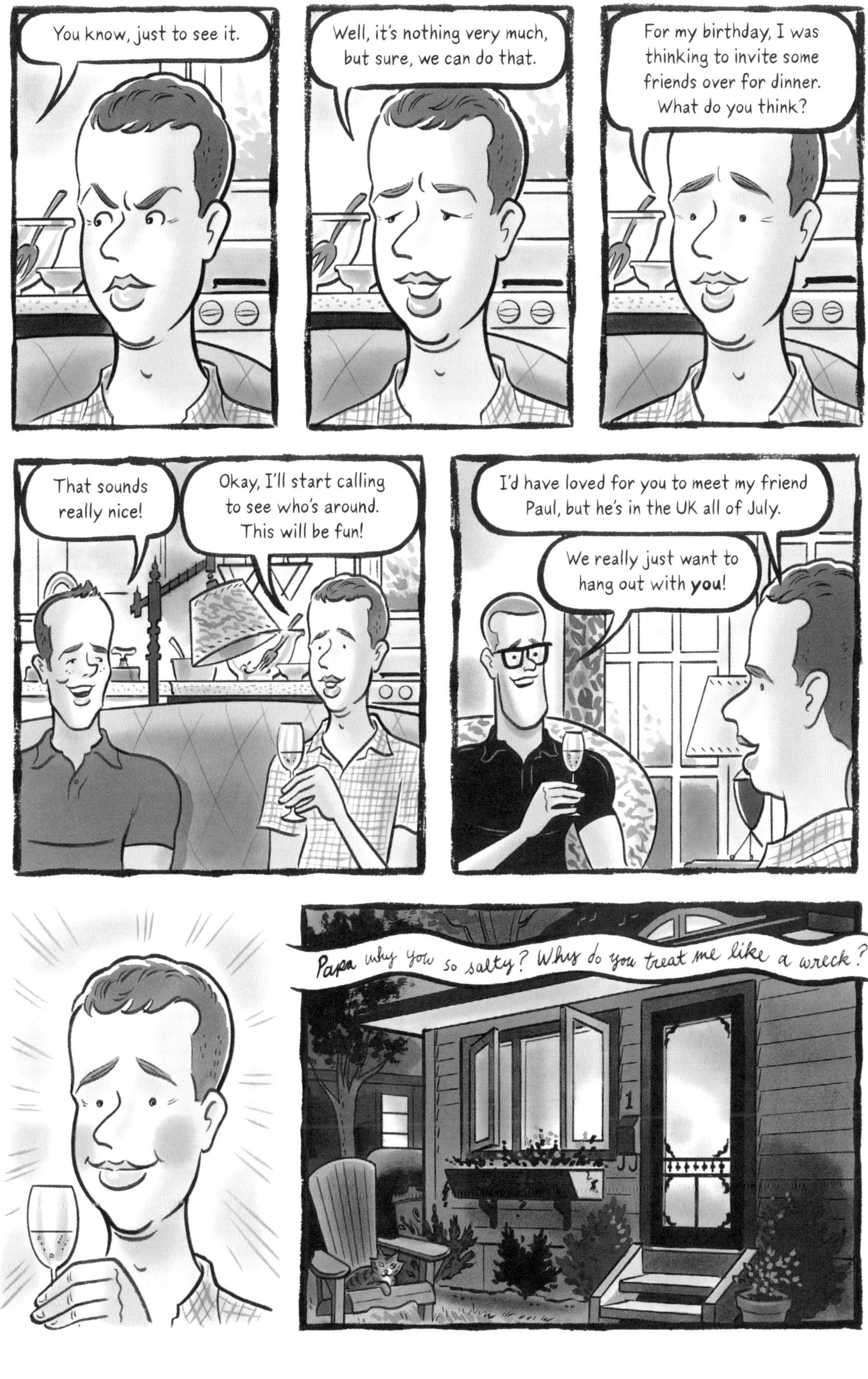
You know, just to see it.
Well, it's nothing very much, but sure, we can do that.
For my birthday, I was thinking to invite some friends over for dinner. What do you think?
That sounds really nice!
Okay, I'll start calling to see who's around. This will be fun!
I'd have loved for you to meet my friend Paul, but he's in the UK all of July.
We really just want to hang out with **you**!
Papa why you so salty? Why do you treat me like a wreck?

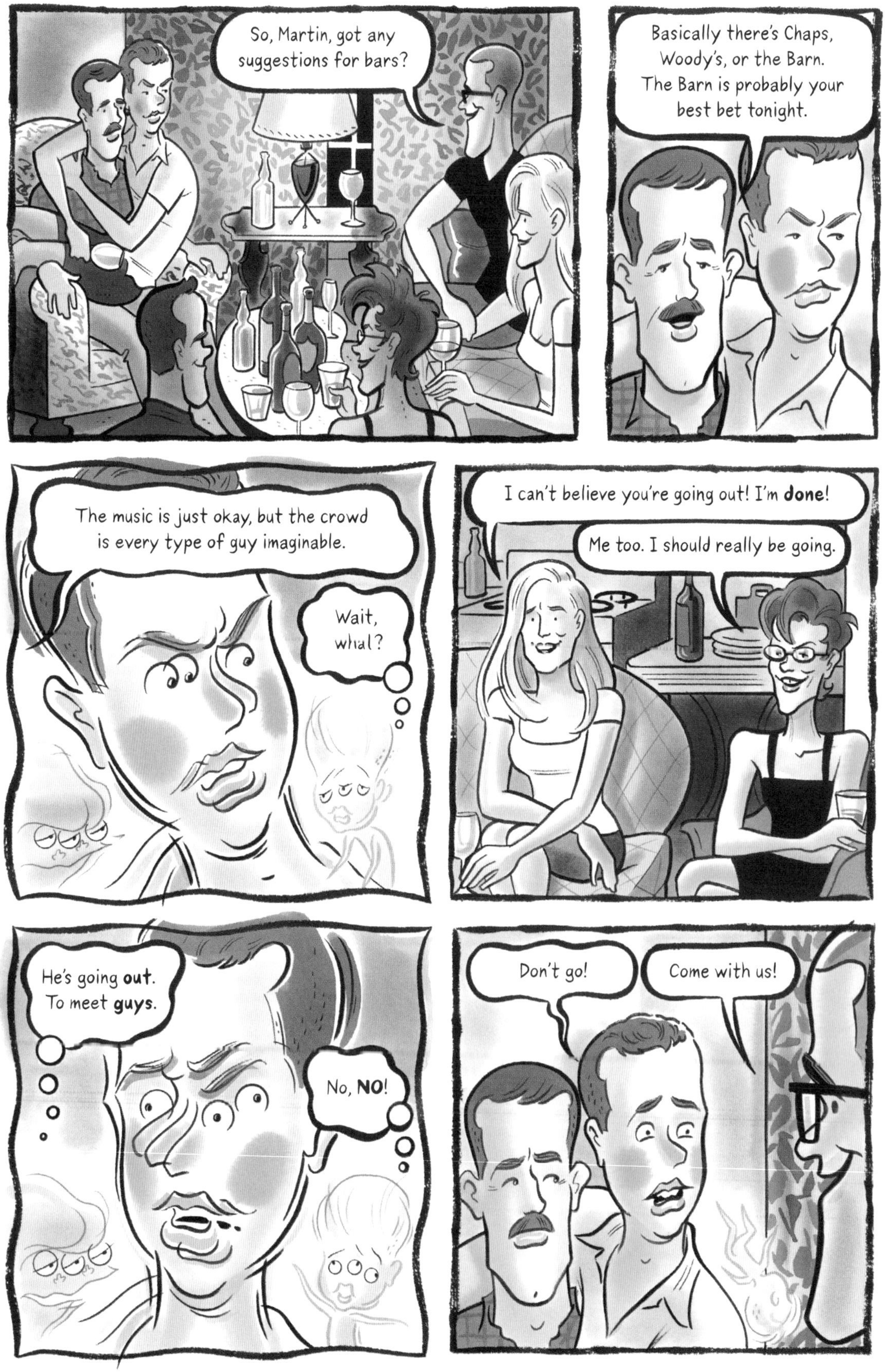
So, Martin, got any suggestions for bars?
Basically there's Chaps, Woody's, or the Barn. The Barn is probably your best bet tonight.
The music is just okay, but the crowd is every type of guy imaginable.
Wait, what?
I can't believe you're going out! I'm **done**!
Me too. I should really be going.
He's going **out**. To meet **guys**.
No, **NO**!
Don't go!
Come with us!

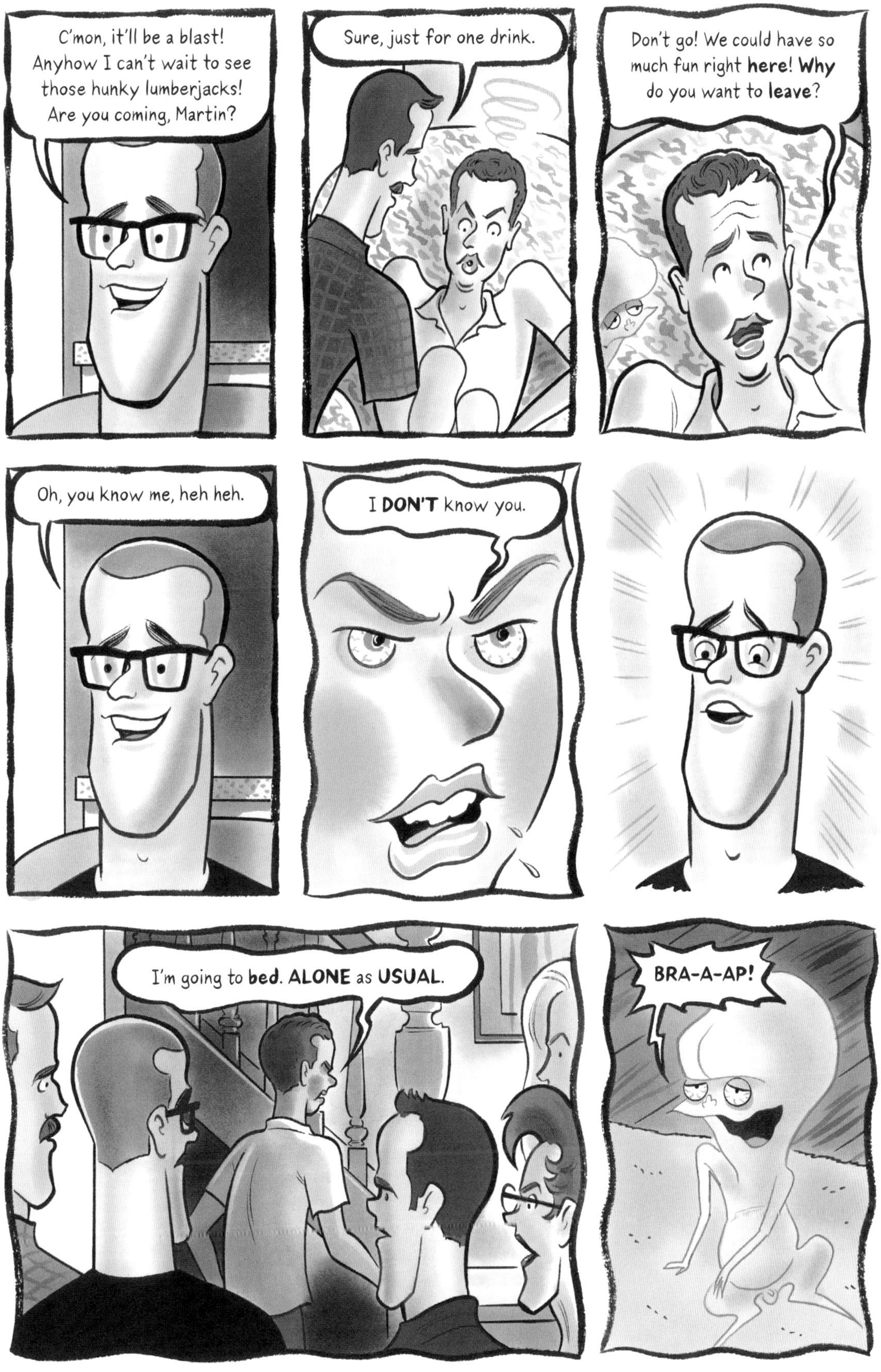
C'mon, it'll be a blast! Anyhow I can't wait to see those hunky lumberjacks! Are you coming, Martin?
Sure, just for one drink.
Don't go! We could have so much fun right **here**! **Why** do you want to **leave**?
Oh, you know me, heh heh.
I **DON'T** know you.
I'm going to **bed**. **ALONE** as **USUAL**.
BRA-A-AP!

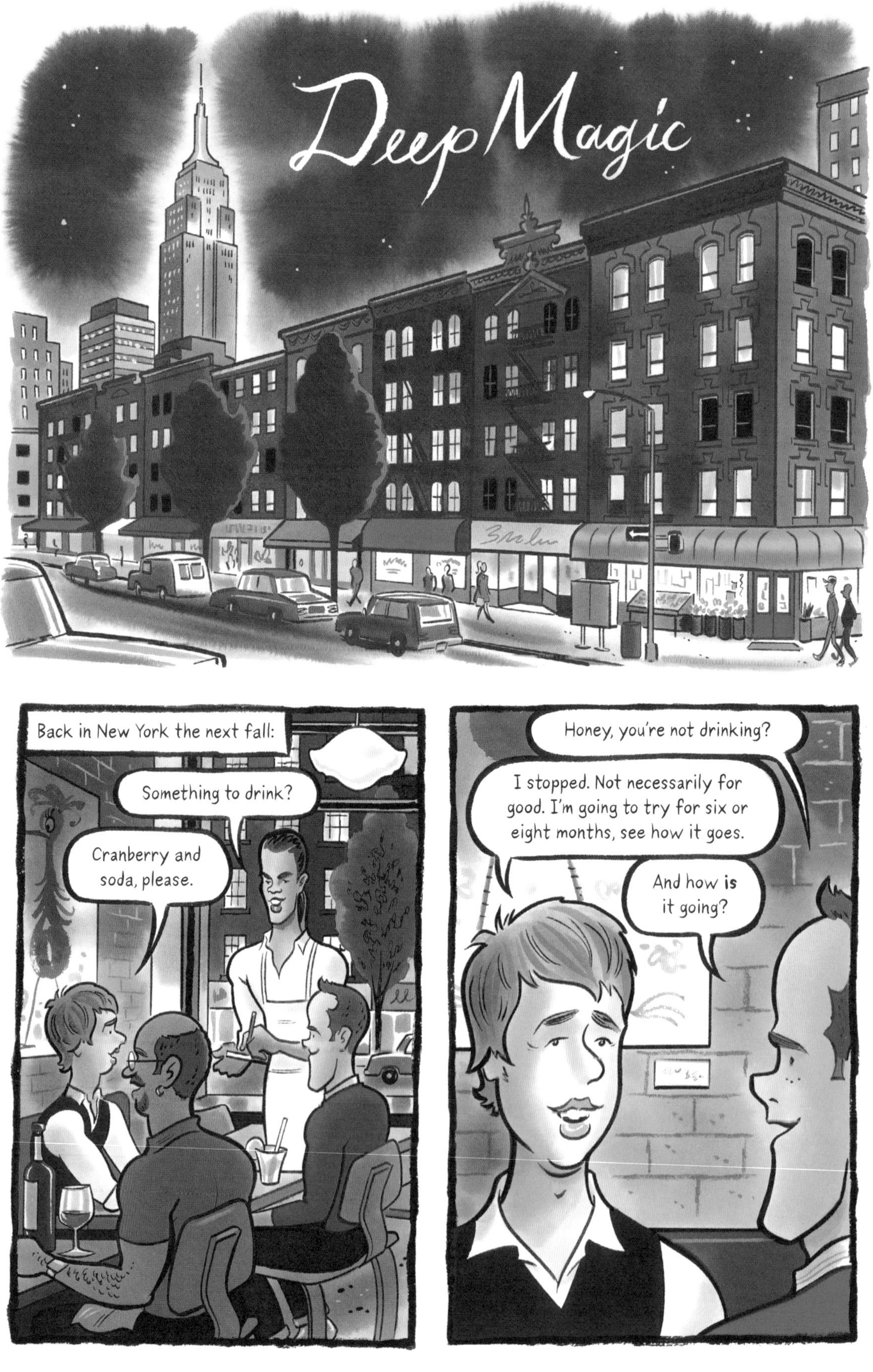
Deep Magic
Back in New York the next fall:
Something to drink?
Cranberry and soda, please.
Honey, you're not drinking?
I stopped. Not necessarily for good. I'm going to try for six or eight months, see how it goes.
And how **is** it going?

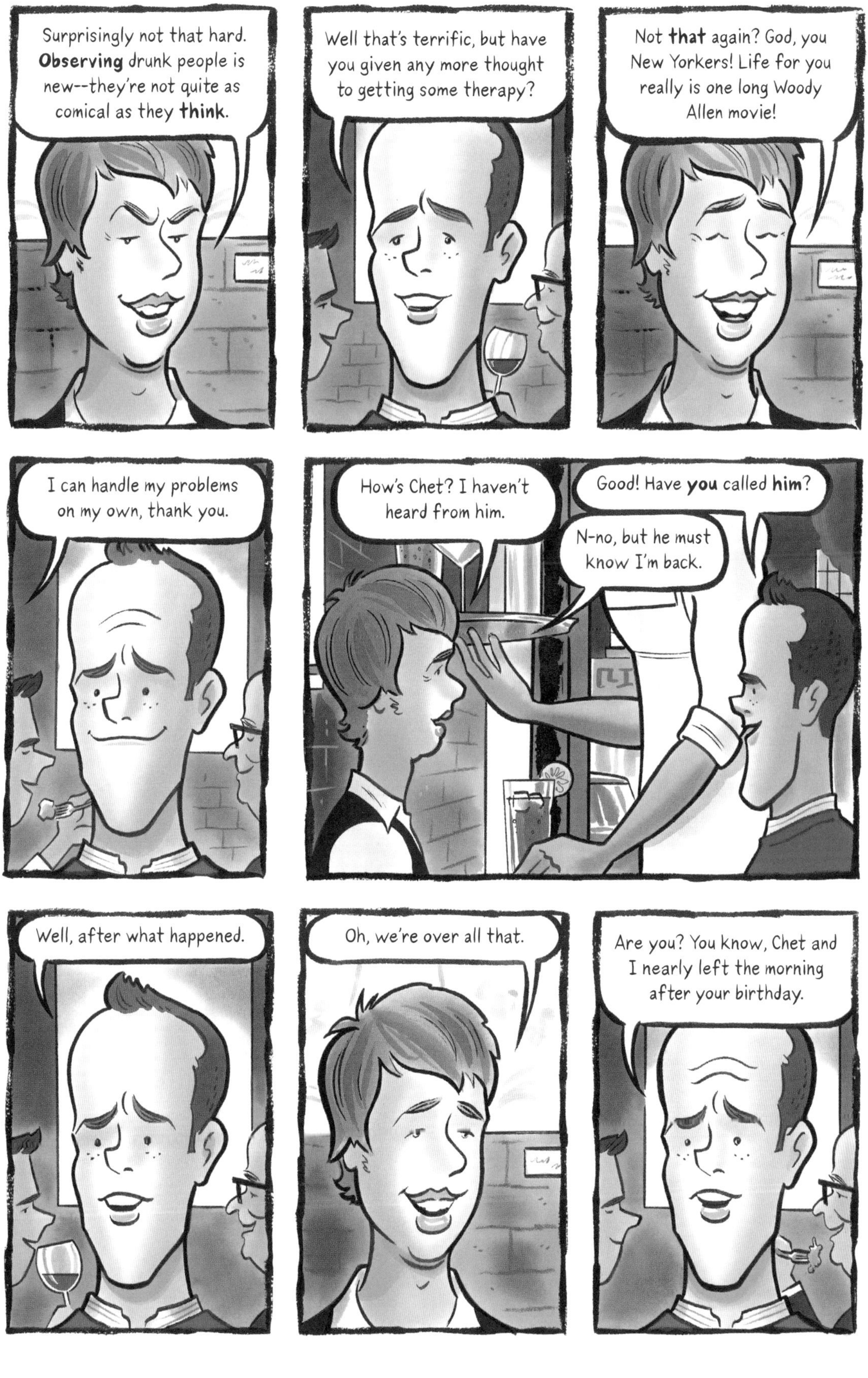
Surprisingly not that hard. **Observing** drunk people is new--they're not quite as comical as they **think**.
Well that's terrific, but have you given any more thought to getting some therapy?
Not **that** again? God, you New Yorkers! Life for you really is one long Woody Allen movie!
I can handle my problems on my own, thank you.
How's Chet? I haven't heard from him.
Good! Have **you** called **him**?
N-no, but he must know I'm back.
Well, after what happened.
Oh, we're over all that.
Are you? You know, Chet and I nearly left the morning after your birthday.

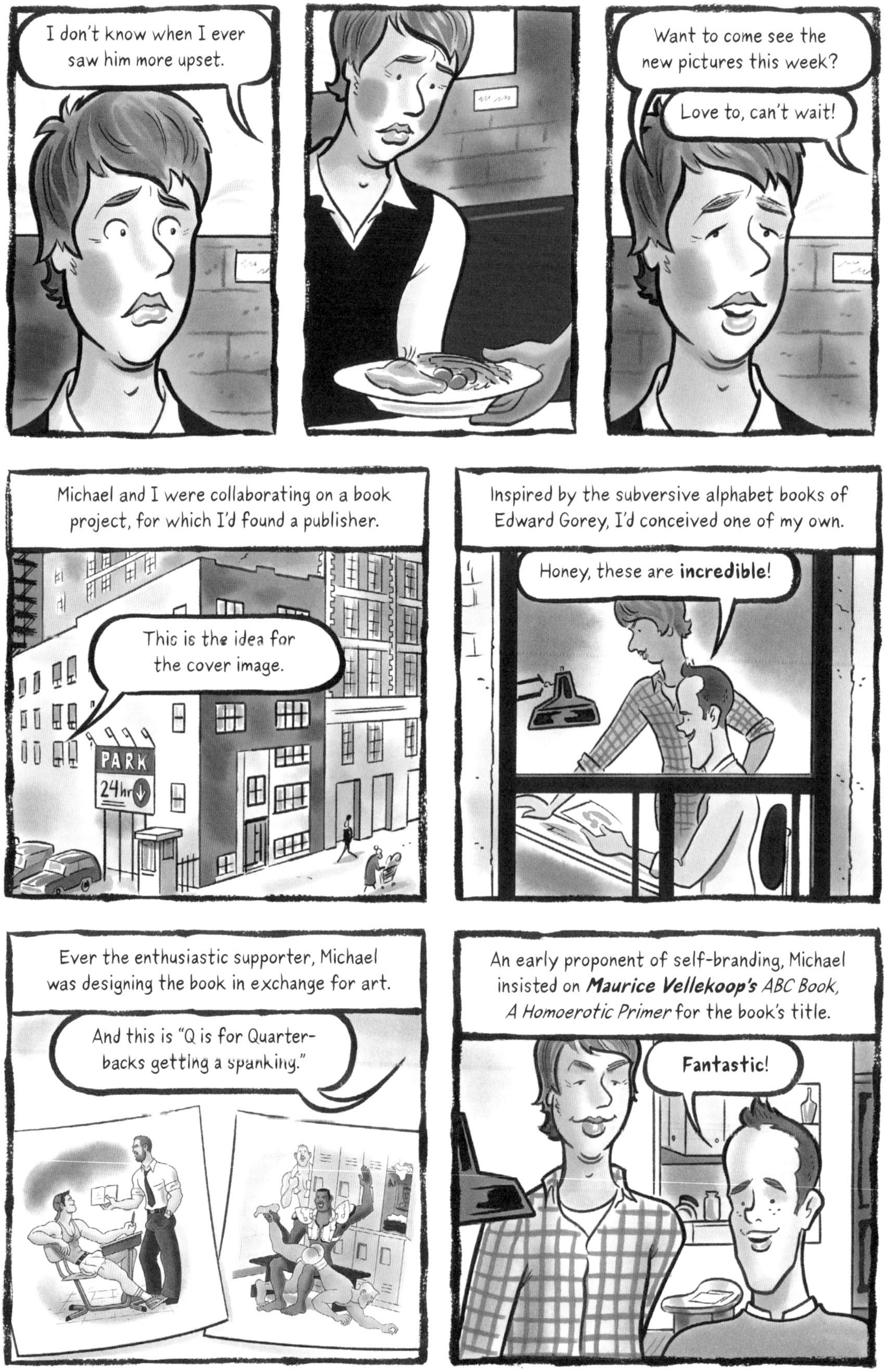

I don't know when I ever saw him more upset.
Want to come see the new pictures this week?
Love to, can't wait!
Michael and I were collaborating on a book project, for which I'd found a publisher.
This is the idea for the cover image.
PARK
24hr
Inspired by the subversive alphabet books of Edward Gorey, I'd conceived one of my own.
Honey, these are **incredible**!
Ever the enthusiastic supporter, Michael was designing the book in exchange for art.
And this is "Q is for Quarter-backs getting a spanking."
An early proponent of self-branding, Michael insisted on ***Maurice Vellekoop's*** *ABC Book, A Homoerotic Primer* for the book's title.
Fantastic!

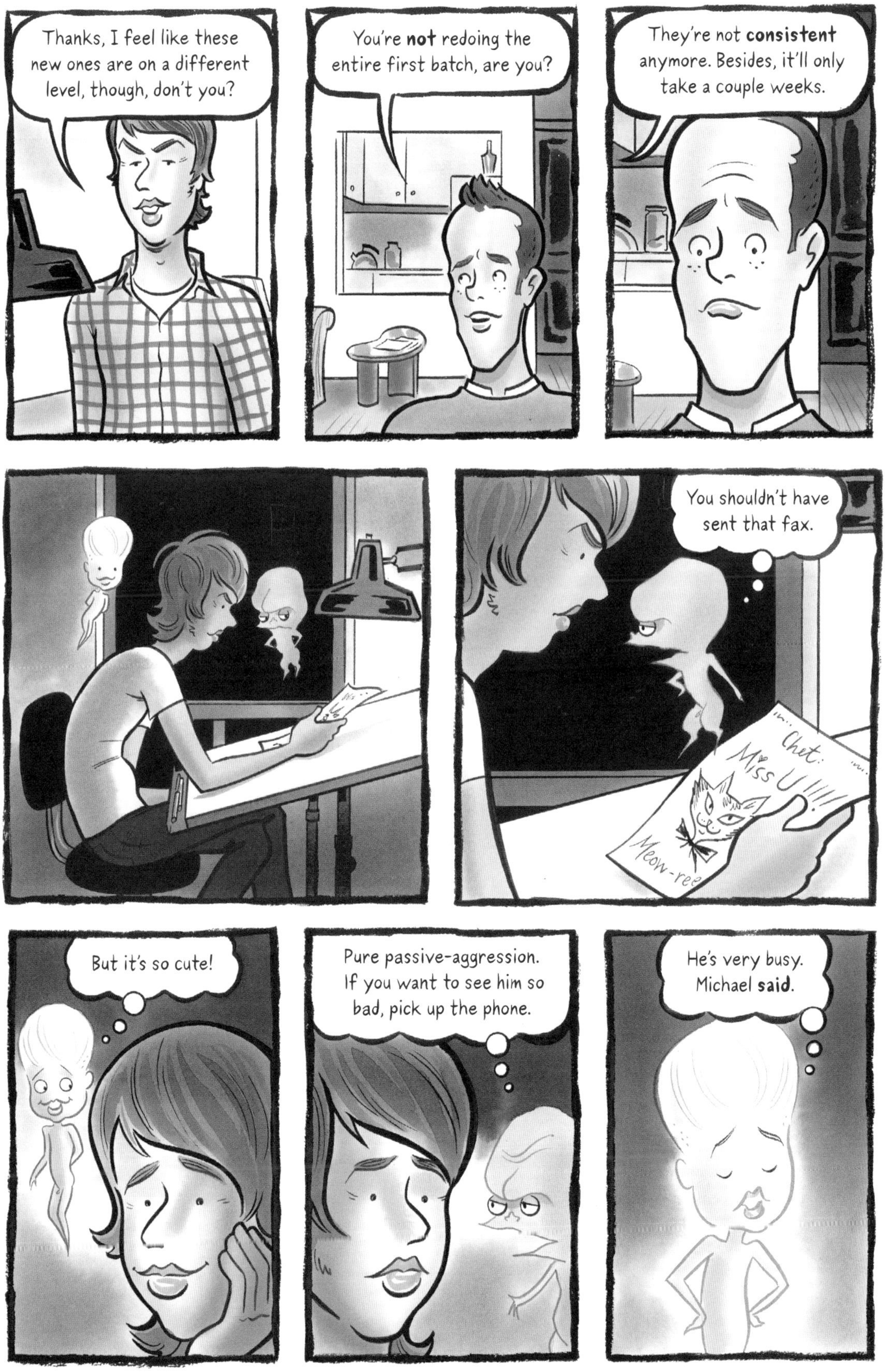
Thanks, I feel like these new ones are on a different level, though, don't you?
You're **not** redoing the entire first batch, are you?
They're not **consistent** anymore. Besides, it'll only take a couple weeks.
You shouldn't have sent that fax.
Chet:
Miss U!!!!
Meow-ree
But it's so cute!
Pure passive-aggression. If you want to see him so bad, pick up the phone.
He's very busy. Michael **said**.

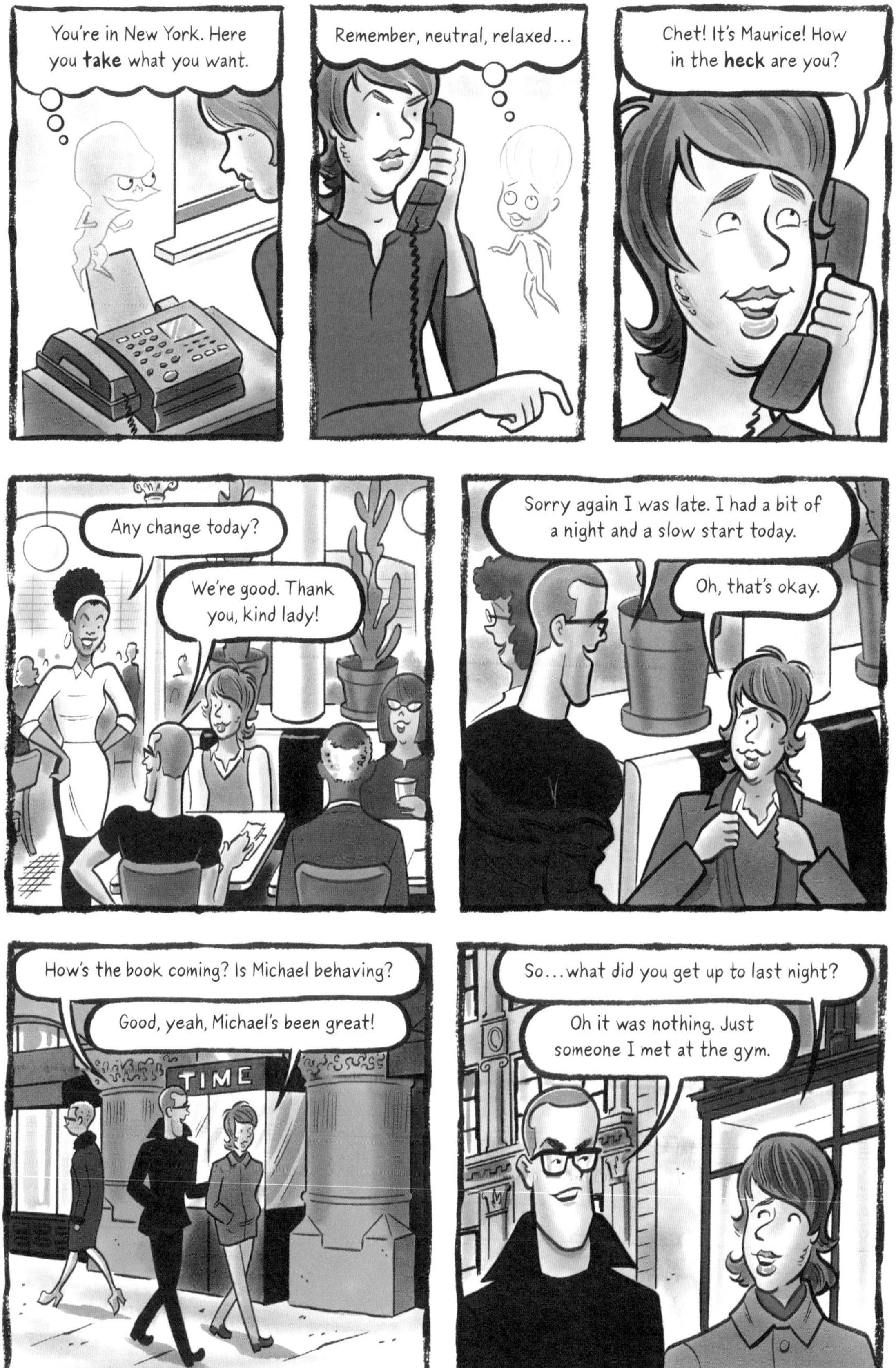
You're in New York. Here you **take** what you want.
Remember, neutral, relaxed...
Chet! It's Maurice! How in the **heck** are you?
Any change today?
We're good. Thank you, kind lady!
Sorry again I was late. I had a bit of a night and a slow start today.
Oh, that's okay.
How's the book coming? Is Michael behaving?
Good, yeah, Michael's been great!
TIME
So...what did you get up to last night?
Oh it was nothing. Just someone I met at the gym.

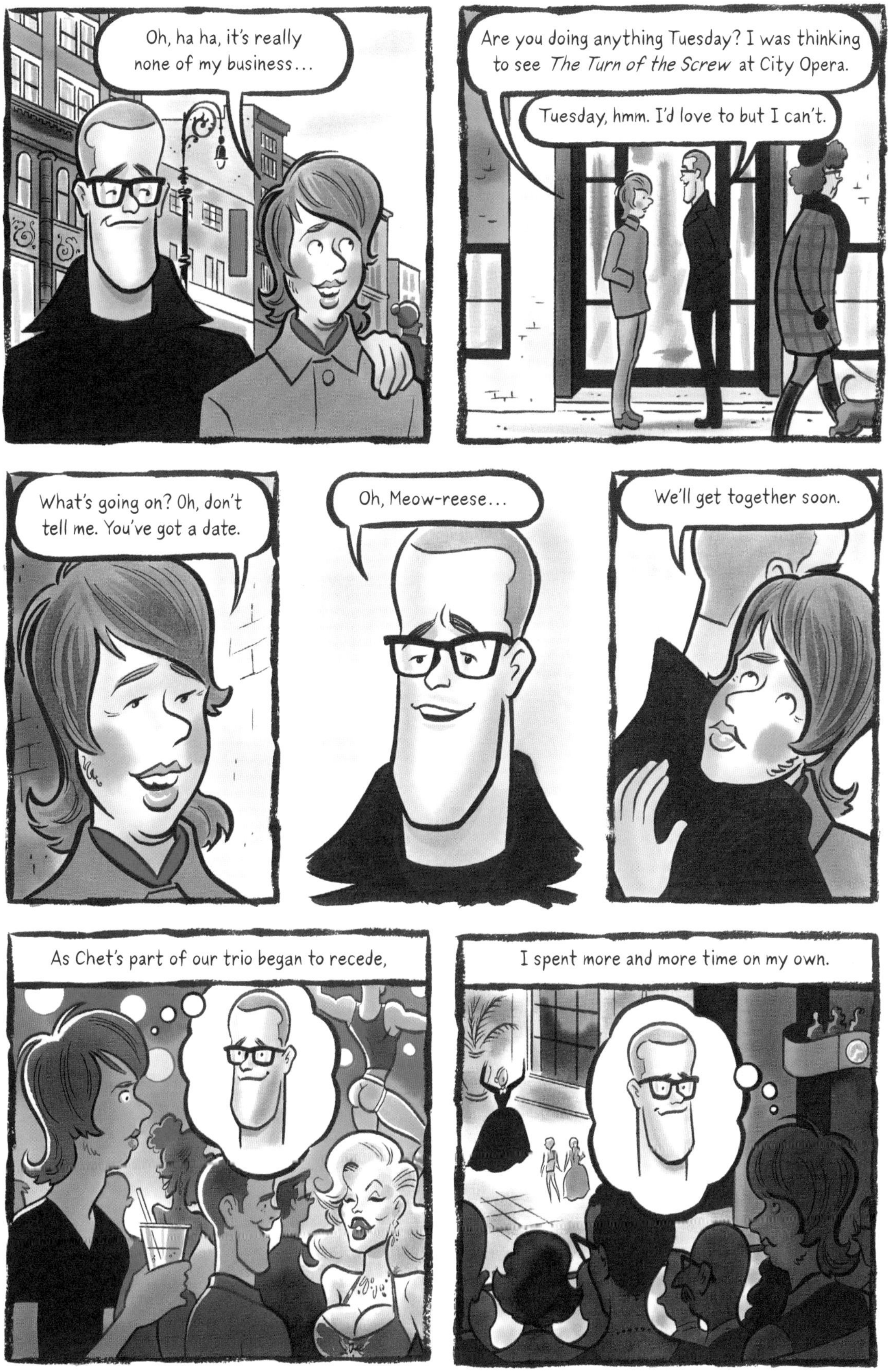
Oh, ha ha, it's really none of my business...
Are you doing anything Tuesday? I was thinking to see *The Turn of the Screw* at City Opera.
Tuesday, hmm. I'd love to but I can't.
What's going on? Oh, don't tell me. You've got a date.
Oh, Meow-reese...
We'll get together soon.
As Chet's part of our trio began to recede,
I spent more and more time on my own.

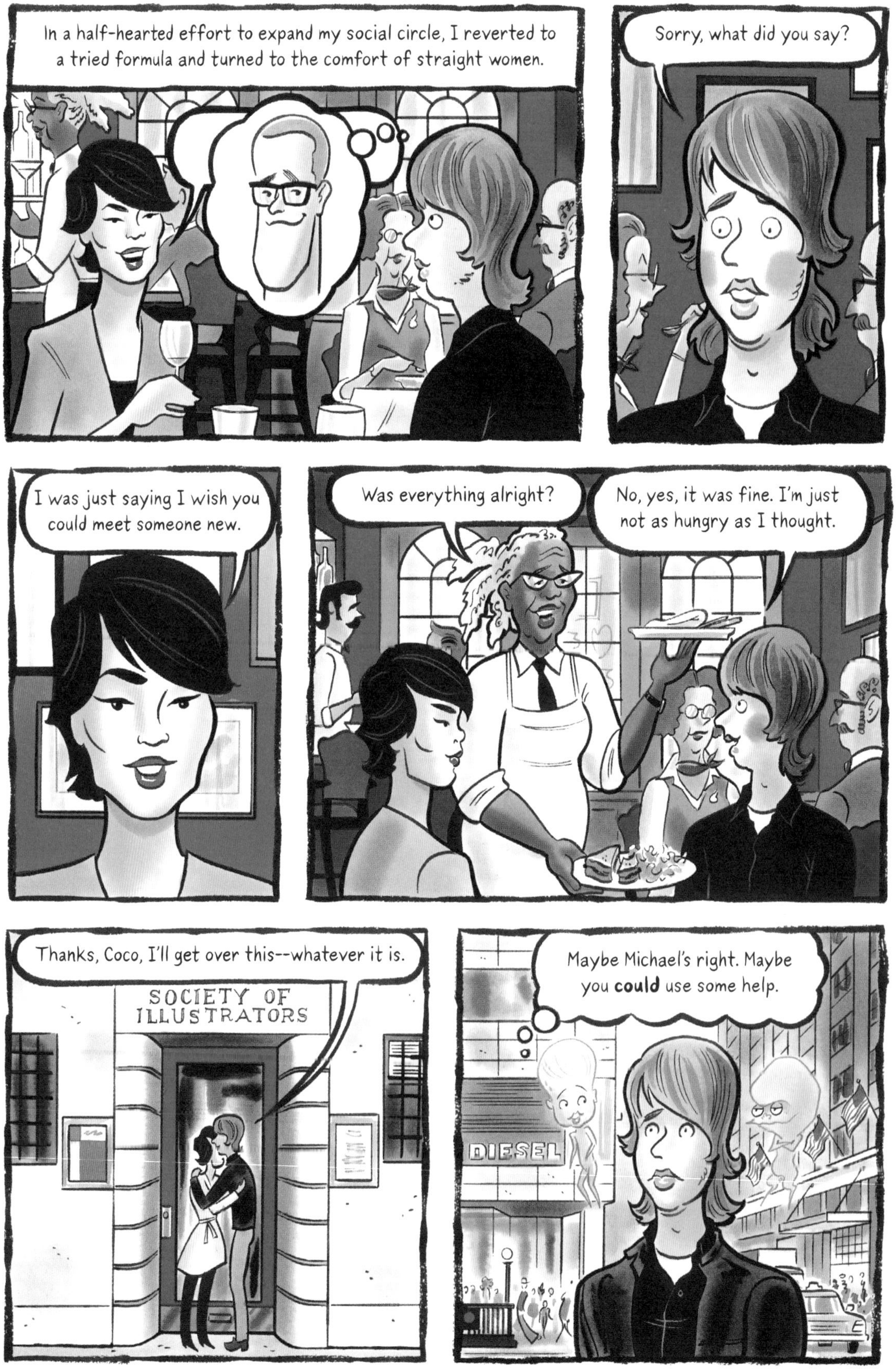
In a half-hearted effort to expand my social circle, I reverted to a tried formula and turned to the comfort of straight women.
Sorry, what did you say?
I was just saying I wish you could meet someone new.
Was everything alright?
No, yes, it was fine. I'm just not as hungry as I thought.
Thanks, Coco, I'll get over this--whatever it is.
SOCIETY OF ILLUSTRATORS
Maybe Michael's right. Maybe you **could** use some help.
DIESEL

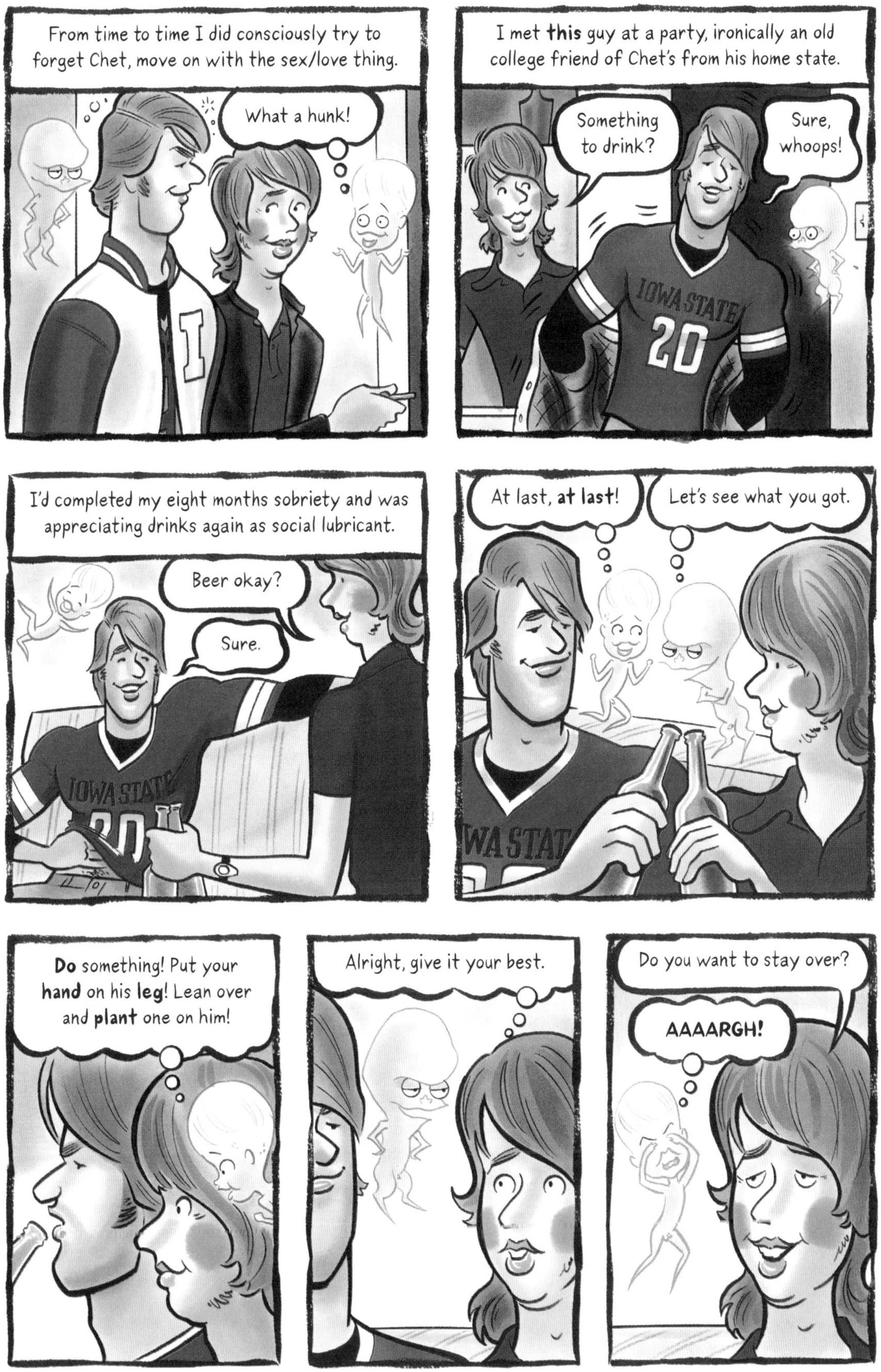
From time to time I did consciously try to forget Chet, move on with the sex/love thing.
What a hunk!
I met **this** guy at a party, ironically an old college friend of Chet's from his home state.
Something to drink?
Sure, whoops!
IOWA STATE
20
I'd completed my eight months sobriety and was appreciating drinks again as social lubricant.
Beer okay?
Sure.
IOWA STATE
At last, **at last**!
Let's see what you got.
Do something! Put your **hand** on his **leg**! Lean over and **plant** one on him!
Alright, give it your best.
Do you want to stay over?
AAAARGH!

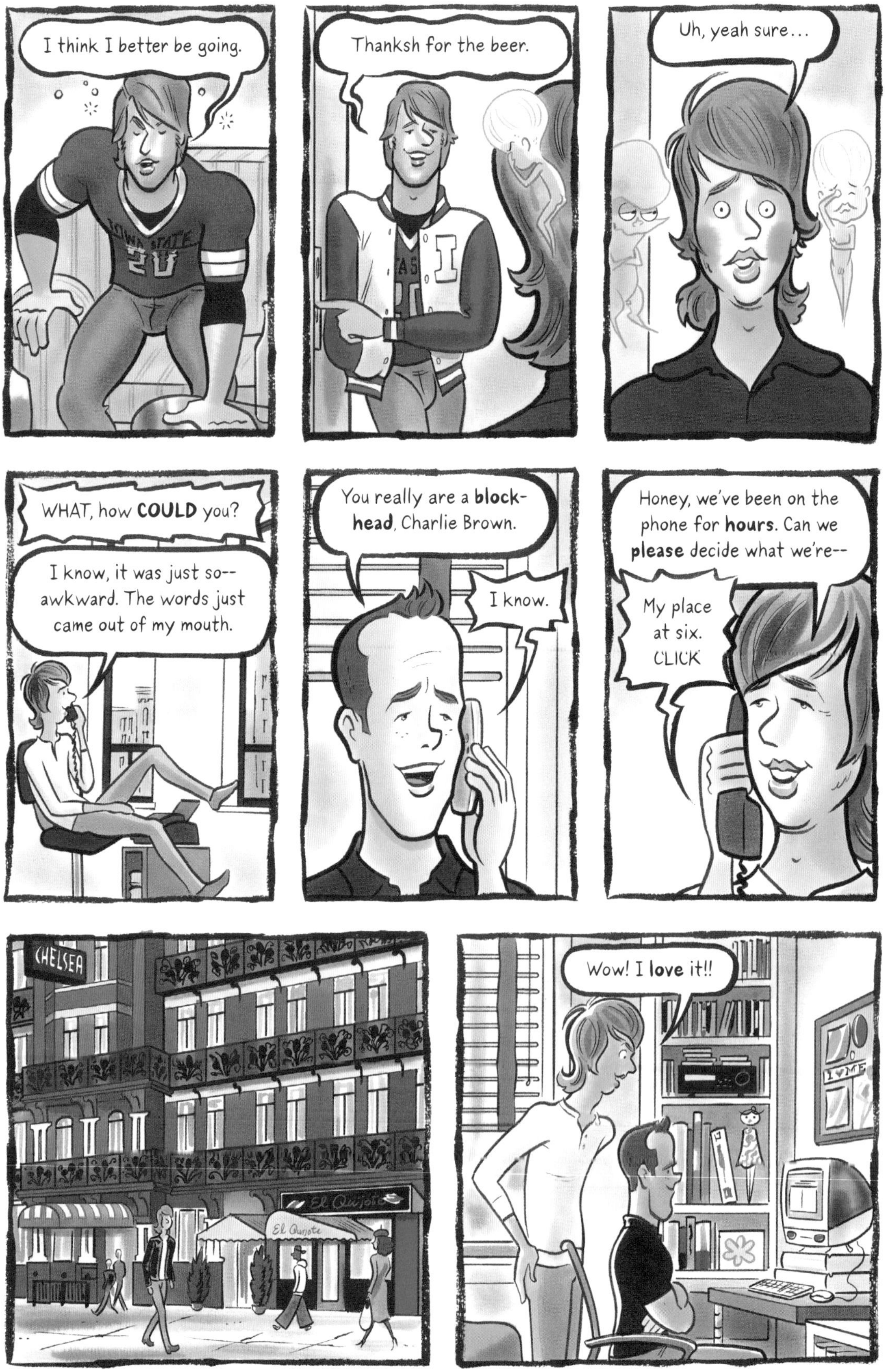
I think I better be going.
Thanksh for the beer.
Uh, yeah sure...
WHAT, how **COULD** you?
I know, it was just so--awkward. The words just came out of my mouth.
You really are a **block-head**, Charlie Brown.
I know.
Honey, we've been on the phone for **hours**. Can we **please** decide what we're--
My place at six. CLICK
CHELSEA
El Quijote
El Quijote
Wow! I **love** it!!

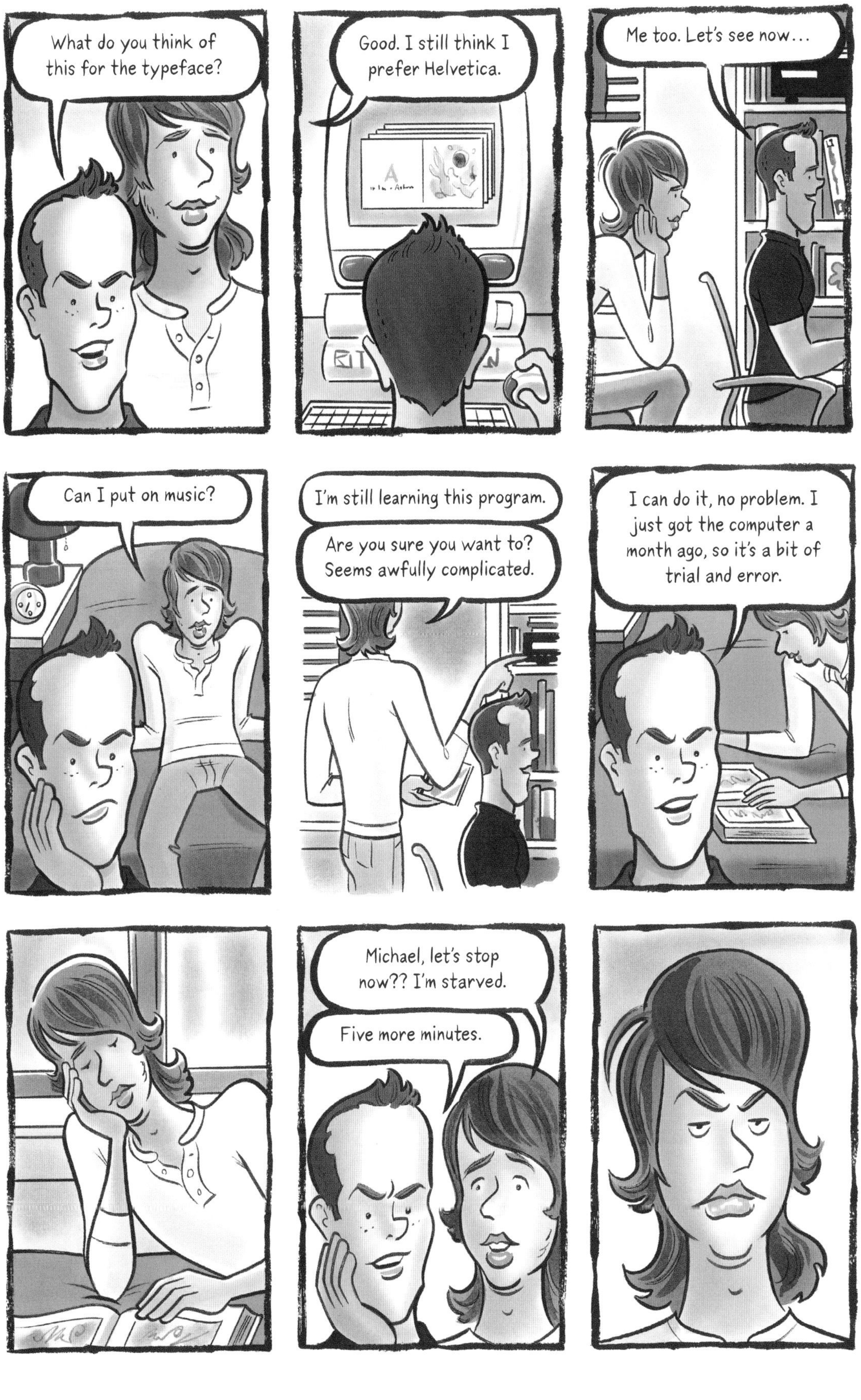
What do you think of this for the typeface?
Good. I still think I prefer Helvetica.
Me too. Let's see now...
Can I put on music?
I'm still learning this program.
Are you sure you want to? Seems awfully complicated.
I can do it, no problem. I just got the computer a month ago, so it's a bit of trial and error.
Michael, let's stop now?? I'm starved.
Five more minutes.

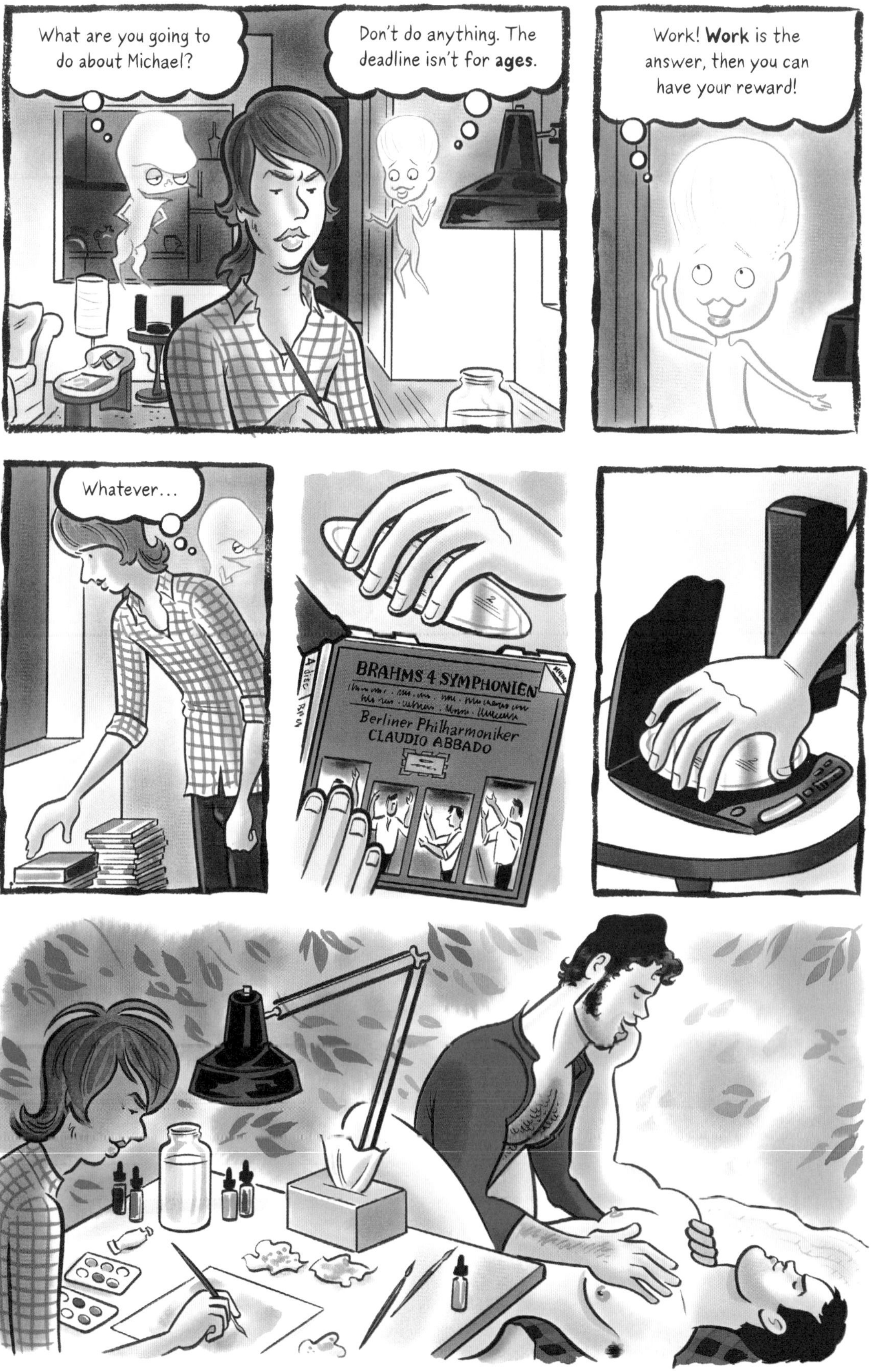
What are you going to do about Michael?
Don't do anything. The deadline isn't for **ages**.
Work! **Work** is the answer, then you can have your reward!
Whatever...
BRAHMS 4 SYMPHONIEN
Berliner Philharmoniker
CLAUDIO ABBADO

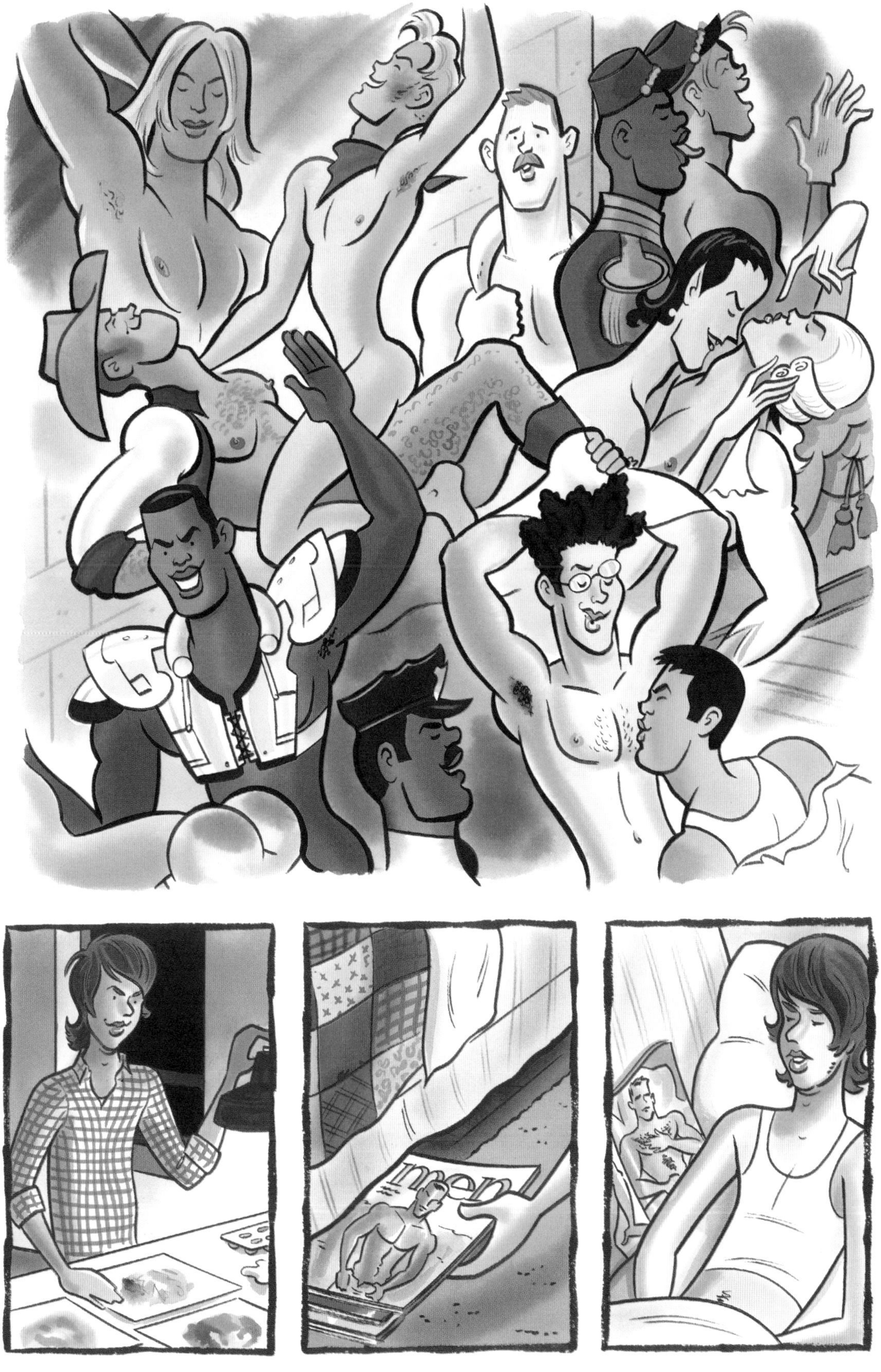
men

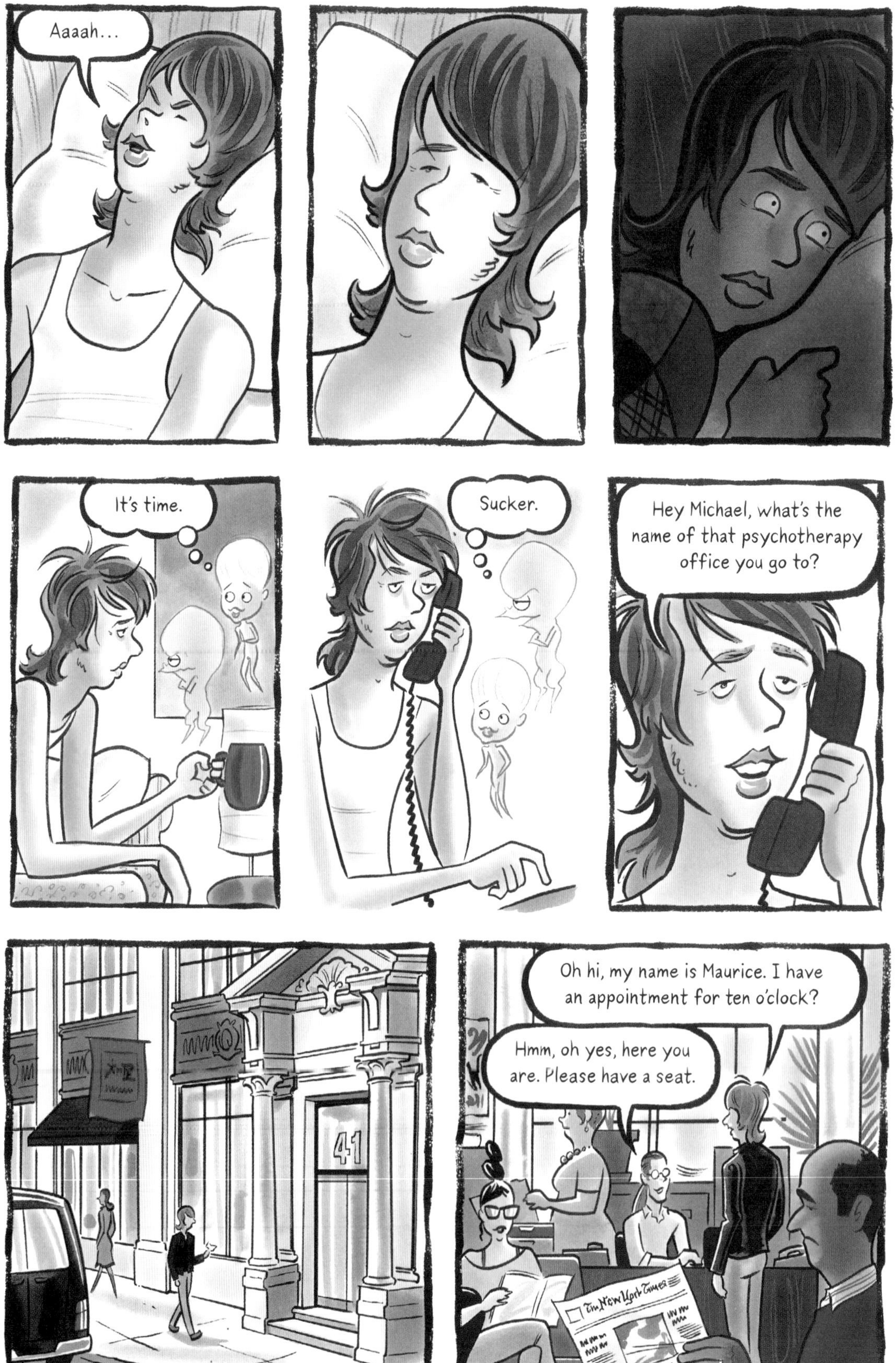
Aaaah...
It's time.
Sucker.
Hey Michael, what's the name of that psychotherapy office you go to?
41
Oh hi, my name is Maurice. I have an appointment for ten o'clock?
Hmm, oh yes, here you are. Please have a seat.

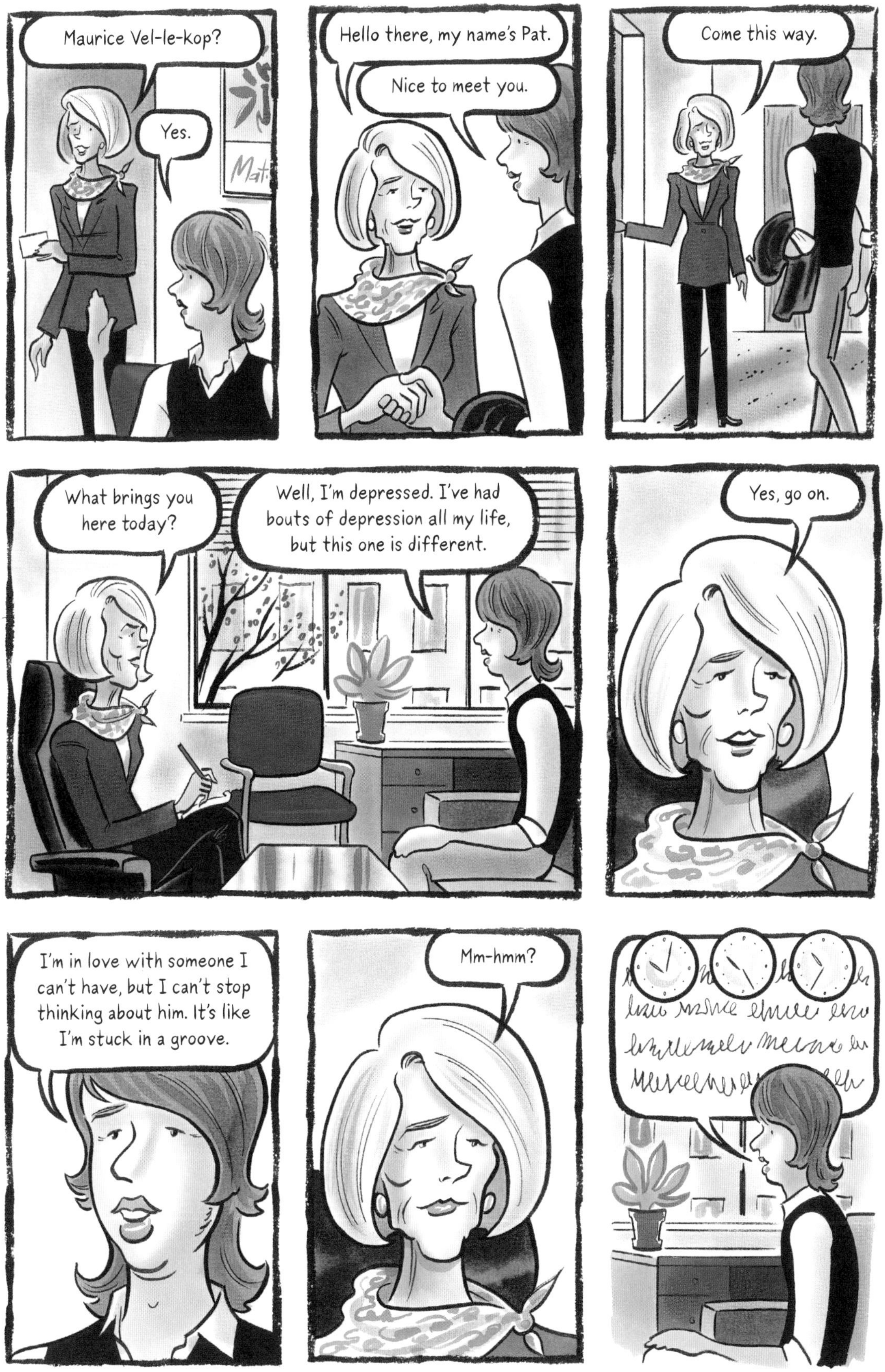
Maurice Vel-le-kop?
Yes.
Hello there, my name's Pat.
Nice to meet you.
Come this way.
What brings you here today?
Well, I'm depressed. I've had bouts of depression all my life, but this one is different.
Yes, go on.
I'm in love with someone I can't have, but I can't stop thinking about him. It's like I'm stuck in a groove.
Mm-hmm?

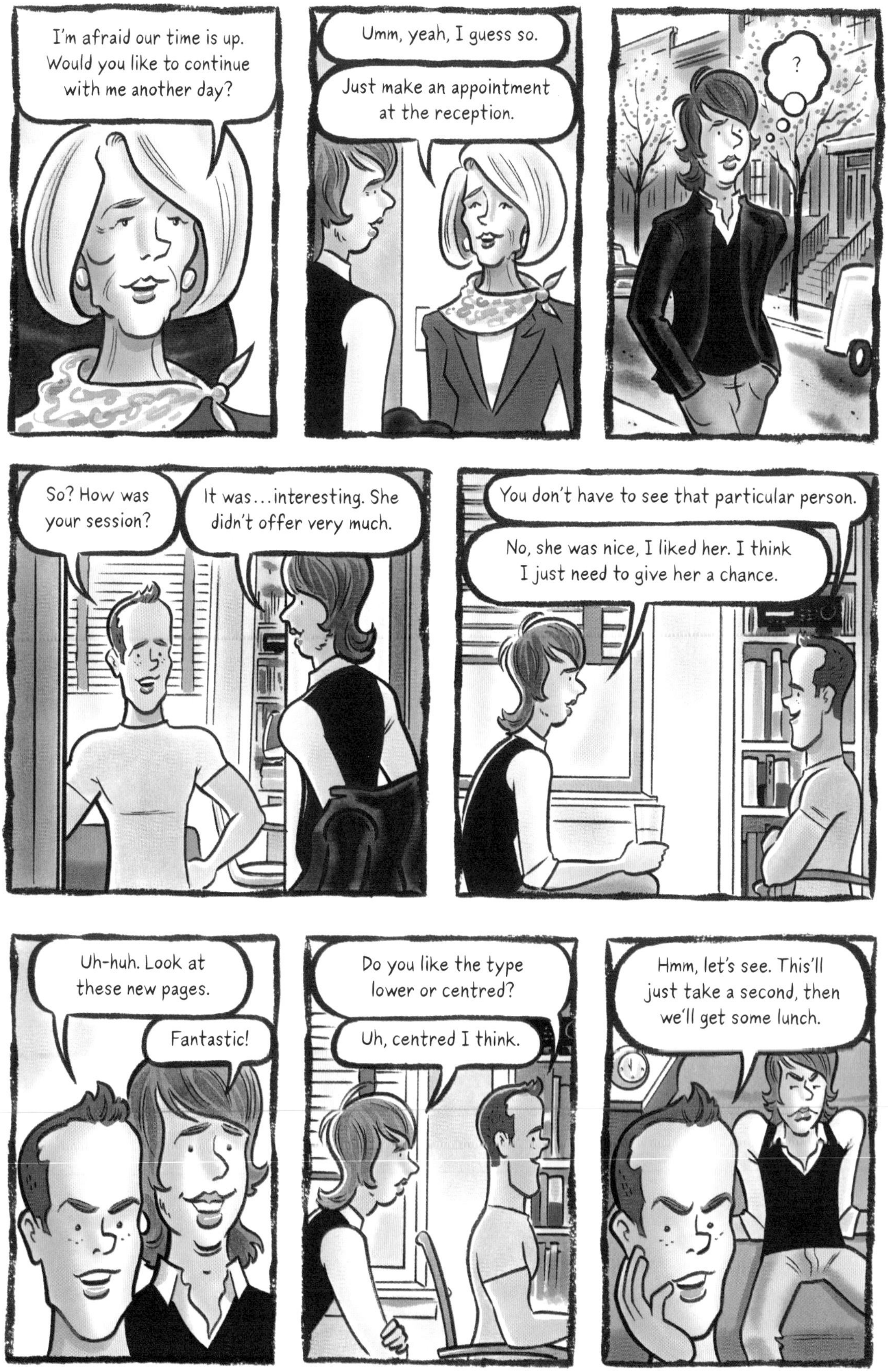

I'm afraid our time is up. Would you like to continue with me another day?
Umm, yeah, I guess so.
Just make an appointment at the reception.
?
So? How was your session?
It was...interesting. She didn't offer very much.
You don't have to see that particular person.
No, she was nice, I liked her. I think I just need to give her a chance.
Uh-huh. Look at these new pages.
Fantastic!
Do you like the type lower or centred?
Uh, centred I think.
Hmm, let's see. This'll just take a second, then we'll get some lunch.

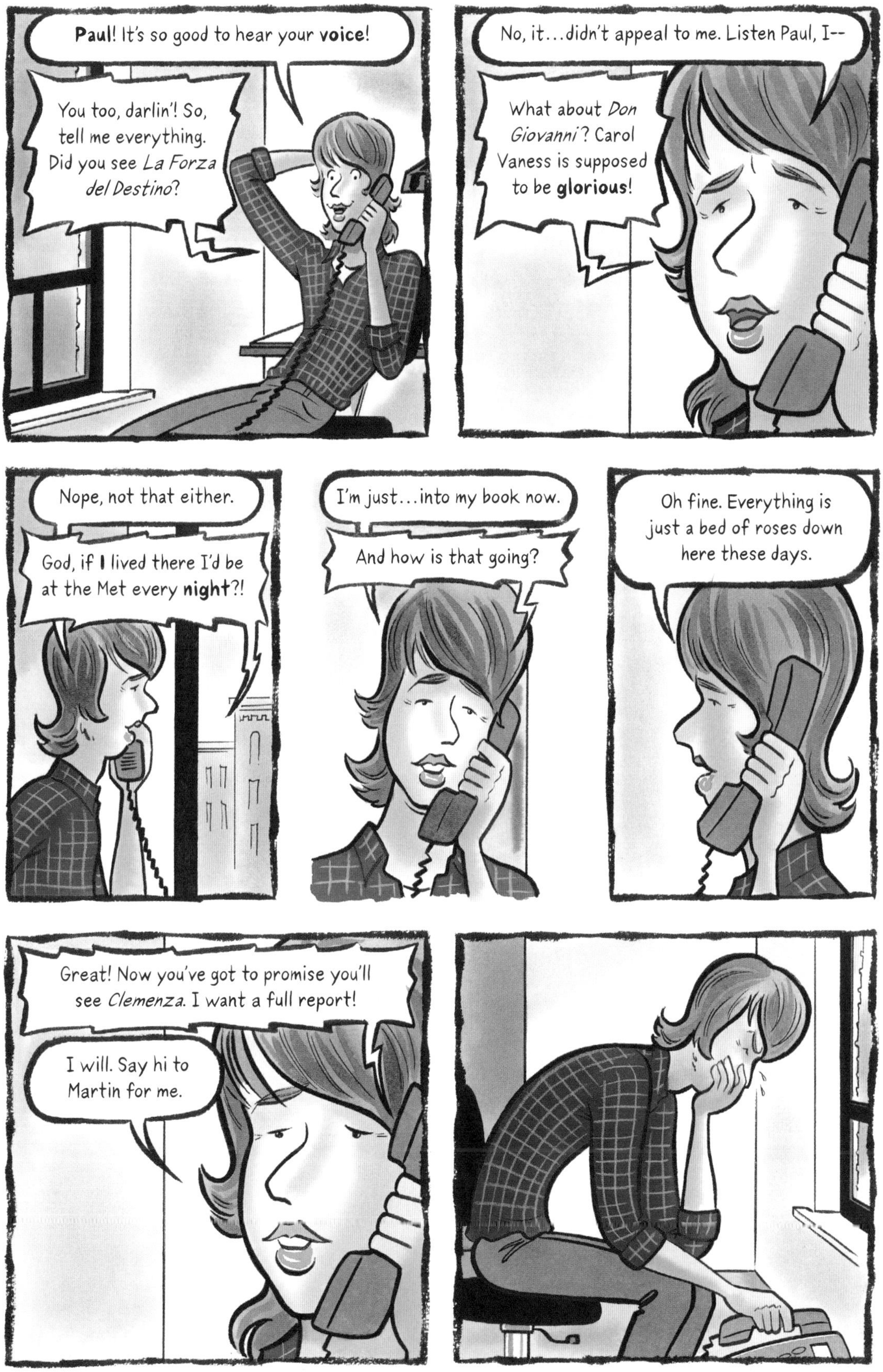

Paul! It's so good to hear your **voice**!
You too, darlin'! So, tell me everything. Did you see *La Forza del Destino*?
No, it...didn't appeal to me. Listen Paul, I--
What about *Don Giovanni*? Carol Vaness is supposed to be **glorious**!
Nope, not that either.
God, if **I** lived there I'd be at the Met every **night**?!
I'm just...into my book now.
And how is that going?
Oh fine. Everything is just a bed of roses down here these days.
Great! Now you've got to promise you'll see *Clemenza*. I want a full report!
I will. Say hi to Martin for me.

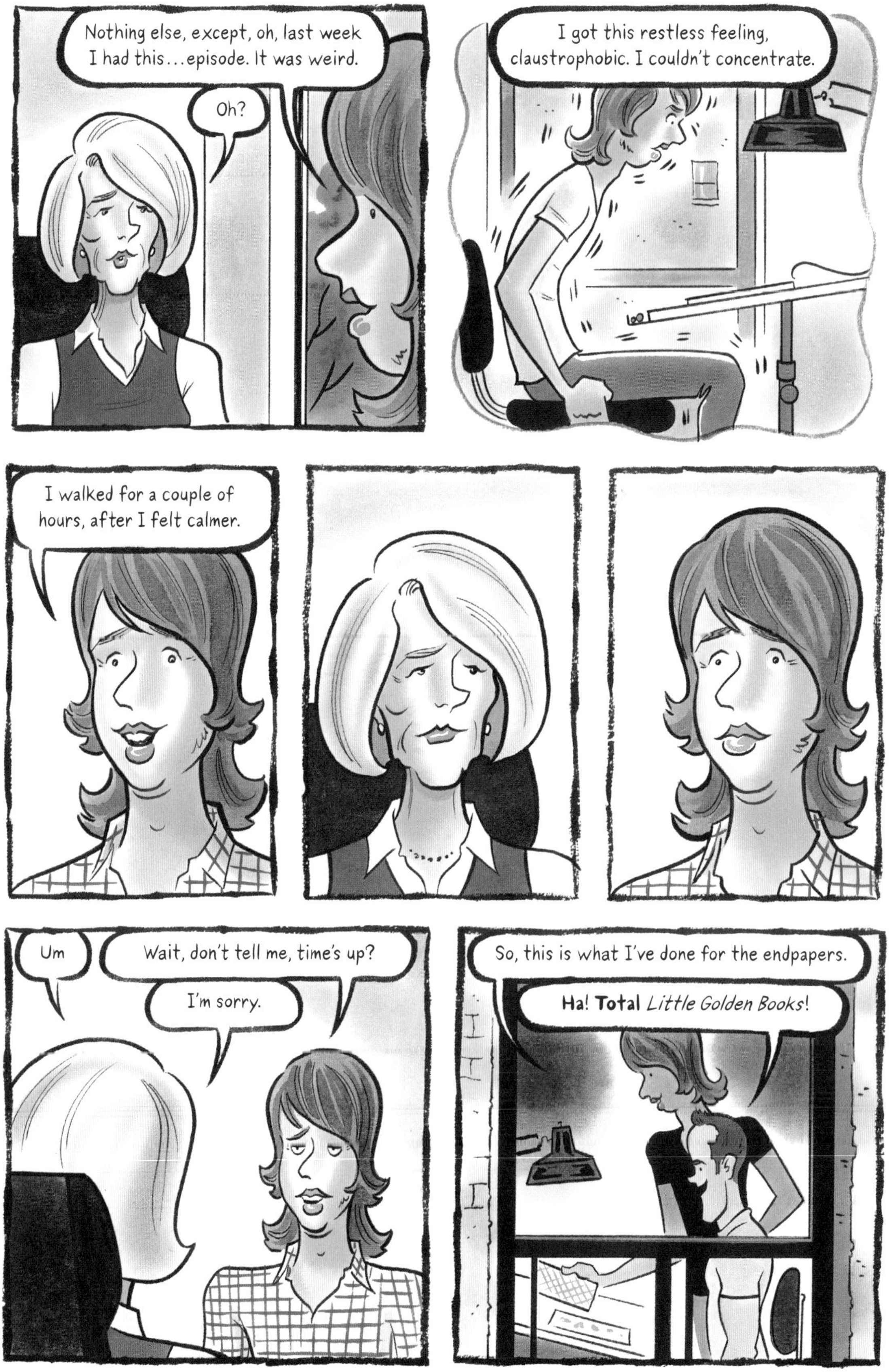
Nothing else, except, oh, last week I had this...episode. It was weird.
Oh?
I got this restless feeling, claustrophobic. I couldn't concentrate.
I walked for a couple of hours, after I felt calmer.
Um
Wait, don't tell me, time's up?
I'm sorry.
So, this is what I've done for the endpapers.
Ha! Total *Little Golden Books*!

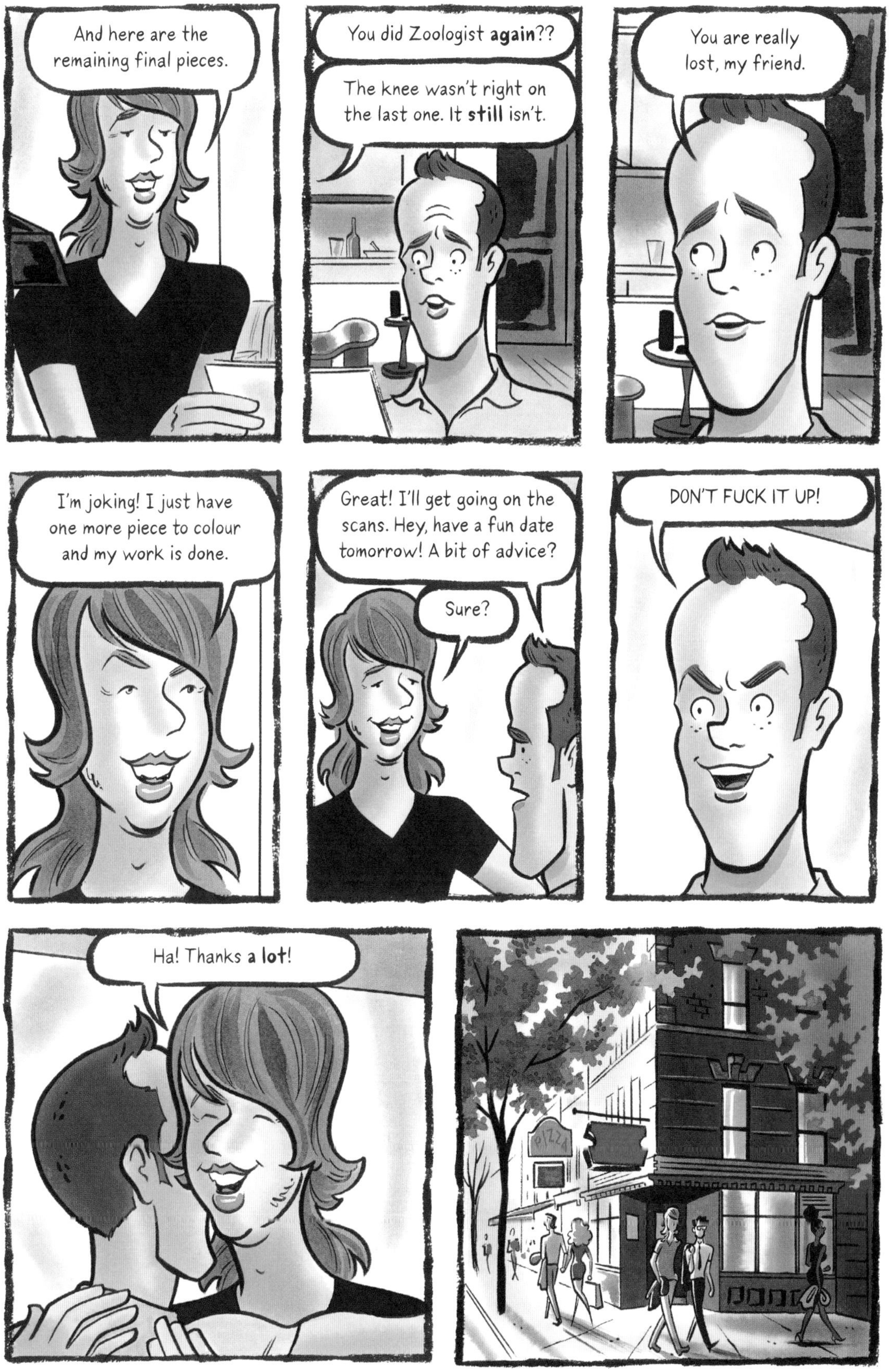
And here are the remaining final pieces.
You did Zoologist **again**??
The knee wasn't right on the last one. It **still** isn't.
You are really lost, my friend.
I'm joking! I just have one more piece to colour and my work is done.
Great! I'll get going on the scans. Hey, have a fun date tomorrow! A bit of advice?
Sure?
DON'T FUCK IT UP!
Ha! Thanks **a lot**!
PIZZA

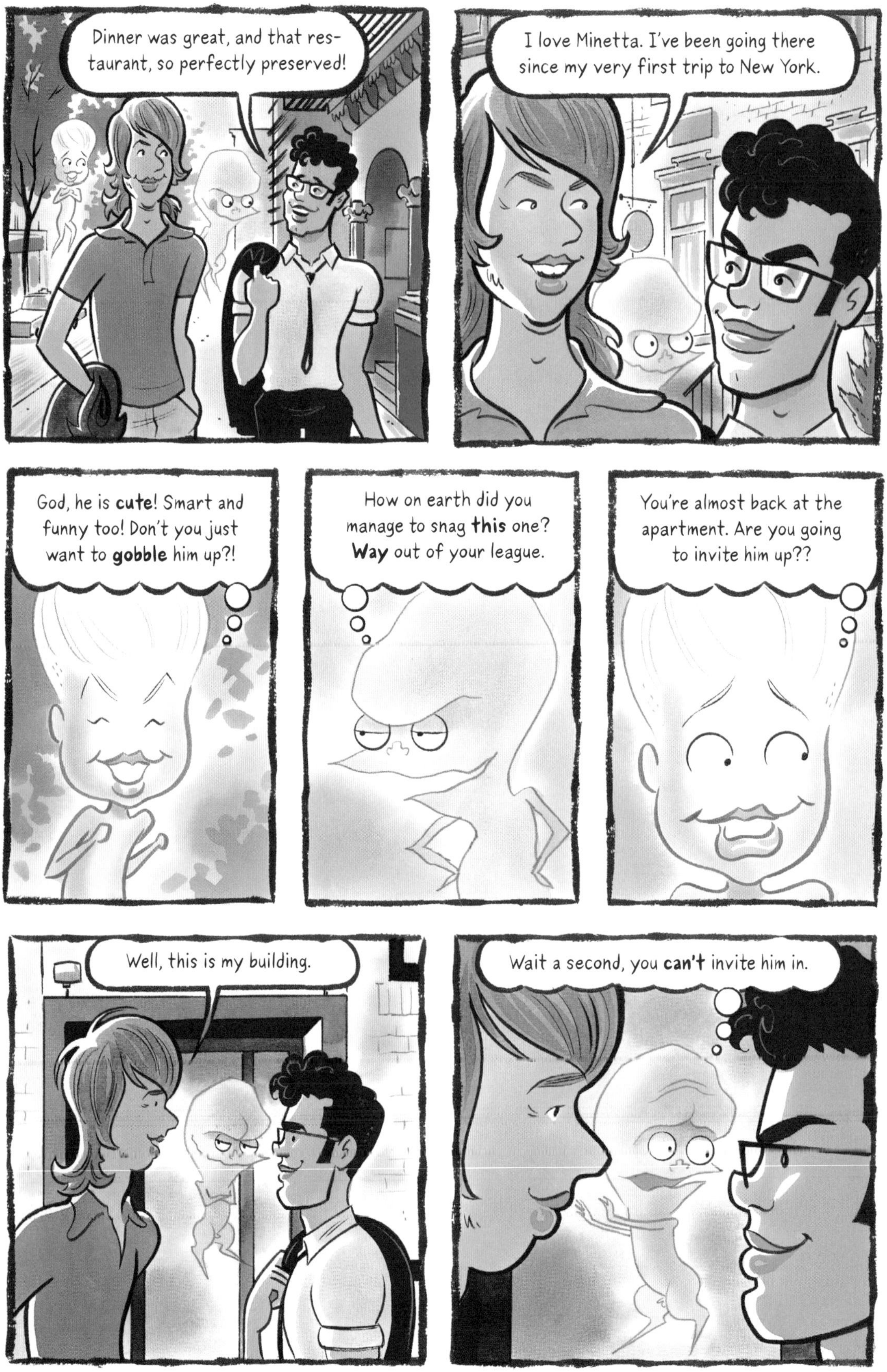
Dinner was great, and that restaurant, so perfectly preserved!
I love Minetta. I've been going there since my very first trip to New York.
God, he is **cute**! Smart and funny too! Don't you just want to **gobble** him up?!
How on earth did you manage to snag **this** one? **Way** out of your league.
You're almost back at the apartment. Are you going to invite him up??
Well, this is my building.
Wait a second, you **can't** invite him in.

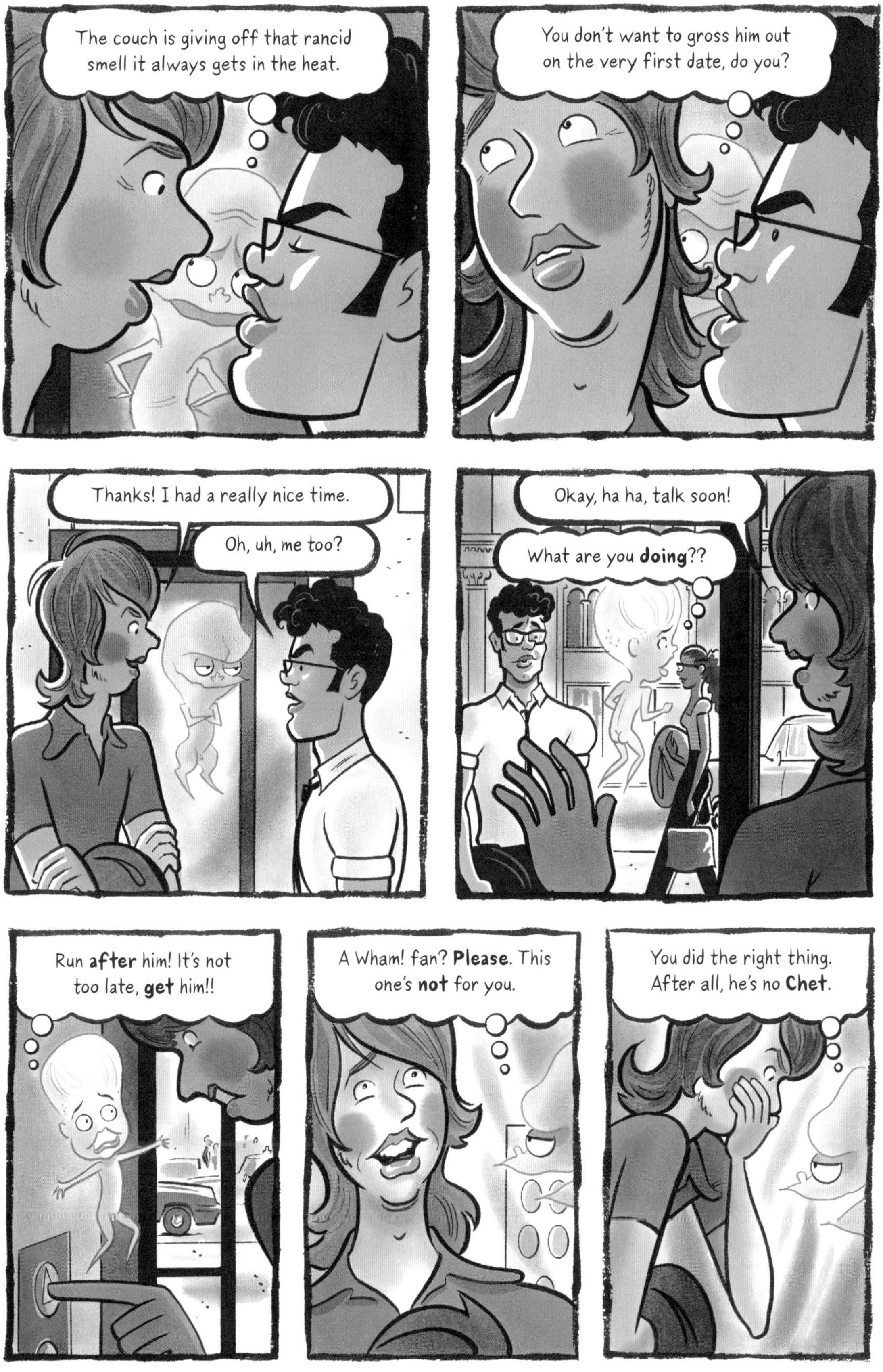
The couch is giving off that rancid smell it always gets in the heat.
You don't want to gross him out on the very first date, do you?
Thanks! I had a really nice time.
Oh, uh, me too?
Okay, ha ha, talk soon!
What are you **doing**??
Run **after** him! It's not too late, **get** him!!
A Wham! fan? **Please**. This one's **not** for you.
You did the right thing. After all, he's no **Chet**.

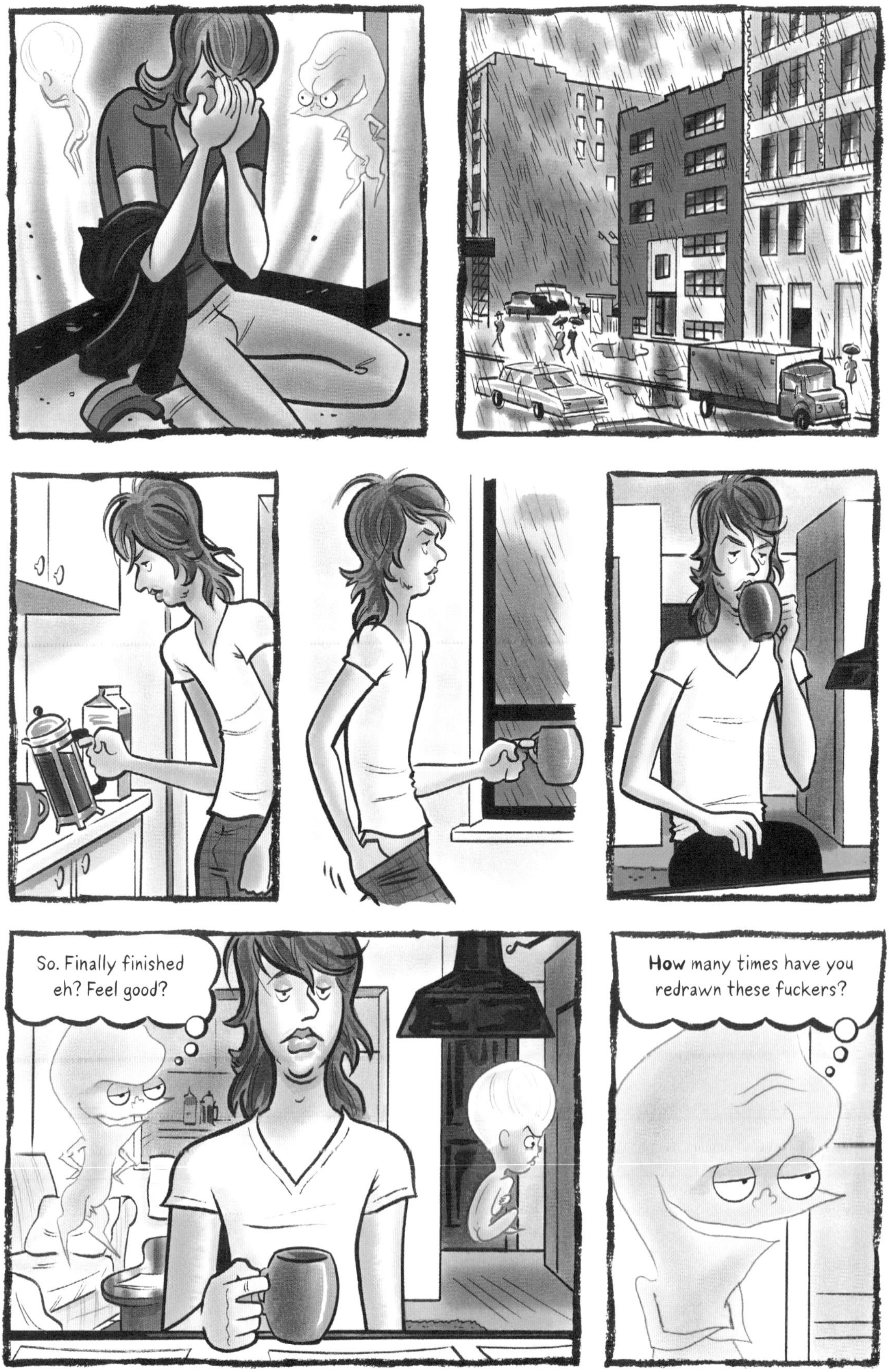
So. Finally finished
eh? Feel good?
How many times have you
redrawn these fuckers?

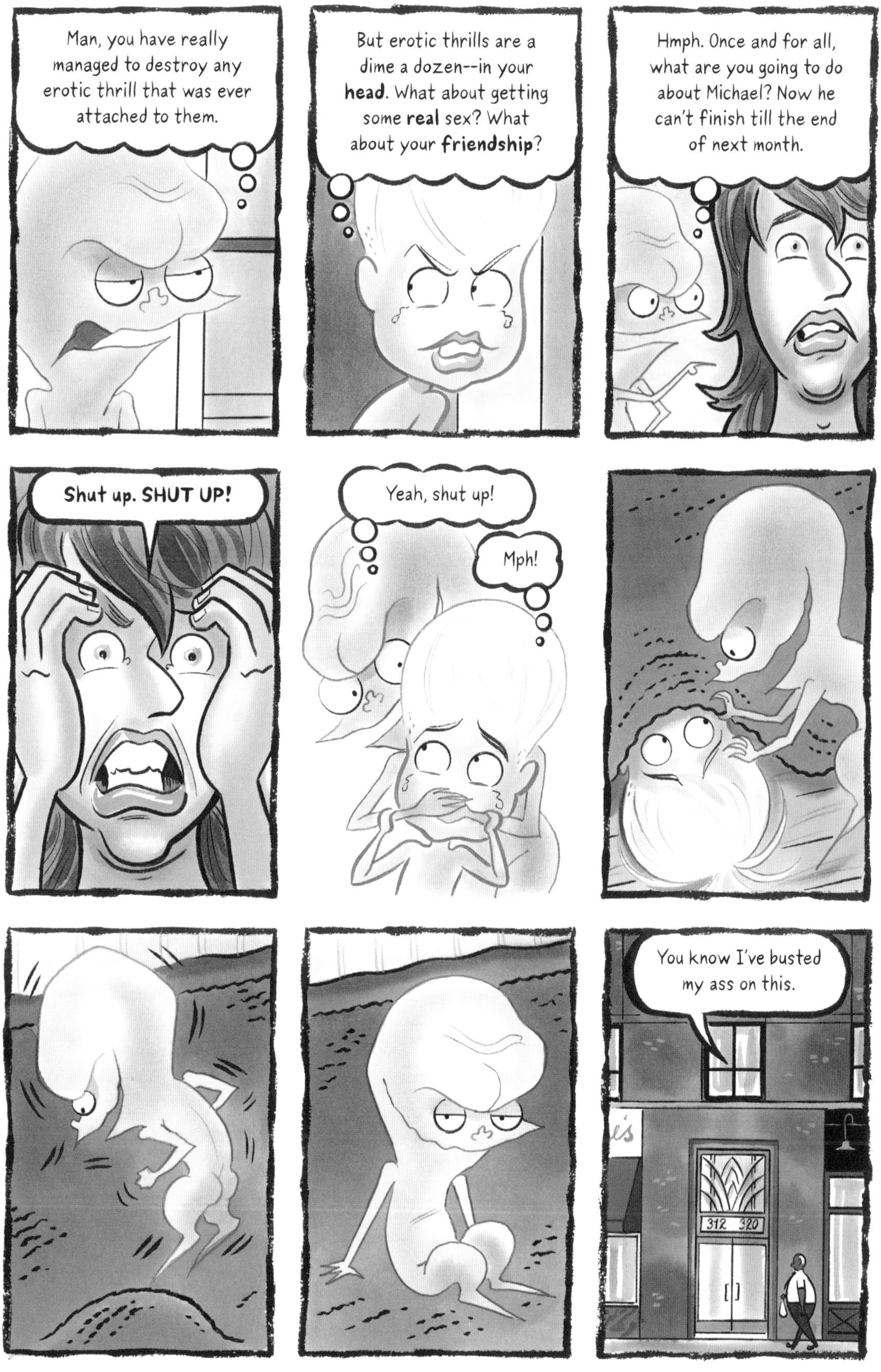
Man, you have really managed to destroy any erotic thrill that was ever attached to them.
But erotic thrills are a dime a dozen--in your head. What about getting some real sex? What about your friendship?
Hmph. Once and for all, what are you going to do about Michael? Now he can't finish till the end of next month.
Shut up. SHUT UP!
Yeah, shut up!
Mph!
You know I've busted my ass on this.

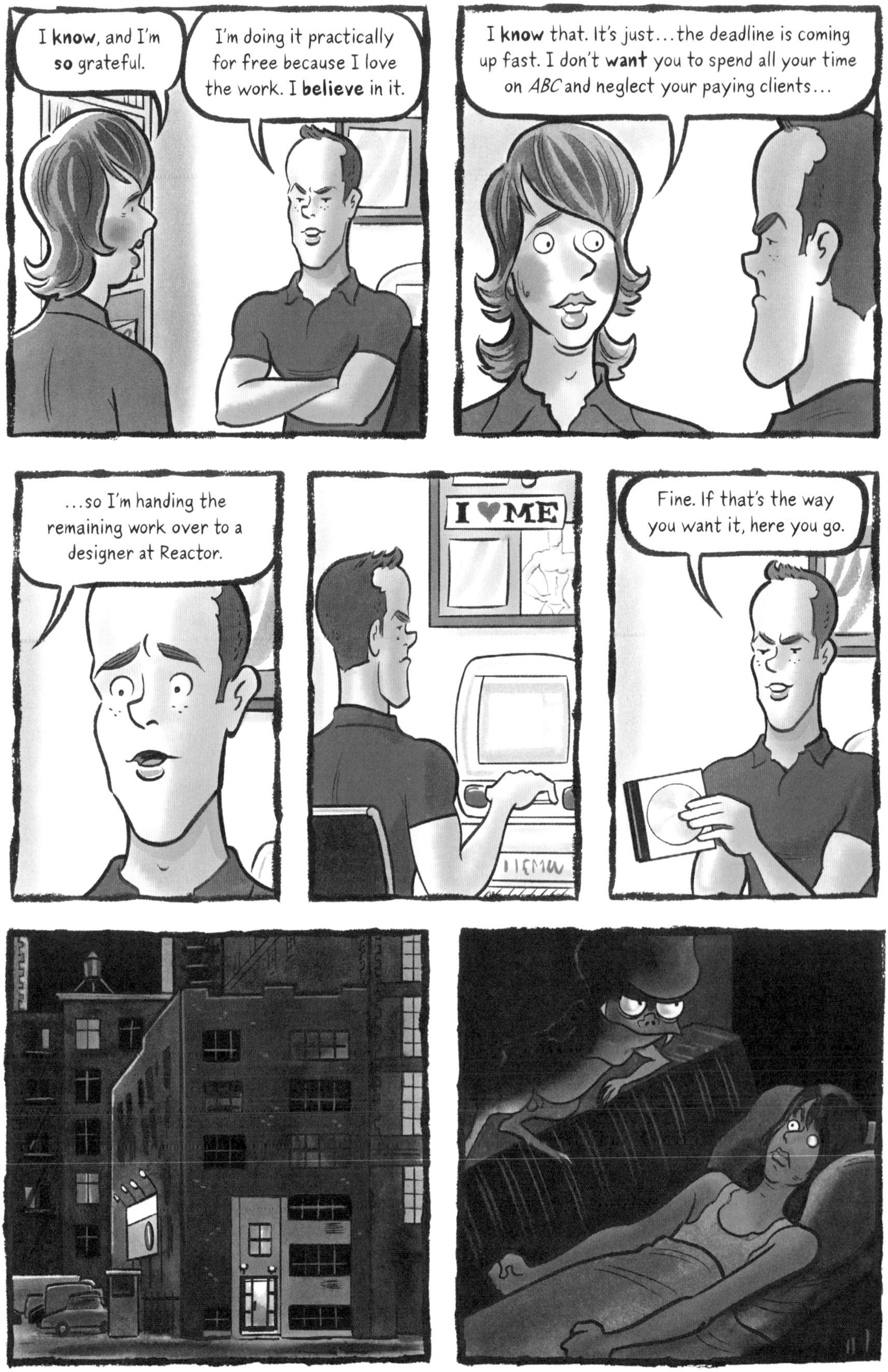
I **know**, and I'm **so** grateful.
I'm doing it practically for free because I love the work. I **believe** in it.
I **know** that. It's just...the deadline is coming up fast. I don't **want** you to spend all your time on *ABC* and neglect your paying clients...
...so I'm handing the remaining work over to a designer at Reactor.
I ♥ ME
Fine. If that's the way you want it, here you go.

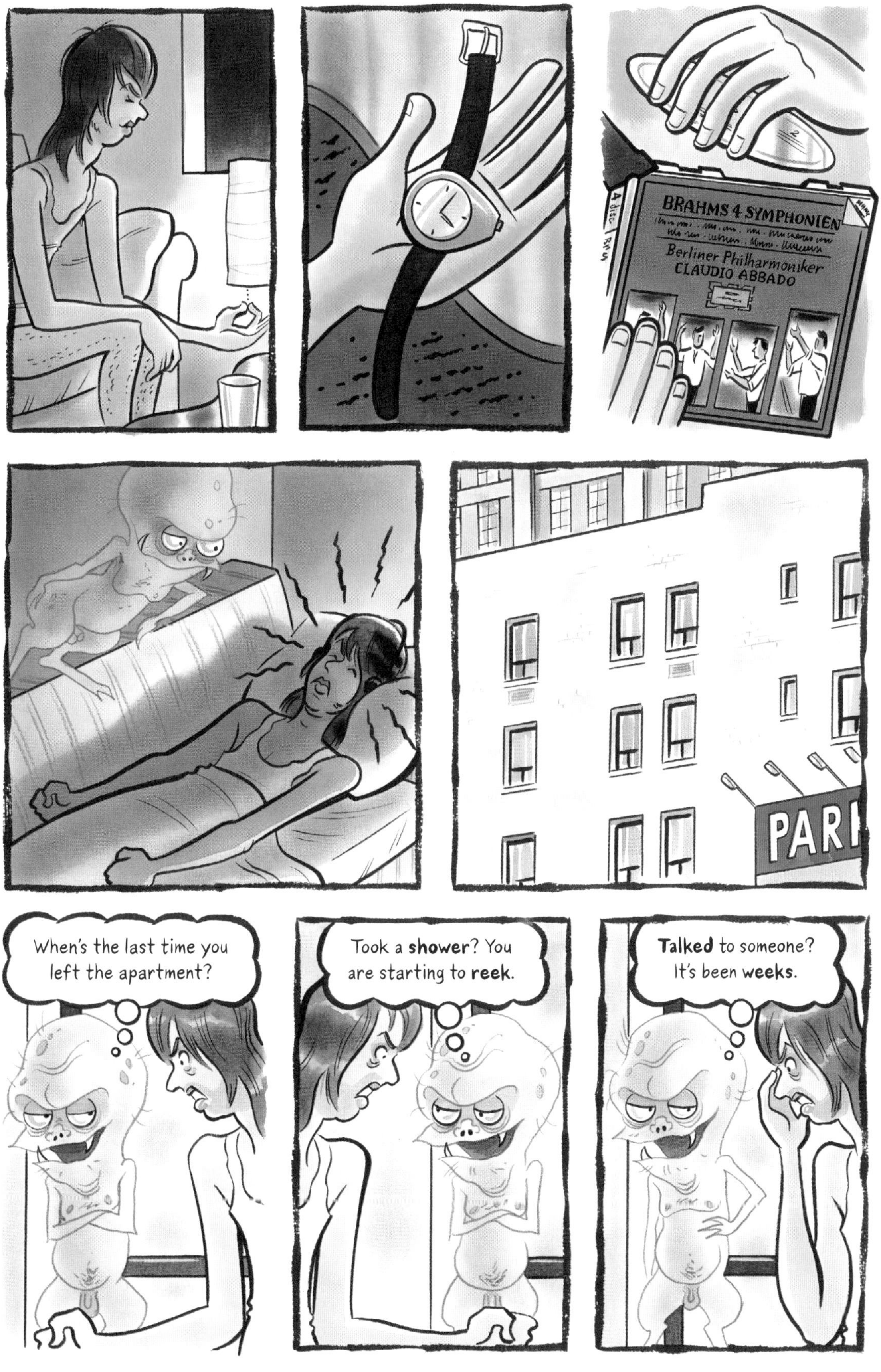
BRAHMS 4 SYMPHONIEN
Berliner Philharmoniker
CLAUDIO ABBADO
When's the last time you left the apartment?
Took a **shower**? You are starting to **reek**.
Talked to someone? It's been **weeks**.

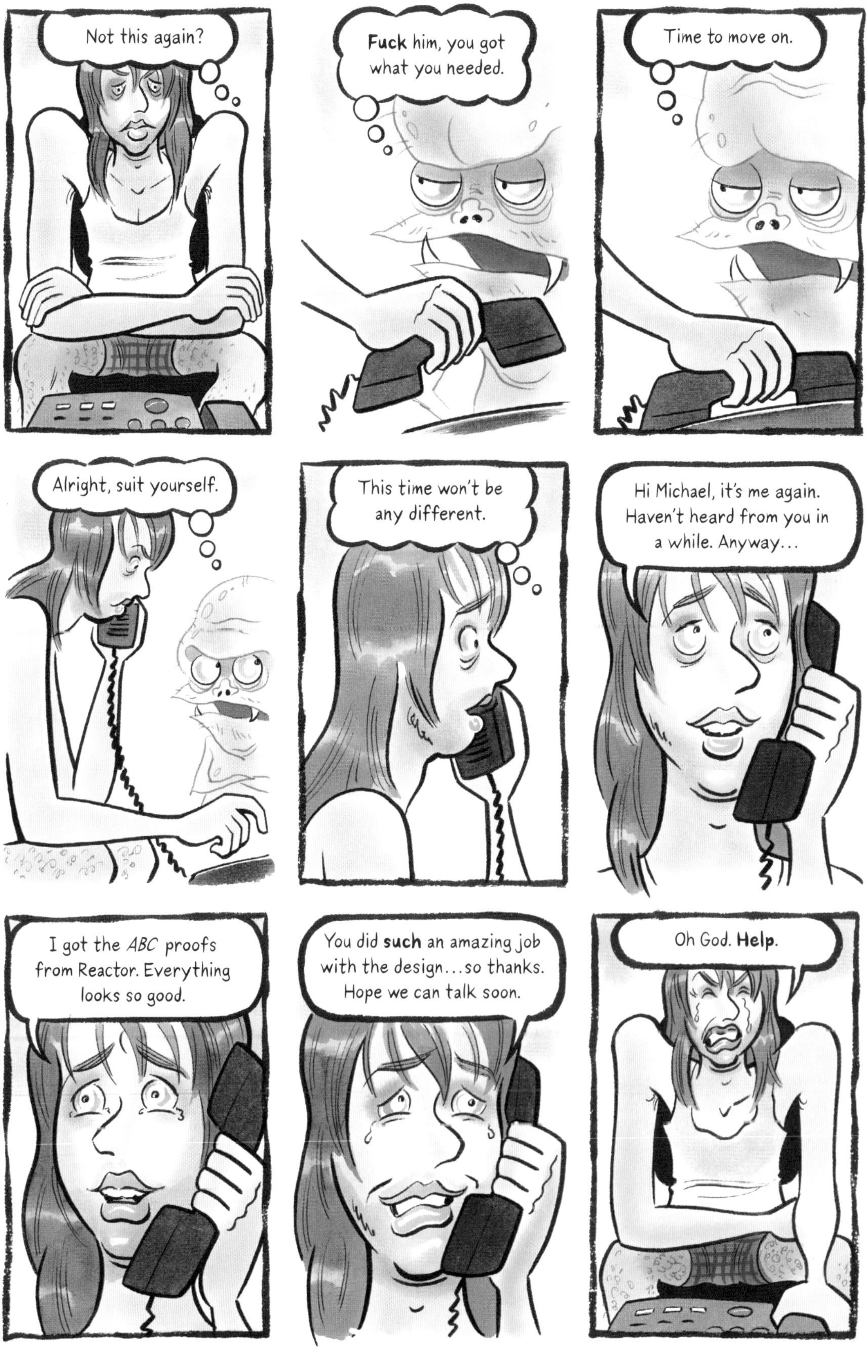
Not this again?
Fuck him, you got what you needed.
Time to move on.
Alright, suit yourself.
This time won't be any different.
Hi Michael, it's me again. Haven't heard from you in a while. Anyway...
I got the *ABC* proofs from Reactor. Everything looks so good.
You did **such** an amazing job with the design...so thanks. Hope we can talk soon.
Oh God. **Help**.

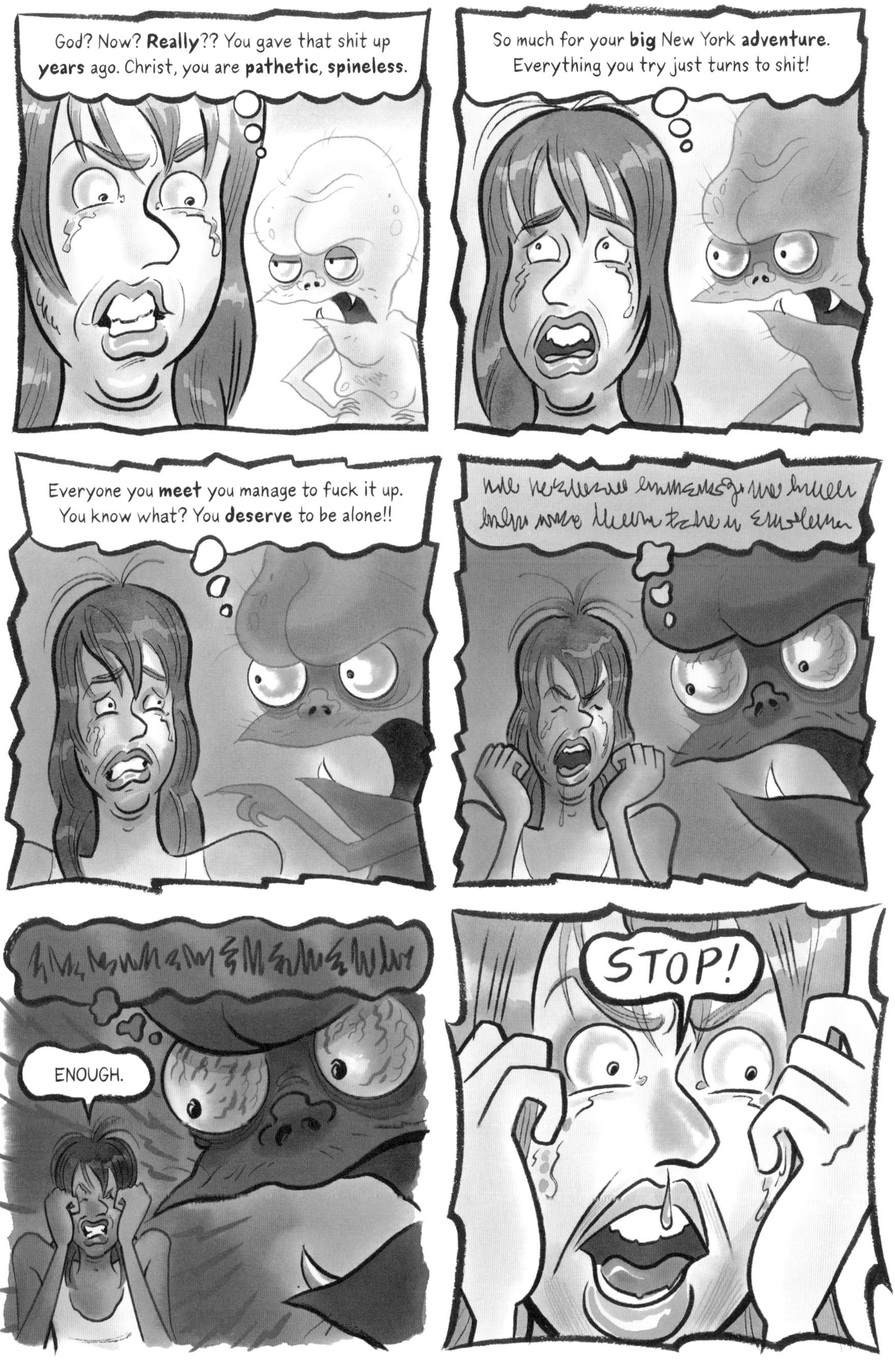
God? Now? **Really**?? You gave that shit up **years** ago. Christ, you are **pathetic**, **spineless**.
So much for your **big** New York **adventure**. Everything you try just turns to shit!
Everyone you **meet** you manage to fuck it up. You know what? You **deserve** to be alone!!
ENOUGH.
STOP!

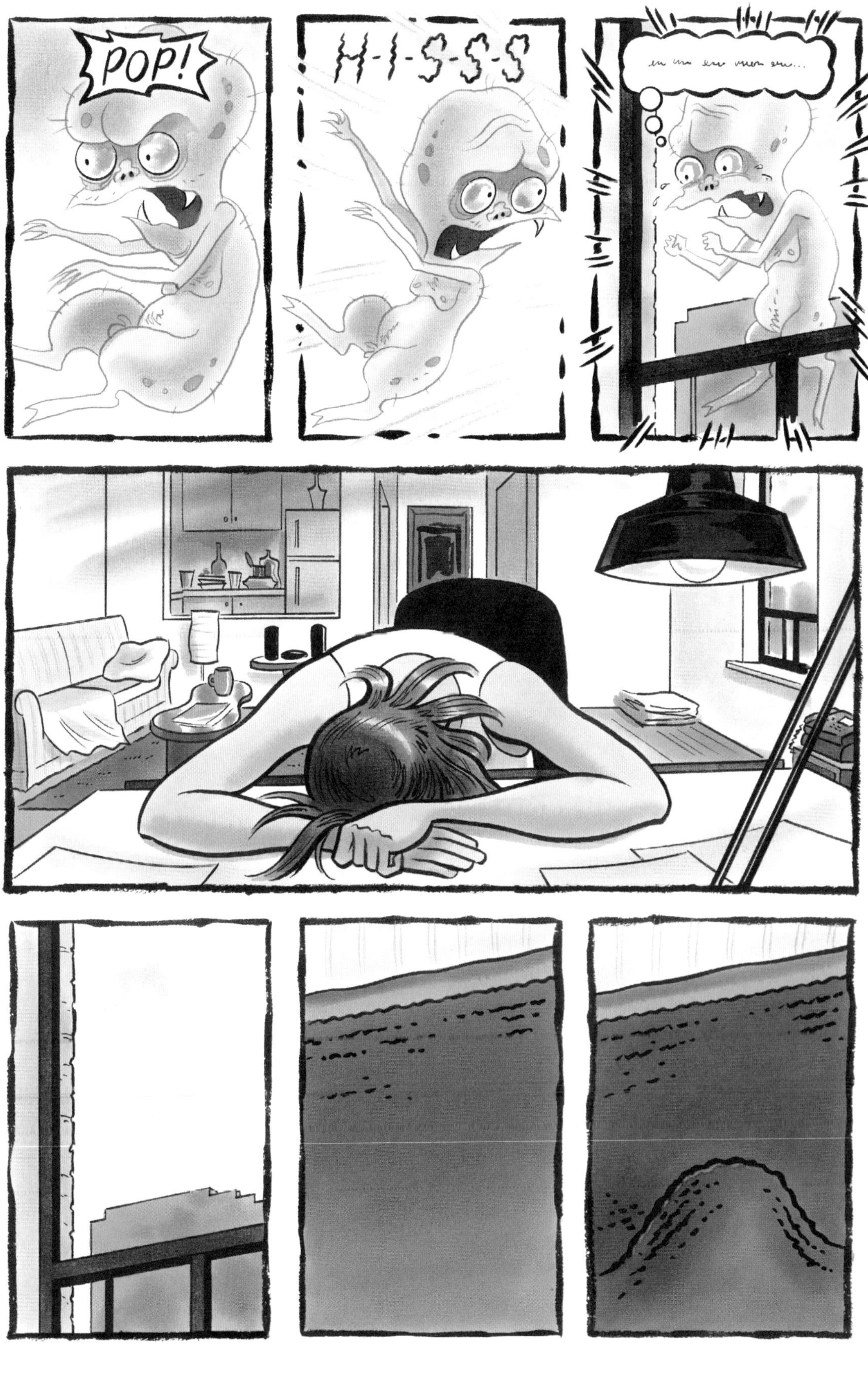
POP!
H-I-S-S-S

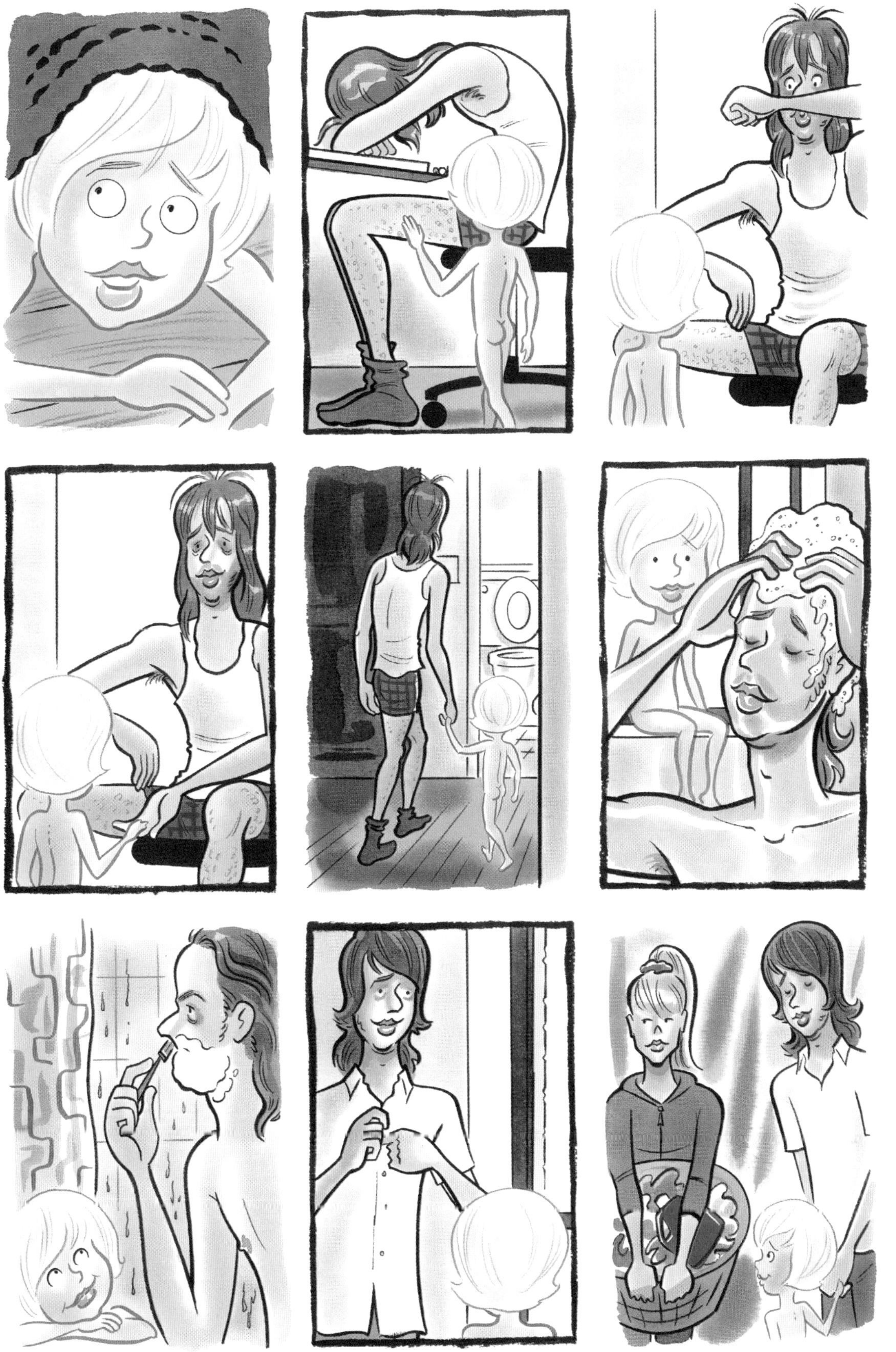

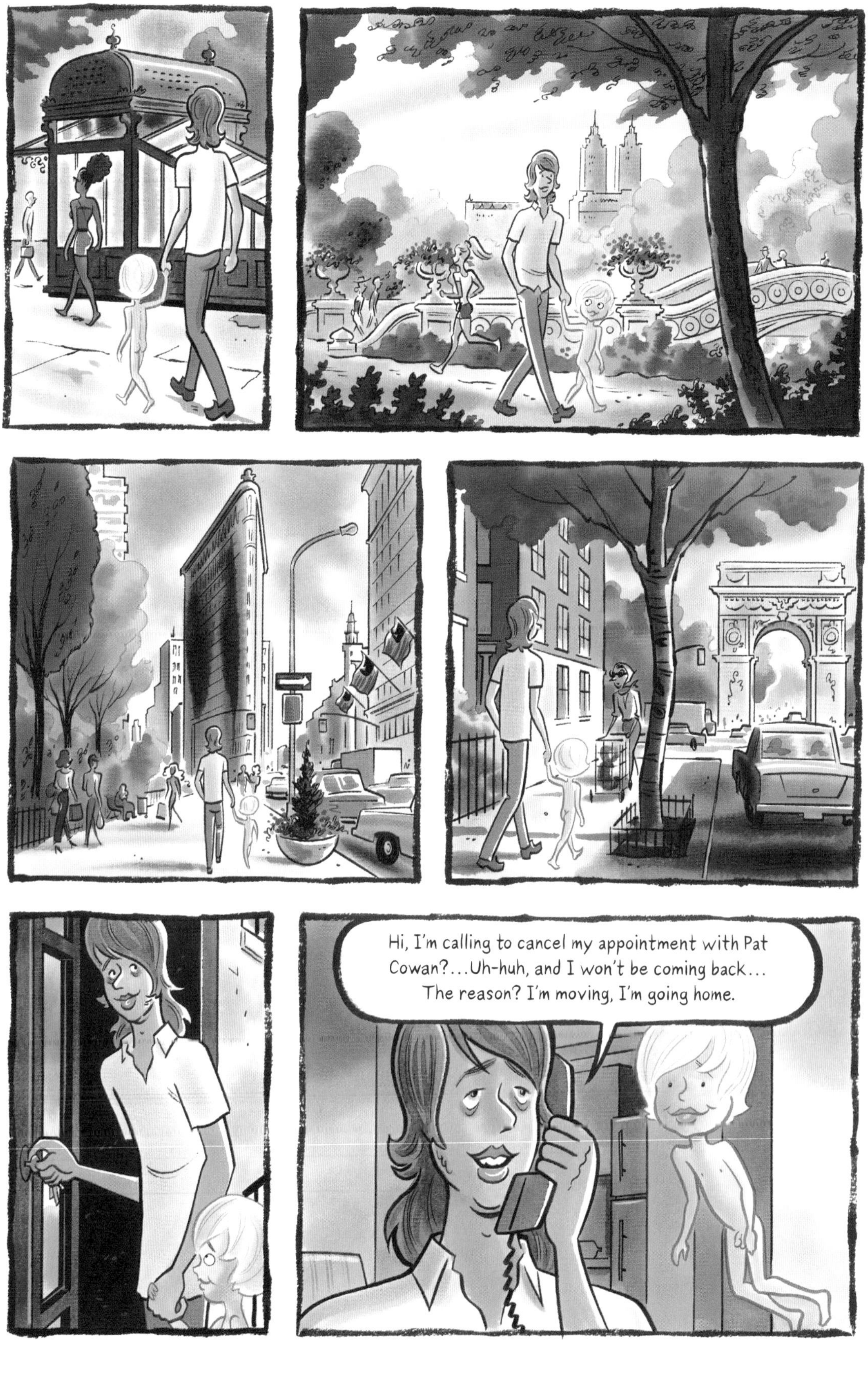
Hi, I'm calling to cancel my appointment with Pat Cowan?...Uh-huh, and I won't be coming back... The reason? I'm moving, I'm going home.

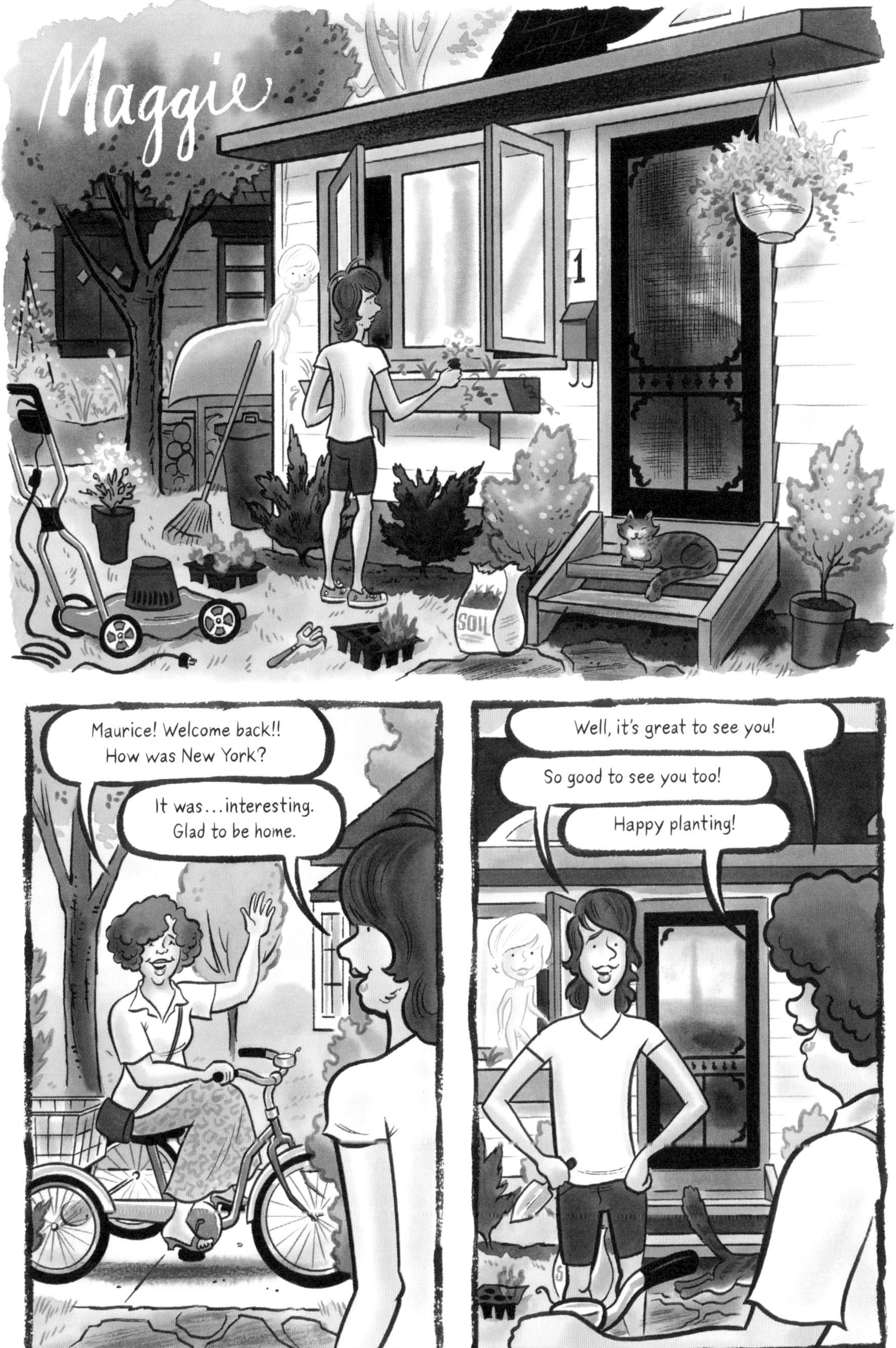
Maggie
1
SOIL
Maurice! Welcome back!! How was New York?
It was...interesting. Glad to be home.
Well, it's great to see you!
So good to see you too!
Happy planting!

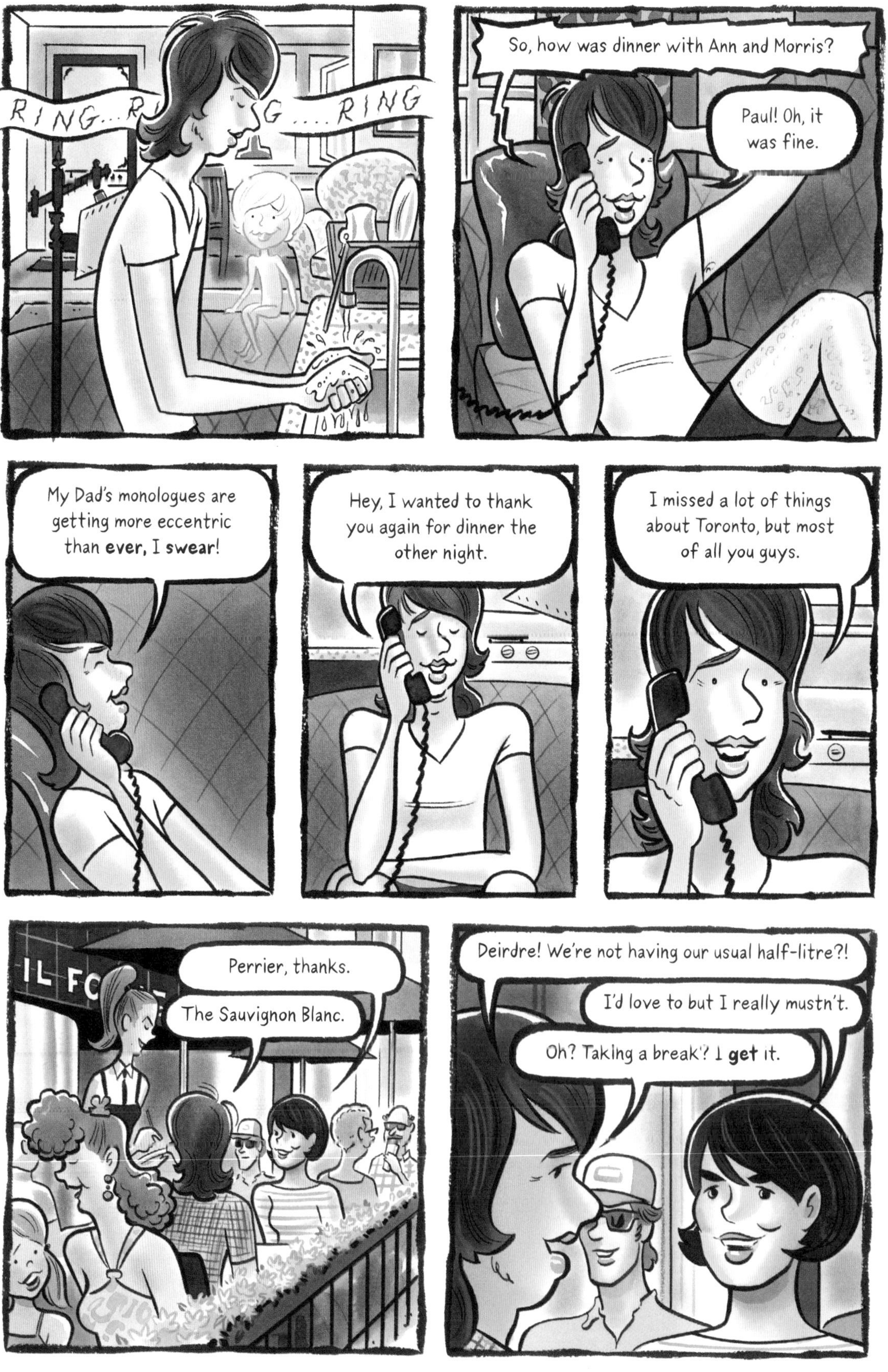
RING...RI
G....RING
So, how was dinner with Ann and Morris?
Paul! Oh, it was fine.
My Dad's monologues are getting more eccentric than **ever**, I **swear**!
Hey, I wanted to thank you again for dinner the other night.
I missed a lot of things about Toronto, but most of all you guys.
Perrier, thanks.
The Sauvignon Blanc.
Deirdre! We're not having our usual half-litre?!
I'd love to but I really mustn't.
Oh? Taking a break? I **get** it.

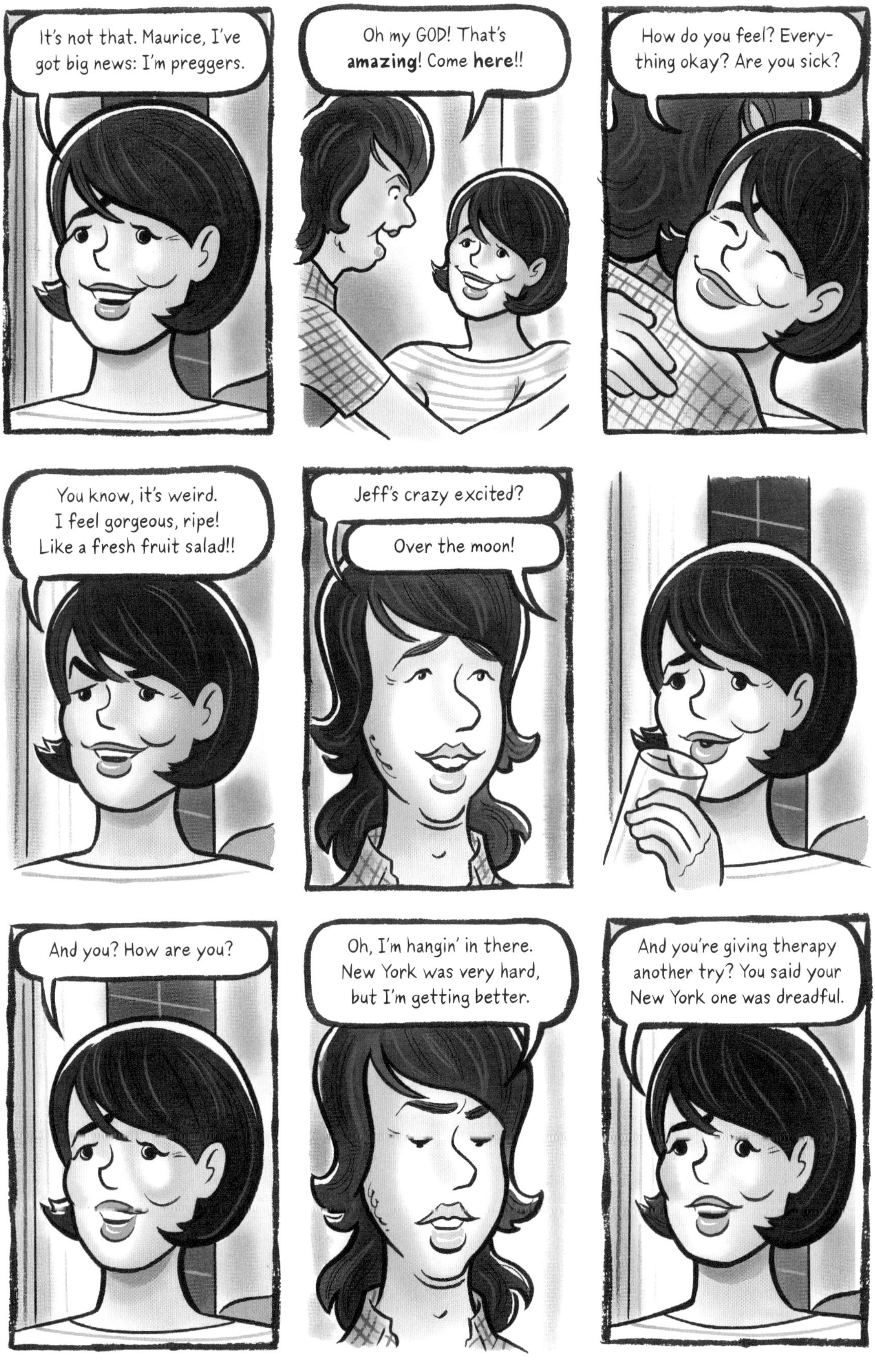
It's not that. Maurice, I've got big news: I'm preggers.
Oh my GOD! That's **amazing**! Come **here**!!
How do you feel? Every-thing okay? Are you sick?
You know, it's weird. I feel gorgeous, ripe! Like a fresh fruit salad!!
Jeff's crazy excited?
Over the moon!
And you? How are you?
Oh, I'm hangin' in there. New York was very hard, but I'm getting better.
And you're giving therapy another try? You said your New York one was dreadful.

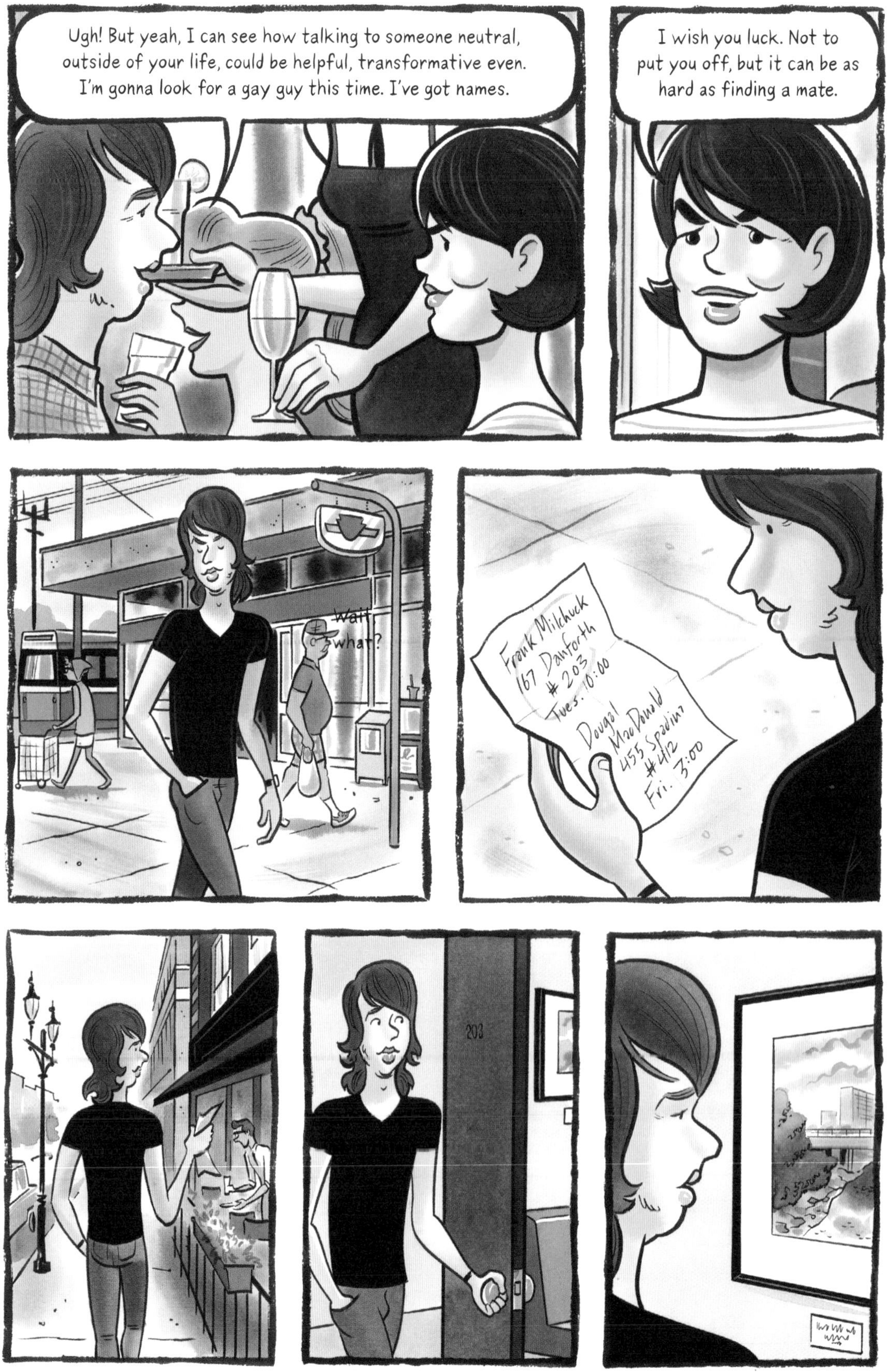
Ugh! But yeah, I can see how talking to someone neutral, outside of your life, could be helpful, transformative even. I'm gonna look for a gay guy this time. I've got names.
I wish you luck. Not to put you off, but it can be as hard as finding a mate.
Wait, what?
Frank Milchuck
167 Danforth
203
Tues. 10:00
Dougal MacDonald
455 Spadina
412
Fri. 3:00
203

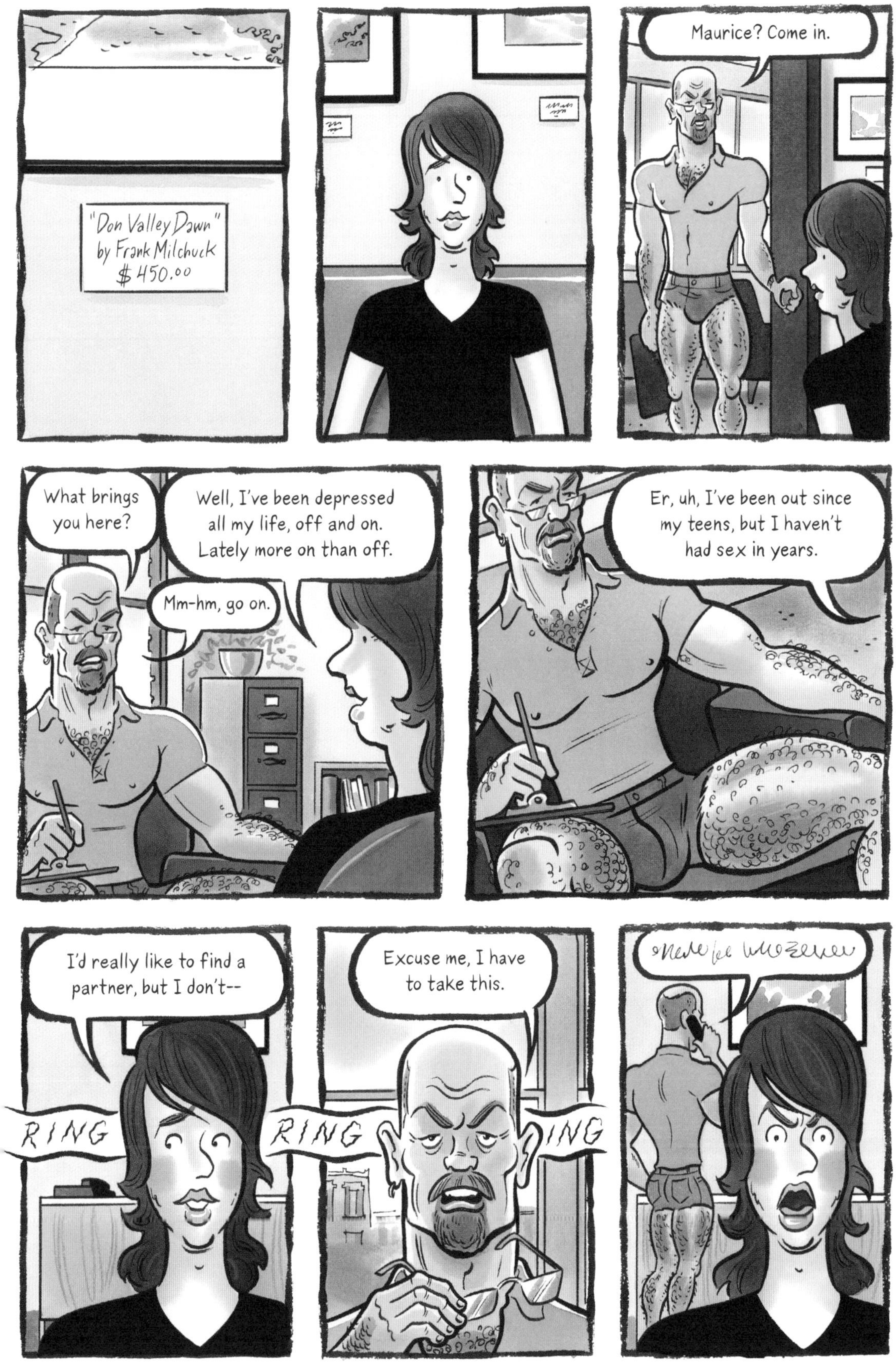
"Don Valley Dawn"
by Frank Milchuck
$450.00
Maurice? Come in.
What brings you here?
Well, I've been depressed all my life, off and on. Lately more on than off.
Mm-hm, go on.
Er, uh, I've been out since my teens, but I haven't had sex in years.
I'd really like to find a partner, but I don't--
RING
RING
ING
Excuse me, I have to take this.

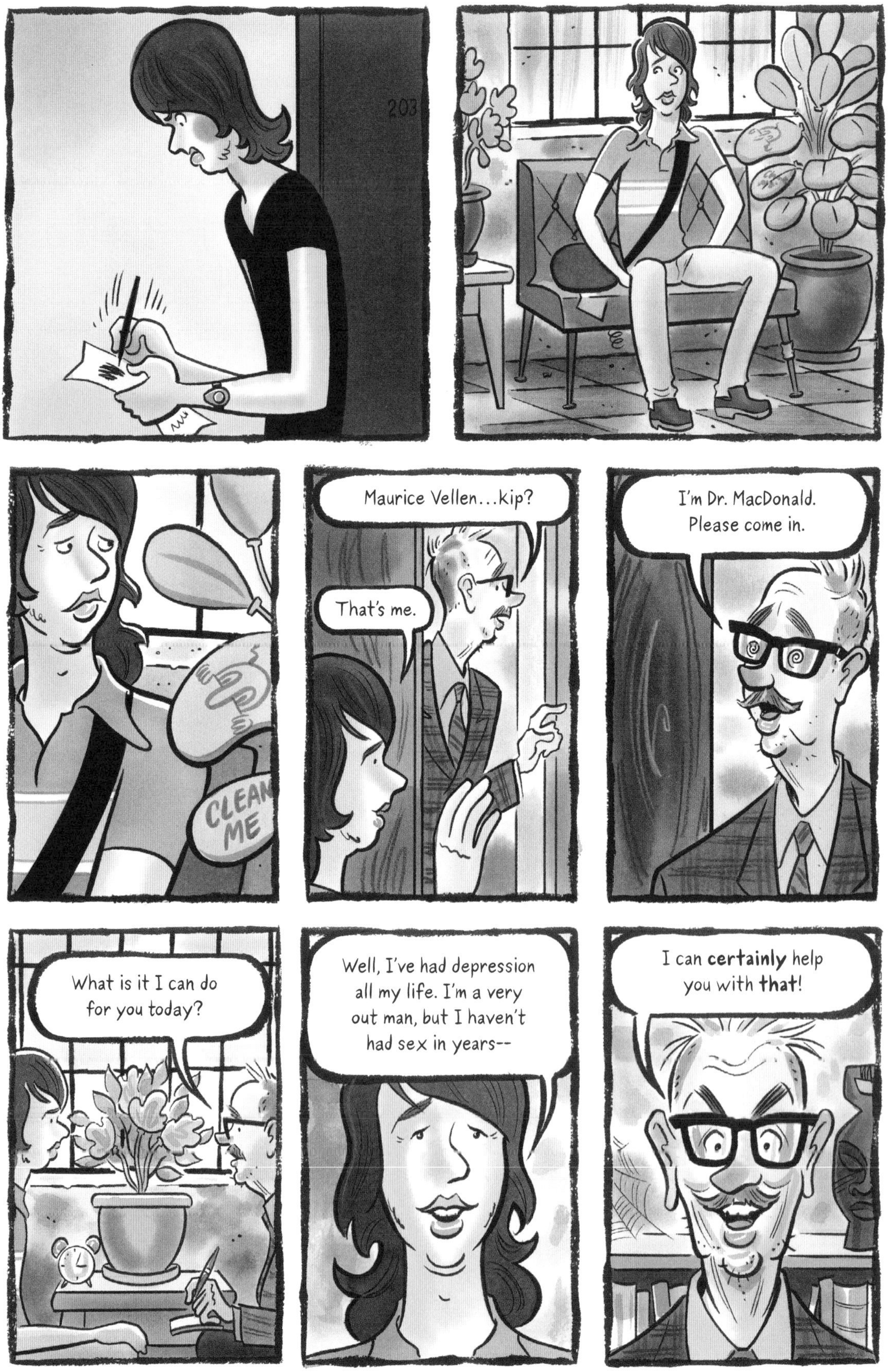

203
Maurice Vellen...kip?
That's me.
CLEAN ME
I'm Dr. MacDonald. Please come in.
What is it I can do for you today?
Well, I've had depression all my life. I'm a very out man, but I haven't had sex in years--
I can **certainly** help you with **that**!

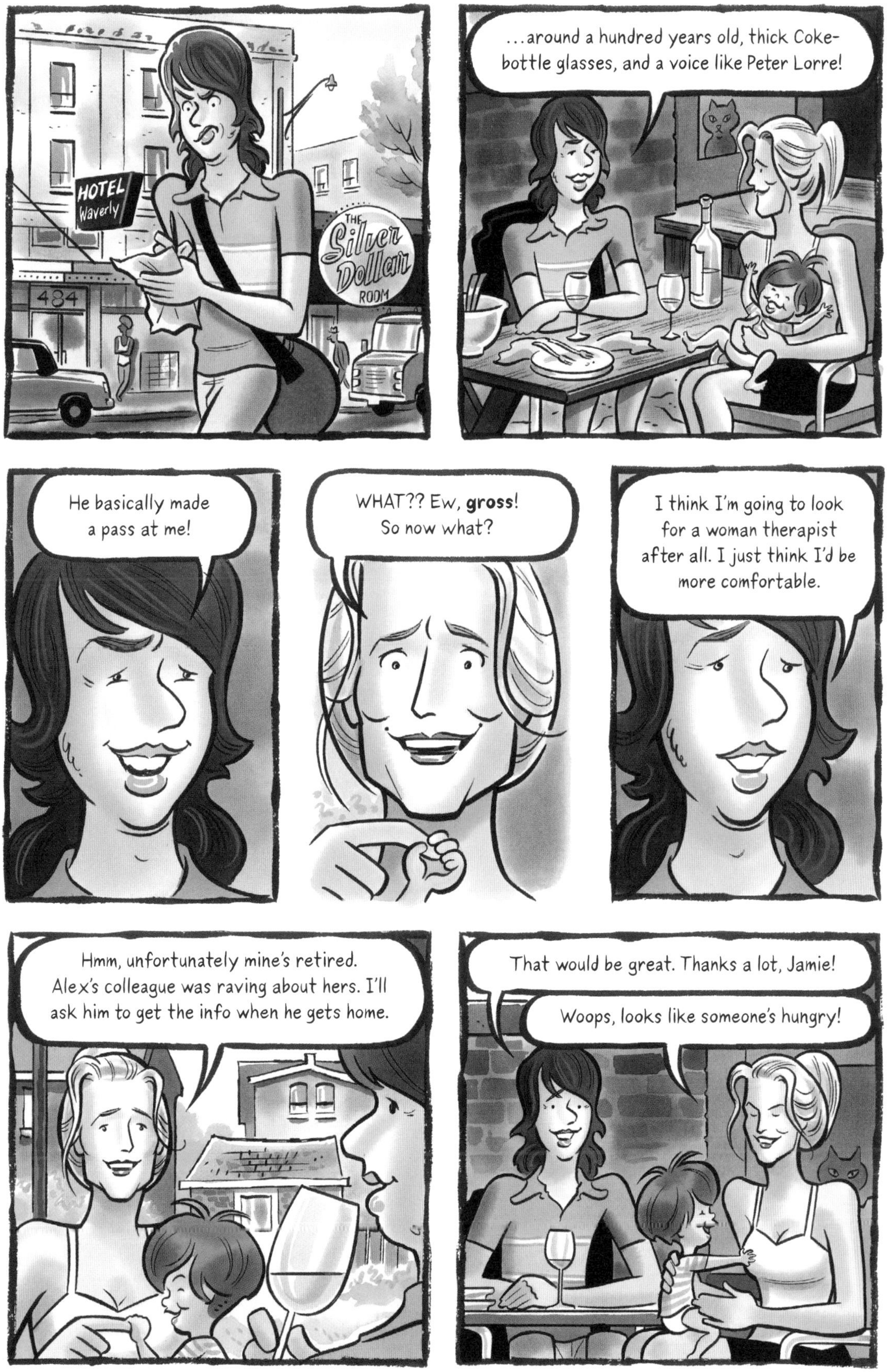
HOTEL
Waverly
484
THE
Silver
Dollar
ROOM
...around a hundred years old, thick Coke-bottle glasses, and a voice like Peter Lorre!
He basically made a pass at me!
WHAT?? Ew, **gross**! So now what?
I think I'm going to look for a woman therapist after all. I just think I'd be more comfortable.
Hmm, unfortunately mine's retired. Alex's colleague was raving about hers. I'll ask him to get the info when he gets home.
That would be great. Thanks a lot, Jamie!
Woops, looks like someone's hungry!

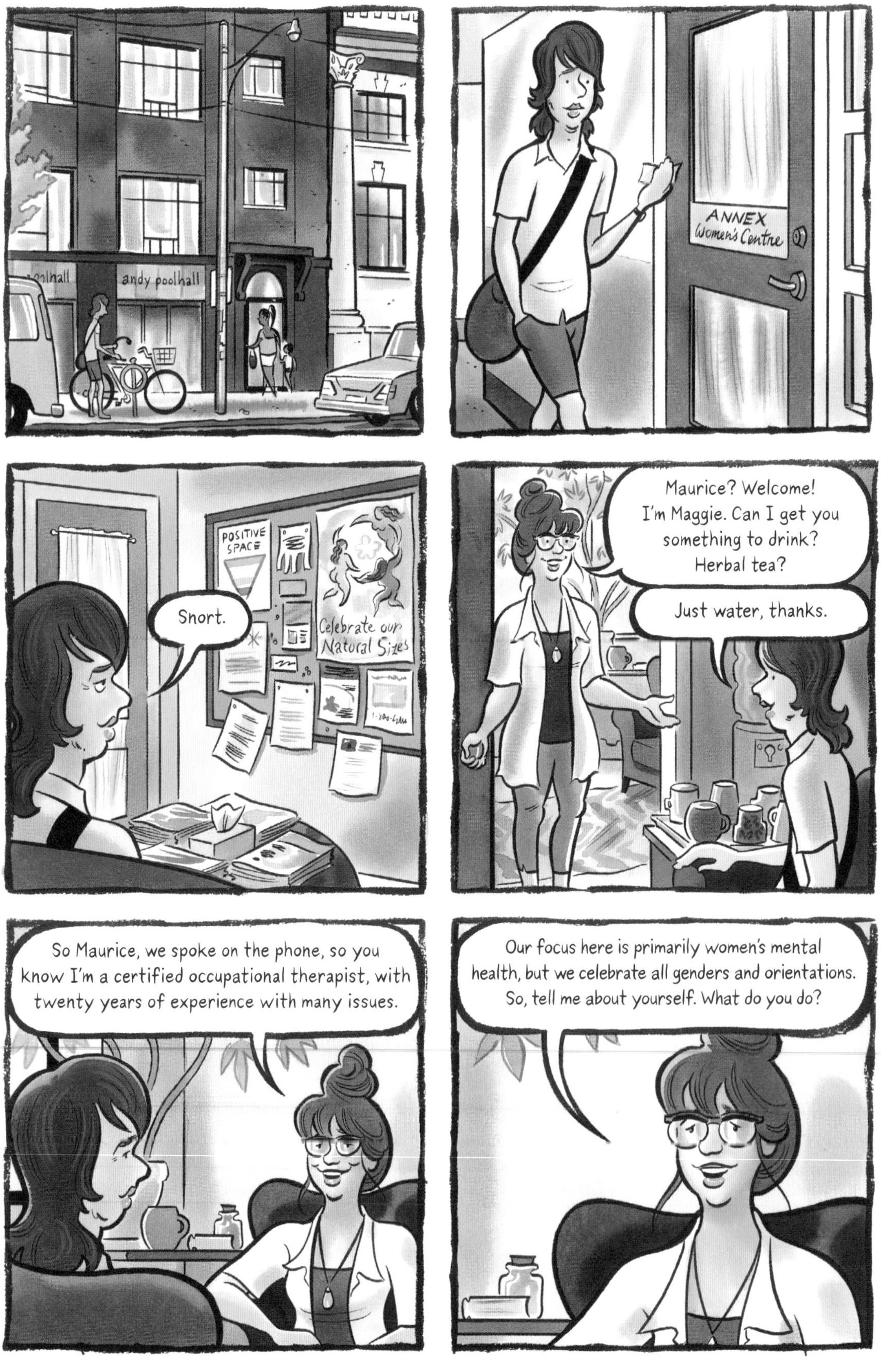
andy poolhall
ANNEX
Women's Centre
POSITIVE SPACE
Celebrate our Natural Sizes
Snort.
Maurice? Welcome! I'm Maggie. Can I get you something to drink? Herbal tea?
Just water, thanks.
So Maurice, we spoke on the phone, so you know I'm a certified occupational therapist, with twenty years of experience with many issues.
Our focus here is primarily women's mental health, but we celebrate all genders and orientations. So, tell me about yourself. What do you do?

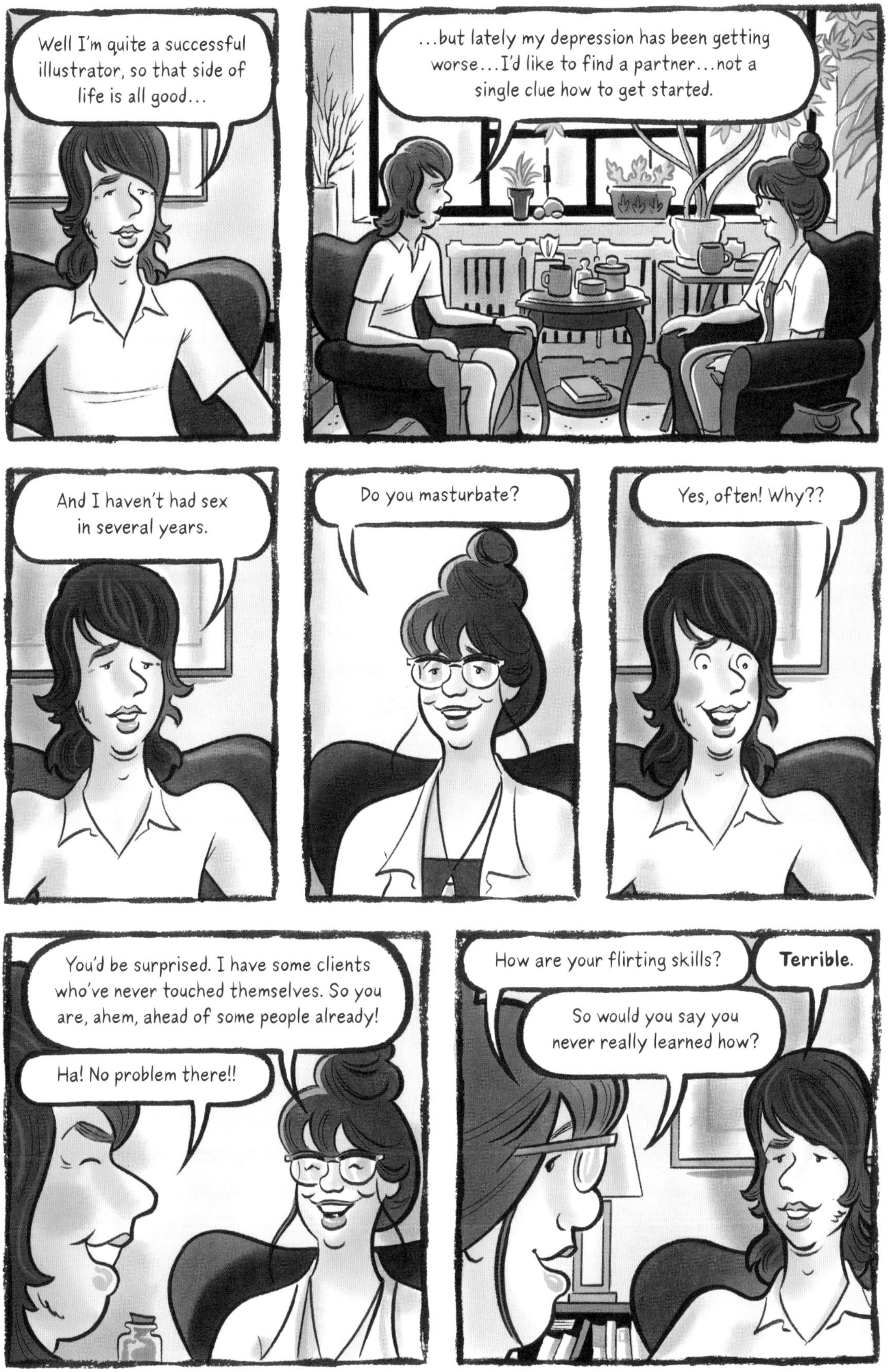
Well I'm quite a successful illustrator, so that side of life is all good...
...but lately my depression has been getting worse...I'd like to find a partner...not a single clue how to get started.
And I haven't had sex in several years.
Do you masturbate?
Yes, often! Why??
You'd be surprised. I have some clients who've never touched themselves. So you are, ahem, ahead of some people already!
Ha! No problem there!!
How are your flirting skills?
Terrible.
So would you say you never really learned how?

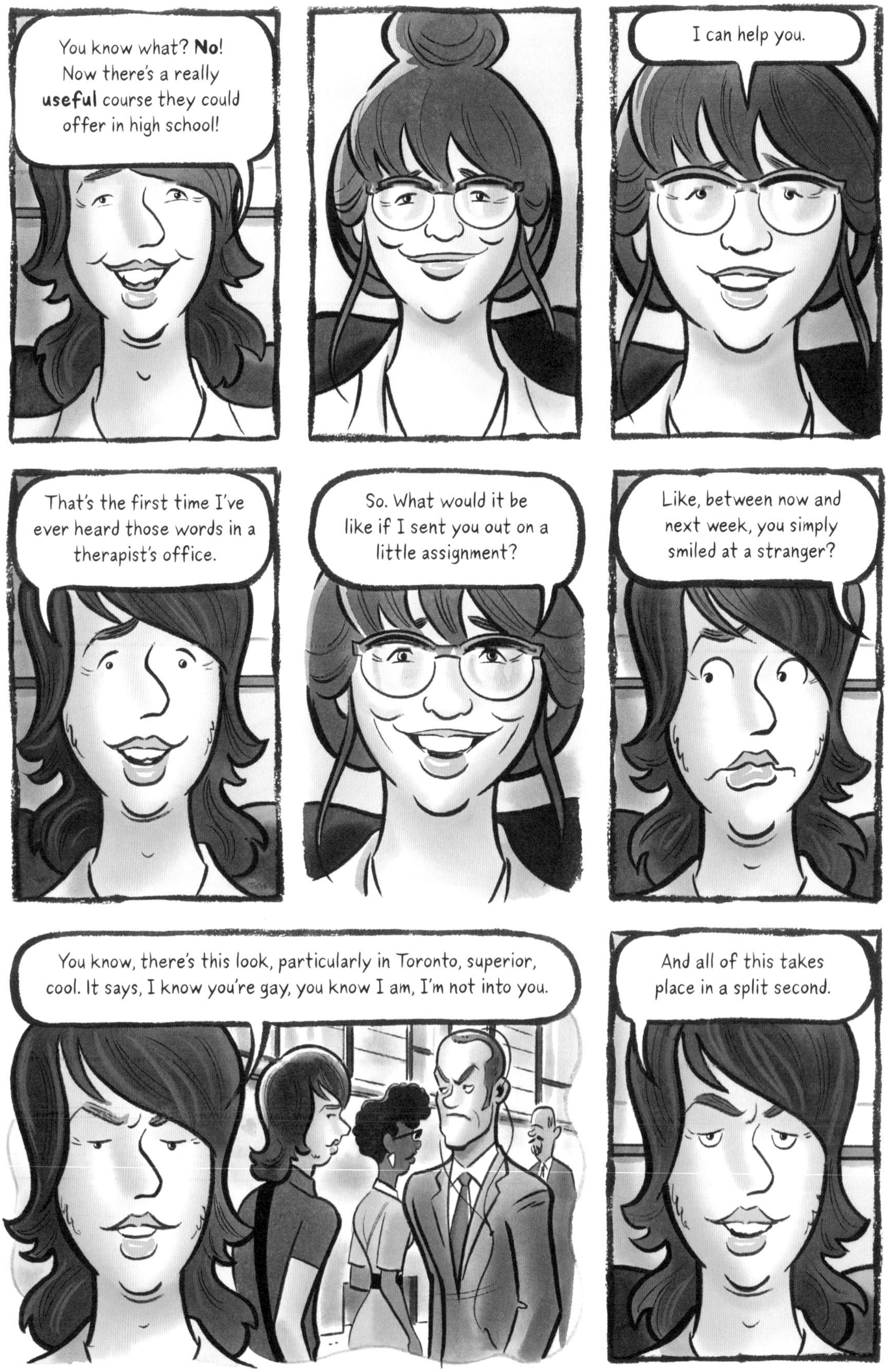
You know what? **No**! Now there's a really **useful** course they could offer in high school!
I can help you.
That's the first time I've ever heard those words in a therapist's office.
So. What would it be like if I sent you out on a little assignment?
Like, between now and next week, you simply smiled at a stranger?
You know, there's this look, particularly in Toronto, superior, cool. It says, I know you're gay, you know I am, I'm not into you.
And all of this takes place in a split second.

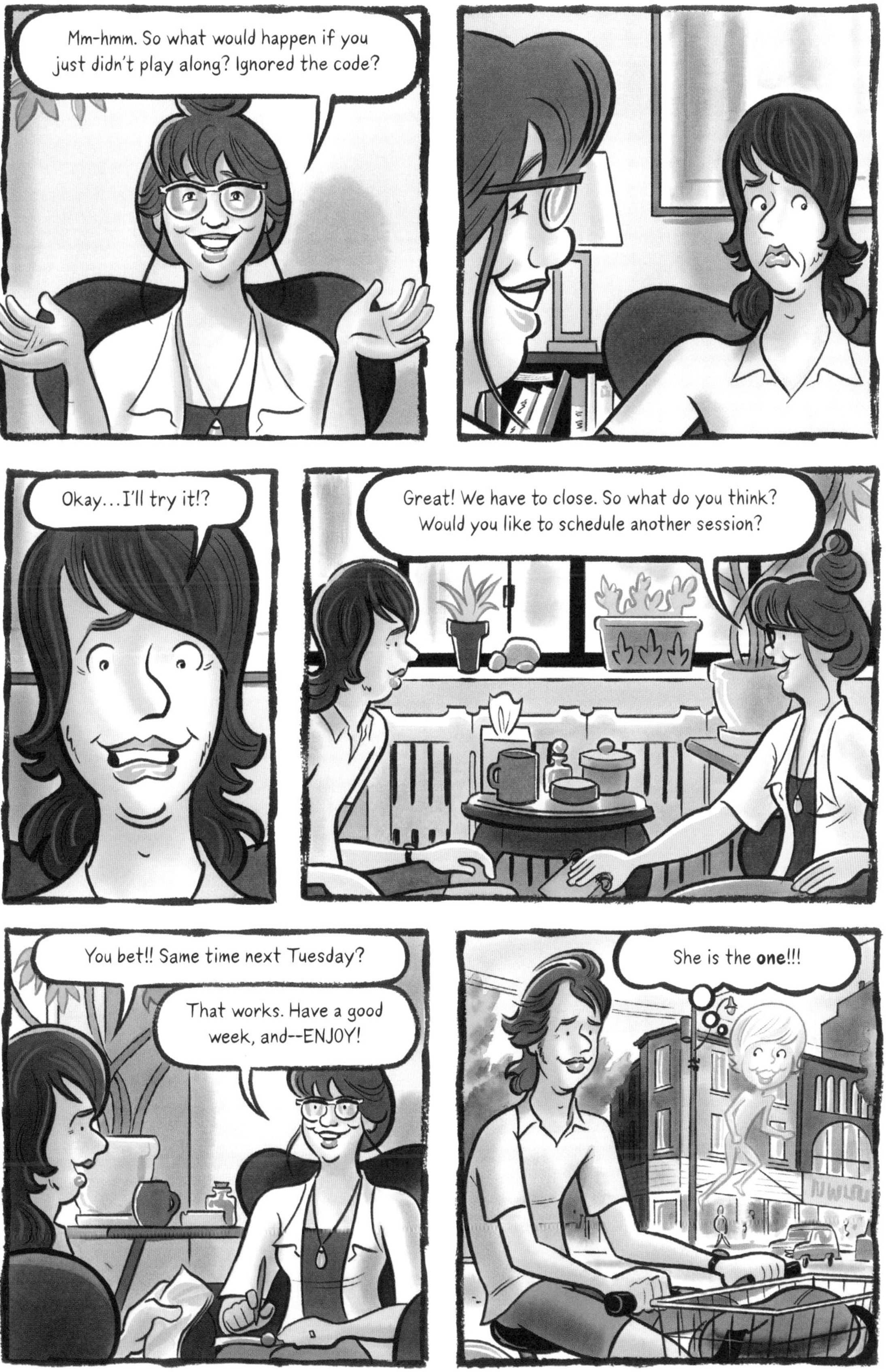
Mm-hmm. So what would happen if you just didn't play along? Ignored the code?
Okay...I'll try it!?
Great! We have to close. So what do you think? Would you like to schedule another session?
You bet!! Same time next Tuesday?
That works. Have a good week, and--ENJOY!
She is the **one**!!!

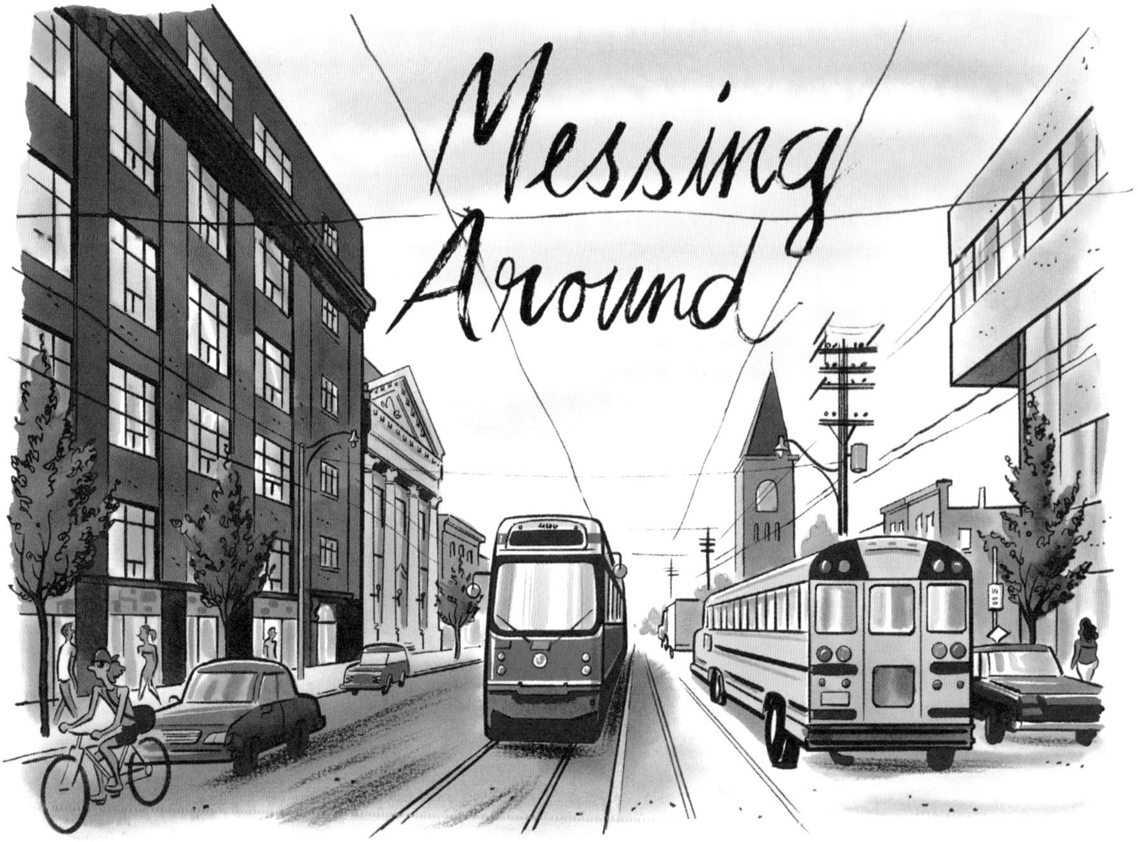
Messing Around

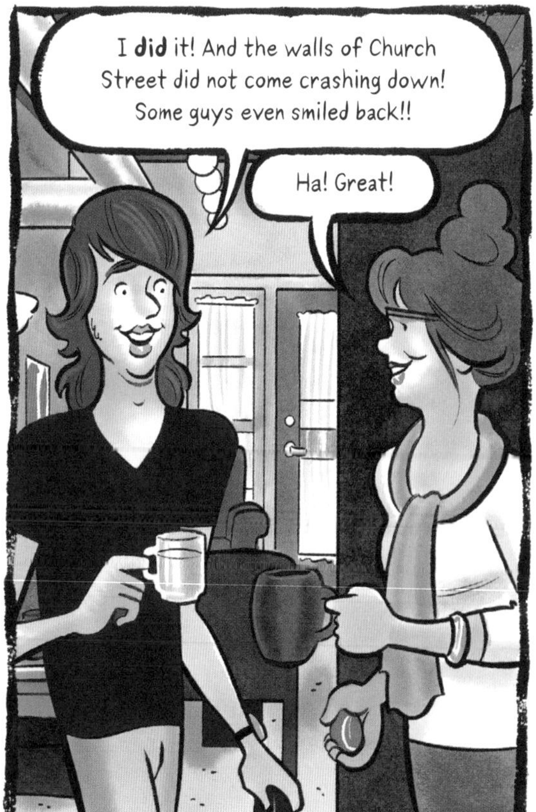
I **did** it! And the walls of Church Street did not come crashing down! Some guys even smiled back!!
Ha! Great!

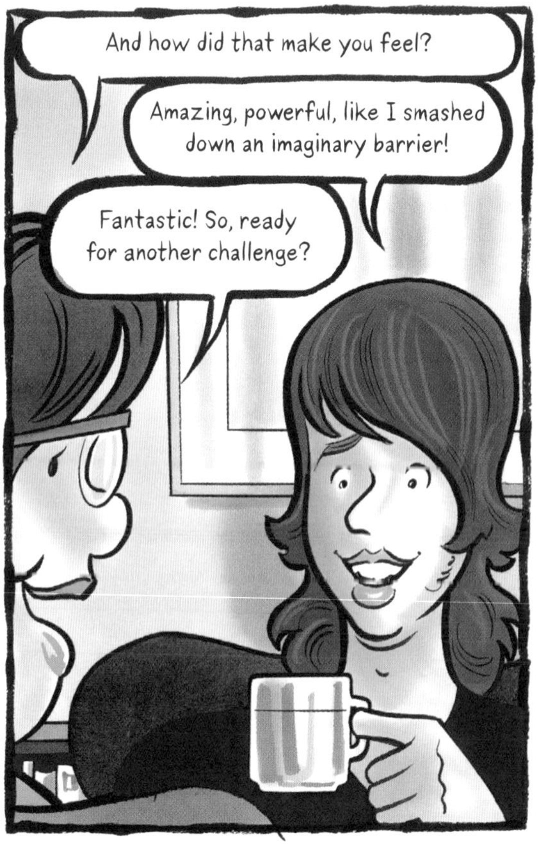
And how did that make you feel?
Amazing, powerful, like I smashed down an imaginary barrier!
Fantastic! So, ready for another challenge?

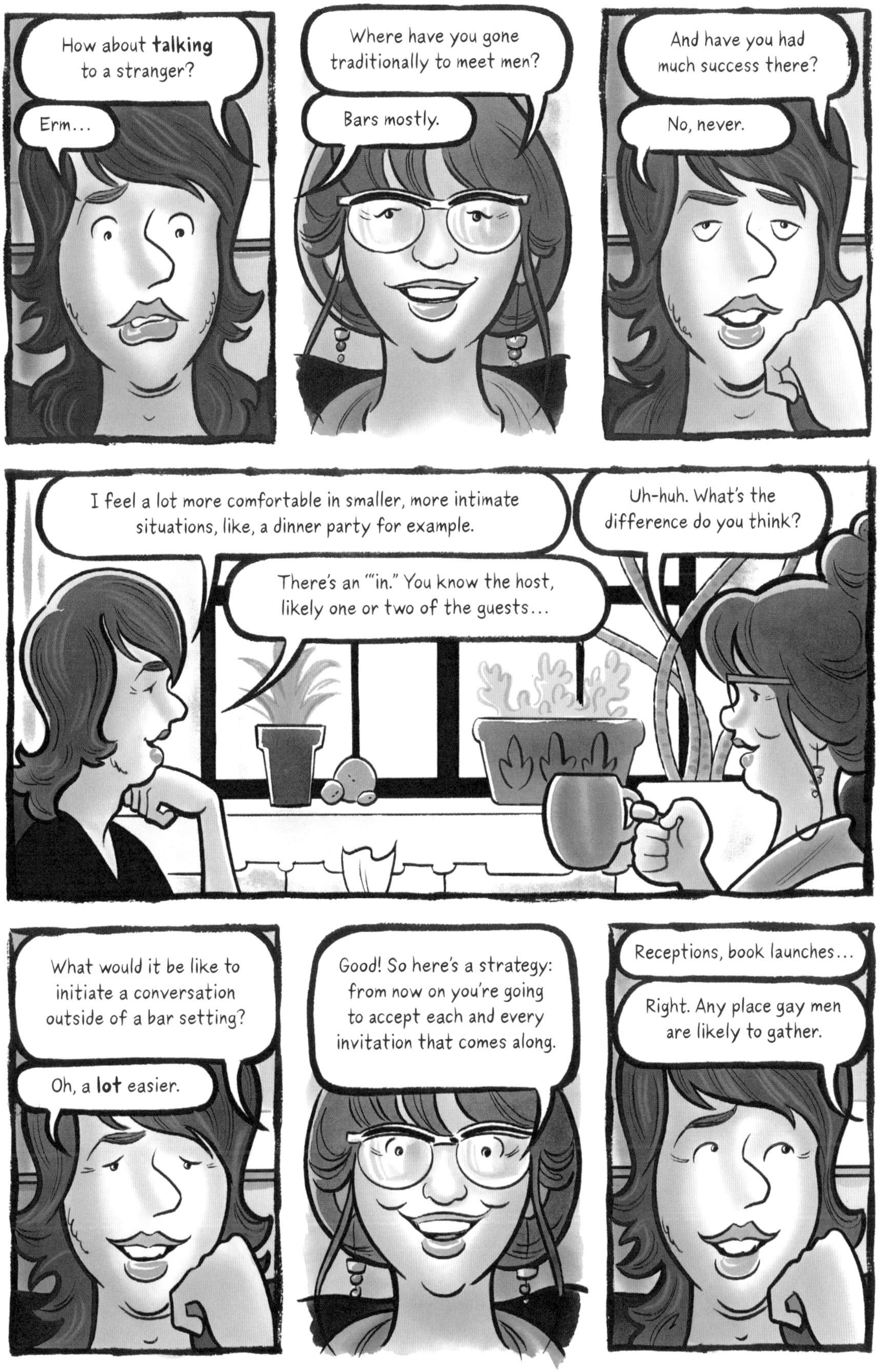
How about **talking** to a stranger?
Erm...
Where have you gone traditionally to meet men?
Bars mostly.
And have you had much success there?
No, never.
I feel a lot more comfortable in smaller, more intimate situations, like, a dinner party for example.
Uh-huh. What's the difference do you think?
There's an ""in." You know the host, likely one or two of the guests...
What would it be like to initiate a conversation outside of a bar setting?
Oh, a **lot** easier.
Good! So here's a strategy: from now on you're going to accept each and every invitation that comes along.
Receptions, book launches...
Right. Any place gay men are likely to gather.

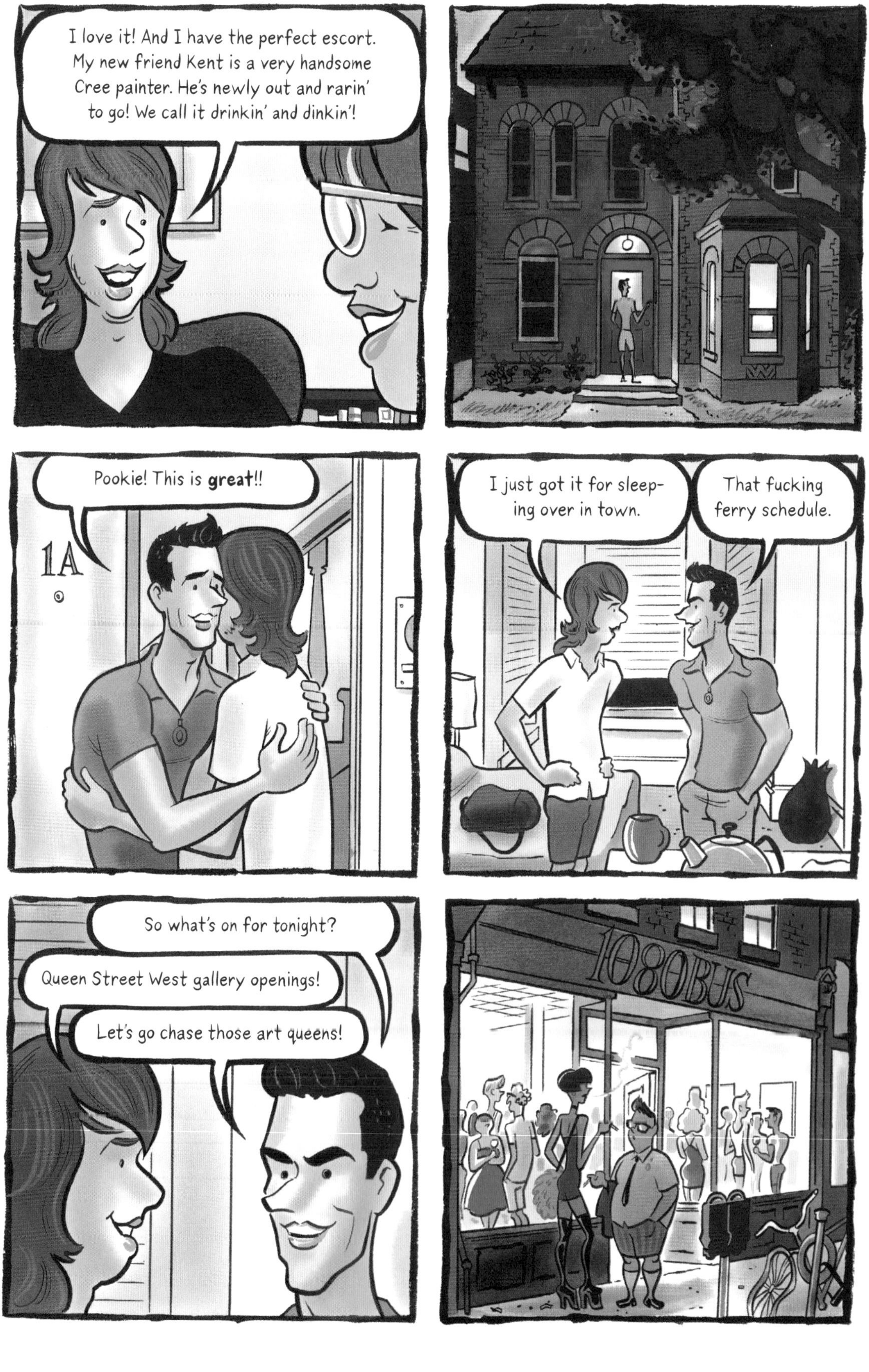
I love it! And I have the perfect escort. My new friend Kent is a very handsome Cree painter. He's newly out and rarin' to go! We call it drinkin' and dinkin'!
Pookie! This is **great**!!
1A
I just got it for sleep-ing over in town.
That fucking ferry schedule.
So what's on for tonight?
Queen Street West gallery openings!
Let's go chase those art queens!
1080BUS

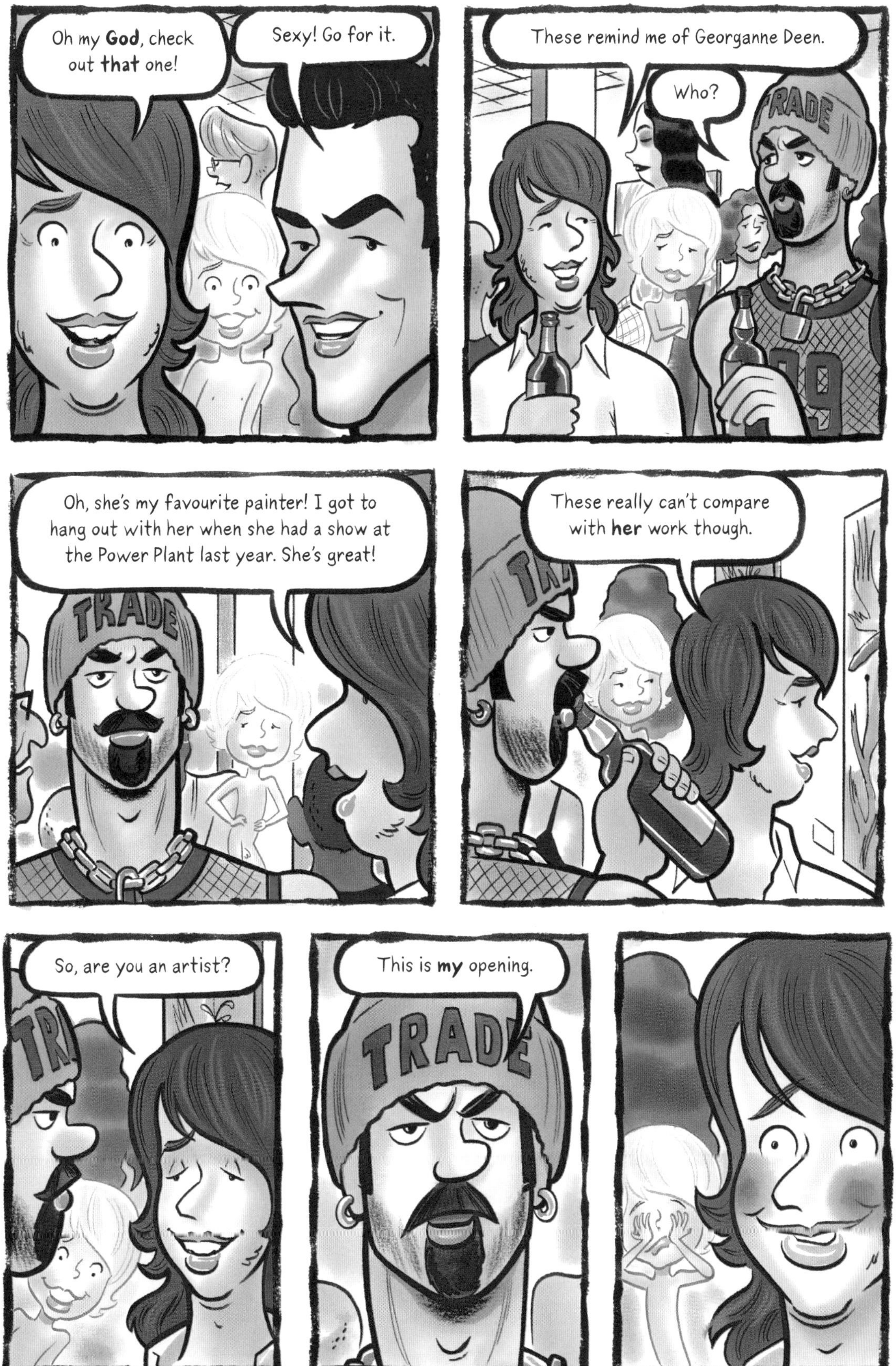
Oh my **God**, check out **that** one!
Sexy! Go for it.
These remind me of Georganne Deen.
Who?
TRADE
Oh, she's my favourite painter! I got to hang out with her when she had a show at the Power Plant last year. She's great!
TRADE
These really can't compare with **her** work though.
So, are you an artist?
This is **my** opening.
TRADE

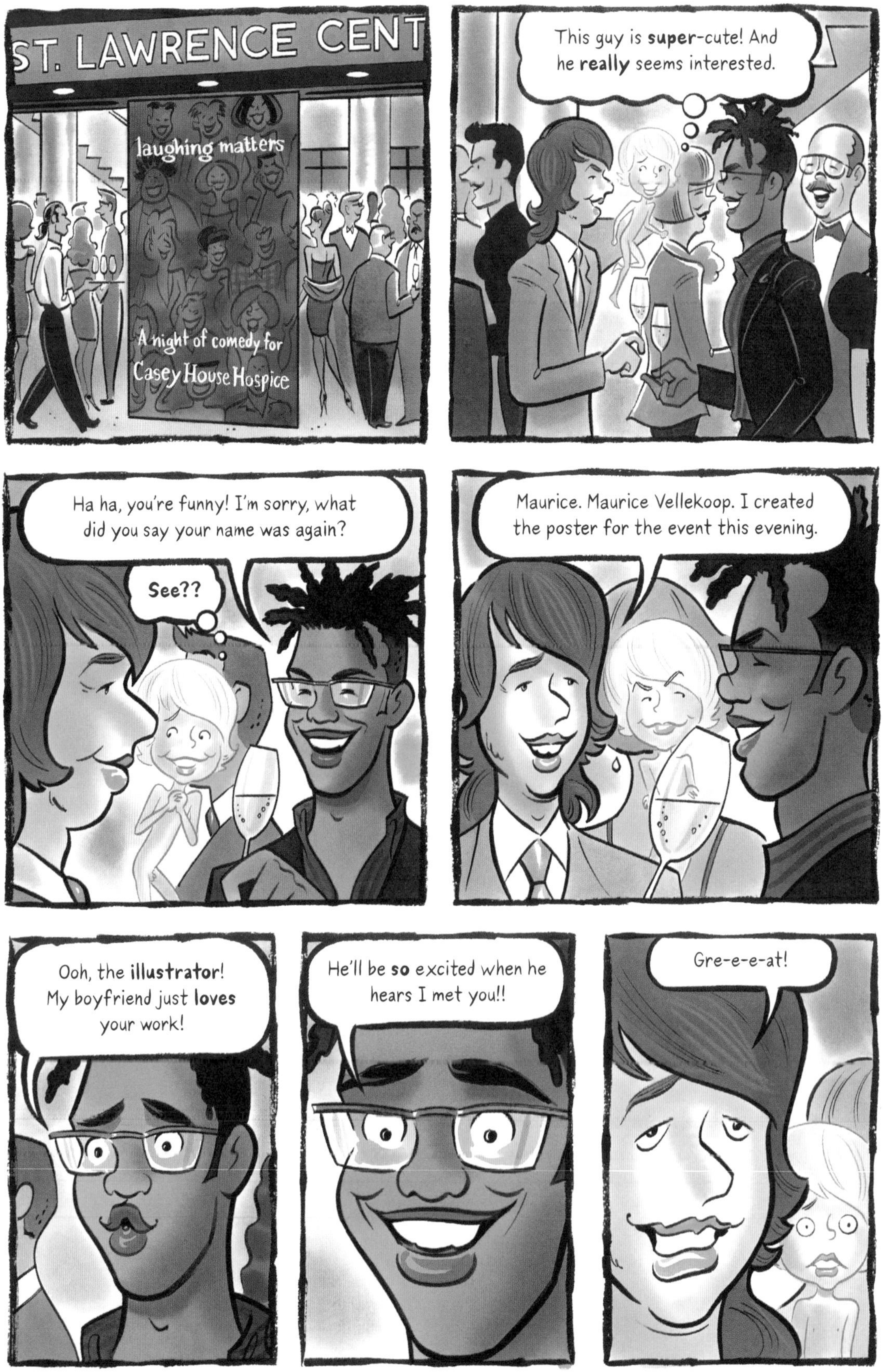
ST. LAWRENCE CENT
laughing matters
A night of comedy for
Casey House Hospice
This guy is **super**-cute! And he **really** seems interested.
Ha ha, you're funny! I'm sorry, what did you say your name was again?
See??
Maurice. Maurice Vellekoop. I created the poster for the event this evening.
Ooh, the **illustrator**! My boyfriend just **loves** your work!
He'll be **so** excited when he hears I met you!!
Gre-e-e-at!

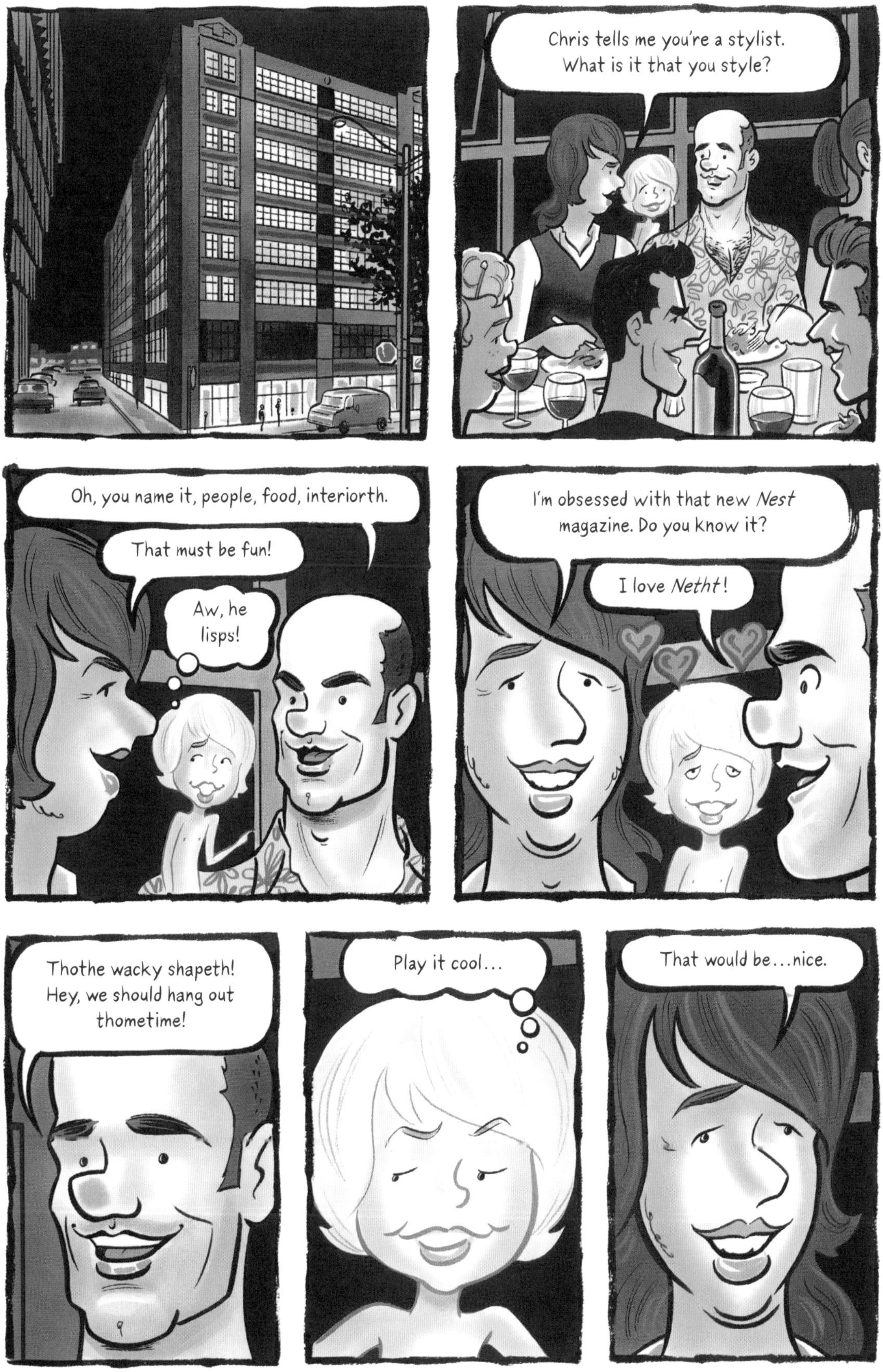
Chris tells me you're a stylist. What is it that you style?
Oh, you name it, people, food, interiorth.
That must be fun!
Aw, he lisps!
I'm obsessed with that new *Nest* magazine. Do you know it?
I love *Netht*!
Thothe wacky shapeth! Hey, we should hang out thometime!
Play it cool...
That would be...nice.

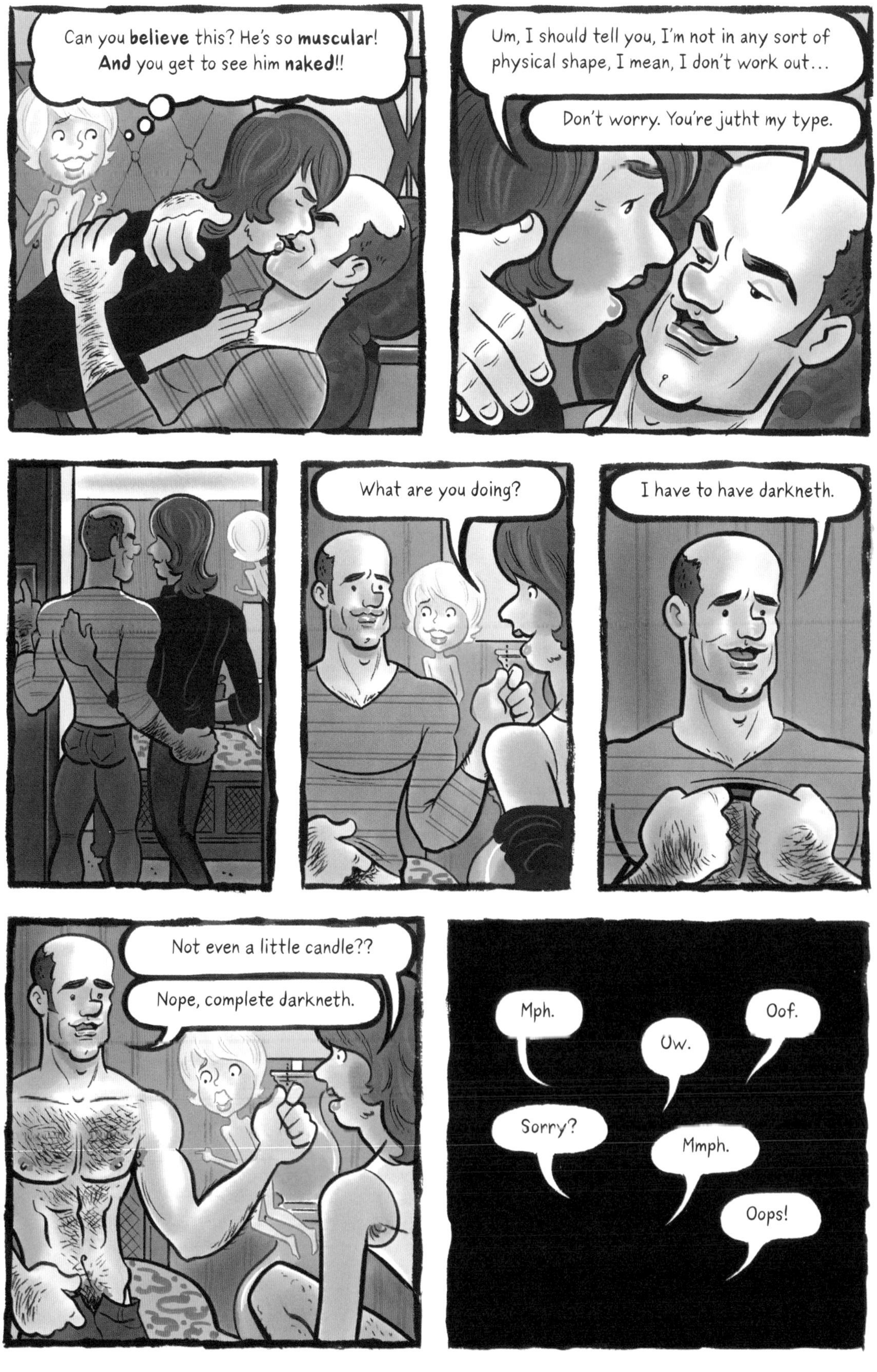
Can you **believe** this? He's so **muscular**! **And** you get to see him **naked**!!
Um, I should tell you, I'm not in any sort of physical shape, I mean, I don't work out...
Don't worry. You're jutht my type.
What are you doing?
I have to have darkneth.
Not even a little candle??
Nope, complete darkneth.
Mph.
Ow.
Oof.
Sorry?
Mmph.
Oops!

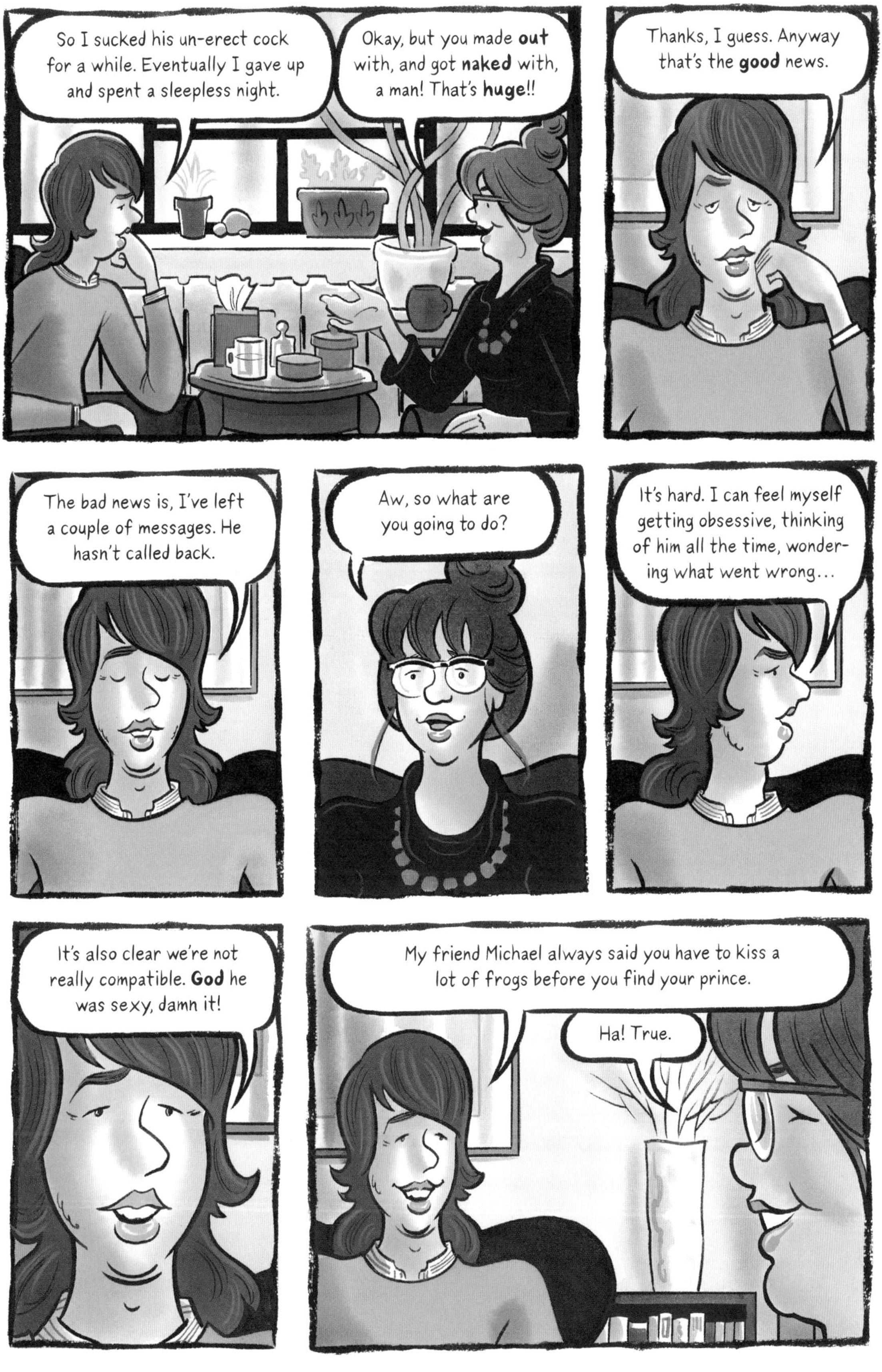
So I sucked his un-erect cock for a while. Eventually I gave up and spent a sleepless night.
Okay, but you made **out** with, and got **naked** with, a man! That's **huge**!!
Thanks, I guess. Anyway that's the **good** news.
The bad news is, I've left a couple of messages. He hasn't called back.
Aw, so what are you going to do?
It's hard. I can feel myself getting obsessive, thinking of him all the time, wondering what went wrong...
It's also clear we're not really compatible. **God** he was sexy, damn it!
My friend Michael always said you have to kiss a lot of frogs before you find your prince.
Ha! True.

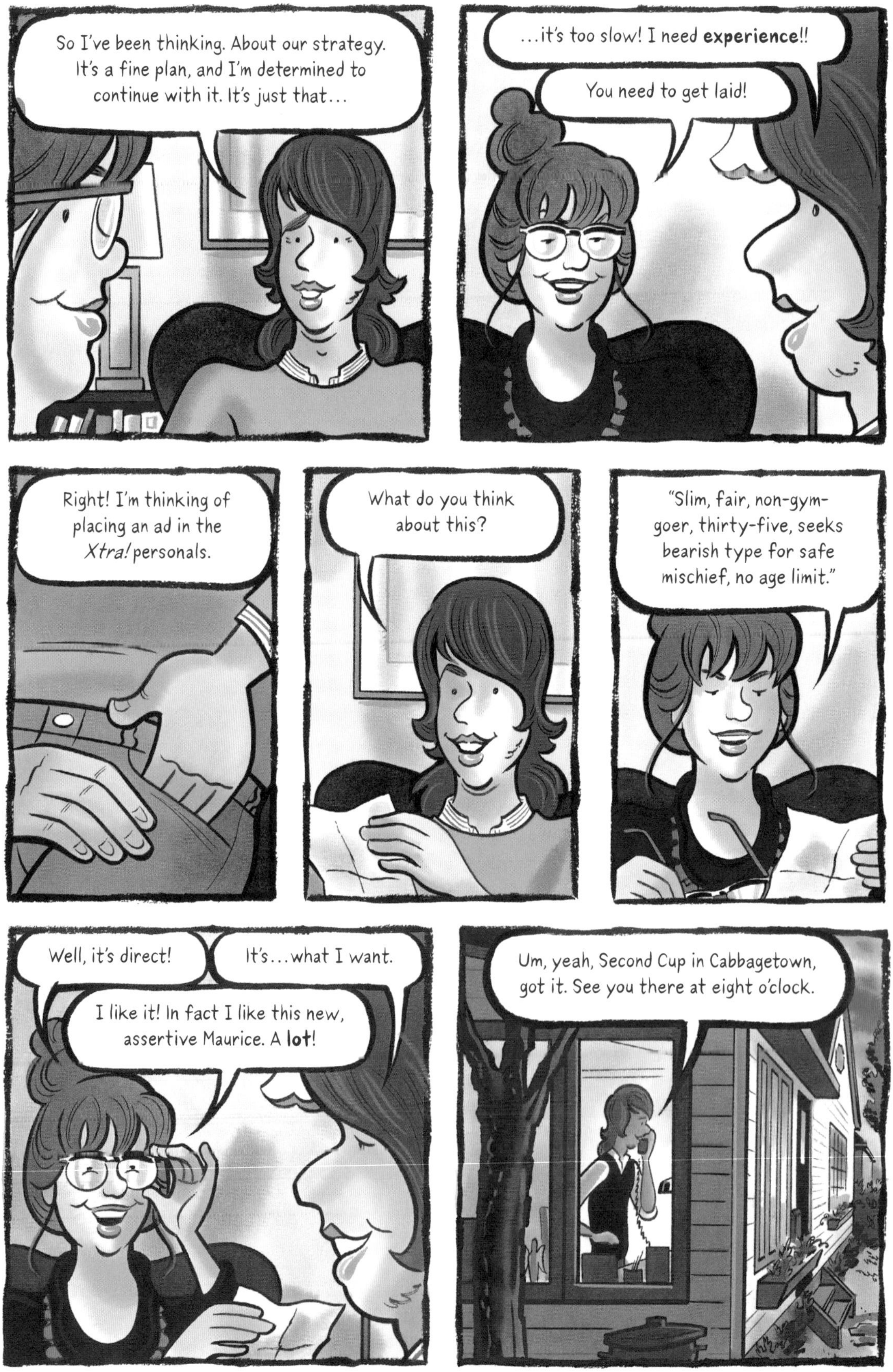
So I've been thinking. About our strategy. It's a fine plan, and I'm determined to continue with it. It's just that...
...it's too slow! I need **experience**!!
You need to get laid!
Right! I'm thinking of placing an ad in the *Xtra!* personals.
What do you think about this?
"Slim, fair, non-gym-goer, thirty-five, seeks bearish type for safe mischief, no age limit."
Well, it's direct!
It's...what I want.
I like it! In fact I like this new, assertive Maurice. A **lot**!
Um, yeah, Second Cup in Cabbagetown, got it. See you there at eight o'clock.

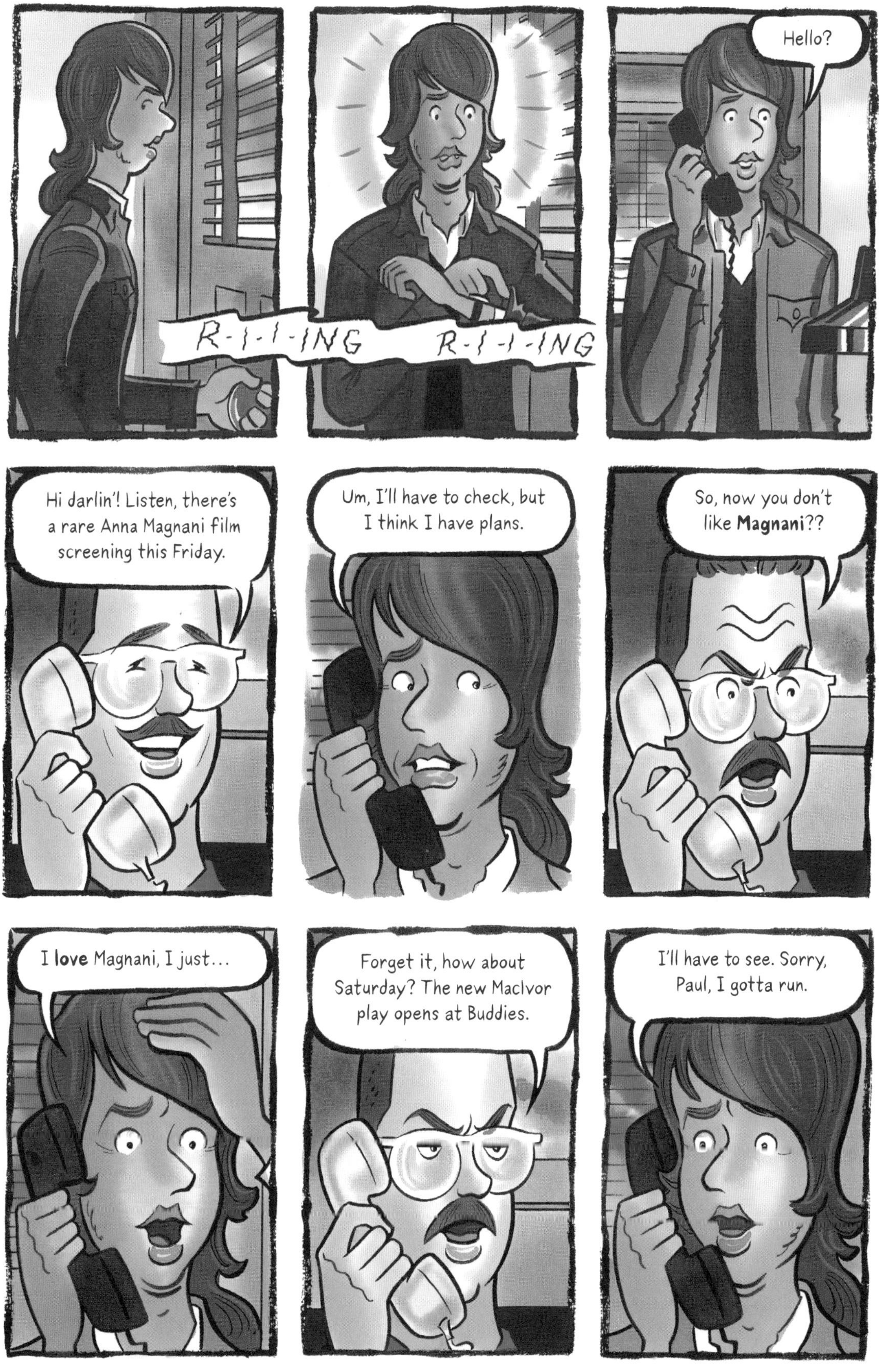
R-I-I-ING
R-I-I-ING
Hello?
Hi darlin'! Listen, there's a rare Anna Magnani film screening this Friday.
Um, I'll have to check, but I think I have plans.
So, now you don't like **Magnani**??
I **love** Magnani, I just...
Forget it, how about Saturday? The new MacIvor play opens at Buddies.
I'll have to see. Sorry, Paul, I gotta run.

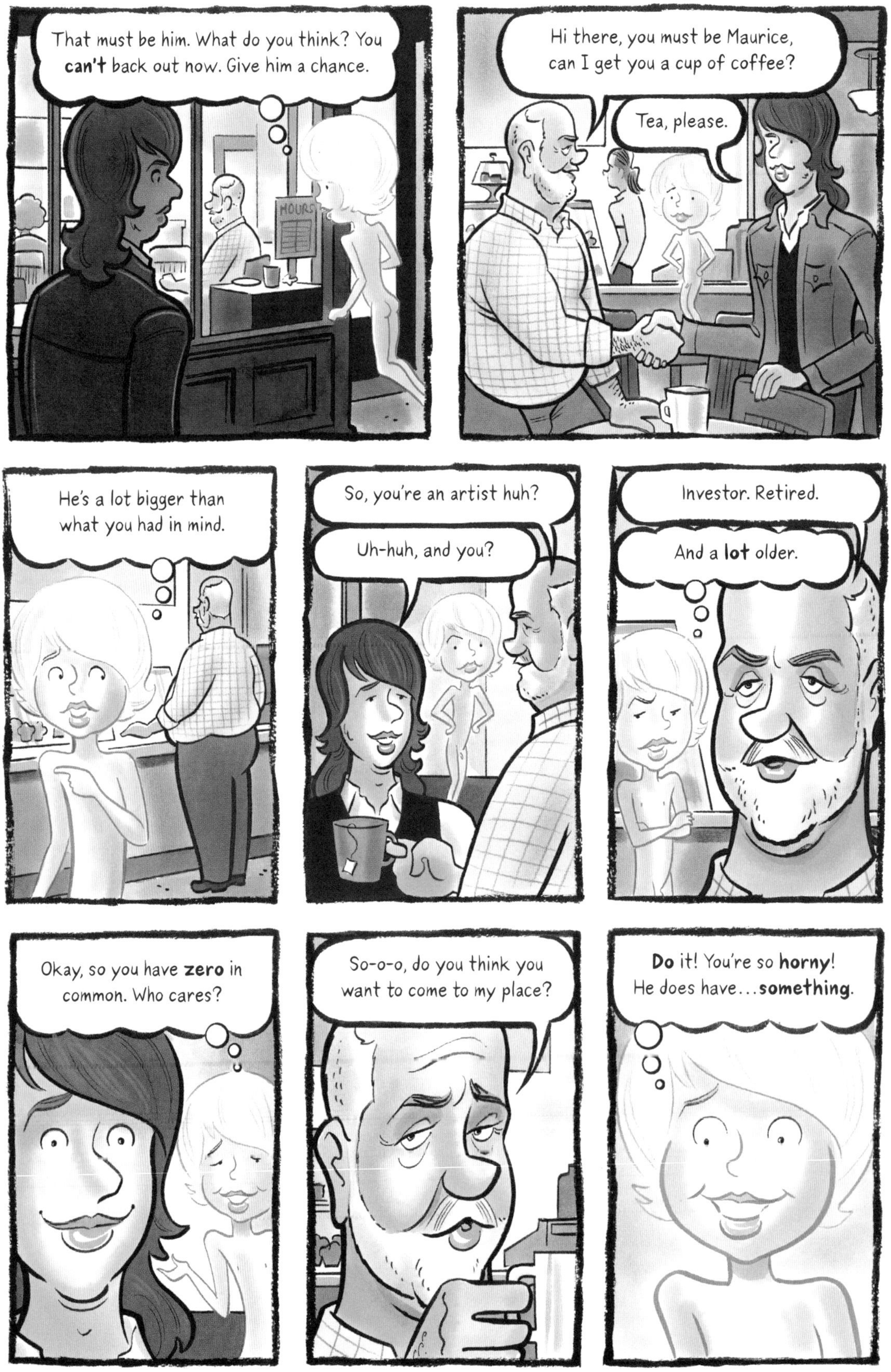
That must be him. What do you think? You **can't** back out now. Give him a chance.
HOURS
Hi there, you must be Maurice, can I get you a cup of coffee?
Tea, please.
He's a lot bigger than what you had in mind.
So, you're an artist huh?
Uh-huh, and you?
Investor. Retired.
And a **lot** older.
Okay, so you have **zero** in common. Who cares?
So-o-o, do you think you want to come to my place?
Do it! You're so **horny**! He does have... **something**.

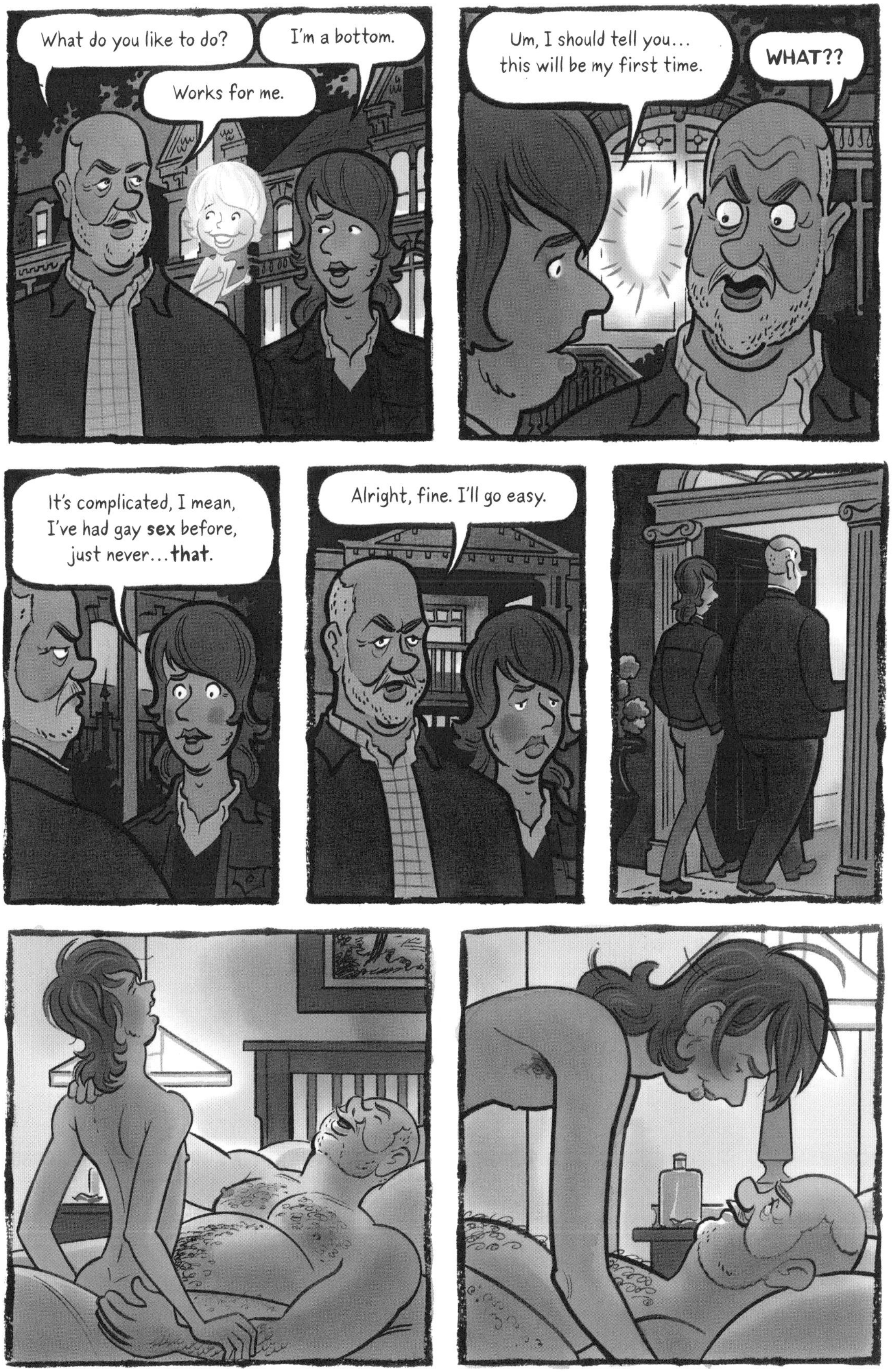
What do you like to do?
I'm a bottom.
Works for me.
Um, I should tell you... this will be my first time.
WHAT??
It's complicated, I mean, I've had gay **sex** before, just never... **that**.
Alright, fine. I'll go easy.

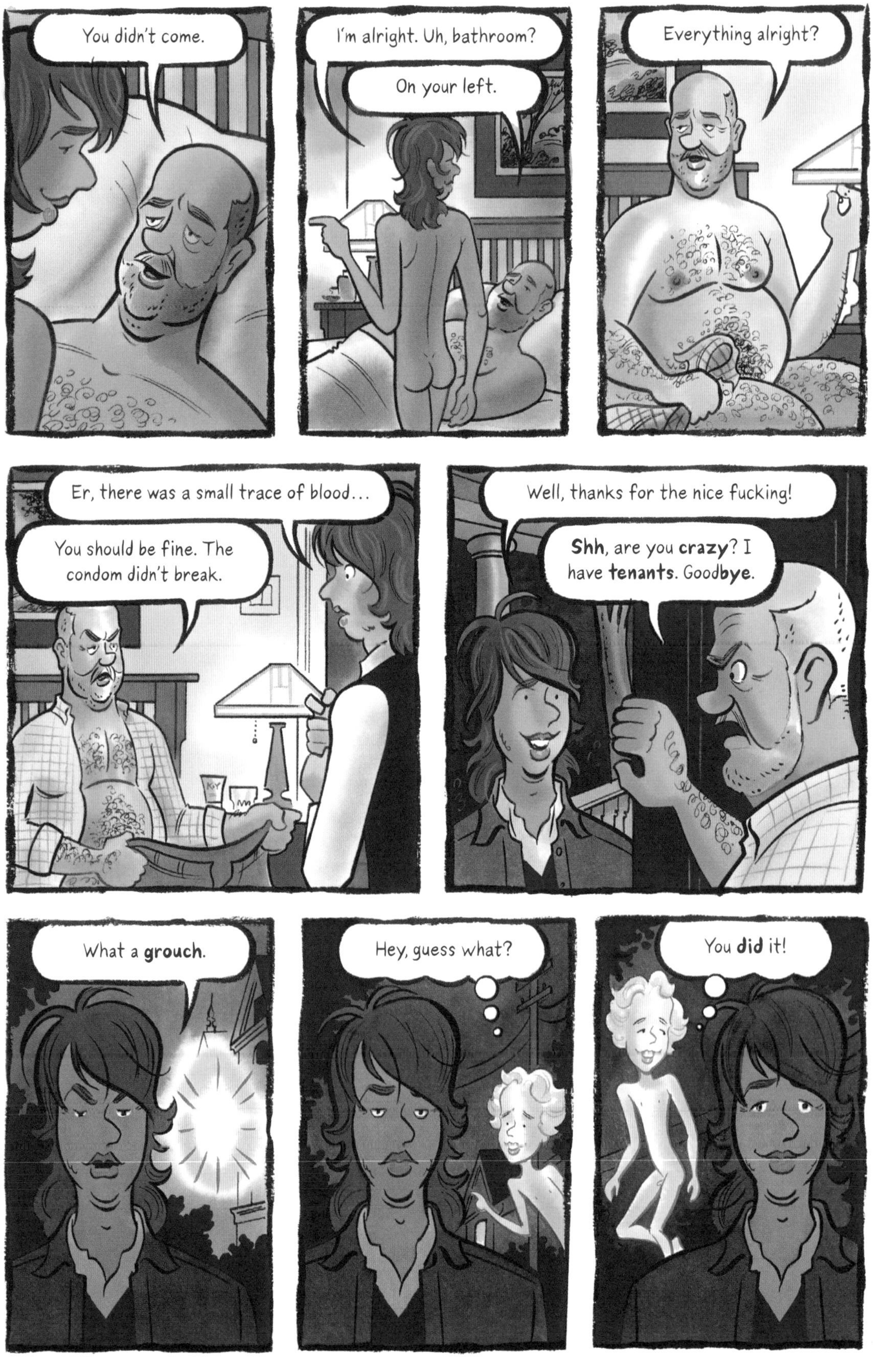
You didn't come.
I'm alright. Uh, bathroom?
On your left.
Everything alright?
Er, there was a small trace of blood...
You should be fine. The condom didn't break.
Well, thanks for the nice fucking!
Shh, are you **crazy**? I have **tenants**. Good**bye**.
What a **grouch**.
Hey, guess what?
You **did** it!

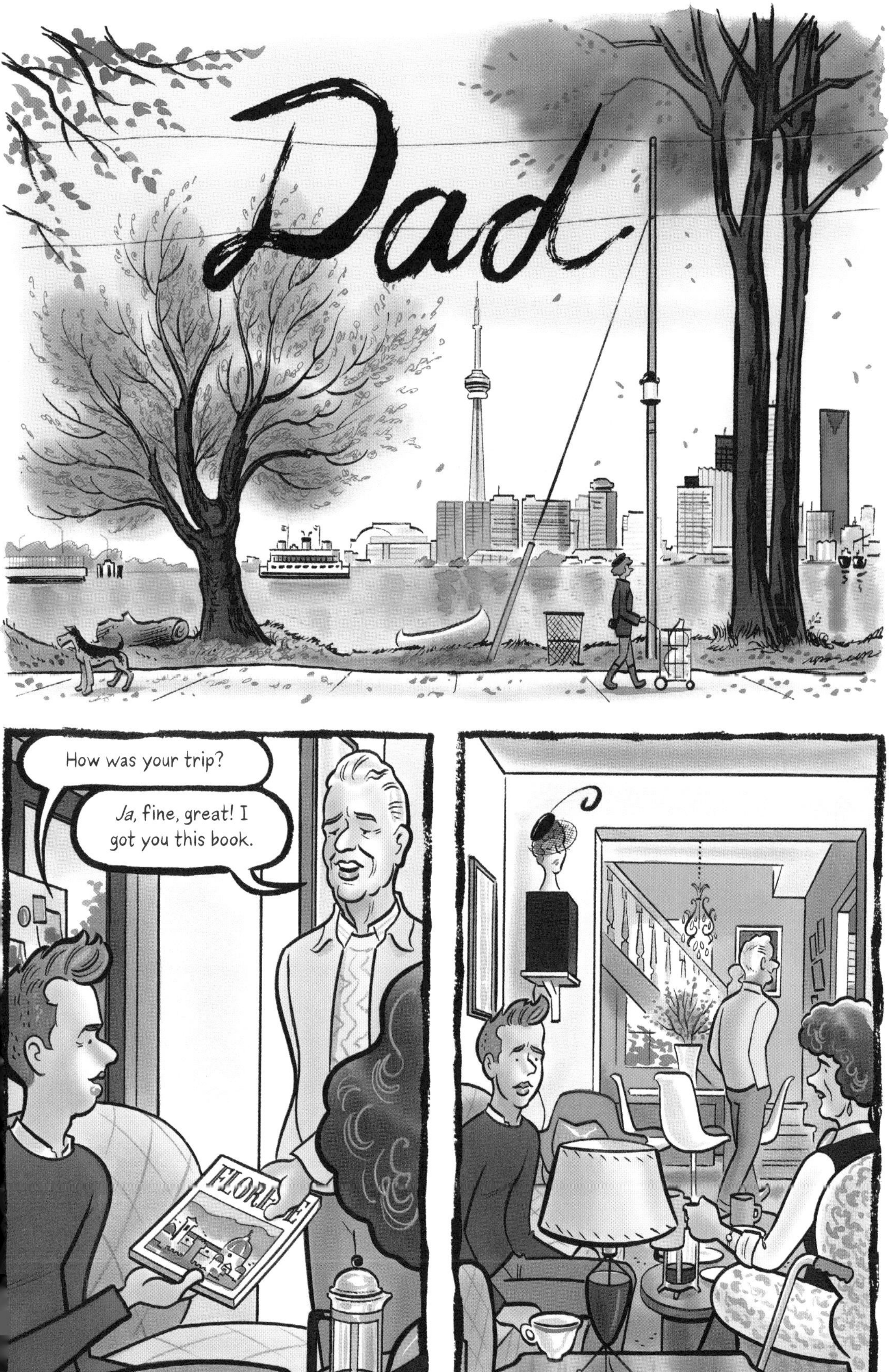
Dad
How was your trip?
Ja, fine, great! I got you this book.

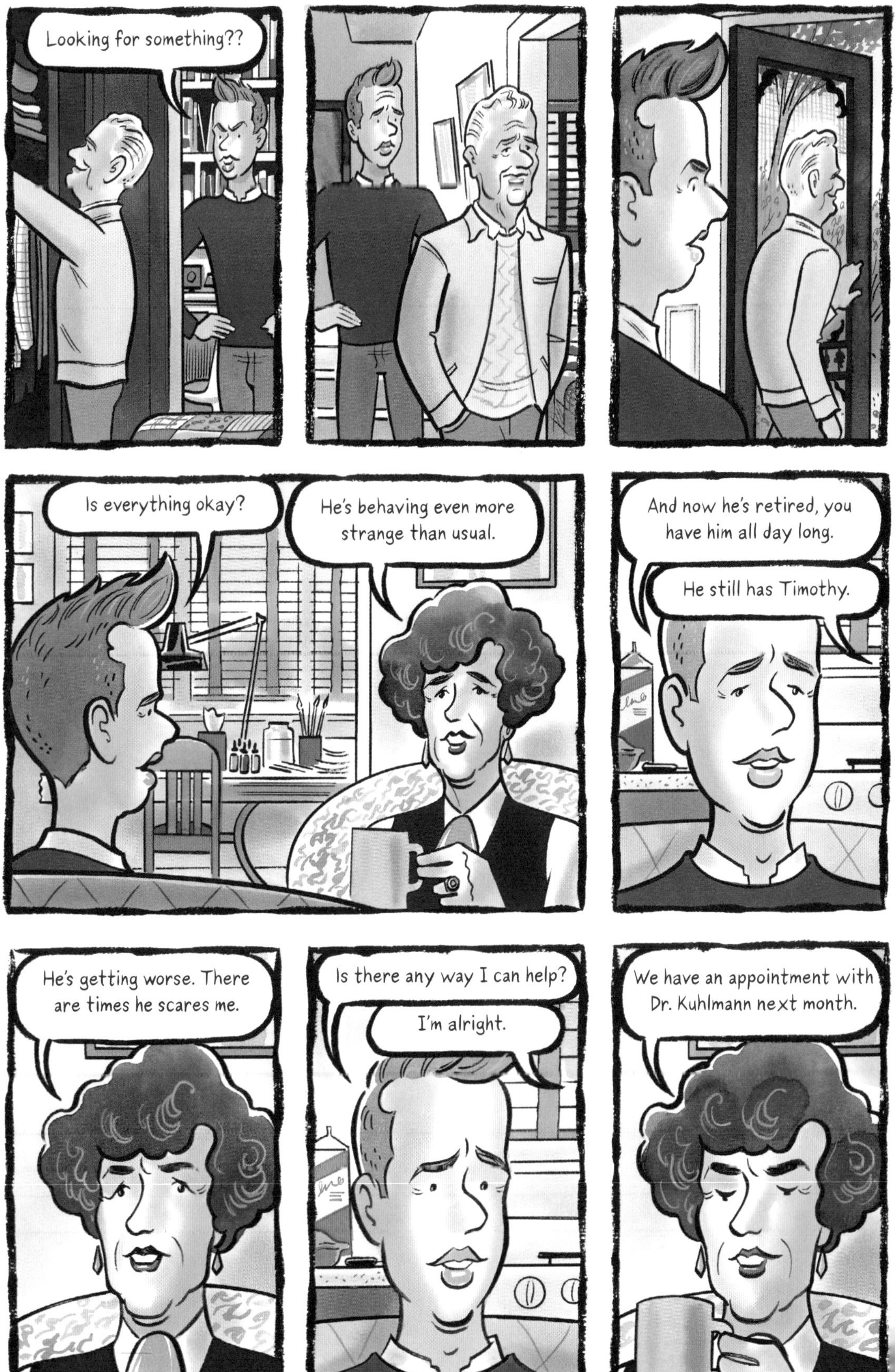
Looking for something??
Is everything okay?
He's behaving even more strange than usual.
And now he's retired, you have him all day long.
He still has Timothy.
He's getting worse. There are times he scares me.
Is there any way I can help?
I'm alright.
We have an appointment with Dr. Kuhlmann next month.

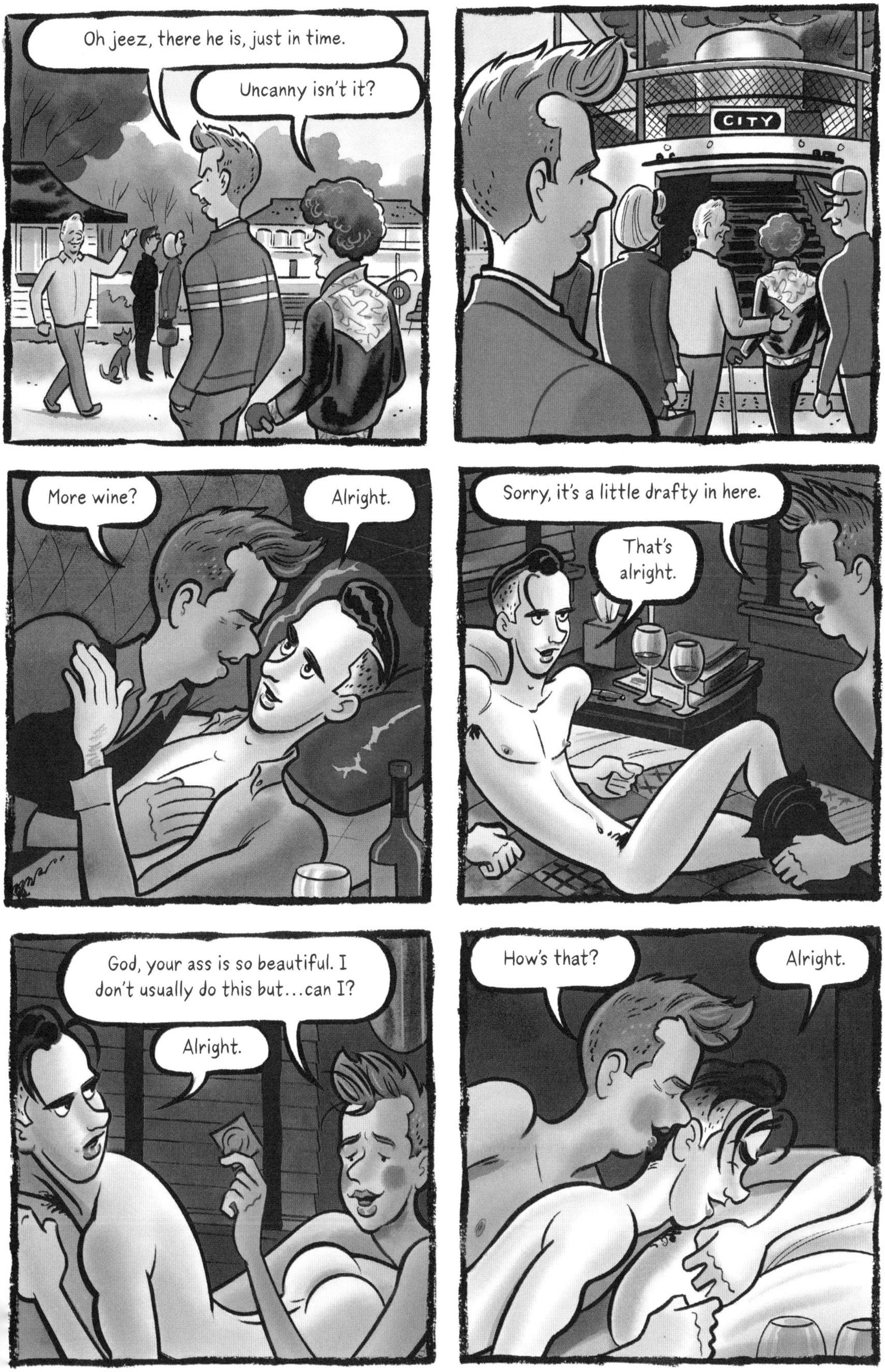
Oh jeez, there he is, just in time.
Uncanny isn't it?
CITY
More wine?
Alright.
Sorry, it's a little drafty in here.
That's alright.
God, your ass is so beautiful. I don't usually do this but...can I?
Alright.
How's that?
Alright.

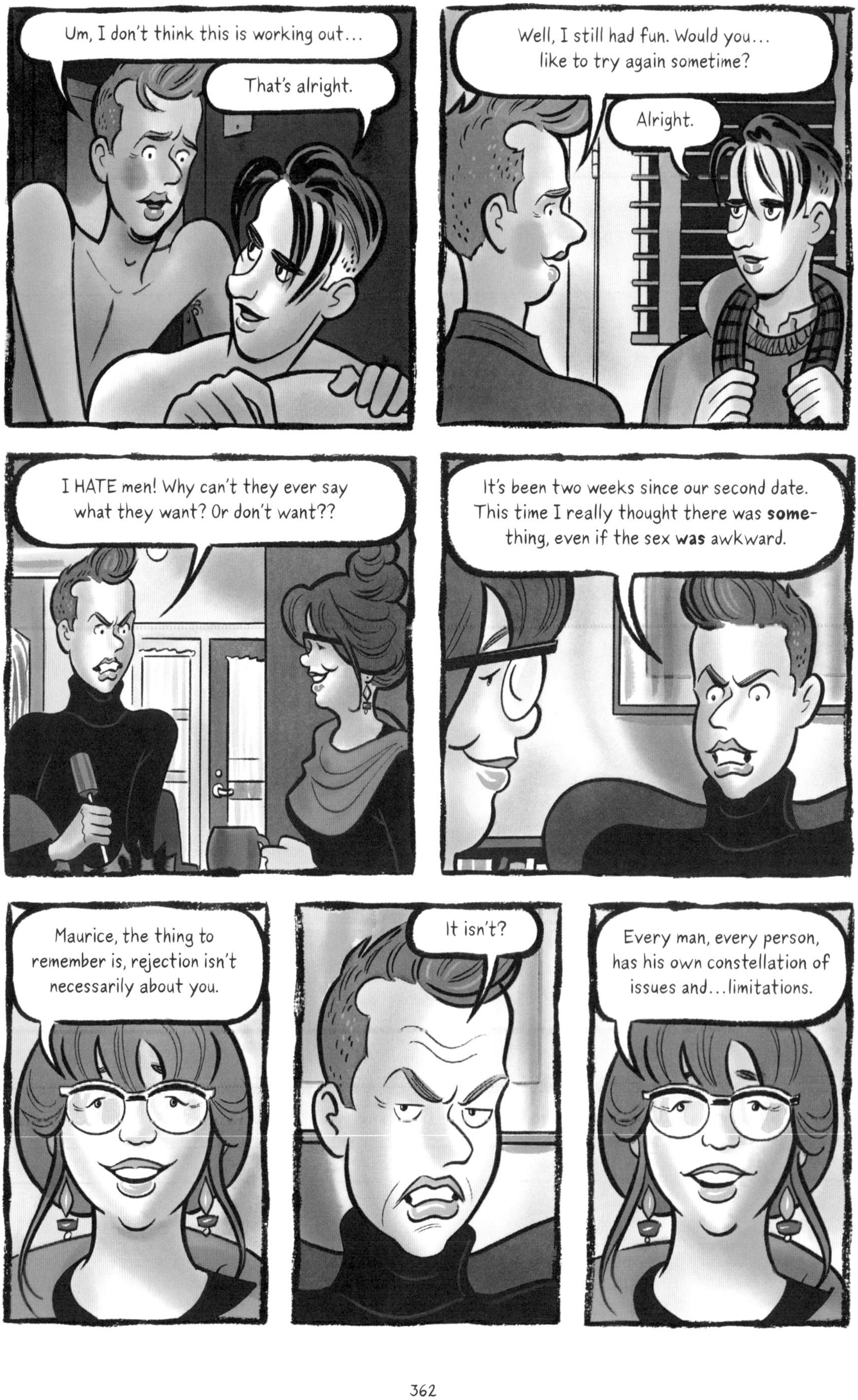
Um, I don't think this is working out...
That's alright.
Well, I still had fun. Would you... like to try again sometime?
Alright.
I HATE men! Why can't they ever say what they want? Or don't want??
It's been two weeks since our second date. This time I really thought there was **some-thing**, even if the sex **was** awkward.
Maurice, the thing to remember is, rejection isn't necessarily about you.
It isn't?
Every man, every person, has his own constellation of issues and... limitations.

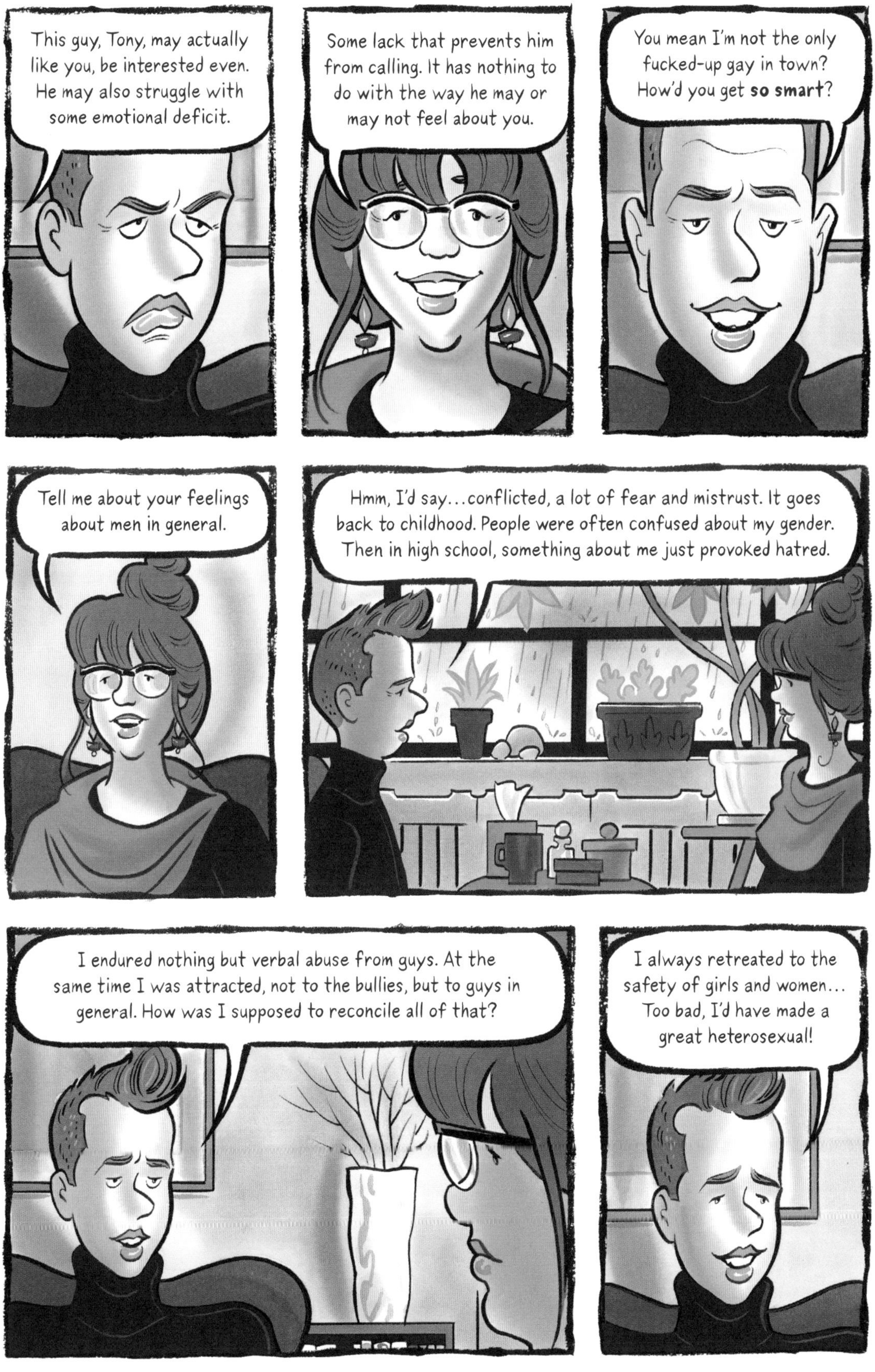
This guy, Tony, may actually like you, be interested even. He may also struggle with some emotional deficit.
Some lack that prevents him from calling. It has nothing to do with the way he may or may not feel about you.
You mean I'm not the only fucked-up gay in town? How'd you get **so smart**?
Tell me about your feelings about men in general.
Hmm, I'd say...conflicted, a lot of fear and mistrust. It goes back to childhood. People were often confused about my gender. Then in high school, something about me just provoked hatred.
I endured nothing but verbal abuse from guys. At the same time I was attracted, not to the bullies, but to guys in general. How was I supposed to reconcile all of that?
I always retreated to the safety of girls and women... Too bad, I'd have made a great heterosexual!

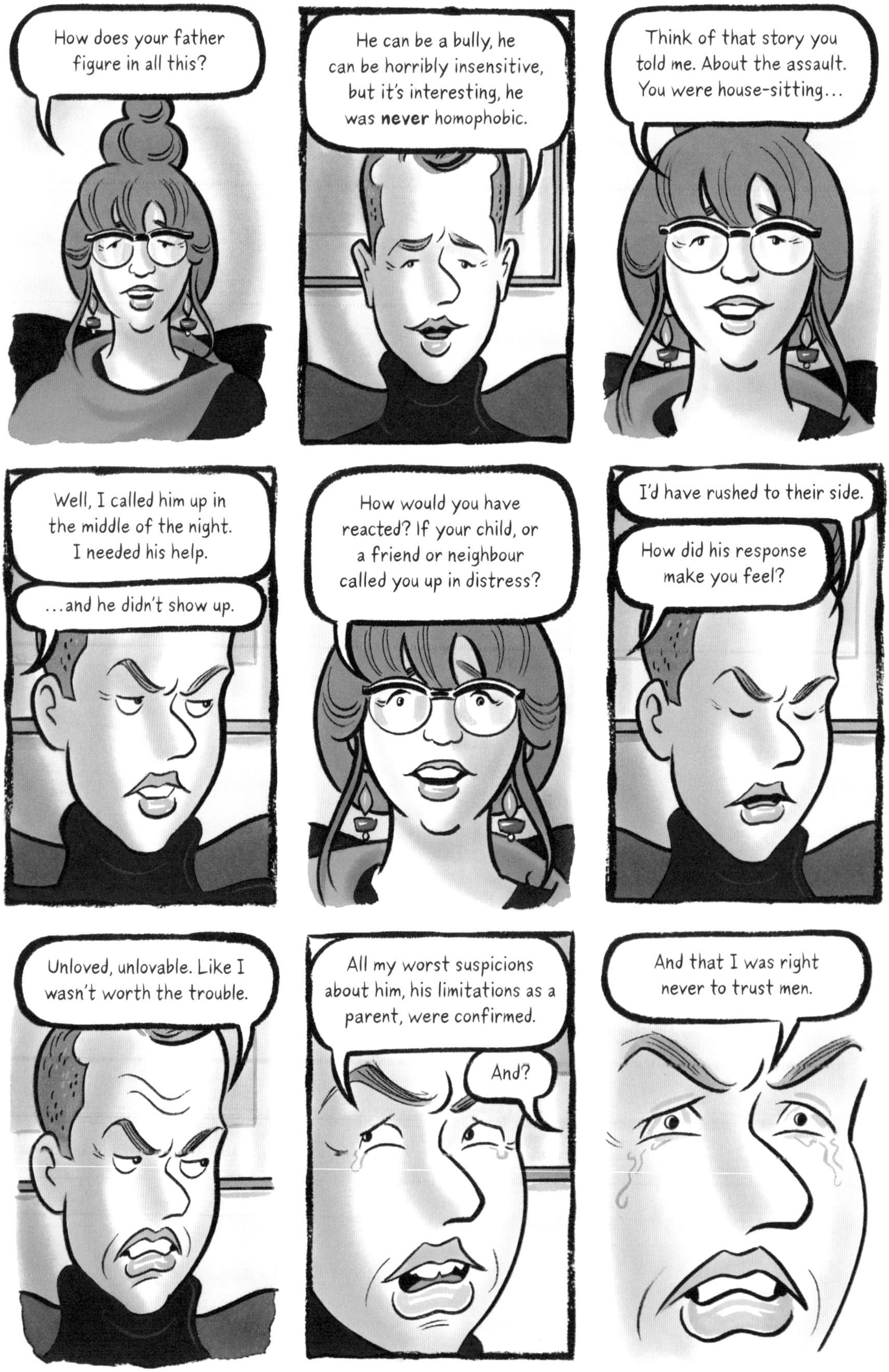
How does your father figure in all this?
He can be a bully, he can be horribly insensitive, but it's interesting, he was **never** homophobic.
Think of that story you told me. About the assault. You were house-sitting...
Well, I called him up in the middle of the night. I needed his help.
...and he didn't show up.
How would you have reacted? If your child, or a friend or neighbour called you up in distress?
I'd have rushed to their side.
How did his response make you feel?
Unloved, unlovable. Like I wasn't worth the trouble.
All my worst suspicions about him, his limitations as a parent, were confirmed.
And?
And that I was right never to trust men.

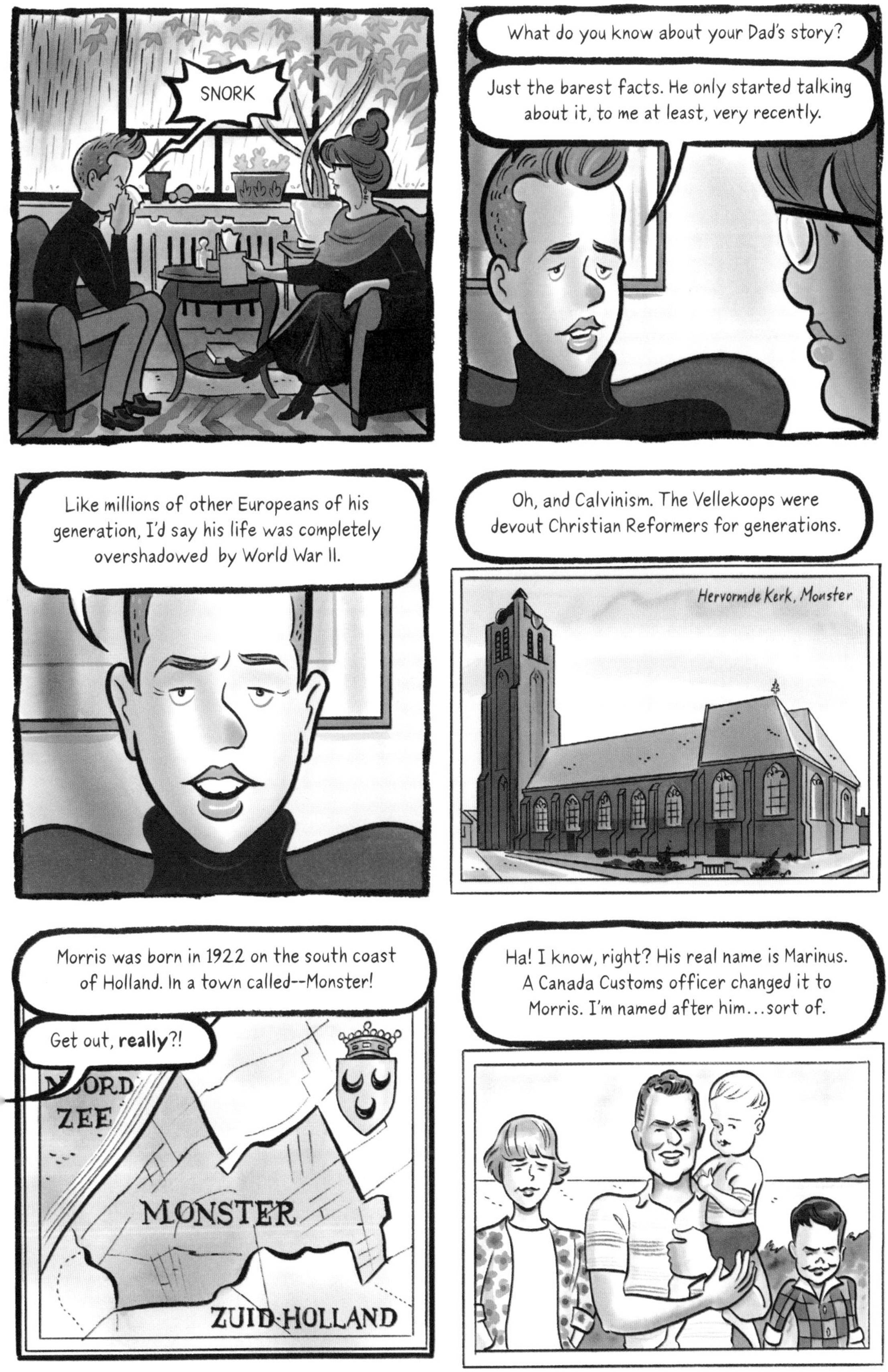
SNORK
What do you know about your Dad's story?
Just the barest facts. He only started talking about it, to me at least, very recently.
Like millions of other Europeans of his generation, I'd say his life was completely overshadowed by World War II.
Oh, and Calvinism. The Vellekoops were devout Christian Reformers for generations.
Hervormde Kerk, Monster
Morris was born in 1922 on the south coast of Holland. In a town called--Monster!
Get out, **really**?!
ZEE
MONSTER
ZUID-HOLLAND
Ha! I know, right? His real name is Marinus. A Canada Customs officer changed it to Morris. I'm named after him...sort of.

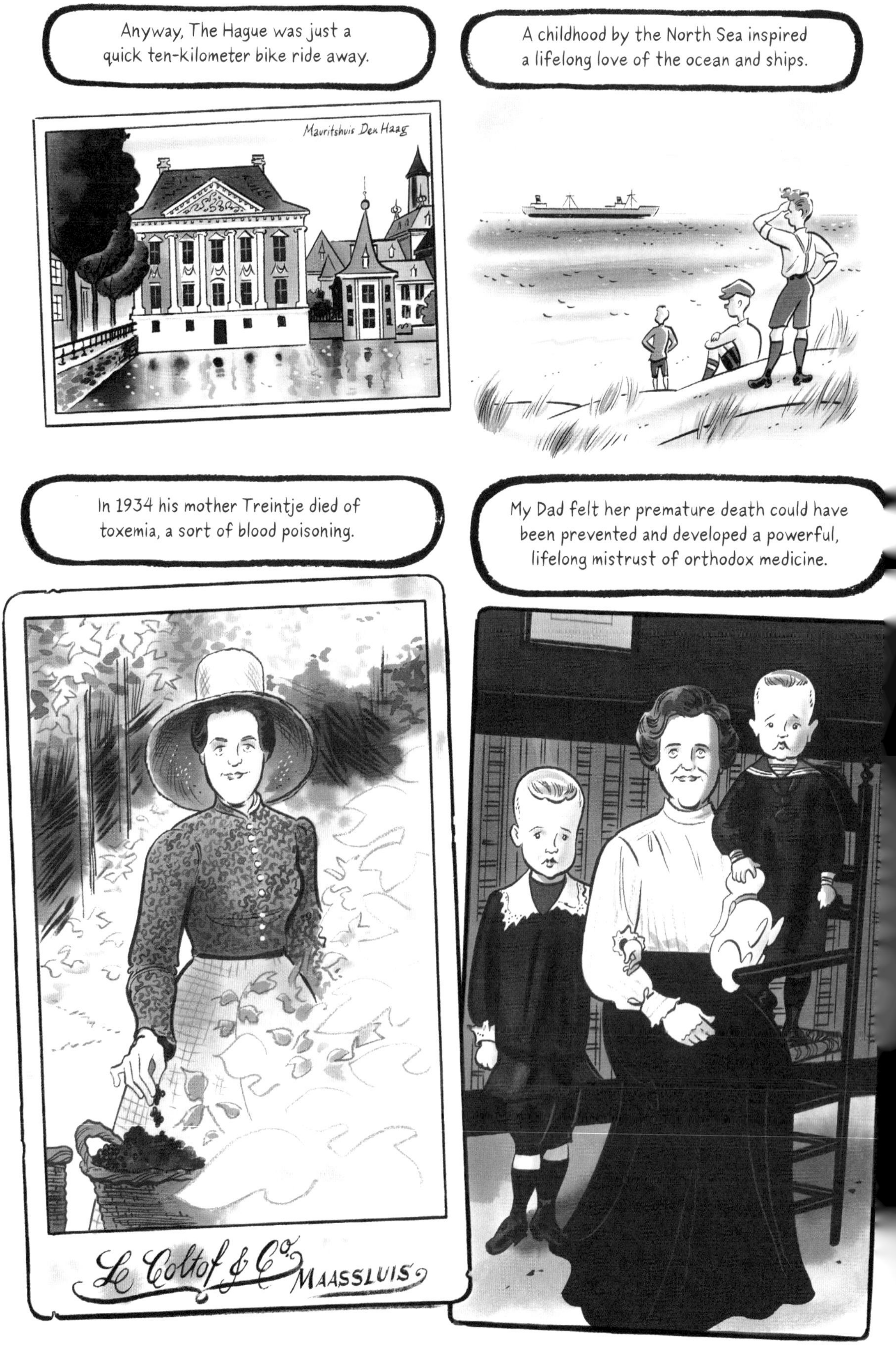
Anyway, The Hague was just a quick ten-kilometer bike ride away.
Mauritshuis Den Haag
A childhood by the North Sea inspired a lifelong love of the ocean and ships.
In 1934 his mother Treintje died of toxemia, a sort of blood poisoning.
Le Coltof & Co.
MAASSLUIS
My Dad felt her premature death could have been prevented and developed a powerful, lifelong mistrust of orthodox medicine.

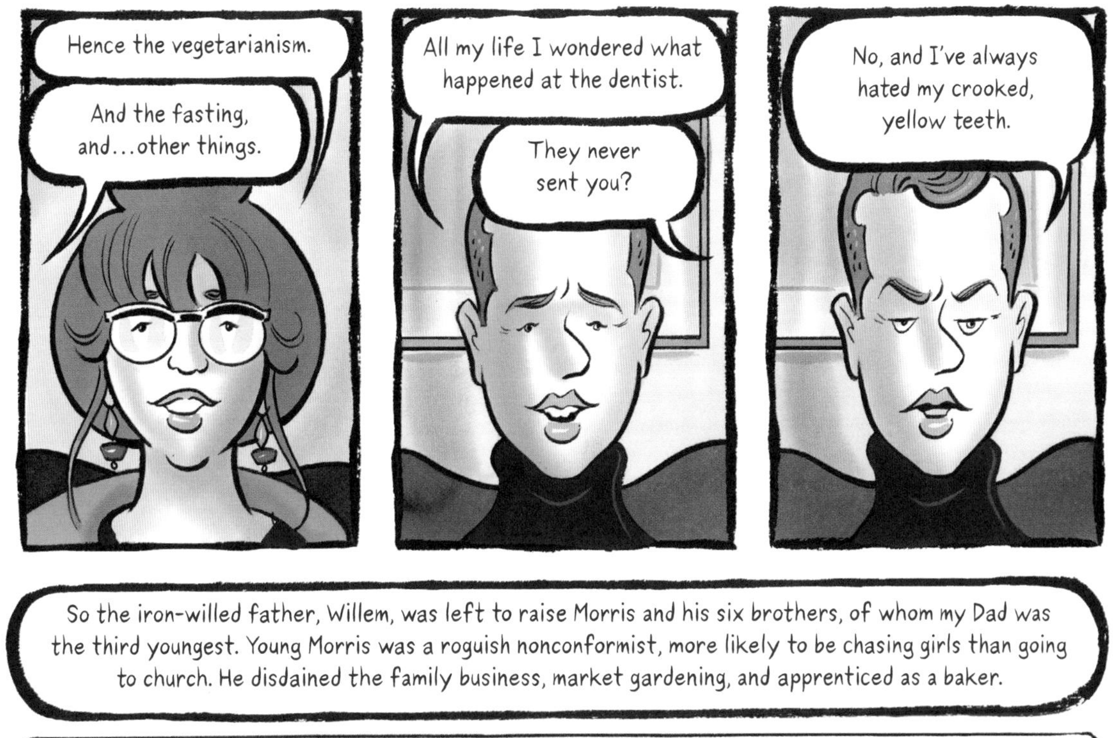
Hence the vegetarianism.
And the fasting, and...other things.
All my life I wondered what happened at the dentist.
They never sent you?
No, and I've always hated my crooked, yellow teeth.

So the iron-willed father, Willem, was left to raise Morris and his six brothers, of whom my Dad was the third youngest. Young Morris was a roguish nonconformist, more likely to be chasing girls than going to church. He disdained the family business, market gardening, and apprenticed as a baker.

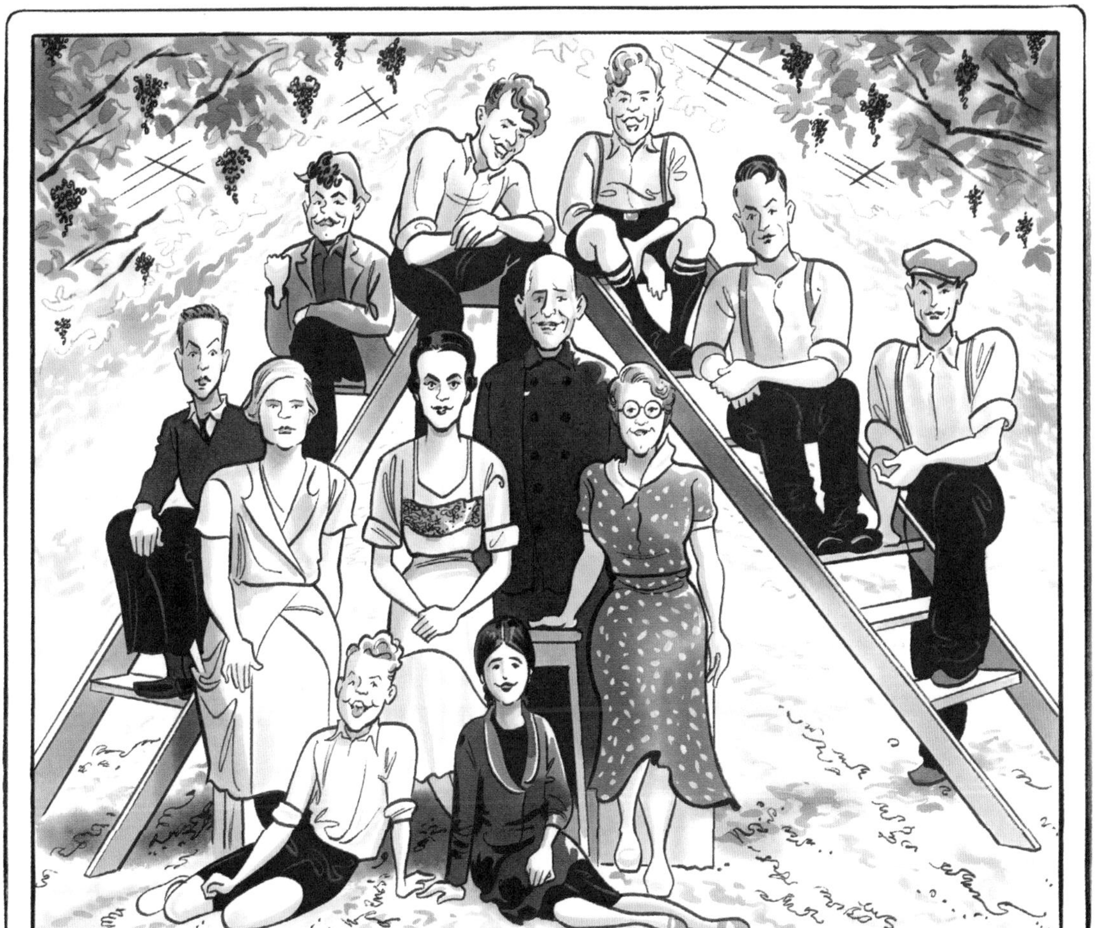

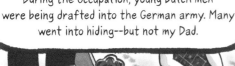

During the Occupation, young Dutch men were being drafted into the German army. Many went into hiding--but not my Dad.

He blithely went about his business till one day a former friend, now a police officer with the Nazis, turned him in.

He was rounded up and sent to do forced labour in a German arms factory.

Eventually the factory was bombed, and the commander let all his charges go free.

All of this is very murky, no dates, no idea where in Germany this took place.

One detail I do remember: anytime soup was offered, my Dad would decline. "Salt water," he called it.

Wow, memories of work camp food, huh?

Exactly.

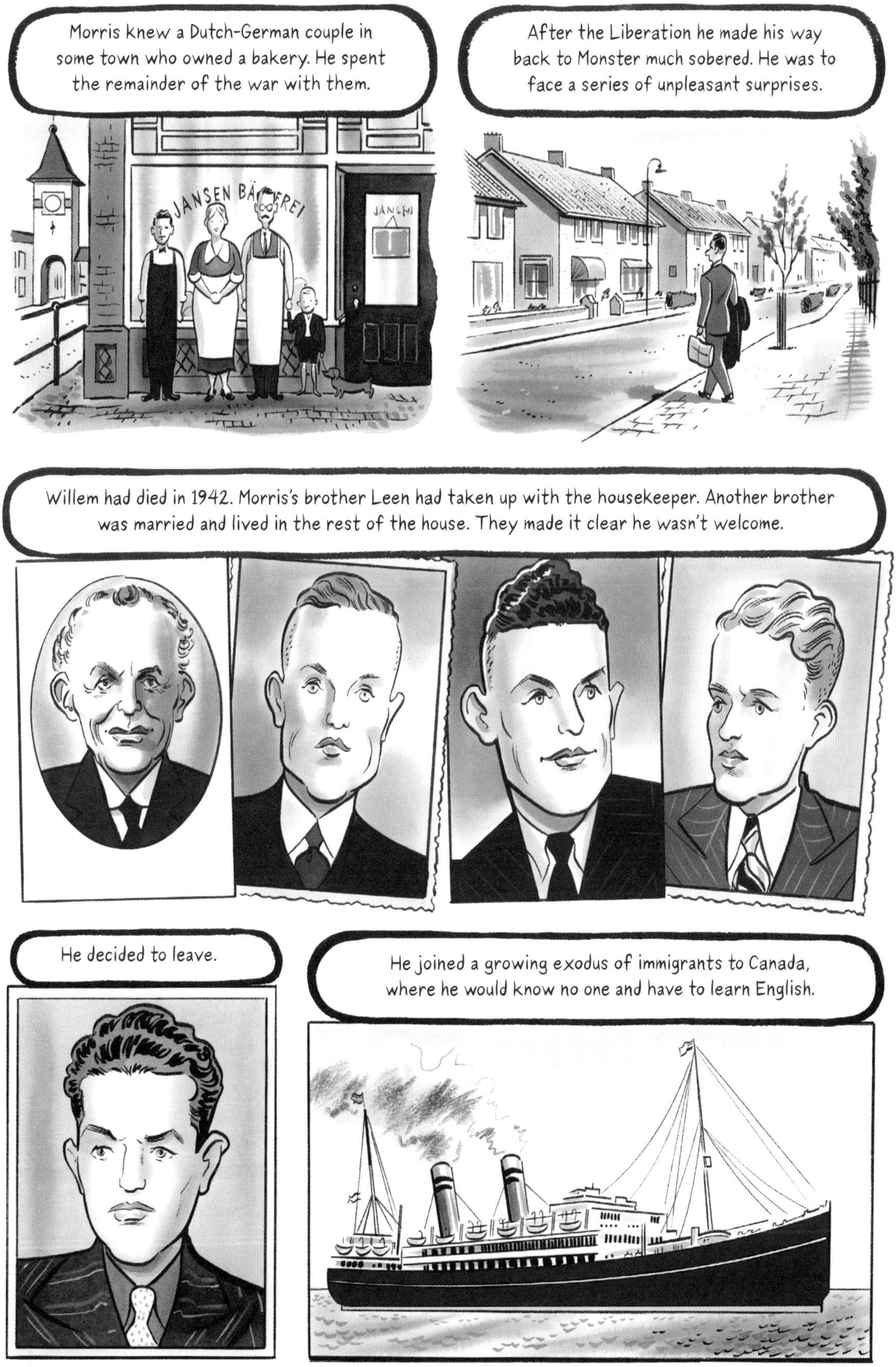
Morris knew a Dutch-German couple in some town who owned a bakery. He spent the remainder of the war with them.
JANSEN
After the Liberation he made his way back to Monster much sobered. He was to face a series of unpleasant surprises.
Willem had died in 1942. Morris's brother Leen had taken up with the housekeeper. Another brother was married and lived in the rest of the house. They made it clear he wasn't welcome.
He decided to leave.
He joined a growing exodus of immigrants to Canada, where he would know no one and have to learn English.

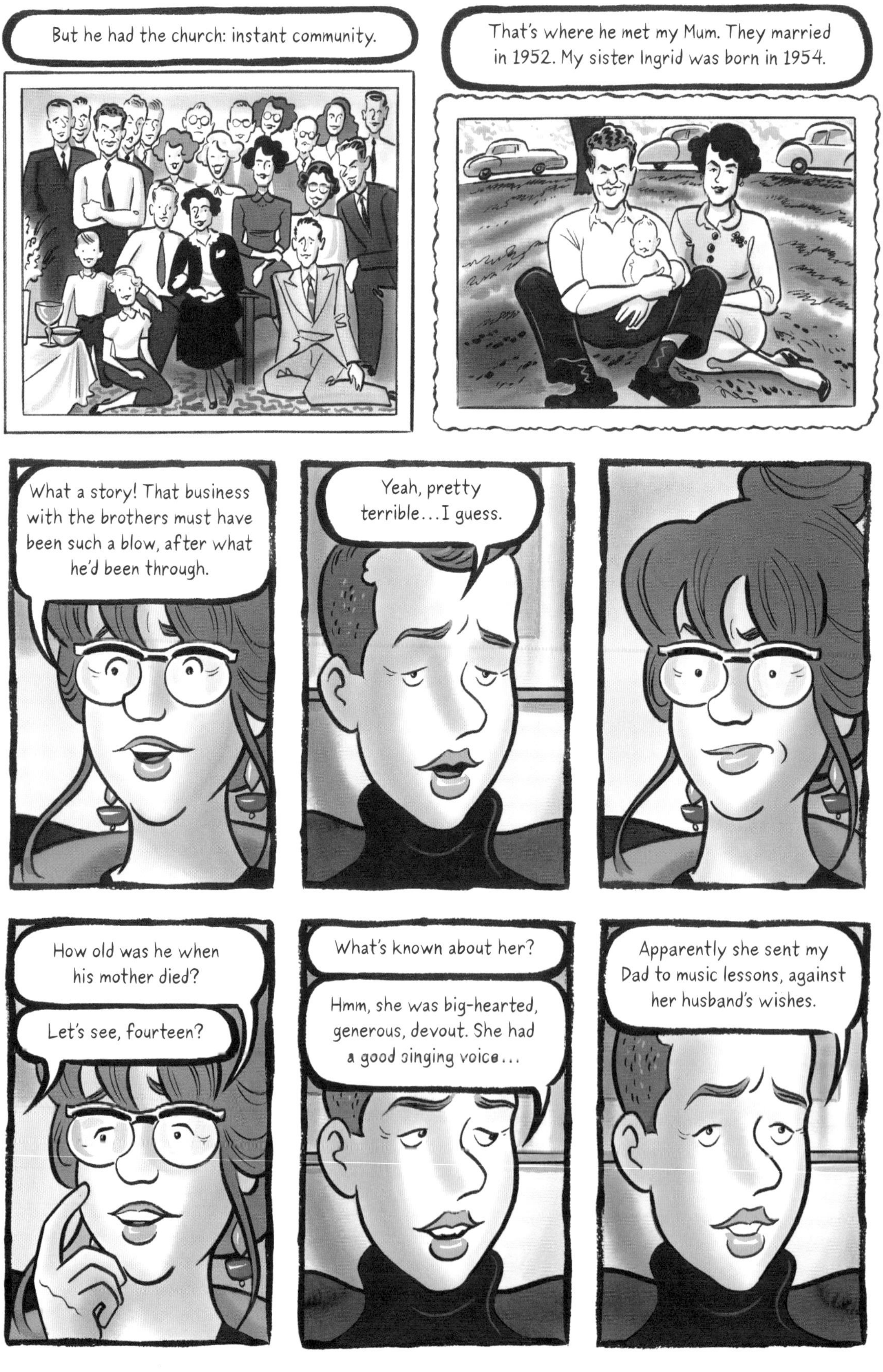

But he had the church: instant community.
That's where he met my Mum. They married in 1952. My sister Ingrid was born in 1954.
What a story! That business with the brothers must have been such a blow, after what he'd been through.
Yeah, pretty terrible...I guess.
How old was he when his mother died?
Let's see, fourteen?
What's known about her?
Hmm, she was big-hearted, generous, devout. She had a good singing voice...
Apparently she sent my Dad to music lessons, against her husband's wishes.

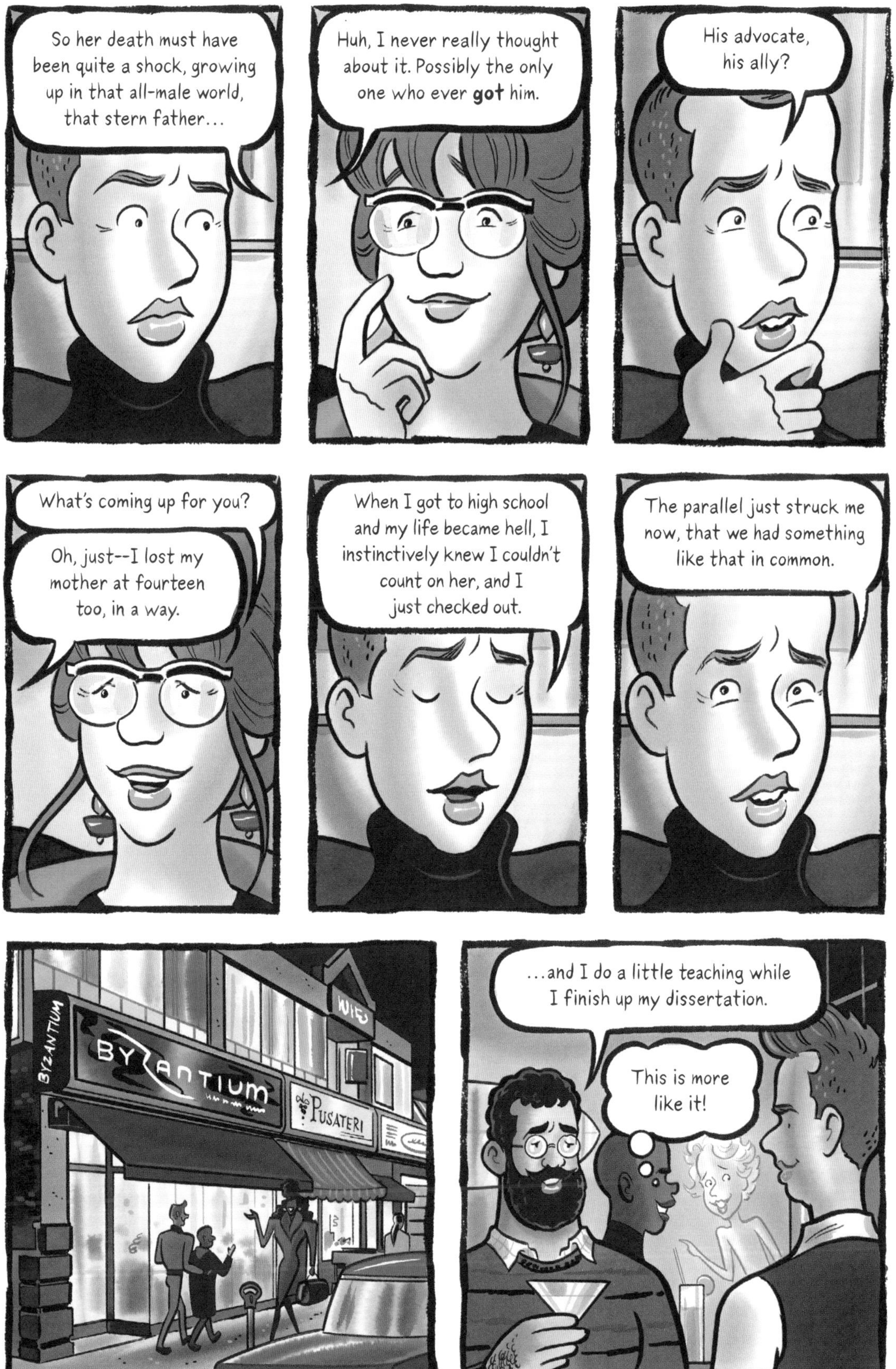
So her death must have been quite a shock, growing up in that all-male world, that stern father...
Huh, I never really thought about it. Possibly the only one who ever **got** him.
His advocate, his ally?
What's coming up for you?
Oh, just--I lost my mother at fourteen too, in a way.
When I got to high school and my life became hell, I instinctively knew I couldn't count on her, and I just checked out.
The parallel just struck me now, that we had something like that in common.
BYZANTIUM
PUSATERI
...and I do a little teaching while I finish up my dissertation.
This is more like it!

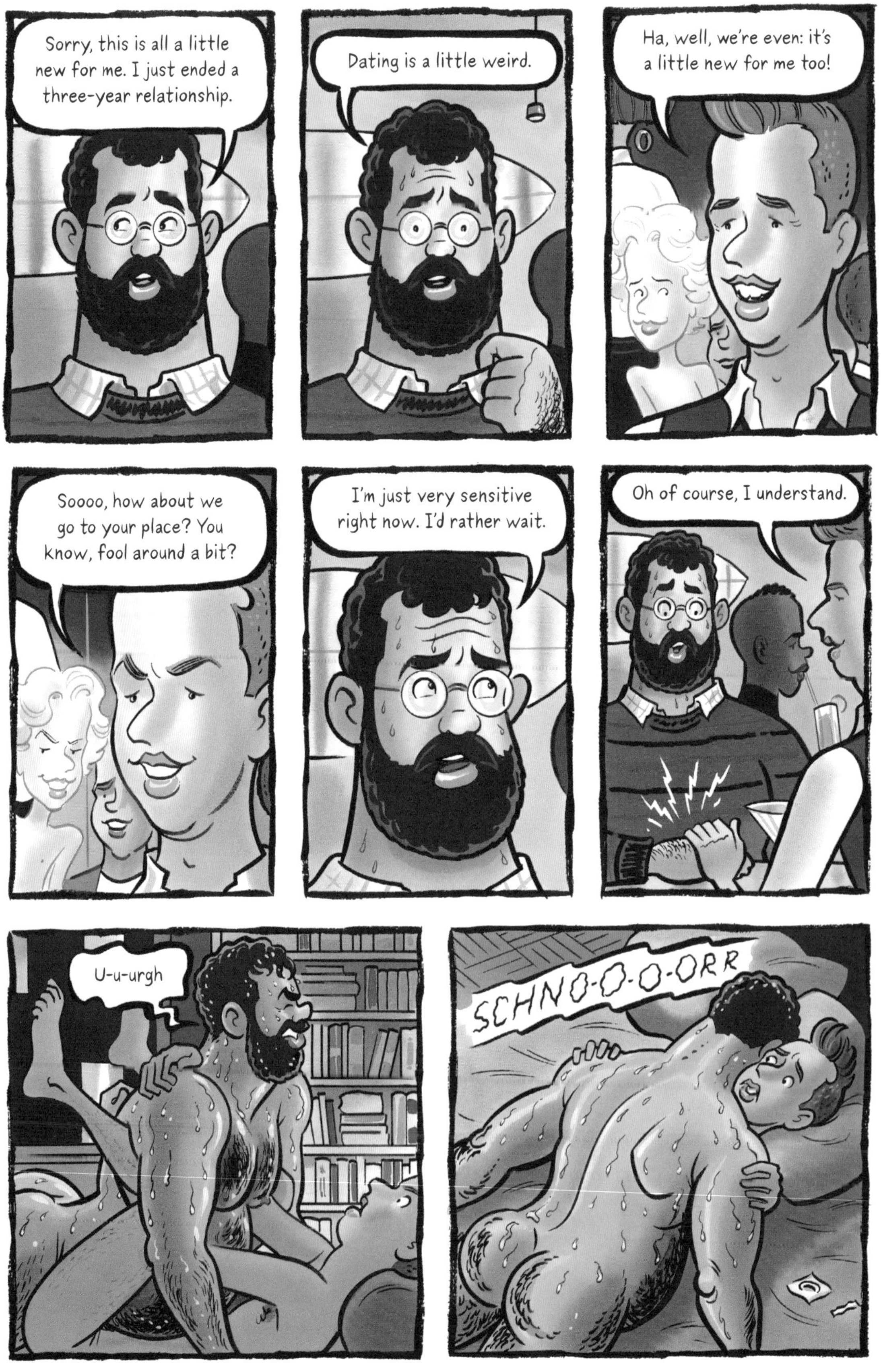
Sorry, this is all a little new for me. I just ended a three-year relationship.
Dating is a little weird.
Ha, well, we're even: it's a little new for me too!
Soooo, how about we go to your place? You know, fool around a bit?
I'm just very sensitive right now. I'd rather wait.
Oh of course, I understand.
U-u-urgh
SCHNO-O-O-ORR

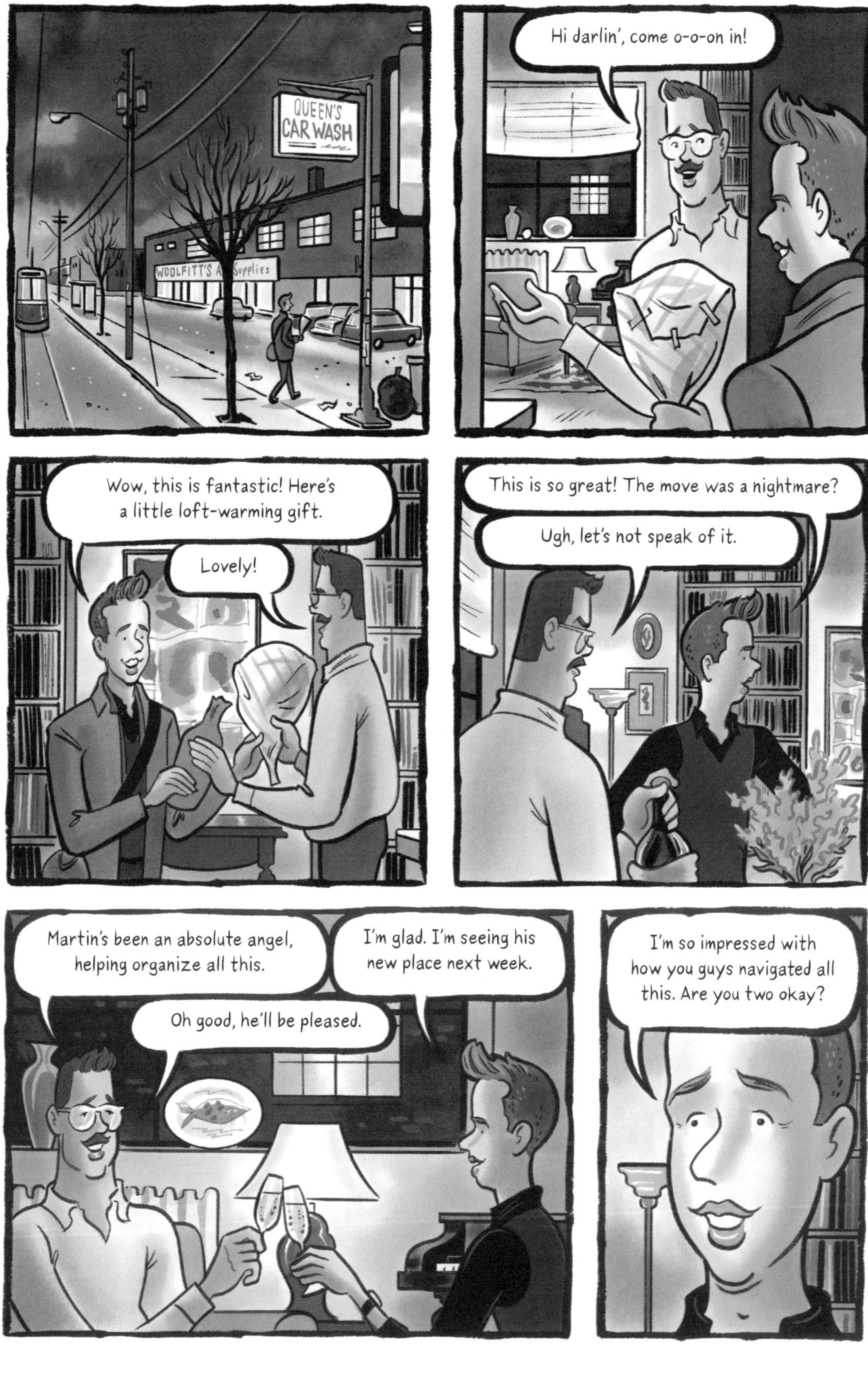
QUEEN'S CAR WASH
WOOLFITT'S A Supplies
Hi darlin', come o-o-on in!
Wow, this is fantastic! Here's a little loft-warming gift.
Lovely!
This is so great! The move was a nightmare?
Ugh, let's not speak of it.
Martin's been an absolute angel, helping organize all this.
I'm glad. I'm seeing his new place next week.
Oh good, he'll be pleased.
I'm so impressed with how you guys navigated all this. Are you two okay?

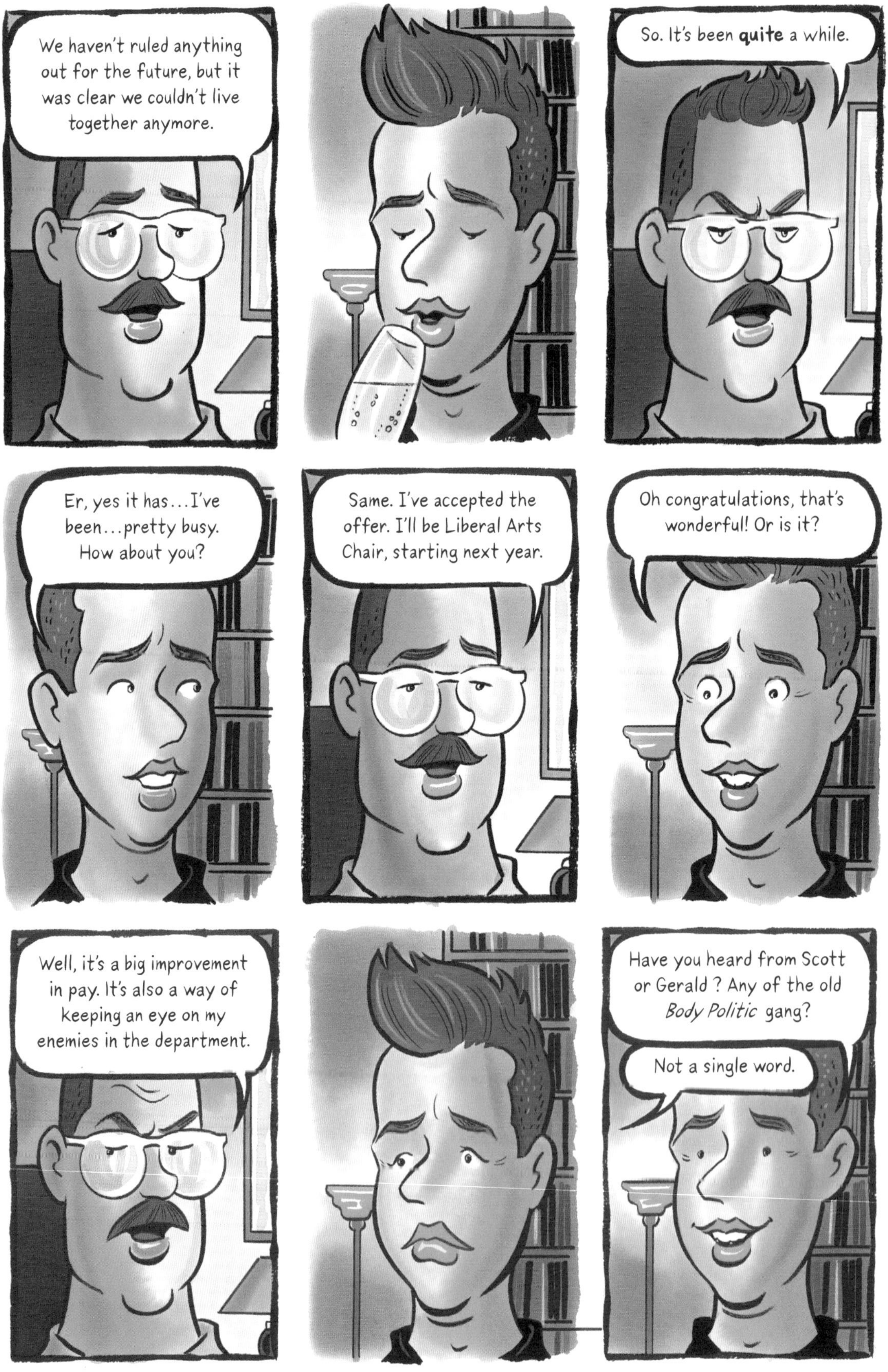
We haven't ruled anything out for the future, but it was clear we couldn't live together anymore.
So. It's been **quite** a while.
Er, yes it has...I've been...pretty busy. How about you?
Same. I've accepted the offer. I'll be Liberal Arts Chair, starting next year.
Oh congratulations, that's wonderful! Or is it?
Well, it's a big improvement in pay. It's also a way of keeping an eye on my enemies in the department.
Have you heard from Scott or Gerald? Any of the old *Body Politic* gang?
Not a single word.

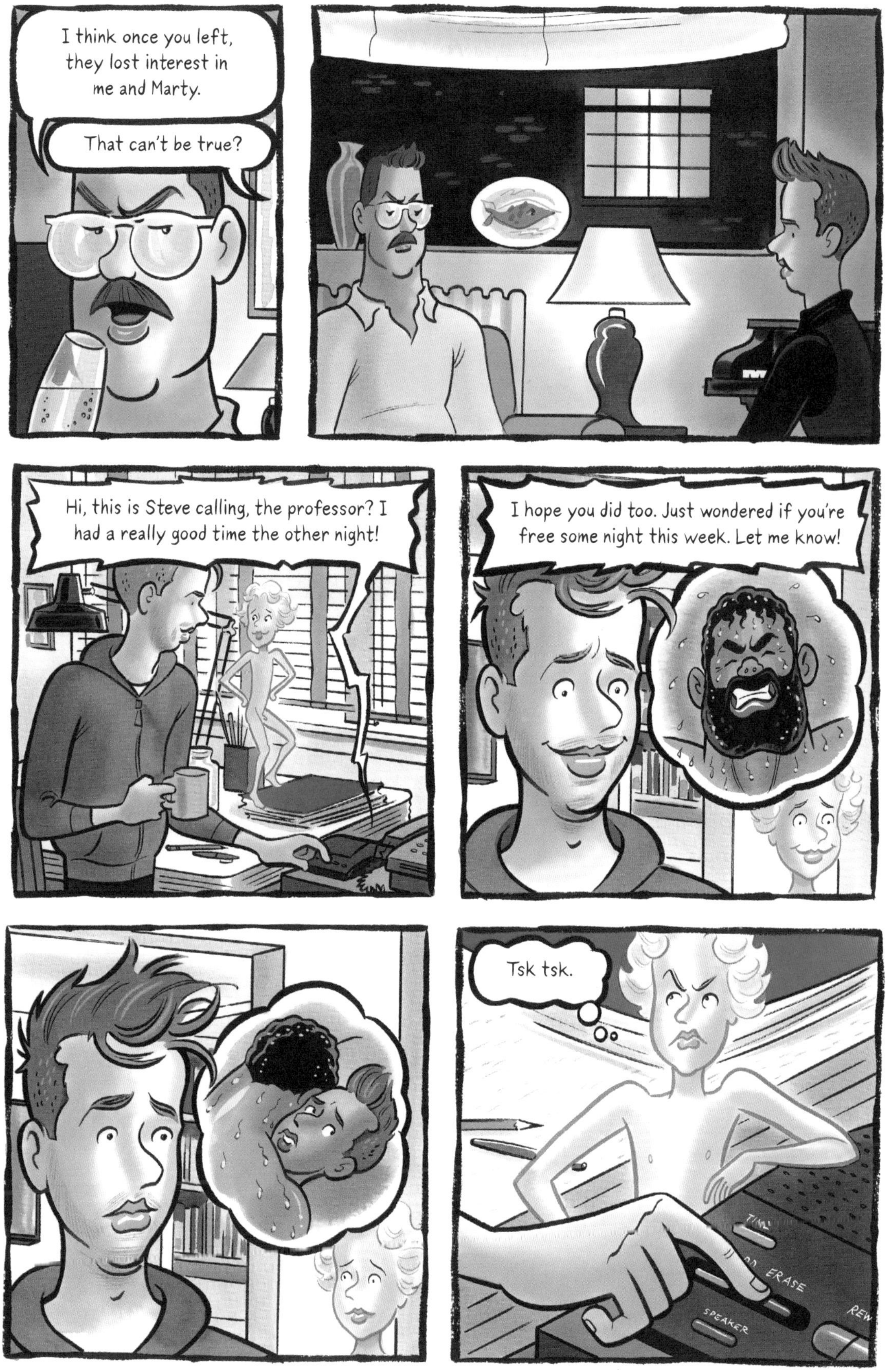
I think once you left, they lost interest in me and Marty.
That can't be true?
Hi, this is Steve calling, the professor? I had a really good time the other night!
I hope you did too. Just wondered if you're free some night this week. Let me know!
Tsk tsk.
ERASE
SPEAKER
REW

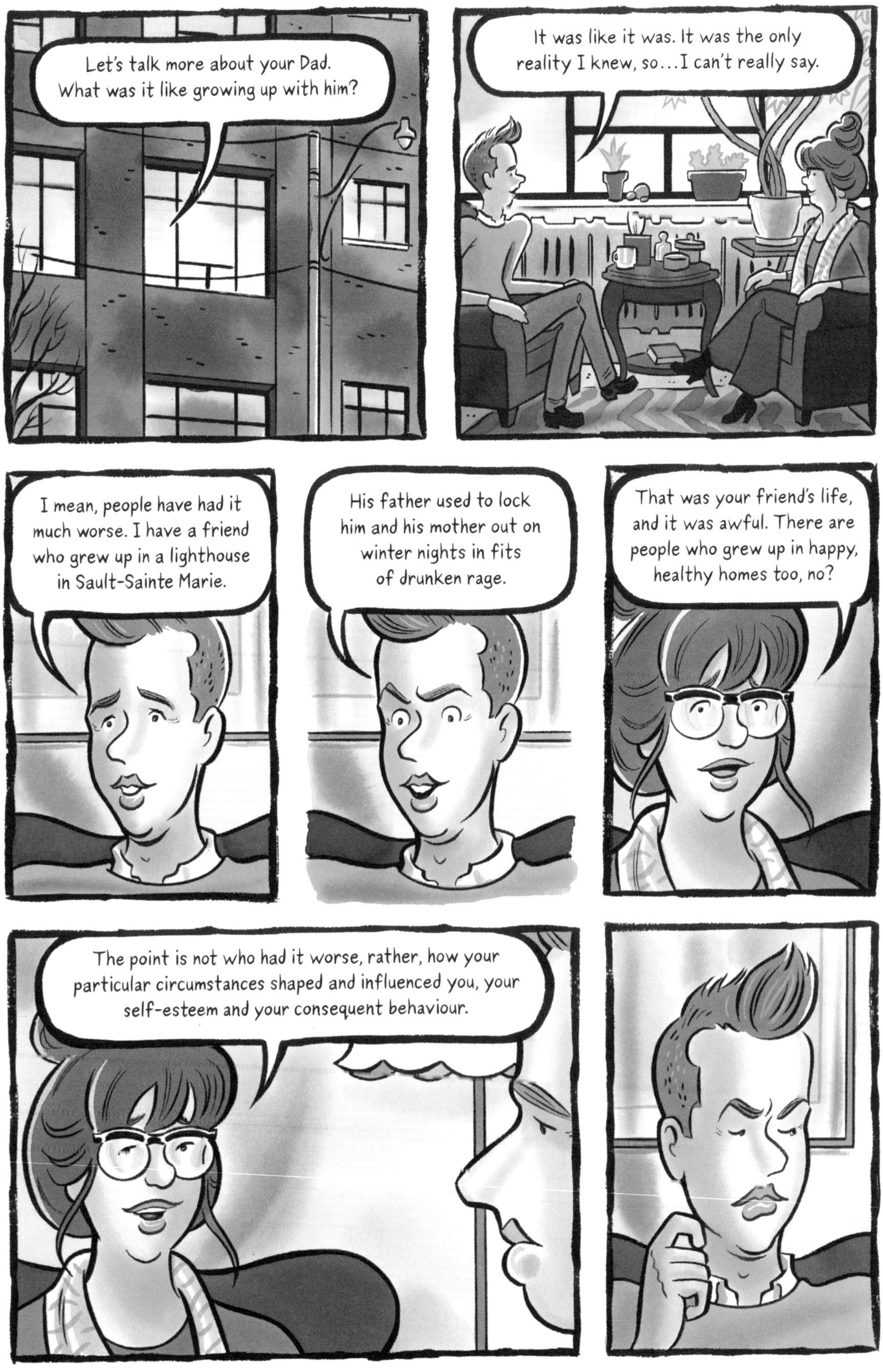
Let's talk more about your Dad. What was it like growing up with him?
It was like it was. It was the only reality I knew, so...I can't really say.
I mean, people have had it much worse. I have a friend who grew up in a lighthouse in Sault-Sainte Marie.
His father used to lock him and his mother out on winter nights in fits of drunken rage.
That was your friend's life, and it was awful. There are people who grew up in happy, healthy homes too, no?
The point is not who had it worse, rather, how your particular circumstances shaped and influenced you, your self-esteem and your consequent behaviour.

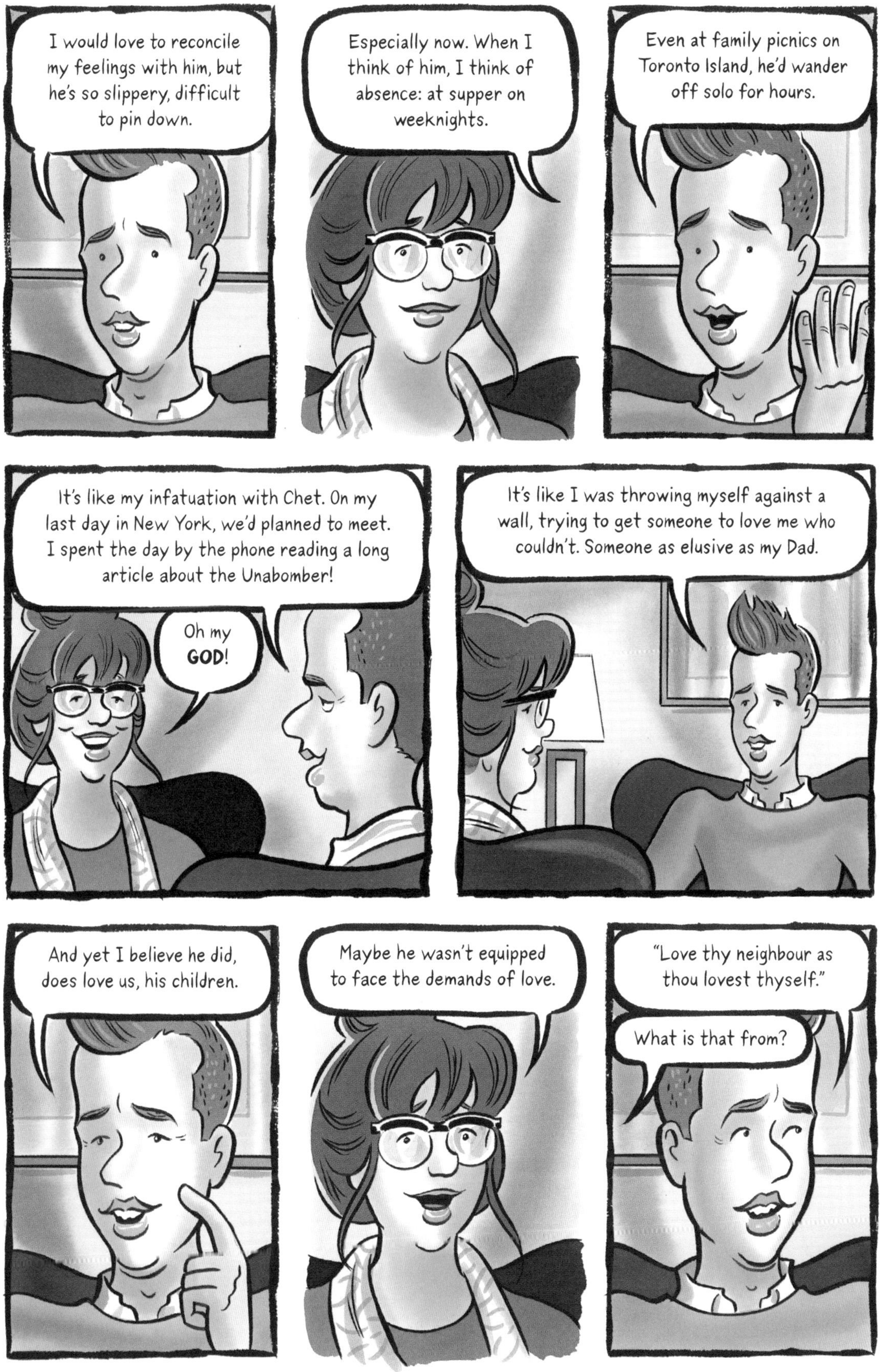
I would love to reconcile my feelings with him, but he's so slippery, difficult to pin down.
Especially now. When I think of him, I think of absence: at supper on weeknights.
Even at family picnics on Toronto Island, he'd wander off solo for hours.
It's like my infatuation with Chet. On my last day in New York, we'd planned to meet. I spent the day by the phone reading a long article about the Unabomber!
Oh my **GOD**!
It's like I was throwing myself against a wall, trying to get someone to love me who couldn't. Someone as elusive as my Dad.
And yet I believe he did, does love us, his children.
Maybe he wasn't equipped to face the demands of love.
"Love thy neighbour as thou lovest thyself."
What is that from?

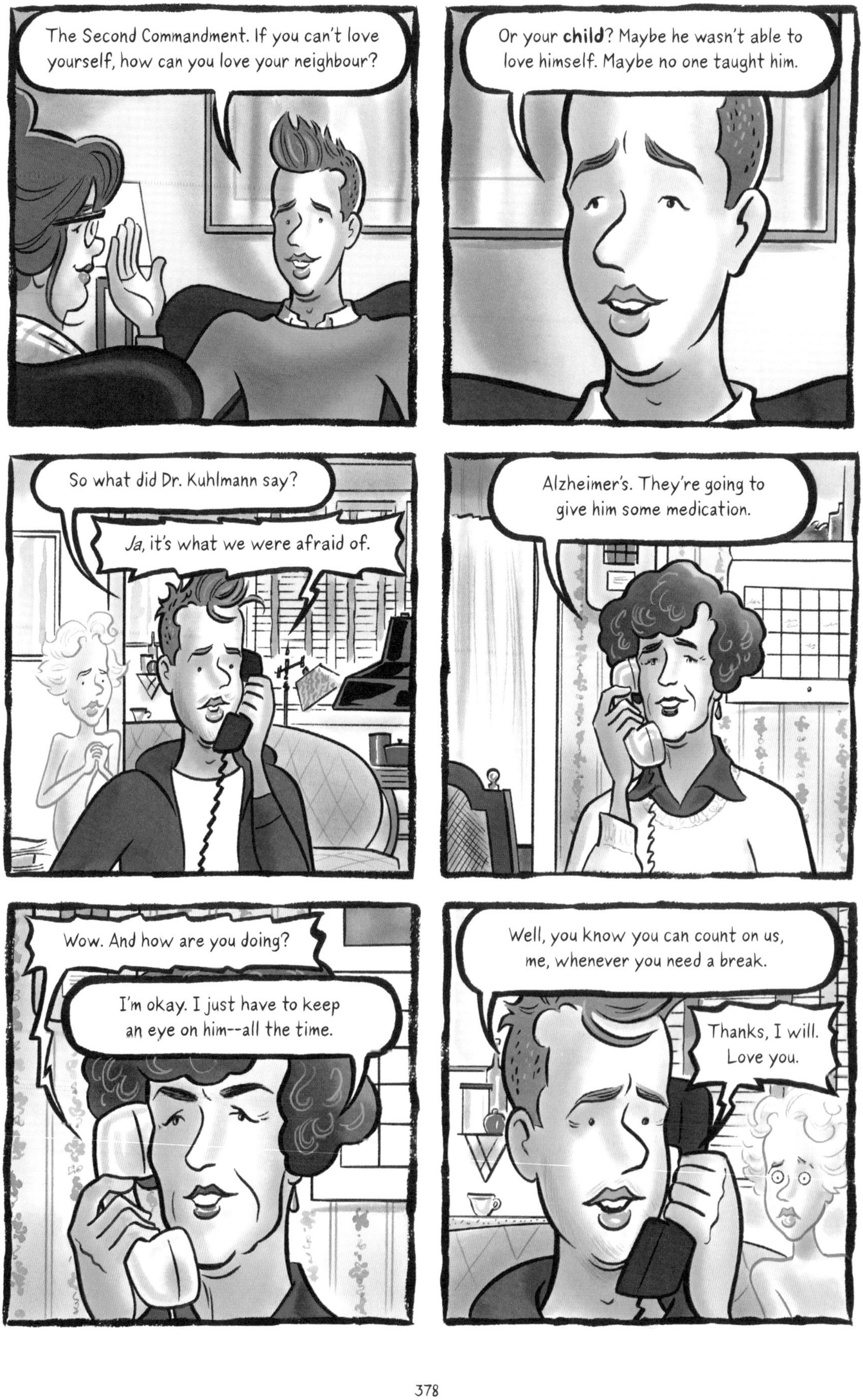
The Second Commandment. If you can't love yourself, how can you love your neighbour?
Or your **child**? Maybe he wasn't able to love himself. Maybe no one taught him.
So what did Dr. Kuhlmann say?
Ja, it's what we were afraid of.
Alzheimer's. They're going to give him some medication.
Wow. And how are you doing?
I'm okay. I just have to keep an eye on him--all the time.
Well, you know you can count on us, me, whenever you need a break.
Thanks, I will. Love you.

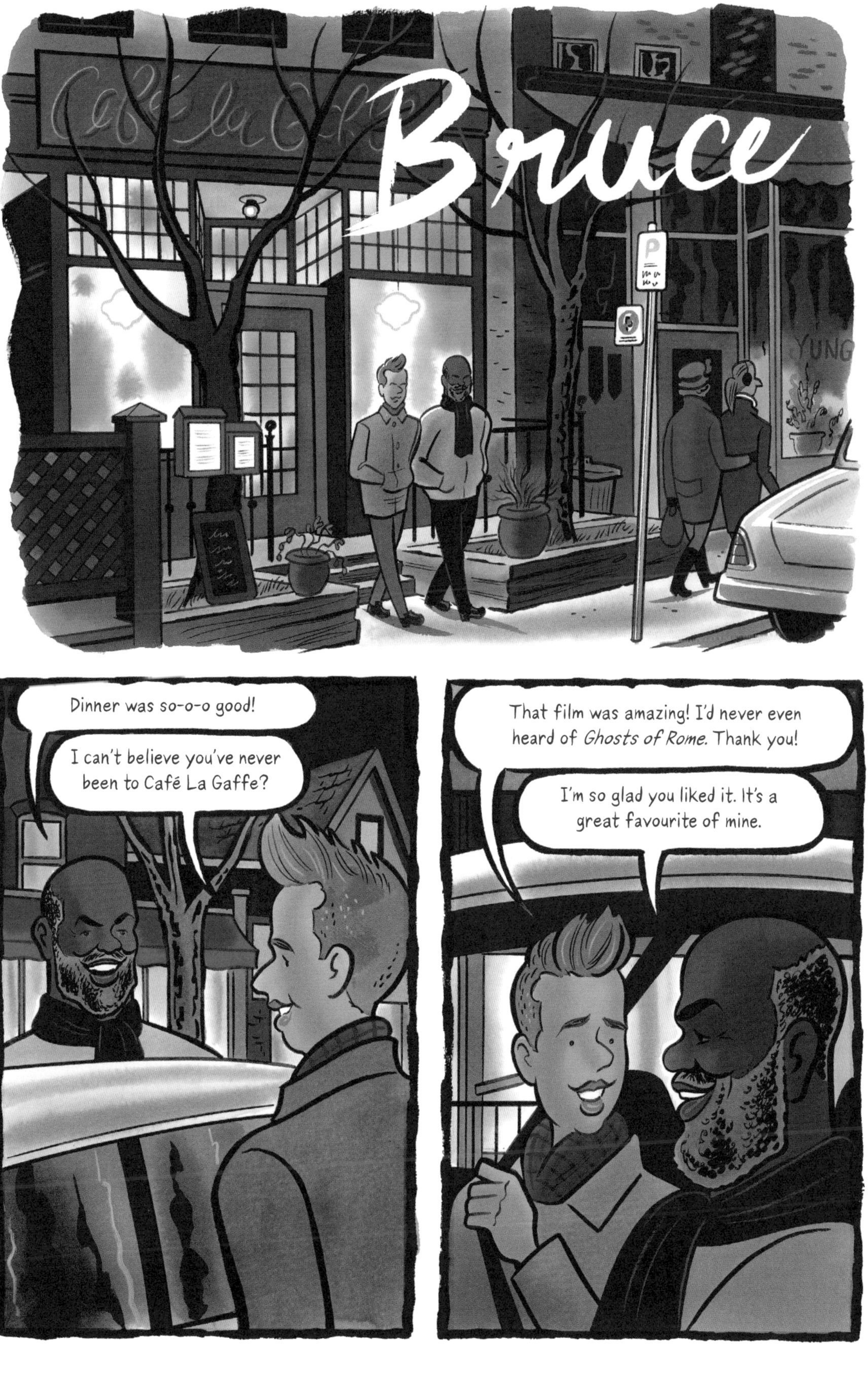
Bruce
YUNG
Dinner was so-o-o good!
I can't believe you've never been to Café La Gaffe?
That film was amazing! I'd never even heard of *Ghosts of Rome.* Thank you!
I'm so glad you liked it. It's a great favourite of mine.

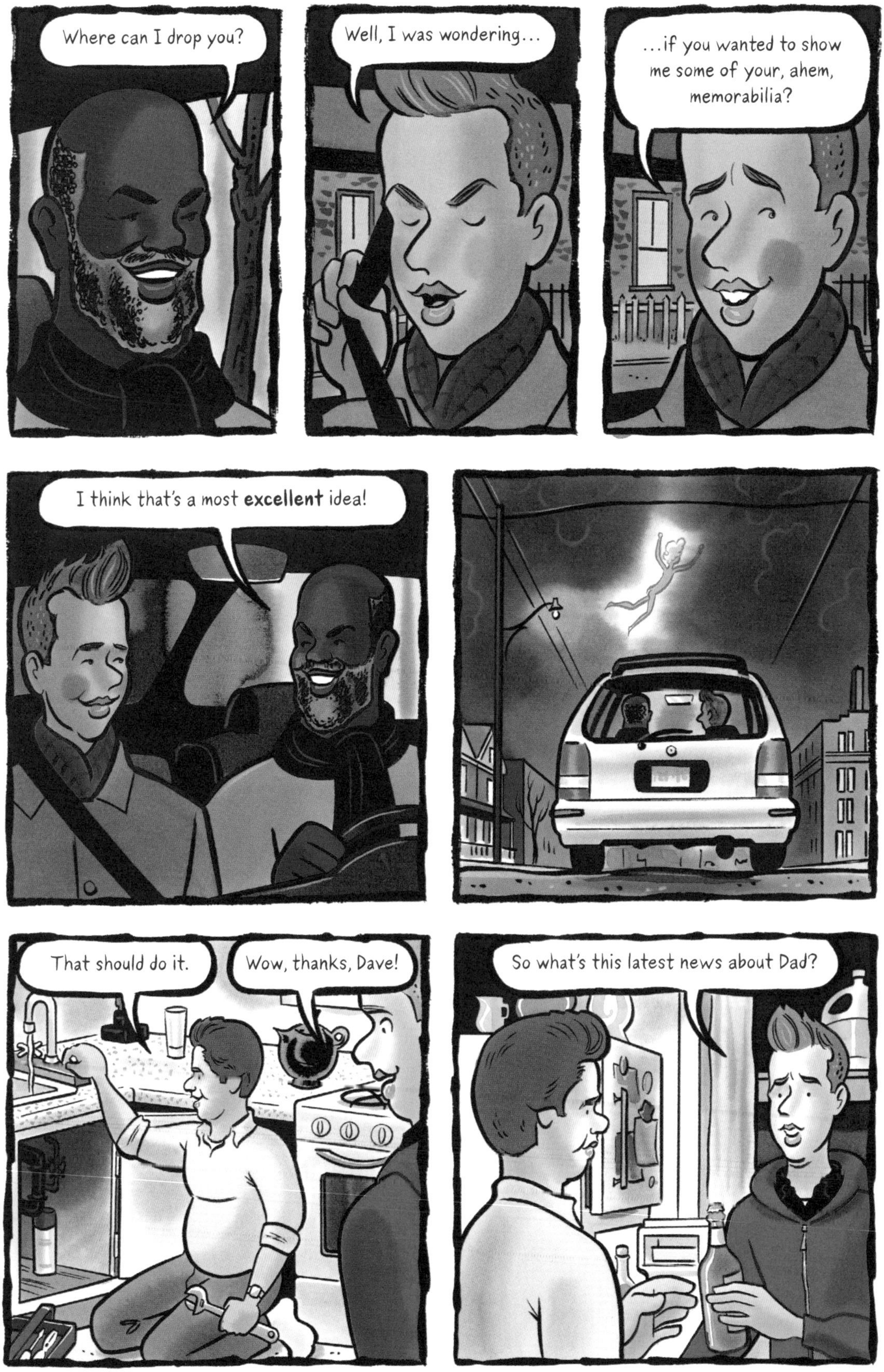

Where can I drop you?
Well, I was wondering...
...if you wanted to show me some of your, ahem, memorabilia?
I think that's a most **excellent** idea!
That should do it.
Wow, thanks, Dave!
So what's this latest news about Dad?

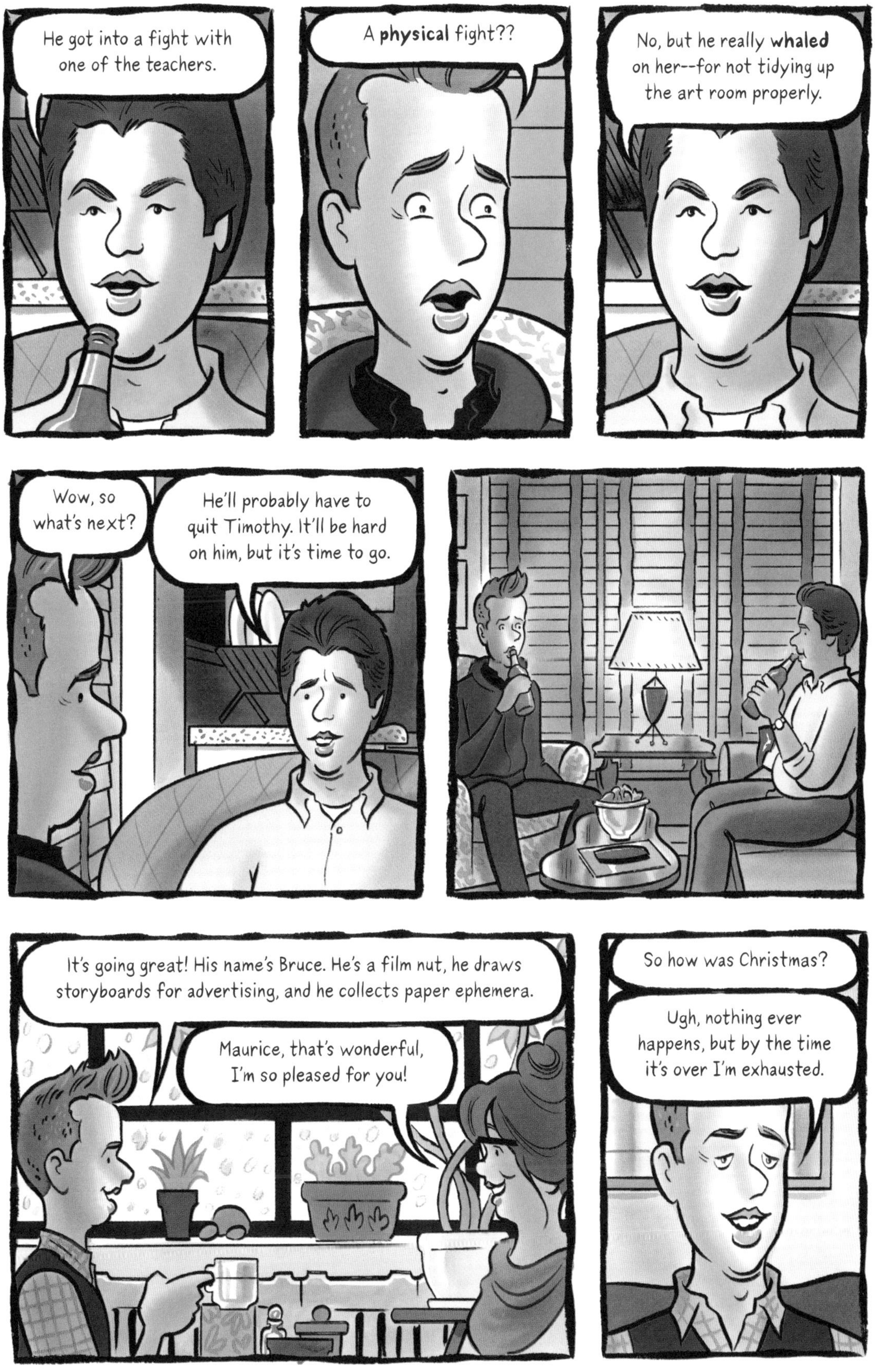
He got into a fight with one of the teachers.
A **physical** fight??
No, but he really **whaled** on her--for not tidying up the art room properly.
Wow, so what's next?
He'll probably have to quit Timothy. It'll be hard on him, but it's time to go.
It's going great! His name's Bruce. He's a film nut, he draws storyboards for advertising, and he collects paper ephemera.
Maurice, that's wonderful, I'm so pleased for you!
So how was Christmas?
Ugh, nothing ever happens, but by the time it's over I'm exhausted.

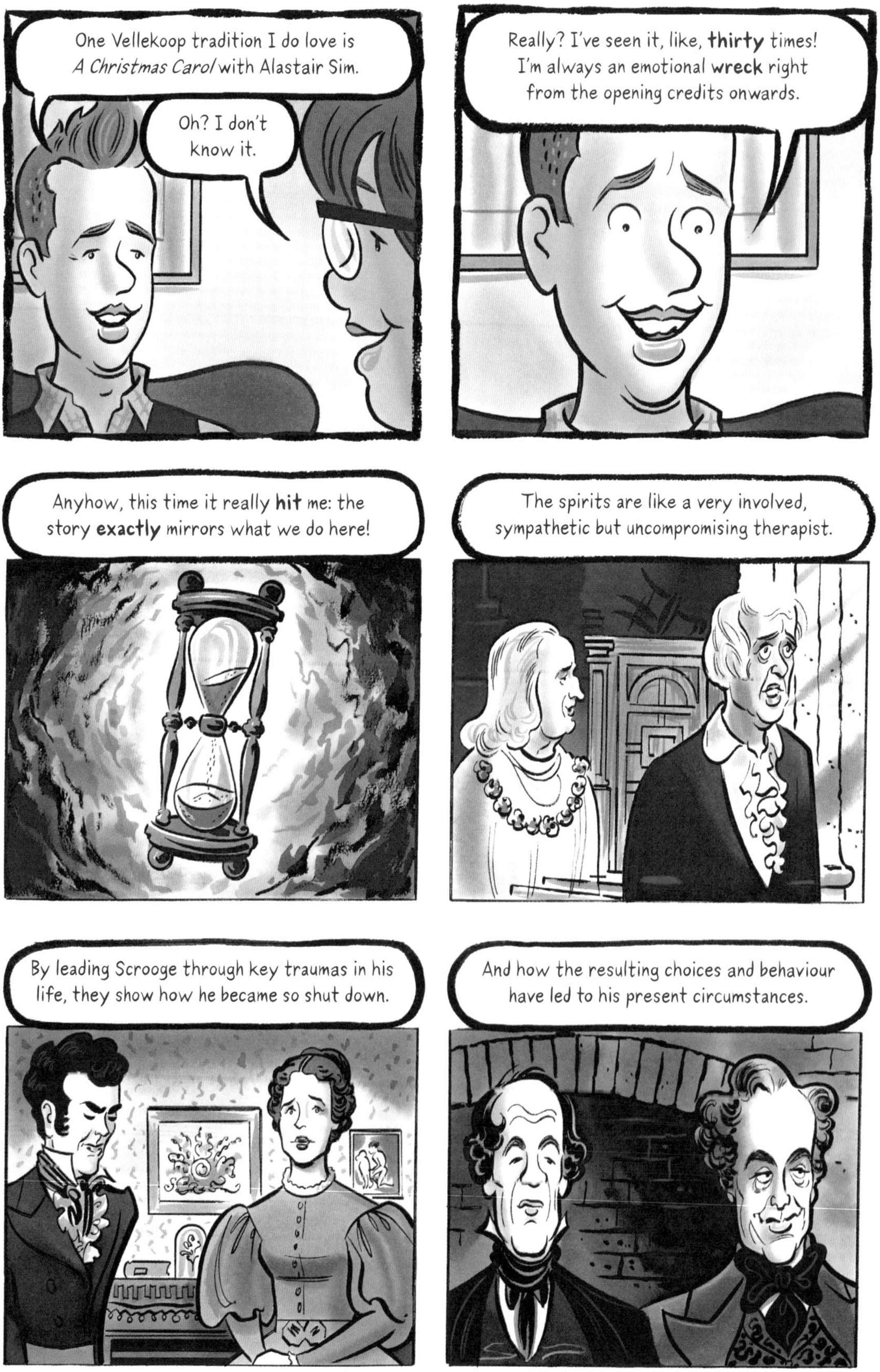

One Vellekoop tradition I do love is *A Christmas Carol* with Alastair Sim.
Oh? I don't know it.
Really? I've seen it, like, **thirty** times! I'm always an emotional **wreck** right from the opening credits onwards.
Anyhow, this time it really **hit** me: the story **exactly** mirrors what we do here!
The spirits are like a very involved, sympathetic but uncompromising therapist.
By leading Scrooge through key traumas in his life, they show how he became so shut down.
And how the resulting choices and behaviour have led to his present circumstances.

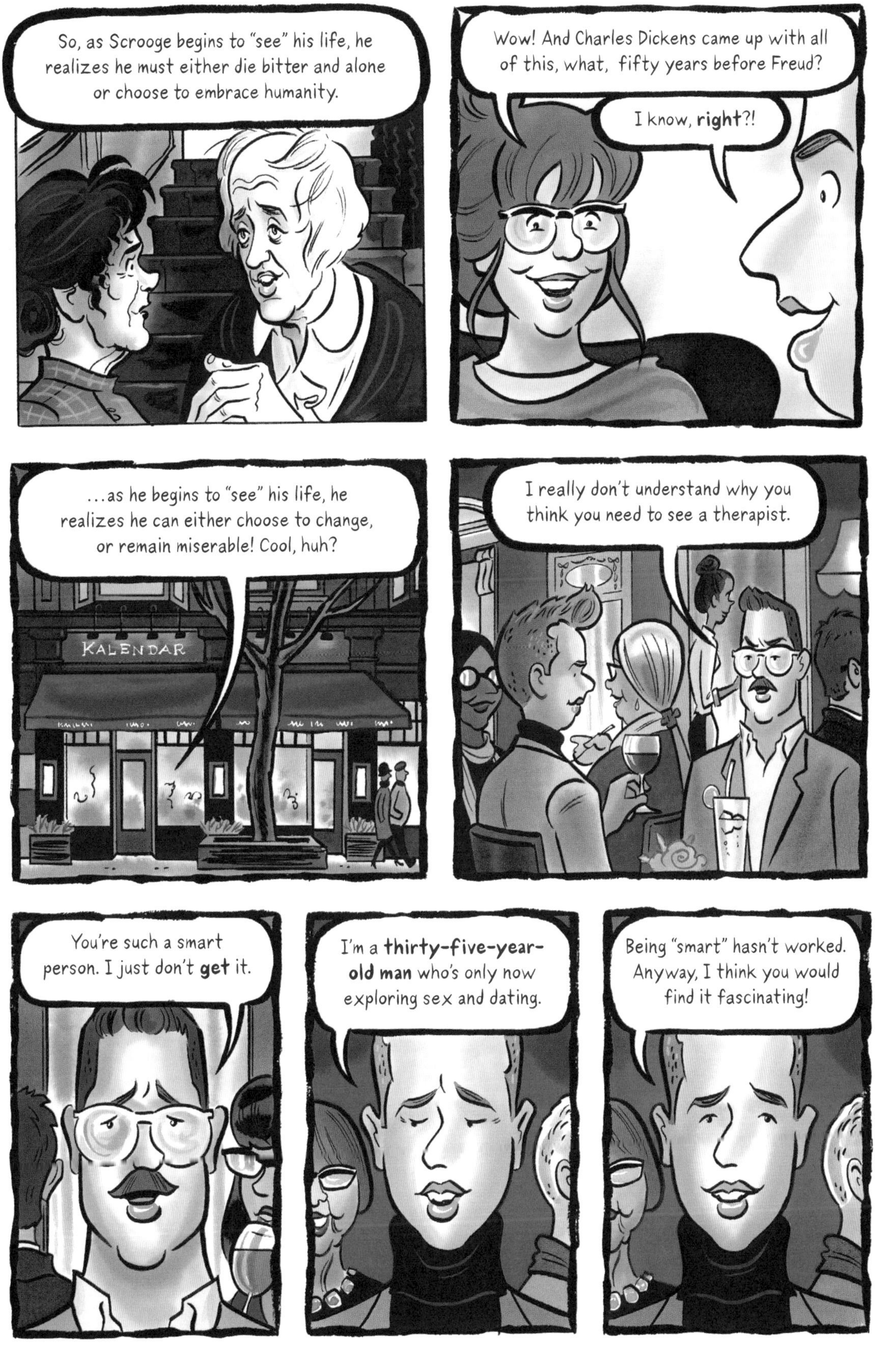
So, as Scrooge begins to "see" his life, he realizes he must either die bitter and alone or choose to embrace humanity.
Wow! And Charles Dickens came up with all of this, what, fifty years before Freud?
I know, **right**?!
...as he begins to "see" his life, he realizes he can either choose to change, or remain miserable! Cool, huh?
KALENDAR
I really don't understand why you think you need to see a therapist.
You're such a smart person. I just don't **get** it.
I'm a **thirty-five-year-old man** who's only now exploring sex and dating.
Being "smart" hasn't worked. Anyway, I think you would find it fascinating!

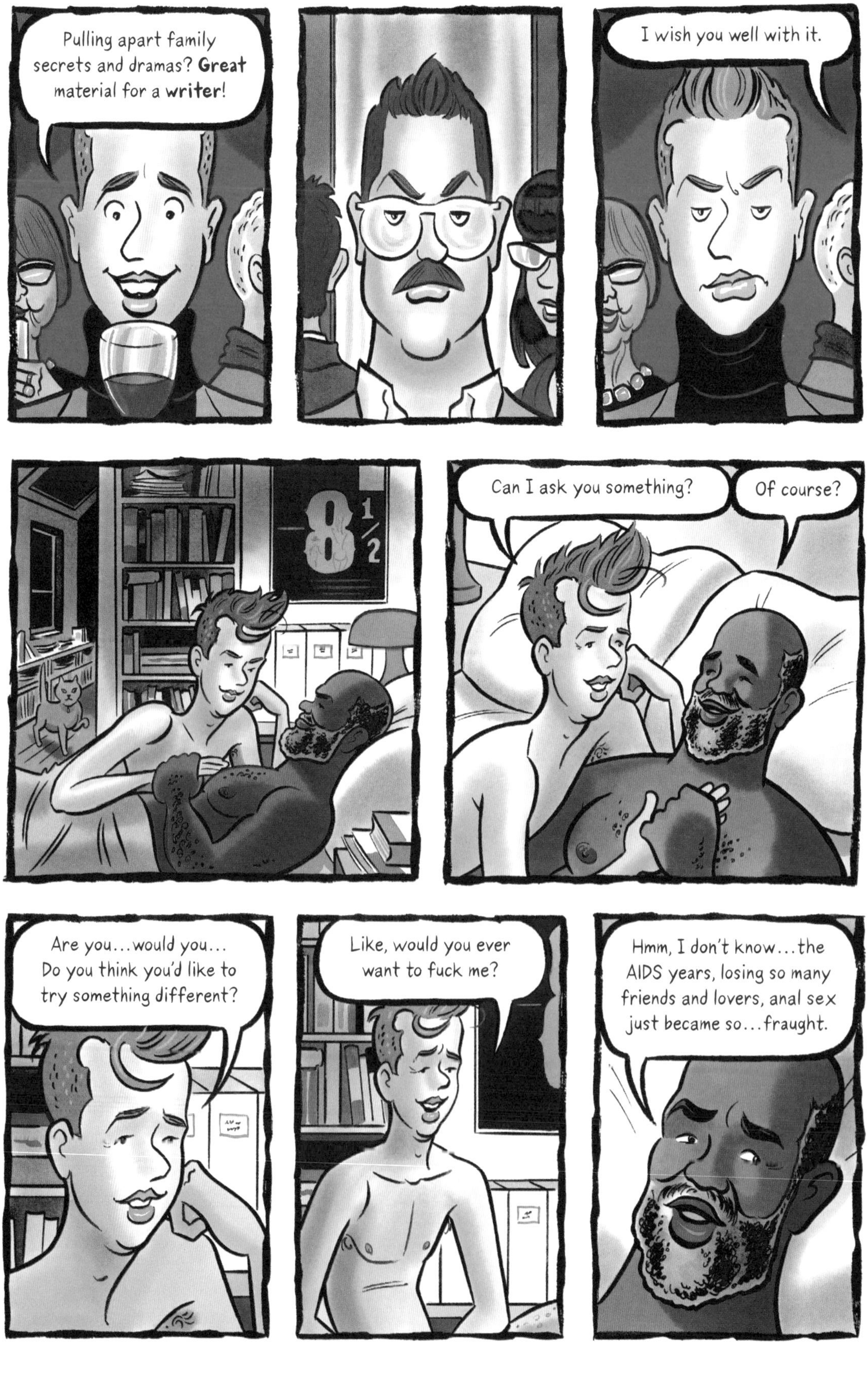

Pulling apart family secrets and dramas? **Great** material for a **writer**!
I wish you well with it.
Can I ask you something?
Of course?
Are you...would you... Do you think you'd like to try something different?
Like, would you ever want to fuck me?
Hmm, I don't know...the AIDS years, losing so many friends and lovers, anal sex just became so...fraught.

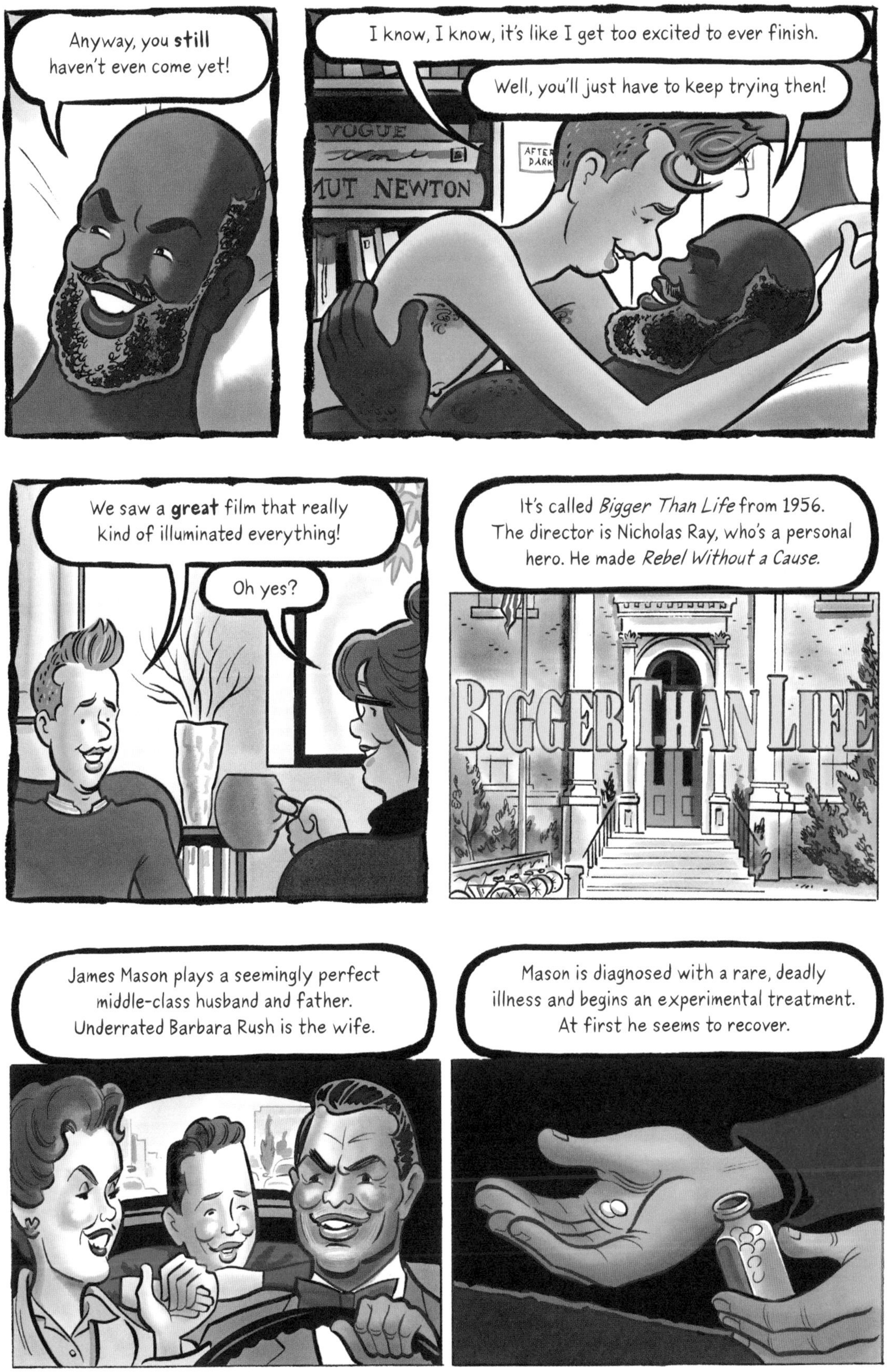

Anyway, you **still** haven't even come yet!
I know, I know, it's like I get too excited to ever finish.
Well, you'll just have to keep trying then!
VOGUE
MUT NEWTON
AFTER DARK
We saw a **great** film that really kind of illuminated everything!
Oh yes?
It's called *Bigger Than Life* from 1956. The director is Nicholas Ray, who's a personal hero. He made *Rebel Without a Cause.*
BIGGER THAN LIFE
James Mason plays a seemingly perfect middle-class husband and father. Underrated Barbara Rush is the wife.
Mason is diagnosed with a rare, deadly illness and begins an experimental treatment. At first he seems to recover.

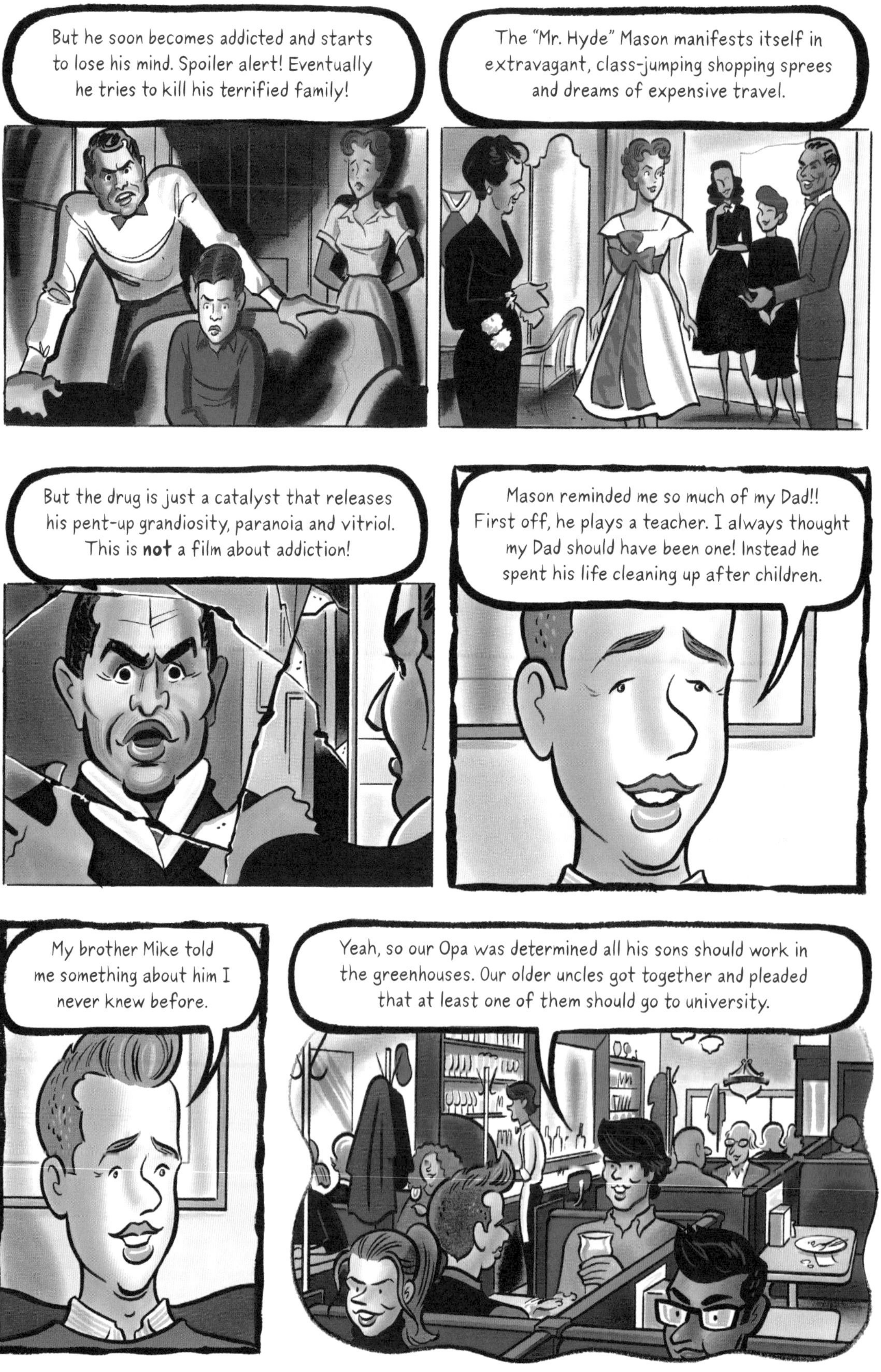
But he soon becomes addicted and starts to lose his mind. Spoiler alert! Eventually he tries to kill his terrified family!
The "Mr. Hyde" Mason manifests itself in extravagant, class-jumping shopping sprees and dreams of expensive travel.
But the drug is just a catalyst that releases his pent-up grandiosity, paranoia and vitriol. This is not a film about addiction!
Mason reminded me so much of my Dad!! First off, he plays a teacher. I always thought my Dad should have been one! Instead he spent his life cleaning up after children.
My brother Mike told me something about him I never knew before.
Yeah, so our Opa was determined all his sons should work in the greenhouses. Our older uncles got together and pleaded that at least one of them should go to university.

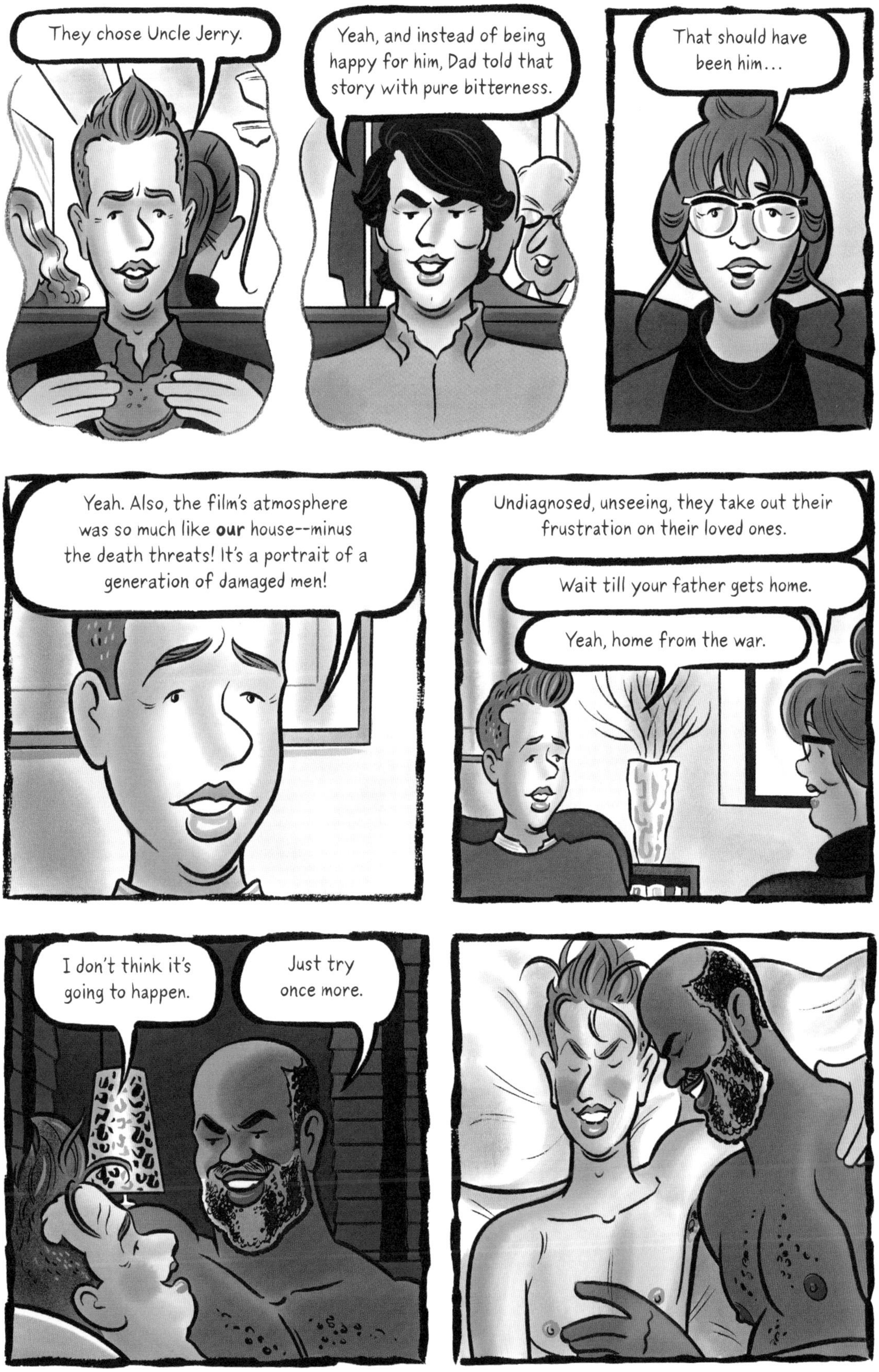
They chose Uncle Jerry.
Yeah, and instead of being happy for him, Dad told that story with pure bitterness.
That should have been him...
Yeah. Also, the film's atmosphere was so much like **our** house--minus the death threats! It's a portrait of a generation of damaged men!
Undiagnosed, unseeing, they take out their frustration on their loved ones.
Wait till your father gets home.
Yeah, home from the war.
I don't think it's going to happen.
Just try once more.

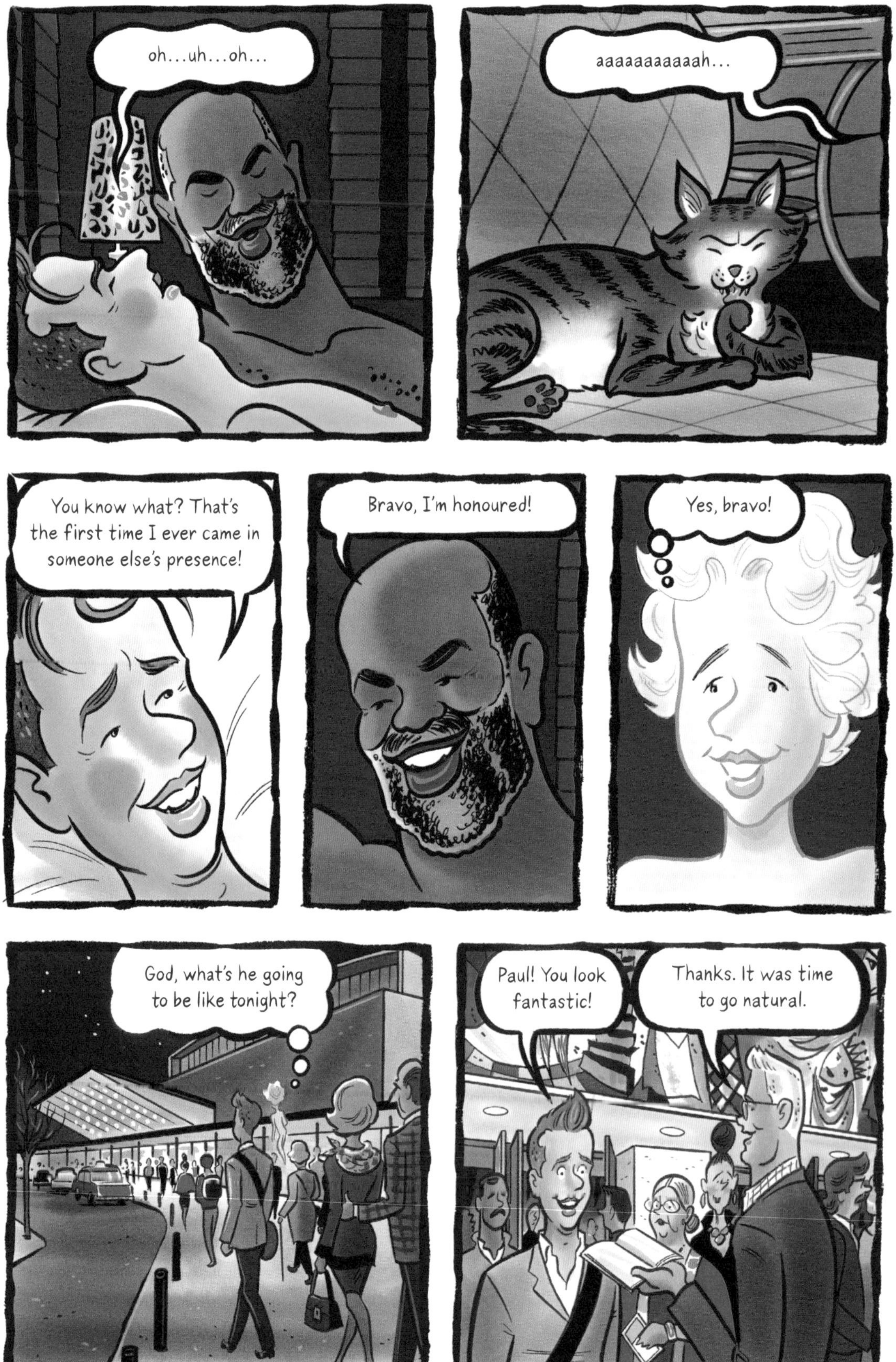
oh...uh...oh...
aaaaaaaaaaah...
You know what? That's the first time I ever came in someone else's presence!
Bravo, I'm honoured!
Yes, bravo!
God, what's he going to be like tonight?
Paul! You look fantastic!
Thanks. It was time to go natural.

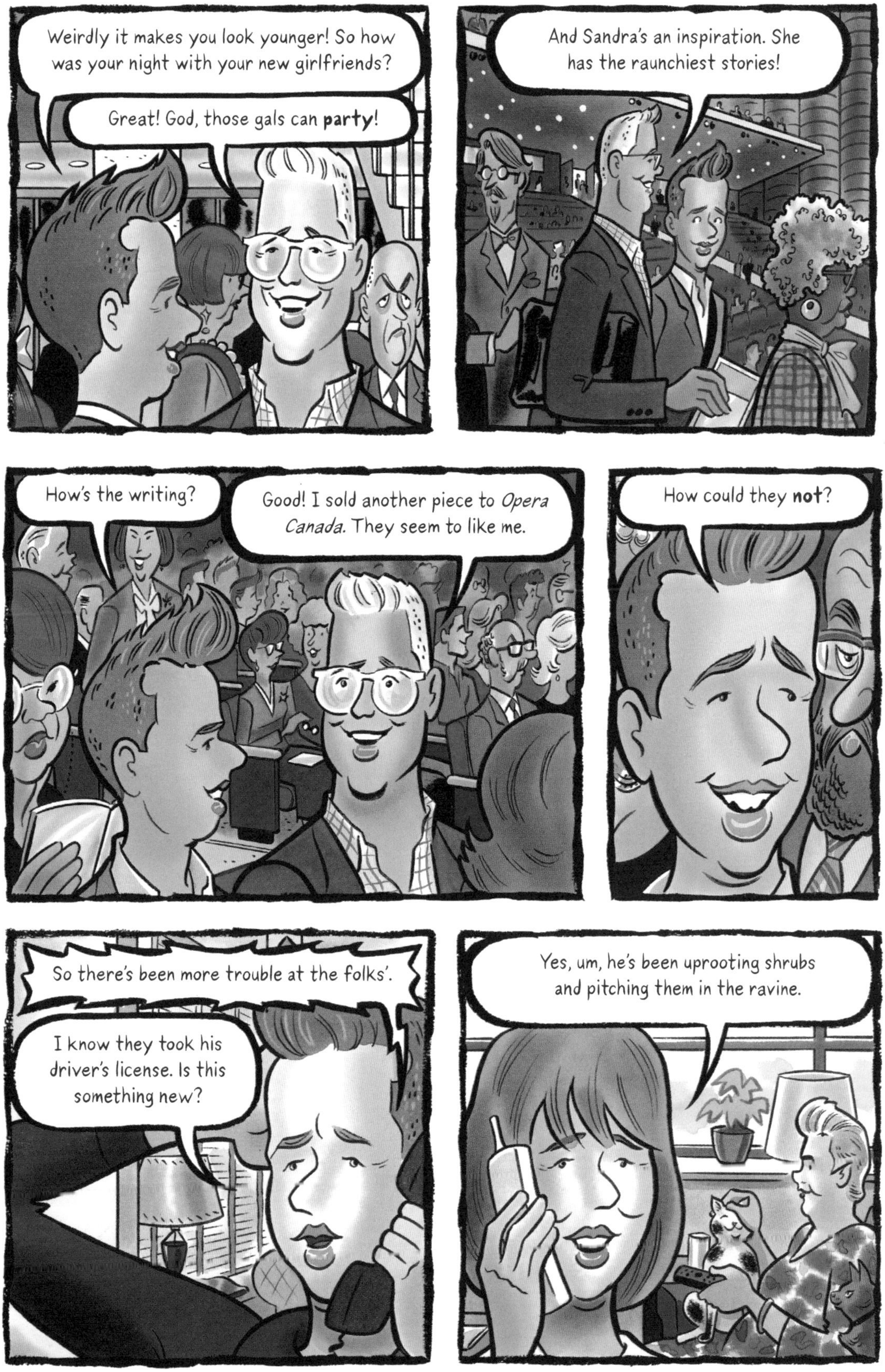
Weirdly it makes you look younger! So how was your night with your new girlfriends?
Great! God, those gals can **party**!
And Sandra's an inspiration. She has the raunchiest stories!
How's the writing?
Good! I sold another piece to *Opera Canada*. They seem to like me.
How could they **not**?
So there's been more trouble at the folks'.
I know they took his driver's license. Is this something new?
Yes, um, he's been uprooting shrubs and pitching them in the ravine.

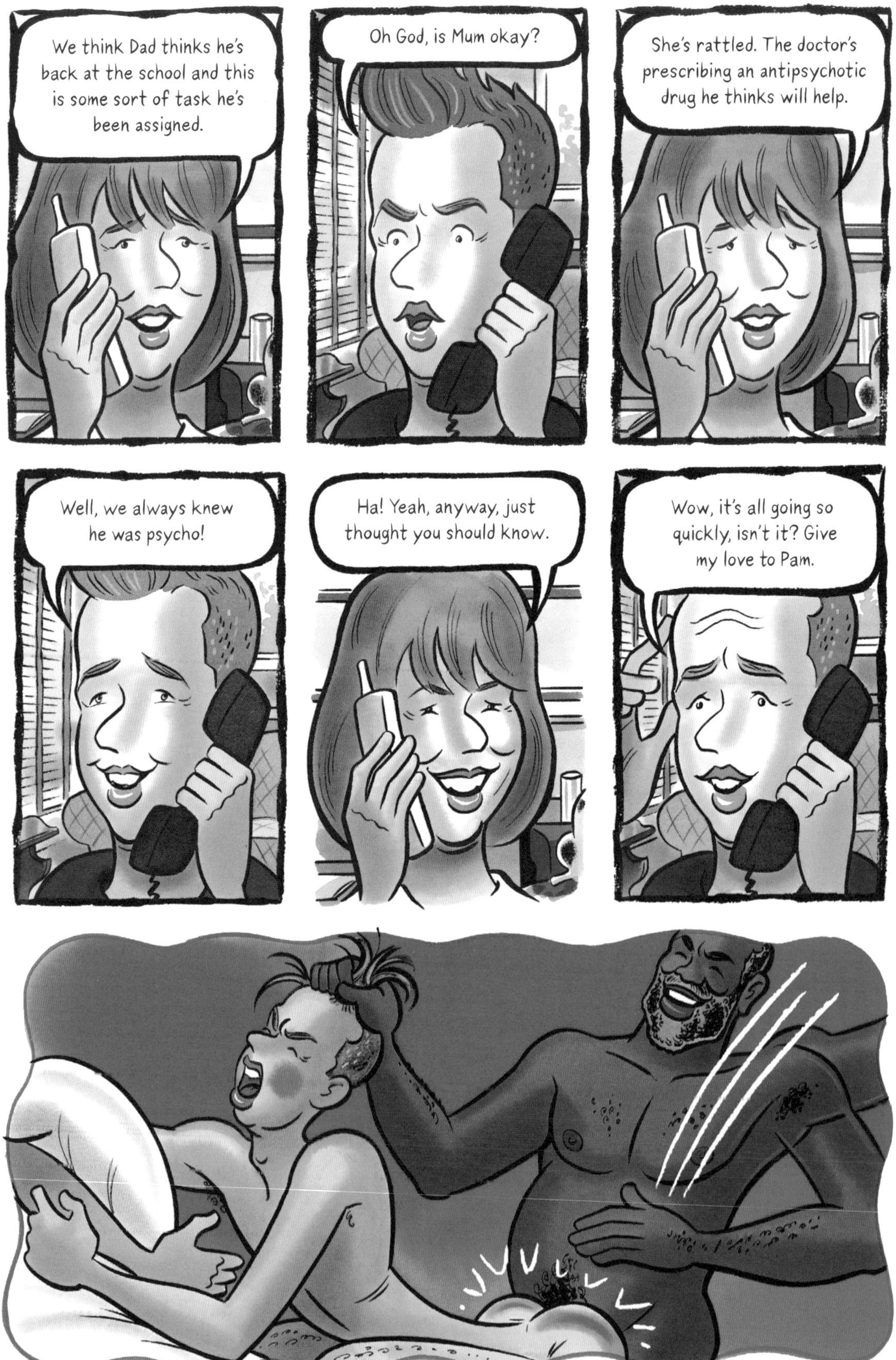
We think Dad thinks he's back at the school and this is some sort of task he's been assigned.
Oh God, is Mum okay?
She's rattled. The doctor's prescribing an antipsychotic drug he thinks will help.
Well, we always knew he was psycho!
Ha! Yeah, anyway, just thought you should know.
Wow, it's all going so quickly, isn't it? Give my love to Pam.

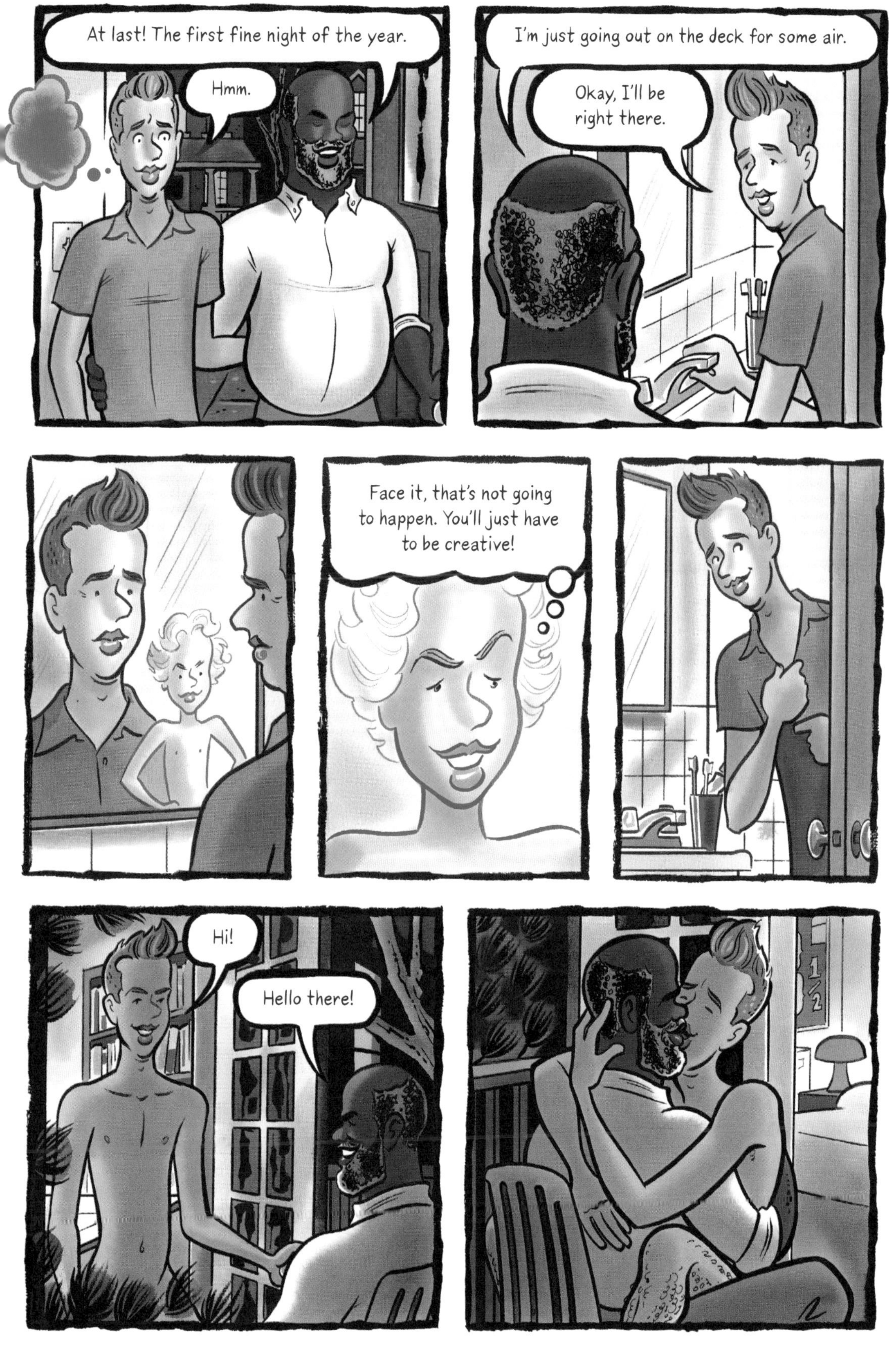

At last! The first fine night of the year.
Hmm.
I'm just going out on the deck for some air.
Okay, I'll be right there.
Face it, that's not going to happen. You'll just have to be creative!
Hi!
Hello there!

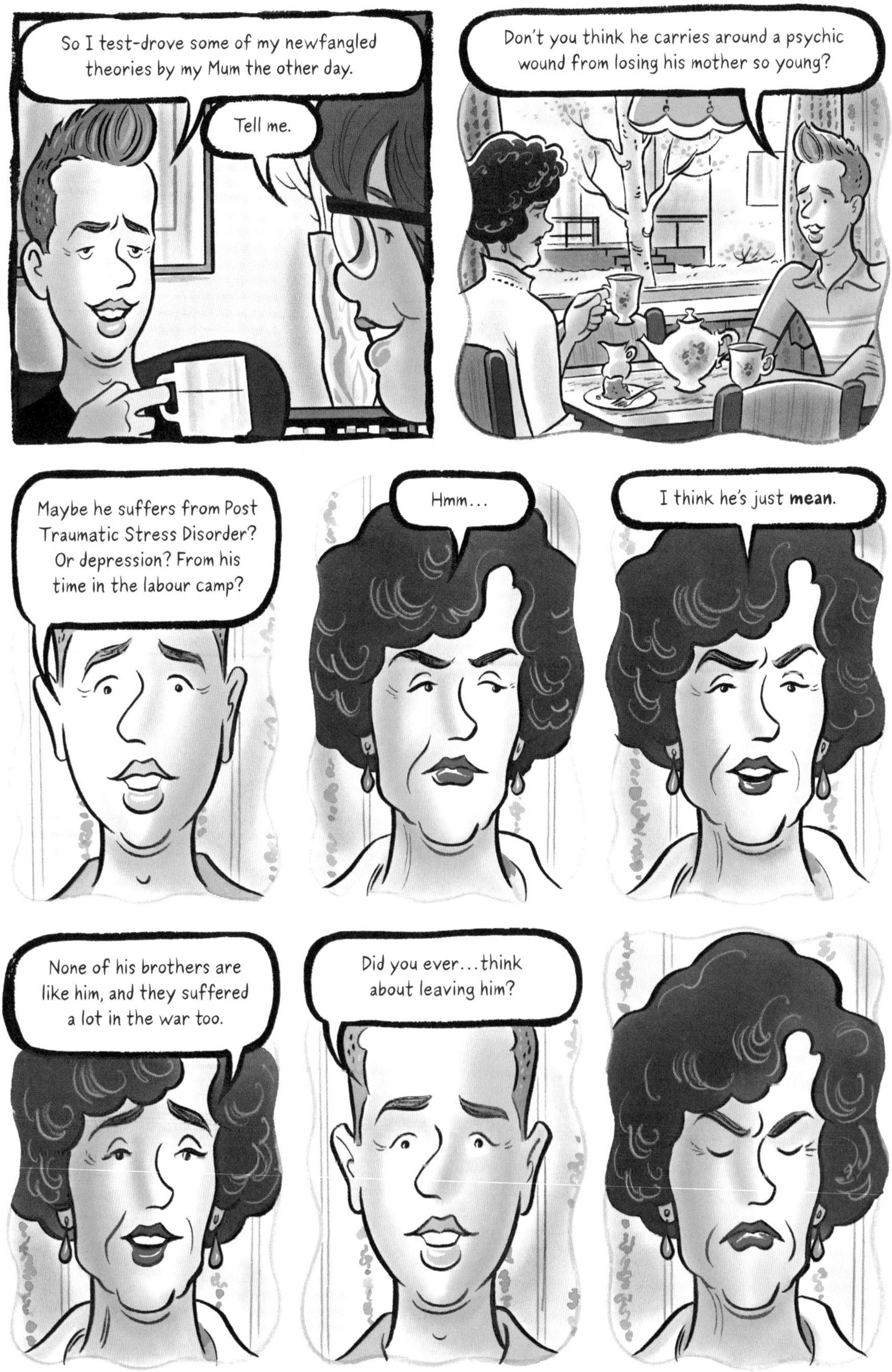
So I test-drove some of my newfangled theories by my Mum the other day.
Tell me.
Don't you think he carries around a psychic wound from losing his mother so young?
Maybe he suffers from Post Traumatic Stress Disorder? Or depression? From his time in the labour camp?
Hmm...
I think he's just **mean**.
None of his brothers are like him, and they suffered a lot in the war too.
Did you ever... think about leaving him?

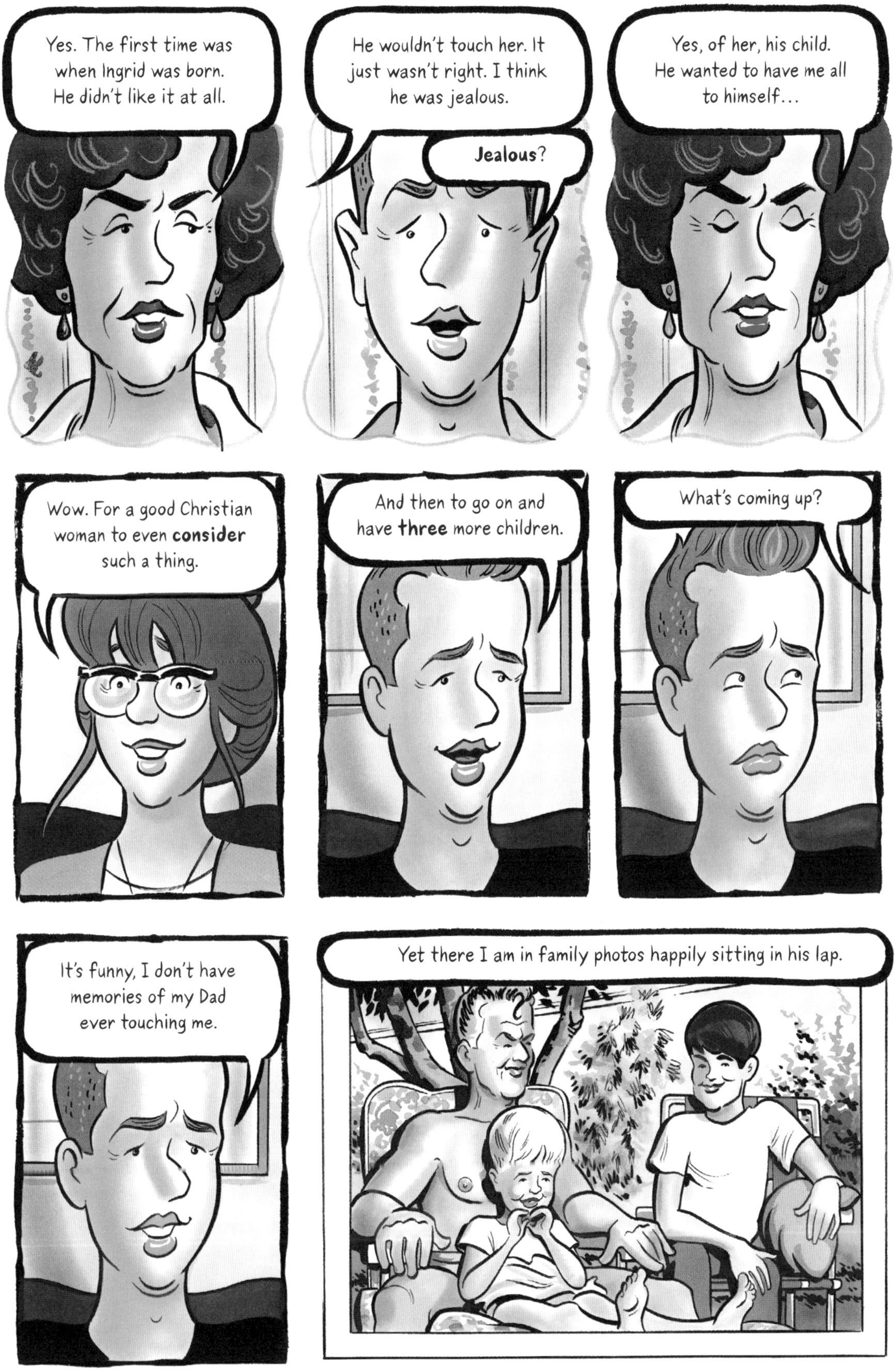
Yes. The first time was when Ingrid was born. He didn't like it at all.
He wouldn't touch her. It just wasn't right. I think he was jealous.
Jealous?
Yes, of her, his child. He wanted to have me all to himself...
Wow. For a good Christian woman to even consider such a thing.
And then to go on and have three more children.
What's coming up?
It's funny, I don't have memories of my Dad ever touching me.
Yet there I am in family photos happily sitting in his lap.

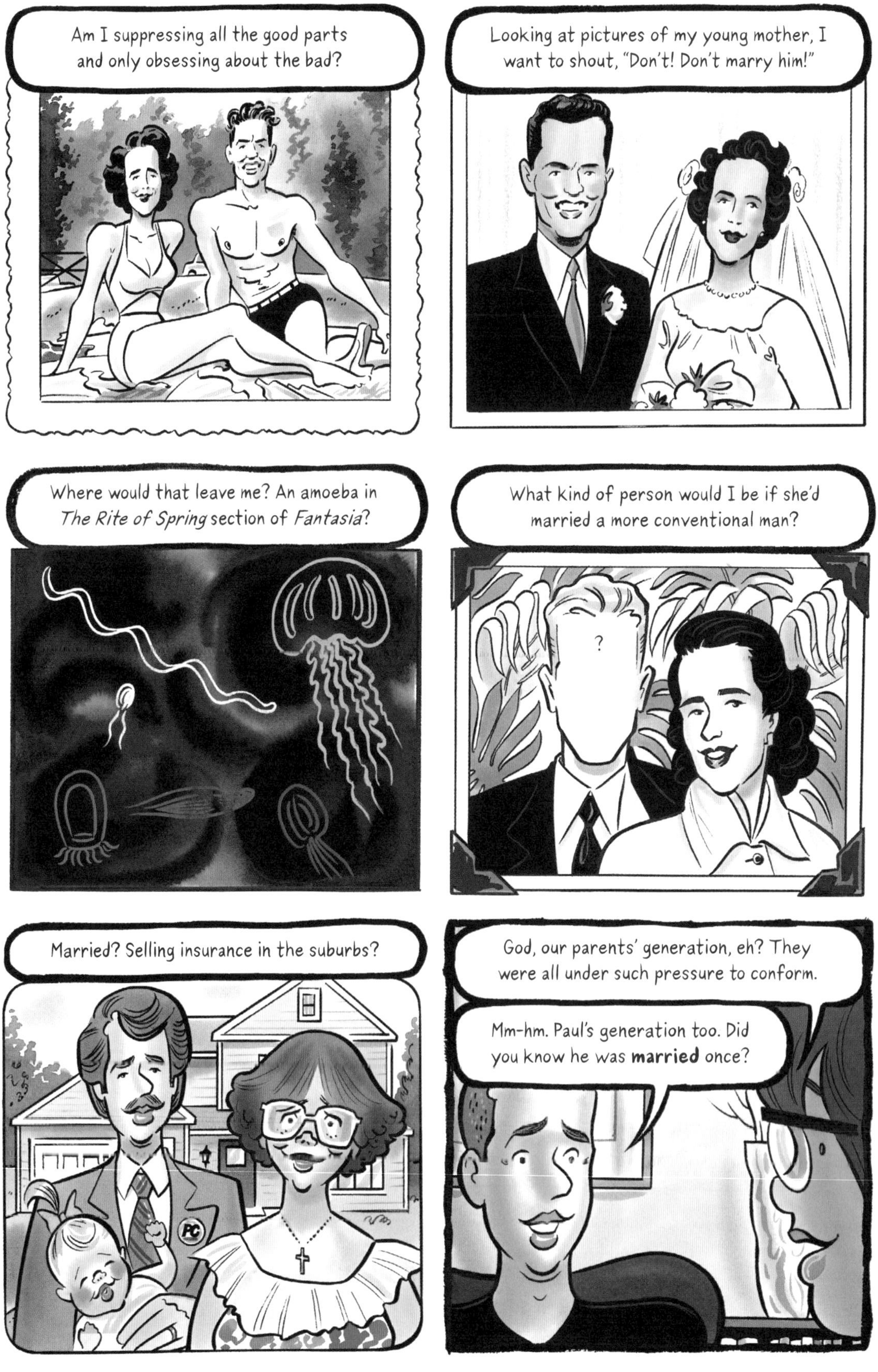
Am I suppressing all the good parts and only obsessing about the bad?
Looking at pictures of my young mother, I want to shout, "Don't! Don't marry him!"
Where would that leave me? An amoeba in *The Rite of Spring* section of *Fantasia*?
What kind of person would I be if she'd married a more conventional man?
?
Married? Selling insurance in the suburbs?
PC
God, our parents' generation, eh? They were all under such pressure to conform.
Mm-hm. Paul's generation too. Did you know he was **married** once?

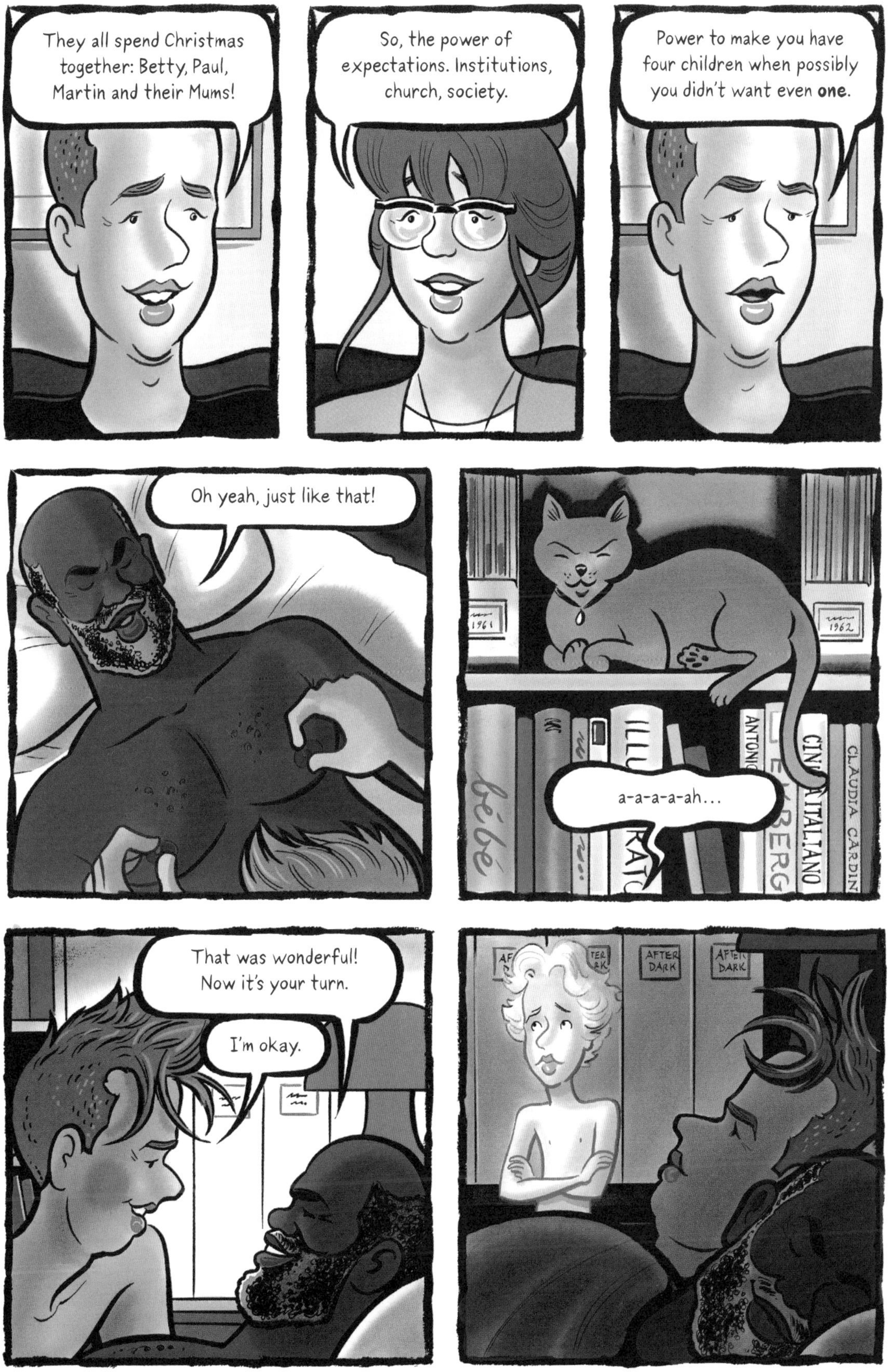
They all spend Christmas together: Betty, Paul, Martin and their Mums!
So, the power of expectations. Institutions, church, society.
Power to make you have four children when possibly you didn't want even **one**.
Oh yeah, just like that!
a-a-a-a-ah...
That was wonderful! Now it's your turn.
I'm okay.

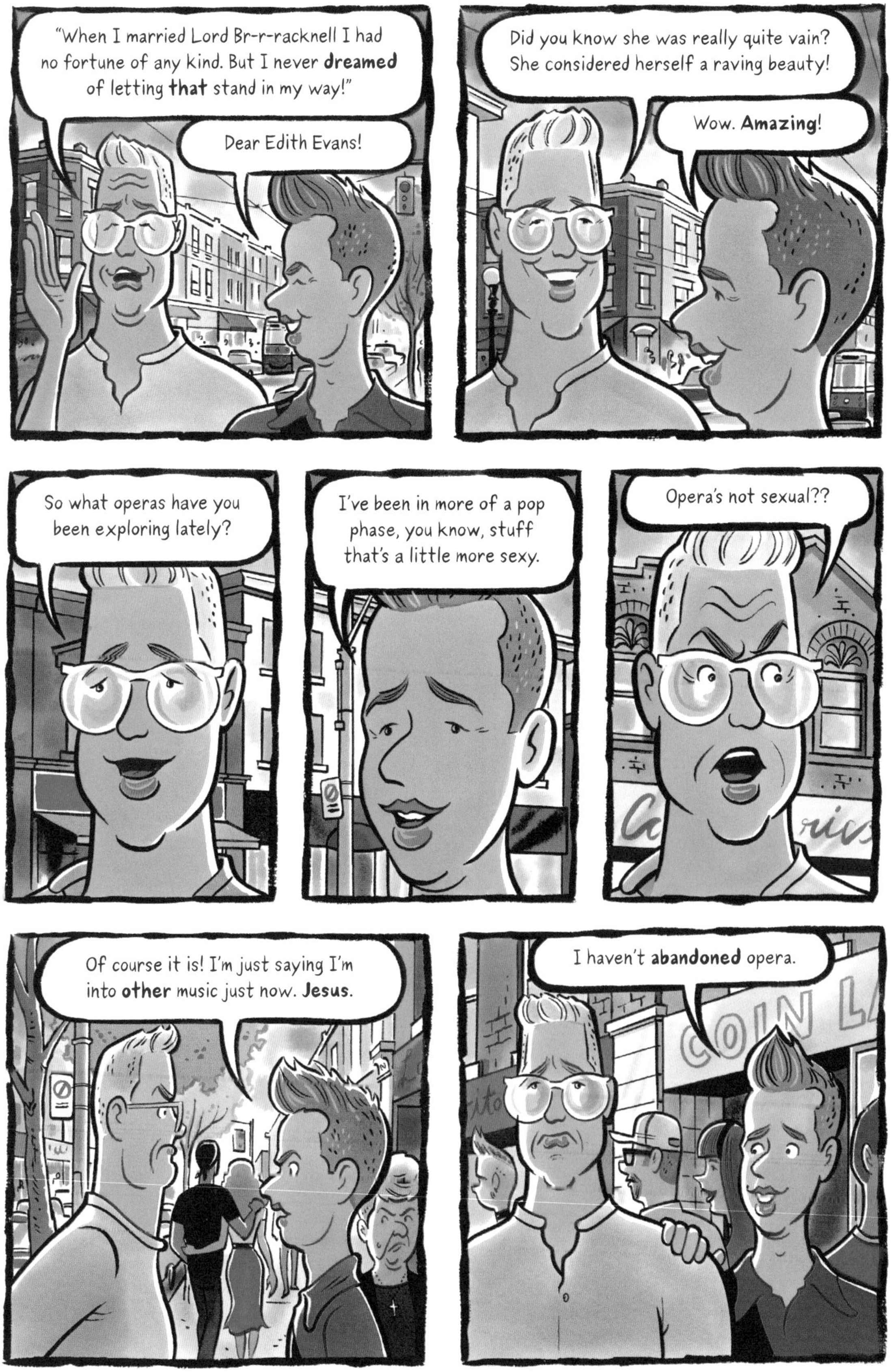
"When I married Lord Br-r-racknell I had no fortune of any kind. But I never **dreamed** of letting **that** stand in my way!"
Dear Edith Evans!
Did you know she was really quite vain? She considered herself a raving beauty!
Wow. **Amazing**!
So what operas have you been exploring lately?
I've been in more of a pop phase, you know, stuff that's a little more sexy.
Opera's not sexual??
Of course it is! I'm just saying I'm into **other** music just now. **Jesus**.
I haven't **abandoned** opera.

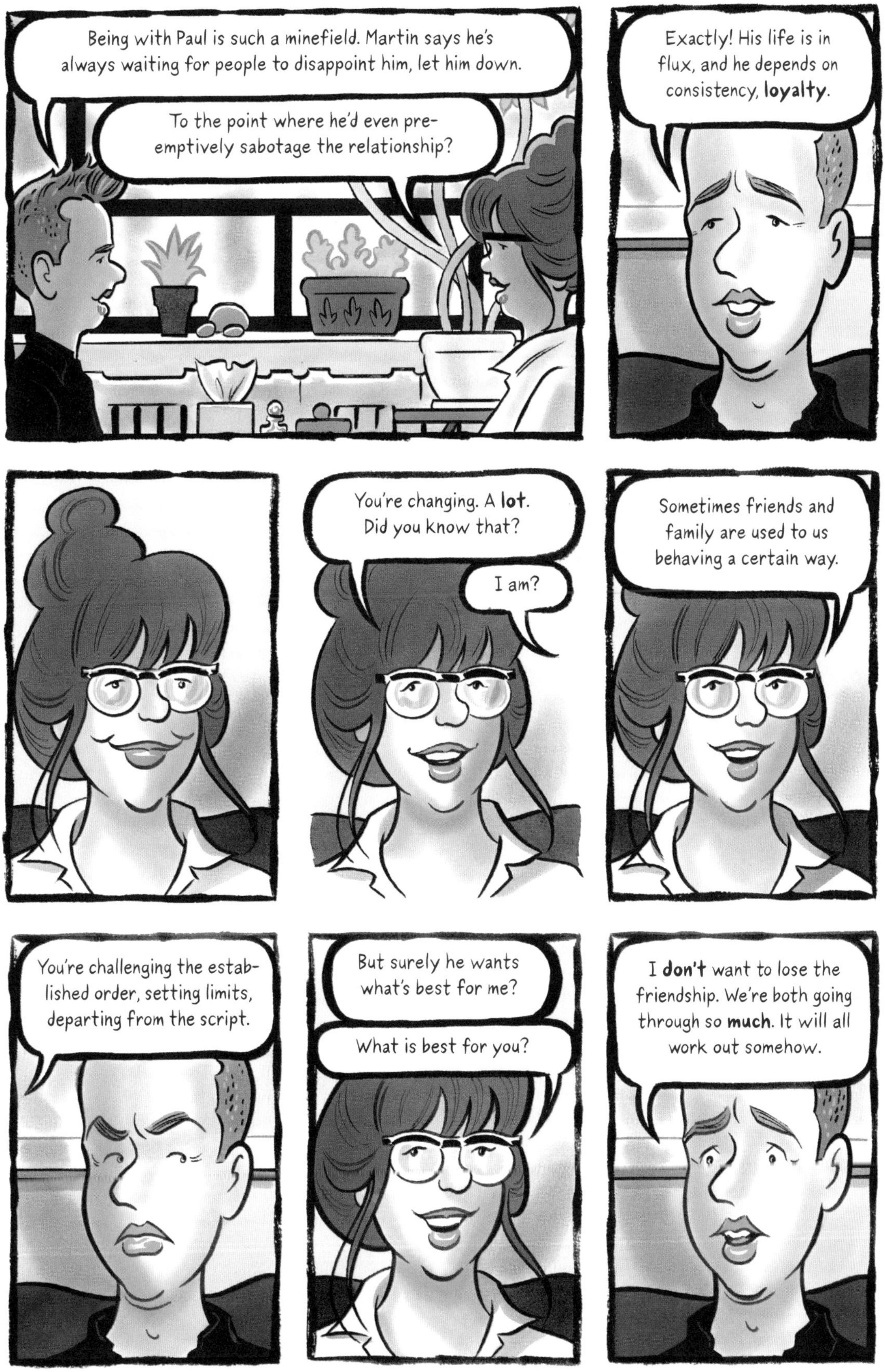
Being with Paul is such a minefield. Martin says he's always waiting for people to disappoint him, let him down.
To the point where he'd even pre-emptively sabotage the relationship?
Exactly! His life is in flux, and he depends on consistency, **loyalty**.
You're changing. A **lot**. Did you know that?
I am?
Sometimes friends and family are used to us behaving a certain way.
You're challenging the established order, setting limits, departing from the script.
But surely he wants what's best for me?
What is best for you?
I **don't** want to lose the friendship. We're both going through so **much**. It will all work out somehow.

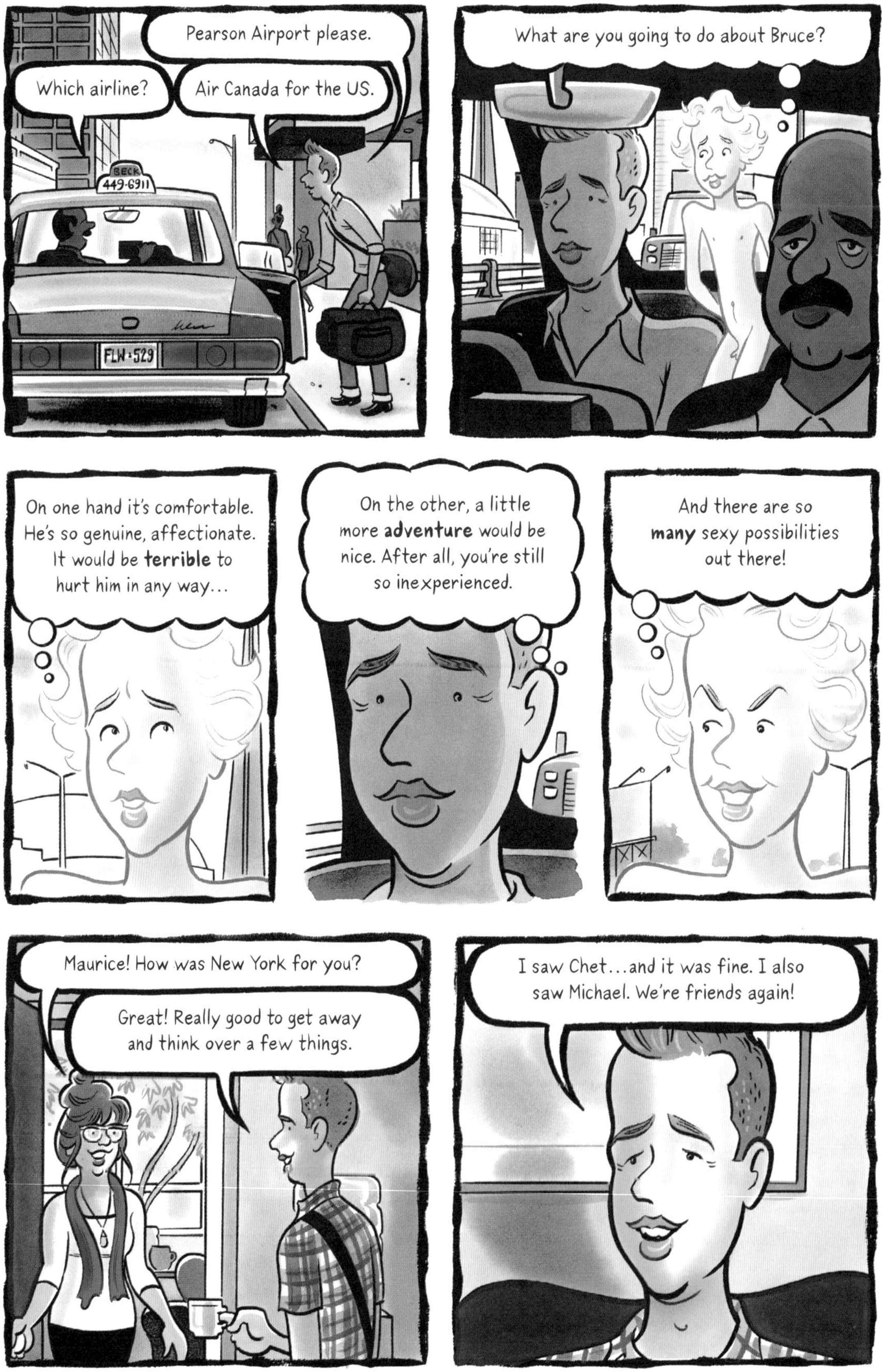
Pearson Airport please.
Which airline?
Air Canada for the US.
BECK
449-6911
FLW•529
What are you going to do about Bruce?
On one hand it's comfortable. He's so genuine, affectionate. It would be **terrible** to hurt him in any way...
On the other, a little more **adventure** would be nice. After all, you're still so inexperienced.
And there are so **many** sexy possibilities out there!
Maurice! How was New York for you?
Great! Really good to get away and think over a few things.
I saw Chet...and it was fine. I also saw Michael. We're friends again!

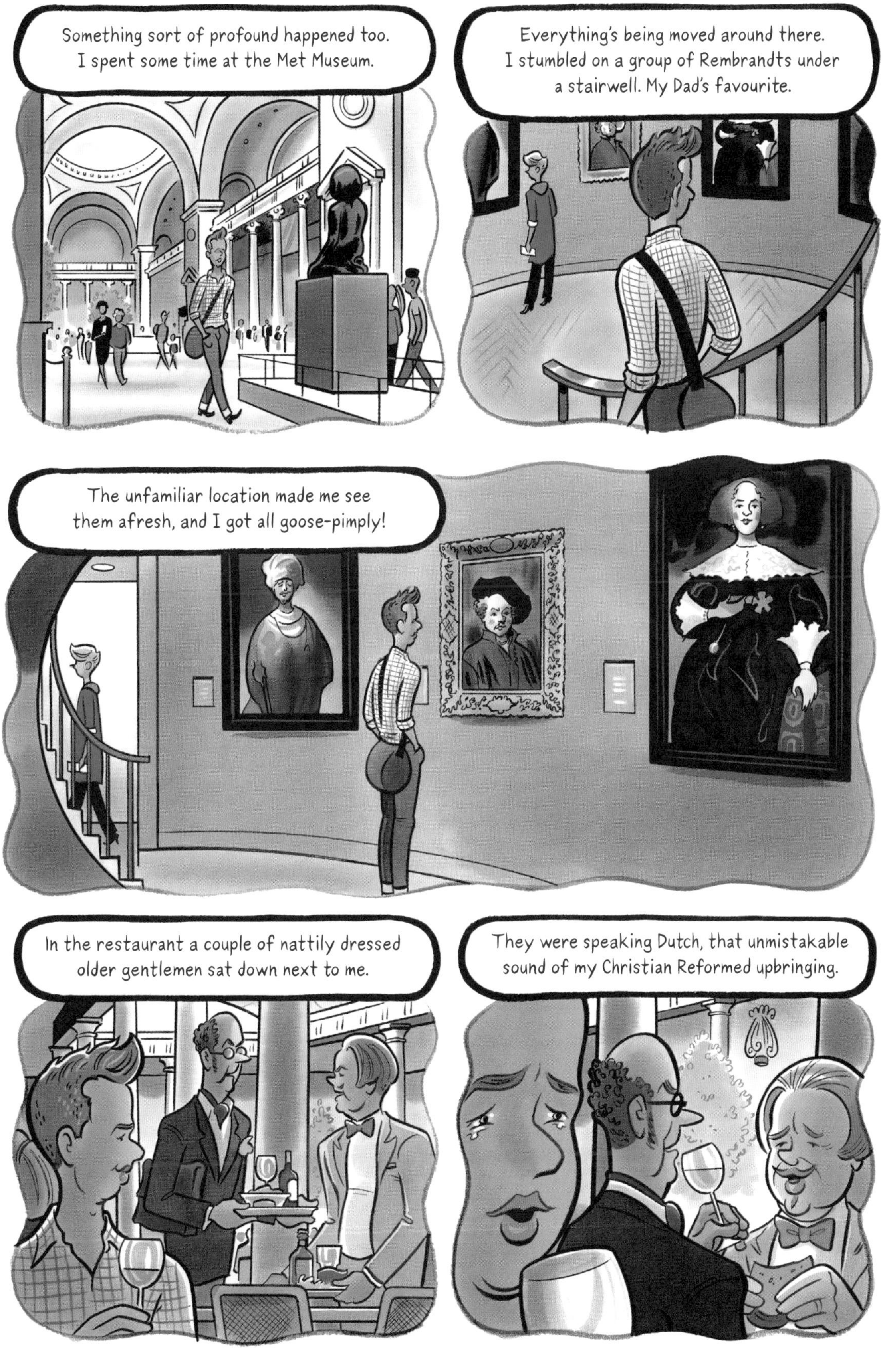
Something sort of profound happened too. I spent some time at the Met Museum.
Everything's being moved around there. I stumbled on a group of Rembrandts under a stairwell. My Dad's favourite.
The unfamiliar location made me see them afresh, and I got all goose-pimply!
In the restaurant a couple of nattily dressed older gentlemen sat down next to me.
They were speaking Dutch, that unmistakable sound of my Christian Reformed upbringing.

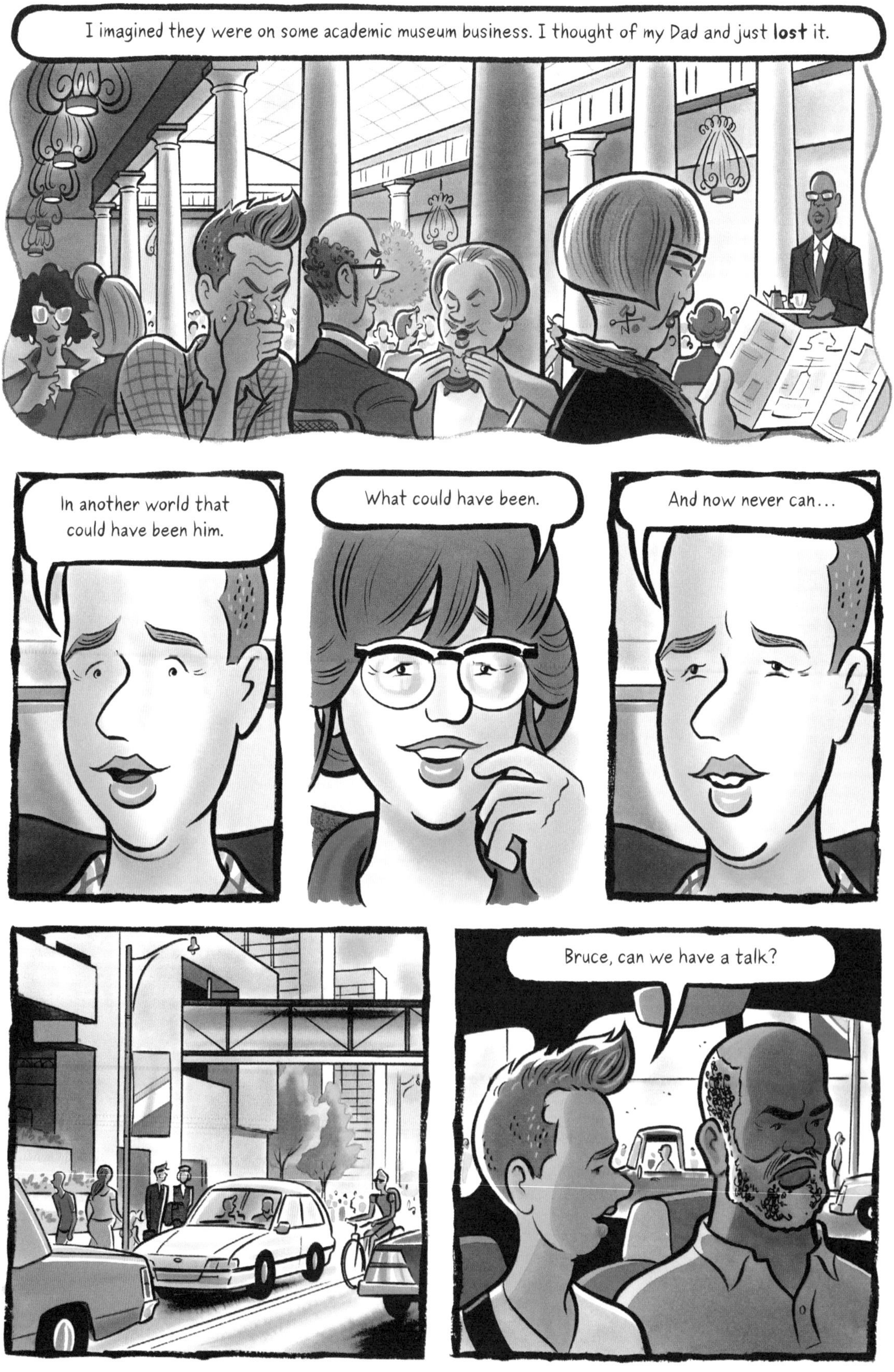
I imagined they were on some academic museum business. I thought of my Dad and just **lost** it.
In another world that could have been him.
What could have been.
And now never can...
Bruce, can we have a talk?

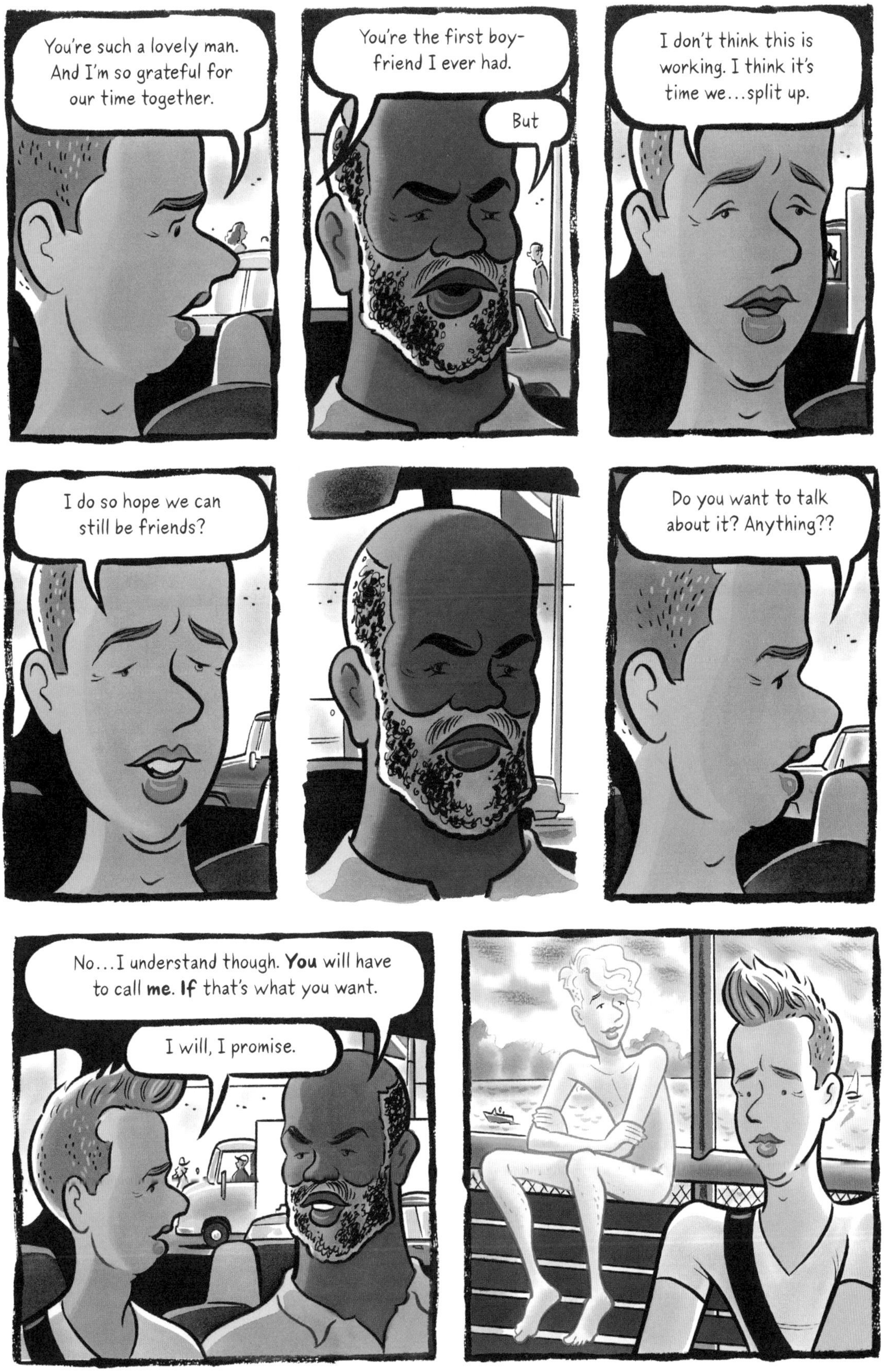
You're such a lovely man. And I'm so grateful for our time together.
You're the first boy-friend I ever had.
But
I don't think this is working. I think it's time we...split up.
I do so hope we can still be friends?
Do you want to talk about it? Anything??
No...I understand though. **You** will have to call **me**. **If** that's what you want.
I will, I promise.

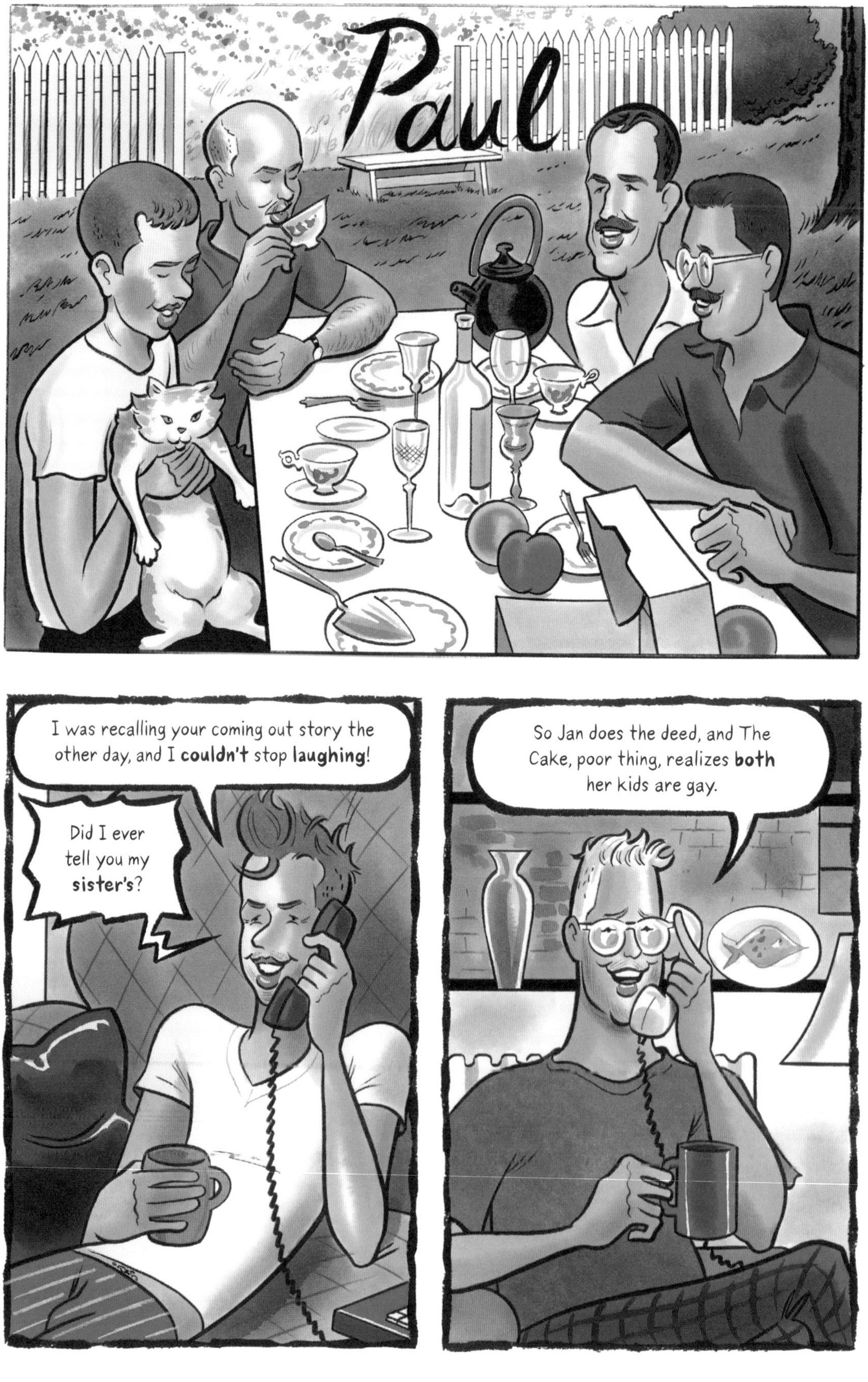
Paul
I was recalling your coming out story the other day, and I **couldn't** stop **laughing**!
Did I ever tell you my **sister's**?
So Jan does the deed, and The Cake, poor thing, realizes **both** her kids are gay.

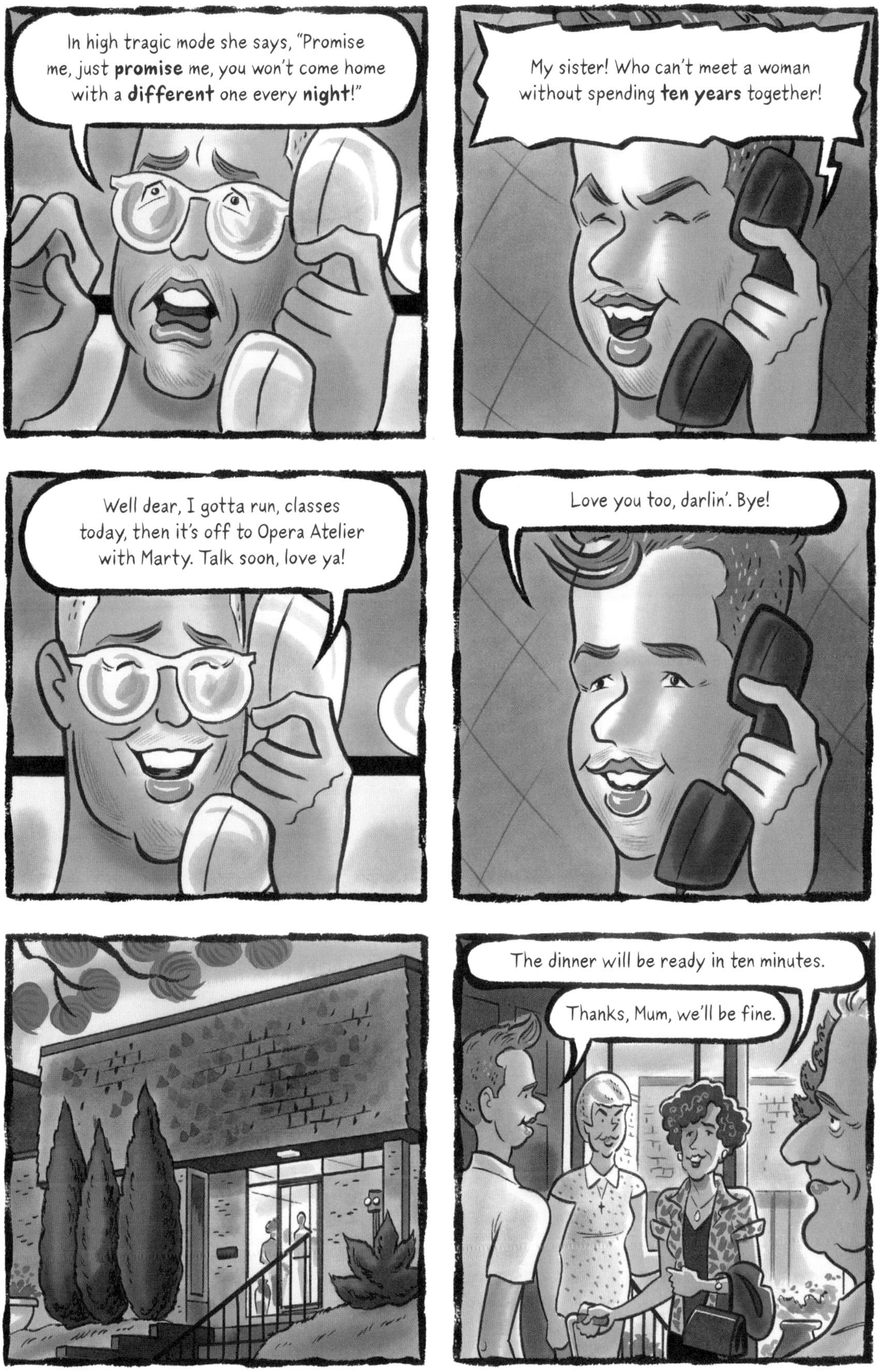
In high tragic mode she says, "Promise me, just **promise** me, you won't come home with a **different** one every **night**!"
My sister! Who can't meet a woman without spending **ten years** together!
Well dear, I gotta run, classes today, then it's off to Opera Atelier with Marty. Talk soon, love ya!
Love you too, darlin'. Bye!
The dinner will be ready in ten minutes.
Thanks, Mum, we'll be fine.

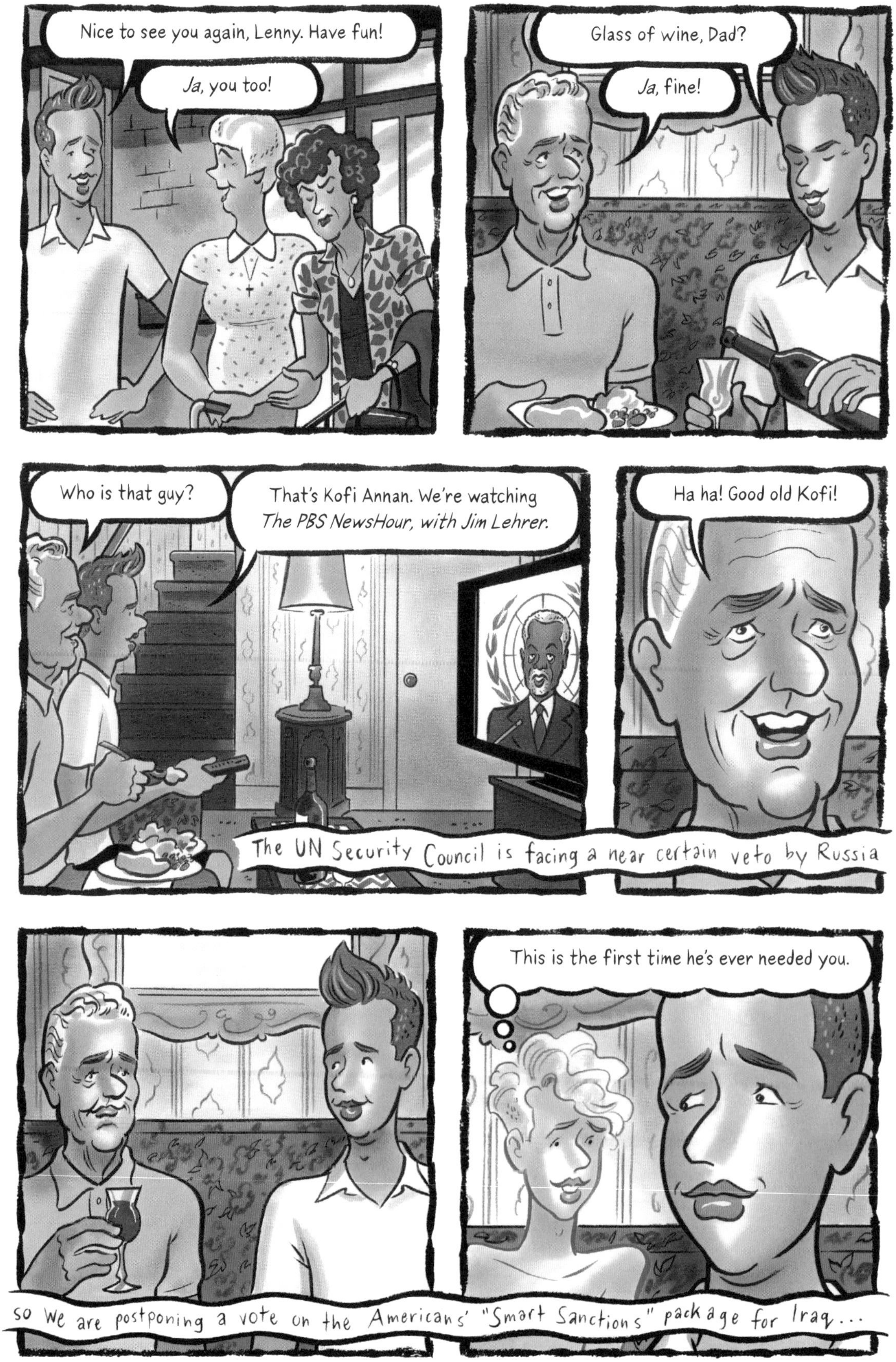

Nice to see you again, Lenny. Have fun!
Ja, you too!
Glass of wine, Dad?
Ja, fine!
Who is that guy?
That's Kofi Annan. We're watching *The PBS NewsHour, with Jim Lehrer.*
Ha ha! Good old Kofi!
The UN Security Council is facing a near certain veto by Russia
This is the first time he's ever needed you.
so we are postponing a vote on the Americans' "Smart Sanctions" package for Iraq...

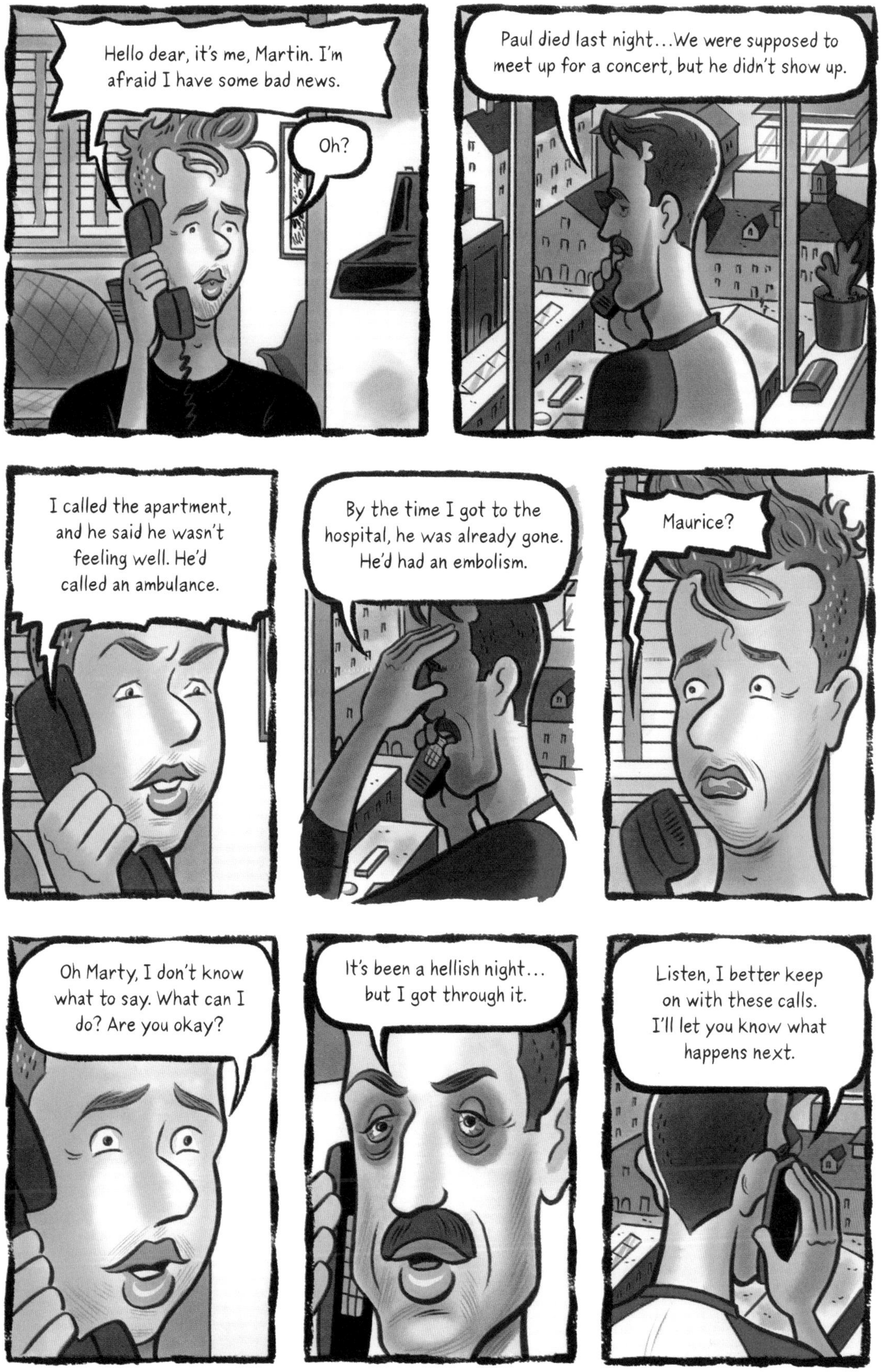
Hello dear, it's me, Martin. I'm afraid I have some bad news.
Oh?
Paul died last night...We were supposed to meet up for a concert, but he didn't show up.
I called the apartment, and he said he wasn't feeling well. He'd called an ambulance.
By the time I got to the hospital, he was already gone. He'd had an embolism.
Maurice?
Oh Marty, I don't know what to say. What can I do? Are you okay?
It's been a hellish night... but I got through it.
Listen, I better keep on with these calls. I'll let you know what happens next.

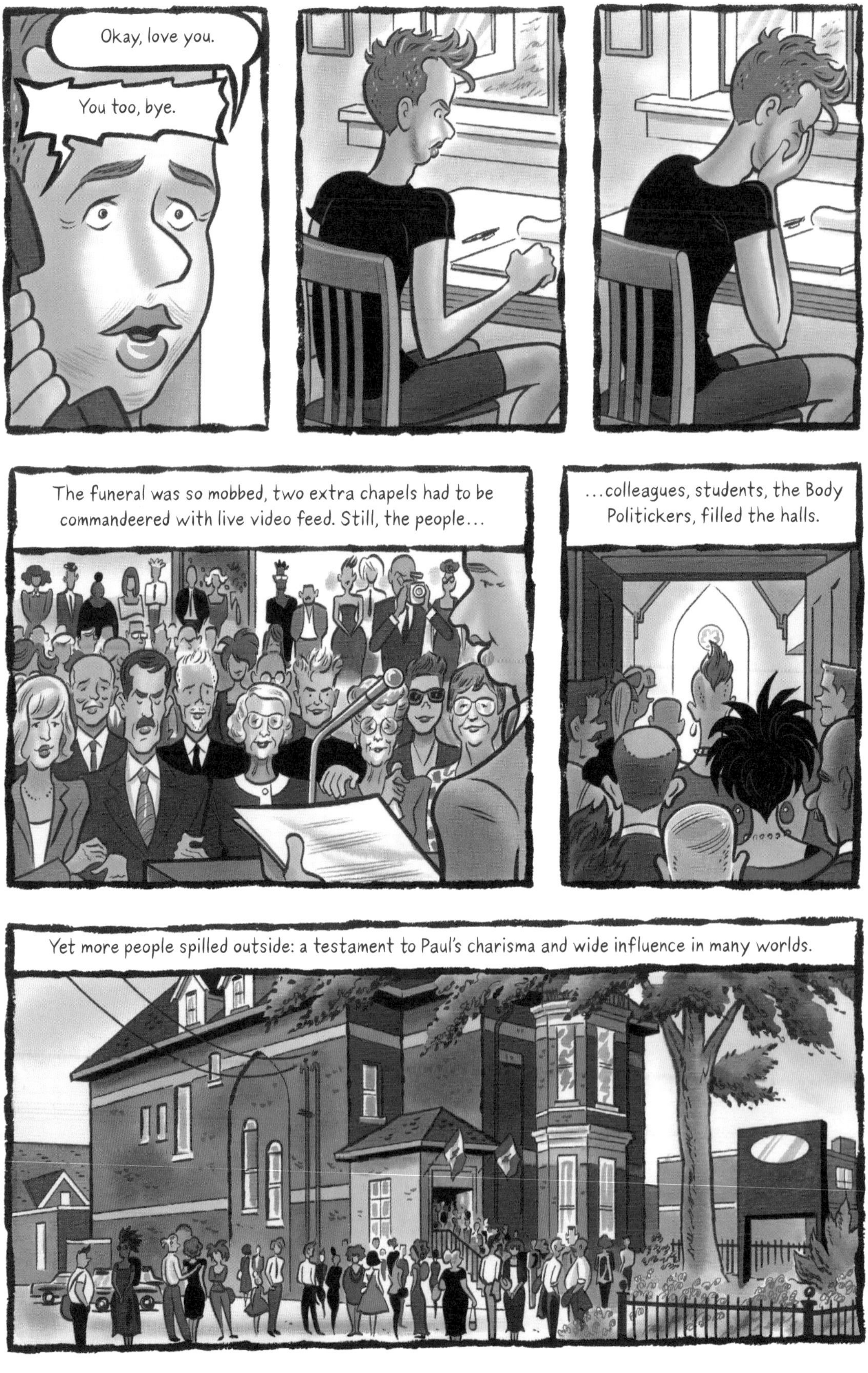

Okay, love you.
You too, bye.
The funeral was so mobbed, two extra chapels had to be commandeered with live video feed. Still, the people...
...colleagues, students, the Body Politickers, filled the halls.
Yet more people spilled outside: a testament to Paul's charisma and wide influence in many worlds.

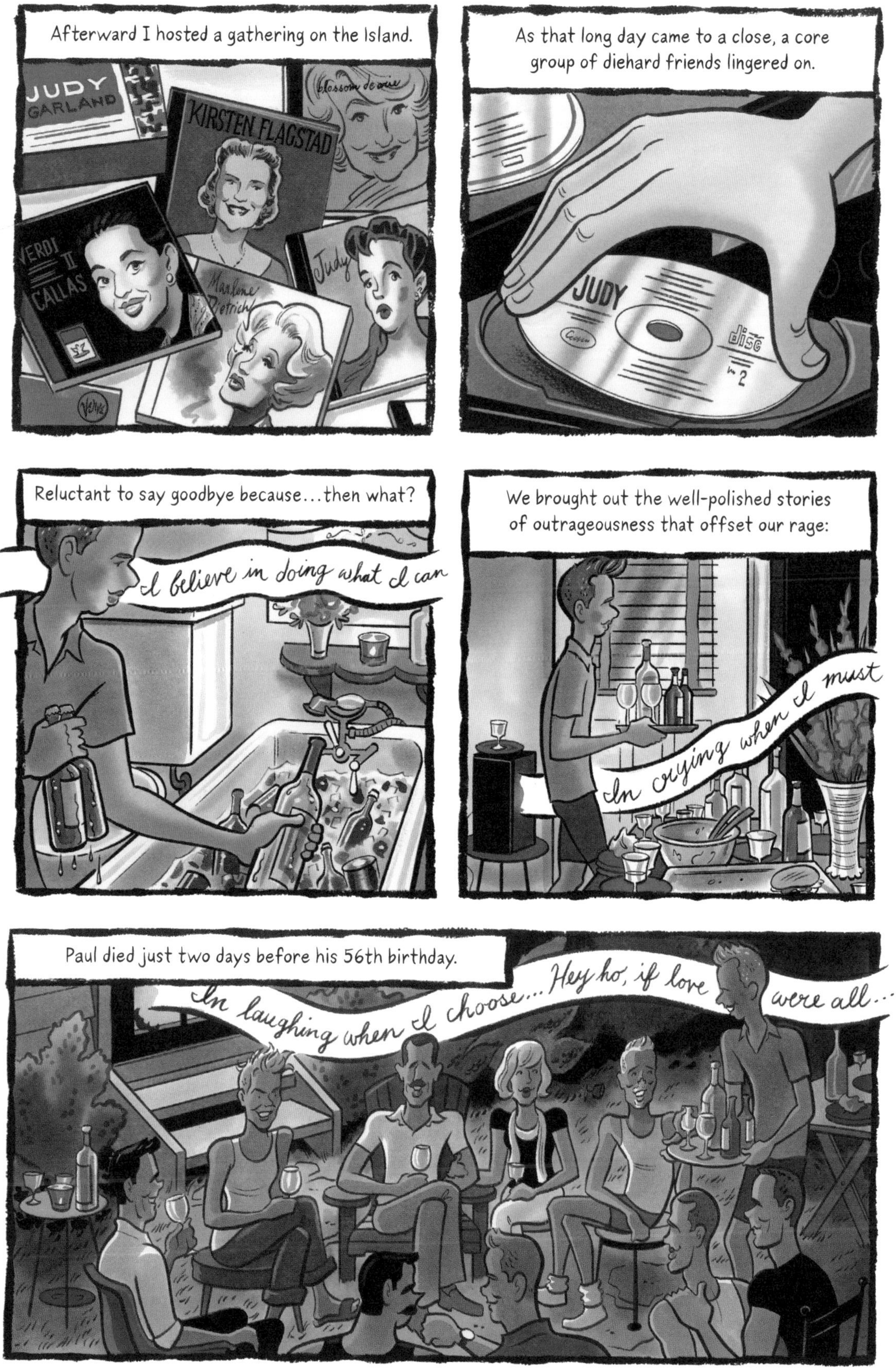
Afterward I hosted a gathering on the Island.
JUDY GARLAND
KIRSTEN FLAGSTAD
VERDI II CALLAS
Marlene Dietrich
Judy
As that long day came to a close, a core group of diehard friends lingered on.
JUDY
disc
2
Reluctant to say goodbye because... then what?
I believe in doing what I can
We brought out the well-polished stories of outrageousness that offset our rage:
In crying when I must
Paul died just two days before his 56th birthday.
In laughing when I choose... Hey ho, if love were all...

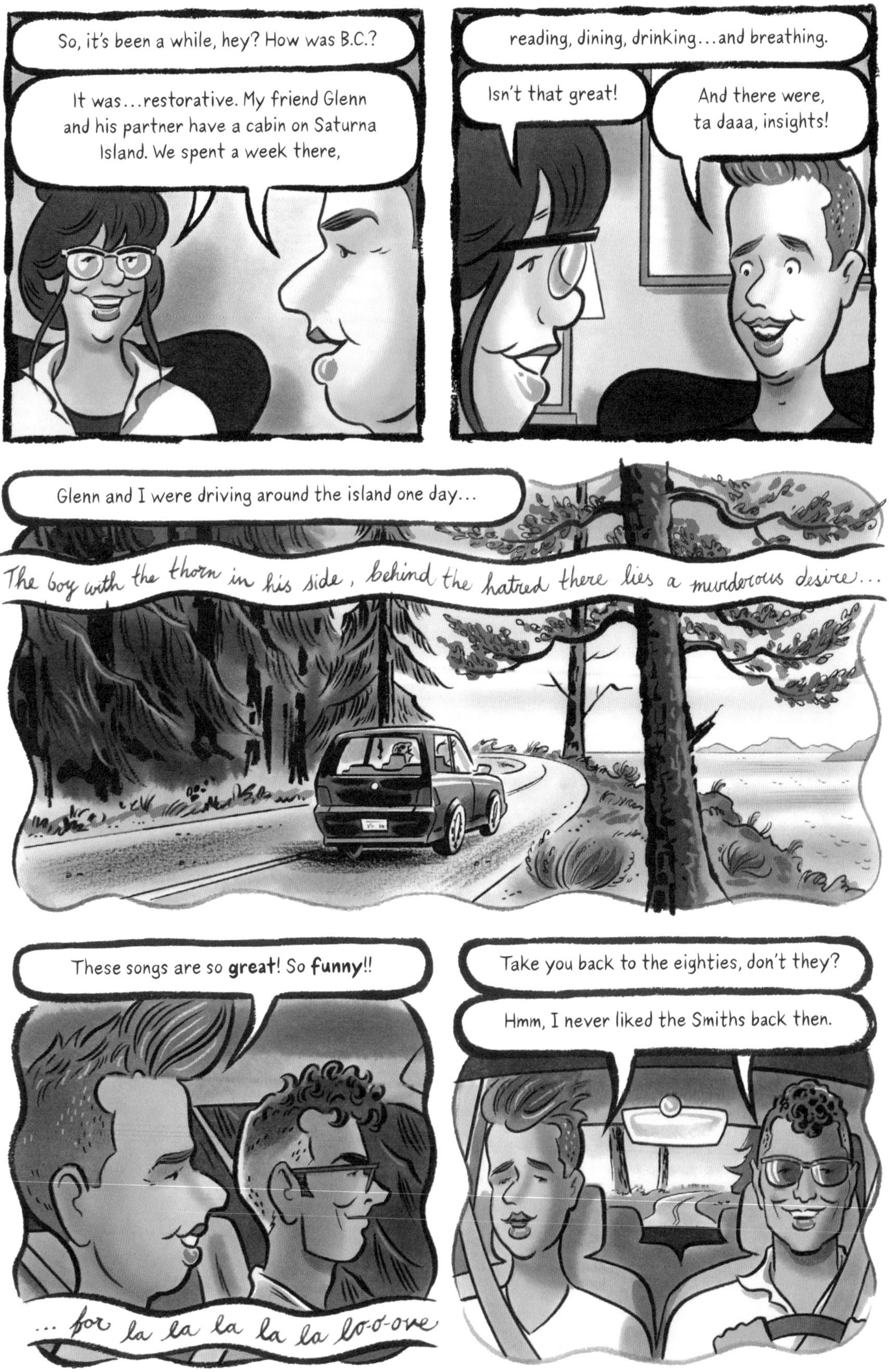
So, it's been a while, hey? How was B.C.?
It was...restorative. My friend Glenn and his partner have a cabin on Saturna Island. We spent a week there,
reading, dining, drinking...and breathing.
Isn't that great!
And there were, ta daaa, insights!
Glenn and I were driving around the island one day...
The boy with the thorn in his side, behind the hatred there lies a murderous desire...
These songs are so **great**! So **funny**!!
... for la la la la la lo-o-ove
Take you back to the eighties, don't they?
Hmm, I never liked the Smiths back then.

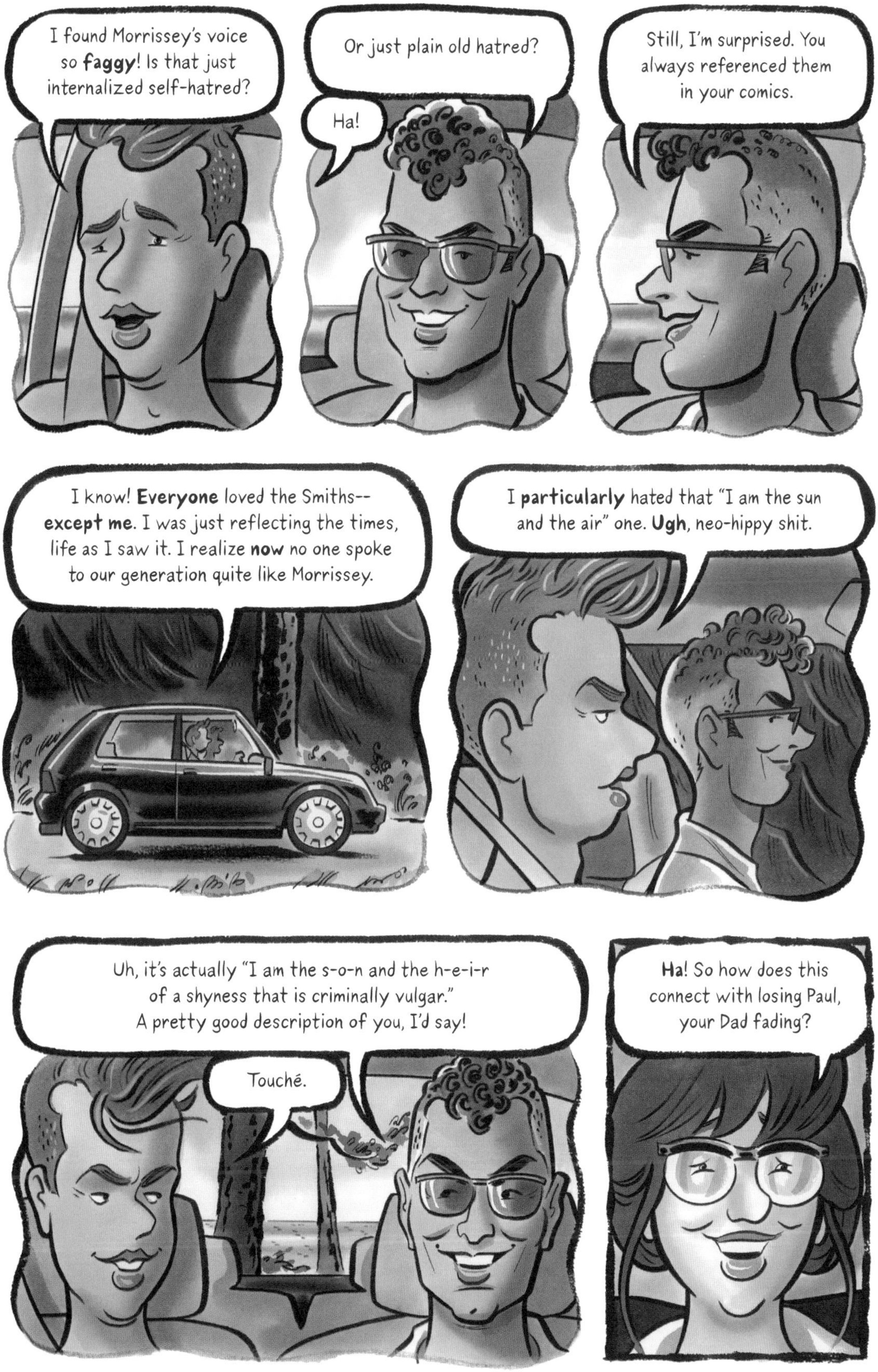
I found Morrissey's voice so **faggy**! Is that just internalized self-hatred?
Or just plain old hatred?
Ha!
Still, I'm surprised. You always referenced them in your comics.
I know! **Everyone** loved the Smiths-- **except me.** I was just reflecting the times, life as I saw it. I realize **now** no one spoke to our generation quite like Morrissey.
I **particularly** hated that "I am the sun and the air" one. **Ugh**, neo-hippy shit.
Uh, it's actually "I am the s-o-n and the h-e-i-r of a shyness that is criminally vulgar." A pretty good description of you, I'd say!
Touché.
Ha! So how does this connect with losing Paul, your Dad fading?

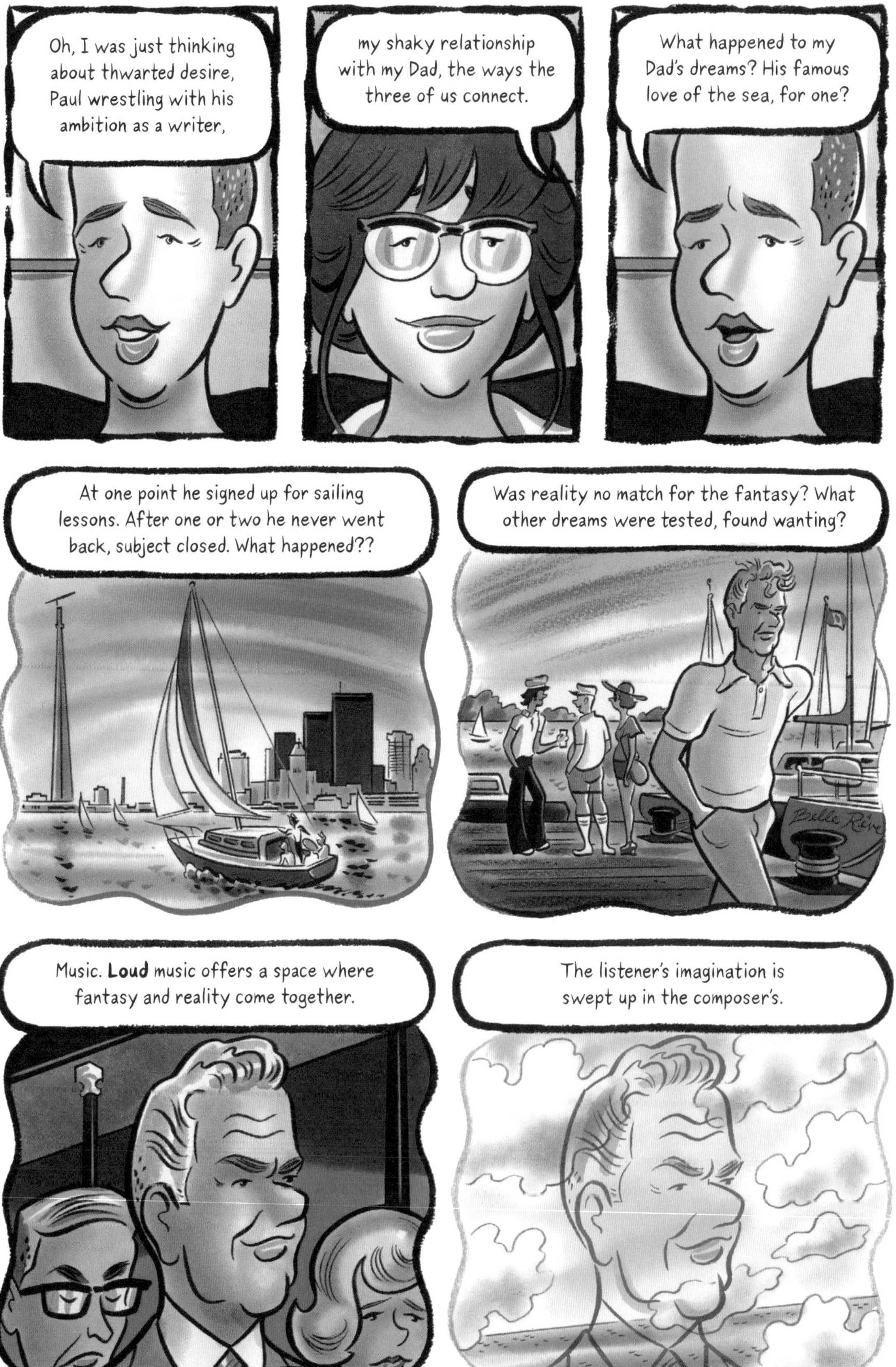
Oh, I was just thinking about thwarted desire, Paul wrestling with his ambition as a writer,
my shaky relationship with my Dad, the ways the three of us connect.
What happened to my Dad's dreams? His famous love of the sea, for one?
At one point he signed up for sailing lessons. After one or two he never went back, subject closed. What happened??
Was reality no match for the fantasy? What other dreams were tested, found wanting?
Belle Rêve
Music. **Loud** music offers a space where fantasy and reality come together.
The listener's imagination is swept up in the composer's.

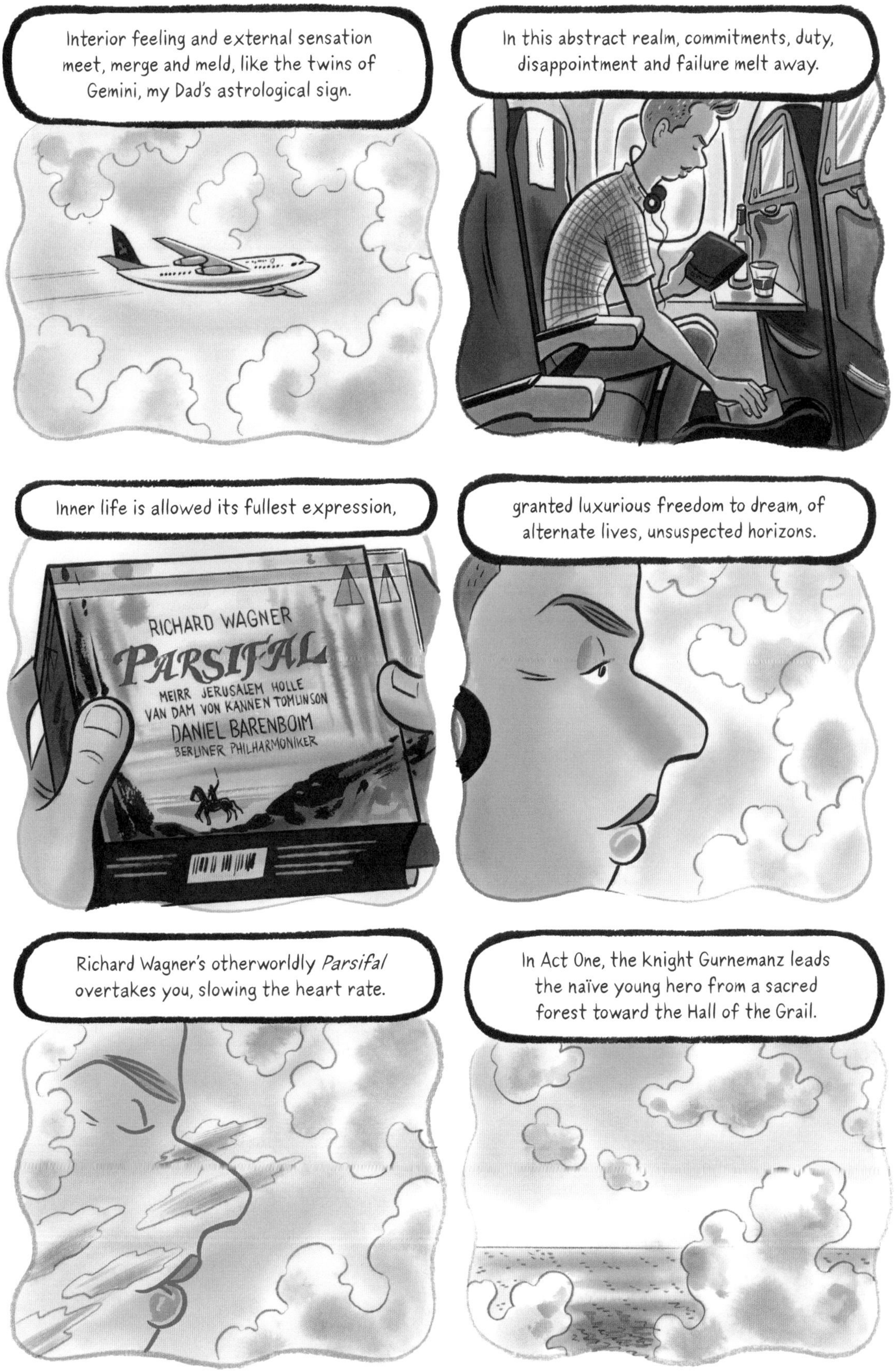
Interior feeling and external sensation meet, merge and meld, like the twins of Gemini, my Dad's astrological sign.
In this abstract realm, commitments, duty, disappointment and failure melt away.
Inner life is allowed its fullest expression,
RICHARD WAGNER
PARSIFAL
MEIRR JERUSALEM HOLLE
VAN DAM VON KANNEN TOMLINSON
DANIEL BARENBOIM
BERLINER PHILHARMONIKER
granted luxurious freedom to dream, of alternate lives, unsuspected horizons.
Richard Wagner's otherworldly *Parsifal* overtakes you, slowing the heart rate.
In Act One, the knight Gurnemanz leads the naïve young hero from a sacred forest toward the Hall of the Grail.

As the scene transforms, Parsifal remarks, "I scarcely move, yet I seem to have travelled a great distance."

"Here time becomes space," the wise elder explains enigmatically.

At one legendary Met performance, Paul had an out-of-body experience.

I picture him there now, soaring upward into that vast, fabled auditorium,

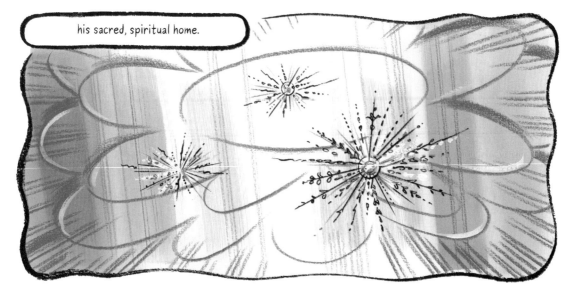

his sacred, spiritual home.

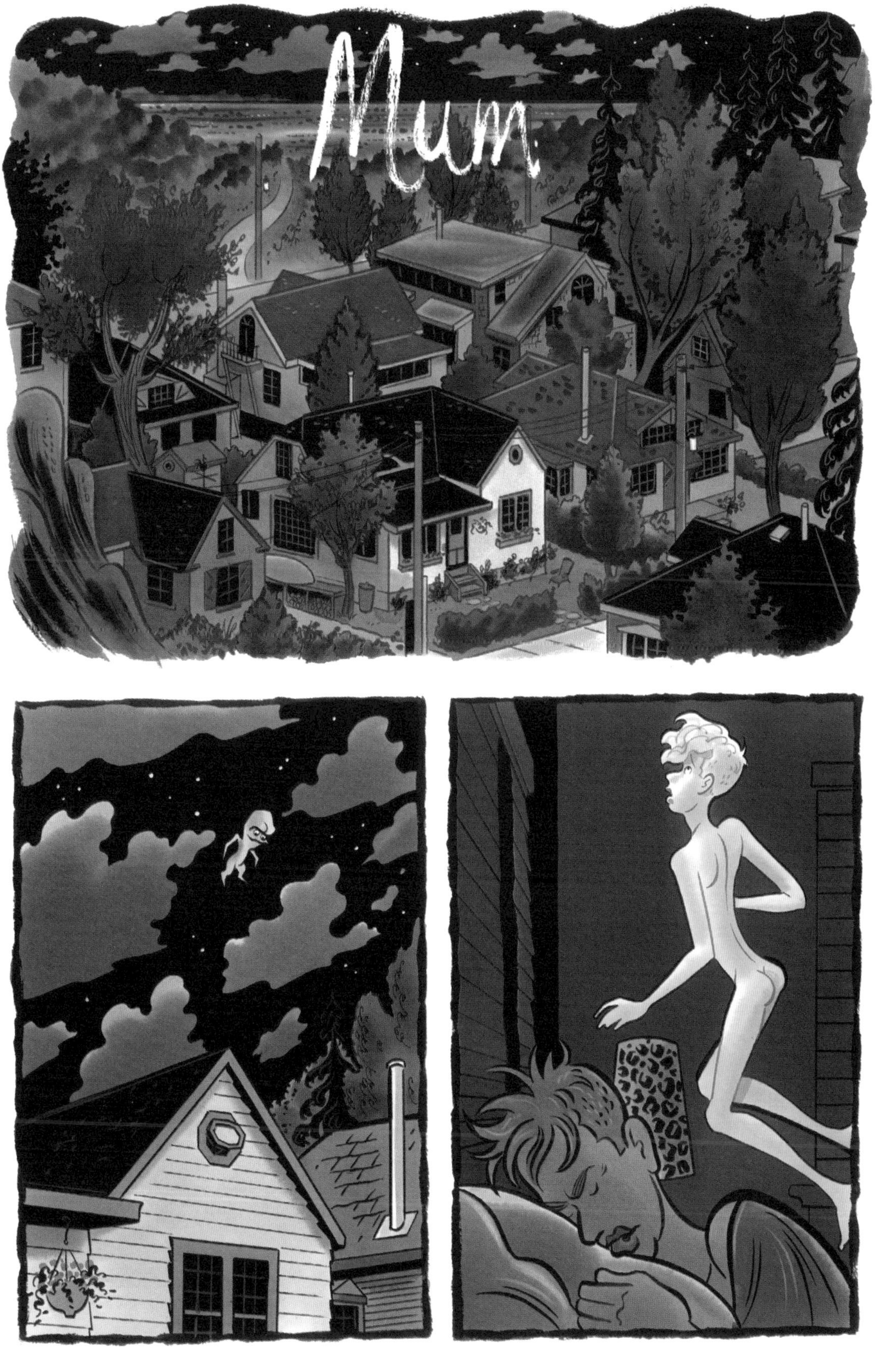
Mum

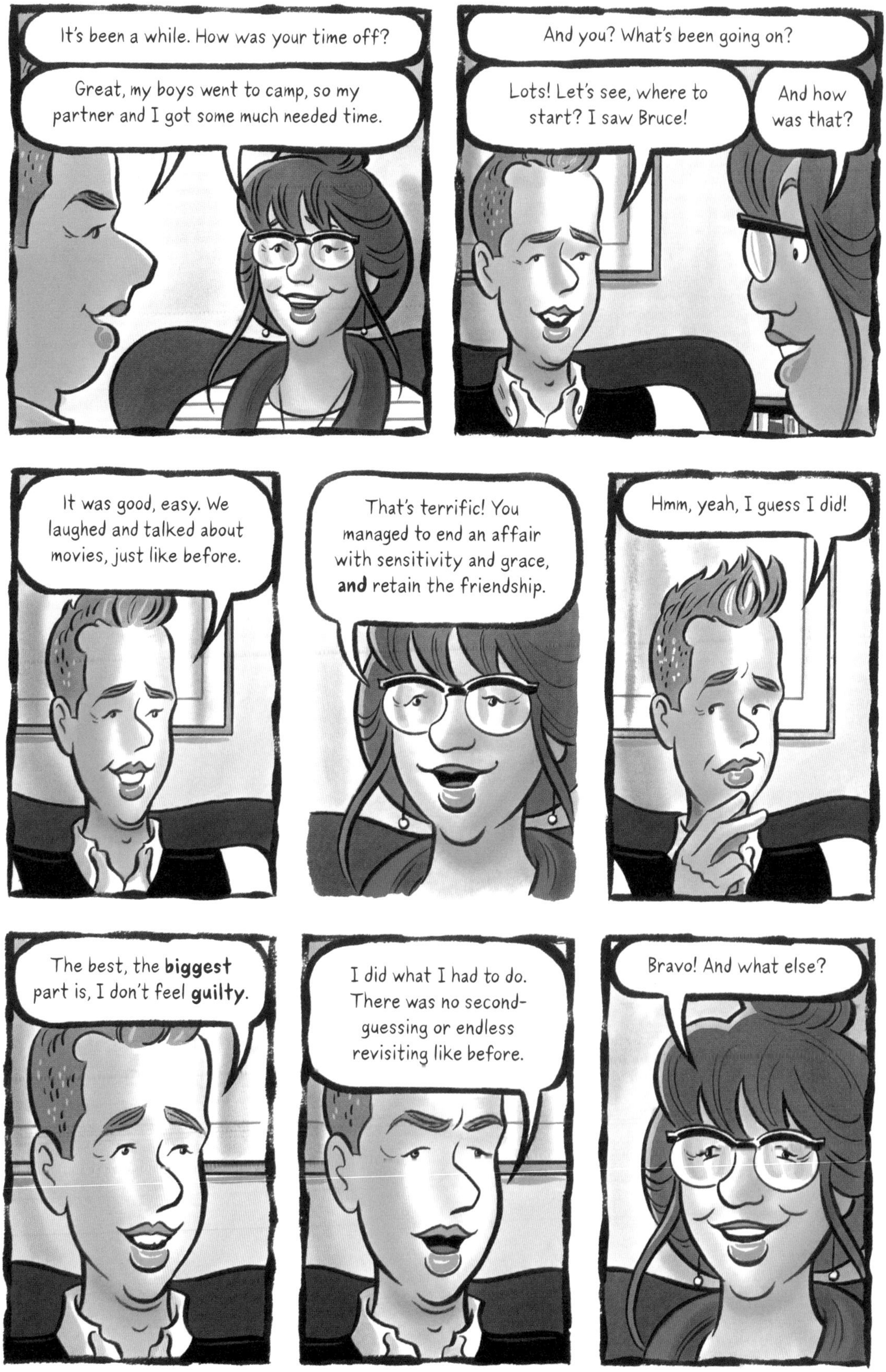
It's been a while. How was your time off?
Great, my boys went to camp, so my partner and I got some much needed time.
And you? What's been going on?
Lots! Let's see, where to start? I saw Bruce!
And how was that?
It was good, easy. We laughed and talked about movies, just like before.
That's terrific! You managed to end an affair with sensitivity and grace, **and** retain the friendship.
Hmm, yeah, I guess I did!
The best, the **biggest** part is, I don't feel **guilty**.
I did what I had to do. There was no second-guessing or endless revisiting like before.
Bravo! And what else?

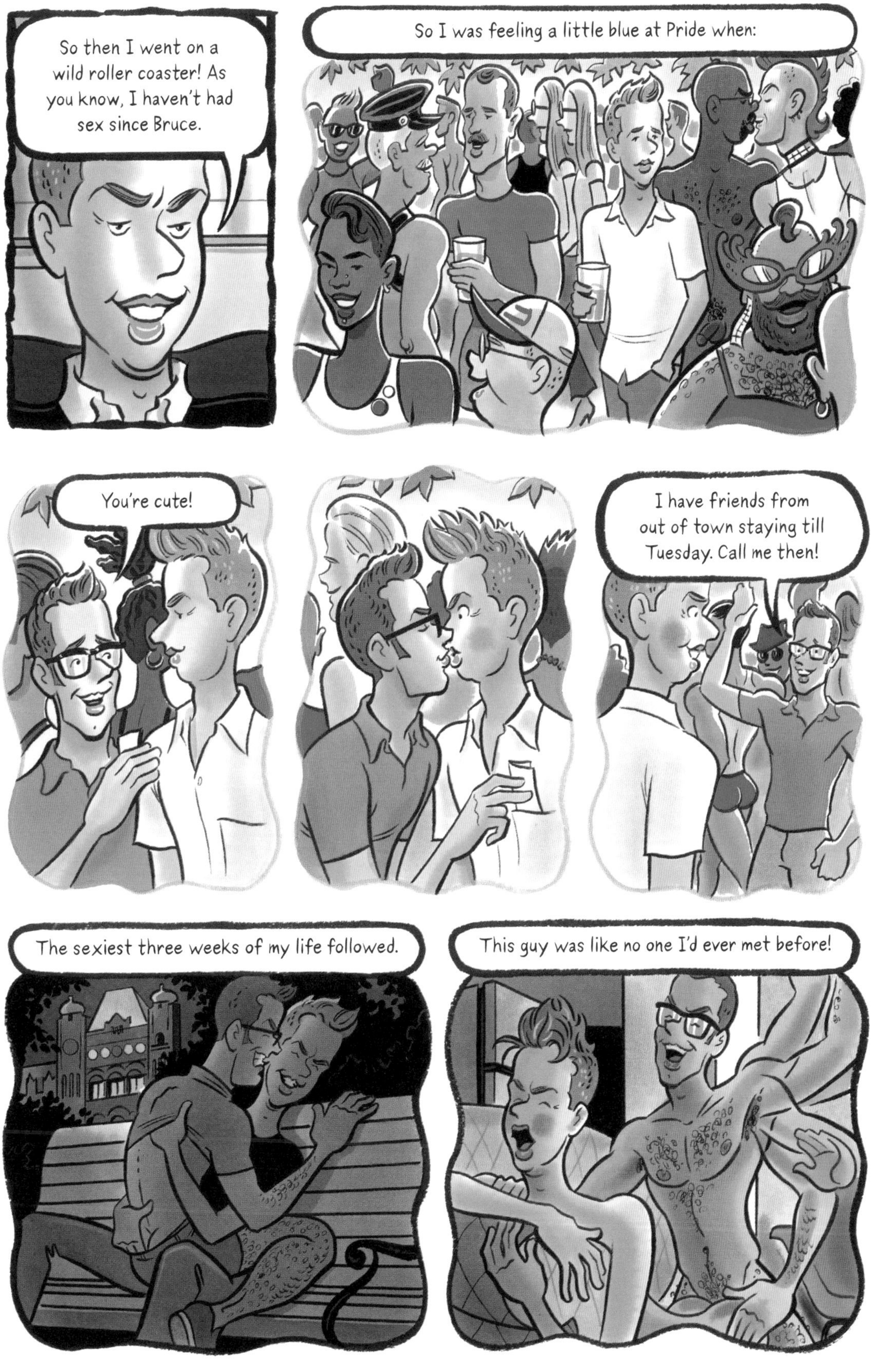
So then I went on a wild roller coaster! As you know, I haven't had sex since Bruce.
So I was feeling a little blue at Pride when:
You're cute!
I have friends from out of town staying till Tuesday. Call me then!
The sexiest three weeks of my life followed.
This guy was like no one I'd ever met before!

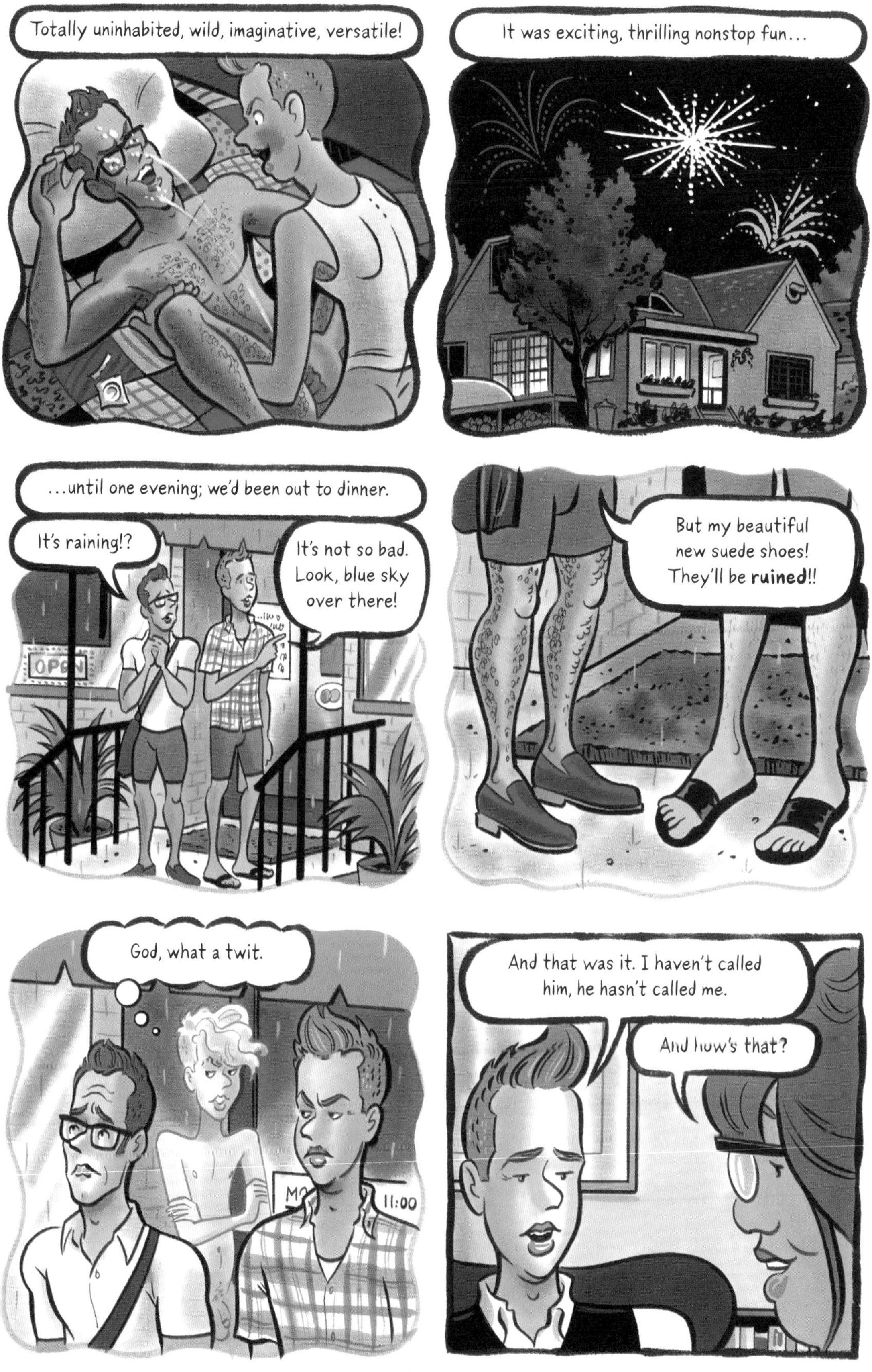
Totally uninhabited, wild, imaginative, versatile!
It was exciting, thrilling nonstop fun...
...until one evening; we'd been out to dinner.
It's raining!?
It's not so bad. Look, blue sky over there!
OPEN
But my beautiful new suede shoes! They'll be **ruined**!!
God, what a twit.
11:00
And that was it. I haven't called him, he hasn't called me.
And how's that?

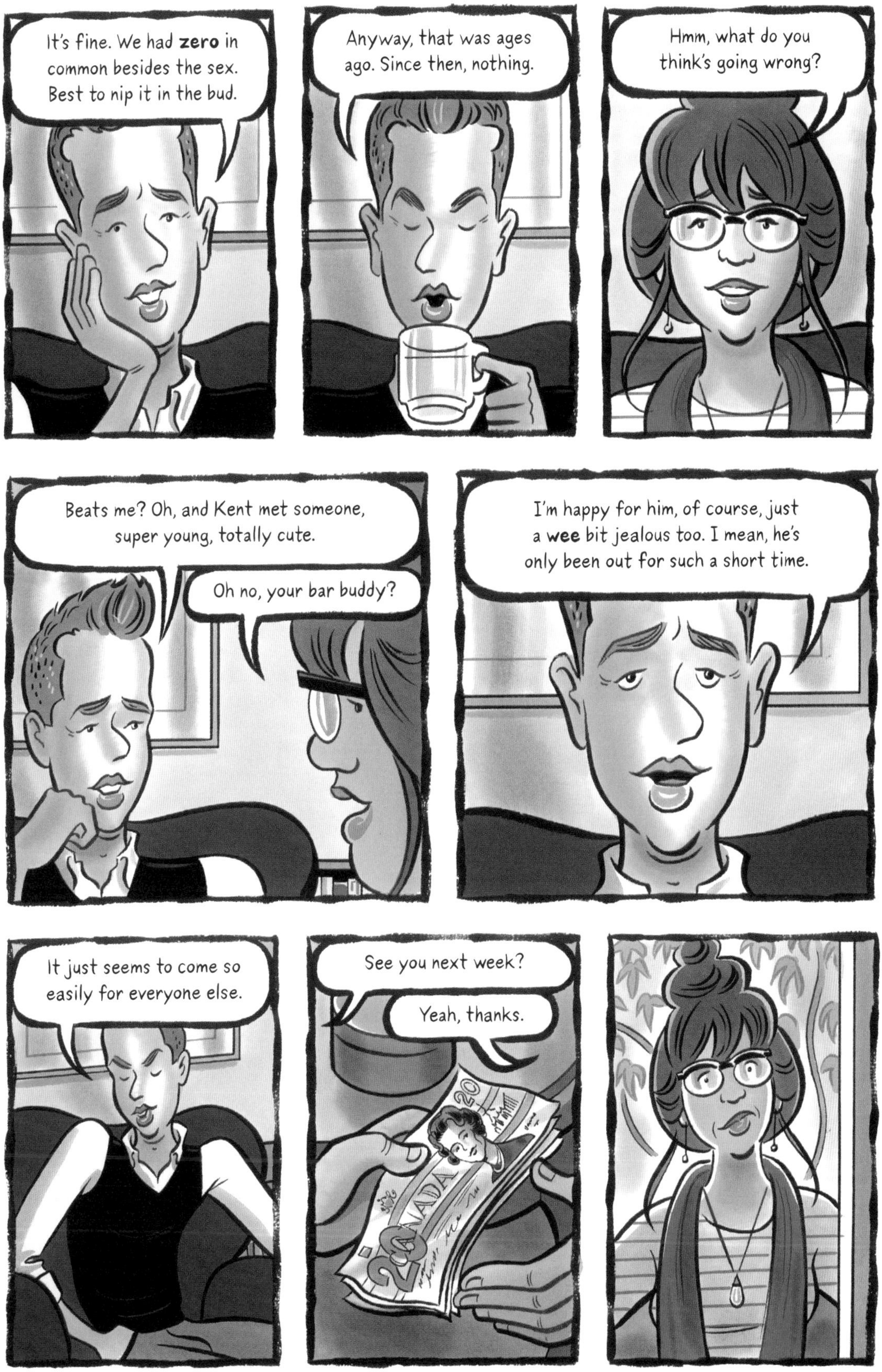
It's fine. We had **zero** in common besides the sex. Best to nip it in the bud.
Anyway, that was ages ago. Since then, nothing.
Hmm, what do you think's going wrong?
Beats me? Oh, and Kent met someone, super young, totally cute.
Oh no, your bar buddy?
I'm happy for him, of course, just a **wee** bit jealous too. I mean, he's only been out for such a short time.
It just seems to come so easily for everyone else.
See you next week?
Yeah, thanks.

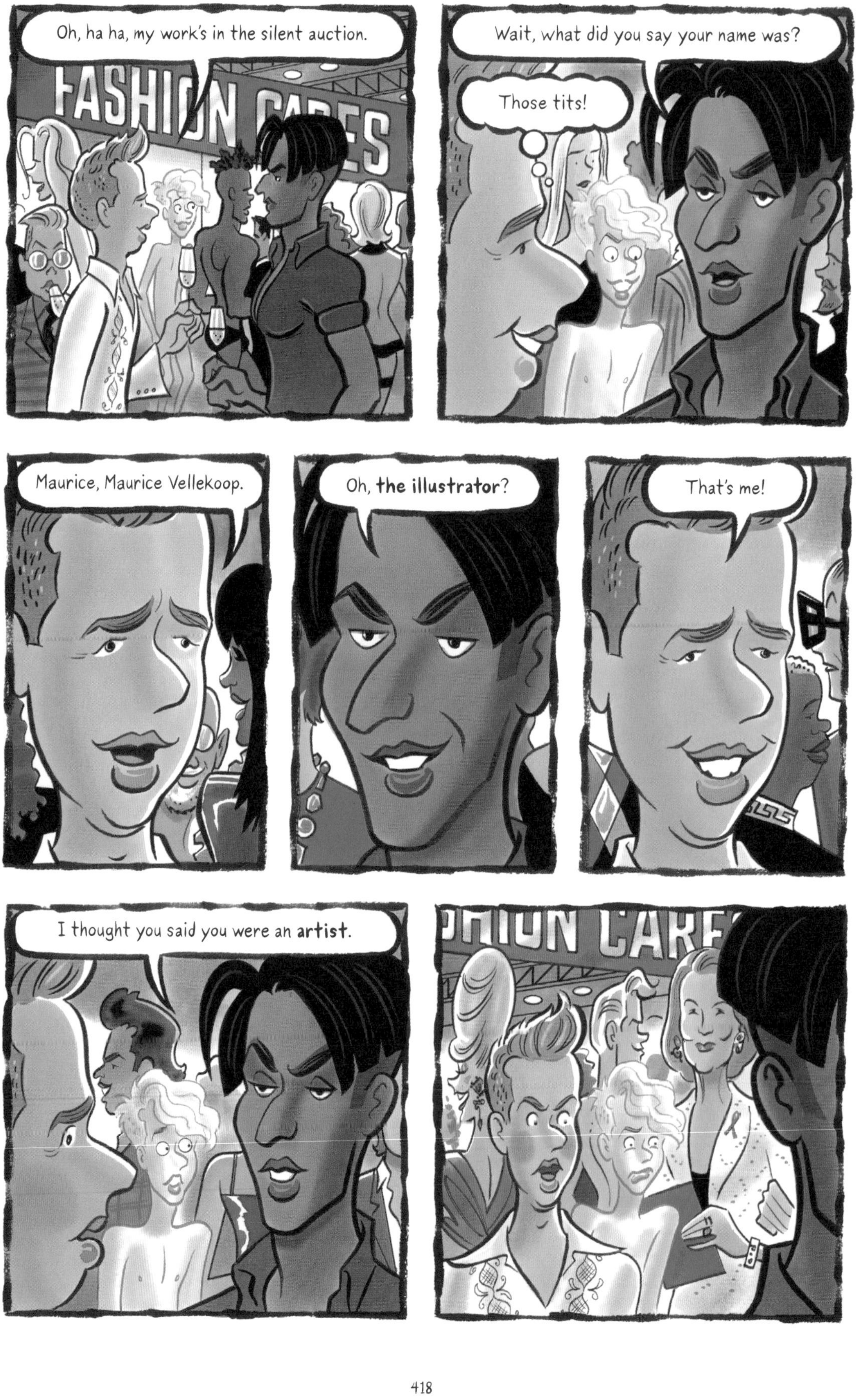
Oh, ha ha, my work's in the silent auction.
Wait, what did you say your name was?
Those tits!
Maurice, Maurice Vellekoop.
Oh, the illustrator?
That's me!
I thought you said you were an artist.

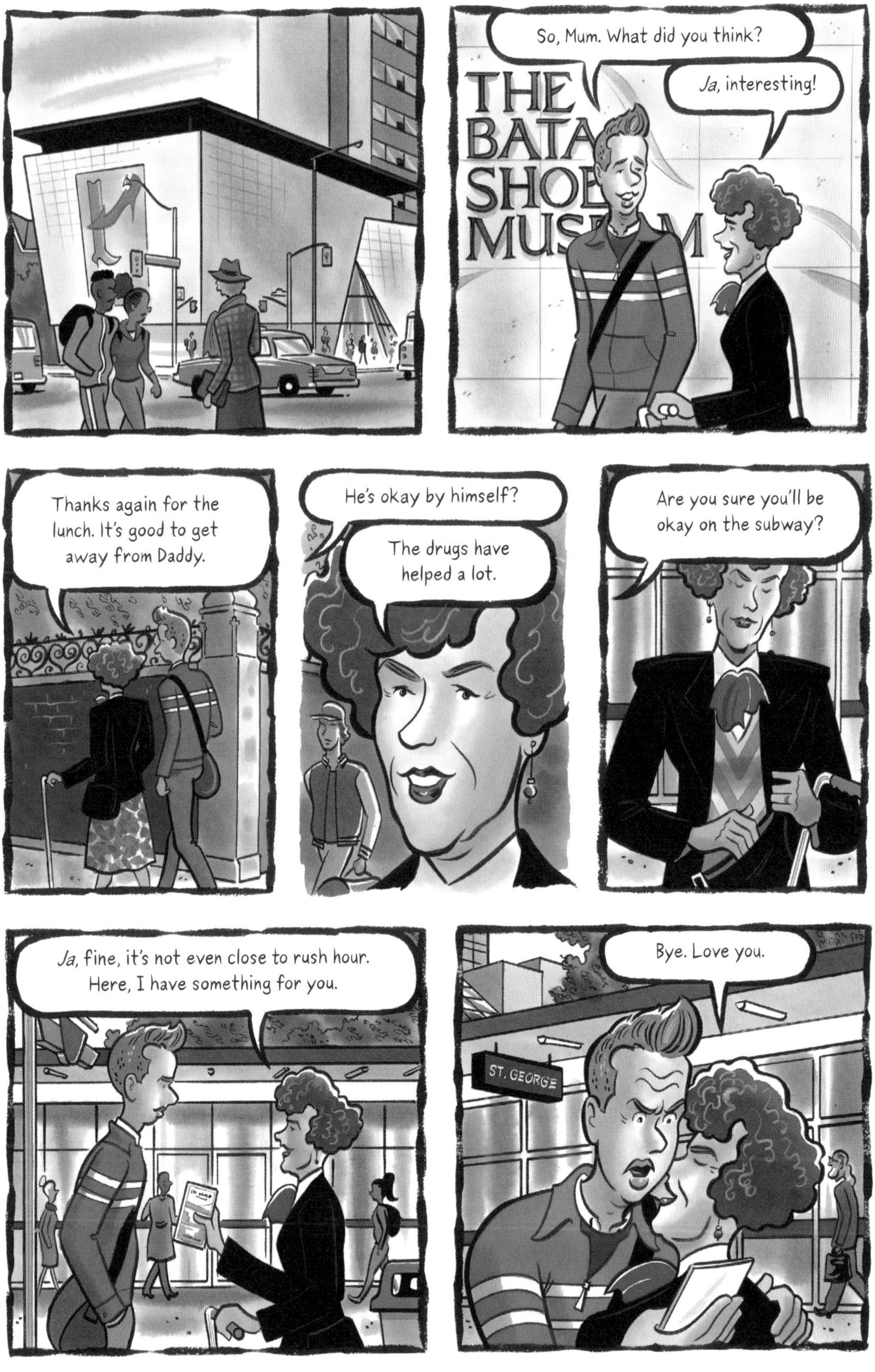
THE BATA SHOE MUSEUM
So, Mum. What did you think?
Ja, interesting!
Thanks again for the lunch. It's good to get away from Daddy.
He's okay by himself?
The drugs have helped a lot.
Are you sure you'll be okay on the subway?
Ja, fine, it's not even close to rush hour. Here, I have something for you.
ST. GEORGE
Bye. Love you.

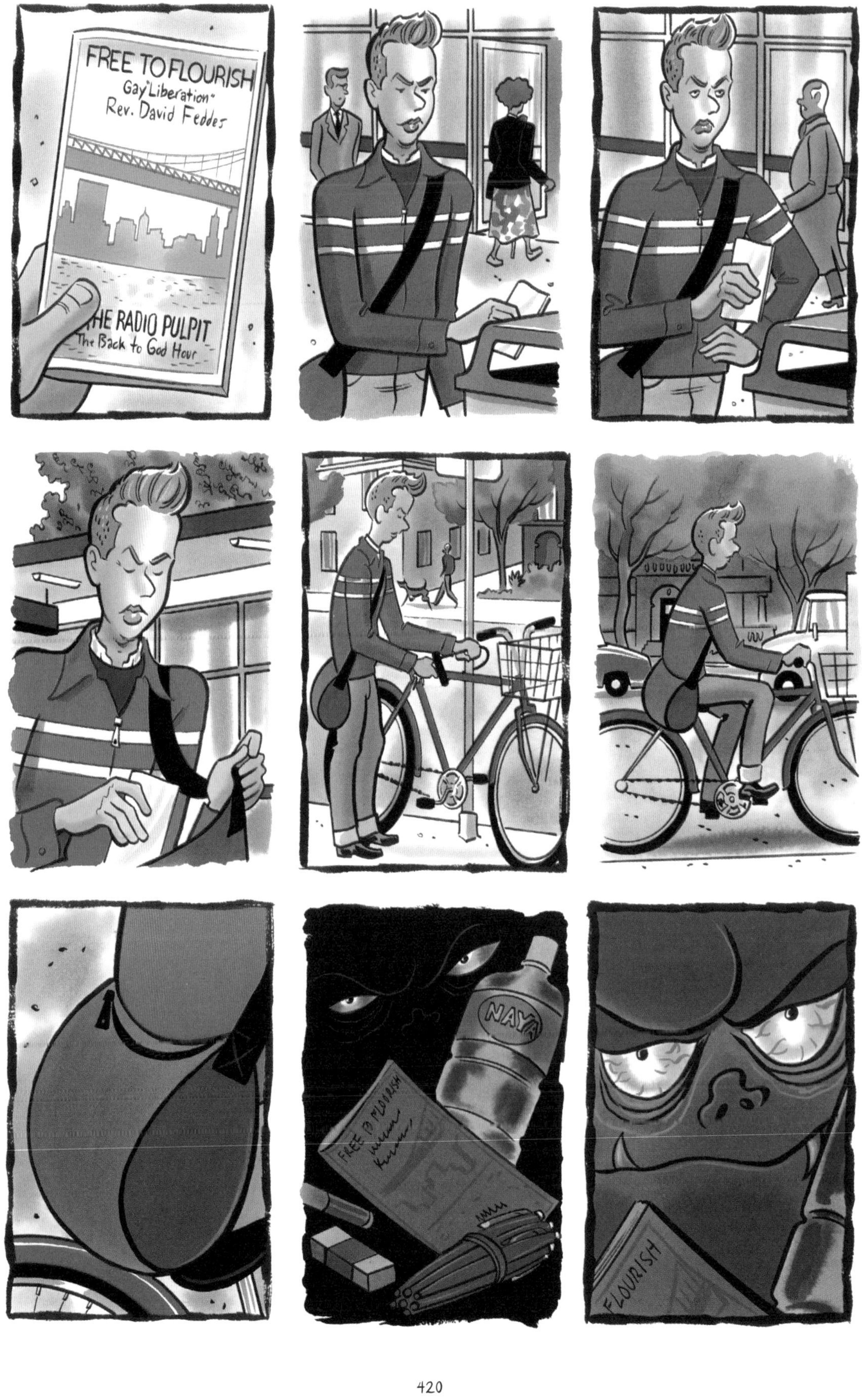
FREE TO FLOURISH
Gay "Liberation"
Rev. David Feddes
HE RADIO PULPIT
The Back to God Hour
NAYA
FREE TO FLOURISH
FLOURISH

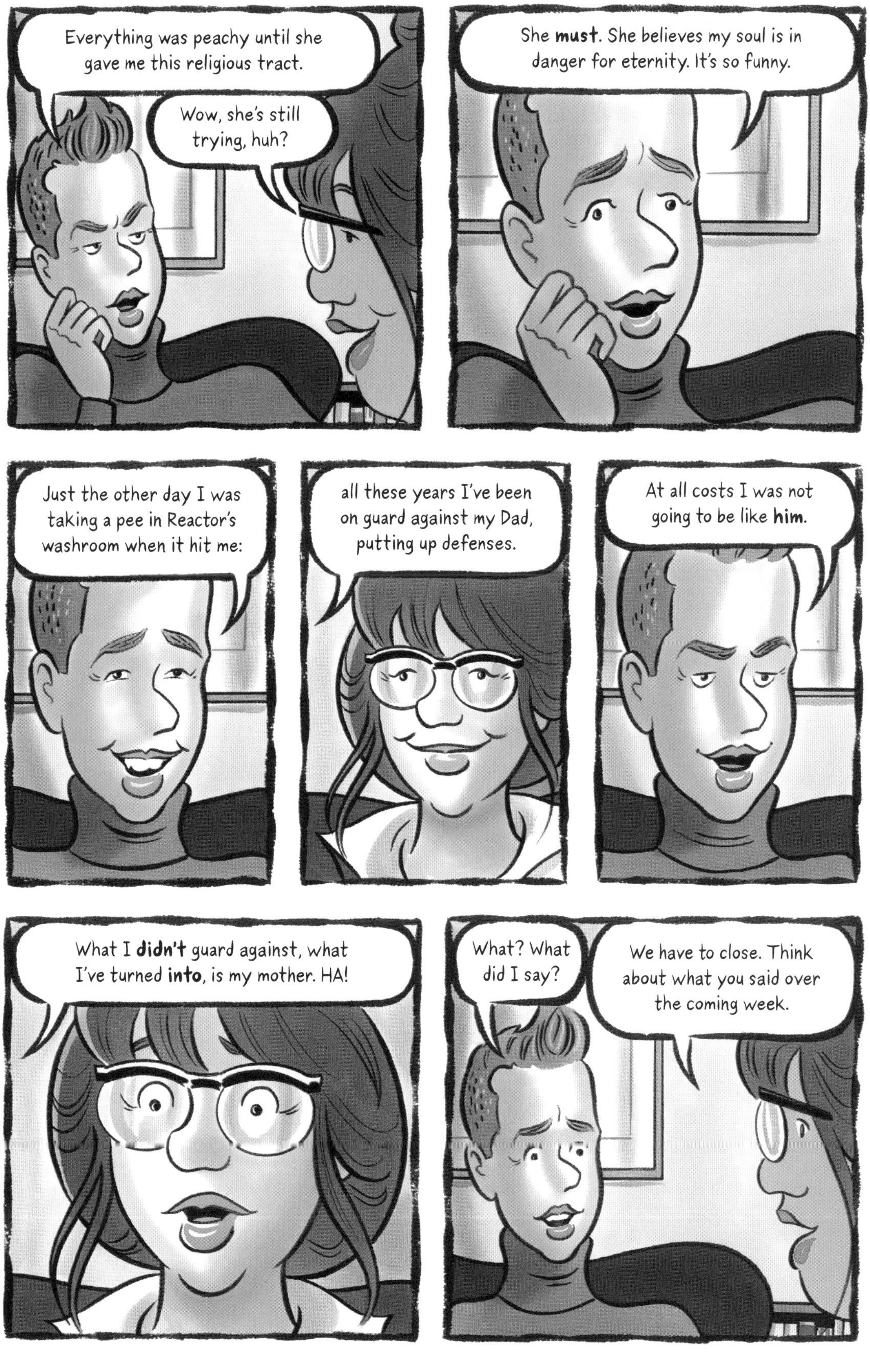
Everything was peachy until she gave me this religious tract.
Wow, she's still trying, huh?
She **must**. She believes my soul is in danger for eternity. It's so funny.
Just the other day I was taking a pee in Reactor's washroom when it hit me:
all these years I've been on guard against my Dad, putting up defenses.
At all costs I was not going to be like **him**.
What I **didn't** guard against, what I've turned **into**, is my mother. HA!
What? What did I say?
We have to close. Think about what you said over the coming week.

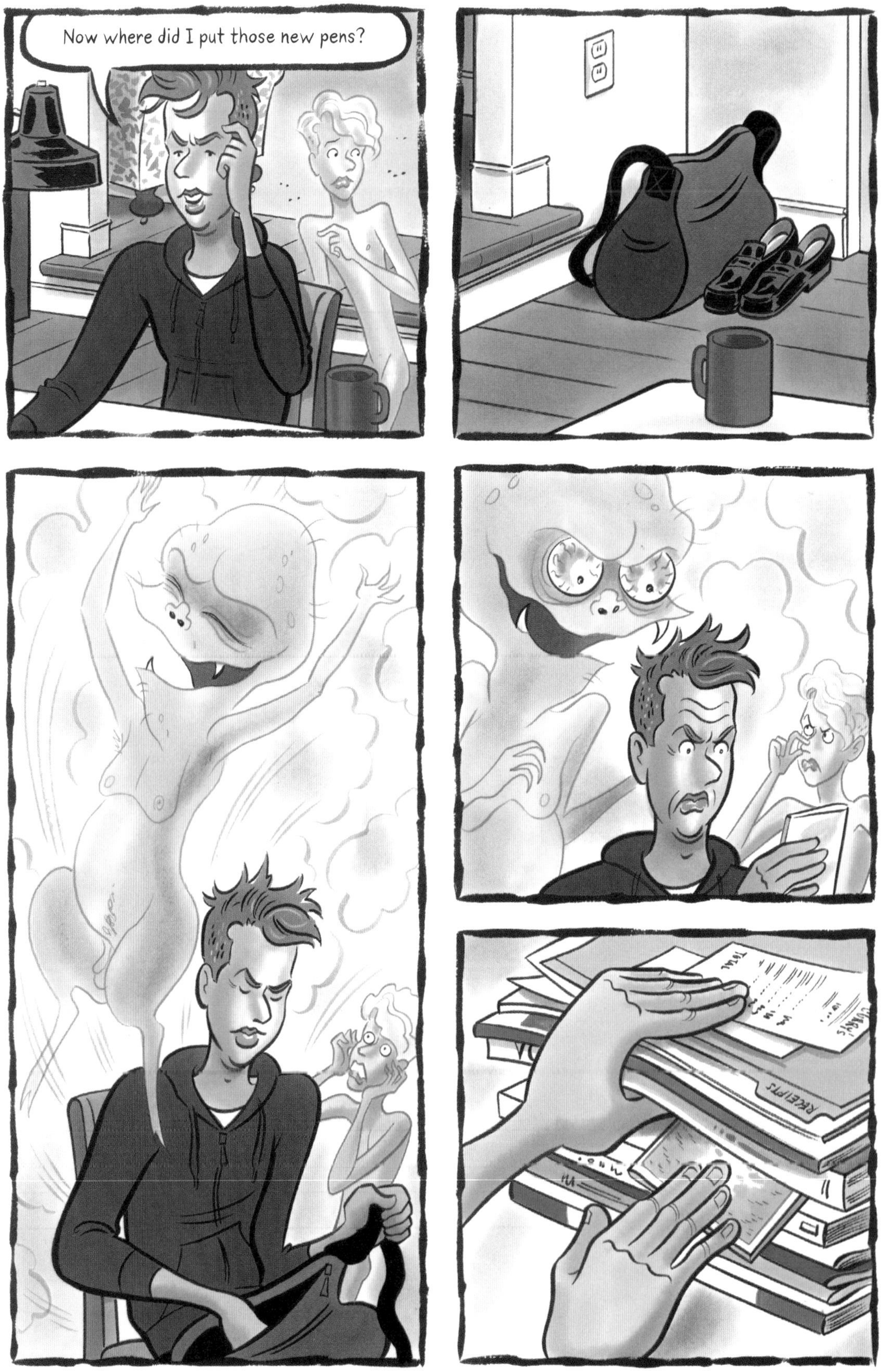
Now where did I put those new pens?

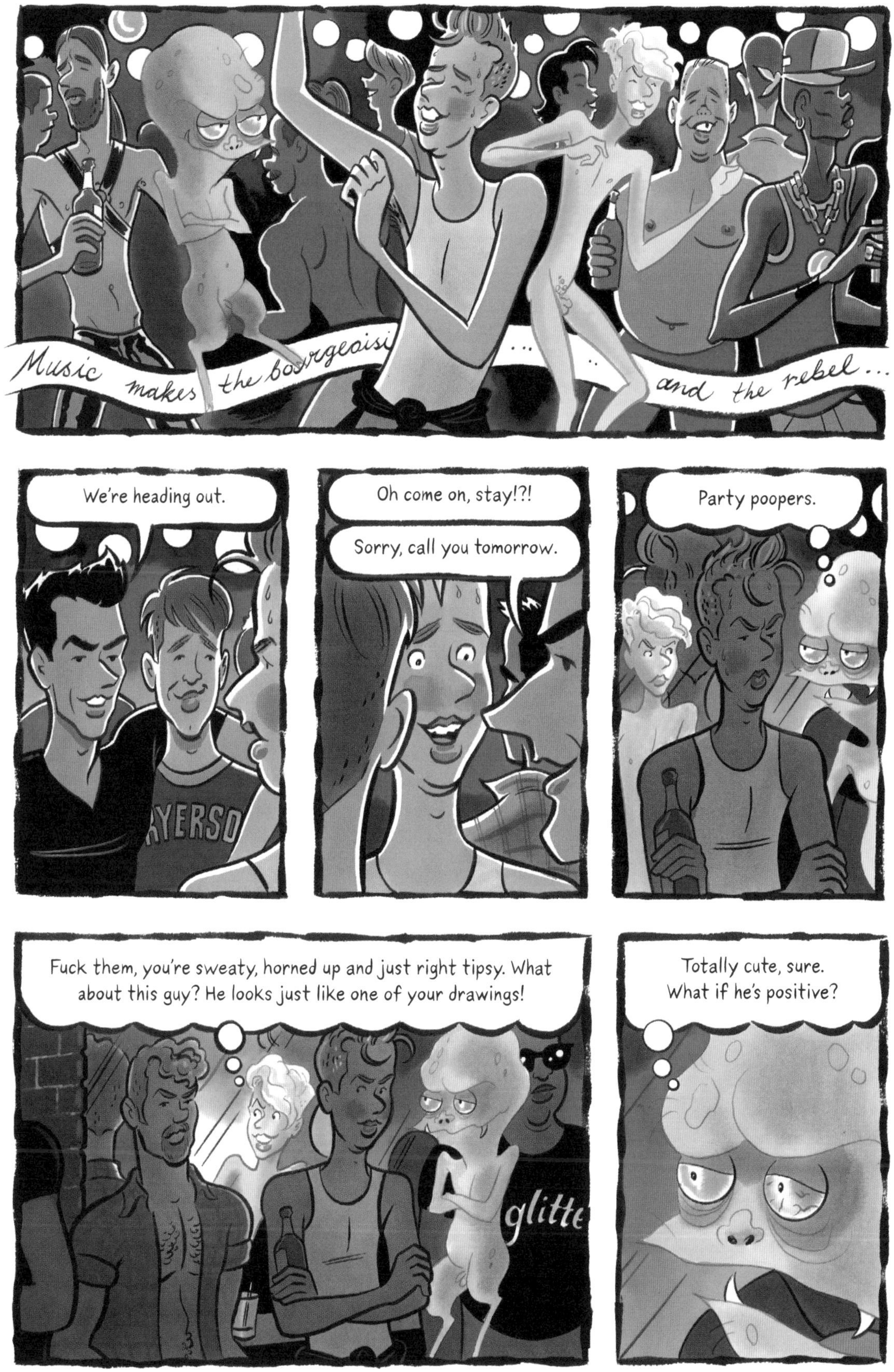
Music makes the bourgeoisi ... and the rebel...
We're heading out.
Oh come on, stay!?!
Sorry, call you tomorrow.
Party poopers.
Fuck them, you're sweaty, horned up and just right tipsy. What about this guy? He looks just like one of your drawings!
Totally cute, sure. What if he's positive?

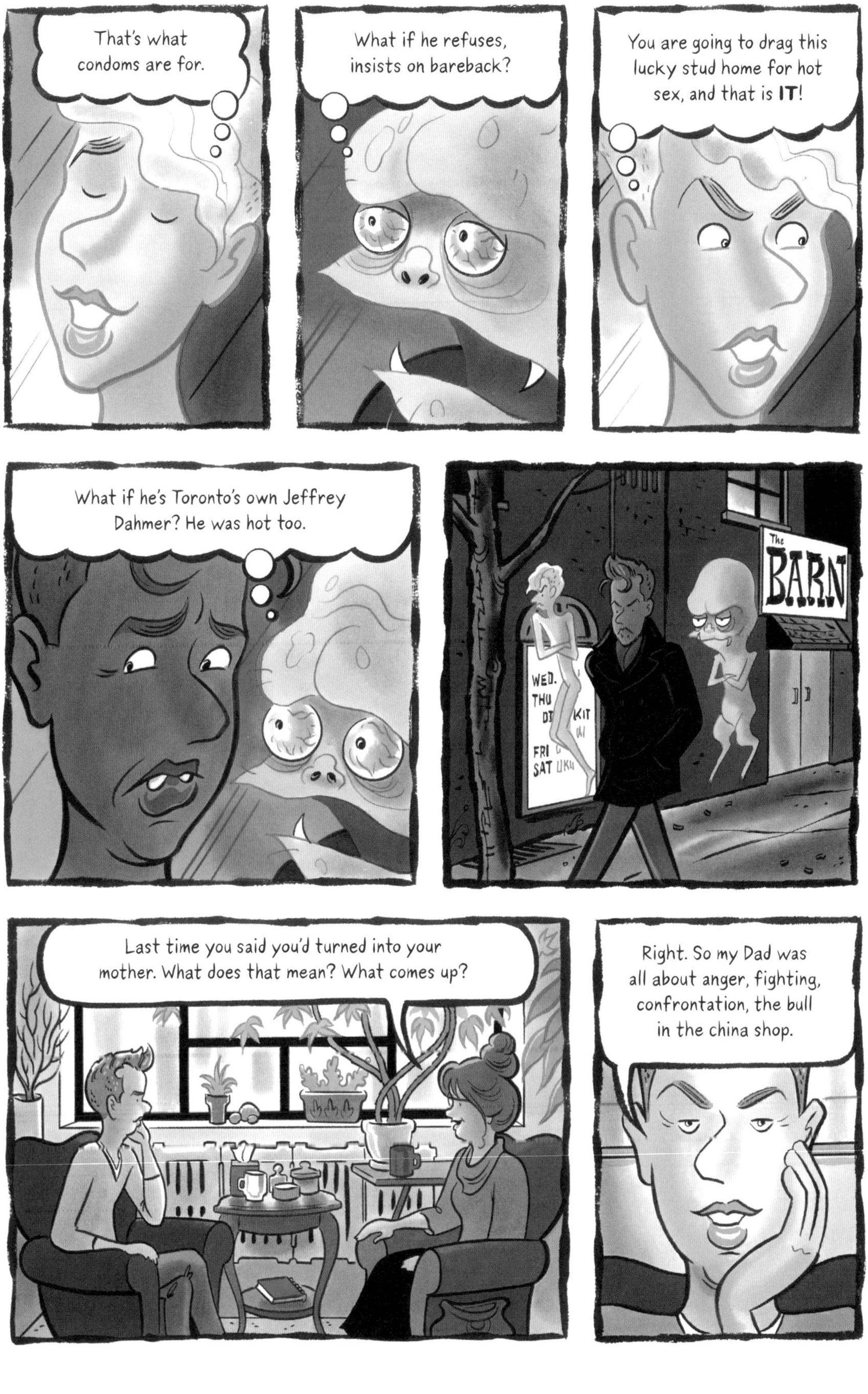
That's what condoms are for.
What if he refuses, insists on bareback?
You are going to drag this lucky stud home for hot sex, and that is **IT**!
What if he's Toronto's own Jeffrey Dahmer? He was hot too.
The BARN
WED.
THU
FRI
SAT
Last time you said you'd turned into your mother. What does that mean? What comes up?
Right. So my Dad was all about anger, fighting, confrontation, the bull in the china shop.

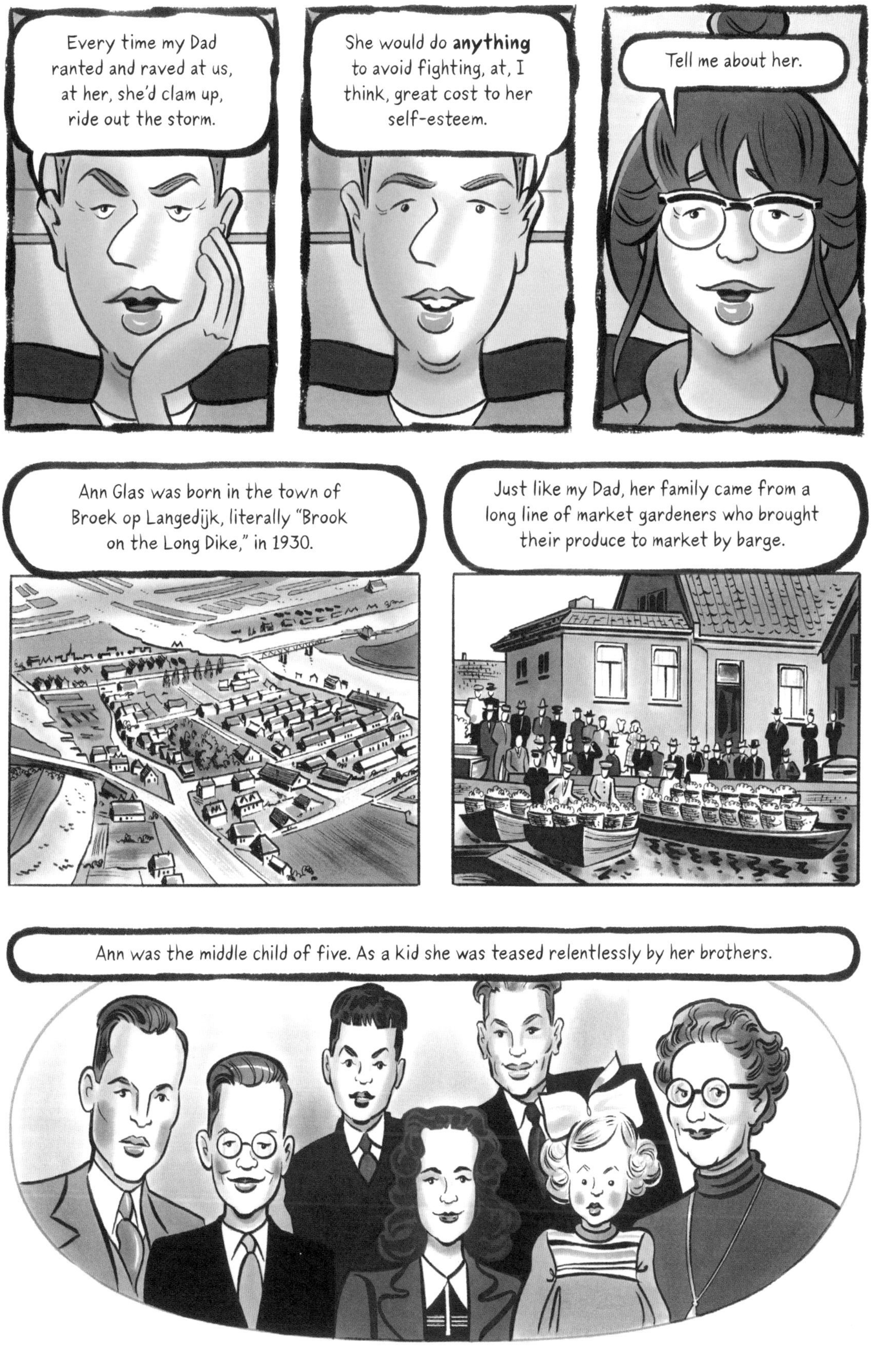
Every time my Dad ranted and raved at us, at her, she'd clam up, ride out the storm.
She would do **anything** to avoid fighting, at, I think, great cost to her self-esteem.
Tell me about her.
Ann Glas was born in the town of Broek op Langedijk, literally "Brook on the Long Dike," in 1930.
Just like my Dad, her family came from a long line of market gardeners who brought their produce to market by barge.
Ann was the middle child of five. As a kid she was teased relentlessly by her brothers.

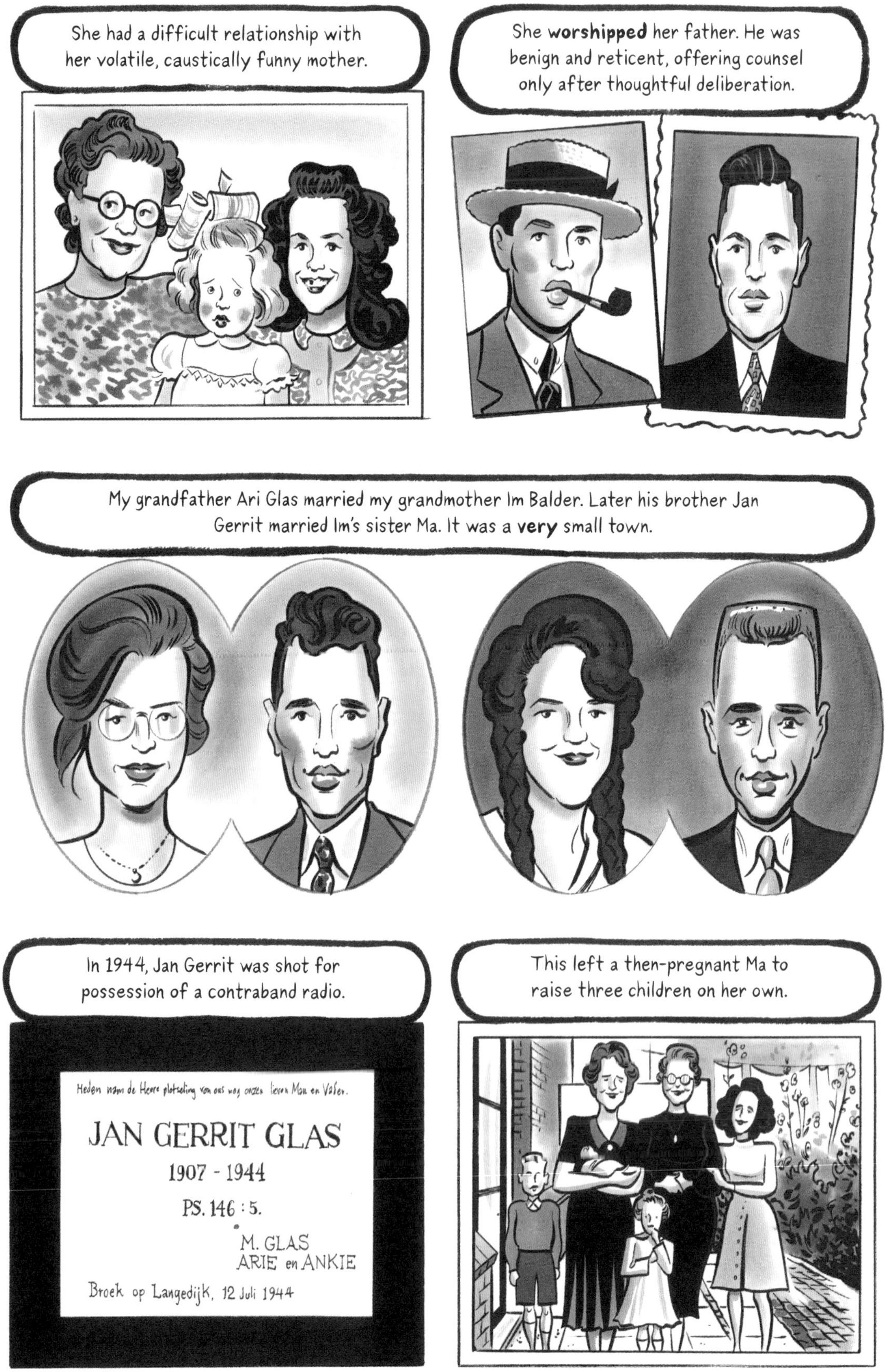
She had a difficult relationship with her volatile, caustically funny mother.
She **worshipped** her father. He was benign and reticent, offering counsel only after thoughtful deliberation.
My grandfather Ari Glas married my grandmother Im Balder. Later his brother Jan Gerrit married Im's sister Ma. It was a **very** small town.
In 1944, Jan Gerrit was shot for possession of a contraband radio.
Heden nam de Heere plotseling van ons weg onzen lieven Man en Vader.
JAN GERRIT GLAS
1907 - 1944
PS. 146 : 5.
M. GLAS
ARIE en ANKIE
Broek op Langedijk, 12 Juli 1944
This left a then-pregnant Ma to raise three children on her own.

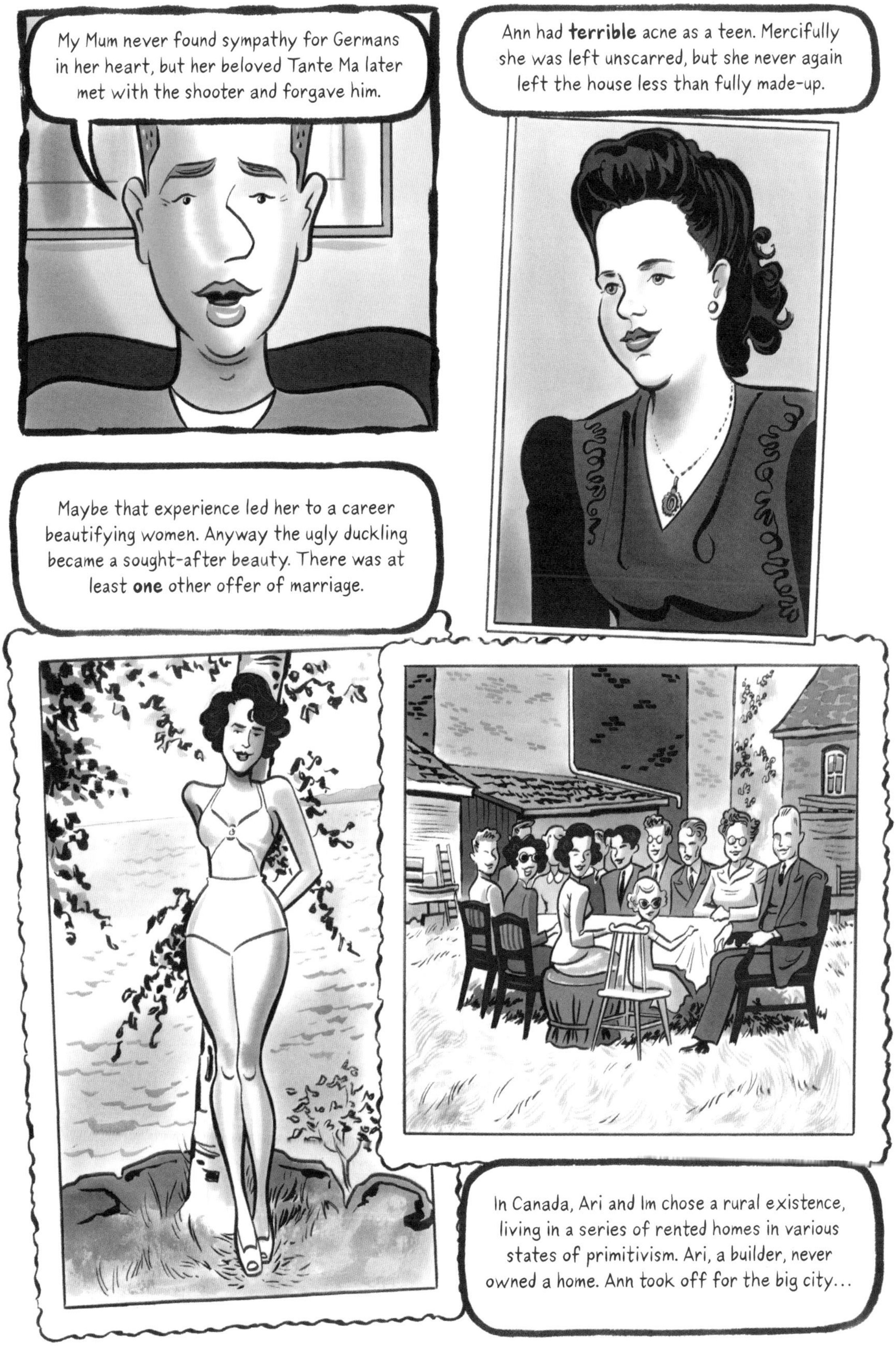
My Mum never found sympathy for Germans in her heart, but her beloved Tante Ma later met with the shooter and forgave him.
Ann had **terrible** acne as a teen. Mercifully she was left unscarred, but she never again left the house less than fully made-up.
Maybe that experience led her to a career beautifying women. Anyway the ugly duckling became a sought-after beauty. There was at least **one** other offer of marriage.
In Canada, Ari and Im chose a rural existence, living in a series of rented homes in various states of primitivism. Ari, a builder, never owned a home. Ann took off for the big city...

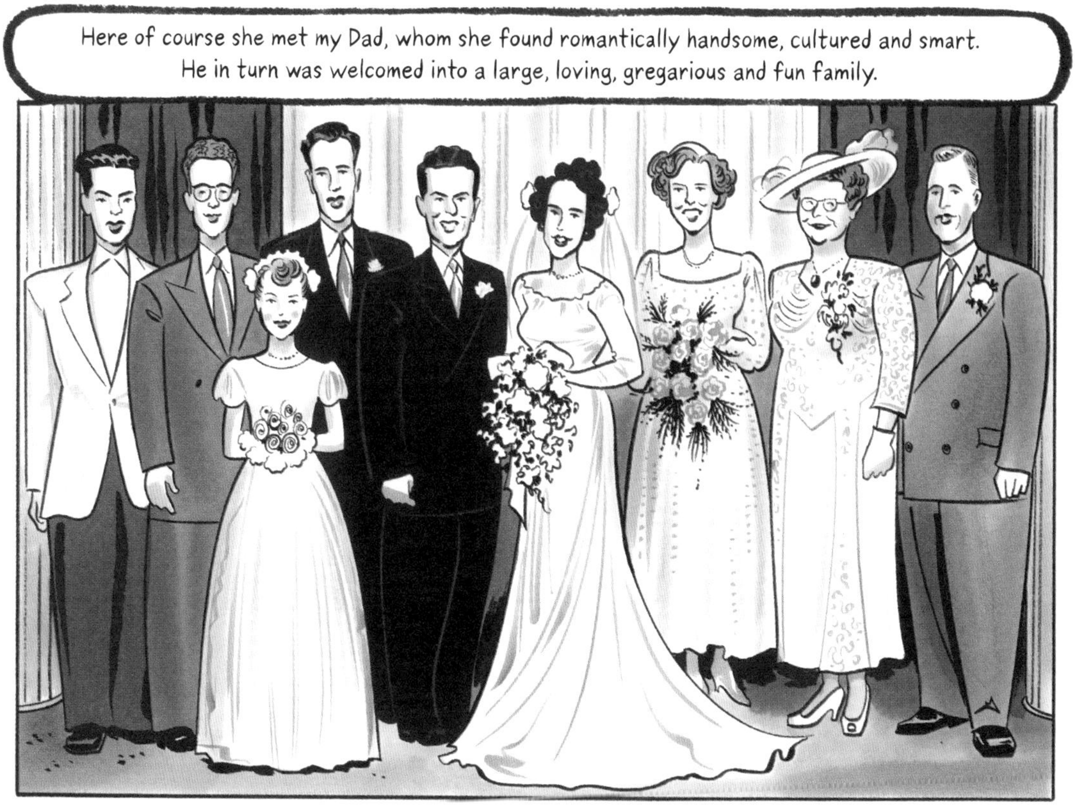
Here of course she met my Dad, whom she found romantically handsome, cultured and smart.
He in turn was welcomed into a large, loving, gregarious and fun family.

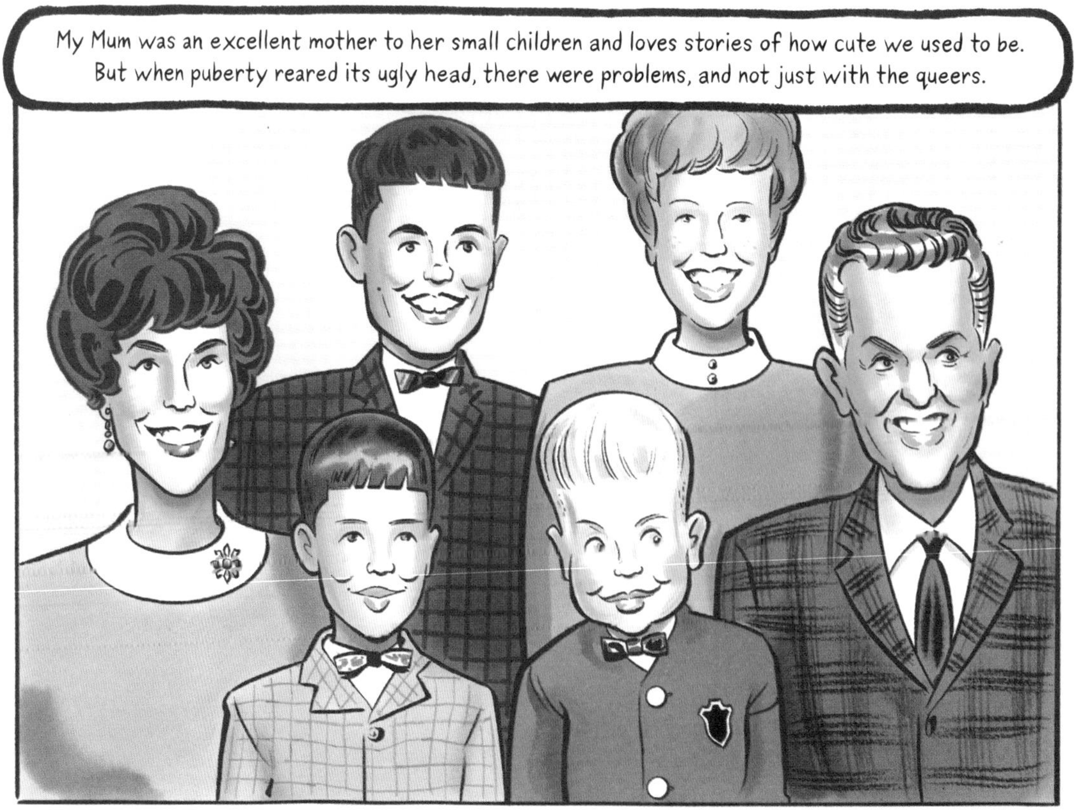
My Mum was an excellent mother to her small children and loves stories of how cute we used to be.
But when puberty reared its ugly head, there were problems, and not just with the queers.

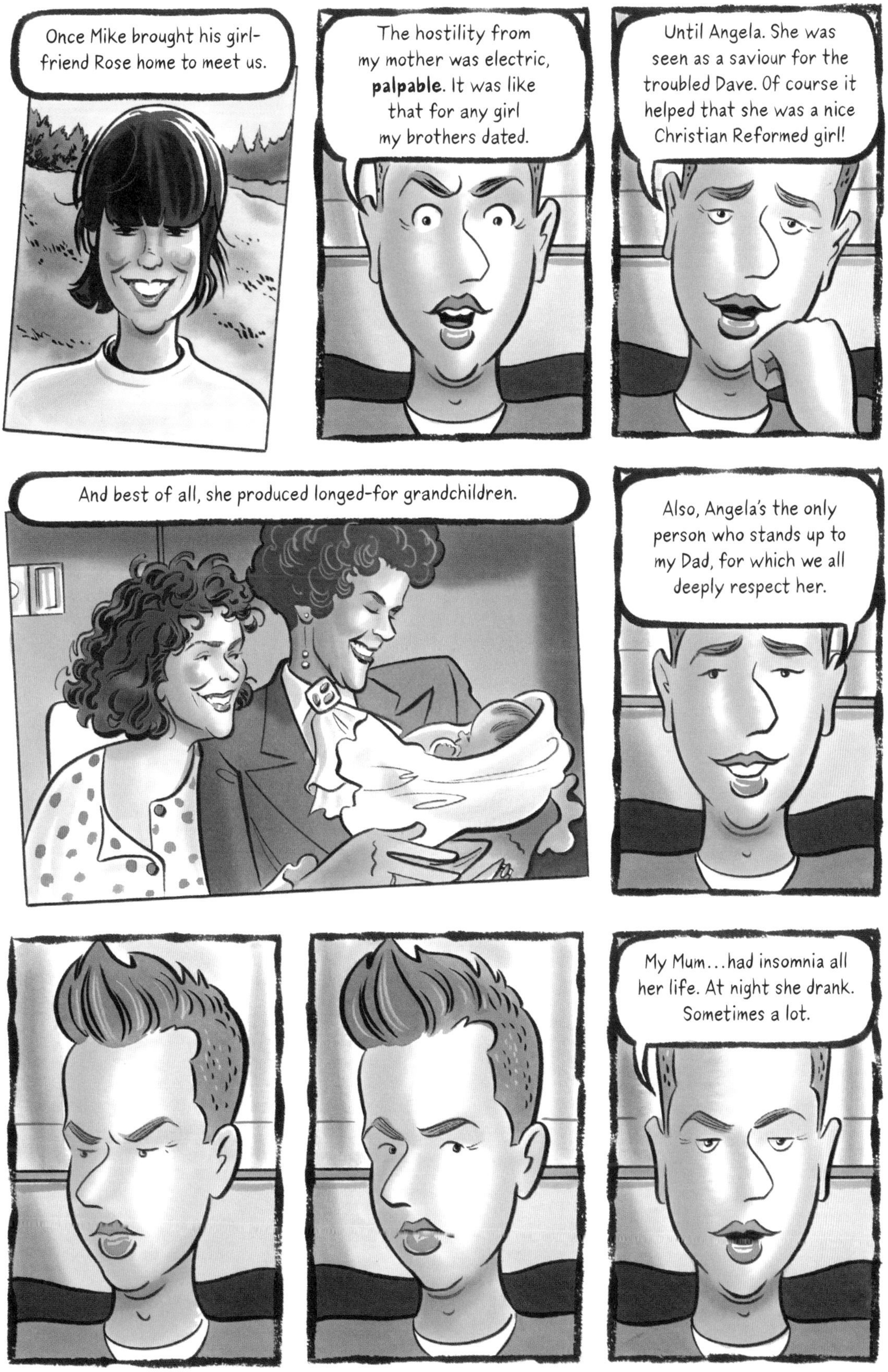
Once Mike brought his girl-friend Rose home to meet us.
The hostility from my mother was electric, **palpable**. It was like that for any girl my brothers dated.
Until Angela. She was seen as a saviour for the troubled Dave. Of course it helped that she was a nice Christian Reformed girl!
And best of all, she produced longed-for grandchildren.
Also, Angela's the only person who stands up to my Dad, for which we all deeply respect her.
My Mum...had insomnia all her life. At night she drank. Sometimes a lot.

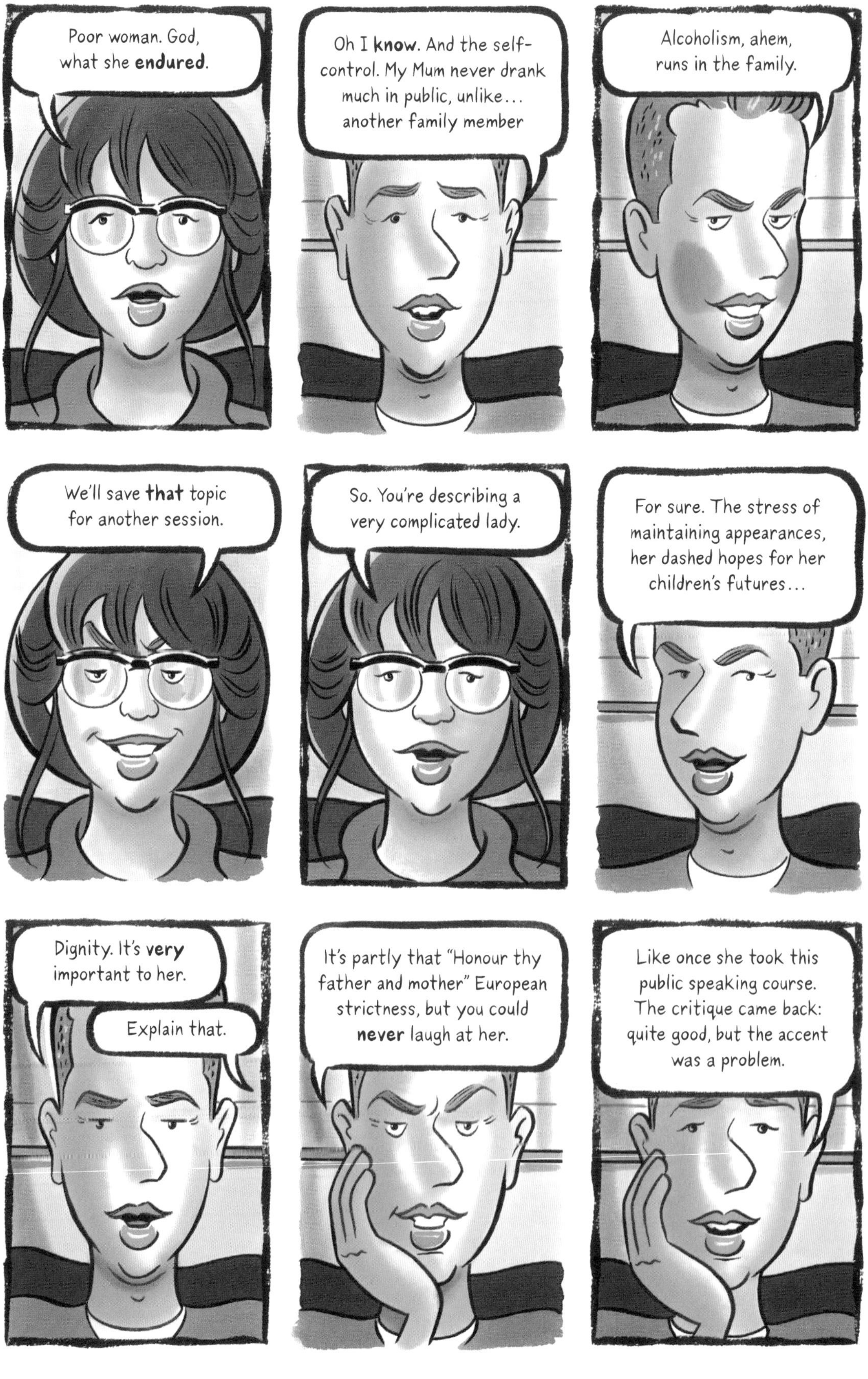
Poor woman. God, what she **endured**.
Oh I **know**. And the self-control. My Mum never drank much in public, unlike... another family member
Alcoholism, ahem, runs in the family.
We'll save **that** topic for another session.
So. You're describing a very complicated lady.
For sure. The stress of maintaining appearances, her dashed hopes for her children's futures...
Dignity. It's **very** important to her.
Explain that.
It's partly that "Honour thy father and mother" European strictness, but you could **never** laugh at her.
Like once she took this public speaking course. The critique came back: quite good, but the accent was a problem.

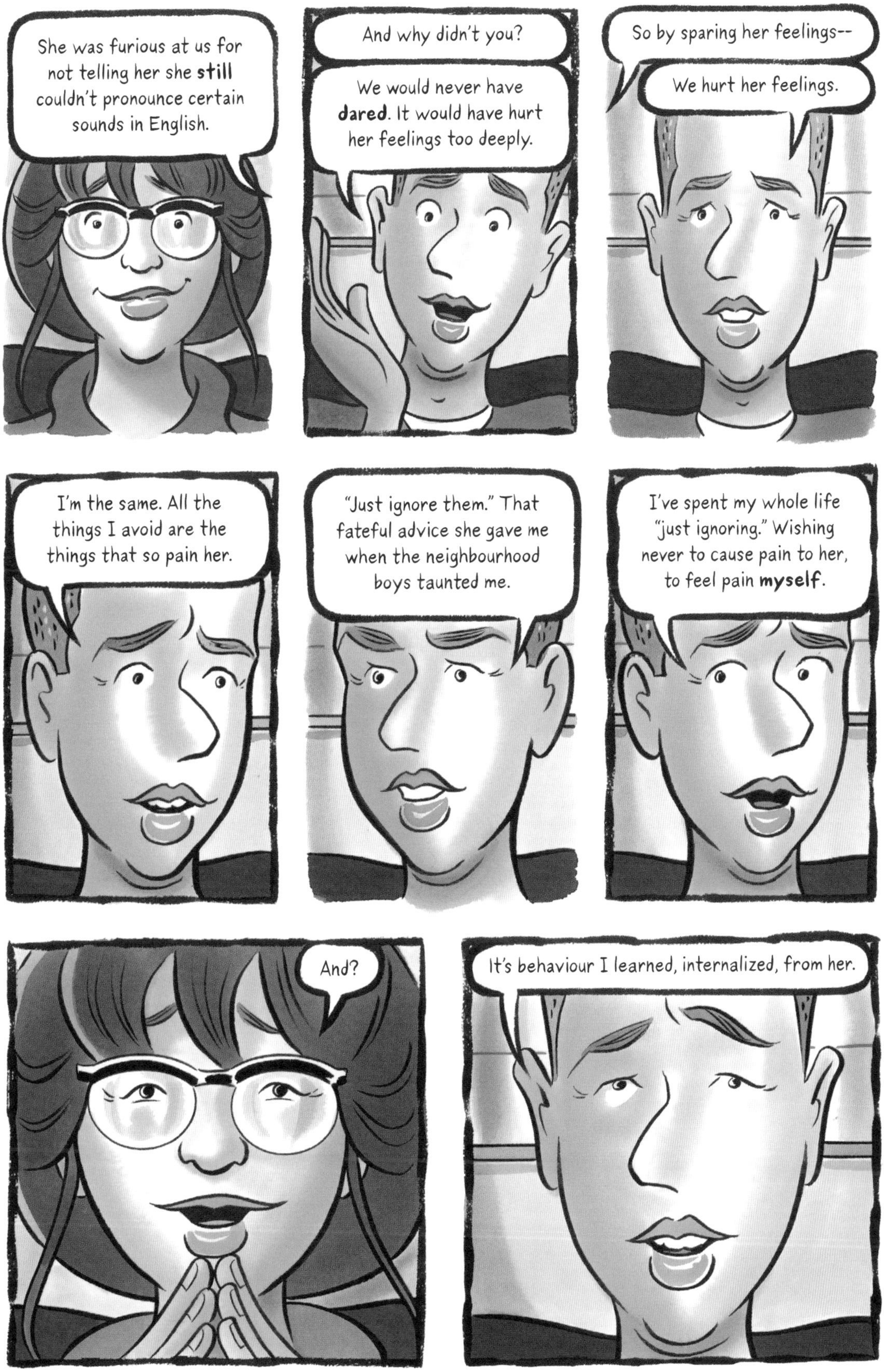
She was furious at us for not telling her she **still** couldn't pronounce certain sounds in English.
And why didn't you?
We would never have **dared**. It would have hurt her feelings too deeply.
So by sparing her feelings--
We hurt her feelings.
I'm the same. All the things I avoid are the things that so pain her.
"Just ignore them." That fateful advice she gave me when the neighbourhood boys taunted me.
I've spent my whole life "just ignoring." Wishing never to cause pain to her, to feel pain **myself**.
And?
It's behaviour I learned, internalized, from her.

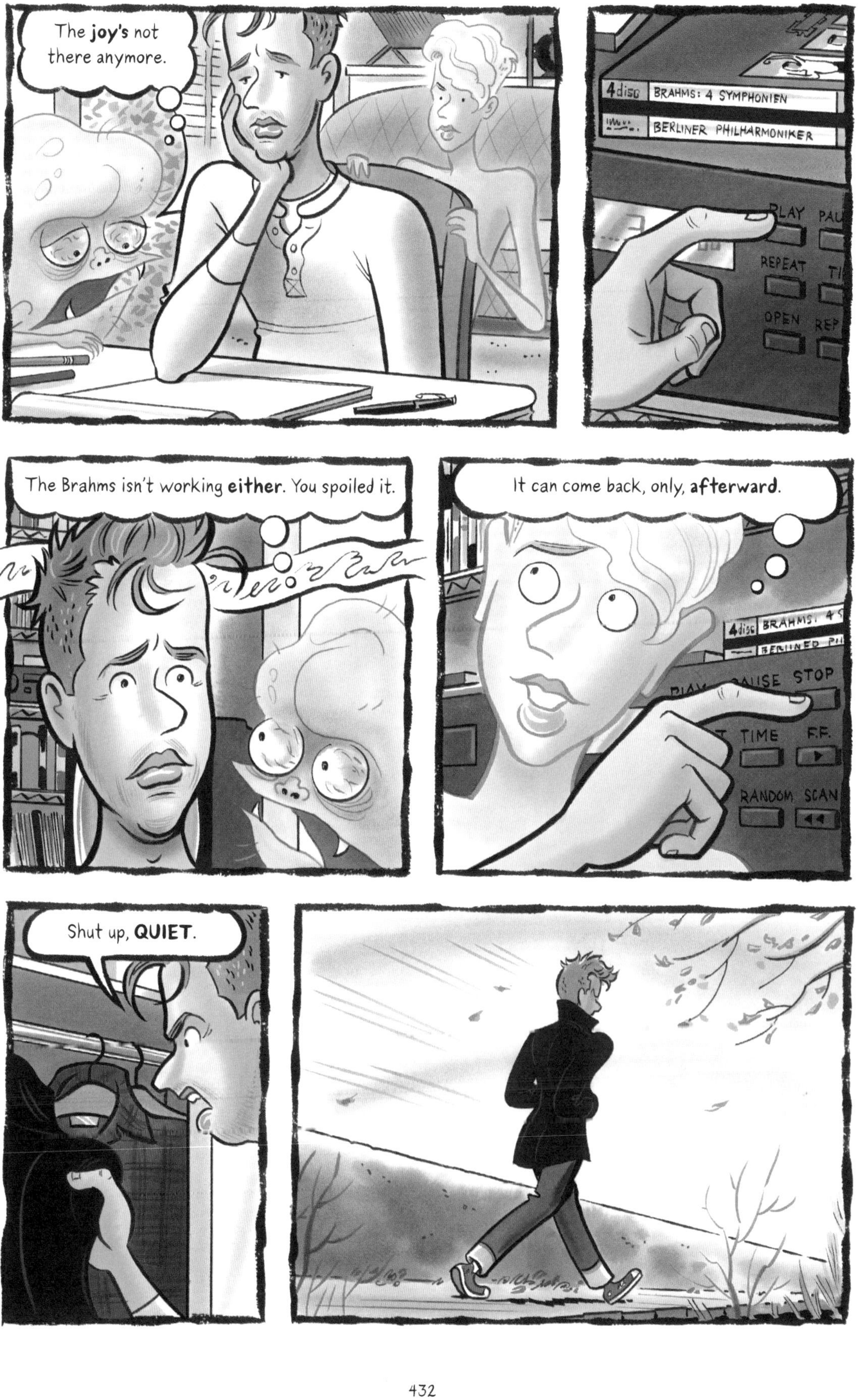
The joy's not there anymore.
4disc BRAHMS: 4 SYMPHONIEN
BERLINER PHILHARMONIKER
PLAY
REPEAT
OPEN
The Brahms isn't working either. You spoiled it.
It can come back, only, afterward.
STOP
TIME
F.F.
RANDOM
SCAN
Shut up, QUIET.

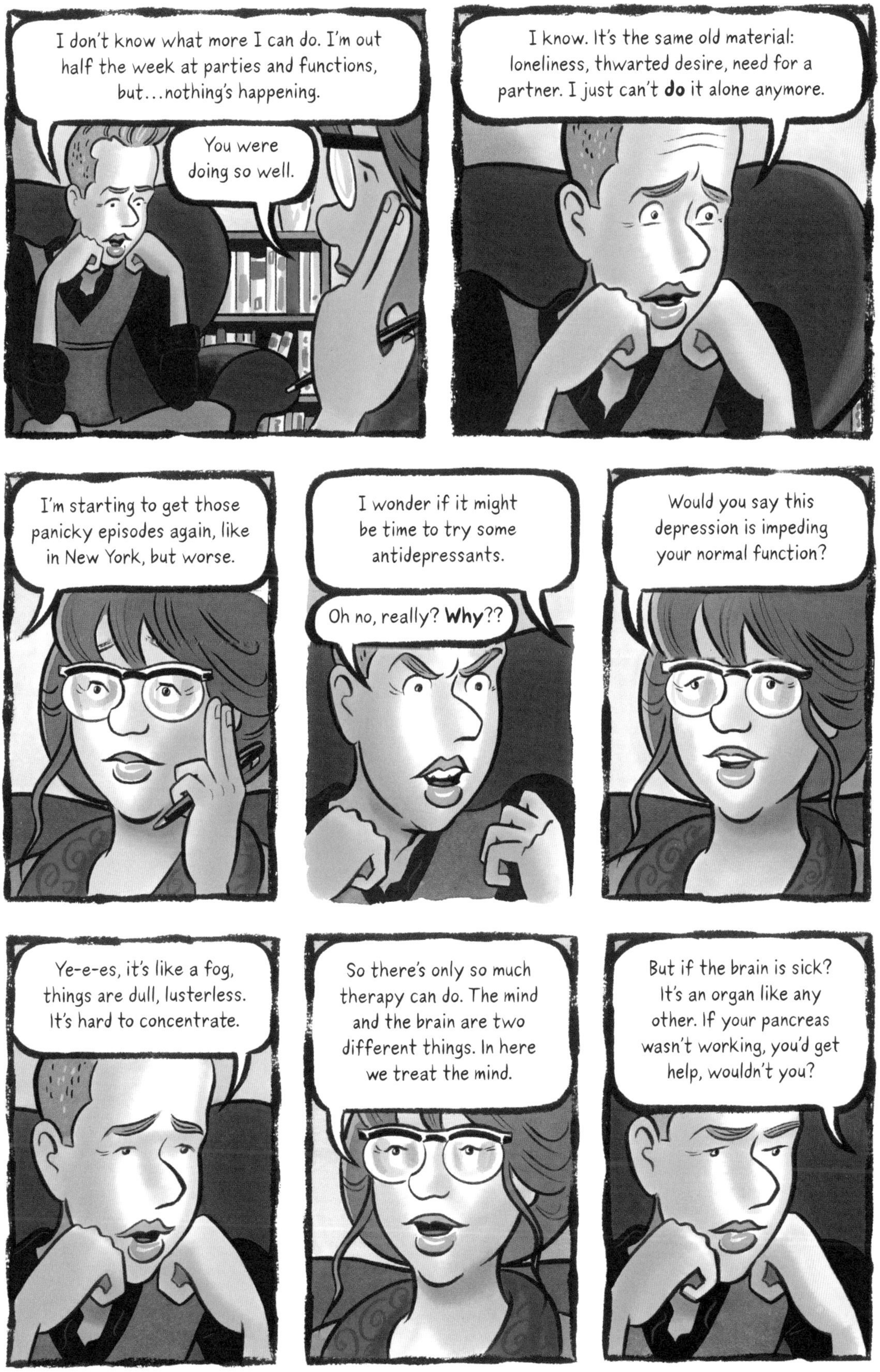
I don't know what more I can do. I'm out half the week at parties and functions, but...nothing's happening.
You were doing so well.
I know. It's the same old material: loneliness, thwarted desire, need for a partner. I just can't **do** it alone anymore.
I'm starting to get those panicky episodes again, like in New York, but worse.
I wonder if it might be time to try some antidepressants.
Oh no, really? **Why**??
Would you say this depression is impeding your normal function?
Ye-e-es, it's like a fog, things are dull, lusterless. It's hard to concentrate.
So there's only so much therapy can do. The mind and the brain are two different things. In here we treat the mind.
But if the brain is sick? It's an organ like any other. If your pancreas wasn't working, you'd get help, wouldn't you?

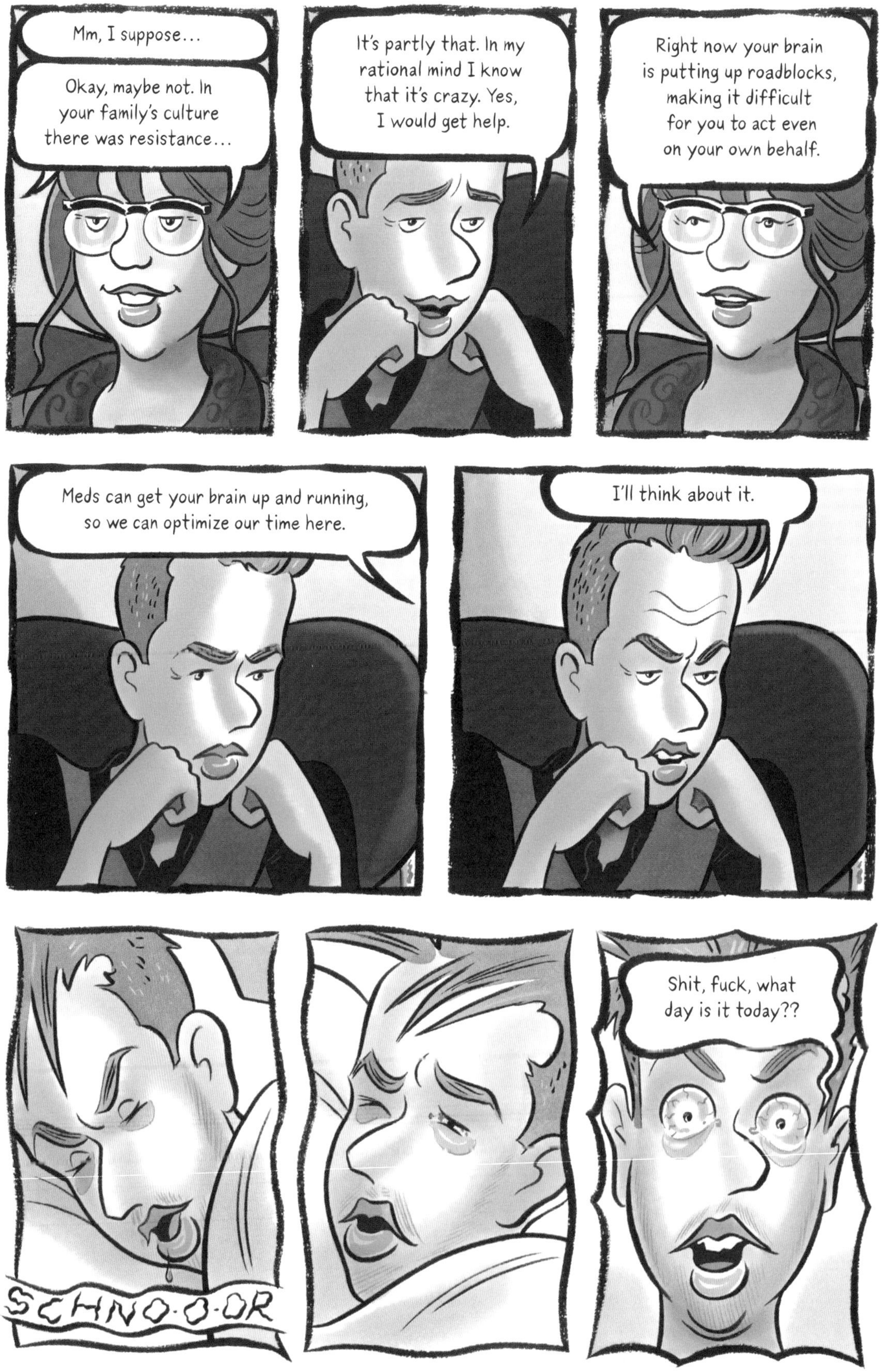
Mm, I suppose...
Okay, maybe not. In your family's culture there was resistance...
It's partly that. In my rational mind I know that it's crazy. Yes, I would get help.
Right now your brain is putting up roadblocks, making it difficult for you to act even on your own behalf.
Meds can get your brain up and running, so we can optimize our time here.
I'll think about it.
SCHNO-O-OR
Shit, fuck, what day is it today??

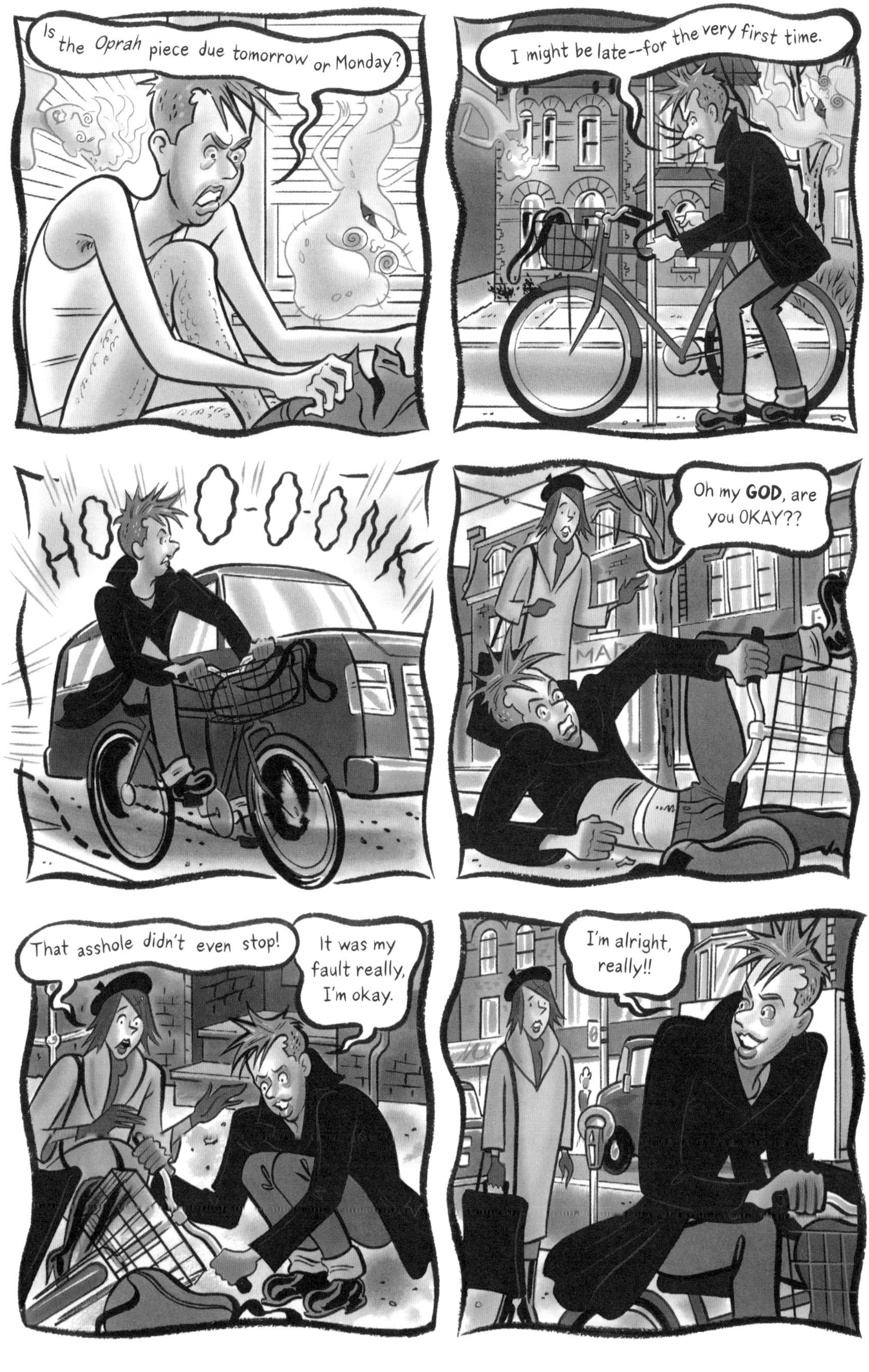
Is the *Oprah* piece due tomorrow or Monday?
I might be late--for the very first time.
HO-O-O-ONK
Oh my **GOD**, are you OKAY??
That asshole didn't even stop!
It was my fault really, I'm okay.
I'm alright, really!!

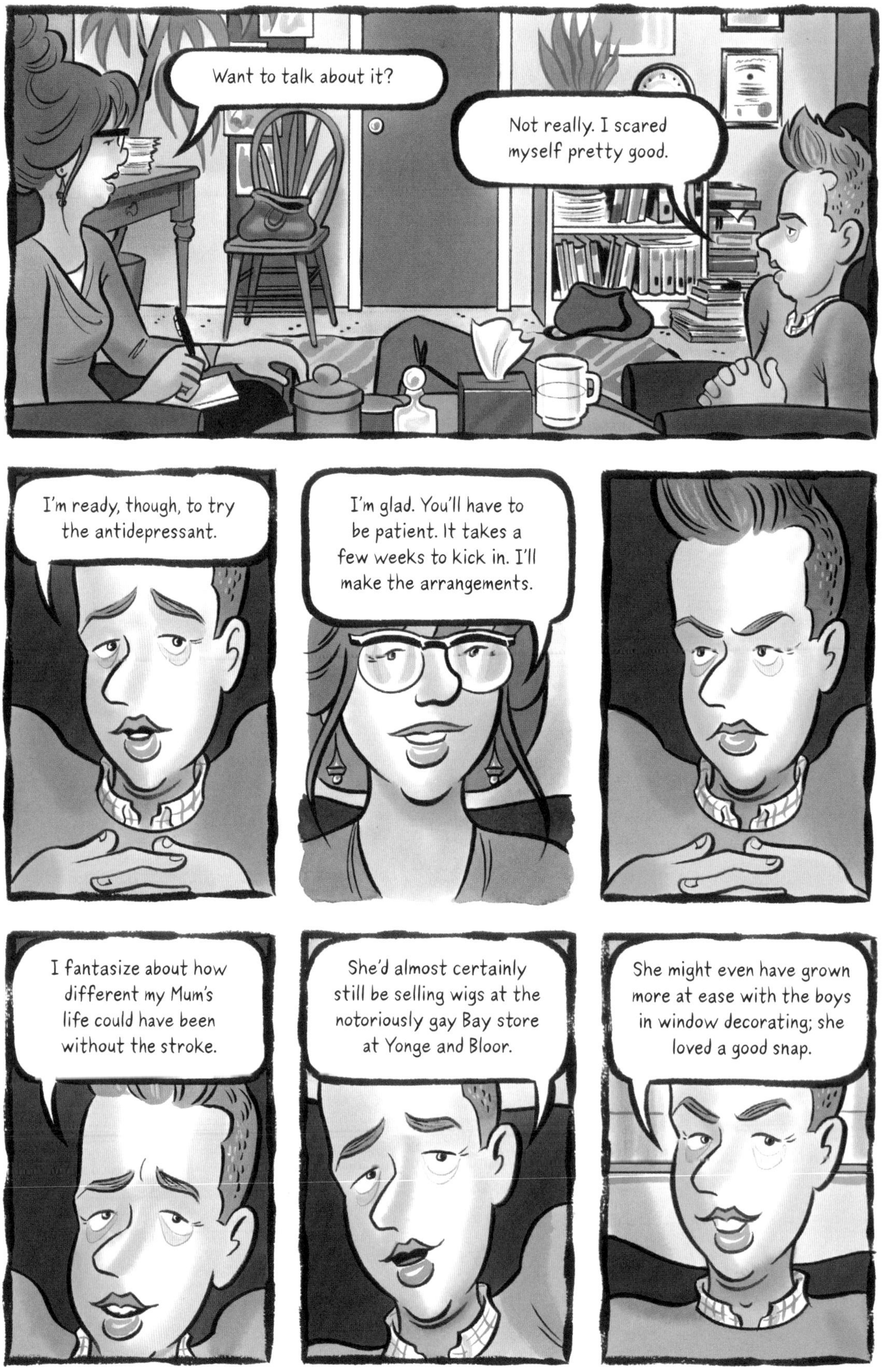
Want to talk about it?
Not really. I scared myself pretty good.
I'm ready, though, to try the antidepressant.
I'm glad. You'll have to be patient. It takes a few weeks to kick in. I'll make the arrangements.
I fantasize about how different my Mum's life could have been without the stroke.
She'd almost certainly still be selling wigs at the notoriously gay Bay store at Yonge and Bloor.
She might even have grown more at ease with the boys in window decorating; she loved a good snap.

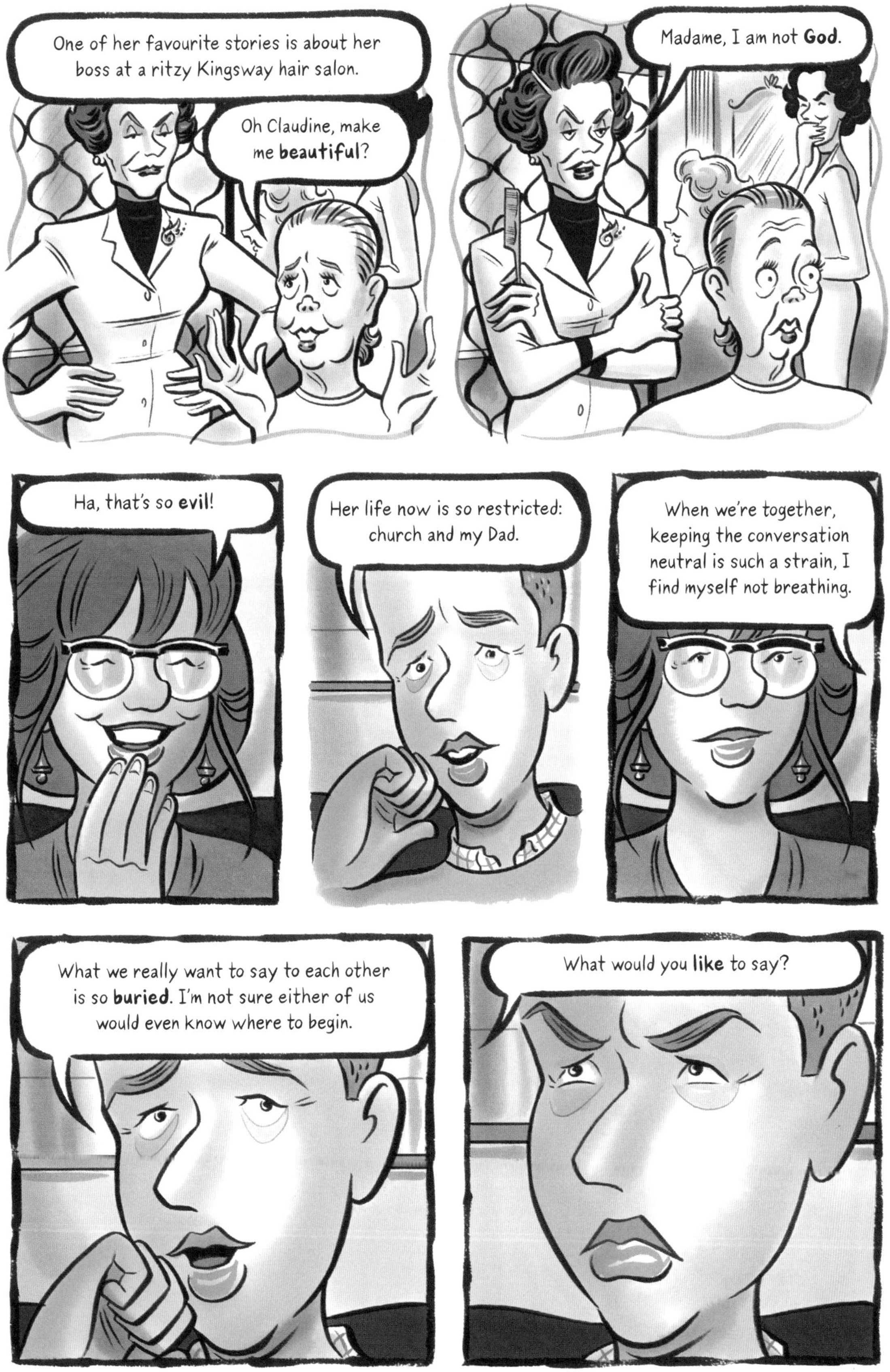
One of her favourite stories is about her boss at a ritzy Kingsway hair salon.
Oh Claudine, make me **beautiful**?
Madame, I am not **God**.
Ha, that's so **evil**!
Her life now is so restricted: church and my Dad.
When we're together, keeping the conversation neutral is such a strain, I find myself not breathing.
What we really want to say to each other is so **buried**. I'm not sure either of us would even know where to begin.
What would you **like** to say?

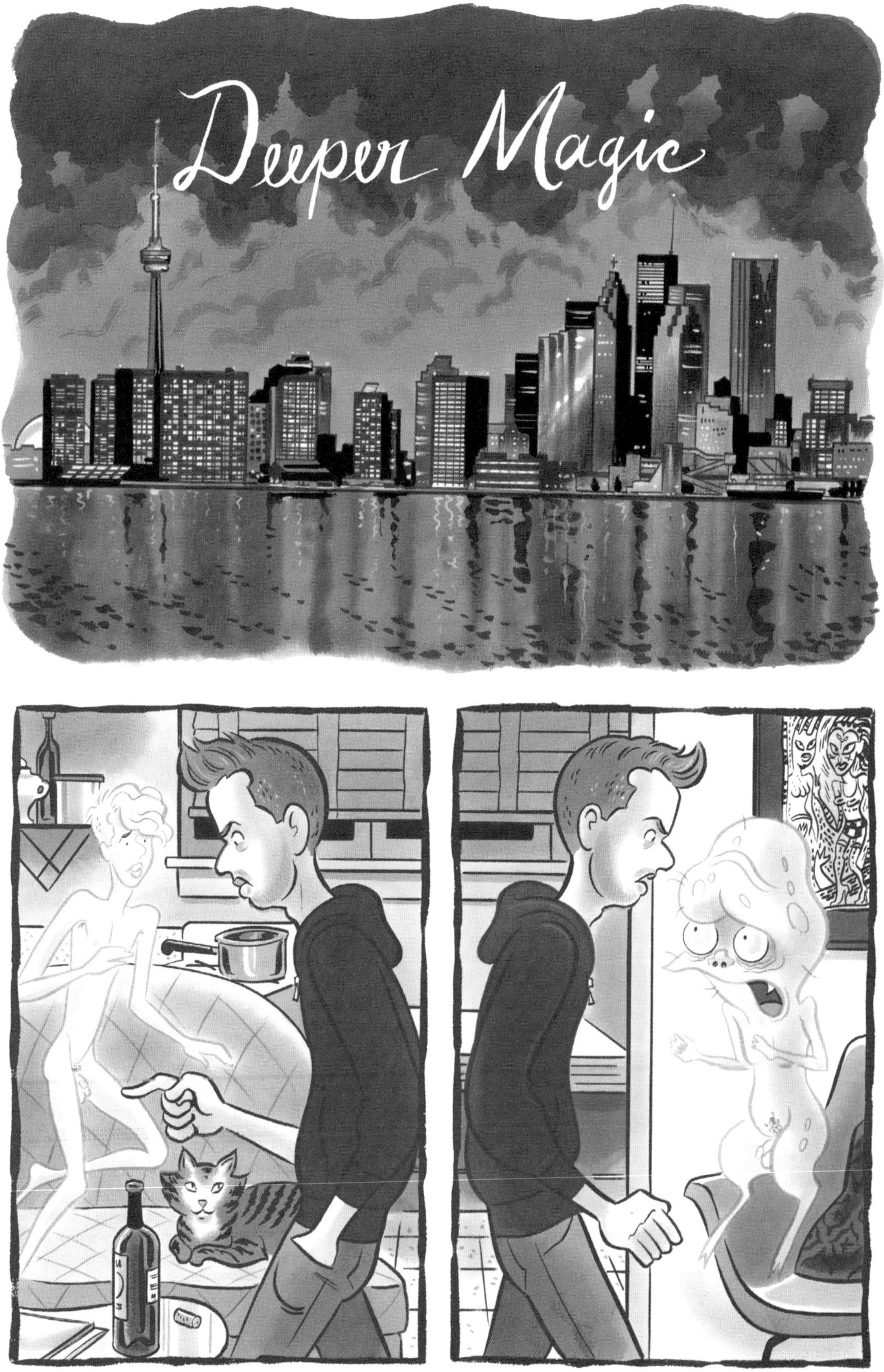
Deeper Magic

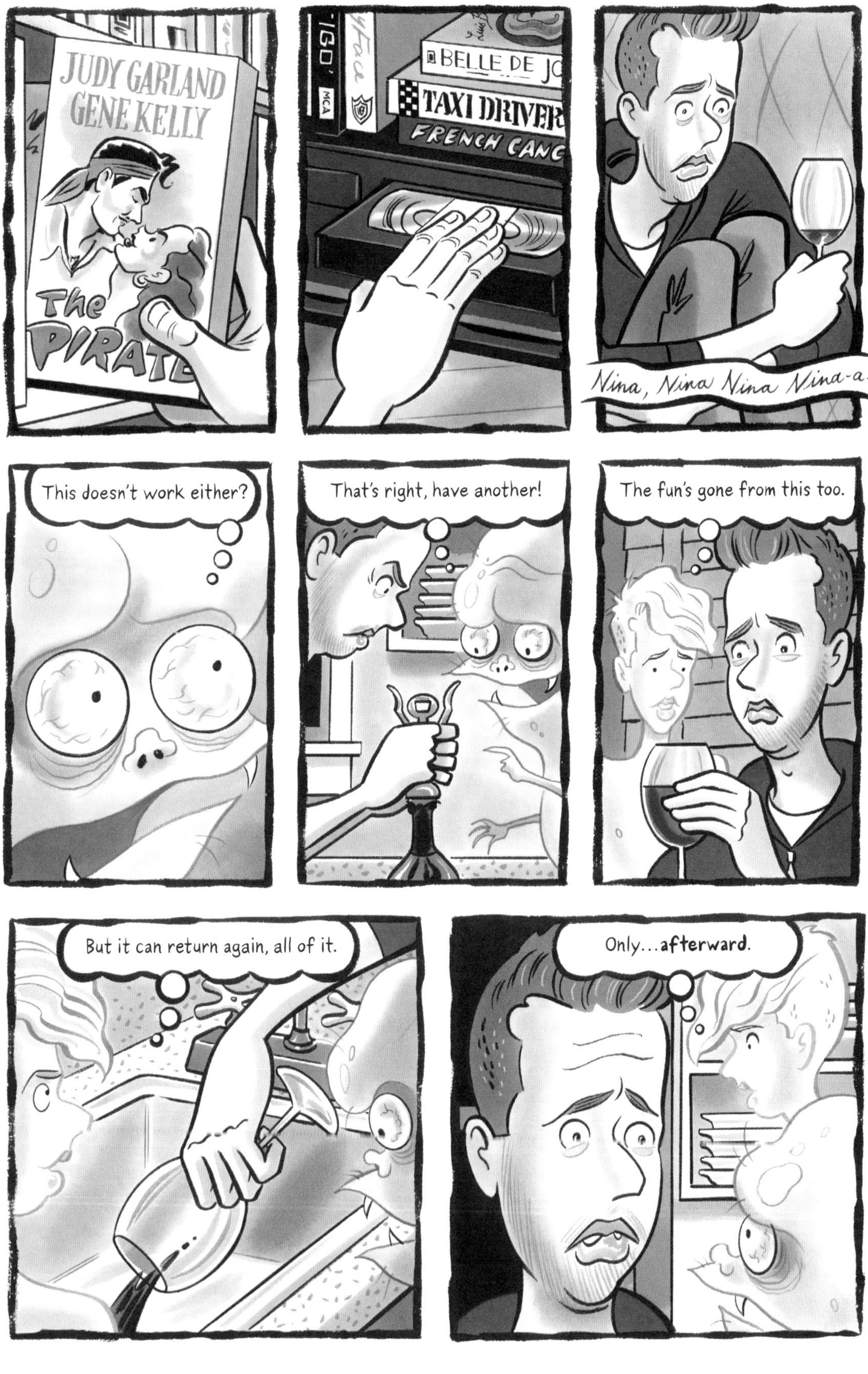
JUDY GARLAND
GENE KELLY
The PIRAT
BELLE DE JO
TAXI DRIVER
FRENCH CANC
MCA
Nina, Nina Nina Nina-a-a
This doesn't work either?
That's right, have another!
The fun's gone from this too.
But it can return again, all of it.
Only...**afterward**.

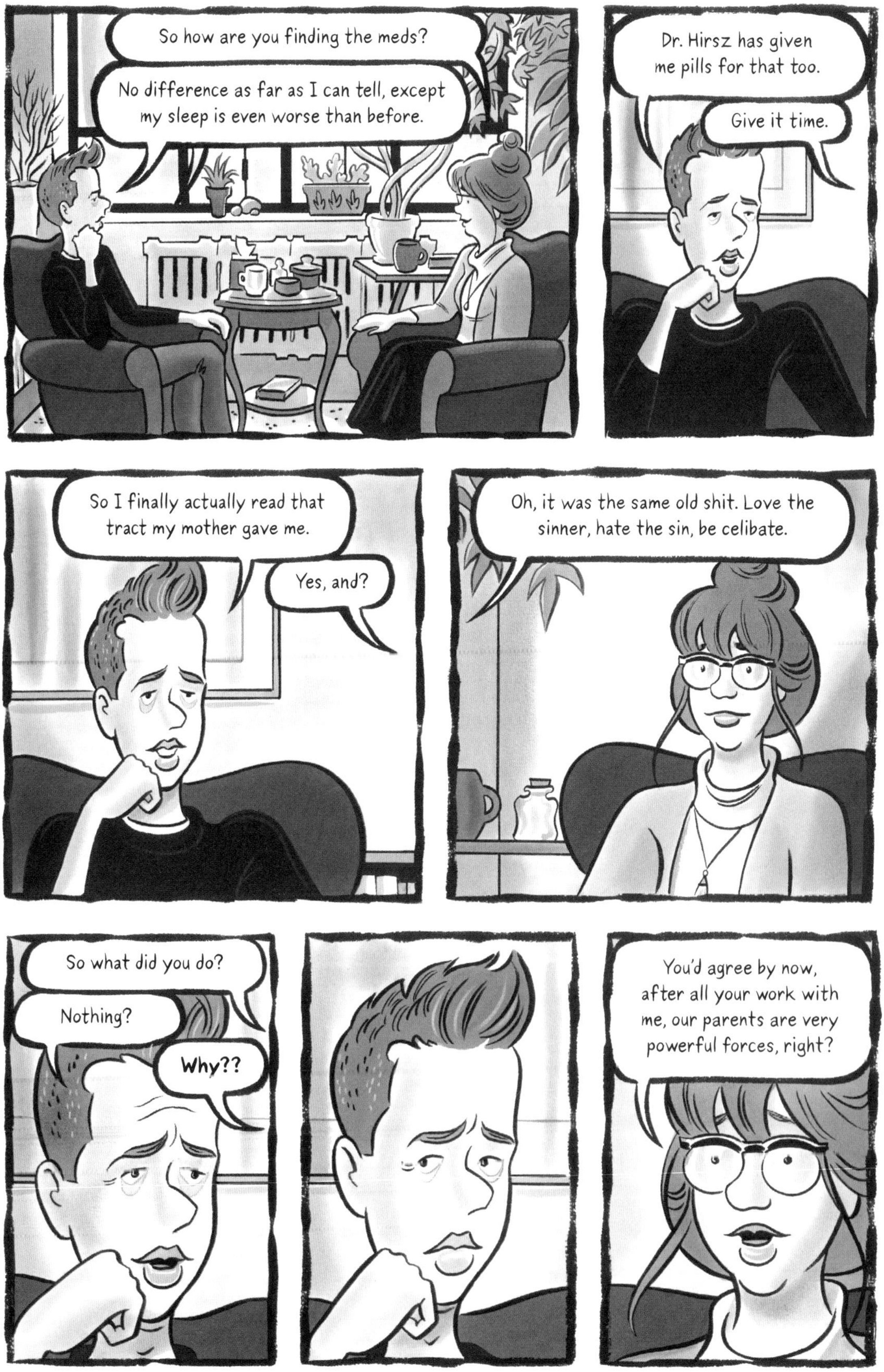
So how are you finding the meds?
No difference as far as I can tell, except my sleep is even worse than before.
Dr. Hirsz has given me pills for that too.
Give it time.
So I finally actually read that tract my mother gave me.
Yes, and?
Oh, it was the same old shit. Love the sinner, hate the sin, be celibate.
So what did you do?
Nothing?
Why??
You'd agree by now, after all your work with me, our parents are very powerful forces, right?

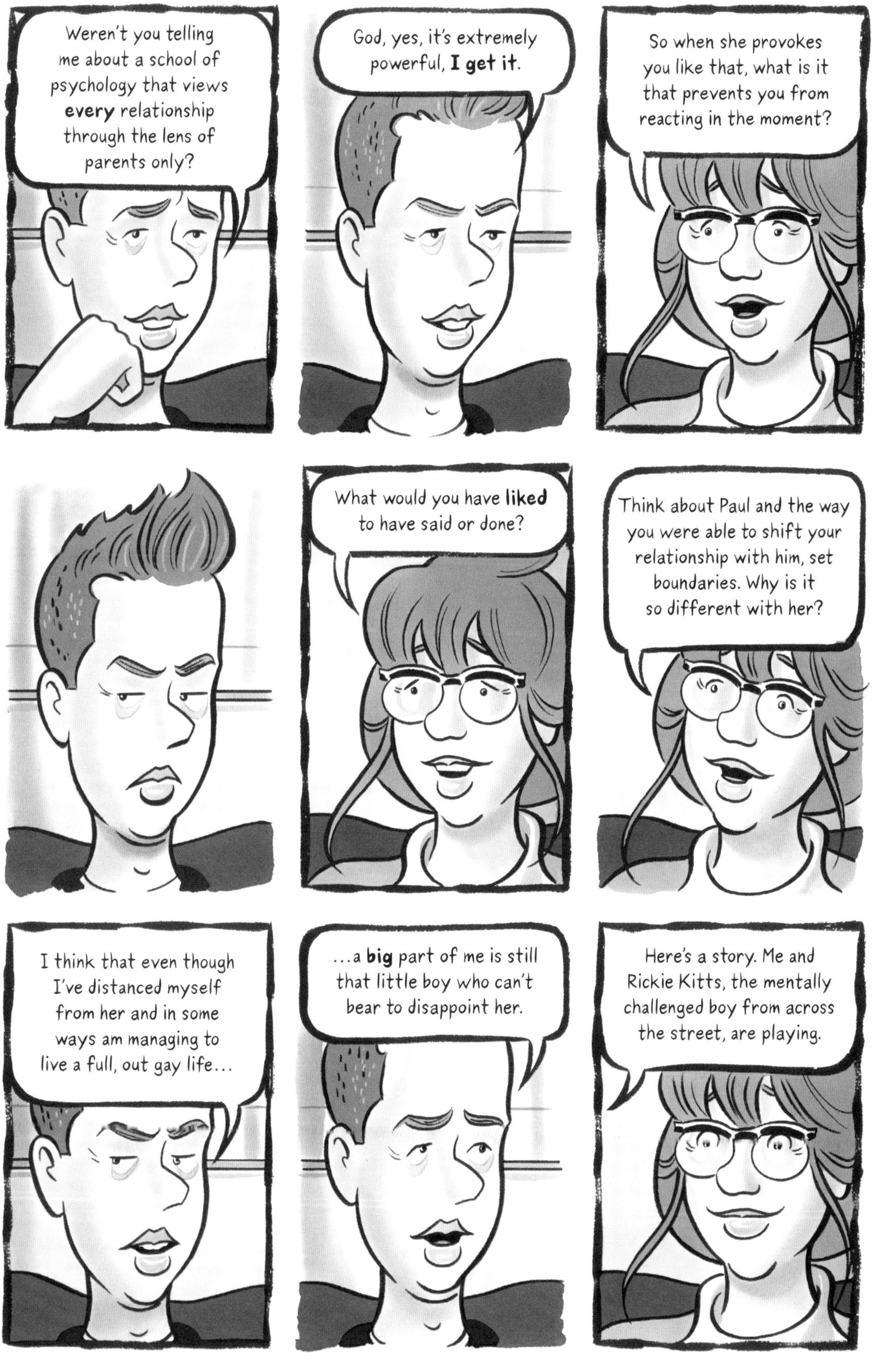

Weren't you telling me about a school of psychology that views **every** relationship through the lens of parents only?
God, yes, it's extremely powerful, **I get it**.
So when she provokes you like that, what is it that prevents you from reacting in the moment?
What would you have **liked** to have said or done?
Think about Paul and the way you were able to shift your relationship with him, set boundaries. Why is it so different with her?
I think that even though I've distanced myself from her and in some ways am managing to live a full, out gay life...
...a **big** part of me is still that little boy who can't bear to disappoint her.
Here's a story. Me and Rickie Kitts, the mentally challenged boy from across the street, are playing.

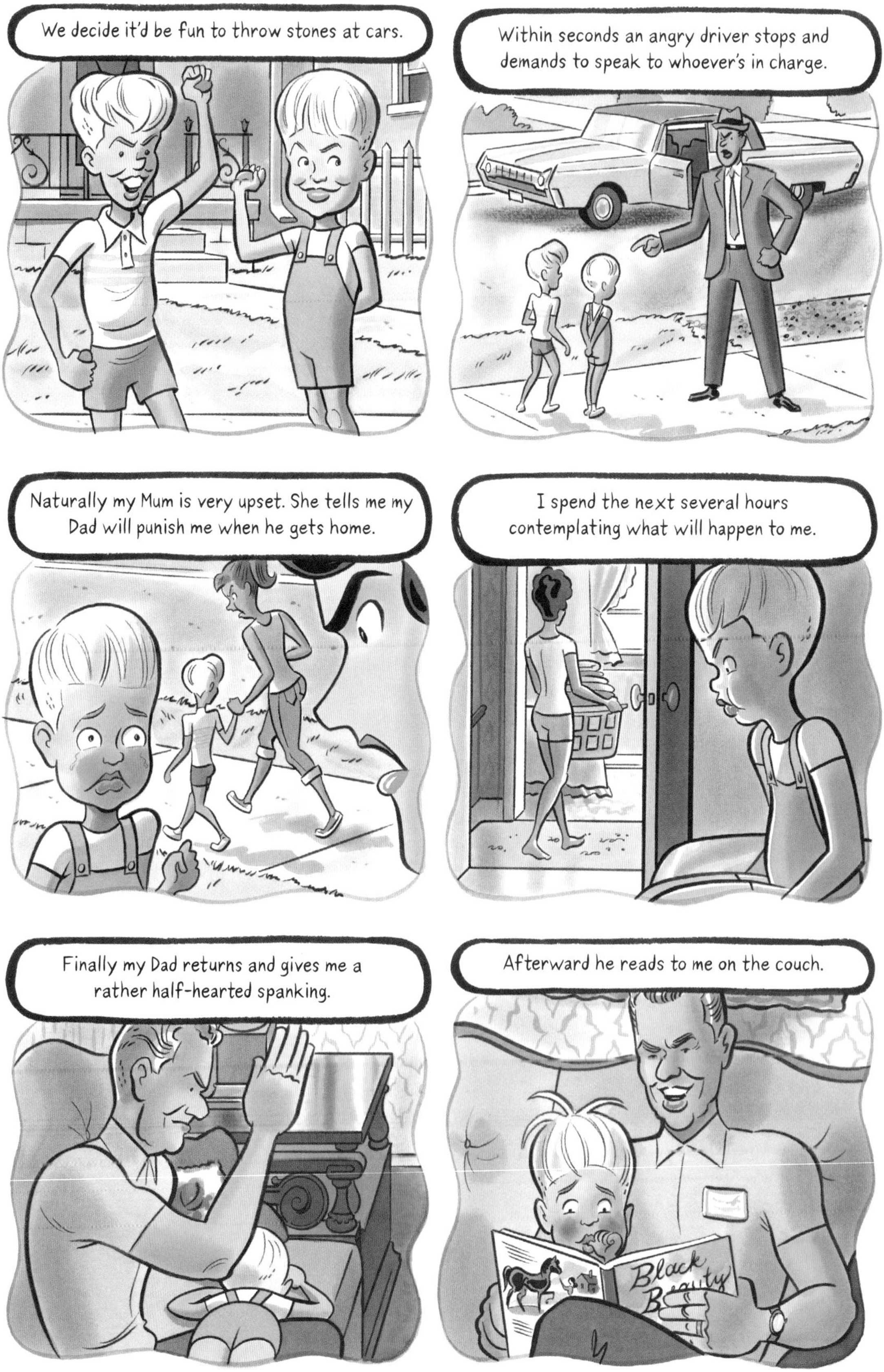
We decide it'd be fun to throw stones at cars.
Within seconds an angry driver stops and demands to speak to whoever's in charge.
Naturally my Mum is very upset. She tells me my Dad will punish me when he gets home.
I spend the next several hours contemplating what will happen to me.
Finally my Dad returns and gives me a rather half-hearted spanking.
Afterward he reads to me on the couch.
Black

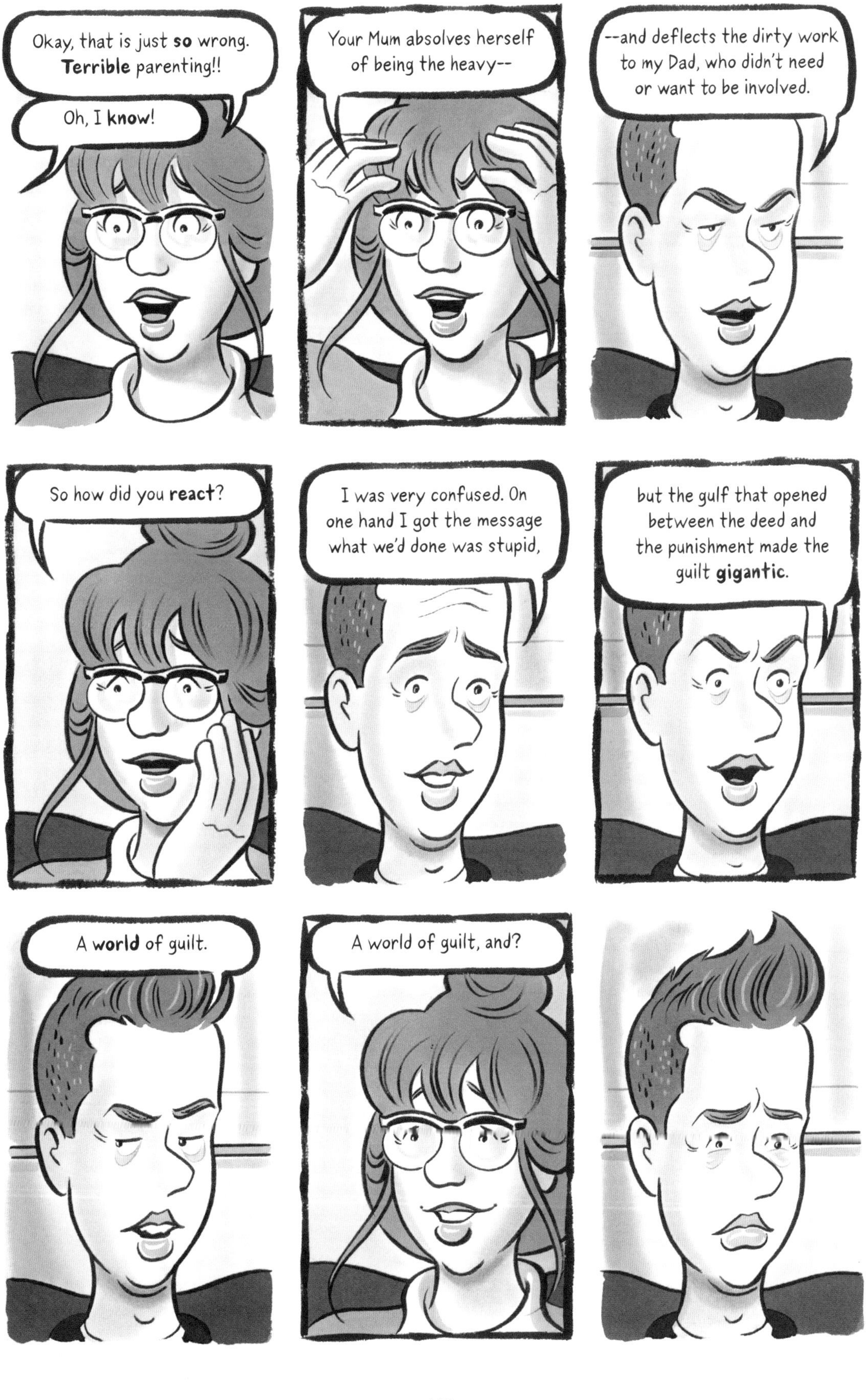
Okay, that is just **so** wrong. **Terrible** parenting!!
Oh, I **know**!
Your Mum absolves herself of being the heavy--
--and deflects the dirty work to my Dad, who didn't need or want to be involved.
So how did you **react**?
I was very confused. On one hand I got the message what we'd done was stupid,
but the gulf that opened between the deed and the punishment made the guilt **gigantic**.
A **world** of guilt.
A world of guilt, and?

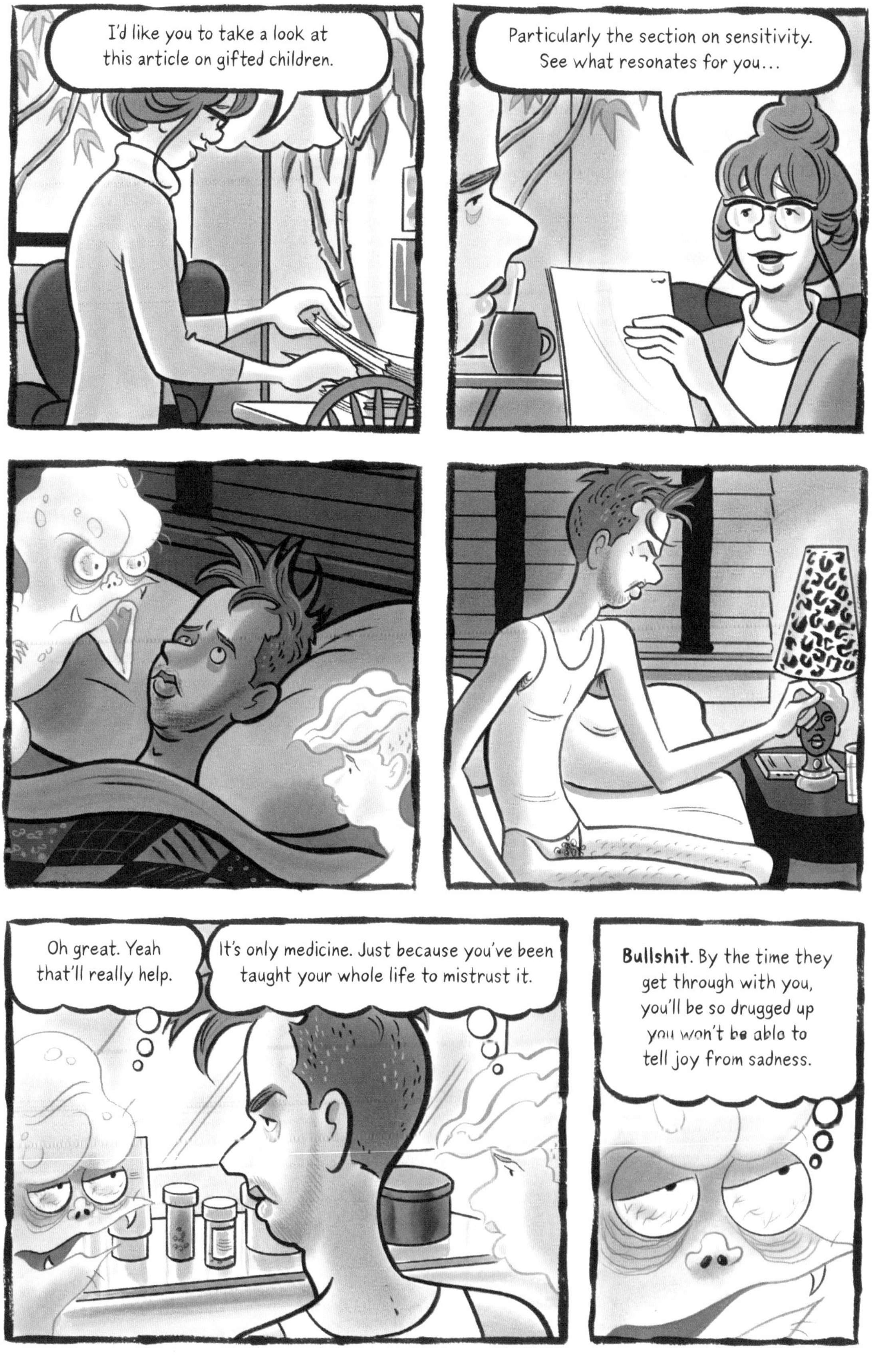
I'd like you to take a look at this article on gifted children.
Particularly the section on sensitivity. See what resonates for you...
Oh great. Yeah that'll really help.
It's only medicine. Just because you've been taught your whole life to mistrust it.
Bullshit. By the time they get through with you, you'll be so drugged up you won't be able to tell joy from sadness.

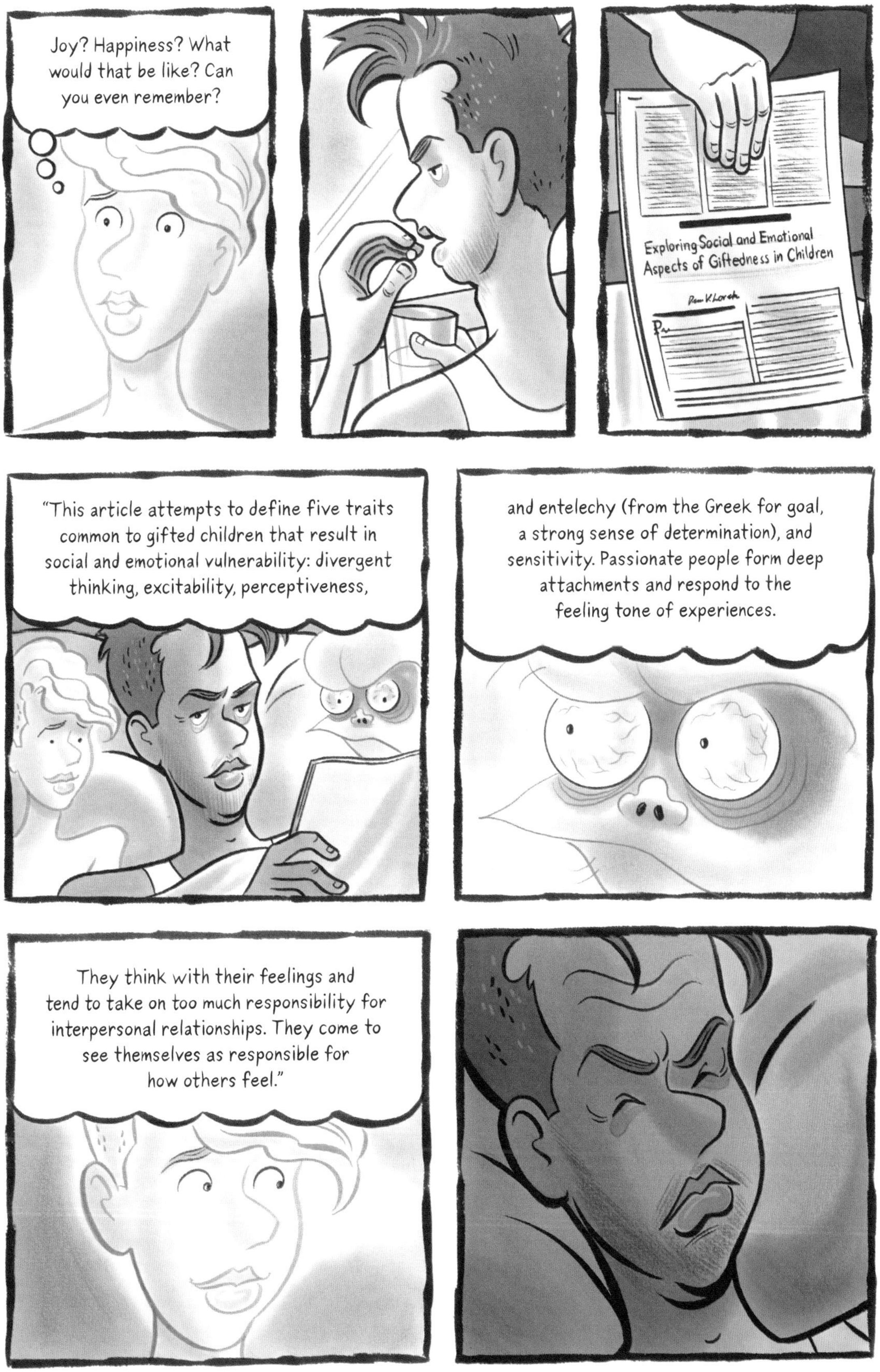
Joy? Happiness? What would that be like? Can you even remember?
Exploring Social and Emotional Aspects of Giftedness in Children
"This article attempts to define five traits common to gifted children that result in social and emotional vulnerability: divergent thinking, excitability, perceptiveness,
and entelechy (from the Greek for goal, a strong sense of determination), and sensitivity. Passionate people form deep attachments and respond to the feeling tone of experiences.
They think with their feelings and tend to take on too much responsibility for interpersonal relationships. They come to see themselves as responsible for how others feel."

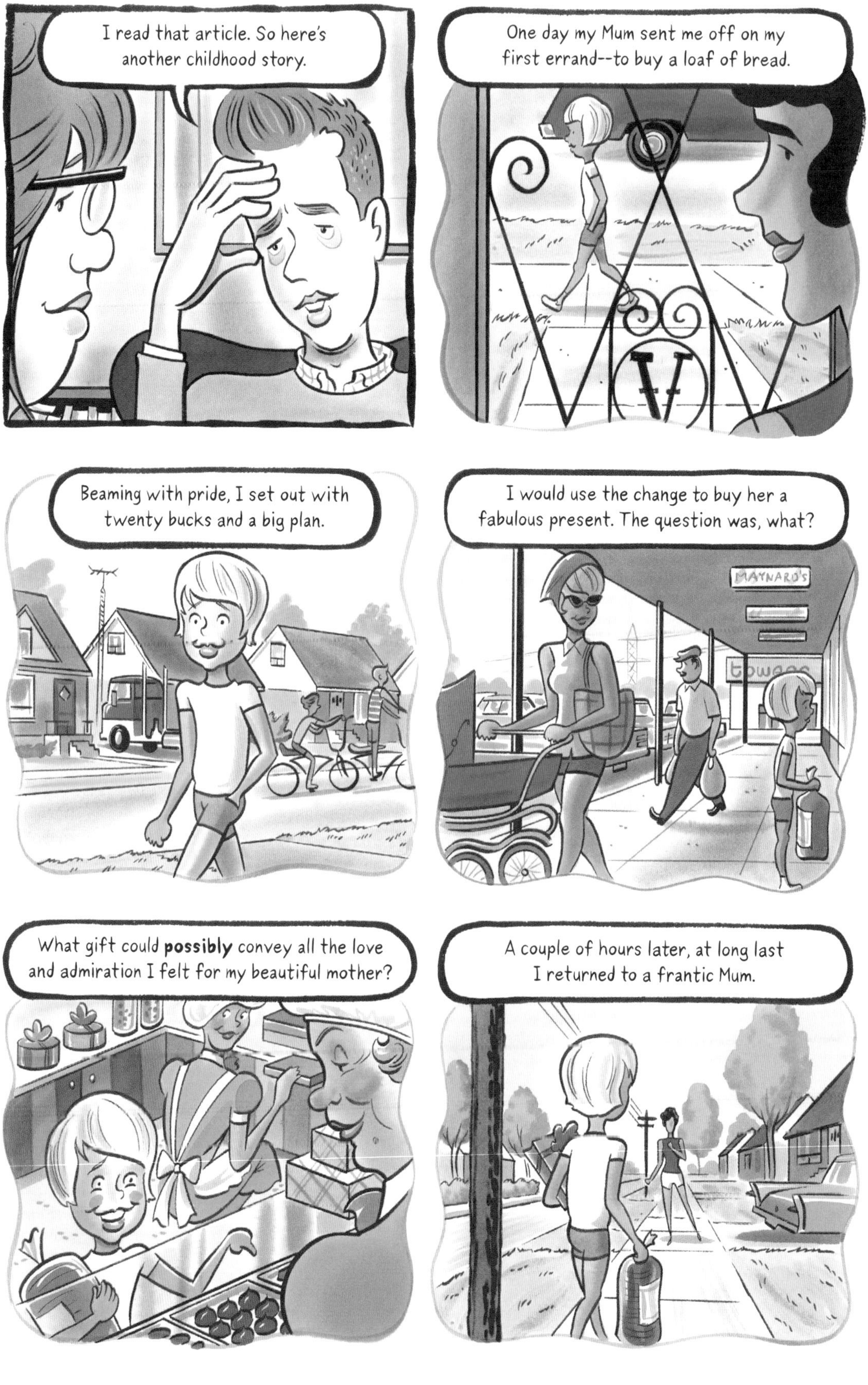
I read that article. So here's another childhood story.
One day my Mum sent me off on my first errand--to buy a loaf of bread.
Beaming with pride, I set out with twenty bucks and a big plan.
I would use the change to buy her a fabulous present. The question was, what?
MAYNARD'S
What gift could **possibly** convey all the love and admiration I felt for my beautiful mother?
A couple of hours later, at long last I returned to a frantic Mum.

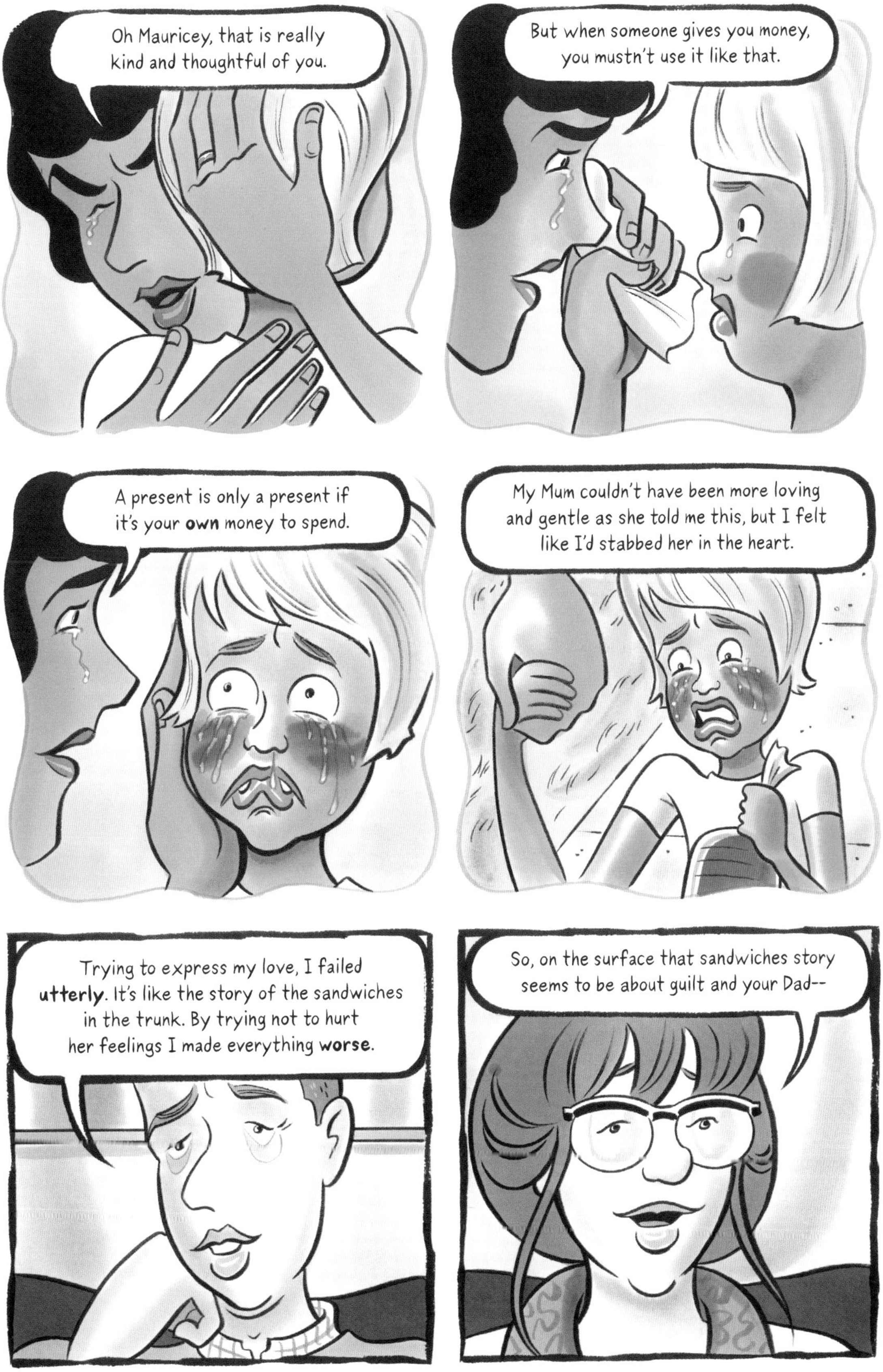
Oh Mauricey, that is really kind and thoughtful of you.
But when someone gives you money, you mustn't use it like that.
A present is only a present if it's your **own** money to spend.
My Mum couldn't have been more loving and gentle as she told me this, but I felt like I'd stabbed her in the heart.
Trying to express my love, I failed **utterly**. It's like the story of the sandwiches in the trunk. By trying not to hurt her feelings I made everything **worse**.
So, on the surface that sandwiches story seems to be about guilt and your Dad--

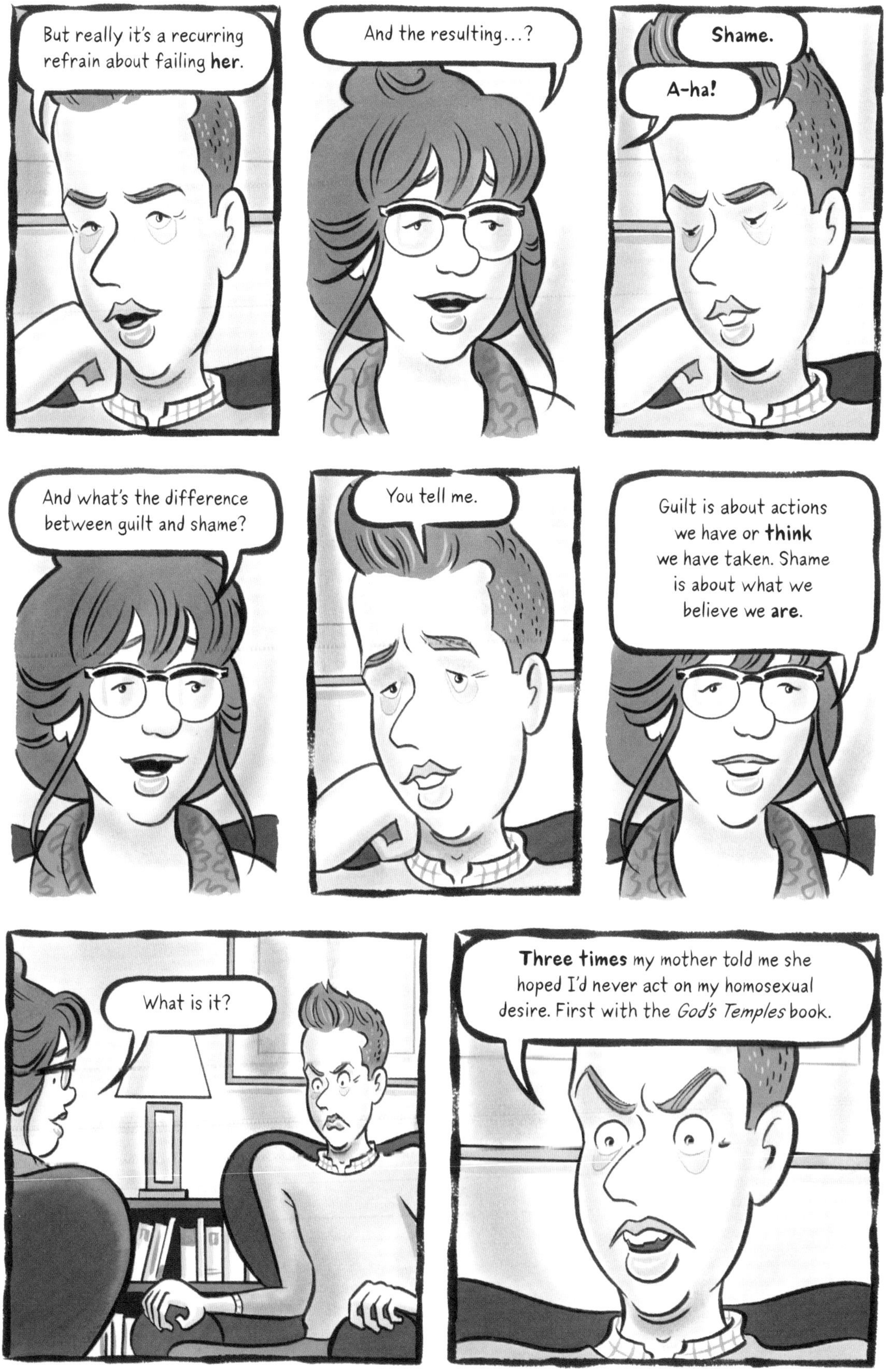
But really it's a recurring refrain about failing **her**.
And the resulting...?
Shame.
A-ha!
And what's the difference between guilt and shame?
You tell me.
Guilt is about actions we have or **think** we have taken. Shame is about what we believe we **are**.
What is it?
Three times my mother told me she hoped I'd never act on my homosexual desire. First with the *God's Temples* book.

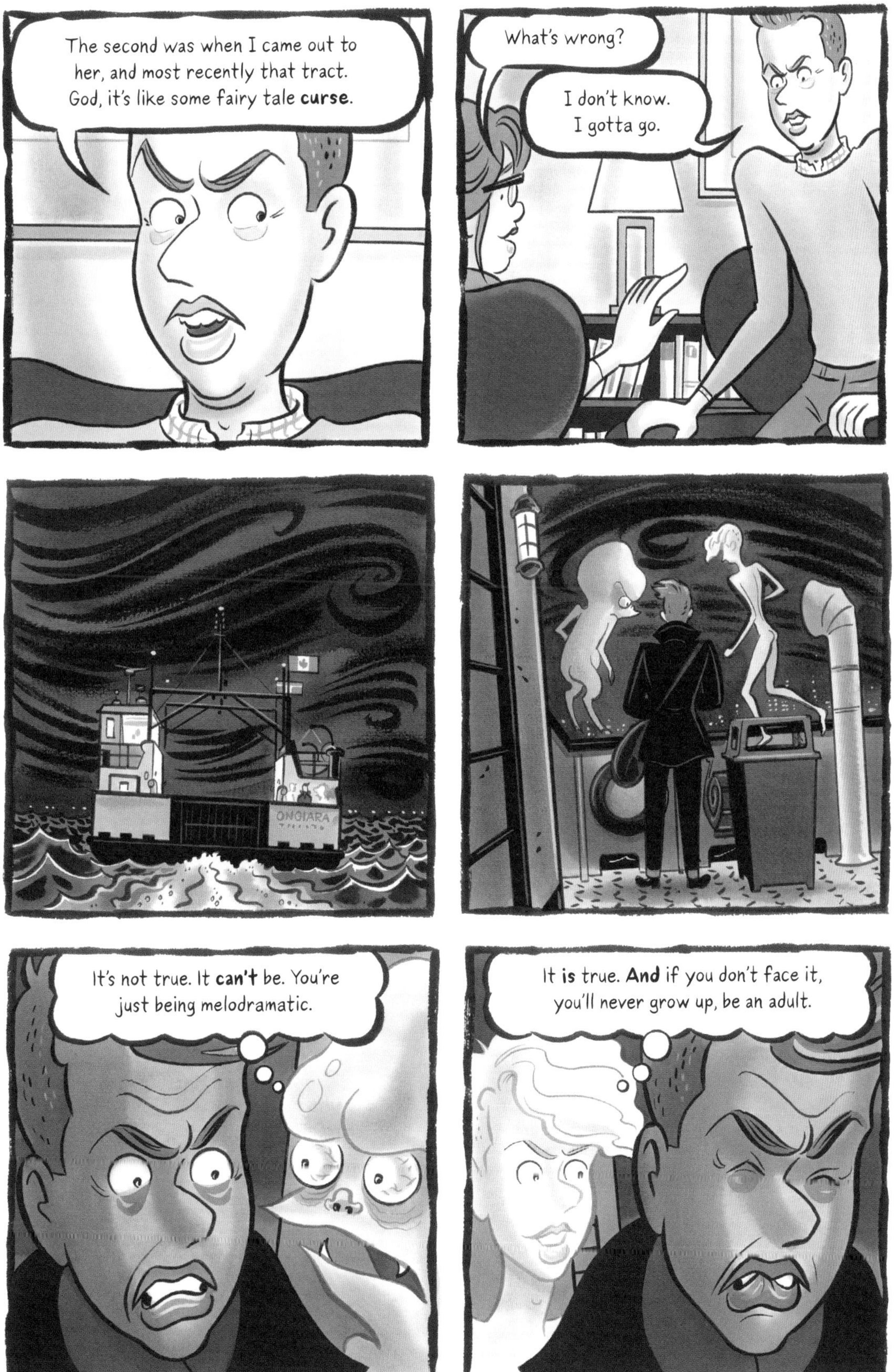
The second was when I came out to her, and most recently that tract. God, it's like some fairy tale **curse**.
What's wrong?
I don't know. I gotta go.
ONGIARA
It's not true. It **can't** be. You're just being melodramatic.
It **is** true. **And** if you don't face it, you'll never grow up, be an adult.

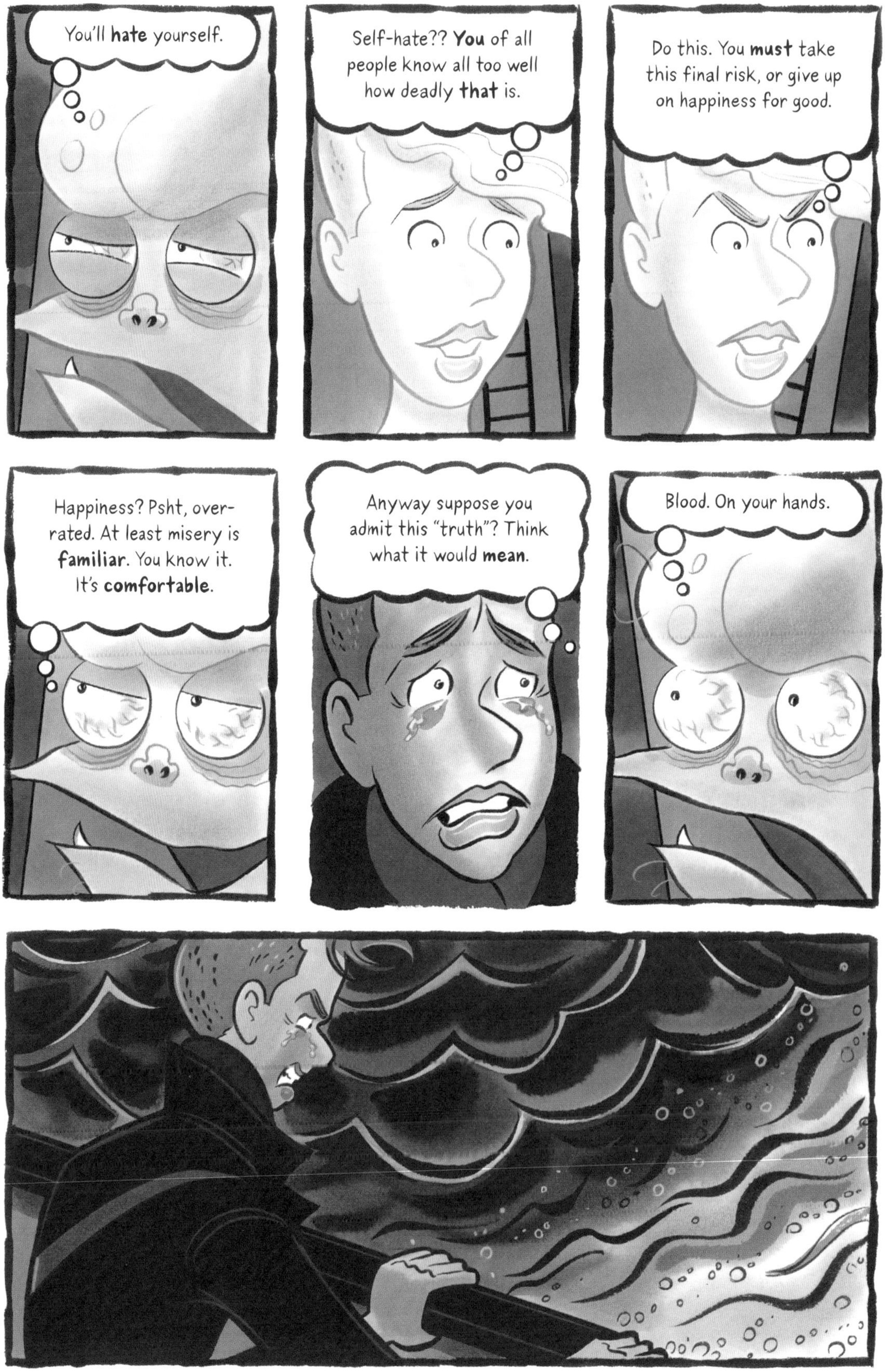
You'll **hate** yourself.
Self-hate?? **You** of all people know all too well how deadly **that** is.
Do this. You **must** take this final risk, or give up on happiness for good.
Happiness? Psht, over-rated. At least misery is **familiar**. You know it. It's **comfortable**.
Anyway suppose you admit this "truth"? Think what it would **mean**.
Blood. On your hands.

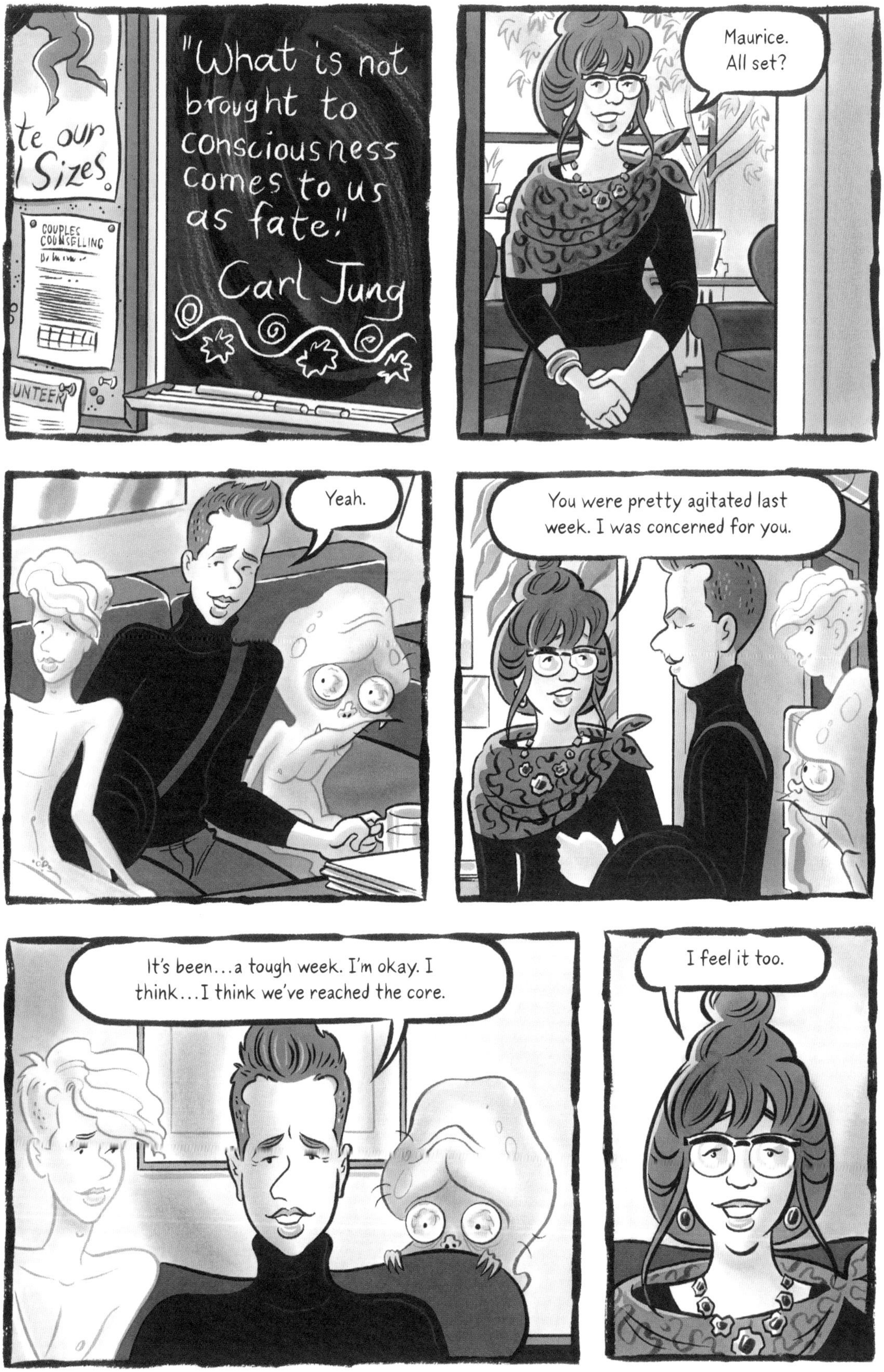
te our
l Sizes.
COUPLES COUNSELLING
UNTEER
"What is not brought to consciousness comes to us as fate!"
Carl Jung
Maurice. All set?
Yeah.
You were pretty agitated last week. I was concerned for you.
It's been...a tough week. I'm okay. I think...I think we've reached the core.
I feel it too.

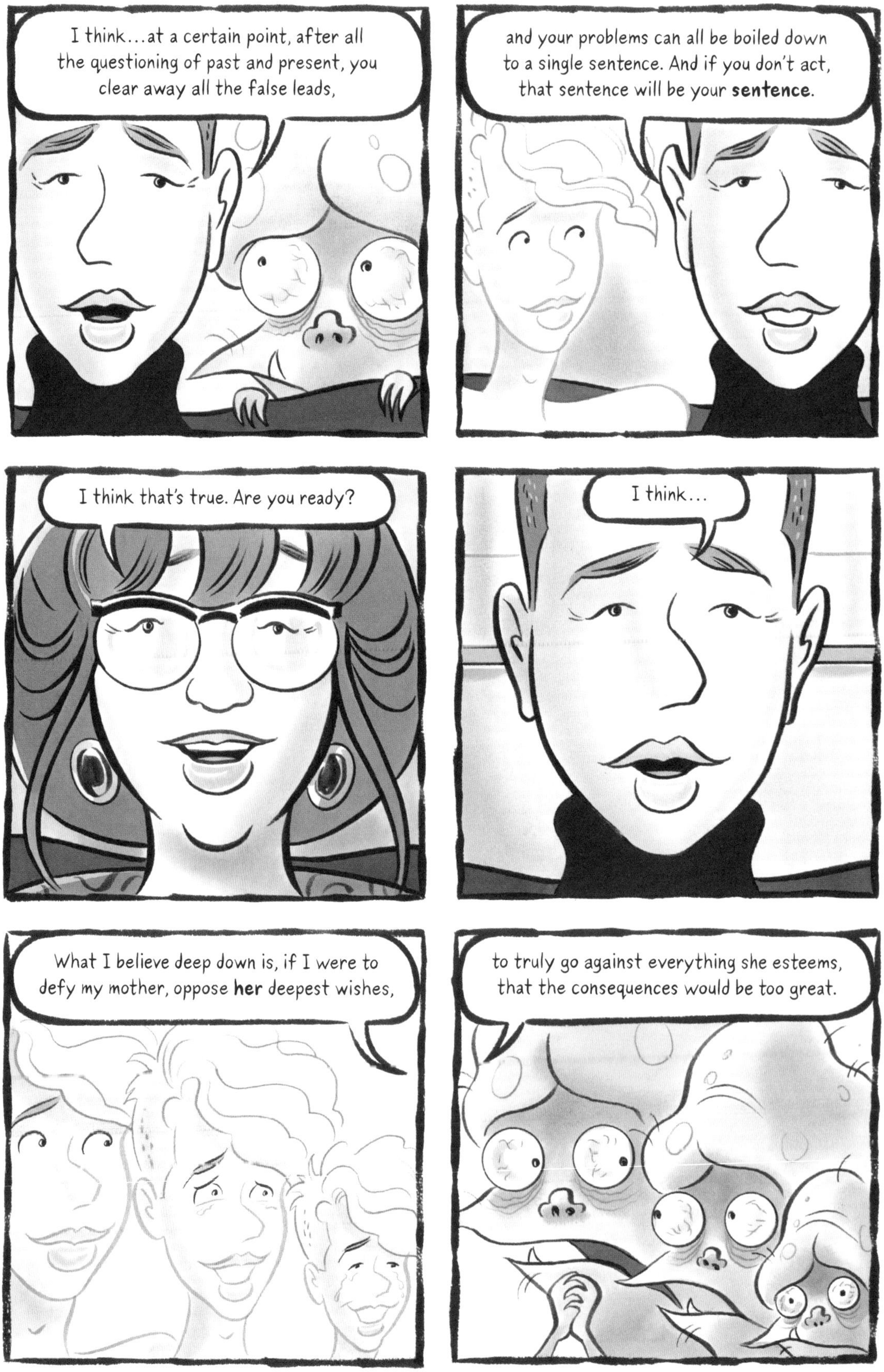
I think...at a certain point, after all the questioning of past and present, you clear away all the false leads,
and your problems can all be boiled down to a single sentence. And if you don't act, that sentence will be your **sentence**.
I think that's true. Are you ready?
I think...
What I believe deep down is, if I were to defy my mother, oppose **her** deepest wishes,
to truly go against everything she esteems, that the consequences would be too great.

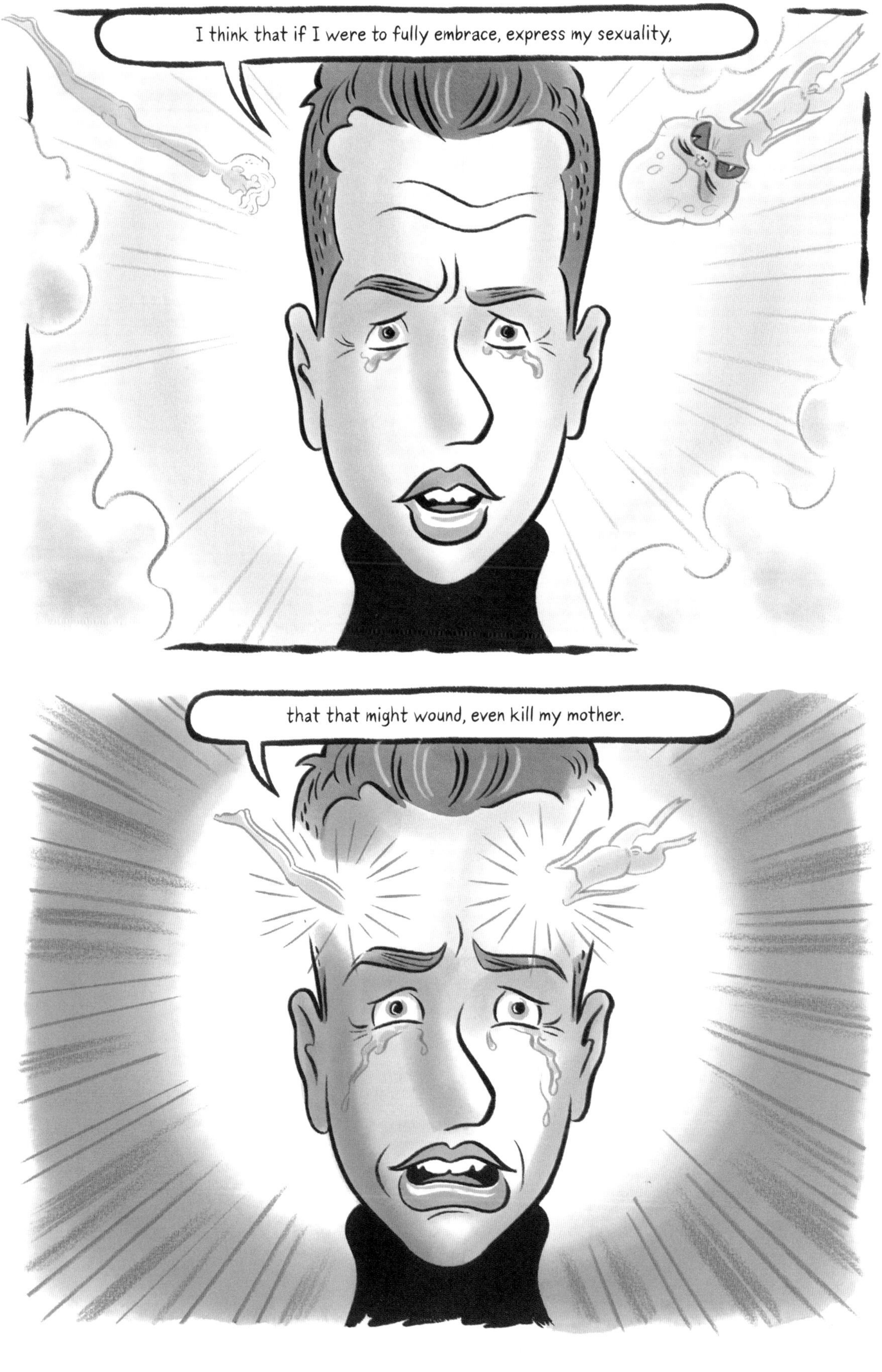
I think that if I were to fully embrace, express my sexuality,
that that might wound, even kill my mother.

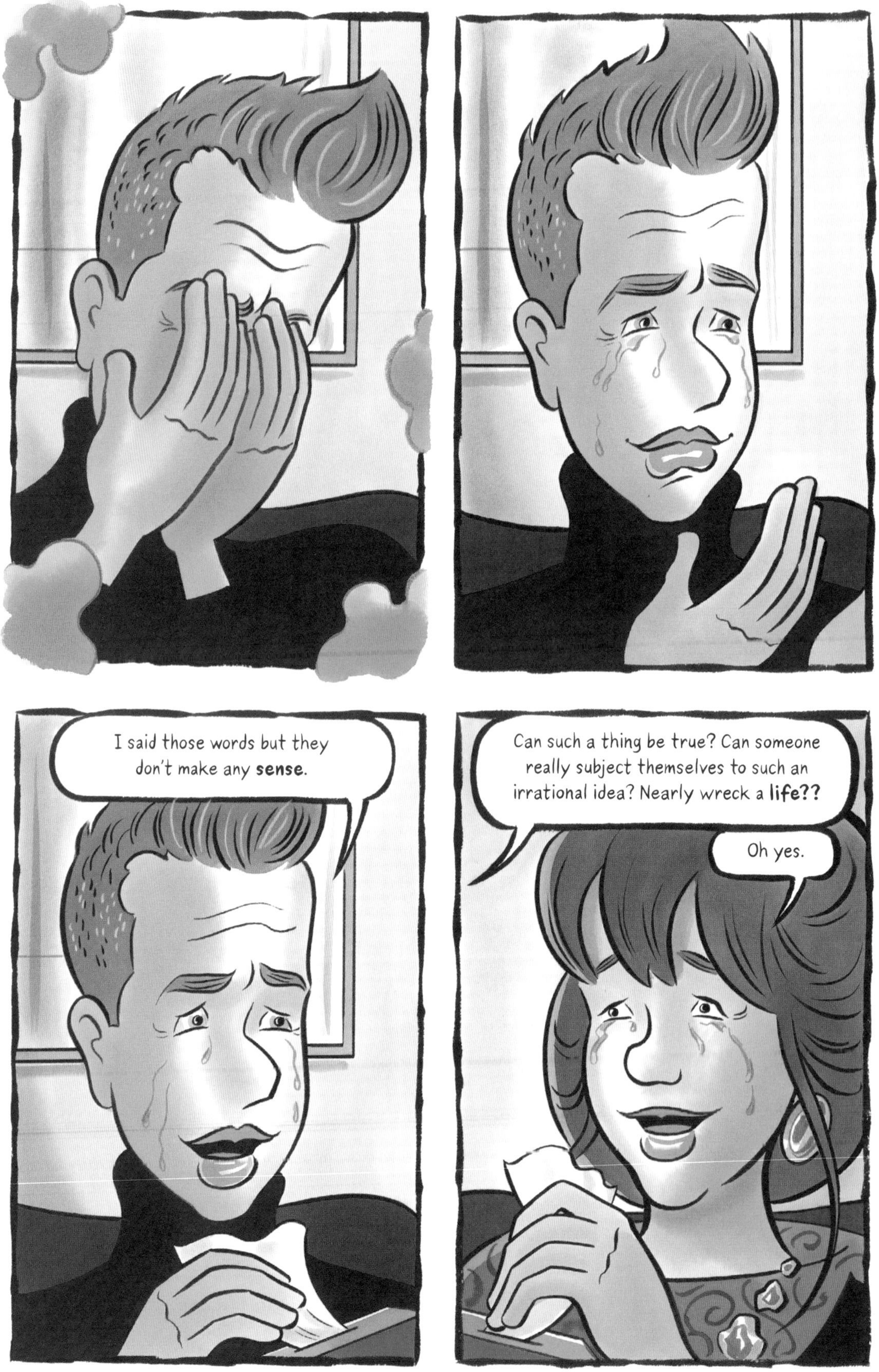
I said those words but they don't make any **sense**.
Can such a thing be true? Can someone really subject themselves to such an irrational idea? Nearly wreck a **life??**
Oh yes.

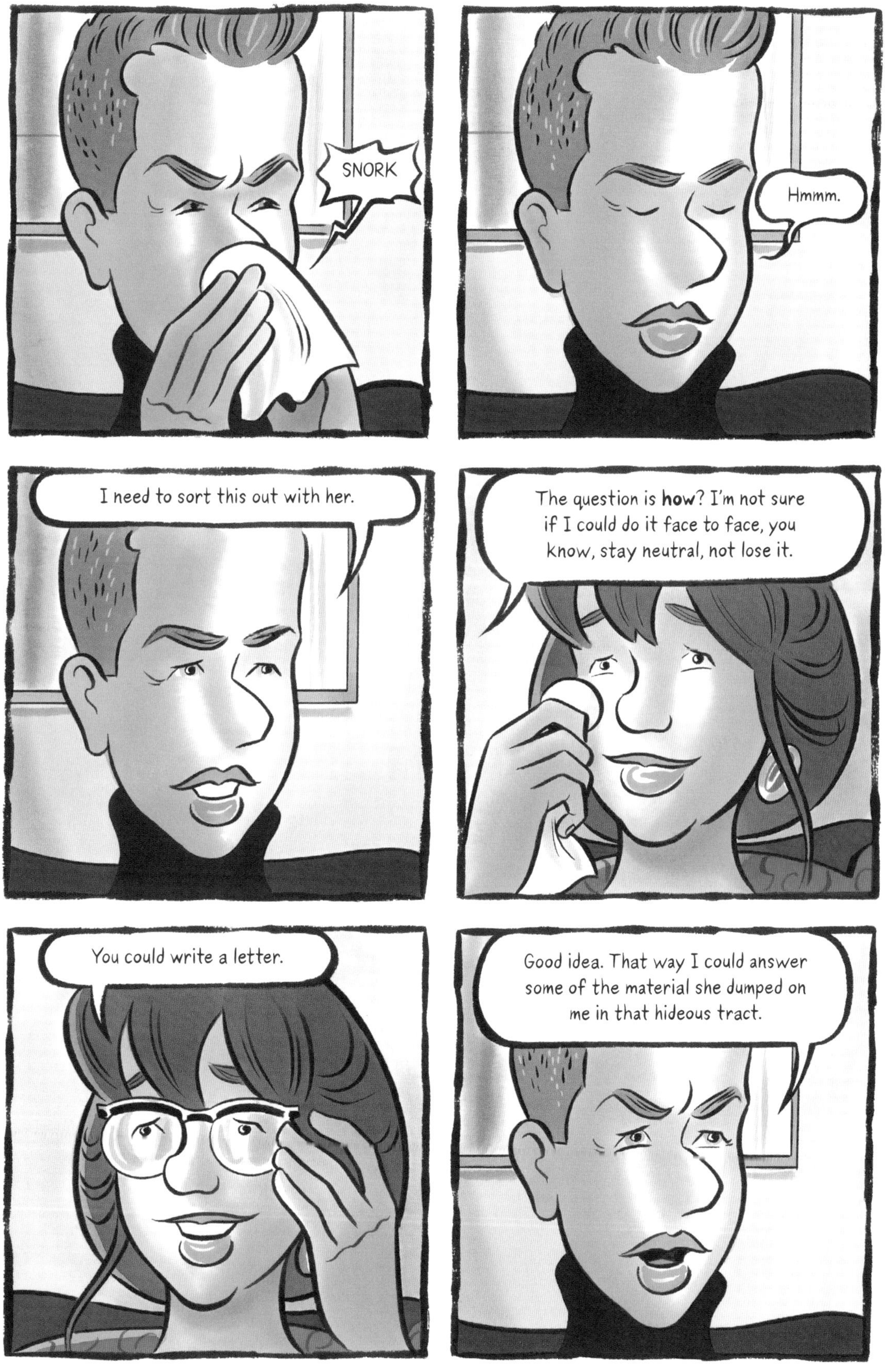
SNORK
Hmmm.
I need to sort this out with her.
The question is **how**? I'm not sure if I could do it face to face, you know, stay neutral, not lose it.
You could write a letter.
Good idea. That way I could answer some of the material she dumped on me in that hideous tract.

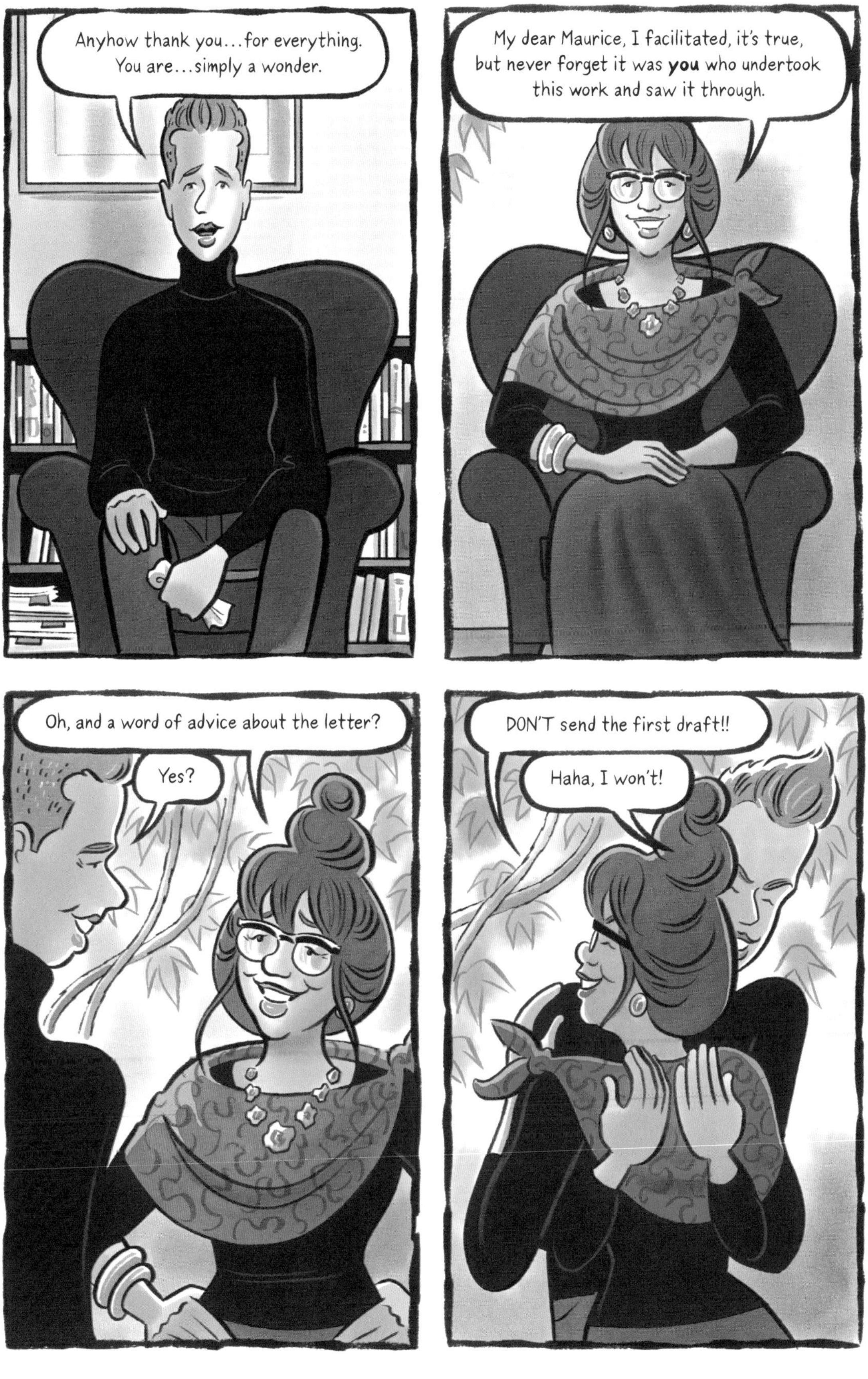
Anyhow thank you...for everything. You are...simply a wonder.
My dear Maurice, I facilitated, it's true, but never forget it was **you** who undertook this work and saw it through.
Oh, and a word of advice about the letter?
Yes?
DON'T send the first draft!!
Haha, I won't!

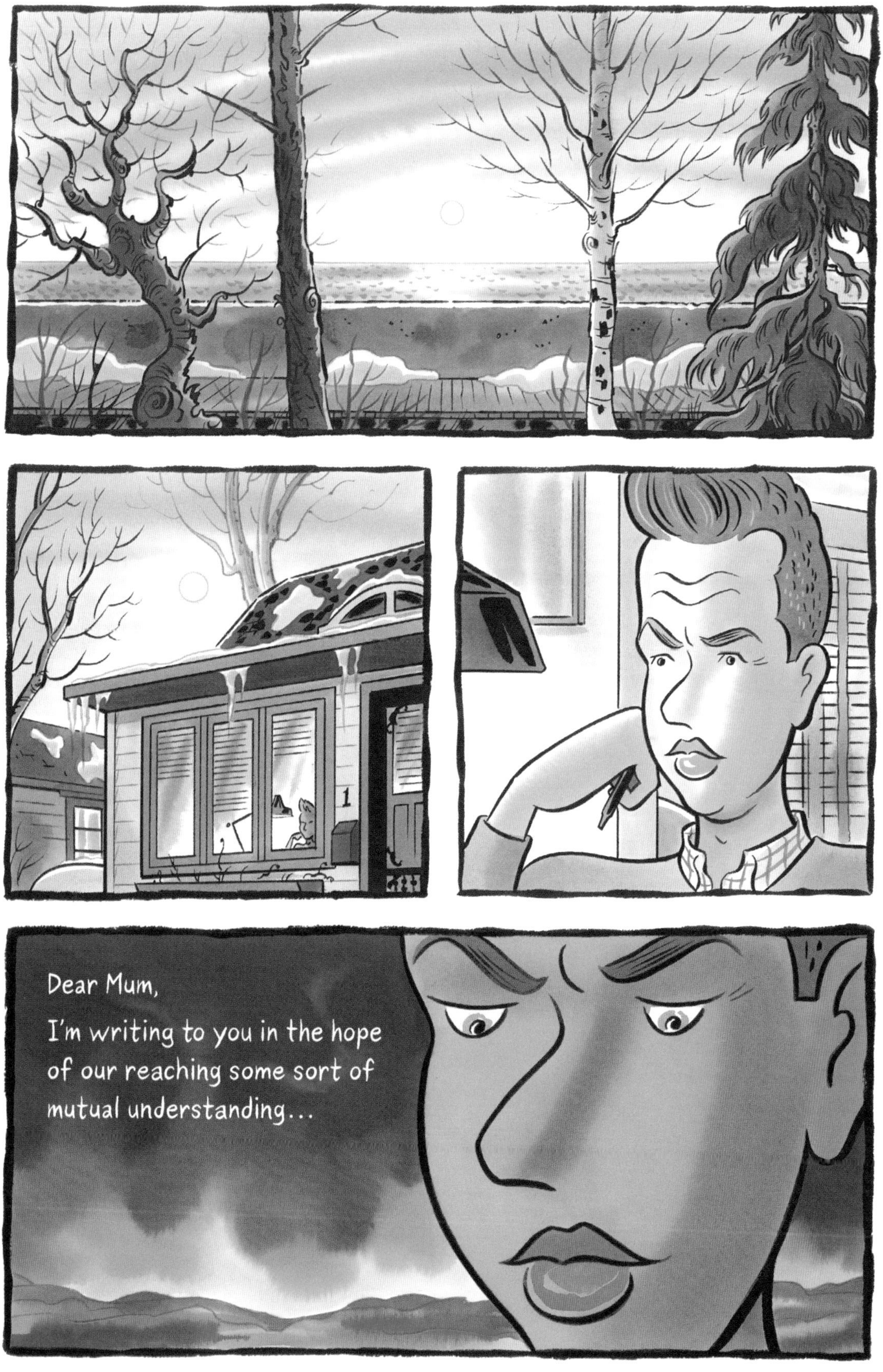
Dear Mum,
I'm writing to you in the hope of our reaching some sort of mutual understanding...

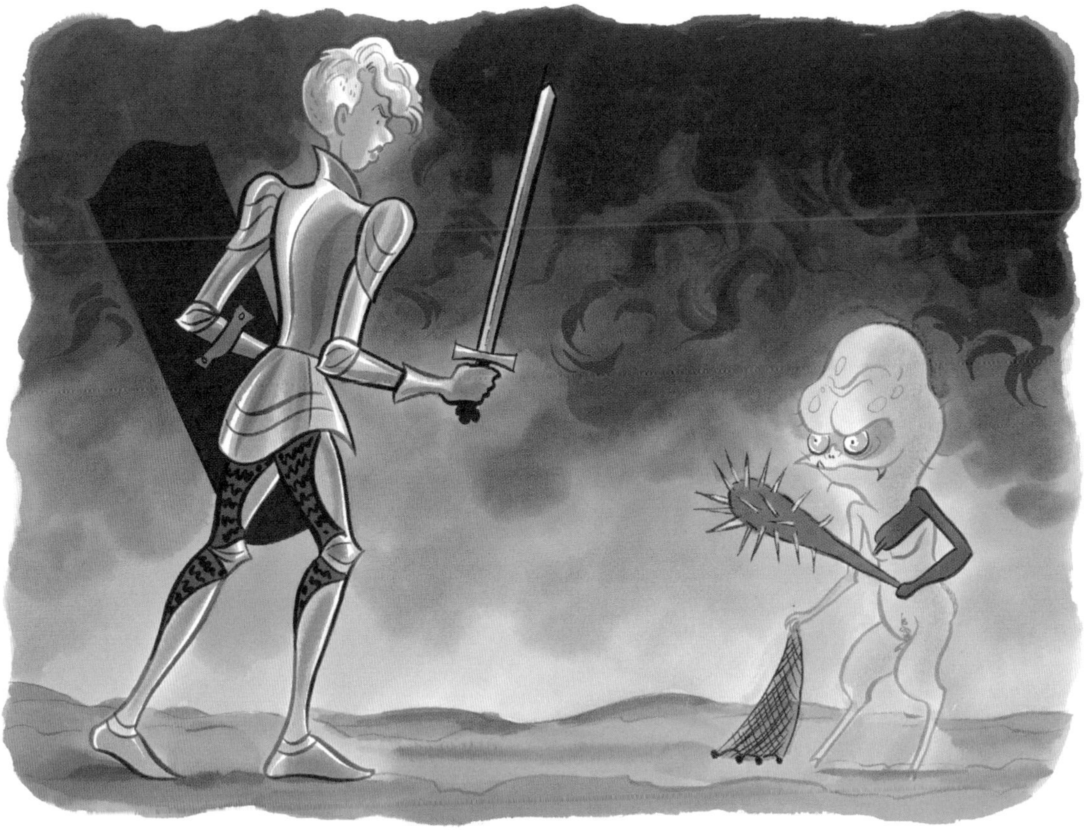

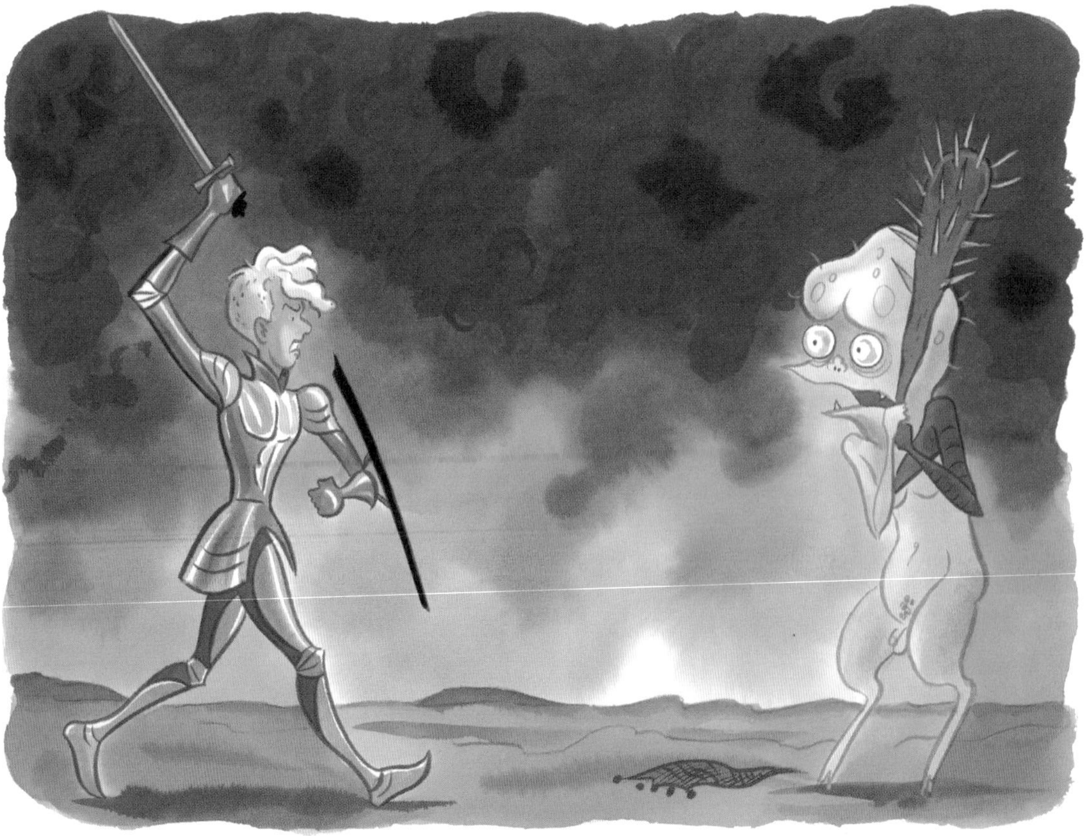

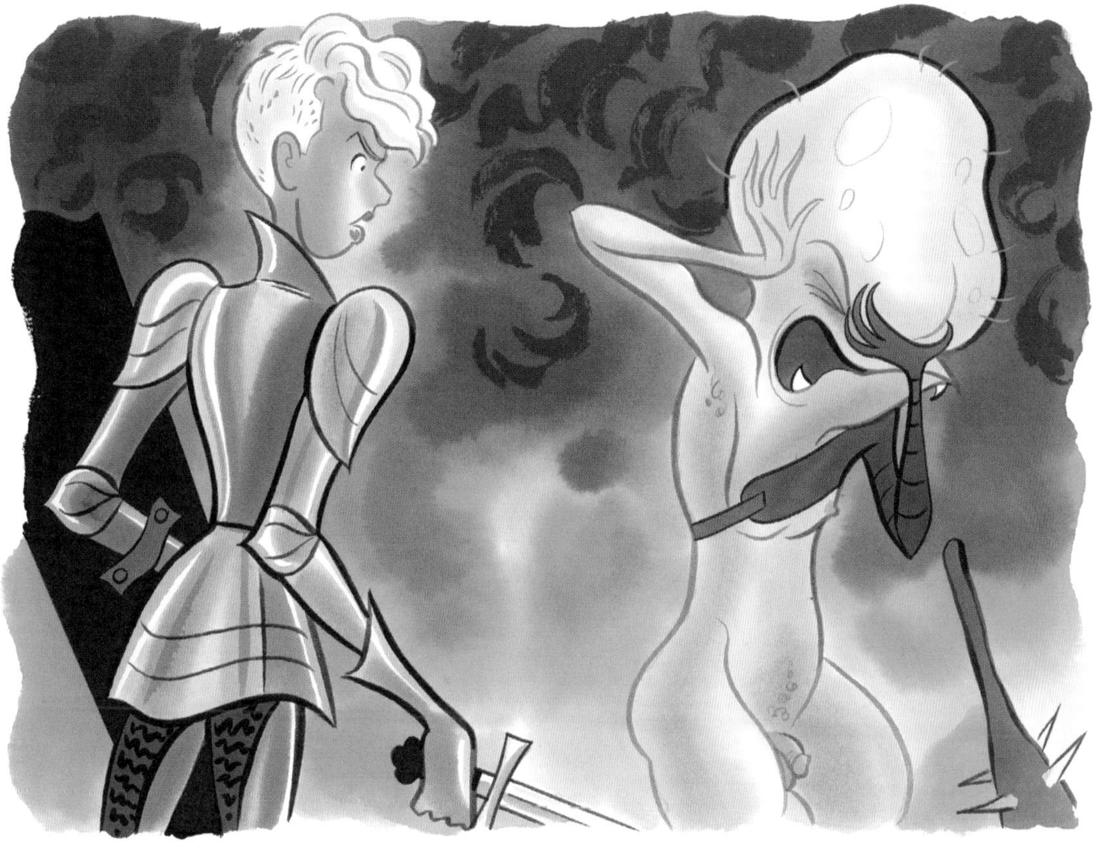

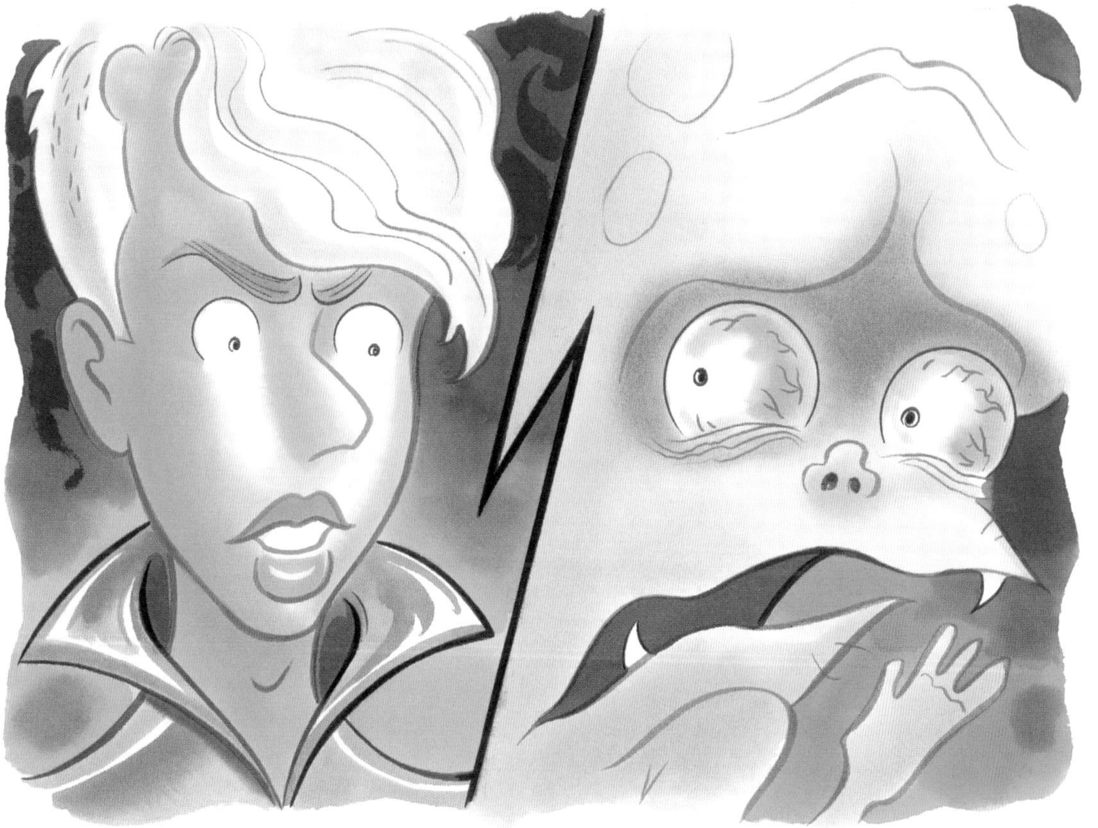

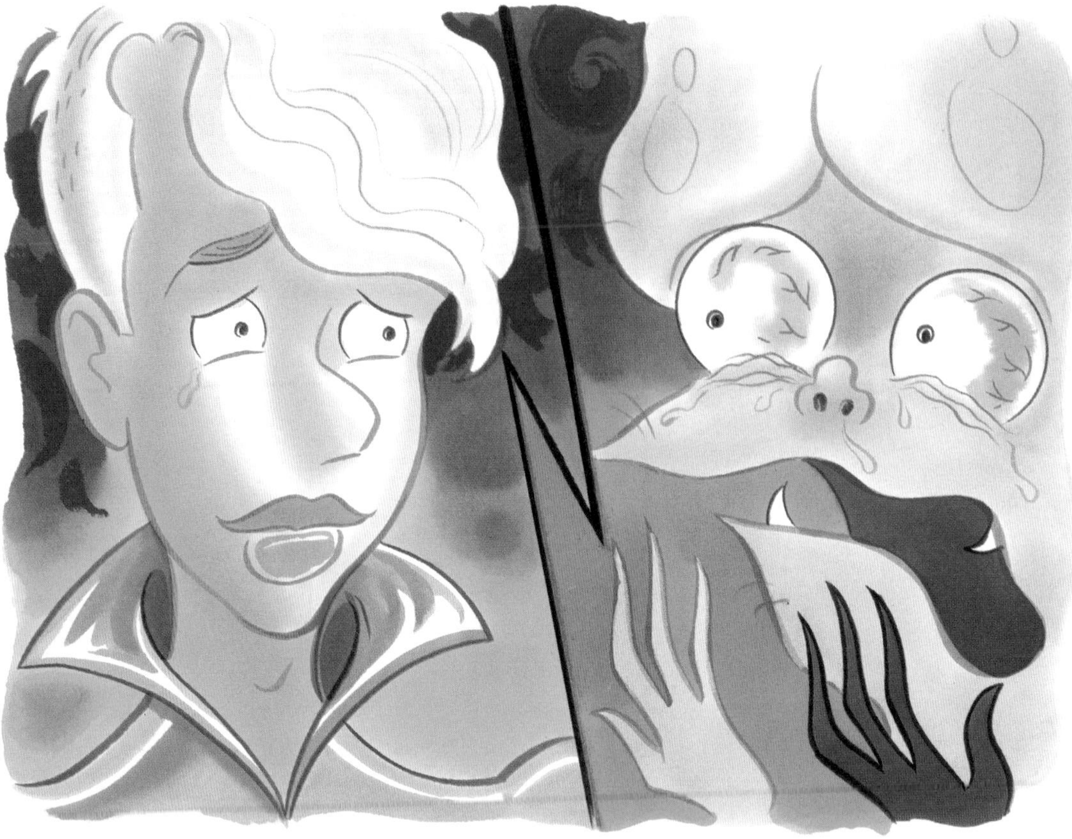

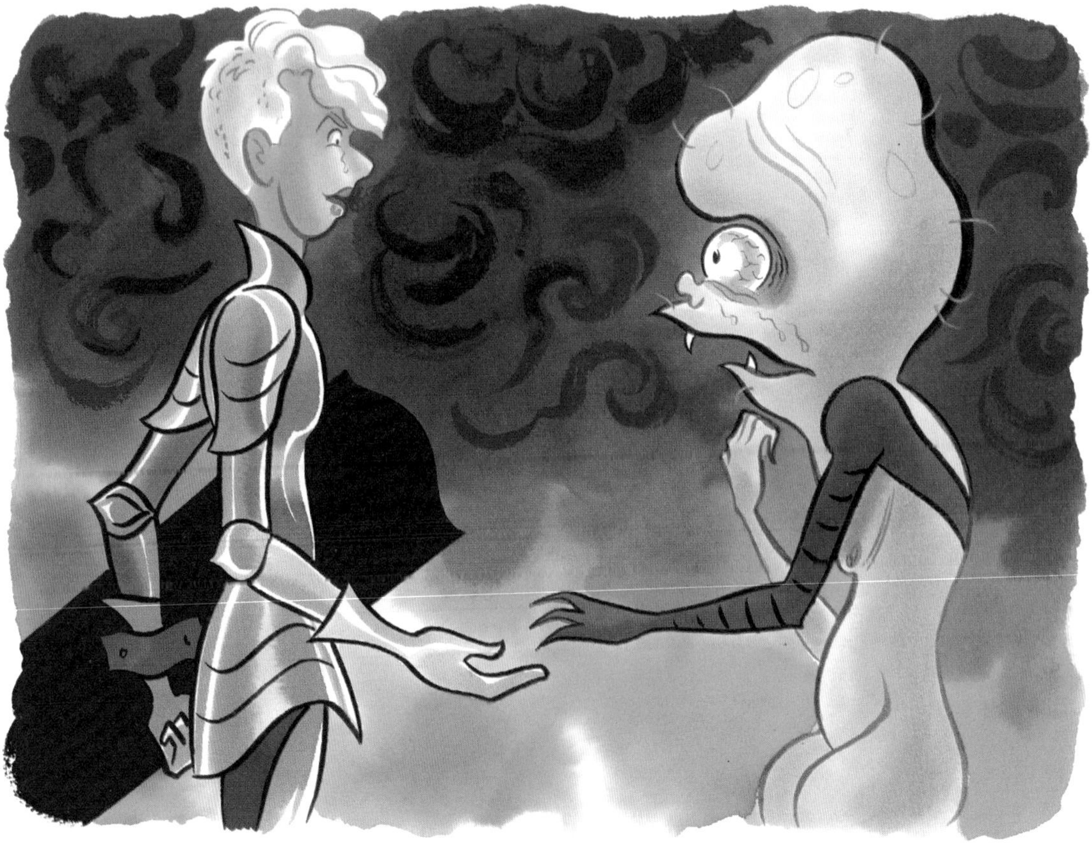

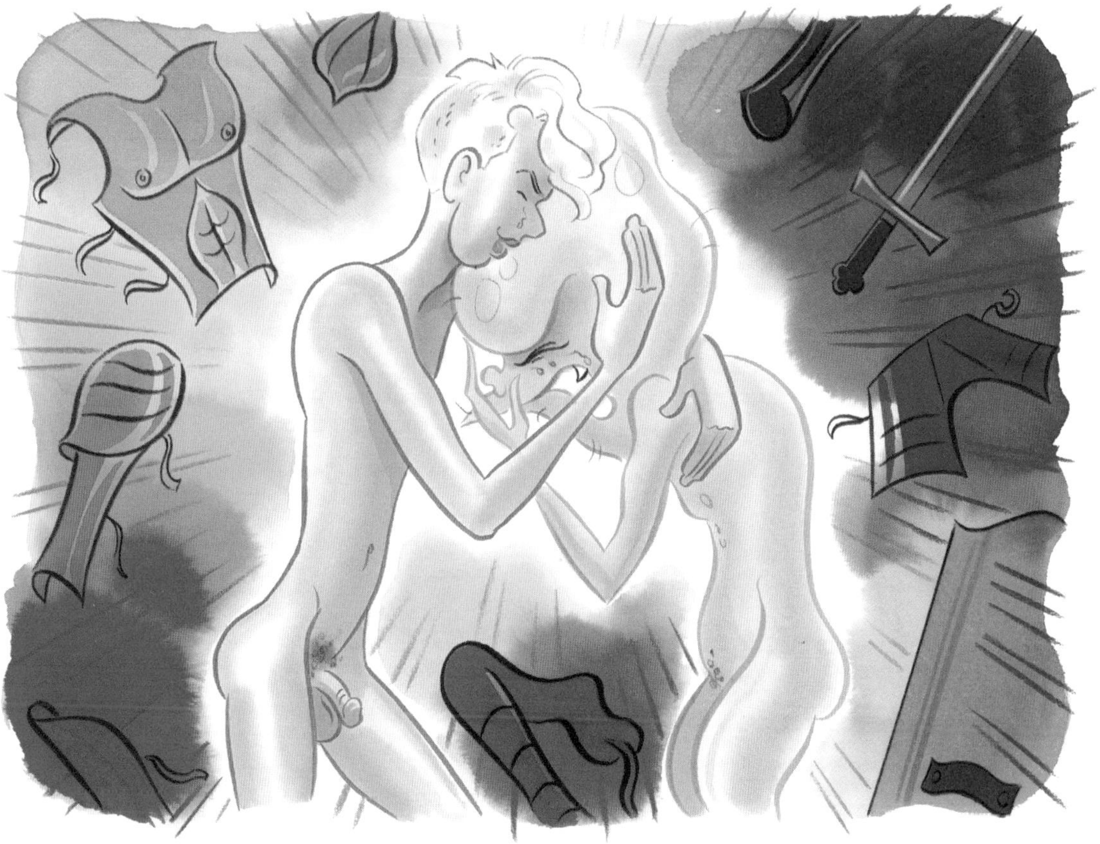

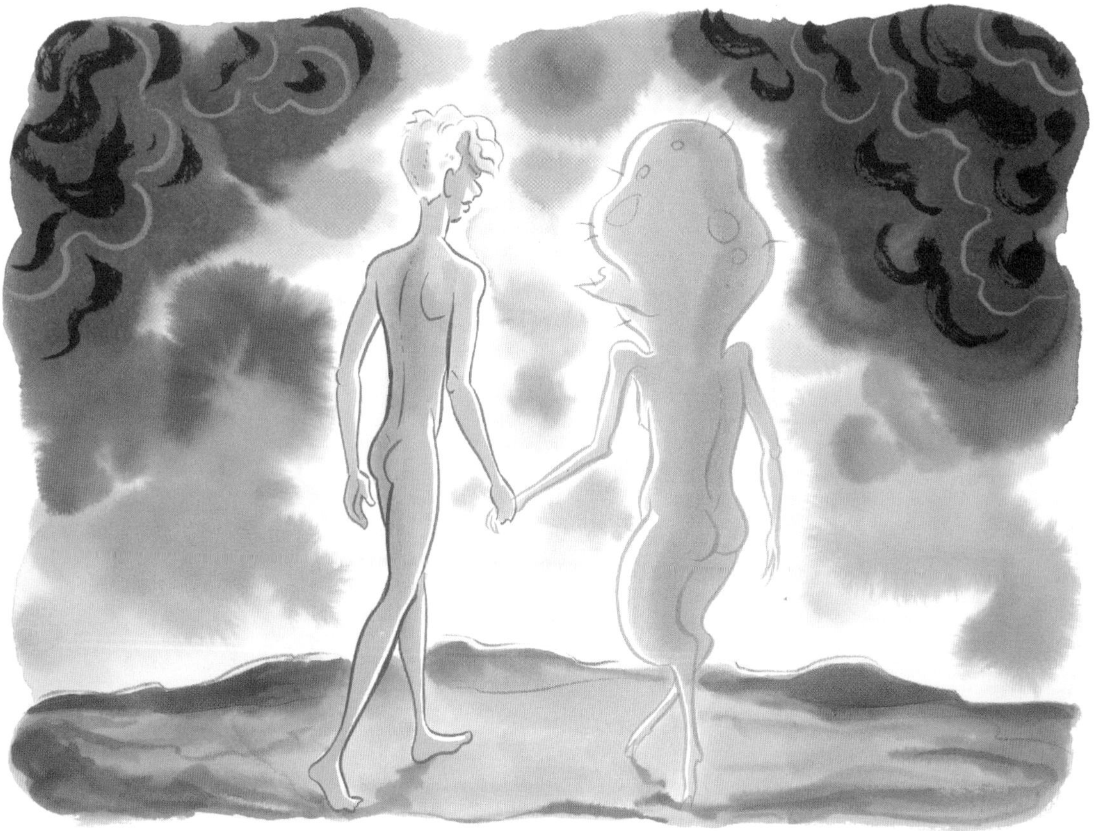

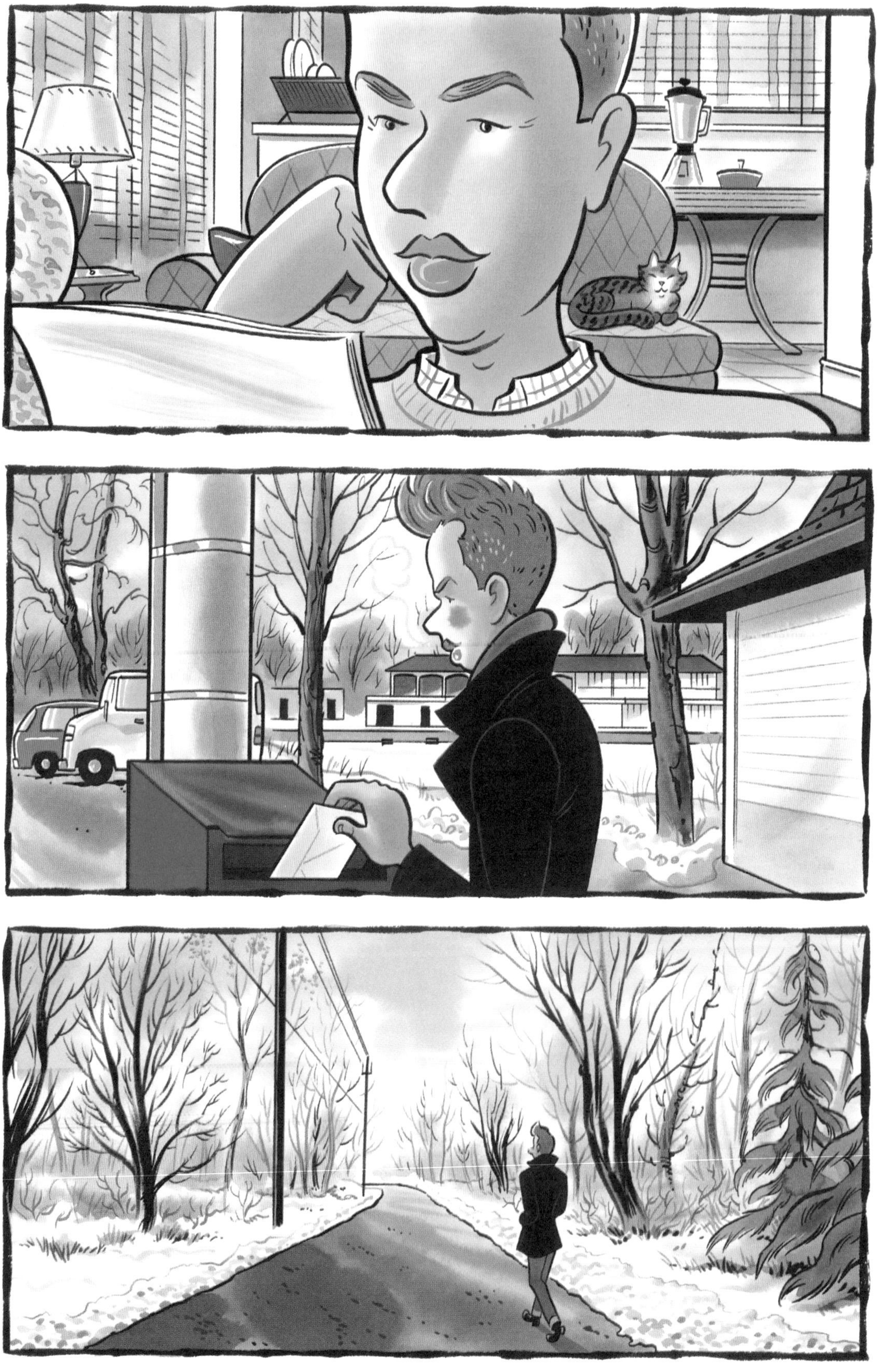

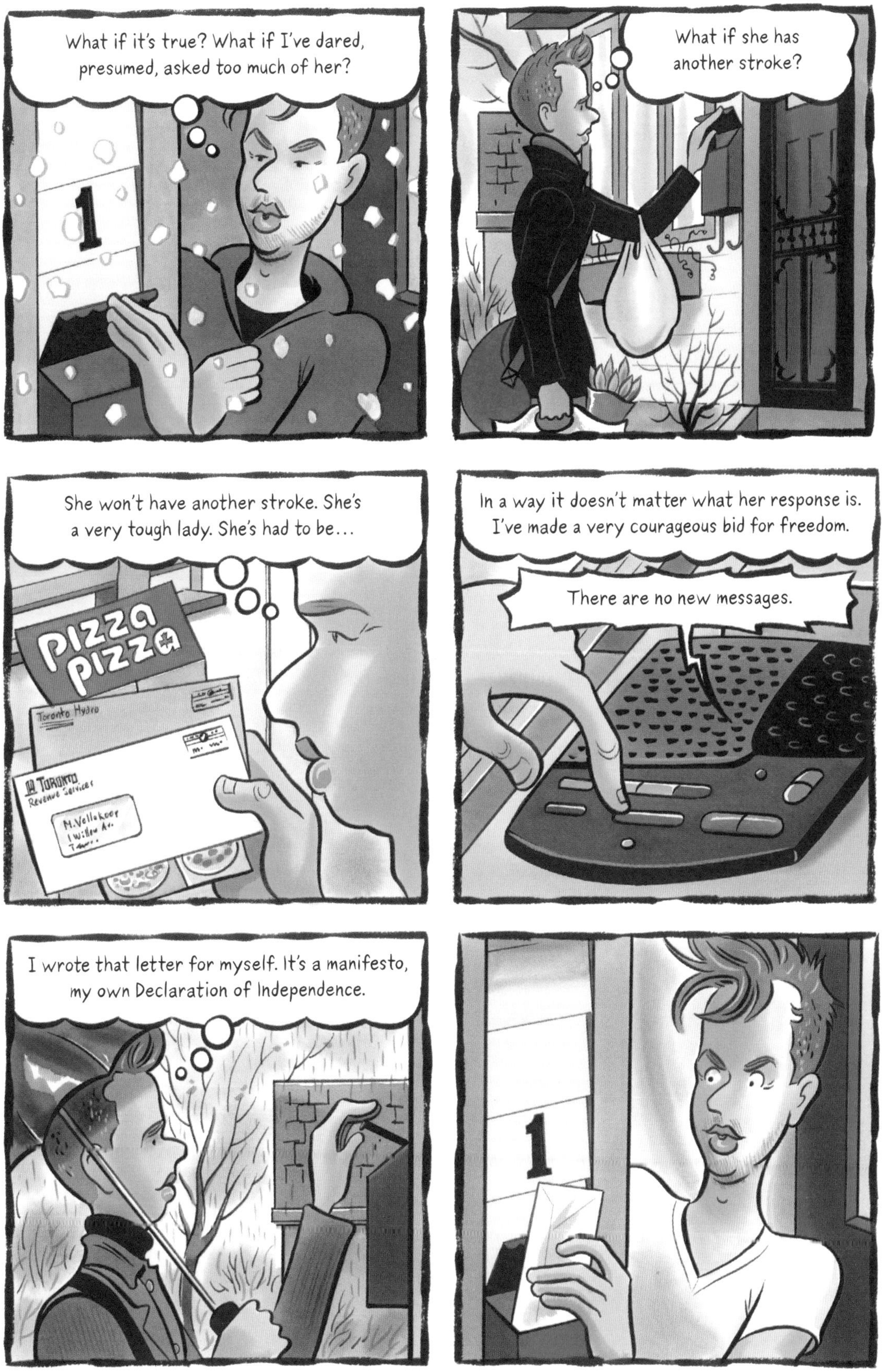
What if it's true? What if I've dared, presumed, asked too much of her?
1
What if she has another stroke?
She won't have another stroke. She's a very tough lady. She's had to be...
pizza pizza
Toronto Hydro
In a way it doesn't matter what her response is. I've made a very courageous bid for freedom.
There are no new messages.
I wrote that letter for myself. It's a manifesto, my own Declaration of Independence.
1

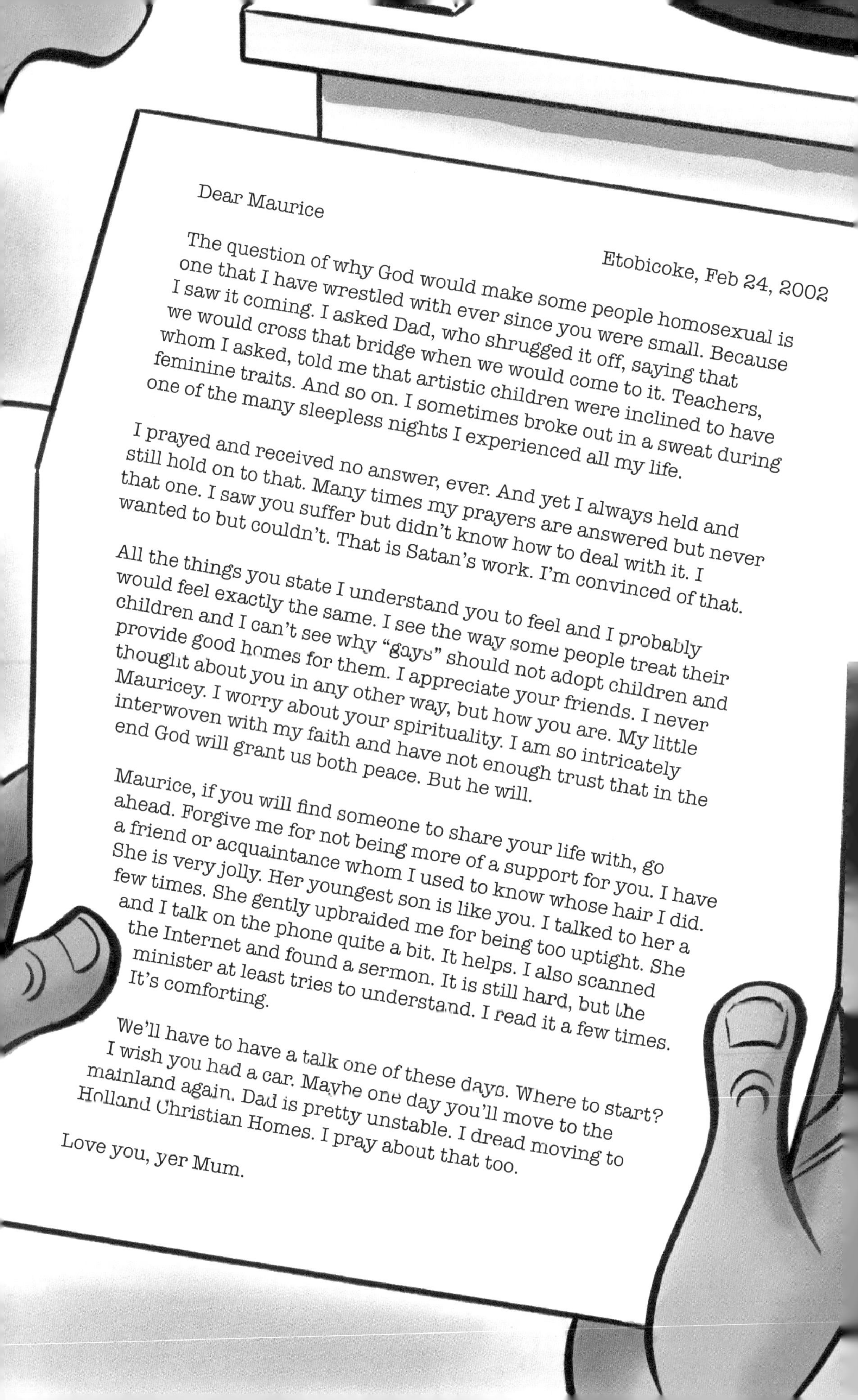

Dear Maurice

Etobicoke, Feb 24, 2002

The question of why God would make some people homosexual is one that I have wrestled with ever since you were small. Because I saw it coming. I asked Dad, who shrugged it off, saying that we would cross that bridge when we would come to it. Teachers, whom I asked, told me that artistic children were inclined to have feminine traits. And so on. I sometimes broke out in a sweat during one of the many sleepless nights I experienced all my life.

I prayed and received no answer, ever. And yet I always held and still hold on to that. Many times my prayers are answered but never that one. I saw you suffer but didn't know how to deal with it. I wanted to but couldn't. That is Satan's work. I'm convinced of that.

All the things you state I understand you to feel and I probably would feel exactly the same. I see the way some people treat their children and I can't see why "gays" should not adopt children and provide good homes for them. I appreciate your friends. I never thought about you in any other way, but how you are. My little Mauricey. I worry about your spirituality. I am so intricately interwoven with my faith and have not enough trust that in the end God will grant us both peace. But he will.

Maurice, if you will find someone to share your life with, go ahead. Forgive me for not being more of a support for you. I have a friend or acquaintance whom I used to know whose hair I did. She is very jolly. Her youngest son is like you. I talked to her a few times. She gently upbraided me for being too uptight. She and I talk on the phone quite a bit. It helps. I also scanned the Internet and found a sermon. It is still hard, but the minister at least tries to understand. I read it a few times. It's comforting.

We'll have to have a talk one of these days. Where to start? I wish you had a car. Maybe one day you'll move to the mainland again. Dad is pretty unstable. I dread moving to Holland Christian Homes. I pray about that too.

Love you, yer Mum.

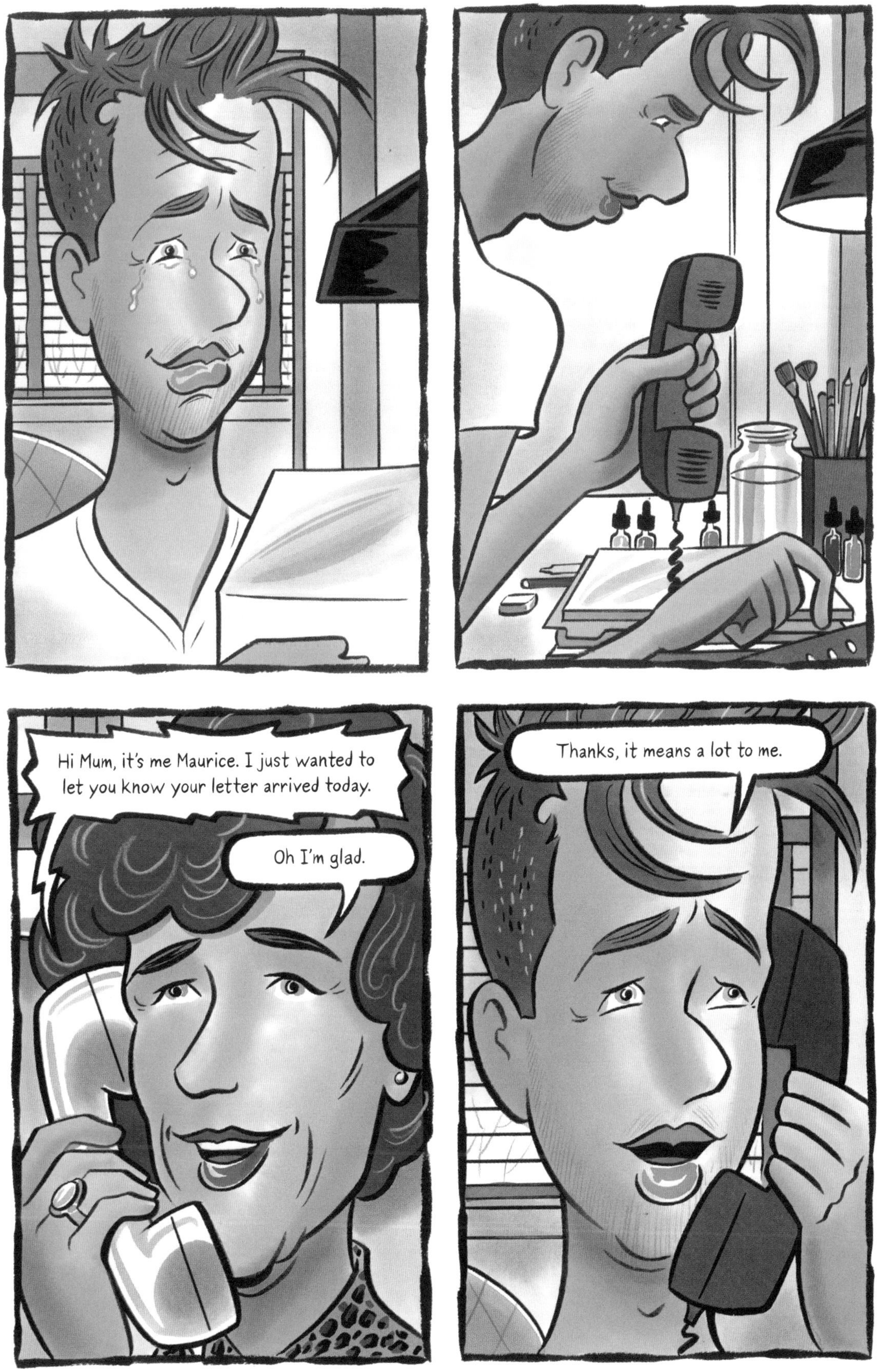
Hi Mum, it's me Maurice. I just wanted to let you know your letter arrived today.
Oh I'm glad.
Thanks, it means a lot to me.

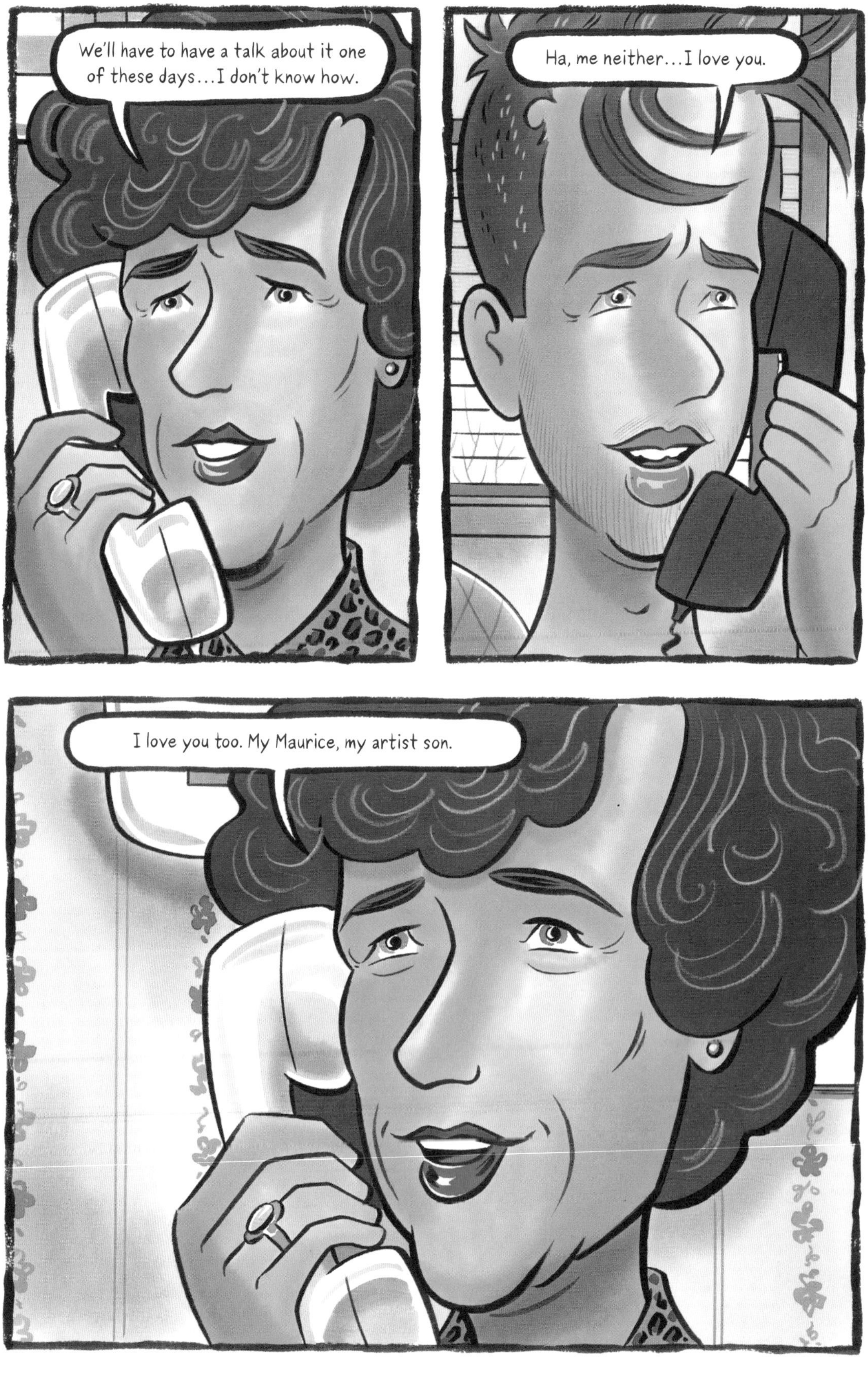
We'll have to have a talk about it one of these days...I don't know how.
Ha, me neither...I love you.
I love you too. My Maurice, my artist son.

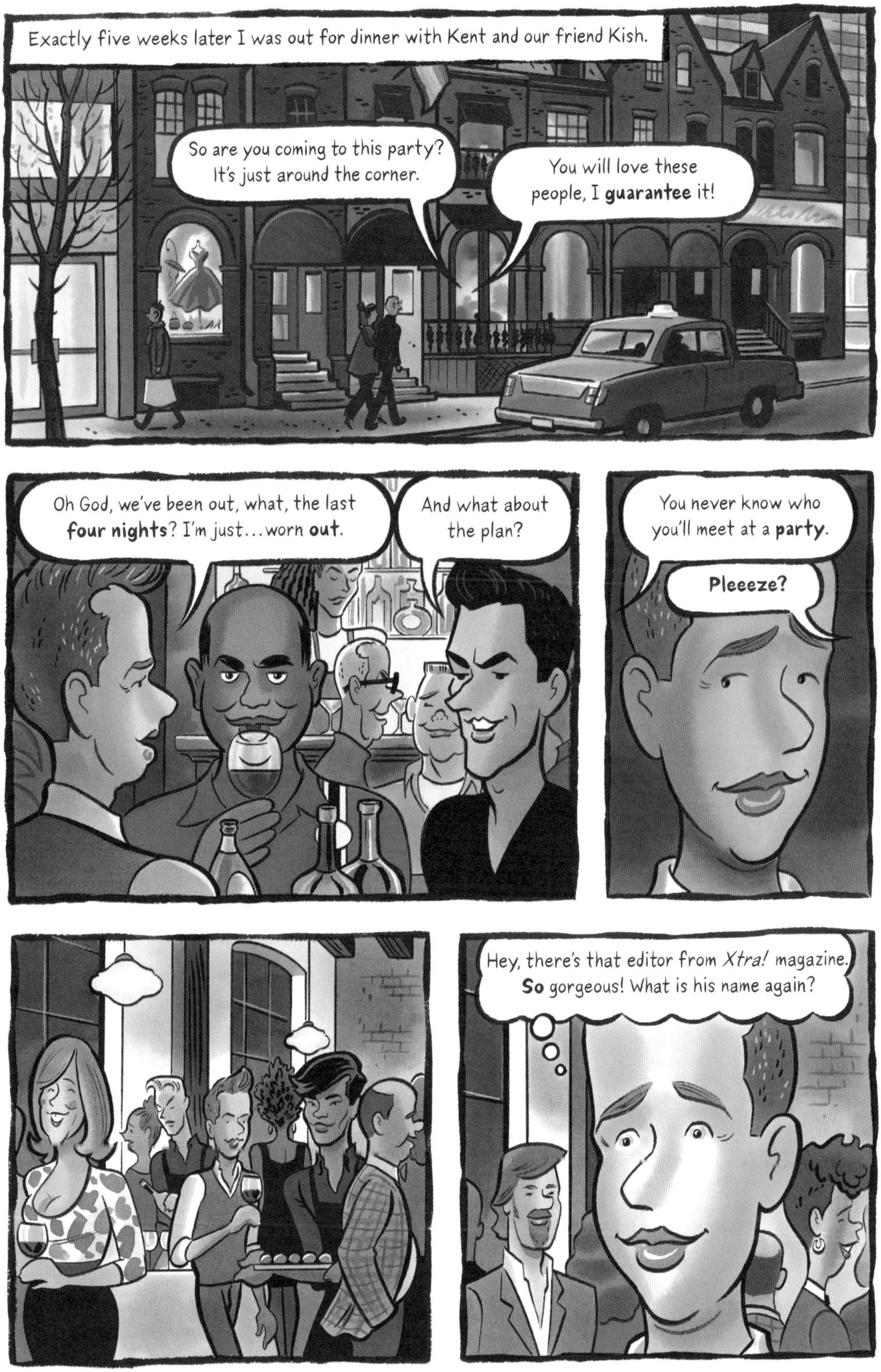
Exactly five weeks later I was out for dinner with Kent and our friend Kish.
So are you coming to this party? It's just around the corner.
You will love these people, I **guarantee** it!
Oh God, we've been out, what, the last **four nights**? I'm just... worn **out**.
And what about the plan?
You never know who you'll meet at a **party**.
Pleeeze?
Hey, there's that editor from *Xtra!* magazine. **So** gorgeous! What is his name again?

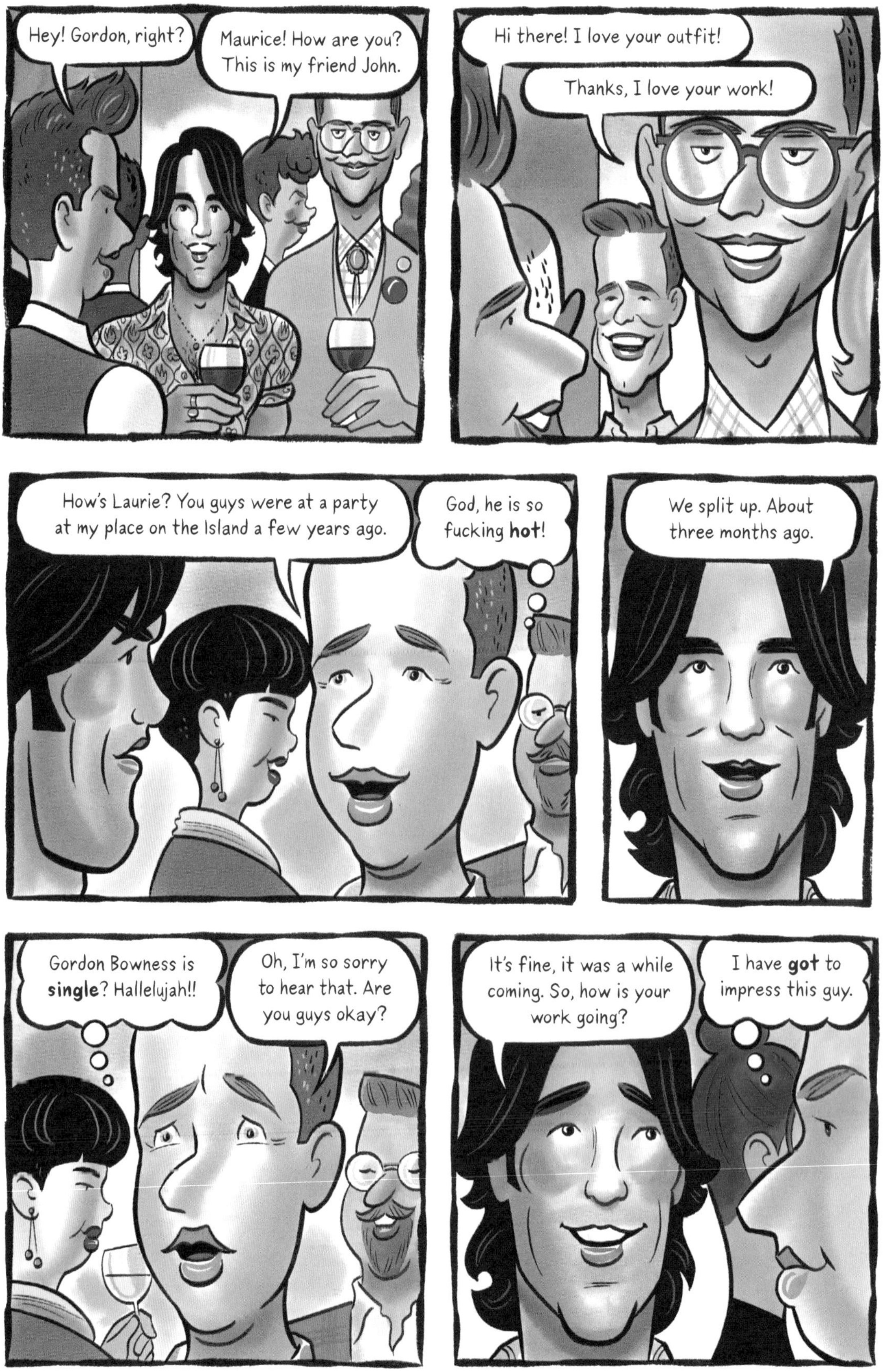
Hey! Gordon, right?
Maurice! How are you? This is my friend John.
Hi there! I love your outfit!
Thanks, I love your work!
How's Laurie? You guys were at a party at my place on the Island a few years ago.
God, he is so fucking **hot**!
We split up. About three months ago.
Gordon Bowness is **single**? Hallelujah!!
Oh, I'm so sorry to hear that. Are you guys okay?
It's fine, it was a while coming. So, how is your work going?
I have **got** to impress this guy.

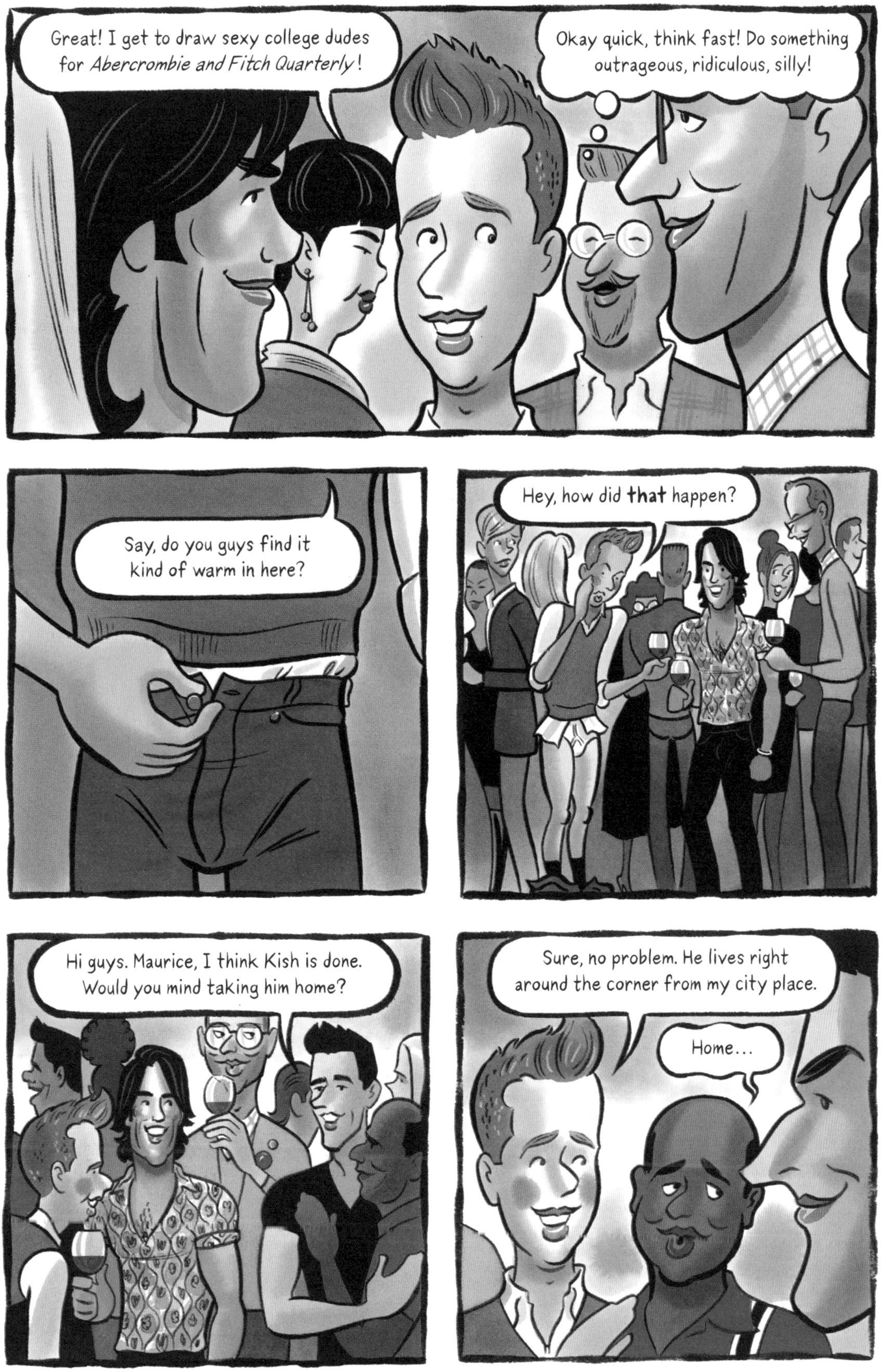

Great! I get to draw sexy college dudes for *Abercrombie and Fitch Quarterly*!
Okay quick, think fast! Do something outrageous, ridiculous, silly!
Say, do you guys find it kind of warm in here?
Hey, how did **that** happen?
Hi guys. Maurice, I think Kish is done. Would you mind taking him home?
Sure, no problem. He lives right around the corner from my city place.
Home...

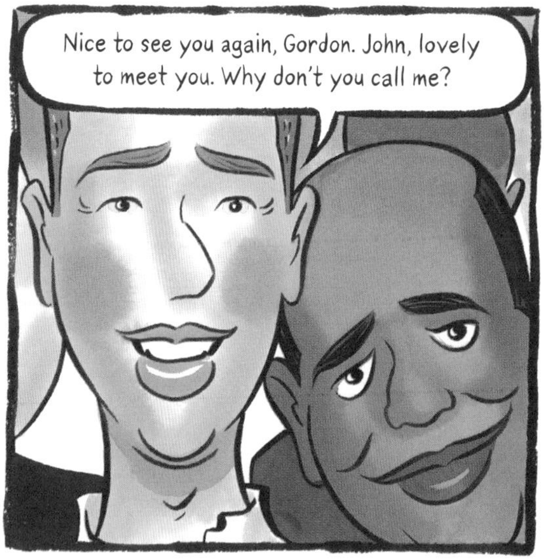
Nice to see you again, Gordon. John, lovely to meet you. Why don't you call me?

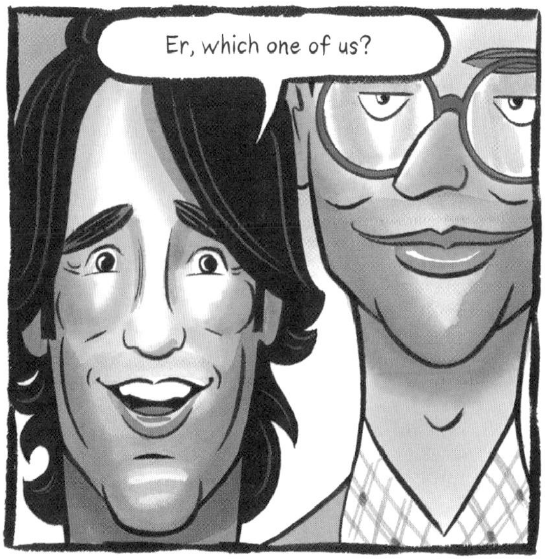
Er, which one of us?

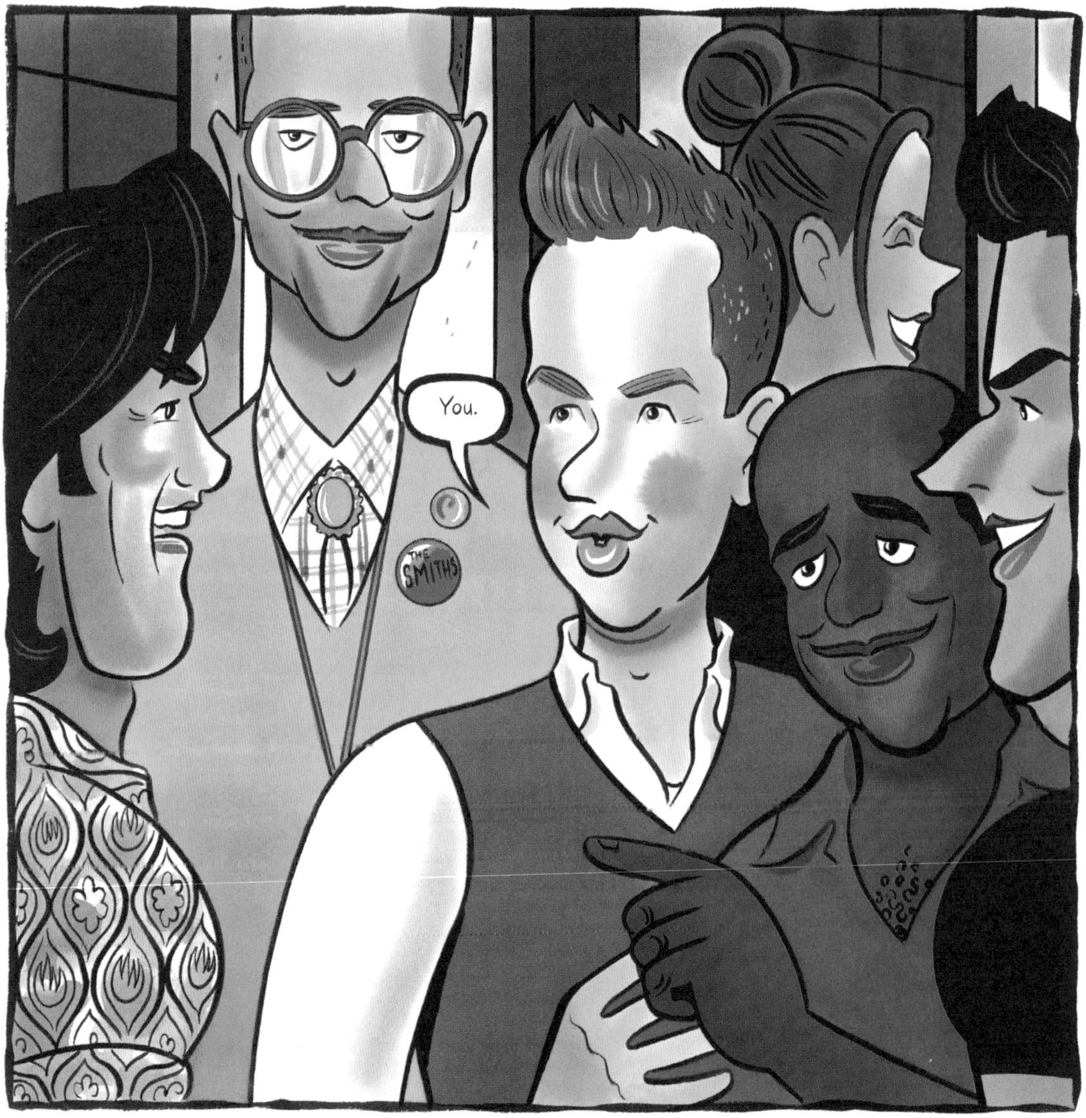
You.
THE SMITHS

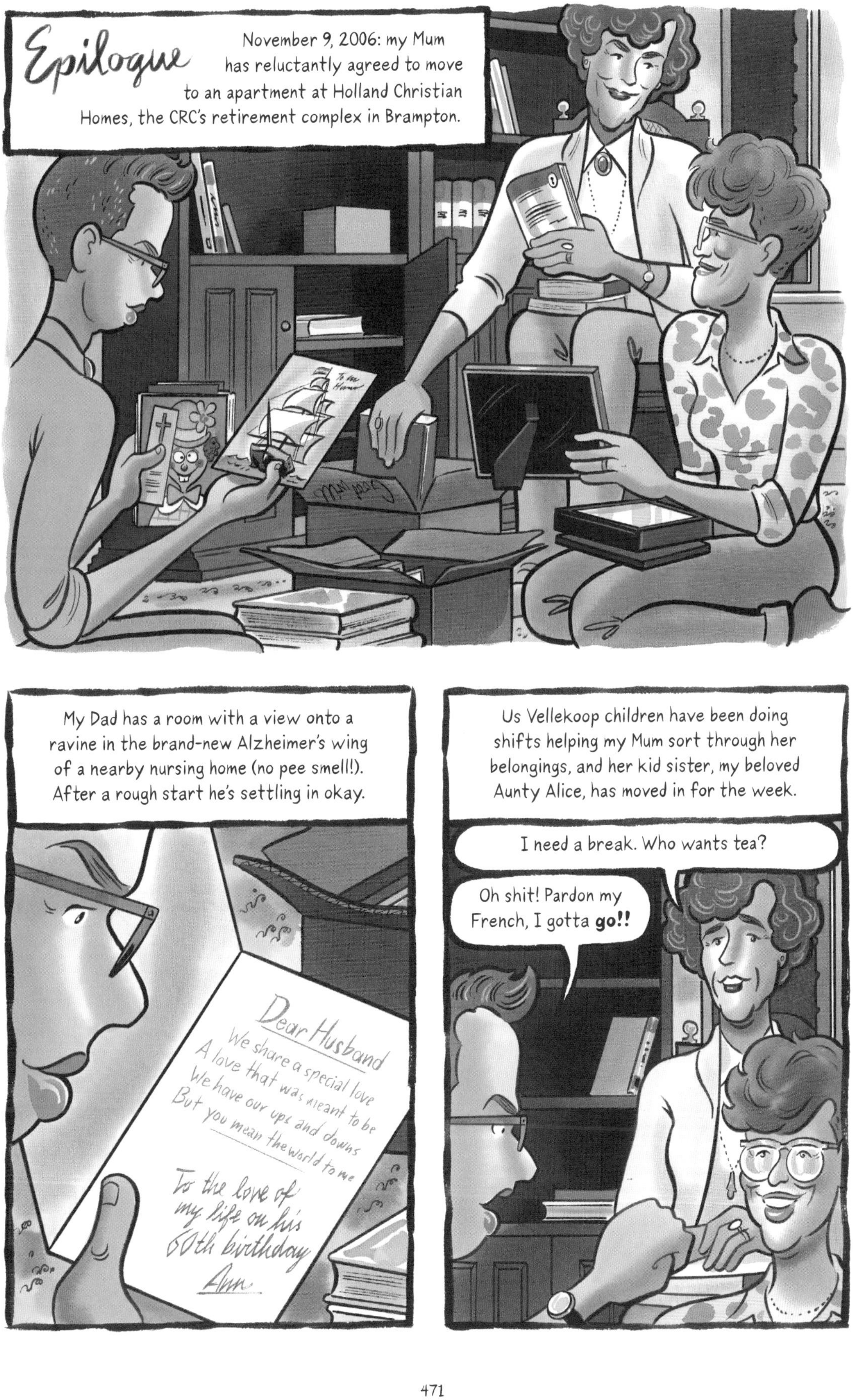
Epilogue
November 9, 2006: my Mum has reluctantly agreed to move to an apartment at Holland Christian Homes, the CRC's retirement complex in Brampton.
My Dad has a room with a view onto a ravine in the brand-new Alzheimer's wing of a nearby nursing home (no pee smell!). After a rough start he's settling in okay.
Dear Husband
We share a special love
A love that was meant to be
We have our ups and downs
But you mean the world to me
To the love of my life on his 60th birthday
Ann
Us Vellekoop children have been doing shifts helping my Mum sort through her belongings, and her kid sister, my beloved Aunty Alice, has moved in for the week.
I need a break. Who wants tea?
Oh shit! Pardon my French, I gotta **go!!**

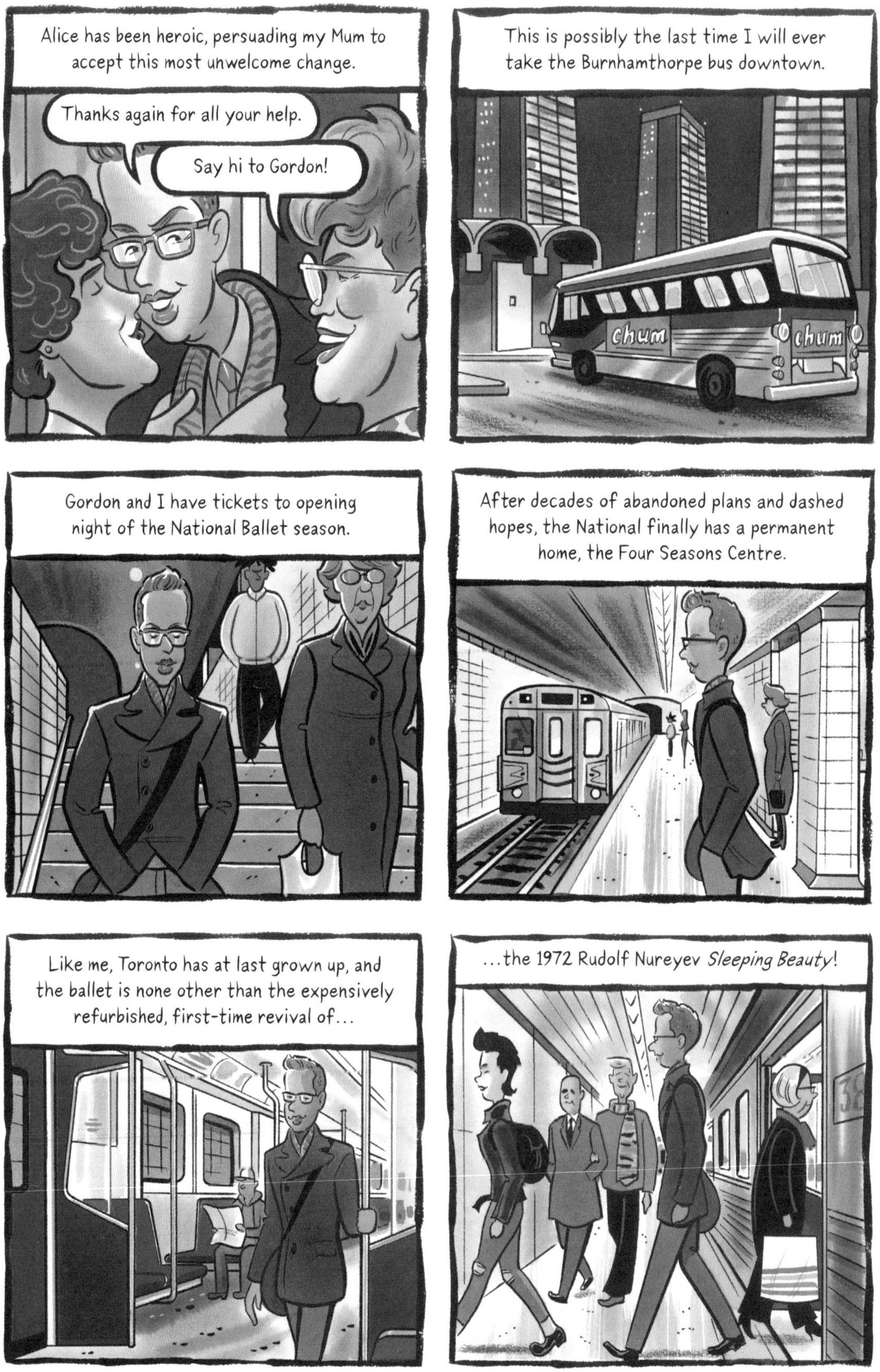
Alice has been heroic, persuading my Mum to accept this most unwelcome change.
Thanks again for all your help.
Say hi to Gordon!
This is possibly the last time I will ever take the Burnhamthorpe bus downtown.
chum
chum
Gordon and I have tickets to opening night of the National Ballet season.
After decades of abandoned plans and dashed hopes, the National finally has a permanent home, the Four Seasons Centre.
Like me, Toronto has at last grown up, and the ballet is none other than the expensively refurbished, first-time revival of...
...the 1972 Rudolf Nureyev *Sleeping Beauty*!

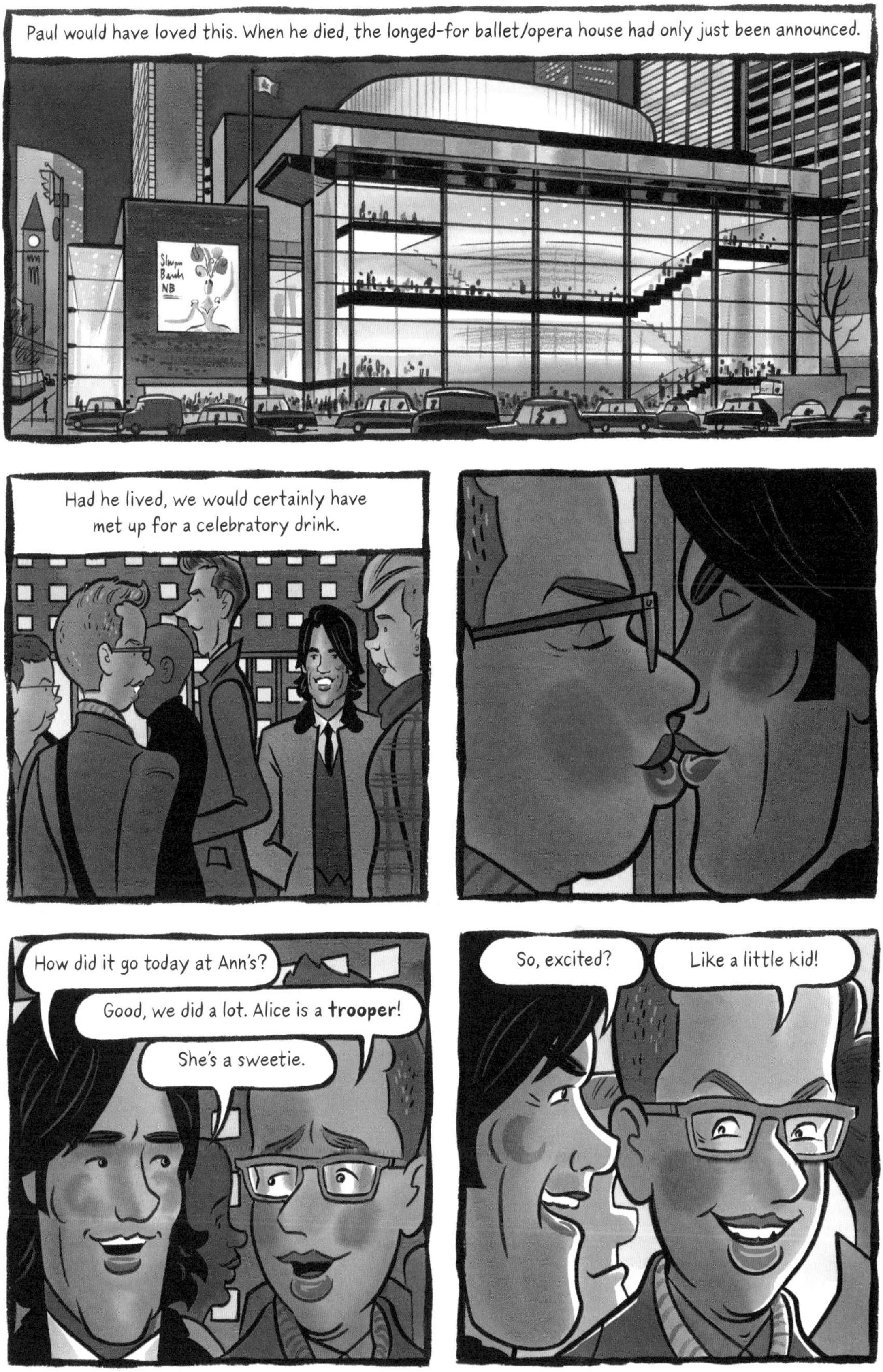
Paul would have loved this. When he died, the longed-for ballet/opera house had only just been announced.
Had he lived, we would certainly have met up for a celebratory drink.
How did it go today at Ann's?
Good, we did a lot. Alice is a **trooper**!
She's a sweetie.
So, excited?
Like a little kid!

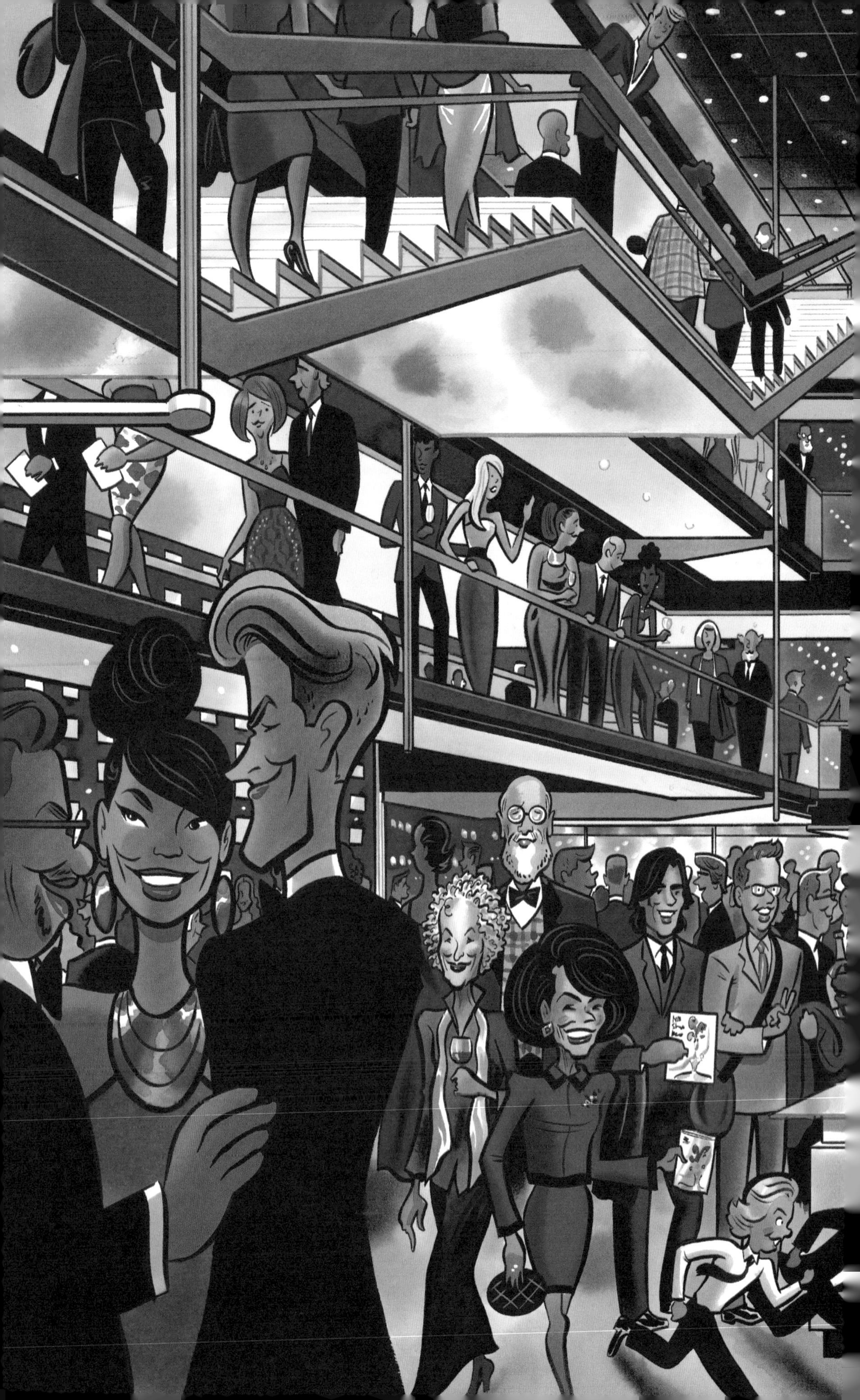

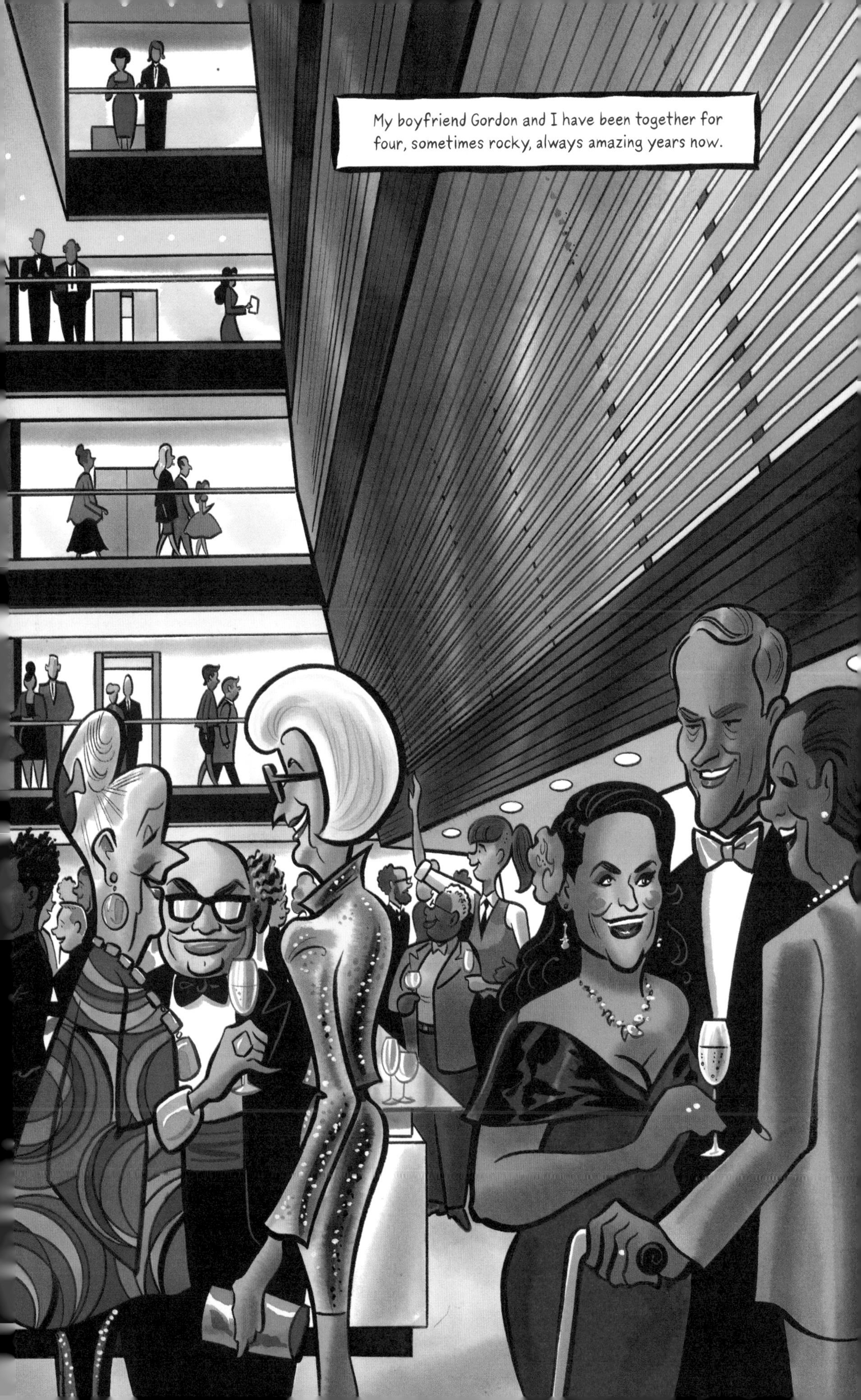
My boyfriend Gordon and I have been together for four, sometimes rocky, always amazing years now.

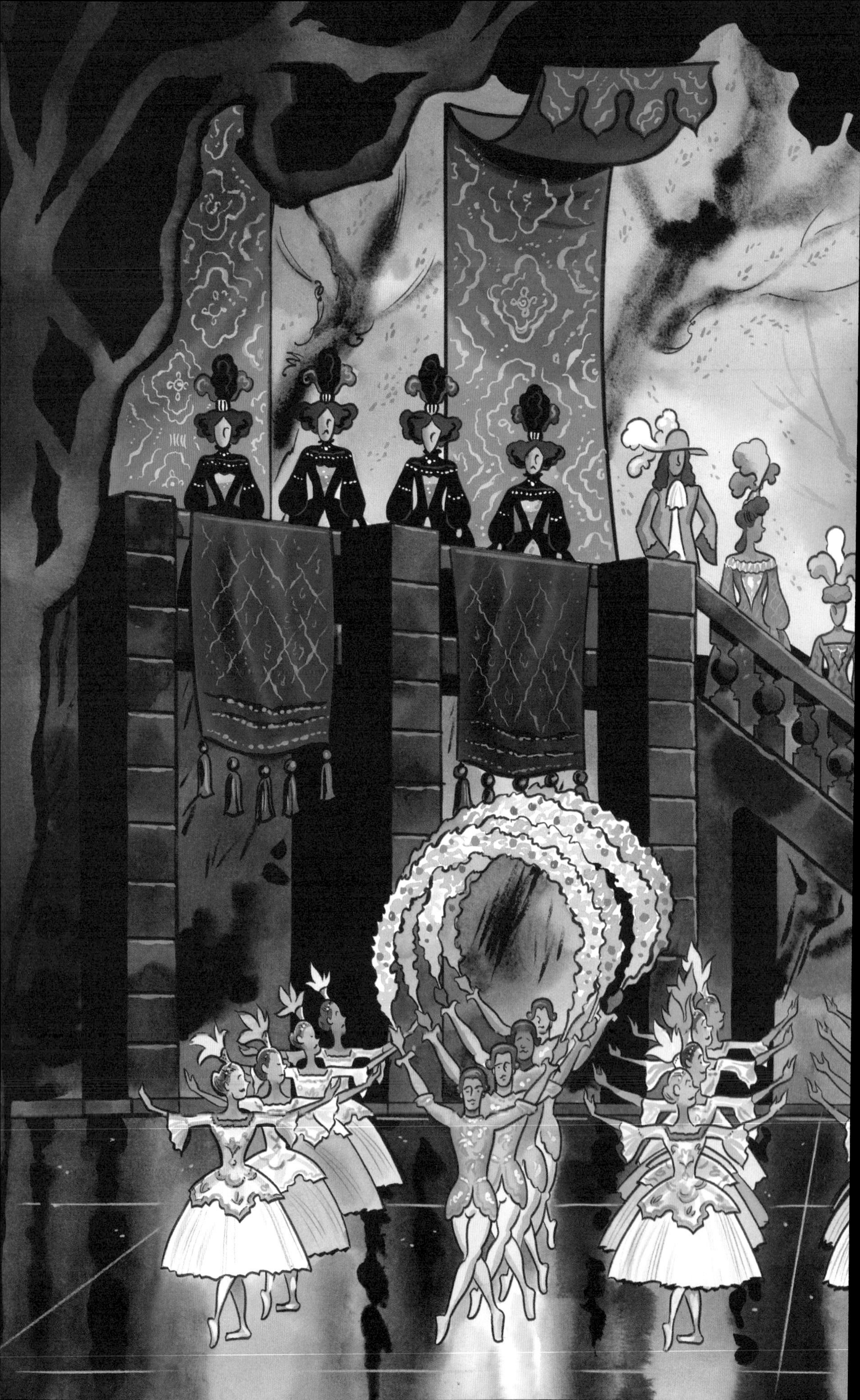

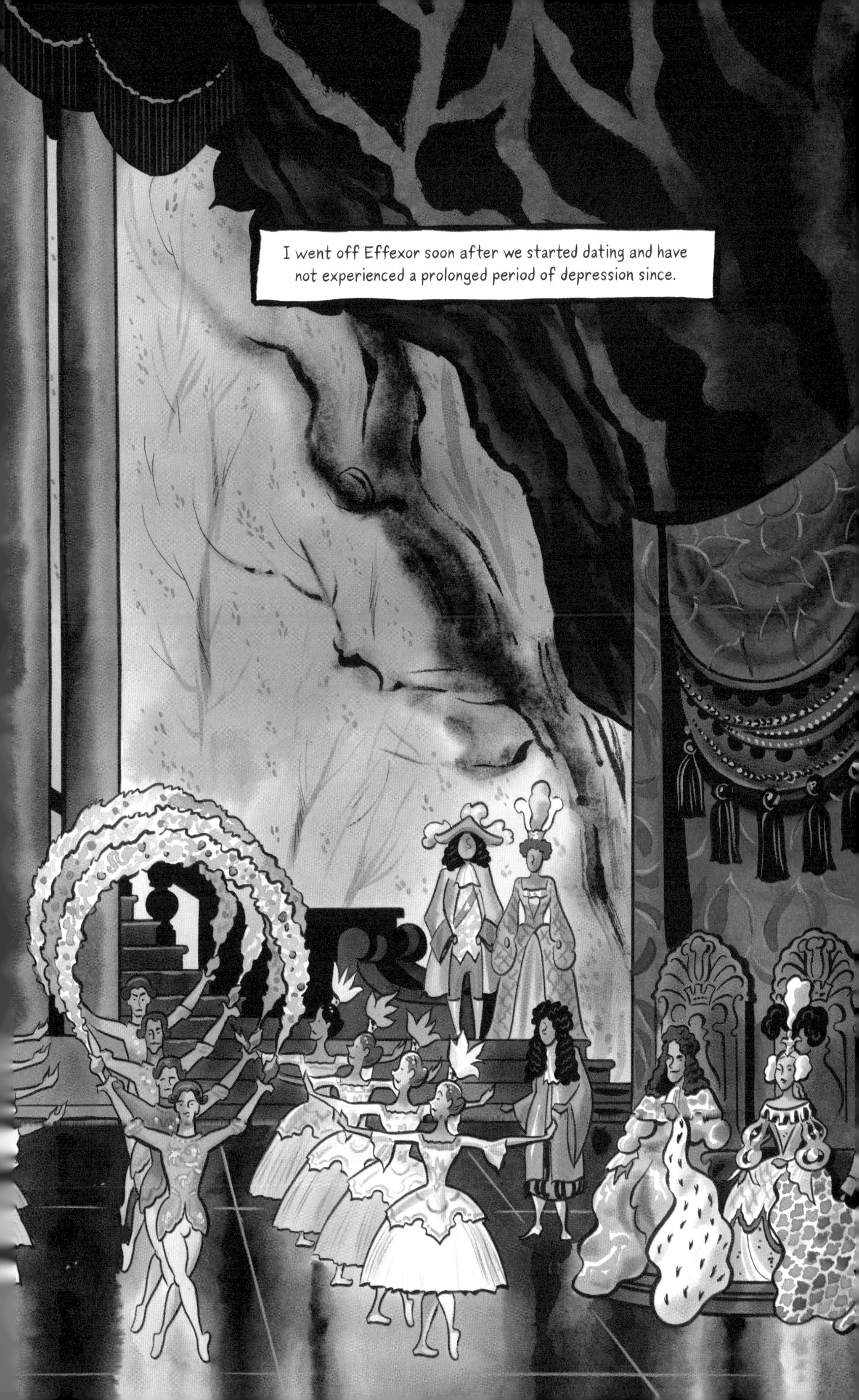
I went off Effexor soon after we started dating and have not experienced a prolonged period of depression since.

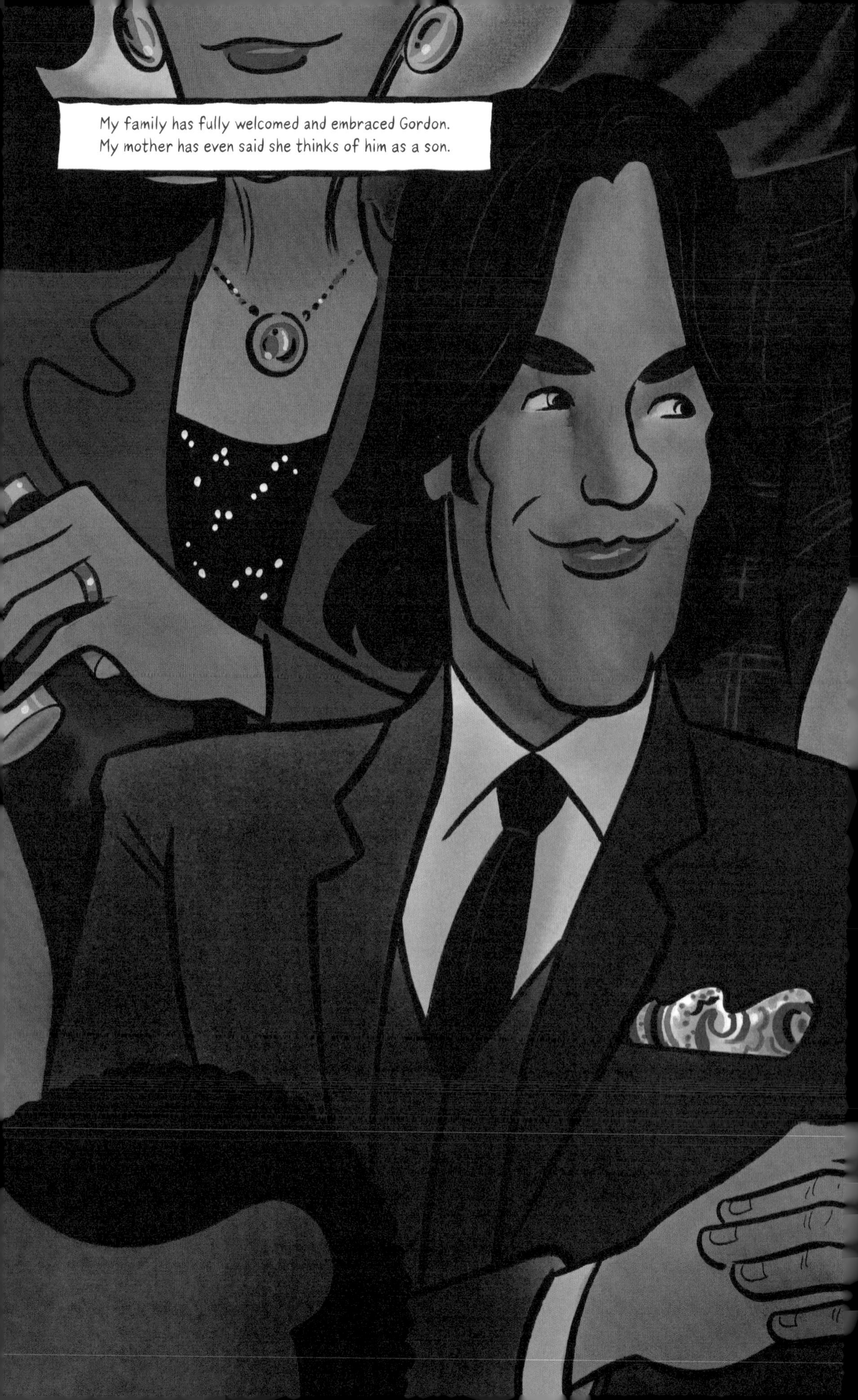
My family has fully welcomed and embraced Gordon.
My mother has even said she thinks of him as a son.

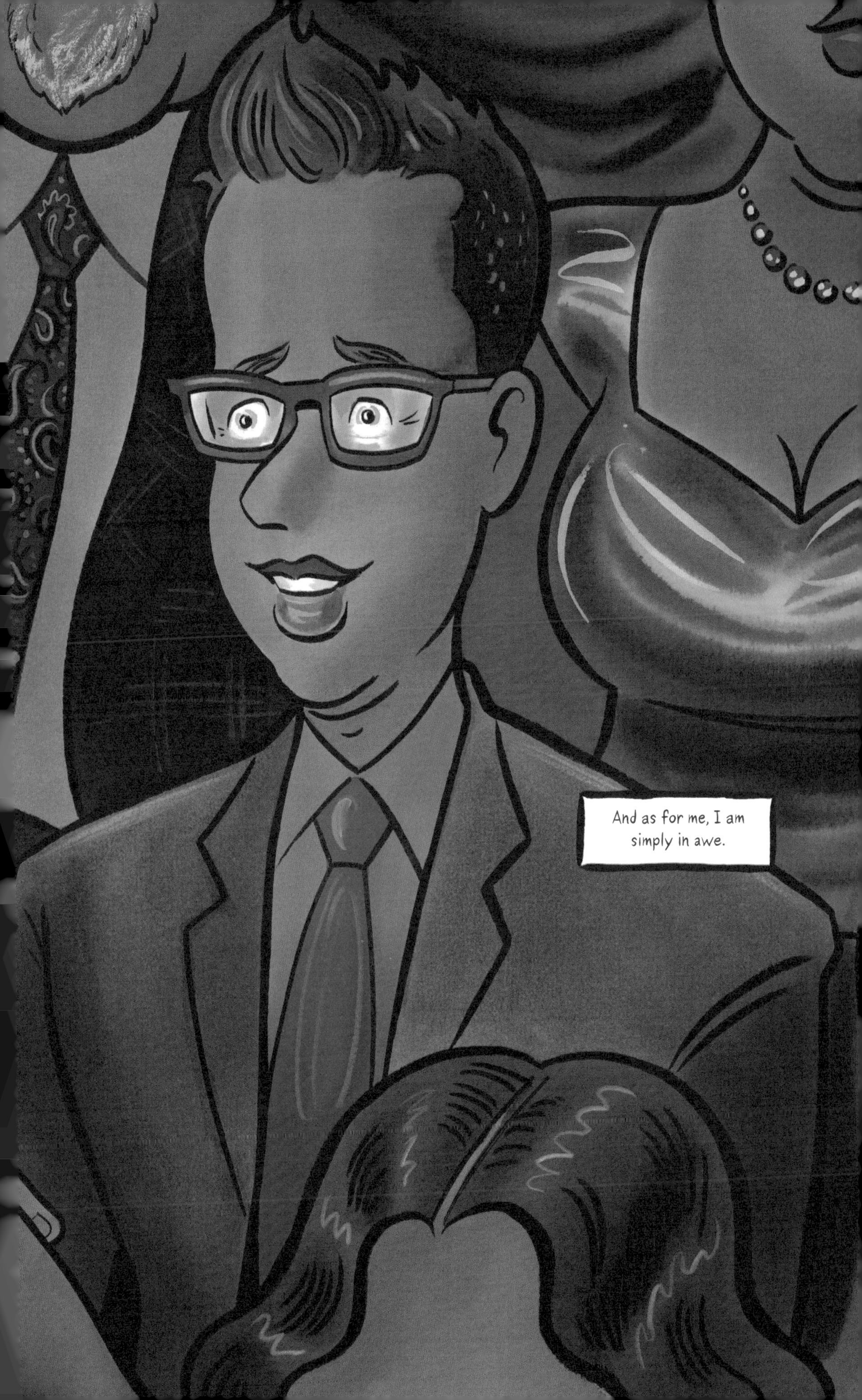
And as for me, I am simply in awe.

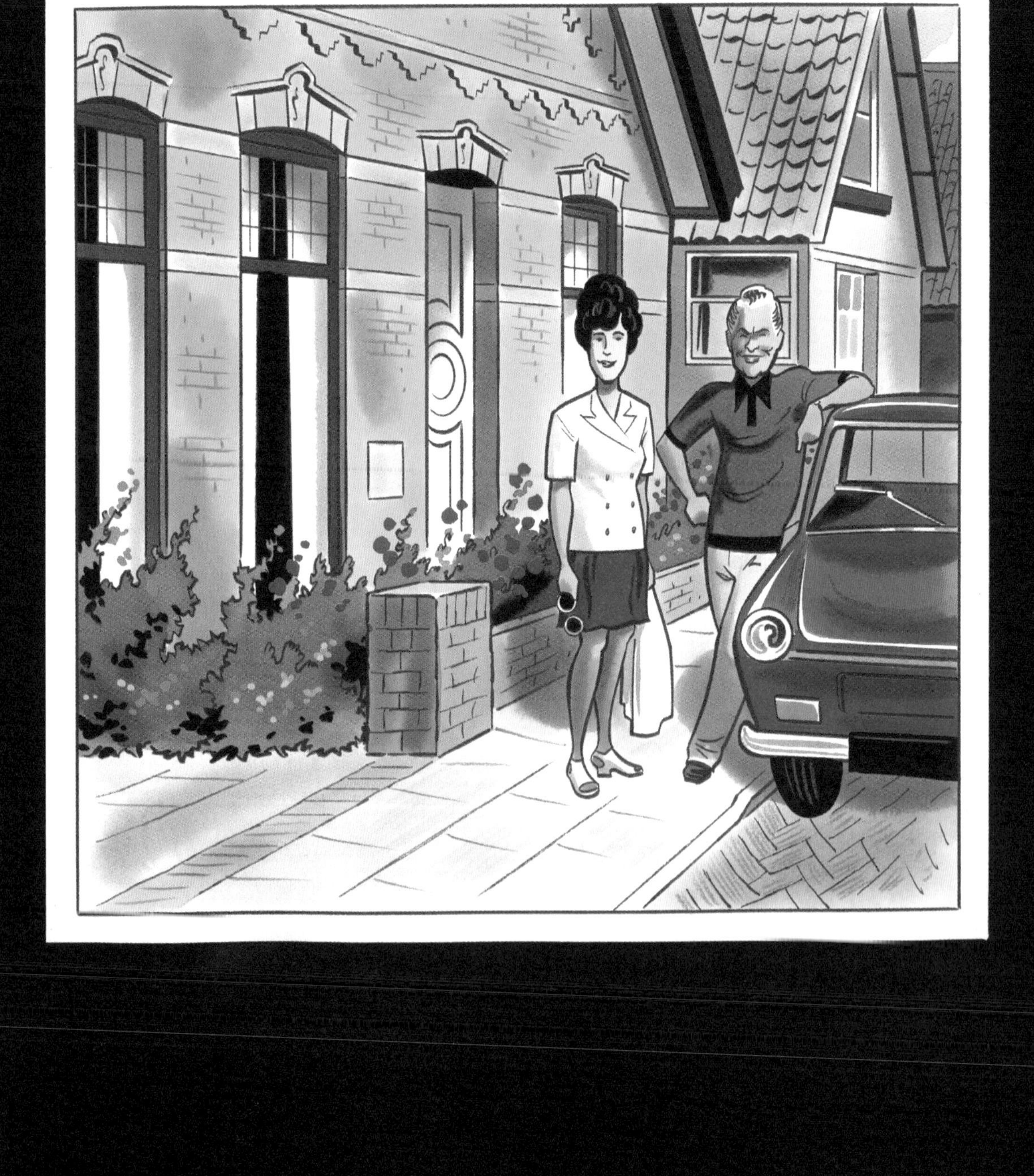

Coda

My Dad spent five years in the care of the amazing staff at Dom Lipa nursing home in Etobicoke. Weakened by a long period of decline brought on by Alzheimer's, he caught pneumonia and died in hospital on April 22, 2007. Perversely the disease causes family and friends to begin a mourning process long before their loved one dies, and this was true for my Mum, Ingrid, Mike, Dave and me. My Dad's relatively quick end was a relief and a blessing.

A series of ministrokes left my Mum confined to bed, unable to care for herself. She moved to Faith Manor, then Grace Manor, the two nursing homes at Holland Christian Homes, the CRC retirement complex in Brampton. She was vaccinated for Covid-19 without side effects and survived two outbreaks of the pandemic in the home. In the spring of 2021 she began refusing food and medication. My siblings and I were incredibly fortunate to be allowed to see her in her final week. She died peacefully on March 13 of that awful year, surrounded by the loving attention of her incredible caregivers. I am so grateful to them and extremely proud of my Mum's courage and determination. She was at peace with her Lord.

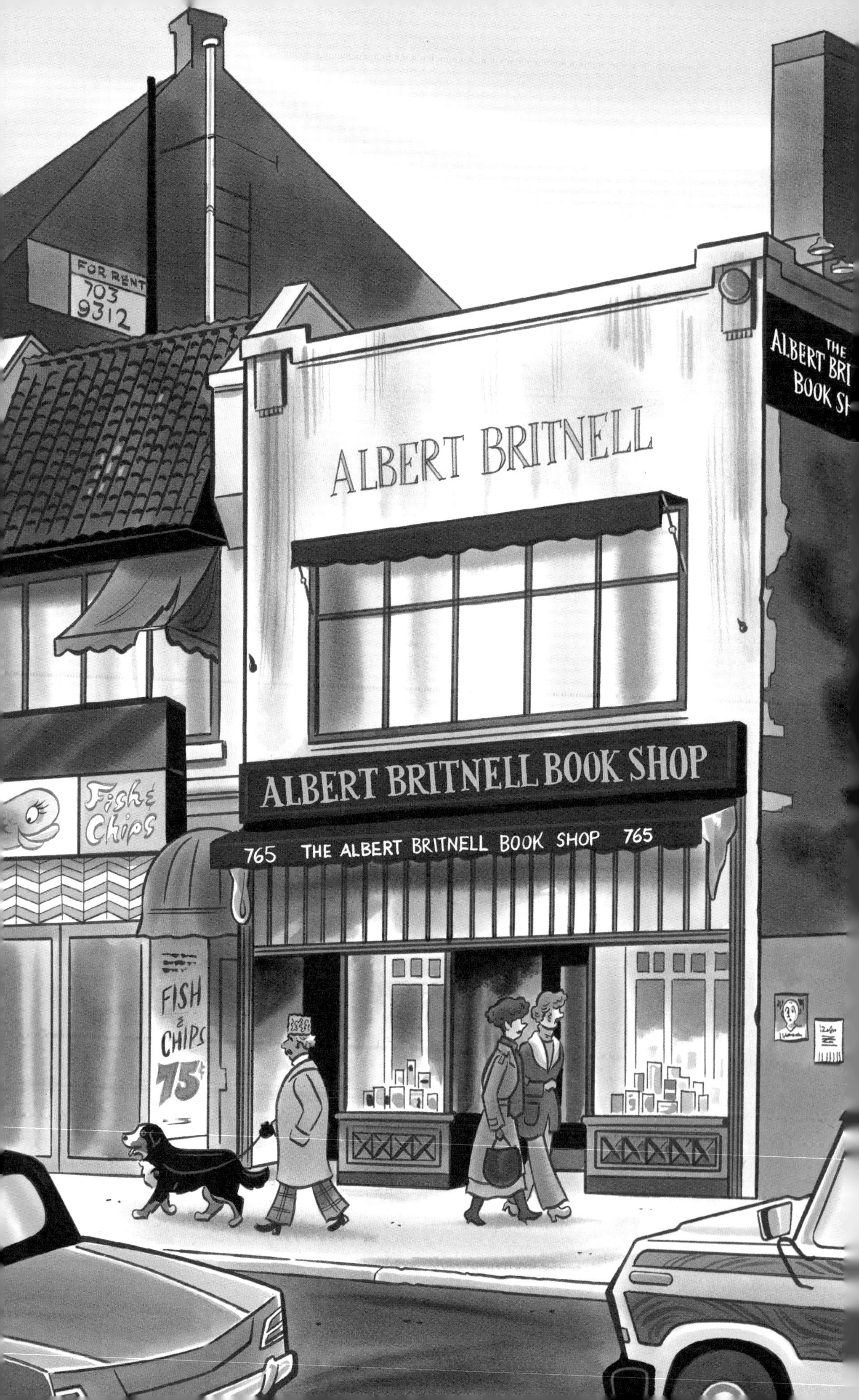
FOR RENT
703
9312
THE
ALBERT BRI
BOOK SH
ALBERT BRITNELL
ALBERT BRITNELL BOOK SHOP
765 THE ALBERT BRITNELL BOOK SHOP 765
Fish & Chips
FISH & CHIPS
75¢

Acknowledgements

Many smart and talented people helped me to create this book with their thoughts, comments and perceptions. Thank you, Anita Kunz, Dick Chin, Jamie Bennett, Deirdre Millin, Jim Belisle, Peter Birkemoe, Fiona Smyth, Michael Economy, Eric Kostiuk Williams, James Burn, Bruce Jones, John Martz, Alice Kooy and Isabel Sousa.

Thanks to Katie Wilson at the National Ballet Archive, John the paper guy at Aboveground Art Supply, and Altie Karper, Kathleen Fridella and Andy Hughes at Pantheon.

Early on Chester Brown gave me some very helpful advice and kindly assisted me in navigating the world of grant proposals.

Many thanks to the Canada Council for the Arts and the Ontario Arts Council for generous grants that relieved money worries for lengthy, luxurious stretches of time.

Laura Shepherd read my manuscript early on and offered wise and thoughtful comments and critique. Likewise, more recently, Jen Whalen and Christopher Richards.

Martin Roebuck, my dear friend of many years, gave invaluable insight into the wild and wonderful mind of Paul Baker.

Thanks to my agent Sam Hiyate for recommending Robert McKee's book *Story*, which helped me tremendously.

My mother Ann was always ready to share memories and insights, despite her misgivings about my project and the invasion of her privacy that it represents. Thanks to my siblings for their insights, vastly different memories and unstinting support and enthusiasm.

Margaret Powell has been generously supportive. I have been extremely lucky to continue to benefit from her matchless humour, imagination, compassion and deep insight.

Thank you, Chip Kidd, for pouncing on what was a very slight proposal back in 2012 and shepherding it through draft after draft with formidable expertise.

Deepest gratitude to my steadfast illustration rep of thirty-seven years, and biggest cheerleader, Bill Grigsby of Reactor Art and Design. Also to his unfailingly calm, patient and generous partner Steve Dunk, and the army of interns and junior designers who worked so hard on production over many years, including Landon Whittaker, Jess Frost, Emily McCourt, Emily Thornton and Taylor Houle.

The quoted material on page 445 comes from "Exploring Social and Emotional Aspects of Giftedness in Children," by Deirdre V. Lovecky, published in *The Roeper Review*, 1992, volume 15, number 1.

Finally, I couldn't have done it without my lovely and loving partner Gordon Bowness. I owe him so much--he has held my spirit high through so many doubts and fears, uppity ups and downest downs. One quick glance from his unerring editorial eye identified the problem I was dumbfounded by in any given passage, and he was right there with an array of imaginative solutions. What can I say? My heart is full.

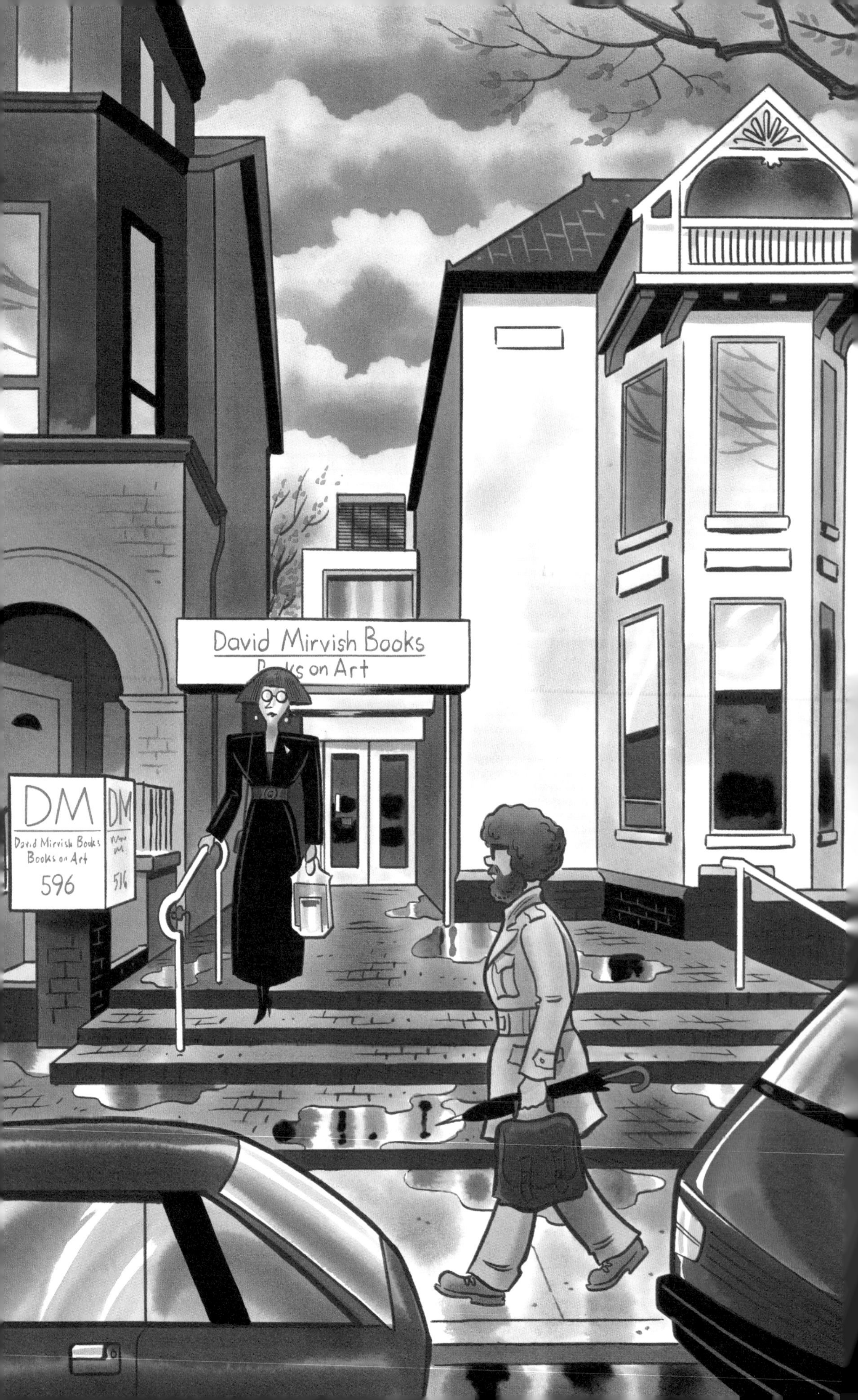
David Mirvish Books
DM
David Mirvish Books
Books on Art
596

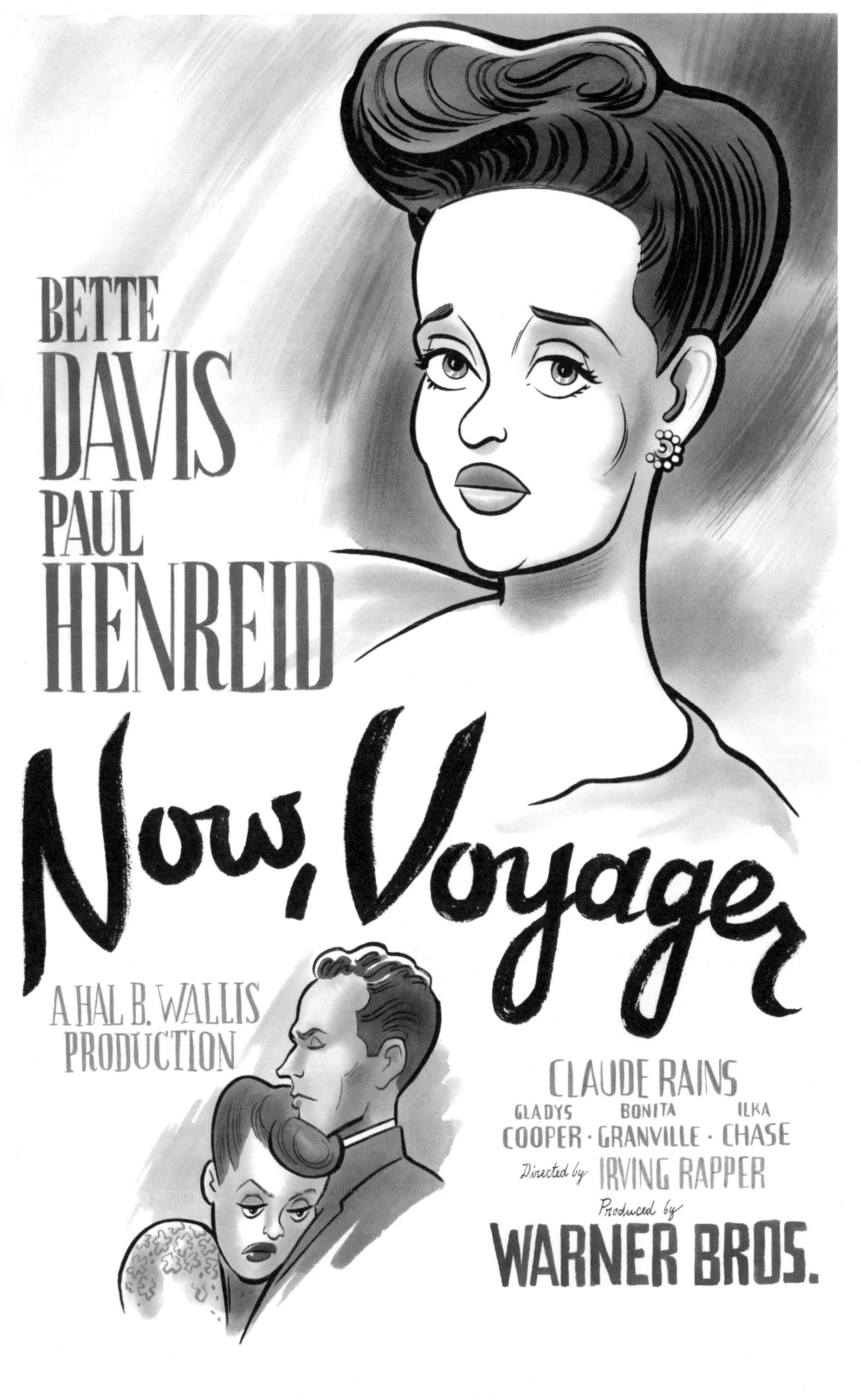
BETTE
DAVIS
PAUL
HENREID
Now, Voyager
A HAL B. WALLIS
PRODUCTION
CLAUDE RAINS
GLADYS
BONITA
ILKA
COOPER · GRANVILLE · CHASE
Directed by IRVING RAPPER
Produced by
WARNER BROS.

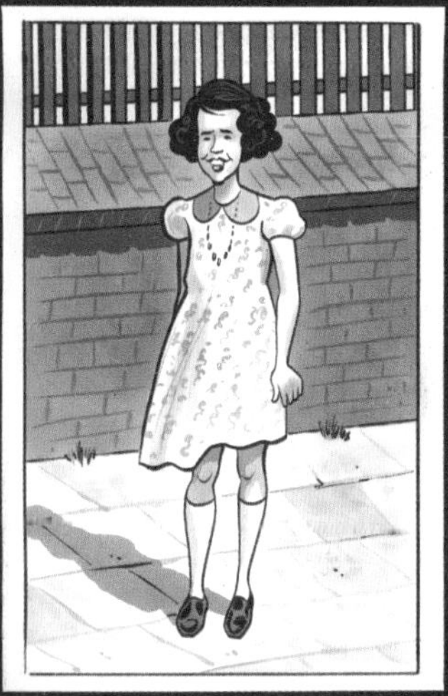
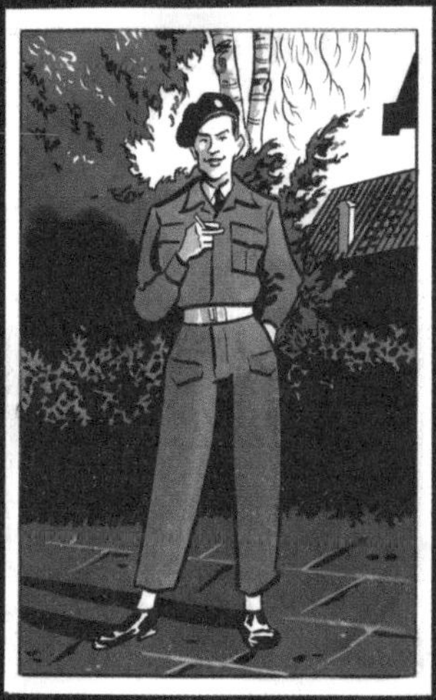
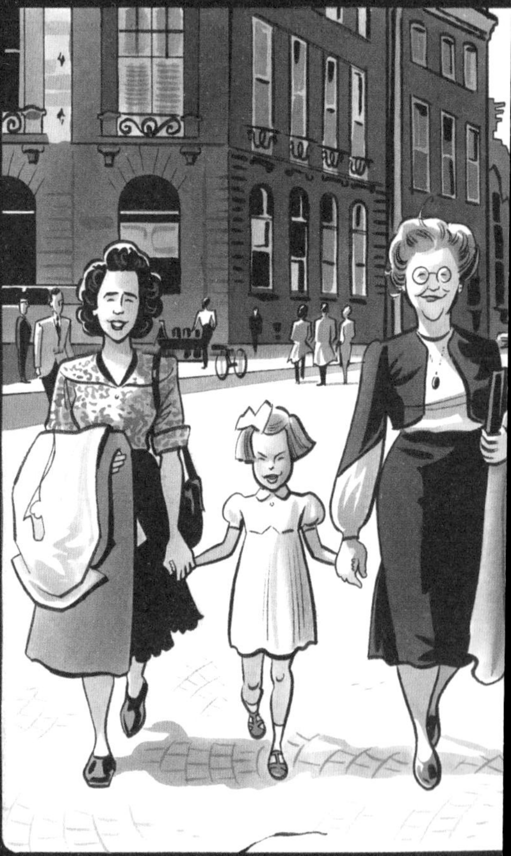
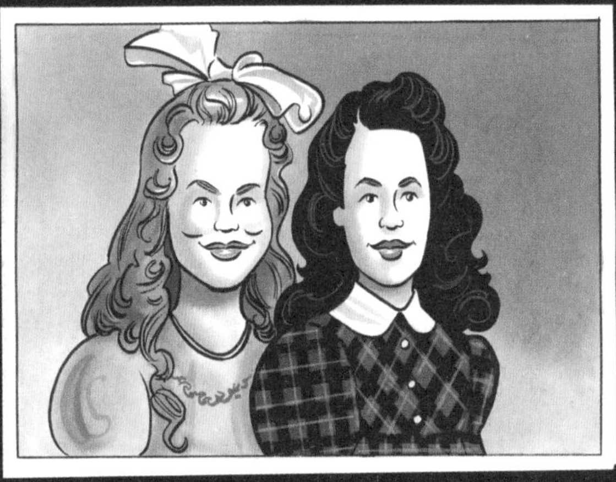
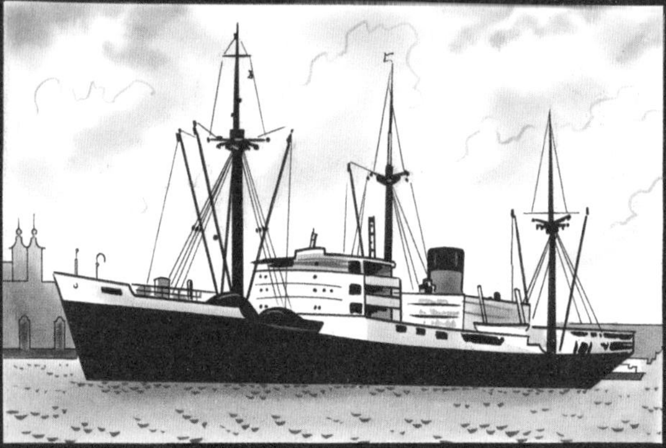
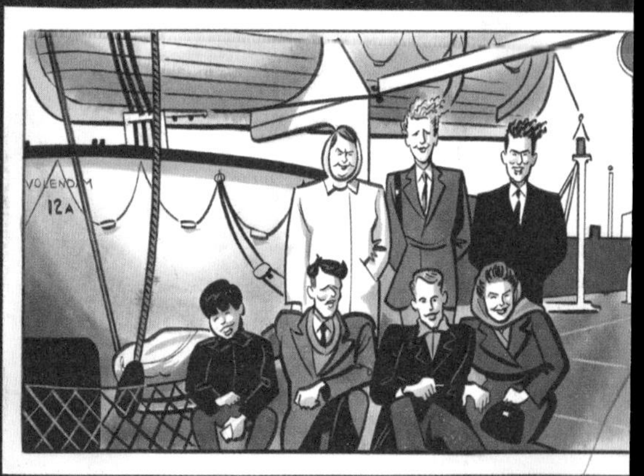
VOLENDAM
12A
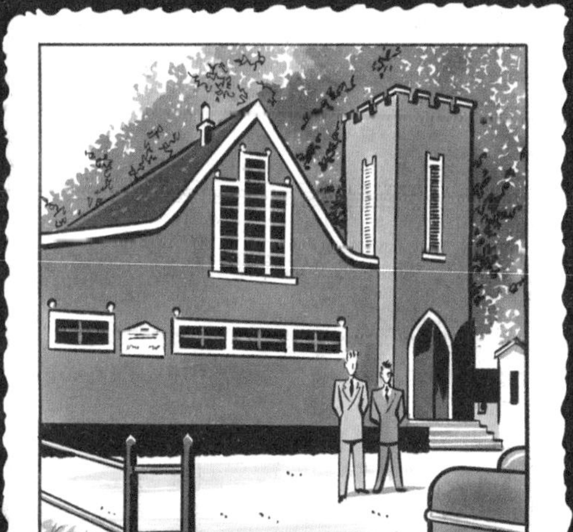
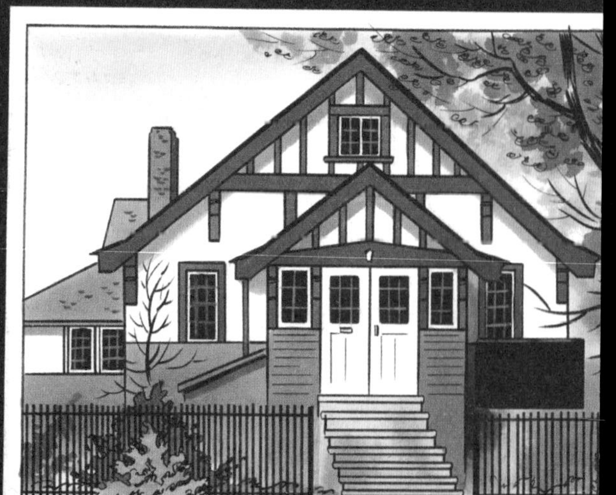